Luther L. Paulson

**Hand-Book and Directory of San Luis Obispo,**

Santa Barbara, Ventura, Kern, San Bernardino, Los Angeles and San Diego counties,

with a list of the post-offices of the Pacific coast

Luther L. Paulson

**Hand-Book and Directory of San Luis Obispo,**
*Santa Barbara, Ventura, Kern, San Bernardino, Los Angeles and San Diego counties, with a list of the post-offices of the Pacific coast*

ISBN/EAN: 9783337384036

Printed in Europe, USA, Canada, Australia, Japan

Cover: Foto ©ninafisch / pixelio.de

More available books at **www.hansebooks.com**

# HAND-BOOK

AND

# DIRECTORY

OF

## San Luis Obispo, Santa Barbara,

## Ventura, Kern, San Bernardino, Los Angeles & San Diego

## COUNTIES,

WITH

A LIST OF THE POST-OFFICES OF THE PACIFIC COAST; WELLS, FARGO & CO'S OFFICES; MONEY ORDER OFFICES; RATES OF DOMESTIC AND FOREIGN POSTAGE; SENATORIAL DISTRICTS OF THE STATE OF CALIFORNIA; MARINE DISTANCES; RAILROAD DISTANCES BETWEEN POINTS EAST AND WEST; THE STATES OF THE UNION, WITH THEIR CAPITALS, POPULATION IN 1870, AND AREA IN SQUARE MILES, ETC., ETC.

---

*SAN FRANCISCO:*
Compiled and Published by L. L. PAULSON.
FRANCIS & VALENTINE, COMMERCIAL STEAM PRESSES, 517 CLAY STREET.
1875.

# PREFACE.

IN compiling the third series of the HAND-BOOK AND DIRECTORY, for the Counties of SAN LUIS OBISPO, SANTA BARBARA, VENTURA, KERN, SAN BERNARDINO, LOS ANGELES, and SAN DIEGO, I have endeavored, as in the preeceding issues, to obtain and give the correct name and residence of all permanent inhabitants, noting occupation, location and post-office address of each.

Much care has been used in obtaining the statistical information, and yet it has been impossible ta avoid all errors. These, however, are comparatively few, and will lead to still more thorough and careful work hereafter.

In order to make my work equally acceptable to the merchant and farmer, the resident and the tourist, I have added a complete description of each County, City, Town, Village, Hamlet and Farming Centre; also of the Watering Places and all points of natural attraction. For the tourist and invalid who may visit California for pleasure, or for sanitary reasons, this feature of my book, I am convinced, will be of great utility.

I desire also to inform the public that this work is one number of a series which will form, when complete, a Hand-Book and Directory of the State, engrossing the names of all residents.

I hope to have the support and patronage of the public in this undertaking, and shall always strive to merit it by making my publications valuable through their completeness and reliability.

THE PUBLISHER.

# TABLE OF CONTENTS.

### General Index.
PAGE.
Descriptive of San Luis Obispo County............ 17
" " Santa Barbara County............... 91
" " Ventura County.......................171
" " Kern County...........................209
" " San Bernardino County............251
" " Los Angeles County.................289
" " San Diego County....................449
Residents of San Luis Obispo County............. 33
" " Santa Barbara County............... 97
" " Ventura County.......................177
" " Kern County...........................215
" " San Bernardino County............257
" " Los Angeles County.................307
" " San Diego..............................455
Post Offices,
Wells, Fargo & Co.'s Offices, } ..................9 to 12
Money Order Offices,
Postage Rates, Domestic and Foreign........12 to 14
Population of the World............................... 15
Senatorial Districts of State......................... 15
Railroad Distances between points East and West 16
Marine Distances....................................... 16
States of the Union,
Capitals,
Population,
Area in miles,                       } .................... 16
Governors' Term Expire,
Time of Election.

### San Francisco Advertisers.
Armes & Dallam, Wood and Willow Ware..........302
Atwood & Bodwell,
  Wind Mills, and Horse Powers, 88 and 89
Baker & Hamilton, Agricultural Implements......240
Bartling & Kimball, Bookbinders...................... x
Beach, Chilion, Stationery.............................. 70
Benjamin & Co., Henry A.,
  Congress and Seltzer Water 84
Berson & Son, Furniture................................ 84
Braverman & Levy, Importers of Jewelry,
  Front Cover
Brittan, Holbrook & Co., Stoves, etc............... 52
Bruce D., Printer...........................Back Cover
Bryan, Wm. & Thos., Hotel............................ 46
Bryant & Taylor, Safes and Locks.......Front Cover
Burkardt, Max, Picture Frames, etc................528
Callaghan, D. & Co., Yeast Powder.................519
Christy & Wise, Commission Wool Merchants... 27
Cox, James, Commission Wool Merchants......528
Daily Evening Post......................60 and Front Cover
Dutard, H., Commission Merchant..................478
Eastman, T. S., Carriages, Coaches, etc.........524
Eitner, Rudolph, Engraver.............................513
Francis & Valentine, Printers....Inside Front Cover
Frank Bros. & Co., Agricultural Implements.... 32
Galo & Co., J. W., Commission Merchants.....528
Gillispie, Zan & Co., Broom Manufacturers...... 70
Golden Gate Academy..............Between 384 and 385
Goodall, Nelson & Perkins, Steamship Co......517
Haines, E. W., Sewing Machines....................214
Harral, E. W., Sewing Machines........236 and 535
Hawley & Co., Marcus C...........Between 320 and 321
Heald's Business College.............Between 272 and 273
Hill, Samuel, Sewing Machines......................454
Hoag, Chas. P., Wind Mills...........................528
Holloway, Joseph E., Wind Mills.................... xiv
Holt, Warren, Patent Gate Hinge...................530
Holt, Warren, Maps.....................................531
I. X. L. Bitters..............................Back Cover
Jarvis, Geo. M., Native Wines and Brandies, etc.306
Johnson & Co., J. C., Harness, etc................226
Keeler & Co., Statuary....................Front Cover
Kittredge, Jonathan, Safes, Vaults, etc........... 66
Landrum & Rodgers, Imported Stock............. 50
Larkins & Co., Carriages..............................446
Liesenfeld, P., Billiard Table Manufacturer,
  Back Cover
Linforth, Kellogg & Co., Agricult'l Implements...418
Locke & Montague, Stoves, etc.........Front Cover

PAGE.
Martin, Wm. H., Real Estate.........................525
Mead & Co., A., Sewing Machines..........iv and 234
Meeker & James, Carriage and Wagon Material, 303
Mendelsohn & Co., Shirt Manufacturers...........528
Mills & Evans, Wagons................................516
Moody & Farish, Wool Commission Merchants... 90
Moore, Mrs. H. A., Hair Producer.................. 52
Moore, H. H., Books....................................529
Moore, James, Wool Commission Merchant..... 90
Nichols & Co., A. C., Commission Merchants... 70
Osborn & Alexander, Mechanics' Tools.......28-29
Pacific Saw Manufacturing Company..............474
Pacific Oil and Lead Works...........................303
Palmer & Knox, Golden State Iron Works......529
Peters, J. H., Photographer..........................523
Read, Ellis, Scotch Type Foundry......Front Cover
Redstone, John H., Patent Solicitor................ 30
Robinson, Alfred, Real Estate........................322
Salamander Felting Company.......................... xi
Sanborn, Vail & Co., Mirrors, etc.,
  Front and Back Cover
San Francisco Chronicle.............Cover and page iii
San Francisco Savings Union......................... 90
Schneider, W. H., Guns, Pistols, etc..............519
Schumacher, A., Leather and Findings........... 62
Shaw & Robinson, Hotel, (Hanna House).......519
Shepman, W. E., Gold and Silver Plating........ 30
Sims, John R., Iron Doors, Safes, etc............520
Skinker, John, Gunpowder, Rifles, etc...........178
Southwick, A. H., Wind Mills........................522
Spaulding, N. W., Saw Smithing, etc.............474
Spaulding & Co., F. M., Paper Warehouse...... xiii
Steele & Co., James G., Squirrel Poison......... 84
Strahle & Co., Jacob, Manufacturers Billiard Tables,
  72
Sweeney & Co., J. P., Seedsmen................... 30
Swett & Co., D. L., Printers.......................... 62
Tustin, W. I., Wind Mills and Horse Powers, 108-109
Vanderslice & Co., Manufacturing Jewelers,
  Back Cover
Waterhouse & Lester, Wagon and Carriage Materials.................................................228
Wellington, B. F., Vegetable, Fruit, and Flower
  Seeds................................................. 70
Wetherbee, G. M., Bee Hives, etc.................529
Wilson, H. H., Firearms, etc.......................... 58
Wilson Sewing Machine................................ 70

### San Francisco Advertisements, Classified.
**Agricultural Implements.**
Baker & Hamilton.......................................240
Frank Bros. & Co........................................ 32
Hawley & Co., Marcus C..........Between 320 and 321
Linforth, Kellogg & Co................................418
**Bank.**
San Francisco Savings Union........................ 90
**Bee Hive Manufacturer.**
Wetherbee, G. M........................................529
**Billiard Table Manufacturers.**
Liesenfeld, P..............................Back Cover
Strahle & Co., Jacob.................................... 72
**Bitters.**
Dr. Henley's I. X. L........................Back Cover
**Bookbinders.**
Bartling & Kimball........................................ x
**Bookseller.**
Moore, H. H..............................................529
**Broom Manufacturers.**
Gillispie, Zan & Co...................................... 70
**Colleges and Academies.**
Haskins & Kellogg.................Between 384 and 385
Heald, E. P..........................Between 272 and 273
**Carriages and Coaches.**
Eastman, T. S...........................................524
Larkins & Co.............................................446
**Carriage and Wagon Material.**
Meeker, James & Co...................................303
Waterhouse & Lester..................................228

L. L. PAULSON'S DIRECTORIES.

| | PAGE. |
|---|---|
| **Commission Merchants (General).** | |
| Dutard, H. | 478 |
| Gale & Co., J. W. | 528 |
| Nichols & Co., A. C. | 70 |
| **Commission Merchants (Wool).** | |
| Christy & Wise | 27 |
| Cox, James W. | 528 |
| Moody & Farish | 90 |
| Moore, James | 90 |
| **Engines, Machinery, etc.** | |
| Baker & Hamilton | 240 |
| Golden State Iron Works | 529 |
| Hawley & Co., Marcus C. Between 320 and 321 | |
| Linforth, Kellogg & Co. | 448 |
| **Engraver (Wood).** | |
| Eitner, Rudolph | 513 |
| **Felting.** | |
| Seward Cole | xi |
| **Firearms, etc.** | |
| Schneider, W. H. | 519 |
| Skinker, John | 176 |
| Wilson, H. H. | 58 |
| **Furniture.** | |
| Berson & Son | 84 |
| **Gold and Silver Plating.** | |
| Shepman, W. E. | 30 |
| **Gunpowder.** | |
| Schneider, W. H. | 519 |
| Skinker, John | 176 |
| Wilson, H. H. | 58 |
| **Hair Producer.** | |
| Moore, Mrs. H. A. | 52 |
| **Hardware.** | |
| Baker & Hamilton | 240 |
| Hawley & Co., Marcus C. Between 320 and 321 | |
| Linforth, Kellogg & Co. | 448 |
| Osborn & Alexander | 28–29 |
| **Harness Manufacturers.** | |
| Johnson & Co., J. C. | 226 |
| **Horse Powers.** | |
| Atwood & Bodwell | 89 |
| Tustin, W. I. | 109 |
| **Hotels.** | |
| Bryan, Wm. & Thos. | 46 |
| Shaw & Robinson | 519 |
| **Imported Stock.** | |
| Landrum & Rodgers | 50 |
| **Jewelers (Manufacturing and Importing).** | |
| Braverman & Levy | Front Cover |
| Vandersilce & Co. | Back Cover |
| **Leather and Findings.** | |
| Schumacher, A. | 62 |
| **Maps.** | |
| Holt, Warren | 531 |
| **Mechanics' Tools.** | |
| Osborn & Alexander | 28–29 |
| Pacific Saw Manufacturing Co. | 474 |
| **Metals.** | |
| Brittan, Holbrook & Co. | 52 |
| **Mineral Water.** | |
| Benjamin & Co., Henry A. | 84 |
| **Newspapers.** | |
| Daily Evening Post | 90 and Front Cover |
| San Francisco Chronicle | Cover and page iii |
| **Paper Warehouse.** | |
| Spaulding & Co., F. M. | xiii |
| **Patent Gate Hinge.** | |
| Holt, Warren | 530 |
| **Patent Solicitor.** | |
| Redstone, John H. | 30 |
| **Photographs.** | |
| Peters, J. H. | 523 |
| **Picture Frames, Mirrors, etc.** | |
| Burkardt, Max | 528 |
| Sanborn, Vail & Co. | Outside Covers |
| **Printers.** | |
| Bruce, D. | Back Cover |
| Francis & Valentine | Inside Front Cover |
| Swett & Co., D. L. | 62 |
| **Printing Material.** | |
| Wetherbee, G. M. | 529 |

| | PAGE. |
|---|---|
| **Real Estate.** | |
| Martin, Wm. H. | 525 |
| Robinson, Alfred | 322 |
| **Rifles.** | |
| Schneider, W. H. | 519 |
| Skinker, John | 176 |
| Wilson, H. H. | 58 |
| **Stationery.** | |
| Beach, Chilion | 70 |
| Spaulding & Co. F. M. | xiii |
| **Statuary.** | |
| Keeler & Co. | Front Cover |
| **Safes, Locks, Vaults, etc.** | |
| Bryant & Taylor | Front Cover |
| Kittredge, Jonathan | 66 |
| Sims, John R. | 520 |
| **Saws (Manufacturing).** | |
| Pacific Saw Manufacturing Co. | 474 |
| Spaulding, N. W. | 474 |
| **Saw Smithing.** | |
| Spaulding, N. W. | 474 |
| **Seeds, etc.** | |
| Pacific Oil and Lead Works | 303 |
| Sweeney & Co., J. P. | 30 |
| Wellington, B. F. | 70 |
| **Sewing Machines.** | |
| Haines, E. W. | 214 |
| Harral, E. W. | 236–535 |
| Hill, Samuel | 454 |
| Mead & Co., A. | iv and 234 |
| Wilson Sewing Machine | 70 |
| **Shirt Manufacturers.** | |
| Mendelsohn & Co. | 528 |
| **Squirrel Poison.** | |
| Steele, James G. | 84 |
| **Steamship Company.** | |
| Goodall, Nelson &. Perkins | 517 |
| **Stoves, Ranges, etc.** | |
| Brittan, Holbrook & Co. | 52 |
| Locke & Montague | Front Cover |
| **Type Founder.** | |
| Read, Ellis | Front Cover |
| **Wagons.** | |
| Baker & Hamilton | 240 |
| Eastman, T. S. | 324 |
| Frank Bros. & Co. | 32 |
| Hawley & Co., Marcus C. Between 320 and 321 | |
| Linforth, Kellogg & Co. | 448 |
| Mills & Evans | 516 |
| **Wind Mills.** | |
| Atwood & Bodwell | 88 |
| Hoag, Chas. P. | 528 |
| Holloway, Joseph E. | xiv |
| Southwick, A. H. | 522 |
| Tustin, W. I. | 168 |
| **Wines, Brandies, etc.** | |
| Jervis, Geo. M. | 306 |
| **Wood and Willow Ware.** | |
| Armes & Dallam | 302 |
| **Yeast Powder Manufacturers.** | |
| Callaghan & Co., D. | 519 |

## San Luis Obispo County Advertisers.

| | |
|---|---|
| Arana, Jesus C., Hair Dressing Emporium | 56 |
| Bank of San Luis Obispo | 512 |
| Bayer, Theobald, Blacksmith | 144 |
| Benrimo, M. A., Hotel | 52 |
| Blackburn & Morris, Hotel | 160 |
| Blake, Harvey B. & Co., Real Estate | 82 |
| Blochman, A. & Co., Commission Merchants | 154 |
| Bouldin, R. C., Attorney | 170 |
| Branch Bros., Millers | 552 |
| Buchart & Sons, Geo., General Mdse and Hotel | 150 |
| Cass, James, Lumber, etc. | 244 |
| Ceribelli, S., Soda Water Manufacturer | 156 |
| Dana Bros., Farm Lands | 408 |
| Farmer, Robert, Livery Stable | 152 |
| Finney & Peterson, Blacksmiths | 250 |
| Frederick, Joseph, Hotel | 248 |
| Goultree Bros., Commission Merchants | 148 |
| Gruble, Benjamin, Carpenter | 167 |
| Grant, Lull & Co., Hardware | 146 |
| Hammerschlag & Levy, General Merchandise | 506 |
| Hammerschlag, M., General Merchandise | 506 |

L. L. PAULSON'S DIRECTORIES. vii

| | PAGE. |
|---|---|
| Harrison, M. B., Attorney | 170 |
| Harris, R. R., Surveyor | 52 |
| Hazen & Sandbrcock, Agricultural Implements | 31 |
| Lindenmayer, Julius, Brewer | 247 |
| Little & Cochran, Lecture Hall | 502 |
| McDonald Bros., Hotel | 68 |
| Miller, F. K., Attorney | 170 |
| Murphy, Lorenzo, Hair Dresser | 532 |
| Newsom, D. F., White Sulphur Springs | 504 |
| Oglesby, A. A., Attorney | 170 |
| Ortega, J. C., Stationery | 508 |
| Osgood, H. M., Watchmaker | 148 |
| Phillips, C. H., Land | 510 |
| Pollard & James, Millers | 167 |
| Preston, R. M., Conveyancer | 148 |
| Rackliffe, L., General Merchandise | 154 |
| Rembaugh, H. S. & Co., Publishers | 56 |
| Schwartz, Harford & Co., Lumber | 256 |
| Schwartz, L. & Co., General Merchandise | 511 |
| Sittenfeld & Co., Commission Merchants | 158 |
| Smallwood, Spurgeon & Staiger, Butchers | 249 |
| Steele Bros., Lands | 510 |
| Stocking, E. B., Wharf and Warehouse | 245 |
| Stocking, J. C., Blacksmith | 245 |
| Sunderland Quicksilver Mining Co. | 527 |
| Turner, J. C., Blacksmith | 62 |
| Williamson, A., Stoves and Tinware | 148 |
| Wobkin, E., Livery | 170 |

### San Luis Obispo Co. Advertisements, Classified.

**Agricultural Implements.**
Grant, Lull & Co. ... 146
Hazen & Sandercock ... 31

**Attorneys.**
Bouldin, R. C. ... 170
Harrison, M. B. ... 170
Miller, F. K. ... 170
Oglesby, A. A. ... 170

**Bank.**
Bank of San Luis Obispo ... 512

**Barbers.**
Arana, Jesus C. ... 53
Murphy, Lorenzo ... 529

**Blacksmiths.**
Bayer, Theobald ... 144
Finney & Peterson ... 250
Stocking, J. C. ... 245
Turner, J. C. ... 62

**Brewer.**
Lindenmayer, Julius ... 247

**Butcher.**
Smallwood, Spurgeon & Staiger ... 249

**Carpenter.**
Grable, Benjamin ... 167

**Commission Merchants.**
Blochman, A. & Co. ... 156
Goldtree Bros. ... 148
Sittenfeld & Co. ... 158

**Conveyancer.**
Preston, R. M. ... 148

**General Merchandise.**
Buchart & Sons, Geo. ... 150
Grant, Lull & Co. ... 146
Hammerschlag & Levy ... 506
Hammerschlag, M. ... 506
Rackliffe, L. ... 154
Schwartz, L. & Co. ... 511

**Hotels.**
Benrimo, M. A. ... 52
Blackburn & Morris ... 160
Buchart & Sons, Geo ... 150
Frederick, Joseph ... 248
McDonald Bros. ... 68

**Livery Stables.**
Farmer, Robt. ... 152
Wobken, E. ... 170

**Lumber.**
Cass, James ... 244
Schwartz, Harford & Co. ... 256

**Medicinal Springs.**
Newsom, D. F. ... 504

**Mills (Flouring).**
Branch Bros. ... 532
Pollard & James ... 167

| | PAGE. |
|---|---|
| **Mine.** | |
| Sunderland Quicksilver Mining Co. | 527 |
| **Publisher.** | |
| Rembaugh, H. S. & Co. | 56 |
| **Real Estate.** | |
| Blake, Harvey B. & Co. | 82 |
| Dana Bros. | 498 |
| Phillips, C. H. | 510 |
| Steele Bros. | 510 |
| **Saloon.** | |
| Little & Cochran | 502 |
| **Soda Water.** | |
| Ceribelli, S. | 156 |
| **Stationery.** | |
| Ortega, J. C. | 508 |
| **Stoves and Tinware.** | |
| Williamson, A. | 148 |
| **Surveyor.** | |
| Harris, R. R. | 52 |
| **Warehouseman.** | |
| Stocking, E. B. | 245 |
| **Watches, etc.** | |
| Osgood, H. M. | 148 |

### Santa Barbara County Advertisers.

Abel, Henry, Harness, etc. ... 248
Abernethy & Co., R., Stoves, etc. ... 134
Adam, Wm. L., General Merchandise ... 112
Bennett, Mrs. A. M., Hotel ... 496
Bradford, W. J., Blacksmith ... 246
Braun, Robert, Blacksmith ... 106
Broughton, W. W., Publisher ... 136
Burke, M. F., Store, Hotel, etc. ... 138
Carteri, L., Hotel ... 246
Cebrian, J. C., Architect ... 472
Clark, Dana B., Nurseries ... 48
Connor & Chaine, Stage Line ... 98
Cook, R. D., Blacksmith, etc. ... 110
Cooley, W. R., Livery Stable ... 130
Crosby, J. A., Real Estate ... 102
Curtiss, Wilbur, Hot Sulphur Springs ... 126
Dockery & Swanton, Livery Stable ... 108
Drake, F. R., Hotel ... 472
Dunbar, John, Book Store ... 120
Foster, Geo. W., Hotel, etc. ... 514
Froom & Co., A. W., Book Store ... 120
Hammell & Adams, Real Estate ... 140
Harkness, F., Groceries, etc. ... 142
Harriman & Co., Lumber ... 475
Hartman & Co., J., General Merchandise ... 532
Hart & Bro., Thos., Wagon Manufacturers ... 104
Hoffman, J., House and Sign Painting ... 136
Hudson, J. W., Livery Stable ... 438
Johnson, J. A., Publisher ... 56
Kæding & Co., Otto, Saloon ... 243
Kaiser, L. M. & Co., General Merchandise ... 154
Laughlin & Co., H. J., General Merchandise ... 478
Liggett & Porter, hotel ... 480
Middlemiss & Co., Joseph, Real Estate ... 241
Miller, Israel, Watch Maker ... 472
Pettygrove, A. L., Publisher ... 140
Porterfield, J. R., Publisher ... 84
Rich, J. A., Blacksmith ... 128
Russell & Co., Publishers ... 56
Santa Maria Valley Farmers' Union ... 515
Sexton, Joseph, Nurseries ... 170
Smith, N. D. & F., Wharf Proprietors ... 124
Stevens, Chas., Stage Line ... 114
Stokum & Cavalli, Restaurant ... 140
Thomasoni, Antonio, Brewery ... 136
Tilley, S. T., Book Store ... 120
Twist, Frank W., Groceries, etc. ... 472
Van Nader Bros., Livery Stable ... 100

### Santa Barbara Co. Advertisements, Classified.

**Architect.**
Cebrian, J. C. ... 472

**Blacksmiths.**
Bradford, W. J. ... 246
Braun, Robert ... 106
Cook, R. D. ... 110
Rich, J. A. ... 128

**Brewer.**
Thomasoni, Antonio ... 131

## L. L. PAULSON'S DIRECTORIES.

### General Merchandise.
| | PAGE |
|---|---|
| Adam, Wm. L. | 112 |
| Burke, M. F. | 138 |
| Foster, Geo. W. | 514 |
| Hartman, & Co., J. | 529 |
| Kaiser & Co., L. M. | 134 |
| Laughlin & Co., H. J. | 478 |
| Santa Maria Valley Farmers' Union | 515 |
| Twist, Frank W. | 472 |

### Groceries.
| | |
|---|---|
| Harkness, F. | 142 |

### Harness Manufacturer.
| | |
|---|---|
| Abel Henry | 248 |

### Hotels.
| | |
|---|---|
| Bennett, Mrs. A. M. | 460 |
| Burke, M. F. | 138 |
| Cartori, L. | 246 |
| Drake, F. R. | 472 |
| Foster, Geo. W. | 514 |
| Liggott & Porter | 480 |

### Liverymen.
| | |
|---|---|
| Cooley, W. R. | 130 |
| Dockery & Swanton | 108 |
| Hudson, J. W. | 468 |
| Van Nader Bros. | 100 |

### Lumber, etc.
| | |
|---|---|
| Harriman & Co. | 476 |

### Medicinal Springs.
| | |
|---|---|
| Curtiss, Wilbur | 126 |

### Nurseries.
| | |
|---|---|
| Clark, Dana B. | 48 |
| Sexton, Joseph | 470 |

### Painter.
| | |
|---|---|
| Hoffman, J. | 130 |

### Publishers.
| | |
|---|---|
| Broughton, W. W. | 130 |
| Johnson, J. A. | 56 |
| Pettygrove, A. L. | 140 |
| Porterfield, J. R. | 84 |
| Russell & Co. | 56 |

### Real Estate.
| | |
|---|---|
| Crosby, J. A. | 102 |
| Hammell & Adams | 140 |
| Middlemiss & Co., Joseph | 246 |

### Restaurant.
| | |
|---|---|
| Stokum & Cavalli | 140 |

### Saloons.
| | |
|---|---|
| Foster, Geo. W. | 514 |
| Kniding & Co., Otto | 243 |

### Stage Lines.
| | |
|---|---|
| Connor & Chaine | 08 |
| Stevens, Chas. | 114 |

### Stationery.
| | |
|---|---|
| Dunbar, John | 120 |
| Froom & Co., A. W. | 120 |
| Tilloy, S. T. | 120 |

### Stoves and Tinware.
| | |
|---|---|
| Abernethy & Co. | 134 |

### Wagons, etc.
| | |
|---|---|
| Hart & Bro., Thos. | 104 |

### Warehousemen.
| | |
|---|---|
| Smith, N. D. & F. | 124 |

### Watches, etc.
| | |
|---|---|
| Miller, Israel | 472 |

### Wharfingers.
| | |
|---|---|
| Smith, N. D. & F. | 124 |

## Ventura County Advertisers.
| | |
|---|---|
| Ayers, William, Hotel | 184 |
| Bank of Ventura | 186 |
| Bard, Thomas R., Real Estate | 178 |
| Blanchard & Bradley, Millers | 518 |
| Edson, C. J., Watchmaker | 186 |
| Edwards, E. A., House Hardware | 200 |
| Gerberding, A., Commission Merchant | 180 |
| Grant, T. P., Wagonmaker | 230 |
| Hobson, W. D., Hotel | 509 |
| Ireland, E. H., Blacksmithing | 170 |
| Livingston, R. G., General Merchandise | 207 |
| McCoy, D. D., Hotel | 246 |
| McKee, W. S., Boarding House | 198 |
| Pietra, Schiappa Antonio, General Merchandise | 232 |
| Pope, H. S., Furniture Manufacturer | 182 |
| Pope, H. S., Gunsmith | 182 |
| Rhoads & Gorden, Groceries, etc. | 130 |

| | PAGE |
|---|---|
| Riggon, H. N., Saddles and Harness | 200 |
| Salisbury & Co., A. J., Lumber Dealers | 180 |
| Scranton, C. B., Blacksmithing | 170 |
| Shepherd & Sheridan, Publishers | 180 |
| Sudden, James, Wharf Proprietor | 196 |
| Wiggin, C. P., Hotel | 44 |
| Wiggin & Carr, Real Estate | 44 |
| Wiley Brothers, General Merchandise | 130 |

## Ventura County Advertisements, Classified.

### Agricultural Implements.
| | |
|---|---|
| Edwards, E. A. | 200 |

### Bank.
| | |
|---|---|
| Bank of Ventura | 186 |

### Blacksmiths.
| | |
|---|---|
| Grant, T. P. | 230 |
| Ireland, E. H. | 170 |
| Scranton, C. B. | 170 |

### Commission Merchant.
| | |
|---|---|
| Gerberding, A. | 180 |

### Furniture.
| | |
|---|---|
| Pope, H. S. | 182 |

### General Merchandise.
| | |
|---|---|
| Livingston, R. G. | 207 |
| Pietra, Schiappa Antonio | 232 |
| Wiley Brothers | 130 |

### Groceries.
| | |
|---|---|
| Rhoads & Gorden | 136 |

### Gunsmith.
| | |
|---|---|
| Pope, H. S. | 182 |

### Harness, etc.
| | |
|---|---|
| Riggon, H. N. | 200 |

### Hotels.
| | |
|---|---|
| Ayers, Wm. | 184 |
| Hobson, W. D. | 509 |
| McCoy, D. D. | 246 |
| McKee, W. S. | 198 |
| Wiggin, C. P. | 44 |

### Lumber.
| | |
|---|---|
| Salisbury & Co., A J. | 180 |
| Sudden, James | 196 |

### Mills (Flouring).
| | |
|---|---|
| Blanchard & Bradley | 518 |

### Publishers.
| | |
|---|---|
| Shepherd & Sheridan | 180 |

### Real Estate.
| | |
|---|---|
| Bard, Thos. R. | 178 |
| Wiggin & Carr | 44 |

### Stoves and Tinware.
| | |
|---|---|
| Edwards, E. A. | 200 |

### Wagon Manufacturer.
| | |
|---|---|
| Grant, T. P. | 230 |

### Watches, etc.
| | |
|---|---|
| Edson, C. J. | 186 |

### Wharfinger.
| | |
|---|---|
| Sudden, James | 196 |

## Kern County Advertisers.
| | |
|---|---|
| Bodon, Fred., Blacksmith | 122 |
| Chunn, N. C., Livery Stable | 156 |
| Cross, Anson, Livery Stable | 224 |
| Durnal, John A., Saloon | 122 |
| Green & Hirshfeld, General Merchandise | 218 |
| Kern Valley Bank | 224 |
| Taylor & Glonn, Blacksmiths | 122 |

## Kern County Advertisements, Classified.

### Bank.
| | |
|---|---|
| Kern Valley Bank | 224 |

### Blacksmiths.
| | |
|---|---|
| Bodon, Fred. | 122 |
| Taylor & Glonn | 122 |

### General Merchandise.
| | |
|---|---|
| Green & Hirschfeld | 218 |

### Liverymen.
| | |
|---|---|
| Chunn, N. C. | 156 |
| Cross, Anson | 224 |

### Saloon.
| | |
|---|---|
| Durnal, John A. | 122 |

## L. L. PAULSON'S DIRECTORIES.  ix

### San Bernardino County Advertisers.
PAGE.
Allen & Drew, Druggists..........................204
American Cash Store, General Merchandise........270
Bank of San Bernardino..................................304
Bowland & Craig, Druggists........................188
Brocker & Reinhold, Furniture.....................194
Brunn & Sherwin, Hotel.............................526
Cunningham, R. F., General Merchandise..........194
Drew Bros., Stoves and Tinware...................208
Emmons, H. R., Druggist............................194
Foy, John M., Harness Manufacturer...............264
Gould, H., Publisher..................................64
Kenniston & Brazelton, Livery Stable.............206
King & Bro., R. H., Harness, etc.................208
Lawson Bros., Cigar Store..........................208
Lawson Bros., Assay Office.........................208
Linville, W. J., Planing Mill.....................288
Lyon & Rosenthal, General Merchandise...........270
McFarlane & Cochran, Thos., Livery Stable......188
Mee & Co., Blacksmiths.............................445
Meyerstein & Co., Dry Goods, etc.................270
Miguel, L., General Merchandise..................204
Mobray, M. E., Watches.............................194
Perris & Isaac, Publishers........................188
Rolfe, Samuel, Lumber Commission Dealer.........270
Russell, P. S. & W. P., Nurseries.................202
Sayward, W. T., Lands..............................xii
Swift & Kats, Real Estate.........................509
Wise, A. B., Blacksmith.............................204

### San Bernardino Co. Advertisements, Classified.
**Assaying.**
Lawson Bros.........................................208
**Bank.**
Bank of San Bernardino.............................304
**Blacksmiths.**
Mee & Co.............................................445
Wise, A. B............................................204
**Cigars.**
Lawson Bros.........................................208
**Druggists.**
Allen & Drew........................................204
Bowland & Craig....................................188
Emmons, H. R........................................194
**Dry Goods.**
Meyerstein & Co....................................270
**Furniture.**
Brocker & Reinhold.................................194
**General Merchandise.**
American Cash Store................................270
Cunningham, R. F....................................194
Lyon & Rosenthal...................................270
Miguel, L............................................204
**Harness, etc.**
Foy, John M.........................................264
King & Bro., R. H...................................208
**Hotel.**
Brunn & Sherwin....................................526

### Los Angeles County Advertisers.
Bacon, F. P., Ranch owner..........................132
Bassett, J. M., Publisher..........................362
Bonestool, C. A., Stationery.........between 368 and 369
Brooks, W. H. J., Examiner of Titles..............417
Burton, C. C., Hair Dresser.........................532
Cabot, C., Real Estate.............................378
Childs, M. W., Stoves, etc..........................118
Farmers and Merchants Bank.........................334
Forst, Anton, Hotel, Feed Stable, etc.............130
Foy, S. C., Harness Manufacturer..................374
Freeman, D., Lands..................................525
Garey, Thomas A., Nurseries........................358
Hayward, D. C., Nurseries..........................404
Jones, Norman C., Real Estate......................458
Kittredge, W., Hotel................................130
Kraszynski, Andrew J...............................243
Liever, John, Gunsmith..............................408
Macy, Wilson & Co., Livery Stable.................305
McRae Bros., Hotel..................................110
Morgan & Monroe, Hotel..............................326
Olden, Wm. R., Real Estate.........................322
Page & Gravel, Carriage and Wagon Manufact'rs... 42

PAGE.
Shorb, J. De Barth., Real Estate..................378
Slotterbek, Henry, Gunsmith.......................408
Spurgeon Bros., Dry Goods..........................408
Stoneman, Gen. Geo., Vintner......................521
Strong, Rev. Robert, Real Estate..................408
Temple & Workman, Bankers.........................330
Temple, F. P. F., Real Estate.....................525
Trudel, J. B., Salt Manufacturer..................354
Vignos, J. M., Nurseries...........................370
Wallace, J. C., Nurseries..........................366
Westminster Co-operative Store, General Mdse....412
Wilson, B. D. & Co., Real Estate..................378
Woodroofe, E., Blacksmith..........................156

### Los Angeles Co. Advertisements, Classified.
**Bank.**
Commercial Bank of San Diego......................462
**Blacksmiths.**
Rostert, P..........................................507
Wescott & Hatloberg................................134
**Carriage Manufacturer.**
Stevens, J..........................................507
**Hotels.**
Craigin, S. W........................................54
Levy, S.............................................142
McKean, A. B........................................120
**Liverymen.**
Bailey & Redman....................................122
Hinton, Gallagher & Co.............................116
**Planing Mill.**
San Diego Mill Co..................................134
**Wagons.**
Rostert, P..........................................507
**Banks.**
Farmers' & Merchants'..............................334
Temple & Workman...................................330
**Barber.**
Burton, C. C........................................532
**Blacksmith.**
Woodroofe, E.......................................156
**Carriage Manufacturers.**
Page & Gravel....................................... 42
**Dry Goods, etc.**
Spurgeon Bros......................................408
**Examiner of Titles.**
Brooks, W. H. J....................................417
**Feed Stable.**
Forst, Anton.......................................130
**General Merchandise.**
Westminster Co-operative Store....................412
**Gunsmiths.**
Liever, John........................................408
Slotterbek, Henry..................................408
**Harness, etc.**
Foy, S. C...........................................374
**Hotels.**
Forst, Anton.......................................130
Kittredge, W.......................................130
Krazynski, Andrew J................................243
McRae Bros.........................................110
Morgan & Monroe....................................326
**Liverymen.**
Macy, Wilson & Co..................................305
**Nurseries.**
Garey, Thos. A.....................................358
Hayward, D. C......................................404
Vignos, J. M.......................................370
Wallace, J. C......................................366
**Publisher.**
Bassett, J. M......................................362
**Real Estate.**
Bacon, F. P........................................132
Cabot, C............................................378
Freeman, D.........................................525
Jones, Norman C....................................458
Olden, Wm. R.......................................322
Shorb, J. DeBarth..................................378
Strong, Rev. Robert................................408
Temple, F. P. F....................................525
Wilson, B. D. & Co.................................378
**Salt Manufacturer.**
Trudel, J. B.......................................354

L. L. PAULSON'S DIRECTORIES.

**Stationery.** PAGE.
Bonesteel & Co., C. A....................between 368 and 360
    **Stoves and Tinware.**
Childs, M. W.....................................................118
    **Vintner.**
Stoneman, Gen. Geo..........................................521
    **Wagons.**
Page & Gravel..................................................... 42

---

### San Diego County Advertisers.

Bailey & Redman, Livery Stable......................122
Commercial Bank of San Diego........................492
Craigue, S. W., Hotel........................................ 54
Hinton, Gallagher & Co., Livery Stable............116
Levy, S., Hotel..................................................142
McKean, A. B., Hotel........................................120
Rostert, P., Blacksmith and Wagonmaker........507
San Diego Mill Co.............................................134
Stevens, J., Carriage Manufacturer..................507
Wescott & Hatleberg, Blacksmiths...................134

**San Diego Co. Advertisements, Classified.**
PAGE.
    **Liverymen.**
Kenniston & Brazelton.....................................206
McFarlane & Cochran, Thos............................188
    **Lumber.**
Rolfe, Samuel...................................................270
    **Nurseries.**
Russell, P. S. & W. P........................................202
    **Planing Mills.**
Linville, W. J....................................................288
    **Publishers.**
Gould, H........................................................... 64
Perris & Isaac...................................................188
    **Real Estate.**
Sayward, W. T.................................................. xii
Swift & Katz.....................................................500
    **Stoves and Tinware.**
Drew Bros........................................................208
    **Watches, etc.**
Mobray, M. E...................................................194

---

WM. BARTLING.      HENRY KIMBALL.

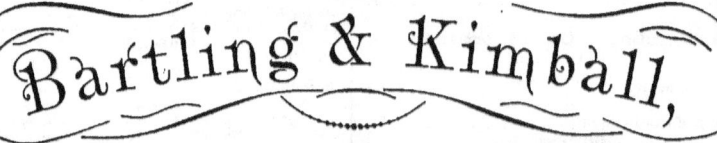

## BOOK-BINDERS, PAPER RULERS

—AND—

Blank-Book Manufacturers,

### 505 CLAY STREET, S. W. CORNER SANSOME,

SAN FRANCISCO.

*Orders from the Country, by Mail or Express, promptly attended to.*

EDWARD BOSQUI. F. M. SPAULDING.

# Wholesale Paper & Twine Warehouse.

## F. M. SPAULDING & CO.

### 411, 413, 415 SANSOME ST.,

Cor. Commercial, San Francisco, Cal.

HAVE CONSTANTLY IN STOCK A LARGE VARIETY OF ALL KINDS AND QUALITIES OF PAPERS AND TWINES.

#### SOLE AGENTS FOR

### Crane's Celebrated Bank and Ledger Paper,

ON THE PACIFIC COAST.

**BOND OR BANK NOTE PAPER, WHITE AND TINTED.**

FLAT PAPER, different Sizes and Grades.
BOOK,      "         "         "         "         "
NEWS,      "         "         "         "         "
POSTER,    "         "         "         "         "
MANILLA, Etc., Etc.             "         "         "

Card-Board, Straw-Board, Leather-Board, Etc.

#### OUR TWINE DEPARTMENT

Will be kept supplied with a full assortment of FLAX, HEMP, LINEN, COTTON and PAPER TWINES.

Prompt and courteous attention to customers, and moderate prices for goods. Consumers of above-named articles are respectfully invited to call and examine our stock before purchasing elsewhere.

# AUTOMATIC PUMPS!

## SOMETHING ENTIRELY NEW!

Water raised to any height and distance by compressed air. Just what every house needs, which is situated outside of cities, where they have not the convenience of running water. Ample supply of water from the well for bath-room, hot and cold-water faucets, hose for the lawn, cattle-yard, etc. The power is an 8 or 10-foot windmill. The whole machine durable; not liable to get out of order. When properly set, runs without any attention. It simply needs oiling once a month. The wind-wheel can be placed any distance from the well or spring, in order to get a good exposure to the wind, if necessary.

CALL ON OR ADDRESS,

## JOSEPH E. HOLLOWAY,

31 BEALE STREET, S. F., where a Machine can be seen in Operation.

## A GENERAL DESCRIPTION

OF

# SAN LUIS OBISPO CO.

SAN LUIS OBISPO COUNTY is bounded on the North by Monterey County; on the South by the counties of Santa Barbara and Ventura; on the East by Kern County, and on the West by the Pacific Ocean. It has an extreme length from North to South of about seventy miles, with an average width of about sixty, giving a total area of 4,200 square miles, or 2,688,000 acres. In the vicinity of 500,000 acres are held by Spanish grants, the residue, more than 2,000,000, being government land, subject to pre-emption under existing laws, except such portions as may be in the possession of actual settlers.

The Santa Lucia range bisects the county, passing through it from North to South, making two unequal divisions, the one to the Eastward being by far the greatest, embracing nearly two-thirds of the entire area of the county. This section possesses a considerable growth of white oak, with some little pine and live oak. It is only adapted for stock-raising, its nutritious grasses, the spontaneous product of its virgin soil, rendering it very valuable for that purpose. To the Westward of the Santa Lucia range lies the smaller division, occupying the slope of the Santa Lucia and the intermediate space, sweeping away to the sea. This is the agricultural portion of the county, and here also is that large dairying interest, which has obtained for San Luis Obispo the *soubriquet* of the "cow county." It also enjoys the reputation of being the best watered portion of the State. Streams approach the valleys and lower lands from every possible spot of hill and mountain, and from mere silver threads broaden into rivulets moving along to a music as of silver bells; then swelling into mountain streams, they rush with the impetuosity of a miniature torrent, until, tumbling into the plain or valley below, with less haste and the more measured dignity of a steady-going creek, they wend their devious way to mingle with the waters of the "vasty deep."

San Luis Obispo County was organized in 1850. The assessed valuation of property in 1874 amounted to $4,505,504, and the population aggregated 9,000. The climate is very mild, there being but a slight thermometical variation throughout the year, vegetables of nearly all descriptions being successfully grown in the open air during the entire twelvemonth. There are no rapid changes of temperature, the atmosphere is perfect in its purity, and its locale is much sought as possessing all the requisites of a sanitarium. The soil is a black vegetable loam, with an underlying stratum of clay. Wheat, barley, oats, beans, corn, potatoes, and all temperate climate fruits are produced, the soil, from its exceeding richness, giving large returns to even the indifferent cultivator, such is the perfect adaptability of the climate, and so thoroughly does nature perform the work of irrigation. Near the base of the mountain range, the semi-tropical fruits are successfully cultivated. The moist lands contiguous to the creeks produce as fine sugar beets as are raised in the State.

The principal streams, by their number, attest the perfection and completeness of the natural irrigation system of this county. They are the Salinas, San Luis Obispo, Arroyo Grande, San Luis Soto, Chorro, Old Creek, Morro, Villa Creek, Torro, Santa Rosa Creek, La Cruz, San Simeon Creek, Pico Creek, Laguna Creek, San Caspojoro Creek, Suey Creek, Berros Creek, Corral de Piedra Creek, Nipomo Creek, Estrella Creek, Nacimiento Creek, and the Santa Margarita. These are mostly small creeks, taking their names from towns which they pass in their flow, or from the valleys through which they ripple, though some are very considerable streams. The most important of these creeks, however, would lend more dignity to the name of river than do some who possess it; nor would the misnomer be so glaring as in the case of many rivers in adjacent counties, whose beds are never moistened except in carrying off the surplus after the winter's rains, and which, ere summer grows old, absolutely die of thirst.

The principal valleys of this county are the San Luis Obispo, Salinas, Santa Marguerita, Arroyo Grande, Osos, Laguna, Chorro, San Jose, Santa Rosa, Nipomo, Huasna, Cholama and Estrella.

The valley of San Luis Obispo, in which is situated the mission giving to the county and town their name, extends in a direction nearly Northwest and Southeast from Estero Bay to the Arroyo Grande; a distance of nearly twenty miles, having a width varying from three to five miles. The greater portion of this valley is good agricultural land. The Cañadas de los Osas and de las Piedras branch from this valley. The San Luis Obispo Creek, which flows through the greater portion of it, empties into the bay below the port of San Luis Obispo.

The Salinas Valley is quite an extensive agricultural district. It is irrigated by the Salinas River, which, having its source among the peaks of the Santa Lucia Mountains, lying toward the Southeast, flows for a distance of twenty-five or thirty miles through this valley, just previous to entering the county of Monterey. It has considerable good agricultural land. Many small arable valleys branch from this to the East and West.

The valley of Santa Marguerita is a broad plateau on the Northeastern side of the Santa Lucia Mountains, some twenty miles to the Northeast of San Luis Obispo. It has an elevation of some 1,200 feet above the sea, and has a much heavier growth of timber than the lower valleys, oak, pine, manzanita and other trees, peculiar to the mountain regions of the State, growing in perfection; evidencing that the air, at this elevation, contains far more moisture than in the lower districts. A branch of the Salinas River flows through this valley.

The Arroyo Grande Valley is watered by a creek of the same name. It has a considerable area, is both level and rolling, and is devoted to agricultural and stock-grazing purposes, the hills being rich with verdure, affording abundant pasturage for thousands of sheep and cattle. The agricultural lands occupy the lower levels, lying immediately along the banks of the creek.

The Osos and Laguna valleys run parallel with the Coast. The Laguna is a continuation of the Osos, they being separated only by a line of peaks almost equi-distant. The Laguna and a portion of the Corral de Piedra lying intermediate between the town and port, are termed plains, from assuming, as they do, their proportions.

The Santa Rosa is said to be the most picturesque and fertile valley in the county. It has a length of about twelve miles; is watered by the Santa Rosa Creek, which flows nearly through its centre. Corn is the principal product of the valley, which from the town of Cambria, its settlement, in the western portion of the valley to the mountain foot upon the East, is almost one continuous farm. Flowers have a spontaneous growth here, and most excellent fruits are raised.

Huasna Valley is some eight or nine miles in length by a width ranging from one-half to three-quarters of a mile. A dense growth of oak forms a living hedge upon either side for its entire length. The soil is very rich. Only a small portion of the valley has been under cultivation, it having been used for many years exclusively for the purpose of stock-grazing, and even now affords pasturage to innumerable sheep, cattle and horses. It is surrounded by lofty mountains. A small stream, bearing the same name as the valley, furnishes the water supply. Branching from the main valley are many of smaller area, bearing the same name as the main valley. The Flora here is wonderfully beautiful and abundant. It dots the hillsides with gold, crimson and azure, and sprinkles the verdure of the lower plain with the variegated hues of a fairy landscape.

Cholama Valley is twenty-five miles in length, with a width of from four to five miles. The soil is a light sandy loam. Stock-raising is the principal resource, all the mountain and

foot-hill lands being devoted to this industry. Considerable cottonwood and oak is scattered throughout its area, and a small quantity of hay is produced.
The valley of Estrella is also devoted principally to the raising of stock, sheep having the preference. The soil is a sandy loam. The valley has a length of seventy-five miles, with an average width of two. The mountains and hills furnish an abundance of pasturage. Cottonwood and oak trees abound in the valley, and hay is raised to some extent. The Salinas River flows through it, furnishing an abundance of water. Two mountains ranges lie between it and the coast, some twenty-three miles distant. - No fogs visit the valley. The atmosphere is pure and the climate conducive to good health. The thermometer indicates about 78° average.
San Luis Obispo County has twenty-four school districts, with a school census aggregating above 1,600. Agriculture and the interest of stock-raising exist side by side, and we regret our utter inability to obtain accurate statistics which would allow of an intelligent comparison between the two. In this county, in 1867, only 12,000 acres were under cultivation.

## LANDS.

Much land is held for sale in the various parts of the county, on most reasonable terms. The Steele Bros. are offering 40,000 acres, in tracts of any size. This land is of various grades, comprising every variety of soil, from the best hill grazing to the richest bottom lands, suitable for producing all kinds of grain, vegetables, hops, sugar beets, tobacco and fruits. It includes improved farms, dairy ranches, and unimproved lands, and is susceptible of irrigation at but slight expense, much of it being magnificently watered by never-failing brooks, abounding in trout, small lakes and springs. Live oak, willow and cottonwood timber is abundant. This property is situated five miles South of San Luis Obispo, on the Santa Barbara Stage Road, and nine miles from San Luis Obispo Landing, one of the best harbors upon the coast, possessing as good shipping accommodations as any port between San Francisco and San Diego. The improved lands and dairy farms will be sold fully stocked and equipped, if preferred.

Messrs. Dana Bros. are holding for sale 37,000 acres of choice land, situated twenty-four miles South of the town of San Luis Obispo. The soil of more than one-half of this large tract is black adobe, the remainder being a sandy loam, suitable for the production of cereals, potatoes, beans, and all kinds of vegetables. It is well irrigated by running streams, which never fail; also by springs. On that portion of the tract which has a sandy soil, water can be obtained by digging to a depth of from fifteen to twenty feet. A large lagoon is also on the property. These lands have been chiefly used for stock-grazing, there being at present on the property flocks aggregating 16,000 sheep, 2,500 head of cattle, and 100 horses. During the dryest year the best of crops can be produced. Any portion of this land can be purchased on reasonable terms, at from $20 to $100 per acre; 17,000 acres are valley land, 17,300 acres hill or grazing land, with 3,000 acres of timber.

There is a large public domain in San Luis Obispo County, comprising lands of every description, subject to pre-emption.

## THE DAIRY INTEREST

Of San Luis Obispo is very large, no county in the State being better adapted for this pursuit. The largest dairy interests are in the vicinity of Cambria, and distributed along the coast nearly the entire length of the county. Dairies in the neighborhood of Cambria have produced, in one season, 200 ℔s. of butter on an average for each cow. The demand for cheese manufactured here is steady, much of it going to the Eastern States, China and Mexico.

The inducements offered by this county to persons wishing to engage in this industry, are manifold. Pasturage is abundant throughout the year, and is obtainable at low rates and on easy terms, while cows can be leased at from $10 to $12 per annum. Profits are large, butter scarcely ever commanding less than 30c. per ℔., the range being from 25c. to 75c. per ℔.

San Luis Obispo County has four flour mills, with an aggregate capacity of 30,000 barrels per annum.

The Arroyo Grande Mills are located on the Arroyo Grande Creek, from which they derive their power, three miles from the town of that name, and twelve miles South of San Luis

Obispo. They are owned by Messrs. Branch Bros.; manufacture a very superior article of flour, and have a capacity of thirty barrels per day. Corn-meal, middlings and ground feed are also among the manufactures of this mill, which has, beside, an extensive grist trade among the farmers of the surrounding country. The proprietors intend adding to the efficiency of their operations soon, by the introduction of improved machinery, and also propose erecting extensive warehouses for the storage of grain.

The Chorro Mill, owned and conducted by Messrs. Pollard & James, are located three miles distant from San Luis Obispo, on Chorro Creek. The creek furnishes a fine motive power, the fall being 190 feet. The wheel in use is a turbine. Twenty-five barrels per day are ground, the article comparing favorably in quality with any brand made upon the coast.

Two miles East from San Luis Obispo is another water-power mill, owned by Mr. C. Sumner; while one and one-half miles North from Cambria is the large steam mill of Messrs. Leffingwell & Sons.

## MINERAL RESOURCES.

San Luis Obispo County numbers among its mineral resources neither gold nor silver mines, though it enjoys the reputation of possessing the richest quicksilver deposits on the Pacific Coast.

The Sunderland Quicksilver Mining Co., the mine being better known as the Santa Cruz, is located Northeast from Cambria eighteen miles. It was incorporated September 14th, 1874, under its present name, the capital stock being $10,000,000, divided into 100,000 shares. This company owns and is operating upon 102 acres of land, the result of the consolodization of the "Santa Cruz," 2,200 feet; "San Lorenzo," 2,000 feet; "European," 1,500 feet; "Arago," 1,500 feet, and "Cuvier," 1,000. Considerable work has been done in the mine, with very satisfactory results. Four tunnels penetrate the hill. The ledge shows croppings for over 3,000 feet in length, and, in one place, over 400 feet wide. All of the tunnels are being worked in ore assaying from one-quarter to two per cent. The ore is reduced in a very perfect Riotte & Luckhardt Furnace, with a capacity of twenty tons per diem; the walls are built of dressed freestone, lined within with fire-brick; attached are three large iron condensers. A twelve-horse power engine runs the blower connected with the furnace. The fire is under perfect control, and the fumes are conveyed to the condensers without any loss. A narrow-gauge road, 1240 feet in length, connects the mine with the furnace, for the transportation of the ore. The supply of wood and water is convenient and inexhaustible, water being conducted to the tank which supplies the furnace through 6,000 feet of pipe.

The Oceanic Mine is situated in the Santa Rosa Valley, some seven miles from the ocean, and about five miles from the village of Cambria. The mine has an elevation of 1,000 feet above the level of the ocean. The ledge lies East and West, varying from a perpendicular to an incline of about fifteen degrees, dipping toward the North. The vein matter is from twelve to twenty feet wide. The cinnabar obtained here reduces fourteen per cent. of quicksilver per ton, having an average marketable value of $150 to the ton. The reduction furnace has a capacity of twenty tons per diem. The Oceanic is an incorporated company, with a capital of $6,000,000, divided into 60,000 shares. Many of the stock-holders are well known business men of San Francisco. Three mines were engulphed in the formation of this, viz.: the "Sulphur Spring," "Bristol and Morse," and the "Second."

The Mahoney Mine is within one mile of the Sunderland. It has been quite well prospected, and has grown into high favor. It has but a small furnace, with the capacity of four tons per day. Many other mines and prospects exist throughout the county, but all of less importance than the ones noticed. Among them are the "Keystone" and "Quien Sabe;" the latter was recently bonded for a large amount, and promises to develop into a very rich property. It is nine miles North of Cambria.

## ASPHALTUM.

On the South fork of the Arroyo Grande Creek, on a ranch of 4,500 acres, owned by Mr. F. Branch, is a fine asphaltum bed, covering an area of full an half mile. It has not been sufficiently worked to ascertain its depth. Tar springs are numerous throughout this bed, two of the largest having a diameter of from twenty to thirty feet, with an unascertainable depth. These have at times acted as a capital bear trap, and have also overwhelmed many more domestic animals, while in search of water. From one of the tar springs in this locality issues a gas with a hissing noise, as of steam escaping from a small vent. On the application of a match it burns readily, though having but slight illuminating power. An abandoned oil well is in this vicinity, the abandonment being due to a breakage of the tools, or their sticking in some mud vein, and the inability of the operators to extract them. A very good show of heavy oil is upon the water at the well top. The asphaltum found here is being taken to San Luis Obispo for the various uses to which it is adapted. The mine has not been worked to any great extent, as the Steele Bros. have one much nearer town. Another bed is in a deep canyon about two miles from that owned by Mr Branch, not so extensive, but producing a better quality of this product.

In the Southern part of the county is an extensive ledge of alabaster, of superior quality, for the working of which preparations have been made.

This county has three mineral springs, which have become quite celebrated as places of pleasure resort, and for the medicinal benefit, too, derivable from the waters.

Newsom's White Sulphur Springs are located fourteen miles South from San Luis Obispo, twelve miles from the steamer landing, and two miles from the Santa Barbara stage station, Arroyo Grande. The springs are situated in a mountain canyon about 600 feet in width. The locality is abundant in heavy undergrowth. The principal spring throws off a sufficient quantity of water to irrigate land at the distance of a mile below. Its temperature is 100° fahrenheit. It holds in solution sulphur, iron and magnesia. Its application is both external and internal, a cure being rapid and certain in cases of paralysis, rheumatism, billiousness, debility, and all diseases of the nerves and skin. At a distance of thirty feet is a spring of soft cold water; about 100 yards further, two of cold water impregnated with iron, one containing sulphur, and one asphaltum. The mean temperature in this little mountain valley is about 65°. Fish and game abound. The mountain sides are heavily wooded with live oak of dense growth, whose foliage is perrennial.

An hotel will soon be completed large enough to entertain, in connection with the cottages, one hundred guests, with excellent camping facilities, unlimited in extent. Mr. Newsom proposes to bring from the Arroyo Grande Creek, by means of a race, sufficient water to run a 20-horse power engine all the year. This water-power he offers to anyone who will establish a manufacturing interest, he taking the value of land and water interest in stock of the institution.

The Paso Robles Hot Springs are situated in an oak grove, thirty miles East of San Luis Obispo. Neither pains nor expense have been spared to render the springs an attractive and comfortable resort. Thousands of people visit these springs from all portions of the State and United States. Messrs. Blackburn & James are the proprietors.

The Pecho Warm Springs are situated fifteen miles Northwest from San Luis Obispo, and two from the coast, in a deep canyon. The temperature of the water is 96°; its properties being about the same as those of Newsom's White Sulphur Springs. The locality has been but little improved, arising from the difficulty experienced in obtaining a title to the property, they being located on a Spanish grant.

The principal towns of the county are: San Luis Obispo, Morro, Cambria, Cambria Landing, Cayucos, San Simeon, Old Creek, Arroyo Grande, Avila, San Marcos and San Miguel.

## SAN LUIS OBISPO,

The county seat, and principal town of the county, occupies the grounds of the old mission, founded by the monks of the order of St. Francis, September 1st, 1772. From it both town and county derive their name. The mission was laid out and built in the usual form of a quadrangle; the work being performed by Indians, rude and unskilled, to be sure, but directed and supplemented by the accomplished Fathers. The material used was such as the immediate neighborhood afforded, and if both labor and material were crude, the one was well adapted for service, the other well and honestly performed, as the present existence of the buildings in a well preserved state fully attest, after the wear and tear of more than a century. The mission had a season of almost unexampled prosperity.  Its flocks and herds roamed over miles upon miles of verdant pasturage; improvement, religious, educational and financial, moved hand in hand to what bade fair to be a peaceful, happy future of pastoral quiet, comfort and independence.  The soil was tilled to the extent rendered necessary by home consumption.  Orchards and vineyards were planted, and everything was done to administer to the welfare of the mission, which persistent toil, guided by energy and intelligence could do.  But although the missions, coeval with this, did for a term of years labor sedulously for the religious advancement and civilization of the savage aborigines of the land, and although the system has many profound admirers, it must be admitted that their energies as evangelists had suffered a severe diminution previous to the blow aimed at the prosperity of the missions by the Mexican Congress of 1826.  After the settlement of the country by the missionaries, sixty years of undisturbed quiet offered an opportunity in which to demonstrate the efficiency of their schemes for the civilization of the native.  Their increasing wealth rendered them unfit for their previous missionary labors, and the moral, religious and physical condition of the Indian became a matter of less consideration with them than the cultivation of their boundless acres, and the increase of their vast flocks and herds. Their acession to wealth was by no gradual progression.  Deriving their labor from the natives who received no largess but the food and clothing their own labor produced, with the virgin pasturage of the limitless hills for their flocks and herds, in a climate so tempered, even to the shorn lamb, as but to develop rapid physical growth, how could they do otherwise than wax thrifty and rich, without the lapse of years, usually necessary for such a metamorphosis?

After founding twenty-one missions along the coast, following its configuration on their Northward journey, they appear to have used no exertions in behalf of the Indians of the interior. That they were left to their fate is by no means doubtful, as proof is wanting that any effort was ever made to explore the interior, either to learn whether the country was inhabitable, or the inhabitant worthy of being included in those promises which they were sent forth to proclaim in the name of God.  The last mission was founded in 1823, ten years previous to the promulgation of secularization by the Mexican Congress.  A complete chain of missions stretched from San Diego to San Francisco, the boundaries of whose lands interlocking, as effectually excluded the settler, as though the entire coast were the fortified wall of a vast principality.  The more so since their decisions were absolute, they being the only authority, temporal or spiritual, of which the land could boast.

From 1800 to 1822, the style of living and the revenues of these lords of the missions was in a measure regal; their church services had degenerated into a mere religious formality; and disguised beneath their priestly robes was the substantial farmer, the prosperous produce speculator, and the opulent stock-raiser.

In 1831, Indians to the number of 18,683 were domesticated at the various missions.

Although this system had given evidences of decay many years previous, its doom was irrevocably sealed by the overthrow of the Spanish dominion in Mexico, in 1822.  The precautions taken by the Fathers tending to prevent the settlement of the territory by white emigrants, was a fatal injury to their cause, leaving them totally bereft of all means of defense, under the changing order of things, and the introduction of a new government; as in the newly framed constitution of the Mexican Republic, population was the basis upon which rested representation, and the missions aggregating but a few white inhabitants, Upper California was denied representation as a State, and declared a territory with a representative in Congress, but even he denied the privilege of a vote.  The law enacted by the Mexican Congress of 1826, deprived the Fathers of both their lands and the labor of the Indians, cut off their salaries, and appropriated the " Pious Fund " to the uses of the Republic.

Then the errors of the system became fully apparent.  The Fathers had simply upheld the Indian, without teaching him to walk alone; they had maintained him in a condition of independence, without showing him how to attain or maintain the position by his own undirected efforts. As a result, when deprived of the guidance to which they had so long been accustomed, they became an enemy, more to be apprehended by the few white settlers, than the savage hordes of the interior, and the Mexican Congress was induced, within two years from the enaction of the law regarding the missions, to repeal that portion relating to the natives, and they were allowed to return to the missions. Their labor, however, was not as efficient as formerly, and they were controlled with far more difficulty.

In the year 1833, a law was enacted by Congress for the entire abolition of the missions, with the removal of the missionaries, and a division of the lands and cattle among the settlers and natives. The law was repealed before it could be carried into effect, by Santa Ana, who succeeeded to power through the aid of the church party. The succeeding years, up to 1840, when Congress assumed control of the missions, was a stormy, trying period for the Fathers. Mexico was distracted by internal political broils and convulsions, and the Fathers were stripped of their privileges one after another by the various parties succeeding to the government control. In 1845, the remaining missions were sold at auction to the highest bidder.

In the year 1825, the mission of San Luis Obispo had 87,000 cattle, 2,000 tame horses, 3,500 mares, 3,700 mules, and 72,000 sheep. One of the Fathers of the mission carried with him, in 1828, when he left for Spain, $100,000.

In reviewing the history of this period we cannot but admire the zeal which led these Fathers to so meritorious an undertaking in a new and unexplored country, where they had every reason to expect but a succession of hardships and a period of deprivation extending probably over a long term of years. We cannot but glorify them for the unexampled courage and determination with which they leveled every obstacle which barred their progress, and the firmness with which they marched on to a glorious and complete victory. Yet must we deplore the after usurpation of high, noble resolves, and pure, worthy motives, by so mean a successor as love of wealth, and lust for power.

The town of San Luis Obispo occupies a nook at one extremity of the valley of the same name, nine miles from the coast, and on the stage road leading from the terminus of the S. P. R. R. through the coast counties to Los Angeles. It was incorporated some five years since, the corporate limits including an area of four square miles. Its suburbs are fast being lost in the improvements which are being rapidly carried forward. Its population numbers in the vicinity of 2,000. Two streams pass through it, constantly supplied by the numerous springs and rivulets flowing down from the Santa Lucia Range. One, the Stenner Creek, flows in from the North, through the fertile fields of the Chorro Valley, and in the lower portion of the town forms a coalition with San Luis Creek, which rises near the Summit of the Santa Marguerita Pass, and flows immediately through the town, touching the boundary of the old mission garden, now the site of beautiful and tasteful residences. The thermometer indicates an average of 65° fahrenheit.

There are three private and three public schools in the town, with an aggregate attendance of about five hundred pupils. Teachers are carefully selected, rigidly examined, and adequately recompensed.

The town has four hotels and six livery stables, and commands a large trade from both directions upon the coast, and for at least one hundred miles toward the interior. A large amount of capital is invested in merchandising, and there are quite a number of wealthy and responsible mercantile houses.

The San Luis Obispo Bank is a very prosperous institution, with a paid-up cash capital of $200,000. It has been paying monthly dividends of one and one-half per cent.

Water Works, very creditable to the young city, have been erected at a cost of $40,000. The reservoir is built of stone, and is situated upon a sidehill, 160 feet above the town, giving a pressure which would enable it to render effective service during a conflagration. The supply is derived from a branch of San Luis Creek, and is conveyed in an open flume for two miles, around the side of a neighboring mountain, before reaching the reservoir. The distributing pipes, taking the water from the reservoir, have a diameter of eleven inches. The mains, laid through the streets, are seven inches in diameter, with which the smaller supply pipes connect. There are now upwards of five miles of street mains, to which the company is still constantly adding. The capacity of the works will allow of the distribution of 600,000 gallons daily.

Quite a number of handsome churches assist in beautifying the town. The Methodist, Methodist Episcopal, Episcopal and Catholic denominations have church edifices, which are both neat in appearance and comfortable in their interior arrangement. The observance of the Sabbath is very general in this community. To the stranger who strolls along the streets upon this day, the fact is very apparent, and the contrast offered between it and the average California town is very marked.

The Masonic fraternity, also the Odd Fellows, have lodges here, as well as the Good Templars, and a recently organized lodge of Knights of Pythias. Two Literary Clubs hold weekly sessions, and a well organized Grange meets fortnightly.

In some portions of the town, those most improved, the streets are well shaded. The character of the private residences has changed for the better during a year or two past, and many fine buildings grace the surroundings. All those now in process of erection are vastly superior to the ones erected in times past. Door yards are beautified, too, by flowers of all descriptions, gladdening the senses with their brilliancy of coloring, and the fragrance of their delicious perfumes.

The rapid growth of this town has necessitated, from time to time, the addition of more territory. The old mission garden was first used to supply this need, some two years since, and was divided into lots which were quickly sold.

The Phillips Addition of fifty acres is situated about 900 yards East of the Court House. The tract is somewhat elevated in position, is sheltered from the coast winds, and commands a fine view of the surrounding country. Palm street cuts through the entire tract. Water from the city water works will be supplied to every portion of the ground. The situation as a site for residences could not be better chosen. Mr. Phillips has erected here, as his private dwelling, one of the finest buildings, of that class, in the town. The lots are 50x150 feet. Through this tract will be opened an avenue 100 feet in width.

One mile from the business center is the Beebe and Phillips Addition of 400 acres, subdivided into five and ten-acre lots.

West from the Court House, three-quarters of a mile, is the Laguna Tract, comprising 1,200 acres. The soil of this tract is a vegetable loam, of exceeding richness, suitable for the most diverse cultivation. The lots each include ten acres.

The Coast Line Stage arrives and departs daily, North and South. Coaches run between the town and harbor, which is nine miles distant. The stage between San Luis Obispo and Cambria, by way of Morro, Old Creek and Cayucos, runs three times per week, each way.

The Telegraph Line from San Francisco to Santa Barbara, is laid by way of San Luis Obispo, and grants unreserved and rapid communication with all portions of the land. An independent line connects the town with the harbor.

San Luis Obispo has one paper, the weekly *Tribune*.

## MORRO

Is situated on the Eastern shore of a bay of the same name, on a nearly level table land of light, sandy soil, with a gradual slope to the West and South. Good soft water can be obtained by sinking wells to a moderate depth. There is a perfect absence of trees of natural growth, but those of any species or variety, transplanted, become thrifty growers in this rich soil, as is evidenced by the fine appearance of those which, from time to time, have been planted by the resident townspeople. The soil, though light, has not yet failed to return fair crops, the crop of 1873 being better than usual, and excelling the crops of many portions of the county, possessing heavier soil. Grain of all kinds, all descriptions of fruits, and potatoes, are cultivated to advantage.

The town site was laid out in 1870, but owing to a lack of capital, there has not been as much growth or improvement as those most interested in the place could wish.

The situation of the town is one of rare beauty. A perfect view of the ocean is obtained for fifteen miles Northwest and Southwest, vessels being apparent while yet a long distance out at sea. The chief attraction is the grand old rock, from which the early Spanish settlers named the bay, and from which also the town is named. Morro Rock lies midway in the entrance to Morro Bay, dividing the channel. It lifts up an area of barren rock, equal to about eighty acres, 600 feet above the level of the surrounding waters. It forms a very prominent land mark. Vessels of light draft have no difficulty in entering Morro Bay, where they can discharge their freights at a wharf, completely protected from damage by the elements. The bay is the port of entry for a prosperous back country, and it is not at all unreasonable to anticipate for Morro a bustling future. It has a wharf, warehouse, two stores, hotel, and a population of about 100.

## CAMBRIA,

Thirty-two miles North of San Luis Obispo, is situated in Santa Rosa Valley. It is a town settled and inhabited by Americans. The adobe structure has no existence here. A school building, of generous proportions, crowns one of the loftiest eminences in the town. The school session is maintained through about eight months in the year. A grove of sugar pine of natural growth occupies the grounds surrounding the school. The region of country contiguous to Cambria is very irregular, being uneven, and broken by numerous hills. Its resources are stock-raising and dairying.

The town contains two hotels, several dry goods and grocery stores, drug stores, saloons, butcher shop, blacksmith and harness shop, and one livery stable. It numbers among its population 300 inhabitants. There are two sawmills in this vicinity, one located in town, the other distant one and one-half miles North. A scarcity of choice timber, close at hand, has materially lessened their operations.

CAMBRIA LANDING is two miles West from the town. A commodious warehouse and substantial wharf have been constructed here, allowing even large vessels to lie alongside, at all stages of the tide. This port will eventually receive a large amount of freight, the product of the mines working in the vicinity, as well as the agricultural production of a large circuit.

## CAYUCOS,

Of which Old Creek is the post office, is situated in the Northeastern bight of Estero Bay, twenty-two miles Southwest from Paso Robles Hot Springs, and fourteen miles East from Cambria. The landing was located in 1869, by James Cass, who still resides there. The principal resource of the place is dairying. The dairy product shipped during the month of February, 1875, amounted to 35,000 lbs. The soil of the locality is adobe. From Point Buchon to Point Pinos, near Cambria, the hill side on the shore of Estero Bay which faces the South, is said to be among the most fertile land in the county. The dairying is conducted principally by Swiss. A large amount of cheese is manufactured here. This is a school district, although a very young settlement. The town has been laid out and many lots staked off on the Moro y Cayucos Rancho. Mr. Cass has erected warehouses, suitable for the storage of grain, and has perfected arrangements with Messrs. Goodall, Nelson & Perkins, for a regular visit of one of their steamers every eight days. Every improvement which can facilitate the unloading and shipping of freight has been made, and additions will be made to the wharf and warehouses as often as may be necessary to meet the demands of an increasing business.

## SAN SIMEON

Is located upon the bay of the same name. The village comprises two stores, hotel, saloon and warehouse. The settlement is a small one, distant from San Luis Obispo forty-four miles Northward. Whale-fishing is prosecuted by a company formed for the purpose, and the port has gained some notoriety for the opportunities it affords in this direction. The harbor is considered a good one, although lighters are required in loading and discharging cargoes. San Simeon is ten miles above the village of Cambria.

## OLD CREEK

Has no settlement to speak of; only a wayside house of entertainment, post office and saloon. It is situated in a beautiful valley, as fertile as it is picturesque. Old Creek flows through the valley, furnishing water adequate for all the needs of cultivation. Cayucos is only one mile distant.

## SAN MIGUEL,

Whose more recent name is San Marcos, commands the ancient site of the mission of San Miguel, founded July 25th, 1797.

The present settlement is situated on the bank of the Salinas River, thirty-eight miles North of San Luis Obispo, and about 40 miles from the headwaters of the Salinas.

The town comprises two hotels, two stores, two saloons, one blacksmith and wagon shop; with a population of about fifty persons. Two mountain ranges separate it from the ocean, which is twenty-three miles distant. It has daily communication with Soledad (Monterey County,) by stage, also with San Luis Obispo. Merchandise is freighted over from San Luis Obispo Landing by wagons, the distance being forty-seven miles. It is in the center of a large stock-raising district. The old mission church and accompanying buildings yet exist in a comparatively sound condition, the outer walls exposing the ravages of time. There is considerable government land in this vicinity, awaiting those who are seeking homesteads.

## ARROYO GRANDE

Is a small settlement, some three or four years old. It lies about twelve miles South of San Luis Obispo, on the West bank of the Arroyo Grande Creek. It is also on the stage road leading through to Santa Barbara. Arroyo Grande has two hotels, two stores, two saloons, and a wagon and blacksmith shop. It has also a good school. The resources of the contiguous country are pastoral and agricultural. Much fallow arable land adjoins the creek upon its either bank. The land farther back is rolling, its surface being broken into hills, which are utilized by the stock-raiser.

The Arroyo Grande Creek possesses admirable facilities for manufacturing purposes, facilities which some shrewd capitalist will some day take advantage of. There is a fall of about 100 feet to the mile, and 150-horse power, at least, is running to waste, simply for the want of application. The Arroyo Grand Flour Mills, elsewhere mentioned, and owned by Branch Bros., is the only manufacturing establishment on the stream. This is a living stream, and the power derivable from it would be a perpetual one.

The banks of this stream are quite heavily wooded, which furnish an endless supply of timber, consisting of cottonwood, sycamore, box elder and willow.

Excellent locations can be found here for the establishment of mills of any description, or for a tannery. A woolen or beet sugar factory especially would find this an advantageous situation, from the heavy wool-producing interest, not of this section alone, but of the entire county, and from the adaptability of the soil and climate to the production of the sugar beet, which were grown at the rate of fifty tons per acre one season, on the property of Dana Bros., in the Southern portion of the county.

The Newsom White Sulphur Springs are but three miles from the village of Arroyo Grande. West of the village, two miles, the beach forms one of the most enjoyable drives on the coast. It is both firm and hard, with a length of thirteen miles.

## AVILA

is the name of a new town laid out by the Avila Bros. It is identical with that of the settlement at San Luis Obispo Landing.

The site is a very advantageous one, and quite a town is expected to spring up here, not without reason, as its advantages are manifold.

The climate is very uniform, the western sea breezes being entirely broken by a huge promontory, which extends far into the sea. On the Northeast and South it is equally as well protected by hills, which almost environ it on the landward side. None of the extremes of heat and cold are felt here, which are so prevalent in coast towns.

The town is well laid out, having five broad streets, eighty feet in width, the main one called San Luis, after the county seat.

The projectors of the settlement are inviting and inducing settlers by using extreme generosity in the disposition of their lots.

The harbor is of sufficient size to accommodate a large fleet; it is safe from most winds, with an utter absence of breezes from off land. Within the bay about one and one-half miles, is a small cove of great depth, protected by bluffs, which offers absolute safety to vessels of large tonnage and unusual draft, at all seasons of the year. A good wharf has been erected here by Mr. John Harford, a respected and enterprising resident of San Luis Obispo, who is also constructing a narrow-guage railroad between this point and the county seat. Several miles of the road have been graded, bridges and trestle-works have been built for the spanning of chasms, and all this effected by the meagre capital and uncompromising energy and courage of one man, who in view of the obstacles to be overcome, could find no one to assist in bearing the burdens of his enterprise. One mile and one-quarter of the road has been in operation for some time, transporting freight to the wharf from the warehouse of Mr. Harford, located at about that distance inland. This gentleman's pluck and foresight will result in the possession of a piece of property which will eventually enrich him. The coast steamers of Messrs. Goodall, Nelson & Perkins call here regularly.

The future prosperity of San Luis Obispo County is fully assured. The rich resources of her agricultural wealth; the immensity of her wool-producing interest; the magnitude of her inexhaustible mineral treasures; the certain income from the legitimate direction of her large dairying industry; and her possibilities as a manufacturing center, when her vast resources in that direction are fully utilized; all set the seal of unmistakable, perfect and permanent success upon its future.

The rich fertility of its fields, with a salubrity of climate so perfectly adapted to lead both vegetable and physical growth to an expression of its most perfect maturity, is attracting an immigration which will speedily develop its every interest.

Its magnificent valleys, under the influence of the sturdy arm of this new comer, will be made to pay a tribute to production, the richness of which has been undreamed of as within the realms of its possibilities.

The flocks and herds which now crop the luxuriant herbage of its hills, as compared with those of the future, are but as a fleck upon an unclouded sky to the mass of vapors which enshroud it.

Within the bowels of its loftiest peaks, will delve, with the energies of giants, the thousands who will be tempted hither by the luring hope of a brighter fortune.

The homestead of the settler will dot every available portion of the magnificent public domain of 2,000,000 acres.

The rushing murmur of the creeks will be drowned by the noisy clatter of ponderous machinery, to which the strong-armed mechanic will give direction.

The product of the then trebly enhanced dairies will be transported to all quarters of the globe, and this county named among those of Herkimer, Orange, Oneida, and Westchester, for the similarity, excellence and magnitude of its manufacture. Long ere this, too, the question of rapid transportation will have been satisfactorily settled, and over the iron rails will thunder, at their prodigious speed, the trains which bear to the markets of the world, the fruits of a labor magnificently compensated.

Then peace and happiness will be the only dwellers upon its mountains. Joy clothed in plenty will be hidden in every recess of the hills, and the grain-clad valleys will be alone inhabited by the rich, the prosperous and the happy.

---

J. H. WISE.                THOS. DENIGAN.

# CHRISTY & WISE,

—AGENTS FOR—

# WOOL GROWERS & COMMISSION MERCHANTS,

—FOR THE SALE OF—

### HIDES, TALLOW, ETC.

607 FRONT STREET,             Bet. Jackson and Pacific,

SAN FRANCISCO.

**LIBERAL ADVANCES MADE AND SUPPLIES FURNISHED.**

## OSBORN & ALEXANDER,
## MECHANICS' TOOLS AND HARDWARE,
### 624 MARKET STREET,

Opposite Palace Hotel, - - SAN FRANCISCO.

## "BOSS" WASHING MACHINE

Acknowledged by all who have used Washing Machines to be

**THE BEST IN USE.**

The only Machine made that has the Lateral Motion. It will Wash

**BLANKETS, SPREADS,**

QUILTS, CARPETS, Etc.

**A Child Can Work It.**

EVERY FAMILY SHOULD HAVE ONE.

No more Blue Mondays. No more Hard Wash Days.

*A LIBERAL DISCOUNT TO THE TRADE.*

I feel just as happy as a big sun-flower;
The secret is plain to be seen,
For I get through my work in half the time
By using the "Boss" Washing Machine.

**PARLOR AIR PISTOL,**
OR RIFLE.

**NO NOISE. NO OFFENSIVE ODOR**

The best indoor amusement for old or young.

*You Can Become a Crack Shot.*

**JUST THE THING FOR A CHRISTMAS PRESENT.**

## $5.00.

Orders Sent by Express C. O. D. Send for Circular.

DIRECTORY OF SAN LUIS OBISPO COUNTY. 33

| Name. | Occupation. | Place of Business. | Residence. | Town or P. O. |
|---|---|---|---|---|
| Abrego, J J | Carpenter | San Luis Obispo | San Luis Obispo | S Luis Obispo. |
| Acuna, J | Farmer | San Luis Obispo Co. | nr San Luis Obispo. | S Luis Obispo. |
| Acuna, M | Ranchero | nr Cholamie | San Luis Obispo Co. | Cholamie. |
| **Acuna, A** | Merchant | Cholamie | Cholamie | Cholamie. |
| Adams, H | Farmer | San Luis Obispo Co. | | San Simeon. |
| Agard, W A T | Railroad surveyor | Avila | Avila | S Luis Obispo. |
| Agnellini, Pedro & Co | Variety store | Monterey st | Monterey st | S Luis Obispo. |
| **Agnellini, Peter & Co** | Groceries | Chorro st | cor Monterey st | S Luis Obispo. |
| Aguayo, G | Laborer | nr San Luis Obispo. | San Luis Obispo Co. | S Luis Obispo. |
| Aguila, V | Laborer | San Luis Obispo Co. | | San Simeon. |
| Aguiar, S | Laborer | San Luis Obispo Co. | nr San Luis Obispo. | S Luis Obispo. |
| Aguilar, A M | Saddlery&harness | Monterey st | Morro st | S Luis Obispo. |
| Ahern, J | Laborer | nr Paso Robles | San Luis Obispo Co. | Paso Robles. |
| Ahlert, F | Farmer | San Luis Obispo Co. | nr San Luis Obispo. | S Luis Obispo. |
| Albert, Mrs Lucy | | Santa Rosa st. | Santa Rosa st | S Luis Obispo. |
| Alegria, J | Laborer | nr San Luis Obispo. | San Luis Obispo Co. | S Luis Obispo. |
| **Alford, Geo S.** | Farmer | Mono Creek | 8 m N E Morro | Morro. |
| Allen, James | Farmer | San Bernado | 4¾ m N E Morro | Morro. |
| Allen, Jas | Farmer | San Luis Obispo Co. | nr San Luis Obispo. | S Luis Obispo. |
| **Allen, H.** | Farmer | nr Arroyo Grande | San Luis Obispo Co. | Arroyo Grande. |
| Allen, J W | Minister | San Luis Obispo Co. | | San Simeon. |
| Allen, J C | Boot maker | San Luis Obispo Co. | San Luis Obispo | S Luis Obispo. |
| **Alva, M** | Farmer | | San Luis Obispo Co. | San Simeon. |
| Alviso, C | Saloon keeper | San Luis Obispo Co. | nr San Luis Obispo. | S Luis Obispo. |
| Alviso, J | Laborer | | San Luis Obispo Co. | S Luis Obispo. |
| Amador, C | Farmer | San Luis Obispo Co. | | Piedgas Blancas |
| **Anderson, Kitty** | Millinery | Monterey st | San Luis Obispo | S Luis Obispo. |
| Anderson, Mrs Kitty | Millinery | Monterey st | San Luis Obispo | S Luis Obispo. |
| Anderson, J F | Farmer | nr San Luis Obispo. | San Luis Obispo Co. | S Luis Obispo. |
| **Anderson, T** | Farmer | nr San Luis Obispo. | San Luis Obispo Co. | S Luis Obispo. |
| Anderson, R | Farmer | San Luis Obispo Co. | nr San Luis Obispo. | S Luis Obispo. |
| Anderson, D | Farmer | nr San Luis Obispo. | San Luis Obispo Co. | S Luis Obispo. |
| Anderson, J E | Farmer | San Luis Obispo Co. | nr San Luis Obispo. | S Luis Obispo. |
| **Anderson, W L** | Farmer | nr San Luis Obispo. | San Luis Obispo Co. | S Luis Obispo. |
| Anderson, O | Farmer | nr Salinas | San Luis Obispo Co. | Salinas. |
| Andrews, N D | Farmer | San Luis Obispo Co. | | San Simeon. |
| **Andrews, J P** | Dairyman | San Luis Obispo Co. | nr San Luis Obispo. | S Luis Obispo. |
| **Andrews, N D** | Farmer | Morro | Morro | Morro. |
| Andrews, Nathan | Farmer | Morro | Morro | Morro. |
| Andrews, J P | Capitalist | San Luis Obispo | San Luis Obispo | S Luis Obispo. |
| Andrews, J | Farmer | San Luis Creek | E San Luis Obispo. | S Luis Obispo. |
| **Auger, A W** | Farmer | San Luis Obispo Co. | nr San Luis Obispo. | S Luis Obispo. |
| Anthony, C | Teamster | San Luis Obispo Co. | nr Cambria | Cambria. |
| Aparicio, L | Laborer | San Luis Obispo Co. | nr San Luis Obispo. | S Luis Obispo. |
| Apsey, J E | Liquor dealer | Monterey st | San Luis Obispo | S Luis Obispo. |
| **Aragon, J** | Farmer | nr San Luis Obispo. | San Luis Obispo Co. | S Luis Obispo. |
| Aragon, T | Laborer | nr Santa Margarita | San Luis Obispo Co. | S Margarita. |
| **Arana, J C** | Barber | Monterey st | Morro st | S Luis Obispo. |
| Arbuckle, W B | Farmer | | San Luis Obispo Co. | San Simeon. |
| Arce, R, Jr | Laborer | nr San Luis Obispo. | San Luis Obispo Co. | S Luis Obispo. |
| Arce, R | Laborer | San Luis Obispo Co. | nr San Luis Obispo. | S Luis Obispo. |
| **Archer, W C** | Farmer | | San Luis Obispo Co. | San Simeon. |
| Arcos, J | Restaurant | Palm st | Palm st | S Luis Obispo. |
| Arias, A | Laborer | San Luis Obispo Co. | nr San Luis Obispo. | S Luis Obispo. |
| Armstrong, G W | Farmer | San Luis Obispo Co. | | San Simeon. |
| **Armstrong, D** | Farmer | San Luis Obispo Co. | | San Simeon. |
| Arujo, F | Laborer | San Luis Obispo Co. | nr San Luis Obispo. | S Luis Obispo. |
| Ash, W J | Engineer | San Luis Obispo | San Luis Obispo | S Luis Obispo. |
| Asher, C | Merchant | San Luis Obispo | San Luis Obispo | S Luis Obispo. |
| Alencio, R | Laborer | nr San Jose | San Luis Obispo Co. | San Jose. |
| Atencio, J | Laborer | San Luis Obispo Co. | nr San Jose | San Jose. |
| Atension, J | Laborer | San Luis Obispo Co. | nr San Luis Obispo. | S Luis Obispo. |

| Name. | Occupation. | Place of Business. | Residence. | Town or P. O. |
|---|---|---|---|---|
| Austin, W H | Painter | Monterey st | San Luis Obispo | S Luis Obispo. |
| Austin, G. T | Farmer | Morro Creek | 2 m N Morro | Morro. |
| Austin, E | Farmer | | San Luis Obispo Co. | San Simeon. |
| Austin G T | Farmer | nr Morro | San Luis Obispo Co. | Morro. |
| Avila, J V | Farmer | San Luis Obispo Co. | nr San Luis Obispo. | S Luis Obispo. |
| Avilez, J A | Laborer | San Luis Obispo Co. | | San Jose. |
| Avila, Francisco | Farmer | Avila | Avila | S Luis Obispo. |
| Avila, Juan V | Farmer | Avila | Avila | S Luis Obispo. |
| Avila, Santana | Laborer | Avila | Avila | S Luis Obispo. |
| Avila, J A | Farmer | San Luis Obispo Co. | nr San Luis Obispo. | S Luis Obispo. |
| Aylett, W D | Physician | Paso Robles | San Luis Obispo Co. | Paso Robles. |
| Azbill, N | Farmer | San Luis Obispo Co. | | San Simeon. |
| Baca, Y | Farmer | San Luis Obispo Co. | nr Arroyo Grande | Arroyo Grande. |
| Bahan, M V B | Farmer | nr Arroyo Grande | San Luis Obispo Co. | Arroyo Grande. |
| Bailey, W | Farmer | nr San Luis Obispo | nr San Luis Obispo. | S Luis Obispo. |
| Bailey, W T | Dairyman | Los Osos | 7 m S E Morro | Morro. |
| Bains, J | Farmer | nr San Luis Obispo | San Luis Obispo Co. | S Luis Obispo. |
| Bains, John | Saloon keeper | Morro | Morro | Morro. |
| Baker, A J | Carpenter | | San Luis Obispo Co. | San Simeon. |
| Baker, J C | Farmer | San Luis Obispo Co. | | San Simeon. |
| Baker, D F | Stock raiser | San Luis Obispo Co. | nr Paso Robles | Paso Robles. |
| Baker, H A | Farmer | | 12 m S Arroyo Gr'de | Arroyo Grande. |
| Balaam, J S | Farmer | San Luis Obispo Co. | nr Cambria | Cambria. |
| Balaam, Geo, Jr | Farmer | | San Luis Obispo Co. | San Simeon. |
| Balch, W H | Stage driver | San Luis Obispo | San Luis Obispo | S Luis Obispo. |
| Balderrama, Y | Laborer | nr San Luis Obispo | San Luis Obispo Co. | S Luis Obispo. |
| Balenzuela, J | Farmer | San Luis Obispo Co. | nr Paso Robles | Paso Robles. |
| Balenzuela, T | Laborer | San Luis Obispo Co. | nr Arroyo Grande | Arroyo Grande. |
| Barbero, — | Baker | Santa Rosa st | Santa Rosa st | S Luis Obispo. |
| Barbier, J | Laborer | San Luis Obispo Co. | nr San Luis Obispo. | S Luis Obispo. |
| Barba, J | Laborer | nr San Luis Obispo | San Luis Obispo Co. | S Luis Obispo. |
| Barelas, J | Laborer | nr San Luis Obispo | San Luis Obispo Co. | S Luis Obispo. |
| Barger, Dr D E | Physician | Monterey st | Cosmopolitan Hotel | S Luis Obispo. |
| Barnes, S | Cook | San Luis Obispo | San Luis Obispo | S Luis Obispo. |
| Barnes, G W | Carpenter | San Luis Obispo | San Luis Obispo | S Luis Obispo. |
| Barnstead, T S | Ship builder | San Luis Obispo | San Luis Obispo | S Luis Obispo. |
| Barnebery, J W | Farmer | San Luis Obispo Co. | nr San Luis Obispo. | S Luis Obispo. |
| Barney, M | Laborer | nr San Jose | San Luis Obispo Co. | San Jose. |
| Barnell, W R | Farmer | nr Cambria | San Luis Obispo Co. | Cambria. |
| Barnes, J H | Farmer | San Luis Obispo Co. | nr San Luis Obispo. | S Luis Obispo. |
| Barneberg, J | Farmer | nr San Luis Obispo | San Luis Obispo Co. | S Luis Obispo. |
| Barneberg, A | Farmer | nr San Luis Obispo | San Luis Obispo Co. | S Luis Obispo. |
| Barnet, Thos | Farmer | Cambria road | 1 m N W San L O'po | S Luis Obispo. |
| Barneburg, Aaron | Machine shop | Broad & Higuerra sts | Garden st | S Luis Obispo. |
| Barneburg, A | Farmer | | Moash st | S Luis Obispo. |
| Barnes, G W | Justice of peace | Morro st | Monterey st | S Luis Obispo. |
| Barron, B T | Carpenter | San Luis Obispo | Cosmopolitan Hotel | S Luis Obispo. |
| Barrios, J | Farmer | San Luis Obispo Co. | nr Santa Margarita | S Margarita. |
| Barron, W T | Carpenter | San Luis Obispo | San Luis Obispo Co. | S Luis Obispo. |
| Barrickman, J N | Farmer | | San Luis Obispo Co. | San Simeon. |
| Barrett, T | Laborer | nr San Luis Obispo | San Luis Obispo Co. | S Luis Obispo. |
| Barrington, E | Miner | San Luis Obispo Co. | nr Arroyo Grande | Arroyo Grande. |
| Barron, C H | Farmer | San Luis Obispo Co. | nr San Luis Obispo. | S Luis Obispo. |
| Bartlett, J R | Farmer | San Luis Obispo Co. | nr San Simeon | San Simeon. |
| Barton, J | Farmer | San Luis Obispo Co. | | San Simeon. |
| Bassett, G F | Carpenter | San Luis Obispo | Monterey st | S Luis Obispo. |
| Bates, S B | Teamster | | San Luis Obispo Co. | San Simeon. |
| Bates, J T | Farmer | nr Paso Robles | San Luis Obispo Co. | Paso Robles. |
| Batran, W | Laborer | nr Santa Margarita | San Luis Obispo Co. | S Margarita. |
| Bauman, F J | Painter | San Luis Obispo | San Luis Obispo | S Luis Obispo. |
| Baume, J | Teamster | nr San Luis Obispo | San Luis Obispo Co. | S Luis Obispo. |
| Bayer, T | Blacksmith | Monterey st | San Luis Obispo | S Luis Obispo. |
| Beach, W | Carpenter | Broad & Higuerra sts | Cosmopolitan Hotel | S Luis Obispo. |
| Bean, R M | Sheep raiser | nr San Luis Obispo | San Luis Obispo Co. | S Luis Obispo. |

DIRECTORY OF SAN LUIS OBISPO COUNTY. 35

| Name. | Occupation. | Place of Business. | Residence. | Town or P. O. |
|---|---|---|---|---|
| Bean, E P | Sheep raiser | nr La Panza | San Luis Obispo Co. | La Panza. |
| Beattie, A C | Stock raiser | San Luis Obispo Co. | nr San Miguel | San Miguel. |
| Beavers, J W | Laborer | nr Morro | San Luis Obispo Co. | Morro. |
| Bebee, Judge | | | Broad st | S Luis Obispo. |
| Beck, H J | Farmer | nr San Luis Obispo | San Luis Obispo Co. | S Luis Obispo. |
| Beckett, L J | Teacher | Morro | Morro | Morro. |
| Beckett, J T | Dairyman | nr Morro | San Luis Obispo Co. | Morro. |
| Beckett, F B | Nursery | Higuerra st | Higuerra st | S Luis Obispo. |
| Beebee, Wm L | Farmer | Montgomery st | Marsh and Broad sts. | S Luis Obispo. |
| Beebee, J R | Stock raiser | San Luis Obispo Co. | nr Cambria | Cambria. |
| Beebee, G W | Stock raiser | nr Cambria | San Luis Obispo Co. | Cambria. |
| Beem, A J | Laborer | San Luis Obispo Co. | nr Morro | Morro. |
| Behannon, W I | Laborer | nr San Luis Obispo | San Luis Obispo Co. | S Luis Obispo. |
| Bejil, J J | Farmer | San Luis Obispo Co. | nr San Luis Obispo | S Luis Obispo. |
| Bellah, S | Farmer | San Luis Obispo Co. | Arroyo Grande | Arroyo Grande. |
| Bell, J | Farmer | San Luis Obispo Co. | nr San Luis Obispo | S Luis Obispo. |
| Beltran, J | Laborer | San Luis Obispo Co. | nr Morro | Morro. |
| Benjamin, J D | Hog raiser | Paso Robles Ranch | San Luis Obispo Co. | Paso Robles. |
| Benjamin, J D | Lumberman | San Luis Obispo Co. | nr Morro | Morro. |
| Bennett, J B | Tel operator | Monterey st | Marsh st | S Luis Obispo. |
| Bennett, A M | Carpenter | San Luis Obispo | San Luis Obispo | S Luis Obispo. |
| Bennett, J | Blacksmith | Santa Margarita | San Luis Obispo Co. | S Margarita. |
| Benrimo, M A | Hotel keeper | Avila | Avila | S Luis Obispo. |
| Benton, A F | Grocer | Hot Springs | Hot Springs | Paso Robles. |
| Benton, A F | Sheep raiser | 5 m E P R Hot Sp's. | San Luis Obispo Co. | Paso Robles. |
| Berger, G | Farmer | | San Luis Obispo Co | San Simeon. |
| Bermudes, T | Laborer | nr San Luis Obispo | San Luis Obispo Co. | S Luis Obispo. |
| Bernal, G | Clerk | San Luis Obispo | San Luis Obispo | S Luis Obispo. |
| Bichard, D H | Farmer | San Luis Obispo Co. | nr Morro | Morro. |
| Bickmore, J H | Laborer | nr San Luis Obispo | San Luis Obispo Co. | S Luis Obispo. |
| Bidamon, J C | Carpenter | San Luis Obispo | Buchon st | S Luis Obispo. |
| Biddle, P | Stock raiser | nr Estrella | San Luis Obispo Co. | Estrella. |
| Biddle, J | Ranchero | nr Estrella | San Luis Obispo Co. | Estrella. |
| Biggs, D, Jr | Farmer | nr San Luis Obispo | San Luis Obispo Co. | S Luis Obispo. |
| Biggs, J | Farmer | San Luis Obispo Co. | nr San Luis Obispo | S Luis Obispo. |
| Bilamon, J C | Carpenter | San Luis Obispo | San Luis Obispo | S Luis Obispo. |
| Billa, Mrs Jesus | | | Santa Rosa st | S Luis Obispo. |
| Billa, Francisco | Laborer | Palm st | Mill st | S Luis Obispo. |
| Bishop, W B | Farmer | nr Morro | San Luis Obispo Co. | Morro. |
| Blackburn, D D | Carpenter | Hot Springs | P R Hot Springs | Paso Robles. |
| Blackburn, J H | Farmer | nr Hot Springs | San Luis Obispo Co. | Paso Robles. |
| Black, J M | Blacksmith | San Miguel | San Miguel | San Miguel. |
| Black, J T | Farmer | nr San Miguel | San Luis Obispo Co. | San Miguel. |
| Black, James M | Blacksmith | Monterey st | Monterey st | S Luis Obispo. |
| Blackburn, James | Stock raiser | Paso Robles Road | | Paso Robles. |
| Blackburn & Morris | Cosmopol'n hotel | Monterey st | | S Luis Obispo. |
| Blackburn, J H | Ranchero | 23 m N San Luis Ob | | Paso Robles. |
| Blackburn, D D | Proprietor | P R Hot Springs | San Luis Obispo Co. | Paso Robles. |
| Blackburn, J H | Stock raiser | Paso Robles Ranch | San Luis Obispo Co. | Paso Robles. |
| Blake, J | Clerk | Monterey st | Monterey st | S Luis Obispo. |
| Blake, H B & Co | Real estate | Monterey st | | S Luis Obispo. |
| Blake, H B | Real estate | Monterey st | Miss'n Building | S Luis Obispo. |
| Blanco, J | Farmer | San Luis Obispo Co. | nr San Luis Obispo | S Luis Obispo. |
| Blanco, Jose | Teamster | San Luis Obispo | Chorro st | S Luis Obispo. |
| Blanch, C | Farmer | nr Morro | San Luis Obispo Co. | Morro. |
| Bloch, L | Clerk | Monterey st | Monterey st | S Luis Obispo. |
| Blochman & Co, A | Gen merchandise | Monterey st | | S Luis Obispo. |
| Blochman, A | Gen merchandise | 405-407 Sansome st. | San Francisco | San Francisco. |
| Blumenthal, A | Merchant | San Miguel | San Miguel | San Miguel. |
| Blunt, L | Dairyman | San Luis Obispo Co. | nr San Simeon | San Simeon. |
| Bode, W | Seaman | San Luis Obispo Co. | nr P R Hot Springs | Paso Robles. |
| Boll, M | Boot maker | Monterey st | Broad & Monterey sts | S Luis Obispo. |
| Bonilla, J M | Farmer | San Luis Obispo Co. | nr San Luis Obispo | S Luis Obispo. |

| NAME. | OCCUPATION. | PLACE OF BUSINESS. | RESIDENCE. | TOWN OR P. O. |
|---|---|---|---|---|
| Bonilla, M | Stock | San Luis Creek | 1½ m N E S Luis O | S Luis Obispo. |
| Boody, Geo | Teacher | San Jose | San Jose | San Jose. |
| Borden, H H | Farmer | San Luis Obispo Co. | nr San Miguel | San Miguel. |
| Borgues, R | Laborer | nr San Luis Obispo. | San Luis Obispo Co. | S Luis Obispo. |
| Borland, W E | Carpenter | San Luis Obispo | San Luis Obispo | S Luis Obispo. |
| Borland, W J | Contractor | Avila | Avila | S Luis Obispo. |
| Bornilla, M | Farmer | nr San Luis Obispo. | San Luis Obispo Co. | S Luis Obispo. |
| Boronda, E | Saloon and farm. | Summit of S M M'n | 6 m N E San Luis O | S Luis Obispo. |
| Bosse, Henry | Dairyman | Arroyo Grande | Arroyo Grande | Arroyo Grande. |
| Bosse & Hemphill | Dairymen | Arroyo Grande | Arroyo Grande | Arroyo Grande. |
| Bosworth, B | Seaman | San Luis Obispo | San Luis Obispo | S Luis Obispo. |
| Bouldin, R C | Attorney at law | Call Building | Monterey st | S Luis Obispo. |
| Bradley, Amos | Stage driver | San Luis Obispo. | Nipomo st | S Luis Obispo. |
| Branch, A W | Hotel proprietor. | Higuerra st | Higuerra st | S Luis Obispo. |
| Branch, L R | Stock | Arroyo Grande | 3½ m N E Arroyo G | Arroyo Grande. |
| Branch Mill | Flour mill | Arroyo Grande | | Arroyo Grande. |
| Branch, Fredk | Stock | Arroyo Grande Cr'k | 3 m N E Arroyo G'e | Arroyo Grande. |
| Branch, Ramon | Stock | Arroyo Grande | 4 m N E Arroyo G'e | Arroyo Grande. |
| Branch, Frank | Stock | Arroyo Grande | 3¼ m N E Arroyo G | Arroyo Grande. |
| Branch, R J | Ranchero | San Luis Obispo Co. | nr Arroyo Grande | Arroyo Grande. |
| Brandið, I | Seaman | San Luis Obispo Co. | | San Simeon. |
| Brant, Geo | Laborer | nr San Luis Obispo. | San Luis Obispo Co. | S Luis Obispo. |
| Bray, F T | Farmer | nr Cambria | San Luis Obispo Co. | Cambria. |
| Brennan, James | Farmer | Santa Barbara Road. | 5 m S Arroyo Grande | Arroyo Grande. |
| Bresette, E | Cooper | Cambria | Cambria | Cambria. |
| Brewster, S R | Saddler | San Simeon | San Simeon | San Simeon. |
| Brian, A | Farmer | San Luis Obispo Co. | nr Arroyo Grande | Arroyo Grande. |
| Brian, L D | Dairyman | nr Morro | San Luis Obispo Co. | Morro. |
| Brian, G W | Dairyman | | San Luis Obispo Co. | San Simeon. |
| Brian, M | Farmer | | San Luis Obispo Co. | San Simeon. |
| Brian, A T | Farmer | nr San Luis Obispo. | San Luis Obispo Co. | S Luis Obispo. |
| Briefner, P | Dep postmaster | Branch st | Arroyo Grande | Arroyo Grande. |
| Brierley, W C | Laborer | San Luis Obispo Co. | nr Cambria | Cambria. |
| Bristoll, J | Farmer | San Luis Obispo Co. | nr Cambria | Cambria. |
| Brizzolara, L | Groceries | Monterey st | Monterey st | S Luis Obispo. |
| Brizzolara, S | Saloon | San Luis Obispo. | Monterey st | S Luis Obispo. |
| Brizzolara & Co, S. | Saloon | Monterey st | Monterey st | S Luis Obispo. |
| Brizzolara, J | Merchant | Monterey st | Monterey st | S Luis Obispo. |
| Brizzolara, B | Merchant | Monterey st | Monterey st | S Luis Obispo. |
| Brizzolara, S | Merchant | San Luis Obispo | San Luis Obispo | S Luis Obispo. |
| Brown, R S | Dairyman | Toro Creek | 9 m N E Morro | Morro. |
| Brown, Samuel | Capitalist | Petaluma | Petaluma | Petaluma. |
| Brown, L | Farmer | nr Hot Springs | San Luis Obispo Co. | Paso Robles. |
| Brown, W | Laborer | San Luis Obispo Co. | nr San Luis Obispo. | S Luis Obispo. |
| Brown, D W | Laborer | nr San Luis Obispo. | San Luis Obispo Co. | S Luis Obispo. |
| Brown, H L | Carpenter | San Luis Obispo | San Luis Obispo | S Luis Obispo. |
| Brown, M M | Teamster | San Luis Obispo Co | nr San Luis Obispo. | S Luis Obispo. |
| Brown, W A | Butcher | Arroyo Grande | Arroyo Grande | Arroyo Grande. |
| Brown, G F | Farmer | nr San Luis Obispo. | San Luis Obispo Co. | S Luis Obispo. |
| Brown, R F | Carpenter | Morro | Morro | Morro. |
| Brumley, C R | Drayman | San Luis Obispo Co. | nr La Panza | La Panza. |
| Bryan, A | Farmer | Oso Flaco | 3½ m N E Guadalupe | Guadalupe. |
| Bryan, E W | Teamster | nr Oso Flaco | San Luis Obispo Co. | Oso Flaco. |
| Bryant, I | Farmer | nr Hot Springs | San Luis Obispo Co. | Paso Robles. |
| Budar, Antonio | Saddler | Palm st | Palm st | S Luis Obispo. |
| Buelna, Luis | Painter | San Luis Obispo | Santa Rosa st | S Luis Obispo. |
| Buelna, J A | Farmer | San Luis Obispo Co. | nr Morro | Morro. |
| Buelna, R | Laborer | nr Morro | San Luis Obispo Co. | Morro. |
| Buelna, G | Farmer | nr Morro | San Luis Obispo Co. | Morro. |
| Buffington, J Q | Dairyman | nr Cambria | San Luis Obispo Co. | Cambria. |
| Buffington, A C | Farmer | San Luis Obispo Co. | | San Simeon. |
| Buffum, J M | Farmer | nr Cambria | San Luis Obispo Co. | Cambria. |
| Bump, J | Policeman | San Luis Obispo | Cosmopolitan Hotel | S Luis Obispo. |
| Bunce, I H | Carpenter | San Luis Obispo | San Luis Obispo | S Luis Obispo. |

DIRECTORY OF SAN LUIS OBISPO COUNTY. 37

| Name. | Occupation. | Place of Business. | Residence. | Town or P. O. |
|---|---|---|---|---|
| Burdie, E B | Miner | Cambria | Cambria | Cambria. |
| Burden, A | Farmer | nr Morro | San Luis Obispo Co.. | Morro. |
| Burgess, T H | Dairyman | nr San Luis Obispo.. | San Luis Obispo Co.. | S Luis Obispo. |
| Burke, M | Laborer | nr San Luis Obispo.. | San Luis Obispo Co.. | S Luis Obispo. |
| Burke, J | Gardener | San Luis Obispo Co.. | nr San Luis Obispo... | S Luis Obispo. |
| Burneson, A J | Farmer | San Luis Obispo Co.. | nr Oso Flaco | Oso Flaco. |
| Burnett, J B | Hotel | Arroyo Grande | Branch st | Arroyo Grande. |
| Burnett, W | Stock raiser | San Luis Obispo Co.. | nr Morro | Morro. |
| Burnett, J B | Carpenter | Santa Margarita | Santa Margarita | S Margarita. |
| Burneson, A W | Farmer | nr Oso Flaco | San Luis Obispo Co.. | Oso Flaco. |
| Burnett, T J | Miller | Arroyo Grande | Arroyo Grande | Arroyo Grande. |
| Burt, T F | Carpenter | San Miguel | San Miguel | San Miguel. |
| Burton, A H | Minister | San Luis Obispo Co.. | | San Simeon. |
| Burtnett, W C | Farmer | San Luis Obispo Co.. | nr San Luis Obispo... | S Luis Obispo. |
| Butchart, J B | Merchant | San Miguel | San Miguel | San Miguel. |
| Butchart, G | Merchant | San Miguel | San Miguel | San Miguel. |
| Butchart, N | Merchant | San Miguel | San Miguel | San Miguel. |
| Buton, A | Farmer | San Luis Obispo Co.. | nr Morro | Morro. |
| Buzzolara, B | Gen merchandise. | Monterey st | Monterey st | S Luis Obispo. |
| Byers, R | Farmer | | San Luis Obispo Co.. | San Simeon. |
| Byrne, J F | Architect | P R Hot Springs | San Luis Obispo Co.. | Paso Robles. |
| Caake, C | Steward | Avila | Avila | S Luis Obispo. |
| Cabral, J | Barber | San Luis Obispo | San Luis Obispo | S Luis Obispo. |
| Caley, H R | Livery keeper | P R Hot Springs | San Luis Obispo Co.. | Paso Robles. |
| Caley, H R | Locksmith | P R Hot Springs | San Luis Obispo Co.. | Paso Robles. |
| Call, S B | Saddle & harness. | Monterey st | Morro & Higuerra sts | S Luis Obispo. |
| Calloway, W D | Farmer | San Luis Obispo Co.. | nr San Luis Obispo... | S Luis Obispo. |
| Camon, P | Miner | San Luis Obispo Co.. | Salinas | Salinas. |
| Campbell, J B | Farmer | Campbell's Station | San Luis Obispo Co.. | Paso Robles. |
| Campbell, — | Farmer | S B Road | 3 m S Arroyo Gr'de. | Arroyo Grande. |
| Campbell, G O | Dairyman | San Luis Obispo Co.. | nr Morro | Morro. |
| Campbell, J D | Farmer | San Luis Obispo Co.. | nr Cambria | Cambria. |
| Campbell, A E | Dairyman | Cayucos | San Luis Obispo Co.. | Cayucos. |
| Camp, Frank | Bar keeper | San Miguel | San Luis Obispo Co.. | San Miguel. |
| Camp, D | Laborer | San Luis Obispo Co.. | San Luis Obispo Co.. | S Luis Obispo. |
| Campbell, J B | Carpenter. | Santa Margarita | San Luis Obispo Co.. | S Margarita. |
| Campbell, J O | Farmer | San Luis Obispo Co.. | nr Morro | Morro. |
| Canet, J | Farmer | nr San Luis Obispo.. | San Luis Obispo Co.. | S Luis Obispo. |
| Canet, Jose | Ranchero | Cañada Canet | 5 m E Morro | Morro. |
| Canizales, B | Laborer | San Luis Obispo | San Luis Obispo | S Luis Obispo. |
| Cano, R | Teamster | San Luis Obispo | San Luis Obispo | S Luis Obispo. |
| Cantua, G | Farmer | San Luis Obispo Co.. | nr Morro | Morro. |
| Cantrell, J M | Farmer | San Luis Obispo Co.. | nr Cambria | Cambria. |
| Cantua, J | Farmer | nr San Simeon | San Luis Obispo Co.. | San Simeon. |
| Cardoza, F | Sheep raiser | 15 m W Paso Robles | San Luis Obispo Co.. | Paso Robles. |
| Cardoza, J S | Stock raiser | nr P R Hot Springs.. | San Luis Obispo Co.. | Paso Robles. |
| Cardona, J L | Farmer | San Luis Obispo Co.. | nr Oso Flaco | Oso Flaco. |
| Cardoza, F R | Stock raiser | San Luis Obispo Co.. | nr P R Hot Springs.. | Paso Robles. |
| Carey, L | Farmer | San Luis Obispo Co.. | nr Cambria | Cambria. |
| Carey, W | Farmer | San Luis Obispo Co.. | nr Arroyo Grande | Arroyo Grande. |
| Carlon, J M | Farmer | nr San Luis Obispo.. | San Luis Obispo Co.. | S Luis Obispo. |
| Carlon, J A | Farmer | nr San Luis Obispo.. | San Luis Obispo Co.. | S Luis Obispo. |
| Carlon, R A | Farmer | nr San Luis Obispo.. | San Luis Obispo Co.. | S Luis Obispo. |
| Carlon, F | Farmer | nr San Luis Obispo.. | San Luis Obispo Co.. | S Luis Obispo. |
| Carlon, J M | Farmer | nr San Luis Obispo.. | San Luis Obispo Co.. | S Luis Obispo. |
| Carlon, P | Farmer | San Luis Obispo Co.. | nr San Luis Obispo... | S Luis Obispo. |
| Carlon, P O | Farmer | San Luis Obispo Co.. | nr San Luis Obispo... | S Luis Obispo. |
| Carnwell, J | Stage driver | P R Hot Springs | San Luis Obispo Co.. | Paso Robles. |
| Carpenter, Ezra | Surveyor | P R Hot Springs | San Luis Obispo Co.. | Paso Robles. |
| Carrillo, J R | Laborer | San Luis Obispo | San Luis Obispo Co.. | S Luis Obispo. |
| Carranzo, R | Farmer | Morro | San Luis Obispo Co.. | Morro. |
| Carrisoza, G | Laborer | San Luis Obispo Co.. | nr San Jose | San Jose. |
| Carroll, T | Farmer | nr San Jose | San Luis Obispo Co.. | S Luis Obispo. |
| Carson, L O | Plasterer | San Luis Obispo | Cosmopolitan Hotel.. | S Luis Obispo. |

| Name. | Occupation. | Place of Business. | Residence. | Town or P. O. |
|---|---|---|---|---|
| Carter, J | Clerk | San Luis Obispo Co. | San Miguel | San Miguel. |
| Casey, Alvin | Laborer | Paso Robles | Paso Robles | Paso Robles. |
| Case, G W | Laborer | San Luis Obispo Co. | nr San Simeon | San Simeon. |
| Casner, J | Cigar manufact'g | Monterey st | Monterey st | S Luis Obispo. |
| Cass, J | Farmer | San Luis Obispo Co. | nr Morro | Morro. |
| Cassner, N | Watch maker | Monterey st | French Hotel | S Luis Obispo. |
| Castile, Jesse | Farmer | Berros Creek | 1½ S Arroyo G'e Cr'k | Arroyo Grande. |
| Castro, F | Farmer | Avila Road | 6 m S S Luis Obispo. | San Jose. |
| Castro, Mrs | | | Buchon st | S Luis Obispo. |
| Castro, Cesareo | Saloon | Avila | Avila | S Luis Obispo. |
| Castro, J | Saloon | Avila | Avila | S Luis Obispo. |
| Castro, M | Saloon | Avila | Avila | S Luis Obispo. |
| Castro, M R. | Farmer | nr Arroyo Grande | San Luis Obispo Co. | Arroyo Grande. |
| Castro, P | Laborer | San Luis Obispo | San Luis Obispo | S Luis Obispo. |
| Castro, C | Laborer | San Luis Obispo | San Luis Obispo | S Luis Obispo. |
| Castillo, A M | Farmer | nr San Luis Obispo | San Luis Obispo Co. | S Luis Obispo. |
| Castro, F | Farmer | San Luis Obispo Co. | nr San Luis Obispo | S Luis Obispo. |
| Castro, E | Farmer | nr San Luis Obispo | San Luis Obispo Co. | S Luis Obispo. |
| Castro, R | Laborer | San Luis Obispo Co. | nr Oso Flaco | Oso Flaco. |
| Castro, W D | Farmer | nr Piedro Blanca | San Luis Obispo Co. | Piedgas Blancas |
| Castro, M | Musician | San Luis Obispo | San Luis Obispo | S Luis Obispo. |
| Castro, D | Farmer | nr Morro | San Luis Obispo Co. | Morro. |
| Castro, J | Laborer | San Jose | San Luis Obispo Co. | San Jose. |
| Castillo, G | Laborer | San Luis Obispo | San Luis Obispo | S Luis Obispo. |
| Castro, J | Farmer | nr San Simeon | San Luis Obispo Co. | San Simeon. |
| Castro, J | Laborer | San Luis Obispo | San Luis Obispo | S Luis Obispo. |
| Castillo, J | Laborer | San Luis Obispo | San Luis Obispo | S Luis Obispo. |
| Castro, B | Laborer | Estrella | San Luis Obispo Co. | Estrella. |
| Castro, J | Farmer | nr San Luis Obispo | San Luis Obispo Co. | S Luis Obispo. |
| Castro, F | Real estate agt. | San Luis Obispo | San Luis Obispo Co. | S Luis Obispo. |
| Castro, R | Laborer | San Luis Obispo Co. | San Jose | Arroyo Grande. |
| Castillo, J D | Laborer | San Luis Obispo | San Luis Obispo Co. | S Luis Obispo. |
| Casteel, J | Farmer | San Luis Obispo, Co. | nr Arroyo Grande | Arroyo Grande. |
| Castanos, J M | Silversmith | Morro | San Luis Obispo Co. | Morro. |
| Castro, B A | Farmer | San Luis Obispo Co. | nr San Luis Obispo | S Luis Obispo. |
| Caswell, J H | Engineer | San Simeon | San Simeon | San Simeon. |
| Catalinat, H | Butcher | San Luis Obispo | San Luis Obispo | S Luis Obispo. |
| Cavasso, R J | Clerk | Monterey st | Monterey st | S Luis Obispo. |
| Cerf, M | Gen merchandise. | Monterey st | 1203 Sutter st | San Francisco. |
| Cerf, E | Gen merchandise. | Monterey st | San Luis Obispo | S Luis Obispo. |
| Ceribelli, S | Soda factory | Monterey st | Monterey st | S Luis Obispo. |
| Cervantes, Leon | Surveyor | Summit of S M M'n. | 6 m N E S Luis Ob'o | S Luis Obispo. |
| Cervantes, Refugio | Laborer | San Luis Obispo | San Luis Obispo | S Luis Obispo. |
| Cervantes, A L | Surveyor | San Luis Obispo | San Luis Obispo | S Luis Obispo. |
| Chamblin, J L | Merchant | Cambria | San Luis Obispo Co. | Cambria. |
| Chandler, J P | Mechanic | San Simeon | San Luis Obispo Co. | San Simeon. |
| Chapin, E M | Pork packer | Cambria | San Luis Obispo Co. | Cambria. |
| Chapin, G M | Pork packer | San Luis Obispo Co. | Cambria | Cambria. |
| Charvez, V | Farmer | Cambria Road | 3 m N W S Luis O. | S Luis Obispo. |
| Charawell, J | Farmer | San Luis Obispo Co. | nr San Luis Obispo | S Luis Obispo. |
| Chavoya, F | Farmer | San Luis Obispo Co. | nr P R Hot Springs. | Paso Robles. |
| Chaves, A | Laborer | Morro | San Luis Obispo Co. | Morro. |
| Chaves, J | Laborer | San Luis Obispo | San Luis Obispo | S Luis Obispo. |
| Chaves, J A | Farmer | San Luis Obispo Co. | nr San Luis Obispo | S Luis Obispo. |
| Chaves, V | Farmer | nr San Luis Obispo | San Luis Obispo | S Luis Obispo. |
| Chaves, A | Farmer | San Luis Obispo Co. | nr San Luis Obispo | S Luis Obispo. |
| Chesney, J W | Sheep raiser | 14 m W P R Spr'gs. | San Luis Obispo Co. | Paso Robles. |
| Childs, J E | Liquor dealer | San Luis Obispo | San Luis Obispo | S Luis Obispo. |
| Chipman, W | Farmer | nr P R Hot Springs. | San Luis Obispo Co. | Paso Robles. |
| Chism, G P | Laborer | Cambria | San Luis Obispo Co. | Cambria. |
| Christie, P | Washerman | San Luis Obispo | Chorro st | S Luis Obispo. |
| Christie, Frank | Laborer | San Luis Obispo | McDougal's Hotel | S Luis Obispo. |
| Christie, F | Mason | San Luis Obispo | San Luis Obispo | S Luis Obispo. |
| Clark, R M | Teacher | San Luis Obispo | San Luis Obispo | S Luis Obispo. |

## DIRECTORY OF SAN LUIS OBISPO COUNTY. 39

| Name. | Occupation. | Place of Business. | Residence. | Town or P. O. |
|---|---|---|---|---|
| Clarke, A K | Farmer | nr San Luis Obispo | San Luis Obispo Co. | S Luis Obispo. |
| Clarke, W A | Blacksmith | P R Hot Springs | San Luis Obispo Co. | Paso Robles. |
| Clarke, A J | Farmer | nr San Simeon | San Luis Obispo Co. | San Simeon. |
| Clarke, J A | Dairyman | nr Cambria | San Luis Obispo Co. | Cambria. |
| Clarke, C L | Farmer | nr Morro | San Luis Obispo Co. | Morro. |
| Clark, Joseph | Whaleman | San Simeon | San Simeon | San Simeon. |
| Claussen, J | Farmer | nr San Luis Obispo | San Luis Obispo Co. | S Luis Obispo. |
| Claussen, E | Farmer | San Luis Obispo Co. | nr San Luis Obispo | S Luis Obispo. |
| Cleary, R | Laborer | Arroyo Grande | San Luis Obispo Co. | Arroyo Grande. |
| Cloud, John | Farmer | Cambria Road | 1¼ m N W S L Ob'po | S Luis Obispo. |
| Cloud, J C | Farmer | nr San Luis Obispo | San Luis Obispo Co. | S Luis Obispo. |
| Clough, F | Carriage man'ftr. | San Luis Obispo | San Luis Obispo | S Luis Obispo. |
| Cloudo, J | Whaleman | San Luis Obispo Co. | Cambria | Cambria. |
| Cochran, J T | Saloon | Monterey st | Monterey st | S Luis Obispo. |
| Cochran, A | Carpenter | San Luis Obispo | San Luis Obispo | S Luis Obispo. |
| Cochran, E | Blacksmith | San Luis Obispo Co. | Morro | Morro. |
| Cocke, Jas H | Dairyman | Little Morro. | 5 m N E Morro | Morro. |
| Cocke, F N | Dairyman | Oso Flaco | 3 m N W Guadalupe | Guadalupe. |
| Cocke, W J | Dairyman | Oso Flaco | 3 m N W Guadalupe | Guadalupe. |
| Cocke, G C | Dairyman | Oso Flaco | 3 m N W Guadalupe | Guadalupe. |
| Cocke, C | Farmer | nr Morro | San Luis Obispo Co. | Morro. |
| Cocke, J H | Farmer | nr Morro | San Luis Obispo Co. | Morro. |
| Cocke, J | Farmer | nr Morro | San Luis Obispo Co. | Morro. |
| Cocke, G C | Farmer | Morro | San Luis Obispo Co. | Morro. |
| Cocke, W J | Farmer | San Luis Obispo Co. | nr Morro | Morro. |
| Cocke, N F | Farmer | San Luis Obispo Co. | nr Morro | Morro. |
| Cofer, E M | Dairyman | nr Cambria | San Luis Obispo Co. | Cambria. |
| Cofer, R D | Farmer | nr San Miguel | San Luis Obispo Co. | San Miguel. |
| Coffee, G H | Miner | Cambria | San Luis Obispo Co. | Cambria. |
| Coffee, E | Dairyman | Cambria | San Luis Obispo Co. | Cambria. |
| Coffee, J S | Farmer | nr Cambria | San Luis Obispo Co. | Cambria. |
| Coffee, W | Farmer | San Luis Obispo Co. | nr San Simeon | San Simeon. |
| Cole, E | Farmer | nr Cambria | San Luis Obispo Co. | Cambria. |
| Cole, G M | Saddler | Cambria | San Luis Obispo Co. | Cambria. |
| Cole, J | Laborer | San Luis Obispo Co. | San Jose | San Jose. |
| Cole, B | Farmer | San Luis Obispo Co. | nr San Luis Obispo | S Luis Obispo. |
| Collins, Chas | Carpenter | San Luis Obispo | Palm st. | S Luis Obispo. |
| Collins, C | Cooper | San Luis Obispo | San Luis Obispo | S Luis Obispo. |
| Collins, D G | Farmer | nr San Luis Obispo | San Luis Obispo Co. | S Luis Obispo. |
| Compher, J B | Farmer | nr San Simeon | San Luis Obispo Co. | San Simeon. |
| Conley, L | Bar keeper | Cambria | San Luis Obispo Co. | Cambria. |
| Conley, A B | Farmer | San Luis Obispo Co. | nr Cambria | Cambria. |
| Conley, W | Farmer | nr Cambria | San Luis Obispo | Cambria. |
| Conley, S | Laborer | San Luis Obispo | San Luis Obispo | S Luis Obispo. |
| Connelly, T | Farmer | nr San Luis Obispo | San Luis Obispo Co. | S Luis Obispo. |
| Contreras, S A | Laborer | San Luis Obispo | San Luis Obispo Co. | S Luis Obispo. |
| Conway, E N | Bookkeeper | Cambria | San Luis Obispo Co. | Cambria. |
| Cook, E F | Farmer | Guadalupe Road | 2 m S Arroyo Grande | Arroyo Grande. |
| Cook, C | Porter | Cosmopolitan Hotel. | Monterey st | S Luis Obispo. |
| Cook, C D | Laborer | San Luis Obispo | San Luis Obispo | S Luis Obispo. |
| Cook, S | Farmer | nr San Luis Obispo | San Luis Obispo Co. | S Luis Obispo. |
| Cook, A | Bricklayer | San Luis Obispo | San Luis Obispo | S Luis Obispo. |
| Cook, A | Farmer | San Luis Obispo Co. | San Simeon | San Simeon. |
| Cooper, D | Lawyer | San Luis Obispo | San Luis Obispo | S Luis Obispo. |
| Copperes, L | Farmer | nr San Luis Obispo | San Luis Obispo Co. | S Luis Obispo. |
| Corales, F | Laborer | San Luis Obispo | San Luis Obispo | S Luis Obispo. |
| Corales, J | Laborer | San Luis Obispo | San Luis Obispo | S Luis Obispo. |
| Corbit, John | Postmaster | Arroyo Grande | ½ m N E A Grande | Arroyo Grande. |
| Corbit, John | Dairyman | San Luis Obispo Rd. | 3 m N E A Grande | Arroyo Grande. |
| Corbit, J | Blacksmith | Arroyo Grande | San Luis Obispo Co. | Arroyo Grande. |
| Cordova, B | Laborer | San Luis Obispo | San Luis Obispo | S Luis Obispo. |
| Cordova, P | Laborer | San Luis Obispo | San Luis Obispo | S Luis Obispo. |
| Cordova, T | Farmer | nr Arroyo Grande | San Luis Obispo Co. | Arroyo Grande. |
| Coronwell, O N | Farmer | nr Arroyo Grande | San Luis Obispo Co. | Arroyo Grande. |

## L. L. PAULSON'S HAND-BOOK AND

| NAME. | OCCUPATION. | PLACE OF BUSINESS. | RESIDEN |
|---|---|---|---|
| Coronado, J | Laborer | San Luis Obispo | San Luis Obi |
| **Correa, Frank** | Groceries | Monterey | Santa Rosa s |
| Correa, Francisco | Saloon & groceries | Monterey st | cor Santa Ro |
| Correa, F | Merchant | San Luis Obispo | San Luis Obi |
| Covington, W | Farmer | San Luis Obispo Co. | nr San Simeo |
| Cox, F O | Seaman | San Luis Obispo | San Luis Obi |
| Cramer, S L | Tinsmith | Cambria | San Luis Obi |
| **Crane, R S** | Farmer | nr Huasna | San Luis Obi |
| Crawford, D P | Dairyman | San Luis Obispo Co. | Cambria |
| Creason, A | Farmer | San Luis Obispo Co. | nr Cambria |
| Creason, T | Laborer | San Luis Obispo Co. | Piedro Blanc |
| Crew, W M | Carpenter | San Luis Obispo Co. | Cambria |
| Croley, D | Wheelwright | San Luis Obispo Co. | San Miguel |
| Cromwell, H B | Laborer | San Luis Obispo Co. | Arroyo Gran |
| Croxford, A | Farmer | San Luis Obispo Co. | nr P R Hot |
| Cummings, Geo | Farmer | nr Old Creek | San Luis Obi |
| Cummins, L E | Teamster | Arroyo Grande | San Luis Obi |
| Cunningham, J C | Farmer | 5 m NE of P R H S | San Luis Obi |
| **Cunningham, P** | Hostler | Monterey st | Monterey st |
| Cunningham, J | Teamster | P R Hot Springs | San Luis Obi |
| Cupis, L | Laborer | Morro | San Luis Obi |
| Currier, J C | Sheep raiser | St Helena Ranch | San Luis Ob |
| **Currier, J C** | Merchant | San Miguel | San Luis Ob |
| **Cushing, J F** | Farmer | nr Cambria | San Luis Ob |
| Dahlke, C | Teacher | San Luis Obispo | San Luis Ob |
| Dait, C K | Tel operator | P R Hot Springs | San Luis Ob |
| Dallidet, P H | Vintner | Toro st | Toro st |
| Damas, A | Bar keeper | San Luis Obispo | San Luis Ob |
| Dana, Fred | Deputy assessor | Court House | 24 m S San ] |
| **Dana, Charles W** | County clerk | Court House | San Luis Ob |
| **Dana Bros** | Stock raisers | Santa Barbara Road | 9 m Arroyo |
| **Dana, I** | Stock raiser | Nipoma Ranch | 24 m S San ] |
| **Dana, A G** | Stock raiser | Nipoma Ranch | 24 m S San ] |
| **Dana, W C** | Stock raiser | Nipoma Ranch | 24 m S San ] |
| **Dana, E C** | Stock raiser | Nipoma Ranch | 24 m S San ] |
| **Dana, F A** | Stock raiser | Nipoma Ranch | 24 m S San ] |
| **Dana, D A** | Stock raiser | Nipoma Ranch | 24 m S San ] |
| **Dana, S M** | Stock raiser | Nipoma Ranch | 24 m S San ] |
| **Dana, J F** | Stock raiser | Nipoma Ranch | 24 m S San ] |
| **Dana, H C** | Stock raiser | Nipoma Ranch | 24 m S San ] |
| Daniels, L | Laborer | San Luis Obispo Co. | nr P S Hot |
| Darke, F E | Teacher | San Luis Obispo | San Luis Ob |
| Daugherty, R | Laborer | nr San Luis Obispo | San Luis Ob |
| Daurence, James | Farmer | Morro | Morro |
| Davis, F | Waiter | Cosmopolitan Hotel | Monterey st |
| **Davidson, S M** | Farmer | nr Cambria | San Luis Ob |
| Davis, J B | Farmer | nr San Miguel | San Luis Ob |
| Davis, Geo | Stock raiser | nr San Miguel | San Luis Ob |
| Davis, J P | Trader | San Luis Obispo Co. | nr San Luis |
| **Davis, G S** | Blacksmith | Cambria | Cambria |
| Davis, J | Laborer | nr Cambria | San Luis Ob |
| **Davis, David** | Farmer | San Luis Obispo Co. | nr San Sime |
| Day, E M | Carpenter | Higuerra st | Higuerra st |
| **Day, L W** | Farmer | San Luis Obispo Co. | nr San Simeo |
| Dayton, J W | Laborer | San Luis Obispo Co. | nr San Luis |
| **Deane, W J** | Farmer | nr Cambria | San Luis Ob |
| DeBrun, J Y | Laborer | nr Josephine | San Luis Ob |
| DeCruz, J | Whaleman | San Luis Obispo Co. | nr Piedro B |
| Deffner, Geo | Saloon | Chorro st | Chorro st |
| Deffner, J | Laborer | nr San Luis Obispo | San Luis Ob |
| Deffner, G | Boot maker | San Luis Obispo | San Luis Ob |
| Defossett, Martin | Steward | Monterey st | Monterey st |
| Defosset, Louis | Waiter | Monterey st | Monterey st |
| De la Guerra, F | Clerk | San Luis Obispo | San Luis Ol |

DIRECTORY OF SAN LUIS OBISPO COUNTY. 41

| Name. | Occupation. | Place of Business. | Residence. | Town or P. O. |
|---|---|---|---|---|
| Delapierre, Henry... | Paper hanger...... | Monterey st............ | Monterey st............. | S Luis Obispo. |
| Delapierre H......... | Upholsterer. ....... | San Luis Obispo...... | San Luis Obispo...... | S Luis Obispo. |
| De la Rosa, A........ | Fisherman .......... | San Luis Obispo...... | San Luis Obispo...... | S Luis Obispo. |
| Deliseguez, Albert.. | Clerk. ...... ......... | .................................. | 1 m S E S L Obispo | S Luis Obispo. |
| De Leon, F P......... | Bar keeper........... | San Luis Obispo...... | Palm st.................... | S Luis Obispo. |
| Delgado, F.. ......... | Saloon...... ........... | nr San Luis Obispo... | San Luis Obispo Co.. | S Luis Obispo. |
| Deliseguez, Albert. | Bartender........... | Cosmopolitan Hotel.. | 1 m E San L Obispo | S Luis Obispo. |
| Deliseguez, Alexander............... | Farmer ............... | Muñoz Place......... | 1 m E San L Obispo | S Luis Obispo. |
| Demint, G S......... | Teamster ........... | nr P R Hot Springs.. | San Luis Obispo Co.. | Paso Robles. |
| Deming, R...:..... | Stock raiser ....... | San Luis Obispo Co.. | nr San Luis Obispo... | S Luis Obispo. |
| Dempsey, W......... | Farmer ............... | nr San Luis Obispo... | San Luis Obispo Co.. | S Luis Obispo. |
| Denice, C E .......... | Farmer ............... | San Luis Obispo Co.. | nr Cambria............. | Cambria. |
| Denise, W H......... | Stock raiser........ | nr Cambria............ | San Luis Obispo Co.. | Cambria. |
| Denman, C E ........ | Laborer................ | San Luis Obispo Co.. | nr San Luis Obispo... | S Luis Obispo. |
| Dennis, John......... | Druggist............., | Monterey st............ | San Luis Obispo...... | S Luis Obisbo. |
| Dennis, T.............. | Carpenter............ | San Luis Obispo...... | Cosmopolitan Hotel.. | S Luis Obispo. |
| Dennis, J D .......... | Druggist............... | Monterey st............ | Buchon st................ | S Luis Obispo. |
| Dennis, W A......... | Miner ................... | San Luis Obispo Co.. | nr Josephine........... | Josephine. |
| Dennis, N.............. | Laborer................ | San Luis Obispo Co.. | nr San Miguel......... | San Miguel. |
| Dennis, J D........... | Druggist............... | San Luis Obispo...... | San Luis Obispo...... | S Luis Obispo. |
| De Boco, Jose Simon | Saloon................. | Broad st................. | Broad st.................. | S Luis Obispo. |
| Detro, M............... | Farmer ............... | nr Cambria............. | San Luis Obispo Co.. | Cambria. |
| Devine, P.............. | Farmer ............... | San Luis Obispo Co.. | nr San Miguel......... | San Miguel. |
| Devoto, G.............. | Grocer.................. | Monterey st............ | Monterey st............. | S Luis Obispo. |
| Deweese, W H ..... | Farmer ............... | nr P R Hot Springs.. | San Luis Obispo Co.. | Paso Robles. |
| Dewitt, C C........... | Farmer ............... | nr Oso Flaco........... | San Luis Obispo Co.. | Oso Flaco. |
| Dias, F.................. | Farmer ............... | San Luis Obispo Co.. | nr Morro................. | Morro. |
| Dickerson, O E...... | Sheep raiser........ | San Luis Obispo Co.. | nr San Luis Obispo... | S Luis Obispo. |
| Dickerson, J ...!..... | Farmer................. | San Luis Obispo Co.. | nr San Luis Obispo... | S Luis Obispo. |
| Dillard, W B.......... | Lawyer................. | San Luis Obispo...... | San Luis Obispo...... | S Luis Obispo. |
| Dillon, Mrs............ | ............................ | San Luis Obispo...... | San Luis Obispo...... | S Luis Obispo. |
| Dillon, E................ | Stock raiser ....... | San Luis Obispo Co.. | nr San Luis Obispo... | S Luis Obispo. |
| Divoto, G.............. | Groceries............. | Monterey st............ | Monterey st............. | S Luis Obispo. |
| Dobbs, W R.......... | Farmer ............... | nr San Luis Obispo... | San Luis Obispo Co.. | S Luis Obispo. |
| Dodge, M C........... | Carpenter............ | Paso Robles........... | P S Hot Springs...... | Paso Robles. |
| Dodson, R............. | Painter................. | San Luis Obispo Co.. | nr Cambria............. | Cambria. |
| Dodson, M............. | Farmer ............... | San Luis Obispo Co.. | nr San Simeon........ | San Simeon. |
| Dominguez, T....... | Farmer ............... | nr Arroyo Grande... | San Luis Obispo Co.. | Arroyo Grande. |
| Domingues, J M.... | Farmer ............... | San Luis Obispo Co.. | nr Arroyo Grande... | Arroyo Grande. |
| Dominguez, E....... | Farmer ............... | San Luis Obispo Co.. | nr San Jose............ | San Jose. |
| Donaldson, D........ | Plasterer.............. | San Luis Obispo...... | Monterey st............ | S Luis Obispo. |
| Donnelly, J............ | Farmer ............... | San Luis Obispo Co.. | nr Morro................. | Morro. |
| Donohue, P........... | Farmer ............... | San Luis Obispo Co.. | nr San Luis Obispo... | S Luis Obispo. |
| Dorame, J............. | Farmer ............... | nr Arroyo Grande... | San Luis Obispo Co.. | Arroyo Grande. |
| Doring, E P........... | Dairyman............. | Toro Creek............. | 9 m N E Morro...... | Morro. |
| Dorsey, S J............ | Carriage painter.. | P R Hot Springs .... | San Luis Obispo Co.. | Paso Robles. |
| Doty, B F............... | Farmer ............... | nr Cambria............. | San Luis Obispo Co.. | Cambria. |
| Dougherty, J H..... | Farmer ............... | nr San Luis Obispo... | San Luis Obispo Co.. | S Luis Obispo. |
| Douglass, T........... | Laborer................ | nr San Luis Obispo... | San Luis Obispo Co.. | S Luis Obispo. |
| Douglass, W......... | Farmer ............... | San Luis Obispo Co.. | nr Arroyo Grande... | Arroyo Grande. |
| Douglass, B H ...... | Farmer ............... | nr San Luis Obispo... | San Luis Obispo Co.. | S Luis Obispo. |
| Doulin, M.............. | Stock raiser ........ | nr Huasna.............. | San Luis Obispo Co.. | Huasna. |
| Dovemir, H........... | Cook.................... | P R Hot Springs..... | San Luis Obispo Co.. | Paso Robles. |
| Dover, J................ | Farmer................. | San Luis Obispo...... | nr Morro................. | Morro. |
| Dowdle, D T.......... | Farmer ............... | nr San Simeon....... | San Luis Obispo Co.. | San Simeon. |
| Downing, W......... | Farmer................. | nr San Luis Obispo... | San Luis Obispo Co.. | S Luis Obispo. |
| Doyle, J M............. | Laborer................ | nr San Luis Obispo... | San Luis Obispo Co.. | S Luis Obispo. |
| Draper, L H.......... | Farmer ............... | nr Morro................. | San Luis Obispo Co.. | Morro. |
| Dughi, G............... | Gardener............. | nr San Luis Obispo... | San Luis Obispo Co.. | S Luis Obispo. |
| Dunbar, D ............ | Saloon keeper..... | Monterey st........... | Monterey st............ | S Luis Obispo. |
| Dunbar, J A.......... | Farmer ............... | nr San Luis Obispo... | San Luis Obispo Co.. | S Luis Obispo. |
| Dunbar, C............. | Farmer ............... | nr San Simeon........ | San Luis Obispo Co.. | San Simeon. |
| Dunbar, J M.......... | Farmer................. | nr San Luis Obispo... | San Luis Obispo Co.. | S Luis Obispo. |

42                L. L. PAULSON'S HAND-BOOK AND

LOUIS EMERY PAGE.                               FELIX

# PAGE & GRAV

—MANUFACTURERS OF—

## Carriages and W

OF ALL KINDS, OF THE BEST MA

THEY ALSO KEEP ON HAND A COMPLETE STOC

## Carriages, Buggies, Light

### AND HEAVY WAGO

OF THEIR OWN MAKE, WHICH THEY WARRAN
RESPECT.

They have determined to sell their work at prices as low
worthless work that is frequently being palmed off upon t
in Los Angeles and elsewhere. Call and see the b
ment of Carriages and Buggies ever offered in Los
All Carriages and Buggies manufactured by us
fitted with Page's Celebrated Patent Adjust
able

**SPRING LAZYBACK, SO WELL ADAPTED**

## DIRECTORY OF SAN LUIS OBISPO COUNTY. 43

| Name. | Occupation. | Place of Business. | Residence. | Town or P. O. |
|---|---|---|---|---|
| Dunbar, A............ | Farmer............... | San Luis Obispo Co.. | nr San Luis Obispo... | S Luis Obispo. |
| Dunbar, A M......... | Farmer............... | nr San Luis Obispo... | San Luis Obispo Co.. | S Luis Obispo. |
| Dunbar, D............ | Farmer............... | San Luis Obispo Co.. | nr San Luis Obispo... | S Luis Obispo. |
| Duncan, N P......... | Physician............ | San Miguel............. | San Miguel............. | San Miguel. |
| Dunn, Jose........... | Hostler................ | Monterey st............ | Monterey st............ | S Luis Obispo. |
| Dunn, P H............ | Manager.............. | P R Hot Springs....... | San Luis Obispo Co.. | Paso Robles. |
| Dunn, F J.............. | Farmer................ | nr Morro................ | San Luis Obispo Co.. | Morro. |
| Durazoz, Mrs R...... | ........................ | ........................ | Nipoma st............ | S Luis Obispo. |
| Durazo, J............. | Laborer............... | nr San Luis Obispo.. | San Luis Obispo Co.. | S Luis Obispo. |
| Durfee, J S........... | Laborer............... | nr Arroyo Grande.... | San Luis Obispo Co.. | Arroyo Grande. |
| **Dwiggins, J**...... | Farmer................ | San Luis Obispo Co.. | nr P R Hot Springs... | Paso Robles. |
| Ecline, J F............ | Farmer................ | nr P R Hot Springs... | San Luis Obispo Co.. | Paso Robles. |
| Ecline, B.............. | Farmer................ | 3 m W P R H Sp'gs | San Luis Obispo Co.. | Paso Robles. |
| Edgerly, C L.......... | Carpenter............ | San Luis Obispo...... | San Luis Obispo...... | S Luis Obispo. |
| Edmund, J............ | Carpenter............ | Cambria............... | Cambria............... | Cambria. |
| Edwards, W.......... | Blacksmith.......... | Monterey st............ | San Luis Obispo..... | S Luis Obispo. |
| **Edwards, D**........ | Farmer................ | Cambria road......... | 1 m N W S L Obispo | S Luis Obispo. |
| Edwards, Eli......... | Farmer................ | San Luis Obispo Rd | 5 m N A Grande..... | Arroyo Grande. |
| Edwards, W P....... | Mechanic............ | San Luis Obispo..... | San Luis Obispo..... | S Luis Obispo. |
| Eely, R................. | Moulder.............. | Broad & Higuerra sts | ........................ | S Luis Obispo. |
| Elliott, John.......... | Bar keeper.......... | Higuerra & Morro sts. | Higuerra & Morro sts. | S Luis Obispo. |
| Ellingsworth, S...... | Laborer............... | nr San Luis Obispo.. | San Luis Obispo Co.. | S Luis Obispo. |
| Elliott, J............... | Liquor dealer....... | San Luis Obispo..... | San Luis Obispo..... | S Luis Obispo. |
| **Elliott, R**........... | Farmer................ | nr San Miguel........ | San Luis Obispo Co.. | San Miguel. |
| Ely, D H............... | Farmer................ | nr San Luis Obispo.. | San Luis Obispo Co.. | S Luis Obispo. |
| Emerson, J........... | Farmer................ | nr Arroyo Grande... | San Luis Obispo Co.. | Arroyo Grande. |
| **Emert, C G**......... | Farmer................ | nr Cambria............ | San Luis Obispo Co.. | Cambria. |
| Emerson, E S........ | Farmer................ | San Luis Obispo Co.. | San Luis Obispo Co.. | Cambria. |
| Emrich, John........ | Farmer................ | Oso Flaco.............. | 2 m N Guadalupe.... | Guadalupe. |
| **English, S**........... | Farmer................ | nr Cambria............ | San Luis Obispo Co.. | Cambria. |
| Enos, L................ | Miner.................. | San Luis Obispo..... | San Luis Obispo..... | S Luis Obispo. |
| Epperson, W........ | Farmer................ | San Luis Obispo Co.. | nr Cambria............ | Cambria. |
| Epperly, T S......... | Farmer................ | San Luis Obispo Co.. | nr Morro............... | Morro. |
| **Epperly, W H**...... | Farmer................ | nr Cambria............ | San Luis Obispo Co.. | Cambria. |
| Era, J.................. | Miner.................. | Cambria............... | Cambria............... | Cambria. |
| Ernest, H............. | Cook................... | P R Hot Springs...... | San Luis Obispo Co.. | Paso Robles. |
| Escamilla, J.......... | Laborer............... | nr San Luis Obispo.. | nr San Luis Obispo.. | S Luis Obispo. |
| Escalanta, E......... | Laborer............... | San Luis Obispo Co.. | nr San Luis Obispo.. | S Luis Obispo. |
| **Escarsega, J**....... | Farmer................ | San Luis Obispo Co.. | nr Arroyo Grande... | Arroyo Grande. |
| Eslinger, W F........ | Farmer................ | San Luis Obispo Co.. | nr Morro............... | Morro. |
| Espinoza, E.......... | Laborer............... | San Luis Obispo Co.. | nr San Luis Obispo.. | S Luis Obispo. |
| **Espinosa, V**......... | Farmer................ | San Luis Obispo Co.. | nr San Jose........... | San Jose. |
| Esquerr, Ygnacio... | Groceries............ | Chorro st.............. | Chorro st.............. | S Luis Obispo. |
| Esquer, Y............. | Hatter.................. | San Luis Obispo..... | San Luis Obispo Co.. | S Luis Obispo. |
| Esquer, G............. | Laborer............... | nr San Luis Obispo.. | San Luis Obispo Co.. | S Luis Obispo. |
| **Estener, Wm**....... | Farmer................ | San Luis Obispo..... | Chorro st.............. | S Luis Obispo. |
| Estrade, Joaquin... | Stock raiser......... | San Luis Creek...... | 2 m N E S L Obispo | S Luis Obispo. |
| Estrada, M........... | Laborer............... | San Luis Obispo Co.. | nr Cambria............ | Cambria. |
| Estrada, B............ | Laborer............... | nr San Jose........... | San Luis Obispo Co.. | San Jose. |
| Estrada, F............ | Ranchero............ | nr San Simeon....... | San Luis Obispo Co.. | San Simeon. |
| Estrado, R............ | Farmer................ | nr San Luis Obispo.. | San Luis Obispo Co./ | S Luis Obispo. |
| Estrado, P............ | Farmer................ | San Luis Obispo Co.. | nr San Luis Obispo.. | S Luis Obispo. |
| **Estrado, J**........... | Farmer................ | nr San Luis Obispo.. | San Luis Obispo Co.. | S Luis Obispo. |
| Estudillo, J R........ | Stock raiser......... | Oso Flaco.............. | 3¼ m N E Guadalupe | Guadalupe. |
| Estudillo, L D........ | Stock raiser......... | Oso Flaco.............. | 3½ m N E Guadalupe | Guadalupe. |
| Estudillo, L.......... | Farmer................ | nr Arroyo Grande... | San Luis Obispo Co.. | Arroyo Grande. |
| Estudillo, J K........ | Farmer................ | San Luis Obispo Co.. | nr Arroyo Grande... | Arroyo Grande. |
| Estudillo, M......... | Farmer................ | San Luis Obispo Co.. | nr Arroyo Grande... | Arroyo Grande. |
| **Evans, T J**........... | Farmer................ | nr Cambria............ | San Luis Obispo Co.. | Cambria. |
| Evans, W............. | Carpenter............ | San Luis Obispo..... | San Luis Obispo..... | S Luis Obispo. |
| Everett, A............ | Farmer................ | nr Cambria............ | San Luis Obispo Co.. | Cambria. |
| **Everett, E A**........ | Farmer................ | nr Cambria............ | San Luis Obispo Co.. | Cambria. |
| Exline, B.............. | Miner.................. | San Luis Obispo..... | San Luis Obispo..... | S Luis Obispo. |
| Fairbanks, A D..... | Dairyman............ | San Luis Obispo Co.. | 3 m S E Morro....... | Morro. |

# TOURISTS IN SEARCH OF HEALTH,

## OR PLEASURE,

### WILL FIND BOTH BY VISITING

# THE OJAI VALLEY,

IN VENTURA COUNTY, 15 MILES NORTH OF SAN BUENAVENTURA, AND 30 MILES EAST OF SANTA BARBARA.

This beautiful valley is shut in by high mountain ranges, which prevent the rough sea breezes and fogs from reaching it.

Its elevation above the sea level renders the air dry and bracing, and its climate is peculiarly adapted to those suffering from

### Asthma, Bronchitis, and all Pulmonary Complaints.

Having recently purchased the Hotel at

# NORDHOFF,

#### IN THE CENTRE OF THIS VALLEY,

I have completely refitted and furnished it in the best manner, and the house is now open for the reception of guests. Invalids and others will find comfortably furnished sunny rooms, with open fires, and a table supplied with the best the market affords.

Parties taken to the celebrated Matlija Hot Springs, the Petroleum Wells, and other points of interest.

The Valley and neighboring mountain canyons abound with game of all kinds, and the mountain streams are stocked with trout.

Cottages will be rented to parties desiring more accommodation than can be had in the Hotel.     **C. P. WIGGIN, Proprietor.**

---

**C. P. WIGGIN.**                                                                 **MORTIMER CARR.**

# WIGGIN & CARR,

### DEALERS IN

# REAL ESTATE.

#### MONEY LOANED ON APPROVED SECURITIES.

### Agency of the
# FIREMEN'S FUND INSURANCE CO. OF CALIFORNIA

Information relating to the climate, resources, and attractions of the OJAI VALLEY and vicinity, freely furnished on application. Call on or address,

*C. P. WIGGIN, Nordhoff, Ventura County,*     -     -     *Cal.*

# DIRECTORY OF SAN LUIS OBISPO COUNTY. 45

| Name. | Occupation. | Place of Business. | Residence. | Town or P. O. |
|---|---|---|---|---|
| Fairbanks, A D | Farmer | San Luis Obispo Co. | nr Cambria | Cambria. |
| Farbish, J S | Clerk | San Miguel | 38 m N San Luis Ob | San Miguel. |
| Farmer, Robt | Livery stable | Arroyo Grande | Branch st | Arroyo Grande. |
| Farmer, W | Farmer | San Luis Obispo Co. | nr Arroyo Grande | Arroyo Grande. |
| Farrell, W | Merchant | Santa Margarita | Santa Margarita | S Margarita. |
| Farrell, Geo | Stage driver | San Luis Obispo | San Luis Obispo | S Luis Obispo. |
| Fancher, J | Farmer | San Luis Obispo Co. | nr Cambria | Cambria. |
| Fancher, A | Farmer | San Luis Obispo Co. | nr Cambria | Cambria. |
| Fancher, J K P | Farmer | San Luis Obispo Co. | nr Cambria | Cambria. |
| Faustino, M | Laborer | San Luis Obispo | San Luis Obispo | S Luis Obispo. |
| Feliz, Jose | Ranchero | | | Morro. |
| Feliz, Joaquin | Stock raiser | Atascadero Ranch | 17 m N San Luis Ob | S Margarita. |
| Feliz, Ramon | Ranchero | Morro Creek | 7½ m N E Morro | Morro. |
| Feliz, A M | Farmer | San Luis Obispo Co. | nr San Luis Obispo | S Luis Obispo. |
| Feliz, J | Farmer | nr San Luis Obispo. | San Luis Obispo Co. | S Luis Obispo. |
| Feliz, J Y | Farmer | San Luis Obispo Co. | nr San Luis Obispo | S Luis Obispo. |
| Feliz, N | Farmer | San Luis Obispo Co. | nr Morro | Morro. |
| Feliz, A | Farmer | nr Cambria | San Luis Obispo Co. | Cambria. |
| Feliz, J R | Farmer | San Luis Obispo Co. | nr Morro | Morro. |
| Feliz, Jose | Farmer | nr Morro | San Luis Obispo Co. | Morro. |
| Feliz, V C | Farmer | San Luis Obispo Co. | nr San Luis Obispo | S Luis Obispo. |
| Felix, F | Teamster | San Luis Obispo. | San Luis Obispo. | S Luis Obispo. |
| Felt, Everett | Laborer | San Luis Obispo | nr San Simeon | San Simeon. |
| Felts, J M | Teacher | Cambria | Cambria | Cambria. |
| Fenton, J | Merchant | Estrella | Estrella | Estrella. |
| Fernandez, N | Whaleman | nr San Simeon | San Luis Obispo Co. | San Simeon. |
| Fernandez, B | Farmer | nr San Luis Obispo | San Luis Obispo Co. | S Luis Obispo. |
| Fernandez, M | Laborer | San Luis Obispo | San Luis Obispo | S Luis Obispo. |
| Feydora, L | Whaleman | San Luis Obispo Co. | nr San Simeon | San Simeon. |
| Filey, W | Farmer | San Luis Obispo Co. | nr Morro | Morro. |
| Filipponi, C | Laborer | San Luis Obispo Co. | Piedgas Blancas | Pied's Blancas. |
| Findley, J J | Stock raiser | nr Cambria | San Luis Obispo Co. | Cambria. |
| Fine, F F | Dairyman | Huasna Ranch | 9 m N W Arroyo G. | Arroyo Grande. |
| Fine, I H | Farmer | San Luis Obispo Co. | nr Morro | Morro. |
| Fine, Joff | Farmer | nr Morro | San Luis Obispo Co. | Morro. |
| Fine, J M | Farmer | San Luis Obispo Co. | nr Old Creek | Old Creek. |
| Fink, Charles | Hotel proprietor | Fink's Hotel | Monterey st | S Luis Obispo. |
| Finly, J J | Farmer | nr San Luis Obispo | San Luis Obispo Co. | S Luis Obispo. |
| Fisher, E S | Gunsmith | Monterey st | Monterey st | S Luis Obispo. |
| Fisher, J F | Gunsmith | Monterey st | Palm st | S Luis Obispo. |
| Fitch, A | Butcher | P R Hot Springs | San Luis Obispo Co. | Paso Robles. |
| Fitzpatrick, T | Millwright | Morro | Morro | Morro. |
| Fleck, John | Millwright | San Luis Obispo | San Luis Obispo | S Luis Obispo. |
| Fleisher, M | Clerk | Monterey st | Monterey st | S Luis Obispo. |
| Fletcher, J R | Farmer | nr Cambria | San Luis Obispo Co. | Cambria. |
| Fletcher, J H | Farmer | San Luis Obispo Co. | nr Cambria | Cambria. |
| Flint, B T | Stock raiser | nr San Luis Obispo | San Luis Obispo Co. | S Luis Obispo. |
| Flint, J W | Stock raiser | nr San Luis Obispo | San Luis Obispo Co. | S Luis Obispo. |
| Flint, R G | Stock raiser | San Luis Obispo Co. | nr Estrella | Estrella. |
| Flood, I | Dairyman | San Luis Obispo | nr Morro | Morro. |
| Flood, C | Miller | Cambria | Cambria | Cambria. |
| Flood, J A | Farmer | nr Morro | San Luis Obispo Co. | Morro. |
| Flores, L G | Laborer | nr San Luis Obispo | San Luis Obispo Co. | S Luis Obispo. |
| Flores, F | Farmer | nr San Luis Obispo | San Luis Obispo Co. | S Luis Obispo. |
| Flores, J | Farmer | nr Josephine | San Luis Obispo Co. | Josephine. |
| Flynn, J D | Steward | San Luis Obispo Co. | P R Hot Springs | Paso Robles. |
| Forbes, Mrs L | | | Higuerra st | S Luis Obispo. |
| Ford, Mrs | Laundress | Morro | Morro | Morro. |
| Ford, J W | Farmer | nr Cambria | San Luis Obispo Co | Cambria. |
| Ford, A R | Farmer | nr Morro | San Luis Obispo Co. | Morro. |
| Ford, I N | Farmer | nr Cambria | San Luis Obispo Co. | Cambria. |
| Ford, B F | Farmer | nr Morro | San Luis Obispo Co. | Morro. |
| Foreman, J H | Farmer | nr P R Hot Springs | San Luis Obispo Co. | Paso Robles. |
| Foreman, S W | Civil engineer | San Luis Obispo | San Luis Obispo | S Luis Obispo. |

# AMERICAN EXCHANGE HOTEL,

## SAN FRANCISCO.

This old and popular Hotel, which has for the last twenty-four years extended to the traveling public a cordial welcome and the comfort of a home, and so favorably known to old Californians and the traveling public, that it requires no comment on our part further than to say that the BRYAN BROS., who also are old Californians, and know how to cater to the wants of the traveling public, have taken the full proprietorship of the above hotel, and shall leave nothing undone to make this hotel second to none in San Francisco, for

## COMFORT, GOOD LIVING AND CLEANLINESS.

Our sole aim shall be to the comfort and welfare of our guests; our table is furnished with the best the market affords; the house has been thoroughly renovated and newly furnished throughout; two hundred rooms well ventilated.

Gentlemanly and obliging clerks, and clean and attentive waiters, will always be found in our hotel.

The hotel is the most centrally located of any in the city, being in the centre of the business portion of the city; the Street Cars pass the door every two minutes to all parts of the city; our Coach, with Red Lights, will be at the railroad depots and wharfs to convey passengers to the house free of charge; our Runners wear Silver Badges on left breast, with the name of the house on.

☞ BEWARE OF OTHER RUNNERS. ☜

## OUR PRICES ARE FROM $1.50 TO $2.00 PER DAY.

GIVE US A CALL, AND JUDGE FOR YOURSELVES.

**WM. and THOS. BRYAN, Proprietors.**

## DIRECTORY OF SAN LUIS OBISPO COUNTY. 47

| Name. | Occupation. | Place of Business. | Residence. | Town or P. O. |
|---|---|---|---|---|
| Forest, John | Laborer | Morro | Morro | Morro. |
| Forrester, P A | Sawyer | Cambria | Cambria | Cambria. |
| Forrester, P | | San Luis Obispo Co. | nr Cambria | Cambria. |
| Forrester, A J | Liquor dealer | San Luis Obispo | San Luis Obispo | S Luis Obispo. |
| Forsyth, D | Contractor | Monterey st | Monterey st | S Luis Obispo. |
| Fossit, R T | Farmer | nr Cambria | San Luis Obispo Co. | Cambria. |
| Foster, C | Bar keeper | P R Hot Springs | P R Hot Springs | Paso Robles. |
| Foster, A T | Farmer | nr Cambria | San Luis Obispo Co. | Cambria. |
| Fotterdale, W | Farmer | nr Estrella | San Luis Obispo Co. | Estrella. |
| Fourcade, M | Laborer | nr Morro | San Luis Obispo Co. | Morro. |
| Fourcade, R | Farmer | San Luis Obispo Co. | nr San Luis Obispo | S Luis Obispo. |
| Foute, Y | Whaleman | nr San Luis Obispo | San Luis Obispo Co. | S Luis Obispo. |
| Fowler, T J | Farmer | Santa Barbara Road. | 4 m S E Arroyo G'e | Arroyo Grande. |
| Fowler & Washburn | Farmers | Berros Creek | 2 m S Ar'o Gr'de C'k | Arroyo Grande. |
| Fowler, Albert | Farmer | Berros Creek | 2½m S Ar'o Gr'de C'k | Arroyo Grande. |
| Fowler, W, Sr | Farmer | nr Arroyo Grande. | San Luis Obispo Co. | Arroyo Grande. |
| Fowler, H C | Farmer | nr Morro | San Luis Obispo Co. | Morro. |
| Fraga, Francisco | Saddle & harness. | Monterey st | | S Luis Obispo. |
| Fraga, Luis | Teamster | San Luis Obispo | Chorro st | S Luis Obispo. |
| Frame, D H | Ranchero | Morro | Morro | Morro. |
| Francis, Henry | Livery stable | Monterey st | Monterey st | S Luis Obispo. |
| Frankl, L | Merchant | Piedgas Blancas | Piedgas Blancas | Piedgas Blancas. |
| Francisco, M | Whaleman | San Luis Obispo Co. | nr San Luis Obispo | S Luis Obispo. |
| Frazer, S S | Teacher | San Jose | San Jose | San Jose. |
| Frederick, J | Hotel keeper | San Luis Obispo | San Luis Obispo | S Luis Obispo. |
| Frederick, Jos | French hotel | Monterey st | Monterey st | S Luis Obispo. |
| Freeman, J | Farmer | San Luis Obispo Co. | nr Josephine Mine | Paso Robles. |
| Freeman, J S | Farmer | nr P R Hot Springs | San Luis Obispo Co. | Paso Robles. |
| Freeborn, W S | Farmer | San Luis Obispo Co. | nr San Luis Obispo | S Luis Obispo. |
| Freeborn, W | Farmer | nr San Luis Obispo | San Luis Obispo Co. | S Luis Obispo. |
| Freeborn, J M | Farmer | San Luis Obispo Co. | nr San Luis Obispo | S Luis Obispo. |
| Freeborn, R | Teamster | Santa Margarita | San Luis Obispo Co. | S Margarita. |
| Freites, F | Farmer | Oso Flaco | 2½ m N Guadalupe | Guadalupe. |
| Freshour, C C | Farmer | San Luis Obispo Co. | nr P R Hot Springs | Paso Robles. |
| Freshour, A | Farmer | San Luis Obispo Co. | nr P R Hot Springs | Paso Robles. |
| Fresquiz, J C | Laborer | nr Arroyo Grande | San Luis Obispo Co. | Arroyo Grande. |
| Freytus, F | Farmer | San Luis Obispo Co. | nr Oso Flaco | Oso Flaco. |
| Frick, A | Farmer | nr P R Hot Springs. | San Luis Obispo Co. | Paso Robles. |
| Friedlander P | Clerk | Monterey st | Monterey st | S Luis Obispo. |
| Froom, T H | Blacksmith | San Luis Obispo | San Luis Obispo Co. | S Luis Obispo. |
| Frost, J J | Grocery store | Nipoma st | Nipoma st | S Luis Obispo. |
| Frost, J G | Wheelwright | San Luis Obispo | San Luis Obispo | S Luis Obispo. |
| Fuller, C E | Laborer | San Luis Obispo | San Luis Obispo | S Luis Obispo. |
| Fulton, J R | Farmer | San Luis Obispo Co. | nr San Luis Obispo | S Luis Obispo. |
| Gagiola, Philip | Laborer | San Luis Obispo | Monterey st | S Luis Obispo. |
| Gajiola, F, Jr | Farmer | San Luis Obispo Co. | nr Arroyo Grande | Arroyo Grande. |
| Galindo, Francisco. | Saloon | Morro st | Morro st | S Luis Obispo. |
| Galindo, F | Miner | San Luis Obispo Co. | nr San Luis Obispo | S Luis Obispo. |
| Galloway, J | Sawyer | San Luis Obispo | San Luis Obispo | S Luis Obispo. |
| Gallagher, D | Farmer | nr San Luis Obispo | San Luis Obispo Co. | S Luis Obispo. |
| Gallego, C | Farmer | nr San Luis Obispo | San Luis Obispo Co. | S Luis Obispo. |
| Gambel, Isaac | Carpenter | San Luis Obispo | Chorro st | S Luis Obispo. |
| Gamble, R, Sr | Physician | San Luis Obispo | San Luis Obispo | S Luis Obispo. |
| Gambill, N R | Miner | Cambria | Cambria | Cambria. |
| Gamboa, L | Laborer | San Luis Obispo | nr San Luis Obispo | S Luis Obispo. |
| Gamble, R, Jr | Farmer | nr San Luis Obispo | San Luis Obispo Co. | S Luis Obispo. |
| Ganoung, Ed | Contractor | San Luis Obispo | Nipoma st | S Luis Obispo. |
| Ganoung, H J | Farmer | San Luis Obispo Co. | nr San Luis Obispo | S Luis Obispo. |
| Gans, A | Merchant | Cambria | Cambria | Cambria. |
| Garcia, Guadalupe. | Laborer | San Luis Obispo | Palm st | S Luis Obispo. |
| Garcia, L | Whaleman | San Luis Obispo Co. | nr San Luis Obispo | S Luis Obispo. |
| Garcia, J .M | Laborer | nr Morro | San Luis Obispo Co. | Morro. |
| Garcia, J A | Teamster | nr San Luis Obispo | San Luis Obispo Co. | S Luis Obispo. |
| Garcia, J | Farmer | San Luis Obispo Co. | nr San Luis Obispo | S Luis Obispo. |

# DANA B. CLARK'S
## Tropical, Semi-Tropical,
### AND
## TEMPERATE CLIMATE
# NURSERIES

IN THE MONTECITO,

FOUR MILES EAST FROM TOWN,

## SANTA BARBARA, CAL.

---

Have the best stock of

### ORANGE, LEMON, LIME AND CITRON,

ON THE COAST.

---

## LARGE QUANTITIES OF LAQUAT and GUAVA.

---

Makes a Specialty of introducing and experimenting with new and rare kinds of Fruit and Ornamental Trees, Shrubs and Plants. Propagates everything in the open ground.

**NOT A HOT-HOUSE OR GLASS-HOUSE ON THE PLACE.**

## PRICE LISTS FREE, IN NOVEMBER

DIRECTORY OF SAN LUIS OBISPO COUNTY.

| Name. | Occupation. | Place of Business. | Residence. |
|---|---|---|---|
| Garcia, F | Laborer | nr San Luis Obispo | San Luis Obispo Co.. |
| Garcia, V | Farmer | nr San Jose | San Luis Obispo Co.. |
| Garcia, D | Laborer | San Luis Obispo Co. | nr San Luis Obispo... |
| Garcia, J M | Laborer | San Luis Obispo Co.. | nr Morro |
| Garcia, C | Laborer | nr San Luis Obispo .. | San Luis Obispo Co.. |
| Garcia, J A | Stock raiser | San Luis Obispo Co.. | nr San Luis Obispo.. |
| Garcia, J | Farmer | San Luis Obispo Co.. | nr San Luis Obispo.. |
| Garcia, T | Laborer | nr San Luis Obispo.. | San Luis Obispo Co.. |
| Garcia, P | Farmer | San Luis Obispo Co.. | nr San Luis Obispo... |
| Garcia, I | Farmer | nr San Luis Obispo... | San Luis Obispo Co.. |
| Garcia, A C | Butcher | San Luis Obispo | San Luis Obispo..... |
| Garcia, S | Laborer | nr San Luis Obispo... | San Luis Obispo Co.. |
| Gardner, P | Farmer | San Luis Obispo Co.. | nr San Luis Obispo.. |
| Garrett, E | Laborer | San Luis Obispo Co.. | nr San Luis Obispo... |
| Gatta, J N | Dairyman | Huasna Ranch | 10 m N W Arroyo G |
| Gaver, G J | Dairyman | nr Cambria | San Luis Obispo Co.. |
| Gaxiola, V | Silversmith | San Luis Obispo | San Luis Obispo..... |
| Gaxiola, F | Laborer | San Luis Obispo | San Luis Obispo ..... |
| Gaxiola, G | Farmer | nr Cambria | San Luis Obispo Co.. |
| Gaxiola, J | Farmer | San Luis Obispo Co.. | nr San Luis Obispo.. |
| Gaylord, J W | Dentist | Cambria | Cambria |
| Gergis, H | Farmer | nr San Luis Obispo.. | San Luis Obispo Co.. |
| Gettings, S A | Farmer | San Luis Obispo | nr San Luis Obispo.. |
| Gibson, J W | Farmer | San Luis Obispo Co.. | nr Cambria |
| Gibson, J D | Farmer | San Luis Obispo Co.. | nr San Simeon |
| Gibson, F M | Farmer | nr Cambria | San Luis Obispo Co.. |
| Giddings, S | Farmer | Oso Flaco | 3 m N Guadalupe.... |
| Gilbert, M | Capitalist | San Luis Obispo | San Luis Obispo..... |
| Gilbert, M | Farmer | nr Morro | San Luis Obispo Co.. |
| Gilbert D W | Farmer | 4 m W P R Spr'gs | San Luis Obispo Co.. |
| Gilliss, P | Farmer | San Luis Obispo Co.. | 4 m W Hot Springs. |
| Gillis, F A | Farmer | San Luis Obispo Co.. | nr Piedgas Blancas .. |
| Gill, W | Laborer | San Luis Obispo Co.. | nr Estrella |
| Gillespy, J | Laborer | nr San Miguel | San Luis Obispo Co.. |
| Gillis, N B | Teamster | nr Piedgas Blancas.. | San Luis Obispo Co.. |
| Gillis, P, Sr | Farmer | nr Piedgas Blancas... | San Luis Obispo Co.. |
| Gillis, P, Jr | Farmer | San Luis Obispo Co.. | nr Piedgas Blancas .. |
| Gillespie, N | Farmer | San Luis Obispo Co.. | nr Cambria |
| Gillen, W | Painter | Santa Margarita | Santa Margarita |
| Gillespie, W M | Farmer | nr Cambria | San Luis Obispo Co.. |
| Gillis, P | Teamster | nr Piedgas Blancas.. | San Luis Obispo Co.. |
| Gilmore, J H | Clerk | San Luis Obispo | San Luis Obispo |
| Gilroy, K | Farmer | nr San Luis Obispo.. | San Luis Obispo Co.. |
| Gilroy, J G | Stock raiser | Santa Isabel Ranch.. | San Luis Obispo Co.. |
| Gilroy, R H | Stock raiser | Santa Isabel Ranch.. | San Luis Obispo Co.. |
| Glass, T | Laborer | San Luis Obispo Co.. | nr San Luis Obispo.. |
| Glenn, R | Laborer | San Luis Obispo Co.. | nr San Luis Obispo.. |
| Glover, M W | Minister | San Luis Obispo | San Luis Obispo..... |
| Godfrey, H | Stock raiser | San Luis Obispo Co.. | nr Hot Springs |
| Goeggel, Wm | Watch maker | Monterey st | San Luis Obispo..... |
| Goldtree, N | Gen merchandise | | Pine st |
| Goldtree Bros | Gen merchandise | San Luis Obispo | San Luis Obispo |
| Goldtree, M | Clerk | San Luis Obispo | San Luis Obispo..... |
| Goldsworthy, G E | Miner | San Luis Obispo Co.. | nr Josephine |
| Goldsworthy, W | Butcher | Josephine | Josephine |
| Gomes, J B | Whaleman | Piedgas Blancas | Piedgas Blancas |
| Gomes, J | Whaleman | Piedgas Blancas | Piedgas Blancas |
| Gooch, — | Carpenter | | |
| Goodman, I | Stock raiser | San Luis Obispo Co.. | nr Estrella |
| Goodman, A J | Farmer | nr San Luis Obispo.. | San Luis Obispo Co.. |
| Goodman, J H | Banker | Napa | Napa |
| Gorduno, T | Laborer | nr San Luis Obispo.. | San Luis Obispo Co.. |
| Gordon, E H | Farmer | nr San Luis Obispo.. | San Luis Obispo Co.. |
| Gordon, T | Laborer | nr Estrella | San Luis Obispo Co.. |

WILLIAM M. LANDRUM.                  JAMES. M. RODGERS.

# LANDRUM & RODGERS,

### THE PIONEER BREEDERS AND FIRST IMPORTERS OF

## Angora Goats & Cotswold Sheep,

### On the Pacific Coast,

Have Constantly on Hand the Largest and Finest Flocks in America, of Pure Breeds and Grades.

**WATSONVILLE,**    -    -    **SANTA CRUZ COUNTY.**

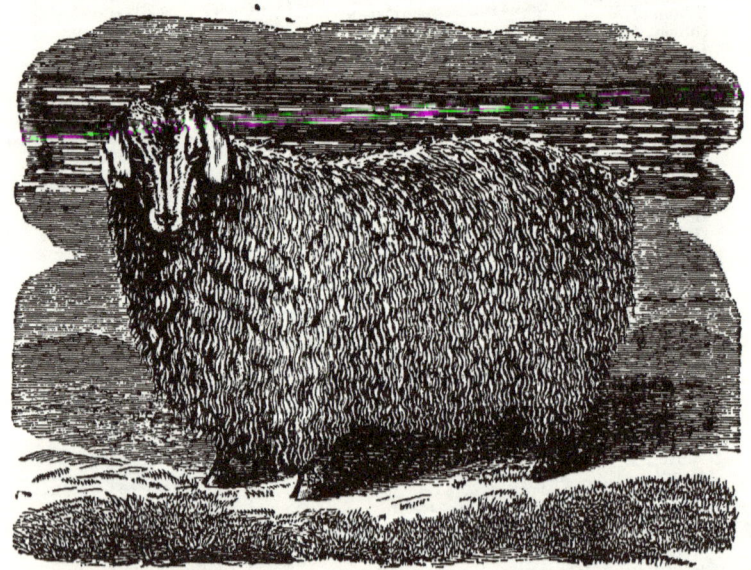

This Cut is from a Photograph of Imported NELLY, 9 years old; won the Sweepstakes Prize at the California State Fair in 1873, and sheared 7 lbs. of fine Mohair. We have others nearly as good. Parties owning Mountain Lands will do well to see our Flocks and investigate the ANGORA GOAT BUSINESS.

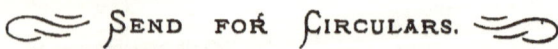

SEND FOR CIRCULARS.

We price everything according to merit.

## DIRECTORY OF SAN LUIS OBISPO COUNTY.

| Name. | Occupation. | Place of Business. | Residence. |
|---|---|---|---|
| Gould, A W | Laborer | San Luis Obispo Co. | nr Cambria |
| Grable, B | Undertaker | Broad st | Nipomo st |
| Gracy, Robert | Principal of sch'l. | San Luis Obispo | Cosmopolitan Hotel.. |
| Grady, Frank | Saloon | Morro st | cor Palm st |
| Grady, F | Farmer | nr Santa Margarita .. | San Luis Obispo Co.. |
| Grafins, J | Farmer | San Luis Obispo Co.. | nr San Luis Obispo .. |
| Grandstaff, J | Blacksmith | Cambria Road | San Luis Obispo Co.. |
| Grandstaff, J | Blacksmith | San Luis Obispo | San Luis Obispo |
| Grant, Geo E | Capitalist | San Francisco | Oakland |
| Grant, Lull & Co .. | Gen merchandise. | Main and Bridge | |
| Grassan, C | Laborer | nr San Luis Obispo.. | San Luis Obispo Co.. |
| Graves, W J | Attorney | Monterey st | Monterey st |
| Graves, E | Lawyer | San Luis Obispo | San Luis Obispo |
| Graves, C | Farmer | nr Cambria | San Luis Obispo Co.. |
| Gray, W M | Bar tender | Higuerra st | Higuerra st |
| Gray, W | Liquor dealer | San Luis Obispo | San Luis Obispo |
| Green, Joseph | Farmer | Santa Rosa st | Santa Rosa st |
| Green, J | Farmer | nr San Miguel | San Luis Obispo Co.. |
| Green, O | Farmer | nr Oso Flaco | San Luis Obispo Co.. |
| Greenberg, D | Stock raiser | San Luis Obispo Co.. | nr Hot Springs |
| Griep, Conrad | Farmer | | 1½ m S Arroyo Gr'de |
| Grier, M C | Farmer | nr Hot Springs | San Luis Obispo Co.. |
| Griffith, J E | | Morro | Morro |
| Griffin, J D | Farmer | nr San Miguel | San Luis Obispo Co.. |
| Griffith, J R | Farmer | San Luis Obispo | nr San Luis Obispo .. |
| Grigsby, W G | Farmer | nr Santa Margarita .. | San Luis Obispo Co.. |
| Grigsby, G W | Laborer | nr San Luis Obispo.. | San Luis Obispo Co.. |
| Gross, Chas | Teamster | San Luis Obispo | Mill st |
| Gross, F | Teamster | San Luis Obispo Co.. | nr Piedgas Blancas... |
| Grose, P | Farmer | nr San Luis Obispo.. | San Luis Obispo Co.. |
| Grose, C | Laborer | nr San Luis Obispo.. | San Luis Obispo Co.. |
| Groves, B T | Farmer | 8 m W P R Hot Sp's | San Luis Obispo Co.. |
| Gruell, H | Hotel keeper | Willows | 1 m N Morro |
| Gruell, J G | Farmer | nr Cambria | San Luis Obispo Co.. |
| Gruell, W S | Dairyman | nr Cambria | San Luis Obispo Co.. |
| Gruell, L H | Farmer | nr San Luis Obispo.. | San Luis Obispo Co.. |
| Grunert, Lewis | Tinsmith | Monterey st | Monterey st |
| Grunert, Mrs W | Doctress | San Luis Obispo | Monterey st |
| Guerrero, Blas | | | Chorro st |
| Guerra, J D | Laborer | San Luis Obispo Co.. | nr San Luis Obispo.. |
| Guerrero, B | Farmer | San Luis Obispo Co.. | nr San Luis Obispo.. |
| Guffy, W G | Farmer | San Luis Obispo Co.. | nr P R Hot Springs.. |
| Guhlstorff, J | Farmer | San Luis Obispo Co.. | nr San Miguel |
| Gullman, Francois | Farmer and stock | Tasajera Creek | 12 m N S Luis Ob'o |
| Gulnac, E | Laborer | nr Piedgas Blancas.. | San Luis Obispo Co.. |
| Gurole, J | Laborer | nr San Luis Obispo.. | San Luis Obispo Co.. |
| Haas, C | Teamster | | San Luis Obispo Co.. |
| Hackney, J | Blacksmith | Morro | Morro |
| Haines, W R | Dairyman | nr San Luis Obispo.. | San Luis Obispo Co.. |
| Halcom, C C | Laborer | San Luis Obispo Co.. | |
| Haley, B | Carpenter | San Luis Obispo | |
| Haley, Wm | Carpenter | San Luis Obispo | Monterey st |
| Hale, W J | Hunter | P R Hot Springs | San Luis Obispo Co.. |
| Hale, G | Carpenter | San Luis Obispo Co.. | |
| Haley, B | Teamster | | San Luis Obispo Co.. |
| Haley, W B | Carpenter | San Luis Obispo | San Luis Obispo |
| Hale, W J | Miner | San Luis Obispo Co.. | |
| Hall, Mrs M | Hotel keeper | Morro | Morro |
| Haller, J S | Farmer | San Luis Obispo Co.. | nr San Luis Obispo.. |
| Hall, I C | Farmer | San Luis Obispo Co | nr Cambria |
| Hall, W | Dairyman | San Luis Obispo Co.. | nr San Luis Obispo.. |
| Hallett, D | Carpenter | Morro | Morro |
| Hall, M M | Teacher | San Luis Obispo Co.. | |
| Halsel, H S | Farmer | San Luis Obispo Co.. | nr San Luis Obispo.. |

# BRITTAN, HOLBROOK & CO.,
#### — IMPORTERS OF —
# STOVES & METALS
### TINNERS' STOCK, TOOLS AND MACHINES,
## NOS. 111 & 113 CALIFORNIA, AND 17 & 19 DAVIS ST.
### SAN FRANCISCO.

---

## MRS. H. A. MOORE,
## The Great Scientific Hair Producer,
### NO. 523 KEARNY STREET, ROOMS NOS. 4 & 5, S. F.

Mrs. H. A. Moore would announce to ladies and gentlemen who desire the personal adornment of a fine suit of hair, that she has opened parlors for its express treatment. They are emphatically assured she possesses the skill to produce a full, flowing crop of hair on all stages of baldness. A few treatments will convince the most skeptical; this is no exaggeration. No mineral or damaging substances used. I have in my parlors photographs of well known citizens, exhibiting the contrast before and after treatment, which can be seen by those desiring it. No better evidence can be furnished. When they are seen, doubt vanishes. Preparations sent to all parts of the country.

---

# BAY HOTEL AND RESTAURANT

Avila.

**T**HE PUBLIC is informed that the undersigned has opened, at the People's Landing, the above designated Hotel, Restaurant, and Saloon, where he will endeavor to cater to the taste and comfort of his friends and the public at large, to the best of his ability.

Good and Clean beds; Meals at all hours. The best of Wines, Liquors and Cigars.

M. A. BENRIMO, Proprietor.

---

# R. R. Harris,
## COUNTY
# SURVEYOR

### OFFICE, IN COURT HOUSE
### SAN LUIS OBISPO.

### New and Reliable COUNTY MAPS
Made from my own surveys
### FOR SALE AT REASONABLE RATES

## DIRECTORY OF SAN LUIS OBISPO COUNTY. 53

| Name. | Occupation. | Place of Business. | Residence. | Town or P. O. |
|---|---|---|---|---|
| Hammerschlag, M | Genl merchant.... | Arroyo Grande........ | Arroyo Grande........ | Arroyo Grande. |
| Hammerschlag & Levy............... | Gen merchandise. | Monterey st............. | ....................... | S Luis Obispo. |
| Hammell, D R...... | Stock raiser......... | San Luis Obispo Co... | ........................ | Estrella. |
| Hampton, G W..... | Farmer............... | Cambria Road......... | 1 m N W S L Ob'po | S Luis Obispo. |
| Hanlon, J............. | Gardener .......... | San Luis Obispo Co... | nr San Luis Obispo... | S Luis Obispo. |
| Hanna H............... | Farmer............... | San Luis Obispo Co... | nr Arroyo Grande.... | Arroyo Grande. |
| Hanson, W J......... | Stock raiser ....... | San Luis Obispo Co... | nr Morro................ | Morro. |
| Hardie, A M......... | Farmer............... | San Luis Obispo Co... | nr Morro................ | Morro. |
| Hardie, T............. | Farmer............... | nr Morro................ | San Luis Obispo Co.. | Morro. |
| Hardy, J C........... | Farmer............... | nr San Luis Obispo.. | San Luis Obispo Co.. | S Luis Obispo. |
| Harford, John...... | Farmer............... | San Luis Obispo...... | San Luis Obispo...... | S Luis Obispo. |
| Harford, J........... | Lumber dealer.... | Railroad Landing... | Railroad Landing.... | S Luis Obispo. |
| Harford, F........... | Farmer............... | nr San Luis Obispo.. | San Luis Obispo Co.. | S Luis Obispo. |
| Harford, J........... | Stock raiser......... | San Luis Obispo Co... | nr San Luis Obispo.. | S Luis Obispo. |
| Harlow&Meachum | Farmers ............. | Huasna Ranch........ | 24 m S E San L O'po | Arroyo Grande. |
| Harlow, Capt M..... | Farmer............... | Huasna Ranch........ | 24 m S E San L O'po | Arroyo Grande. |
| Harper, H W........ | Laborer............... | San Luis Obispo Co... | nr Arroyo Grande.... | Arroyo Grande. |
| Harrison, M B...... | Attorney at law... | Calls Building........ | San Luis Obispo..... | S Luis Obispo. |
| Harris, R R.......... | Surveyor ........... | Court House........... | Broad st................. | S Luis Obispo. |
| Harrington, D...... | Saddlery&harness | Monterey st............ | Morro st................ | S Luis Obispo. |
| Harrold, Michel..... | Dairyman........... | Little Morro........... | 5 m N E Morro ...... | Morro. |
| Harris, A............. | Farmer............... | nr Morro............... | San Luis Obispo Co.. | Morro. |
| Harris, E S.......... | Farmer ...... ........ | San Luis Obispo Co... | nr Cambria............. | Cambria. |
| Harriman, J F...... | Farmer ............... | nr Cambria............ | San Luis Obispo Co.. | Cambria. |
| Harris, W............ | Teamster............ | ........................ | San Luis Obispo Co.. | S Luis Obispo. |
| Hartford, J.......... | Lumber............... | Monterey st............ | San Luis Obispo...... | S Luis Obispo. |
| Hart, A............... | Laborer............... | San Luis Obispo Co... | nr San Luis Obispo... | S Luis Obispo. |
| Hart, C............... | Blacksmith......... | San Luis Obispo...... | San Luis Obispo...... | S Luis Obispo. |
| Hartly, W B......... | Farmer ............. | nr Arroyo Grande... | San Luis Obispo Co.. | Arroyo Grande. |
| Hart, C............... | Dairyman........... | nr Cambria............ | San Luis Obispo Co.. | Cambria. |
| Hartnell, A.......... | Ranchero........... | nr San Luis Obispo... | San Luis Obispo Co.. | S Luis Obispo. |
| Hartnell, A ......... | Musician............ | San Luis Obispo...... | San Luis Obispo...... | S Luis Obispo. |
| Harvey, W .......... | Miner................. | Cambria............... | San Luis Obispo Co.. | Cambria. |
| Hasbrouck, A B..... | Laborer .............. | San Luis Obispo Co... | ........................ | S Luis Obispo. |
| Haskins, H C........ | Pastor ME church | San Luis Obispo...... | Garden st.............. | S Luis Obispo. |
| Haskin, J ............ | Blacksmith......... | Cambria................ | San Luis Obispo Co.. | Cambria. |
| Haskins, J H........ | Laborer .............. | San Luis Obispo Co... | ........................ | S Luis Obispo. |
| Haskell, A W....... | Insurance agent... | San Luis Obispo...... | San Luis Obispo Co.. | S Luis Obispo. |
| Hassen, Esteban... | Groceries............ | Chorro st............... | Chorro st............... | S Luis Obispo. |
| Hathway, A R ...... | Sheep raiser........ | San Luis Obispo...... | Peach st................ | S Luis Obispo. |
| Haworth, J K....... | Carpenter .......... | San Luis Obispo Co... | ........................ | S Luis Obispo. |
| Hayes, T C........... | Carpenter........... | Cambria............... | Cambria............... | Cambria. |
| Hayes, James ....... | Bridge builder .... | Avila................... | Avila................... | S Luis Obispo. |
| Hayes, Danl......... | Laborer............... | San Luis Obispo...... | Broad st................ | S Luis Obispo. |
| Hayes, Wm W....... | Physician........... | Monterey st............ | Monterey st............ | S Luis Obispo. |
| Hazard, R J......... | Dairyman........... | Cayucos............... | 8 m N Morro.......... | Morro. |
| Hazard, A............ | Dairyman........... | Los Osos............... | 10 m S Morro......... | Morro. |
| Hazard, A S......... | Farmer................ | nr Morro............... | San Luis Obispo Co.. | Morro. |
| Hazen, J B........... | Hardware store... | Broad st................ | Broad st................ | S Luis Obispo. |
| Hazen&Sandercock | Lumber yard...... | Broad st................ | ........................ | S Luis Obispo. |
| Hazkin, E............ | Blacksmith......... | Cambria............... | San Luis Obispo Co.. | Cambria. |
| Heald, O W. ....... | Farmer............... | ........................ | San Luis Obispo Co.. | Estella. |
| Hearne, R............ | Laborer............... | San Luis Obispo Co... | ........................ | Cambria. |
| Hearst, G W........ | Farmer............... | nr Cambria............ | San Luis Obispo Co.. | Cambria. |
| Hecox, A H......... | Stage driver........ | San Luis Obispo...... | Santa Rosa st......... | S Luis Obispo. |
| Hector, G W........ | Blacksmith......... | Cambria............... | Cambria............... | Cambria. |
| Hedrick, W C....... | Farmer............... | San Luis Obispo Co... | ........................ | Paso Robles. |
| Hemmi, P............ | Merchant............ | San Luis Obispo...... | San Luis Obispo...... | S Luis Obispo. |
| Hempton, G W..... | Farmer............... | Cnmbria Road........ | 1 m N W San L O'po | S Luis Obispo. |
| Hemphill, Wm..... | Dairyman........... | Arroyo Grande....... | Arroyo Grande........ | Arroyo Grande. |
| Henderson, W A.... | General store....... | Higuerra st............ | Nipoma st.............. | S Luis Obispo. |
| Henderson, M...... | Contractor ......... | San Luis Obispo...... | Nipoma st.............. | S Luis Obispo. |
| Hendricks, A J...... | Stage driver........ | P R Hot Springs..... | San Luis Obispo Co.. | Paso Robles. |

## SAN DIEGO, CALIFORNIA.

## THE FINEST HOTEL IN SOUTHERN CALIFORNIA

### 100 ROOMS.

FIRST-CLASS IN EVERY RESPECT.

S. W. CRAIGUE,　　　　　J. A. GORDON,
*PROPRIETOR.*　　　　　　*MANAGER.*

DIRECTORY OF SAN LUIS OBISPO COUNTY. 55

| Name. | Occupation. | Place of Business. | Residence. | Town or P. O. |
|---|---|---|---|---|
| Hendon, A P | Minister | Cambria | San Luis Obispo Co. | Cambria. |
| Hendrickson, G | Blacksmith | San Luis Obispo | San Luis Obispo Co. | S Luis Obispo. |
| Henderson M | Carpenter | San Luis Obispo | San Luis Obispo | S Luis Obispo. |
| Henry, D | Farmer | Stage Road | 3 m S Arroyo Grande | Arroyo Grande. |
| Hernandez, Torivio | Laborer | San Luis Obispo | Santa Rosa st | S Luis Obispo. |
| Hernandez, Juan | Ranchero | San Bernado | 6 m N E Morro | Morro. |
| Hernandez, S | Miner | nr Morro | San Luis Obispo Co. | Morro. |
| Herrera, Thomas | Farmer | Toro st | Toro st | S Luis Obispo. |
| Herrera, Antonio | Job wagon | San Luis.Obispo | Monterey st | S Luis Obispo. |
| Herrera, J B | Farmer | San Luis Obispo Co. | nr San Luis Obispo | S Luis Obispo. |
| Herrera, A | Farmer | nr San Luis Obispo | San Luis Obispo Co. | S Luis Obispo. |
| Herrera, T, Jr | Laborer | nr San Luis Obispo | San Luis Obispo Co. | S Luis Obispo. |
| Herrera, D | Farmer | nr San Luis Obispo | San Luis Obispo Co. | S Luis Obispo. |
| Herrera, R | Farmer | nr San Luis Obispo | San Luis Obispo Co. | S Luis Obispo. |
| Hess, Henry | Farmer | Arroyo Grande | Branch st | Arroyo Grande. |
| Hess, J | Farmer | nr P R Hot Springs | San Luis Obispo Co. | Paso Robles. |
| Hickman, J | Cook | P R Hot Springs | San Luis Obispo Co. | Paso Robles. |
| Higgins, E W | Farmer | nr Cambria | San Luis Obispo Co. | Cambria. |
| Higuerra, Thos | Farmer | San Luis Obispo | Nipoma st | S Luis Obispo. |
| Higuera, J J | Laborer | nr San Luis Obispo | San Luis Obispo Co. | S Luis Obispo. |
| Higuera, T E | Laborer | nr Morro | San Luis Obispo Co. | Morro. |
| Higuera, J R | Stock raiser | nr San Luis Obispo | San Luis Obispo Co. | S Luis Obispo. |
| Higuera, J A | Laborer | San Luis Obispo Co. | | S Luis Obispo. |
| Higuera, T B | Farmer | San Luis Obispo Co. | nr San Luis Obispo | S Luis Obispo. |
| Hilderbrand, Jas. | Boot maker | Monterey st | Monterey st | S Luis Obispo. |
| Hildebrand, J | Farmer | nr Cambria | San Luis Obispo Co. | Cambria. |
| Hill, J | Farmer | San Luis Obispo Co. | nr Cambria | Cambria. |
| Hill, R R | Carpenter | Arroyo Grande | Arroyo Grande | Arroyo Grande. |
| Hilliard, F | Farmer | San Luis Obispo Co. | nr San Luis Obispo | S Luis Obispo. |
| Hill, J W | Farmer | nr Cambria | San Luis Obispo Co. | Cambria. |
| Hinchliffe, B F | Surveyor | San Luis Obispo | San Luis Obispo Co. | S Luis Obispo. |
| Hinkle, P | Carpenter | San Luis Obispo | San Luis Obispo | S Luis Obispo. |
| Hoffman, Peter | Farmer | San Luis Obispo | Higuerra st | S Luis Obispo. |
| Hoffman, P V | Teamster | nr San Luis Obispo | nr San Luis Obispo | S Luis Obispo. |
| Hogan, J | Laborer | San Luis Obispo | nr San Luis Obispo | S Luis Obispo. |
| Hoge, G F | Farmer | nr Santa Margarita | San Luis Obispo Co. | S Margarita. |
| Holstadt, J W | Stock raiser | nr San Luis Obispo | San Luis Obispo Co. | S Luis Obispo. |
| Holcomb, R R | Farmer | nr Morro | San Luis Obispo Co. | Morro. |
| Holder, W | Blacksmith | San Luis Obispo | | S Luis Obispo. |
| Hollister, J | Farmer and stock | Cambria Road | 6 m N W San L O'po | S Luis Obispo. |
| Holloway, P | Farmer | nr San Simeon | San Luis Obispo Co. | San Simeon. |
| Hollinbeck, J D S | Farmer | nr Cambria | San Luis Obispo Co. | Cambria. |
| Holloway, C L | Stock raiser | nr San Luis Obispo | San Luis Obispo Co. | S Luis Obispo. |
| Holladay, W | Laborer | San Luis Obispo Co. | | S Luis Obispo. |
| Holmes, R R R | Photographer | Morro st | Morro st | S Luis Obispo. |
| Holt, James | Plasterer | San Luis Obispo | Monterey st | S Luis Obispo. |
| Holt Bros | Farmers | Huasna Ranch | 24 m S E San L O'po | Arroyo Grande. |
| Holt, W F | Laborer | | San Luis Obispo Co. | Arroyo Grande. |
| Hooper, John | Farmer | San Luis Obispo Co. | nr San Luis Obispo | S Luis Obispo. |
| Hopper, J B | Farmer | San Luis Obispo Co. | nr P R Hot Springs | Paso Robles. |
| Hopper, W | Farmer | San Miguel | San Luis Obispo Co. | San Miguel. |
| Hoskin, A J | Farmer | nr Morro | San Luis Obispo Co. | Morro. |
| Hottell, H H | Teacher | Arroyo Grande | Arroyo Grande | Arroyo Grande. |
| Houghton, J | Stock raiser | San Luis Obispo Co. | nr Estrella | Estrella. |
| Howe, E W | Ranchero | Mono Creek | 7 m N E Morro | Morro. |
| Howe, Isaac | Farmer & stock | Morro Creek | 16 m N W S L O'po | Morro. |
| Howell, I L | Farmer | nr San Luis Obispo | San Luis Obispo Co. | S Luis Obispo. |
| Hoyt, W H | Laborer | San Luis Obispo Co. | | S Luis Obispo. |
| Huasna,— | Farmer | Huasna Ranch | 24 m S E San L O'po | Arroyo Grande. |
| Hudson, A J | Stock raiser | nr Morro | San Luis Obispo Co. | Morro. |
| Hudson, W | Laborer | San Luis Obispo Co. | | S Luis Obispo. |
| Hughes, A J | Farmer | San Luis Obispo Co. | nr P R Hot Springs | Paso Robles. |
| Humphreys, W S | Farmer | nr Cambria | San Luis Obispo Co. | Cambria. |
| Humphreys, A P | Farmer | nr San Luis Obispo | San Luis Obispo Co. | S Luis Obispo. |

## THE
# Santa Barbara Press

**IS PUBLISHED DAILY AND WEEKLY,**

—BY—

## J. A. JOHNSON,

SANTA BARBARA, CAL.

OFFICE IN PRESS BUILDING, STATE ST.

---

**TERMS OF SUBSCRIPTION.**

Daily, per annum, in advance, . . $5.00
" six months, " . . 2.50
" three " " . . 1.50
Weekly, per annum, in advance, . 2.50
" six months, " . 1.25

Postage on WEEKLY prepaid by Publisher.

---

# SANTA BARBARA INDEX,

WM. F. RUSSELL, VIRGINIA F. RUSSELL,

EDITORS AND PUBLISHERS,

UNDER THE FIRM NAME OF

## RUSSELL & CO.

OFFICE ON STATE ST.,

BETWEEN COTA AND HALEY.

---

**TERMS OF SUBSCRIPTION.**

One Year. . . . . . . $4.00
Six Months, . . . . . . 2.00
Three Months, . . . . . . 1.00

---

# SAN LUIS OBISPO TRIBUNE.

**PUBLISHED EVERY SATURDAY**

—AT—

San Luis Obispo, - California,

BY

H. S. REMBAUGH and O. F. THORNTON,

**TERMS IN ADVANCE:**

For Three Months, . . . . . $1.50
For Six Months, . . . . . 2.50
For One Year, . . . . . 4.00

**ADVERTISING RATES:**

One Square (1 inch), first insertion, . . $1.50
Each subsequent insertion up to four, . - 1.00
Thereafter, for each insertion, . . - 35 Cts.

A liberal deduction from the above rates will be made on advertisements inserted by the year. Transient, Election and Legal Advertisements must be accompanied by the cash. All communications should be addressed to

## H. S. REMBAUGH & CO.

"TRIBUNE OFFICE," San Luis Obispo.

---

## COSMOPOLITAN
# Hair Dressing Emporium,

MONTEREY STREET,

San Luis Obispo, - California,

Is the place to go for a

**FASHIONABLE HAIRCUT, AN EASY SHAVE, OR A LUXURIOUS SHAMPOO.**

---

HAIR AND WHISKERS DYED IN ARTISTIC STYLE. HOT AND COLD BATHS AT ALL HOURS.

JESUS C. ARANA, - - Proprietor.

## DIRECTORY OF SAN LUIS OBISPO COUNTY. 57

| NAME. | OCCUPATION. | PLACE OF BUSINESS. | RESIDENCE. | TOWN OR P. O. |
|---|---|---|---|---|
| Hunter, G L............ | ...................... | San Luis Obispo...... | Bouchon st............... | S Luis Obispo. |
| Hunter, Mrs C...... | Milliner ............... | Morro st.................. | San Luis Obispo...... | S Luis Obispo. |
| Hunter, Geo........... | Bath tender......... | P R Hot Springs ..... | San Luis Obispo Co.. | Paso Robles. |
| Hurley, J................ | Farmer ................ | nr Santa Margarita... | San Luis Obispo Co.. | S Margarita. |
| Hutchinson, S M... | Farmer ................ | nr Morro................ | San Luis Obispo Co.. | Morro. |
| Ingalls, J N............ | Seaman................ | San Luis Obispo...... | San Luis Obispo...... | S Luis Obispo. |
| Isom, Hugh............ | Farmer ................ | Morro Creek ......... | 4 m N E Morro........ | Morro. |
| Ivens, C H............. | Farmer ................ | San Luis Obispo Co.. | nr Cambria............. | Cambria. |
| Jackson, J H.......... | Miner.................. | Cambria................ | Cambria................ | Cambria. |
| Jackson, A............. | Farmer ................ | San Luis Obispo Co.. | nr Santa Margarita... | S Margarita. |
| Jack, W D.............. | Merchant............. | San Luis Obispo..... | San Luis Obispo...... | S Luis Obispo. |
| Jackson, W........... | Farmer ................ | nr Cambria........... | San Luis Obispo Co.. | Cambria. |
| Jack, R E............... | Stock raiser ........ | San Luis Obispo Co.. | nr Estrella............... | Estrella. |
| James, John......... | Farmer ................ | San Luis Obispo Co.. | Paso Robles Ranch... | Paso Robles. |
| James, D W........... | Capitalist............. | P R Hot Springs...... | San Luis Obispo Co.. | S Luis Obispo. |
| James, S L, Jr....... | Stock raiser........ | nr Arroyo Grande... | San Luis Obispo Co.. | Arroyo Grande. |
| James, W B........... | Stock raiser ........ | San Luis Obispo Co.. | nr Arroyo Grande.... | Arroyo Grande. |
| James, C F............. | Stock raiser ........ | San Luis Obispo Co.. | nr Santa Margarita... | S Margarita. |
| Jaramillo, R.......... | Farmer ................ | San Luis Obispo Co.. | nr Santa Margarita... | S Margarita. |
| Jasper, G............... | Farmer................ | San Luis Obispo Co.. | nr San Luis Obispo.. | S Luis Obispo. |
| Jatta, J N............... | Dairyman ........... | nr Arroyo Grande.... | San Luis Obispo Co.. | Arroyo Grande. |
| Jaurez, L............... | Laborer................ | San Luis Obispo Co.. | nr P R Hot Springs.. | Paso Robles. |
| Jeffreys, W M........ | Stock raiser........ | San Luis Obispo Co.. | nr San Miguel......... | San Miguel. |
| Jelingsmith, J....... | Farmer ................ | 10 m W of P R H S.. | San Luis Obispo Co.. | Paso Robles. |
| Jennings, J M....... | Farmer ................ | nr Cambria........... | San Luis Obispo Co.. | Cambria. |
| Jerome, W............. | Carpenter ........... | San Luis Obispo..... | San Luis Obispo...... | S Luis Obispo. |
| Jessie, J................. | Farmer ................ | San Luis Obispo Co.. | nr San Luis Obispo.. | S Luis Obispo. |
| Jessee, J L............. | Dairyman............ | San Luis Obispo Co.. | nr Arroyo Grande ... | Arroyo Grande. |
| Jessee, A C............ | Dairyman............. | nr Santa Margarita .. | San Luis Obispo Co.. | S Margarita. |
| Jewett, Henry....... | Musician............. | Santa Rosa st......... | Santa Rosa st......... | S Luis Obispo. |
| Jewett, H............... | Laborer................ | San Luis Obispo Co.. | nr San Luis Obispo.. | S Luis Obispo. |
| Jimenez, N............ | Farmer ................ | San Luis Obispo Co.. | nr Estella............... | Estrella. |
| Joaquin, A............. | Farmer ................ | nr Las Tablas......... | San Luis Obispo Co.. | Las Tablas. |
| Johe, W................. | Farmer ................ | nr San Luis Obispo.. | San Luis Obispo Co.. | S Luis Obispo. |
| Johe, G.................. | Shoe maker........ | San Luis Obispo..... | San Luis Obispo...... | S Luis Obispo. |
| Johnson, Albert.... | Farmer ................ | Cambria Road........ | 1¼ m N W S L O'po | S Luis Obispo. |
| Johnson, W........... | Teamster ............ | San Luis Obispo Co.. | Paso Robles Ranch... | Paso Robles. |
| Johnson, Anderson | Farmer ................ | Oso Flaco.............. | 1½ m N Guadalupe.. | Guadalupe. |
| Johnson, Irvine..... | Farmer ................ | Oso Flaco.............. | 1 m N Guadalupe.... | Gaudalupe. |
| Johnson, J R......... | Carpenter ........... | San Luis Obispo..... | Nipoma st ............. | S Luis Obispo. |
| Johnson, H H........ | Dairyman............ | Berros Creek ......... | 6 m SE A Grande.... | Arroyo Grande. |
| Johnson, Thos...... | Farmer................ | Cambria Road........ | ¾ m N W S L Ob'po | S Luis Obispo. |
| Johnson, David..... | Contractor .......... | Monterey st........... | Monterey st........... | S Luis Obispo. |
| Johnson, Chas H... | Farmer ................ | Cambria Road........ | 1¼ m N W S L Ob'po | S Luis Obispo. |
| Johnson, John...... | Carpenter ........... | San Luis Obispo..... | Toro st.................. | S Luis Obispo. |
| Johnson, C H........ | Merchant............. | San Luis Obispo..... | San Luis Obispo...... | S Luis Obispo. |
| Johnson, C A........ | Farmer ................ | nr San Luis Obispo.. | San Luis Obispo Co.. | S Luis Obispo. |
| Johnson, J............ | Farmer ................ | nr Cambria........... | San Luis Obispo Co.. | Cambria. |
| Johnson, J N......... | Blacksmith......... | San Luis Obispo..... | San Luis Obispo...... | S Luis Obispo. |
| Johnson, T W........ | Farmer ................ | nr San Luis Obispo.. | San Luis Obispo Co.. | S Luis Obispo. |
| Johnson, J S.......... | Teamster............. | San Luis Obispo Co.. | nr San Luis Obispo.. | S Luis Obispo. |
| Johnson, A........... | Miner.................. | San Luis Obispo..... | San Luis Obispo...... | S Luis Obispo. |
| Johnson, J A......... | Merchant............. | Arroyo Grande....... | Arroyo Grande........ | Arroyo Grande. |
| Johnson, D M........ | Laborer................ | nr San Luis Obispo.. | San Luis Obispo Co.. | S Luis Obispo. |
| Johnson, N A........ | Farmer ................ | nr San Luis Obispo.. | San Luis Obispo Co.. | S Luis Obispo. |
| Johnson, J J.......... | Farmer ................ | nr San Luis Obispo.. | San Luis Obispo Co.. | S Luis Obispo. |
| Johnson, E H........ | Farmer ................ | San Luis Obispo Co.. | nr Santa Margarita... | S Margarita. |
| Johnson, W E ...... | Teamster............. | nr Cambria ........... | San Luis Obispo Co.. | Cambria. |
| Johnson, I............. | Farmer ................ | San Luis Obispo Co.. | nr San Luis Obispo.. | S Luis Obispo. |
| Johnson, J............ | Laborer................ | San Luis Obispo Co.. | nr Cambria............. | Cambria. |
| Johnston, H H....... | Dairyman............ | nr Arroyo Grande.... | San Luis Obispo Co.. | Arroyo Grande. |
| Johnson, T B......... | Dairyman........... | San Luis Obispo Co.. | nr Santa Margarita... | S Margarita. |
| Johnson, J............ | Stock raiser ........ | nr Cambria............ | San Luis Obispo Co.. | Cambria. |
| Joice, W................ | Laborer ............... | nr San Luis Obispo.. | San Luis Obispo Co.. | S Luis Obispo. |

# H. H. WILSON,

—LATE—

# WILSON & EVANS

——IMPORTER OF——

## Breech and Muzzle-Loading Shot Guns

Of the Best English and American Makers, and Agent of the Latest and Best Style Rifles.

Importers of  every description of

## Fire Arms, Fishing Tackle

### AND GUN MATERIALS.

COLT'S, SMITH AND WESSON, SHARP'S, HENRY'S AND SPENCER'S RIFLES AND PISTOLS. DIXON'S POWDER FLASKS, SHOT POUCHES, &C. WOSTENHOLM'S POCKET CUTLERY, ELEY'S CAPS, WADS, AND ALL KINDS OF BREECH-LOADING AMMUNITION.

## NO. 513 CLAY STREET,

### SAN FRANCISCO.

New Work made to order. Repairing done in the best manner, and warranted to give satisfaction.

DIRECTORY OF SAN LUIS OBISPO COUNTY. 59

| NAME. | OCCUPATION. | PLACE OF BUSINESS. | RESIDENCE. | TOWN OR P. O. |
|---|---|---|---|---|
| Jones, W S | Stock | Arroyo Grande | 2 m N Arroyo Gr'de | Arroyo Grande. |
| Jones, F P | Farmer | Avila | Avila | S Luis Obispo. |
| Jones, J M | Stock raiser | San Luis Obispo | Cosmopolitan Hotel | S Luis Obispo. |
| Jones, C D P | Stock raiser | San Luis Obispo Co | nr Estrella | Estrella. |
| Jones, H B | Carpenter | Cambria | Cambria | Cambria. |
| Jones, J M | Stock raiser | nr La Panza | San Luis Obispo Co | La Panza. |
| Jones, J W | Laborer | San Luis Obispo Co | nr Oso Flaco | Oso Flaco. |
| Jones, B | Carpenter | Morro | Morro | Morro. |
| Jones, T B | Farmer | nr San Luis Obispo | San Luis Obispo Co | S Luis Obispo. |
| Jones, G F | Farmer | nr San Luis Obispo | San Luis Obispo Co | S Luis Obispo. |
| Jones, W L | Painter | San Luis Obispo Co | nr Arroyo Grande | Arroyo Grande. |
| Jones, F P | Hotel keeper | San Luis Obispo | San Luis Obispo | S Luis Obispo. |
| Jones, H M | Laborer | nr San Miguel | San Luis Obispo Co | San Miguel. |
| Juarez, A F | Laborer | nr San Luis Obispo | San Luis Obispo Co | S Luis Obispo. |
| Judson, W A | Dairyman | San Luis Obispo Co | nr Cambria | Cambria. |
| Kaetzel, P | Farmer | San Luis Obispo Co | nr Cambria | Cambria. |
| Kaiser, Sol | Clerk | Monterey st | Monterey st | S Luis Obispo. |
| Kaiser, L M | Gen merchandise | | Guadalupe | Guadalupe. |
| Kamerling, W | Laborer | nr Oso Flaco | San Luis Obispo Co | Oso Flaco. |
| Kammaline, W | Farmer | Oso Flaco | 2½ m N Guadalupe | Guadalupe. |
| Kastan, L | Clerk | Monterey st | Monterey st | S Luis Obispo. |
| Kastan, L | Merchant | San Luis Obispo | San Luis Obispo | S Luis Obispo. |
| Keane, J | Carpenter | San Luis Obispo | San Luis Obispo | S Luis Obispo. |
| Kearney, James | Teamster | 7 m W P R H Sp'gs | San Luis Obispo Co | Paso Robles. |
| Keating, T | Carpenter | San Luis Obispo | San Luis Obispo | S Luis Obispo. |
| Keeler, J | Farmer | San Luis Obispo Co | nr San Luis Obispo | S Luis Obispo. |
| Kelley, B | Laborer | nr Arroyo Grande | San Luis Obispo Co | Arroyo Grande. |
| Kelley, J | Laborer | San Luis Obispo Co | nr San Luis Obispo | S Luis Obispo. |
| Kelsey, A | Carpenter | Cambria | Cambria | Cambria. |
| Kelsey, I | Farmer | San Luis Obispo Co | nr Morro | Morro. |
| Kemp, Wm | Farmer | Oso Flaco | | Guadalupe. |
| Kennedy, R D | Lumberman | nr Morro | San Luis Obispo Co | Morro. |
| Kent, H A | Stock raiser | nr San Luis Obispo | San Luis Obispo Co | S Luis Obispo. |
| Kent, C C | Farmer | nr Piedgas Blancas | San Luis Obispo Co | Piedgas Bl'cas. |
| Kernan, Peter A | Blacksmith | Monterey st | Monterey st | S Luis Obispo. |
| Kester, J F | Hotel keeper | Morro Willows | 1 m N Morro | Morro. |
| Kester, J G | Farmer | San Luis Obispo | nr Morro | Morro. |
| Kester, J F | Stock raiser | San Luis Obispo Co | nr Morro | Morro. |
| Kester, J B | Farmer | San Luis Obispo Co | nr Morro | Morro. |
| Kester, J L | Farmer | nr Morro | San Luis Obispo Co | Morro. |
| Ketchum, Yank | Horse breaker | San Luis Obispo Co | P R Hot Springs | Paso Robles. |
| Ketchum, E B | Farmer | Arroyo Grande | Arroyo Grande | Arroyo Grande. |
| Ketchum, Fred'k | Farmer | Arroyo Grande | Arroyo Grande | Arroyo Grande. |
| Ketchum, T | Farmer | San Luis Obispo Co | nr Arroyo Grande | Arroyo Grande. |
| Ketchum, M B | Laborer | San Luis Obispo Co | P R Hot Springs | Paso Robles. |
| Kilbride, T | Miner | San Luis Obispo | San Luis Obispo | S Luis Obispo. |
| Kimball, Fred H | Genl merchant | Higuerra st | Monterey st | S Luis Obispo. |
| Kimball, J | Carpenter | San Luis Obispo | Nipoma st | S Luis Obispo. |
| Kimball, W | Carpenter | | Nipoma st | S Luis Obispo. |
| Kimmel, L | Farmer | nr Cambria | San Luis Obispo Co | Cambria. |
| King, D | Farmer | San Luis Obispo Co | nr Arroyo Grande | Arroyo Grande. |
| King, E | Farmer | nr Cambria | San Luis Obispo Co | Cambria. |
| King, N | Teamster | San Luis Obispo Co | nr San Luis Obispo | S Luis Obispo. |
| Kingery, S | Farmer | nr Morro | San Luis Obispo Co | Morro. |
| Kink, W F | Farmer | San Luis Obispo | nr Cambria | Cambria. |
| Kinney, S S | Farmer | nr Arroyo Grande | San Luis Obispo Co | Arroyo Grande. |
| Kirby, C H | Farmer | nr Morro | San Luis Obispo Co | Morro. |
| Kirkendall, T | Farmer | nr San Miguel | San Luis Obispo Co | San Miguel. |
| Kirkpatrick, J M | Miner | San Luis Obispo | San Luis Obispo | S Luis Obispo. |
| Kirk, R | Stock raiser | San Luis Obispo Co | P R Hot Springs | Paso Robles. |
| Kirkpatrick, A | Farmer | San Luis Obispo Co | nr Cambria | Cambria. |
| Kleher, J | Wagon maker | San Miguel | San Miguel | San Miguel. |
| Kline, H | Farmer | Oso Flaco | | Guadalupe. |
| Klippel, C P | Farmer | nr San Miguel | San Luis Obispo Co | San Miguel. |

# Daily Evening Post

### The Popular Journal of San Francisco.

THE EVENING POST is published every afternoon (Sundays excepted) at 2 p. m., 3:30 p. m., and 4:30 p. m., thus furnishing the latest news up to the time of departure of each mail.

The EVENING POST is now in the fourth year of its publication, and has attained a larger circulation than all the other Evening Papers on the Coast combined.

The POST publishes the best and fullest Telegraphic Reports of any San Francisco Paper, while in the fullness and reliability of its Local Reports, the freshness and vigor of its Editorials, and the reliability of its Stock Articles, it is confessedly ahead of all its contemporaries.

Its Market Reports are prepared by Special Reporters, and it contains full details of all Commercial Intelligence, while it is the only Afternoon Paper in San Francisco publishing the

## COMPLETE SALES OF THE STOCK BOARD,

A special Telegraphic Wire connecting the Stock Exchange with its office, by means of which sales are instantaneously reported up to the latest minute.

### TERMS.

The POST is served by Carriers in San Francisco, Oakland, Sacramento and other large towns for 12½ cents per week, and is sent by mail for $5 per year.

Owing to the time of departure of the mails, the POST reaches many parts of the State with twelve hours later news than any other San Francisco Paper.

DIRECTORY OF SAN LUIS OBISPO COUNTY. 61

| NAME. | OCCUPATION. | PLACE OF BUSINESS. | RESIDENCE. | TOWN OR P. O. |
|---|---|---|---|---|
| Knapp, — | Merchant | San Jose Ranch | 30 m E San L O'po.. | S Margarita. |
| Knapp, J | Farmer | San Luis Obispo Co.. | nr San Jose | San Jose. |
| Kohn, F | Blacksmith | San Luis Obispo | San Luis Obispo | S Luis Obispo. |
| Krebs, Ernst | Druggist | Monterey st | cor Geary st | S Luis Obispo. |
| Krebs & Co, E | Druggists | Monterey st | | S Luis Obispo. |
| Krebs, Julius | Dep co clerk | Court House | Garden st | S Luis Obispo. |
| Kutnow, H | Clerk | Monterey st | Monterey st | S Luis Obispo. |
| Kurtz, C A | Brewer | San Luis Obispo | San Luis Obispo | S Luis Obispo. |
| Labish, O | Blacksmith | San Luis Obispo | San Luis Obispo | S Luis Obispo. |
| Lacy, H | Laborer | San Luis Obispo Co.. | nr San Luis Obispo.. | S Luis Obispo. |
| Laff, Girard | Farmer | Santa Barbara S R.. | 2 m S San Luis Ob.. | S Luis Obispo. |
| Laflandre. Alex | Tailor | Monterey st | Monterey st | S Luis Obispo. |
| Laguna, E | Farmer | nr San Luis Obispo.. | San Luis Obispo Co.. | S Luis Obispo. |
| Lahey, P | Farmer | nr San Miguel | San Luis Obispo Co. | San Miguel. |
| Laird, H S | Carpenter | Higuerra st | Nipoma st | S Luis Obispo. |
| Laird, J M | Farmer | nr Cambria | San Luis Obispo Co. | Cambria. |
| Lake, C G | Farmer | nr Piedgas Blancas.. | San Luis Obispo Co. | Pied's Blancas. |
| Lakin, G W | Surveyor | San Luis Obispo | San Luis Obispo | S Luis Obispo. |
| Lally, J | Farmer | nr P R Hot Springs.. | San Luis Obispo Co. | Paso Robles. |
| Lambert, D | Teacher | Morro | Morro | Morro. |
| Lameda, T | Laborer | San Luis Obispo Co.. | nr Morro | Morro. |
| Landecker, Wm B. | Clerk | Monterey st | Monterey st | S Luis Obispo. |
| Landeker, Lazare.. | Book keeper | Monterey st | Broad st | S Luis Obispo. |
| Lane, W T | Physician | Cambria | Cambria | Cambria. |
| Lane, E M | Laborer | San Luis Obispo Co.. | nr San Luis Obispo.. | S Luis Obispo. |
| Lang, Geo | Plumber | San Luis Obispo | Monterey st | S Luis Obispo. |
| Langhery, Henry | | nr Cambria | Morro st | S Luis Obispo. |
| Langlois, Wm | Farmer | Morro Creek | 8 m N E Morro | Morro. |
| Langhery, C A | Dairyman | nr Cambria | San Luis Obispo Co. | Cambria. |
| Larias, O | Laborer | nr San Luis Obispo.. | San Luis Obispo Co. | Cambria. |
| Lasar, M | Gen merchandise. | Chorro st | Chorro st | S Luis Obispo. |
| Lasar, Emanuel | Gen merchandise. | Monterey st | Chorro st | S Luis Obispo. |
| Latham, R W | Farmer | nr Cambria | San Luis Obispo Co. | Cambria. |
| Lawler, W B | Clerk | Piedgas Blancas | Piedgas Blancas | Piedgas Bl'cas. |
| Lawrence, M A | Barber | Chorro st | Monterey st | S Luis Obispo. |
| Lazcano, Bernardo. | Co treasurer | Court House | San Jose Valley | S Luis Obispo. |
| Lazcano, M | Farmer | San Luis Obispo Co.. | nr San Luis Obispo.. | San Jose. |
| Leach, J W | Minister | San Luis Obispo | San Luis Obispo | S Luis Obispo. |
| Leary. J | Farmer | San Luis Obispo Co.. | nr San Simeon | San Simeon. |
| Lee, W W | Painter | Morro st | Mill st | S Luis Obispo. |
| Lee, R F | Blacksmith | Higuerra st | | S Luis Obispo. |
| Lee, Henry | Blacksmith | Higuerra st | Cambria Road | S Luis Obispo. |
| Lee, W | Blacksmith | San Luis Obispo | San Luis Obispo | S Luis Obispo. |
| Lee, C | Farmer | nr San Luis Obispo.. | San Luis Obispo Co. | S Luis Obispo. |
| Leff, Gerard | Farmer | Santa Barbara Rd ... | 1½ m S San Luis Ob | S Luis Obispo. |
| Leffingwell, A C | Carpenter | Cambria | Cambria | Cambria. |
| Leffingwell, J L | Dairyman | nr Cambria | San Luis Obispo Co. | Cambria. |
| Leffingwell, W, Jr. | Engineer | Cambria | Cambria | Cambria. |
| Leffingwell, W, Sr | Farmer | San Luis Obispo Co.. | nr Cambria | Cambria. |
| Leighton, Danl | Dep assessor | San Simeon | Cambria | S Luis Obispo. |
| Leighton, D | Farmer | nr Cambria | San Luis Obispo Co. | Cambria. |
| Leman, F | Dairyman | San Luis Obispo Co.. | nr Cambria | Cambria. |
| Le Prince, V A | Bar keeper | San Luis Obispo | San Luis Obispo | S Luis Obispo. |
| Levy, A | Watch maker | Monterey st | San Luis Obispo | S Luis Obispo. |
| Levy, I D | Gen merchandise | Monterey st | Monterey st | S Luis Obispo. |
| Levy, I D | Clerk | San Luis Obispo | San Luis Obispo | S Luis Obispo. |
| Lewelling, J P | Policeman | San Luis Obispo | San Luis Obispo | S Luis Obispo. |
| Lewis, Thos | Carpenter | San Luis Obispo | Chorro st | S Luis Obispo. |
| Lewis, N | Farmer | San Luis Obispo Rd.. | 2 m N Arroyo G'e... | Arroyo Grande. |
| Lewis, T | Carpenter | San Luis Obispo Co.. | San Luis Obispo | S Luis Obispo. |
| Lewis, J M | Teamster | San Luis Obispo Co.. | nr San Luis Obispo.. | S Luis Obispo. |
| Lightner, H F | Farmer | nr San Luis Obispo.. | San Luis Obispo Co. | S Luis Obispo. |
| Limas, A | Laborer | nr San Luis Obispo.. | San Luis Obispo Co. | S Luis Obispo. |
| Linbridge, R C | Seaman | San Luis Obispo | San Luis Obispo | S Luis Obispo. |

## A. SCHUMACHE[R]

Importer of and Dealer in

## LEATHER & FIND[INGS]

Manufacturer of BOOT LEGS & SHOE UPPE[RS]

Depot of Crist & Rued's Skirting, Harness, Bridle and Sol[e]

417 Battery Street, Corner Me[rchant]

P. O. BOX 1767.

## J. C. TURNE[R]

## BLACKSMITH AND HORSE[SHOER]

5 MILES SOUTH FROM SAN LUIS OBIS[PO]

Horseshoeing, Repairing of all kinds of Agricultural Implements. General
and durably. All work done in the best manner.

## Book & Job Pr[inter]

AND BLANK BOOK MANUFACTURER

420 CLAY ST., BELOW SANSOME, SAN [FRANCISCO]

*Every Variety of Job Printing Promptly Exe[cuted]*

Orders from the interior receive the same attention as if the parties were

## DIRECTORY OF SAN LUIS OBISPO COUNTY. 63

| NAME. | OCCUPATION. | PLACE OF BUSINESS. | RESIDENCE. | TOWN OR P. O. |
|---|---|---|---|---|
| Lincoln, Wearmouth & Co | Carpenters | Higuerra st | Broad st | S Luis Obispo. |
| Lincoln, Geo W | Clerk | Monterey st | Broad st | S Luis Obispo. |
| Lincoln, E W | Carpenter | San Luis Obispo | Broad st | S Luis Obispo. |
| Lincholin, E W | Carpenter | San Luis Obispo | San Luis Obispo | S Luis Obispo. |
| Lindenmayer, Julius | Brewer | Monterey st | Monterey st | S Luis Obispo. |
| Lindner, J D | Carpenter | Cambria | Cambria | Cambria. |
| Lingo, G W | Hotel keeper | Cambria | Cambria | Cambria. |
| Liqueiro, Francisco | Stock raiser | Liqueiro Ranch | 16 m N San Luis Ob. | S Margarita. |
| Littenfeldt, M | Clerk | Monterey st | Monterey st | S Luis Obispo. |
| Little, H W | Saloon and hall | Monterey st | Osos st | S Luis Obispo. |
| Little & Cochran | Saloon and hall | Monterey st |  | S Luis Obispo. |
| Lobe, — | Farmer | Guadalupe Road | 2 m S Arroyo Gr'de. | Arroyo Grande. |
| Lockwood, M H | Teacher | Morro Creek | 4¼ m N E Morro | Morro. |
| Lockhart, W T | Mining sup't | San Luis Obispo Co. | nr P R Hot Springs | Josephine. |
| Lockhart, J T | Ass mining sup't. | nr P R Hot Springs | San Luis Obispo Co. | Josephine. |
| Lockwood, J N | Farmer | San Luis Obispo Co. | nr Morro | Morro. |
| Loewenstein, J | Tailor | Monterey st | Marsh st | S Luis Obispo. |
| Loewenstein, G | Tailor | Monterey st | Monterey st | S Luis Obispo. |
| Loewenstein, Julius | Tailor | Monterey st | Pacific st | S Luis Obispo. |
| Logan, R | Dairyman | San Luis Obispo Co. | nr Cambria | Cambria. |
| Logan, D A | Dairyman | nr Old Creek | San Luis Obispo Co. | Old Creek. |
| Lonchrey, J | Farmer | San Luis Obispo Co. | nr P R Hot Springs | Paso Robles. |
| Long, W | Stage driver | San Luis Obispo | San Luis Obispo | S Luis Obispo. |
| Long, R | Laborer | San Luis Obispo Co. | nr Cambria | Cambria. |
| Loobliner, H | Gen merchandise | Monterey st | Monterey st | S Luis Obispo. |
| Loomis, A M | Supt S L W Co. | Santa Rosa st | Monterey st | S Luis Obispo. |
| Lopez, T | Laborer | San Luis Obispo Co. | nr San Luis Obispo. | S Luis Obispo. |
| Lopez, J M | Dairyman | San Luis Obispo Co. | nr Piedgas Blancas | Piedgas Bl'cas. |
| Lopez, G J | Laborer | nr Arroyo Grande | San Luis Obispo | Arroyo Grande. |
| Lopez, J M | Farmer | San Luis Obispo Co. | nr San Luis Obispo. | S Luis Obispo. |
| Lopez, L | Merchant | San Luis Obispo | San Luis Obispo | S Luis Obispo. |
| Lorenzana, A | Farmer | nr Estrella | San Luis Obispo Co. | Estrella. |
| Loring, E P | Dairyman | nr Old Creek | San Luis Obispo Co. | Old Creek. |
| Lossius, Rudolph | Clerk | Cosmopolitan Hotel | Monterey st | S Luis Obispo. |
| Louvell, Paul | Saloon | Santa Margarita Rd. | 4 m NE San L O'po. | S Luis Obispo. |
| Louvel, P P | Farmer | San Luis Obispo Co. | nr San Luis Obispo. | S Luis Obispo. |
| Lovett, C M | Teacher | San Luis Obispo | San Luis Obispo | S Luis Obispo. |
| Low, W M | Laborer | San Luis Obispo Co. | nr San Luis Obispo. | S Luis Obispo. |
| Lowell, P | Laborer | San Luis Obispo Co. | nr Arroyo Grande | Arroyo Grande. |
| Lucano, P | Laborer | nr San Luis Obispo. | San Luis Obispo Co. | S Luis Obispo. |
| Lucas, W B | Laborer | San Luis Obispo Co. | nr San Luis Obispo. | S Luis Obispo. |
| Lucero, J | Laborer | nr San Jose | San Luis Obispo Co. | San Jose. |
| Lucero, P A | Laborer | nr Morro | San Luis Obispo Co. | Morro. |
| Lucero, J | Laborer | nr Morro | San Luis Obispo Co. | Morro. |
| Lugo, J Y | Laborer | nr San Luis Obispo. | San Luis Obispo Co. | S Luis Obispo. |
| Lull, — | Gen merchandise. | Main and Bridge sts | Main st | Cambria. |
| Lunceford, W | Farmer | nr San Luis Obispo. | San Luis Obispo Co. | S Luis Obispo. |
| Lunceford, W | Farmer | San Luis Obispo Co. | nr Santa Margarita. | S Margarita. |
| Lunceford, W T | Stock raiser | San Luis Obispo Co. | nr P R Hot Springs. | Paso Robles. |
| Lurick, H | Carpenter | San Luis Obispo | San Luis Obispo | S Luis Obispo. |
| Luthrill, W | Laborer | San Luis Obispo Co. | nr San Luis Obispo. | S Luis Obispo. |
| Luther, R | Blacksmith | Cambria | Cambria | Cambria. |
| Lynch, W J | Saddler | Arroyo Grande | Arroyo Grande | Arroyo Grande. |
| Lynch, J | Merchant | Cambria | Cambria | Cambria. |
| Lynch, J | Laborer | nr P R Hot Springs | San Luis Obispo Co. | Paso Robles. |
| Lynn, G D | Laborer | San Luis Obispo | San Luis Obispo | S Luis Obispo. |
| Lyon, J M | Blacksmith | Arroyo Grande | Branch st | Arroyo Grande. |
| Machado, H | Whaleman | Piedgas Blancas | Piedgas Blancas | Piedgas Bl'cas. |
| Machado, J | Whaleman | Piedgas Blancas | Piedgas Blancas | Piedgas Bl'cas. |
| Madariaga, J A | Musician | San Luis Obispo | San Luis Obispo | S Luis Obispo. |
| Madigan, J | Laborer | nr San Luis Obispo. | San Luis Obispo Co. | S Luis Obispo. |

## SAN BERNARDINO.

H. GOULD, - - Proprietor.

## THREE DOLLARS PER ANNUM.

DIRECTORY OF SAN LUIS OBISPO COUNTY. 65

| Name. | Occupation. | Place of Business. | Residence. | Town or P. O. |
|---|---|---|---|---|
| Madrid, L | Laborer | San Luis Obispo Co.. | nr San Luis Obispo... | S Luis Obispo. |
| Maggi, K | Clerk | Monterey st | Monterey st | S Luis Obispo. |
| Maguire, Mrs | Laundry | San Luis Obispo | Chorro st | S Luis Obispo. |
| Mahoney, J B | | Mahoney Mine | San Luis Obispo Co.. | Paso Robles. |
| Mahony, J F | Miner | Josephine | Josephine | Josephine. |
| Muhurin, T | Farmer | San Luis Obispo Co.. | nr Cambria | Cambria. |
| Major, E D | Constable | Monterey st | | S Luis Obispo. |
| Major, J F | Laborer | San Luis Obispo Co.. | nr San Luis Obispo.. | S Luis Obispo. |
| Mallagh, D P | Livery stable | Avila | Avila | S Luis Obispo. |
| Mallagh, David | Agent | G N & P S S Co | Avila | S Luis Obispo. |
| Malzacher, S | Brewer | San Luis Obispo | San Luis Obispo | S Luis Obispo. |
| Mannahan, Geo | Painter | San Luis Obispo | Monterey st | S Luis Obispo. |
| Mandersheld, C | Druggist | Cambria | Cambria | Cambria. |
| Manning, J S | Farmer | San Luis Obispo Co.. | nr Salinas | Salinas. |
| Munson, J M | Teacher | Cambria | Cambria | Cambria. |
| Manning, B | Farmer | San Luis Obispo Co.. | nr San Luis Obispo.. | S Luis Obispo. |
| Mansillas, Valentine | Teamster | San Luis Obispo | Chorro st | S Luis Obispo. |
| Marguez, S | Laborer | San Luis Obispo Co.. | nr San Luis Obispo.. | S Luis Obispo. |
| Marguez, P | Laborer | San Luis Obispo Co.. | nr San Luis Obispo.. | S Luis Obispo. |
| Mark, Chris | Sheep herder | Monterey st | San Luis Obispo | S Luis Obispo. |
| Marks, M C | Farmer | nr Cambria | San Luis Obispo Co.. | Cambria. |
| Martinez, B | Ranchero | Los Osos | 2½ m E Morro | Morro. |
| Martinez, A | Laborer | nr Santa Margarita... | San Luis Obispo Co.. | S Margarita. |
| Martinez, P | Farmer | San Luis Obispo Co.. | nr San Luis Obispo... | S Luis Obispo. |
| Martinez, Juan | Farmer | nr San Luis Obispo.. | San Luis Obispo Co.. | S Luis Obispo. |
| Martinez, R | Laborer | San Luis Obispo Co.. | San Luis Obispo Co.. | S Luis Obispo. |
| Martin, Barney | Laborer | San Luis Obispo Co.. | San Jose Valley | S Margarita. |
| Martin, Luther | | San Luis Obispo | Monterey st | S Luis Obispo. |
| Martin, C C | Carpenter | | Beach | S Luis Obispo. |
| Martin, H W | Farmer | nr Cambria | San Luis Obispo Co.. | Cambria. |
| Martinez, B | Laborer | nr San Luis Obispo | San Luis Obispo Co.. | S Luis Obispo. |
| Martin, H | Laborer | nr San Miguel | San Luis Obispo Co.. | San Miguel. |
| Martinez, A | Laborer | San Luis Obispo Co.. | nr San Luis Obispo.. | S Luis Obispo. |
| Martin, M B | Farmer | nr Cambria | San Luis Obispo Co.. | Cambria. |
| Martinez, Jose | Farmer | nr Morro | San Luis Obispo Co.. | Morro. |
| Martinez, F | Laborer | nr San Luis Obispo.. | San Luis Obispo Co.. | S Luis Obispo. |
| Martin, C C | Carpenter | San Luis Obispo | San Luis Obispo | S Luis Obispo. |
| Martin, E | Laborer | San Luis Obispo Co.. | nr San Luis Obispo.. | S Luis Obispo. |
| Martin, J | Laborer | San Luis Obispo Co.. | nr San Luis Obispo.. | S Luis Obispo. |
| Martin, L | Blacksmith | San Luis Obispo Co.. | San Luis Obispo | S Luis Obispo. |
| Martin, H W | Farmer | nr Morro | San Luis Obispo Co.. | Morro. |
| Martel, C | Laborer | nr San Luis Obispo... | San Luis Obispo Co.. | S Luis Obispo. |
| Martinez, L | Farmer | San Luis Obispo Co.. | nr Morro | Morro. |
| Maso, J | Farmer | San Luis Obispo Co.. | nr P R Hot Springs.. | Paso Robles. |
| Mason, A T | Miner | San Luis Obispo | San Luis Obispo | S Luis Obispo. |
| Mathies, B | Farmer | San Luis Obispo Co.. | 2 m E P R H Sp'gs.. | Paso Robles. |
| Matos, G | Farmer | nr San Luis Obispo.. | San Luis Obispo Co.. | S Luis Obispo. |
| Mathews, D J | Teamster | San Luis Obispo | Nipoma st | S Luis Obispo. |
| Mauk, Franklin | Blacksmith | | Marsh st | S Luis Obispo. |
| Mauk, G W | Under sheriff | Court House | Marsh st | S Luis Obispo. |
| Maxwell, L | Capitalist | San Luis Obispo | Nipoma st | S Luis Obispo. |
| Mayer, J B | Farmer | nr San Luis Obispo.. | San Luis Obispo Co.. | S Luis Obispo. |
| Mayfield, B F | Farmer | San Luis Obispo Co.. | nr Cambria | Cambria. |
| McAdam, P | Farmer | nr San Miguel | San Luis Obispo Co.. | San Miguel. |
| McCane, W A | Farmer | nr Cambria | San Luis Obispo Co.. | Cambria. |
| McClelland, J | Farmer | San Luis Obispo Co.. | nr P R Hot Springs.. | Paso Robles. |
| McClure, E | Laborer | San Luis Obispo Co.. | nr Estrella | Estrella. |
| McCollister, J | Laborer | San Luis Obispo Co.. | nr San Luis Obispo.. | S Luis Obispo. |
| McCollom, J C | Physician | | | S Luis Obispo. |
| McCrea, C | Farmer | nr Piedgas Blancas.. | San Luis Obispo Co.. | Piedgas Bl'cas. |
| McCune, J | Laborer | nr San Luis Obispo.. | San Luis Obispo Co.. | S Luis Obispo. |
| McDonald, L | Farmer | San Luis Obispo Co.. | nr Estrella | Estrella. |
| McDonald, M | Laborer | nr San Luis Obispo.. | San Luis Obispo Co.. | S Luis Obispo. |
| McDougall, S P | Hotel | Monterey st | Monterey st | S Luis Obispo. |

# Phoenix Iron Works,

### Nos. 18 AND 20 FREMONT ST.,
#### SAN FRANCISCO, CAL.

## JONATHAN KITTREDGE, - Proprietor.

**ESTIMATES FOR BANK WORK FURNISHED ON SHORT NOTICE.**

**MY SAFES ARE Superior to any in Use, AND I CHALLENGE COMPETITION.**

### MANUFACTURER OF
# IRON DOORS AND SHUTTERS,
#### Wrought-Iron Girders, Prison Cells, Fence and Railing
# BRIDGE AND BOLT WORK,
#### And all Kinds of Housesmith Work.

Bank Vaults, Bank Locks, Vault Necks and Doors. A Large Stock of Safes constantly on hand. Send for Catalogue.

## DIRECTORY OF SAN LUIS OBISPO COUNTY.

| Name. | Occupation. | Place of Business. | Residence. |
|---|---|---|---|
| McEntee, J | Dairyman | San Luis Obispo Co. | nr San Luis Obispo... |
| McFadden, O P | Farmer | nr Cambria | San Luis Obispo Co.. |
| McFarland, D K | Farmer | nr San Luis Obispo... | San Luis Obispo Co.. |
| McFersan, J C | Farmer | San Luis Obispo Co. | nr Cambria |
| McGee, H J | Laborer | nr Estrella | San Luis Obispo Co.. |
| McGee, J | Laborer | San Luis Obispo Co.. | nr Estrella |
| McGee, W A | Laborer | San Luis Obispo Co. | nr Estrella |
| McGinnis, W T | Laborer | nr San Luis Obispo... | San Luis Obispo Co.. |
| McGinnis, W J | Farmer | San Luis Obispo Co.. | nr San Luis Obispo... |
| McGinnis, J F | Plasterer | San Luis Obispo | San Luis Obispo |
| McGonan, J | Porter | P R Hot Springs | San Luis Obispo Co.. |
| McGrew, J | Laborer | San Luis Obispo Co. | nr Cambria |
| McGuire, I N | Stock raiser | San Luis Obispo Co.. | nr San Luis Obispo.. |
| McHenry, P | Dairyman | nr San Luis Obispo... | San Luis Obispo Co.. |
| McHenry, J | Dairyman | nr San Luis Obispo... | San Luis Obispo Co.. |
| McHenry, F | Farmer | San Luis Obispo Co. | nr San Luis Obispo... |
| McKay, James | Carpenter | San Luis Obispo | Monterey st |
| McKay, R | Laborer | nr P R Hot Springs. | San Luis Obispo Co.. |
| McKean, O E | Farmer | nr Cambria | San Luis Obispo Co.. |
| McKee, M D | Farmer | San Luis Obispo Co. | nr Morro |
| McKee, J F | Farmer | San Luis Obispo Co. | nr Huasna |
| McKeen, W A | Farmer | nr San Luis Obispo... | San Luis Obispo Co.. |
| McKinney, H G | Farmer | nr P R Hot Springs.. | San Luis Obispo Co.. |
| McKio, G | Farmer | San Luis Obispo Co.. | P R Hot Springs |
| McLeish, R M | Laborer | San Luis Obispo Co. | nr Santa Margarita |
| McLeod, Alex | Livery stable | Monterey st | Monterey st |
| McLeod, A C | Farmer | nr Huasna | San Luis Obispo Co.. |
| McMurry, W J | Laborer | nr San Luis Obispo.. | San Luis Obispo Co.. |
| McSorley, C | Bar keeper | San Luis Obispo | San Luis Obispo |
| McTalbert, J | Miner | San Jose | San Jose |
| McWilliams, G | Miner | Cambria | Cambria |
| Meacham, J B | Dairyman | San Luis Obispo Co. | Huasna |
| Mend, Geo | Dairyman | Huasna Road | 8 m N W A Grande |
| Mead, A | Farmer | nr Huasna | San Luis Obispo Co.. |
| Medino, M | Laborer | nr San Luis Obispo... | San Luis Obispo Co.. |
| Mehlmann, H | Restaurant | Higuerra st | Higuerra st |
| Melendez, J | Laborer | nr San Jose | San Luis Obispo Co.. |
| Melvine, D B | Laborer | nr Arroyo Grande | San Luis Obispo Co.. |
| Mendez, A | Laborer | San Luis Obispo Co. | nr San Luis Obispo.. |
| Merrill, C S, Jr | Stock raiser | nr La Panza | San Luis Obispo Co.. |
| Merrill, R P | Farmer | San Luis Obispo Co.. | nr San Miguel |
| Merritt, C W | Farmer | nr Huasna | San Luis Obispo Co.. |
| Mertz, J H | Carpenter | | Fink's Hotel |
| Mesa, Simona | | | Mill st |
| Mesquita, R | Farmer | San Luis Obispo Co. | nr Cambria |
| Messer, W W | Capitalist | P R Hot Springs | P R Hot Springs |
| Metzger, Chas | Clerk | Monterey st | Monterey st |
| Meuton, W | Farmer | 8 m E P R H Sp'gs.. | San Luis Obispo Co. |
| Meuton, H D | Merchant | San Miguel | San Miguel |
| Meuton, W H | Farmer | San Luis Obispo Co. | nr San Miguel |
| Michael, G W | Miller | Chorro Mills | Chorro Creek |
| Michael, Geo | Farmer | Morro Creek | 4½ m N E Morro |
| Middagh, G | Farmer | San Luis Obispo Co.. | nr San Miguel |
| Mideiro, J E | Barber | Chorro st | Monterey st |
| Mighell, M E | Farmer | nr Morro | San Luis Obispo Co.. |
| Miles, W T | Saloon keeper | Monterey st | Mill st |
| Miles, E | Stock raiser | nr Estrella | San Luis Obispo Co.. |
| Miller, J W | Farmer | Oso Flaco | 3½ m N E Guadalupe |
| Miller, J M | Dairyman | Oso Flaco | 3 m N Guadalupe.... |
| Miller, C | Waiter | Cosmopolitan Hotel.. | Monterey st |
| Miller, S R | Farmer | Monterey st | Broad st |
| Miller, F K | Attorney at law | Call's building | Higuerra st |
| Miller, Mrs | | | Buchon st |
| Miller, P | Laborer | nr Estrella | San Luis Obispo Co.. |

# McDonald Bros.,

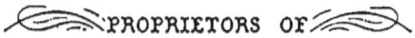PROPRIETORS OF

## SAN MARCOS,

### SAN LUIS OBISPO CO., CAL.

---

A roomy and well conducted hotel for the accommodation of the traveling public.

The appointments of table and sleeping apartments are such as cannot fail in ministering to the perfect comfort of guests.

A Saloon is connected with the hotel, where can be obtained,

## LIQUORS & CIGARS

**OF THE FINEST QUALITY.**

---

Messrs. McDONALD BROS. have in addition a large stock farm, and are actively engaged in stock-farming upon the most approved principles.

## DIRECTORY OF SAN LUIS OBISPO COUNTY. 69

| Name. | Occupation. | Place of Business. | Residence. | Town or P. O. |
|---|---|---|---|---|
| Miller, J............. | Whaleman......... | Piedgas Blancas...... | Piedgas Blancas...... | Piedgas Bl'cas. |
| Miller, N S........ | Farmer............. | nr Oso Flaco........... | San Luis Obispo Co... | Oso Flaco. |
| Miller, D S........ | Teamster.......... | San Luis Obispo Co.. | nr San Luis Obispo... | S Luis Obispo. |
| Miller, J F........ | Laborer............. | San Luis Obispo Co.. | nr San Luis Obispo.. | S Luis Obispo. |
| Miller, H............ | Stock raiser....... | San Luis Obispo Co.. | nr Estrella............. | Estrella. |
| Miller, I............. | Farmer............. | nr Morro.............. | San Luis Obispo Co.. | Morro. |
| Miller, M............ | Boot maker....... | Arroyo Grande........ | Arroyo Grande........ | Arroyo Grande. |
| Minor, H A........ | Farmer............. | nr San Jose............ | San Luis Obispo Co.. | San Jose. |
| Minoli, Louis..... | Boarding house... | Rincon Mine........... | 22 m E San L Ob'po.. | S Luis Obispo. |
| Mira, M............ | Whaleman......... | Piedgas Blancas...... | Piedgas Blancas...... | Piedgas Bl'cas. |
| Misenheimer, J.... | Farmer............. | Cambria road......... | San Luis Obispo Co.. | Paso Robles. |
| Misenheimer, H S.. | Farmer............. | San Luis Obispo Co.. | nr Cambria............. | Cambria. |
| Mitchell, W B..... | Insurance agent... | San Luis Obispo...... | San Luis Obispo...... | S Luis Obispo. |
| Mitchell, W........ | Laborer............. | nr San Miguel......... | San Luis Obispo Co.. | San Miguel. |
| Mitchell, J......... | Farmer............. | San Luis Obispo Co.. | nr P R Hot Springs.. | Paso Robles. |
| Mohrin, J J........ | General mdse...... | Arroyo Grande........ | Branch st.............. | Arroyo Grande. |
| Moisa, F............. | Laborer............. | San Luis Obispo Co.. | nr San Luis Obispo.. | S Luis Obispo. |
| Mojica, P............ | Farmer............. | nr San Jose............ | San Luis Obispo Co.. | San Jose. |
| Molina, J............ | Laborer............. | nr San Luis Obispo.. | San Luis Obispo Co.. | S Luis Obispo. |
| Molino, J B........ | Laborer............. | San Luis Obispo Co.. | nr San Luis Obispo.. | S Luis Obispo. |
| Molina, C........... | Farmer............. | nr San Luis Obispo.. | San Luis Obispo Co.. | S Luis Obispo. |
| Monroe, J T....... | Teamster.......... | nr San Luis Obispo.. | San Luis Obispo Co.. | S Luis Obispo. |
| Montgomery, H S... | Laborer............. | nr Estrella............. | San Luis Obispo Co.. | Estrella. |
| Montana, R........ | Cook................ | San Luis Obispo...... | San Luis Obispo...... | S Luis Obispo. |
| Moody, Henry..... | Farmer............. | 7 m E Paso Robles S | San Luis Obispo Co.. | Paso Robles. |
| Moody, J S......... | Farmer............. | 7 m E Paso Robles S | San Luis Obispo Co.. | Paso Robles. |
| Moore, Hugh....... | Dairyman.......... | Cambria Road......... | 1 m N W S Luis O.. | S Luis Obispo. |
| Moore, W, Jr...... | Farmer............. | nr San Luis Obispo.. | San Luis Obispo Co.. | S Luis Obispo. |
| Moraga, A.......... | Laborer............. | nr San Jose............ | San Luis Obispo Co.. | San Jose. |
| Morales, G.......... | Laborer............. | San Luis Obispo Co.. | nr San Jose............ | San Jose. |
| Moraga, J........... | Laborer............. | San Luis Obispo Co.. | nr San Luis Obispo.. | S Luis Obispo. |
| Moraga, F........... | Laborer............. | nr San Luis Obispo.. | San Luis Obispo Co.. | S Luis Obispo. |
| Mora, W W........ | Butcher............. | Morro................. | Morro................. | Morro. |
| Moreno, Luis...... | Butcher............. | Monterey st........... | San Luis Obispo...... | S Luis Obispo. |
| Moreno, J........... | Laborer............. | San Luis Obispo Co.. | nr Huasna............. | Huasna. |
| Morehouse, N B... | Farmer............. | nr San Miguel......... | San Luis Obispo Co.. | San Miguel. |
| Morelock, T........ | Carpenter.......... | Cambria.............. | Cambria.............. | Cambria. |
| Moreno, Y.......... | Laborer............. | nr San Luis Obispo.. | San Luis Obispo Co.. | S Luis Obispo. |
| Moreno, F........... | Laborer............. | nr San Luis Obispo.. | San Luis Obispo Co.. | S Luis Obispo. |
| Morehouse, C D... | Farmer............. | P R Hot Springs...... | San Luis Obispo Co.. | Paso Robles. |
| Morehouse, W L... | Farmer............. | San Luis Obispo Co.. | P R Hot Springs...... | Paso Robles. |
| Morehouse, H B... | Farmer............. | San Luis Obispo Co.. | P R Hot Springs...... | Paso Robles. |
| Morris, E B........ | Hotel proprietor.. | Cosmopolitan Hotel.. | Monterey st........... | S Luis Obispo. |
| Morris, B F........ | Farmer............. | nr Cambria............ | San Luis Obispo Co.. | Cambria. |
| Morris, J F......... | Farmer............. | nr Huasna............. | San Luis Obispo Co.. | Huasna. |
| Morris, E........... | Farmer............. | nr P R Hot Springs.. | San Luis Obispo Co.. | Paso Robles. |
| Morrell, W......... | Blacksmith......... | San Luis Obispo...... | San Luis Obispo...... | S Luis Obispo. |
| Morriss, J........... | Farmer............. | San Luis Obispo Co.. | nr Morro.............. | Morro. |
| Morris, C D........ | Farmer............. | San Luis Obispo Co.. | nr Cambria............ | Cambria. |
| Morris, G W....... | Farmer............. | nr Cambria............ | San Luis Obispo Co.. | Cambria. |
| Morss, J............. | Farmer............. | San Luis Obispo Co.. | nr Cambria............ | Cambria. |
| Morse, E M........ | Physician.......... | P R Hot Springs...... | San Luis Obispo Co.. | Paso Robles. |
| Morse, W........... | Farmer............. | nr San Luis Obispo.. | San Luis Obispo Co.. | S Luis Obispo. |
| Morss, J W......... | Farmer............. | nr Cambria............ | San Luis Obispo Co.. | Cambria. |
| Morton, R B....... | Teacher............ | Morro................. | Morro................. | Morro. |
| Mortell, C.......... | Laborer............. | San Luis Obispo...... | Monterey st........... | S Luis Obispo. |
| Moss, B............. | Laborer............. | San Luis Obispo Co.. | nr San Luis Obispo.. | S Luis Obispo. |
| Moss, F.............. | Farmer............. | San Luis Obispo Co.. | nr San Luis Obispo.. | S Luis Obispo. |
| Mothersead, A J... | Farmer............. | Morro Creek.......... | 5 m N E Morro....... | Morro. |
| Mowatt, W C...... | Farmer............. | San Luis Obispo Co.. | nr Cambria............ | Cambria. |
| Mowatt, C.......... | Butcher............. | Cambria.............. | Cambria.............. | Cambria. |
| Moxley, R M....... | Farmer............. | nr San Luis Obispo.. | San Luis Obispo Co.. | S Luis Obispo. |
| Muir, J F........... | Farmer............. | nr Cambria............ | San Luis Obispo Co.. | Cambria. |
| Mullen, R........... | Farmer............. | San Luis Obispo Co.. | nr Santa Margarita... | S Margarita. |

## A. C. NICHOLS & CO.

**400 & 402 BATTERY STREET, COR. CLAY, - - SAN FRANCISCO.**

### COMMISSION MERCHANTS,

AND DEALERS IN

## HIDES, TALLOW, PELTS, OIL, LEATHER,

Of all kinds, including French, Eastern and California. Importers of Tanners' and Curriers' Tools, Materials and Machinery. **Also, AGENTS FOR TANNERIES.** Pay the highest cash market price for Hides, Tallow and Pelts.

M. ZAN,     J. GILLESPIE.     F. ZAN,

## GILLESPIE, ZAN & CO.

⌒ EUREKA BROOM FACTORY, ⌒

Sole owners and Manufacturers of

## PATENT SPIRAL & CORRUGATED BROOMS

And Ordinary BROOMS, BRUSHES and WISPS.

**Dealers in Wooden and Willow Ware, Broom Corn, Handles, Wire, Twine, Etc.,**

**114 Sacramento St., bet. Davis and Drumm, San Francisco.**

---

### B. F. WELLINGTON,

Importer and Dealer in all kinds of

### Vegetable, Flower, Fruit & Tree Seeds

PLANTS AND TREES,

425 Washington St., nearly opposite the Post Office, S. F.

### CHILION BEACH,

—IMPORTER OF—

### BOOKS AND FINE STATIONERY

No. 5 Montgomery St., Masonic Temple, San Francisco.

Monograms and Crests artistically designed and engraved. Constantly in receipt of new books and the very latest style of Stationery. Special attention given to Wedding and Visiting Cards.

---

### THE WILSON

## Sewing Machine

General Office, 337 Kearny St. S. F.

LOCK STITCH,
STRAIGHT NEEDLE.

Prices,

## $20 LOWER

Than any other first-class Machine.

**WARRANTED FOR FIVE YEARS.**

### HIGHEST PREMIUM

At World's Fair, Vienna, 1873, and at most of the State and County Fairs in the United States.

**Send for Circulars and Samples.**

**AGENTS WANTED.**

## DIRECTORY OF SAN LUIS OBISPO COUNTY. 71

| Name. | Occupation. | Place of Business. | Residence. | Town or P. O. |
|---|---|---|---|---|
| Mullin, J | Teamster | San Luis Obispo Co. | nr San Luis Obispo | S Luis Obispo. |
| Mungin, J | Laborer | nr San Luis Obispo | San Luis Obispo Co. | S Luis Obispo. |
| Mungilla, L V | Laborer | San Luis Obispo Co. | nr San Luis Obispo | S Luis Obispo. |
| Munoz, Benj | Saloon | Chorro st | Monterey st | S Luis Obispo. |
| Muñoz, Mrs C | Farming | | 1 m E S Luis Obispo. | S Luis Obispo. |
| Muñoz, J G | Clerk | Post Office | 1 m S E San Luis Ob | S Luis Obispo. |
| Minor, R A | Tel operator | Avila | Avila | S Luis Obispo. |
| Munson, A | Farmer | nr San Luis Obispo | San Luis Obispo Co. | S Luis Obispo. |
| Murdock, J C | Stock raiser | Oso Flaco | 3 m N Guadalupe | Guadalupe. |
| Murphy, P W | Capitalist | San Luis Obispo | Santa Margarita | S Margarita. |
| Murphy, Patrick | Stock raiser | Santa Margarita | 12 m N S Luis Ob'o. | S Margarita. |
| Murphy, L V | Barber | Monterey st | Monterey st | S Luis Obispo. |
| Murphy, G W | Farmer | San Luis Obispo Co. | nr Cambria | Cambria. |
| Murphy, L V | Barber | San Luis Obispo | San Luis Obispo | S Luis Obispo. |
| Murphy, T | Saloon | San Luis Obispo Co. | nr San Luis Obispo | S Luis Obispo. |
| Murphy, J E | Farmer | nr Cambria | San Luis Obispo Co. | Cambria. |
| Murrey, Walter | Attorney at law | | Monterey st | S Luis Obispo. |
| Murray, W R | Laborer | San Luis Obispo Co. | nr San Luis Obispo | S Luis Obispo. |
| Muscio, J | Laborer | San Luis Obispo Co. | nr Piedgas Blancas | Piedgas Bl'cas. |
| Musick, L W | Printer | Huasna | Huasna | Huasna. |
| Musick, B F | Minister | Cambria | Cambria | Cambria. |
| Musick, L T | Farmer | San Luis Obispo Co. | nr Huasna | Huasna. |
| Musick, B T | Farmer | San Luis Obispo Co. | nr Huasna | Huasna. |
| Musick, R B | Farmer | nr Huasna | San Luis Obispo Co. | Huasna. |
| Myers, E G | Farmer | nr Cambria | San Luis Obispo Co. | Cambria. |
| Najar, J | Laborer | San Luis Obispo Co. | nr Arroyo Grande | Arroyo Grande. |
| Najar, F | Laborer | nr San Luis Obispo | San Luis Obispo Co. | S Luis Obispo. |
| Najar, J D | Laborer | nr Arroyo Grande | San Luis Obispo Co. | Arroyo Grande. |
| Narvaez, Jose | Ranchero | Morro Creek | 7 m N E Morro | Morro. |
| Navarro, M | Laborer | San Luis Obispo Co. | nr San Luis Obispo | S Luis Obispo. |
| Navarro, F | Laborer | nr San Luis Obispo | San Luis Obispo Co. | S Luis Obispo. |
| Nelson, David | Laborer | Los Osos | | Morro. |
| Nelson, Wm | Farmer | | 5 m SE Arroyo G'de. | Arroyo Grande. |
| Nelson, J M | Farmer | Guadalupe Road | ½ m S Arroyo Grande | Arroyo Grande. |
| Nelson, W H | Farmer | Los Osos | | Morro. |
| Nelson, H | Farmer | San Luis Obispo Co. | nr San Luis Obispo | S Luis Obispo. |
| Nelson, G S | Farmer | San Luis Obispo Co. | nr San Luis Obispo | S Luis Obispo. |
| Nellis, A R | Blacksmith | San Luis Obispo | San Luis Obispo | S Luis Obispo. |
| Nesbit, J W | Farmer | San Luis Obispo Co. | nr Morro | Morro. |
| Newhouse, C D | Farmer | Cambria Road | San Luis Obispo Co. | Paso Robles. |
| Newhouse, H B | Farmer | San Luis Obispo Co. | Cambria Road | Paso Robles. |
| Newhouse, N B | Farmer | Cambria Road | San Luis Obispo Co. | Paso Robles. |
| Newhall, — | Stock raiser | Suey Ranch | 20 m S S Luis Ob'po. | Arroyo Grande. |
| Newlove, John | Farmer | Oso Flaco | ¾ m N W Guadalupe | Guadalupe. |
| Newman, D | Dry goods | Monterey st | Monterey st | S Luis Obispo. |
| Newsom, D F | | Newsom Springs | 1½ m S Arroyo Gr'de | Arroyo Grande. |
| Nichols, J | Farmer | nr Santa Margarita | San Luis Obispo Co. | S Margarita. |
| Nickerson, M J | Dairyman | P R Hot Springs | San Luis Obispo Co. | Paso Robles. |
| Nickerson, T | Blacksmith | San Luis Obispo | San Luis Obispo | S Luis Obispo. |
| Noah, D M | Book keeper | Monterey st | Higuerra st | S Luis Obispo. |
| Noah, M | Butcher | Monterey st | Higuerra st | S Luis Obispo. |
| Nobel, R | Farmer | nr Cambria | San Luis Obispo Co. | Cambria. |
| Noe & Co, Juan | Variety store | | | Guadalupe. |
| Noe, J | Laborer | San Luis Obispo Co. | nr San Luis Obispo | S Luis Obispo. |
| Noe, J S | Butcher | San Miguel | San Miguel | San Miguel. |
| Norcross, David C | Sheriff | Court House | Higuerra st | S Luis Obispo. |
| Norcross, John | Sheep raiser | San Luis Obispo | Higuerra st | S Luis Obispo. |
| Norcross, J C | Insurance agent | Estrella | Estrella | Estrella. |
| Norman, Jas H | Farmer | nr Arroyo Grande | ¾ m N E Arroyo G'e | Arroyo Grande. |
| Norris, G S | Farmer | nr Cambria | San Luis Obispo Co. | Cambria. |
| Nosker, B F | Laborer | San Luis Obispo Co. | nr Estrella | Estrella. |
| Nuckols, N | Farmer | nr Morro | San Luis Obispo Co. | Morro. |
| Nuckols, C M | Farmer | San Luis Obispo Co. | nr Morro | Morro. |
| Nuckols, N H | Farmer | nr San Luis Obispo | nr Morro | Morro. |

## FIRST PREMIUM AT SACRAMENTO STATE FAIR, 1874.
### For the Best Tables and Cushions.
## STANDARD CALIFORNIA BILLIARD TABLES.

# JACOB STRAHLE & CO.
### 533 Market Street - - - SAN FRANCISCO.

**Patented Nov. 23d, 1869. Improved. Nov., 1873.**

Endorsed by GARNIER, UBASSY, JOSEPH and CYRILLE DION, A. P. RUDOLPH, A. KRAKER, and all the CHAMPIONS of the WORLD. These cushions are without doubt the best in existence; the most reliable for accuracy, elasticity, and all purposes of scientific play. They are used exclusively in all matches for the championship, and can only be bought at our Warerooms.

First-Class New Bevel Tables, compelte, 10 ft. x 5...............$350 and upward.
" " " " " 9 ft. x 4½...............300 " "
" " " " " 8 ft. x 4...............250 " "
" " " " " 7 ft. x 3½...............200 " "
Bagatelle Tables, each......................................................................50 " "
Pigeon Hole Tables, each...............................................................100 " "
Jenny Lind " "............................................................................150 " "

## BILLIARD GOODS and Trimmings of Every Description.
### THE LARGEST BILLIARD HOUSE ON THE COAST.
## 150 BILLIARD TABLES,
**OF ALL SIZES, STYLES AND FINISH, READY FOR DELIVERY.**

Tables repaired, transformed into Bevels, or exchanged. Purchasers will find it greatly to their advantage to call and examine our immense stock before purchasing elsewhere. Our facilities for manufacturing are such that we have succeeded in bringing the price of Billiard Tables within the reach of every lover of the game.

### ALL TABLES OF OUR MANUFACTURE GUARANTEED FOR YEARS.
**TIME SALES ON THE MOST LIBERAL TERMS.**

☞ For further particulars, send for Catalogue and Price List.

## JACOB STRAHLE & CO.
*533 Market Street, San Francisco, Cal.*

RECTORY OF SAN LUIS OBISPO COUNTY. 73

| Occupation. | Place of Business. | Residence. | Town or P. O. |
|---|---|---|---|
| erk ............... | Monterey st,........... | Chorro st. ............... | S Luis Obispo. |
| irmer ............. | San Luis Obispo Co.. | nr P R Hot Springs... | Paso Robles. |
| irmer ............. | nr San Miguel......... | San Luis Obispo Co.. | San Miguel. |
| age driver........ | San Luis Obispo...... | San Luis Obispo ...... | S Luis Obispo. |
| iborer ............. | nr San Luis Obispo... | San Luis Obispo Co.. | S Luis Obispo. |
| iiryman.......... | Osos Road ............. | 5 m W S Luis Ob'o | S Luis Obispo. |
| iiryman.......... | San Luis Obispo Co.. | nr San Luis Obispo.. | S Luis Obispo. |
| irmer............. | nr Morro............... | San Luis Obispo Co.. | Morro. |
| st attorney...... | Court House........... | San Luis Obispo...... | S Luis Obispo. |
| irmer............. | San Bernardo Cr'k .. | 4½ m E Morro......... | Morro. |
| harf hand ...... | Avila................... | Avila.................... | S Luis Obispo. |
| harf hand ...... | Avila................... | Avila.................... | S Luis Obispo. |
| ason............... | San Luis Obispo ...... | San Luis Obispo...... | S, Luis Obispo. |
| erk................ | Avila................... | Avila.................... | S Luis Obispo. |
| otel keeper ...... | Morro................... | Morro................... | Morro. |
| iborer............. | nr Morro............... | San Luis Obispo Co.. | Morro. |
| irmer............. | nr Morro............... | San Luis Obispo Co.. | Morro. |
| iborer............. | nr San Luis Obispo.. | San Luis Obispo Co.. | S Luis Obispo. |
| iborer............. | nr Huasna.............. | San Luis Obispo Co.. | Huasna. |
| iborer............. | San Luis Obispo Co.. | nr San Luis Obispo.. | S Luis Obispo. |
| irmer............. | nr Cambria ............ | San Luis Obispo Co,. | Cambria. |
| irmer............. | San Luis Obispo Co.. | nr Cambria ............ | Cambria. |
| irmer............. | nr San Luis Obispo.. | San Luis Obispo Co.. | S Luis Obispo. |
| irmer............. | San Luis Obispo Co.. | nr Arroyo Grande.... | Arroyo Grande. |
| irmer............. | San Luis Obispo Co.. | nr San Luis Obispo.. | S Luis Obispo. |
| ock raiser....... | San Luis Obispo Co.. | nr San Luis Obispo.. | S Luis Obispo. |
| irmer............. | San Luis Obispo Co.. | nr San Luis Obispo.. | S Luis Obispo. |
| irmer............. | nr San Luis Obispo.. | San Luis Obispo Co.. | S Luis Obispo. |
| irmer............. | nr San Luis Obispo.. | San Luis Obispo Co.. | S Luis Obispo. |
| irmer............. | San Luis Obispo Co.. | nr Cambria ............ | Cambria. |
| iborer............. | San Luis Obispo Co.. | nr San Miguel......... | San Miguel. |
| gt W F & Co.. | Monterey st............ | Garden st ............. | S Luis Obispo. |
| irmer............. | San Luis Obispo Co.. | nr San Luis Obispo.. | S Luis Obispo. |
| irmer............. | San Luis Obispo Co.. | nr San Luis Obispo.. | S Luis Obispo. |
| irmer............. | nr Morro............... | San Luis Obispo Co.. | Morro. |
| irmer............. | nr Morro............... | San Luis Obispo Co.. | Morro. |
| irmer............. | San Luis Obispo Co.. | nr Morro............... | Morro. |
| irmer............. | nr Arroyo Grande.... | San Luis Obispo Co.. | Arroyo Grande. |
| ock raiser....... | San Luis Obispo Co.. | P R Hot Springs...... | Paso Robles. |
| lerk................ | San Luis Obispo...... | San Luis Obispo...... | S Luis Obispo. |
| iborer............. | San Luis Obispo Co.. | nr San Jose............ | San Jose. |
| rchitect .......... | Monterey st............ | ......................... | S Luis Obispo. |
| iweller............ | Monterey st............ | Morro and Peach sts | S Luis Obispo. |
| irpenter .......... | San Luis Obispo...... | Osos st................. | S Luis Obispo. |
| irmer............. | San Luis Obispo Co.. | nr Morro............... | Morro. |
| ioe maker........ | Higuerra st............. | San Luis Obispo...... | S Luis Obispo. |
| irmer............. | San Luis Obispo Co.. | nr Cambria ............ | Cambria. |
| air maker........ | San Luis Obispo...... | San Luis Obispo...... | S Luis Obispo. |
| iloon............... | Cambria Road......... | San Luis Obispo...... | S Luis Obispo. |
| ock raiser ....... | nr San Jose............ | San Luis Obispo Co.. | San Jose. |
| irmer............. | San Luis Obispo Co.. | nr Morro............... | Morro. |
| irmer............. | nr Arroyo Grande.... | San Luis Obispo Co.. | Arroyo Grande. |
| irmer............. | San Luis Obispo Co.. | nr San Luis Obispo .. | S Luis Obispo. |
| irmer............. | nr Piedgas Blancas... | San Luis Obispo Co.. | Piedgas Bl'cas. |
| nion restaurant. | Monterey st............ | Monterey st............ | S Luis Obispo. |
| iborer............. | Avila................... | Avila.................... | S Luis Obispo. |
| umber dealer... | Morro................... | Morro................... | Morro. |
| apitalist.......... | San Francisco......... | San Francisco......... | San Francisco. |
| irmer............. | nr San Simeon......... | San Luis Obispo Co.. | San Miguel. |
| ep treasurer..... | Court House........... | San Luis Obispo...... | S Luis Obispo. |
| arpenter.......... | Cambria................ | Cambria................ | Cambria. |
| airyman.......... | San Luis Obispo Co.. | nr Cambria ............ | Cambria. |
| iborer............. | nr Cholamie........... | San Luis Obispo Co.. | Cholamie. |
| iloon............... | Monterey st............ | Morro st............... | S Luis Obispo. |

5

| Name. | Occupation. | Place of Business. | Residence. | Town or P. O. |
|---|---|---|---|---|
| Parker & Block | Blacksmiths | Monterey st | Monterey st | S Luis Obispo. |
| Parker, C | Blacksmith | Monterey st | Monterey st | S Luis Obispo. |
| Parker, F W | Farmer | Morro | Morro | Morro. |
| Parker, B D | Laborer | San Luis Obispo Co. | nr Cambria | Cambria. |
| Parrish, G W | Farmer | San Luis Obispo Co. | nr San Miguel | San Miguel. |
| Parr, Ramon | Teacher | nr Cambria | San Luis Obispo Co. | Cambria. |
| Patchell, J A | Stock raiser | San Luis Obispo Co. | nr San Miguel | San Miguel. |
| Pate, D | Farmer | San Luis Obispo Co. | nr P R Hot Springs | Paso Robles. |
| Patrick, James | Dairyman | Los Osos | 10 m S Morro | Morro. |
| Patrick, B | Stock raiser | P R Hot Springs | San Luis Obispo Co. | Paso Robles. |
| Patterson&Purcell | Stock raiser | Estrella Valley | 11 m E San Miguel | San Miguel. |
| Patterson, A J | Stock raiser | Estrella Valley | 11 m E San Miguel | San Miguel. |
| Patterson, N G | Sheep raiser | 15 m E P R Hot Sp's | San Luis Obispo Co | Paso Robles. |
| Patterson, T | Major domo | Santa Isabel Ranch | San Luis Obispo Co. | Paso Robles. |
| Payne, G J | Engle stable | Monterey st | Broad st | S Luis Obispo. |
| Pellerier, Chas | Groc's & bath h'se | Monterey st | Monterey st | S Luis Obispo. |
| Pellerier, C B T | Carpenter | San Luis Obispo | San Luis Obispo | S Luis Obispo. |
| Pena, J | Whaleman | San Luis Obispo | San Luis Obispo | S Luis Obispo. |
| Pennington, Alfred | Carpenter | Morro st | Higuerra st | S Luis Obispo. |
| Pennington, J | Farmer | nr San Luis Obispo. | San Luis Obispo Co. | S Luis Obispo. |
| Pepperman, M | Jeweler | Monterey st | Monterey st | S Luis Obispo. |
| Peralta, P | Laborer | San Luis Obispo Co. | nr San Luis Obispo. | S Luis Obispo. |
| Peralta, J V | Laborer | nr San Luis Obispo. | San Luis Obispo Co. | S Luis Obispo. |
| Peralta, J | Laborer | nr San Luis Obispo. | San Luis Obispo Co. | S Luis Obispo. |
| Peralta, J M | Farmer | nr San Luis Obispo. | San Luis Obispo Co. | S Luis Obispo. |
| Perez, J A | Laborer | nr San Luis Obispo. | San Luis Obispo Co. | S Luis Obispo. |
| Perfumo, P | Saloon keeper | San Luis Obispo | San Luis Obispo | S Luis Obispo. |
| Periera, J | Whaleman | Piedgas Blancas | Piedgas Blancas | Piedgas Bl'cas. |
| Perry, N | Farmer | nr Old Creek | San Luis Obispo Co. | Old Creek. |
| Peters, J D | Farmer | nr San Miguel | San Luis Obispo Co. | San Miguel. |
| Petit, B F | Stock raiser | nr Arroyo Grande | San Luis Obispo Co. | Arroyo Grande. |
| Pezzoni, B | Laborer | San Luis Obispo Co. | nr Piedgas Blancas | Piedgas Bl'cas. |
| Phelan, J | Dairyman | nr Cambria | San Luis Obispo Co. | Cambria. |
| Philbrick, R | Blacksmith | | Fink's Hotel | S Luis Obispo. |
| Philbrick & Barneburg | Machine shop | Broad & Higuerra sts | | S Luis Obispo. |
| Philbrick, Geo W | Farmer | S B Road | 3 m S A Grande | Arroyo Grande. |
| Phillips, C H | Cashier | S L O Bank | Monterey st | S Luis Obispo. |
| Philips, J | Tailor | Monterey st | Monterey st | S Luis Obispo. |
| Phillips, W | Farmer | nr Cambria | San Luis Obispo Co. | Cambria. |
| Phillips, M E | Farmer | San Luis Obispo Co. | nr Cambria | Cambria. |
| Phillips, R | Stock raiser | San Luis Obispo Co. | nr Cambria | Cambria. |
| Phillips, F | Farmer | San Luis Obispo Co. | nr Cambria | Cambria. |
| Phillips, T | Farmer | nr Morro | San Luis Obispo Co. | Morro. |
| Phoenix, W | Dairyman | Huasna Ranch | 4 m N Arroyo G'e | Arroyo Grande. |
| Phoenix, C | Farmer | nr Huasna | San Luis Obispo Co. | Huasna. |
| Phoenix, G | Farmer | San Luis Obispo Co. | nr Huasna | Huasna. |
| Pico, Z A | Merchant | San Luis Obispo | San Luis Obispo | S Luis Obispo. |
| Pico, F | Merchant | San Luis Obispo | San Luis Obispo | S Luis Obispo. |
| Pico, J J | Farmer | San Luis Obispo Co. | nr San Luis Obispo | S Luis Obispo. |
| Pico, F | Farmer | nr Cambria | San Luis Obispo Co. | Cambria. |
| Pico, B | Farmer | San Luis Obispo Co. | nr Piedgas Blancas | Piedgas Bl'cas. |
| Pico, A B | Laborer | nr San Luis Obispo. | San Luis Obispo Co. | S Luis Obispo. |
| Pico, T | Laborer | nr San Luis Obispo | San Luis Obispo Co. | S Luis Obispo. |
| Pierson, S P | Stock raiser | nr Cambria | San Luis Obispo Co. | Cambria. |
| Pierce, J | Teamster | nr Cambria | San Luis Obispo Co. | Cambria. |
| Pierce, G W | Dairyman | San Luis Obispo Co. | nr Old Creek | Old Creek. |
| Pierce, W, Jr | Farmer | San Luis Obispo Co. | nr San Luis Obispo. | S Luis Obispo. |
| Pilant, J W | Stock raiser | San Luis Obispo Co. | nr San Miguel | San Miguel. |
| Pilkey, M | Farmer | San Luis Obispo Co. | nr Cambria | Cambria. |
| Pillard, L | Baker | San Jose | San Jose | San Jose. |
| Pollard & James | PropsChorro F M | Monterey st | | S Luis Obispo. |
| Pollard, S A | Chorro fl'g mills | Monterey st | Monterey st | S Luis Obispo. |
| Pollard, R | Clerk | San Luis Obispo | San Luis Obispo | S Luis Obispo. |

DIRECTORY OF SAN LUIS OBISPO COUNTY. 75

| Name. | Occupation. | Place of Business. | Residence. | Town or P. O. |
|---|---|---|---|---|
| Ponce, A | Farmer | San Luis Obispo Co. | nr San Jose | San Jose. |
| Pond, R H | Sheep raiser | Eureka Ranch | San Luis Obispo Co. | Paso Robles. |
| Pond, E S | Sheep raiser | Eureka Ranch | San Luis Obispo Co. | Paso Robles. |
| Pond, Geo | Sheep raiser | Eureka Ranch | San Luis Obispo Co. | Paso Robles. |
| Pound, J | Farmer | nr San Luis Obispo | San Luis Obispo Co. | S Luis Obispo. |
| Pool Bros. | Farmers | Stage Road | 2¼ m S Arroyo Gr'de | Arroyo Grande. |
| Pool, James | Farmer | Stage Road | 2¼ m S Arroyo Gr'de | Arroyo Grande. |
| Pool, John | Farmer | Stage Road | 2½ m S Arroyo Gr'de. | Arroyo Grande. |
| Poorman, H W | Farmer | San Luis Obispo Co. | nr San Luis Obispo | S Luis Obispo. |
| Popp, G | Miller | Arroyo Grande | Arroyo Grande | Arroyo Grande. |
| Porcher, C P | Stock raiser | San Luis Obispo Co. | nr San Luis Obispo. | S Luis Obispo. |
| Porter, James | Carpenter | San Luis Obispo | | S Luis Obispo. |
| Potter, D | Hardware store | Monterey st | Chorro st | S Luis Obispo. |
| Potter, D C | Stock raiser | Monterey st | Chorro st | S Luis Obispo. |
| Potter, L | Farmer | Oso Flaco | 1 m W Guadalupe | Guadalupe. |
| Potter, L L | Farmer | nr San Luis Obispo. | San Luis Obispo Co. | S Luis Obispo. |
| Powell, D C | Farmer | nr Morro | San Luis Obispo Co. | Morro. |
| Pratt, T C | Farmer | San Bernado | 4½ m N E Morro | Morro. |
| Pratt, J E | Farmer | San Luis Obispo Co. | nr Cambria | Cambria. |
| Pratt, T G | Farmer | San Luis Obispo Co. | nr San Luis Obispo. | S Luis Obispo. |
| Preston, R M | Notary public | Morro | Morro | Morro. |
| Pressey, A E | Farmer | nr San Luis Obispo. | San Luis Obispo Co. | S Luis Obispo. |
| Price, J M | Stock | Landing Road | 5 m W A Grande | Arroyo Grande. |
| Price, H P | Farmer | nr Cambria | San Luis Obispo Co. | Cambria. |
| Price, J S | Farmer | San Luis Obispo Co. | nr Arroyo Grande | Arroyo Grande. |
| Priest, R A G | Clerk | Court House | San Luis Obispo | S Luis Obispo. |
| Proctor, G E | Farmer | San Luis Obispo Co. | nr Cambria | Cambria. |
| Proctor, F L | Stock raiser | San Luis Obispo Co. | nr Cambria | Cambria. |
| Proctor, G W | Blacksmith | Cambria | Cambria | Cambria. |
| Pinham, C W | Dairyman | San Luis Obispo Co. | nr Cambria | Cambria. |
| Puenta, F | Stock raiser | nr San Luis Obispo. | San Luis Obispo Co. | S Luis Obispo. |
| Pullen, A W W | Farmer | nr San Luis Obispo | San Luis Obispo Co. | S Luis Obispo. |
| Purcell, A E | Stock raiser | Estrella Valley | 11 m E San Miguel. | San Miguel. |
| Purcell, T D | Carpenter | Estrella | Estrella. | Estrella. |
| Quintana, P | Stock raiser | Cambria Road | 8 m N San L Obispo | S Luis Obispo. |
| Quintana, E | Farmer | nr San Luis Obispo | San Luis Obispo Co. | S Luis Obispo. |
| Quintana, J M | Farmer | San Luis Obispo Co. | nr San Luis Obispo. | S Luis Obispo. |
| Quintana, Stevan | Farmer | Cambria Road | 3 m N W San L O'po | S Luis Obispo. |
| Quinteros, J D | Laborer | San Luis Obispo Co. | nr San Luis Obispo. | S Luis Obispo. |
| Rackliffe, L | Gen merchandise | Monterey st | Monterey st | S Luis Obispo. |
| Rackliffe, S | Teacher | San Luis Obispo | San Luis Obispo | S Luis Obispo. |
| Rader, John | Farmer | Arroyo Grande Creek | 28 m Arroyo Grande | Arroyo Grande. |
| Rader, J | Blacksmith | Cambria | Cambria | Cambria. |
| Rady, Phil | Blacksmith | Higuerra st | Higuerra st | S Luis Obispo. |
| Rainey, R S | Dairyman | nr San Luis Obispo | San Luis Obispo Co. | S Luis Obispo. |
| Raishley, W | Farmer | nr Salinas | San Luis Obispo Co. | Salinas. |
| Raishleigh, W | Ranchero | San Luis Obispo Co. | nr La Panza | La Panza. |
| Ramage, J A | Farmer | San Luis Obispo Co. | nr San Miguel | San Miguel. |
| Ramage, G W | Merchant | Cambria | Cambria | Cambria. |
| Rameriz, Antonio | Laborer | San Luis Obispo | San Luis Obispo | S Luis Obispo. |
| Ramirez, J M | Laborer | San Luis Obispo Co. | nr San Luis Obispo. | S Luis Obispo. |
| Ramsy, W R | Laborer | San Luis Obispo Co. | nr San Luis Obispo. | S Luis Obispo. |
| Ramsey, A | Carpenter | San Luis Obispo | San Luis Obispo | S Luis Obispo. |
| Randall, J W | Laborer | San Luis Obispo Co. | nr San Luis Obispo. | S Luis Obispo. |
| Ransdell, Miss L V | Teacher | San Luis Obispo | Monterey st | S Luis Obispo. |
| Ransom, Dr J | Physician | Monterey st | Monterey st | S Luis Obispo. |
| Rathbone, W B | Wool | San Luis Obispo | Monterey st | S Luis Obispo. |
| Ray, G | Farmer | nr San Miguel | San Luis Obispo Co. | San Miguel. |
| Ready, P F | Blacksmith | San Luis Obispo | San Luis Obispo | S Luis Obispo. |
| Rebitaille, P | Farmer | nr Arroyo Grande | San Luis Obispo Co. | Arroyo Grande. |
| Rector, W H | Farmer | nr Cambria | San Luis Obispo Co. | Cambria. |
| Rector, T J | Farmer | nr Morro | San Luis Obispo Co. | Morro. |
| Rector, J P | Farmer | nr San Jose | San Luis Obispo Co. | San Jose. |
| Rector, W A | Blacksmith | Morro | Morro | Morro. |

# 76   L. L. PAULSON'S HAND-BOOK AND

| NAME. | OCCUPATION. | PLACE OF BUSINESS. | RESIDENCE. | TOWN OR P. O. |
|---|---|---|---|---|
| Rector, G W | Farmer | nr San Jose | San Luis Obispo Co | San Jose. |
| Redmond, H | Engineer | Cambria | Cambria | Cambria. |
| **Reed, E L** | Feed stable | Higuera st | Higuerra st | S Luis Obispo. |
| Reed, T | Farmer | San Luis Obispo Co | nr San Luis Obispo | S Luis Obispo. |
| Reed, J C | Farmer | nr Cambria | San Luis Obispo Co | Cambria. |
| Reed, G | Clerk | San Luis Obispo | San Luis Obispo | S Luis Obispo. |
| Reed, J T | Farmer | San Luis Obispo Co | nr Cambria | Cambria. |
| Reimenschreider H | Laborer | nr San Luis Obispo | San Luis Obispo Co | S Luis Obispo. |
| **Reembaugh, H S** | Publisher | S L O Tribune | Morro st | S Luis Obispo. |
| **Rembaugh, H S & Co** | Publishers | S L O Tribune | Morro st | S Luis Obispo. |
| Remick, J D | Farmer | San Luis Obispo Co | nr Estrella | Estrella. |
| Remick, W L | Farmer | San Luis Obispo Co | nr Estrella | Estrella. |
| Remick, A C | Stockman | nr Estrella | San Luis Obispo Co | Estrella. |
| Renoult, Frank | Sign painter | Monterey st | Monterey st | S Luis Obispo. |
| **Renoult, J** | Painter | San Luis Obispo | San Luis Obispo | S Luis Obispo. |
| Renwick, W S | Farmer | San Luis Obispo Co | nr Arroyo Grande | Arroyo Grande. |
| Reynolds, A J | Barber | San Luis Obispo | San Luis Obispo | S Luis Obispo. |
| Reynolds, H C | Laborer | nr San Luis Obispo | San Luis Obispo Co | S Luis Obispo. |
| Rhyne, H W | Farmer | nr San Miguel | San Luis Obispo Co | San Miguel. |
| **Rice, G S** | Farmer | Arroyo Grande | Arroyo Grande | Arroyo Grande. |
| Rice, Danl | Speculator | Arroyo Grande | Arroyo Grande | Arroyo Grande. |
| **Rice, C** | Farmer | San Luis Obispo Co | nr Morro | Morro. |
| Rice, D | Farmer | nr San Luis Obispo | San Luis Obispo Co | S Luis Obispo. |
| Richmond, G | Stage driver | San Luis Obispo | San Luis Obispo | S Luis Obispo. |
| Richards, W | Farmer | nr Cambria | San Luis Obispo Co | Cambria. |
| Ridge, Thos | Hostler | Higuerra st | Higuerra st | S Luis Obispo. |
| Ridge, T R | Farmer | nr San Luis Obispo | San Luis Obispo Co | S Luis Obispo. |
| **Riffe, J D** | Farmer | San Luis Obispo Co | nr San Luis Obispo | S Luis Obispo. |
| Riffe, J | Farmer | San Luis Obispo Co | nr San Luis Obispo | S Luis Obispo. |
| Rigdon, R | Farmer | nr Cambria | San Luis Obispo Co | Cambria. |
| Riggs, A | Whaleman | San Luis Obispo | San Luis Obispo | S Luis Obispo. |
| Righetti, R | Laborer | nr Old Creek | San Luis Obispo Co | Old Creek. |
| Righette, S | Laborer | nr Piedgas Blancas | San Luis Obispo Co | Piedgas Blancas |
| Righetti, P | Laborer | San Luis Obispo Co | nr Piedgas Blancas | Piedgas Blancas |
| **Riley, Franklin** | Farmer | Morro | Morro | Morro. |
| Rios, E | Farmer | nr San Miguel | San Luis Obispo Co | San Miguel. |
| Rios, F | Stock raiser | San Luis Obispo Co | nr P R Hot Springs | Paso Robles. |
| **Rios, Camilo** | Stock raiser | San Luis Obispo Co | nr San Miguel | San Miguel. |
| Rival, A | Laborer | nr San Luis Obispo | San Luis Obispo Co | S Luis Obispo. |
| Rivera, J A | Laborer | nr San Miguel | San Luis Obispo Co | San Miguel. |
| Rivera, F | Laborer | nr San Luis Obispo | San Luis Obispo Co | S Luis Obispo. |
| Robbins, Geo W | Hotel keeper | Arroyo Grande | Branch st | Arroyo Grande. |
| Robbins, T G | Farmer | nr Cambria | San Luis Obispo Co | Cambria. |
| Roberts, G J | Carpenter | San Luis Obispo | San Luis Obispo | S Luis Obispo. |
| Robertson, J B | Teacher | Cambria | Cambria | Cambria. |
| Roberts, J G | Farmer | nr Arroyo Grande | San Luis Obispo Co | Arroyo Grande. |
| Robinson, F C | Laborer | Higuerra & Morro | Higuerra & Morro | S Luis Obispo. |
| Robinson, J T | Farmer | San Luis Obispo Co | nr P R Hot Springs | Paso Robles. |
| **Robinson, W** | Blacksmith | Arroyo Grande | Arroyo Grande | Arroyo Grande. |
| Robinson, J | Farmer | nr San Luis Obispo | San Luis Obispo Co | S Luis Obispo. |
| Roco, J S | Teacher | San Luis Obispo | San Luis Obispo | S Luis Obispo. |
| Rodgers, J P E | Collector | San Jose | San Jose | San Jose. |
| Rodgers, H | Farmer | nr Old Creek | San Luis Obispo Co | Old Creek. |
| Rodgers, M | Farmer | nr San Jose | San Luis Obispo Co | San Jose. |
| Rodriguez, Z | Laborer | San Luis Obispo Co | nr San Luis Obispo | S Luis Obispo. |
| **Rodriguez, J** | Farmer | San Luis Obispo Co | nr San Luis Obispo | S Luis Obispo. |
| Rodriguez, J D | Laborer | San Luis Obispo Co | nr San Luis Obispo | S Luis Obispo. |
| Rodriguez, R | Laborer | San Luis Obispo Co | nr Arroyo Grande | Arroyo Grande. |
| Rodriguez, J M | Farmer | San Luis Obispo Co | nr Morro | Morro. |
| Rodriguez, F | Printer | San Luis Obispo | San Luis Obispo | S Luis Obispo. |
| Rodriguez, J | Farmer | San Luis Obispo Co | nr San Luis Obispo | S Luis Obispo. |
| Rodriguez, J | Farmer | nr San Luis Obispo | San Luis Obispo Co | S Luis Obispo. |
| Rodriguez, J D A | Farmer | San Luis Obispo Co | nr San Luis Obispo | S Luis Obispo. |

# DIRECTORY OF SAN LUIS OBISPO COUNTY. 77

| Name. | Occupation. | Place of Business. | Residence. | Town or P. O. |
|---|---|---|---|---|
| Rodriguez, F S | Farmer | nr San Luis Obispo | San Luis Obispo Co. | S Luis Obispo. |
| Rodriguez, A | Farmer | San Luis Obispo Co. | nr San Luis Obispo. | S Luis Obispo. |
| Rodriguez, J R | Farmer | San Luis Obispo Co. | nr San Luis Obispo. | S Luis Obispo. |
| Rodriguez, J | Farmers | San Luis Obispo Co. | nr Morro | Morro. |
| Rodriguez, F | Laborer | nr San Luis Obispo | San Luis Obispo Co. | S Luis Obispo. |
| Rodriguez, M | Laborer | nr Morro | San Luis Obispo Co. | Morro. |
| Rodriguez, A M | Laborer | nr San Luis Obispo | San Luis Obispo Co. | S Luis Obispo. |
| Rogers, E P | Dentist | Monterey st | Monterey st | S Luis Obispo. |
| Rogers, H | Farmer | nr San Luis Obispo | San Luis Obispo Co. | S Luis Obispo. |
| Roquette, P P | Stock raiser | nr P R Hot Springs | San Luis Obispo Co. | Paso Robles. |
| Romero, Juan | Ranchero | | | Morro. |
| Romero, R | Laborer | nr San Jose | San Luis Obispo Co. | San Jose. |
| Romero, L | Laborer | San Luis Obispo Co. | nr San Jose | San Jose. |
| Romero, J J | Stock raiser | nr Morro | San Luis Obispo Co. | S Margarita. |
| Romero, P | Farmer | San Luis Obispo Co. | nr San Jose | San Jose. |
| Romero, F | Laborer | San Luis Obispo Co. | nr Estrella | Estrella. |
| Romero, P, Jr | Laborer | San Luis Obispo Co. | nr Arroyo Grande | Arroyo Grande. |
| Romero, J | Farmer | nr San Luis Obispo | San Luis Obispo Co. | S Luis Obispo. |
| Romero, J | Farmer | nr San Luis Obispo | San Luis Obispo Co. | S Luis Obispo. |
| Romero, P | Farmer | San Luis Obispo Co. | nr San Luis Obispo | S Luis Obispo. |
| Romero, J | Laborer | San Luis Obispo Co. | nr San Luis Obispo | S Luis Obispo. |
| Romero, L | Farmer | San Luis Obispo Co. | nr Cambria | Cambria. |
| Romero, I | Laborer | San Luis Obispo Co. | San Luis Obispo | S Luis Obispo. |
| Romero, J L | Laborer | San Luis Obispo Co. | nr Arroyo Grande | Arroyo Grande. |
| Romero, A | Laborer | nr San Luis Obispo | San Luis Obispo Co. | S Luis Obispo. |
| Rommick, N B | Farmer | nr Estrella | San Luis Obispo Co. | Estrella. |
| Romo, J M | Farmer | nr Morro | San Luis Obispo Co. | Morro. |
| Romo, J M | Stock raiser | nr Morro | San Luis Obispo Co. | Morro. |
| Roof, H | Saddler | Cambria | Cambria | Cambria. |
| Root, D | Farmer | nr San Luis Obispo | San Luis Obispo Co. | S Luis Obispo. |
| Root, L B | Farmer | San Luis Obispo Co. | nr Cambria | Cambria. |
| Rosas, Guadalupe | Saddler | Chorro st | Santa Rosa st | S Luis Obispo. |
| Rose, A W | Ranchero | Los Osos | 2 m S E Morro | Morro. |
| Ross, J D | Farmer | nr Arroyo Grande | San Luis Obispo Co. | Arroyo Grande. |
| Rudesill, J A | Farmer | San Luis Obispo Co. | nr Morro | Morro. |
| Rudesill, W T | Farmer | San Luis Obispo Co. | nr Morro | Morro. |
| Ruis, V | Laborer | nr San Jose | San Luis Obispo Co. | San Jose. |
| Ruis, F | Laborer | nr Arroyo Grande | San Luis Obispo Co. | Arroyo Grande. |
| Ruis, F | Farmer | San Luis Obispo Co. | nr Cambria | Cambria. |
| Ruiz, R | Farmer | nr San Luis Obispo | San Luis Obispo Co. | S Luis Obispo. |
| Ruiz, J G | Laborer | San Luis Obispo Co. | nr San Luis Obispo | S Luis Obispo. |
| Russell, B | Merchant | Cholamie | Cholamie | Cholamie. |
| Russel, C J | Merchant | Cambria | Cambria | Cambria. |
| Russel, J C | Dairyman | San Luis Obispo Co. | nr San Luis Obispo | S Luis Obispo. |
| Rutherford, John | Farmer | Oso Flaco | | Guadalupe. |
| Rutherford, S | Farmer | Oso Flaco | | Guadalupe. |
| Rutherford, A J | Farmer | San Luis Obispo Co. | nr San Luis Obispo | S Luis Obispo. |
| Rutherford, S T | Laborer | nr Oso Flaco | San Luis Obispo Co. | Oso Flaco. |
| Ryan, W H | Saloon | Arroyo Grande | Branch st | Arroyo Grande. |
| Safley, J H | Farmer | nr Santa Margarita | San Luis Obispo Co. | S Margarita. |
| Saint, S A | Laborer | San Luis Obispo Co. | nr San Luis Obispo | S Luis Obispo. |
| Salas, J | Laborer | nr San Luis Obispo | San Luis Obispo Co. | S Luis Obispo. |
| Salazar, Y | Laborer | nr San Luis Obispo | San Luis Obispo Co. | S Luis Obispo. |
| Salgado, Francisco | Farmer | Cambria Road | ½ m N W S L Obispo | S Luis Obispo. |
| Salgado, J | Farmer | San Luis Obispo Co. | nr San Luis Obispo | S Luis Obispo. |
| Salgado, F | Saddler | San Luis Obispo | San Luis Obispo | S Luis Obispo. |
| Salgado, P | Farmer | San Luis Obispo Co. | nr San Luis Obispo | S Luis Obispo. |
| Salvador M | Gardener | San Luis Obispo Co. | nr San Luis Obispo | S Luis Obispo. |
| Samsel, W A | Farmer | San Luis Obispo Co. | nr San Luis Obispo | S Luis Obispo. |
| Sanabria, Francisco | Carpenter | Monterey st | Monterey st | S Luis Obispo. |
| Sanborn, E F | Carpenter | San Luis Obispo | San Luis Obispo | S Luis Obispo. |
| Sanches, Bernabe | Teamster | San Luis Obispo Co. | Chorro st | S Luis Obispo. |
| Sanchez, A | Mason | San Luis Obispo | San Luis Obispo | S Luis Obispo. |
| Sanchez, B | Farmer | San Luis Obispo Co. | nr San Luis Obispo | S Luis Obispo. |

| Name. | Occupation. | Place of Business. | Residen |
|---|---|---|---|
| Sandercock, Wm... | Hardware............ | Broad st............... | Beach st...... |
| Sanderson, Geo...... | Merchant........... | P R Hot Springs...... | San Luis Obi |
| Sanderson, G R...... | Lawyer............... | P R Hot Springs.... | P R Hot Spr |
| Sandercock, W...... | Farmer............. | nr San Luis Obispo.. | San Luis Obi |
| Sanford, J............. | Miner................ | San Luis Obispo...... | San Luis Ob |
| Sankey, C C......... | Farmer............. | San Luis Obispo Co.. | nr San Migu |
| San Luis Water Co | ........................ | Santa Rosa st.......... | .................. |
| Sansome, E......... | Farmer............. | nr San Luis Obispo.. | San Luis Obi |
| Santa Cruz, J....... | Laborer............. | nr San Luis Obispo... | San Luis Obi |
| Santillanes, N....... | Laborer............. | San Luis Obispo Co.. | nr San Luis |
| Sarber, F A......... | Barber.............. | San Luis Obispo...... | Monterey st. |
| Sargent, R K......... | Laborer............. | nr San Luis Obispo... | San Luis Obi |
| Sasalez, N ........... | Gardener ......... | San Luis Obispo Co.. | nr San Luis |
| Sauer, Andrew ...... | Baker............... | Chorro st............... | Chorro st.... |
| Sauer, Trenida...... | Lodging house.... | Chorro st............... | Chorro st.... |
| Saules, J............... | Laborer............. | nr Cambria............. | San Luis Obi |
| Saunders, D G...... | Farmer............. | San Luis Obispo Co.. | nr Cambria.. |
| Sausloro, D ....... | Painter ............. | San Luis Obispo...... | San Luis Ob |
| Sautter, E F......... | Clerk................ | San Miguel............ | 38 m N San |
| Saxton, G W....... | Miner................ | San Luis Obispo...... | San Luis Obi |
| Saylor, F............... | Laborer............. | San Luis Obispo Co.. | nr Cambria.. |
| Scales, W I......... | Farmer............. | nr San Miguel......... | San Luis Obi |
| Schafer, C............ | Machinist........... | San Luis Obispo...... | San Luis Ob |
| Scharch, Jos......... | Cook ................ | Monterey st........... | Monterey st. |
| Scherrer, J............ | Farmer............. | San Luis Obispo Co.. | nr San Jose. |
| Schein, S ............. | Clerk................ | San Luis Obispo...... | San Luis Ob |
| Scheiffarley, J J.... | Farmer............. | nr San Luis Obispo... | San Luis Obi |
| Schein, Salo.......... | Clerk................ | Monterey st........... | Monterey st. |
| Schindler, W......... | Farmer............. | nr Cambria............. | San Luis Obi |
| Schiebig, C........... | Farmer............. | San Luis Obispo Co.. | nr San Luis |
| Schiefferly, J J... | Co assessor........ | Court House .......... | 6 m S S Luis |
| Scribner, J H ...... | Laborer............. | nr Cambria............. | San Luis Ob |
| Schrimsher, G..... | Farmer ............. | nr San Luis Obispo... | San Luis Obi |
| Schulze, W H...... | Farmer............. | San Luis Obispo Co. | nr San Luis |
| Schwartz, I........... | Clerk................ | Monterey st........... | Monterey st. |
| Schwaub, J........... | Laborer............. | San Luis Obispo Co.. | nr Estrella.. |
| Schwartz, I ........ | Gen merchandise | Guadalupe.............. | .................. |
| Schwartz, L......... | Gen merchandise. | Monterey st........... | Monterey st. |
| Schwartz & Co, L.. | Gen merchandise. | Monterey st........... | .................. |
| Schwartz, K........ | Gen merchandise. | Monterey st........... | Monterey st. |
| Schwartz, S........ | Clerk................ | Monterey st........... | Monterey st. |
| Schwarz, Harford & Co............. | Lumber dealers... | San Luis Obispo...... | .................. |
| Schwartz, L......... | Lumber dealer.... | San Luis Obispo...... | Santa Cruz.. |
| Scott, H A............ | Clerk................ | San Luis Obispo...... | San Luis Ob |
| Scott, W J............ | Farmer............. | San Luis Obispo Co.. | nr San Luis |
| Scott, J................ | Farmer............. | San Luis Obispo Co.. | nr Cambria. |
| Scott, P M........... | Farmer............. | San Luis Obispo Co.. | nr Cambria.. |
| Seabury, P A........ | Seaman............. | Cambria................ | Cambria...... |
| Seabury, F A....... | Farmer............. | San Luis Obispo Co.. | nr Estrella... |
| Seberiano, B ........ | Laborer............. | San Luis Obispo Co.. | nr San Luis |
| See, J................ | Farmer............. | San Luis Obispo Co.. | nr San Luis |
| Seely, T............... | Farmer............. | San Luis Obispo Co.. | nr San Luis |
| Seely, H J............ | Farmer............. | nr San Luis Obispo... | San Luis Ob |
| Selby, T E........... | Farmer............. | San Luis Obispo Co.. | nr Cambria. |
| Selby, J................ | Farmer............. | Cambria Road......... | San Luis Ob |
| Selm, L............... | Brewer............. | San Luis Obispo...... | San Luis Obi |
| Sepulveda, J......... | Farmer............. | nr Arroyo Grande.... | San Luis Ob |
| Seradel, L............. | Laborer............. | nr San Luis Obispo... | San Luis Ob |
| Serrappio, D......... | Laborer............. | nr P R Hot Springs... | San Luis Ob |
| Serradel, J E......... | Laborer............. | nr Cambria............. | San Luis Ob |
| Serrano, F............ | Laborer............. | San Luis Obispo Co.. | nr P R Hot |
| Serrano, M........... | Laborer............. | San Luis Obispo Co.. | nr San Luis |
| Servia, P............. | Farmer............. | San Luis Obispo Co.. | nr San Luis |

## DIRECTORY OF SAN LUIS OBISPO COUNTY. 79

| Name. | Occupation. | Place of Business. | Residence. | Town or P. O. |
|---|---|---|---|---|
| Sesena, E............... | Laborer............... | nr San Luis Obispo.. | San Luis Obispo Co.. | S Luis Obispo. |
| Sesma, R............... | Laborer............... | nr San Jose............. | San Luis Obispo Co.. | San Jose. |
| Shannon, R........... | Farmer............... | 6 m E Paso Robles S | San Luis Obispo Co.. | Paso Robles. |
| Shang, N W........... | Dentist.................. | San Luis Obispo...... | San Luis Obispo..... | S Luis Obispo. |
| Sharren, C V.......... | Farmer............... | Morro Creek........... | 3 m N Morro........... | Morro. |
| Sharwood, T H...... | Clerk.................. | Avila..................... | Avila..................... | S Luis Obispo. |
| Sharp, H................. | Farmer............... | nr Cambria............. | San Luis Obispo Co.. | Cambria. |
| Shauge, N W.......... | Dentist.................. | Monterey st............. | Monterey st............. | S Luis Obispo. |
| Shaw, E S............... | Farmer............... | Santa Barbara Rd ... | 4 m S Arroyo G'e.... | Arroyo Grande. |
| Sheehan, J.............. | Farmer............... | San Luis Obispo Co.. | nr San Miguel......... | San Miguel. |
| Sheid, W T............. | Stock raiser.......... | nr Estrella............... | San Luis Obispo Co.. | Estrella. |
| Shelton, S................ | Laborer............... | San Luis Obispo Co.. | nr San Miguel......... | San Miguel. |
| Sheppard, J............. | Wheelwright....... | Monterey st............. | Monterey st............. | S Luis Obispo. |
| Shepherd, B J......... | Blacksmith........... | Morro..................... | Morro..................... | M... . |
| Shepherd, L............ | Last maker.......... | Cayucos.................. | San Luis Obispo Co.. | C.. ncos. |
| Sherman, T............. | Wheelwright....... | Cambria.................. | Cambria.................. | Cambria. |
| Shipp, T B............... | Farmer............... | San Luis Obispo Co.. | nr Cambria............. | Cambria. |
| Shipp, G F............... | Farmer............... | nr Cambria............. | San Luis Obispo Co.. | Cambria. |
| Shoof, John............. | Farmer............... | Morro Bay............... | ½ m S Morro........... | Morro. |
| Short, M S............... | Mason.................. | Morro..................... | Morro..................... | Morro. |
| Short, I M............... | Laborer............... | San Luis Obispo Co.. | nr Morro................. | Morro. |
| Short, J B................ | Dairyman............. | San Luis Obispo Co.. | nr Morro................. | Morro. |
| Short, Miss Willey | Dress maker......... | Monterey st............. | Monterey st............. | S Luis Obispo. |
| Short, L H............... | Chief engineer..... | Avila..................... | Avila..................... | S Luis Obispo. |
| Sierras, J F J........... | Farmer............... | nr San Luis Obispo.. | San Luis Obispo Co.. | S Luis Obispo. |
| Sigueiro, F.............. | Farmer............... | nr Santa Margarita.. | San Luis Obispo Co.. | S Margarita. |
| Sigueiro, J D........... | Farmer............... | nr Santa Margarita.. | San Luis Obispo Co.. | S Margarita. |
| Silva, J.................... | Laborer............... | San Luis Obispo Co.. | nr San Luis Obispo.. | S Luis Obispo. |
| Silvera, Antonio..... | Restaurant............ | Higuerra st............. | cor Nipoma st......... | S Luis Obispo. |
| Silverira, J N.......... | Whaleman............ | San Luis Obispo Co.. | nr Piedgas Blancas .. | Piedgas Blancas |
| Silveira, J............... | Laborer............... | nr San Luis Obispo.. | San Luis Obispo Co.. | S Luis Obispo. |
| Simmler, J J............ | Postmaster........... | Monterey st............. | Monterey st............. | S Luis Obispo. |
| Simmons, J B.......... | Stock raiser.......... | San Luis Obispo Co.. | nr San Miguel......... | San Miguel. |
| Simpson, E.............. | Farmer............... | nr San Luis Obispo.. | San Luis Obispo Co.. | S Luis Obispo. |
| Sinchimer, B........... | Clerk.................. | Monterey st............. | Monterey st............. | S Luis Obispo. |
| Sinfuegos, J M........ | Laborer............... | nr San Luis Obispo.. | San Luis Obispo Co.. | S Luis Obispo. |
| Sittenfeld, Arnold... | Gen merchandise. | San Miguel.............. | 38 m N San L O'po.. | San Miguel. |
| Sittenfeld & Co...... | Gen merchandise. | San Miguel.............. | 38 m N San L O'po.. | San Miguel. |
| Sitton, S P............... | Farmer............... | San Luis Obispo Co.. | nr Cambria............. | Cambria. |
| Skuaw, H L............. | Farmer............... | San Luis Obispo Co.. | nr Estrella............... | Estrella. |
| Slack, J W............... | Farmer............... | San Luis Obispo Co.. | nr San Luis Obispo.. | S Luis Obispo. |
| Slack, U................... | Millwright........... | Cambria.................. | Cambria.................. | Cambria. |
| Slaughter, J C.......... | Brewer.................. | San Luis Obispo Co.. | nr Oso Flaco........... | Oso Flaco. |
| Slaysman, C R........ | Harness manuf'r | San Luis Obispo...... | Cosmopolitan Hotel.. | S Luis Obispo. |
| Sloan, J R................ | Farmer............... | nr Cambria............. | San Luis Obispo Co.. | Cambria. |
| Smallwood, A B..... | Butcher................. | Fulton Market......... | cor Mill & Torro sts.. | S Luis Obispo. |
| Smallwood, Staiger & Spurgeon | Butchers............... | Fulton Market......... | Monterey & Chorro.. | S Luis Obispo. |
| Smiley, H A............ | Mechanic.............. | San Luis Obispo...... | San Luis Obispo...... | S Luis Obispo. |
| Smith, E H.............. | Dairyman............. | Toro Creek............. | 10 m N E Morro..... | Morro. |
| Smith, A C............... | Dairyman............. |                      |                      | Morro. |
| Smith, F.................. | Stage proprietor... | San Luis Obispo...... | Higuerra st............. | S Luis Obispo. |
| Smith, J S................ | Dairyman............. | Cambria Road......... | 2½ m NW S L O'po... | S Luis Obispo. |
| Smith, M J.............. | Deputy assessor... | Court House........... | Monterey st............. | S Luis Obispo. |
| Smith, F L............... | Blacksmith........... |                      |                      | S Luis Obispo. |
| Smith, D A.............. | Tinsmith............... | Monterey st............. | Fink's Hotel............ | S Luis Obispo. |
| Smith, A G.............. | Trader.................. | P R Hot Springs...... | San Luis Obispo Co.. | Paso Robles. |
| Smith, D B.............. | Miner.................. | Morro..................... | Morro..................... | Morro. |
| Smith, P W.............. | Farmer............... | San Luis Obispo Co.. | nr San Luis Obispo... | S Luis Obispo. |
| Smith, E H.............. | Farmer............... | nr Morro................. | San Luis Obispo Co.. | Morro. |
| Smith, Z B............... | Dairyman............. | nr Cambria............. | San Luis Obispo Co.. | Cambria. |
| Smith, I C................ | Farmer............... | nr Morro................. | San Luis Obispo Co.. | Morro. |
| Smith, W................. | Laborer............... | San Luis Obispo Co.. | P R Hot Springs...... | Paso Robles. |
| Smith, J P................ | Stock raiser.......... | nr Cambria............. | San Luis Obispo Co.. | Cambria. |

| Name. | Occupation. | Place of Business. | Reside? |
|---|---|---|---|
| Smith, Levi | Farmer | San Luis Obispo Co. | nr San Luis |
| Smith, T. | Stage driver | San Luis Obispo | San Luis Ob |
| Snyder, W W | Farmer | San Luis Obispo Co. | nr Cambria. |
| Soberanes, J Y | Laborer | nr Cambria | San Luis Ob |
| Sohlke, J A | Druggist | Monterey st | Monterey st. |
| Somers, J | Water cart | San Luis Obispo | |
| Soto, J | Farmer | nr Palo Prieto | San Luis Obi |
| Soto, B | Laborer | San Luis Obispo Co. | nr San Luis |
| Soto, J | Laborer | nr San Luis Obispo | San Luis Obi |
| Soto, Y E | Farmer | San Luis Obispo Co. | nr San Luis |
| Soto, A | Farmer | San Luis Obispo Co. | nr Morro |
| Soto, B | Farmer | nr Cambria | San Luis Ob |
| Spaulding, E R | Clerk | San Miguel | San Luis Ob |
| Spaulding, L F | Farmer | nr Cambria | San Luis Ob |
| Speegle, J J | Laborer | nr San Luis Obispo | San Luis Ob |
| Sperry, J H | Farmer | Morro | Morro |
| Sperry, H A | Clerk | nr Arroyo Grande | San Luis Ob |
| Spessey, J A | Farmer | San Luis Obispo Co. | nr Morro |
| Speyer, D | Clerk | Monterey st | Monterey st. |
| Spooner, A B, Jr | Stable keeper | San Luis Obispo | San Luis Ob |
| Spooner, A B, Sr | Minister | Morro | Morro |
| Sproul, F S | Lumberman | Nipoma st | Beach st |
| Spurgeon, Chas R. | Butcher | Fulton Market | Monterey st |
| Spurgeon, C H | Butcher | Fulton Market | Monterey st. |
| Stahr, A | Clerk | Monterey st | Monterey st. |
| Staley, J W | Laborer | nr San Miguel | San Luis Ob |
| Stanley, H Y | Dairyman | San Bernado | 2½ m E Mor |
| Stanuseich, John | S L O Market | Monterey st | |
| Stanuseich, A | Stock raiser | nr San Luis Obispo | San Luis Obi |
| Stanton, Fred'k | Contractor | Monterey st | Beach st |
| Stanton, F | Stock raiser | nr Cambria | San Luis Obi |
| Staiger, J J | Butcher | Fulton Market | Monterey st |
| Stearnes, E C | Cook | San Luis Obispo | San Luis Ob |
| Steele, E W | Capitalist | San Luis Obispo | San Luis Ob |
| Steele, Geo | Stock | Santa Barbara Road | 7 m S San L |
| Steele Bros. | Fulton Market | Monterey st | |
| Steiger, J J | Butcher | San Luis Obispo | San Luis Ob |
| Stenner, Wm | Farmer | Santa Rosa st | Santa Rosa s |
| Stephens. T J | Farmer | San Luis Obispo Co. | nr Morro |
| Stephenson, W | Laborer | nr San Luis Obispo | San Luis Obi |
| Stevens, S J | Farmer | Los Osos | 5 m S E Mo |
| Stevens, W E | Clerk | Cambria | San Luis Obi |
| Stevenson, J O | Farmer | San Luis Obispo Co. | nr San Luis |
| Stewart, W E. | Merchant | Morro | Morro |
| Stewart, N | Dairyman | nr Cambria | San Luis Obi |
| Stewart, J Y | Farmer | San Luis Obispo Co. | nr Morro |
| Stewart, J C | Farmer | San Luis Obispo Co. | nr Morro |
| Stewart, J J | Farmer | nr Cambria | nr Cambria |
| Still, T C | Farmer | nr San Luis Obispo | San Luis Obi |
| Stiner, F | Farmer | nr Cambria | San Luis Obi |
| St John, John | Mason | San Luis Obispo | Morro st |
| St John, W H | Brick layer | San Luis Obispo | San Luis Obi |
| Stockdale, D F | Farmer | 5 m N P R Spr'gs | San Luis Obi |
| Stockwell, J H | Painter & grainer | Monterey st | Monterey st |
| Stocking, J C | Blacksmith | Morro | Morro |
| Stocking, E B | Warehouseman | Morro | Morro |
| Stoe, W | Farmer | San Luis Obispo Co. | nr San Luis |
| Stone, G | Farmer | nr San Luis Obispo | San Luis Ob |
| Stone, W H | Laborer | nr Morro | San Luis Obi |
| Stoughton, E | Farmer | nr San Luis Obispo | San Luis Obi |
| Stow, W W | Capitalist | San Francisco | San Francisc |
| Stowell, G W | Farmer | nr Morro | San Luis Obi |
| Stringham, E. | Blacksmith | San Luis Obispo | San Luis Obi |
| Strong, Charles | Laborer | San Luis Obispo | Monterey st. |

DIRECTORY OF SAN LUIS OBISPO COUNTY. 81

| Name. | Occupation. | Place of Business. | Residence. | Town or P. O. |
|---|---|---|---|---|
| Sullens, R............ | Farmer............... | nr Cambria............... | San Luis Obispo Co.. | Cambria. |
| Sullivan, J........... | Blacksmith......... | San Luis Obispo...... | San Luis Obispo...... | S Luis Obispo. |
| Sullivan, J H........ | Laborer............... | nr P R Hot Springs.. | San Luis Obispo Co.. | Paso Robles. |
| Summers, Jas, Jr.. | Blacksmith....... | San Luis Obispo...... | San Luis Obispo...... | S Luis Obispo. |
| Summerville, S...... | Laborer............... | nr San Luis Obispo.. | San Luis Obispo Co.. | S Luis Obispo. |
| Summers, J........... | Laborer............... | San Luis Obispo Co.. | nr San Luis Obispo.. | S Luis Obispo. |
| Summers, J W...... | Farmer............... | San Luis Obispo Co.. | nr San Luis Obispo... | S Luis Obispo. |
| Sumner, Sandy...... | Miller and stock.. | Santa Margarita Rd.. | 3 m N E S L Ob'po.. | S Luis Obispo. |
| Summers, J, Jr..... | ............................. | Monterey st............ | Monterey st............ | S Luis Obispo. |
| Sumner, B F........ | Farmer................ | San Luis Obispo Co.. | nr San Luis Obispo.. | S Luis Obispo. |
| Sumner, G............ | Laborer............... | nr San Luis Obispo.. | San Luis Obispo Co.. | S Luis Obispo. |
| Sutherland, J B..... | Miller................. | San Luis Obispo...... | San Luis Obispo...... | S Luis Obispo. |
| Sutherland, —..... | Farmer............... | Cambria Road........ | 2½ m N W S L Ob'po | S Luis Obispo. |
| Sutton, John........ | Teamster............. | Monterey st............ | Monterey st............ | S Luis Obispo. |
| Sutton, James...... | Contractor.......... | Monterey st............ | Monterey st............ | S Luis Obispo. |
| Swann, J.............. | Farmer............... | nr Morro............... | San Luis Obispo Co. | Morro. |
| Swain, R C........... | Farmer............... | San Luis Obispo Co.. | nr Morro............... | Morro. |
| Switzer, J R......... | Farmer............... | nr Cambria............ | San Luis Obispo Co.. | Cambria. |
| Swarover, C V...... | Farmer .............. | San Luis Obispo Co.. | nr Morro............... | Morro. |
| Sweet, T.............. | Wheelwright....... | Cambria................. | Cambria................. | Cambria. |
| Sweeney, F O....... | Farmer............... | nr San Luis Obispo.. | San Luis Obispo Co.. | S Luis Obispo. |
| Sweeney, J H....... | Farmer............... | San Luis Obispo Co.. | nr San Luis Obispo.. | S Luis Obispo. |
| Sylva, A............... | Whaleman........... | Piedgas Blancas...... | Piedgas Blancas...... | Piedgas Blancas |
| Sylvera, P............ | Hotel keeper....... | San Luis Obispo...... | San Luis Obispo...... | S Luis Obispo. |
| Talbot, J.............. | Farmer............... | Cambria Road........ | 1 m N W S L O'po.. | S Luis Obispo. |
| Tanner, H C......... | Laborer............... | nr San Luis Obispo.. | San Luis Obispo Co.. | S Luis Obispo. |
| Tanner, T............. | Teamster............. | nr San Luis Obispo.. | San Luis Obispo Co.. | S Luis Obispo. |
| Tapia, J............... | Stock raiser........ | nr San Luis Obispo.. | San Luis Obispo Co.. | S Luis Obispo. |
| Tapia, Nabor........ | Feed stable.......... | Monterey st............ | Monterey st............ | S Luis Obispo. |
| Tate, C................ | Carpenter............ | Morro................... | Morro................... | Morro. |
| Tatum, A C.......... | Blacksmith......... | San Luis Obispo...... | San Luis Obispo...... | S Luis Obispo. |
| Taubert, C........... | Bar keeper.......... | Cosmopolitan Hotel. | ............................ | S Luis Obispo. |
| Taujour, W......... | Butcher.............. | San Luis Obispo...... | San Luis Obispo ..... | S Luis Obispo. |
| Taylor, E F.......... | Farmer............... | San Luis Obispo Co.. | nr Cambria............ | Cambria. |
| Taylor, P............. | Farmer............... | nr Cambria............ | San Luis Obispo Co.. | Cambria. |
| Taylor, J.............. | Farmer............... | San Luis Obispo Co.. | nr Arroyo Grande ... | Arroyo Grande. |
| Taylor, P H......... | Carpenter............ | San Jose................ | San Jose................ | San Jose. |
| Taylor, J F........... | Laborer............... | San Luis Obispo Co.. | nr San Jose............ | San Jose. |
| Taylor, J W......... | Laborer............... | San Luis Obispo Co.. | nr Estrella............. | Estrella. |
| Taylor, W H........ | Stage driver....... | San Luis Obispo...... | San Luis Obispo...... | S Luis Obispo. |
| Taylor, P H......... | Carpenter............ | San Luis Obispo...... | San Luis Obispo...... | S Luis Obispo. |
| Taylor, D............. | Farmer............... | nr Morro............... | San Luis Obispo Co.. | Morro. |
| Taylor, John........ | Farmer............... | Morro Creek.......... | 3½ m N Morro........ | Morro. |
| Taylor, H............. | Farmer............... | San Luis Obispo Co.. | nr Santa Margarita.. | S Margarita. |
| Taylor, David....... | Farmer............... | Morro Creek.......... | 3½ m N Morro........ | Morro. |
| Tercis, F.............. | Painter............... | San Luis Obispo...... | San Luis Obispo...... | S Luis Obispo. |
| Thaler, D............. | Laborer............... | San Luis Obispo Co.. | nr San Luis Obispo.. | S Luis Obispo. |
| Thompson, J L..... | Mason................ | nr P R Hot Springs.. | San Luis Obispo Co.. | Paso Robles. |
| Thompson, A W... | Laborer............... | nr Arroyo Grande... | San Luis Obispo Co.. | Arroyo Grande. |
| Thompson, J........ | Farmer............... | nr San Miguel........ | San Luis Obispo Co.. | San Miguel. |
| Thompson, J........ | Stock raiser........ | San Luis Obispo Co.. | nr San Miguel........ | San Miguel. |
| Thompson, J D.... | Capitalist............ | San Luis Obispo...... | San Luis Obispo...... | S Luis Obispo. |
| Thompson, J........ | Capitalist............ | San Luis Obispo...... | San Luis Obispo...... | S Luis Obispo. |
| Thornton, O F..... | Editor................ | S L O Tribune....... | Cosmopolitan Hotel.. | S Luis Obispo. |
| Tibbets, B P........ | Laborer............... | nr San Luis Obispo.. | San Luis Obispo Co.. | S Luis Obispo. |
| Tibbetts, —......... | Brick maker....... | San Luis Obispo...... | Buchon st.............. | S Luis Obispo. |
| Tico, P................ | Laborer............... | nr San Luis Obispo.. | San Luis Obispo Co.. | S Luis Obispo. |
| Tierney, Frank..... | R R overseer....... | Avila................... | Avila................... | S Luis Obispo. |
| Tinkey, D............ | Farmer............... | nr Morro............... | San Luis Obispo Co.. | Morro. |
| Titus, J............... | Teacher.............. | San Luis Obispo...... | Monterey st............ | S Luis Obispo. |
| Titus, Mrs L........ | Music teacher..... | Monterey st............ | Monterey st............ | S Luis Obispo. |
| Tonino, A............ | Laborer............... | San Luis Obispo Co.. | nr Old Creek.......... | Old Creek. |
| Torres, V............. | Farmer............... | nr Morro............... | San Luis Obispo Co.. | Morro. |
| Townsend, J B..... | Barber................ | San Luis Obispo...... | San Luis Obispo...... | S Luis Obispo. |

5½

# HARVEY B. BLAKE & CO.

### SAN LUIS OBISPO, CAL.

## Real Estate, Collection

### AND GENERAL AGENTS

HAVE FOR SALE, AND TO RENT,

## 100,000 Acres of Farming Land,

IN

### SAN LUIS OBISPO AND SANTA BARBARA COUNTIES.

---

## COLLECTIONS MADE, LOANS NEGOTIATED.

SEARCHERS OF RECORDS, CONVEYANCERS,

—AND A—

## GENERAL BUSINESS AGENCY CONDUCTED.

REFER BY PERMISSION TO

| | | |
|---|---|---|
| Bank of San Luis Obispo, | Lewis T. Burton, | Santa Barbara. |
| Hon. W. I. Graves, San Luis Obispo. | Hon. T. I. Maguire, | " |
| I. C. Ortega, Agent W. F. & Co. " | F. W. Frost, Esq. | " |
| P. W. Murphy, Esq. " | Coast Line Stage Co., | " |

### P. O. Address, SAN LUIS OBISPO, BOX 29.

# DIRECTORY OF SAN LUIS OBISPO COUNTY. 83

| Name. | Occupation. | Place of Business. | Residence. | Town or P. O. |
|---|---|---|---|---|
| Trabucco, J B | Gardener | nr San Luis Obispo | San Luis Obispo Co. | S Luis Obispo. |
| Tracey, James | Farmer | Los Osos | 5 m S Morro | Morro. |
| Tracy, J | Farmer | San Luis Obispo Co. | nr San Luis Obispo | S Luis Obispo. |
| Trejo, J | Laborer | San Luis Obispo Co. | nr San Luis Obispo | S Luis Obispo. |
| Tripp, R B | Physician | Morro | Morro | Morro. |
| Tromer, F | Farmer | San Luis Obispo Co. | nr San Luis Obispo | S Luis Obispo. |
| Troy, P | Teacher | San Luis Obispo | San Luis Obispo | S Luis Obispo. |
| Truesdell, G E | Farmer | San Luis Obispo Co. | | Beach. |
| Trujillo, M | Farmer | nr San Luis Obispo | San Luis Obispo Co. | S Luis Obispo. |
| Tuley, H, Sr | Farmer | nr San Luis Obispo | San Luis Obispo Co. | S Luis Obispo. |
| Tuley, H, Jr | Farmer | San Luis Obispo Co. | nr San Luis Obispo | S Luis Obispo. |
| Tule, J | Compositor | Morro st | Higuerra st | S Luis Obispo. |
| Tule, G B | Compositor | Morro st | Morro st | S Luis Obispo. |
| Tull, J R | Farmer | San Luis Obispo Co. | nr San Simeon | San Simeon. |
| Tull, J M | Farmer | nr San Simeon | San Luis Obispo Co. | San Simeon. |
| Turner, R B | Laborer | nr Estrella | San Luis Obispo Co. | Estrella. |
| Turner, E | Tinsmith | San Luis Obispo | San Luis Obispo | S Luis Obispo. |
| Turner, W A | Farmer | San Luis Obispo Co. | nr San Luis Obispo | S Luis Obispo. |
| Turner, S M | Farmer | nr San Luis Obispo | San Luis Obispo Co. | S Luis Obispo. |
| Turner & Potter | Stoves & tinw're | Monterey st | | S Luis Obispo. |
| Turner, S M | Tinsmith | Monterey st | Nipoma st | S Luis Obispo. |
| Uloah, L | Laborer | nr San Luis Obispo | San Luis Obispo Co. | S Luis Obispo. |
| Ungert, A | Clerk | Higuerra st | Monterey st | S Luis Obispo. |
| Ungren, Frank | Palace saloon | Monterey st | Monterey st | S Luis Obispo. |
| Upchurch, R D | Farmer | Beach Road | 3 m S W San Luis Ob | S Luis Obispo. |
| Urtado, F | Farmer | San Luis Obispo Co. | nr San Luis Obispo | S Luis Obispo. |
| Utley, F W | Dairyman | nr Cambria | San Luis Obispo Co. | Cambria. |
| Utley, M | Farmer | nr Cambria | San Luis Obispo Co. | Cambria. |
| Utley, L | Farmer | San Luis Obispo Co. | nr Cambria | Cambria. |
| Utter, D | Farmer | nr Cambria | San Luis Obispo Co. | Cambria. |
| Valdies, J N | Dairyman | Landing Road | 3 m W Arroyo Gr'de | Arroyo Grande. |
| Valdez, A | Laborer | San Luis Obispo Co. | nr San Luis Obispo | S Luis Obispo. |
| Valdez, J J | Laborer | nr San Luis Obispo | San Luis Obispo Co. | S Luis Obispo. |
| Valdez, J J | Farmer | nr Arroyo Grande | San Luis Obispo Co. | Arroyo Grande. |
| Valencia, R | Farmer | nr San Luis Obispo | San Luis Obispo Co. | S Luis Obispo. |
| Valencia, J A | Farmer | nr Arroyo Grande | San Luis Obispo Co. | Arroyo Grande. |
| Valenzuela, J M | Farmer | nr San Jose | San Luis Obispo Co. | San Jose. |
| Valenzuela, Y | Laborer | San Luis Obispo Co. | nr San Luis Obispo | S Luis Obispo. |
| Valencia, J D | Farmer | San Luis Obispo Co. | nr San Luis Obispo | S Luis Obispo. |
| Van Campen, A | R R overseer | Avila | Avila | S Luis Obispo. |
| Van Gorden, I | Farmer | nr San Luis Obispo | San Luis Obispo Co. | S Luis Obispo. |
| Van Gorden, G | Farmer | San Luis Obispo Co. | nr Cambria | Cambria. |
| Van Gorden, J | Farmer | nr Cambria | San Luis Obispo Co. | Cambria. |
| Van Gundy, H | Farmer | Oso Flaco | | Guadalupe. |
| Van Gundy, Wm | Farmer | Oso Flaco | | Guadalupe. |
| Vanier, E | Carpenter | San Luis Obispo | San Luis Obispo | S Luis Obispo. |
| Vasquez, S | Stock raiser | San Luis Obispo Co. | nr Cambria | Cambria. |
| Vasquez, J A | Farmer | nr Morro | San Luis Obispo Co. | Morro. |
| Vaughan, D | Stock raiser | San Luis Obispo Co. | nr Morro | Morro. |
| Vaughan, J V | Stock raiser | nr Morro | San Luis Obispo Co. | Morro. |
| Vaughan, G W | Stock ratser | San Luis Obispo Co. | nr Morro | Morro. |
| Vega, Enrique | Teamster | San Luis Obispo | Chorro st | S Luis Obispo. |
| Velarde, J L | Farmer | San Luis Obispo Co. | nr San Luis Obispo | S Luis Obispo. |
| Venable, Judge McD R | County judge | | Monterey st | S Luis Obispo. |
| Venable, H C | Farmer | San Luis Obispo Co. | nr San Luis Obispo | S Luis Obispo. |
| Verlague, S | Groceries | Monterey st | cor Broad st | S Luis Obispo. |
| Viera, J | Whaleman | nr San Luis Obispo | San Luis Obispo Co. | S Luis Obispo. |
| Villa, J R | Farmer | San Luis Obispo Co. | nr San Luis Obispo | S Luis Obispo. |
| Villa, F | Farmer | San Luis Obispo Co. | nr San Luis Obispo | S Luis Obispo. |
| Villa, C | Farmer | San Luis Obispo Co. | nr San Luis Obispo | S Luis Obispo. |
| Villa, J | Farmer | nr San Luis Obispo | San Luis Obispo Co. | S Luis Obispo. |
| Villa, J Y | Farmer | nr San Luis Obispo | San Luis Obispo Co. | S Luis Obispo. |
| Villa, A | Laborer | nr San Luis Obispo | San Luis Obispo Co. | S Luis Obispo. |

## STEELE'S SQUIRREL POISON

### SURE DEATH

—TO—

SQUIRRELS, GOPHERS, RATS, MICE,

And all such

**TROUBLESOME PESTS.**

MILLIONS OF DOLLARS

Saved annually to the farmers of California by the free use of

### STEELE'S SQUIRREL POISON

For sale by all Druggists, Grocers and General Dealers. Price $1 per box. Made by JAS. G. STEELE & CO., San Francisco, Cal. Liberal discount to the trade.

---

## THE

PLACE TO BUY A GOOD ARTICLE CHEAP.

### BERSON & SON,

Nos. 710 & 712 WASHINGTON ST.,

Above Kearny, - SAN FRANCISCO.

DEALERS IN

### Carpets, Oil Cloths,

FURNITURE, BEDDING, MATTRESSES.

**UPHOLSTERERS' GOODS,**

LACE CURTAINS,

And Everything Usually Included in the Stock of a First-Class Carpet and Furniture Establishment.

☞ Give us a call and test the truth of the above statement.

---

HENRY H. BENJAMIN & CO.

Office—162 NEW MONTGOMERY ST.,

Near Howard, SAN FRANCISCO.

A Refreshing Beverage and Invigorating Tonic. Highly recommended by Physicians for Invalids and Family Use.

---

## THE GUADALUPE TELEGRAPH

IS PUBLISHED

### EVERY SATURDAY

—AT—

### GUADALUPE,

SANTA BARBARA CO., - CAL.

—BY—

### J. R. PORTERFIELD,

PUBLISHER AND PROPRIETOR

TERMS IN ADVANCE:

| | |
|---|---|
| One Year | $3 00 |
| Six Months | 2 00 |
| Three Months | 1 50 |
| Single Copies | 10 |

DIRECTORY OF SAN LUIS OBISPO COUNTY. 85

| NAME. | OCCUPATION. | PLACE OF BUSINESS. | RESIDENCE. | TOWN OR P. O. |
|---|---|---|---|---|
| Villar, F............ | Mason............ | San Luis Obispo...... | San Luis Obispo...... | S Luis Obispo. |
| Villa, J A........... | Laborer............ | San Luis Obispo Co.. | nr San Luis Obispo... | S Luis Obispo. |
| Villa, J M........... | Laborer............ | nr San Luis Obispo.. | San Luis Obispo Co.. | S Luis Obispo. |
| Villa, Federico..... | Farmer........... | San Luis Obispo Co.. | nr San Luis Obispo.. | S Luis Obispo. |
| Villa, C............... | Laborer............ | nr San Luis Obispo... | San Luis Obispo Co.. | S Luis Obispo. |
| Villa, E............... | Laborer............ | San Luis Obispo Co.. | nr San Luis Obispo... | S Luis Obispo. |
| Villa, F............... | Farmer............ | San Luis Obispo Co.. | nr San Luis Obispo.. | S Luis Obispo. |
| Villa, Ramon A.... | Farmer............ | nr San Luis Obispo... | San Luis Obispo Co.. | S Luis Obispo. |
| Villa, Roberto...... | Farmer............ | San Luis Obispo Co.. | nr Morro............... | Morro. |
| Villa, Y.............. | Farmer............ | nr Morro............... | San Luis Obispo Co.. | Morro. |
| Villa, J A........... | Farmer............ | San Luis Obispo Co.. | nr Morro............... | Morro. |
| Villa, R J........... | Farmer............ | San Luis Obispo Co.. | nr Morro............... | Morro. |
| Villa, V.............. | Laborer............ | San Luis Obispo Co.. | nr San Luis Obispo.. | S Luis Obispo. |
| Villavicencio, F..... | Farmer........... | nr San Luis Obispo... | San Luis Obispo Co.. | S Luis Obispo. |
| Villegas, F........... | Farmer........... | San Luis Obispo...... | nr San Luis Obispo.. | S Luis Obispo. |
| Vincent, J............ | Carpenter......... | San Luis Obispo...... | San Luis Obispo...... | S Luis Obispo. |
| Voss, J................ | Farmer............ | nr Cambria........... | San Luis Obispo Co.. | Cambria. |
| Wade, J C........... | .......................... | San Luis Obispo...... | San Luis Obispo...... | S Luis Obispo. |
| Wagers, F........... | Boarding house... | Higuerra st........... | Higuerra st........... | S Luis Obispo. |
| Waler, J.............. | Farmer............ | San Luis Obispo Co.. | nr San Miguel......... | San Miguel. |
| Waldo, C F......... | Farmer............ | San Luis Obispo Co.. | nr Cambria............ | Cambria. |
| Walker, A........... | Carpenter......... | San Luis Obispo...... | San Luis Obispo...... | S Luis Obispo. |
| Walker, J R........ | Farmer............ | nr Cambria........... | San Luis Obispo Co.. | Cambria. |
| Walker, J T........ | Stage driver...... | Cambria............... | Cambria............... | Cambria. |
| Walker, M W...... | Farmer............ | nr San Luis Obispo... | San Luis Obispo Co.. | S Luis Obispo. |
| Walker, W W...... | Farmer............ | San Luis Obispo Co.. | nr Morro............... | Morro. |
| Walker, J........... | Farmer............ | San Luis Obispo Co.. | nr Cambria............ | Cambria. |
| Walker, J A........ | Physician.......... | Cambria............... | Cambria............... | Cambria. |
| Walker, J S........ | Farmer............ | San Luis Obispo Co.. | nr San Luis Obispo.. | S Luis Obispo. |
| Wallace, A M...... | Farmer............ | San Luis Obispo Co.. | nr San Miguel......... | San Miguel. |
| Wall, John.......... | .......................... | San Luis Obispo...... | Beach st.............. | S Luis Obispo. |
| Wallace, J........... | Sheep raiser....... | Cambria Road........ | San Luis Obispo Co.. | Paso Robles. |
| Wallace, H.......... | Blacksmith........ | San Luis Obispo...... | San Luis Obispo...... | S Luis Obispo. |
| Wallace, W G...... | Farmer............ | San Luis Obispo Co.. | nr Morro............... | Morro. |
| Walsh, John........ | Water carrier..... | Avila.................. | Avila.................. | S Luis Obispo. |
| Walsworth, A B... | Farmer............ | nr P R Hot Springs.. | San Luis Obispo Co.. | Paso Robles. |
| Ward, Thos......... | Teamster.......... | Higuerra st........... | Broad st.............. | S Luis Obispo. |
| Ward, H C.......... | Surveyor.......... | San Luis Obispo...... | Cosmopolitan Hotel.. | S Luis Obispo. |
| Warden, L M...... | Stock raiser....... | San Luis Obispo Co.. | nr San Luis Obispo.. | S Luis Obispo. |
| Ward, L H.......... | Farmer............ | nr Cambria........... | San Luis Obispo Co.. | Cambria. |
| Ward, J.............. | Farmer............ | San Luis Obispo Co.. | nr Cambria............ | Cambria. |
| Ward, M A......... | Farmer............ | nr Cambria........... | San Luis Obispo Co.. | Cambria. |
| Warden, W H..... | Laborer............ | San Luis Obispo Co.. | nr Santa Margarita... | S Margarita. |
| Warden, A P....... | Farmer............ | nr P R Hot Springs.. | San Luis Obispo Co.. | Paso Robles. |
| Ward, J S........... | Laborer............ | nr San Luis Obispo... | San Luis Obispo Co.. | S Luis Obispo. |
| Ward, A P.......... | Bookkeeper....... | Cambria............... | Cambria............... | Cambria. |
| Warden, H M...... | Farmer............ | San Luis Obispo Co.. | nr San Luis Obispo.. | S Luis Obispo. |
| Warren, M N...... | Stock raiser....... | nr San Luis Obispo... | San Luis Obispo Co.. | San Miguel. |
| Washburn, P J.... | Farmer............ | Berros Creek......... | 2 m S Arroyo Grande | Arroyo Grande. |
| Waters, W W...... | Farmer............ | nr P R Hot Springs.. | San Luis Obispo Co.. | Paso Robles. |
| Waters, W W...... | Compositor........ | Morro st.............. | Monterey st.......... | S Luis Obispo. |
| Watkins, J........... | Farmer............ | San Luis Obispo Co.. | nr Cambria............ | Cambria. |
| Watkins, E.......... | Stock raiser....... | nr San Luis Obispo... | San Luis Obispo Co.. | S Luis Obispo. |
| Watson, J A........ | Laborer............ | nr Cambria........... | San Luis Obispo Co.. | Cambria. |
| Watts, W P......... | Farmer............ | nr Cambria........... | San Luis Obispo Co.. | Cambria. |
| Watts, W P K..... | Farmer............ | nr Cambria........... | San Luis Obispo Co.. | Cambria. |
| Waugh, J J......... | Farmer............ | nr San Luis Obispo... | San Luis Obispo Co.. | S Luis Obispo. |
| Wayne, W........... | Laborer............ | nr San Luis Obispo... | San Luis Obispo Co.. | S Luis Obispo. |
| Wearmouth, Thos.. | Carpenter......... | San Luis Obispo...... | Broad st.............. | S Luis Obispo. |
| Webb, W............ | Farmer............ | nr San Miguel........ | San Luis Obispo Co.. | San Miguel. |
| Webb, M L D...... | Farmer............ | San Luis Obispo Co.. | nr Cambria............ | Cambria. |
| Webb, E............. | Farmer............ | San Luis Obispo Co.. | nr Cambria............ | Cambria. |
| Weidernell, F...... | Blacksmith........ | San Luis Obispo...... | San Luis Obispo...... | S Luis Obispo. |
| Weimer, J........... | Carpenter......... | San Luis Obispo...... | San Luis Obispo...... | S Luis Obispo. |

| Name. | Occupation. | Place of Business. | Residence. | Town or P. O. |
|---|---|---|---|---|
| Weir, H | Sheep raiser | Estrella | San Luis Obispo Co. | Estrella. |
| Weir, J | Sheep raiser | Estrella | San Luis Obispo Co. | Estrella. |
| Weir, N | Farmer | San Luis Obispo Co. | nr San Miguel | San Miguel. |
| Weldon, C | Farmer | San Luis Obispo Co. | nr Huasna | Huasna. |
| Wells, A | Stock raiser | nr San Miguel | San Luis Obispo Co. | San Miguel. |
| Welsh, C E C | Carpenter | San Luis Obispo | San Luis Obispo | S Luis Obispo. |
| Welsh, J | Miner | San Luis Obispo | San Luis Obispo | S Luis Obispo. |
| **Westfall, Dr O D.** | Physician | Monterey st | Monterey st | S Luis Obispo. |
| Wheeler, J H | Clerk | Broad st | Broad st | S Luis Obispo. |
| Wheeler, Mrs M | Millinery | Morro st | San Luis Obispo | S Luis Obispo. |
| Wheelock, D T | Farmer | San Luis Obispo Co. | nr San Luis Obispo | S Luis Obispo. |
| Whitsel, A S | Carpenter | San Luis Obispo | Monterey st | S Luis Obispo. |
| White, James | Saloon | Higuerra st | Higuerra st | S Luis Obispo. |
| Whitney, B C | Saloon keeper | Morro | Morro | Morro. |
| **Whitney, D H** | Farmer | Morro | 1 m E Morro | Morro. |
| **White, G W** | Farmer | San Luis Obispo Co. | nr Cambria | Cambria. |
| **Whitsitt, S B** | Farmer | San Luis Obispo Co. | nr Cambria | Cambria. |
| White, M C | Physician | Morro | Morro | Morro. |
| Whitely, Thos, Jr. | Shoe maker | San Luis Obispo | San Luis Obispo | S Luis Obispo. |
| Whitely, Thos Sr. | Boot maker | San Luis Obispo | San Luis Obispo | S Luis Obispo. |
| White, J T | Laborer | nr Cambria | San Luis Obispo Co. | Cambria. |
| **Whitaker, S L** | Farmer | nr Morro | San Luis Obispo Co. | Morro. |
| White, C | Printer | San Luis Obispo | San Luis Obispo | S Luis Obispo. |
| Whitely, W | Laborer | San Luis Obispo Co. | nr San Luis Obispo | S Luis Obispo. |
| White, H G | Machinist | Cambria | Cambria | Cambria. |
| White, D | Laborer | San Luis Obispo Co. | nr San Miguel | San Miguel. |
| **White, J S** | Farmer | nr San Luis Obispo | San Luis Obispo | S Luis Obispo. |
| Whitrow, C | Teamster | San Luis Obispo Co. | nr San Luis Obispo | S Luis Obispo. |
| Whitesell, J | Teamster | San Luis Obispo Co. | nr San Luis Obispo | S Luis Obispo. |
| Whitaker, W S | Merchant | Cambria | Cambria | Cambria. |
| White, C | Carpenter | nr Estrella | San Luis Obispo Co. | Estrella. |
| Whitaker, J M | Farmer | nr Cambria | San Luis Obispo Co. | Cambria. |
| Whitsell, A S | Carpenter | San Luis Obispo | San Luis Obispo | S Luis Obispo. |
| Wickersham, J G | Banker | Petaluma | Petaluma | Petaluma. |
| Wiggins, S F | Farmer | nr Morro | San Luis Obispo Co. | Morro. |
| **Wightman, John** | Assessor | Court House | Broad st | S Luis Obispo. |
| Wilcox, Mason | Attorneys at law | San Luis Obispo | San Luis Obispo | S Luis Obispo. |
| Wilcox, C E | Saddler | Morro | Morro | Morro. |
| **Wilke, U** | Restaurant | Higuerra st | Higuerra st | S Luis Obispo. |
| **Wilke & Mehlmann** | Restaurant | Higuerra st | Higuerra st | S Luis Obispo. |
| **Wilke, Wm** | Attorney | Court House | Monterey st | S Luis Obispo. |
| Wilkerson, J | Farmer | Cambria Road | San Luis Obispo Co. | Paso Robles. |
| **Wilkinson, J M** | Farmer | San Luis Obispo Co. | nr P R Hot Springs | Paso Robles. |
| Wilkerson, A | Laborer | nr San Luis Obispo | San Luis Obispo Co. | S Luis Obispo. |
| **Wilkenson, J** | Farmer | San Luis Obispo Co. | nr Huasna | Huasna. |
| Wilkenson, J W | Farmer | nr Huasna | San Luis Obispo Co. | Huasna. |
| Wilkes, W | Laborer | San Luis Obispo Co. | nr San Luis Obispo | S Luis Obispo. |
| Wilkinson, J P | Farmer | San Luis Obispo Co. | nr Cambria | Cambria. |
| **Willard, H P** | Farmer | Guadalupe | 3 m S Arroyo Gr'de | Arroyo Grande. |
| Williams, C | Saloon keeper | Morro Willows | 1 m N Morro | Morro. |
| **Williams, R** | Farmer | nr Morro | San Luis Obispo Co. | Morro. |
| Williams, W | Farmer | San Luis Obispo Co. | nr Morro | Morro. |
| Willis, E F | Farmer | nr Cambria | San Luis Obispo Co. | Cambria. |
| **Williamson, A** | Stoves & tinware | Monterey st | Monterey st | S Luis Obispo. |
| Williams, S | Laborer | San Luis Obispo Co. | nr San Luis Obispo | S Luis Obispo. |
| Williams, J W | Mason | San Luis Obispo Co. | San Luis Obispo | S Luis Obispo. |
| **Willard, H P** | Farmer | San Luis Obispo Co. | nr Arroyo Grande | Arroyo Grande. |
| Williams, F | Whaleman | San Luis Obispo | San Luis Obispo | S Luis Obispo. |
| **Williams, M B** | Stock raiser | San Luis Obispo Co. | nr Cambria | Cambria. |
| Williams, C A | Farmer | San Luis Obispo Co. | nr San Luis Obispo | S Luis Obispo. |
| Williams, J | Miner | Arroyo Grande | Arroyo Grande | Arroyo Grande. |
| **Wilmerding, H** | Capitalist | San Francisco | San Francisco | San Francisco. |
| **Wilson, I L** | Carpenter | San Luis Obispo | San Luis Obispo | S Luis Obispo. |
| Wilson, J | Farmer | nr San Luis Obispo | San Luis Obispo Co. | S Luis Obispo. |

| )ccupation. | Place of Business. | Residence. | Town or P. O. |
|---|---|---|---|
| rmer, | San Luis Obispo Co.. | nr P R Hot Springs.. | Paso Robles. |
| rmer, | San Luis Obispo Co.. | nr San Luis Obispo.. | S Luis Obispo. |
| uggist | P R Hot Springs | P R Hot Springs | Paso Robles. |
| rmer | nr Cambria | San Luis Obispo Co.. | Cambria. |
| rmer | San Luis Obispo Co.. | nr Cambria | Cambria. |
| eep raiser | Mud Springs | San Luis Obispo Co.. | Paso Robles. |
| borer | San Luis Obispo Co.. | nr San Luis Obispo... | S Luis Obispo. |
| orney | Monterey st | Monterey st | S Luis Obispo. |
| iryman. | Huasna Ranch | 10 m N W Arroyo G | Arroyo Grande. |
| iryman | Huasna Ranch | 10 m N W Arroyo G | Arroyo Grande. |
| iryman. | Huasna Ranch | 10 m N W Arroyo G | Arroyo Grande. |
| iryman. | Huasna Ranch | 10 m N W Arroyo G | Arroyo Grande. |
| iryman. | Huasna Ranch | 10 m N W Arroyo G | Arroyo Grande. |
| iryman. | San Luis Obispo Co.. | nr Arroyo Grande | Arroyo Grande. |
| wyer | San Luis Obispo | San Luis Obispo | S Luis Obispo. |
| shion Stable... | Monterey st | | S Luis Obispo. |
| borer | nr San Luis Obispo | San Luis Obispo Co.. | S Luis Obispo. |
| rmer | San Luis Obispo Co.. | nr Arroyo Grande | Arroyo Grande. |
| rmer | San Luis Obispo Co.. | nr Arroyo Grande.... | Arroyo Grande. |
| rpenter | San Luis Obispo | Monterey st | S Luis Obispo. |
| rmer | nr P R Hot Springs.. | San Luis Obispo Co.. | Paso Robles. |
| rmer | San Luis Obispo Co.. | nr Cambria | Cambria. |
| mster | nr Cambria | San Luis Obispo Co.. | Cambria. |
| rpenter | Arroyo Grande | Arroyo Grande | Arroyo Grande. |
| puty sheriff | San Luis Obispo | San Luis Obispo | S Luis Obispo. |
| rmer | nr Cambria | San Luis Obispo Co.. | Cambria. |
| rpenter | Arroyo Grande | Branch st | Arroyo Grande. |
| rmer | nr San Luis Obispo | San Luis Obispo Co.. | S Luis Obispo. |
| nker | Monterey st | Higuerra st | S Luis Obispo. |
| rmer | Sunderland Mine | San Luis Obispo Co.. | Paso Robles. |
| nister | Los Osos | 10 m S Morro | Morro. |
| rmer | Cambria Road | San Luis Obispo Co.. | Paso Robles. |
| mer | San Luis Obispo Co.. | nr Morro | Morro. |
| rmer | San Luis Obispo Co.. | nr San Miguel | San Miguel. |
| mer | nr P R Hot Springs.. | San Luis Obispo Co.. | Paso Robles. |
| mer | San Luis Obispo Co.. | nr P R Hot Springs.. | Paso Robles. |
| mer | nr Cambria | San Luis Obispo Co.. | Cambria. |
| mer | nr Morro | San Luis Obispo Co.. | Morro. |
| mer | San Luis Obispo Co.. | nr Estrella | Estrella. |
| mer | San Luis Obispo Co.. | nr Estrella | Estrella. |
| orer | San Luis Obispo Co.. | nr San Luis Obispo.. | S Luis Obispo. |
| ck raiser | nr P R Hot Springs.. | San Luis Obispo Co.. | Paso Robles. |
| fitter | San Luis Obispo | San Luis Obispo | S Luis Obispo. |
| mer | nr Josephine | San Luis Obispo Co.. | Josephine. |
| mster | nr Estrella | San Luis Obispo Co.. | Estrella. |
| mer | San Luis Obispo Co.. | nr San Luis Obispo... | S Luis Obispo. |
| mer. | Morro | San Luis Obispo Co.. | Morro. |
| ep raiser | 16 m W P R Spr'gs.. | San Luis Obispo Co.. | Paso Robles. |
| ep raiser | 16 m W P R Spr'gs.. | San Luis Obispo Co.. | Paso Robles. |
| orer | nr San Luis Obispo... | San Luis Obispo Co.. | S Luis Obispo. |
| orer | nr San Luis Obispo... | San Luis Obispo Co... | S Luis Obispo. |
| orer | San Luis Obispo Co.. | nr San Luis Obispo... | S Luis Obispo. |
| orer | nr San Luis Obispo... | San Luis Obispo Co.. | S Luis Obispo. |
| orer | San Luis Obispo Co.. | nr San Luis Obispo... | S Luis Obispo. |
| rk | Monterey st | Monterey st | S Luis Obispo. |
| ok raiser | San Luis Obispo Co.. | nr San Luis Obispo .. | S Luis Obispo. |
| ok raiser | nr Estrella | San Luis Obispo Co.. | Estrella. |
| ok raiser | San Luis Obispo Co.. | nr Estrella | Estrella. |
| ok raiser | nr Cambria | San Luis Obispo Co.. | Cambria. |

# EXCELSIOR IMPROVED WIND-MILL.

The opinion has become too prevalent that wind-mills are not to be relied upon, either to withstand violent storms, or to perform their work in very light winds. Such opinion is doubtless true in regard to many, perhaps a majority, of mills; nevertheless, it is an injustice to the few mechanics who have made the wind-power a study and a specialty for many years, to class their productions with those of a larger number, who pretend to be wind-mill makers, but who comparatively have little experience, or practical knowledge of the business.

We were the inventors, more than ten years ago, of the single, cross-vane wind-mill. The demand for them gradually increased until they have come into more general use than any other mills. Of course, other parties were induced to make an imitation of them, and some to make use of its name, "EXCELSIOR." A man is desirous of purchasing a wind-mill, and starts in pursuit of the factory. Presently he sees a sign "WIND-MILLS," walks in and inquires, "is this the place where they make the EXCELSIOR WIND-MILL?" The answer is, "Yes, sir; O, yes, we make them," or words to that effect, and the gentleman really thinks he is purchasing an EXCELSIOR. We have recently caused the name to be registered in the U. S. Patent Office as our Trade Mark, and hereby caution all persons not to make unlawful use of the same.

The EXCELSIOR was awarded the first and cash premium at the Cal. State Agricultural Fair in 1872—the only time ever exhibited there. It has taken a larger number of premiums at the Mechanics' Institute Fairs in San Francisco, than any other wind-mill.

The EXCELSIOR is adjustable, and self-regulating, is very substantially built, and with reasonable care will last twenty or twenty-five years. Its construction is simple, and can be easily erected by those who are not mechanics. They will run in lighter winds than any other wind-mill, and violent storms will seldom injure them. They are always under perfect control, a child being able to operate them.

The cut, engraved from a photograph—represents their style and appearance. They are made in twelve sizes, from twelve feet to forty feet diameter of wheel. A larger stock and assortment kept on hand than can be found in the State. Every mill fully guaranteed. Address,

## EXCELSIOR WIND-MILL WORKS,

### 211 AND 213 MISSION STREET, SAN FRANCISCO.

*ATWOOD & BODWELL, Pro's.*

# HORSE-POWERS.

**LITTLE GIANT TRIPLE GEARS AND DOUBLE LEVERS,**
For Two Horses.

**EXCELSIOR DOUBLE-GEARED**
HEAVY ONE-HORSE.

**FARMERS' SINGLE-GEARED,**
FOR ONE HORSE.

These machines are complete in every detail, and possess every improvement and advantage that can be combined in Sweep Horse-Powers. They have an advantage over *any* other horse power in this market, viz: our application of the patent rubber draw-spring, which prevents any breakage of the gears by any sudden start, or jumping, or fractiousness of the horse; and when used for pumping, materially lessens the jerking motion on the lever, caused by the change of motion of the piston.

We use the external gears in these machines. They are universally used on all kinds of geared machinery where internal gears can be dispensed with, being more easily lubricated and cleaned, and less liable to break the periphery of the wheels.

These Powers have dust-proof and self-oiling journals; are simple, strong, durable and cheap. Having succeeded in making them much superior to those which have been imported from the East, we have virtually stopped their importation.

We furnish with these powers, when desired, any size of belt wheels, or style, or weight of balance-wheels, combined with a movable crank-pin for pumping, and counter-balance when needed.

---

## ATWOOD & BODWELL'S
## Windmill Brass Pumps.

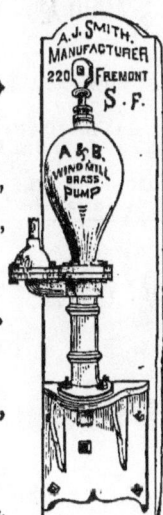

These Pumps were designed especially for Windmill work.

They are superior to any pump of Eastern make, both in weight, strength, and inside finish.

They are constructed in the simplest form of a lift and force pump, and are not liable to get out of order.

### ALL KINDS OF PIPING, FITTINGS, ETC.
Furnished at Lowest Rates. Also Water Tanks, of all Sizes.

## EXCELSIOR WINDMILL WORKS,
### 211 AND 213 MISSION STREET,
### SAN FRANCISCO.
ATWOOD & BODWELL,  -  -  *Proprietors.*

# SAN FRANCISCO SAVINGS UNION

### 532 CALIFORNIA STREET.

Corner of Webb,                  SAN FRANCISCO.

**DEPOSITS 30th JUNE, 1875,**   -  -  -  -   **$6,918,789.61**

**GUARANTEE CAPITAL AND RESERVE FUND,**  -  **$230,781.41**

## DIRECTORS.

JAMES DeFREMERY, President.     ALBERT MILLER, Vice-President.
C. ADOLPHE LOW,                CHARLES BAUM,
GEORGE C. POTTER,            WASHINGTON BARTLETT,
CHARLES PAGE,                  DENIS J. OLIVER,
          ALEXANDER CAMPBELL, Sen.
LOVELL WHITE, Cashier and Secretary.    JOHN ARCHBALD, Surveyor

Receives Deposits and Loans Money on Real Estate Security. Country Remittances may be sent by Wells, Fargo & Co., or by checks of reliable parties, payable in San Francisco, but the responsibility of the Union commences only with the actual receipt of the money.
The signature of the depositor should accompany the first deposit. No charge is made for pass-book or entrance fee.
Office Hours—9 A. M. TO 3 P. M. Open Saturday Evenings from 6½ to 8½.

---

Fullest Prices Obtained.                     Returns Promptly Made.

## JAMES MOORE,
### Wool Commission Merchant and Growers' Agent,
### 321 and 323 FRONT ST.,

SAN FRANCISCO.                                   Mark—J. MOORE, S. F.

### REFERENCES.

D. CALLAGHAN, Esq., Hon. L. CUNNINGHAM, San Francisco; W. H. KNIGHT, Esq., Marysville; PERKINS, LOGAN & CO., Butte County; HOWELL DAVIS, Esq., Colusa County; C. H. SCHROEBEL, Calaveras County; J. R. TRIBBLE, Esq., Tulare County; ROBERT ECCLESTON, Esq., Kern County; R. de la CUESTA, Santa Barbara County; J. C. HAGERMAN, Nevada, Etc., Etc., Etc.

---

## MOODY & FARISH,
## WOOL COMMISSION MERCHANTS
### No. 210 DAVIS STREET, SAN FRANCISCO.

### FOR SALE:
## WOOL BAGS & TWINE, SHEEP SHEARS,

*EUREKA SHEEP-WASH,*
**GLYCERINE SHEEP-WASH, CARBOLIC SHEEP-WASH.**

Cash advances made on consignments.                 Please send shipping receipts.

## A GENERAL DESCRIPTION
### OF
# SANTA BARBARA CO.

SANTA BARBARA COUNTY is bounded on the North by San Luis Obispo County; on the South by the Santa Barbara Channel; West by the Pacific Ocean; and on the East by the County of Ventura.

It was organized in 1850, but until recently has made small advancement in an agricultural direction, her entire territory being devoted to grazing purposes, development in other departments having only recently been inaugurated.

### AREA.

The area of Santa Barbara County, including the islands of Santa Rosa, San Miguel, Santa Cruz and Santa Barbara, with the main land, amounts to about 3,200 square miles, or 2,048,-000 acres.

### THE ASSESSED VALUATION

Of property for 1874 reaches the sum of $6,010,309.

### RESOURCES.

Its resources are agricultural, grazing, and mining. Agriculture, embracing also horticulture, at present leads the industries, and is the principal resource. Many of the great previously undivided grants have been broken up into smaller sections, and from pastoral uses have been turned over to the cultivator. Much of the land forming these great tracts has been unproductive, and even unused for grazing, for years. The soil and climate of the county possess all the advantages required for purposes of cultivation. Fruits indigenous to the tropics, and to the cold, frozen climes of the North, thrive side by side, mingling the delicate perfume of their blossoms and vieing with each other in the realization of the deepest blush.

The grazing interest of Santa Barbara County is probably greater than that of any other portion of the State.

Col. Hollister, the pioneer American engaged in this industry, in 1853 came overland from Ohio, with a flock of 3,000 sheep. He had visited the State a year previous; had been struck with the advantages offered in the direction of sheep-raising by a country where pasturage was perennial, and where, favored by a temperature of unchanging mildness, shelter was rendered unnecessary, and returned to Ohio for the necessary stock with which to establish himself in this new production, in a new country. The flock of 3,000 sheep, with which he reached the State, was a joint stock, of which his individual portion, after the partition, amounted to 800. The partition was effected in San Bernardino County, by way of which they brought in their flocks. From here Col. Hollister drove his flock to Monterey County, passing up the coast through San Bernardino, Los Angeles, Santa Barbara, and San Luis Obispo. Starting with this small beginning, he has persistently led this industry, with a result the perfect success of which is attested by the present magnitude of his possessions. The interests of which he is now the head and front represent millions of dollars, in flocks and real estate. At one time he was the proprietor of flocks aggregating 80,000 head, while his right to the title of a landed proprietor may be said to be vested in one peice of real estate which will survey over one hundred and fifty thousand acres. This forms but one item in the schedule of this gentleman's vast possessions, he owning, privately and conjointly with his numerous partners, both real estate and flocks in various portions of the country.

Its mineral resources, if not large, are varied. Quicksilver, asphaltum and petroleum are the mineral products delved for.

Two ranges of mountains cross the county from West to East, the most Northerly range being the Sierra San Rafael; the one toward the South, the Sierra Santa Ynez. Their altitudes are in the vicinity of from 4,000 to 6,000 feet.

The country between these ranges forms a series of low, irregular hills with scarcely any level land.

Santa Barbara is the only county of the State possessing so large a Southern coast line. This topographical peculiarity is thought to exert great influence upon the climate and productions not only of this county, but also of those to the South and East of it.

North of Point Concepcion, which forms the Northern extremity of the county, the entire coast is subject to cold winds which sweep inland from the Northwest, laden with fogs, while during the winter violent rain-storms prevail from the South. South of the point there is an utter absence of fog, the atmosphere being much drier and warmer than to the North. It seldom rains from May to November, frost is almost unknown, and snow rarely visits the loftiest mountains.

Extending from Point Concepcion in an Easterly direction, to the Southward of the Santa Ynez Mountains, is a belt of land stretching away for one hundred miles along the sea shore, of a width of about three miles, which in advantages of soil and climate will bear favorable comparison with any portion of the State. The climate is almost tropical; the soil possessing unusual richness, with adaptibilities so varied as to ensure perfect maturity for the most dissimilar growths.

There is but little timber in the county, if we except the oak willow and sycamore, which grow in the valleys or upon the plains which skirt the mountains, even the loftiest of which are covered with a heavy growth of nutritious grasses and wild oats, which luxuriate throughout the winter and spring, furnishing the best of pasturage for sheep and cattle through the entire year.

The mountains are much lower in the Western portions of the county than in the Eastern, where occurs the conjunction of the Sierra Nevadas with the coast range. The loftiest peak where this conjunction culminates is Mount Pinos, in the Western portion of Ventura, the adjoining county upon the West, recently formed from Santa Barbara County. Mount Pinos towers to an altitude of nearly 7,500 feet above the sea-level.

## WATER COURSES.

Santa Barbara County has no great number of water courses, although the supply they furnish would prove sufficiently abundant if properly utilized. Little activity seems to have been displayed with the view of supplementing nature, or preparing against emergencies by husbanding a water supply upon which the agriculturist might rely in time of need. Irrigating ditches are as rare in this county as they are plentiful in counties adjacent, and the limpid element is allowed to run its idle course, uninterrupted, to the sea, thus wasting that which, through the medium of intersecting ditches and conveniently located reservoirs, might render prosperous many a dry season, in spite of nature's failing to fill her implied compact with the cultivator of the soil. The Santa Ynez River traverses the county for more than one hundred miles, from East to West, having its outlet in the Pacific Ocean at Santa Lucia. For ten miles from its outlet, it has more the character of a creek than a river.

The Cuyamas, or Santa Maria, has its source in a canyon of the Sierra Nevadas, near the Northeastern boundary of Santa Barbara County; the Northwestern boundary of the county of Ventura, and the extreme Southern boundary of San Luis Obispo County. It is a considerable stream, and forms the Northern boundary of the county for more than one hundred miles, extending Northward of Point Sal nearly as far as Fort Tejon. Gundalupe Lagoon forms its outlet.

These streams have many tributary creeks, which maintain a greater or less flow of water during the entire year. In the summer season the water is very low, scarcely any streams maintaining a flow but for a short distance after leaving the mountains on their way to the sea.

## VALLEY LAND.

Santa Barbara County has not the area of level land to be found in Lós Angeles County. Her valleys are extremely fertile, as are the terraces reaching back and encroaching upon the territory of her hills.

DIRECTORY OF SANTA BARBARA COUNTY. 93

In the Santa Ynez Valley is located the old mission of that name, the buildings of which are still in good preservation, the old bell still serving the purpose to which it was dedicated so many years since, of calling to the worship of God the denizens of its neighborhood.

The valley possesses this topographical feature in common with all upon this portion of the coast. It forms a succession of terraces, marking the uprisal of the land, the result of the geological processes of the present era.

The lowest terrace, of which this valley has three, is at an elevation of twenty-five feet above the river bed; the one occupying the medium position is twenty feet higher than the lowest, while the upper one is still fifty feet above the central one, giving it an extreme height of ninety-five feet from the level of the river.

These terraces were undoubtedly all cut or formed by the river, at widely different periods.

On the south side of the Santa Ynez Mountains the coast line forms a terrace, extending from Santa Barbara to the Gaviota Pass, some eighty feet above the ocean level.

## PRINCIPAL VALLIES.

The principal valleys of the county are the Santa Maria, Santa Barbara Carpenteria, and Lompoc.

We append some figures giving industrial and other statistics for the year 1874, from a report to the Surveyor General of the State by the County Assessor.

In that year (1874) Santa Barbara County had of wheat 15,717 acres, 168,229 bushels ; barley, 8,474 acres, making 286,365 bushels ; corn, 1,094 acres, 43,496 bushels ; beans, 476 acres, 11,360 bushels ; potatoes, 133 acres, 332 tons ; hay, 1,017 acres, 6,108 tons. The number of acres under cultivation, 28,390 ; enclosed, 26,773.

The number of sheep in the county amounted to 431,486 ; giving a wool product of 1,725,-944 lbs.

The number of cows amounted to 4,603 ; calves, 3,717 ; beef cattle, 5,371 ; neat cattle, 13,-598 ; horses, 4,076 ; mules, 369, and 1,394 hogs.

Of trees in bearing there were 6,423 apple ; 1,025 peach ; 3,045 pear ; 802 plum ; 145 cherry; 226 nectarine ; 425 quince ; 1,824 apricot ; 1,373 fig ; 1,489 lemon ; 3,856 orange ; 2,056 olive ; 106 prune ; 1,083 mulberry ; 38,311 almond, and 10,274 walnut.

Grape vines, 213,984. The wine product amounted to 2,825 gallons.

One distillery was running, producing of brandy 1,100 gallons ; one brewery, producing 35,000 gals. beer.

One grist mill was in the county, deriving its power from steam, which turned out during that year 1,500 bbls. of flour, and ground 1,700 bushels of corn.

The value of real estate in the county in 1874 was $3,452,433. Improvements, $768,469. Personal property, $1,789,407. Total valuation of real and personal property in the county, $6,-010,309. The poll-tax collected reached the sum of $3,000, while the number of registered voters amounted to 2,345.

The United States census of 1870 gave the population of the county as 7,784. This census was taken previous to the division of the county, for the purpose of forming the new county of Ventura.

The estimated population of the County of Santa Barbara in 1874 was 11,000.

## TOWNS.

The principal towns of Santa Barbara County are Santa Barbara, Central City, Carpenteria, Guadalupe, La Gaviota, La Graciosa, La Patera, Las Cruces, Lompoc, Montecito, and Santa Ynez.

## SANTA BARBARA,

The county seat, occupies a position on the Southern coast line, about the centre of the county. It is in the vicinity of four hundred and forty miles South of the State capital. It occupies the land formerly tenanted by one of the early missions founded in 1780, whose buildings even yet occupy an eminence about one mile and an half from the beach. The eminence has an elevaion of above two hundred feet, and commands a fine view of the adjacent country and sea coast. The church, which is still in a good state of preservation, is a long, low, dazzlingly white building, with a frontage of about three hundred feet. From this old mission the town and county derive their name.

The harbor is an open roadstead, exposed to winds from the Southward, but realizing some safety from the sea-weed which grows in enormous quantities between the waters of the harbor and the open deep, affording an excellent substitute, and answering in nearly all essential respects the purpose of an effectual breakwater.

A thoroughly serviceable wharf extends 2,000 feet into the water, allowing close moorage to sailing vessels and steamers, which receive and discharge cargo immediately upon the wharf, thus avoiding the trouble, labor and expense concomitant upon lightering.

The assessed valuation of property in the town of Santa Barbara is $2,500,000. The rate of taxation for the years 1875-6 is 75 cents per $100. Its population will aggregate about 4,000.

The streets are laid out in squares, the intermediate blocks measuring 450 feet each way. There are four public plazas, and the streets are sixty feet in width, excepting the two main thoroughfares, State and Carrillo streets, each of which have a breadth of eighty feet.

Water is furnished by the Santa Barbara Water Company, from sources formerly controlled by the mission.

Gas of good quality is furnished by a company established for that purpose.

A good fire department has been organized, possessing one Hook and Ladder Company, as a much needed auxiliary.

During the past year only fifty delinquents were arraigned before the criminal courts.

Among the notable buildings of the town are The Arlington House (nearly completed), Santa Barbara College, Lobero's Theater, City Hall, Occidental Hotel, Morris House, Odd Fellows' Hall, as well as many of the church edifices.

The Arlington House occupies an entire block, with a frontage of 160 feet on State street, and a frontage of 120 feet on each of two side streets. The building is forty-four feet in height to the roof, with a surmounting tower still thirty-six feet higher. It will contain 100 rooms, fifty of which contain marble mantels and fire-places. The dining room is detached, and in the rear of the main building, the kitchen also standing independent of the other buildings.

A verandah surrounds the whole building. The front entrance opens to a circular enclosure. All modern improvements have been introduced, and the entire appointments of the establishment are perfect.

It is owned by a joint stock company, composed entirely of residents of Santa Barbara. The expense attached to the enterprise, independent of upholstering and otherwise furnishing it, amounts to $80,000.

The buildings of the Santa Barbara College are among the best in the State. The Odd Fellows' building is a fine piece of work, and cost in its erection $26,000. The City Hall, built last year, is an ornament to the town. The finest church structure in the town, and one of the best in this portion of the State, is one just completed by the Presbyterian Church. It is built of wood, its steeple reaching upward to the height of one hundred and thirty feet.

## NEWSPAPERS.

Santa Barbara has two daily papers, the *Press* and *News*, and one weekly, the *Index*. The dailies also publish weekly editions. These well-conducted and ably-edited papers have a large circulation, with a good advertising patronage.

## SCHOOLS.

Santa Barbara has a good public school system. One school building is large and roomy, well conducted, provided with efficient teachers. Its departments are graded. Four small buildings in various portions of the town accommodate the less advanced classes. Two two-story school-houses are in process of erection in the upper portion of the town.

## CHURCHES.

The Baptist, Presbyterian, Congregational, Methodist South, Episcopal and Catholic denominations are represented here, not as in some communities, with church edifices alone, but, what in California is rare, with actual worshippers. The good old New England element has carried its Plymouth Rock ideas, somewhat modified, into this locality, and the party who cannot sit through one hour and an half of nasal pulpit utterances, without putting in practice that stale old theatrical dodge of "going out to see a man," had better remain in San Francisco, go to Los Angeles, or strike a mining camp; he can never hope to wedge in his stake in this community.

## PUBLIC CONVEYANCES.

Goodall, Nelson & Perkins S. S. leave Santa Barbara three times per week, each way.

The stages of the Coast Line Stage Company arrive daily from San Francisco and Los Angeles.

Four miles East of Santa Barbara, in the Montecito, are the nurseries of Dana B. Clark. All kinds of tropical, semi-tropical, and temperate climate fruit trees are here in fullest stock, finest varieties, and every stage of growth. Mr. Clark makes a specialty of introducing and experimenting with new and rare species of fruit and ornamental trees, shrubs and plants. He propagates very largely, and has beautiful grounds, well adapted for this purpose.

To the West of Santa Barbara, seven miles, Joseph Sexton is conducting the Santa Barbara Nursery. He is cultivating fruit trees of every species and variety, as well as hardy evergreen shrubbery, pot plants, and all descriptions of ornamental growth. He has also a depot, for sale of his goods, in Santa Barbara.

## CARPENTERIA

Is situated twelve miles east of Santa Barbara. It is a thriving settlement, occupying a valley of the same name containing about sixteen square miles, or in the vicinity of 100,000 acres of land, either altogether level or slightly undulating. A great portion of it is covered with heavy oak forests. Agricultural land here is thought to be equally as arable as any in the State, irrigation being unnecessary and frosts unknown. Corn, barley and beans are the chief products.

Fruit-raising has become a prominent feature in the cultivation of this district, the semi-tropical fruits being largely grown, as well as the almond and walnut. One of the residents of the settlement, Mr. Ormstead, has upon his place the largest asphaltum beds upon the coast. The population of the settlement amounts to about 200. Land is held at $100 per acre, and at this price is considered cheap. The settlement has also three schools, two churches, three stores, two blacksmith and wagon shops, an express and post office, and grange.

In the upper portion of the settlement is the landing, a very essential point in a producing community, as affording the means of marketing their goods without outside aid or intervention. The wharf property is owned by Messrs. N. D. and F. Smith. The wharf is 600 feet in length, with a warehouse capacity of 15,000 sacks. It is the intention to extend the wharf during the present year, giving it an extreme length of one thousand feet. From this point was shipped during 1874, of corn and barley, 40,000 sacks ; of beans, 12,000 sacks ; together with 4,000 sacks potatoes. They also shipped 500,000 feet of lumber from their yard, which they conduct in connection with the wharf at this point.

## MONTECITO

Is four miles from Santa Barbara, and the same distance from Carpenteria; it is on the road to the Hot Springs, and only two miles distant therefrom. It is a very beautiful spot, and appears to much advantage when viewed from the Hot Springs, lying so high above it. Its attractions are scarcely apparent as viewed from the stage road, while merely passing through it. Quite a number of very wealthy gentlemen have made their homes here, erected costly dwellings, and surrounded themselves with every purchaseable elegance. One gentlemen, Col. Bond, has devoted himself to obtaining and perfecting every known exotic growth, and upon his grounds, probably more nearly than upon any spot of earth, center the four quarters of the globe. Here are grouped the results of nature's work in every clime, as expressed in tree, in shrub, in flower, or in fruit. This, too, is the vicinity noted for the magnitude of its celebrated grape vine, grown from a grape vine switch, which only in its eighty-fourth year began to languish, and after it had attained a circumference of nearly four and one-half feet. Because it was thought to have about finished its earthly career, it was determined to exhume it and place it on exhibition at the centennial, as an instance of California abnormal growth.

## HOT SULPHUR SPRINGS.

The Santa Barbara Hot Sulphur Springs lie to the Eastward of Santa Barbara, six miles, at the head of a mountain canyon, 1,450 feet above tide-water level. Here are twenty-two hot springs, varying in temperature from 60° to 122°. Although the waters have been examined by chemists and physicians, no analysis has ever been made. They contain in solution both black and white sulphur, and are also heavily charged with iron. The springs were discovered by Mr. Wilbur Curtiss, in 1855, since which time he has resided on the premises, he having immediately taken the proper steps to secure the property, after having satisfactorily tested the curative powers of the water in his own person, he being at that time in poor health. A four-horse stage runs daily between the Springs and Santa Barbara. Visitors will find the best of hotel accommodations here, with courteous and polite attention. A number of cottages are scattered about, well finished and furnished. The medicinal value of the waters is undoubted, and many are the remarkable cures performed through their agency.

## GUADALUPE

Is the principal town of the Santa Maria Valley, one of the largest and richest sections of the county. This town is about seventy miles Northwest of Santa Barbara, and is a thriving, fast-growing settlement. It numbers in the vicinity of 400 inhabitants; has six stores, two hotels, a livery stable, two meat markets, two blacksmith shops, harness and paint shop, and a newly erected Odd Fellows' Hall; a good school, with an average attendance of sixty pupils; two churches, with another soon to be erected. A weekly paper, *The Guadalupe Weekly Telegraph*, is published here, and is one of the most enterprising and best edited of the interior weeklies.

POINT SAL is the landing for this region. Messrs. Harriman & Co, have a wharf here 1,250 feet in length, with a depth of water varying from 20 to 35 feet. Point Sal is ten miles distant from Guadalupe, eight miles from Central City, seventeen miles from Lompoc, and fifteen miles from La Graciosa.

The shipments of grain from this point during the past year amounted to 110,000 sacks, and 3,000 bales wool. Three warehouses of large capacity are located here, belonging to the above named firm. Harriman & Co. have a large stock of lumber at this point, as well as a large yard at Guadalupe, their sales for last year having amounted to 1,500,000 feet.

LA GRACIOSA and LAS CRUCES are small villages, respectively sixty-eight and forty-three miles northwest from Santa Barbara. Both are post office towns.

LA GAVIOTA is a small settlement also, forty miles northwest from Santa Barbara. Las Cruces is its post office town. At Gaviota Landing some of the smaller sailing vessels and coast steamers call to leave freight for the upper portion of the valley, and bear to market the product of the neighborhood.

## LOMPOC.

This new town is distant from Santa Barbara forty miles, in a northwesterly direction. It was founded by a colony, which possessed 33,000 acres of land, divided and sold in tracts of from five to eighty acres, in November, 1874. It is situated inland but a short distance from Point Concepcion, on the Santa Ynez River and Miguelito Creek. The colony is founded on strict temperance principles. A good hotel, the Lompoc House, has recently been opened here. One paper is published, the *Weekly Record*.

## CENTRAL CITY.

A short distance to the eastward of Guadalupe is the present town of Central City, more generally known as Santa Maria. It is situated on the banks of the Santa Maria River, which irrigates the fertile valley of the same name. It has about 300 inhabitants, one of the best hotels in the interior of the State, three stores, two blacksmith shops, a livery stable, harness shop, and several of those "'round-the-corner" establishments, where the thirsty are provided for and the *weary* are at rest—under the table.

Central City is a most prosperous, enterprising little town, occupying one of the best portions of the county.

DIRECTORY OF SANTA BARBARA COUNTY. 97

| NAME. | OCCUPATION. | PLACE OF BUSINESS. | RESIDENCE. | TOWN OR P. O. |
|---|---|---|---|---|
| Abadie, Guillermo.. | Ranchero............ | ............................ | Santa Barbara......... | Santa Barbara. |
| Abbott, William... | Hostler................ | Santa Barbara......... | Santa Barbara Co..... | Santa Barbara. |
| Abbot, Orrin Lee... | Attorney............. | Santa Barbara......... | Santa Barbara Co..... | Santa Barbara. |
| Abbott, O L.......... | Lawyer............... | State st.................. | Vineyard st............ | Santa Barbara. |
| Abel, H............... | Saddler............... | Central City.......... | Central City........... | Central City. |
| Abernethy, R....... | Stoves & hardw're | Main st.................. | Main st.................. | Guadalupe. |
| Abernethy, R & Co | Stoves & hardw're | Main st.................. | Main st.................. | Guadalupe. |
| Abernethy, James. | Blacksmith.......... | Guadalupe st......... | Guadalupe st......... | Guadalupe. |
| Abercrombie, Alex R........... | Books & station'y | State st.................. | Haley st.................. | Santa Barbara. |
| Abernethy, Wm..... | Carpenter........... | Guadalupe st......... | Guadalupe st......... | Guadalupe. |
| Abernethy, Robert. | Blacksmith.......... | Guadalupe st......... | Guadalupe st......... | Guadalupe. |
| Abercrombie, Rev. Jas................... | Pastor................. | Episcopal Church.... | Gutierrez st........... | Santa Barbara. |
| Abila, Felipe Santiago......... | Vaquero.............. | Santa Barbara Co.... | Santa Lucia............ | |
| Ablett, Charles Ed. | Saloon keeper...... | Santa Barbara Co.... | Carpenteria........... | Carpenteria. |
| Abram, A J........... | Clerk.................. | State st.................. | State st.................. | Santa Barbara. |
| Adams, D M......... | Merchant............ | La Graciosa........... | Guadalupe Valley.... | La Graciosa. |
| Adams, Asa.......... | Real estate.......... | State st.................. | Montecito st........... | Santa Barbara. |
| Adam, Wm L....... | Gen mdse............ | Santa Maria Valley.. | 1½ m W Central City | Santa Maria. |
| Adams, Asa.......... | Farmer................ | Carpenteria........... | Santa Barbara Co.... | Carpenteria. |
| Adams, Ira Winchell .......... | Laborer............... | Santa Barbara Co.... | Santa Maria............ | Santa Maria. |
| Adams, Newton C.. | Stage agent.......... | Santa Barbara ....... | Santa Barbara Co..... | Santa Barbara. |
| Aguilar, Jose Maria | Vaquero............... | Santa Barbara Co.... | Santa Barbara......... | Santa Barbara. |
| Aguilar, Jesus....... | Ranchero............. | Santa Maria........... | Santa Barbara Co..... | Santa Marin. |
| Aguilar, Jose Julian | Laborer............... | Santa Ynez............ | Santa Barbara Co..... | Las Cruces. |
| Alabama, William. | Laborer............... | Santa Barbara Co.... | Santa Barbara......... | Santa Barbara. |
| Albert, Albert C... | Farmer................ | 1st Township......... | Santa Barbara Co..... | |
| Alipaz, Manuel..... | Laborer............... | Santa Barbara........ | Santa Barbara Co..... | Santa Barbara. |
| Allen, James......... | Farmer................ | Santa Barbara Co.... | Santa Barbara......... | Santa Barbara. |
| Allen, Gabriel...... | Farmer................ | Santa Barbara Co.... | 1st Township. | |
| Alling, Franklin S.. | Roofer................. | Santa Barbara........ | Santa Barbara Co..... | Santa Barbara. |
| Alvord, C E.......... | Assessor.............. | Santa Barbara........ | Yanonali st ........... | Santa Barbara. |
| Altrada, Salvador... | Laborer............... | Santa Ynez Road..... | 4 m N Las Cruces.... | Las Cruces. |
| Altrada, Salvador... | Laborer............... | Las Cruces............ | Santa Barbara Co..... | Las Cruces. |
| Alvares, Jose Maria | Laborer............... | Santa Barbara Co.... | Santa Barbara......... | Santa Barbara. |
| Alves, Francisco.... | Miner................. | Santa Barbara........ | Santa Barbara Co.. . | Santa Barbara. |
| Alves, Frank......... | Laborer............... | Santa Barbara........ | Haley st.................. | Santa Barbara. |
| Alvord, Chas E..... | Mechanic............ | Arroyo Burro......... | Santa Barbara Co..... | |
| Ames, Oths Nathaniel........... | Teamster............. | ............................ | Santa Barbara......... | Santa Barbara. |
| Anderson, Robert... | Laborer............... | Santa Maria........... | Santa Barbara Co..... | Santa Maria. |
| Andersen, David ... | Laborer............... | Santa Barbara Co.... | Santa Barbara......... | Santa Barbara. |
| Anderson, Samuel A........ | Painter............... | Santa Barbara........ | Santa Barbara Co..... | Santa Barbara. |
| Anderson, Lary .... | Laborer............... | Santa Barbara........ | Santa Barbara Co..... | Santa Barbara. |
| Andersen, Wm...... | Saloon................. | Carpenteria Valley... | Carpenteria ........... | Carpenteria. |
| Andonague, J M & Son........... | Gen merchandise | State st.................. | State st.................. | Santa Barbara. |
| Andonague, F C.... | Gen merchandise | State st.................. | State st.................. | Santa Barbara. |
| Andonague, Francisco......... | Clerk.................. | Santa Barbara Co..... | Santa Barbara......... | Santa Barbara. |
| Andonague, J M.... | Gen Merchandise | State st.................. | State st.................. | Santa Barbara. |
| Antonio, F............ | Farmer................ | ............................ | ............................ | |
| Antimiramo, Jose... | Farmer................ | 3d Township.......... | Santa Barbara Co..... | Las Cruces. |
| Arata, Gregoire..... | Farmer................ | ............................ | Santa Barbara......... | Santa Barbara. |
| Arata, Juan ......... | Ranchero............. | Los Alamos............ | Los Alamos............ | Guadalupe. |
| Archer, J............. | Bee raiser............ | Santa Barbara ....... | Victoria st.............. | Santa Barbara. |
| Arellanes, —........ | Laborer............... | Santa Barbara........ | Chapala st.............. | Santa Barbara. |
| Arellanes, Felipe.... | Laborer............... | ............................ | Santa Barbara......... | Santa Barbara. |
| Arellanes, Francisco, Jr...... | Laborer............... | 3d Township.......... | ............................ | |

EUGENE CHAINE. W. J. CONNOR.

# CONNOR & CHAINE,

PROPRIETORS OF

# GUADALUPE AND LOMPOC STAGE CO.

CENTRAL CITY, SANTA BARBARA COUNTY, CAL.

Stage Route by way of La Graciosa.

---

GOOD STOCK, EXCELLENT COACHES, AND QUICK TIME.

RECTORY OF SANTA BARBARA COUNTY. 99

| Occupation. | Place of Business. | Residence. | Town or P. O. |
|---|---|---|---|
| nchero | 3d Township | Santa Barbara Co | |
| nchero | Santa Barbara Co | 3d Township | |
| nchero | Santa Barbara Co | San Julian | |
| quero | San Julian | | |
| rmer | Santa Barbara Co | Santa Barbara | Santa Barbara. |
| borer | Carpenteria | Santa Barbara Co | Carpenteria. |
| borer | Santa Barbara Co | Santa Barbara | Santa Barbara. |
| quero | Santa Barbara Co | Todos Santos | |
| nchero | Casmoli | Santa Barbara Co | |
| nchero | Santa Barbara Co | Casmoli | |
| borer | Santa Barbara Co | Santa Barbara | Santa Barbara. |
| nchero | Casmoli | Santa Barbara Co | |
| borer | Santa Barbara Co | Santa Barbara | Santa Barbara. |
| borer | Santa Barbara | Santa Barbara Co | Santa Barbara. |
| borer | Santa Barbara | Santa Barbara Co | Santa Barbara. |
| nchero | San Julian Road | 1½ m W Las Cruces | Las Cruces. |
| quero | San Julian Road | Santa Barbara Co | Las Cruces. |
| eep raiser | 3d Township | Santa Barbara Co | |
| ctor | Santa Barbara Co | Santa Barbara | Santa Barbara. |
| rmer | Santa Barbara Co | 1st Township | |
| ysician | Milpas st | Milpas st | Santa Barbara. |
| ilor | Santa Barbara | Santa Barbara Co | Santa Barbara. |
| rmer | Santa Barbara Co | Carpenteria | Carpenteria. |
| borer | Carpenteria | Santa Barbara Co | Carpenteria. |
| rmer | 3d Township | Santa Barbara Co | |
| son | Santa Barbara Co | Santa Barbara | Santa Barbara. |
| e raiser | | Grey st | Santa Barbara. |
| e raiser | | Grey st | Santa Barbara. |
| oceries | State st | Anacapa st | Santa Barbara. |
| oceries | State st | Victoria st | Santa Barbara. |
| ck raiser | 2d Precinct | Santa Barbara Co | |
| ck raiser | Santa Barbara Co | Santa Barbara | Santa Barbara. |
| rchant | Santa Barbara Co | Santa Barbara | Santa Barbara. |
| erk | Santa Barbara Co | Santa Barbara | Santa Barbara. |
| | Santa Barbara | Santa Barbara Co | Santa Barbara. |
| borer | Santa Barbara | Santa Barbara Co | Santa Barbara. |
| borer | Santa Barbara Co | Santa Barbara | Santa Barbara. |
| borer | Santa Barbara Co | Santa Barbara | Santa Barbara. |
| rmer | Santa Barbara | Santa Barbara Co | Santa Barbara. |
| borer | Santa Barbara Co | Santa Barbara | Santa Barbara. |
| borer | Santa Barbara Co | Carpenteria | Carpenteria. |
| borer | Carpenteria | Santa Barbara Co | Carpenteria. |
| borer | Santa Barbara | Santa Barbara Co | Santa Barbara. |
| borer | Santa Barbara | Santa Barbara Co | Santa Barbara. |
| uggist | Guadalupe st | 3d st | Guadalupe. |
| borer | Guadalupe | Olivera st | Guadalupe. |
| rmer | Guadalupe | Olivera st | Guadalupe. |
| rmer | Santa Barbara | Santa Barbara Co | Santa Barbara. |
| ther | Santa Barbara | Santa Barbara Co | Santa Barbara. |
| inter | Santa Barbara | Vineyard st | Santa Barbara. |
| | | | Santa Barbara. |
| borer | Santa Barbara | Santa Barbara Co | |
| borer | Santa Barbara | Santa Barbara Co | Santa Barbara. |
| cidental hotel | State st | State st | Santa Barbara. |
| rmer | Carpenteria | Santa Barbara Co | Carpenteria. |
| rmer | Carpenteria | Santa Barbara Co | Carpenteria. |
| rmer | Carpenteria Valley | 2½ m E Carpenteria | Carpenteria. |

W. P. VAN NADER.            ISAAC VAN NADER.

# VAN NADER BROS.

## Livery, Feed and Sale Stable,

### HOTEL AND SALOON.

**MAIN STREET, - - - - CENTRAL CITY,**

Santa Barbara Co., Cal.

---

**Private Conveyances and Saddle Horses on Hire at All Times.**

---

HORSES BOARDED AT LOWEST RATES.

COMMODIOUS CORRALS, LARGE SHEDS.

---

The Hotel and Saloon offer the Best of Entertainment. Guests Accommodated by the Day, Week or Month.

---

RATES LOW, FARE GOOD.

## DIRECTORY OF SANTA BARBARA COUNTY. 101

| Name. | Occupation. | Place of Business. | Residence. | Town or P. O. |
|---|---|---|---|---|
| Bailard, A............ | Farmer ............. | Carpenteria Valley.. | 3 m E Carpenteria... | Carpenteria. |
| Baker, Melville Cox | Mechanic ........... | Saticoy ............... | Santa Barbara Co..... | Saticoy. |
| Baker, F N............ | Station keeper..... | Bell's Station. ... .... | Los Alamos............. | Guadalupe. |
| Baker, Robert La F | Farmer ............... | Santa Barbara Co..... | La Patera................ | Santa* Barbara. |
| Baker, Andrew J... | Carpenter............ | Santa Barbara Co..... | La Patera............... | Santa Barbara. |
| Ball, William........ | Laborer............... | Santa Barbara Co..... | La Patera............... | Santa Barbara. |
| Bamford, W James | Blacksmith.......... | Montecito.............. | Santa Barbara Co..... | Santa Barbara. |
| Barber, Peter J...... | Carpenter............ | Santa Barbara......... | Santa Barbara Co..... | Santa Barbara. |
| Barber, P J........... | Architect............. | Ortega st............... | Vineyard st............ | Santa Barbara. |
| Bargolia, Angel..... | Farmer ............... | Santa Barbara Co..... | Santa Rita.............. | Santa Barbara. |
| Barkley, A S......... | Farmer ............... | Santa Barbara......... | Santa Barbara Co..... | Santa Barbara. |
| **Barker, Jas Lawrence**........ | Surveyor............. | Santa Barbara Co..... | Santa Barbara......... | Santa Barbara. |
| Barker, J L........... | Insurance agent... | State st................. | Bath st................. | Santa Barbara. |
| Barker, John......... | Farmer .............. | Santa Maria Valley.. | 2½ m S Guadalupe... | Guadalupe. |
| Barker, F I............ | Carpenter............ | Santa Barbara......... | Bath st................. | Santa Barbara. |
| Barker, Fred......... | Carpenter ........... | Santa Barbara......... | Anellago st............ | Santa Barbara. |
| Barker, James....... | Attorney............. | State st................. | Bath st................. | Santa Barbara. |
| Barnstead, T D..... | Toll collector...... | Stearn's Wharf...... | State st................. | Santa Barbara. |
| **Barnard, Wm**...... | Farmer .............. | Carpenteria Valley... | 1½ m E Carpenteria.. | Carpenteria. |
| **Barnard, W E**...... | Real estate......... | State st................. | Santa Barbara......... | Santa Barbara. |
| **Barnes, John W**.... | Hotel keeper....... | Santa Barbara Co..... | Santa Barbara......... | Santa Barbara. |
| Barnstead, Thomas D......... | Clerk.................. | Santa Barbara Co..... | Santa Barbara......... | Santa Barbara. |
| Barrow, James..... | Laborer.............. | Santa Maria Valley.. | 2 m S Guadalupe..... | Guadalupe. |
| Barron, Pedro....... | Genl merchant.... | Santa Barbara Road. | 11 m S E Las Cruces | Las Cruces. |
| Barreras, Antonio... | Laborer............. | Santa Barbara Co..... | Santa Barbara......... | Santa Barbara. |
| Barros, Pedro....... | Laborer............. | 3d Township ......... | Santa Barbara Co..... | Santa Barbara. |
| Bartch, Jacob........ | Laborer............. | Santa Barbara Co..... | First Precinct......... | Santa Barbara. |
| **Barth, P J**........... | Furniture........... | Ortega st............... | Haley st................ | Santa Barbara. |
| Bartlett, F A......... | Printer ............. | State st................. | Ortega st................ | Santa Barbara. |
| Bartlett, Fred Eli... | Painter ............. | Santa Barbara Co..... | 1st Township.......... | Santa Barbara. |
| **Bartlett, J Edward** | Stock raiser........ | Santa Barbara......... | Santa Barbara Co..... | Santa Barbara. |
| Barton, Thomas A... | Farmer .............. | Santa Barbara Co..... | Santa Maria............ | Santa Maria. |
| Bassett, R S.......... | Musician............ | Santa Barbara......... | Bath st................. | Santa Barbara. |
| Bassett, John P..... | Carpenter........... | Santa Barbara......... | Carrillo st............. | Santa Barbara. |
| **Basye, Joseph**...... | Farmer .............. | Santa Barbara Co..... | San Marcos............ | Santa Barbara. |
| **Bates, Dr Chas Bell** | Physician............ | Ortega st............... | Chapala st............. | Santa Barbara. |
| Bates, Asa Byron... | Farmer............... | Santa Barbara Co..... | Santa Barbara......... | Santa Barbara. |
| Bates, Joseph....... | Wagon maker..... | Cota st................. | Anapamu st............ | Santa Barbara. |
| Bates, H G............ | Clerk.................. | State st................. | State st................ | Santa Barbara. |
| **Bates, T** ............. | Furniture........... | State st................. | De la Vira st.......... | Santa Barbara. |
| Bates, C R............ | Wheelwright....... | Cota st................. | Anapamu st............ | Santa Barbara. |
| **Batt, P J**............. | Furniture........... | Ortega st............... | Santa Barbara Co..... | Santa Barbara. |
| Battin, Joseph C.... | Farmer .............. | Santa Barbara Co..... | Yanonali st............ | Santa Barbara. |
| Battle, — ............ | ...................... | Santa Barbara Co..... | Anapamu st............ | Santa Barbara. |
| Batten, Hiram...... | Farmer .............. | Santa Barbara Co..... | Montecito.............. | Santa Barbara. |
| **Battles, Rollins E.** | Farmer .............. | Santa Maria........... | Santa Barbara Co..... | Santa Maria. |
| Battles, G W......... | Farmer .............. | ........................ | Santa Barbara Co..... | Santa Barbara. |
| Beach, G W.......... | Carpenter........... | Carpenteria........... | Carpenteria........... | Carpenteria. |
| Beals, R............... | Contractor......... | Santa Barbara Co..... | Vineyard st............ | Santa Barbara. |
| Beal, Lucien......... | Shepherd............ | 3d Township ......... | Santa Barbara Co..... | Santa Barbara. |
| Beardsley, Melvin W.......... | Mechanic ........... | Santa Barbara Co..... | Santa Barbara......... | Santa Barbara. |
| **Bebee, David**...... | Farmer .............. | Santa Barbara Co..... | Arroyo Buerro........ | Santa Barbara. |
| Becerra, T............ | Saloon................ | Carpenteria Valley... | Carpenteria........... | Carpenteria. |
| Bechtell, W F....... | Painter .............. | Santa Barbara Co..... | Montecito.............. | Santa Barbara. |
| Beckwith, Huron... | Farmer .............. | Santa Barbara Co..... | Santa Barbara......... | Santa Barbara. |
| **Beckwith, Milton**.. | Farmer .............. | Santa Barbara Co..... | Goleta................... | Santa Barbara. |
| Bede, J T.............. | Farmer .............. | Guadalupe............. | Olivera st............. | Guadalupe. |
| Behn, A............... | Tinsmith............ | State st................. | Carrillo st............. | Santa Barbara. |
| Behrens, Christopher....... | Shoe maker........ | Santa Barbara Co..... | Santa Barbara......... | Santa Barbara. |
| Bell, J S............... | Stock raiser......... | Los Alamos............ | Santa Barbara Co..... | Guadalupe. |

# REAL ESTATE AGENT

## OFFICES:

No. 624 MARKET ST., - - San Francisco,

—AND—

## MAIN STREET,

SANTA BARBARA COUNTY, CAL.

ALSO, AGENT FOR

## J. E. PARKER,

Of Sacramento, Manufacturer and Dealer in

## SADDLERY, HARNESS,

### WHIPS, SPURS, ETC.,

MAIN STREET, CENTRAL CITY.

DIRECTORY OF SANTA BARBARA COUNTY. 103

| OCCUPATION. | PLACE OF BUSINESS. | RESIDENCE. | TOWN OR P. O. |
|---|---|---|---|
| ot maker | State st | State st | Santa Barbara. |
| oon | State st | Anacapa st | Santa Barbara. |
| iryman | Point Sal | 10 m S W Guadalupe | Guadalupe. |
| nchero | Los Alamos | Santa Barbara Co | Santa Barbara. |
| | | | Santa Barbara. |
| rmer | Santa Barbara Co | La Patera | Santa Barbara. |
| rpenter | Santa Barbara Co | Santa Barbara | Santa Barbara. |
| ean view house | Ocean Beach | Foot of Bath st | Santa Barbara. |
| | Santa Barbara Co | | Santa Barbara. |
| rmer | Carpenteria Valley | 1 m E Carpenteria | Carpenteria. |
| rmer | Carpenteria Valley | 3 m W Carpenteria | Carpenteria. |
| rmer | Point Sal | 10 m S W Guadalupe | Guadalupe. |
| rpenter | Santa Barbara Co | San Buenaventura | Santa Barbara. |
| chanic | Carpenteria | Santa Barbara Co | Carpenteria. |
| rmer | Carpenteria | Santa Barbara Co | Carpenteria. |
| rmer | Carpenteria | 1½ m N Carpenteria | Carpenteria. |
| nister | Santa Barbara | Santa Barbara Co | Santa Barbara. |
| rmer | Santa Barbara Co | Santa Clara | Santa Barbara. |
| borer | Santa Barbara | Santa Barbara Co | Santa Barbara. |
| borer | Santa Barbara Co | Santa Barbara | Santa Barbara. |
| rmer | 2d Precinct | Santa Barbara Co | Santa Barbara. |
| borer | Santa Barbara Co | Santa Barbara | Santa Barbara. |
| rmer | Santa Barbara | Santa Barbara Co | Santa Barbara. |
| tcher | Guadalupe st | Guadalupe st | Guadalupe. |
| ckman | Santa Barbara | Haley st | Santa Barbara. |
| rmer | | Santa Barbara Co | Santa Barbara. |
| borer | Santa Barbara Co | Santa Barbara | Santa Barbara. |
| amster | Santa Barbara Co | Santa Barbara | Santa Barbara. |
| rk | State st | Santa Barbara | Santa Barbara. |
| amster | Santa Barbara | Santa Barbara st | Santa Barbara. |
| oe maker | Montecito | Santa Barbara Co | Santa Barbara. |
| rmer | Carpenteria Valley | 3 m W Carpenteria | Carpenteria. |
| borer | Santa Barbara Co | Montecito | Santa Barbara. |
| rmer | Montecito | Santa Barbara Co | Santa Barbara. |
| rk | State st | De la Guerra st | Santa Barbara. |
| rmer | 1st Precinct | Santa Barbara Co | Santa Barbara. |
| eculator | 1st Township | Santa Barbara Co | Santa Barbara. |
| rmer | Santa Barbara Co | Carpenteria | Carpenteria. |
| rk | State st | Garden & Victoria sts | Santa Barbara. |
| rniture dealer | State st | Garden & Victoria sts | Santa Barbara. |
| oceries | State st | | Santa Barbara. |
| ocery | State st | Milpas st | Santa Barbara. |
| cksmith | Santa Barbara Co | Santa Maria | Santa Maria. |
| mberman | Santa Maria | Santa Barbara Co | Santa Maria. |
| gineer | Santa Barbara Co | Santa Barbara | Santa Barbara. |
| rber shop | State st | Haley st | Santa Barbara. |
| amster | Santa Barbara | Vineyard st | Santa Barbara. |
| rdware | State st | Ortega st | Santa Barbara. |
| rber | Santa Barbara | Santa Barbara Co | Santa Barbara. |
| borer | Point Sal | 10 m S W Guadalupe | Guadalupe. |
| rmer | Santa Barbara Co | Santa Barbara | Santa Barbara. |
| rmer | Montecito | Santa Barbara Co | Santa Barbara. |
| rmer | Santa Barbara Co | Santa Barbara | Santa Barbara. |
| borer | Santa Barbara | Santa Barbara Co | Santa Barbara. |
| borer | Santa Barbara | Santa Barbara | Santa Barbara |
| rchant | 1st Precinct | Santa Barbara Co | Santa Barbara. |
| cksmith | Canyon Perdida | Carrillo st | Santa Barbara. |
| smith | Santa Barbara Co | Santa Barbara | Santa Barbara. |
| | | Victoria st | Santa Barbara. |
| rmer | Santa Barbara | Santa Barbara Co | Santa Barbara. |
| ood yard | Santa Barbara | Milpas st | Santa Barbara. |
| amster | Santa Barbara | Santa Barbara Co | Santa Barbara. |
| ner | Guadalupe st | Guadalupe st | Guadalupe. |

THOMAS HART. REUBEN HART.
# THOMAS HART & BROTHER,
GUADALUPE, SANTA BARBARA CO., - - - - CAL.

## Blacksmiths

And Manufacturers of

## Carriages, Farm, Express & Lumber Wagons,

PLOWS, HARROWS, CULTIVATORS,

AND ALL KINDS OF AGRICULTURAL IMPLEMENTS.

### Turning done,
And All Kinds of Machinery Repaired.

**HORSE**  **SHOEING**

And General Job Work done in the best manner and with the greatest dispatch.

*All work guaranteed.*     *No material used but the best.*

# DIRECTORY OF SANTA BARBARA COUNTY.

| NAME. | OCCUPATION. | PLACE OF BUSINESS. | RESIDENCE. | TOWN OR P. O. |
|---|---|---|---|---|
| Bowen, S............... | Clerk ............... | State st.................... | Santa Barbara.......... | Santa Barbara. |
| Bowers, Rev. Stephen...... | Pastor............ ......... | Methodist Church.... | De la Guerra st........ | Santa Barbara. |
| **Bowers, John**....... | Farmer ............ | Pleasant Valley....... | Santa Barbara Co.... | Santa Barbara. |
| Boyle, John... | Laborer ... ........... | Santa Barbara Co.... | Santa Barbara.......... | Santa Barbara. |
| **Bracken, James**.... | Farmer .......... | Santa Barbara Co.... | Cañada................... | |
| **Bradford, W J**...... | Blacksmith.......... | Main-st................... | Main st............ ....... | Carpenteria. |
| Bradbury, A K P... | Druggist ........... | State st .................. | Santa Barbara.......... | Santa Barbara. |
| Bradbury, Dr........ | Physician ........... | State st .................. | De la Guerra st........ | Santa Barbara. |
| Brady, Thomas...... | Hostler.. ............. | Santa Barbara Co.... | Santa Maria............. | Santa Maria. |
| Bradshaw, J A...... | Laborer................ | 1st Township.......... | Santa Barbara Co..... | Santa Barbara. |
| Bradley, John........ | Farmer ............ | Santa Barbara......... | Santa Barbara Co.... | Santa Barbara. |
| **Brady, W H**......... | Attorney............. | Santa Barbara Co.... | La Graciosa... ........... | La Graciosa. |
| Bradbury, H K...... | Attorney............. | Santa Barbara Co.... | Santa Barbara.......... | Santa Barbara. |
| Bradley, Paul........ | Farmer ............ | Santa Maria............ | Santa Barbara Co.... | Santa Maria. |
| Brady, Felipe........ | Laborer ... ........... | Santa Barbara......... | Santa Barbara Co.... | Santa Barbara. |
| Bralich, L C........... | Variety store....... | State st .................. | State st.................... | Santa Barbara. |
| Brand & Stewart.... | Millinery............. | State st .................. | Santa Barbara.......... | Santa Barbara. |
| Brand, Mrs G E..... | Millinery............. | State st .................. | De la Guerra st........ | Santa Barbara. |
| Brand, G E............ | Dry goods............ | State st .................. | De la Guerra st........ | Santa Barbara. |
| **Braun, Robert**..... | Blacksmith.......... | Main st ................... | Central City............ | Santa Maria. |
| Brayant, Francis M | Laborer................ | Santa Barbara Co..... | Santa Maria............. | Santa Maria. |
| Breck, William....... | Gunsmith............. | Santa Barbara Co..... | Santa Barbara.......... | Santa Barbara. |
| Brecht, August...... | Barber ................ | State st .................. | State st.................... | Santa Barbara. |
| **Brechtel, Wm F**... | Groceries............. | State st .................. | State st.................... | Santa Barbara. |
| Brechtel, W E ....... | .............................. | .............................. | .............................. | Santa Barbara. |
| Breck, Wm............ | Gunsmith............. | De la Guerra st........ | De la Guerra st........ | Santa Barbara. |
| Breen, Thomas ..... | Laborer................ | Santa Barbara......... | Santa Barbara Co.... | Santa Barbara. |
| Bren, John G......... | Farmer ............ | 1st Township ......... | Santa Barbara Co.... | Santa Barbara. |
| **Breitzmann, Robt.**| Chemist & apoth. | State st .................. | State st.................... | Santa Barbara. |
| Brewster, J A........ | Librarian ............ | Odd Fellows' Library| Gutierrez st ............ | Santa Barbara. |
| Brinkerhauf, G ..... | Farmer ............ | Santa Barbara......... | Milpas st.................. | Santa Barbara. |
| Brink, Andrew ..... | Laborer ... ........... | Santa Barbara......... | Santa Barbara Co.... | Santa Barbara. |
| **Brinkerhoff, S B**... | Doctor ............ | Santa Barbara......... | Santa Barbara Co.... | Santa Barbara. |
| Bristol, H, Jr......... | Clerk ................... | State st .................. | De la Guerra st........ | Santa Barbara. |
| Bristol, Henry........ | Merchant ............ | .............................. | Vineyard st............. | Santa Barbara. |
| Brock, Benj F........ | Butcher................ | State st .................. | Gutierrez st ............ | Santa Barbara. |
| Bronson, Mrs........ | Bdg house............ | Garden st ............... | Garden st................. | Santa Barbara. |
| **Bronshea, Peter I.**| Farmer ............ | Santa Barbara Co..... | Montecito................ | Santa Barbara. |
| Bronshea, Peter J... | Farmer ............ | Montecito.............. | Santa Barbara Co.... | Santa Barbara. |
| Brookline, T J ...... | Merchant ............ | Santa Barbara Co..... | Los Alisos ............... | Los Alisos. |
| Brookshire, Thos ... | Saloon .................. | Guadalupe st........... | 3d st........................ | Guadalupe. |
| Brophy, Michael.... | Laborer ............ | Santa Barbara Co..... | Santa Barbara.......... | Santa Barbara. |
| Broughton, John R. | Ranchero ............ | Santa Ynez............. | Santa Barbara Co.... | Ballard's Sta. |
| Broughton, John R. | Ranchero ............ | San Julian Ranch.... | 8 m W Las Cruces... | Las Cruces. |
| **Brown, Andrew J.**| Planing mill ........ | .............................. | Quarentena st.......... | Santa Barbara. |
| Brown, — ............. | Furniture............. | State st .................. | Garden st................. | Santa Barbara. |
| Brown, T S ........... | Farmer ............ | Santa Maria Valley.. | 2 m S E Gaudalupe.. | Guadalupe. |
| Brown, Hamblet R. | Furniture store ... | State st .................. | Garden st................. | Santa Barbara. |
| **Brown & Bates**.... | Furniture store ... | State st .................. | Santa Barbara.......... | Santa Barbara. |
| Brown, T A............ | Farmer ............ | Santa Maria Valley.. | 2 m S E Guadalupe.. | Guadalupe. |
| Brown, Chester F .. | Painter................. | Cota st .................. | Bath st..................... | Santa Barbara. |
| Brown, Mrs E R ... | .............................. | .............................. | Bath st..................... | Santa Barbara. |
| **Brown, Franklin B**| Farmer ............ | La Patera............... | Santa Barbara.......... | |
| Brown, John.......... | Mechanic ......... .,... | Santa Barbara Co..... | Santa Barbara.......... | Santa Barbara. |
| Brown, B H Case... | Mariner ............ | Santa Barbara Co....,| Santa Barbara.......... | Santa Barbara. |
| Brown, John Sumner............... | Laborer ............ | Santa Barbara......... | Santa Barbara Co..... | Santa Barbara. |
| Bruse, Luinon....... | Laborer................ | Santa Barbara Co..... | Los Alisos ............... | Los Alisos. |
| Bryant, Andrew J.. | Farmer ............,.,... | Ojai Ranch ............. | Santa Barbara Co..... | |
| Bryerly, Newman W............................. | Farmer ............ | Hueneme...............,... | Santa Barbara Co..... | Hueneme. |
| **Buchanan, A W** ... | Wells Fargo's agt | State st .................. | Haley st ................... | Santa Barbara. |
| Buchanan, Michael.| Farmer ............ | Santa Barbara......... | Santa Barbara Co.... | Santa Barbara. |

# ROBERT BRAUN,

## BLACKSMITH,

Central City, Santa Barbara Co., - - Cal.

Wagon Making and Repairing, and Wood Work of all descriptions.

Repairing of all kinds of Agricultural Implements.

*General Job Work done with neatness, durability and dispatch.*

## HORSESHOEING A SPECIALTY.

*All work done in the best manner, and guaranteed to give satisfaction.*

# DIRECTORY OF SANTA BARBARA COUNTY. 107

| Name. | Occupation. | Place of Business. | Residence. | Town or P. O. |
|---|---|---|---|---|
| Buck, Henry | Barber | Santa Barbara | Santa Barbara Co | Santa Barbara. |
| Buck, George | Farmer | La Pelas | Santa Barbara Co | |
| Buckingham, J | Brick layer | Santa Barbara | De la Guerra st | Santa Barbara. |
| Buding, John T | Farmer | Santa Barbara Co | Santa Barbara | Santa Barbara. |
| Budron, C A | Farmer | Santa Barbara | Santa Barbara Co | Santa Barbara. |
| Buelna, Jose | Merchant | Santa Barbara | Santa Barbara Co | Santa Barbara. |
| Buell, Alonzo W | Dairyman | Santa Barbara Co | Las Llagas | |
| Buelna, Joaquin | Farmer | Cañada | Santa Barbara Co | |
| Buell, Henry J | Farmer | Santa Barbara | Santa Barbara Co | Santa Barbara. |
| Buell, H P | Dairyman | Las Cruces | Las Cruces | Las Cruces. |
| Buell, Alonzo Wilcox | Dairyman | Las Llagas | 20 m S E Las Cruces | Las Cruces. |
| Buell, R T | Dairyman | Juanita Ranch | 5 m S Ballard's Sta | Ballard's Sta. |
| Buelna, Jose | Hotel | Santa Ynez Road | 4 m N E Las Cruces | Las Cruces. |
| Buell, Hailan Page | Dairyman | Santa Barbara Co | Las Cruces | Las Cruces. |
| Buell, Harvey J | Farmer | Santa Barbara Co | Santa Barbara | Santa Barbara. |
| Bulger, Henry | Farmer | Santa Barbara Co | Santa Barbara | Santa Barbara. |
| Bun, William | Carpenter | Santa Barbara Co | Santa Barbara | Santa Barbara. |
| Burch, Levi | Laborer | Santa Barbara | Santa Barbara Co | Santa Barbara. |
| Burke, M F | Gen'l merchant | Gaviota Landing | 3 m S Las Cruces | Las Cruces. |
| Burke, Miguel F | Clerk | Santa Barbara Co | Santa Barbara | Santa Barbara. |
| Burke, James Walker | Ranchero | Santa Ynez | Santa Barbara Co | Ballard's Sta. |
| Burrows, Josiah | Farmer | Dos Pueblos | Santa Barbara Co | |
| Burrus, Jas | Hostler | Cota st | Cota st | Santa Barbara. |
| Burrola, G | Laborer | La Laguna | Santa Barbara Co | |
| Burton, Louis F | Farmer | Santa Barbara | Santa Barbara Co | Santa Barbara. |
| Burton, Benj Jos | Merchant | Santa Barbara Co | Santa Barbara | Santa Barbara. |
| Burton, Solomon | Machinist | Santa Barbara | Santa Barbara Co | Santa Barbara. |
| Burton, Santa Anna | Laborer | Santa Barbara Co | Santa Barbara | Santa Barbara. |
| Burton, John | Laborer | Santa Ynez | 10 m N E Las Cruces | Las Cruces. |
| Burton, Benj | Clerk | State st | Ortega st | Santa Barbara. |
| Buster, Wm | Farmer | Carpenteria Valley | Carpenteria | Carpenteria. |
| Buster, John | Farmer | Carpenteria | Carpenteria | Carpenteria. |
| Bustos, Bernardino | Laborer | Santa Barbara Co | Santa Barbara | Santa Barbara. |
| Butler, Chas W | Farmer | Carpenteria Valley | 2¼ m W Carpenteria | Carpenteria. |
| Butler, J A | Farmer | Carpenteria Valley | 2 m W Carpenteria | Carpenteria. |
| Butler, Mrs R | Plain sewer | | Montecito | Santa Barbara. |
| Butler, W Mayhew | Farmer | Santa Barbara Co | Arroyo Burro | |
| Butts, Norman | Laborer | Santa Barbara Co | La Patera | |
| Byrnes, Jas | Harness maker | State st | Vinegar st | Santa Barbara. |
| Caballi, F | Restaurant | State st | State st | Santa Barbara. |
| Cadwell, O N | Orchard | Carpenteria Valley | 2 m E Carpenteria | Carpenteria. |
| Cagle, William | Farmer | Santa Barbara Co | 1st Township | Santa Barbara. |
| Calderon, Valentin | Vaquero | Santa Barbara | Santa Barbara Co | Santa Barbara. |
| Calderon, Jose de J | Laborer | Santa Barbara Co | Santa Barbara | Santa Barbara. |
| Caldwell, Oren N | Farmer | Carpenteria | Santa Barbara Co | Carpenteria. |
| Caldom, — | Farmer | Carpenteria Valley | 3¼ m W Carpenteria | Carpenteria. |
| Calder, J | Dentist | State st | Santa Barbara Co | Santa Barbara. |
| Callas, E C | Farmer | Carpenteria Valley | 3 m W Carpenteria | Carpenteria. |
| Callis, Wm Sterling | Farmer | Santa Barbara | Santa Barbara Co | Santa Barbara. |
| Callett, Ezra | Farmer | La Patera | Santa Barbara Co | |
| Callis, Wm | Farmer | Carpenteria Valley | 2¼ m W Carpenteria | Carpenteria. |
| Cambell, John | Farmer | Carpenteria | Santa Barbara Co | Carpenteria. |
| Campe, Hy | Laborer | Santa Barbara | Santa Barbara Co | Santa Barbara. |
| Campbell, Ed A | Mechanic | Santa Barbara | Santa Barbara Co | Santa Barbara. |
| Campbell, A B | Dentist | Santa Barbara Co | Santa Barbara | Santa Barbara. |
| Canedo, Narcisco | Laborer | Santa Barbara | Santa Barbara Co | Santa Barbara. |
| Caneda, N A | Ranchero | Santa Barbara | Santa Barbara Co | Santa Barbara. |
| Caneda, Conrado | Hostler | State st | | Santa Barbara. |
| Canfield, A W | Water works | Santa Barbara | Fig ave | Santa Barbara. |
| Cannon, W L | Hunter | Santa Barbara Co | Santa Maria | Santa Maria. |
| Cantua, Santiago | Vaquero | Santa Barbara | Santa Barbara Co | Santa Barbara. |
| Caranza, Feliz | Laborer | Santa Maria | Santa Barbara Co | Santa Maria. |

C. W. SWANTON.                                                  JOHN DOCKERY.

# LOMPOC
# LIVERY AND FEED STABLE.

Southwest corner of G Street and Ocean Avenue,

## LOMPOC,

SANTA BARBARA CO., - - - - - - - CAL.

DOCKERY & SWANTON, Proprietors.

This establishment, being complete in all its branches, is now ready to accommodate the public in the best manner. The finest of

**BUGGIES, CARRIAGES AND HORSES,**

With careful drivers, by the DAY or WEEK. Horses boarded and groomed by the day, week or month.

We respectfully solicit a share of public patronage, pledging in return attention to business, and a determination to satisfy our customers.

# DIRECTORY OF SANTA BARBARA COUNTY. 109

| Name. | Occupation. | Place of Business. | Residence. | Town or P. O. |
|---|---|---|---|---|
| Cardon, Elijio | Laborer | Santa Barbara Co | Santa Barbara | Santa Barbara. |
| Cardenas, F. | | 3d Precinct | Santa Barbara Co | |
| Carillo, Jose M. | Laborer | Santa Barbara | Santa Barbara Co | Santa Barbara. |
| Carillo, Anastuscio A | Laborer | Santa Barbara | Santa Barbara Co | Santa Barbara. |
| Carilla, Francisco | Laborer | Santa Barbara | Santa Barbara Co | Santa Barbara. |
| Carillo, Guillermo | Musician | Santa Barbara Co | Santa Barbara | Santa Barbara. |
| Carillo, Juan Jose | Laborer | Santa Barbara | Santa Barbara Co | Santa Barbara. |
| Carner, W A | Laborer | Los Alamos | 40 m S Guadalupe | Guadalupe. |
| Carnes, H Steven | U S assessor | Santa Barbara | Santa Barbara Co | Santa Barbara. |
| Carnahan, Robert | Laborer | Santa Barbara Co | Cañada | |
| Carnes, Henry | | | Chapala st | Santa Barbara. |
| Carnes, John | Hostler | State st | State st | Santa Barbara. |
| Carillo, P | Butcher | Santa Barbara | | Santa Barbara. |
| Carrillo, Jose A | Laborer | Santa Barbara Co | Santa Ynez | Ballard's Sta. |
| Carrillo, Plutarco | Laborer | Santa Barbara Co | Santa Barbara | Santa Barbara. |
| Carrillo, Alfredo | Laborer | Santa Barbara Co | Santa Barbara | Santa Barbara. |
| Carrell, Peter Lang | Farmer | 1st Precinct | Santa Barbara Co | Santa Barbara. |
| Carrillo, F U | Clerk | Santa Barbara Co | Santa Barbara | Santa Barbara. |
| Carrall, Pattle | Laborer | Santa Barbara Co | Ojai Ranch | |
| Carrillo, Romuldo | Clerk | Santa Barbara Co | Santa Barbara | Santa Barbara. |
| Carty, Daniel | Laborer | Santa Barbara | Santa Barbara Co | Santa Barbara. |
| Cartery, Henri | Ranchero | Santa Ynez | 10 m E Las Cruces | Las Cruces. |
| Carter, Francis | Laborer | Santa Barbara | Santa Barbara | Santa Barbara. |
| Caryl, Wm Barron | Farmer | Montecito | Santa Barbara Co | Santa Barbara. |
| Case, Geo Carter | Farmer | Santa Barbara | Santa Barbara Co | Santa Barbara. |
| Castro, Jose A | Laborer | Santa Barbara | Santa Barbara | Santa Barbara. |
| Castro, Miguel, Jr | Laborer | Santa Barbara Co | Santa Barbara | Santa Barbara. |
| Castro, Jose R T | Shoe maker | Santa Barbara Co | San Jose | |
| Castorneo, Pascale | Sheep raiser | Santa Barbara Co | Montecito | Santa Barbara. |
| Castanos, Luis | Clergyman | Santa Barbara | Baños st | Santa Barbara. |
| Cauch, Dr R | Homeopathic phy | Carpenteria Valley | 1½ m E Carpenteria | Carpenteria. |
| Cavallier, N V | Laborer | Santa Barbara Co | Santa Barbara | Santa Barbara. |
| Cavallero, Vincent | Variety store | State st | State st | Santa Barbara. |
| Cave, Joseph | Laborer | Santa Barbara | Anapamu st | Santa Barbara. |
| Cebrian, J C | C E & architect | State st | State st | Santa Barbara. |
| Center, H | Farmer | Santa Barbara | Yanonali st | Santa Barbara. |
| Chaine, E | Stage proprietor | Guad'pe&LompocSL | Central City | Central City. |
| Chappell, E | Farmer | La Graciosa | 2 m E La Graciosa | La Graciosa. |
| Chappell, Edwin | Farmer | Santa Barbara Co | Los Alamos | |
| Chase, Sydney | Farmer | Santa Barbara | 1st Precinct | |
| Chase, George W | Seaman | Santa Barbara | Santa Barbara Co | Santa Barbara. |
| Chase, A R | Clerk | State st | Chapala st | Santa Barbara. |
| Chism, John R | Seaman | Santa Barbara Co | Santa Barbara | Santa Barbara. |
| Church, N | Farmer | La Patera | Santa Barbara Co | |
| Clapp, Ed Lewis | Laborer | La Patera | Santa Barbara Co | |
| Clark, C N | Grocer | Santa Barbara | Santa Barbara Co | Santa Barbara. |
| Clark, Dana B | Farmer | Santa Barbara | Santa Barbara Co | Santa Barbara. |
| Clark, John | Stage driver | Santa Barbara Co | Santa Barbara | Santa Barbara. |
| Clark, Isaac N | Laborer | La Patera | Santa Barbara Co | |
| Clark, L C | Carpenter | Santa Barbara Co | Santa Barbara | Santa Barbara. |
| Clarke, Mrs Sarah | | | Anacapa st | Santa Barbara. |
| Clark, L K | Clerk | State st | Santa Barbara | Santa Barbara. |
| Clark, — | Laborer | Santa Barbara Co | Victoria st | Santa Barbara. |
| Clark, Chas H | Farmer | Point Sal | 10 m SW Guadalupe | Guadalupe. |
| Clark, E | | | | Santa Barbara. |
| Clark, L C | Clerk | State st | Cota st | Santa Barbara. |
| Clark, J W | Clerk | Guadalupe st | Guadalupe st | Guadalupe. |
| Clayton, B F | Lumber&wareh'e | Point Sal | 10 m SW Guadalupe | Guadalupe. |
| Clifton, Henry | Deputy sheriff | Court House | Chapala st | Santa Barbara. |
| Cline, Joseph H | Plasterer | Santa Barbara | Santa Barbara Co | Santa Barbara. |
| Cline, William | Carpenter | Santa Barbara Co | Santa Barbara | Santa Barbara. |
| Coak, Larken I | Laborer | Santa Barbara Co | 3d Township | |
| Coats, Newton M | Farmer | Santa Barbara Co | Montecito | |

# R. D. COOK,
# BLACKSMITH

And Manufacturer of

## WAGONS

And all kinds of

## AGRICULTURAL
## IMPLEMENTS

**MAIN STREET, Central City,**

SANTA BARBARA COUNTY, CAL.

## BAIN WAGONS

### FOR SALE.

Orders for all kinds of Machinery and Implements promptly filled.

**WOOD WORK AND ALL KINDS OF TURNING DONE.**

RECTORY OF SANTA BARBARA COUNTY. 111

| CCUPATION. | PLACE OF BUSINESS. | RESIDENCE. | TOWN OR P. O. |
|---|---|---|---|
| rney at law... | State st............... | State st................ | Santa Barbara. |
| chero............ | Las Cruces............. | Las Cruces........... | Las Cruces. |
| uero............ | Santa Barbara......... | Santa Barbara Co.... | Santa Barbara. |
| orer............. | Santa Barbara......... | Santa Barbara Co.... | Santa Barbara. |
| chero........... | Santa Barbara Co..... | 3d Township.......... | |
| uero............ | Santa Barbara Co..... | Santa Barbara........ | Santa Barbara. |
| chero........... | 3d Township.......... | Santa Barbara Co..... | |
| chero........... | Santa Barbara Co..... | 3d Township.......... | |
| icher............ | Carpenteria............ | Carpenteria........... | Carpenteria. |
| 'k ............... | Santa Barbara Co..... | Santa Barbara........ | Santa Barbara. |
| chant........... | Santa Barbara......... | Santa Barbara Co.... | Santa Barbara. |
| mer............. | Santa Maria Valley.. | 2 m E Guadalupe..... | Guadalupe. |
| mer............. | Carpenteria Valley... | 4 m E Carpenteria... | Carpenteria. |
| mer ............. | Carpenteria Valley... | 4 m E Carpenteria... | Carpenteria. |
| mer............. | Santa Barbara Co..... | Santa Barbara........ | Santa Barbara. |
| mster........... | Santa Barbara Co..... | Santa Barbara........ | Santa Barbara. |
| man............ | Santa Barbara......... | Santa Barbara........ | Santa Barbara. |
| mster........... | Santa Barbara......... | Santa Barbara Co.... | Santa Barbara. |
| iner.............. | Santa Barbara Co..... | Santa Barbara........ | Santa Barbara. |
| tender.......... | Guadalupe st......... | Guadalupe st......... | Guadalupe. |
| orer............. | Santa Barbara......... | Santa Barbara Co.... | Santa Barbara. |
| mer ............. | Santa Barbara Co..... | 2d Precinct............ | |
| cksmith........ | Cota st.................. | Quinientos st......... | Santa Barbara. |
| cksmith........ | Cota st................. | Haley st................ | Santa Barbara. |
| penter ......... | Guadalupe st.......... | Olivera st.............. | Guadalupe. |
| :k ............... | State st................. | Milpas st .............. | Santa Barbara. |
| orer ............. | 1st Township.......... | Santa Barbara Co.... | |
| orer............. | Santa Barbara......... | Santa Barbara Co.... | Santa Barbara. |
| .................. | .......................... | Vineyard st........... | Santa Barbara. |
| mer ............. | Montecito.............. | Santa Barbara Co.... | |
| penter ......... | Santa Barbara......... | Santa Barbara Co.... | Santa Barbara. |
| mer ............. | Santa Maria Valley.. | 2 m S E Guadalupe.. | Guadalupe. |
| mer ............. | Santa Maria Valley.. | 2 m S E Guadalupe.. | Guadalupe. |
| mer ............. | Santa Maria Valley . | 2 m S E Guadalupe.. | Guadalupe. |
| cher............. | Santa Barbara Co..... | Santa Barbara........ | Santa Barbara. |
| cher............. | Santa Barbara Co..... | Los Alamos........... | |
| mer ............. | Montecito.............. | Santa Barbara Co.... | |
| cher............. | Santa Maria............ | Santa Barbara Co.... | Santa Maria. |
| ister............ | Santa Barbara......... | Santa Barbara Co.... | Santa Barbara. |
| sident .......... | National Gold Bank.. | Chapala st ........... | Santa Barbara. |
| penter.......... | Gutierrez st............ | Gutierrez st........... | Santa Barbara. |
| ringe maker .. | Main st.................. | Central City........... | Santa Maria. |
| gistrate ........ | City Hall................ | De la Guerra st....... | Santa Barbara. |
| ery stable...... | Cota st................... | Chapala st............. | Santa Barbara. |
| mer ............. | Cota st................... | Chapala st............. | Santa Barbara. |
| ble keeper..... | Santa Barbara......... | Santa Barbara Co.... | Santa Barbara. |
| rk................ | Santa Barbara Co..... | Santa Barbara........ | Santa Barbara. |
| :k raiser........ | Santa Barbara Co..... | 3d Township.......... | |
| mer ............. | Santa Barbara Co..... | Dos Pueblos........... | |
| :tor .............. | Saticoy.................. | Santa Barbara Co.... | Saticoy. |
| veyor .......... | State st.................. | De la Guerra st....... | Santa Barbara. |
| mster........... | Santa Barbara......... | Ortega st............... | Santa Barbara. |
| mer............. | La Graciosa............ | 2 m S La Graciosa... | La Graciosa. |
| chero........... | Santa Rosa Ranch.... | 12m S W Ball'ds sta'n | Ballard's Sta'n. |
| mer ............ | Beach Road............ | 1½ m W Guadalupe.. | Guadalupe. |
| mer ............. | Santa Barbara Co.... | 1st Township.......... | |
| orer............. | Santa Barbara......... | Santa Barbara Co..... | Santa Barbara. |
| cher............. | Santa Barbara......... | Santa Barbara........ | Santa Barbara. |
| orer............. | Santa Barbara Co..... | Santa Barbara........ | Santa Barbara. |
| orer............. | Santa Barbara......... | Santa Barbara........ | Santa Barbara. |

# WILLIAM L. ADAM,

Wholesale and Retail Dealer in

## GENERAL MERCHANDISE,

SANTA MARIA, SANTA BARBARA CO., CAL.

## DRY GOODS,

## GROCERIES & PROVISIONS

## BOOTS, SHOES, TINWARE,

### HARDWARE, CROCKERY,

## Wines and Liquors

TOBACCO, CIGARS, ETC.

The Public is invited to call and examine this large and finely selected stock of goods before purchasing elsewhere.

Guaranteed to suit with respect to Quality and Price.

# DIRECTORY OF SANTA BARBARA COUNTY.

| NAME. | OCCUPATION. | PLACE OF BUSINESS. | RESIDENCE. | TOWN OR P. O. |
|---|---|---|---|---|
| Cordero, Juan de Jesus | Laborer | Las Cruces | Sant Barbara Co | Las Cruces. |
| Cordero, Salvador | Laborer | Santa Barbara | Sant Barbara Co | Santa Barbara. |
| Cordero, Jose A | Shoe maker | Santa Barbara Co | Sant Barbara | Santa Barbara. |
| Cordero, Tomas R | Laborer | Santa Barbara | Santa Barbara Co | Santa Barbara. |
| **Cordero, Vicente** | Ranchero | Las Cruces | Santa Barbara Co | Las Cruces. |
| Cordero, J G | Laborer | Santa Barbara Co | San Francisquito | |
| Cordero, Miguel | Laborer | Refugie | Santa Barbara Co | |
| Cordero, Mariano | Luborer | Santa Barbara Co | Santa Barbara | Santa Barbara. |
| Cordero, Romualdo | Laborer | Las Cruces | Las Cruces | Las Cruces. |
| Cordero, Frank | Laborer | Santa Barbara | De la Guerra st | Santa Barbara. |
| Cordero, Francisco N | Ranchero | Las Cruces | Las Cruces | Las Cruces. |
| Cordero, Estanislaro C | Ranchero | Las Cruces | Las Cruces | Las Cruces. |
| Corkery, John | Laborer | Santa Barbara | Haley st | Santa Barbara. |
| Correa, Jos G | Farmer | 3d Township | Santa Barbara Co | |
| Corrales, Jesus | Laborer | Santa Ynez | 10 m N E L Cruces | Las Cruces. |
| Correa, Jose | Vaquero | Santa Ynez | 10 m N E L Cruces | Las Cruces. |
| Corrales, Francisco | Laborer | Santa Ynez | 10 m N E L Cruces | Santa Ynez. |
| Cota, Jesus | Farmer | Carpenteria | Carpenteria | Carpenteria. |
| Cota, Joaquin | Physician | Las Cruces | Las Cruces | Las Cruces. |
| **Cota, Manuel** | Farmer | Santa Barbara Co | Carpenteria | Carpenteria. |
| **Cota, Victor** | Ranchero | Santa Barbara | Santa Barbara Co | Santa Barbara. |
| Cota, Jose Manuel | Ranchero | Santa Barbara | Santa Barbara Co | Santa Barbara. |
| Cota, Benito | Laborer | Santa Barbara | Santa Barbara Co | Santa Barbara. |
| **Cota, Jose de Jesus** | Farmer | Santa Barbara Co | Santa Barbara | Santa Barbara. |
| Cota, Valentine | Farmer | Santa Barbara Co | Santa Barbara | Santa Barbara. |
| Cota, Jose de Jesus | Laborer | Carpenteria | Santa Barbara Co | Carpenteria. |
| Cota, JoseRomualdo | Vaquero | Santa Barbara Co | Santa Barbara | Santa Barbara. |
| Cota, Jose Ramon | Vaquero | Santa Barbara | Santa Barbara Co | Santa Barbara. |
| Cota, Jose Maria, Jr | Vaquero | Santa Barbara Co | Carpenteria | Carpenteria. |
| Cota, Manual A | Vaquero | Santa Barbara Co | Santa Barbara Co | Santa Barbara. |
| Cota, Pacifico del E S | Laborer | Santa Barbara | Santa Barbara | Santa Barbara. |
| **Cota, Jose Maria** | Farmer | Santa Barbara Co | Carpenteria | Carpenteria. |
| Cota, Ynocente | Vaquero | Santa Barbara Co | Santa Barbara | Santa Barbara. |
| Cota, Luis | Vaquero | Santa Barbara Co | Santa Barbara | Santa Barbara. |
| **Cota, Leonardo** | Ranchero | Los Alamos | Santa Barbara Co | |
| Cota, Juan | Laborer | Santa Barbara Co | Santa Barbara | Santa Barbara. |
| Cota, Manuel de Jesus | Laborer | Santa Barbara Co | Santa Barbara | Santa Barbara. |
| Cota, Juan de Jesus | Laborer | Montecito | Santa Barbara Co | |
| Cota, Francisco | Laborer | Santa Barbara | Santa Barbara | Santa Barbara. |
| Cota, Emido | Vaquero | Santa Barbara Co | Santa Barbara | Santa Barbara. |
| Cotton, David | Piano tuner | State st | Haley st | Santa Barbara. |
| Coulter, Martin L | Farmer | Santa Barbara Co | 1st Precinct | |
| **Courtwright, John** | Saloon keeper | Santa Barbara | Santa Barbara Co | Santa Barbara. |
| Covarrubias, C J | Painter | Santa Barbara | Santa Barbara Co | Santa Barbara. |
| Covarubias, O | Laborer | Santa Barbara | Santa Barbara | Santa Barbara. |
| Covarrubias, N A | Clerk | Santa Barbara | Santa Barbara Co | Santa Barbara. |
| **Covarrubias, N A** | Livery stable | State st | Canyon Perdido st | Santa Barbara. |
| **Covarrubias, O M** | Livery stable | State st | Santa Barbara | Santa Barbara. |
| Coyle, Patrick | Farmer | Santa Barbara | Santa Barbara Co | Santa Barbara. |
| Coyle, Peter | Farmer | Santa Barbara | Santa Barbara | Santa Barbara. |
| Cox, Richard | Mariner | Santa Barbara Co | | |
| Crabb, James M | Laborer | Santa Barbara | Santa Barbara Co | Santa Barbara. |
| **Crabtree, E J** | Farmer | Santa Barbara | Santa Maria | Santa Maria. |
| Crane, H G | Farmer | Santa Barbara Co | Santa Barbara | Santa Barbara. |
| Crane, — | | | Vineyard st | Santa Barbara. |
| **Crane & Barker** | Real estate | State st | State st | Santa Barbara. |
| **Crane, H G** | Real estate | State st | Vineyard st | Santa Barbara. |
| Crane, J L | Farmer | Carpenteria Valley | 3¼ m W Carpenteria | Carpenteria. |
| Craviota, A | Carpenter | Santa Barbara | Bath st | Santa Barbara. |
| **Cravins, Thos A** | Farmer | Carpenteria Valley | 1 m W Carpenteria | Carpenteria. |

8

# U. S. MAIL LINE

### FROM

# Guadalupe to Lompoc

(CONNECTING WITH COAST LINE STAGE CO.)

### STAGES OF THE

# LOMPOC STAGE CO.

Leave Guadalupe every morning, at 6, from the Revere House, for

## SANTA MARIA,
## GRACIOSA AND LOMPOC

### RETURNING.

## LEAVE LOMPOC EVERY NOON

CHARLES STEVENS, Proprietor.

I. SCHWARTZ, Agent, Guadalupe.

# DIRECTORY OF SANTA BARBARA COUNTY. 115

| Name. | Occupation. | Place of Business. | Residence. | Town or P. O. |
|---|---|---|---|---|
| Crawford, M G | Teamster | Santa Barbara | Haley st | Santa Barbara. |
| Crondoni, D | Vintner | Santa Barbara | | Santa Barbara. |
| Cross, John | Laborer | Santa Barbara Co | Carpenteria | Carpenteria. |
| Cross, Mrs J | Boarding house | | Chapala st | Santa Barbara. |
| Cross, John | Farmer | Carpenteria Valley | 4½ m E Carpenteria | Carpenteria. |
| Crosby, J A | Real estate agt | Main st | Central City | Santa Maria. |
| Crowell, Chas D | Stage driver | Santa Barbara | Santa Barbara Co | Santa Barbara. |
| Crumrine, H | Teacher | Sespe | Santa Barbara Co | |
| Cruz, Juan Reyes | Laborer | Santa Barbara | Santa Barbara Co | Santa Barbara. |
| Cuesta, J De la | Farmer | 3 m N Santa Ynez | Santa Barbara Co | Ballard's Sta'n. |
| Cuesta, B De la | Farmer | 3 m N Santa Ynez | Santa Barbara Co | Ballard's Sta'n. |
| Cuesta, L De la | Farmer | 3 m N Santa Ynez | Santa Barbara Co | Ballard's Sta'n. |
| Cuesta, Joaq De la | Farmer | 3 m N Santa Ynez | Santa Barbara Co | Ballard's Sta'n. |
| Cuesta, E De la | Farmer | 3 m N Santa Ynez | 3 m N Santa Ynez | Ballard's Sta'n. |
| Cuesta, John De la | Farmer | 3 m N Santa Ynez | Santa Barbara Co | Ballard's Sta'n. |
| Cuesta, J De la | Gen merchandise | Santa Ynez | Santa Ynez Mission | Ballard's Sta'n. |
| Cuesta, R De la | Ranchero | Najahni Ranch | 6 m S Bal'd's Stat'n | Ballard's Sta'n. |
| Cuesta & Moll | Gen merchandise | Santa Ynez | | Ballard's Sta'n. |
| Cuesta, RomanDela | Gen merchandise | 3 m N Santa Ynez | 3 m N Santa Ynez | Ballard's Sta'n. |
| Curley, T B | Auction & comm | State st | State st | Santa Barbara. |
| Curley & Sherman | Auction & comm | State st | | Santa Barbara. |
| Curran, John | Laborer | Santa Barbara | Garden st | Santa Barbara. |
| Curran, John | Farmer | Montecito | Santa Barbara Co | |
| Curtiss, Wilbur | Prop. hot s. sp'gs | Santa Barbara Co | 6 m from S. B | Santa Barbara. |
| Cushing, Stephen | Laborer | Santa Barbara Co | Santa Barbara | Santa Barbara. |
| Cushing, Mrs | | | Garden st | Santa Barbara. |
| Cutler, Edward | Hostler | Santa Barbara Co | La Patera | |
| Dailey, Elias | Stock raiser | Carpenteria Valley | 3 m E Carpenteria | Carpenteria. |
| Dalley, Henry | Carpenter | Santa Barbara | Chapala st | Santa Barbara. |
| Dalley, Henry J | Cooper | Santa Barbara | Santa Barbara Co | Santa Barbara. |
| Daniels, John | Laborer | Santa Barbara Co | Las Cruces | Las Cruces. |
| Davis, Peter | Farmer | Santa Barbara Co | Santa Barbara | Santa Barbara. |
| Davis, Alfred | Butcher | State st | State st | Santa Barbara. |
| Davis, Francis C | Farmer | La Patera | Santa Barbara Co | |
| Davis, Gray Van B | Farmer | Santa Paula | Santa Barbara | |
| Davis, Giles | Boot & shoe mkr | State st | Anacapa st | Santa Barbara. |
| Davison & Shepard | Pion'r plan'g mill | Montecito st | | Santa Barbara. |
| Davison, M T | Pion'r plan'g mill | Montecito'st | Anacapa st | Santa Barbara. |
| Dayton, Pulaski G | Farmer | Santa Barbara Co | 1st Township | |
| Dean, — | | Santa Barbara | Garden st | Santa Barbara. |
| Dechman, W C | Merchant | Santa Barbara | Santa Barbara Co | Santa Barbara. |
| Degeme, P | Cooper | | Rancheria st | Santa Barbara. |
| Degener, H | Painter | State st | State st | Santa Barbara. |
| De La Guerra, Chas | Clerk | State st | De la Guerra st | Santa Barbara. |
| Delaney, Wm | Farmer | | Santa Barbara st | Santa Barbara. |
| Dement, Mrs Olive | | | De la Guerra st | Santa Barbara. |
| Den, Emanuel R | Ranchero | Santa Barbara | Santa Barbara Co | |
| Den, Guillermo A | Farmer | Dos Pueblos | Santa Barbara Co | |
| Dennis, Thomas | Carpenter | Santa Barbara | Santa Barbara Co | Santa Barbara. |
| Denning, Hiram M | Farmer | Carpenteria | Santa Barbara Co | Carpenteria. |
| Detmon, Chas | Carpenter | Santa Barbara Co | Santa Barbara | Santa Barbara. |
| Deunn, Peter J | Farmer | 2d Precinct | Santa Barbara Co | |
| Dewlancy, R W | Farmer | La Patera | Santa Barbara Co | |
| Dial, Isaac | Watch maker | State st | De la Guerra Plaza | Santa Barbara. |
| Diblee, Carmi | Blacksmith | Santa Barbara | Santa Barbara | Santa Barbara. |
| Dibblee, Thos B | Lawyer | Santa Barbara Co | Santa Barbara | Santa Barbara. |
| Dickinson, George | Dairyman | Osco Flaco | Santa Barbara Co | |
| Dictman, C | Carpenter | State st | State st | Santa Barbara. |
| Dillard, Robt M | Attorney | Santa Barbara Co | Santa Barbara | Santa Barbara. |
| Dimmick, W | Clerk | State st | State st | Santa Barbara. |
| Dimmick, Dr L N | Physician | State st | Garden st | Santa Barbara. |
| Dimmick, Milton | Farmer | Carpenteria Valley | 4 m E Carpenteria | Carpenteria. |
| Dinsmore, A I | Farmer | Santa Barbara Co | Montecito | |
| Dinsmore, B T | Farmer | Montecito | Santa Barbara Co | |

# FASHION
## Livery and Feed Stable

## HINTON, GALLAGHER & CO.

### CORNER
### SECOND AND D STREETS,

## SAN DIEGO.

# DIRECTORY OF SANTA BARBARA COUNTY. 117

| NAME. | OCCUPATION. | PLACE OF BUSINESS. | RESIDENCE. | TOWN OR P. O. |
|---|---|---|---|---|
| Dobson, Jesse | Doctor | Santa Paula | Santa Barbara Co | |
| Dockery, John | Livery stable | Ocean Ave | G st | Lompoc. |
| Dockery & Swauton | Livery stable | Ocean Ave | | Lompoc. |
| Dockhorn, F | Laborer | Santa Rosa Ranch | 12 m S W Bal'd's Stn | Ballard's Sta'n. |
| Doe, Charles | Farmer | Santa Barbara Co | La Patera | |
| Dominguez, Ed | Laborer | Santa Barbara Co | Carpenteria | Carpenteria. |
| Dominguez, Josede J | Laborer | Santa Barbara Co | Santa Barbara | Santa Barbara. |
| Dominguez, Stephen | Cooper | Santa Barbara | Carmelos | |
| Dominguez, Jose A | Laborer | Montecito | Santa Barbara Co | |
| Dominguez, F A | Laborer | Santa Barbara Co | Santa Barbara | Santa Barbara. |
| Dominguez, Robert | Farmer | La Patera | Santa Barbara Co | |
| Dominguez, Martin | Farmer | Santa Barbara Co | La Patera | |
| Dominguez, Feliciano | Musician | Santa Barbara | Santa Barbara Co | Santa Barbara. |
| Dominguez, Jose | Laborer | Santa Barbara Co | Montecito | |
| Dominguez, Jose M | Laborer | Montecito | Santa Barbara Co | |
| Dominguez, Francisco | Vaquero | Santa Barbara Co | Santa Barbara Co | Santa Barbara. |
| Dominguez, Nemecio | Farmer | Montecito | Santa Barbara Co | |
| Dominguez, Pedro | Vaquero | Santa Barbara Co | Santa Barbara | Santa Barbara. |
| Donavau, J | Farmer | Santa Maria Valley | 2 m S Guadalupe | Guadalupe. |
| Donuellan, J | Flour packer | Chapala st | Chapala st | Santa Barbara. |
| Doran, Nicholas | Teacher | Santa Ynez | 10 m N E Las Cruces | Santa Ynez. |
| Dorncott, Thomas | Mariner | Santa Barbara | Santa Barbara Co | Santa Barbara. |
| Dorricott, Thos | Butcher | State st | Chapala st | Santa Barbara. |
| Doty, Albert C | Farmer | Santa Barbara | Yanonali st | Santa Barbara. |
| Doud, Chas Edward | Butcher | Santa Barbara Co | Montecito | |
| Douglas, Wm | Farmer | Santa Maria Road | 1 m E Guadalupe | Guadalupe. |
| Douglas, C | Farmer | Santa Maria Valley | 1 m E Guadalupe | Guadalupe. |
| Douglas, E | Farmer | Santa Maria Valley | 1 m E Guadalupe | Guadalupe. |
| Doulton, Josiah | | | Carrillo st | Santa Barbara. |
| Dover, Wm | Fisherman | Santa Barbara | Yanonali st | Santa Barbara. |
| Dowell, Richard | Lather | Santa Barbara | Santa Barbara Co | Santa Barbara. |
| Drain, James | Farmer | 1st Township | Santa Barbara Co | |
| Drake, F K | Prop union house | Bath & Gutierrez sts | | Santa Barbara. |
| Driscoll, J F | Printer | | Santa Barbara Co | |
| Dugdale, George | | | Sola st | Santa Barbara. |
| Dunbar, John | Variety store | Guadalupe st | Guadalupe st | Guadalupe. |
| Duncan, R H | Lawyer | Santa Barbara Co | Santa Barbara | Santa Barbara. |
| Dunne, Hugh | Farmer | Santa Barbara Co | | Santa Barbara. |
| Dunshee, John | Wheelwright | Canyon Perdido st | Del Vino st | Santa Barbara. |
| Dunshee, R | Wagon maker | Canyon Perdido st | Vineyard st | Santa Barbara. |
| Dupuy, Mathew | Hotel keeper | Santa Barbara Co | Santa Barbara | Santa Barbara. |
| Durr, Julius | Farmer | Los Alamos | Santa Barbara Co | |
| Dutard, H | Comm merchant | 217 and 219 Clay st | Howard, bet 21st&22d | San Francisco. |
| Dutton, J R | Carpenter | Santa Barbara | Carrillo st | Santa Barbara. |
| Ealand, Wm | Butcher | State st | Haley st | Santa Barbara. |
| Ealand, Joseph | Butcher | State st | Chapala st | Santa Barbara. |
| Easley, Pleasant C | Farmer | Santa Barbara Co | Sespe | |
| Eason, Chas Horace | Superintendent | Santa Barbara Co | Santa Barbara | Santa Barbara. |
| Ebberling, Wm | Blacksmith | Cota st | Santa Barbara | Santa Barbara. |
| Eddleman, J J | Saddle & harness | Guadalupe st | Guadalupe st | Guadalupe. |
| Edmundson, A G | Farmer | Santa Ynez | Santa Barbara Co | Santa Barbara. |
| Edwards, J Brooks | Farmer | Santa Ynez | Santa Barbara Co | Ballard's Statn. |
| Edwards, Cullen W | Stock raiser | Sespe | Santa Barbara Co | |
| Edwards, John | Hardware | State st | Sola st | Santa Barbara. |
| Effinger, A | Carpenter | Santa Barbara | Vineyard st | Santa Barbara. |
| Efner, Joseph | Blacksmith | Santa Barbara | Santa Barbara Co | Santa Barbara. |
| Elizalde, J J | Clerk | State st | Garden st | Santa Barbara. |
| Elizalde, Francisco | Laborer | Santa Barbara Co | Santa Barbara | Santa Barbara. |
| Elizalde, Marcus A | Ranchero | Santa Barbara Co | La Laguna | |
| Elizalde, Jose de J | Stock raiser | Santa Barbara Co | Santa Barbara | Santa Barbara. |
| Ellis, N | Gen merchandise | State st | State st | Santa Barbara. |

# M. W. CHILDS,

—— IMPORTER AND DEALER IN ——

# STOVES, RANGES,

## Hardware, Agricultural Implements,

FORCE and LIFT PUMPS, RUBBER HOSE, CROCKERY, GLASSWARE, IRON and LEAD PIPE, FARMING and MINING TOOLS, HOUSEKEEPING GOODS, HYDRAULIC RAMS, etc.

Manufacturer of all kinds of

Tin, Copper, Sheet Iron Ware,

—— AND ——

ARTESIAN WELL PIPE.

—— SOLE AGENT FOR THE ——

## Celebrated Richmond & Richmond Double Oven Palace Ranges

COPPER RESERVOIRS can be attached to these Ranges to heat water for Bath Rooms, Wash Trays, &c. Hundreds of them have been sold by us, in this and adjoining towns, and have given entire satisfaction.

We are also Sole Agents for the NORMAN RANGE and EMPIRE CITY STOVES.

### PLUMBING & GASFITTING A SPECIALTY

None but first-class workmen employed, and satisfaction guaranteed. All sizes Gas and Water Pipe for sale and laid, if desired, in the best manner. All orders promptly attended to. Remember the place,

## No. 21 Los Angeles St., Los Angeles, Cal.

DIRECTORY OF SANTA BARBARA COUNTY. 119

| Name. | Occupation. | Place of Business. | Residence. | Town or P. O. |
|---|---|---|---|---|
| Ellis, John J......... | Farmer............. | Santa Barbara Co.... | Montecito............ | |
| Emerson, Jordan R | Farmer.............. | Carpenteria .......... | Santa Barbara Co.... | Carpenteria. |
| Emes, Jonathan W | Doctor ..... ..... | Santa Barbara Co.... | Santa Barbara......... | Santa Barbara. |
| Emigh, Henry....... | Cabinet maker.... | Haley st............... | Santa Barbara....... | Santa Barbara. |
| Emile, — ........... | Cook................ | State st............... | State st............... | Santa Barbara. |
| Engels, Fredk P..... | Saloon.............. | Guadalupe st......... | Olivera st.............. | Guadalupe. |
| Erfurt, Julius........ | Bookkeeper........ | State st............... | Haley st............... | Santa Barbara. |
| Esperon, D.......... | Bakery.... ........ | State st............... | State st............... | Santa Barbara. |
| Espinosa, Jose....... | Laborer............. | Santa Ynez........... | 10 m N E Las Cruces | Santa Ynez. |
| Espinosa, Joaquin A | Vaquero... ......... | Montecito............. | Santa Barbara Co.... | |
| Espinosa, Francisco | Laborer............. | La Laguna............ | Santa Barbara Co.... | |
| Espinosa, Jose G.... | Vaquero............. | Santa Barbara Co.... | La Laguna............. | |
| Espinosa, Gasper.... | Laborer............. | Santa Barbara........ | Santa Barbara Co.... | Santa Barbara. |
| Espinosa, Jose Ramon...... | Laborer ..... ......... | Santa Barbara Co.... | Santa Barbara........ | Santa Barbara. |
| Espinosa, Jose del C | Laborer............. | Santa Barbara........ | Santa Barbara Co.... | Santa Barbara. |
| Estorga, S............ | Butcher.............. | Carpenteria Valley... | Carpenteria ........... | Carpenteria. |
| Estrada, Jose A..... | Ranchero........... | Santa Barbara........ | Santa Barbara Co.... | Santa Barbara. |
| Estrada, Manuel..... | Laborer............. | Santa Barbara........ | Santa Barbara Co.... | Santa Barbara. |
| Estrade, Jose A.. ... | Ranchero .......... | Santa Barbara........ | Santa Barbara Co.... | Santa Barbara. |
| Estudillo, Jose V... | Farmer ............. | 3d Township......... | Santa Barbara Co.... | |
| Estudillo, Lewis..... | Farmer ............. | Santa Barbara Co.... | Los Alamos........... | |
| Estudillo, Jose Ramon...... | Farmer ............. | Santa Barbara Co.... | Santa Maria......... | Santa Maria. |
| Etchas, Martin...... | Merchant .......... | Santa Barbara........ | Santa Barbara Co.... | Santa Barbara. |
| Evain, Lewis......... | Laborer ... ........ | Santa Barbara........ | Santa Barbara Co.... | Santa Barbara. |
| Evans, John Emmet..... | Laborer............. | Santa Barbara Co..... | 1st Township......... | |
| Evans, Samuel...... | Blacksmith.......... | Santa Barbara........ | Santa Barbara Co.... | Santa Barbara. |
| Evans, A............. | Waiter............... | State st............... | Anacapa st............ | Santa Barbara. |
| Everett, Hiram..... | Farmer ............. | Santa Barbara Co.... | 2d Precinct............ | |
| Everett, Oratus...... | Farmer ............. | Santa Barbara ....... | Santa Barbara Co..... | Santa Barbara. |
| Ewery, Wm J...... | Ranchero .......... | 1st Township......... | Santa Barbara Co..... | |
| Faber, George....... | Farmer ............. | Santa Barbara Co.... | Arroyo Burro......... | |
| Fairbanks, Mrs A... | | | Chapala st............ | Santa Barbara. |
| Fairbanks, John C.. | Seaman.............. | Santa Barbara........ | Santa Barbara Co.... | Santa Barbara. |
| Farris, William R | Sheep raiser........ | Cañada................ | Santa Barbara Co.... | |
| Farrell, James....... | Laborer............. | Santa Barbara Co..... | 1st Township......... | |
| Faulkner, Jacob H. | Farmer ............. | Santa Barbara Co.... | Gutierrez st ........... | Santa Barbara. |
| Fawcett & O'Brien | Attorneys at law.. | State st............... | Santa Barbara........ | Santa Barbara. |
| Fawcett, Eugene... | Attorney............ | State st............... | Garden st............. | Santa Barbara. |
| Fuker, Nicholas..... | Blacksmith......... | 1st Township ........ | Santa Barbara Co.... | |
| Feliz, Jose........... | Laborer............. | Santa Barbara........ | Santa Barbara Co.... | Santa Barbara. |
| Feliz, Martin........ | Laborer............. | Santa Barbara Co.... | Santa Barbara........ | Santa Barbara. |
| Feliz, Jose H....... | Ranchero .......... | Santa Barbara Co.... | Los Alamos........... | |
| Feliz, Dolores........ | Laborer............. | Santa Barbara Co.... | 3d Township.......... | |
| Fellows, Richard.... | Laborer ............ | Santa Barbara........ | Santa Barbara Co.... | Santa Barbara. |
| Fender, Eli.......... | Laborer............. | Santa Barbara ....... | Santa Barbara........ | Santa Barbara. |
| Ferguson, George... | Stage driver........ | Santa Barbara ....... | Santa Barbara Co.... | Santa Barbara. |
| Ferl, F W........... | Carpenter........... | Santa Barbara Co... | Santa Barbara........ | Santa Barbara. |
| Fernald & Richards | Attorneys at law.. | State st............... | Santa Barbara........ | Santa Barbara. |
| Fernald, Chas....... | Attorney at law... | State st............... | Santa Barbara st..... | Santa Barbara. |
| Ferris, David........ | Clerk................ | Main st, Guadalupe. | Main st, Guadalupe.. | Guadalupe. |
| Farrier, George...... | Farmer ............. | Santa Barbara ....... | Santa Barbara Co.... | Santa Barbara. |
| Ferran, Patrick...... | Laborer ... ....... | | Santa Barbara Co.... | Santa Barbara. |
| Fesler, James K..... | Farmer ............. | Santa Barbara Co.... | Santa Maria........... | Santa Maria. |
| Fesler, Isaac ........ | Farmer ............. | Santa Barbara Co.... | 3d Township.......... | |
| Field, Edwin.. ..... | Watchmaker....... | State st............... | Santa Barbara st...... | Santa Barbara. |
| Flugger, Harvey... | Druggist............ | State st............... | State st............... | Santa Barbara. |
| Finny, Samuel...... | Farmer ............. | | Santa Barbara Co.... | Santa Barbara. |
| Fisher, I K......... | Butcher............. | State st............... | Laguna st............. | Santa Barbara. |
| Fish, Henry........ | Farmer ............. | Carpenteria Valley... | 1½ m E Carpenteria.. | Carpenteria. |
| Fish, Chas........... | Farmer ............. | Carpenteria Valley... | 1½ m E Carpenteria.. | Carpenteria. |
| Flake, John.......... | Miller...... ........ | Guadalupe............ | Guadalupe st......... | Guadalupe. |

## A. W. FROOM & CO.,
STATE STREET, Santa Barbara,

Keep the largest stock of

### Books, Stationery, Toys,
NOTIONS, and

## MUSICAL INSTRUMENTS!
To be found in the City.

Also, Black Walnut, Rosewood and Bronzed PICTURE FRAMES.

**STEREOSCOPIC VIEWS OF SANTA BARBARA.**

PIANOS or ORGANS sold on the INSTALLMENT PLAN, or Rented. Also, agents for the Celebrated

**GROVER & BAKER SEWING MACHINES**

Picture Frames made to order. Currency taken at par.

☞ Remember the place, sign of the Big Book, *Press* building, State street, Santa Barbara.

---

## S. T. TILLEY'S
## Book Store!
—AND—
## NEWS DEPOT,
STATE STREET, SANTA BARBARA.

I keep constantly on hand a large assortment of

Miscellaneous Books, | Pocket-Knives,
School Books, | Chromos,
Toy Books, | Picture Frames,
Blank Books, | Tissue Papers,
Pocket-Books, | Card Board,
Initial Stationary, | Drawing Paper,
Gold Pens, | Copy Books,
Stereoscopes, | Blank Notes,
Stereoscopic Views, | Drafts and Receipts,
Etc., Etc.

**STATIONERY.**

Any Book not in the store can be ordered. Books sold at catalogue prices in gold.
☞ Subscriptions received for the San Francisco Daily and Weekly papers, at publishers' rates.
☞ Papers and Magazines from all parts of the Eastern States.

---

# PIONEER HOTEL!
Julian, San Diego Co., Cal.,

## A. B. McKEAN
~~PROPRIETOR.~~

The above Hotel furnishes the best accomodations for travelers and tourists.

**Apartments Comfortably & Neatly Furnished**

TABLE WELL AND ABUNDANTLY SUPPLIED.

---

POST OFFICE

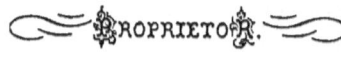
Book Store
—AND—
## NEWS DEPOT,
JOHN DUNBAR, Proprietor,
GUADALUPE, CAL.

School Books, Blank Books,
Composition Books,
Note and Letter Paper,
Foolscap, Legal Cap,
Bill Paper,
Violin and Guitar Strings,
Pocket Knives and Cutlery,
Confectionery, Toys, Etc.

### A CIRCULATING LIBRARY

Of Standard Authors is connected with the Bookstore. Agency for most of the California and Eastern Publications.
☞ Books in any language supplied on short notice.

## DIRECTORY OF SANTA BARBARA COUNTY.

| Name. | Occupation. | Place of Business. | Residence. | Town or P. O. |
|---|---|---|---|---|
| Flaying, Daniel..... | Blacksmith ........ | Santa Barbara Co..... | Santa Barbara.......... | Santa Barbara. |
| Flaying, Andrew... | Blacksmith.......... | Los Alamos............. | Santa Barbara Co.... | |
| Fletcher, Nathan, Jr | Farmer .............. | Santa Barbara.......... | Santa Barbara Co.... | Santa Barbara. |
| Flint, L. ...... ...... | Carpenter........... | Santa Barbara.......... | Gutierrez st ............ | Santa Barbara. |
| Flinn, James.......... | Laborer.............. | Santa Barbara.......... | Santa Barbara Co.... | Santa Barbara. |
| Fletcher, Nathan, Sr....... | Farmer .... ........... | Santa Barbara Co..... | Santa Barbara.......... | Santa Barbara. |
| Fletcher, Sam W... | Hotel keeper ...... | | Santa Barbara Co.... | |
| Flores, Juan.......... | Laborer............. | Santa Barbara Co..... | Santa Maria............. | Santa Maria. |
| Flores, Anastacio... | Laborer.............. | Santa Barbara.......... | Santa Barbara Co.... | Santa Maria. |
| Flores, F M.......... | Laborer.............. | Santa Barbara Co..... | La Patera................ | |
| Flores, William.... | Farmer .............. | Sespe ................... | Santa Barbara Co.... | |
| Fluche, A............. | Merchant tailor... | State st................. | Ortega st................ | Santa Barbara. |
| Flying, D............. | Blacksmith......... | Santa Barbara......... | Cota st................... | Santa Barbara. |
| Flynn, James........ | Brick maker...... | Gutierrez st........... | Guiterrez st............. | Santa Barbara. |
| Forbush, R........... | Furniture store... | State st................. | State st.................. | Santa Barbara. |
| Forbes, John......... | Drayman .......... | Santa Barbara......... | Castle st................. | Santa Barbara. |
| Ford, John Phillip | Farmer .............. | Los Alamos............. | Santa Barbara Co.... | |
| Formby, James R... | Farmer .............. | Pleasant Valley........ | Santa Barbara Co.... | |
| Formby, Andrew J | Farmer .............. | 1st Township........... | Santa Barbara Co.... | |
| Forney, S............. | Surveyor ........... | Carpenteria ........... | Santa Barbara Co.... | Carpenteria. |
| Forsythe, P G........ | Blacksmith......... | Rich Hunt............. | Garden st................ | Santa Barbara. |
| Forsythe, George W | Gen merchandise | La Graciosa............ | | La Graciosa. |
| Foster, Malcom...... | Farmer .............. | Santa Marcus Ranch | 4 m S E Santa Ynez. | Santa Ynez. |
| Foster, Eugene P... | Farmer.............. | La Patera............... | Santa Barbara Co .... | |
| Foster, Isaac G..... | Farmer .............. | Santa Barbara Co.... | La Patera................ | |
| Foster, W E.......... | Farmer .............. | Santa Barbara Co.... | Montecito................ | |
| Foster, Marion S.... | Teamster............ | Santa Ynez............. | Santa Barbara Co.... | Ballard's Statn. |
| Foxen, G J J....... | Ranchero .......... | Santa Barbara Co.... | Tenaquai................. | |
| Foxen, A J John... | Ranchero .......... | Santa Barbara Co.... | Tenaquai................. | |
| Foxen, Reyes........ | Laborer ............. | Montecito.............. | Santa Barbara Co.... | |
| Foxen, R F........... | Ranchero .......... | Foxon's Ranch....... | Santa Barbara Co.... | |
| Foxen, Thomas F... | Farmer.... .......... | 3d Township .......... | Santa Barbara Co.... | |
| Francis, W M....... | Attorney at law... | State st................. | Santa Barbara......... | Santa Barbara. |
| France, T............. | Farmer .............. | | Santa Barbara st...... | Santa Barbara. |
| Franklin, M.......... | Farmer .............. | Carpenteria Valley... | 1¾ m E Carpenteria. | Carpenteria. |
| Franklin, Jessie..... | Farmer.............. | Carpenteria Valley... | 1¾ m E Carpenteria.. | Carpenteria. |
| Franklin, Richd G.. | Farmer.............. | Carpenteria Valley... | 2 m E Carpenteria... | Carpenteria. |
| Franklin, James H. | Farmer.............. | Santa Barbara Co.... | Carpenteria............ | Carpenteria. |
| Franklin, W A...... | Farmer .............. | Santa Barbara......... | Santa Barbara Co.... | Santa Barbara. |
| Freeman, Chas J.... | Doctor ....... ...... | Santa Barbara......... | Santa Barbara Co.... | Santa Barbara. |
| Freeton, Thomas W | Lawyer.............. | Santa Barbara Co.... | Santa Barbara Co.... | Santa Barbara. |
| French, Charles Lee | Farmer .............. | Santa Barbara Co.... | 1st Precinct... ......... | |
| Frisius & Heinster. | Liquor dealers..... | State st................ | Santa Barbara......... | Santa Barbara. |
| Frisius, A............. | Liquor dealer...... | State st................ | State and Cota sts.... | Santa Barbara. |
| Frisius, P............. | Clerk ................ | State st................. | State st.................. | Santa Barbara. |
| Frisius, John F C A | Merchant .......... | Santa Barbara Co.... | San Jose................. | |
| Fromby, M L........ | Farmer .............. | Santa Barbara Co.... | Pleasant Valley........ | |
| Froom, A W & Co.. | Books&stationery | State st................. | Santa Barbara......... | Santa Barbara. |
| Frost, F W........... | Gen merchandise. | State st................ | De la Vina st.......... | Santa Barbara. |
| Frowzer, J............ | Grainer & marbl'r | Montecito st........... | Montecito st............ | Santa Barbara. |
| Frye, Alfred ........ | Farmer .............. | Santa Barbara Co.... | Carpenteria ........... | Carpenteria. |
| Fugler, Francis...... | Farmer .............. | Santa Maria............ | Santa Barbara Co..... | Santa Maria. |
| Furlong, Mathew W | Seaman.............. | Santa Barbara......... | Santa Barbara Co.,... | Santa Barbara. |
| Furst, Benj F....... | Farmer .............. | Santa Barbara Co.... | 1st Township.... ..... | |
| Furst, Martin I..... | Merchant .......... | Santa Barbara......... | Santa Barbara......... | Santa Barbara. |
| Gabelda, Samuel.... | Laborer............. | Santa Barbara Co.... | Santa Barbara Co.... | Santa Barbara. |
| Gaffney, James...... | Laborer............. | Santa Barbara......... | Santa Barbara Co.... | Santa Barbara. |
| Gallardo, F F....... | Lawyer............. | Santa Barbara......... | Santa Barbara Co..... | Santa Barbara. |
| Gambel, Isaac....... | Farmer .............. | Santa Maria............ | Santa Barbara Co.... | Santa Maria. |
| Games, Antonio .... | Mason ............... | Santa Barbara Co.... | Santa Barbara......... | Santa Barbara. |
| Gann, W Andrew .. | Carpenter .......... | Santa Barbara......... | Santa Barbara Co..... | Santa Barbara. |
| Ganong, Henry...... | Carpenter........... | Santa Barbara......... | Rosa st.................. | Santa Barbara. |
| Garcia, Jose A ...... | Laborer............. | Santa Barbara......... | Santa Barbara Co.... | Santa Barbara. |

## PIONEER BLACKSMITH SHOP,

FRED BODEN, - Proprietor,

**TEHICHIPA,**
KERN COUNTY, - CAL.

### Blacksmithing, Wagon Work

And general Repairing done with

Neatness, Durability and Dispatch.

## HORSE - SHOEING
A SPECIALTY.

## TAYLOR & GLENN,
**BLACKSMITHS**
—AND—

### WAGON MANUFACTURERS
TEHICHIPA, KERN CO., CAL.

Horse-Shoeing, Iron and Wood Work of all kinds.
Dispatch is used in the performance of Job Work, and all work is guaranteed to be of a superior quality.

## Grand Hotel Saloon
### MAIN ST.
TEHICHIPA, KERN COUNTY, CAL.

JOHN A. DURNAL, - Propr.

None sold but the Best of

### Wines, Liquors and Cigars.

D. D. BAILEY.    L. B. REDMAN.

## BAILEY & REDMAN,
—PROPRIETORS OF—

### JULIAN
### Livery, Feed and Sale Stable

65 MILES N. E. SAN DIEGO, CAL.

Teams, single and double, Buggies and Carriages, and Saddle Horses always on hand and let at lowest rates.
Tourists conveyed to the Agua Calienta Hot Springs, in quick time and at small cost.
A large corral in connection with the stable. Good Pasturage in abundance.

**DAILY STAGE TO BANNER.**

DIRECTORY OF SANTA BARBARA COUNTY. 123

| NAME. | OCCUPATION. | PLACE OF BUSINESS. | RESIDENCE. | TOWN OR P. O. |
|---|---|---|---|---|
| Garcia, Avalina | Laborer | Las Cruces | Las Cruces | Las Cruces. |
| Garcia, Jose D | Laborer | Santa Barbara | Santa Barbara Co | Santa Barbara. |
| Garcia, Manuel | Laborer | Montecito | Santa Barbara Co | |
| Garcia, Pedro | Laborer | Santa Barbara Co | Santa Barbara | Santa Barbara. |
| Garcia, Vicente | Laborer | Santa Barbara | Santa Barbara Co | Santa Barbara. |
| Garcia, Liberato | Laborer | Santa Barbara Co | Santa Barbara | Santa Barbara. |
| Garcia, Curtiss M. | Laborer | Santa Barbara Co | Santa Barbara | Santa Barbara. |
| Garcia, Tomas | Laborer | Santa Barbara Co | | |
| Garcia, Jose | Saloon keeper | Santa Barbara Co | Santa Barbara | Santa Barbara. |
| Garcia, Jesus | Laborer | Simi | Santa Barbara Co | |
| Garcia, Jose M | Laborer | Santa Barbara | Santa Barbara Co | Santa Barbara. |
| Garcia, Manuel F. | Laborer | Carpenteria | Santa Barbara Co | Carpenteria. |
| Garland, Addison | Trader | Montecito Valley | Anapamu st | Santa Barbara. |
| Gardiner, Randolph | Farmer | Santa Barbara Co | 1st Township | |
| Garner, Willis S | Farmer | Santa Barbara Co | Pleasant Valley | |
| Garrett, Robert | Carpenter | Santa Barbara Co | Santa Barbara | Santa Barbara. |
| Gay, G A | Saloon keeper | Santa Barbara | Santa Barbara Co | Santa Barbara. |
| Gaylord, Saml W. | Druggist | Santa Barbara Co | Santa Barbara | Santa Barbara. |
| Gaylord, Geo S W. | Farmer | Santa Barbara Co | Santa Barbara | Santa Barbara. |
| Gedney, James E | Carpenter | Santa Barbara Co | Santa Barbara | Santa Barbara. |
| Gening, Henry W. | Farmer | Santa Barbara | Santa Barbara Co | Santa Barbara. |
| Gerard, Emile | Laborer | Santa Barbara Co | Santa Barbara | Santa Barbara. |
| German, C | Ranchero | Las Cruces | Santa Barbara Co | Las Cruces. |
| German, B | Ranchero | Las Cruces | Santa Barbara Co | Las Cruces. |
| German, Manuel | Laborer | Santa Barbara | Santa Barbara Co | Santa Barbara. |
| Gettings, Saml A | Farmer | Santa Barbara Co | 1st Township | |
| Gibson, John | Blacksmith | 1st Township | Santa Barbara Co | |
| Giddings, Mrs | | | Garden st | Santa Barbara. |
| Gilbert, David W. | Farmer | 1st Township | Santa Barbara Co | |
| Gilchrist, Chas | Carpenter | Santa Barbara | Haley st | Santa Barbara. |
| Gilchrist, I N | Carpenter | Santa Barbara | Anapamu st | Santa Barbara. |
| Giles, Frank | Farmer | Carpenteria | 1½ m N Carpenteria. | Carpenteria. |
| Giltner, Michael | Farmer | Santa Maria | Santa Barbara Co | Santa Maria. |
| Gleason, Henry | Clerk and agent | Guadalupe st | Guadalupe st | Guadalupe. |
| Godfrey, R | Laborer | Carpenteria | Carpenteria | Carpenteria. |
| Goland, George | Laborer | Santa Barbara | Rancheria st | Santa Barbara. |
| Goland, John | Agt sew machine | Santa Barbara | Bath st | Santa Barbara. |
| Gonzales, A | Miner | Santa Barbara | Santa Barbara Co | Santa Barbara. |
| Gonzales, Henrique | Mechanic | Santa Barbara Co | Santa Barbara | Santa Barbara. |
| Gonzales, Felipe | Musician | Santa Barbara | Santa Barbara Co | Santa Barbara. |
| Gonzales, Ramon | Ranchero | Santa Barbara Co | Santa Barbara | Santa Barbara. |
| Goodfellow, C | Carpenter | Guadalupe st | Guadalupe st | Guadalupe. |
| Gordon, David A | Printer | Santa Barbara Co | Santa Barbara | Santa Barbara. |
| Gormley, Thos | Stock raiser | Guadalupe Ranch | 3 m S Guadalupe | Guadalupe. |
| Goss, W F M | Boots and shoes | State st | 9½ m N Santa Barb | Santa Barbara. |
| Gourley, E T | Clerk | Stearn's Lumber Y'd | Anacapa st | Santa Barbara. |
| Goux, A G | Grocer | Haley st | State st | Santa Barbara. |
| Goux, John Emilio | Merchant | Santa Barbara Co | Santa Barbara | Santa Barbara. |
| Goux, J E | Liquor dealer | State st | State st | Santa Barbara. |
| Graham, Saml C | Teacher | Santa Barbara Co | Santa Maria | Santa Maria. |
| Graham, Charles | Laborer | Santa Barbara | Gutierrez st | Santa Barbara. |
| Graham, — | Pastor | Presbyterian Church | State st | Santa Barbara. |
| Graham, Chas | Teamster | Santa Barbara | Anacapa st | Santa Barbara. |
| Gratiot, Chas C | Carpenter | Santa Barbara | Haley st | Santa Barbara. |
| Gray, Clarence | Teacher | Santa Barbara Co | Santa Maria | Santa Maria. |
| Gray, Nicholas, Jr. | Farmer | Santa Barbara Co | Santa Maria | Santa Maria. |
| Green, John A | Plumber | Cota st | Santa Barbara | Santa Barbara. |
| Green, Henry Bell | Farmer | Santa Barbara Co | 2d Precinct | |
| Green, John Pugh. | Lawyer | Santa Barbara Co | 1st Township | |
| Greenwell, W E | Engineer | Santa Barbara Co | Santa Barbara | Santa Barbara. |
| Green, Chas Henry | Laborer | Santa Maria | Santa Barbara Co | Santa Maria. |
| Green, John W | Farmer | 3d Township | Santa Barbara Co | |
| Greenwell, W E | U S surveyor | Bath st | Montecito st | Santa Barbara. |

N. D. SMITH.                                      F. SMITH.

# N. D. & F. SMITH,

PROPRIETORS OF

## CARPINTERIA WHARF

*Santa Barbara Co., Cal.*

Good Deep Water Berths.          Landing Safe in Heaviest Weather.

---

ALSO, DEALERS IN

## LUMBER, DOORS

BLINDS, MOULDINGS, BRACKETS,

## CORD and STOVE WOOD

ETC., ETC.

## DIRECTORY OF SANTA BARBARA COUNTY.

| NAME. | OCCUPATION. | PLACE OF BUSINESS. | RESIDENCE. | TOWN OR P. O. |
|---|---|---|---|---|
| Green, Mrs Mary... | | | Santa Barbara st...... | Santa Barbara. |
| Green, H H.......... | Blacksmith ........ | Montecito Valley..... | 4 m N E S Barbara.. | Santa Barbara. |
| Grey, R H............ | Gardener........... | Santa Barbara......... | Bath st................. | Santa Barbara. |
| Groin, John......... | Carriage maker... | Santa Barbara Co..... | Anacapa st............. | Santa Barbara. |
| Grubb, Martin....... | Cigar maker ...... | | Carpenteria............. | Carpenteria. |
| Grunig, Henry...... | Carpenter.......... | Montecito st............ | Montecito st........... | Santa Barbara. |
| Guerasa, Jose........ | Laborer............. | Santa Barbara......... | Santa Barbara Co.... | Santa Barbara. |
| Guerrara, Francisco | Vaquero ............ | Las Cruces............. | Santa Barbara Co.... | Las Cruces. |
| Guerra, Alex de la.. | Ranchero .......... | Santa Barbara Co.... | Los Alamos............ | |
| Guerara, Camilo ... | Laborer............. | Santa Barbara Co..... | Santa Barbara ... .... | Santa Barbara. |
| Guerra, A M de la. | Notary public..... | Santa Barbara......... | Santa Barbara......... | Santa Barbara. |
| Guerra, Miguel de la | Ranchero........... | Santa Barbara Co.... | Santa Barbara......... | Santa Barbara. |
| Guerra, F J de la... | Ranchero .......... | Santa Barbara......... | Santa Barbara Co.... | Santa Barbara. |
| Guerra, Juan J de la | Teacher............. | Santa Barbara Co..... | Santa Barbara......... | Santa Barbara. |
| Guerra, Jose A de la | Ranchero........... | Los Alamos............ | Santa Barbara Co.... | |
| Guerra, G de la..... | Ranchero........... | | Santa Barbara Co.... | |
| Guerra, F T de la... | Ranchero .......... | Santa Barbara Co.... | Santa Barbara......... | Santa Barbara. |
| Guerra, Pablo de la | Dist judge......... | Santa Barbara......... | Santa Barbara Co.... | Santa Barbara. |
| Guinard, B.......... | Watch maker..... | State st................ | 110 State st............ | Santa Barbara. |
| Gunterman, Henry.. | Carpenter.......... | Santa Barbara........ | Anacapa st............. | Santa Barbara. |
| Guthrie, Richd ..... | Liquors............. | Guadalupe st.......... | Guadalupe st.......... | Guadalupe. |
| Gutierrez, L R...... | Clerk................ | State st................ | | Santa Barbara. |
| Gutierrez, B......... | Druggist........... | State st................ | Utah and Ortega sts. | Santa Barbara. |
| Gutierrez, A......... | Gardener........... | Santa Barbara......... | Gutierrez st........... | Santa Barbara. |
| Gutierrez, O, Jr .... | Ranchero........... | Santa Barbara......... | Santa Barbara Co.... | Santa Barbara. |
| Gutierrez, Jose ..... | Ranchero........... | Santa Barbara Co..... | San Barbara........... | Santa Barbara. |
| Gutierrez, Miguel. | Saloon keeper..... | Santa Barbara Co..... | Santa Barbara......... | Santa Barbara. |
| Gutierrez, A M...... | Ranchero .......... | La Laguna............. | Santa Barbara Co.... | |
| Gutierrez, Miguel... | Laborer............. | Santa Barbara......... | Santa Barbara Co..... | Santa Barbara. |
| Gutierrez, Beuiguo | Druggist........... | Santa Barbara......... | Santa Barbara Co.... | Santa Barbara. |
| Gutierrez, F N ..... | Translator ........ | Santa Barbara........ | Santa Barbara Co.... | Santa Barbara. |
| Gutierrez, Luis J... | Clerk ............... | Santa Barbara........ | Santa Barbara Co.... | Santa Barbara. |
| Hadley, Stephen.... | Teamster .......... | Point Sal ............. | 10 m W Guadalupe.. | Guadalupe. |
| Haese, Wm A....... | Tailor ............... | State st................ | Carrillo st............. | Santa Barbara. |
| Haese, Chas A...... | Tailor ............... | State st................ | Carrillo st............. | Santa Barbara. |
| Haines, J H.......... | W U tel operator | Guadalupe st.......... | Guadalupe st.......... | Guadalupe. |
| Hails, R.............. | Merchant tailor... | | Bath st ................ | Santa Barbara. |
| Hall, J C............. | Clerk ............... | State st................ | Garden & Victoria sts | Santa Barbara. |
| Halloway, Cyrus.... | Carpenter ......... | Santa Barbara........ | Santa Barbara Co..... | Santa Barbara. |
| Hall, Reuben R..... | Dairyman.......... | Ojai Rancho.......... | Santa Barbara Co.... | |
| Ham, James.......... | Laborer ............ | Santa Barbara Co..... | Santa Barbara......... | Santa Barbara. |
| Hames, Joseph C... | Farmer ............. | Santa Barbara Co..... | Santa Barbara......... | Santa Barbara. |
| Hamer, Mrs M F.. | Millinery store.... | State st................ | Mission st............. | Santa Barbara. |
| Hamilton, A S...... | Bee raiser.......... | Montecito Valley.... | 3½ m N S Barbara... | Santa Barbara. |
| Hamilton, Wm...... | Ranchero .......... | Carpenteria......... ....... | Santa Barbara Co.... | Carpenteria. |
| Hamilton, J P....... | | Santa Barbara........ | Haley st .............. | Santa Barbara. |
| Hamilton, J W...... | Butcher............. | State st................ | Haley st .............. | Santa Barbara. |
| Hammell & Adams | Real estate........ | State st................ | Santa Barbara........ | Santa Barbara. |
| Hammell, James... | Real estate........ | State st................ | Haley st .............. | Santa Barbara. |
| Hampton, William | Laborer ............ | Santa Barbara Co..... | Santa Barbara......... | Santa Barbara. |
| Hanford, Jesse...... | Farmer............. | Santa Barbara........ | Haley st .............. | Santa Barbara. |
| Hanson, Jesse G.... | Dairyman ......... | Santa Barbara Co..... | Las Cruces............ | Las Cruces. |
| Hanover, S.......... | Variety store...... | State st................ | State st................ | Santa Barbara. |
| Hardiss, John A..... | Farmer............. | Santa Barbara Co.... | La Patera............. | |
| Hargan, Geo W..... | Farmer ............. | La Patera............. | Santa Barbara Co.... | |
| Harkness, Fredk & Co...... | Grocery store...... | State st................ | State st................ | Santa Barbara. |
| Harkness, L........ | Clerk................ | State st................ | State st...... .......... | Santa Barbara. |
| Harlow, John D..... | Mariner............. | La Patera............. | Santa Barbara Co.... | |
| Harmon, Silas S.... | Teacher............. | Santa Barbara Co..... | Santa Barbara ....... | Santa Barbara. |
| Harmon, S H....... | Lumber dealer.... | San Francisco........ | | San Francisco. |
| Harris, Amos........ | | | Cota st................ | Santa Barbara. |
| Harris, James Hanby... | Farmer ............. | Santa Barbara Co..... | Cincquitas............ ...... | |

## Santa Barbara
# Hot Sulphur Springs.

This famous SANITARIUM, and celebrated HEALTH and PLEASURE RESORT, is six miles from Santa Barbara, in the mountains, at an altitude of 1450 feet above tide-water; affording one of the grandest views in the world, especially from POINT LOOK OUT, near the Springs, overlooking the city of Santa Barbara, Carpenteria, Montecito, and the beautiful Valley beneath. The grand old Pacific, with her islands, and the shipping lie before you. But greater by far is the value of these waters to health! Here are twenty-two Springs, spouting forth their waters from the rocks, varying in temperature from 60° to 122°. Chemists from all parts of the world have examined them, and unite in pronouncing them of a superior and unrivaled medicinal character. Some of the most wonderful cures on record have here been performed simply by their use.

Invalids, Tourists and Pleasure-seekers should visit them. Good accommodations and all city comforts offered.

Board, including Steam and Hot Water Baths, $2 50 to $3 00 per day.
*A Daily Four-Horse Stage runs to and from Santa Barbara, from Wells, Fargo's Express Office. Fare $1.00 each way; Ely Rundell, Agent.*

**WILBUR CURTISS,** = = **Proprietor.**

DIRECTORY OF SANTA BARBARA COUNTY. 127

| NAME. | OCCUPATION. | PLACE OF BUSINESS. | RESIDENCE. | TOWN OR P. O. |
|---|---|---|---|---|
| Harris, John M...... | Farmer............ | Santa Barbara Co..... | Santa Maria............ | Santa Maria. |
| Harris, Henry T..... | Farmer............ | Santa Barbara Co..... | 1st Township........... | |
| Harron, Daniel...... | Farmer............ | Santa Barbara Co..... | Santa Barbara.......... | Santa Barbara. |
| Harrington, John W | Mariner............ | Santa Barbara Co..... | Santa Barbara.......... | Santa Barbara. |
| Harrison, Phares... | Minister........... | Cañada................... | Santa Barbara Co..... | |
| Harris, B............. | Gen merchandise. | State st................. | State st.................. | Santa Barbara. |
| Harris, H H......... | Barber............. | Guadalupe st........... | Guadalupe st........... | Guadalupe. |
| Harrington, Capt J W......... | Sea captain........ | Santa Barbara......... | Montecito st............ | Santa Barbara. |
| Harriman & Co..... | Lumber dealers... | Main st................. | Guadalupe.............. | Guadalupe. |
| Harriman, W S..... | Lumber dealer..... | Main st................. | Main st.................. | Guadalupe. |
| Hartshorn, E F..... | Miner............... | Santa Barbara Co..... | 1st Township........... | |
| Hartnell, G A....... | Ranchero ......... | Santa Barbara Co..... | Todos Santos........... | |
| Hartmann, J........ | Gen merchandise. | Main st................. | Olivera st................ | Guadalupe. |
| Hart, Thos.......... | Blacksmith........ | Guadalupe st........... | Olivera st................ | Guadalupe. |
| Hart, R.............. | Wagon maker....: | Guadalupe st........... | Olivera st................ | Guadalupe. |
| Hartman & Co, J.. | Genl merchandise | Guadalupe st........... | | Guadalupe. |
| Hartshorn, Frank... | Farmer............. | Carpenteria Valley... | 3½ m W Carpenteria | Carpenteria. |
| Hart, Thomas....... | Stone mason....... | Santa Barbara......... | Haley st.................. | Santa Barbara. |
| Hart, J V............ | Merchant tailor... | State st................. | Garden st................ | Santa Barbara. |
| Hartley, George S | Livery stable....... | State st................. | Gutierrez st............. | Santa Barbara. |
| Haskell, John W... | Laborer............. | Santa Barbara Co..... | Santa Barbara.......... | Santa Barbara. |
| Haskell, John...... | Teamster .......... | Santa Barbara......... | Vineyard st............. | Santa Barbara. |
| Hastings, — ....... | Architect........... | | Haley st.................. | Santa Barbara. |
| Hathaway, D F..... | Laborer............. | Santa Barbara Co..... | Santa Barbara.......... | Santa Barbara. |
| Hathaway, S R..... | Farmer............. | La Patera.............. | Santa Barbara Co..... | |
| Havens, Frances D | Farmer............. | Santa Barbara Co..... | Santa Barbara.......... | Santa Barbara. |
| Haverly, Wm J..... | Farmer............. | Santa Barbara......... | Milpas st................ | Santa Barbara. |
| Hawkins, — ....... | Engineer ........... | Chapala st............. | Haley st.................. | Santa Barbara. |
| Hawkins, Wm...... | Expressman....... | Santa Barbara......... | Nopal st................. | Santa Barbara. |
| Hawkes, John E... | Miller............... | Chapala st............. | Vineyard st............. | Santa Barbara. |
| Hawley, Mathew E | Carpenter.......... | Santa Barbara......... | Santa Barbara Co..... | Santa Barbara. |
| Hay, J D............. | Real estate ........ | Haley st................ | Sola st................... | Santa Barbara. |
| Hayman, Albert... | | | Haley st.................. | Santa Barbara. |
| Hayne, Chas........ | Teamster........... | Santa Barbara......... | Anacapa st.............. | Santa Barbara. |
| Haynes, John...... | Laborer............. | Point Sal.............. | 10 m S W Gaudalupe | Guadalupe. |
| Hayne, William O.. | Farmer............. | Montecito ............. | Santa Barbara Co..... | |
| Haynes, William W | Farmer............. | Santa Barbara Co..... | Montecito............... | |
| Hays, Jacob......... | Carpenter.......... | 1st Township......... | Santa Barbara Co..... | |
| Hayward&Muzzall | Photographers.... | State st................. | | Santa Barbara. |
| Hayward, E J...... | Photographer..... | State st................. | Bath st .................. | Santa Barbara. |
| Hayward, F......... | Lumber dealer... | San Francisco........ | | San Francisco. |
| Heacock, John C... | Farmer............. | Santa Barbara Co..... | Los Alamos............. | |
| Heacock, Josiah... | Clerk................ | State st................. | Ortega st................. | Santa Barbara. |
| Heath, Russell...... | Lawyer............. | Carpenteria ........... | Santa Barbara Co..... | Carpenteria. |
| Heath, Joseph I.... | Laborer............. | Santa Barbara......... | Santa Barbara.......... | Santa Barbara. |
| Hector, John, Jr.... | Farmer............. | Santa Barbara Co..... | 2d Precinct............. | |
| Hector, Wilson..... | Blacksmith........ | 2d Precinct............ | Santa Barbara Co..... | |
| Hector, John, Sr... | Blacksmith........ | Santa Barbara Co..... | 2d Precinct............. | |
| Hector, Zachary.... | Farmer............. | Santa Barbara Co..... | Santa Paula............. | |
| Hedrick, Joseph.... | Laborer............. | Santa Barbara Co..... | La Patera............... | |
| Hedrick, Geo P..... | Farmer............. | Santa Barbara........ | Santa Barbara Co..... | Santa Barbara. |
| Hedrick, David E.. | Farmer............. | Santa Barbara Co..... | Arroyo Burro.......... | |
| Hedrick, Chas...... | Clerk................ | Santa Barbara........ | Anacapa st.............. | Santa Barbara. |
| Hedrick, Mrs M L.. | | | Anacapa st.............. | Santa Barbara. |
| Hellmer, Geo........ | Miss'n water bath | State st................. | Ortega st................. | Santa Barbara. |
| Hellmer&Strecker | Miss'n water bath | State st................. | | Santa Barbara. |
| Hemenes, J......... | Farmer............. | Carpenteria ........... | Carpenteria ............ | Carpenteria. |
| Henderson, Milton.. | Farmer............. | Carpenteria Valley... | 4 m W Carpenteria. | Carpenteria. |
| Henley, Thomas.... | Farmer............. | Santa Barbara Co..... | Santa Maria............ | Santa Maria. |
| Henricks, F P....... | Farmer............. | Santa Maria........... | Santa Barbara Co..... | Santa Maria. |
| Heppner & Co...... | Merchant tailors.. | State st................. | Santa Barbara......... | Santa Barbara. |
| Heppner, J P........ | Merchant tailor... | State st................. | State st.................. | Santa Barbara. |
| Herdman, Robert... | Farmer............., | Montecito.............. | Santa Barbara Co..... | |

# J. A. RICH

# BLACKSMITH
## And General Iron Worker,

Canyon Perdido Street, near State.

**SANTA BARBARA, CAL.**

Particular Attention Paid to Horse and Mule Shoeing,

Family Carriages,

Rockaways,

**TOP AND OPEN BUGGIES,
LIGHT AND HEAVY EXPRESS WAGONS,**

Made of the best selected and thoroughly-seasoned Timber. Jobbing, Carriage Trimming, Painting and Blacksmithing neatly done.
Orders will receive prompt attention.

## DIRECTORY OF SANTA BARBARA COUNTY.

| NAME. | OCCUPATION. | PLACE OF BUSINESS. | RESIDENCE. |
|---|---|---|---|
| Hernandez, Olago de J....... | Farmer............. | Ojai Ranch ......... | Santa Barbara Co..... |
| Hernandez, Jose G.. | Farmer............ ........ | Santa Barbara........ | Santa Barbara Co..... |
| **Hernster, Geo**....... | Liquor dealer...... | State st............ | State and Cota sts..... |
| Hernandez, J........ | Farmer............. | Carpenteria .......... | Carpenteria ............ |
| Herrick, Alonzo..... | Farmer.. ............ | Santa Barbara Co..... | La Patera............ |
| Herting, F............ | Butcher............ ... | Guadalupe st....... | Guadalupe st........... |
| Hester, T R........... | Night watchman.. | Stearn's Wharf...... | Chapala st.......... |
| **Hester, Thos**......... | Painter............... | Santa Barbara........ | Chapala st....... ...... |
| Hewes, Geo........... | Bar tender......... | State st............ | Haley st................. |
| Hewlett, Frank M.. | Farmer............. | Santa Barbara Co..... | La Patera............. |
| Hickox, Seth Hart.. | Farmer............. | Santa Barbara Co..... | Montecito............ |
| **Hickok, Amos W**... | Carpenter .......... | Santa Barbara........ | Santa Barbara Co.... |
| Hicks, Thos H...... | Farmer............. | La Patera............ | Santa Barbara Co..... |
| Hickox, John Scott | Farmer............. | Montecito........... | Santa Barbara Co..... |
| Hicks, Beverly A... | Farmer............. | La Patera............ | Santa Barbara Co.... |
| Higby, Chas J........ | Farmer............. | La Patera............ | Santa Barbara Co.... |
| **Higgins, Leslie T**.. | Farmer............. | Santa Barbara........ | Santa Barbara Co.... |
| Higuera, Manuel.... | Laborer............. ...... | Santa Barbara........ | Santa Barbara Co.... |
| **Higuera, Ygnacio**.. | ............ | Santa Barbara........ | Santa Barbara Co..... |
| Higuerra, Reugio... | Carpenter............ | Santa Barbara........ | Santa Barbara Co..... |
| Higuera, Miguel..... | Laborer............. | Santa Barbara Co.... | Santa Barbara.......... |
| Hilgers, M............ | Porter............... | State st............ | State st..... ............. |
| **Hill, Dr**............. | Physician.. ......... | Ortega st................ | ............ ............... |
| Hill, Ensigne N.... | Laborer............ ...... | Tepequi............ | Santa Barbara Co.... |
| **Hill, Jesse**........... | Stock............... | Santa Barbara Co..... | Victoria st............ |
| Hill,Jesse Ramon M | Ranchero........... | Santa Barbara Co..... | La Patera............ |
| Hill, Mora Jose..... | Farmer............. | La Patera............ | Santa Barbara Co..... |
| Hill, Vicente........ | Ranchero .. ......... | La Patera............ | Santa Barbara Co..... |
| Hill, Daniel F....... | Farmer............. | La Patera............ | Santa Barbara Co..... |
| Hill, Hiram H....... | Blacksmith........ | La Patera............ | Santa Barbara Co..... |
| Hilton, Saml H..... | Farmer............. | Santa Barbara........ | Santa Barbara Co..... |
| **Hobbs, Samuel**...... | Farmer............. | Santa Barbara Co..... | Santa Maria............ |
| **Hoffman, S J**........ | Painter............... | Guadalupe st....... | Olivera st............ |
| **Hoit, Wm**........... | Real estate......... | State st............ | Mason st.............. |
| **Hoit, E M**........... | Notary public..... | State st............ | Mason st............... |
| **Hollister, W W**..... | Sheep raiser......... | Santa Barbara Co..... | Santa Barbara......... |
| Hollingshead, Daniel........ ...... | Miner............... | Santa Barbara Co..... | La Patera............ |
| Hollister, Edgar A.. | Farmer............. | Santa Barbara Co..... | La Patera............ |
| Hollister, Albert D. | Farmer............. | La Patera............ | Santa Barbara Co..... |
| **Holloway, John J**. | Stock raiser......... | Cañada Gato......... | ........... ............... |
| Holloway, Thos J... | Farmer............. | Cañada Gato.. ...... | ............ ............. |
| Holloway, Huester.. | Stock raiser......... | Cañada Gato......... | ............ ............. |
| **Holmes, Jacob T**.. | Farmer. ............ | Santa Barbara........ | Santa Barbara Co.... |
| Holmes, Jacob...... | Carpenter........... | Santa Barbara ........ | Victoria st............ |
| Holmberg, L A...... | Carpenter........... | Santa Barbara........ | Santa Barbara Co.... |
| **Holmes, Thos W**... | Farmer ............ | Los Alamos......... | Santa Barbara Co.... |
| Holser, John......... | Butcher............ | Santa Barbara........ | Santa Barbara Co.... |
| Home, Chas Henry | Mechanic........... | Las Cruces.......... | Santa Barbara Co.... |
| Hoolin, Thomas..... | Stage driver........ | Santa Barbara........ | Santa Barbara Co.... |
| **Hope, Thomas**...... | Ranchero ........... | Santa Barbara Co..... | Santa Barbara.......... |
| Hope, John........... | Carpenter........... | Santa Barbara........ | De la Guerra st........ |
| Hopper, John.. ...... | Farmer............. | Santa Maria......... | Santa Barbara Co.... |
| Hopper, John T..... | Farmer ............ | Santa Maria......... | Santa Barbara Co.... |
| Horn, Andrew....... | Stage driver........ | Santa'Barbara Co..... | Santa Barbara.......... |
| Horn, William....... | Butcher............ | 1st Township....... | Santa Barbara Co.... |
| **Hosmer, Richard N** | Merchant........... | Santa Barbara Co..... | Santa Barbara.......... |
| Hosmer, Thomas... | Mechanic .......... | Santa Barbara........ | Santa Barbara Co.... |
| Hough, Rev J W... | Pastor.............. | Cong Church....... | Anacapa st............ |
| **Houx, Octave**....... | Gen merchandise. | State st............ ......... | State st................ |
| Houx, F W.......... | Laborer.... ......... | Santa Barbara ........ | Vineyard st............ |
| Howard, Wm........ | Farmer............. | Carpenteria Valley... | 4½ m W Carpenteria |
| Howard, E A........ | Hostler............. | La Patera............. ...... | Santa Barbara Co.... |

9

## W. R. COOLEY,
―PROPRIETOR―
# Livery Stable,
## COTA STREET,
**SANTA BARBARA,   -   CALIFORNIA.**

Carriages, open and covered, Wagons, Matched Teams, Single and Saddle Horses let at reasonable rates. Parties conveyed to any part of the county, cheaply and quickly. Boarding Horses given careful attention, and good grooming. Corral and Sheds connected with the Stable.

---

## ANTON FORST,
PROPRIETOR OF
# Hotel, Feed Stable and Hall,
**ELLIS STATION, EL MONTE,**
12 Miles South-East Los Angeles, Los Angeles County, Cal.

Best Accommodations furnished to the Traveling Public

Boarders taken by the Week or Month. Table Boarders and Transient Lodgers accommodated. The finest Wines, Liquors and Cigars at the Bar.

### A GOOD FEED STABLE

Connected with the house, with spacious corral attached. Horses carefully and well provided for. Feed for sale in large or small quantities. A commodious Hall for the use of Traveling Shows, Exhibitions, Lectures, Etc.

**TERMS REASONABLE.**

---

## WILEY BROTHERS,
Santa Paula, Ventura County, Cal.
DEALERS IN
# General Merchandise
## DRY GOODS,
Provisions, Tobacco and Cigars,
## BOOTS AND SHOES
HARDWARE, CLOTHING,
# DRUGS,
—AND—
Gentlemen's and Ladies' Furnishing Goods.

**CALL AND EXAMINE.**

---

## W. KITTREDGE,
PROPRIETOR OF THE
# RAILROAD HOUSE,
**SAN FERNANDO,**
LOS ANGELES COUNTY, - CALIFORNIA.

Eating Station for Passengers both by Rail and Stage.

Every attention shown to guests, and every advantage offered to travelers, in the way of a Good Table and Comfortable Sleeping Apartments.

**BOARD BY THE WEEK OR MONTH.**
Lodgers taken over Night.
**DAY BOARDERS ACCOMMODATED.**

## DIRECTORY OF SANTA BARBARA COUNTY.

| Name. | Occupation. | Place of Business. | Residence. |
|---|---|---|---|
| Howe, R D | Tinsmith | State st | Moore's Hotel |
| Howell, J | Clerk | State st | State st |
| Hoyt, Ed More | Speculator | Santa Barbara | Santa Barbara Co |
| Hubbell, D W | Printer | Guadalupe Telegraph | Guadalupe st |
| Hubert, P | Carpenter | Santa Barbara | Valerio st |
| Hubel, J C | Clerk | Cota st | Cota st |
| Hudson, John | Farmer | Santa Maria Valley | 3½ m E Guadalupe |
| Hudson, J Wm | Fashion liv'y st'e | Guadalupe st | 3d st |
| Hudson, And J | Farmer | 1st Township | Santa Barbara Co |
| Hughes, James P | Teamster | 3d Township | Santa Barbara Co |
| Hulburt, Seth | Painter | Santa Barbara Co | 1st Township |
| Hulett, Nathan | Farmer | La Patera | Santa Barbara Co |
| Hulett, Henry | Farmer | Santa Barbara Co | La Patera |
| Hull, John Rufus | Laborer | Santa Barbara Co | Santa Barbara |
| Hunter, John M | Farmer | Montecito | Santa Barbara Co |
| Hunt, Wm | Carpenter | Santa Barbara | Anacapa st |
| Huntington, J | Feed store | Cota st | Gutierrez st |
| Hunt, R O | Blacksmith | Cota st | Anacapa st |
| Hunt, C L | Clerk | State st | Anacapa st |
| Hunt & Austin | Grocers | State st | |
| Hunt, W L | Clerk | State st | Anacapa st |
| Hunt, C C | Grocery | State st | State st |
| Hunt & Bates | Blacksmiths | Cota st | |
| Hurburt, Willard | Laborer | Santa Barbara Co | La Patera |
| Huse, Chas E | Attorney at law | Montecito st | Santa Barbara st |
| Huston, John | Farmer | Santa Barbara Co | Santa Maria |
| Idison, Edward | Capitalist | Santa Barbara | Anacapa st |
| Ireland, S | Blacksmith | Cota st | Cota st |
| Irwin, I N | Janitor court h'se | | Santa Barbara |
| Jacinto, Manuel | Seaman | Santa Barbara | Santa Barbara Co |
| Jackson, Amos | Stock raiser | Santa Barbara Co | Cañada |
| Jacobs, James J | Farmer | Santa Barbara | Santa Barbara Co |
| James, Samuel T | Mechanic | Santa Barbara | Santa Barbara Co |
| Jamison, T B | Farmer | Santa Maria Valley | 2 m E Guadalupe |
| Janssens, Jos | Clerk | State st | State st |
| Janssens, John | | Santa Barbara Co | Santa Barbara |
| Janssens, A E | Grocer | State st | State st |
| Janssens, A | Groceries | State st | State st |
| Jansen, Lars | Wagon maker | Guadalupe st | Olivera st |
| Jarvis, Alfred | Farmer | Santa Barbara Co | 2d Precinct |
| Jayne, John M | Carpenter | Santa Barbara Co | Carpenteria |
| Jefferys, Thos | Sailor | Santa Barbara | Montecito st |
| Jeffrys, Thomas | Laborer | Santa Barbara | Santa Barbara Co |
| Jenkins, Richard | Seaman | Santa Barbara Co | Santa Barbara |
| Johnson, R | Painter | Main st | |
| Johnson, Wm Henry | Carpenter | Santa Barbara | Santa Barbara Co |
| Johnson, Thomas B | Farmer | Santa Barbara | Santa Barbara |
| Johnson, Servine T | Farmer | Santa Barbara Co | Carpenteria |
| Johnson, James | Farmer | Goleta | Santa Barbara Co |
| Johnson, Jasper N | Farmer | Santa Barbara Co | La Patera |
| Johns, Hugh L | Blacksmith | Santa Barbara Co | |
| Johnson, Richard | Carpenter | Santa Barbara | Santa Barbara Co |
| Johnson, Geo | Confectionery | State st | Haley st |
| Johnson, J A | Editor | State st | Anacapa & Ortega sts |
| Johns, D V | Farmer | Guadalupe | Olivera st |
| Johnson, Jerome | Freight clerk | Stearn's Wharf | State st |
| Joiner, Wm E | Mason | Santa Barbara Co | Santa Barbara |
| Joiner, James A | Printer | Santa Barbara Co | Santa Barbara |
| Joiner, Joseph F | Clerk | Santa Barbara | Santa Barbara Co |
| Jones, Miles H | Laborer | Santa Barbara Co | Santa Barbara |
| Jones, J Frederick | Cook | Las Cruces | Santa Barbara Co |
| Jones, Douglas W | Merchant | Carpenteria | Santa Barbara Co |
| Jones, Fredk F | Laborer | Las Cruces | Santa Barbara Co |
| Jones, Amos K | Dentist | Santa Barbara Co | Pleasant Valley |

# F. P. BACON,

—— PROPRIETOR OF ——

# Marengo Ranche

**SITUATED SEVEN MILES NORTH-EAST FROM LOS ANGELES,**

## CONTAINING 8000 ACRES.

**VINEYARD, 40 ACRES.**    **ORCHARDS, 150 ACRES.**

---

There are in good growth, 1,500 Orange Trees, 800 Walnut Trees, besides Lemon, Almond, Peach, Pear, Apple and Fig Trees, in full and best varieties.

The water facilities grant a supply greater than is necessary to satisfy all demands, whether for irrigating or domestic purposes. The springs from which the water is derived are situated at an elevation, giving sufficient fall to allow of its conduct to any portion of the property.

Extensive Timber Lands, with the best qualities of timber, 300 acres of White Oak, Live Oak, Red Oak and Black Oak.

Elevation above the sea level, one thousand feet. The soil varies in character from a sandy and gravelly loam to a black adobe, while at this altitude and in this locality frost is positively unknown.

# DIRECTORY OF SANTA BARBARA COUNTY. 133

| Name. | Occupation. | Place of Business. | Residence. | Town or P. O. |
|---|---|---|---|---|
| Jones, Wm Rutliff | Dentist | Santa Barbara Co | 1st Township | |
| Jones, A W | Proprietor | Revere House | Guadalupe st | Guadalupe. |
| Jones, Charles | Machinist | Pioneer Mill | Bath st | Santa Barbara. |
| Jordon, Charles | Butcher | | Santa Barbara Co | Santa Barbara. |
| Joycifer, Jose | Laborer | Santa Barbara | Santa Barbara Co | Santa Barbara. |
| Joyner, — | Brick mason | Santa Barbara | Santa Barbara | Santa Barbara. |
| Juarez, Ben T | Bricklayer | Santa Barbara Co | Santa Barbara | Santa Barbara. |
| Juarez, Joaquin | Vaquero | Santa Barbara Co | Santa Barbara | Santa Barbara. |
| Juarez, Joaquin | Laborer | Montecito | Santa Barbara Co | |
| Jurez, Leandro | Farmer | Montecito | Santa Barbara Co | |
| Kaeding, Otto | Sailor | State st | Haley st | Santa Barbara. |
| Kaeding & Co | Saloon | State st | Santa Barbara | Santa Barbara. |
| Kaeintz, J | Barber | State st | State st | Santa Barbara. |
| Kahn, Lazard | Clerk | Santa Barbara Co | Santa Barbara | Santa Barbara. |
| Kahn, Moise | Merchant | Santa Barbara | Santa Barbara Co | Santa Barbara. |
| Kaiser, Solomon | Clerk | Guadalupe st | Guadalupe st | Guadalupe. |
| Kaiser, L M | Gen merchandise | Guadalupe st | Guadalupe st | Guadalupe. |
| Kaiser, L M & Co | Gen merchandise | Guadalupe st | | Guadalupe. |
| Kaiser, J | | | Guadalupe | Guadalupe. |
| Kays, John Charles | Merchant | Santa Barbara | Santa Barbara Co | Santa Barbara. |
| Kays, Thomas C | Ranchero | Santa Barbara Co | Santa Ynez | Ballard's Statn. |
| Kays, John | Clerk | Santa Barbara Co | Carpenteria | Carpenteria. |
| Keeler, B B | Farmer | Carpenteria Valley | 1½ m E Carpenteria | Carpenteria. |
| Keep, Wm B | Printer | State st | Anacapa st | Santa Barbara. |
| Keyser, — | Milkman | Santa Barbara | Milpas st | Santa Barbara. |
| Keith, Emilia M | Musician | Santa Barbara | Santa Barbara Co | Santa Barbara. |
| Keller, N J | Blacksmith | Los Alamos | Santa Barbara Co | |
| Kelley, Horace A | Printer | Santa Barbara Co | Santa Barbara | Santa Barbara. |
| Keller, M | Plasterer | State st | State st | Santa Barbara. |
| Kellogg, L F | Attorney | State st | State st | Santa Barbara. |
| Kelton, C H | Restaurant | State st | State st | Santa Barbara. |
| Kelton, Mrs C H | Milliner | State st | State st | Santa Barbara. |
| Kennedy, Henry M | Farmer | Santa Barbara Co | Pleasant Valley | |
| Kennedy, Cyrus | Farmer | Santa Barbara Co | Montecito | |
| Kennedy, W D | Printer | State st | Ortega st | Santa Barbara. |
| Kent, F Wm | Farmer | Santa Barbara Co | Santa Barbara | Santa Barbara. |
| Kent, Henry A, Jr | Stock raiser | Santa Maria | Santa Barbara Co | Santa Maria. |
| Kerston, Karl | Laborer | Santa Barbara | Micheltorena st | Santa Barbara. |
| Ketchum, John | | | Bath st | Santa Barbara. |
| Key, Allen L | Farmer | La Patera | Santa Barbara Co | |
| Keiser, Thomas J | Miner | Santa Barbara Co | La Patera | |
| Keysee, Joseph | Farmer | Santa Barbara | Grey st | Santa Barbara. |
| Keyzer, John W | Farmer | Santa Barbara | Santa Barbara Co | Santa Barbara. |
| Kilgore, M M | Farmer | Santa Ynez Road | 8 m N E L Cruces | Santa Ynez. |
| Kimberley, M M | Ranchero | Santa BarbaraCo | Santa Barbara | Santa Barbara. |
| Kincaid, Jos H | Attorney | Santa Barbara | Santa Barbara Co | Santa Barbara. |
| Kindrid, Ed | Hostler | Los Alamos | Santa Barbara Co | |
| Kinervane, Patrick | Watchman | Santa Barbara | Santa Barbara Co | Santa Barbara. |
| King, Richard | Hotel keeper | Rincon | Santa Barbara Co | Rincon. |
| King, Thomas | Laborer | Santa Barbara Co | Santa Barbara | Santa Barbara. |
| King, Manuel | Carriage maker | Santa Barbara Co | 1st Township | |
| King, Richd | Farmer | Carpenteria | | Carpenteria. |
| Kirk, Francis M | Laborer | Santa Barbara Co | Santa Barbara | Santa Barbara. |
| Knapp, Eugene J | Grocer | Santa Barbara st | Santa Barbara Co | Santa Barbara. |
| Knapp, J B | Painter | Cota st | State st | Santa Barbara. |
| Knapp & Brown | Painters | Cota st | | Santa Barbara. |
| Knapp, Geo | Carpenter | Santa Barbara | Haley st | Santa Barbara. |
| Knapp, E J | Farmer | Carpenteria Valley | | Carpenteria. |
| Knectle, F R | Mariner | Santa Paula | Santa Barbara Co | |
| Knight, Francis | | 4 m E Carpenteria | Vineyard st | Santa Barbara. |
| Kraft, J M | Shoe maker | Guadalupe st | Guadalupe st | Guadalupe. |
| Kynerson & Tilley | Flouring mill | Chapala st | | Santa Barbara. |
| Lacey, J | Bricklayer | Santa Barbara | Bath st | Santa Barbara. |
| Ladd, Mrs | | | Anacapa st | Santa Barbara. |

## R. ABERNETHY & CO.

### GUADALUPE,

DEALERS IN

## Pumps, Pump Pipe,

And Manufacturers of

### TIN, COPPER AND SHEET IRON WARE

Of every description.

DAIRY FIXTURES MANUFACTURED TO ORDER. ARTESIAN WELL PIPE CONSTANTLY ON HAND. PUMPS REPAIRED. JOBBING PROMPTLY ATTENDED TO.

---

## L. M. KAISER & CO.

Guadalupe, Santa Barbara Co. Cal.

Dealers in

## General Merchandise,

Dry Goods, Provisions,

LIQUORS, TOBACCOS, CIGARS,

### BOOTS, SHOES, HARDWARE,

CLOTHING, DRUGS,

—AND—

FURNISHING GOODS OF ALL DESCRIPTIONS.

---

D. W. BRIANT.  E. F. MAXFIELD.  W. W. TERRY.

## SAN DIEGO MILL COMPANY

Furnish all kinds of

# MILL WORK

On Shortest Notice.

### Sawing, Planing, Turning

AND EVERY VARIETY OF HOUSE FINISH.

A good assortment of

### Molding Always On Hand.

We also manufacture

Bee Hives, Section Boxes, Honey Cases, Etc., Cheap for Cash. Call and see.

Or we will grind your Corn and Barley.

---

J. W. WESCOTT.    J. O. HATLEBERG.

## The Big Shoe Blacksmith & Wagon Shop

### Wescott & Hatleberg,

Manufacturers of all kinds of

## BUGGIES & CARRIAGES,

Also, Spring and Lumber Wagons.

Cor. 8th and J Sts., San Diego, Cal.

Also, Patent right for the Goodenough Horseshoe.

# DIRECTORY OF SANTA BARBARA COUNTY. 135

| Name. | Occupation. | Place of Business. | Residence. | Town or P. O. |
|---|---|---|---|---|
| LaForce, Lewis | Carpenter | Santa Barbara Co | Santa Barbara | Santa Barbara. |
| Lage, F H | | Los Alamos | 40 m S Guadalupe | Guadalupe. |
| Lagnas, Juan | Farmer | Carpenteria Valley | 1 m W Carpenteria | Carpenteria. |
| LaGrange, Miss N. | Editor | State st | Ortega Hotel | Santa Barbara. |
| Laird, D | Farmer | Santa Maria Road | 1 m S E Guadalupe | Guadalupe. |
| Lake, Wingate N | Teamster | Santa Barbara | Santa Barbara Co | Santa Barbara. |
| Lakey, Andrew | Farmer | Casmalia Ranch | 6 m S Guadalupe | Guadalupe. |
| Lamb, Chas C | Clerk | Santa Barbara Co | Santa Barbara | Santa Barbara. |
| Lambert, Nicholas | Farmer | Santa Barbara | Garden st | Santa Barbara. |
| Lambert, Henry | Farmer | Carpenteria Valley | 4 m W Carpenteria | Carpenteria. |
| Landes, James S | Dairyman | Santa Barbara | Santa Barbara Co | Santa Barbara. |
| Lane, Joseph | Farmer | Santa Barbara Co | Arroyo Burro | |
| Lane, Dallas | Farmer | La Patera | Santa Barbara Co | |
| Lane, Miles Hinton | Farmer | Santa Barbara Co | Arroyo Burro | |
| Larcombe, Mr S E. | Tel operator | Ortega st | Haley st | Santa Barbara. |
| Lardner, S B | Stock raiser | Corallitos | 6 m S Guadalupe | Guadalupe. |
| Larny, Peter | Laborer | Santa Barbara | Santa Barbara Co | Santa Barbara. |
| Lasalle, Charles | Farmer | Santa Barbara Co | La Patera | |
| Lasalle, Charles | Ranchero | Santa Barbara Co | 3d Township | |
| Lataillade, C E | Hardware | State st | State st | Santa Barbara. |
| Latimer, W H | Farmer | Santa Barbara Co | 1st Township | |
| Laughlin, H J & Co | General store | Main st, Guadalupe | Guadalupe | Guadalupe. |
| Laughlin, H J | General store | Main st | Guadalupe | Guadalupe. |
| Laurie, Mrs L | | | State st | Santa Barbara. |
| Lavies, Wm | Agent | La Patera | Santa Barbara Co | |
| Lea, Benjamin | Farmer | Carpenteria | Santa Barbara Co | Carpenteria. |
| Leach, Chas W | Carpenter | Santa Barbara | Santa Barbara Co | Santa Barbara. |
| Lebendelfer, D S | Painter | Santa Barbara | Santa Barbara Co | Santa Barbara. |
| Lee, P W | Butcher | State st | State st | Santa Barbara. |
| Leighton, Rufus | | Santa Barbara | Anacapa st | Santa Barbara. |
| Leitner, Samuel | Bricklayer | Santa Barbara | De la Guerra st | Santa Barbara. |
| Leiva, R J | Clerk | State st | State st | Santa Barbara. |
| Leland, Geo W | Butcher | Santa Barbara Co | Santa Barbara | Santa Barbara. |
| Leland, Wm | Butcher | State st | Santa Barbara | Santa Barbara. |
| Lemon, L | Painter | Cota st | Haley st | Santa Barbara. |
| Leon, Cleofas Ponce de | Laborer | Santa Barbara | Santa Barbara Co | Santa Barbara. |
| Leonard, S | Tailor | State st | Castella st | Santa Barbara. |
| Lesher, Mrs C | Fruit store | State st | De la Guerra st | Santa Barbara. |
| Leslie, A | Supt bell's ranch | Los Alamos | | Guadalupe. |
| Lestee, Wm | Stone mason | Santa Barbara | Haley st | Santa Barbara. |
| Levi, J | Watchmaker | State st | State st | Santa Barbara. |
| Levia, Guadalupe | Laborer | Santa Barbara | Santa Barbara st | Santa Barbara. |
| Levy, J | Clerk | State st | State st | Santa Barbara. |
| Levy, A | Groceries | Carpenteria Valley | Carpenteria | Carpenteria. |
| Levy, Samuel | Merchant | Santa Barbara Co | Santa Barbara | Santa Barbara. |
| Leives, Thomas | Farmer | La Patera | Santa Barbara Co | |
| Lewis, Jos M | Farmer | Santa Barbara Co | Santa Maria | Santa Maria. |
| Lewis, Frank | Butcher | Guadalupe st | Guadalupe st | Guadalupe. |
| Lewis, Geo W | Farmer | Ballard's Station | Ballard's Ranch | Ballard's Sta. |
| Lewis, Henry | Farmer | Carpenteria Valley | 1¼ m W Carpenteria | Carpenteria. |
| Lewty, D | Machinist | Guadalupe st | Olivera st | Guadalupe. |
| Leyba, Rafael E | Ranchero | Najahni | 3 m N E L Cruces | Las Cruces. |
| Leyba, Jose R | Laborer | Las Cruces | Las Cruces Ranch | Las Cruces. |
| Leyba, Jose de Jesus | Laborer | Santa Barbara Co | Santa Barbara | Santa Barbara. |
| Leyba, Francisco, Jr | Carpenter | Santa Barbara Co | Santa Barbara | Santa Barbara. |
| Loyba, Quirno | Laborer | Santa Barbara | Santa Barbara Co | Santa Barbara. |
| Leyba, Guadalupe | Laborer | Santa Barbara Co | Santa Barbara | Santa Barbara. |
| Libbey, Chas D | Fisherman | Santa Barbara | Grey st | Santa Barbara. |
| Liggett & Porter | Lompoc hotel | I and Ocean Ave | cor I and Ocean Ave | Lompoc. |
| Liggett, Mrs May | Lompoc hotel | I and Ocean Ave | cor I and Ocean Ave | Lompoc. |
| Lillie, Henry | Farmer | Santa Barbara | Santa Barbara Co | Santa Barbara. |
| Lillard, William T | Laborer | La Patera | Santa Barbara Co | |
| Linahe, Cornelius | Boot & shoe store | State st | State st | Santa Barbara. |

## J. HOFFMAN
### GUADALUPE, CAL.

### PAINTING,

DONE IN THE MOST APPROVED STYLE.

### GRAINING & MARBLING
Done with Neatness and Skill.

### Carriage & Wagon Painting a Specialty
Shop Next Door to Hart Bros.

---

## BREWERY.

### The Pioneer Brewery of the County

ANTONIO TOMASONI, Proprietor,

Guadalupe, Santa Barbara Co., Cal.

Patronize Home Manufacture and purchase

 The Best Lager Beer

Made in the State.

**Agreeable to the taste, nourishing to the system, and a healthy Beverage.**

Warranted entirely free from all poisonous Compounds.

Orders received at Brewery, and Beer delivered free of charge.

---

## ☞ THE ☜
# LOMPOC RECORD!

——ORGAN OF THE——

### "Lompoc Temperance Colony."

PUBLISHED EVERY SATURDAY AT

### Lompoc, Santa Barbara County, Cal.

W. W. BROUGHTON,

EDITOR AND PUBLISHER.

**Subscription Price $4 Per Annum.**

**Weekly Circulation 2,000.**

The RECORD sends free papers to all who desire reliable information concerning the Lompoc Colony, and is the best advertising medium South of San Francisco.

---

# RHOADS & GORDEN

SANTA PAULA, Ventura Co., Cal.

——DEALERS IN——

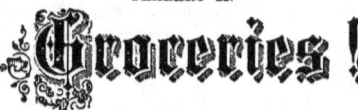

Of all descriptions.

### CANNED FRUITS, TOBACCO

CIGARS, NOTIONS, ETC.

A Saloon connected with the Store, at the bar of which will be found

### Wines & Liquors

OF THE FINEST BRANDS.

## DIRECTORY OF SANTA BARBARA COUNTY. 137

| Name. | Occupation. | Place of Business. | Residence. | Town or P. O. |
|---|---|---|---|---|
| Lincoln, Barny...... | Bar tender............ | State st...................... | State st..................... | Santa Barbara. |
| Lincoln, A L.......... | Cashier................ | National Gold Bank. | Victoria st................. | Santa Barbara. |
| Lind, Mathew......... | Carpenter ........... | Guadalupe st............. | Guadalupe st............. | Guadalupe. |
| Linville, H H......... | Farmer ................ | Santa Barbara........... | Milpas st.................... | Santa Barbara. |
| Little, Miss M E..... | Tel operator ......... | Ortega st.................... | State st....................... | Santa Barbara. |
| Lloy, Geo A............ | Painter ................. | State st....................... | Micheltorena st.......... | Santa Barbara. |
| Lloyd, E C.............. | Painter.................. | State st....................... | Micheltorena st.......... | Santa Barbara. |
| Lobaugh, Jacob...... | Laborer................ | Santa Barbara........... | Santa Barbara Co..... | Santa Barbara. |
| Lockwood, S G....... | Pres S M V F Un | Santa Maria Valley... | ½ m S Central City... | Santa Maria. |
| Lockwood, Nathan. | Carpenter ........... | Santa Barbara........... | Anacapa st................. | Santa Barbara. |
| Lofthouse, Ralph.. | Farmer ................ | Sespe.......................... | Santa Barbara Co.... | |
| Logo, Charles......... | Tailor .................. | Santa Barbara........... | Santa Barbara Co..... | Santa Barbara. |
| Lombard, H L......... | Farmer ............... | La Patera................... | Santa Barbara Co..... | |
| Loney, Thomas....... | Farmer ............... | Santa Barbara........... | Santa Barbara Co..... | Santa Barbara. |
| Longdon, Benj C.... | Clerk.................... | La Patera................... | Santa Barbara Co..... | |
| Long, Geo Henry.... | Farmer ............... | San Julian Ranch..... | 8 m W L Cruces...... | Las Cruces. |
| Long, N C................ | Farmer ............... | Carpenteria Valley... | 1½ m E Carpenteria. | Carpenteria. |
| Loomis, Sherman.. | Saddlery&harness | State st....................... | Ortega st.................... | Santa Barbara. |
| Loomis, Frank........ | Clerk................... | State st....................... | State st....................... | Santa Barbara. |
| Lopez, Jose de Jesus | Laborer............... | Santa Barbara Co.... | 1st Precinct............... | |
| Lopez, Feliz............. | Vaquero .............. | Santa Barbara Co.... | Cañada....................... | |
| Lopez, Jesus........... | Farmer ............... | Montecito................... | Santa Barbara Co .... | |
| Lopez, Ramon A..... | Laborer............... | Montecito................... | Santa Barbara Co.... | |
| Lopez, Doroteo....... | Vaquero.............. | Santa Barbara Co.... | Santa Barbara........... | |
| Lopez, Mariano...... | Justice of peace... | Santa Barbara Co.... | Santa Barbara........... | Santa Barbara. |
| Lopez, Antonio Y... | Vaquero............... | Los Alamos............... | Santa Barbara Co.... | |
| Lopez, Juan............ | Laborer............... | Santa Barbara Co.... | Tecolotito................... | |
| Lopez, Solomon...... | Vaquero .............. | Santa Barbara........... | Santa Barbara Co.... | Santa Barbara. |
| Lopez, Jose Maria.. | Vaquero .............. | Santa Barbara Co.... | Carmelos ................... | |
| Lopez, Maximo....... | Laborer............... | Santa Barbara Co.... | Santa Barbara........... | Santa Barbara. |
| Lopez, Jose Antonio | Laborer............... | Santa Barbara Co.... | Santa Barbara........... | Santa Barbara. |
| Lopez, Gregoire..... | Vaquero .............. | Santa Barbara Co.... | Santa Barbara........... | Santa Barbara. |
| Lopez, Bernardino.. | Vaquero .............. | Santa Barbara........... | Santa Barbara Co.... | Santa Barbara. |
| Lopez, Francisco.... | Vaquero............... | Santa Barbara Co.... | Santa Barbara........... | Santa Barbara. |
| Lord, Mrs F C......... | ........................... | ........................... | Guiterrez st................ | Santa Barbara. |
| Lord, J N................. | Gunsmith ........... | State st....................... | Gutierrez st............... | Santa Barbara. |
| Lorenzana, Jose..... | Saloon keeper...... | Santa Barbara Co.... | Santa Barbara........... | Santa Barbara. |
| Loureyro, Jose M... | Merchant ............ | Santa Barbara........... | Santa Barbara Co..... | |
| Love, John.............. | Seaman............... | Santa Barbara Co.... | Santa Barbara........... | Santa Barbara. |
| Lovett, C M............. | Gen merchandise.. | Main st...................... | Central City.............. | Santa Barbara. |
| Low, Winfield Scott | Teamster............. | Santa Barbara Co.... | Santa Barbara........... | Santa Maria. |
| Lowe, E S................ | Variety store....... | State st....................... | De la Guerra st......... | Santa Barbara. |
| Loweberger, Luis... | Farmer ............... | 2d Precinct................ | Santa Barbara Co.... | |
| Lown, John............. | Clerk.................... | Main st....................... | Main st....................... | Guadalupe. |
| Lowry, Spencer E.. | Laborer ............... | Santa Barbara Co.... | Santa Barbara........... | Santa Barbara. |
| Loza, S..................... | Farmer ............... | Carpenteria............... | Carpenteria .............. | Carpenteria. |
| Lucas, C Bralish... | Groceries&liquors | State st....................... | State st....................... | Santa Barbara. |
| Lucas, Jas T............ | Real estate .......... | State st....................... | Fig ave....................... | Santa Barbara. |
| Lucas Bros.............. | Real estate agents | State st....................... | Santa Barbara........... | Santa Barbara. |
| Lucas, C F............... | Real estate .......... | State st....................... | Anacapa st................. | Santa Barbara. |
| Luce, Benj M.......... | Farmer ............... | Montecito................... | Santa Barbara Co..... | |
| Lugio, Eugenio....... | Vaquero .............. | Santa Barbara Co.... | Santa Barbara........... | Santa Barbara. |
| Lugo, Francisco M. | Laborer ............... | Santa Barbara........... | Santa Barbara Co.... | Santa Barbara. |
| Lugo, Jose A........... | Laborer ............... | Las Cruces................ | Las Cruces Ranch.... | Las Cruces. |
| Lugo, Jose Y........... | Laborer ............... | Santa Barbara........... | Santa Barbara Co.... | Santa Barbara. |
| Lugo, Guillermo..... | Laborer ............... | Montecito................... | Santa Barbara Co.... | |
| Lugo, Saturnino..... | Laborer ............... | Santa Barbara........... | Santa Barbara Co.... | Santa Barbara. |
| Lugo, Francisco .... | Vaquero .............. | Santa Barbara........... | Santa Barbara Co.... | Santa Barbara. |
| Lugo, Ygnacio........ | Ranchero............. | Santa Barbara Co.... | Santa Barbara........... | Santa Barbara. |
| Lugo, Francisco .... | Laborer ............... | Santa Barbara Co.... | Mallego...................... | |
| Lugo, Pedro............ | Laborer ............... | Santa Barbara........... | Santa Barbara Co.... | |
| Lugo, Jose.............. | Laborer ............... | Santa Barbara Co.... | Montecito................... | |
| Lugo, Jose de Garcia.... ............ | Laborer................. | Montecito................... | Santa Barbara Co..... | |

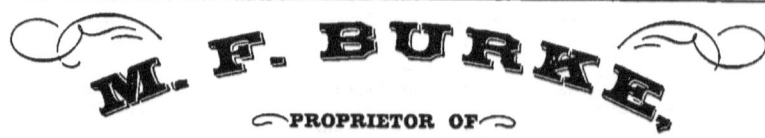

### PROPRIETOR OF

# GAVIOTA STORE AND HOTEL,

## Dry Goods, Groceries,

### PROVISIONS, BOOTS, SHOES,

Cigars, Tobaccos, Wines, Liquors,

**HARDWARE, TINWARE,**

**Willow Goods, Glass and Crockeryware, Etc.**

HOTEL WELL FURNISHED. TABLE AND SLEEPING APARTMENTS UNEXCEPTIONABLE.

PROPRIETOR OF

## STAGE LINE FROM LAS CRUCES TO SANTA BARBARA.

### Also, Manager of Gaviota Wharf,

Where will be found good shipping facilities. Western Union Telegraph Office at the Store.

DIRECTORY OF SANTA BARBARA COUNTY. 139

| Name. | Occupation. | Place of Business. | Residence. | Town or P. O. |
|---|---|---|---|---|
| Lugo, Juan | Laborer | Santa Barbara Co | 2d Precinct | |
| Luis, Amado | Laborer | Santa Barbara Co | Santa Barbara | Santa Barbara. |
| Lunceford, Sam'l J | Farmer | 3d Township | Santa Barbara Co | |
| Lyman, C C L | Harness maker | State st | Morris House | Santa Barbara. |
| Lyman, Walter | Carpenter | Santa Barbara | Santa Barbara Co | Santa Barbara. |
| Lyall, A | Carpenter | Santa Barbara | State st | Santa Barbara. |
| Macklin, N | Carpenter | Carpenteria | Santa Barbara Co | Carpenteria. |
| Madrueno, Jose de J | Blacksmith | Carpenteria | Santa Barbara Co | Carpenteria. |
| MaGuire, H F | Clerk | State st | Eaten st | Santa Barbara. |
| Maguire, Francis John | County judge | Santa Barbara | Santa Barbara Co | Santa Barbara. |
| Main, W E | Stock | | Santa Barbara | Santa Barbara. |
| Maldonado, Jose M | Cigar maker | Santa Barbara | Santa Barbara Co | Santa Barbara. |
| Mallorquin, Jose | Saloon keeper | Santa Barbara | Santa Barbara Co | Santa Barbara. |
| Malo, Ramon Jose | Ranchero | Santa Barbara | Santa Barbara Co | Santa Barbara. |
| Manning, J | Laborer | Point Sal | 10 m S W Gaudalupe | Guadalupe. |
| Manter, William O | Seaman | Santa Barbara | Santa Barbara Co | Santa Barbara. |
| Marchan, D | Ranchero | Santa Barbara Co | 3d Township | |
| Marcy, Harvy | Clerk | State st | Montecito st | Santa Barbara. |
| Marcum, Leroy | Teamster | Point Sal | 10 m S W Gaudalupe | Guadalupe. |
| Marcey, Cyrus | Plasterer | Santa Barbara | Montecito st | Santa Barbara. |
| Marcy, W C | Farmer | | Bath st | Santa Barbara. |
| Maris, W S | Clerk | State st | Haley st | Santa Barbara. |
| Markhum, L | Teamster | Point Sal | 10 m S W Gaudalupe | Guadalupe. |
| Marshall, R | Carriage ironer | Canyon Perdido st | State st | Santa Barbara. |
| Marshall, Cyrus | Stone mason | Santa Barbara | Montecito st | Santa Barbara. |
| Marston, — | Dairyman | Santa Barbara | Bath st | Santa Barbara. |
| Martin, H H | Clerk | I and Ocean Ave | I and Ocean Ave | Lompoc. |
| Martler, John W | Hunter | Santa Barbara Co | Santa Maria | Santa Maria. |
| Martinez, Bernube | Farmer | 2d Precinct | Santa Barbara Co | |
| Martin, Franklin | Laborer | Santa Barbara Co | Montecito | |
| Martin, Peter P | Farmer | La Patera | Santa Barbara Co | |
| Martinez, Leandro | Cook | Santa Barbara Co | Santa Barbara | Santa Barbara. |
| Martin, Joaquin | Liquor dealer | State st | State st | Santa Barbara. |
| Martin, Mrs A D | Dress maker | De la Guerra st | De la Guerra st | Santa Barbara. |
| Martin, Andrew | Farmer | Carpenteria Valley | 2 m E Carpenteria | Carpenteria. |
| Martin, T S | Saloon | State st | State st | Santa Barbara. |
| Martin, Thomas W | Carpenter | Santa Barbara | Santa Barbara Co | Santa Barbara. |
| Martin, Era E | Farmer | Santa Barbara Co | La Patera | |
| Martinez, Alex G | Farmer | Los Alamos | Santa Barbara Co | |
| Martin, John H | Farmer | Santa Barbara Co | Ojai Rancho | |
| Martinez, Luis | Farmer | San Jose | Santa Barbara Co | |
| Martin, Charles | Farmer | Santa Barbara Co | Goleta | |
| Martin, Charles | Laborer | Montecito | Santa Barbara Co | |
| Masa, Alonzo | Saddler | State st | De la Guerra st | Santa Barbara. |
| Mathison, C P | Farmer | Santa Maria Valley | 2 m S E Guadalupe | Guadalupe. |
| Maxwell, Walter | Printer | Telegraph | Guadalupe st | Guadalupe. |
| Maxwell, J K | Stock raiser | Guadalupe | Guadalupe | Guadalupe. |
| Mayhew, Jonathan | Farmer | Santa Barbara | Santa Barbara Co | Santa Barbara. |
| Maxfield, D C | Miner | Santa Barbara Co | Santa Barbara | Santa Barbara. |
| Maxfield, Ezra F | Carpenter | Santa Barbara Co | Santa Barbara | Santa Barbara. |
| Maxim, John King | Farmer | Santa Barbara Co | Santa Barbara | Santa Barbara. |
| McAllister, Robert | Farmer | Santa Barbara Co | Carpenteria | Carpenteria. |
| McAllister, Jacob | Laborer | La Patera | Santa Barbara Co | |
| McCaffrey, Hugh | Saloon keeper | Santa Barbara Co | Santa Barbara | Santa Barbara. |
| McCaffrey, James | Vintner | San Jose | Santa Barbara Co | |
| McCaffrey, Charles | Laborer | Santa Barbara Co | Santa Barbara | Santa Barbara. |
| McCardle, Patrick | Farmer | Santa Maria | Santa Barbara Co | Santa Maria. |
| McCaughey, William | Laborer | Santa Barbara Co | Santa Barbara | Santa Barbara. |
| McCaffrey, James J | Farmer | La Patera | Santa Barbara Co | |
| McCall, Samuel M | Farmer | Santa Barbara Co | Santa Barbara | Santa Barbara. |
| McCarty, Edward W | Farmer | Sespe | Santa Barbara Co | |

J. HAMMELL.    ASA ADAMS.

## HAMMELL & ADAMS,

—DEALERS IN—

# REAL ESTATE

**Office opposite Press Building, State Street, Santa Barbara.**

Doing, in connection with their Real Estate Business, a General Commission Business, and are also engaged in the collection of Rents, Negotiation of Loans, and the Payment of Taxes for non-residents.

And have for sale, choice lots in the upper part of town, improved and unimproved,

Also, lots in the lower part of town, 50x100 feet, of excellent land, for $50, $100 and $150 each.

Especial attention is directed to a large tract of land which we will sell to actual settlers at small prices.

### COUNTRY PROPERTY.

We have lands in the Centinela Tract, and also own a fine portion of "El Conejo" Rancho, for sale in lots to suit.

### NEW COMERS

Are invited to call and see what fine chances for investment we offer in Montecito. We have in that beautiful valley, several tracts.

### A CARRIAGE

Is always in readiness for the convenience of parties desiring to look at our lands.

---

## Stokum & Cavalli,

# RESTAURANT

### CONFECTIONERY,

## Ice Cream & Oyster Saloon

Orders for Balls, Parties and Soirees promptly attended to.

### STATE STREET,

SANTA BARBARA,    -    -    CAL.

---

# THE
## DAILY AND WEEKLY

Published in Santa Barbara,

—BY—

## AL. PETTYGROVE,

## TERMS.

DAILY, PER ANNUM,  -  -  $6.00

WEEKLY,    "    -    $3.00

---

W. McRAE.    D. McRAE.

## McRAE BROTHERS,

PROPRIETORS OF THE

### SAN FERNANDO,

Los Angeles County,  -  -  California.

Tourists and Travelers will find good accommodations and conveniences at this house.

Our Table is well supplied and served, rooms well furnished and neat, and Bar well stocked and supervised.

IRECTORY OF SANTA BARBARA COUNTY.    141

| )CCUPATION. | PLACE OF BUSINESS. | RESIDENCE. | TOWN OR P. O. |
|---|---|---|---|
| 'mer............ | Santa Barbara Co..... | Casmali..................... | |
| 'mor............ | Santa Maria Valley.. | 2 m N E Guadalupe. | Guadalupe. |
| stler........... | 3d Township.. ......... | Santa Barbara Co..... | |
| .................. | ............................... | Anacapa st............ | Santa Barbara. |
| ge stand....... | Carpenteria ............ | Carpenteria ............ | Carpenteria. |
| imster ........ | Santa Barbara Co..... | Santa Barbara......... | Santa Barbara. |
| rmer............ | Santa Barbara Co.... | 1st Township........... | |
| rmer............ | Santa Maria Valley.. | 2¼ m E Guadalupe... | Guadalupe. |
| rmer............ | Santa Maria Valley.. | 2¼ m E Guadalupe... | Guadalupe. |
| rmer............ | Santa Barbara......... | Santa Barbara Co..... | Santa Barbara. |
| rmer............ | Santa Barbara Co..... | La Patera................. | |
| rmer............ | Santa Barbara......... | Santa Barbara Co..... | Santa Barbara. |
| son............. | Santa Barbara Co..... | 1st Precinct............. | |
| ick layer...... | Santa Barbara......... | Santa Barbara Co..... | Santa Barbara. |
| borer........... | Guadalupe ............... | Guadalupe st........... | Guadalupe. |
| rpenter ........ | Santa Barbara......... | Santa Barbara st...... | Santa Barbara. |
| gineer.......... | Santa Barbara......... | Santa Barbara Co..... | Santa Barbara. |
| ....................... | ................................. | Garden st............... | Santa Barbara. |
| rmer............ | Santa Barbara Co.... | Rincon.................... | Rincon. |
| borer........... | Santa Barbara......... | Vineyard st............. | Santa Barbara. |
| nchero ........ | Carpenteria ............ | Santa Barbara Co..... | Carpenteria. |
| ner............. | Santa Barbara Co..... | Rincon.................... | Rincon. |
| lesman......... | S M V F U Store..... | ............................... | Santa Maria. |
| amster......... | Las Cruces.............. | Las Cruces.............. | Las Cruces. |
| ok keeper..... | Santa Barbara......... | Santa Barbara Co..... | Santa Barbara. |
| irmer........... | Santa Maria Valley.. | 3½ m E Guadalupe... | Guadalupe. |
| rpenter....... | Santa Barbara Co..... | Santa Barbara......... | Santa Barbara. |
| iborer......... | Santa Barbara Co..... | Santa Barbara......... | Santa Barbara. |
| irmer........... | Montecito ............... | Santa Barbara Co..... | |
| ick layer....... | Santa Barbara......... | Santa Barbara Co..... | Santa Barbara. |
| acher.......... | Santa Barbara Co..... | Santa Barbara......... | Santa Barbara. |
| acher .......... | Carpenteria ............ | Santa Barbara Co..... | Carpenteria. |
| al estate....... | State st.................... | Victoria st.............. | Santa Barbara. |
| erk............. | Santa Barbara Co..... | 3d Township ........... | |
| erk............. | State st.................... | Victoria st.............. | Santa Barbara. |
| irmer........... | Santa Maria............ | Santa Barbara Co..... | Santa Maria. |
| irmer........... | Santa Barbara Co..... | La Patera................ | |
| torney......... | State st.................... | Cota st.................... | Santa Barbara. |
| ock raiser ..... | Santa Maria Valley.. | 3 m S E Guadalupe... | Guadalupe. |
| irmer........... | Santa Barbara Co..... | 1st Township........... | |
| iborer.......... | Santa Barbara......... | Santa Barbara Co..... | Santa Barbara. |
| erk ............ | Santa Barbara Co..... | Santa Barbara......... | Santa Barbara. |
| erk............. | Stearn's Lumber Y'd | Anacapa st............. | Santa Barbara. |
| .................... | ................................ | Montecito st........... | Santa Barbara. |
| one cutter..... | Santa Barbara......... | Chapala st............... | Santa Barbara. |
| lerk............ | State st.................... | Haley st.................. | Santa Barbara. |
| erchant ....... | Santa Barbara......... | Santa Barbara Co.... | Santa Barbara. |
| iddler.......... | Santa Barbara......... | Santa Barbara Co.... | Santa Barbara. |
| aquero ........ | Santa Barbara Co..... | Santa Barbara......... | Santa Barbara. |
| ainter .......... | State st.................... | Rose Ave................ | Santa Barbara. |
| ................... | ................................ | Rose Ave................ | Santa Barbara. |
| arber........... | Santa Barbara Co..... | Santa Barbara......... | Santa Barbara. |
| armer .......... | Santa Barbara Co..... | 1st Township........... | |
| nrmer........... | 1st Township........... | Santa Barbara Co..... | |
| eal estate...... | Haley st.................. | Sola st.................... | Santa Barbara. |
| eal estate...... | Haley st.................. | Sola st.................... | Santa Barbara. |
| lerk............. | State st.................... | State st................... | Santa Barbara. |
| ssistant P M.. | State st.................... | Santa Barbara......... | Santa Barbara. |
| ec S M V F U.. | Santa Maria Valley.. | 2½ m N E Central C'y | Santa Maria. |
| Vatch maker... | State st.................... | State st................... | Santa Barbara. |

# TEMECULA HOTEL,
## FEED STABLE AND GENERAL STORE

### S. LEVY, Proprietor.

Half Way Bet. San Bernardino and San Diego.

---

Good accommodations for Wayfarers, Tourists, and the Traveling Public generally. Parties conveyed to any point quickly and at low rates.

The Temescal Hot Springs are 33 miles distant; Los Angeles, 100 miles; Julian, 55 miles, and San Luis Rey, 25 miles.

The Post Office is at the store, where will be found a full assortment of Merchandise, appertaining to the stock of a country store.

Hay and Grain for sale in large and small quantities.

---

# F. HARKNESS,
—DEALER IN—

## Groceries, Provisions

### BOTTLED WINES AND LIQUORS,

(FOR FAMILY USE,)

### CROCKERY, GLASSWARE, WOOD & WILLOWWARE

TOBACCO, CIGARS, ETC.

State Street, Bet. the Morris House and Occidental Hotel,

**SANTA BARBARA, CAL.**

# DIRECTORY OF SANTA BARBARA COUNTY.

| NAME. | OCCUPATION. | PLACE OF BUSINESS. | RESIDENCE. |
|---|---|---|---|
| Miller Bros............ | Brewery................ | Vineyard st............... | ............................ |
| Miller & Lovett..... | General mdse...... | Main st.................... | Central City........... |
| Miller, Orrine....... | General mdse...... | Main st.................... | Central City........... |
| Miller, J M........... | General mdse...... | Main st.................... | 3½ m N W Guadalupe |
| Milligan, James B.. | Ranchero............ | Santa Barbara Co..... | Santa Barbara......... |
| Miller, Joel............ | Farmer............... | 3d Township............ | Santa Barbara Co..... |
| Miller, H R........... | Brewery............... | Vineyard st.............. | Vineyard st............. |
| Miller, Henry....... | Brewery............... | Vineyard st.............. | Vineyard st............. |
| Miller, Isaac.......... | Farmer................ | Cineguitas................ | Santa Barbara Co.... |
| Miller, John Wolf. | Apiarian.............. | Santa Maria............. | Santa Barbara Co.... |
| Mills, Howard W... | Sheep raiser........ | Santa Barbara Co.... | Santa Barbara......... |
| Mills, Hiram W.... | Seaman................ | Santa Barbara Co.... | Santa Barbara......... |
| Miller, Richd D..... | Carpenter............ | Santa Barbara......... | Laguna st................ |
| Minor, Irthamer..... | Teamster.............. | Santa Barbara......... | Gutierrez st............. |
| Mitchell, David..... | Horse trainer....... | Santa Barbara......... | Grey st.................... |
| Mitchell, W F....... | Farmer................ | Santa Barbara Co.... | La Patera................ |
| Mitchell, John....... | Laborer................ | Santa Ynez............. | Santa Barbara Co.... |
| Mix, James............ | Carpenter............ | Santa Barbara Co.... | Santa Barbara......... |
| Moffitt, Dr............ | Physician............. | Juanita Ranch......... | 5 m S Bal'd's Stat'n |
| Molera, P B........... | Surveyor.............. | State st................... | State st................... |
| Moley, N J............ | Merchant tailor... | State st................... | Anapamu st............ |
| Moll, John............. | Gen merchandise | Santa Ynez............. | Santa Ynez Mission.. |
| Mollay, Thomas.... | Laborer................ | Santa Barbara......... | Santa Barbara Co..... |
| Monroe, William... | Farmer............... | Pleasant Valley...... | Santa Barbara Co.... |
| Moon, David......... | Teamster.............. | Juanita Ranch......... | 5 m S Ballard's Stn... |
| Moore, Capt E...... | Blacksmith.......... | Santa Barbara Co.... | Santa Maria............. |
| Moore, John.......... | Laborer................ | La Patera................ | Santa Barbara Co..... |
| Moore, A P............ | Speculator............ | San Francisco......... | Grand Hotel............ |
| Moore, H H........... | Speculator............ | Oakland................... | ............................ |
| Moore, John F...... | Ranchero............. | Moore's Island......... | 30 m S S Barbara.... |
| Moore, Thos W.... | Ranchero............. | Santa Ynez............. | 10 m N E L Cruces.. |
| Moore,Lawrence W | Stock raiser......... | ............................ | Rancheria st............ |
| Moore, G W........... | ............................ | ............................ | Vineyard st.............. |
| Moore, P L............ | Tobacconist.......... | State st................... | De la Guerra st........ |
| Moore, T Wallace.. | Ranchero............. | Santa Barbara......... | Micheltorena st........ |
| Moore, Robert T.... | Hostler................. | Santa Barbara Co.... | Santa Barbara......... |
| Morani, Bantista.. | Saddler................ | State st................... | State st................... |
| Morani, Jacovo..... | Saddler................ | State st................... | State st................... |
| Moraga, P.............. | Clerk................... | State st................... | State st................... |
| Morales, Jose........ | Mechanic............. | Santa Barbara Co.... | Las Cruces.............. |
| Moraga, Jose G..... | Farmer................ | Santa Barbara Co.... | Santa Barbara......... |
| Morago, Gaivaso... | Laborer................ | Santa Barbara......... | Santa Barbara Co.... |
| Moraga, Mrs R...... | ............................ | ............................ | Chapala st.............. |
| Moreno, F.............. | Saddle & harness. | State st................... | State st................... |
| Morenlini, B......... | Ocean view saloon | State st................... | State st................... |
| Moreno, Pio.......... | Laborer................ | Santa Barbara Co.... | Carpenteria............ |
| Morris, James F... | Morris hotel......... | State st................... | cor State and Haley sts |
| Morris, Dr J D.... | Physician............. | State st................... | Anacapa st.............. |
| Morrison, Duncan W.................. | Farmer................ | La Patera................ | Santa Barbara Co.... |
| Morse, James Jr.... | Carpenter............ | Guadalupe st.......... | Guadalupe st........... |
| Morse, Wm........... | Stock raiser......... | Carpenteria Valley.. | 5½ m E Carpenteria.. |
| Mudd, S J............. | Farmer................ | Santa Maria Valley.. | 2½ m E Guadalupe.... |
| Mullin, James....... | Ranchero............ | Santa Barbara......... | Santa Barbara Co..... |
| Murat, Joseph....... | Brewer................ | Santa Barbara......... | Santa Barbara Co..... |
| Murchada, P......... | Laborer................ | Las Cruces............. | Santa Barbara Co.... |
| Murray, Philo....... | Farmer................ | Santa Barbara......... | Santa Barbara Co..... |
| Murray, John........ | Carpenter............ | Santa Barbara......... | Santa Barbara Co..... |
| Muzzall, H............ | Photographer...... | State st................... | Bath st.................... |
| Myerben, Pedro... | Grocery store....... | Santa Ynez Road..... | 3 m N E Las Cruces |
| Meyers, James L... | Stage driver........ | Santa Barbara Co.... | Santa Barbara......... |
| Nandle, —............ | Farmer................ | State st................... | Quinientos st........... |
| Nandle, George D.. | Farmer................ | Santa Barbara......... | Santa Barbara Co..... |
| Neal, Mrs S........... | Dress maker......... | ............................ | Milpas st................. |

# THEOBALD BAYER,
## BLACKSMITH & WAGON MAKER,
Opposite Post Office, San Luis Obispo, Cal.

  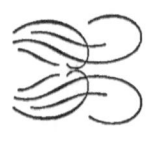

All work in this line done in the best manner, and on the most reasonable terms. Constantly on hand and for sale,

## IRON, COAL, HARDWOOD, LUMBER
### Plows, Agricultural Implements
And Farming Tools of all descriptions, at all prices.

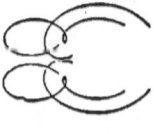  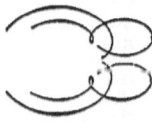

## CARRIAGES AND BUGGIES Made to Order
—— OR NEATLY REPAIRED. ——

# HORSESHOEING
## DONE IN A SUPERIOR MANNER.
All work guaranteed to give satisfaction.

# DIRECTORY OF SANTA BARBARA COUNTY. 145

| NAME. | OCCUPATION. | PLACE OF BUSINESS. | RESIDENCE. | TOWN OR P. O. |
|---|---|---|---|---|
| Neal, John P | Farmer | Santa Barbara Co | Montecito | |
| Neely, William | Mason | Montecito | Santa Barbara Co | |
| Nelson, John D | Clerk | Santa Barbara | Santa Barbara Co | Santa Barbara. |
| Neumayer, Prof A | Musician | S Barbara College | Chapala st | Santa Barbara. |
| Newburg, E S | Ranchero | Santa Barbara Co | Santa Barbara | Santa Barbara. |
| Newcomb, Mrs M J | | Anacapa st | Anacapa st | Santa Barbara. |
| Newell, T N | Grocer | State st | Haley st | Santa Barbara. |
| Newell & Shotwell | Grocers | State st | | Santa Barbara. |
| Newman, N W | Laborer | Santa Maria Valley | 2 m S Guadalupe | Guadalupe. |
| Newton, George | Laborer | Santa Barbara | Santa Barbara Co | Santa Barbara. |
| Niblet, Edward | Laborer | Santa Barbara Co | Santa Barbara | Santa Barbara. |
| Nicholson, Melford P | Farmer | Santa Barbara Co | Santa Maria | Santa Maria. |
| Nicholson, N P | Vice president | S M V F U | 3½ m E Central City | Santa Maria. |
| Nichols, Dr G B | Physician | Main st | Olivera st | Guadalupe. |
| Nichols, G | Barber | State st | | Santa Barbara. |
| Nidever, G | | | | Santa Barbara. |
| Nidever, John | Farmer | Carpenteria Valley | 2¼ m W Carpenteria | Carpenteria. |
| Nidever, John, Sr | Farmer | Santa Barbara | Santa Barbara Co | Santa Barbara. |
| Nidever, George E | Mariner | Santa Barbara | Santa Barbara Co | Santa Barbara. |
| Nidever, Jacob | Farmer | Santa Barbara | Santa Barbara Co | Santa Barbara. |
| Nidever, David A | Farmer | Santa Barbara Co | Santa Barbara | Santa Barbara. |
| Nidever, George, Sr | Stock raiser | Santa Barbara Co | Santa Barbara | Santa Barbara. |
| Nidever, Marcus | Seaman | Santa Barbara | Santa Barbara Co | Santa Barbara. |
| Nidever, J R | Laborer | Santa Barbara | Santa Barbara Co | Santa Barbara. |
| Nidever, Mrs Alice | Farmer | | | Santa Barbara. |
| Nixon, Thos | Carpenter | Santa Barbara | Vineyard st | Santa Barbara. |
| Noe, John | Variety store | Main st | Main st | Guadalupe. |
| Noe & Co, John | Fruit | Guadalupe st | Guadalupe st | Guadalupe. |
| Nolan, George H | Painter | Santa Barbara | Santa Barbara Co | Santa Barbara. |
| Nolan, William T | Teacher | Santa Ynez | Santa Barbara Co | Ballard's Sta'n. |
| Noponlo, Peter | Variety store | State st | Santa Barbara | Santa Barbara. |
| Norris, James A | Farmer | Guadalupe | Guadalupe | Guadalupe. |
| Norris, J R | Farmer | Santa Maria Valley | 4 m E Guadalupe | Guadalupe. |
| Norris, Benj | Farmer | Carpenteria Valley | 4½ m W Carpenteria | Carpenteria. |
| Norway & Cooper | R E and surveyors | State st | De la Guerra st | Santa Barbara. |
| Norway, W H | R E and surveyor | State st | Vineyard st | Santa Barbara. |
| Noyes, Arthur T | Brick maker | Santa Barbara Co | Santa Barbara | Santa Barbara. |
| Noyes, Edward T | Farmer | 3d Township | Santa Barbara Co | |
| Nutt, W J | Farmer | Santa Barbara Co | Santa Paula | |
| O'Brien, John | Laborer | Santa Barbara | Santa Barbara Co | Santa Barbara. |
| O'Brien, Wm | Attorney | State st | Garden st | Santa Barbara. |
| Oconnor, Jas | Blacksmith | Cota st | | Santa Barbara. |
| Ogan, James | Farmer | Carpenteria Valley | 1½ m E Carpenteria | Carpenteria. |
| Ogan, John | Farmer | Carpenteria Valley | 1½ m E Carpenteria | Carpenteria. |
| Ogan, James S | Farmer | Carpenteria | Santa Barbara Co | Carpenteria. |
| Oglesby, O O | Capitalist | Santa Barbara | Victoria st | Santa Barbara. |
| Oglesby, D F | Farmer | Carpenteria | 2 m E Carpenteria | Carpenteria. |
| Ogle, Munroe | Farmer | Los Alamos | Santa Barbara Co | |
| Oglesby, A A | Farmer | Santa Barbara Co | Santa Barbara | Santa Barbara. |
| Ohlmeyer, Henry | Stock | Santa Barbara | Vineyard st | Santa Barbara. |
| Olivera, Juan N | Laborer | Santa Ynez | 10 m N E Las Cruces | Santa Ynez. |
| Oliver, J C | Principal | Public School | Laguna st | Santa Barbara. |
| Olivera, E M | Farmer | Santa Barbara Co | Santa Maria | Santa Maria. |
| Olivera, Juan | Vaquero | Santa Barbara Co | Casmali | |
| Olivas, L G | Farmer | Santa Barbara Co | Santa Barbara | Santa Barbara. |
| Olivera, Thomas | Laborer | Santa Barbara Co | Santa Maria | Santa Maria. |
| Olivas, Francisco | Laborer | Santa Barbara Co | Santa Barbara | Santa Barbara. |
| Olivera, Jose R | Farmer | Casmali | Santa Barbara Co | |
| Olivera, Juan P | Ranchero | Santa Barbara Co | La Patera | |
| Olivas, Luis | Ranchero | 1st Township | Santa Barbara Co | |
| Olivas, Jose V | Vaquero | Santa Barbara Co | Santa Barbara | Santa Barbara. |
| Olivera, Juan de Dios | Ranchero | Santa Barbara Co | Tepusque | |

10

# PIONEER STORE!
## Grant, Lull & Co.
### PROPRIETORS,
Importers and Dealers in

# General Merchandise,
CAMBRIA & SAN SIMEON BAY, S. L. O. CO., CAL.

## HARDWARE, TINWARE,
### STOVES, CROCKERY, GLASSWARE,
## DOORS, WINDOWS,
## PAINTS, BRUSHES & OILS, FURNITURE

**Bedding and Household Furnishing Goods,**

## LUMBER
—— OF ALL KINDS, ——

### SHAKES, SHINGLES, POSTS, ETC.,
—— ALSO, AGENTS FOR THE CELEBRATED ——

## SCHUTTLER FARM WAGON

Call and examine our stock before purchasing elsewhere, as we will not be undersold by any house in the county.

### GRANT, LULL & CO.,
Agents for San Simeon Bay Wharf.

# DIRECTORY OF SANTA BARBARA COUNTY. 147

| Name. | Occupation. | Place of Business. | Residence. | Town or P. O. |
|---|---|---|---|---|
| Olivera, M............... | Laborer............... | Santa Barbara........... | Santa Barbara Co...... | Santa Barbara. |
| Olivera, Juan de Jesus................. | Vaquero............... | Santa Barbara........... | Santa Barbara Co..... | Santa Barbara. |
| Olivera, Jose A...... | Teamster............. | Las Cruces............... | Santa Barbara Co..... | Las Cruces. |
| Olivera, Cecilio..... | Ranchero............. | Santa Barbara Co.... | Santa Barbara........ | Santa Barbara. |
| Olivas, Juan Sr...... | Laborer............... | Santa Barbara........... | Santa Barbara Co.... | Santa Barbara. |
| Olivas, Juan deJesus | Laborer............... | Santa Barbara........... | Santa Barbara Co.... | Santa Barbara. |
| Olivas, Felipe........ | Ranchero............ | Santa Barbara........... | Santa Barbara Co.... | Santa Barbara. |
| Olivas, Juan .......... | Laborer............... | Santa Barbara Co.... | 2d Precinct.............. | |
| Olivas, Antonio...... | Laborer............... | Santa Barbara Co.... | Montecito............... | |
| Olivas, Blas........... | Laborer ............... | Montecito............... | Santa Barbara Co..... | |
| Olmstead, S H ...... | Farmer................ | Carpenteria Valley... | 1½ m E Carpenteria. | Carpenteria. |
| Olmstead, Seth R... | Farmer................ | Santa Barbara Co.... | Carpenteria............. | Carpenteria. |
| O'Loughlin, C........ | Miner.................. | Santa Barbara Co.... | Santa Barbara.......... | Santa Barbara. |
| O'Neil, O H.......... | Doctor.................. | Santa Barbara........... | Santa Barbara Co.... | Santa Barbara. |
| O'Neil, Patrick..... | General store......... | Guadalupe................ | La Graciosa............. | La Graciosa. |
| O'Neil, M.............. | Farmer................ | Beach Road............. | 1 m W Guadalupe.... | Guadalupe. |
| O'Neil, Joseph B ... | Farmer................ | Santa Barbara Co.... | Sespe...................... | |
| Ontiveras, Ramon... | Vaquero............... | Tepusqui ................ | Santa Barbara Co .... | |
| Ontiveras, F.......... | Ranchero............ | Tepusqui................. | Santa Barbara Co.... | |
| Ontiveras, Juan...... | Ranchero............ | Santa Maria............. | Santa Barbara Co.... | Santa Maria. |
| Ontiveras, A.......... | Farmer................ | 3d Township............ | Santa Barbara Co.... | |
| Opdyke, C M........ | Gardener.............. | Santa Barbara.......... | Chapala st.............. | Santa Barbara. |
| Orcutt, Jacob H.... | Sheep raiser......... | 3d Township............ | Santa Barbara Co.... | |
| Ord, James L......... | Doctor.................. | Santa Barbara Co.... | Santa Barbara.......... | Santa Barbara. |
| Ord, R B .............. | Justice of peace... | State st................... | Vineyard st............. | Santa Barbara. |
| Ordaz, Vicente ...... | Laborer............... | Santa Barbara Co.... | Refugio................... | |
| Orella, B................ | Ranchero............ | Cañada Corral ......... | 16 m S E Las Cruces | Santa Barbara. |
| Orellano, N............ | Laborer................ | Santa Barbara Co.... | Santa Barbara.......... | Santa Barbara. |
| Orella, Bruno......... | Ranchero............ | Santa Barbara Co.... | 3d Township............ | |
| Oreña, Gasper ...... | Ranchero............ | Santa Barbara Co.... | 3d Township............ | |
| Orford, Julius........ | Bookkeeper.......... | State st................... | Haley st.................. | Santa Barbara. |
| Ormsby, Levi......... | Farmer................ | Carpenteria Valley... | 4½ m W Carpenteria | Carpenteria. |
| Ormsby, L W........ | Farmer................ | Santa Barbara Co.... | Montecito............... | |
| Orr, Edward.......... | Farmer................ | Santa Barbara Co.... | La Patera................ | |
| Orr, Joshua W...... | Carriage maker .. | Santa Barbara ......... | Santa Barbara Co..... | Santa Barbara. |
| Orr, Jas W ........... | Groceries............. | State st................... | Chapala st............. | Santa Barbara. |
| Orr, James E......... | Carpenter............ | Santa Barbara.......... | Figueroa st............. | Santa Barbara. |
| Orr, David............. | Carpenter............ | Santa Barbara.......... | Santa Barbara st...... | Santa Barbara. |
| Orrelas, Yalro ....... | Laborer............... | Santa Barbara Co.... | Carpenteria............. | Carpenteria. |
| Ortega, Jose D....... | Laborer............... | Cineguitas............... | Santa Barbara Co..... | |
| Ortega, Jose Maria.. | Vaquero............... | Santa Barbara ......... | Santa Barbara Co..... | Santa Barbara. |
| Ortega, Miguel A... | Laborer............... | Santa Barbara Co.... | Los Alamos............. | |
| Ortega, D A de la S | Laborer............... | Santa Anita............. | Santa Barbara Co..... | |
| Ortega, E C........... | Vaquero .............. | Santa Barbara Co.... | Dos Pueblos............ | |
| Ortega, Jose Maria.. | Laborer............... | Santa Barbara Co.... | Santa Barbara........... | Santa Barbara. |
| Ortega, Vicente...... | Laborer............... | Santa Barbara.......... | Santa Barbara Co..... | Santa Barbara. |
| Ortega, E.............. | Laborer ............... | Las Cruces.............. | Santa Barbara Co..... | Las Cruces. |
| Ortega, F.............. | Teamster.............. | Santa Barbara Co.... | Las Cruces.............. | Las Cruces. |
| Ortega, F ............. | Teamster.............. | Santa Barbara Co.... | Santa Barbara Co..... | Santa Barbara. |
| Ortega, Gaudalupe.. | Laborer............... | Santa Barbara Co.... | Santa Barbara Co..... | Santa Barbara. |
| Ortega, P............... | Ranchero............ | Santa Barbara......... | Santa Barbara Co..... | Santa Barbara. |
| Ortega, Lewis ....... | Clerk................... | State st................... | State st................... | Santa Barbara. |
| Ortega, P R J F..... | Ranchero............ | Arroyo Honda......... | 10 m S E L Cruces... | Las Cruces. |
| Ortega, Ezekiel...... | Laborer............... | San Julian Ranch.... | 8 m W Las Cruces... | Las Cruces. |
| Ortega, Jose F....... | Ranchero............ | Las Cruces.............. | Las Cruces Ranch.... | Las Cruces. |
| Owen, W M ......... | Farmer................ | Santa Maria Valley.. | 2 m E Guadalupe..... | Guadalupe. |
| Owen, Benj F........ | Farmer................ | Santa Barbara.......... | La Patera................ | |
| Owen, William...... | Farmer................ | Santa Barbara Co.... | Santa Barbara.......... | Santa Barbara. |
| Packard, Albert ... | Attorney.............. | State st................... | Rancheria st........... | Santa Barbara. |
| Packwood, I L...... | Hotel keeper......... | Santa Barbara Co.... | Santa Barbara.......... | Santa Barbara. |
| Paddock, B J ........ | Carpenter............ | Santa Barbara.......... | Anacapa st.............. | Santa Barbara. |
| Paddock, C H........ | ............................ | ............................ | Anapamu st............ | Santa Barbara. |
| Paddock, C L........ | Clerk................... | State st................... | Victoria st.............. | Santa Barbara. |

# H. M. OSGOOD,

## Watchmaker & Jeweler

**MONTEREY ST., SAN LUIS OBISPO,**

Has a first-class stock of

WATCHES, CLOCKS & JEWELRY,

Spectacles of Every Kind,

Silver and Silver-Plated Ware.

Repairing Fine Watches a Specialty.

## GOLDTREE BRO'S,

**SAN LUIS OBISPO, CAL.**

## COMMISSION MERCHANTS

And Wholesale and Retail Dealers in

**GENERAL MERCHANDISE.**

---

CORRESPONDENTS:

**SITTENFELD & CO.,**
San Miguel, San Luis Obispo Co., Cal.

**I. SCHWARTZ & CO.,**
Guadalupe, Santa Barbara Co., Cal.

---

# R. M. PRESTON,

## NOTARY PUBLIC

—AND—

## CONVEYANCER,

Office of Justice of the Peace,

MORO.

SAN LUIS OBISPO CO., - CALIFORNIA.

# A. WILLIAMSON,

DEALER IN

## STOVES, TINWARE,

Hardware, House Furnishing Goods, Storage and Commission Merchant.

**MONTEREY STREET,**

SAN LUIS OBISPO, - CALIFORNIA.

## DIRECTORY OF SANTA BARBARA COUNTY.

| Name. | Occupation. | Place of Business. | Residence. |
|---|---|---|---|
| Paddock, Wm | Carpenter | Santa Barbara | Laguna st |
| Paddock, E L | Merchant | Santa Barbara | Anapamu st |
| Palmley, Mrs | | | Haley st |
| Pardee, R G | Farmer | Carpenteria Valley | 5 m E Carpenteria |
| Parr, Thomas | Saddler | Santa Barbara | Santa Barbara Co |
| Park, Joseph | Ranchero | Santa Barbara Co | Carpenteria |
| Parkinson, J D | Doctor | Santa Barbara | Santa Barbara Co |
| Parker, Rev | Pastor | Ortega and Vineyard | Garden st |
| Parma, V | Variety store | State st | State st |
| Parmer, G B | Variety store | State st | State st |
| Parish, W B | Tailor | State st | Victoria st |
| Parsons, Jacob | | | Chapala st |
| Pasque, Emil | Farmer | Point Sal | 8 m S W Guadalupe |
| Patch, Wm Y | | | Santa Barbara st |
| Paulsel, N | Farmer | Santa Barbara | Santa Barbara Co |
| Pearce, James G | Carpenter | Santa Barbara | Grey st |
| Peck, Wm | Blacksmith | Santa Barbara | Haley st |
| Peña, Felipe | Laborer | Santa Barbara Co | Santa Barbara |
| Pendola, J | Grocery | State st | Bath st |
| Pendola & Bralich | Variety store | State st | State st |
| Pendola, L | Variety store | State st | State st |
| Pendola, Antonio | Clerk | State st | State st |
| Pendola, Bavastrello | Liquors | State st | State st |
| Penfield, — | | | |
| Penny, E | Farmer | Carpenteria Valley | 1¼ m E Carpenteria |
| Penner, James | Farmer | Santa Barbara Co | San Marcos |
| Penny, H | Laborer | Santa Barbara | Vineyard st |
| Peralta, Juana | Laborer | Santa Barbara Co | Santa Barbara |
| Percival, W | Seaman | Santa Barbara Co | Santa Barbara |
| Perez, Manez | Farmer | Santa Barbara Co | Santa Maria |
| Perry, Antonio | Laborer | Point Sal | 10 m S W Guadalupe |
| Perry, Thomas L | Painter | Santa Barbara | Santa Barbara Co |
| Perry, William | Engineer | Santa Barbara | Santa Barbara Co |
| Peters, James R | Farmer | Santa Barbara Co | Los Alamos |
| Peterson, J O | Harness maker | State st | Morris Hotel |
| Pettigrove, Chas | Editor | State st | Gutierrez st |
| Pettinger, John | Carpenter | Santa Barbara | Santa Barbara Co |
| Pettygrove, Al | Publisher | State st | Gutierrez st |
| Pettinger, J | Farmer | Carpenteria Valley | 5 m E Carpenteria |
| Phelps, — | Physician | | Garden st |
| Phelps, H Wright | Engineer | State st | |
| Pico, Raphael | Musician | Santa Barbara | Guiterrez st |
| Pico, Miguel | Laborer | Santa Barbara Co | Carpenteria |
| Pico, Manuel | Laborer | Carpenteria | Santa Barbara Co |
| Pico, Marino | Laborer | Santa Barbara Co | Santa Barbara |
| Pico, Jose de J | Laborer | Santa Barbara | Santa Barbara Co |
| Pico, Ventura | Laborer | Santa Barbara | Santa Barbara Co |
| Pico, M A | Laborer | Carpenteria | Santa Barbara Co |
| Pico, Juan de Mata | Laborer | Santa Barbara Co | Santa Barbara |
| Pico, Jose Manuel | Vaquero | Santa Barbara | Santa Barbara |
| Pico, Miguel | Vaquero | Santa Barbara | Santa Barbara Co |
| Pico, Jose R | Vaquero | Santa Barbara Co | Santa Barbara |
| Pico, Gregorio | Laborer | Santa Barbara Co | Santa Barbara |
| Pico, Juan | Laborer | Santa Barbara | Santa Barbara Co |
| Pierce, Ira | Ranchero | Najahni | 7 m S Ballard's Sta |
| Pierce, T | Carpenter | Santa Barbara | De la Guerra st |
| Pierce, C | Lumber dealer | State st | State st |
| Pierce, A M | Cigar store | State st | State st |
| Pierce, — | Farmer | Santa Barbara | Garden st |
| Pierce, E H | Farmer | Carpenteria Valley | 3 m E Carpenteria |
| Pierce, Isaac B | Farmer | Santa Barbara Co | Santa Barbara |
| Pike, John F | Farmer | Carpenteria | Santa Barbara Co |
| Pilcher, John A | Stone mason | Santa Barbara | Santa Barbara st |
| Pinkham, R D | Farmer | La Patera | Santa Barbara Co |

### SAN MARCOS,

San Luis Obispo County, - - - California.

—IMPORTERS AND DEALERS IN—

# General Merchandise.

## HOUSE FURNISHING AND HOUSEHOLD GOODS,

IN EVERY VARIETY,

## WOOL, HIDES AND PRODUCE BOUGHT.

### A HOTEL

Containing every convenience for guests; also, ten cottages for use of families, in connection with the Hotel.

The Best of Entertainment at Low Rates.

**A WELL APPOINTED STABLE,**

*Giving the best of care to Transient and Boarding Stock.*

HAY AND GRAIN ALWAYS ON HAND AND FOR SALE IN LARGE OR SMALL QUANTITIES.

DIRECTORY OF SANTA BARBARA COUNTY. 151

| Name. | Occupation. | Place of Business. | Residence. | Town or P. O. |
|---|---|---|---|---|
| Placher, Soul | Farmer | Carpenteria | Santa Barbara Co | Carpenteria. |
| Platt, John C | Dep co clerk | Santa Barbara | Santa Barbara Co | Santa Barbara. |
| Pleasant, J W | Carpenter | Santa Barbara Co | Santa Ynez | Ballard's Sta'n. |
| Plummer, Mrs Soul | Books, stationery | State st | State st | Santa Barbara. |
| Polloreno, G | Teamster | Montecito | Santa Barbara Co | |
| Porter, Arza | Sheriff | Santa Barbara | Chapala st | Santa Barbara. |
| Porterfield, J H | Carpenter | Guadalupe | 2d st | Guadalupe. |
| Porterfield, J R | Publisher | Guadalupe Telegraph | 2d st | Guadalupe. |
| Porter, John A | Lompoc hotel | I and Ocean Ave | I and Ocean Ave | Lompoc. |
| Potter, George | Farmer | Santa Barbara Co | Pleasant Valley | |
| Powell, Rich'd | Teamster | Point Sal | 10 m S W Guadalupe | Guadalupe. |
| Preston, E J | Farmer | Beach Road | 2 m W Guadalupe | Guadalupe. |
| Price, W R | Clerk | State st | Union Hotel | Santa Barbara. |
| Price, R-uben | Farmer | Santa Barbara Co | Santa Paula | |
| Prior, Thomas | Painter | Santa Barbara | Gutierrez st | Santa Barbara. |
| Proctor, W C | Teamster | Santa Barbara | Santa Barbara Co | Santa Barbara. |
| Prosser, W | Carpenter | Santa Barbara | Haley st | Santa Barbara. |
| Prose, D W | Farmer | Cañada | Santa Barbara Co | |
| Purdy, Byron | Printer | Santa Barbara | Santa Barbara Co | Santa Barbara. |
| Pyster, John | Farmer | Carpenteria Valley | 5 m E Carpenteria | Carpenteria. |
| Quijada, Pedro | Laborer | Santa Barbara | Chapala st | Santa Barbara. |
| Quintero, S | Vaquero | La Patera | Santa Barbara Co | |
| Quizado, T | Teamster | Santa Barbara | Santa Barbara Co | Santa Barbara. |
| Quizado, Felipe | Vaquero | Santa Barbara Co | Santa Barbara | Santa Barbara. |
| Quizado, Juan | Laborer | Santa Barbara Co | Santa Barbara | Santa Barbara. |
| Rader, John | Butcher | Guadalupe st | | Guadalupe. |
| Raffour, Louis | Hotel keeper | Santa Barbara | Santa Barbara Co | Santa Barbara. |
| Rall, A L | Clerk | State st | State st | Santa Barbara. |
| Ramirez, Juan | Laborer | Carpenteria | Santa Barbara Co | Carpenteria. |
| Randall, Eli | Harness maker | State st | Haley st | Santa Barbara. |
| Randolph, G C | Farmer | Carpenteria | Santa Barbara Co | Carpenteria. |
| Rawles, M L | Farmer | Santa Barbara Co | La Patera | |
| Raymond, Henry | Speculator | Santa Barbara Co | Santa Barbara | Santa Barbara. |
| Raymond, T W | Druggist | State st | Ortega st | Santa Barbara. |
| Reddick, John | Farmer | Santa Barbara Co | Santa Barbara | Santa Barbara. |
| Remington, W B | Laborer | Santa Barbara | Santa Barbara Co | Santa Barbara. |
| Renhart, Morris | Laborer | Santa Barbara | Santa Barbara Co | Santa Barbara. |
| Resser, Hartman | Doctor | Santa Barbara | Santa Barbara Co | Santa Barbara. |
| Reyes, Juan | Laborer | Santa Barbara | Santa Barbara Co | Santa Barbara. |
| Reyes, Martin | Laborer | Santa Barbara | Santa Barbara Co | Santa Barbara. |
| Reynolds, W | Wheelwright | Cota st | Main st | Santa Barbara. |
| Reynolds, M L | Speculator | Santa Barbara | Santa Barbara Co | Santa Barbara. |
| Reyna, Jas | Clerk | State st | Anacapa st | Santa Barbara. |
| Reynolds, A J | Barber | Guadalupe st | Guadalupe st | Guadalupe. |
| Reyser, Thos J | Farmer | Santa Barbara Co | Grey st | Santa Barbara. |
| Rhodehaver, J H | Carp & architect | State st | Santa Barbara st | Santa Barbara. |
| Rhodes, Saml | Mason | Santa Barbara | Laguna st | Santa Barbara. |
| Rhodes, J H | Farmer | Carpenteria | 1½ m N Carpenteria | Carpenteria. |
| Rias, — | Stock | Santa Barbara Co | Chapala st | Santa Barbara. |
| Rice, J H | Farmer | Santa Maria Valley | 2½ m E Guadalupe | Guadalupe. |
| Rice, A | Farmer | 1st Precinct | Santa Barbara Co | |
| Richardson, Geo M | Farmer | 1st Township | Santa Barbara Co | |
| Rich, Addison | Blacksmith | Santa Barbara Co | Santa Barbara | Santa Barbara. |
| Richardson, M | Farmer | Carpenteria Valley | 2 m E Carpenteria | Carpenteria. |
| Richardson, W | Farmer | Carpenteria Valley | 2 m E Carpenteria | Carpenteria. |
| Rich, J A | Blacksmith | Canyon Perdido st | Carrillo st | Santa Barbara. |
| Richards, S | Stone mason | Santa Barbara | Santa Barbara st | Santa Barbara. |
| Richards, Jarrett | Attorney at law | State st | Montecito st | Santa Barbara. |
| Richardson, H | Farmer | Carpenteria Valley | 2 m E Carpenteria | Carpenteria. |
| Richardson, D | Farmer | Carpenteria Valley | 2 m E Carpenteria | Carpenteria. |
| Richardson, Chas | Farmer | Carpenteria Valley | 2 m E Carpenteria | Carpenteria. |
| Richardson, Amos | Farmer | Carpenteria Valley | 2 m E Carpenteria | Carpenteria. |
| Riddell, James | Druggist | 1st Township | Santa Barbara Co | |
| Rider, Benj H | Carpenter | Santa Barbara | Santa Barbara st | Santa Barbara. |

# ARROYO GRANDE
## LIVERY, FEED AND SALE STABLE

ROBERT FARMER, - - - Proprietor.

San Luis Obispo  County, Cal'a.

Has on hand at all times an entirely new and fine stock of

## FANCY TOP AND OPEN BUGGIES,
### CARRIAGES AND WAGONS,
SUITABLE FOR MOUNTAIN TRAVEL.

Brand-New "Stylish Turn Outs,"  The Best in the County,

## Matched Teams and Single Horses
### SADDLE  HORSES,

Equal, if not superior, to the stock of any stable in the interior of the state.

**Parties promptly conveyed to any portion of the Country.**

I have also a large Corral for the accommodation of bands of Cattle or Horses. Particular attention paid to transient stock.

## TERMS LOW.

# DIRECTORY OF SANTA BARBARA COUNTY. 153

| Name. | Occupation. | Place of Business. | Residence. | Town or P. O. |
|---|---|---|---|---|
| Riggs, T C | Farmer | Beach Road | 2½ m W Guadalupe | Guadalupe. |
| Rines, Joshua R | Lighthouse keeper | Santa Barbara Co | 3d Township | |
| Risdon, Dr A D | Homeop'c phy'n | State st | Vineyard st | Santa Barbara. |
| Robbins, Juan G | Miner | Santa Barbara | Santa Barbara Co | Santa Barbara. |
| Robbins, M V | Farmer | Guadalupe | Guadalupe | Guadalupe. |
| Roberts, Mrs M A | | | Vineyard st | Santa Barbara. |
| Roberts, T W | Farmer | Santa Maria Valley | ½ m E Guadalupe | Guadalupe. |
| Roberts, Hugh | Painter | Santa Barbara | Haley st | Santa Barbara. |
| Roberts, W N | Dairyman | La Patera | Santa Barbara Co | |
| Roberts, Peter H | Laborer | Carpenteria | Santa Barbara Co | Carpenteria. |
| Robinson, S S | | | Haley st | Santa Barbara. |
| Robinson, W D | Farmer | Santa Barbara Co | Santa Barbara | Santa Barbara. |
| Robinson, H | Hostler | Santa Barbara Co | Santa Barbara | Santa Barbara. |
| Robinson, Richard | Seaman | Santa Barbara Co | Santa Barbara | Santa Barbara. |
| Robinson, Richard O | Seaman | Santa Barbara | Santa Barbara | Santa Barbara. |
| Robinson, Edward | Farmer | Montecito | Santa Barbara Co | |
| Robles, Gaudalupe | Vaquero | Santa Barbara Co | Santa Barbara | Santa Barbara. |
| Robles, Jose | Laborer | Santa Barbara Co | Montecito | |
| Rodehaver, G H | Carpenter | Santa Barbara Co | Santa Barbara | Santa Barbara. |
| Rodriguez, Loreto | Laborer | Santa Barbara Co | Santa Barbara | Santa Barbara. |
| Rodriguez, Jose de J | Laborer | Santa Barbara Co | Santa Barbara | Santa Barbara. |
| Rodriguez, Jose | Painter | Santa Barbara | Santa Barbara Co | Santa Barbara. |
| Rodriguez, R | Laborer | Santa Barbara Co | Montecito | |
| Rodriguez, C A B de J | Farmer | Santa Barbara Co | Carpenteria | Carpenteria. |
| Rodriguez, A M | Laborer | Santa Barbara | Santa Barbara Co | Santa Barbara. |
| Rodriguez, J A A | Ranchero | Santa Barbara | Santa Barbara Co | Santa Barbara. |
| Rodriguez, A D | Laborer | Santa Barbara | Santa Barbara Co | Santa Barbara. |
| Rodriguez, Juan C | Ranchero | Santa Ynez | Santa Ynez | Santa Ynez. |
| Roderiguez, Jose | Laborer | Santa Barbara | Anacapa st | Santa Barbara. |
| Rodriguez, Juan | Stable keeper | State st | State st | Santa Barbara. |
| Roderiguez, Pedro | Laborer | Santa Barbara | De la Guerra st | Santa Barbara. |
| Roderiguez, A | Laborer | Santa Barbara | Bath st | Santa Barbara. |
| Roderiguez, M | Farmer | Carpenteria Valley | 2 m E Carpenteria | Carpenteria. |
| Roderiguez, C | Butcher | Carpenteria | Carpenteria | Carpenteria. |
| Roder, John | Tailor | State st | Castel st | Santa Barbara. |
| Rodgers, S | Farmer | Beach Road | 2 m W Guadalupe | Guadalupe. |
| Roeder, E C | Clerk | State st | Montecito st | Santa Barbara. |
| Roeder, George | | | Anacapa st | Santa Barbara. |
| Rogers, E F | Agent | | Victoria st | Santa Barbara. |
| Rogers, A | Merchant | | Victoria st | Santa Barbara. |
| Rogers, S P | Farmer | Santa Barbara Co | La Patera | |
| Romans, Henry | Laborer | Los Alamos | Santa Barbara Co | |
| Romero, Jesus | Laborer | Mountain View | Santa Barbara Co | |
| Romero, V P | Laborer | Los Alamos | Santa Barbara Co | |
| Romero, Jose A | Vaquero | Santa Ynez | Santa Barbara Co | |
| Romero, Miguel | Laborer | Santa Barbara | Santa Barbara Co | Santa Barbara. |
| Romero, Francisco | Laborer | Santa Barbara Co | Santa Barbara | Santa Barbara. |
| Romero, Jose R | Vaquero | Santa Barbara Co | Santa Barbara | Santa Barbara. |
| Romero, Pedro A | Vaquero | Montecito | Santa Barbara Co | |
| Romero, Nemecio | Vaquero | Santa Barbara Co | Montecito | |
| Romero, A | Vaquero | Montecito | Santa Barbara Co | |
| Romero, A | Laborer | Montecito | Santa Barbara Co | |
| Romero, Jose Z | Laborer | Santa Barbara Co | Montecito | |
| Romero, J P | Vaquero | Santa Barbara Co | Los Alamos | |
| Romera, P V | Farmer | Santa Barbara Co | 3d Township | |
| Romero, J M | Mason | Santa Barbara | Santa Barbara Co | Santa Barbara. |
| Romero, Juan | Laborer | Montecito | Santa Barbara Co | |
| Romero, Jose A | Laborer | Montecito | Santa Barbara Co | |
| Romero, Mariano | Farmer | Montecito | Santa Barbara Co | |
| Romero, Juan | Farmer | Santa Barbara Co | Santa Barbara | Santa Barbara. |
| Romero, Juan de Dios | Clerk | Santa Barbara | Santa Barbara Co | Santa Barbara. |
| Root, A | Farmer | Santa Barbara Co | La Patera | |

# L. RACKLIFFE

## SAN LUIS OBISPO, CAL.

—— DEALER IN ——

## General Merchandise

### FANCY GOODS, CHEMICALS,

### PAINTS AND OILS,

## Dry Goods, Provisions,

### LIQUORS, TOBACCO & CIGARS,

# BOOTS & SHOES

### HARDWARE, FARMING IMPLEMENTS,

## Crockeryware, Blankets,

### FASHIONABLE CLOTHING,

## GENERAL FURNISHING GOODS

Country Produce taken in Exchange for Goods, at the Highest Market Rates

# DIRECTORY OF SANTA BARBARA COUNTY. 155

| Name. | Occupation. | Place of Business. | Residence. | Town or P. O. |
|---|---|---|---|---|
| Rork, James | Laborer | Santa Barbara Co | Santa Barbara | Santa Barbara. |
| Rosenberg, Isaac | Barber | Santa Barbara Co | Santa Barbara | Santa Barbara. |
| Rosenberg, — | Grain store | Cota st | | Santa Barbara. |
| Rose, W B | Stock raiser | Santa Barbara Co | Sespe | |
| Rose, D W | Farmer | Cañada | Santa Barbara Co | |
| Rosenberg, T H B | Farmer | Carpenteria | Santa Barbara Co | Carpenteria. |
| Rosenberg, T H B | City express | State st | Santa Barbara st | Santa Barbara. |
| Rosenberg & Huntington | Grain store | Cota st | | Santa Barbara. |
| Rossi, Jos | Book maker | State st | State st | Santa Barbara. |
| Ross, George de S | Clerk | Santa Barbara Co | Santa Barbara | Santa Barbara. |
| Rouard, Jose M | Laborer | Santa Barbara | Santa Barbara Co | Santa Barbara. |
| Rourd, Jos | Blacksmith | Canyon Perdido st | Canyon Perdido st | Santa Barbara. |
| Rowe, Benj S | Book keeper | State st | State st | Santa Barbara. |
| Rue, Godfrey | Laborer | Santa Barbara Co | Carpenteria | Carpenteria. |
| Ruiz, Felipe | Laborer | Santa Barbara | Santa Barbara Co | Santa Barbara. |
| Ruiz, Juan B | Laborer | Santa Barbara Co | Cañada | |
| Ruiz, M Jose de la L | Carpenter | Santa Barbara | Santa Barbara Co | Santa Barbara. |
| Ruiz, Jose A | Laborer | Santa Barbara Co | Santa Barbara | Santa Barbara. |
| Ruiz, Jose N | Ranchero | 3d Township | Santa Barbara Co | |
| Ruiz, Jose | Vaquero | Santa Barbara | Santa Barbara Co | Santa Barbara. |
| Ruiz, N A | Farmer | Tepusque | Santa Barbara Co | |
| Ruiz, Jose del Carmen | Vaquero | Santa Barbara Co | Santa Barbara | Santa Barbara. |
| Ruiz, Jose de Jesus | Vaquero | Santa Barbara | Santa Barbara Co | Santa Barbara. |
| Ruiz, Jose M | Laborer | Santa Barbara Co | Carpenteria | Carpenteria. |
| Ruiz, Jose, Jr | Laborer | Santa Barbara Co | Santa Barbara | Carpenteria. |
| Ruiz, Francisco | Laborer | Carpenteria | Santa Barbara Co | Carpenteria. |
| Ruiz, J de la Cruz, Sr | Laborer | Santa Barbara Co | Tepusque | |
| Ruiz, Diego | Vaquero | Santa Barbara | Carpenteria | Carpenteria. |
| Ruiz, G, Jr | Vaquero | Santa Barbara | Santa Barbara Co | Santa Barbara. |
| Ruiz, L A A | Laborer | Santa Barbara Co | Todos Santos | |
| Ruiz, Antonio | Laborer | Carpenteria | Santa Barbara Co | Carpenteria. |
| Ruiz, Carlos, Sr | Farmer | Santa Barbara Co | Carpenteria | Carpenteria. |
| Ruiz, Carlos, Jr | Laborer | Santa Barbara | Santa Barbara Co | Santa Barbara. |
| Ruiz, Jose Lino | Vaquero | Santa Barbara Co | Santa Barbara | Santa Barbara. |
| Ruiz, Pedro | Laborer | Refugio | Santa Barbara Co | |
| Ruiz, Baltazar | Vaquero | Santa Barbara | Santa Barbara Co | Santa Barbara. |
| Ruiz, Jose Antonio | Vaquero | Santa Barbara | Santa Barbara Co | Santa Barbara. |
| Ruiz, Juan de la Cruz | Ranchero | Santa Barbara Co | Santa Barbara | Santa Barbara. |
| Ruiz, J A C | Laborer | Santa Barbara Co | Santa Barbara | Santa Barbara. |
| Ruiz, Jose A | Laborer | Santa Maria | Santa Barbara Co | Santa Maria. |
| Ruiz, Andre | Laborer | Santa Barbara Co | Santa Barbara | Santa Barbara. |
| Ruiz, Geronimo | Farmer | Santa Barbara Co | Chapala st | Santa Barbara. |
| Ruiz, Jose, Sr | Laborer | Santa Barbara | Santa Barbara st | Santa Barbara. |
| Ruiz, Antonio | Druggist | State st | State st | Santa Barbara. |
| Ruiz, Lewis | Clerk | State st | Santa Barbara | Santa Barbara. |
| Ruiz, F | Clerk | State st | Anacapa st | Santa Barbara. |
| Ruiz, Mrs M | | | Figueroa st | Santa Barbara. |
| Rumble, R H | Painter | State st | State st | Santa Barbara. |
| Rundell, Eli | Agt C L S Co | State st | Haley st | Santa Barbara. |
| Rundell, F M | Hotel | Ballard's Station | Ballard's Station | Ballard's Sta'n. |
| Russell, John | Farmer | Carpenteria | Santa Barbara Co | Carpenteria. |
| Russell, A W | Lawyer | Santa Barbara | Santa Barbara Co | Santa Barbara. |
| Russ, Andrew J | Clerk | Santa Barbara Co | Santa Barbara | Santa Barbara. |
| Russ, A | Saloon | State st | Morrison House | Santa Barbara. |
| Russ, Van Valkenburg | Saloon | State st | Santa Barbara | Santa Barbara. |
| Russell, Geo W | Clerk | State st | State st | Santa Barbara. |
| Russell, Wm F | S B index | State st | Santa Barbara | Santa Barbara. |
| Russell, Virginia F | S B index | State st | Santa Barbara | Santa Barbara. |
| Russell & Co | S B index | State st | Santa Barbara | Santa Barbara. |

## S. CERIBELLI,

PROPRIETOR OF

### SAN LUIS OBISPO

### Soda Water

### WORKS.

ALSO DEALER IN

### Wines, Liquors, Tobacco,

CIGARS AND CONFECTIONERY.

Monterey St., San Luis Obispo.

---

## PIONEER
## BRICK STORE,

A. Blochman & Co., Proprs.,

## COMMISSION MERCHANTS

AND DEALERS IN

### General Merchandise.

WOOL, HIDES AND PRODUCE BOUGHT.

**SAN LUIS OBISPO, - CAL.**

---

## BLACKSMITHING
—BY—

### E. WOODROOFE,

ELLIS STATION, EL MONTE
LOS ANGELES CO., CAL.

### HORSESHOEING,

Iron and Wood Work of all kinds.

☞ Dispatch used in the performance of Job Work, and all work is guaranteed to be of a superior quality.

---

### N. C. CHUNN,
—PROPRIETOR OF—

## Caliente Livery, Feed
### AND SALE STABLE,

CALIENTE, KERN COUNTY, CAL.

### Match Teams and Single Horses,
With Vehicles of all Descriptions.

**EXCELLENT SADDLE HORSES**

The best of accommodations for those stopping over. Careful attention paid to boarding horses.

**GOOD CORRAL AND SHED.**

Hay and Grain in large and small quantities. Visitors conveyed to all points of interest.

# DIRECTORY OF SANTA BARBARA COUNTY. 157

| Name. | Occupation. | Place of Business. | Residence. | Town or P. O. |
|---|---|---|---|---|
| Russell, Mrs E L... | .................. | .................. | Cota st.............. | Santa Barbara. |
| Russell, J W......... | Drayman .......... | Santa Barbara...... | Montecito st........ | Santa Barbara. |
| Rust, Geo............. | Paper carrier...... | State st............. | Anacapa st.......... | Santa Barbara. |
| Rust, H H............ | Book keeper....... | Santa Barbara...... | Anacapa st.......... | Santa Barbara. |
| Rutherford, Aaron.. | Farmer ............ | Santa Maria Valley.. | 4 m E Guadalupe.... | Guadalupe. |
| Rutherford, Geo..... | Horse shoer ....... | Canyon Perdido st... | Cordeley st......... | Santa Barbara. |
| Ryan, Mrs J M....... | .................. | ....:................ | Micheltorena st..... | Santa Barbara. |
| Ryder, James H..... | Seaman............ | Santa Barbara Co.... | Santa Barbara...... | Santa Barbara. |
| Rynerson & Tilley | Flour mill ........ | Chapala st........... | .................. | Santa Barbara. |
| Rynerson, C C...... | Flour mill ........ | Chapala st........... | Bath st ............ | Santa Barbara. |
| Rystrom, C F........ | Farmer ............ | Carpenteria Valley... | 1¼ m E Carpenteria. | Carpenteria. |
| Sniotz, John ........ | Butcher............ | Santa Barbara....... | Santa Barbara st.... | Santa Barbara. |
| Saint John, W H... | Mason............. | Santa Barbara....... | Santa Barbara Co.... | Santa Barbara. |
| Sais, Tranquilito..... | Laborer ........... | Santa Barbara Co.... | Santa Barbara...... | Santa Barbara. |
| Salazar, Jose J....... | Laborer............ | 2d Precinct.......... | Santa Barbara Co.... | |
| Salascer, F S ........ | Laborer............ | Santa Barbara Co.... | Santa Maria......... | Santa Maria. |
| Salgado, Juan ....... | Laborer ........... | Santa Barbara Co.... | Montecito........... | |
| Salnzar, Juan........ | Saddler............ | State st.............. | State st............. | Santa Barbara. |
| Salmon, Alijo....... | Tailor .............. | Santa Barbara....... | Santa Barbara Co.... | Santa Barbara. |
| Salomon, Fernando | Gen merchandise. | State st............? | State st............. | Santa Barbara. |
| Salomon & Horix.. | Gen merchandise. | State st.............. | .................. | Santa Barbara. |
| Saltmarsh, J B...... | Miner............... | Santa Barbara Co.... | 3d Township........ | |
| Sanders, John........ | Farmer ............ | La Patera........... | Santa Barbara Co.... | |
| Santa Barbara Bank............... | .................. | .................. | .................. | Santa Barbara. |
| Santa Maria Valley Farmer's Union | Gen'l store........ | Broadway, cor Main. | Central City......... | Santa Maria. |
| Sargent, A W....... | Farmer ........... | La Patera........... | Santa Barbara Co.... | |
| Save, John .......... | St charles hotel ... | State st.............. | State st............. | Santa Barbara. |
| Savies, Leandro..... | Merchant ......... | Santa Barbara....... | Santa Barbara Co.... | Santa Barbara. |
| Savitz, John J....... | Laborer ........... | Santa Barbara....... | Santa Barbara Co.... | Santa Barbara. |
| Sawyer, M........... | .................. | .................. | Bath st ............ | Santa Barbara. |
| Scarsolo, Jos........ | Clerk .............. | State st.............. | Santa Barbara...... | Santa Barbara. |
| Schacht, W.......... | Farmer ............ | Santa Maria Valley.. | ¼ m S E Guadalupe. | Guadalupe. |
| Schnell, W H....... | Farmer ............ | Montecito........... | Santa Barbara Co.... | |
| Schuster, A ......... | Body maker....... | Cota st.............. | Pacific Hotel........ | Santa Barbara. |
| Schultz, John........ | Farmer ........... | Carpenteria Valley... | 2½ m E Carpenteria. | Carpenteria. |
| Scollan, Eugene..... | Farmer ........... | Santa Barbara Co.... | La Patera........... | |
| Scollan, John ....... | Laborer........... | Santa Barbara....... | Santa Barbara Co.... | Santa Barbara. |
| Scott, W F.......... | Farmer............ | Santa Barbara Co.... | Santa Barbara...... | Santa Barbara. |
| Scott, J M........... | Contractor........ | Santa Barbara....... | Fig ave............. | Santa Barbara. |
| Scott, J............... | Farmer ........... | Carpenteria Valley... | 5 m E Carpenteria... | Carpenteria. |
| Scott, J W.......... | Book keeper...... | .................. | Bath st ............ | Santa Barbara. |
| Scriminger, E M.... | Carpenter ........ | Santa Barbara st..... | Santa Barbara st.... | Santa Barbara. |
| Scudder, W H ...... | Fruit, candies, &c | State st.............. | Santa Barbara ..... | Santa Barbara. |
| Scull, Abel .......... | Farmer ........... | 2d Precinct......... | Santa Barbara Co.... | |
| Scull, Charles ...... | Farmer ........... | Santa Barbara....... | Santa Barbara Co.... | Santa Barbara. |
| Seaverens, H H..... | Farmer ........... | Montecito.......... | Santa Barbara Co.... | |
| Seers, M............. | Barber shop...... | State st.............. | Santa Barbara...... | Santa Barbara. |
| Sefton, Waine...... | Printer ............ | State st.............. | Garden st........... | Santa Barbara. |
| Sefton, A W........ | Printer ........... | Santa Barbara....... | Santa Barbara Co.... | Santa Barbara. |
| Seitters, Henry ..... | Tailor ............. | State st.............. | Garden st........... | Santa Barbara. |
| Sellers, Wm ........ | Farmer............ | Carpenteria Valley... | 1 m E Carpenteria.. | Carpenteria. |
| Senter, German..... | Mechanic ........ | Santa Barbara Co.... | Santa Barbara...... | Santa Barbara. |
| Sevay, J.............. | Blacksmith....... | Guadalupe st........ | Olivera st........... | Guadalupe. |
| Sexton, Joseph ..... | Farmer ........... | Santa Barbara Co.... | Santa Barbara...... | Santa Barbara. |
| Sexton, R K........ | Capitalist ........ | Santa Barbara...... | Castle st............ | Santa Barbara. |
| Sexton, L............ | Nurseryman...... | S B Nursery........ | Castle st............ | Santa Barbara. |
| Sexton, J............. | Prop S B nursery | Montecito st........ | 7 m W Santa Barbara | Santa Barbara. |
| Shandrow, Franklin | Carpenter ........ | Santa Barbara....... | Santa Barbara...... | Santa Barbara. |
| Sharky, Andy....... | Horse shoer ...... | Canyon Perdido st... | Garden st........... | Santa Barbara. |
| Shaug, A W ........ | Laborer........... | Santa Barbara Co.... | Santa Maria......... | Santa Maria. |
| Shaw, James........ | Hotel keeper...... | Santa Barbara....... | Santa Barbara Co.... | Santa Barbara. |
| Shaw, Dr Jas B.... | Physician......... | State st.............. | State st............. | Santa Barbara. |

### SAN MIGUEL,

San Luis Obispo County, California.

# COMMISSION MERCHANTS,

*AND DEALERS IN*

## General Merchandise,

**FANCY GOODS, CHEMICALS, DRUGS, MEDICINES,**

PAINTS, OILS, STATIONERY, ETC.

**DRY GOODS, PROVISIONS, LIQUORS,**

TOBACCO,

**CIGARS, BOOTS AND SHOES, HARDWARE,**

CROCKERYWARE,

BLANKETS, CLOTHING, AND GENERAL FURNISHING GOODS.

AGENTS FOR WELLS, FARGO & CO., THE COAST LINE U. S. STAGE CO., AND THE WESTERN UNION TELEGRAPH.

## DIRECTORY OF SANTA BARBARA COUNTY. 159

| NAME. | OCCUPATION. | PLACE OF BUSINESS. | RESIDENCE. | TOWN OR P. O. |
|---|---|---|---|---|
| Shaw, Mrs E | | | Victoria st | Santa Barbara. |
| Shaw, C J | Stock raiser | Los Alamos | 40 m S Gaudalupe | Guadalupe. |
| Shaw, Mrs Mary | Hotel prop | White House | Chapala st | Santa Barbara. |
| Shaw, Earl | Farmer | Goleta | Santa Barbara Co | |
| Shaw, Charles W | Farmer | Santa Barbara Co | Santa Barbara | Santa Barbara. |
| Sheffeld, Chas G | Cooper | Santa Barbara Co | Santa Barbara | Santa Barbara. |
| Shenk, Isaac H | Farmer | La Patera | Santa Barbara Co | |
| Shepard, H T | Pioneer pla'g mill | Montecito & State sts | Montecito st | Santa Barbara. |
| Shepherd, Joseph | Laborer | Santa Barbara | Santa Barbara Co | Santa Barbara. |
| Sherman, — | Real estate | State st | | Santa Barbara. |
| Sherman, C | Auction & com | State st | Chapala st | Santa Barbara. |
| Sherman, C E | Butcher | State st | Chapala st | Santa Barbara. |
| Sherman & Ealand | Butchers | State st | | Santa Barbara. |
| Shew, Conrad | Tailor | Montecito | Santa Barbara Co | |
| Shewsbury, N | Dentist | Santa Barbara Co | Santa Barbara | Santa Barbara. |
| Shields, James | Farmer | Carpenteria Valley | 3½ m W Carpenteria | Carpenteria. |
| Shields, Frank | Farmer | Carpenteria Valley | 3½ m W Carpenteria | Carpenteria. |
| Shields, Wm | Farmer | Carpenteria Valley | 3½ m W Carpenteria | Carpenteria. |
| Shields, John | Farmer | Santa Barbara | Santa Barbara Co | Santa Barbara. |
| Shipp, William | Farmer | 1st Township | Santa Barbara Co | |
| Shoemake, John | Farmer | Santa Barbara Co | Santa Barbara | Santa Barbara. |
| Shoemake, Mrs C | | | Vineyard st | Santa Barbara. |
| Short, James M | Clerk | Santa Barbara | Santa Barbara Co | Santa Barbara. |
| Shortig, Augustus | Farmer | La Patera | Santa Barbara Co | |
| Shotwell, C S | Grocery store | State st | Fig Ave | Santa Barbara. |
| Shotwell, Jas | Clerk | State st | Fig Ave | Santa Barbara. |
| Shoults, J W | Farmer | Carpenteria Valley | 1½ m E Carpenteria | Carpenteria. |
| Shotwell G W | Saloon keeper | Santa Barbara | Santa Barbara Co | Santa Barbara. |
| Shoup, Sam'l | Bdg house | De la Guerra st | De la Guerra st | Santa Barbara. |
| Shoults, William | Laborer | Rincon | Santa Barbara Co | |
| Show, Daniel | Farmer | Santa Barbara | Santa Barbara Co | Santa Barbara. |
| Shrewsbury, Dr J N | Dentist | Santa Barbara | De la Guerra st | Santa Barbara. |
| Shuman, John L | Farmer | Santa Barbara Co | 3d Township | |
| Shuster, Louis P | Merchant | Santa Barbara | Santa Barbara | Santa Barbara. |
| Shuster, A A | Merchant | Santa Barbara | Santa Barbara Co | Santa Barbara. |
| Sibley, Hiram C | Laborer | Santa Maria | Santa Barbara Co | Santa Maria. |
| Silbas, Jose | Laborer | Santa Barbara Co | Sahta Barbara | Santa Barbara. |
| Silvas, Jose | Teamster | Santa Barbara Co | Santa Barbara | Santa Barbara. |
| Silvey, John Lester | Farmer | Santa Barbara Co | 2d Precinct | |
| Silveria, C | Teamster | Santa Maria Valley | 1½ m E Guadalupe | Guadalupe. |
| Silveria, T | Teamster | Santa Maria Valley | 1½ m E Guadalupe | Guadalupe. |
| Simmons, George | Farmer | Carpenteria Valley | 4 m E Carpenteria | Carpenteria. |
| Simpson, James | — | | Chapala st | Santa Barbara. |
| Simpson, George | Mason | Santa Barbara Co | Santa Barbara | Santa Barbara. |
| Simpson, J A | Farmer | Santa Barbara | Santa Barbara Co | Santa Barbara. |
| Skelton, James I | Mechanic | Llagas | 20 m S E L Cruces | Las Cruces. |
| Skelton, J I | Carpenter | Santa Barbara | Grey st | |
| Skelton, Mrs | | | Grey st | Santa Barbara. |
| Slattery, John | Laborer | Santa Maria Valley | 2 m S Guadalupe | Guadalupe. |
| Smith, E | Painter | Cota st | nr Santa Barbara st | Santa Barbara. |
| Smith, Wm | Teamster | Santa Barbara | Yanonali st | Santa Barbara. |
| Smith, Fred | Clerk | State st | State and Cota sts | Santa Barbara. |
| Smith Bros | Wharfingers | Carpenteria Valley | 3 m W Carpenteria | Carpenteria. |
| Smith, Milton | Wharfinger | Carpenteria Valley | 3 m W Carpenteria | Carpenteria. |
| Smith, N D | Wharfinger | Carpenteria Valley | 3 m W Carpenteria | Carpenteria. |
| Smith & Edwards | Hardware | State st | | Santa Barbara. |
| Smith, C C | Hardware | State st | Bath st | Santa Barbara. |
| Smith, — | Printer | State st | Castle st | Santa Barbara. |
| Smith, B J | Farmer | Santa Barbara | Santa Barbara | Santa Barbara. |
| Smith, Frank | Bookkeeper | Stearn's Wharf | State st | Santa Barbara. |
| Smith, Mrs J | | | Carrillo st | Santa Barbara. |
| Smith, Albano | Ranchero | Santa Barbara | Santa Barbara Co | Santa Barbara. |
| Smith, George | Ranchero | Santa Barbara Co | Santa Barbara | Santa Barbara. |

J. H. BLACKBURN.                                      E. B. MORRIS.

# COSMOPOLITAN HOTEL,

MONTEREY ST., SAN LUIS OBISPO, CAL.

*HOUSE WELL LOCATED,*

**NEWLY FURNISHED,**

## LIBERALLY CONDUCTED.

Gentlemanly Treatment at the Office,

Appetizing Fare at the Table,

**And PERFECT COMFORT IN THE SLEEPING APARTMENTS**

At the Bar will be found a complete stock of the choicest brands of

**WINES, LIQUORS & CIGARS**

Together with a skillful and courteous attendant.

BLACKBURN & MORRIS,  -  -  Proprietors.

# DIRECTORY OF SANTA BARBARA COUNTY. 161

| NAME. | OCCUPATION. | PLACE OF BUSINESS. | RESIDENCE. | TOWN OR P. O. |
|---|---|---|---|---|
| Smith, John. | Mariner | Santa Barbara Co. | Santa Barbara | Santa Barbara. |
| Smith, August M. | Farmer | 1st Precinct | Santa Barbara Co. | |
| Smith, Nelson D. | Farmer | Carpenteria | Santa Barbara Co. | Carpenteria. |
| Smith, Frank | Farmer | Santa Barbara Co. | Carpenteria | Carpenteria. |
| Smith, John M. | Farmer | Carpenteria | Santa Barbara Co. | Carpenteria. |
| Smith, John F. | Blacksmith | Santa Barbarf | Santa Barbara Co. | Santa Barbara. |
| Smith, Anthony | Brewer | Santa Barbara | Santa Barbara Co. | Santa Barbara. |
| Smith, Bennet | Blacksmith | Santa Barbara Co. | Carpenteria | Carpenteria. |
| Smith, Charles C. | Mariner | Santa Barbara | Santa Barbara Co. | Santa Barbara. |
| Smith, Robert W. | Light h'se k'per | Santa Barbara | Santa Barbara Co. | Santa Barbara. |
| Smith, Crowson | Miner | Santa Barbara Co. | Santa Barbara | Santa Barbara. |
| Smith, B A | Saloon | Guadalupe st | Guadalupe st | Guadalupe. |
| Smith, George | Laborer | Point Sal | 10 m S W Guadalupe | Guadalupe. |
| Smith, G V | Farmer | Point Sal | 8 m S W Guadalupe | Guadalupe. |
| Smythe, Thos. | Groceries | State st | Vineyard st | Santa Barbara. |
| Snedaker, H | Farmer | Santa Barbara | Nopal st | Santa Barbara. |
| Snyder, Thomas | Farmer | Santa Barbara | Santa Barbara Co. | Santa Barbara. |
| Snyder, Jesse | Farmer | Santa Barbara Co. | Goleta | |
| Soberanes, Thos M. | Laborer | Santa Barbara Co. | Santa Barbara | Santa Barbara. |
| Solsbury, Thomas. | Farmer | Beach Road | 1 m W Guadalupe | Guadalupe. |
| Sota, Antonio E. | Farmer | Santa Barbara Co. | Santa Barbara | Santa Barbara. |
| Sota, Jose M de la C | Musician | Santa Barbara | Santa Barbara Co. | Santa Barbara. |
| Soto, Y Jacobo | Musician | Santa Barbara | Santa Barbara Co. | Santa Barbara. |
| Souleus, Emile | Cook | Santa Barbara Co. | Santa Barbara Co. | Santa Barbara. |
| Souse, Cerillo | Laborer | Carpenteria | Santa Barbara Co. | Carpenteria. |
| Southwick, Mrs | | | Vineyard st | Santa Barbara. |
| South, Chas H | Justice of peace | Guadalupe Valley | La Graciosa | La Graciosa. |
| South, Charles H. | Laborer | Los Alamos | Santa Barbara Co. | |
| Sowerwine, George. | Laborer | Santa Barbara Wh'f | Haley st | Santa Barbara. |
| Sparks, John R. | Farmer | Sespe | Santa Barbara Co. | |
| Speed, Wm | Teamster | Point Sal | 10 m S W Guadalupe | Guadalupe. |
| Spencer, G H | Architect | State st | Santa Barbara st | Santa Barbara. |
| Spencer, Thomas | Druggist | Santa Barbara Co. | Santa Barbara | Santa Barbara. |
| Splain, David | Light h'se k'per | Santa Barbara Co. | Point Conception | |
| Splain, Herbert | Laborer | 1st Township | Santa Barbara Co. | |
| Sprague, V B | Carriage maker | Santa Barbara | Santa Barbara | Santa Barbara. |
| Sprague, B L | Carriage maker | Santa Barbara | Santa Barbara | Santa Barbara. |
| Sprague, Thomas | Surveyor | Santa Barbara Co. | Santa Barbara | Santa Barbara. |
| Sprague, Mrs Nettie | Dress maker | Santa Barbara | | Santa Barbara. |
| Sprague, — | Livery stable | Cota st | | Santa Barbara. |
| Sprague, Geo A. | Painter | Santa Barbara | | Santa Barbara. |
| Sproul, W G | Stage driver | Santa Barbara | Santa Barbara Co. | Santa Barbara. |
| Sprout, Wm | Farmer | Santa Barbara | Montecito st | Santa Barbara. |
| Sproul, Wm | Teamster | Santa Barbara | Haley st | Santa Barbara. |
| Staats, Silas D | Carpenter | Santa Barbara | Santa Barbara Co. | Santa Barbara. |
| Stackhouse, Geo F. | Farmer | Santa Maria Valley. | 2 m N La Graciosa | La Graciosa. |
| Stafford, Walter | Soda manuf'r | De la Guerra st | De la Guerra st | Santa Barbara. |
| Stanah, Charles | Mason | Santa Barbara Co. | Santa Barbara | Santa Barbara. |
| Stanton, N R | Constable | State st | Montecito st | Santa Barbara. |
| Stanley, G W | Merchant | Santa Barbara | Fig Ave | Santa Barbara. |
| Stanley, George F. | Clerk | State st | State st | Santa Barbara. |
| Stanwood, W H. | Merchant | Santa Barbara | Santa Barbara Co. | Santa Barbara. |
| Stanton, Elijah | Farmer | Santa Barbara | Santa Barbara Co. | Santa Barbara. |
| Stanton, Thomas E | Farmer | Santa Barbara | Santa Barbara Co. | Santa Barbara. |
| Stark, Andrew J | Farmer | Santa Barbara Co. | 1st Township | |
| Stark, Lewis | | | Anapamu st | Santa Barbara. |
| Stearns, John P. | Lumber | Gutierrez st | Chapala st | Santa Barbara. |
| Stearns, John P. | Lawyer | Santa Barbara | Santa Barbara | Santa Barbara. |
| Stearns, John | Farmer | Santa Barbara Co. | Los Alamos | |
| Steele, Mrs C L | | | Vineyard st | Santa Barbara. |
| Steele, Lafayette | Carpenter | Santa Barbara | Santa Barbara | Santa Barbara. |
| Steele, Sebern | Carpenter | Santa Barbara | Santa Barbara Co. | Santa Barbara. |
| Steigaman, A | Laborer | Santa Barbara | Yanonali st | Santa Barbara. |
| Stephens, Martin H | Farmer | Santa Maria | Santa Barbara Co. | Santa Maria. |

11

| Name. | Occupation. | Place of Business. | Residence. | Town or P. O. |
|---|---|---|---|---|
| Stephenson, W | Laborer | Santa Barbara Co | Santa Barbara | Santa Barbara. |
| Stephens, Ezra F | Miner | Santa Barbara Co | Rincon | Rincon. |
| Stephens, Ed R | Clerk | Santa Barbara Co | Santa Barbara | Santa Barbara. |
| Stergemann, Augustus | Laborer | Santa Barbara Co | Santa Barbara | Santa Barbara. |
| Sterns, Mrs E F | Millinery store | State st | State st | Santa Barbara. |
| Sterling, Geo | Blacksmith | Cota st | | Santa Barbara. |
| Sterns, J G | Merchant | State st | State st | Santa Barbara. |
| Stovans, Robert F | Druggist | Santa Barbara Co | Santa Barbara | Santa Barbara. |
| Stevens, R | | | Garden st | Santa Barbara. |
| Stevens, E R | Groceries | State st | Garden st | Santa Barbara. |
| Stevens, J H | Brick maker | Garden st | Garden st | Santa Barbara. |
| Stevens & Tilley | Groceries | State st | | Santa Barbara. |
| Stevens, C J | U S m stage line. | Guadalupe | Guadalupe st | Guadalupe. |
| Stewart, Mrs | Millinery | State st | Santa Barbara | Santa Barbara. |
| Stewart, J S | Clerk | State st | State st | Santa Barbara. |
| Stewart, Enoch | Farmer | 1st Township | Santa Barbara Co | |
| Stewart, Hamilton | Farmer | 3d Township | Santa Barbara Co | |
| Stoce, Daniel C | Laborer | Santa Barbara Co | Santa Paula | |
| Stillwell, Wm Wilson | Farmer | Santa Barbara Co | Santa Maria | Santa Maria. |
| Stockton, Thomas J | Farmer | Santa Barbara | Santa Barbara Co | Santa Barbara. |
| Stock, Levi | Laborer | Santa Barbara | Haley st | Santa Barbara. |
| Stokum & Cavalli. | Restaurant | State st | State st | Santa Barbara. |
| Stone, F M | Wheelwright | Canyon Perdido st | State st | Santa Barbara. |
| Stone, Oliver | Blacksmith | Canyon Perdido st | State st | Santa Barbara. |
| Stone, S B | Clerk | Point Sal | Santa Barbara Co | Guadalupe. |
| Stone, J M | Farmer | Santa Maria Valley | 2½ m S E Guadalupe | Guadalupe. |
| Stone, H P | County clerk | Court House | Chapala st | Santa Barbara. |
| Stork, Prof | | | Vineyard st | Santa Barbara. |
| Stoudt, Charley | Saloon | State st | State st | Santa Barbara. |
| Stowell, Henry | Laborer | Santa Barbara Co | Santa Maria | Santa Maria. |
| Straithan, Robt | Farmer | Carpenteria Valley | 3¼ m W Carpenteria | Carpenteria. |
| Stratton, W C | Attorney at law | State st | Ortega st | Santa Barbara. |
| Strecker, August | Miss'n wat bath | State st | Ortega House | Santa Barbara. |
| Streeter, E E | Message deliverer | Ortega st | Gutierrez st | Santa Barbara. |
| Streeter, Wm A | Painter | Santa Barbara | Gutierrez st | Santa Barbara. |
| Streeter, W C | Mason | Santa Barbara Co | Santa Barbara | Santa Barbara. |
| Streeter, Albert A | Barber | Santa Barbara | Santa Barbara | Santa Barbara. |
| Street, Jesse | Hostler | Santa Barbara | Santa Barbara Co | Santa Barbara. |
| Strengfield, Sevier | Speculator | Santa Barbara Co | Santa Barbara | Santa Barbara. |
| Striedle, M | Boot & shoe store | State st | Haley st | Santa Barbara. |
| Stringfield, A E | Dairyman | Santa Barbara | Ortega st | Santa Barbara. |
| Stringfield, S | Dairyman | Santa Barbara | Ortega st | Santa Barbara. |
| St. Ores, L | Carpenter | Guadalupe | Guadalupe st | Guadalupe. |
| Strother, W H | Farmer | Santa Barbara Co | Carpenteria | Carpenteria. |
| Struhe, John | Farmer | Santa Barbara Co | Santa Barbara | Santa Barbara. |
| Stubblefield, A | Farmer | Santa Barbara Co | 3d Township | |
| Stubblefield, Robert C | Farmer | Santa Barbara | Santa Barbara Co | Santa Barbara. |
| Sturgeon, Samuel R J | Lawyer | Santa Barbara | Santa Barbara | Santa Barbara. |
| Sullivan, John | Laborer | Santa Barbara Co | Santa Barbara | Santa Barbara. |
| Sullivan, David | Farmer | Santa Barbara Co | Santa Barbara Co | Santa Barbara. |
| Summers, James H | Carpenter | Santa Barbara Co | Santa Barbara | Santa Barbara. |
| Summers, Jas | Stock | Santa Barbara | Anacapa st | Santa Barbara. |
| Suril, Firmin | Farmer | Santa Barbara | Santa Barbara | Santa Barbara. |
| Surila, Juan | Farmer | Santa Barbara | Santa Barbara Co | Santa Barbara. |
| Sutton, Amos | Farmer | Carpenteria Valley | 1 m E Carpenteria | Carpenteria. |
| Sutton, B F | Farmer | Carpenteria | Carpenteria | Carpenteria. |
| Swartz, I & Co | Genl merchandise | Guadalupe st | | Guadalupe. |
| Swartz, Isidor | Gen merchandise. | Guadalupe st | Guadalupe st | Guadalupe. |
| Sweetser, J N | | Santa Barbara | | Santa Barbara. |
| Swift, W D | Farmer | Montecito | Santa Barbara Co | |

# DIRECTORY OF SANTA BARBARA COUNTY.

| Name. | Occupation. | Place of Business. | Residence. | Town or P. O. |
|---|---|---|---|---|
| Swift, C E | Farmer | Santa Barbara Co | Montecito | |
| Swift, James H | Farmer | Santa Barbara Co | Montecito | |
| Swift, Jarvis | Farmer | San Leandro | Santa Barbara Co | |
| Swineburn, Jas | Boot maker | State st | State st | Santa Barbara. |
| Switzer, Leonard | Teamster | Santa Barbara | Santa Barbara Co | Santa Barbara. |
| Tallent, B E | Tinsmith | State st | De La Vina st | Santa Barbara. |
| Tallant, Henry | | | Vineyard st | Santa Barbara. |
| Talley, Edmund | Laborer | Santa Barbara | State st | Santa Barbara. |
| Tapie & Co | St Charles hotel | State st | State st | Santa Barbara. |
| Tapie, Pedro | Merchant | Santa Barbara | Santa Barbara Co | Santa Barbara. |
| Taylor, Wm | Photographer | State st | State st | Santa Barbara. |
| Taylor, E B | Farmer | Santa Barbara Co | Santa Maria | Santa Maria. |
| Taylor, Morgan G | Farmer | 1st Township | Santa Barbara Co | |
| Taylor, Alex S | Farmer | Santa Barbara Co | La Patera | |
| Teague, A G | Laborer | Santa Maria Valley | 3 m E Guadalupe | Guadalupe. |
| Tebbetts, Mrs Dolores | | | Vineyard st | Santa Barbara. |
| Tebbetts, G P | Com & post mas'r | State st | Haley st | Santa Barbara. |
| Tebbetts, Rufus P | Agent | Santa Barbara Co | Santa Barbara | Santa Barbara. |
| Terrell, D | Carpenter | Santa Barbara | Victoria st | Santa Barbara. |
| Terso, Aguire | Ranchero | Santa Barbara | Santa Barbara Co | Santa Barbara. |
| Thaine, Edward L | Stock raiser | Santa Barbara Co | 2d Precinct | |
| Thompson, Arthur W | Laborer | Santa Barbara Co | Santa Barbara | Santa Barbara. |
| Thompson, F W | Clerk | Santa Barbara | Santa Barbara Co | Santa Barbara. |
| Thomas, Geo W | Clerk | Santa Barbara | Santa Barbara Co | Santa Barbara. |
| Thomas & Johnson | Confectionery | State st | Santa Barbara | Santa Barbara. |
| Thomas, G W | Confectionery | State st | Anacapa st | Santa Barbara. |
| Thomas, B F | Attorney at law | Guadalupe st | Guadalupe st | Guadalupe. |
| Thompson, Fred'k | Dairyman | Llagas | 20 m S E Las Cruces | Las Cruces. |
| Thompson, C A | Searcher records | State st | | Santa Barbara. |
| Thompson, Chas Augustus | Clerk | State st | Castle st, cor Haley | Santa Barbara. |
| Thompson, H C | Printer | State st | Ortega st | Santa Barbara. |
| Thompson, John | Painter | Santa Barbara | Anapamu st | Santa Barbara. |
| Thompson, David | Farmer | Santa Barbara | Montecito st | Santa Barbara. |
| Thompson, Francis A | County clerk | Santa Barbara | Santa Barbara Co | Santa Barbara. |
| Thompson, Dixey W | Ranchero | Santa Barbara | Santa Barbara Co | Santa Barbara. |
| Thomas, Pealter | Butcher | Carpenteria | Santa Barbara Co | Carpenteria. |
| Thornberg, Joseph | Farmer | Santa Maria | Santa Barbara Co | Santa Maria. |
| Thornberg, John | Farmer | Santa Barbara Co | Santa Barbara Co | Santa Barbara. |
| Thurmond, John R | Farmer | Santa Barbara Co | Carpenteria | Carpenteria. |
| Thurmond, G E | Gen merchandise | Carpenteria | Carpenteria | Carpenteria. |
| Thurmond, Rich'd | Farmer | Carpenteria | Carpenteria | Carpenteria. |
| Tierney, J | Clerk | Chapala st | De La Vina st | Santa Barbara. |
| Tierney, P J | Carpenter | | Vineyard st | Santa Barbara. |
| Tierney, J | Miller | Chapala st | Vineyard st | Santa Barbara. |
| Tilley, S T | Books & station'y | State st | Chapala st | Santa Barbara. |
| Tilley, W G | Clerk | State st | Anapamu st | Santa Barbara. |
| Tilley, W J | Grocery store | Front st | Sacramento st | San Francisco. |
| Titus, Abner S | Farmer | Santa Barbara Co | Montecito | |
| Tobey, West | Carpenter | Santa Barbara | Santa Barbara Co | Santa Barbara. |
| Todd, Joseph | Carpenter | Santa Barbara | Santa Barbara Co | Santa Barbara. |
| Tompkins, W R | Farmer | Santa Barbara Co | Santa Barbara | Santa Barbara. |
| Tompkins, John G | Farmer | Santa Barbara Co | 1st Township | |
| Tomisaini, A | Brewer | Guadalupe st | Guadalupe st | Guadalupe. |
| Torquini, C | Brewer | Guadalupe st | Guadalupe st | Guadalupe. |
| Torre, Antonio de la | Laborer | San Marcos | Santa Barbara Co | |
| Treussell, Capt H G | | | Castle st | Santa Barbara. |
| Trenwith, G F | Book keeper | State st | Anapamu st | Santa Barbara. |
| Triplet, J K | Farmer | Santa Maria Valley | 2½ m E Guadalupe | Guadalupe. |
| Triplet, Lemuel | Farmer | Santa Barbara Co | La Patera | |
| Trott, Joseph | Farmer | Santa Maria | Santa Barbara Co | Santa Maria. |

L. L. PAULSON'S HAND-BOOK AND

| NAME. | OCCUPATION. | PLACE OF BUSINESS. | RESIDENCE. | TOWN OR P. O. |
|---|---|---|---|---|
| Trout, D H............ | Teacher............ | City school............ | Haley st................. | Santa Barbara. |
| Trussell, Horacio G | Carpenter........... | Santa Barbara......... | Santa Barbara Co..... | Santa Barbara. |
| Tucker, Mrs Carrie | Proprietress........ | Exchange Hotel...... | Guadalupe st........... | Guadalupe. |
| Tucker, H............. | ......................... | ................................ | Montecito st............ | Santa Barbara. |
| Tunnell, Martin L.. | Farmer............. | Santa Maria............ | Santa Barbara Co.... | Santa Maria. |
| Turbett, William... | Cook................ | 1st Township.......... | Santa Barbara Co.... | |
| Turman, James R.. | Carriage maker .. | Santa Barbara Co.... | 1st Township........... | |
| Turman, Benjamin C | Farmer............. | San Marcos........... | Santa Barbara Co.... | |
| Turner, John......... | Laborer............. | Santa Barbara Co.... | San Marcos ............ | |
| Turner, Daniel...... | Miner.... ......... | Santa Barbara Co.... | Santa Barbara......... | Santa Barbara. |
| Tuttle, M E.......... | Fancy goods........ | State st................ | Santa Barbara......... | Santa Barbara. |
| Tuttle, W N......... | Photographic art. | State st................ | Guiterrez st............. | Santa Barbara. |
| Tuttle, John T...... | Merchant........... | Santa Barbara Co.... | Santa Barbara......... | Santa Barbara. |
| Twist, Frank W ... | Groceries............ | State st................ | State st................. | Santa Barbara. |
| Twist, Elias......... | Clerk................ | Haley st................ | State st................. | Santa Barbara. |
| Tyler, Smith C..... | Teamster........... | Santa Barbara Co.... | Santa Barbara......... | Santa Barbara. |
| Tyler, Smith........ | Mechanic............ | Gaviota Landing..... | 3 m S Las Cruces.... | Las Cruces. |
| Tyng, George........ | Sheep raiser........ | Los Alamos............ | Santa Barbara Co.... | |
| Tyng, George........ | ......................... | ................................ | Anacapa st............. | Santa Barbara. |
| Ubiedo, Benito...... | Laborer............. | Santa Barbara Co.... | La Patera............... | |
| Upson, Mrs.......... | ......................... | ................................ | Bath st ................ | Santa Barbara. |
| Urquires, Esteban.. | Laborer............. | Simi.................. | Santa Barbara Co.... | |
| Valdez, Jose Salvador ............ | Laborer............. | Santa Barbara Co.... | Santa Barbara......... | Santa Barbara. |
| Valdez, Raymond.. | Saloon keeper..... | Santa Barbara Co.... | Santa Barbara......... | Santa Barbara. |
| Valdez, Rafael....... | Laborer............. | Santa Barbara........ | Santa Barbara Co.... | Santa Barbara. |
| Valdez, Jose Maria. | Farmer............. | Santa Barbara Co.... | Las Cruces............. | Las Cruces. |
| Valencia, Juan Y... | Vaquero............ | San Julian Ranch.... | 8 m W L Cruces...... | Las Cruces. |
| Valenzuela, Jose M, Jr................... | Laborer............ | Santa Barbara Co.... | Santa Barbara......... | Santa Barbara. |
| Valenzuela, Augustus ......... | Laborer............. | Santa Barbara........ | Santa Barbara Co..... | Santa Barbara. |
| Valencia, Pablo..... | Laborer............ | Santa Barbara........ | Santa Barbara Co..... | Santa Barbara. |
| Valencia, Juan Y... | Vaquero............ | Santa Barbara Co.... | San Julian.............. | Santa Barbara. |
| Valenzuela, Juan Jose ............... | Vaquero.... ......... | Santa Barbara........ | Santa Barbara Co.... | Santa Barbara. |
| Valenzuela, Jose de J .................. | Laborer............ | Santa Barbara Co.... | Santa Barbara......... | Santa Barbara. |
| Valenzuela, —...... | Laborer............. | Santa Barbara........ | Santa Barbara Co.... | Santa Barbara. |
| Valenzuela, Vicento | Vaquero........... | Santa Barbara........ | Santa Barbara Co.... | Santa Barbara. |
| Valenzuela, Narcisso.. ........ | Laborer............. | Santa Barbara........ | Santa Barbara Co.... | Santa Barbara. |
| Valenzuela, Jose M | Laborer............. | Santa Barbara........ | Santa Barbara......... | Santa Barbara. |
| Valenzuela, Casimiro .......... | Vaquero........... | Santa Barbara Co.... | Santa Barbara......... | Santa Barbara. |
| Valenzuela, Cliodo. | Ranchero .. ........ | Santa Barbara Co.... | Las Cruces............. | Las. Cruces. |
| Valencia, J B de J. | Laborer............. | Santa Barbara Co.... | Santa Barbara Co.... | Santa Barbara. |
| Valencia, E.......... | Ranchero........... | Las Cruces............ | Santa Barbara Co.... | Las Cruces. |
| Valenzuela, Jose A | Laborer............. | Santa Barbara........ | Santa Barbara Co.... | Santa Barbara. |
| Valencia, Narcisso A | Vaquero............ | Santa Barbara........ | Santa Barbara Co.... | Santa Barbara. |
| Valencia, Benito.... | Laborer............. | Santa Barbara........ | Santa Barbara Co.... | Santa Barbara. |
| Valle, Thomas del.. | Ranchero........... | Santa Barbara Co.... | Santa Barbara......... | Santa Barbara. |
| Vandelier, W ...... | Farmer............. | Carpenteria Valley... | 1½ m E Carpenteria.. | Carpenteria. |
| Vandecar, J.......... | Farmer............. | Carpenteria Valley... | 2½ m E Carpenteria.. | Carpenteria. |
| Van Doren, Alfred. | Mariner............. | Santa Barbara Co.... | Santa Barbara......... | Santa Barbara. |
| Vanejai, Felipe..... | Vaquero ... ........ | Santa Barbara Co.... | Santa Barbara......... | Santa Barbara. |
| Vanejas, Ramon.... | Laborer............. | Santa Barbara Co.... | Santa Maria............ | Santa Maria. |
| Vannade, I........... | ......................... | ................................ | ........................... | |
| Van Mater, J M... | Hardware........... | State st................ | Ortega st............... | Santa Barbara. |
| Van Mater, Jno McC................ | Farmer............. | Santa Barbara........ | Santa Barbara Co.... | Santa Barbara. |
| Van Vactor, Wm... | Books ............. | Iowa Hill............. | Iowa Hill.............. | Santa Barbara. |
| Van Valkenburg, Edwd ............. | Saloon............... | State st................ | Figueroa st............ | Santa Barbara. |

# DIRECTORY OF SANTA BARBARA COUNTY.

| Name. | Occupation. | Place of Business. | Residence. |
|---|---|---|---|
| Van Winkle, H...... | Dentist............ | Ortega st.................. | Bath st................ |
| Varnum Paschal.... | Laborer............. | Santa Barbara Co..... | 3d Township........... |
| Vasquez, P........... | Hunter............. | Santa Barbara Co..... | Haley st................ |
| Vasquez, Pablo..... | Laborer............. | Las Cruces............... | Las Cruces Ranch.... |
| Vasquez, C V........ | Hunter............. | Santa Barbara Co.... | Santa Barbara........ |
| Vasquez, Pablo..... | Ranchero ......... | Santa Barbara........ | Santa Barbara Co.... |
| Vasquez, Juan ...... | Teamster.......... | Santa Barbara........ | Santa Barbara Co.... |
| Vasquez, Ramon O. | Hunter............. | Santa Barbara........ | Santa Barbara Co.... |
| Vejar, Dolores...... | Ranchero ......... | Santa Barbara Co.... | 1st Township......... |
| Vejar, Salvador..... | Laborer............ | Montecito............... | Santa Barbara Co.... |
| Velerdo, Ascension. | Laborer ........... | Carpenteria............ | Santa Barbara Co.... |
| Venable, H C...... | Farmer............. | Santa Maria Valley.. | 2 m E Guadalupe..... |
| Venable, Thomas... | Farmer............. | Santa Barbara........ | Santa Barbara Co.... |
| Vick, Reuben L..... | Carpenter......... | Santa Barbara Co.... | Santa Barbara........ |
| Vidal, Francisco... | Stock raiser........ | Santa Maria Valley.. | 3 m E Guadalupe..... |
| Vidal, Jose......... | Stock raiser ....... | Santa Maria Valley.. | 3 m E Guadalupe..... |
| Villa, A, Jr......... | Stock raiser....... | Point Sal ............... | 8 m S W Guadalupe. |
| Villa, Antonio...... | Stock raiser....... | Point Sal ............... | 8 m S W Guadalupe. |
| Villalba, Ramon.... | Farmer............. | Santa Barbara Co.... | Carpenteria........ |
| Villa, AntonioMaria | Laborer ............ | Santa Maria........... | Santa Barbara Co.... |
| Villalba, Rafael... | Farmer ............. | Santa Barbara Co.... | Carpenteria ........... |
| Voorhees, Wm...... | Miner............... | Santa Barbara........ | .......................... |
| Wadrinens, J........ | Farmer............. | Carpenteria............ | Carpenteria ........... |
| Wadsworth, Jas.... | Clerk................ | State st.................. | Santa Barbara st...... |
| Wadsworth, Amos. | Carpenter ......... | Santa Barbara........ | Santa Barbara st...... |
| Walcott, John...... | Book keeper....... | State st.................. | Chapala st............. |
| Walcott, John...... | Carpenter.......... | Santa Barbara........ | Santa Barbara Co.... |
| Walker, J P......... | Farmer............. | Carpenteria Valley... | 4 m E Carpenteria... |
| Walker, B O........ | Farmer............. | Beach Road............ | 1¼ m W Guadalupe.. |
| Walker, Edward.... | Laborer............. | Santa Maria Valley.. | 2 m S Guadalupe...... |
| Walker, Frank.... | Architect ......... | Gutierrez st ........... | Chapala st............. |
| Walker, G............ | Expressman........ | Santa Barbara........ | Haley st................ |
| Walker, Mrs ........ | Dress maker....... | State st.................. | Santa Barbara........ |
| Walker, John A..... | Blacksmith......... | Montecito............... | Santa Barbara Co.... |
| Walker, John........ | Blacksmith......... | Santa Barbara........ | Santa Barbara Co.... |
| Walker, Charles.... | Farmer ............. | Santa Barbara Co.... | Carpenteria ........... |
| Wallace, W K...... | Bricklayer ......... | Santa Barbara Co.... | Santa Barbara........ |
| Wallen, Russell... | Farmer ............. | Santa Barbara Co.... | Montecito.............. |
| Wallis, John Lee.. | Farmer ............. | 3d Township .......... | Santa Barbara Co..... |
| Wall, Charles J..... | Painter.............. | Santa Barbara Co.... | Santa Barbara........ |
| Walsh, William.... | Laborer............. | Santa Barbara........ | Santa Barbara Co.... |
| Walters, Chas........ | Engineer............ | Pioneer Mill............ | .......................... |
| Ward, John.......... | Farmer............. | Carpenteria ........... | 1½ m N W Carp'ria... |
| Ward, Francis Y... | Ranchero ......... | Santa Barbara Co.... | 3d Township ........... |
| Ward, James......... | Mason .............. | Santa Barbara........ | Santa Barbara Co.... |
| Warn, N B........... | Blacksmith ........ | Cota st.................. | De la Guerra st........ |
| Warn Bros............ | Blacksmith......... | Cota st.................. | Santa Barbara........ |
| Warn, I C............ | Blacksmith......... | Cota st.................. | De la Guerra st........ |
| Warner, Lewis H... | Clerk................ | Santa Barbara Co.... | Carpenteria ........... |
| Warren, Dr M...... | Dentist.............. | State st.................. | State st................ |
| Warren, W H....... | Dentist.............. | Santa Barbara Co.... | 1st Township.......... |
| Warren, Edward ... | Butcher............. | State st.................. | Cota st................ |
| Washburn, S H..... | Laborer ............ | Alamo Point........... | Santa Barbara Co.... |
| Watts, J N........... | Wheelwright....... | Canyon Perdido st... | State st................ |
| Way, Wm............ | Farmer............. | Carpenteria Valley... | 1 m W Carpenteria.. |
| Webb, Wm S........ | ..................... | ........................... | Vineyard st............ |
| Webb, Andrew S... | Mechanic .......... | Pleasant Valley ...... | .......................... |
| Webster, Lefevre... | Mason .............. | Santa Barbara........ | Santa Barbara Co.... |
| Webster, J R........ | Painter.............. | Santa Barbara........ | Santa Barbara st...... |
| Webster, George D. | Lather............... | Santa Barbara........ | Santa Barbara st...... |
| Wedekind, F........ | Saloon............... | Cota st.................. | Ortega st.............. |
| Wedekind, A....... | Saloon............... | Cota st.................. | Ortega st.............. |
| Weide, George...... | Farmer............. | Carpenteria Valley... | 1½ m E Carpenteria.. |
| Weill, Armand...... | Clerk................ | State st.................. | State st................ |

| Name. | Occupation. | Place of Business. | Residence. | Town or P. O. |
|---|---|---|---|---|
| Welch, Greenleaf C | Gardener | Santa Barbara Co. | Santa Barbara | Santa Barbara. |
| Weldon, S | Cong preacher | | | Santa Barbara. |
| Wentling, Jo B | Clerk | Santa Barbara Co. | Santa Barbara | Santa Barbara. |
| Wescott, Jonas | Attorney & not'y | Guadalupe st. | 3d st | Guadalupe. |
| Wescott, J | Druggist | Main st | Guadalupe | Guadalupe. |
| West, Rodney P | Teamster | Santa Barbara Co. | Las Cruces | Las Cruces. |
| Wharton, T | Shoe store | State st | State st | Santa Barbara. |
| Wheaton, James A. | Laborer | Santa Barbara | Santa Barbara Co. | Santa Barbara. |
| Wheelis, I | Farmer | Santa Maria Valley. | 3½ m E Guadalupe | Guadalupe. |
| Whipple, S | Laborer | Santa Maria Valley. | 1 m S Guadalupe | Guadalupe. |
| White, A W | Laborer | Point Sal | 10 m S W Guadalupe | Guadalupe. |
| White, Guy | Carpenter | Santa Barbara | Victoria st | Santa Barbara. |
| Whitford, D N | Farmer | Carpenteria | 1 m N W Carp'ria. | Carpenteria. |
| Whitford, Wm | Farmer | Carpenteria | 1¼ m N W Carp'ria. | Carpenteria. |
| Whiteted, Mrs L M | | | Vineyard st | Santa Barbara. |
| Wickenden, F | Stock raiser | Tenaquai | Santa Barbara Co. | |
| Wicks, M F | Farmer | Santa Barbara | Santa Barbara Co. | Santa Barbara. |
| Wigmore, A A | Laborer | Los Alamos | 40 m S Guadalupe. | Guadalupe. |
| Wilcox, J W | Farmer | Carpenteria Valley. | 5 m E Carpenteria. | Carpenteria. |
| Wiley, B T | Farmer | Santa Barbara Co. | Ceneguitas | |
| Williams, A B | Ranchero | Las Cruces | Las Cruces | Las Cruces. |
| Williams, I B | Farmer | Santa Maria Valley. | 1 m E Guadalupe | Guadalupe. |
| Williams, Henry | Pacific hotel | State st | State st | Santa Barbara. |
| Williamson, J F | Attorney | Chapala st | Chapala st | Santa Barbara. |
| Willets, George | Farmer | Carpenteria Valley. | 1¼ m E Carpenteria. | Carpenteria. |
| Williams, J P | Farmer | Santa Maria Valley. | 1 m E Guadalupe. | Guadalupe. |
| Williams, Peter | Hackman | Morris House. | Gutierrez st | Santa Barbara. |
| Williams, James | Seaman | 3d Township | Santa Barbara Co. | |
| Williams, Thomas H | | | Santa Barbara Co. | Santa Barbara. |
| Williams, Stephen D | Stock raiser | Las Cruces | Santa Barbara Co. | Las Cruces. |
| Williams, Albert J. | Painter | Santa Barbara Co. | Santa Barbara Co. | Santa Barbara. |
| Williams, G W | Banker | Santa Barbara Co. | Santa Barbara Co. | Santa Barbara. |
| Williams, James G | Clerk | Santa Barbara Co. | Santa Barbara Co. | Santa Barbara. |
| Williams, G M | Farmer | Santa Barbara Co. | Santa Barbara Co. | Santa Barbara. |
| Williford, I N | Farmer | La Patera | Santa Barbara Co. | |
| Williams, James O | Dairyman | La Patera | Santa Barbara Co. | |
| Wilson, John | Laborer | Santa Rosa Ranch | 12 m S W Bal's St'n | Ballard's Sta'n. |
| Wilson, A J C | Stock | Carpenteria Valley. | 4 m E Carpenteria. | Carpenteria. |
| Wilson, Jacob | Farmer | Carpenteria Valley. | ¾ m W Carpenteria. | Carpenteria. |
| Wilson, Thomas | Miner | | | Santa Barbara. |
| Wilson, J E | Gunsmith | Santa Barbara | Santa Barbara Co. | Santa Barbara. |
| Wilson, William J | Farmer | Santa Barbara Co. | | |
| Wilson, Joseph | Printer | Santa Barbara | Santa Barbara | Santa Barbara. |
| Wilson, Charles C. | Teamster | Santa Barbara Co. | Santa Barbara Co. | Santa Barbara. |
| Winchester, Uriah. | Farmer | Santa Barbara Co. | Dos Pueblos | |
| Winchester, Dr R F | Physician | Carrillo st | Chapala st | Santa Barbara. |
| Windle, F W | Carpenter | Santa Barbara Co. | 2d Precinct. | |
| Winemiller, Joseph | Carpenter | Santa Barbara | Grey st | Santa Barbara. |
| Winegni, — | Boarding house | | Garden st | Santa Barbara. |
| Winton, N W | Real estate | State st | Salinas st | Santa Barbara. |
| Wise, Wm. | Carpenter | Santa Barbara | Cota st. | Santa Barbara. |
| Wood, W A | Farmer | Santa Barbara Co. | Santa Barbara | Santa Barbara. |
| Wood, E N | Doctor | Santa Barbara Co. | Santa Barbara | Santa Barbara. |
| Woods, Healy C. | Farmer | Santa Barbara Co. | Carpenteria | Carpenteria. |
| Woods, H D | Farmer | Carpenteria | Santa Barbara Co. | Carpenteria. |
| Wood, N H | Teamster | | | Santa Barbara. |
| Woods, B F | Carpenter | Santa Barbara st | De la Guerra st | Santa Barbara. |
| Wood, L P | Furniture | | Figueroa st | Santa Barbara. |
| Woods, — | | | Victoria st | Santa Barbara. |
| Woods, Mrs E N | | | Victoria st | Santa Barbara. |
| Wood, Thos P | Harness manuf. | Main st | Main st | Guadalupe. |
| Woodbridge, W H. | Real estate | State st | Grey st | Santa Barbara. |
| Woods, Mrs M A | | | Grey st | Santa Barbara. |

## DIRECTORY OF SANTA BARBARA COUNTY.

| NAME. | OCCUPATION. | PLACE OF BUSINESS. | RESIDENCE. | TOWN OR P. O. |
|---|---|---|---|---|
| Wood, Mrs H D..... | Millinery store.... | State st................. | Santa Barbara......... | Santa Barbara. |
| Wolley, E............. | Farmer............. | Santa Maria Valley.. | 3 m S Guadalupe..... | Guadalupe. |
| Wooley, John Forrest............. | Farmer............. | Santa Barbara Co..... | Santa Barbara......... | Santa Barbara. |
| Wormstadt, Henry.. | Laborer............. | Santa Barbara Co..... | Carpenteria ............ | Carpenteria. |
| Wrightington, Joseph............ | Seaman............. | Santa Barbara Co..... | Santa Barbara......... | Santa Barbara. |
| Wright, A V B..... | Farmer............. | Arroyo Burro.......... | Santa Barbara Co..... | |
| Wright, C A........ | Wire worker ...... | ........................... | Haley st................ | Santa Barbara. |
| Wright, Geo D...... | Clerk................ | State st................. | Haley st................ | Santa Barbara. |
| Wurch, Michel...... | Brewery ............ | Cota st................. | Cota st................. | Santa Barbara. |
| Wyatt, Geo.......... | Laborer............. | Sexton's Nursery..... | 7 m W S Barbara..... | Santa Barbara. |
| Wylie, Henry....... | Mariner............. | Santa Barbara........ | Santa Barbara Co..... | Santa Barbara. |
| Yates, Alex......... | Farmer............. | Carpenteria Valley... | Carpenteria............ | Carpenteria. |
| Yates, Alexander... | Miner................ | Santa Barbara........ | Santa Barbara Co..... | Santa Barbara. |
| Yorba, Jose de Jesus | Farmer............. | Santa Barbara Co.... | La Laguna............. | |
| Yost, Francis........ | Laborer............. | Santa Barbara Co.... | 3d Township ......... | |
| Young, L............. | Marble dealer ..... | ........................... | Anapamu st............ | Santa Barbara. |
| Young, George W.. | Ranchero............ | Santa Barbara Co.... | Tahiquis................ | |
| Young, Francis C... | Ranchero............ | Tahiquis............... | Santa Barbara Co..... | |
| Young, Thomas J.. | Farmer............. | Santa Barbara Co.... | Arroyo Burro......... | |
| Young, Ezra........ | Farmer............. | Santa Barbara........ | Santa Barbara Co..... | Santa Barbara. |
| Yudart, Ulpiado..... | Ranchero............ | Santa Barbara ........ | Santa Barbara Co..... | Santa Barbara. |
| Yudart, W........... | Liquor dealer... .. | State st ............... | State st................. | Santa Barbara. |
| Zimmer Thos....... | Miner................ | Ballard's Station...... | Santa Ynez Road..... | Ballard's Sta'n. |
| Zimmerman, Chas.. | Laborer............. | Point Sal............... | 10 m S W Guad'pe.. | Guadalupe. |
| Zurmuhlen, Joseph. | Farmer............. | ........................... | San Jose................ | |
| Zurmuhlen, Augustus........... | Baker................ | ........................... | Santa Barbara......... | |
| Zurmuhlen, Luis.... | Laborer............. | Arroyo Burro.......... | ........................... | |

### MONTEREY STREET, SAN LUIS OBISPO, CAL.

We have constantly on hand and for sale at low rates, wholesale and retail, Extra, Superfine and Graham Flour, Fresh Corn Meal, Cracked Wheat, Middlings, Shorts, Bran, Ground Barley and Chicken Feed. We guarantee in all cases our Extra Flour to give satisfaction, or refund the money.

**POLLARD & JAMES, CHORRO MILLS.**

---

## BENJAMIN GRABLE,
## CARPENTER & BUILDER

Broad Street, bet. Marsh and Pacific,

SAN LUIS OBISPO.

Work of all kinds in this line of business promptly attended to.

Contracts for Building Taken, etc.

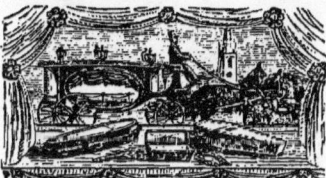

Particular attention paid to

**Undertaker's Work.**

Constantly on hand, Zinc-Lined Coffins of all Sizes.

**A New Hearse.**

Subject to Order. Charges Moderate.

168         L. L. PAULSON'S HAND-BOOK AND

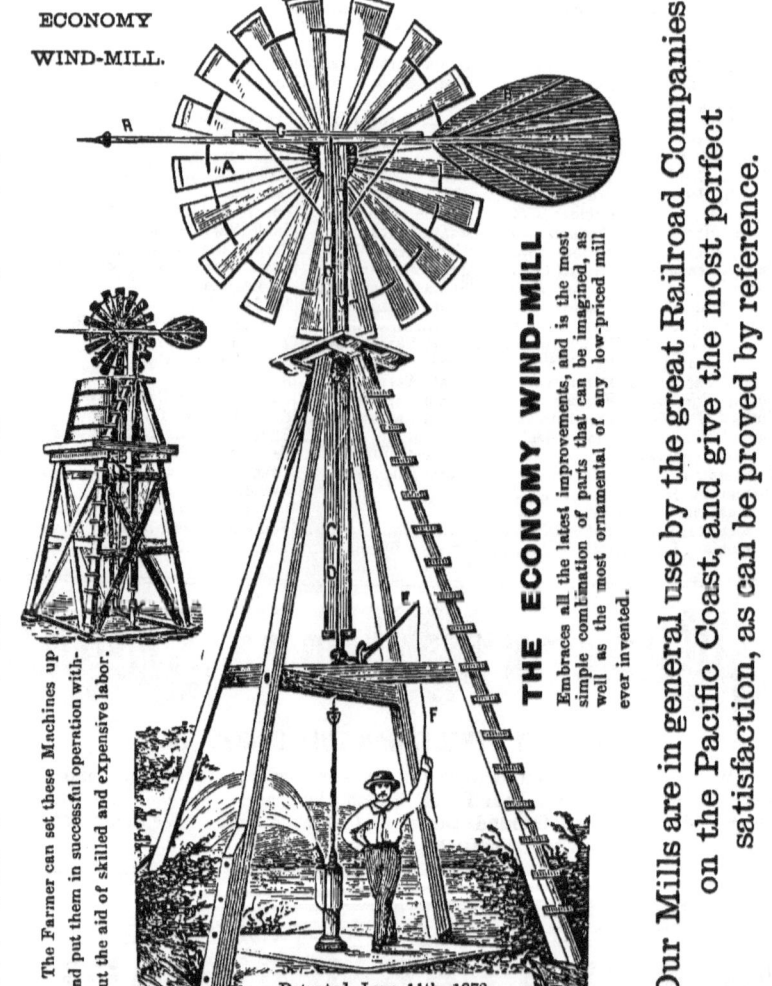

**ECONOMY WIND-MILL.**

Patented June 11th, 1872.

The Farmer can set these Machines up and put them in successful operation without the aid of skilled and expensive labor.

**THE ECONOMY WIND-MILL**
Embraces all the latest improvements, and is the most simple combination of parts that can be imagined, as well as the most ornamental of any low-priced mill ever invented.

Our Mills are in general use by the great Railroad Companies on the Pacific Coast, and give the most perfect satisfaction, as can be proved by reference.

The manufacture of Pumping Machinery has been our specialty for the past twenty-seven years. We are the Pioneer and largest manufacturer in this line on the Pacific Coast, and we say, without the least fear of successful contradiction, that for BEAUTY, SIMPLICITY, CONVENIENCE, DURABILTY AND ECONOMY, these Machines are UNEQUALLED.

We have received all the FIRST PREMIUMS awarded by the MECHANICS' INSTITUTE of this City, in our line, for the past nine years, and every time previous when we exhibited in competition with others, for which we have our Diplomas to show.

**W. I. TUSTIN, Patentee.**

## W. I. TUSTIN'S PATENT
# First Premium Wind-Mills and Horse-Powers

The Simplicity and Perfection of these Machines is the result of 27 years' experience in California.

THE "ECONOMY" AT WORK.

These powers are designed for all purposes, such as pumping water for irrigation, watering stock, chopping feed, churning, sawing wood, running machinery for manufacturing, mechanical or other purposes.

THE ECLIPSE.—For 1 Horse.

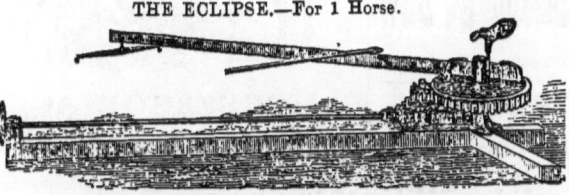

THE ECONOMY.—For 1 or 2 Horses.

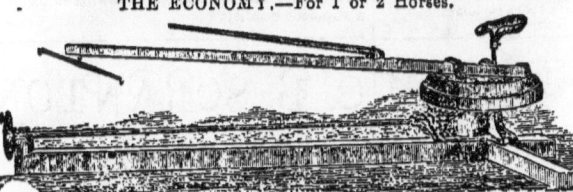

THE MONITOR.—For 2 or 4 Horses.

*Tanks, Pumps, Piping, and every variety of Machinery and goods connected with this line of business, Furnished to Order, at the Lowest Market Prices.*

*ALL WORK GUARANTEED.*
Send for Descriptive Circulars and Price-Lists.
—FACTORY AND OFFICE,—
## Cor. of Market and Beale Streets, S. F.
### W. I. TUSTIN.

## M. B. HARRISON,
### Attorney & Counselor at Law
OFFICE—In Call's Building, San Luis Obispo.

---

  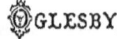GLESBY,

### ATTORNEY AND COUNSELOR AT LAW
OFFICE—In Court House, San Luis Obispo.

---

## F. K. MILLER,
### Attorney & Counselor at Law
OFFICE—In Call's Building, (up stairs) San Luis Obispo.

---

## R. C. BOULDIN,
### ATTORNEY AT LAW
OFFICE—Room No. 4, Call's Building, San Luis Obispo.

---

## FASHION

## LIVERY & FEED STABLES

Opposite Cosmopolitan Hotel,

### MONTEREY ST.,
SAN LUIS OBISPO, CAL.

### E. WOBKEN,
#### PROPRIETOR.

The finest of Buggies, Carriages and Horses, with careful drivers to let by the day or week. Horses boarded and groomed by the day, week or month.

---

## BLACKSMITHING
— BY —
## E. H. IRELAND
MAIN ST., SANTA PAULA, VENTURA CO., CAL.

### HORSESHOEING,
IRON AND WOOD WORK OF ALL KINDS.

☞ Dispatch is used in the performance of Job Work, and all work is guaranteed to be of a superior quality.

---

## C. B. SCRANTON
### BLACKSMITH,
MAIN STREET, SANTA PAULA, VENTURA COUNTY, CAL.

BLACKSMITHING, HORSESHOEING

WAGON WORK, MACHINE WORK,

And repairing of all kinds, at short notice and reasonable rates.

# A GENERAL DESCRIPTION

OF

# VENTURA COUNTY.

VENTURA COUNTY is bounded on the North by San Luis Obispo and Kern counties; on the South and Southwest by the Pacific Ocean; on the East by the county of Los Angeles; and on the West by Santa Barbara County and the Pacific Ocean. It includes also within its boundaries the islands of Anacapa and San Nicholas. It has an

### AREA,

Of from twelve to sixteen hundred square miles, or, in acres, from 768,000 to 1,024,000. The

### POPULATION

Of the county reaches in the aggregate about 7,000.

It originally formed the eastern portion of Santa Barbara County. A division was, however, made in 1873, and Ventura was made a county under a new and separate organization, in January of that year.

In an air line it is two hundred and sixty miles from San Francisco; by ocean, three hundred. In 1874 the

### ASSESSED

Valuation of its property was $3,000,000, since which time, to the present, the increase is thought to be fully $800,000.

Ventura is very mountainous; the range in the northeastern portion of the county rises to a height of from five thousand to six thousand feet. The principal ranges are the Sierras, San Rafael, Santa Ynez, Santa Monica and Santa Susanna. The hilly portion of the county abounds in grasses, which grow luxuriantly and are of an exceedingly nutritious nature. This forms admirable pasturage for vast flocks of sheep, and herds of cattle. The grazing interest here is exceedingly large in consequence of the hilly nature of the greater portion of the county. There are 250,000 sheep in the county.

### THE RESOURCES

Of the county are both agricultural and mineral.

### ITS PRINCIPAL VALLEYS

Are the Simi, Las Posas, Santa Clara, Pleasant and Ojai.

Simi Valley lies at the foot of the Santa Susanna Mountains, entering from Los Angeles. It is nine miles long. A succession of small valleys, all forming the Simi Ranche, owned by Col. Thos. A. Scott, the great railway operator, connect Simi with Las Posas Valley. All this section is rich in agricultural promise. It has the watershed of the Santa Susanna range; frost and snow visit only the highest elevations of the loftiest mountains; and deep plowing seems to answer admirably as a substitute for irrigation beyond that which nature furnishes.

Las Posas is a very rich agricultural valley, ten miles in length, ope[r] *excellence* of the county, and one of the most fertile and promising valleys i[n] Clara Valley, which lies along the Santa Clara River, has an extreme len[g] and, at its widest point, would probably measure twenty miles; at som[e] quite narrow. On the south side of the river is a plain about ten miles squ[are] noted for the productive nature of its soil, and its agricultural wealth. It and offers an opportunity to those desiring to become producers, or to tho[se] land investments. Prices range here from ten dollars upward. Artific[ial] means a necessity, as crops of all kinds mature without that aid, yet in n[o] can artesian water be obtained at as small an expense of labor and mone[y] large number of wells, at least thirty, many of which maintain a continue[d] inch pipe, to a height of from twelve to twenty feet above the surface.

Still south, separated from this plain by only a small ridge of hills, lie[s] taining about eight thousand acres of land. Land is well improved in th[e] a thriving industry, and the settlement a very prosperous one. It is [a] schoolhouse in the county outside of San Buenaventura.

Throughout the entire valley of Santa Clara, a fertile soil and mild cl[i] der its productiveness all that could be desired. As before stated, goo[d] need of irrigation, and crops seldom or never fail. Fruits of all kinds th[r] ially, are very superior in flavor to those grown in most sections of the cou[ntry]

A remarkable fact regarding fruit trees here is the rapidity with whi[ch] ing. In a letter written to the "Resources of California," the writer says than a year old from the bud, in blossom.

The yield of corn in this valley is very large, the average being from to the acre, with a single instance of a yield, on a thirty-five acre piece, of bushels per acre.

Potatoes and barley return very large yields, also; and the wheat c the valley most distant from the ocean fogs, proves a very certain one.

Flax is grown for the seed, the fibre being rejected.

Hog-raising forms one of the important business interests of this l[o] turned into the barley fields, to gain a subsistence until the maturity of t[he]

The yield of barley is something so enormous in the same fruitful vall[ey] sidering, that people called upon to record these statistics scarcely But wonderful as these statements appear, their truth is attested by pe[o] One fact, easily substantiated, is, that from a field in the Santa Clara V[alley] and two acres, there was taken one hundred and six bushels of barley per

Along the borders of the valley is an abundance of wood.

Oranges are grown successfully, and beans yield thirty dollars per acr[e] Experiments are being made with the different varieties of Eastern testing their growing qualities.

Fully 512,000 acres of the land of this county is either adapted to [cultiva] tion, or is well timbered; it is distributed in the proportion of one-twentiet[h] teen-twentieths arable.

The timber is white-oak, live-oak, and sycamore. In these varietie[s] country bordering the streams is very abundant.

The principal ranches of the county are the "Coloñia," "Ojai," " Larga," "Guadalasaa," "Las Posas," "Simi" and "Conejo." In ad[dition] considerable government land and much private land, besides the lands of t[he] sion Company," whose property lies adjacent to, and in fact surrounds the cit[y] The Coloñia Ranch covers an immense tract of splendid valley land, locate[d in] county. It produces about 500,000 centals of grain annually, princ[ipally] wheat and corn are also cultivated to some extent, as well as other cereals year dense fogs prevail, rendering this section, to a great extent, indepe[ndent]

stated, upon the best of authority, that it could absolutely dispense with rain-water if every farmer would only provide for emergencies, by sinking a well upon his premises, a matter of small moment in this locality where artesian water is so easy of obtainance. Farmers on these lands are generally successful, though nearly all are "renters," rendering progress less rapid than would be the case did each farmer till his own soil. Appreciating the many advantages of the location, however, all who are able are purchasing, terms being made easy, only a small advance payment being required, long credit being granted for the balance. Those not devoting themselves to growing grain find profitable employment in sheep and hog-raising, which has proved wonderfully remunerative. All of the stock products of the ranchos "Colonia," "Conejo," "Las Posas," "Simi," and "Calleguas," find their way to market through the town of Hueneme, which has large warehouses, and one of the best wharfs on the southern coast, giving to shippers all the accommodations and advantages connected with transportation.

## THE PRINCIPAL TOWNS

Of Ventura County are San Buenaventura, Hueneme, Nordhoff, Santa Paula, Saticoy and Scenega.

In the county are fifteen Schools. Wine and Brandy manufactories are established in the valleys of Tapo, Cumolas, Santa Clara and Calleguas.

## MINERAL.

Both placer and quartz diggings exist in this county, the gold of both making gratifying assays. Cinnabar croppings have also been discovered. Gypsum has been found in the Ojai valley, in large quantities, as well as a vein of potter's clay, near the beach. Large deposits of asphaltum are found along all the small streams. It finds a local use in serving as roofing, and a great amount of it is reduced, and shipped to San Francisco. The difficulty and cost of transportation prevent the asphaltum beds from being worked to their full capacity. They will prove a great source of wealth when this difficulty is removed. This county has also an immense mountain of nearly pure sulphur.

The principal water courses of the county are the Ventura, Santa Clara, Santa Paula, Sespe and San Antonio Rivers.

## MANUFACTURING.

Ventura has no manufacturing interest, compared with what she might sustain. Wood and crude petroleum are easily attainable and cheap; wood being sold at $5,00 per cord. Water with any desired fall can be obtained, land is cheap, and a market for nearly everything which could result from the establishment of such interests, could be found upon the spot.

## LANDS.

Good improved lands can be purchased in this county at very reasonable figures. Mr. Thomas R. Bard, whose interest in the welfare of the county induced him to furnish us with much information we would otherwise have found it difficult to obtain, is offering splendid tracts of farming and grazing lands, well supplied with water from artesian wells, on terms which may almost be dictated by the purchaser. These tracts range from 10,000 acres to 100, and are for sale in large or small parcels, as may best suit the purchaser, at the lowest of prices, and on the most easy terms. People desiring to locate should look through the magnificent valleys of Ventura, acquaint themselves with the accuracy of the statements regarding its fertility, and before purchasing should consult Mr. Bard, who is ready to offer every inducement to fix the preference of immigrants in his locality. Mr. Bard is a resident of Hueneme, situate in the finest valley of Ventura, which is also one of the garden valleys of the State.

## SAN BUENAVENTURA,

The county seat of Ventura County, was organized March 10th, 1866, and at the present time has a population of about 2,000. It communicates with San Francisco by water, through the medium of the Goodall, Nelson & Perkins S. S. Line. With Santa Barbara and Los Angeles, the communication is by daily stage, each way; with Bakersfield, Kern County, connecting with S. P. R. R. by tri-weekly stage; by tri-weekly stage with both Nordhoff and Hueneme; and by daily, with Santa Paula. San Buenaventura is situated in the northern portion of the valley of the same name. The Ventura River empties into the ocean at this point. It was formerly a Spanish village, adobe built, ruinous, filthy, and otherwise well calculated to gladden the heart of its swarthy denizen. It has long since shaken off that lethargy which it enjoyed by right of birth, and, though many traces of its *Castilian* origin yet linger about its suburbs, has developed into the brisk, stirring, galloping life of an enterprising American city.

The old San Buenaventura Mission Church is still standing, although ninety years have elapsed since its foundation. Rows of adobe buildings still exist in its immediate vicinity.

A Court House and Public School building have recently been erected, at a cost of $12,000 each.

The wharf has an extreme length of 1,400 feet, with warehouse capacity of 150,000 sacks of grain. The shipment of wool from this port is very large. The shipment of grain for last year amounted to 200,000 sacks. Two large lumber yards are established at this point, doing a good business. There are also three carriage manufactories. Bricks of a very good quality are manufactured here. The town contains four hotels, ten mercantile houses, four livery stables, two drug stores, two restaurants, and four blacksmith shops.

The Bank of Ventura is doing a general banking business, and is in a very flourishing condition. It was organized in December, 1874, and represents a capital of $250,000. The management is very efficient. A graded public school has been established, and is progressing very satisfactorily, under the supervision of Mr. F. S. S. Buckman.

The Congregational, Methodist and Presbyterian religious denominations are represented here, as well as an infinite variety of organizations of a secret and social type. The Ventura River flanks the town upon the west, the lower valley of which is called Ventura Canyon. This canyon forms the main street, Ventura Avenue, which from the ocean, for three miles inland, presents a carriage way, which is unexcelled. The town is supplied by water from the Ventura River, conducted by ditches to a reservoir, two hundred feet square, occupying an elevation one hundred and sixty feet above the town. It is expected that a change will soon be made in the mode of conducting the water to the reservoir, pipes being substituted for the ditches now in use.

## HUENEME

Is the town next in size to the county seat, and bids fair some day to strip the honors from her more advanced rival, through the fact of her holding as tributary a much larger amount of farming land, and from the possession of other advantages. Hueneme is located on the coast, in Ventura County, about fifteen miles south of San Buenaventura. It is the shipping point of a vast fertile valley, and sends more barley to the San Francisco market than any other port on the coast. Its shipping facilities consist of a fine wharf and two extensive warehouses, having a capacity of 100,000 centals, possessing all possible conveniences for receiving grain from teamsters and delivering it on board of vessels. Goodall, Nelson & Perkins run regular steamers to this port, and during the harvest months, three boats per week are insufficient to place the grain of this section in market.

Hueneme consists of about fifty houses at present, and is rapidly growing, there being splendid opportunities for all tradesmen and mechanics. A good school, hotels, several stores, postoffice, telegraph office, and the usual number of other country places of business, make up the town. For business advantages it has no equal, as there is no town in Southern California having a finer area of back country, or better communication with the San Francisco market. For mechanics and laborers, there is an unlimited field, as new wants are continually developing from the actual productiveness of the surrounding country.

The artesian well located here is a marvel to all strangers, being situated on the beach, and furnishing sufficient water for the entire town, besides having a large surplus.

DIRECTORY OF VENTURA COUNTY. 175

## SATICOY

Has a central situation in the Santa Clara Valley, North of the Santa Clara River, about eight miles from San Buenaventura, and about the same distance from the ocean.

It was founded but a few years since by Mr. E. B. Higgins, and has a store, blacksmith and wagon shop, school-house and post office.

It is situated upon the famous Briggs Rancho, and near it is the renowned Saticoy Spring, famed for its abundant flow, and the purity of its waters. It is in the centre of a magnificent fruit and grain-growing section.

The only drawback upon Saticoy is the fact that it offers no accomodations to travelers. While passing through there recently, we were obliged to select a "soft spot," while heaven furnished the only canopy which covered us. People would do well to avoid towns where so little enterprise is displayed in a proper direction, and strangers are left totally unprovided for. Good quarters can be found upon either side, at Hueneme, or Santa Paula, and this town should be passed through as one crosses the desert—as speedily as possible.

## SANTA PAULA

Is a small village, eight miles up the valley from Saticoy. It contains a school, two hotels, two stores, two flouring mills, and two blacksmith and wagon shops. Santa Paula Creek passes through the town.

Everything thrives well upon the soil of this locality.

A ditch from the Santa Clara River, twenty miles in length, passes through the valley near Saticoy, to be devoted to any use which may be thought proper.

All along the borders of the valley wood is abundant. Messrs. Blanchard & Bradley have a large flouring interest at this point, and are also holding lots and "tracts" for sale at very reasonable prices, and on very generous terms.

## NORDHOFF

Is the settlement in the famous wheat-growing valley of Ojai. It is sixteen miles north from the county seat, near the head of the Ventura River.

It has an extreme elevation of one thousand feet above the sea level; is one of the most beautiful and picturesque valleys in the State, and is one of the best resorts in the country for those afflicted with pulmonary complaints.

Here is one of nature's grandest solitudes, encompassed by scenery in keeping with the majesty of a position high niched among the fastnesses of her awe-inspiring hills. They tower above us upon all hands, no outlet is perceptible, and we feel as though immured from the entire world. Here no busy hum from the haunts of trade disturbs us, no wranglings from the world, no cry for help, no wail of agony. All is peace; unbroken quiet pervades this mountain dell. Were the mind of man so constituted as to admit of unalloyed contentment, and the happiness arising from it, here might he rest forever, nor wish to conquer the summits of these surrounding hills.

A brick hotel, with all modern conveniences, is to be erected here during the present year, for the accommodation of tourists and invalids. It will cost in the neighborhood of $10,000, and is to be a roomy, fine structure. To the tourist we would say, by all means visit Ventura County; to the immigrant, locate there.

# DUPONT'S GUN-POWDER

### AGENCY, 108 BATTERY STREET,

### SAN FRANCISCO.

**CELEBRATED BRANDS:**

SPORTING,
DIAMOND GRAIN,
1, 2, 3 & 4.
EAGLE DUCK, 1, 2 & 3.
EAGLE RIFLE.
SUPERFINE RIFLE,
Fg. FFg, FFFg.
CRYSTAL GRAIN,
1, 2 & 3.
SUPERIOR RIFLE,
GOLDEN PHEASANT,
F, FF, FFF.
IN KEGS AND CANISTERS.

SUPERIOR BRANDS OF MINING
F, FF & FFF.
BLASTING,
C, F, FF, FFF.
CANNON, MUSKET,
ETC., ETC.,
ALL IN IRON KEGS.
FUSE,
OF ALL THE
VARIOUS BRANDS
IN USE ON
THE PACIFIC COAST.

## From the Eagle Safety Fuse Factory,

LOCATED NEAR SANTA CRUZ, CAL.

## WINCHESTER REPEATING-ARMS COMPANY,

NEW HAVEN, CONN.

Their unrivalled REPEATING SPORTING RIFLES, CARBINES and MUSKETS, Plain or Beautifully Plated and Engraved. Cartridges of their make, for Rifles and Pistols of every kind. A full stock of their New Model Arms 1873, now on hand.

## JOHN SKINKER,

Sole Agent for the Pacific Coast,

No. 108 BATTERY ST., - - - - San Francisco.

## DIRECTORY OF VENTURA COUNTY. 177

| NAME. | OCCUPATION. | PLACE OF BUSINESS. | RESIDENCE. | TOWN OR P. O |
|---|---|---|---|---|
| Ables, B............ | Farmer............ | nr Saticoy............ | Ventura Co............ | Saticoy. |
| Ablett & Stanchfield | Stock................ | Beach Road............ | 10 m W San Buenav. | S Buenaventura |
| Ablett, A............ | Stock................ | Beach Road............ | 10 m W San Buenav | S Buenaventura |
| Adair, G W......... | Stock................ | Sespe Ranch............ | ............................ | Santa Paula. |
| Adams, Geo F....... | Printer............ | Ventura Co............ | San Buenaventura ... | S Buenaventura |
| Adams, G W......... | Stock................ | Ex Mission Ranch... | 14 m N E S Buenav. | S Buenaventura |
| Adams, W G......... | Stock raiser........ | Ventura Co............ | nr Saticoy............ | Saticoy. |
| Addleman, James .. | Laborer............ | Ventura Co............ | East Main st......... | S Buenaventura |
| Akers, John......... | Farmer............ | Sespe Ranch............ | 30 m E San Buenav.. | Scenega. |
| Alberts, A C......... | Farmer............ | Ex Mission Ranch... | 6 m E San Buenav... | S Buenaventura |
| Alberts, A C......... | Farmer............ | Ventura Co............ | nr Saticoy............ | Saticoy. |
| Albert, J ............ | Harness maker.... | Ventura Co............ | San Buenaventura... | S Buenaventura |
| Alderman, Joseph.. | Farmer............ | Santa Paula............ | 12 m E San Buenav.. | S Buenaventura |
| Alexander, W D ... | Farmer............ | Ex Mission Ranch... | 12 m N E S Buenav. | S Buenaventura |
| Alexander, Thos..... | Farmer............ | Colonia Ranch........ | ............................ | S Buenaventura |
| Alexander, B....... | Farmer............ | Santa Clara............ | 4 m W Hueneme..... | Hueneme. |
| Alexander, W S.... | Farmer............ | Ventura Co............ | nr Hueneme............ | Hueneme. |
| Allen, J W......... | Farmer............ | nr Hueneme............ | Ventura Co............ | Hueneme. |
| Allyn, Mrs S L H.. | ............................ | ............................ | Palm st................ | Ventura. |
| Alvord, J B......... | Teacher............ | Pleasant Valley...... | ............................ | S Buenaventura |
| Amaden, A A....... | Laborer............ | Main st................ | Main st................ | Hueneme. |
| Andrew, R........... | Druggist............ | Main st................ | San Buenaventura,.. | S Buenaventura |
| Anquisola, M A.... | Sheep raiser....... | Ventura Co............ | San Buenaventura... | S Buenaventura |
| Armstrong, J........ | Farmer............ | nr Hueneme............ | Ventura Co............ | Hueneme. |
| Arnaz, L............. | Gen merchandise. | Main st................ | Main st........, ......... | Ventura. |
| Arnaz, Jose de...... | Ranchero............ | Ventura................ | Ventura Co............ | S Buenaventura |
| Arnaz, Jose......... | Stock................ | Santa Ana Ranch.... | 7 m N San Buenav,.. | S Buenaventura |
| Arnaz, Luis......... | Gen merchandise. | San Buenaventura.. | Ventura Co............ | S Buenaventura |
| Arellanes, J D....... | Laborer............ | nr Hueneme............ | Ventura Co............ | Hueneme. |
| Arnold, Cutler ..... | Farmer & stock.. | Santa Clara Valley.. | 4 m E Hueneme..... | Hueneme. |
| Arnold, Eugene.... | Farmer............ | Santa Clara Valley. | 4 m E Hueneme..... | Hueneme. |
| Arnold, Edw....... | Farmer............ | Santa Clara Valley. | 4 m E Hueneme..... | Hueneme. |
| Arnold, Henry ..... | Farmer............ | Santa Clara Valley. | 4 m E Hueneme..... | Hueneme. |
| Arnold, H H ....... | Blacksmith ........ | Santa Paula............ | 20 m E San Buenav. | Santa Paula. |
| Arnold, Leroy....... | Farmer............ | Los Angeles Road ... | 4 m E Hueneme..... | Hueneme. |
| Arnold, Thos....... | Stock raiser........ | Sespe Ranch............ | 22 m E San Buenav. | Santa Paula. |
| Arnold, M H....... | Farmer............ | Ventura Co ........... | nr Hueneme............ | Hueneme. |
| Arnold, M T....... | Farmer............ | Santa Clara Valley. | 4 m E Hueneme..... | Hueneme. |
| Arrelanes, Jde la L | Laborer............ | Ventura Co............ | San Buenaventura... | S Buenaventura |
| Arrelanes, J A..... | Vaquero............ | Ventura Co............ | San Buenaventura... | S Buenaventura |
| Arrelanes, S B ..... | Butcher............ | Ventura Co............ | San Buenaventura... | S Buenaventura |
| Arundell, Wm H... | Brick mason ....... | Ventura Co............ | 3 m E San Buenav... | S Buenaventura |
| Arundell, W H..... | Farmer............ | Ventura Co............ | Ventura................ | Ventura. |
| Arundell, Thos..... | Plasterer............ | Santa Paula Ranch .. | 3 m E San Buenav.. | S Buenaventura |
| Ashton, H ........... | Carpenter............ | Ventura Co............ | Saticoy ............... | Saticoy. |
| Atmore, Richard... | Farmer............ | Santa Paula Ranch .. | ............................ | Santa Paula. |
| Ayguisola, M....... | Stock................ | West Main st......... | West Main st......... | S Buenaventura |
| Ayala, A............. | Laborer............ | San Buenaventura ... | Ventura Co............ | S Buenaventura |
| Ayala, Francisco ... | Stock................ | Ventura Co............ | Main st................ | Ventura. |
| Ayala, J ............. | Ranchero............ | nr Hueneme............ | Ventura Co............ | Hueneme. |
| Ayala, J R........... | Laborer............ | nr Hueneme............ | Ventura Co............ | Hueneme. |
| Ayala, J del R..... | Laborer............ | Ventura................ | Ventura Co............ | Ventura. |
| Ayala, Ramon ..... | Stock................ | Ojai................ | 15 m N Ventura..... | Nordhoff. |
| Ayala, V............. | Vaquero............ | Ventura Co............ | San Buenaventura... | S Buenaventura |
| Ayres, J ............. | Hotel keeper ...... | Main st................ | San Buenaventura... | S Buenaventura |
| Ayers, J ............. | Farmer............ | Ventura Co............ | San Buenaventura... | S Buenaventura |
| Ayres, Edward..... | Farmer............ | Ojai Valley............ | Nordhoff............ | Nordhoff. |
| Ayres, J A........... | Farmer............ | Ojai Valley............ | Ojai Valley............ | Nordhoff. |
| Ayres, Robt ........ | Farmer............ | Ojai Valley............ | Nordhoff............ | Nordhoff. |
| Ayres, Wm......... | Proprietor........... | Ayres Hotel............ | Main st................ | Ventura. |
| Babb, R F........... | Blacksmith........ | Ventura Co............ | San Buenaventura... | S Buenaventura |
| Bacon, C W ....... | Carpenter ........... | Hueneme............ | Hueneme ............ | Hueneme. |
| Badal, Edward..... | Clerk................ | 1st and California sts | Ventura............ | Ventura. |
| Bailey, C H......... | Laborer............ | Ventura Co............ | San Buenaventura... | S Buenaventura |

12

# VENTURA COUNTY

## THOS. R. BARD,
# REAL ESTATE AGENT,

—— OFFERS FOR SALE ——

## SPLENDID TRACTS OF LAND:

### Fine Grazing Lands,

# SPLENDID FARMING LANDS,

WELL WATERED ;

### FARMS WITH ARTESIAN WELLS,

In Tracts to suit, from 10,000 Acres to 100 Acres.

### TERMS TO SUIT PURCHASERS.

**PRICES WITHIN THE REACH OF ALL.**

⇜ ADDRESS ⇝

## THOMAS R. BARD,
HUENEME, VENTURA CO., CAL.

## DIRECTORY OF VENTURA COUNTY. 179

| Name. | Occupation. | Place of Business. | Residence. | Town or P. O |
|---|---|---|---|---|
| Baker, Lewis | Stock | Santa Paula | 13 m N E S Buenav | Santa Paula. |
| Baker, W E | Farmer | Santa Paula Ranch | 6 m E San Buenav | Santa Paula. |
| Balcom, Wm E | Farmer | Ventura Co | Ventura | Ventura. |
| Baldase, A | Hostler | Main st | Main st | Ventura. |
| Bank of Ventura | | Main st | San Buenaventura | S Buenaventura |
| Barber, J W | Farmer | nr Hueneme | Ventura Co | Hueneme. |
| Bard, Dr C L | Physician & surg. | Main st | Oak st | Ventura. |
| Bard, Thos R | R estate & lumber | Hueneme Wharf | Hueneme | Hueneme. |
| Barker, J A | Farmer | County Road | 1 m E Santa Paula | Santa Panla. |
| Barker, James A | Farmer | Santa Paula | 21 m N E S Buenav | Santa Paula. |
| Barker, J R | Farmer | nr Saticoy | Ventura Co | Saticoy. |
| Barkla, J S | Farmer | Santa Paula | 16 m E San Buenav. | Santa Paula. |
| Barnard, A D | Real estate | Main st | Ventura | Ventura. |
| Barnard, E A | Carpenter | Ventura Co | San Buenaventura | S Buenaventura |
| Barnard, Irvin | Farmer | Cañada Largo | 4 m N W S Buenav. | S Buenaventura |
| Barnard, Wm | Saloon | Main st | Main st | Ventura. |
| Barnett, — | Farmer | Pleasant Valley | 15 m E San Buenav. | S Buenaventura |
| Barnett, Eli | Farmer | Pleasant Valley | 15 m E San Buenav. | S Buenaventura |
| Barnett, J C | Farmer | nr Hueneme | Ventura Co | Hueneme. |
| Barnett, J Z | County assessor | Pleasant Valley | 15 m E San Buenav. | S Buenaventura |
| Barnett, S, Jr | Blacksmith | Ventura Co | San Buenaventura | S Buenaventura |
| Barnett, W | Saloon keeper | Ventura Co | San Buenaventura | S Buenaventura |
| Barnum, C C | Farmer | Ojai Valley | 2 m E Nordhoff | Nordhoff. |
| Baron, F E | Farmer | Santa Clara Valley | 4 m N E Hueneme | Hueneme. |
| Barron, G D | Farmer | Ventura Ave | 2 m N W S Buenav. | S Buenaventura |
| Barron, Geo A | | Ventura Ave | 2 m N W S Buenav | S Buenaventura |
| Barron, I C | Farmer | Ventura | Ventura Co | S Buenaventura |
| Barry, J A | Stable keeper | Ventura Co | San Buenaventura | Ventura. |
| Barry, John | Farmer | Ventura Co | Poli st | S Buenaventura |
| Bartch, Jacob | Farmer | Santa Paula Ranch | 6 m E San Buenav | S Buenaventura |
| Bartlett Bros | Watch makers | Main st | Ventura | S Buenaventura |
| Bartlett, A G | Watch maker | Main st | | Ventura. |
| Bartlett, C G | Watch maker | Main st | | Ventura. |
| Bartlett, J D | Farmer | Cacitas | 8 m W San Buenav. | Ventura. |
| Bartlett, J E | Stock raiser | Ex Mission Ranch | 12 m E San Buenav. | S Buenaventura |
| Batcheller, H D | Harness maker | Ventura Hotel | Ventura | S Buenaventura |
| Bates, — | Laborer | Santa Paula | Santa Paula | Santa Paula. |
| Bath, Joseph | Farmer | Santa Paula | 2 m E Santa Paula | Santa Paula. |
| Baum, George | Farmer | Pleasant Valley | 15 m E San Buenav. | S Buenaventura |
| Baum, Danl | Farmer | Sespe Ranch | 30 m E San Buenav. | Scenega. |
| Beard, Wm | Farmer | Santa Paula | 16 m E San Buenav. | Santa Paula. |
| Bedell, E W | Clerk | Ventura Co | San Buenaventura | S Buenaventura |
| Beers, George | Teamster | Saticoy | 8 m E San Buenav. | Saticoy. |
| Bell, T | Farmer | Ventura Co | nr Saticoy | Saticoy. |
| Bell, Thomas | Laborer | Santa Paula Ranch | 15 m E San Buenav. | Santa Paula. |
| Bell, R | Farmer | nr Hueneme | Ventura Co | Hueneme. |
| Bellah, C | Farmer | nr Hueneme | Ventura Co | Hueneme. |
| Bellah, J | Liveryman | Ventura Co | Hueneme | Hueneme. |
| Benson, T G | Farmer | nr Hueneme | Ventura Co | Hueneme. |
| Bernheim, H | Gen merchandise | Main st | Santa Clara st | Ventura. |
| Berry, John | Farmer | Ventura Co | Palm st | Ventura. |
| Bevens, Benj | Clerk | 1st st | Oak st | Ventura. |
| Bickford, L H | Wheelwright | Main st | Ventura | Ventura. |
| Bickmore, H | Laborer | Santa Paula | 20 m N E S Buenav | Santa Paula. |
| Bientenholtz, H | Farmer | Santa Clara Valley | 5 m N E Hueneme | Hueneme. |
| Biggs, W | | Main st | Main st | Ventura. |
| Bird, W H | Farmer | nr Hueneme | Ventura Co | Hueneme. |
| Blakeney, T | Laborer | Ventura Co | nr Saticoy | Saticoy. |
| Blakeslee, G A | Farmer | Ventura Co | nr Hueneme | Hueneme. |
| Blanchard & Bradley | Capitalists | S Paula Fl'r Mills | Santa Paula | Santa Paula. |
| Blanchard, N W | Capitalist | S Paula Fl'r Mills | Santa Paula | Santa Paula. |
| Bland, C J | Farmer | nr Saticoy | Ventura Co | Saticoy. |
| Bloomberg, A W | Proprietor | Hotel | Nordhoff | Nordhoff. |

# A. J. SALISBURY & CO.,
# LUMBER DEALERS.

### Every Variety of
### Building Material.

**HUENEME,**

Ventura County, California.

---

# A. GERBERDING,

### Forwarding and General

# Commission Merchant,

**HUENEME,**

Ventura Co., California.

# DIRECTORY OF VENTURA COUNTY. 181

| Name. | Occupation. | Place of Business. | Residence. | Town or P. O. |
|---|---|---|---|---|
| Blum, L P............ | Farmer ............. | Ventura Co............ | San Buenaventura... | S Buenaventura |
| Borchard, C........... | Stock............. ...... | Santa Clara Valley .. | 5 m N Hueneme...... | Hueneme. |
| Borchard, Edwd..... | Farmer ............. | Santa Clara Valley .. | 4 m N Hueneme...... | Hueneme. |
| Borchard, John...... | Farmer ............. | Santa Clara Valley .. | 4 m N E Hueneme... | Hueneme. |
| Bortchard, J E...... | Farmer ............. | nr Hueneme............ | Ventura Co............ | Hueneme. |
| Boyle, P............ | Carpenter........... | Ventura Co............ | Saticoy ........... ......... | Saticoy. |
| Brabo, J de D........ | Farmer ............. | nr Saticoy............ | Ventura Co............ | Saticoy. |
| Bracken, James...... | Farmer ............. | Ojai Valley ............ | 4½ m E Nordhoff..... | Nordhoff. |
| Bradey, A ............ | Cook ............. | Ventura Co............ | Ventura ............ ......... | Ventura. |
| Bradley, J H......... | Printer ...... ........ | Ventura Co............ | San Buenaventura... | S Buenaventura |
| Bradley, E M......... | Mechanic .. ........ | Ventura Co............ | San Buenaventura... | S Buenaventura |
| Bradley, Mrs Nellie | Ldg house............ | Palm st............ ......... | Palm st............ ......... | Ventura. |
| Bradley, W E........ | Saloon ............. | Saticoy ............ ......... | 7 m E San Buenav... | Saticoy. |
| Bradshaw, Chas .... | Preacher............ | Ex Mission Ranch ... | 6 m N E San Buenav | S Buenaventura |
| Bradshaw, Wm R. | Architect ........ | Cañada Largo.......... | 3 m N W S Buenav. | S Buenaventura |
| Brant, K............ | Blacksmith......... | Main st............ ......... | ............ ......... ......... | Ventura. |
| Bravo, Juan ........ | Fruit peddler...... | Main st...... ........ | Main st............ ......... | Ventura. |
| Bravo, Juan de...... | Laborer............ | San Buenaventura.... | Main st............ ......... | S Buenaventura |
| Breen, Thos........... | Stock.. ............ | Santa Paula............ | 13 m N E S Buenav. | Santa Paula. |
| Brewster, J C ...... | Photographer .... | Mission Block......... | Main st............ ......... | S Buenaventura |
| Briggs, Duke......... | Butcher............ | Market st............ | Market st............ ......... | Hueneme. |
| Briggs, H............ | Teacher ............ | Hueneme. ............ | Market st............ ......... | Hueneme. |
| Briggs, W O......... | Bar tender........ | Main st............ | Ventura ............ ......... | Ventura. |
| Brinkerhoff, H B ... | Stock............ | Sespe Ranch......... | 35 m E San Buenav. | Scenega. |
| Bristol, Rev S ...... | Farmer& preach'r | Santa Clara River.... | 5 m E San Buenav... | Ventura. |
| Brock, Wm............ | Farmer ............. | Sespe Ranch............ | 30 m E San Buenav. | Santa Paula. |
| Brooks, C ............ | Farmer ............. | Pleasant Valley........ | 10 m E Hueneme.... | Hueneme. |
| Brooks, E C ......... | Carriage maker .. | Santa Clara st......... | Ventura ............ ......... | Ventura. |
| Brooks, J M......... | Druggist............ | East Main st............ | San Buenaventura... | S Buenaventura |
| Brooks, James S.... | Laborer............ | Santa Paula............ | 16 m E San Buenav. | Santa Paula. |
| Brooks, J M......... | Attorney ............ | Main st............ ......... | Poli st............ ......... | Ventura. |
| Brown, Austin...... | Carpenter........... | Ventura ............ ......... | Front st............ ......... | Ventura. |
| Brown, J C........... | Saddler ............ | ............ ......... ......... | Ventura ............ ......... | Ventura. |
| Brown, John ........ | Laborer ............ | Santa Paula Ranch... | 15 m E San Buenav. | Santa Paula. |
| Brown, R M......... | Dry goods............ | Main st............ ......... | Main st............ ......... | Ventura. |
| Brown, W A......... | Stock ............ | Sespe Ranch............ | 20 m E San Buenav. | Santa Paula. |
| Brown, W W......... | Farmer ............. | nr Saticoy............ | Ventura Co............ | Saticoy. |
| Brown, W A......... | Laborer ............ | Ventura Co............ | nr Hueneme............ | Hueneme. |
| Browning, B......... | Laborer ............ | nr Hueneme............ | Ventura Co............ | Hueneme. |
| Braun, Chas ......... | Music teacher...... | Ventura Co............ | San Buenaventura... | S Buenaventura |
| Buckingham, Robt. | Farmer ............. | Pleasant Valley ...... | ............ ......... ......... | Hueneme. |
| Buckman, F S S ... | Teacher............ | Ventura Co............ | San Buenaventura... | S Buenaventura |
| Buker, Alpha........ | Harness maker.... | Market st............ | Market st............ ......... | Hueneme. |
| Bulfinch, Thos ...... | Saloon ............ | Market st............ | Market st............ ......... | Hueneme. |
| Bull, H............... | Laborer............ | nr Hueneme............ | Ventura Co............ | Hueneme. |
| Burnett, J K......... | Laborer............ | Santa Paula............ | 15 m E San Buenav. | S Buenaventura |
| Burrell, Wm......... | Butcher............ | Market st............ | Market st............ ......... | Hueneme. |
| Burrull, W H......... | Farmer ............. | nr Hueneme............ | Ventura Co............ | Hueneme. |
| Butterfield, J H...... | Minister ............ | Ventura Co............ | Hueneme............ ......... | Hueneme. |
| Buttner, Wm......... | Butcher............ | Market st............ | Market st............ ......... | Hueneme. |
| Bynum, K R......... | Farmer ............. | nr Hueneme............ | Ventura Co............ | Hueneme. |
| Byrd, O P............ | Boot maker......... | Ventura Co............ | Hueneme............ ......... | Hueneme. |
| Byrne, Chas B ...... | Tinsmith ......... | Main st............ ......... | Meta st............ ......... | Ventura. |
| Byrne, Edward..... | Stock ............ | Ex Mission Ranch ... | 13 m N E S Buenav. | S Buenaventura |
| Byrne, P ............ | Stock ............ | Ex Mission Ranch ... | 13 m N E S Buenav. | S Buenaventura |
| Cable, W M......... | Farmer ............. | Ventura Co............ | nr Hueneme............ | Hueneme. |
| Caldwell, C T...... | Farmer ............. | nr Saticoy............ | Ventura Co............ | Saticoy. |
| Caldwell, T......... | Farmer ............. | Ex Mission Ranch ... | 10 m N E S Buenav. | S Buenaventura |
| Caldwell, W H...... | Farmer ............. | nr Hueneme............ | Ventura Co............ | Hueneme. |
| Callis, R A ......... | Farmer ............. | nr Hueneme............ | Ventura Co............ | Hueneme. |
| Calton, David. ...... | Farmer ............. | Sespe Ranch............ | 30 m E San Buenav. | Scenega. |
| Camaeilla, Juan..... | Capitalist ........ | San Buenaventura... | West Main st ......... | S Buenaventura |
| Cameron, A M....... | Farmer ............. | Ex Mission Ranch.... | 10 m N E S Buenav. | S Buenaventura |
| Campo, F M del..... | Store keeper......... | Ventura Co............ | San Buenaventura... | S Buenaventura |

# H. S. POPE,
— DEALER IN —
# FURNITURE and BEDDING

OF EVERY DESCRIPTION.

All kinds of **CABINET WORK** made to Order.

Warerooms, N. W. Cor. Main & California Sts.,

San Buenaventura, Ventura Co., Cal.

# H. S. POPE,
# PRACTICAL GUNSMITH

 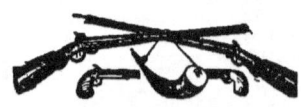

Importer and Dealer in New Improved Breech-Loading SHOTGUNS, RIFLES, PISTOLS, POWDER FLASKS, Etc.

SAN BUENAVENTURA, Ventura County, Cal.

# DIRECTORY OF VENTURA COUNTY. 183

| OCCUPATION. | PLACE OF BUSINESS. | RESIDENCE. | TOWN OR P. O. |
|---|---|---|---|
| 'ice Pres bank | San Buenaventura | Ventura Co | S Buenaventura |
| .................. | Santa Paula Ranch | 6 m E San Buenav. | S Buenaventura |
| 'armer | Santa Clara Valley | 1 m E Hueneme | Hueneme. |
| arpenter | Ventura | Ventura | Ventura. |
| aloon keeper | Ventura Co | San Buenaventura | S Buenaventura |
| teal estate | Ventura Co | Nordhoff | Nordhoff. |
| 'armer | nr Hueneme | Ventura Co | Hueneme. |
| 'armer | nr Hueneme | Ventura Co | Hueneme. |
| 'armer | Sespe Ranch | 30 m E San Buenav. | Scenega. |
| 'armer | Sespe Ranch | 30 m E San Buenav. | Scenega. |
| tock | Sespe Ranch | 35 m E San Buenav. | Scenega. |
| 'armer | Santa Clara Valley | 4 m N E Hueneme | Hueneme. |
| enl merchant | Main st | Santa Clara st | Ventura. |
| en merchandise. | Main st | Ventura | Ventura. |
| en merchandise. | Main st | Ventura Ave | Ventura. |
| lerk | Main st | Ayer's Hotel | Ventura. |
| tock | Santa Clara Valley | 14 m N Hueneme | Hueneme. |
| enl merchants | Main st | Main st | Ventura. |
| tanchero | Ventura | Ventura Co | Ventura. |
| .aborer | San Buenaventura | San Buenaventura | S Buenaventura |
| tock | Sespe Ranch | 20 m E San Buenav. | Scenega. |
| 'ainter | San Buenaventura | Ventura Ave | S Buenaventura |
| 'armer | Ojai Valley | 18 m N Nordhoff | Nordhoff. |
| 'armer | Conejo Road | .................. | Ventura. |
| 'ivil engineer | Ventura Ave | San Buenaventura | S Buenaventura |
| 'armer | 6 m E Ventura | Oak st | Ventura. |
| 'armer | nr Saticoy | Ventura Co | Saticoy. |
| lerk | Main st | Santa Clara st | Ventura. |
| Constable | Ventura Co | Hueneme | Hueneme. |
| 'reight agent | Wharf | Ventura | Ventura. |
| .aborer | Ventura Co | San Buenaventura | S Buenaventura |
| 'armer | Ojai Valley | 2½ m E Nordhoff | Nordhoff. |
| Merchant | Ventura Co | Hueneme | Hueneme. |
| 'armer | Ojai Valley | 18 m N Nordhoff | Nordhoff. |
| 'armer. | Santa Clara Valley | 4 m N Hueneme | Hueneme. |
| 'armer and stock | Santa Clara Valley | 4 m N Hueneme | Hueneme. |
| 'armer | Santa Clara Valley | 3 m E Hueneme | Hueneme. |
| Druggist | Main st | Main st | Hueneme. |
| .aborer | Ventura Co | San Buenaventura | S Buenaventura |
| Carpenter | Ventura | Poli st | Ventura. |
| Dry goods | Main st | Main st | S Buenaventura |
| General mdse | Main st | Main st | Ventura. |
| enl merchant | Saticoy | 7 m E San Buenav. | Saticoy. |
| Blacksmith | Main st | Main st | S Buenaventura |
| Painter | Ventura Co | Saticoy | Saticoy. |
| Carpenter | San Buenaventura | East Main st | S Buenaventura |
| Teaming | Poli st | Ventura | Ventura. |
| Farmer | Pleasant Valley | 10 m E Hueneme | Hueneme. |
| Farmer | Santa Paula Ranch | 12 m N E S Buenav. | S Buenaventura |
| Justice of peace | Market st | Market st | Hueneme. |
| Catholic priest | Mission Church | East Main st | S Buenaventura |
| Farmer | nr Hueneme | Ventura Co | Hueneme. |
| Farmer | nr Hueneme | Ventura Co | Hueneme. |
| Farmer | Santa Clara Valley | 4 m N E Hueneme | Hueneme. |
| Farmer | Sespe Ranch | 30 m E San Buenav. | Scenega. |
| Brewer | Ventura Co | San Buenaventura | S Buenaventura |
| Merchant | .................. | Palm st | Ventura. |
| Farmer | nr Hueneme | Ventura Co | Hueneme. |
| Livery stable | Main st | Main st | S Buenaventura |
| Farmer | Ventura Co | nr Saticoy | Saticoy. |
| Farmer | Ventura Co | nr Hueneme | Hueneme. |
| Farmer | Santa Paula Ranch | 6 m E San Buenav. | S Buenaventura |
| Groceries | East Main st | San Buenaventura | S Buenaventura |

# AYERS HOTEL

## WEST MAIN STREET,

## SAN BUENAVENTURA.

Having completed and furnished my new hotel in the most approved style, I am now prepared to accommodate the traveling public with the best of fare and the neatest and most convenient sleeping apartments. Tourists visiting this part of the coast will find the Ayers Hotel conveniently situated.

## WM. AYERS.

## DIRECTORY OF VENTURA COUNTY. 185

| Name. | Occupation. | Place of Business. | Residence. | Town or P. O. |
|---|---|---|---|---|
| Corey, J A | Grocer | East Main st | San Buenaventura | S Buenaventura |
| Corey, J G | Stock | Santa Paula | 16 m E San Buenav. | Santa Paula. |
| Corey, Milo | Farmer | Ojai Valley | 1¼ m E Nordhoff | Nordhoff. |
| Cornwall, A | Stock raiser | Ventura Co | nr Saticoy | Saticoy. |
| Cornwall, G A | Farmer | Ex Mission Ranch | 13 m N E S B Ven. | Saticoy. |
| Cornwall, Wm | Farmer | Ex Mission Ranch | 12 m E S B Ventura | S Buenaventura |
| Cornwell, P P | Farmer | Sespe ranch | 20 m E S B Ventura | Santa Paula. |
| Cota, G L | Farmer | nr Hueneme | Ventura Co | Hueneme. |
| Covert, E | Druggist | Ventura Co | Hueneme | Hueneme. |
| Crawford, J C | Farmer | Sespe Ranch | 30 m E S B Ventura | Scenega. |
| Cressey, T H | Farmer | Santa Clara Valley | 3 m N E Hueneme | Hueneme. |
| Crinklan, J | Farmer | nr Hueneme | Ventura Co | Hueneme. |
| Criss, I T | | Saticoy | 10 m E S B Ventura | Saticoy. |
| Crissman, E W | Farmer and stock | Ventura Co | Oak st | S Buenaventura |
| Cronk, W S | Painter | Main st | Front st | S Buenaventura |
| Crumline, H | Teacher | Santa Paula | 16 m E S B Ventura | Santa Paula. |
| Cruson, Robt | Farmer | Santa Paula Ranch | | Santa Paula. |
| Cuella, W | Carpenter | Ventura Co | San Buenaventura | S Buenaventura |
| Cullis, R | Farmer | Beach road | | S Buenaventura |
| Cummings, J F | Farmer | Santa Paula Ranch | 11 m E S B Ventura | S Buenaventura |
| Cuniff, M | Stock | Saticoy | Ventura Co | Saticoy. |
| Cunningham, P | Farmer | Ventura Ave | 1 m W Ventura | S Buenaventura |
| Cunningham, P H | Gardener | Ventura Co | Hueneme | Hueneme. |
| Curchill, J S | Farmer | Santa Paula Ranch | 16 m E S B Ventura | Santa Paula. |
| Curlee, John | Farmer | Sespe Ranch | 30 m E S B Ventura | Scenega. |
| Currahan, R | Engineer | Main st | Main st | S B Ventura. |
| Cuslee, J T | Farmer | Ventura Co | nr Saticoy | Saticoy. |
| Cutter, J P | Mechanic | Ventura Co | San Buenaventura | S Buenaventura |
| Dalbert, Chas | Laborer | Ventura | Gray House | S Buenaventura |
| Daley, James | Lumber | Ventura | Ventura Co | S Buenaventura |
| Daley, P H | Livery stable | Main st | Meta st | S Buenaventura |
| Dalley, W | Carpenter | Ventura Co | Saticoy | Saticoy. |
| Dalley, Wm | Stock | Santa Paula | 20 m E S B Ventura | Santa Paula. |
| Daly & Rodgers | Lumber | San Buenaventura | Ventura Co | S Buenaventura |
| Daly, James | Lumber | cor Cal and Front sts | Ventura Co | S Buenaventura |
| Daly, — | Stable | East Main st | San Buenaventura | S Buenaventura |
| Darnul, J J | Farmer | Ventura Co | nr Hueneme | Hueneme. |
| Davenport, H G | Preacher | Pleasant Valley | 15 m E Hueneme | Hueneme. |
| Davenport, Joseph | Farmer | Pleasant Valley | 15 m E Hueneme | Hueneme. |
| Davis, F M | Farmer | Ventura Co | nr Hueneme | Hueneme. |
| Davis, Wm H | Blacksmith | Hueneme | Main st | Hueneme. |
| Davis, Wm | Blacksmith | Hueneme | Main st | Hueneme. |
| Davisson, J I | Farmer | Santa Clara Valley | 4 m N E Hueneme | Hueneme. |
| Day, James A | Farmer | Ventura Co | Santa Clara st | S Buenaventura |
| Dean, D C | Clerk | | Ventura | S Buenaventura |
| Dean, M | Clerk | Main st | Meta st | S Buenaventura |
| Decker, C H | Postmaster | Sespe Ranch | Sespe Ranch | Scenega. |
| Decker, C H | Farmer | nr Hueneme | Ventura Co | Hueneme. |
| De la Guerra, S | Stock | Tapo Ranch | | S Buenaventura |
| De La Guera, Osbaldo | Clerk | Main st | Ventura | S Buenaventura |
| Del Campo, F M | Gen'l merchant | Main st | Ventura Ave | |
| Delmont, F | Physician | Main st | Main st | S Buenaventura |
| Del Valle, Ignacio | Stock | Sespe Ranch | | Scenega. |
| Del Valle, J Y | Farmer | Sespe Ranch | | Scenega. |
| Delvalle, J | Stock | Sespe Ranch | | Scenega. |
| Dempsey, John | Farmer | Santa Clara Valley | 5 m N Hueneme | Hueneme. |
| Dennis, B F | Farmer | Olivas Ranch | 1½ m S E S B Ven | S Buenaventura |
| Dennison, H J | Stock | Ojai Valley | 18 m N Nordhoff | Nordhoff. |
| De Nure, D D | Teacher & farmer | Santa Clara Valley | 3 m N E Hueneme | Hueneme. |
| Detroy Bros | Butchers | West Main st | San Buenaventura | S Buenaventura |
| Detroy, J | Butcher | Main st | Main st | S Buenaventura |
| Detroy, George | Butcher | Main st | Ventura | S Buenaventura |
| Detroy, Joseph | Butcher | Main st | Ventura | S Buenaventura |

## THE
# BANK OF VENTURA,

Main Street, San Buenaventura, Cal.

## AUTHORIZED CAPITAL STOCK, $250,000

### OFFICERS.

L. SNODGRASS—*President.*  M. CANNON—*Vice President.*
M. H. GAY—*Cashier.*

### DIRECTORS.

L. SNODGRASS.  T. R. BARD.  M. CANNON.
W. S. CHAFFEE.  M. H. GAY.  G. W. CHRISMAN
J. M. BROOKS.

### CORRESPONDENTS.

NATIONAL GOLD BANK AND TRUST CO—*San Francisco.*
FARMERS' NATIONAL GOLD BANK—*San Jose.*
FARMERS AND MERCHANTS BANK—*Los Angeles.*
COMMERCIAL BANK—*San Diego.*

☞ Transacts a general banking business, buys and sells Exchange and Currency, and receives general and special deposits. Prompt attention given to collections. Interest allowed on Time Deposits. Vault and Safes are large and first-class, and well adapted for the safe keeping of papers, jewelry, etc., at a trifling cost.

---

W. E. SHEPHERD.  J. J. SHERIDAN.

### VENTURA

# Weekly Signal,

*San Buenaventura, Cal.*

## Ventura Signal,

PUBLISHED WEEKLY BY

### SHEPHERD & SHERIDAN

East Main Street,

San Buenaventura,  California.

Subscription, $3 per annum.

---

C. J. EDSON,

PRACTICAL

# WATCHMAKER,

**Main Street,**

One door west of Wells, Fargo & Co.,

**SAN BUENAVENTURA, CAL.**

Keeps constantly on hand a full and complete assortment of

Clocks, Watches and Jewelry,

SILVER AND PLATED WARE, ETC.

Agent for the World-renowned

**Domestic Sewing Machine,**

Commercial Insurance Co.,

And Ticket Agent for

**G. N. P. S. S. CO.**

## DIRECTORY OF VENTURA COUNTY.

| NAME. | OCCUPATION. | PLACE OF BUSINESS. | RESIDENCE. |
|---|---|---|---|
| Dickerson, Thos | Stock | Ventura Co | Meta st |
| Dickey, F M | Farmer | Santa Clara Valley | 1 m E Hueneme |
| Diehl, A | Farmer | nr Hueneme | Ventura Co |
| Dinsmore, W H | Farmer | Santa Clara Valley | 3 m S E Hueneme |
| Dodson, Jesse | Hotel | Santa Paula | 16 m E S B Ventura |
| Dodson, J R | Farmer | Ventura Co | nr Saticoy |
| Dolittle, Ira P | Stock | Laguna | 7 m E Hueneme |
| Dollar, J W | Farmer | Ojai Valley | 9 m N S B Ventura. |
| Dollar, Saml | Teamster | Ventura | Front st |
| Dollar, Wm | Farmer | Ojai Valley | 9 m N S B Ventura. |
| Dominguez, E | Stock | Sespe Ranch | 35 m E S B Ventura |
| Dominguez, Fred | Stock | Saticoy | 8 m E S B Ventura. |
| Dominguez, Juan | Farmer | Sespe Ranch | |
| Domingues, P | Farmer | Ventura Co | nr Saticoy |
| Domingues, R | Farmer | nr Hueneme | Ventura Co |
| Donlon, Peter | Farmer and stock | Santa Clara Valley | 2 m N Hueneme |
| Douglass, John | Hostler | Santa Clara st | Ventura |
| Drake, E | Farmer | nr Hueneme | Ventura Co |
| Dubbers, Henry | Farmer | Main st | Main st |
| Dunlap, R R | Minister | Ventura Co | Hueneme |
| Dunn, Hugh | Farmer | Olivas Ranch | 6 m S E S B Ventura |
| Dunne, E | Farmer | nr Saticoy | Ventura Co |
| Durrand, Joseph | Laborer | Nordhoff | Nordhoff |
| Durazo, R | Butcher | Ventura Co | San Buenaventura |
| Dutch, John | Gardener | Santa Clara Valley | 3 m N Hueneme |
| Duval, E A | Farmer | nr Saticoy | Ventura Co |
| Duval, E A | Clerk | Main st | Ventura |
| Easley, S I | Farmer | nr Saticoy | Ventura Co |
| Easley, S M W | Deputy assessor | Ventura | Ventura Ave. |
| Easley, Wm | Gardener | Santa Paula | 16 m E S B Ventura |
| Easton, L F | Dep clerk &sheriff | Ventura | Oak st |
| Eaton, C P | Stock | Santa Paula Ranch | |
| Eaton, H P | Sheep raiser | Ventura Co | nr Saticoy |
| Edson, C J | Jeweler | Main st | San Buenaventura |
| Edwards, C W | Farmer | Sespe Ranch | |
| Edwards, E A | Hardware | Main st | Santa Clara st |
| Egbert, J M | Gardener | Ventura | Ventura |
| Egbert, J M | Carpenter | Ventura Co | San Buenaventura |
| Eherne, Thomas | Farmer | Santa Paula Ranch | |
| Einstein. D | Merchant | Ventura Co | San Buenaventura |
| Einstein& Bernheim | Genl merchandise | cor Front and Cal sts | San Buenaventura |
| Elmore, B | Laborer | Ventura | Ventura Co |
| Elsworth, D | Farmer | Ventura Co | nr Saticoy |
| Elwell, Guadalupe | Deputy sheriff | Ventura | Figueroa st |
| Elwell, G | Teamster | Ventura Co | San Buenaventura |
| Elwell, J | Bar keeper | Ventura Co | San Buenaventura |
| Emerson, J R | Farmer | nr Hueneme | Ventura Co |
| Enderlin, Marks | Teacher | Main st | Main st |
| Ensign, Saml | Lighthouse keeper | Hueneme Lighthouse | Hueneme |
| Escandon & Williams | Real estate agents | Ventura Co | San Buenaventura |
| Escandon, A G | Lawyer | Ventura Co | San Buenaventura |
| Escandon, A | Saloon | Main st | Main st |
| Esperanca, Joseph | Baker | Main st | Main st |
| Evans, Harvey | Farmer | Pleasant Valley | |
| Evans, James | Farmer | San Buenaventura | |
| Evans, T J | Farmer | San Buenaventura | |
| Evans, Wm | Farmer | San Buenaventura | |
| Everett, A | Farmer | Santa Paula Ranch | |
| Everett, E | Farmer | Ventura Co | nr Saticoy |
| Fagan, M | Stock | Santa Paula Ranch | 8 m E S B Ventura. |
| Fales, Thos | Blacksmith | Ventura Co | San Buenaventura |
| Farley, W L | Laborer | nr Hueneme | Ventura Co |
| Farrell, A R | Farmer | nr Saticoy | Ventura Co |

# CITY PHARMACY.

## BOWLAND & CRAIG,

## DRUGGISTS AND  APOTHECARIES,

Opposite Post Office, San Bernardino, Cal.

Drugs, Paints, Oils, Glass, Varnishes, Brushes, Patent Medicines, Trusses, Braces, Essential Oils, Concentrated Preparations, and everything usually found in a Drug Store. School Books, Cap, Letter and Note Papers; Inks, Pens, Holders, Card Boards, Pass and Memorandum Books, Slates, Flat and News Paper, etc., etc. Hair, Tooth and Nail Brushes; Handkerchief Extracts, Colognes, Pomades, Hair Oils, Pocket, Dressing, Fine and Round Combs; Hand Mirrors, Puff Boxes, Lily Whites, Rouges, Fine Soaps, and all Toilet Appliances.

## CITY PHARMACY SODA WORKS.

SODA WATER, SARSAPARILLA, MINERAL WATER, ETC.,
on Draught, and bottled in Patent Glass-
Stoppered Bottles.

☞ The Trade supplied in any quantity and at the lowest rates.

---

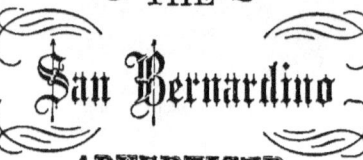

### ADVERTISER.

**BEST ADVERTISING MEDIUM IN SAN BERNARDINO COUNTY.**

1,000 COPIES WEEKLY, DISTRIBUTED GRATUITOUSLY.

☞ *Send for Advertising Rates.* ☜

A COMPLETE

### Book and Job Printing Office.

Every Style of Work executed with promptness.

**PERRIS & ISAAC.**

---

## TURF
## LIVERY & FEED STABLE,

THOS. McFARLANE & COCHRAN, Pro'rs.

Good Teams constantly on hand. Buggies, Carriages and Wagons, Single and Double, Open and Covered.

## THIRD STREET,

San Bernardino, Cal.

## DIRECTORY OF VENTURA COUNTY. 189

| Name. | Occupation. | Place of Business. | Residence. | Town or P. O. |
|---|---|---|---|---|
| Farris, J T | Farmer | nr Hueneme | Ventura Co | Hueneme. |
| Fay, Norman | Stock | Santa Clara Valley | 1 m N Hueneme | Hueneme. |
| Fenlon, J | Farmer | nr Hueneme | Ventura Co | Hueneme. |
| Ferrall, Alex | Laborer | Santa Paula | Santa Paula | Santa Paula. |
| Fessenden, — | | | Nordhoff | Nordhoff. |
| Figueroa, D | Laborer | Ventura Co | San Buenaventura | S Buenaventura |
| Figueroa, Mrs | | | Main st | S Buenaventura |
| Figueroa, S | Laborer | Ventura Co | San Buenaventura | S Buenaventura |
| Finley, J C | Teamster | San Buenaventura | Ventura Co | S Buenaventura |
| Finley, Joseph | Teamster | Ventura | | S Buenaventura |
| Finlon, James | Farmer | Santa Clara Valley | 3 m S Hueneme | Hueneme. |
| Finney, C G | Farmer | Ventura Co | Santa Clara st | S Buenaventura |
| Flanigan, John | Laborer | San Buenaventura | Mission Garden | S Buenaventura |
| Flanegan, J | Farmer | Ventura Co | San Buenaventura | S Buenaventura |
| Flint, H P | Stock | | 3 m N Hueneme | Hueneme. |
| Flores, A | Laborer | Ventura Co | Ventura | S Buenaventura |
| Follett, A D | Gardener | Ventura Co | Ventura Ave | S Buenaventura |
| Fooshea, A C | Farmer | Santa Clara Valley | 3½ m N E Hueneme | Hueneme. |
| Forrest, W H | Farmer | Santa Paula Ranch | | Santa Paula. |
| Foster, E P | Stock | Conejo Valley | 25 m E Hueneme | Hueneme. |
| Fouks, Irwin | Farmer | Santa Paula Ranch | 1¼ m S W S Paula | Santa Paula. |
| Foulks, A M | Farmer | nr Saticoy | Ventura Co | Hueneme. |
| Francis, S A | Carpenter | Ventura Co | San Buenaventura | S Buenaventura |
| Franz, E | Variety store | Main st | Main st | S Buenaventura |
| Freer, James | Stock | Sespe Ranch | | Scenega. |
| Fritch, A | Farmer | nr Hueneme | Ventura Co | Hueneme. |
| Fuller, J D | Farmer | Ventura Co | nr Saticoy | Saticoy. |
| Fry, Wm | Farmer | Sespe Ranch | 20 m E San Buenav. | Scenega. |
| Gardner, Dr John | Physician | Main st | Oak st | S Buenaventura |
| Gardner, — | Farmer | Saticoy | | Saticoy. |
| Garrett, Mrs B | | | Santa Clara st | S Buenaventura |
| Gay, M H | | Main st | Poli st | S Buenaventura |
| Gay, — | Carpenter | Ventura | Ventura Co | S Buenaventura |
| George, I B | Farmer | nr Hueneme | Ventura Co | Hueneme. |
| Gerberding, A | Merchant | Ventura Co | Hueneme | Hueneme. |
| Gerry, W | Bee raiser | Ex Mission Ranch | Santa Clara st | S Buenaventura |
| Gibson, S | Farmer | Ventura Co | nr Saticoy | Saticoy. |
| Gilber, M | Vaquero | Ventura Co | Ventura | S Buenaventura |
| Gilber, J V | Laborer | Ventura Co | Ventura | S Buenaventura |
| Gilbert, Geo S | Book keeper | Main st | Ventura | S Buenaventura |
| Gilbert, Thos | Clerk | Main st | Ventura | S Buenaventura |
| Giles, M P | Huen'e light h'se | Huen'e Light House | Light House | Hueneme. |
| Glenn, Joseph | Blacksmith | Market st | Market st | Hueneme. |
| Glonner, G G | Farmer | Santa Clara Valley | 5 m N E Hueneme | Hueneme. |
| Goddard, Jesse | Farmer | Ojai Valley | 3 m E Nordhoff | Nordhoff. |
| Golding, Thos | Carpenter | Santa Paula | | Santa Paula. |
| Gomez, Julian | Laborer | Ventura | Ventura Ave | S Buenaventura |
| Gomez, J F | Laborer | Ventura Co | Ventura | S Buenaventura |
| Gonzales, A | Laborer | Ventura Co | nr Saticoy | Saticoy. |
| Gonzales, J | Ranchero | nr Hueneme | Ventura Co | Hueneme. |
| Gonzales, M | Laborer | Ventura | Ventura Co | S Buenaventura |
| Gonzales, Mrs | | | Main st | S Buenaventura |
| Goodman, A | General mdse | Main st | Main st | S Buenaventura |
| Goodwin, Jas W | Books & station'y | Main st | Oak st | S Buenaventura |
| Goodwin, E W | P M & var'y st'e | Main st | Oak st | S Buenaventura |
| Gordon, A B | Saloon | Santa Paula | | Santa Paula. |
| Gordon, Wm A | Saloon | Santa Paula | | Santa Paula. |
| Gordon, W A | Farmer | nr Saticoy | Ventura Co | Saticoy. |
| Granger & Williams | Attorneys | Main st | San Buenaventura | S Buenaventura |
| Granger, L C | Attorney | Main st | San Buenaventura | S Buenaventura |
| Granger, Wm | Clerk | Main st | Ayer's Hotel | S Buenaventura |
| Grant, T P | Blacksmith | Main and 1st sts | Ventura | S Buenaventura |
| Grant, K P | Blacksmith | Ventura Co | San Buenaventura | S Buenaventura |

## L. L. PAULSON'S HAND-BOOK AND

| Name. | Occupation. | Place of Business. | Residence. | Town or P. O. |
|---|---|---|---|---|
| Graves, Frank | Teamster | Santa Paula | 16 m E San Buenav. | Santa Paula. |
| Gray, Alexander | Nurseryman | Santa Paula | | Santa Paula. |
| Gray, Thomas | Farmer | Ojai | | Nordhoff. |
| Gray, T C | Farmer | Ventura | Ventura Co | S Buenaventura |
| Green, — | Farmer | Sespe Ranch | 8 m E Santa Paula | Santa Paula. |
| Green, Jacob | Laborer | San Buenaventura | Main st | S Buenaventura |
| Gries, J K | Farmer | Santa Paula Ranch | | Santa Paula. |
| Griffin, Wm | Nurseryman | San Buenaventura | West Main st | S Buenaventura |
| Grimes, Brice | Hardware | Main st | Meta st | S Buenaventura |
| Grout, F S | Carpenter | Hueneme | Market st | Hueneme. |
| Grow, Chas | Carpenter | Ventura | Meta st | S Buenaventura |
| Growall, O P | Shoe maker | Santa Paula | | Santa Paula. |
| Guess, H T | Stock raiser | nr Saticoy | Ventura Co | Saticoy. |
| Guggenheim, H | Clerk | Main st | Ayer's Hotel | S Buenaventura |
| Guiberson, J W | Farmer | Santa Paula | | Santa Paula. |
| Guiberson, S A | Stock | Sespe | | Scenega. |
| Guiberson, S P | Physician | Oak st | Santa Clara st | S Buenaventura |
| Guiberson, W McK | Teamster | Ventura Co | nr Saticoy | Saticoy. |
| Gunn, S R | Carpenter | Ventura | Ventura Co | S Buenaventura |
| Gurrera, S de la | Manufacturer | Ventura Co | Hueneme | Hueneme. |
| Guthrie, R M | Farmer | Pleasant Valley | 13 m E Hueneme | Hueneme. |
| Haines, A | Farmer | Santa Paula | | Santa Paula. |
| Hall, Geo | Livery stable | Main st | Ventura | S Buenaventura |
| Hall, G A | Stock raiser | Ventura Co | San Buenaventura | S Buenaventura |
| Hall, R R | Stock | Santa Paula Ranch | 2 m E San Buenav. | S Buenaventura |
| Hall, R O | Stock raiser | Ventura Co | Ventura | S Buenaventura |
| Halser, J | Stock raiser | Ventura Co | nr Saticoy | Saticoy. |
| Hammond, S | Teamster | Ventura Co | Ventura | S Buenaventura |
| Hampton, H | Physician | Ventura Co | Saticoy | Saticoy. |
| Hampton, Mrs Lue | Dairy | Santa Clara Valley | 5 m N Hueneme | Hueneme. |
| Hampton, Wade | Stock | Ex Mission Ranch | | S Buenaventura |
| Hankinson, T V | Farmer | Ventura Co | nr Saticoy | Saticoy. |
| Hanson, M L | Carpenter | Ventura | California st | S Buenaventura |
| Harbard, John | Stock | Ex Mission | | Santa Paula. |
| Hare, Ed T | Co surveyor | Court House | Oak st | S Buenaventura |
| Harkey, J S | Farmer | Ventura Co | nr Hueneme | Hueneme. |
| Harrer, D H | Farmer | nr Hueneme | Ventura Co | Hueneme. |
| Harrer, Enos | Farmer | Pleasant Valley | 10 m E Hueneme | Hueneme. |
| Harrer, Evan | Farmer | Santa Clara Valley | 4 m N E Hueneme | Hueneme. |
| Harrer, N G | Farmer | Santa Clara Valley | 4 m N E Hueneme | Hueneme. |
| Harrer, Rev Wilson | Pastor | Methodist Church | Pleasant Valley | Hueneme. |
| Harrer, W J | Farmer | nr Hueneme | Ventura Co | Hueneme. |
| Harrington, A J | Blacksmith | Main st | California st | S Buenaventura |
| Harris, C W | Minister | Ventura Co | Hueneme | Hueneme. |
| Harris, Isaac | Farmer | Ventura Co | nr Hueneme | Hueneme. |
| Harris, M K | Farmer | Pleasant Valley | | S Buenaventura |
| Hartman, F | Brewer | Main st | Main st | S Buenaventura |
| Harvey, Wm | Cabinet maker | Main st | California st | S Buenaventura |
| Haskins, H C | Farmer | Sespe Ranch | | Scenega. |
| Harkey, J S | Farmer | Pleasant Valley | 13 m E San Buenav. | S Buenaventura |
| Hattery, E | Farmer | Ventura Co | nr Hueneme | Hueneme. |
| Hattery, H | Farmer | Santa Clara Valley | 4 m E Hueneme | Hueneme. |
| Hatton, John | Farmer | Santa Paula Ranch | | Santa Paula. |
| Hatton, J M | Farmer | Ventura Co | nr Saticoy | Saticoy. |
| Hawkins, P B | Farmer & stock | Santa Clara Valley | 4 m S Hueneme | Hueneme. |
| Hawkins, W L | Farmer | nr Hueneme | Ventura Co | Hueneme. |
| Hayes, — | Farmer | Ventura Co | Poli st | S Buenaventura |
| Hayes, L K | Farmer | Ventura | Ventura Co | S Buenaventura |
| Hayes, Mrs | | | Front st | S Buenaventura |
| Heam, N | Clerk | Main st | Ayer's hotel | S Buenaventura |
| Hemenway, O | Laborer | nr Hueneme | Ventura Co | Hueneme. |
| Henderson, M M | Stock | Main st | California st | S Buenaventura |
| Henney, James | Stock | Sespe Ranch | | Scenega. |
| Henshaw, G H | Carpenter | Santa Paula | | Santa Paula. |

# DIRECTORY OF VENTURA COUNTY. 191

| Name. | Occupation. | Place of Business. | Residence. | Town or P. O. |
|---|---|---|---|---|
| Herbert, L R | Merchant | | Meta st | S Buenaventura |
| Herrett, G M F | Moulder | Ventura Co | Hueneme | Hueneme. |
| Hester, N W | Carpenter & joiner | San Buenaventura | Main st | S Buenaventura |
| Hickerson, N H | Carpenter | Ventura | Front st | S Buenaventura |
| Hicks, J | Farmer | nr Hueneme | Ventura Co | Hueneme. |
| Higgins, C T | Farmer | Saticoy | 7 m E San Buenav | Saticoy. |
| Higgins, E B | Farmer | Saticoy | 7 m E San Buenav | Saticoy. |
| Higuera, M | Farmer | nr Hueneme | Ventura Co | Hueneme. |
| Hill, Mrs | | Ventura | California st | S Buenaventura |
| Hill, J G | Farmer & stock | | 3½ m N Hueneme | Hueneme. |
| Hill, J J | Laborer | Santa Clara Valley | 3½ m N Hueneme | Hueneme. |
| Hill, John S | Miner | Santa Clara Valley | 12 m E Hueneme | Hueneme. |
| Hill, M A | Farmer | nr Hueneme | Ventura Co | Hueneme. |
| Hill, W R | Farmer | nr Hueneme | Ventura Co | Hueneme. |
| Hilpert, Rich'd | Barber | Main st | Main st | S Buenaventura |
| Hines & Brooks | Attorneys | Ventura Co | San Buenaventura | S Buenaventura |
| Hines, J L | Lawyer | Main st | Main st | S Buenaventura |
| Hobart, J | Farmer | Ventura | Ventura Co | S Buenaventura |
| Hobert, J L | Farmer | Ojai | | Nordhoff. |
| Hobson, W D | Hotel prop | Ventura House | Cal'a & S Clara sts | S Buenaventura |
| Hobson, Mrs E | | | cor Front & Palm sts | S Buenaventura |
| Hodges, E | Farmer | nr Saticoy | Ventura Co | Saticoy. |
| Hodgkins, G E | Blacksmith | Saticoy | | Saticoy. |
| Hohlbauch, John | Laborer | Hueneme Wharf | Hueneme Wharf | Hueneme. |
| Holster, J | Stock | Santa Paula Canyon | 3 m N Santa Paula | Santa Paula. |
| Hopkins, W L | Teamster | nr Saticoy | Ventura Co | Saticoy. |
| Hopper, A | Stock | Sespe Ranch | | Scenega. |
| Horton, Wm | Farmer | Sespe Ranch | | Scenega. |
| Horton, J M | Farmer | Sespe Ranch | | Scenega. |
| Hubbard, F A | Farmer | Beach Road | | S Buenaventura |
| Hubbard, G F | Farmer | Ventura | Ventura Co | S Buenaventura |
| Hubbell, D S | Farmer | nr Hueneme | Ventura Co | Hueneme. |
| Hubbell, H C | Bar keeper | Ventura Co | San Buenaventura | S Buenaventura |
| Hughes, W A | Farmer | nr Hueneme | Ventura Co | Hueneme. |
| Hughes, W G | Merchant | Ventura Co | Hueneme | Hueneme. |
| Hund, — | Apiarian | Ojai Valley | 3 m E Nordhoff | Nordhoff. |
| Hunt, W H | Bee raiser | Sespe Ranch | | Scenega. |
| Hutchinson, L | Carpenter | Ventura | Ventura Co | S Buenaventura |
| Huston, W S | Stock | | Front st | S Buenaventura |
| Hyde & Daley | Livery stable | Main st | | S Buenaventura |
| Hyde, Wm | Livery stable | Main st | Oak st | S Buenaventura |
| Ireland, Eugene H | Blacksmith | Santa Paula | | Santa Paula. |
| Ireland, N J | Blacksmith | Santa Paula | | Santa Paula. |
| Isbell, I C | Farmer | Santa Paula | | Santa Paula. |
| Jackson, A | Blacksmith | Ventura Co | Hueneme | Hueneme. |
| James, W B | Blacksmith | Ventura Co | San Buenaventura | S Buenaventura |
| Jenifer, J M | Farmer | Hueneme | Hueneme | Hueneme. |
| Jenifer, Mat | Farmer | Santa Clara Valley | 1 m E Hueneme | Hueneme. |
| Jenness, R S | General mdse | Nordhoff | Nordhoff | Nordhoff. |
| Jopson, A A | Bee raiser | Sespe Ranch | | Scenega. |
| Jimenez, M E | Conveyancer | Ventura Co | San Buenaventura | S Buenaventura |
| Johnson & Sutton | Santa Clara Ho | Main st | San Buenaventura | S Buenaventura |
| Johnson, — | Santa Clara Ho | Main st | San Buenaventura | S Buenaventura |
| Jones, E H | Farmer | Ojai Valley | | Nordhoff. |
| Jones, E S | Blacksmith | Ventura Co | Saticoy | Saticoy. |
| Jones, E M | Hotel keeper | Ventura Co | San Buenaventura | S Buenaventura |
| Jones, J N | Farmer | Ojai | | Nordhoff. |
| Jones, J M | Laborer | Santa Paula | 16 m E San Buenav | Santa Paula. |
| Jones, John | Teamster | Santa Paula | | Santa Paula. |
| Jones, N M | Laborer | Ventura Co | San Buenaventura | S Buenaventura |
| Jones, N M | Com merchant | East Main st | San Buenaventura | S Buenaventura |
| Jones & Hall | Stable | Main st | San Buenaventura | S Buenaventura |
| Jones, — | Stable | Main st | San Buenaventura | S Buenaventura |
| Jones, V M | Stock | Ventura | Front st | S Buenaventura |

| Name. | Occupation. | Place of Business. | Residence. |
|---|---|---|---|
| Joy, Alfred | Farmer | Sespe Ranch | |
| Judkins, Mrs Rosa | | | Main st |
| Jurgensen, H | Blacksmith | Main st | Ayres Hotel |
| Karr, John | Farmer | Ojai Valley | 1 m E Nordhoff |
| Kaufman, M | Farmer | nr Hueneme | Ventura Co |
| Kaultmeyer, H | Farmer | Santa Clara Valley | 6 m N E Hueneme |
| Kearns, J | Laborer | Ventura Co | nr Saticoy |
| Kearney, Wm | Stock | Ex Mission Ranch | 11 m N E S Buenav. |
| Keene, Josiah | Clerk | | Ventura Ave |
| Keith, John | Farmer | Ojai | |
| Keller, N H | Farmer | nr Hueneme | Ventura Co |
| Kelley, M | Stock | Ex Mission Ranch | |
| Kelsey, J B | Farmer | Santa Paula Ranch | 7 m E San Buenav |
| Kelsey, T A | Farmer | nr Saticoy | Ventura Co |
| Kennedy, J L | Stock | Los Posas Ranch | 20 m E San Buenav. |
| Kenney, Cyrus | Bee raiser | Sespe Ranch | |
| Kerns, John | Laborer | Ventura Co | 3 m W Santa Paula, |
| Killfoyle, F | Laborer | Sespe Ranch | 20 m E San Buenav. |
| Kirkpatrick, J N | Laborer | Santa Paula Ranch | 15 m E San Buenav. |
| Kittredge, Wm T | Farmer | Cañada Largo | |
| Knighting, Rev W A | Pastor | Methodist Church | Oak st |
| Koklow, Henry | Farmer | Santa Clara Valley | 5 m N E Hueneme |
| Kuhlman, C W | Genl mdse | Main st | San Buenaventura |
| Kuhlman, J A | Merchant | Ventura Co | San Buenaventura |
| Kuhn, Chas | Farmer | Hueneme Township | |
| Kyle, S | Miner | | Main st |
| Larmer, John | Farmer | Ojai Valley | 15 m N San Buenav. |
| Larson, E | Farmer | County Road | 3 m W Santa Paula. |
| Larson, E C | Farmer | nr Saticoy | Ventura Co |
| La Rue, — | Apiarian | Sespe Ranch | 2 m E Santa Paula |
| Lauranzana, M | Stock | Ventura | Ventura Ave |
| Laurent, M J | Farmer | Santa Clara Valley | 3 m N E Hueneme |
| Lee, G M | Laborer | Ventura Co | San Buenaventura |
| Leech, F S | Carriage maker | Ventura Co | San Buenaventura |
| Lehman, B | Carpenter | Ventura | Poli st |
| Leonard, James | Farmer | Colonia Ranch | 7 m S E San Buenav |
| Lenord, James | Farmer | Santa Clara Valley | 5 m N Hueneme |
| Leveck, Wm | Teamster | Ventura | Poli st |
| Levio, F C | Farmer | Ventura Co | nr Hueneme |
| Levy & Wolf | Genl merchants | Main st | |
| Levy, A | General mdse | Santa Paula | 16 m E San Buenav. |
| Levy, A | Genl merchant | Main st | Market st |
| Lewis, J | Farmer | Ventura Co | nr Hueneme |
| Ley, H D | Painter | California st | Main st |
| Ley, T A | Painter | California st | Santa Clara st |
| Lillie, J | Saloon keeper | Ventura Co | Hueneme |
| Limbacher, P | Barber | Ventura Co | San Buenaventura |
| Linebarger, W | Farmer | Ventura Co | nr Saticoy |
| Lineberger, F M | Farmer | nr Saticoy | Ventura Co |
| Lineberger, J | Laborer | nr Saticoy | Ventura Co |
| Livingston, R G | Genl merchant | Main st | Main st |
| Lopez, Alex | Laborer | Ventura Co | nr Hueneme |
| Lopez, F | Vaquero | Ventura | Ventura Co |
| Lopez, J W | Laborer | Ventura Co | San Buenaventura |
| Lopez, J F | Ranchero | Ventura | Ventura Co |
| Lopez, Ramon | Vaquero | Ventura | Ventura |
| Lopez, Rafael | Ranchero | Ventura | Ventura Co |
| Lopez, Teo | Vaquero | Ventura | Ventura |
| Loranzana, R | Stock | Ventura Co | Ventura Ave |
| Lord, J D | Stock | Sespe Ranch | 25 m E San Buenav. |
| Lorenza, F | Ranchero | Ventura | Ventura Co |
| Lorenza, M | Ranchero | Ventura Co | San Buenaventura |
| Lorenza, R | Laborer | Ventura Co | San Buenaventura |
| Louderback, H | Stock raiser | Ventura Co | San Buenaventura |

## DIRECTORY OF VENTURA COUNTY.

| NAME. | OCCUPATION. | PLACE OF BUSINESS. | RESIDENCE. |
|---|---|---|---|
| Lumbargo, F | Laborer | Main st | Main st |
| Lyon, Robt | Farmer | Ventura Co | Ventura Ave |
| McAdams, J C | Stock raiser | nr Saticoy | Ventura Co |
| McCarty, P V | Shoe maker | | Main st |
| McClinchey, John | Farmer | Santa Clara Valley | 4 m N E Hueneme |
| McCloskey, N | Hostler | Rincon Point | 15 m W San Buenav |
| McCoy, D D | Hotel proprietor | Pioneer Hotel | Market st |
| McDonald, A D | Carpenter | Ventura | Ventura Co |
| McGraw, — | Farmer | Santa Clara Valley | 5 m N Hueneme |
| McGreel, Michael | Teamster | Ventura | |
| McKee, W S | Private board'g | Ojai Valley | Ventura Co |
| McKeeby, C B | Clerk | Main st | Ventura |
| McKeeby, L C | Genl merchandise | Main st | California st |
| McLaughlin, Mark | Farmer & stock | Santa Clara Valley | 4½ m N E Hueneme |
| McMillen, Peter | Carpenter | Santa Paula | 16 m E San Buenav |
| McMordie, Henry | Farmer | Ex Mission Ranch | 5 m N E S Buenav |
| Maddux, J F | Farmer & stock | Santa Clara Valley | 4 m N E Hueneme |
| Maddox, P | Farmer | nr Hueneme | Ventura Co |
| Maddux, R A | Farmer | Ventura Co | nr Hueneme |
| Mahan, John | Farmer | Pleasant Valley | 14 m E San Buenav |
| Marcellaine, W H | Laborer | Nordhoff | Ventura Co |
| Marks, Henry | Gen merchandise | East Main & Cal'a sts | San Buenaventura |
| Marks, M H | Clerk | Main st | California st |
| Marple, Thos | Stock | Sespe Ranch | 30 m E San Buenav |
| Marroquin, M | Ranchero | Ventura | Ventura Co |
| Marsh, W F | Plasterer | Ventura | Ventura Co |
| Martin, F | Laborer | Ventura Co | San Buenaventura |
| Martinez & Co, F | General mdse | Main st | |
| Martines, Flavio | Groceries | Main st | Cañada st |
| Martinez, F P | Painter | Ventura Co | Ventura |
| Maxwell, J W | Druggist | Ventura Co | San Buenaventura |
| May, J | Boot maker | Main st | Ventura |
| Mears, John | Stock | Santa Paula | 4 m S Santa Paula |
| Mehan, Jas | Gardener | Ventura Co | San Buenaventura |
| Meletta, Julius | Wine maker | Ventura Co | Saticoy |
| Melrose, K | Farmer | Santa Ana Ranch | 14 m N W S Buenav |
| Melrose, T W | Farmer | Ventura Co | Ventura |
| Merrideth, Chas T | Teacher | Ojai Valley | 2 m N E Nordhoff |
| Merry, O | Farmer | 2 m N San Buenav | Ventura Ave |
| Methvin, L P | Farmer | nr Hueneme | Ventura Co |
| Middleton, J | Farmer | Ventura Co | nr Saticoy |
| Middleton, W | Blacksmith | Ventura Co | Saticoy |
| Middleswart, Jasper | Laborer | Santa Paula | 1 m W Santa Paula |
| Miller, George | Farmer | Santa Ana Ranch | 8 m N San Buenav |
| Miller, H H | Saloon keeper | Ventura Co | Hueneme |
| Miller, Henry | | San Buenaventura | Ventura Co |
| Miller, H H | Carpenter | Main st | Main st |
| Miller, J M | Comm merchant | East Main st | San Buenaventura |
| Miller & Jones | Comm merchants | East Main st | San Buenaventura |
| Millhouse, G E | Farmer | Ex Mission Ranch | 15 m N E S Buenav |
| Mills, Howard W | Stock | Conejo Grant | 25 m E Hueneme |
| Mitchell, Peter | Laborer | San Buenaventura | San Buenaventura |
| Montgomery, J H | Capitalist | Ojai Valley | Nordhoff |
| Moraga, G | Ranchero | Ventura Co | Ventura |
| Moraga, J S | Ranchero | Ventura Co | Ventura |
| Moraga, Jose | Farmer | Cañada Largo | 4 m N San Buenav |
| Moraga, Vecinte | Ranchero | nr Ventura | Ventura Co |
| Moraga, Miguel | Ranchero | nr Ventura | Ventura Co |
| Morales, J B | Saddler | Ventura Co | San Buenaventura |
| Morales, M | Ranchero | Ventura | Ventura Co |
| Moore, E | Farmer | Santa Paula | 19 m E San Buenav |
| Moore, E W | Farmer | nr Saticoy | Ventura Co |
| Moore, L W | Ranchero | nr Saticoy | Ventura Co |
| Morrison, J Z | Farmer | Sespe Ranch | 30 m E San Buenav |

## R. F. CUNNINGHAM,

RIVERSIDE, San Bernardino Co., Cal.

—DEALER IN—

# General Merchandise

## DRY GOODS,

## Provisions, Liquors,

*TOBACCO and CIGARS,*

Boots & Shoes, Hardware, Clothing, Drugs, and Gentlemen's and Ladies' Furnishing Goods.

---

## Brocker & Reinhold,
# FURNITURE
### DEALERS

THIRD ST., San Bernardino, Cal.

Chamber Sets, Parlor Sets, Bedroom Sets, Matresses, Spring Beds, Chairs and Bureaus constantly on hand. Upholstering done to order. Furniture repaired. Store and Office Fixtures supplied.

---

## RIVERSIDE
# Drug Store

H. R. EMMONS, M. D.

Proprietor,

RIVERSIDE, SAN BERNARDINO COUNTY, CAL'A.

FULL STOCK OF

# DRUGS AND CHEMICALS

Constantly on hand.

Prescriptions prepared at all hours.

---

## M. E. MOWBRAY,

DEALER IN

*GOLD and SILVER*

# WATCHES

FINE JEWELRY,

## SPECTACLES, CHAINS,

Rings, Silverware, Etc.

Jewelry made to order, and the Repairing of Watches a SPECIALTY.

*ALL WORK WARRANTED.*

## SAN BERNARDINO, CAL.

# DIRECTORY OF VENTURA COUNTY. 195

| Name. | Occupation. | Place of Business. | Residence. | Town or P. O. |
|---|---|---|---|---|
| Moulton, J............ | Bookkeeper........ | Santa Paula Mills.... | 16½ m San Buenav... | Santa Paula. |
| Mungaray, F......... | Laborer............ ........ | Ventura Co............ | San Buenaventura... | S Buenaventura |
| Murphy, T H....... | Blacksmith............ | Ventura Co............ | San Buenaventura... | S Buenaventura |
| Murray & Co........ | Painters................... | Main st...... ............ | Santa Clara st........ | S Buenaventura |
| Murray, Chas E.... | Painter............... | Main st.................. | Santa Clara st........ | S Buenaventura |
| Murray, Wm E..... | Painter ............ | Main st.................. | Santa Clara st........ | S Buenaventura |
| Myers, J B........... | Farmer........ | Cañada Largo......... | 4 m N San Buenav... | S Buenaventura |
| Myers, J K.......... | Farmer........ ............ | Cañada Largo......... | 3 m N San Buenav... | S Buenaventura |
| Nash, R............... | Farmer............. | nr Hueneme............ | Ventura Co............ | Hueneme. |
| Naylor, J B.......... | Farmer............. | Ventura Co............ | nr Saticoy............. | Saticoy. |
| Neale, W R.......... | Farmer............. | nr Hueneme............ | Ventura Co............ | Hueneme. |
| Neanby, —.......... | Laborer............. | Ventura ..... .......... | Poli st...... ............ | S Buenaventura |
| Neece, A M.......... | Stock.................. | Santa Clara Valley .. | 5 m N E Hueneme... | Hueneme. |
| Nelson, Peter....... | ,.................... ........ | Oak st.................. | Ventura................ | S Buenaventura |
| Newbury, E S....... | Stock.................. | Conejo Ranch ......... | 20 m E Hueneme..... | Hueneme. |
| Newby, Frank ..... | Gardener............. | Ventura ............... | Poli st.................. | S Buenaventura |
| Newby, T J.......... | Contributor......... | Ojai Valley............. | ........................... | S Buenaventura |
| Newby, Thos........ | Farmer............. | Ojai Valley............. | 3 m N E Nordhoff... | Nordhoff. |
| Newell, Thos ...... | Miller................ | Santa Paula Mills ... | 16 m E San Buenav.. | Santa Paula. |
| Nidever, H F........ | Stock................ | Sespe Ranch .......... | 35 m E San Buenav.. | Scenega. |
| Niederfer, Jacob.... | Clerk................. | Main st................. | Ventura ............... | S Buenaventura |
| Nogues, B............ | Baker................ | West Main st......... | West Main st......... | S Buenaventura |
| Norwood, Thos...... | Clerk................ | Main st................. | California st........... | S Buenaventura |
| Nyñas, Francisco... | Vaquero ............ | Ventura ............... | Main st................. | S Buenaventura |
| Obiols, Y............. | Farmer............. | San Buenaventura... | Ventura Ave.......... | S Buenaventura |
| O'Hara, C ............ | Constable........... | Ventura Co............ | Saticoy ............... | Saticoy. |
| O'Hara, Chas........ | Farmer ....,........ | Ex Mission Ranch... | ........................... | S Buenaventura |
| O'Hara, Hugh...... | Farmer............. | Ex Mission Ranch... | ........................... | S Buenaventura |
| O'Harra, Wm....... | Farmer............. | Ex Mission Ranch... | ........................... | S Buenaventura |
| Old, H W............. | Farmer & stock.. | Santa Clara Valley .. | 3 m E Hueneme ..... | Hueneme. |
| Olivas, J de la S.... | Ranchero .......... | Ventura Co............ | San Buenaventura... | S Buenaventura |
| Olivas, Nicholas..... | Stock................ | Olivas Ranch.......... | 5 m S E S Buenav.. | S Buenaventura |
| Olivas, R............. | Stock................ , | Olivas Ranch.......... | 5 m S E S Buenav.. | S Buenaventura |
| Olivas, Santiago.... | Musician ............ | Ventura Co............ | Saticoy ............... | Saticoy. |
| Oliveras, Estevan... | Ranchero .......... | nr Hueneme............ | Ventura Co............ | Hueneme. |
| Olmsted, R H....... | Farmer............. | Santa Paula Ranch .. | 1¼ m W Santa Paula | Santa Paula. |
| Ortega, Emilo....... | Ranchero .......... | Ventura Co............ | Main st................. | S Buenaventura |
| Ortega, Jose. ....... | Stock................ | San Buenaventura... | Ventura Co............ | S Buenaventura |
| Ortega, Ramon .... | Stock................ | Ventura Co............ | Main st................. | S Buenaventura |
| Ortega, M E......... | Vaquero ............ | Ventura Co............ | San Buenaventura... | S Buenaventura |
| Otero, J M........... | Laborer............. | Ventura Co............ | nr Hueneme............ | Hueneme. |
| Oviols, Y............. | Farmer............. | Ventura Co............ | San Buenaventura... | S Buenaventura |
| Park, J ............... | Farmer............. | Ventura Co............ | nr Hueneme............ | Hueneme. |
| Parsons, Isaac W... | Teamster........... | Ventura Co............ | nr Hueneme............ | Hueneme. |
| Parsons, J W........ | Farmer............. | Santa Paula........... | Santa Paula........... | Santa Paula. |
| Pearson, R C........ | Saloon............... | Main st................. | Main st................. | S Buenaventura |
| Pelzer, F ............ | Vaquero ............ | Ventura ............... | Ventura Co............ | S Buenaventura |
| Peña, R............... | Carpenter........... | Ventura Co............ | San Buenaventura... | S Buenaventura |
| Peralta, Julio........ | Stock................ | Ventura Co............ | Main st................. | S Buenaventura |
| Peralta, Julio........ | Stock................ | Santa Paula Canyon | 2½ m N Santa Paula | Santa Paula. |
| Perkins, Frank...... | Stock................ | Ventura Co............ | Oak & S Clara sts... | S Buenaventura |
| Perkins, E H........ | Harness maker ... | Ventura Co............ | Hueneme ............. | Hueneme. |
| Perkins, S D........ | Merchant .......... | Ventura Co............ | Hueneme ............. | Hueneme. |
| Perkins, T E ....... | Proprietor ......... | Perkins' Hotel......... | Market st ............. | Hueneme. |
| Peterson, J C....... | Farmer............. | nr Saticoy............. | Ventura Co............ | Saticoy. |
| Pfiler, J............... | Farmer............. | Santa Clara Valley.. | 6 m N E Hueneme... | Hueneme. |
| Phillard, —.......... | Carpenter........... | Ventura Co............ | Nordhoff............... | Nordhoff. |
| Pico, J E............. | Carpenter........... | Ventura Co............ | San Buenaventura... | S Buenaventura |
| Pieron, R C......... | Saloon............... | Main st................. | Ventura ............... | S Buenaventura |
| Pierpont, D W...... | Farmer............. | nr Hueneme............ | Ventura Co ........... | Hueneme. |
| Pierson, R C........ | Farmer............. | nr Hueneme,........... | Ventura Co............ | Hueneme. |
| Pinkard, S D........ | Farmer............. | Colonia Ranch........ | 7 m S E S Buenav.. | S Buenaventura |
| Pinkard, S D........ | Farmer............. | Santa Clara Valley.. | 5 m N Hueneme...... | Hueneme. |
| Pinkerton, J ........ | Farmer............. | Ventura Co............ | Ventura ............... | S Buenaventura |

# WHARF PROPRIETOR,

### SAN BUENAVENTURA, CAL.

## GOOD DEEP-WATER BERTHS

AND THE BEST FACILITIES GIVEN TO VESSELS, EITHER FOR LADING OR DISCHARGING CARGOES. A LARGE WAREHOUSE FOR THE STORING OF ALL KINDS OF GOODS.

---

CONTRACTS MADE FOR FURNISHING

### Lumber, Wood and Cargoes

OF ALL DESCRIPTIONS.

---

## WHARF RATES LOW.

## DIRECTORY OF VENTURA COUNTY.

| NAME. | OCCUPATION. | PLACE OF BUSINESS. | RESIDENCE. |
|---|---|---|---|
| Pirie, Wm | Stock | Ojai Valley | ¾ m S Nordhoff |
| Poll, Simon | Stock | Sespe Ranch | 22 m E San Buenav.. |
| Pond, J H | Hotel | Santa Paula | 16 m E San Buenav. |
| Poor, I L | Laborer | Nordhoff | Nordhoff |
| Pope, H S | Gunsmith | Main st | California st |
| Porter, J A C | Wheelwright | Main st | Ayres Hotel |
| Portman, F | Stock | Sespe Ranch | 25 m E San Buenav.. |
| Powell, J T | Farmer | nr Hueneme | Ventura Co |
| Pratt, Wm | Laborer | Ventura Co | Ventura Ave |
| Preble, C S | Lumberman | San Buenaventura | Ventura Ave |
| Preble, Chas | Lumber | Ventura Co | ½ m N Ventura |
| Price, Stillman | Farmer | Santa Clara Valley | 1 m E Hueneme |
| Price, T | Farmer | nr Hueneme | Ventura Co |
| Prince, M | | Santa Paula Ranch | |
| Procter, Thos | Farmer | Ojai Valley | 5 m E Nordhoff |
| Purcell, M | Farmer | Santa Paula Ranch | 7 m E San Buenav... |
| Putnam, L | Carpenter | Ventura Co | Ventura |
| Rae, Wm | Boot maker | Main st | North Main st |
| Ralston, Mrs P | Farmer | Santa Paula | 16 m E San Buenav.. |
| Ramsauer, W P | Farmer | nr Hueneme | Ventura Co |
| Ramsauer, R S | Farmer | nr Hueneme | Ventura Co |
| Ramsey, Andrew | Carpenter | Ojai Valley | 2½ m N E Nordhoff.. |
| Randolph, G | Farmer | Sespe Ranch | 26 m E San Buenav. |
| Randolph, J B | Farmer | Sespe Ranch | 26 m E San Buenav.. |
| Randolph, K | Farmer | Sespe Ranch | 26 m E San Buenav.. |
| Randolph, S | Blacksmith | Main st | Main st |
| Ranuart, L | Saloon | Main st | Main st |
| Read, J J | Farmer | nr Hueneme | Ventura Co |
| Read, S H | Farmer | Pleasant Valley | 12 m E San Buenav. |
| Reaggin, N W | Merchant | Main st | Front st |
| Redman, — | Blacksmith | | Santa Paula |
| Rehart, J | Stock raiser | Ventura Co | nr Saticoy |
| Reiley, Michael | Farmer | Ventura Co | Meta, cor Oak st |
| Reed, G | Laborer | nr Hueneme | Ventura Co |
| Renck, T | Farmer | nr Saticoy | Ventura Co |
| Rennert, L | Bar tender | Main st | San Buenaventura |
| Reyes, R | Vaquero | Ventura Co | San Buenaventura |
| Rhehart, Jacob | Stock | Santa Paula Ranch | 14 m N E San Buena |
| Rhoads & Gordon | Groceries & saloon | Santa Paula | |
| Rhoads, Washington | Groceries & saloon | Santa Paula | 16 m E San Buenav.. |
| Rice, C M | Farmer | Pleasant Valley | 14 m E San Buenav.. |
| Rice, John | Farmer | Pleasant Valley | 14 m E San Buenav.. |
| Rice, Peter | Farmer | Pleasant Valley | 17 m E San Buenav.. |
| Rice, W I | Farmer | Ventura Co | East Main st |
| Richards, W D F | Farmer | Santa Paula Ranch | 10 m E San Bnenav.. |
| Richardson, A L | Farmer | Ventura Co | nr Saticoy |
| Richardson, David | Stock | Santa Paula Canyon | 4 m N Santa Paula.. |
| Richardson, Fred | Stock | Santa Paula Ranch | 17 m E San Buenav.. |
| Richardson, Geo N | Farmer | Santa Paula Ranch | 4 m S E Santa Paula |
| Richardson, Joseph | Furniture | Main st | California st |
| Richardson, J, Jr | Furniture dealer | Main st | California st |
| Richter, Wm M | Farmer | Ojai Valley | 18 m N San Buenav. |
| Ricker, J G | Farmer | Santa Paula Ranch | 13 m E San Buenav. |
| Rienart, Chas | Clerk | Main st | California st |
| Rietzke, Th | Hair dresser | San Buenaventura | San Buenaventura |
| Riggs, J | Farmer | Ventura Co | nr Hueneme |
| Riggs, R N | Farmer | Ventura Co | nr Hueneme |
| Riggen & Co | Drug store | East Main st | San Buenaventura |
| Riggen, S B | Drug store | East Main st | San Buenaventura |
| Riggen, H N | Saddlery&harness | Main st | Ventura |
| Riggen, J P | Saddlery&harness | Main st | Ventura |
| Righetto, F | Variety store | Ventura | Main st |
| Riley, C C | Minister | Sespe Ranch | 30 m E San Buenav.. |

# W. S. McKEE,

# Private Boarding House,

## OJAI VALLEY, VENTURA CO., CAL.

15 Miles N. E. from San Buenaventura.

Rooms comfortably furnished and the Table supplied with the best the market affords.

## Fare, Plain and Home-like.

Close Attention paid to the Wants of Guests.

Travelers will find good accommodations, and every care will be used to render their stay comfortable.

## Guests Received by the Day, Week or Month.

## DIRECTORY OF VENTURA COUNTY. 199

| Name. | Occupation. | Place of Business. | Residence. | Town or P. O. |
|---|---|---|---|---|
| Riley, Wm S. | Livery stable | Santa Clara st | Oak st | S Buenaventura |
| Riley, W S. | Druggist | Ventura Co | San Buenaventura | S Buenaventura |
| Riley, West | Farmer | Sespe Ranch | 30 m E San Buenav. | Scenega. |
| Riva, Gustave | Clerk | Main st | Ayers Hotel | S Buenaventura |
| Rivas, Jose de la | Ranchero | Santa Ana Ranch | 7 m N W San Buena | S Buenaventura |
| Rivas, R de la G | Ranchero | Ventura Co | Ventura | S Buenaventura |
| Robbins, J B | Farmer | Pleasant Valley | 12 m E San Buenav. | S Buenaventura |
| Roberts, L D | Farmer | Ojai Valley | Nordhoff | Nordhoff. |
| Robertson, B J | Farmer | Sespe Ranch | 25 m E San Buenav. | Scenega. |
| Robertson, B J, Jr. | Farmer | Sespe Ranch | 25 m E San Buenav. | Scenega. |
| Robertson, Wm D. | Farmer | Sespe Ranch | 25 m E San Buenav. | Scenega. |
| Robertson, W H | Farmer | Sespe Ranch | 25 m E San Buenav. | Scenega. |
| Robinson, Richard | Stock | Ojai Valley | 4 m E Nordhoff | Nordhoff. |
| Robison, Henry | Attorney | Main st | Oak st | S Buenaventura |
| Rodriguez, J Y A. | Ranchero | Ventura Co | Ventura | S Buenaventura |
| Rodgers, Owen | Lumber | cor Cal and Front sts | Ventura Co | S Buenaventura |
| Rodgers, S | Farmer | nr Hueneme | Ventura Co | Hueneme. |
| Rodrigues, D | Vaquero | Ventura Co | San Buenaventura | S Buenaventura |
| Rodriguez, J W | Ranchero | Ventura Co | San Buenaventura | S Buenaventura |
| Rondebush, Danl | Farmer | Pleasant Valley | 13 m E San Buenav. | S Buenaventura |
| Rosenburgh, J W | Farmer | Sespe Ranch | 23 m E San Buenav. | Santa Paula. |
| Ross, C F | Laborer | Ojai Valley | 18 m N San Buenav. | Nordhoff. |
| Roth & Arnaz | Gen merchandise. | cor Main and Oak sts | San Buenaventura | S Buenaventura |
| Roth, Isaac F | Gen merchandise. | San Buenaventura | Ventura Co | S Buenaventura |
| Roth, J | Shoe dealer | Main st | San Buenaventura | S Buenaventura |
| Rotsler, G F | Farmer | Ventura Co | Saticoy | Saticoy. |
| Ruiz, J del C | Laborer | Ventura Co | San Buenaventura | S Buenaventura |
| Ruiz, Saturnio | Farmer | Ventura | Ventura Co | S Buenaventura |
| Rush, J N | Farmer | nr Hueneme | Ventura Co | Hueneme. |
| Rowell, G W | Farmer | Sespe Ranch | 28 m E San Buenav. | Scenega. |
| Salazar, Alfredo | Farmer | nr Saticoy | Ventura Co | Saticoy. |
| Salazar, Jose | Farmer | nr Saticoy | Ventura Co | Saticoy. |
| Sallisberry, A J & Co | Lumber | Hueneme Wharf | | Hueneme. |
| Sallisberry, A J. | Lumber merchant | Hueneme Wharf | Main st | Hueneme. |
| Salmaron, J | Vaquero | Ventura Co | Ventura | S Buenaventura |
| Saltmarsh, J B | Oilman | Ventura Co | Saticoy | Saticoy. |
| Salvas, Augustine | | Main st | Main st | S Buenaventura |
| Sanches, Mrs | | | Main st | S Buenaventura |
| Sanchez, Juan | Farmer | nr Hueneme | Ventura Co | Hueneme. |
| Sanchez, J V | Barber | Main st | San Buenaventura | S Buenaventura |
| Sanchez, T | Bar keeper | West Main st | San Buenaventura | S Buenaventura |
| Sanchez, Pacifico | Farmer | Ventura Co | nr Hueneme | Hueneme. |
| Saultmarsh, J | Laborer | Santa Paula | 16 m E San Buenav. | Santa Paula. |
| Saviers, John | Farmer | Pleasant Valley | 15 m E Hueneme | Hueneme. |
| Saviers, J Y | Farmer | nr Hueneme | Ventura Co | Hueneme. |
| Savin, A | Clerk | Ventura Co | San Buenaventura | S Buenaventura |
| Saxby, Walton Preble | Lumber dealer | Santa Clara st | Ventura | S Buenaventura |
| Saxby, I T | Lumber yard | Palm st | Oak st | S Buenaventura |
| Scarlett, John | Farmer | Colonia Ranch | 7 m S E San Buenav | S Buenaventura |
| Schearer, R | Wharfinger | Hueneme Wharf | Main st | Hueneme. |
| Schiap, Pietra Antonio | Stock raiser | Ventura Co | San Buenaventura | S Buenaventura |
| Schiappa, Pietra A | General mdse | Main st | San Buenaventura | S Buenaventura |
| Scidmore, G B | Ins & realestate agt | San Buenaventura | Ventura Co | S Buenaventura |
| Schmite, Peter | Farmer | Pleasant Valley | | S Buenaventura |
| Scofield, Benj | Teamster | San Buenaventura | Ventura Ave. | S Buenaventura |
| Scranton, C B | Blacksmith | Santa Paula | 16 m E San Buenav. | Santa Paula. |
| Sebastian, Chas | Farmer | Pleasant Valley | 14 m E San Buenav. | S Buenaventura |
| Sebastian, Chas | Farmer | nr Hueneme | Ventura Co | Hueneme. |
| Sebastian, Geo | Merchant | Ventura Co | Hueneme | Hueneme. |
| Sebastian, J W | Blacksmith | Ventura Co | Hueneme | Hueneme. |
| Sebastian, Robt | Farmer | Santa Paula Ranch | 6 m E San Buenav. | S Buenaventura |
| Secor, Wm | Carpenter | Ventura Co | Ventura Ave. | S Buenaventura |

## H. N. RIGGEN,
# Saddle and Harness Maker,

EAST MAIN STREET,

San Buenaventura,        Ventura Co., Cal.

I wish to call the particular attention of all parties desiring to purchase, to my large and complete stock of

### HEAVY AND LIGHT HARNESS,

Which cannot be excelled for Strength and Durability. I have also on hand a large and fine stock of

### Men's Saddles, Side Saddles, Saddle Trees,

AT SAN FRANCISCO PRICES.

**Halters, Hobbles, Bridles, Buggy Cushions, Synches, Whips, Etc., Etc.**

☞ REPAIRING promptly and carefully done. All orders attended to in person and with dispatch. Prices to suit the times. Give me a call and examine my stock before sending off for articles in my line.

---

## E. A. EDWARDS,
(Agent Wells, Fargo & Co.)
—DEALER IN—

# General House Hardware,

Farming Implements, Mechanics' Tools, Etc.

East Main Street, San Buenaventura, Ventura Co., Cal.

Always on hand a large supply of

## FIRST-CLASS STOVES,

INCLUDING

### FILLEY'S FAMOUS
### "GRANGER,"
—AND—
### CHARTER OAK
### STOVES.

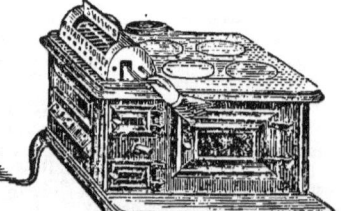

☞ All kinds of Tin and Sheet-Iron work done to order. ARTESIAN WELL and Water Pipes a Specialty.

## DIRECTORY OF VENTURA COUNTY.

| NAME. | OCCUPATION. | PLACE OF BUSINESS. | RESIDENCE. |
|---|---|---|---|
| Sentenac, Paul | Stock | Cañada Largo | |
| Serrano, J de J | Ranchero | Ventura Co | San Buenaventura |
| Sewell, G G | Farmer | Santa Paula Ranch | 13½ m E San Buenav |
| Shaul, J M | Farmer | Santa Clara Valley | 3 m N E Hueneme |
| Shaw, F | Clerk | Main st | Santa Clara st |
| Shaw, J A | Builder | Santa Clara st | Santa Clara st |
| Shaw, Henry | Nursery | Ventura Ave | San Buenaventura |
| Shaw, Selwin | Carpenter | Ventura | Oak st |
| Shepherd & Sheridan | Pub ventu signal | Main st | San Buenaventura |
| Shepherd, W E | Editor ven signal | Main st | |
| Sheppy, A C | Farmer | Ojai Valley | 18 m N San Buenav |
| Sheppy, — | Farmer | Ojai Valley | 3 m E Nordhoff |
| Sheridan, J J | Publisher | Main st | Main st |
| Sheridan, E & M | Printers | Main st | California st |
| Sheridan, S N, Jr | Printer | Main st | California st |
| Sheridan, S N | Brick mason | San Buenaventura | California st |
| Shields, B E | Minister | Ventura Co | Saticoy |
| Sifford, L M | Teamster | Ventura | Meta, cor Cal st |
| Simpson, Geo | Clerk | Main st | Ventura |
| Simpson, M | Carpenter | Ventura Co | Saticoy |
| Simpson, V A | Farmer | Ventura Co | San Buenaventura |
| Sisson, J | Farmer | Pleasant Valley | |
| Skaggs, E | Farmer | Santa Paula Ranch | 16 m E San Buenav |
| Smith, A B | Farmer | Santa Paula Ranch | 6 m E San Buenav |
| Smith, H J | Physician | Ventura Co | Hueneme |
| Smith, H W | Grocers | Main st | Santa Clara st |
| Smith, J C | | | |
| Smith, — | Farmer | Ventura Co | Main st |
| Snider, W W | Farmer | Sespe Ranch | 27 m E San Buenav |
| Snodgrass, A J | Farmer | nr Hueneme | Ventura Co |
| Snodgrass, A | Clerk | Main st | Main st |
| Snodgrass, C | Farmer | Olivas Ranch | 5 m S E S Buenav |
| Snodgrass, Cyrenus | Farmer | Ventura Co | nr Hueneme |
| Snodgrass, L | President V B | Main st | Ventura Ave |
| Snodgrass, L | Farmer | Ventura Co | nr Hueneme |
| Solare, A | Merchant | West Main st | West Main st |
| Soule, C E | Farmer | Ojai Valley | Nordhoff |
| Sparks, J R | Book binder | Ventura Co | Saticoy |
| Spear, Henry | Wines and liquors | Main st | San Buenaventura |
| Spencer, B J | Carpenter | Ventura | Oak st |
| Spragle, A | Stock | Sespe Ranch | |
| Spragle, Theodore | Stock | Sespe Ranch | |
| Sprague, T A | Farmer | Sespe Ranch | |
| Squiers, T A | Tinsmith | Main st | Front st |
| Stackpole, Henry | Harness maker | | Ayers Hotel |
| Stanchfield, L G | Stock | Beach Road | |
| Stark, T J | Farmer | Ventura Co | nr Saticoy |
| Steele, A T | Farmer | Santa Clara Valley | 9 m E San Buenav |
| Steele, J H | Farmer | Santa Clara Valley | 9 m E San Buenav |
| Steepleton, T B | Carpenter | Ojai Valley | 1½ m N E Nordhoff |
| Stephens, Anson | Farmer | Pleasant Valley | 10 m E Hueneme |
| Stephens, M H | Farmer | Pleasant Valley | 10 m E Hueneme |
| Stephens, S D | Clerk | Main st | Ventura |
| Stevens, Anson | Stock raiser | Ventura Co | nr Hueneme |
| Stevens, H C | Sheep raiser | nr Saticoy | Ventura Co |
| Stevens, J E | Farmer | Ventura | Ventura Co |
| Stevens, John | Farmer | nr Hueneme | Ventura Co |
| Stevens, J W | Saloon | Santa Clara st | Santa Clara st |
| Stevens, J W | Carpenter | Ventura Co | San Buenaventura |
| Stilwell, R | Civil engineer | Ventura Co | Saticoy |
| Stone, Horatio | Farmer | nr Saticoy | Ventura Co |
| Stone, J E | | Sespe Ranch | 25 m E San Buenav |

### PROPRIETORS OF

# Russell's Semi-Tropical Nurseries,

12 Miles Northwest of San Bernardino, and
1-2 Mile North of Riverside,

SAN BERNARDINO CO.  -  -  CAL.

**Northern Fruit and Ornamental Trees,**

AT WHOLESALE AND RETAIL.

P. O. ADDRESS, RIVERSIDE,

San Bernardino Co.,  ▪  ▪  ▪  Cal.

DIRECTORY OF VENTURA COUNTY. 203

| Name. | Occupation. | Place of Business. | Residence. | Town or P. O. |
|---|---|---|---|---|
| Stone, J R | Sheriff | San Buenaventura | East Main st | S Buenaventura |
| Stone, J R | Harness maker | Ventura Co | San Buenaventura | S Buenaventura |
| Stoval, Alfred B | Stock | Ventura Co | Front st | S Buennventura |
| Stowe, John | Surveyor | San Buenaventura | Oak st | S Buenaventura |
| Stowe, John T | County clerk | Court House | Oak st | S Buenaventura |
| Strickland, G A | Stock | Santa Clara Valley | Hueneme | Hueneme. |
| Stuart, O | Ranchero | nr Hueneme | Ventura Co | Hueneme. |
| Sturtevant, Mrs | Millinery store | Main st | Ventura | S Buenaventura |
| Sudden, James | Clerk & engineer | Sudden's Warehouse | Front st | S Buenaventura |
| Sudden, Robt | Prop of wharf | Sudden's Warehouse | Front st | S Buenaventura |
| Suhren, Geo H | Farmer | Ojai Valley |  | Nordhoff. |
| Surdam, R G | Oil superintendent | Ventura Co | San Buenaventura | S Buenaventura |
| Surter, W H | Farmer | Santa Paula Ranch | 7 m E San Buenav | S Buenaventura |
| Susman, — | Gen merchandise | Santa Paula | 16 m E San Buenay. | Santa Paula. |
| Sutton, — | S Clara house | Ventura Co | San Buenaventura | S Buenaventura |
| Swanson, J A | Farmer | Sespe Ranch | 27 m E San Buenav. | Scenega. |
| Sweeney, W | Blacksmith | Main st | Oak st | S Buenaventura |
| Sweeney, — | Proprietor | Oak Street Hotel | Oak st | S Buenaventura |
| Swinney, W G | Farmer | nr Hueneme | Ventura Co | Hueneme. |
| Swinney, H G | Farmer | Pleasant Valley |  | Hueneme. |
| Tannatt, Thos | Attorney at law | Main st | Main st | Hueneme. |
| Tanner, A M | Teamster | County Road | 2¼ m N E S Paula | Santa Paula. |
| Tanner, Geo | Farmer | Ventura Co | nr Hueneme | Hueneme. |
| Taylor, Alex | Farmer | Ventura Co | San Buenaventura | S Buenaventura |
| Taylor, David | Farmer | Ventura | Ventura Co | S Buenaventura |
| Taylor, G B | Stock raiser | Ventura | Ventura Co | S Buenaventura |
| Taylor, J. | Stock | Ventura | Ventura Co Road | S Buenaventura |
| Taylor, J B | Stock raiser | Ventura Co | Santa Barbara Road | S Buenaventura |
| Taylor, J L | Carpenter | Main st | Main st | Hueneme. |
| Taylor, Rev T E | Pastor | Presb Church | Oak st | S Buenaventura |
| Templeton, George | Farmer | Ventura Co | Ventura | S Buenaventura |
| Teeters, E H | Farmer | Ventura Co | San Buenaventura | S Buenaventura |
| Thacker, C W | Farmer | Pleasant Valley | 13 m E San Buenav. | S Buenaventura |
| Thayer, F | Druggist | Ventura Co | Saticoy | Saticoy. |
| Thomas, Chas | Farmer | Pleasant Valley | 10 m E Hueneme | Hueneme. |
| Thomas, C K | Farmer | nr Hueneme | Ventura Co | Hueneme. |
| Thomas, J W | Farmer | Pleasant Valley |  | Hueneme. |
| Thompson, J H | Farmer | Santa Clara Valley | 3 m N Hueneme | Hueneme. |
| Thompson, J A | Blacksmith | Main st | Main st | S Buenaventura |
| Thorne, M | Farmer | nr Saticoy | Ventura Co | Saticoy. |
| Tibatts, Edward | Laborer | Santa Clara Valley | 7 m N E Hueneme | Hueneme. |
| Tico, Joaquin | Vaquero | Ventura Co | Ventura | S Buenaventura |
| Tico, Fernando | Vaquero | Ventura | Main st | S Buenaventura |
| Tico, F A | Deputy sheriff | Ventura Co | San Buenaventura | S Buenaventura |
| Tico, J de J | Vaquero | Ventura Co | San Buenaventura | S Buenaventura |
| Tico, Pacifico | Laborer | Ventura Co | San Buenaventura | S Buenaventura |
| Tico, Porfirio | Vaquero | Ventura Co | San Buenaventura | S Buenaventura |
| Tico, R G | Vaquero | Ventura Co | San Buenaventura | S Buenaventura |
| Tillman, Joseph | Merchant | Ventura Co | San Buenaventura | S Buenaventura |
| Todd, C D | Stoves & hardware | Main st | Oak st | S Buenaventura |
| Todd, Edward | Farmer | County Road | 1¾ m W Santa Paula | Santa Paula. |
| Todd, M D L | Farmer | Santa Paula | 1½ m E Santa Paula | Santa Paula. |
| Todd, Saml | Farmer | Santa Paula Canyon | 1 m N Santa Paula | Santa Paula. |
| Tompkins, J G | Farmer | Ventura Co | nr Saticoy | Saticoy. |
| Townsend, C H | Farmer | Santa Paula Ranch | 18 m E San Buenav. | Santa Paula. |
| Townsend, Henry | Farmer | Ventura Co | nr Hueneme | Hueneme. |
| Trotter, J | Farmer | Santa Paula |  | Santa Paula. |
| Turbett, Wm | Farmer | nr Hueneme | Ventura Co | Hueneme. |
| Underhill, G | Teamster | Ventura Co | San Buenaventura | S Buenaventura |
| Ustueaustigui, V | Stock | Ventura Co | Ventura Ave | S Buenaventura |
| Van Bibber, Albert | Capitalist | Santa Clara Valley | 4 m N E Hueneme | Hueneme. |
| Vance, C W | Painter | California st | Poli st | S Buenaventura |
| Vance, J R | Stock raiser | Ventura Co | Ventura | S Buenaventura |
| Vancuren, R O | Clerk | San Buenaventura | Ventura Co | S Buenaventura |

## GO TO THE
# SAN BERNARDINO DRUG STORE,

**THIRD ST.,**  **San Bernardino,**

**CALIFORNIA.**

**ALLEN & DREW,** - - - **Proprietors,**

For Drugs, Chemicals, Dye Stuffs, Genuine Patent Medicines, Sponges, Brushes, Fancy Articles, Perfumery, Toilet Soaps, School Books and Stationery, Garden and Field Flower Seeds, Pure Wines and Liquors; also a fine assortment of Candies.

**Prescriptions Carefully Compounded Day or Night.**

---

**L. MIGUEL,**
DEALER IN
## General Merchandise,
JACKSON'S BLOCK,
3rd St. - San Bernardino, Cal.

**HARDWARE,**

Clothing, Dry Goods, Boots and Shoes,

Hats, Caps,

**CROCKERYWARE, GLASSWARE,**

**TOBACCO AND CIGARS.**

Furnishing Goods in endless variety. The Stock is large and complete. Goods excellent in quality, and Prices low.

---

**A. B. WISE,**

## Blacksmithing AND Horseshoeing

Manufactures to Order, all kinds of

## WAGONS, CARRIAGES,

**Buggies, Etc., Etc,**

Also, all kinds of

**REPAIRING DONE NEATLY AND CHEAPLY.**

**UTAH STREET,**

San Bernardino, - California.

Near the San Bernardino Bank.

## DIRECTORY OF VENTURA COUNTY.

| NAME. | OCCUPATION. | PLACE OF BUSINESS. | RESIDENCE. |
|---|---|---|---|
| Van Curan, — | Laborer | Ventura | Poli st |
| Vail, J L | Laborer | Ventura Co | San Buenaventura |
| VanKuern, Andrew | Mail driver | Nordhoff | Nordhoff |
| Van Winkle, H | Dentist | Main st | San Buenaventura |
| Valdes, A | Laborer | Ventura | Main st |
| Valdez, J de J | Laborer | Ventura | Ventura Co |
| Valdez, J del R | Laborer | Ventura Co | San Buenaventura |
| Valdez, R A | Laborer | Ventura Co | Ventura |
| Valle, J del | Farmer | Ventura Co | nr Saticoy |
| Valle, Y del | Farmer | nr Saticoy | Ventura Co |
| Valenzulla, A | Vaquero | Ventura | Ventura Co |
| Valensula, J M | Farmer | Ventura | Ventura Co |
| Vanigas, J C | Vaquero | Ventura | Ventura Co |
| Vineyard, J A | Farmer | nr Hueneme | Ventura Co |
| Viuson, A W | Farmer | Ventura Ave | Ventura Ave |
| Vinyard, Rev W H | Pastor | Methodist Church | 3½ m N E Hueneme |
| Voegtlen, J J | Farmer | Ventura Co | San Buenaventura |
| Wade, A W | Shoe maker | Ventura Co | San Buenaventura |
| Wagner, C C | Gardener | Ventura Co | Hueneme |
| Wagner, J B | Druggist | Main st | Santa Clara House |
| Wagner, Edward | Clerk | | Main st |
| Wagner, Wm | Farmer | Santa Paula Ranch | 3 m E San Buenav |
| Wakefield, H A | Carpenter | Ventura | Ventura |
| Walbridge, Henry F | | Pleasant Valley | |
| Walbridge, H | Farmer | Ventura Co | nr Hueneme |
| Walker, S E | Farmer | Pleasant Valley | 14 m E San Buenav |
| Walker, W H | Farmer | Pleasant Valley | 14 m E San Buenav |
| Wallace, B L | Carpenter | Ventura | Ventura Co |
| Wallace, D | Farmer | nr Hueneme | Ventura Co |
| Walnut, N | Laborer | Ventura Co | Ojai Valley |
| Walter, D | Farmer | Santa Clara Valley | 4 m N E Hueneme |
| Walton, Amos | Farmer | Santa Paula Ranch | 9 m E San Buenav |
| Walton, W J | Lumber yard | Palm st | Oak st |
| Warfield, — | Carpenter | Ventura | Ventura Co |
| Warner, M | Sea captain | Ventura Co | San Buenaventura |
| Warren, Andrew | Bartender | Main st | San Buenaventura |
| Warring, B F | Farmer | Sespe Ranch | |
| Wasley, T T | Farmer | Ojai | |
| Wason, M | County judge | Ventura Co | San Buenaventura |
| Wassen, W D | Farmer | nr Hueneme | Ventura Co |
| Waters, Geo L | Farmer | Ojai Valley | 1 m S Nordhoff |
| Waters, Jos | Farmer | Ventura Co | San Buenaventura |
| Welch, J F | Carpenter | Ventura Co | Hueneme |
| Welch, John | Farmer | nr Hueneme | Ventura Co |
| Welchman, W H | Farmer | Santa Paula | 20 m E San Buenav |
| Wells, James | Farmer | Ojai Valley | |
| White, Frank | Laborer | Nordhoff | Nordhoff |
| White, H L | Butcher | Ventura Co | Saticoy |
| White, S T | | Saticoy | |
| White & Hixon | Stable | Ventura Co | Saticoy |
| Whitesides, O | Farmer | nr Saticoy | Ventura Co |
| Whitney, C H | Merchant | | Front st |
| Whittemore, E W | Farmer | Ojai | |
| Wickard, Isaac | Laborer | Main st | Main st |
| Wiggin & Carr | Real estate | Ventura Co | Nordhoff |
| Wiggins, Col Chas P | Farmer | Ojai Valley | Nordhoff |
| Wilburn, Hugh | Farmer | Sespe Ranch | 23 m E San Buenav |
| Wiley, B H | Merchant | Santa Paula | 16 m E San Buenav |
| Wiley, J A & Bro | Genl merchants | Santa Paula | 16 m E San Buenav |
| Wiley, J A | Merchant | Santa Paula | 16 m E San Buenav |
| Wiley, J S | Farmer | Ex Mission Ranch | 9 m E San Buenav |
| Willey, B H | Farmer | Ventura Co | Saticoy |
| Willey, J B | Farmer | nr Saticoy | Ventura Co |

# KENNISTON & BRAZELTON,

Fashion  HACK

## AND LIVERY STABLE,

Third St., opp. Post Office,    San Bernardino, Cal.

### Horses and Carriages,

Single or Double, and Saddle Horses kept constantly on hand for the accommodation of the Public. Horses Boarded by the Day, Week, or
Month, at reasonable rates. Conveyances furnished for private
or public occasions at the shortest notice, and upon as
reasonable terms as any first-class establishment in Southern California.

### Outfits for the Principal Mining Camps,

Furnished at the Shortest Notice, and most Reasonable Prices.

*The undersigned will, on and after date, run a Hack for the
accommodation of the public. Orders left at all of
the hotels will receive prompt attention.*

KENNISTON & BRAZELTON,

PROPRIETORS.

## DIRECTORY OF VENTURA COUNTY.

| Name. | Occupation. | Place of Business. | Residence. | Town or P. O. |
|---|---|---|---|---|
| Willey, W H | Farmer | nr Saticoy | Ventura Co | Saticoy. |
| Willett, J | Farmer | 2 m N San Buenav | Ventura Ave | S Buenaventura |
| Willard, C H | Dairyman | Ventura Co | Saticoy | Saticoy. |
| Williams, B T | Dist attorney | Court House | Palm st | S Buenaventura |
| Williams, Caswell | Ranchero | Ventura Co | nr Hueneme | Hueneme. |
| Williams, E B | Farmer | Ventura Co | nr Saticoy | Saticoy. |
| Williams, T H | Farmer | Domingus Ranch | 8 m E San Buenav | S Buenaventura |
| Williams, T H | Farmer | nr Hueneme | Ventura Co | Hueneme. |
| Williams, W T | Attorney | Main st | | S Buenaventura |
| Williamson, John | Laborer | Ventura Co | nr Hueneme | Hueneme. |
| Wilson, Jacob | Farmer | Ventura Co | Ventura | S Buenaventura |
| Wiseman, Theodore | Farmer | Ojai Valley | 2 m E Nordhoff | Nordhoff. |
| Wolf, M L | Genl merchant | Main st | Market st | Hueneme. |
| Wolfson, Joseph | Dealer in hides | Cañada st | Main st | S Buenaventura |
| Wood, L B | Bee raiser | Ojai | 18 m N San Buenav | Nordhoff. |
| Wood, W O | | Pleasant Valley | | S Buenaventura |
| Wood, W O | Minister | Ventura Co | Hueneme | Hueneme. |
| Woodford, — | Laborer | Cameron Ranch | 4 m S W Santa Paula | Santa Paula. |
| Woodruff, J C | Farmer | Santa Clara Valley | 4 m N E Hueneme | Hueneme. |
| Wooley, E B | Farmer | Ventura Co | nr Hueneme | Hueneme. |
| Woolley, Mrs J F | Farmer | Santa Clara Valley | 3½ m N E Hueneme | Hueneme. |
| Wooley, W R | Farmer | Ventura Co | nr Hueneme | Hueneme. |
| Wright, P | Hostler | Ventura Co | San Buenaventura | S Buenaventura |
| Wright, P W | | | Front st | S Buenaventura |
| Wyman, Fred | Farmer | Santa Paula Ranch | 6 m E San Buenav | S Buenaventura |
| Wyman, F P | Farmer | nr Saticoy | Ventura Co | Saticoy. |
| Wyman, Wm | Farmer | Pleasant Valley | 14 m E San Buenav | S Buenaventura |
| Yarbrough, Geo | Carpenter | San Buenaventura | Main st | S Buenaventura |
| Ysoardy, B | Saloon | Main st | San Buenaventura | S Buenaventura |

# R. G. LIVINGSTON

### DEALER IN

# General Merchandise,

## HUENEME, VENTURA COUNTY, CAL.

HAS A COMPLETE STOCK, CONSISTING OF

Dry Goods, Clothing, Boots and Shoes, Hardware, Crockery and Glassware,

Paints, Oils, Etc.

# GROCERIES & PROVISIONS,

Tobacco and Cigars, Wines, Liquors, Etc.

## R. H. KING & BRO.

# Harness and Saddle Manufacturers,

### STEWART'S BUILDING, THIRD STREET,

San Bernardino, - - - California.

### Carriage Trimming to Order.

REPAIRING NEATLY AND PROMPTLY DONE.

---

C. A. LAWSON.　　　　J. E. LAWSON.

## LAWSON BROS.

DEALERS IN

## TOBACCO, CIGARS,

And Smoker's Articles Generally.

Choice Havanas a Specialty.

In connection with the above, we carry on an

### ASSAY OFFICE,

Where we are prepared to make assays of ores of all descriptions. Gold and Silver Bullion, Gold Dust, etc., melted and assayed.
All assays attended to promptly, and returns made at the earliest possible moment. Charges as low as any reliable assayer. Your patronage is respectfully solicited. All work guaranteed.

UTAH ST., bet 3d and 4th,

SAN BERNARDINO,　　CALIFORNIA.

---

P. G. DREW.　　　　H. L. DREW

## DREW BROS.

DEALERS IN

## STOVES, TINWARE

### AND HARDWARE,

Lead and Iron Pipe,

FORCE AND LIFT PUMPS,

And Agricultural Implements;

Also, a General Assortment of House Furnishing Hardware on hand, or furnished to order. We also keep constantly on hand a good assortment of Hard Wood Lumber.

ALL KINDS OF JOBBING PROMPTLY ATTENDED TO.

Cor. Utah and Fourth Sts.

SAN BERNARDINO,　-　CAL.

# A GENERAL DESCRIPTION

OF

# KERN COUNTY

KERN COUNTY is bounded on the North by Tulare; on the East by San Bernardino; on the South by Los Angeles; and on the Southwest by San Luis Obispo. It is of

## AN AREA

Of about eight thousand square miles, and contains about one million nine hundred and twenty thousand acres. Of this about seven hundred and fifty thousand acres are well adapted for agricultural and grazing purposes, though, comparatively speaking, but a small portion is under cultivation. Want of transportation facilities, distance from the markets of the State, and the scanty population of the County, are causes which tend to give sheep-raising and mining a predominence over the farming interest.

## THE COUNTY

Was organized in 1866, and contains nearly two-thirds of the territory formerly included in Tulare County. It comprises portions of the Sierra Nevada, the Coast Range, and the valley lying between them, as well as a portion of the desert valley lying to the eastward of the Sierras.

## THE ASSESSED VALUATION

Of its property, in 1874, was $3,603,316.

## ITS PRINCIPAL TOWNS

Are Bakersfield—the County seat, Havilah, Kernville, and Glenville. The other towns, of which there are many, are small and unimportant.

## IN POSITION

Kern County is almost inaccessible, the lofty mountain wall being without a break, except at the north. Were it not for its inaccessibility, it would probably ere this have become one of the most important, in population and developed resources, of the interior counties.

Its mineral deposits are rich and varied. It has gold mines, both quartz and placer, large salt deposits, sulphur, and other minerals. Petroleum is also one of its products, though here, as elsewhere in California, its production has not been attended with very profitable results.

Along the western border of the County, from its southern extremity to the Kern River, are salt marshes, brine and petroleum springs, covering an area of about four hundred square miles. These really vast resources are, as it were, locked up, from the fact of their interior position and a scarcity of roads, which sadly interfere with the process by which the producer exchanges his product for value received.

## THE PETROLEUM

And asphaltum deposits occupy an extent of country nearly forty miles in length, extending from the eastern corner of Santa Barbara County to Buena Vista Lake on the north. Buena Vista Lake is a sheet of alkaline water, about seven miles in length by two in width.

The most extensive of the petroleum deposits lies to the southeast of this lake, a distance of about eighteen miles. Here is a spring, covering nearly an acre, of thick, heavy oil, termed maltha. The surface is constantly agitated by the escape of gas. Works were erected here in 1864, for the purpose of refining oil for the San Francisco market. After manufacturing some thousands gallons of oil of good quality, the work was abandoned, as the cost of sending it to market enhanced its value to such a degree as to render successful competition with the article shipped from the Eastern States impossible. This belt of oil springs lies parallel to that extending along the coast in Santa Barbara County, the coast ranges alone intervening.

## THE MOUNTAIN RANGES,

Which almost enclose the great plain forming the centre of this County, tower to a height of from eight to ten thousand feet. The buttresses of the Sierra Nevada and the spurs of the coast range project in some places nearly across the plain. There is only one pass to the West, the Paso Robles, which reaches an extreme elevation of four thousand eight hundred feet. On the South is the Tejon Pass, which achieves an elevation of five thousand two hundred and eighty-five feet above the sea. During the Winter and Spring the higher peaks are covered with snow. The lower elevations are well timbered with oak, pine and fir.

Mount Pinos and Mount El Dorado, two of the highest peaks in the Southern division of the Coast Range, have an altitude of nearly eight thousand feet. The San Emidio Canyon heads between these two mountains.

Nearly the entire Western portion of the County is valueless for purposes of agriculture. On the South and East many of the mountains and the low hills are covered with a luxuriant growth of grasses and shrubbery.

On the East, spurs of the Sierra Nevada, called the Tehichipa Mountains, rise to the height of nearly eight thousand feet.

Over these mountains the pass is four thousand feet above the sea level.

To the Eastward of these mountains is the fertile, well-timbered valley of Tehichipa. It covers an area of about twenty-four square miles, and contains fifteen thousand three hundred and sixty acres. It is completely shut in by mountains averaging from seven to eight thousand feet in height. It contains a small salt water lake, from which, by the process of solar evaporation, a large quantity of unusually fine salt is manufactured. Although this manufacture could be increased to almost any extent, still the causes which paralyze the production of petroleum, and the cultivation of cereals to any extent, operate equally against this, and the largest amount obtained in any year was that of one hundred tons, aggregated in 1867. Through this valley lies the stage road leading from Los Angeles into Inyo County.

## JOE WALKER'S VALLEY,

So named in honor of the first settler in the County, who arrived in 1835, lies to the Northward of the Tehichipa Range. This valley, like the other, is completely surrounded by lofty mountains. It contains two thousand four hundred acres of very fertile land, yielding from forty to sixty bushels of wheat, from fifty to sixty bushels of corn, or sixty bushels of barley, to the acre. All kinds of vegetables and hardy fruits grow here luxuriantly. The hills are well timbered, and the supply of pure water is abundant. There are numbers of these mountain-locked valleys in various parts of the County. The valley of the

## SOUTH FORK OF THE KERN RIVER

Is one of the finest in the County, containing about nine thousand six hundred acres of most arable land, well watered and timbered. This valley is about eight miles North of Havilah, the former County seat.

## LINN'S VALLEY,

Lying a few miles to the Southward of that previously mentioned, offers climatic and agricultural inducements to those desiring a good farming locality. The fertility of the soil is such that the cultivator is richly repaid; the thermometer rarely runs above 90° in the Summer, or below 50° during the Winter months. The water is good, and the supply bountiful.

It is quite a thriving settlement, and boasts a grist and saw mill.

The hills and rivers along the entire Eastern and Northern portions of the County are rich in gold-bearing quartz and placer gold, the production of which forms the leading industry of the County, and gives employment to by far the largest portion of its inhabitants.

## KERN RIVER,

From which the County derives its name, was formerly termed by the Mexicans Rio Bravo. It derived its present name from a Lieutenant Kern, formerly one of Fremont's exploring party. It is one of the largest of the Sierra rivers, and gives to this region, in a system of interior lakes, a notoriety arising from so peculiar a characteristic. It traverses nearly the entire County, passing from East to West, entering it near Walker's Pass on the East, and emptying into Goose Lake at the base of the Coast Range on the West. It receives numerous tributaries, and waters a large agricultural district. By numerous and repeated experiments it has been ascertained that this portion of the County is well adapted to cotton cultivation. Several good crops were produced as early as ten years since, being disposed of at good figures. The cost of labor and transportation rendered its cultivation still less profitable than other crops, which was reason sufficient for its abandonment.

There are numerous mining districts among the mountains and along the creeks, near which to meet the demand, villages have sprung up. They have that straggling appearance of hasty and imperfect growth which fixes its unmistakeable stamp upon all such communities. Society is simply conglomerated for the time being. Everything is temporary and subject to rapid and repeated change; no thought is ever taken about harmonizing the surroundings either of place or society; all is rank, absolute conservativism, in the worst phase of its slip-shod, down-at-the-heel existence. No law, save that of the heaviest hand; no order, save the dis-order of the barroom brawler; no church, not even the unseasoned pine structure which enjoys the honor of the first cleared place in the wilderness, which by its meek teachings would at least serve to exercise a slight restraining influence; no school system, and few if any schools. How many such can one call to mind, peopled with the "Colonel Starbottles" and "Jedge Phinns," the omnipresent and exultant heroes of the bowie knife and gin flask, whose knowledge reaches its climax in that they are able to distinguish "their own whiskey skins," and whose high-toned qualities impel them towards the most extreme measures with those rash enough to dispute with them the question of ownership. Yes, we can see it now, the rough board shanties, marching at will down the uneven street, paved with red flannel shirts, old socks and tin cans. Occasionally a squalid, wretched looking woman shows her disheveled head at door or window. Now and then a human form, bearing a pick or shovel, swaggers his superabundance of beard and his scantiness of attire towards the Magnolia Saloon, where, before his array of cut glass, stands the only man in the town whose appearance augurs prosperity.

The Colonel stands upon the porch, that effulgent and proudly swelling feature, which was presumably once a nose, shedding rays not so benignant nor so odorless as those from that rival luminary, which in his presence seems to undergo a partial eclipse. This is the seventy-fifth time since sunrise that providence has sent a messenger to minister to his liquid wants. Number seventy-five does not shatter the Colonel's confidence in human nature, by drinking alone, but suavely asks him to "jine." Mr. Bland serves out the compound, twirling the spoon gracefully and deftly in his be-diamonded fingers, while his richly caparisoned shirt-frill dances approvingly to the effort. The Colonel talks for a moment pensively regarding the nobililty of his early-day associates. What men they were, and what "carving" they did upon the slightest opportunity. He drops in his glass a tear or two, to their memory, glides upon the porch to wait for number seventy-six, and life at Squalor Hollow moves on in its even tenor, each day repeat-

Such was the mining town of a few years since. Let us hope that time has worked a desirable change, straightened the street, evened-up the houses, removed the fragments of cast-off garments, taken a spoke from the wheel of friend Bland's prosperity, added a neat little house of worship to the structures of the town, where the man of God presides on Sunday, and the "schoolmarm" during the week; and let us hope that the Colonel's ruby beak may have bleached to its pristine whiteness, that his self respect, which fled long ago before the stress of evil associations and strong temptation, may have returned, taken him by the hand and led him back through the forgotten paths; past the fragments of his early resolves; over the abandoned hopes and unfulfilled aspirations of his early manhood; to a life more in consonance with whitened hair and ripened years.

The production of

## QUARTZ AND PLACER GOLD

In Kern County is very large, the County honestly earning its reputation as one of the most important mining section in the southern portion of the State.

The causes which have long militated against the prosperity of this County are rapidly being removed.

## THE RAILROAD,

Which has its temporary terminus at Caliente has already given an impetus to all established industries, has suggested the introduction of new interests, and by the time the road is completed, which is being rapidly built, having the southern sea coast at one extremity, and San Francisco at the other, all the benefits which result from rapid land and cheap water communication, will be at the service of this community, and will give an impulse to endeavor which will ultimately enrich the individual, and add materially to the productive wealth of the State.

## BAKERSFIELD,

The principal town and County seat of Kern County, is located one mile from the San Joaquin branch of the Southern Pacific Railroad. It is one hundred and forty miles north of Los Angeles, and two hundred and ninety-eight miles southeast of San Francisco. The town has an eligible and pleasant situation upon the banks of the Kern River. The surrounding country is exceedingly rich in soil resources. The railroad has given large accessions to its population, and to that of the neighboring valleys. Gold mining in the adjacent mountains, together with the silver mining interest of Inyo County, adds largely to the importance of its trade. The Kern furnishes a sufficient water-power to induce the establishment of large manufacturing interests, and will, no doubt, at no distant day, be fully utilized.

## A NARROW-GAUGE

Railroad to Santa Barbara, has been projected, and a company already formed in that city for its construction. Santa Barbara is ninety miles distant.

## HAVILAH

Is situated forty-five miles Northeast of Bakersfield, was once the most important town in the County and the County seat. It is situated on Clear Creek, a small stream tributary to Kern River, which it enters from the south. Its position is inaccessible, it lying in a cleft or defile of the mountains. Its resources are entirely of a mineral character, and it is the center of a large and richly paying mining region. Since a branch of the Southern Pacific Railroad was extended to Bakersfield, the mines in this vicinity are attracting much notice.

Havilah is named from a place mentioned in Genesis, where a land of gold is for the first time alluded to. It has communication with the railroad points of Tipton, Tulare City, and Bakersfield, by daily stage.

## GLENVILLE

Is a small town situated in Linn's Valley. It is altogether unimportant in every respect, except that it is a postoffice.

## CANFIELD

Is twelve miles southwest of Bakersfield, which latter place is its postoffice.

## KERNVILLE

Lies sixty miles Northeast of Bakersfield. It is quite a thriving place. Near it are a dozen or more important quartz ledges, on many of which extensive mills have been in operation for several years, the yield being handsome.

## KERN ISLAND,

Situated in a delta of the Kern River, is a large tract of fertile country, offering decided advantages to those desiring to settle. The Kern Island Irrigating Canal is a work which is now attracting considerable attention. It has for its object the rendering productive, lands which are now in a condition of almost absolute sterility, from the fact of their possessing no natural irrigating facilities. Another work of this nature was some time since commenced by a company calling themselves the San Francisco Canal Company. Their ditch begins upon the North side of the river, moving along the plains on the highest lands practicable. It is stated that it will be thirty miles in length, having a width of one hundred feet. If this work be successfully terminated it will redeem from perfect waste many thousands of acres, which but need this advantage to render them of almost incalculable value.

# PRICES REDUCED!
## SAVE $50. WHY PAY $80.
### THE NEW IMPROVED
# Home Shuttle Sewing Machine,

PRICE $35.00

This Machine, being much Improved, is as good as any in the Market. We also sell the

## Home Sewing Machine.

This Machine is entirely New, and is very Superior, combining ALL the points of excellence of the Older Machines. The above are the

### LIGHTEST RUNNING

and by far the most easily operated Machines in the Market, and so simple that a child readily comprehends them and can operate them.

### CHARTS, $2.00
SEND FOR CIRCULARS,

### E. W. HAINES, General Agent,
17 NEW MONTGOMERY STREET, (Grand Hotel Building.)

Active Agents Wanted.

DIRECTORY OF KERN COUNTY.                                215

| NAME. | OCCUPATION. | PLACE OF BUSINESS. | RESIDENCE. | TOWN OR P. O. |
|---|---|---|---|---|
| Acklin, J K | Printer | Havilah | Kern Co | Havilah. |
| Aconia, K | Laborer | nr Walker's Basin | Kern Co | Havilah. |
| Acuñia, Francisco | Ranchero | Tejon | Kern Co | Tejon. |
| Adams, A J | Farmer | Kern Co | nr Kern Island | Bakersfield. |
| Adams, H | Miner | nr Long Tom | Kern Co | Bakersfield. |
| Adams, W | Farmer | Kern Co | nr Bakersfield | Bakersfield. |
| Adams, W S | Miner | Kern Co | nr Kelsoe | Havilah. |
| Aguan, J | Miller | Kern Co | nr Havilah | Havilah. |
| Ahalt, Isaac | Farmer | Kern Island | Kern Co | Bakersfield. |
| Ahern, D | Miner | nr Havilah | Kern Co | Havilah. |
| Allen, G H | Miner | Kern Co | nr Kernville | Kernville. |
| Allen, H L | Farmer | Kern Co | nr Linn's Valley | Glenville. |
| Allen, J G | Farmer | nr Bakersfield | Kern Co | Bakersfield. |
| Allen, J H | Miner | nr Long Tom | Kern Co | Bakersfield. |
| Allen, W G, Jr | Farmer | nr Bakersfield | Kern Co | Bakersfield. |
| Allison, J T | Farmer | Kern Co | nr Bakersfield | Bakersfield. |
| Anderson, A F | Teamster | Kern Co | nr Bakersfield | Bakersfield. |
| Anderson, J R | Farmer | Kern Co | nr Kern Island | Bakersfield. |
| Anderson, S H | Farmer | Kern Co | nr Bakersfield | Bakersfield. |
| Andrews, W F | Miner | Kern Co | nr Havilah | Havilah. |
| Andrews, W | Stage driver | Kernville | Kern Co | Kernville. |
| Aranjo, T | Farmer | nr Bakersfield | Kern Co | Bakersfield. |
| Arny, Victor | Merchant | Sumner | Kern Co | |
| Ashby, B F | Farmer | nr Tehichipa | Kern Co | Tehichipa. |
| Atkins, H | Stock raiser | Linn's Valley | Kern Co | Glenville. |
| Aud, W J | Miner | nr Posa Creek | Kern Co | Bakersfield. |
| Ault, Amos | Saloon | Caliente | Caliente | Caliente. |
| Awalt, Wm T | Laborer | Walker's Basin | Kern Co | Havilah. |
| Ayers, M | Teamster | nr Bakersfield | Kern Co | Bakersfield. |
| Ayers, W P | Vaquero | nr Agua Caliente | Kern Co | Caliente. |
| Bachman, H S | Physician | 2d st | Bakersfield | Bakersfield. |
| Bahten, D | Miner | nr Piute | Kern Co | |
| Bahten, Henry | Miner | Kern Co | nr Piute | |
| Bahten, John | Miner | Kern Co | nr Havilah | Havilah. |
| Baird, A M | Farmer | nr Tejon | Kern Co | Tejon. |
| Baird, Jas | Farmer | nr Bakersfield | Kern Co | Bakersfield. |
| Baker, Constantine | Lodging house | Caliente | Kern Co | Caliente. |
| Baker, C W | Farmer | Kern Co | nr Kernville | Kernville. |
| Baker & Muehe | Lodging house | Caliente | Kern Co | Caliente. |
| Baker, James | Teamster | Kern Co | nr Linn's Valley | Glenville. |
| Baker, S | Farmer | Kern Island | Kern Co | Bakersfield. |
| Baker, W | Vintner | Bakersfield | Kern Co | Bakersfield. |
| Banfield, J A | Ranchero | Kern Co | nr Santa Maria | |
| Barker, John | Farmer | Bakersfield | Kern Co | Bakersfield. |
| Barker, V | Farmer | Kern Island | | Bakersfield. |
| Barnes, T W | Farmer | Kern Co | nr Bakersfield | Bakersfield. |
| Bassett, Ralph | Farmer | Kern Island | Kern Co | Bakersfield. |
| Bassett, W C | Carpenter | Bakersfield | Kern Co | Bakersfield. |
| Bates, C S | Farmer | Kern Co | nr Kernville | Kernville. |
| Batz, John B | Carpenter | Weldon | Kern Co | Weldon. |
| Bauer, Frederick | Sheep raiser | Bakersfield | Kern Co | Bakersfield. |
| Baulen, W W | Farmer | nr Bakersfield | Kern Co | Bakersfield. |
| Beall, Wm E | Stock raiser | Long Tom | Kern Co | Bakersfield. |
| Bean, John | Farmer | Kern Island | Kern Co | Bakersfield. |
| Beardsley, L A | Teacher | Linn's Valley | Kern Co | Glenville. |
| Beaseley, Jacob | Engineer | Havilah | Kern Co | Havilah. |
| Beaty, Ezra W | Miner | Caliente | Kern Co | Caliente. |
| Beaty, Joseph | Miner | Linn's Valley | Kern Co | Glenville. |
| Beaty, John | Farmer | Kern Co | Hot Spring Valley | Tehichipa. |
| Beck, John | Farmer | Tehichipa Canyon | Kern Co | Tehichipa. |
| Beck, I N | Teamster | Kern Co | Kern Island | Bakersfield. |
| Begli, Chas | Miner | Piute | Kern Co | |
| Behn, Peter | Farmer | Tehichipa | Kern Co | Tehichipa. |
| Belasquez, Joseph | Vaquero | Kern Island | Kern Co | Bakersfield. |

| Name. | Occupation. | Place of Business. | Residence. | Town or P. O. |
|---|---|---|---|---|
| Belding, O | Millwright | Kernville | Kern Co | Kernville. |
| Bell, T N | Mechanic | Bakersfield | Kern Co | Bakersfield. |
| Belshaw, M W | Freighting | Caliente | Kern Co | Caliente. |
| Belt Jas H | Farmer | Tehichipa | Kern Co | Tehichipa. |
| Bemis, E H | Clerk | Bakersfield | Kern Co | Bakersfield. |
| Bennett, J L | Minister | South Fork | Kern Co | Weldon. |
| Bennett, Joseph | Farmer | nr Bakersfield | Kern Co | Bakersfield. |
| Benninger, Geo J | Miner | Tehichipa | Kern Co | Tehichipa. |
| Bequette, H D | County clerk | Havilah | Kern Co | Havilah. |
| Berry, J H | Teacher | Linn's Valley | Kern Co | Glenville. |
| Best, O W | Laborer | nr Bakersfield | Kern Co | Bakersfield. |
| Bevis, G W | Farmer | nr Bakersfield | Kern Co | Bakersfield. |
| Biais, C | Carpenter | Havilah | Kern Co | Havilah. |
| Bickford, Geo W | Shepherd | New River | Kern Co | |
| Bickmore, G | Wheelwright | Bakersfield | Kern Co | Bakersfield. |
| Biggs, David | Farmer | nr Bakersfield | Kern Co | Bakersfield. |
| Bigole, Levy | Farmer | Kern Co | nr Tejon | Tejon. |
| Binnix, T H | Millwright | Havilah | Kern Co | Havilah. |
| Bishop, James | Miner | Kernville | Kern Co | Kernville. |
| Bizzel, L | Teamster | Kern Co | nr Bakersfield | Bakersfield. |
| Black, I S | Mechanic | Woody Precinct | Kern Co | |
| Blade, S P | Miner | nr Havilah | Kern Co | Havilah. |
| Blake, M P | Farmer | Havilah | Kern Co | Havilah. |
| Blanchard, H M | Machinist | Bear Valley | Kern Co | Tehichipa. |
| Bloom, G | Farmer | Kern Co | nr Tehichipa | Tehichipa. |
| Bohm, H | Miner | nr Linn's Valley | Kern Co | Glenville. |
| Bonsel, C M | Farmer | South Fork | Kern Co | Weldon. |
| Boquet, A | Miner | Kern Co | nr Havilah | Havilah. |
| Borgwardt, H | Miner | nr Kelsoe | Kern Co | Havilah. |
| Bostwick, E | Wagon maker | 3d st | Bakersfield | Bakersfield. |
| Bower, W R | Miner | nr Havilah | Kern Co | Havilah. |
| Boyle, C R | Blacksmith | Kernville | Kern Co | Kernville. |
| Bradley, D B | Miner | nr Linn's Valley | Kern Co | Glenville. |
| Brady, Peter | Blacksmith | Kernville | Kern Co | Kernville. |
| Brady, Patrick | Blacksmith | Havilah | Kern Co | Havilah. |
| Brandt, J E | Farmer | nr Bakersfield | Kern Co | Bakersfield. |
| Bratton, A C | Physician | Chester Ave | Bakersfield | Bakersfield. |
| Bridger, James | Miner | Kern Co | nr Havilah | Havilah. |
| Bridger, T D | Miner | Kern Co | nr Havilah | Havilah. |
| Bright, J M | Farmer | nr Tehichipa | Kern Co | Tehichipa. |
| Brite, Joseph H | Farmer | Tehichipa | Kern Co | Tehichipa. |
| Brittain, J S | Printer | Bakersfield | Kern Co | Bakersfield. |
| Brooks, Wm H | Printer | Bakersfield | Kern Co | Bakersfield. |
| Brooks, J, Jr | Farmer | nr Kern Island | Kern Co | Bakersfield. |
| Brown, Andrew | Merchant | Kernville | Kern Co | Kernville. |
| Brown, B E | Blacksmith | Tehichipa | Kern Co | Tehichipa. |
| Brown, Clarence | Farmer | Kern Co | nr South Fork | Weldon. |
| Brown, C F | Farmer | nr Bakersfield | Kern Co | Bakersfield. |
| Brown, Edwd T | Farmer | South Fork | Kern Co | Weldon. |
| Brown, E J | Carpenter | Walker's Basin | Kern Co | Havilah. |
| Brown, J K | Farmer | Kern Co | nr South Fork | Weldon. |
| Brown, Jerry | Farmer | nr Linn's Valley | Kern Co | Glenville. |
| Brown, L | Physician | Havilah | Kern Co | Havilah. |
| Brown, N M | Blacksmith | Kern Island | Kern Co | Bakersfield. |
| Brown, Peter | Farmer | nr Kernville | Kern Co | Kernville. |
| Brown, Wm | | Bakersfield | Kern Co | Bakersfield. |
| Brown, W H | Miner | nr Long Tom | Kern Co | Bakersfield. |
| Brown, Wm S | Teamster | Kern Island | Kern Co | Bakersfield. |
| Brower, C | Book keeper | Bakersfield | Kern Co | Bakersfield. |
| Brundage, B | Lawyer | Havilah | Kern Co | Havilah. |
| Brush, J B | Carpenter | Bakersfield | Kern Co | Bakersfield. |
| Bryant, Joseph | Shepherd | New River | Kern Co | |
| Bryant, P M | Sheep raiser | Kern Island | Kern Co | Bakersfield. |
| Bryson, Thos | Farmer | nr Bakersfield | Kern Co | Bakersfield. |

## DIRECTORY OF KERN COUNTY. 217

| Name. | Occupation. | Place of Business. | Residence. | Town or P. O. |
|---|---|---|---|---|
| Buhn, F L | Farmer | Kern Co | nr Tehichipa | Tehichipa. |
| Burchard, D | Farmer | nr Tehichipa | Kern Co | Tehichipa. |
| Burdett, H | Miner | Kern Co | nr Havilah | Havilah. |
| **Burk, Danl** | Farmer | Kern Co | nr Posa Creek | Bakersfield. |
| Burke, John | Laborer | Kernville | Kern Co | Kernville. |
| Burke, T F | Farmer | Kern Co | nr Bakersfield | Bakersfield. |
| Burker, E R | Miner | Kern Co | nr Walker's Basin | Havilah. |
| Burmuden, A W | Miner | nr Havilah | Kern Co | Havilah. |
| Burnap, Silas A | Farmer | Panama | Kern Co | Panama. |
| **Burr, L W** | Farmer | Kern Island | Kern Co | Bakersfield. |
| Burt, J E | Blacksmith | Bakersfield | Kern Co | Bakersfield. |
| Bushill, J B | Miner | Kern Co | nr Piute | Piute. |
| Busick, Mathew | Miner | Havilah | Kern Co | Havilah. |
| Buskirk, R V | Shoe maker | Kernville | Kern Co | Kernville. |
| **Butler, Alexander** | Farmer | New River | Kern Co | |
| Butler, G W | Miner | nr Havilah | Kern Co | Havilah. |
| Butler, J S | Farmer | nr Bakersfield | Kern Co | Bakersfield. |
| Butler, J S | Miner | nr Kernville | Kern Co | Kernville. |
| Butler, W P | Farmer | Kern Co | nr Bakersfield | Bakersfield. |
| **Butts, A H** | Stock raiser | Bear Valley | Kern Co | Tehichipa. |
| Butterbredt, F | Ranchero | nr Kelsoe Valley | Kern Co | Havilah. |
| Cahoon, G W | Miner | Kern Co | nr Greenhorn | Kernville. |
| Caldwell, J W V | Sheep raiser | Willow Spring | Kern Co | |
| **Calhoun, E E** | Lawyer | Havilah | Kern Co | Havilah. |
| Cameron, G W | Ranchero | nr Havilah | Kern Co | Havilah. |
| **Campbell, Jas** | Pro arlington ho | Bakersfield | Kern Co | Bakersfield. |
| Canfield, W | Stock raiser | Kern Co | Bakersfield | Bakersfield. |
| **Carleton, C C** | Merchant | Kernville | Kern Co | Kernville. |
| **Carlock & Robb** | Lumber | Bakersfield | Kern Co | Bakersfield. |
| Carlock, F M | Lumberman | Sumner | Kern Co | Bakersfield. |
| Carlock, G H | Farmer | Kern River Island | Kern Co | Bakersfield. |
| Carlock, J | Farmer | nr Bakersfield | Kern Co | Bakersfield. |
| **Carlock, W E** | Farmer | Bakersfield | Kern Co | Bakersfield. |
| Carlian, M | Laborer | Caliente | Kern Co | Caliente. |
| Carmichael, D | Farmer | Kern Island | Kern Co | Bakersfield. |
| **Carpenter, Chancey** | Manufacturer | Kern Co | Bakersfield | Bakersfield. |
| Carpenter, Lewis | Laborer | Kern Co | Cross Mill | |
| Carpenter, Philip | Farmer | Kern Co | Cross Mill | |
| Carr, Thos | Miner | nr Greenhorn | Kern Co | Kernville. |
| **Carver, Joel** | Stock raiser | Long Tom | Kern Co | Bakersfield. |
| **Castagneto, Frank** | Fruit store | Caliente | Caliente | Caliente. |
| Castagnetto, Francisco | Gardener | Kern Co | Bakersfield | Bakersfield. |
| Castello, H C | Farmer | Kern Co | nr Bakersfield | Bakersfield. |
| Caughran, C E | Farmer | Sageland | Kern Co | Sageland. |
| Caughran, J W | Farmer | Kern Co | nr Kelsoe Valley | Havilah. |
| Cavenac, J | Miner | Kern Co | nr Havilah | Havilah. |
| **Cerrogordo Freighting Co** | Freighting | Caliente | | Caliente. |
| Chamberlin, J B | Conductor | Cummings Valley | Kern Co | Tehichipa. |
| Chamberlin, J B | Farmer | Tehichipa | Kern Co | Tehichipa. |
| **Chambers, Wm A** | Engineer | Kernville | Kern Co | Kernville. |
| Chandler, S | Farmer | Kern Co | nr Havilah | Havilah. |
| Chaney, E | Miner | Kern Co | Kern Co | |
| Chapman, M E | Miner | nr Havilah | Kern Co | Havilah. |
| **Chappell, J D** | Farmer | Kern Co | nr Bear Valley | Tehichipa. |
| Chappell, J F | Vaquero | Tehichipa | Kern Co | Tehichipa. |
| Charlton, Abm | Farmer | Kern Co | nr Bakersfield | Bakersfield. |
| Charlton, Robert | Farmer | Kern Co | nr Bakersfield | Bakersfield. |
| Chester, D S | Farmer | Buena Vista | Kern Co | |
| Chester, Geo B | Post master | 3d & Chestnut ave | 1 m S Bakersfield | Bakersfield. |
| **Chester, Julius** | Pro So californi'n | North st | Bakersfield | Bakersfield. |
| Childs, P G | Book keeper | Kernville | Kern Co | Kernville. |

## L. L. PAULSON'S HAND-BOOK AND

| Name. | Occupation. | Place of Business. | Residence. | Town or P. O. |
|---|---|---|---|---|
| Christiansen, C...... | Carpenter............ | Kern Co................. | Bakersfield............ | Bakersfield. |
| Christy, R G......... | Sailor ............... | Kern Co................. | Bakersfield............ | Bakersfield. |
| Chubb, O T .......... | Miner ............... | nr Kern Island ....... | Kern Co................ | Bakersfield. |
| Chumm, W C......... | Livery stable........ | Caliente................. | Kern Co................ | Caliente. |
| Churchman, Geo E. | Butcher............... | Kernville .............. | Kern Co................ | Kernville. |
| Chynoweth, W...... | Miner ............... | Kern Co................. | nr Kernville........... | Kernville. |
| Clancy, Geo......... | Farmer .............. | nr So Fork............. | Kern Co................ | Weldon. |
| Clarke, James....... | Miner ............... | Bakersfield............. | Kern Co................ | Bakersfield. |
| Clark, J M........... | Farmer .............. | nr Bakersfield......... | Kern Co................ | Bakersfield. |
| Clark, J J............ | Stock raiser......... | Kern Co................ | Linn's Valley ......... | Glenville. |
| Clark, Lewis......... | Hotel keeper ....... | Kernville .............. | Kern Co................ | Kernville. |
| Clark, R A........... | Carpenter............ | Havilah................. | Kern Co................ | Havilah. |
| Clarke, Robt F...... | Sheep raiser......... | Coyote Springs....... | Kern Co................ | |
| Clark, Wm........... | Laborer............... | Kernville .............. | Kern Co................ | Kernville. |
| Clark, W B L ...... | Stock raiser......... | Kern Co................ | Linn's Valley ......... | Glenville. |
| Clendinin, T H..... | Farmer .............. | nr Bakersfield......... | Kern Co................ | Bakersfield. |
| Cleve, Peter......... | Millwright .......... | Kernville............... | Kern Co................ | Kernville. |
| Closner, David ..... | Farmer .............. | nr Bakersfield......... | Kern Co................ | Bakersfield. |
| Cochran, A A....... | Farmer .............. | Kern Co................ | nr Bakersfield......... | Bakersfield. |
| Cochrane, James.... | Farmer .............. | nr Kernville........... | Kern Co................ | Kernville. |
| Cochran, J D....... | Miner ............... | Kern Co................. | nr Kernville........... | Kernville. |
| Cochran, H F....... | Farmer .............. | nr Bakersfield......... | Kern Co................ | Bakersfield. |
| Cohn, E.............. | Clerk................. | Kern Co................ | Havilah................ | Havilah. |
| Colby, P J........... | Attorney ............. | Chester Ave.......... | Bakersfield............ | Bakersfield. |
| Cole, I McD......... | Teamster............. | nr Walker's Basin... | Kern Co................ | Havilah. |
| Cole, J O............ | Miner ............... | nr Bakersfield......... | Kern Co................ | Bakersfield. |
| Coley, H C........... | | | | |
| Collins, A O......... | Butcher .............. | Bakersfield............. | Kern Co................ | Bakersfield. |
| Collins, Chas ....... | Teamster............. | Kernville .............. | Kern Co................ | Kernville. |
| Collins, C S......... | ...................... | Bakersfield............. | Kern Co................ | Bakersfield. |
| Collier, G M ........ | Farmer .............. | nr Tehichipa ......... | Kern Co................ | Tehichipa. |
| Collins, J C......... | Teamster............. | Kern Co................ | nr Bakersfield......... | Bakersfield. |
| Collins, J T......... | Farmer............... | Kern Co................ | nr Linn's Valley...... | Glenville. |
| Collins, J S......... | Wagon maker...... | Bakersfield............. | Kern Co................ | Bakersfield. |
| Collins, Thos ....... | Miner ............... | Kernville .............. | Kern Co................ | Kernville. |
| Collom, Danl D .... | Laborer............... | Bakersfield............. | Kern Co................ | Bakersfield. |
| Combs, T J.......... | Miner................ | nr White River...... | Kern Co................ | |
| Comstock, D ....... | Farmer .............. | Kern Co................ | nr Bakersfield......... | Bakersfield. |
| Condict, H F....... | Hotel................ | Bakersfield............. | Kern Co................ | Bakersfield. |
| Connelly, J T....... | Blacksmith.......... | Kern Co................ | Bakersfield............ | Bakersfield. |
| Contreras, V ....... | Farmer .............. | Kern Co................ | nr Bakersfield......... | Bakersfield. |
| Cooke, B............. | Barber ............... | Caliente................. | Caliente............... | Caliente. |
| Cook, H L........... | Lumberman......... | Summit Mill.......... | Kern Co................ | Kernville. |
| Coons, Alonzo....... | Telegraph op. ..... | Bakersfield............. | Kern Co................ | Bakersfield. |
| Coons, T J........... | Farmer .............. | Kern Co................ | nr Havilah............. | Havilah. |
| Coons, W H ........ | Clerk................. | Havilah................. | Kern Co................ | Havilah. |
| Cooper, Philip...... | Laborer............... | Kernville .............. | Kern Co................ | Kernville. |
| Corbett, John....... | Butcher .............. | Havilah................. | Kern Co................ | Havilah. |
| Cornelius, J C...... | Laborer............... | nr Havilah............. | Kern Co................ | Havilah. |
| Couse, Wm.......... | Miner ............... | nr Erskin Creek...... | Kern Co................ | |
| Cover, Eli ........... | Hotel keeper ....... | Kernville .............. | Kern Co................ | Kernville. |
| Cover, Jacob W.... | Hotel keeper ....... | Kernville .............. | Kern Co................ | Kernville. |
| Craig, F W ......... | Merchant ........... | Kernville .............. | Kern Co................ | Kernville. |
| Crane, Wm J....... | Laborer............... | Weldon................. | Kern Co................ | Weldon. |
| Crawford, Wm..... | Farmer .............. | Kern Island .......... | Kern Co................ | Bakersfield. |
| Crites, A M L...... | Millwright .......... | Havilah................. | Kern Co................ | Havilah. |
| Crocker, E M ...... | Ranchero ............ | Kern Co................ | nr Bakersfield......... | Bakersfield. |
| Crocker, James C.. | Stock raiser......... | Panama................ | Kern Co................ | Panama. |
| Croslin, R B ........ | Farmer .............. | nr Linn's Valley...... | Kern Co................ | Glenville. |
| Cross, Anson........ | Lumberman......... | nr Havilah............. | Kern Co................ | Havilah. |
| Cross, E D .......... | Farmer .............. | Kern Co................ | nr Bakersfield......... | Bakersfield. |
| Cross, Joel........... | Farmer .............. | nr Linn's Valley...... | Kern Co................ | Glenville. |
| Cross, H H.......... | Clerk................. | Havilah................. | Kern Co................ | Havilah. |
| Crumwell, A W..... | Farmer .............. | nr Bear Valley....... | Kern Co................ | Tehichipa. |

## DIRECTORY OF KERN COUNTY. 219

| Name. | Occupation. | Place of Business. | Residence. | Town or P. O. |
|---|---|---|---|---|
| Cudeback, G P | Farmer | nr Tehichipa | Kern Co | Tehichipa. |
| Cuevas, Leonardo | Laborer | Kernville | Kern Co | Kernville. |
| Cummins, J M | Farmer | Kern Co | nr Tehichipa | Tehichipa. |
| Cummins, John W | Teamster | nr Tehichipa | Kern Co | Tehichipa. |
| Cummings, Wm J | Miner | Kern Co | nr Linn's Valley | Glenville. |
| Curless, C D | Stock raiser | Kern Co | South Fork | Weldon. |
| Cusack, P W | Laborer | nr Havilah | Kern Co | Havilah. |
| Cussac, John | Laborer | Kern Co | nr Havilah | Havilah. |
| Cwen, V | Farmer | Kern Co | nr Bakersfield | Bakersfield. |
| Dampman, J | Farmer | nr Linn's Valley | Kern Co | Glenville. |
| Danprey, Danl'. | Farmer | nr Bakersfield | Kern Co | Bakersfield. |
| Darden, G W | Farmer | nr Bakersfield | Kern Co | Bakersfield. |
| Darnul, Jno J | Farmer | Kern Island | Kern Co | Bakersfield. |
| Davenport, Danl | Farmer | Kern Co | nr Cummin's Valley | Tehichipa. |
| Davenport, Jesse | Farmer | Cummin's Valley | Kern Co | Tehichipa. |
| Davies, A H | Attorney | Chester Ave | Bakersfield | Bakersfield. |
| Davis, A G | Contractor | Bakersfield | Kern Co | Bakersfield. |
| Davis, Brook | Miner | nr Green Horn | Kern Co | Kernville. |
| Davis, I A | Clerk | South Fork | Kern Co | Weldon. |
| Davis, I W | Mail carrier | Kern Co | Kernville | Kernville. |
| Davis, Joseph | Teamster | Kernville | Kern Co | Kernville. |
| Davis, I T | Farmer | nr Bakersfield | Kern Co | Bakersfield. |
| Davis, O S | Farmer | Kern Co | nr Bakersfield | Bakersfield. |
| Davis, W L | Painter | Kern Co | Bakersfield | Bakersfield. |
| Davis, W H | Farmer | Kern Co | nr Bakersfield | Bakersfield. |
| Dawes, J G | Stockman | Bakersfield | Kern Co | Bakersfield. |
| Dawson, W F | Miner | Kern Co | nr Linn's Valley | Glenville. |
| Dearborn, Elias | Farmer | Tejon Canyon | Kern Co | Tejon. |
| Deen, J W | Farmer | nr South Fork | Kern Co | Weldon. |
| Deen, W T | Farmer | nr South Fork | Kern Co | Weldon. |
| Degman, A J | Miner | nr Tehichipa | Kern Co | Tehichipa. |
| Denker, A H | Hotel keeper | Kern Co | Havilah | Havilah. |
| Denker, Chas | Clerk | Kern Co | Havilah | Havilah. |
| Denker, H H | Hotel keeper | Kern Co | Havilah | Havilah. |
| Dernuit, Geo S | Miner | Sageland | Kern Co | Sageland. |
| Dennis, O H | Stock raiser | Kern Co | Linn's Valley | Glenville. |
| Derbon, Adolphus | Laborer | Kern Co | nr Cummin's Valley | Tehichipa. |
| De Silva, Manuel | Laborer | ? | South Fork | Kern Co | Weldon. |
| Despain, Wm | Mechanic | Kern Co | Linn's Valley | Glenville. |
| Devine, Andrew | Laborer | Kern Co | nr Walker's Basin | Havilah. |
| De Witt, J C | Hostler | Kern Co | Havilah | Havilah. |
| Dietz, Chas | Hotel keeper | Bakersfield | Kern Co | Bakersfield. |
| Dimock, H C | Physician | Bakersfield | Kern Co | Bakersfield. |
| Dixon, J P | Stockman | Kern Co | Bakersfield | Bakersfield. |
| Dockerty, Jas | Laborer | Kern Co | nr Bakersfield | Bakersfield. |
| Dolores, Antonio | Farmer | Kern Co | nr Bakersfield | Bakersfield. |
| Donald, John | Farmer | nr Tehichipa | Kern Co | Tehichipa. |
| Donaldson, A M | Carpenter | | Kern Co | Bakersfield. |
| Donez, Wm | Miner | Woody's | Kern Co | |
| Donnell, R R | Saloon | Bakersfield | Kern Co | Bakersfield. |
| Dooly, O D | Minister | Kern Co | Linn's Valley | Glenville. |
| Doriot, C H | Miner | Kern Co | nr Tehichipa | Tehichipa. |
| Dorsey, R B | Mining engineer | Kern Co | Havilah | Havilah. |
| Doshier, J | Farmer | Tehichipa | Kern Co | Tehichipa. |
| Dougherty, J J | Teamster | Kern Co | nr Long Tom | Bakersfield. |
| Dougherty, M McMaley | Farmer | Spout Spring | Kern Co | |
| Dougherty, Thos | Miner | nr Kernville | Kern Co | Havilah. |
| Dow, Edward | Miner | Walker's Basin | Kern Co | Havilah. |
| Dowden, Thos | Farmer | nr Bakersfield | Kern Co | Bakersfield. |
| Drury, W W | Farmer | Kern Co | nr Bakersfield | Bakersfield. |
| DuBratz, A B | Lawyer | Kern Co | Linn's Valley | Glenville. |
| Duke, Geo A | Sheepman | Paso Precinct...' | Kern Co | |
| Dumble, E H | Farmer | Kern Co | nr Bakersfield | Bakersfield. |

| Name. | Occupation. | Place of Business. | Residence. | Town or P. O. |
|---|---|---|---|---|
| Dunlap, J E | Farmer | nr Linn's Valley | Kern Co | Glenville. |
| Dunlap, Calvin | Farmer | Kern Co | nr Linn's Valley | Glenville. |
| Dunlavy, Jas | Laborer | nr Walker's Basin | Kern Co | Havilah. |
| Dunn, James | Farmer | Bear Valley | Kern Co | Tehichipa. |
| Durnal, J A | Saloon | Kern Co | Tehichipa | Tehichipa. |
| Dutty, Wm | Farmer | nr Tehichipa | Kern Co | Tehichipa. |
| Dysert, Joseph C | Farmer | Kern Island | Kern Co | Bakersfield. |
| Dysert, Stephen | Farmer | Kern Island | Kern Co | Bakersfield. |
| Eastman, O | Laborer | Kern Co | nr Bakersfield | Bakersfield. |
| Eckhoff, F J | Miner | Piute | Kern Co | |
| Eddsy, J C | Miner | Kernville | Kern Co | Kernville. |
| Edwards, Nelson | Farmer | Kern Co | nr Bakersfield | Bakersfield. |
| Ehrich, Frederick | Miner | Kern Co | nr Havilah | Havilah. |
| Eldon, John | Carpenter | Dead Ox Springs | Kern Co | |
| Elise, D | Laborer | Walker's Basin | Kern Co | Havilah. |
| Ellington, Jas | Laborer | nr Cross Mill | Kern Co | |
| Ellington, J L | Farmer | Walker's Basin | Kern Co | Havilah. |
| Elliott, C P | Miner | nr Kelsoe | Kern Co | Havilah. |
| Elliott, C H | Physician | Kern Co | Linn's Valley | Glenville. |
| Elliott, G B | Sheep herder | Kern Co | nr Tejon | Tejon. |
| Ellis, A H | Farmer | Tehichipa | Kern Co | Tehichipa. |
| Ellis, A P | Farmer | nr Linn's Valley | Kern Co | Glenville. |
| Ellis, B W | Farmer | Tehichipa | Kern Co | Tehichipa. |
| Ellis, F | Farmer | nr Linn's Valley | Kern Co | Glenville. |
| Ellis, J M | Farmer | Tehichipa | Kern Co | Tehichipa. |
| Ellis, J S | Farmer | nr Kern Island | Kern Co | Bakersfield. |
| Engle, David | Ranchero | nr Long Tom | Kern Co | Bakersfield. |
| Escaiche, Francis | Baker | Kern Co | Havilah | Havilah. |
| Estes, Hark | Miner | Caliente | Kern Co | Caliente. |
| Evans, John | Stage driver | Kern Co | Havilah | Havilah. |
| Evans, P H | Engineer | Kern Co | Kernville | Kernville. |
| Evans, S E | Laborer | Kernville | Kern Co | Kernville. |
| Evecith, John | Ranchero | nr Fort Tejon | Kern Co | Tejon. |
| Eveleth, Thos | Clerk | Kern Co | Fort Tejon | Tejon. |
| Everts, M E | Printer | Kern Co | Havilah | Havilah. |
| Ewing, John N | Tel operator | Fort Tejon | Kern Co | Tejon. |
| Ewing, James | Miner | Kernville | Kern Co | Kernville. |
| Fairchilds, N A | Carpenter | Kern Co | Kernville | Kernville. |
| Fanning, J M | Miner | nr Havilah | Kern Co | Havilah. |
| Farmer, S M | Farmer | nr Linn's Valley | Kern Co | Glenville. |
| Farrell, Michael | Tinsmith | Kern Co | Bakersfield | Bakersfield. |
| Farris, J F | Farmer | Caliente | Kern Co | Caliente. |
| Fawcett, Milton | Teamster | nr Bakersfield | Kern Co | Bakersfield. |
| Ferguson, R N | Farmer | nr Bakersfield | Kern Co | Bakersfield. |
| Fetterman, I L | Farmer | New River | Kern Co | Kernville. |
| Fickert, Frederick | Stable keeper | Kern Co | Havilah | Havilah. |
| Fickert, Louis | Farmer | nr Tchichipa | Kern Co | Tehichipa. |
| Fink, H | Laborer | Kern Co | nr Havilah | Havilah. |
| Finn, H W | Farmer | Kern Co | nr Linn's Valley | Glenville. |
| Finney, Saml | Farmer | Kern Co | nr Bakersfield | Bakersfield. |
| Fisher, F | Machinist | Kern Co | Kelsoe | Havilah. |
| Fisher, F F | Miner | Sageland | Kern Co | Sageland. |
| Fisher, Wm W | Miner | Sageland | Kern Co | Sageland. |
| Fite, Geo | Carpenter | Kern Co | Kernville | Kernville. |
| Fitzgerald, Mathew | Saloon | Caliente | Kern Co | Caliente. |
| Fitzgerald, Richd | Saloon | Caliente | Caliente | Caliente. |
| Flanagan, Timothy | Miner | nr Kernville | Kern Co | Kernville. |
| Fleck, Thos | Stock raiser | Kern Co | San Emedio | Bakersfield. |
| Flinn, M | Engineer | Kern Co | Kernville | Kernville. |
| Flougher, J D | Miner | Kern Co | nr Petersburgh | |
| Flynn, James | Cook | Kern Co | Kernville | Kernville. |
| Foley, F M | Farmer | Kern Co | nr Tehichipa | Tehichipa. |
| Foley, G W | Farmer | Kern Co | nr Tehichipa | Tehichipa. |
| Follansbee, J | Car repairer | Delano | Kern Co | Delano. |

DIRECTORY OF KERN COUNTY. 221

| Name. | Occupation. | Place of Business. | Residence. | Town or P. O. |
|---|---|---|---|---|
| Fontaine, J............ | Miner............... | nr Havilah............ | Kern Co................. | Havilah. |
| Fontaine, J B........ | Farmer............. | Kern Co................. | nr Allen's Camp...... | Caliente. |
| Ford, John............ | Miner............... | nr Havilah............ | Kern Co................. | Havilah. |
| Forgens, IS A........ | Miner............... | Kernville............. | Kern Co................. | Kernville. |
| Forsyth & Moyer... | Saloon.............. | Caliente.............. | Kern Co................. | Caliente. |
| Forsyth, Alex........ | Saloon.............. | Caliente.............. | Kern Co................. | Caliente. |
| Fowler, Tilman..... | Stock raiser....... | Kern Co............... | Tejon.................... | Tejon. |
| Fowler, Wm F....... | Merchant........... | Tehichipa............ | Kern Co................. | Tehichipa. |
| Fox, Alfred L........ | Farmer............. | Kernville............. | Kern Co................. | Kernville. |
| Franklin, Edwd..... | Teamster........... | nr Kern Island..... | Kern Co................. | Bakersfield. |
| Frankville, R........ | Farmer............. | Tehichipa............ | Kern Co................. | Delano. |
| Fraser, John......... | Farmer............. | Sageland............. | Kern Co................. | Sageland. |
| Frazer, H H.......... | Farmer............. | Tehichipa............ | Kern Co................. | Tehichipa. |
| Frazier, M G......... | Farmer............. | Kern Co............... | nr Bakersfield........ | Bakersfield. |
| Frazier, O M......... | Farmer............. | nr Kern Island..... | Kern Co................. | Bakersfield. |
| Free, Frederick.... | Saloon.............. | Caliente.............. | Caliente................ | Caliente. |
| Freed, S W............ | Miner............... | Kern Co............... | nr Kelsoe.............. | Havilah. |
| Freeman, John...... | Laborer............. | nr Cummin's Valley | Kern Co................. | Tehichipa. |
| Freeman, J W....... | Attorney........... | Bakersfield.......... | Kern Co................. | Bakersfield. |
| Freeman, M S....... | Farmer............. | Cummin's Valley... | Kern Co................. | Tehichipa. |
| Frey & Free.......... | Saloon.............. | Caliente.............. | Caliente................ | Caliente. |
| Frey, Wm............. | Saloon.............. | Caliente.............. | Caliente................ | Caliente. |
| Frietsch, J J......... | Merchant........... | Kern Co............... | Havilah................. | Havilah. |
| Frieburgh, T B..... | Farmer............. | Tehichipa............ | Kern Co................. | Tehichipa. |
| Friery, Patrick..... | Farmer............. | nr Long Tom....... | Kern Co................. | Bakersfield. |
| Frieze, G A........... | Carpenter.......... | Kern Co............... | Havilah................. | Havilah. |
| Frink, B............... | Farmer............. | San Emidio.......... | Kern Co................. | Bakersfield. |
| Fugit, Francis....... | Stock raiser....... | Kern Co............... | Linn's Valley........ | Glenville. |
| Fugit, T S............. | Stock raiser....... | Kern Co............... | Linn's Valley........ | Glenville. |
| Fugit, Wm............ | Stock raiser....... | Kern Co............... | Linn's Valley........ | Glenville. |
| Fuller, Jos............ | Laborer............. | Tehichipa............ | Kern Co................. | Tehichipa. |
| Funk, John........... | Stock raiser....... | Kern Co............... | San Emidio........... | Bakersfield. |
| Gabaldine, R........ | Farmer............. | nr Bakersfield..... | Kern Co................. | Bakersfield. |
| Gage, A F............. | Bar keeper........ | Kern Co............... | Bakersfield........... | Bakersfield. |
| Gage, O C............. | Painter............. | Kern Co............... | Bakersfield........... | Bakersfield. |
| Gaitland, Pat........ | Laborer............. | Caliente.............. | Kern Co................. | Caliente. |
| Galtes, P.............. | Gen merchandise. | Bakersfield.......... | Kern Co................. | Bakersfield. |
| Gardett, Peter...... | Farmer............. | Kern Co............... | Posa Flat.............. | Bakersfield. |
| Garner, T R.......... | Farmer............. | Kern Co............... | nr Linn's Valley.... | Glenville. |
| Garrett, J M......... | Farmer............. | nr Kelsoe............ | Kern Co................. | Havilah. |
| Garrett, Matthew.. | Carpenter.......... | Kern Co............... | Bakersfield........... | Bakersfield. |
| Gates, Lafayette... | Farmer............. | Kern Co............... | nr Bakersfield....... | Bakersfield. |
| Gates, M W........... | Farmer............. | nr Bakersfield..... | Kern Co................. | Bakersfield. |
| Gaydon, G............ | Farmer............. | Kern Co............... | nr Linn's Valley.... | Glenville. |
| Geldersleeve, W S.. | Carpenter.......... | Kern Co............... | Bakersfield........... | Bakersfield. |
| George, B............. | Mechanic........... | Kern Co............... | Bakersfield........... | Bakersfield. |
| George, Wm H...... | Physician.......... | Kernville............. | Kern Co................. | Kernville. |
| Gibson, S P.......... | Laborer............. | nr Havilah........... | Kern Co................. | Havilah. |
| Gideon, J P.......... | Miner............... | nr Linn's Valley... | Kern Co................. | Glenville. |
| Gigey, Geo........... | Teamster........... | Kern Co............... | nr Havilah............ | Havilah. |
| Gillian, J A.......... | Stock raiser....... | Woody's.............. | Kern Co................. |  |
| Gilliman, R.......... | Farmer............. | Kern Co............... | nr Linn's Valley.... | Glenville. |
| Gilmac, H C......... | Musician........... | Kern Co............... | Kernville.............. | Kernville. |
| Gilman, Peter...... | Farmer............. | Kern Co............... | nr Kern Island...... | Bakersfield. |
| Gilpin, J M........... | Miner............... | Kernville............. | Kern Co................. | Kernville. |
| Ginwell, G W....... | Stock raiser....... | Bakersfield.......... | Kern Co................. | Bakersfield. |
| Gist, J W.............. | Farmer............. | nr Bakersfield..... | Kern Co................. | Bakersfield. |
| Glasscock, G F..... | Butcher............. | Kern Co............... | Kernville.............. | Kernville. |
| Glenn, Alex.......... | Farmer............. | Kern Co............... | nr Linn's Valley.... | Glenville. |
| Glenn, J A............ | Stock raiser....... | Kern Co............... | Tehichipa............. | Tehichipa. |
| Glenn, J M........... | Farmer............. | nr Linn's Valley... | Kern Co................. | Glenville. |
| Glenn, J N............ | Blacksmith........ | Kern Co............... | Tehichipa............. | Tehichipa. |
| Glenn, J O............ | Farmer............. | nr Tehichipa........ | Kern Co................. | Tehichipa. |
| Glenn, S C............ | Farmer............. | Kern Co............... | nr Tehichipa......... | Tehichipa. |

| Name. | Occupation. | Place of Business. | Residence. | Town or P. O. |
|---|---|---|---|---|
| Glenn, R F | Vaquero | nr Tehichipa | Kern Co | Tehichipa. |
| Glennon, Richard | Miner | Kern Co | nr Claraville | Havilah. |
| Godey, Alexis | Ranchero | Kern Co | nr Tejon | Tejon. |
| Godwin, T H | Farmer | nr Tehichipa | Kern Co | Tehichipa. |
| Goff, Hugh | Miner | nr Kernville | Kern Co | Kernville. |
| Goldworthy, John | Miner | Kernville | Kern Co | Kernville. |
| Goodale, F W | Teamster | Kern Co | nr Havilah | Havilah. |
| Goodhart, P | Farmer | Kern Co | nr Bakersfield | Bakersfield. |
| Gordon, J F | Farmer | nr Bakersfield | Kern Co | Bakersfield. |
| Gorse, Geo | Laborer | Tehichipa | Kern Co | Tehichipa. |
| Grace, John | Teamster | nr Havilah | Kern Co | Havilah. |
| Graham, Isaac | Farmer | nr Linn's Valley | Kern Co | Glenville. |
| Graham, M | Farmer | nr Walker's Basin | Kern Co | Havilah. |
| Graham, Wm | Farmer | Kern Co | nr Tehichipa | Tehichipa. |
| Gram, D C | Miner | nr Linn's Valley | Kern Co | Glenville. |
| Grant, W J | Farmer | Kern Co | nr Linn's Valley | Glenville. |
| Graves, S R | Farmer | New River | Kern Co | |
| Gray, A W | Farmer | Tehichipa | Kern Co | Tehichipa. |
| Gray, J T H | Farmer | Kern Co | nr South Fork | Weldon. |
| Gray, James | Farmer | Kern Island | Kern Co | Bakersfield. |
| Gray, R J | Farmer | nr Linn's Valley | Kern Co | Glenville. |
| Green, A D | Merchant | Kernville | Kern Co | Kernville. |
| Green, Edwd | Merchant | Kern Co | Bakersfield | Bakersfield. |
| Green, E R | Clerk | Kern Co | Kern Island | Bakersfield. |
| Green, Geo Wm | Miner | Kernville | Kern Co | Kernville. |
| Green, Jas | Farmer | Kern Co | nr Tehichipa | Tehichipa. |
| Green, L D | Farmer | Kern Co | nr Tehichipa | Tehichipa. |
| Green & Hirshfield | Gen merchandise | Tehichipa | Kern Co | Tehichipa. |
| Green, — | Genl merchandise | Tehichipa | Kern Co | Tehichipa. |
| Green, P D | Miner | nr Tehichipa | Kern Co | Tehichipa. |
| Greer, Jas | Laborer | nr Bear Valley | Kern Co | Tehichipa. |
| Greer, J W | Teamster | nr Walker's Basin | Kern Co | Havilah. |
| Gregg, Edgar A | Cooper | Kernville | Kern Co | Kernville. |
| Gregory, J H | Farmer | Kern Island | Kern Co | Bakersfield. |
| Groshing, Uriah | Farmer | New River | Kern Co | |
| Groves, G W | Blacksmith | Kern Island | Kern Co | Bakersfield. |
| Grover, J F | Farmer | nr Bakersfield | Kern Co | Bakersfield. |
| Halbert, A J | Farmer | nr Linn's Valley | Kern Co | Glenville. |
| Halbert, G W | Miner | nr Linn's Valley | Kern Co | Glenville. |
| Hale, Chas | Laborer | Caliente | Kern Co | Caliente. |
| Hale, Moses | Farmer | Kern Co | nr Tehichipa | Tehichipa. |
| Hail, G W | Farmer | nr Kern Island | Kern Co | Bakersfield. |
| Hall, Edmund | Blacksmith | Kern Co | Fort Tejon | Tejon. |
| Hall, J T | Harness maker | Kern Co | Long Tom | Bakersfield. |
| Hall, Miller | Clerk | 3d & Chestnut Ave | 3d & Chestnut Ave | Bakersfield. |
| Hamilton, J J | Carpenter | Kern Co | Tehichipa | Tehichipa. |
| Hamilton, J P | Operator | Delano | Kern Co | Delano. |
| Hammer, E D | Druggist | Havilah | Kern Co | Havilah. |
| Hammer, Jesse M | Miner | Havilah | Kern Co | Havilah. |
| Hanhan, John | Farmer | Kern Co | nr Bakersfield | Bakersfield. |
| Hankinson, J | Farmer | Kern Co | nr Bakersfield | Bakersfield. |
| Hanna, W P | Saloon keeper | Havilah | Kern Co | Havilah. |
| Hannan, R | Miner | Kern Co | nr Bakersfield | Bakersfield. |
| Harding, C T | Farmer | Kern Co | Kern Island | Bakersfield. |
| Hare, L H | Farmer | New River | Kern Co | |
| Hare, T R | Engineer | Kern Co | Linn's Valley | Glenville. |
| Harman, D W | Miner | nr Kernville | Kern Co | Kernville. |
| Harman, M E | Lumberman | Kern Co | Summit Mill | Kernville. |
| Harris, Edwd | Farmer | nr Bakersfield | Kern Co | Bakersfield. |
| Harris, Geo | Cook | Havilah | Havilah | Havilah. |
| Harris, Hiram | Farmer | nr Bakersfield | Kern Co | Bakersfield. |
| Harris, James | Farmer | Kern Co | nr Bakersfield | Bakersfield. |
| Harris, J B | R R superinten't | Caliente | Kern Co | Caliente. |
| Harris, W J | Stock raiser | Kern Co | Bakersfeld | Bakersfeld. |

# DIRECTORY OF KERN COUNTY. 223

| Name. | Occupation. | Place of Business. | Residence. | Town or P. O. |
|---|---|---|---|---|
| Hart, Isaac | Stock raiser | Kern Co | Bear Valley | Tehichipa. |
| Hart, Moses | Farmer | nr Tehichipa | Kern Co | Tehichipa. |
| Hart, Meredith | Farmer | Kern Co | nr Tehichipa | Tehichipa. |
| Hart, Saml | Machinist | Kern Co | Bakersfield | Bakersfield. |
| Hasey John | Hotel keeper | Kern Co | Bakersfield | Bakersfield. |
| Haskell, W H | Teamster | Kern Co | Hot Springs | Tehichipa. |
| Haslam, J | Teamster | Kern Co | nr Kelsoe | Havilah. |
| Hatch, Wm O | Shoe maker | Bakersfield | Kern Co | Bakersfield. |
| Haughton, Wm E | Book keeper | Bakersfield | Kern Co | Bakersfield. |
| Haupt, Peter | Miner | Kern Co | Havilah | Havilah. |
| Hausser, G D | Butcher | Kern Co | nr Tehichipa | Tehichipa. |
| Haydon, Thos | Farmer | New River | Kern Co | |
| Hayes, J | Farmer | Kern Co | nr Bakersfield | Bakersfield. |
| Heath, E W | Farmer | Kern Co | nr Havilah | Havilah. |
| Heldman, Chas | Miner | Havilah | Kern Co | Havilah. |
| Hele, E J | Teamster | Kern Co | Summit Mill | Kernville. |
| Helmerigh, H C | Farmer | Kern Co | nr Linn's Valley | Glenville. |
| Henderson, J T | Miner | Kern Co | nr Havilah | Havilah. |
| Henderson, Wm J | Laborer | Allen's Camp | Kern Co | Caliente. |
| Henderson, W H | Butcher | Kern Co | Havilah | Havilah. |
| Henderson, W H | Farmer | Kern Co | nr Havilah | Havilah. |
| Hendricks, C A | Physician | Caliente | Kern Co | Caliente. |
| Hendrickson, J J | Miner | nr Tehichipa | Kern Co | Tehichipa. |
| Henly, J H | Farmer | South Fork | Kern Co | Weldon. |
| Henry, Edwin | Miner | nr Kelsoe | Kern Co | Havilah. |
| Henry, J F | Farmer | Tehichipa | Kern Co | Tehichipa. |
| Henry, Wm | Teamster | Kern Co | nr Bakersfield | Bakersfield. |
| Hepburn, J W | Farmer | Kern Island | Kern Co | Bakersfield. |
| Herndon, D W | Miner | nr Tehichipa | Kern Co | Tehichipa. |
| Herrington, W | Farmer | South Fork | Kern Co | Weldon. |
| Hicks, Chas | Tinsmith | Kern Co | Bakersfield | Bakersfield. |
| Hicks, Jas | Miner | Kern Co | nr Walker's Basin | Havilah. |
| Hickerson, A A | Vaquero | nr Tehichipa | Kern Co | Tehichipa. |
| Hickish, C | Miner | Kern Co | nr Havilah | Havilah. |
| Hickox, S H | Farmer | nr Kern Island | Kern Co | Bakersfield. |
| Higgins, J | Farmer | nr Tehichipa | Kern Co | Tehichipa. |
| Higgins, P W | Farmer | nr Tehichipa | Kern Co | Tehichipa. |
| Higgins, Wm | Miner | nr Greenhorn | Kern Co | Kernville. |
| Hight, C H | Miner | nr Greenhorn | Kern Co | Kernville. |
| Hill, J S | Farmer | Kern Co | nr Tejon | Tejon. |
| Hirschfield & Jacoby | Merchants | Bakersfield | Kern Co | Bakersfield. |
| Hirschfield, — | Merchant | Bakersfield | Kern Co | Bakersfield. |
| Hirshfield, — | Gen merchandise | Tehichipa | Kern Co | Tehichipa. |
| Hirshfield, L | Gen merchandise | Panama | Kern Co | Panama. |
| Hirshfield, H | Clerk | Kern Co | Havilah | Havilah. |
| Hobart, J H | Civil engineer | Caliente | Kern Co | Caliente. |
| Hodges, S J | Ranchero | Kern Co | nr Bakersfield | Bakersfield. |
| Hoffmeister, H | Miner | nr Sageland | Kern Co | Sageland. |
| Hoffman, C F | Miner | nr Havilah | Kern Co | Tehichipa. |
| Hoffman, Z | Farmer | nr Tehichipa | Kern Co | Tehichipa. |
| Hogden, E F | Farmer | Kern Co | Kern Island | Bakersfield. |
| Hoke, W T | Farmer | Kern Co | nr Bakersfield | Bakersfield. |
| Holtby, R M | Sheep raiser | Kern Co | Posa Creek | Bakersfield. |
| Hooper, R | Carpenter | Kern | Kern Co | |
| Hope, Jas | Farmer | nr Bakersfield | Kern Co | Bakersfield. |
| Hopkins, S W | Carpenter | Kern Co | Havilah | Havilah. |
| Hossack, J L | Farmer | Kern Co | nr Tehichipa | Tehichipa. |
| Hower, Manuel | Physician | Kernville | Kern Co | Kernville. |
| Howe, Jas H | Teamster | Walker's Basin | Kern Co | Havilah. |
| Howlett, John | Farmer | nr Bakersfield | Kern Co | Bakersfield. |
| Hucaby, Nathan | Farmer | nr Bakersfield | Kern Co | Bakersfield. |
| Hudnut, J McE | Miner | Kern Co | nr Greenhorn | Kernville. |
| Hudnut, R | Farmer | Kern Co | Lower Kern River | |

# KERN VALLEY BANK,

## BANK BUILDING,

### Cor. Chester Avenue and Second St. North,

**BAKERSFIELD, CAL.**

INCORPORATED, - - - FEBRUARY, 24th 1874.

## CAPITAL, - - $50,000

*DIRECTORS:*

SOL. JEWETT, President.        S. J. LANSING, Secretary.
F. A. TRACY.        P. T. COLBY.        JOHN FUNK.

Buy and Sell Exchange on San Francisco and principal cities of Pacific Coast. Deposits received. Eastern Exchange and Legal Tenders bought and sold. Collections made, State and County Bonds and Warrants bought, and every kind of legitimate Banking Business transacted.

---

# ADOBE STABLE.

## ANSON CROSS,

**THIRD STREET NORTH, WEST OF FRENCH HOTEL,**

*BAKERSFIELD, KERN CO. CAL.*

## Saddle and Carriage Horses,

### And Vehicles of all kinds to Let.

My Stables are among the largest and best arranged in the State. Teamsters and others will find the spacious sheds and corrals adjoining, the greatest convenience. Hay and Grain will be kept constantly on hand for sale at the lowest prices, wholesale and retail.

## DIRECTORY OF KERN COUNTY. 225

| Name. | Occupation. | Place of Business. | Residence. | Town or P. O. |
|---|---|---|---|---|
| Hudson, F C | Laborer | Havilah | Kern Co | Havilah. |
| Hudson, W W | Ranchero | nr Fort Tejon | Kern Co | Tejon. |
| Hughes, Danl | Farmer | nr Bakersfield | Kern Co | Bakersfield. |
| Hughes, Hiram | Farmer | nr Bakersfield | Kern Co | Bakersfield. |
| Hughes, Jas | Miner | Kern Co | nr Havilah | Havilah. |
| Hughes, Thos F | Miner | Havilah | Kern Co | Havilah. |
| Hull, Z T | Teamster | nr Bakersfield | Kern Co | Bakersfield. |
| Hulverson, C | Farmer | Kern Co | nr Greenhorn | Kernville. |
| Humiston, L F | Miner | nr Havilah | Kern Co | Havilah. |
| Hunt, F C | Wheelwright | Bakersfield | Kern Co | Bakersfield. |
| Hunter, J M | Teamster | nr Kernville | Kern Co | Kernville. |
| Hunter, Leonidas | Farmer | Kern Co | nr Fort Tejon | Tejon. |
| Huntsman, Jacob | Farmer | Kern Island | Kern Co | Bakersfield. |
| Hurlburt, C M | Farmer | Linn's Valley | Kern Co | Glenville. |
| Hurlburt, Julius | Farmer | Walker's Basin | Kern Co | Havilah. |
| Hutching, J F | Farmer | nr Sageland | Kern Co | Sageland. |
| Ingraham, P | Carpenter | Kern Co | Havilah | Havilah. |
| Inman, D S | Farmer | Kern Co | Kern Island | Bakersfield. |
| Inman, S B | Farmer | nr Bakersfield | Kern Co | Bakersfield. |
| Jackman, E | Farmer | Kern Co | nr Bakersfield | Bakersfield. |
| Jackson, A R | Engineer | Kern Co | Bakersfield | Bakersfield. |
| Jackson, J G | Farmer | Kern Co | nr Bakersfield | Bakersfield. |
| Jackson, M A | Farmer | Kern Co | Agua Caliente | Caliente. |
| Jacob, Albrecht | Farmer | nr Havilah | Kern Co | Havilah. |
| Jacobs, J E | Tailor | Kern Co | Bakersfield | Bakersfield. |
| Jacoby, Morris | Merchant | Kern Co | Havilah | Havilah. |
| Jacoby, — | Merchant | Bakersfield | Kern Co | Bakersfield. |
| James, E W | Miner | nr Greenhorn | Kern Co | Kernville. |
| James, M E | Miner | Kern Co | nr Bakersfield | Bakersfield. |
| James, Robert | Miner | Kern Co | nr Kernville | Kernville. |
| James, S N | Teamster | nr Bakersfield | Kern Co | Bakersfield. |
| James, Walter | County surveyor | Bakersfield | Kern Co | Bakersfield. |
| Jamison, F M | Farmer | Oak Creek | Kern Co | Bakersfield. |
| Jamison, James | Sheep raiser | Bakersfield | Kern Co | Bakersfield. |
| Jamison, Jno M | Sheep raiser | Bakersfield | Kern Co | Bakersfield. |
| Jamison, S L | Farmer | Tehichipa | Kern Co | Tehichipa. |
| Jastra, H A | Brewer | Kern Co | Bakersfield | Bakersfield. |
| Jeffries, E P | Physician | Kern Co | Fort Tejon | Tejon. |
| Jewett Bros | Ranch | Bakersfield | Kern Co | Bakersfield. |
| Jewett, Sol | Pres kern val bnk | Bakersfield | Kern Co | Bakersfield. |
| Jewett, P D | Stock raiser | Kern Co | Rio Bravo | Bakersfield. |
| Johnson, E A | Farmer | Kern Co | nr Linn's Valley | Glenville. |
| Johnson, Elias | Ranchero | nr Tehichipa | Kern Co | Tehichipa. |
| Johnson, H W | Teamster | Kernville | Kern Co | Kernville. |
| Johnson, Isaac | Farmer | nr Fort Tejon | Kern Co | Tejon. |
| Johnson, J H | Teacher | Kern Co | Tehichipa | Tehichipa. |
| Johnson, J B | Clerk | Kern Co | Bakersfield | Bakersfield. |
| Johnson, J T | Farmer | nr Bakersfield | Kern Co | Bakersfield. |
| Johnson, M N | Miner | Kern Co | nr Walker's Basin | Havilah. |
| Johnson, R M | Farmer | nr Bakersfield | Kern Co | Bakersfield. |
| Johnson, Wm A | Civil engineers | Bakersfield | Kern Co | Bakersfield. |
| Johnson & MacMurdo | Real estate agents | Campbell's Building | | Bakersfield. |
| Johnston, L W | Laborer | Tehichipa | Kern Co | Tehichipa. |
| Jones, H M | Agent | Delano | Kern Co | Delano. |
| Jones, James | Miner | Caliente | Kern Co | Caliente. |
| Jones, S F | Teamster | nr Havilah | Kern Co | Havilah. |
| Jones, Thomas | Miner | Kernville | Kern Co | Kernville. |
| Joy, Thos A | Sheep herder | Bakersfield | Kern Co | Bakersfield. |
| Judd, S M | Carpenter | Kern Co | Bakersfield | Bakersfield. |
| Judson, E | Freighting | San Francisco | San Francisco | San Francisco. |
| Jurgensen, Jno C | Farmer | Tehichipa | Kern Co | Tehichipa. |
| Kane, J | Laborer | nr Bear Valley | Kern Co | Tehichipa. |
| Keating, John | Miner | Kernville | Kern Co | Kernville. |

15

## The Grangers' Copper-Riveted
# HORSE  COLLARS

## Farmers & Teamsters, Examine them.

*Horse Collars put together with Copper Rivets will outwear two of the ordinary kind, and cost no more.*

**FOR SALE BY ALL SADDLERS.**

Manufactured only by

# J. C. JOHNSON & CO.,
### 104 and 106 Front Street,
SAN FRANCISCO.

MANUFACTURERS OF

## Harness, Saddlery, Whips, Lashes, Saddle-Trees
MEN'S, BOYS', LADIES' AND MISSES' SADDLES.

SOLE AGENT FOR

**Kirby's Genuine Santa Cruz Harness Leather.**

## DIRECTORY OF KERN COUNTY. 227

| Name. | Occupation. | Place of Business. | Residence. | Town or P. O. |
|---|---|---|---|---|
| Keith, M C | Farmer | Tehichipa | Kern Co | Tehichipa. |
| Kelly, Jeremiah | Miner | Kernville | Kern Co | Kernville. |
| Keller, Chas | Laborer | nr Bakersfield | Kern Co | Bakersfield. |
| Kelley, A C | Farmer | nr Bakersfield | Kern Co | Bakersfield. |
| **Kern Valley Bank** | Chester ave & 2d st | Bakersfield | Kern Co | Bakersfield. |
| Kerr, T F | Teamster | nr Bakersfield | Kern Co | Bakersfield. |
| **Kerr, T A** | Stock raiser | Kern Co | Havilah | Havilah. |
| Keyes, Rufus | Teamster | Kern Co | nr Walker's Basin | Havilah. |
| Keyser, Joseph | Farmer | Kern Co | nr Tehichipa | Tehichipa. |
| Kimberland, W | Farmer | Kern Co | nr Kern Island | Bakersfield. |
| **King, H C** | Saloon | Caliente | Kern Co | Caliente. |
| King, Jos E | Farmer | New River | Kern Co | |
| King, W J | Miner | Kern Co | nr Long Tom | Bakersfield. |
| Kiser, J H | Farmer | nr Tehichipa | Kern Co | Tehichipa. |
| Kness, Adam | Miner | Kern Co | nr Kernville | Kernville. |
| Lamonte, F A | Miner | nr Havilah | Kern Co | Havilah. |
| **Lamontaine, E** | Millwright | Kern Co | Havilah | Havilah. |
| Lamotte, W | Farmer | nr South Fork | Kern Co | Weldon. |
| Landers, W W | Stock raiser | Kern Co | South Fork | Weldon. |
| Lane, Wm | Farmer | Kern Co | Kern Island | Bakersfield. |
| **Lansing, S J** | Secretary | Kern Valley Bk | Chester Ave | Bakersfield. |
| Laughlin, Jno | Boot maker | Caliente | Kern Co | Caliente. |
| Lavers, D | Farmer | nr Linn's Valley | Kern Co | Glenville. |
| Lavers, J L | Farmer | nr Linn's Valley | Kern Co | Glenville. |
| **Lawrence & Davies** | Attorneys | Chester Ave | Bakersfield | Bakersfield. |
| **Lawrence, A C** | Attorney | Chester Ave | Bakersfield | Bakersfield. |
| Lawrence, D | Sawyer | Kern Co | Kelsoe | Havilah. |
| Lawser, C | Farmer | Kern Co | nr Walker's Basin | Havilah. |
| Lee, Alex | Teamster | nr Tejon | Kern Co | Tejon. |
| **Lee, B F** | Farmer | Kern Co | nr Tejon | Tejon. |
| Lee, J H | Clerk | 3d & Chestnut Ave | Bakersfield | Bakersfield. |
| Lee, Lysander | Ranchero | Kern Co | nr Tejon | Tejon. |
| Lennox, A | Butcher | Kern Co | Bakersfield | Bakersfield. |
| Leonard, B F | Clerk | Kern Co | Keysville | |
| **Ler, John H** | Printer | Bakersfield | Kern Co | Bakersfield. |
| Levan, F C | Miner | Sageland | Kern Co | Sageland. |
| Lewis, C B | Shoe maker | Kernville | Kern Co | Kernville. |
| Lewis, John | Miner | Kern Co | nr Kernville | Kernville. |
| **Lewis, J F** | Stock raiser | Kern Co | Linn's Valley | Glenville. |
| Lewis, J M | Miner | Kern Co | nr Greenhorn | Kernville. |
| Lewis, S C | Miner | Kern Co | nr Tehichipa | Tehichipa. |
| Lightner, A T | Farmer | nr Walker's Basin | Kern Co | Havilah. |
| **Lightner, D S** | Butcher | Kern Co | Havilah | Havilah. |
| Lightner, W | Farmer | Kern Co | nr Walker's Basin | Havilah. |
| Linn, Jackson | Miner | Kernville | Kern Co | Kernville. |
| Litchenberger, A C | Miner | Walker's Basin | Kern Co | Havilah. |
| Little, John | Farmer | Kern Co | nr Bakersfield | Bakersfield. |
| **Livelady, A J** | Saloon | Kernville | Kern Co | Kernville. |
| Lively, Joseph | Physician | Kern Co | Linn's Valley | Glenville. |
| Lochmeyer, F W | Farmer | Kern Co | nr Kelsoe Valley | Havilah. |
| Lock, S D | Butcher | Kern Co | Bakersfield | Bakersfield. |
| **Loftin, S** | Farmer | nr Cummin's Valley | Kern Co | Tehichipa. |
| Logan, Wm O | Boatman | Bakersfield | Kern Co | Bakersfield. |
| Lopez, F | Farmer | nr Bakersfield | Kern Co | Bakersfield. |
| **Lopez, M** | Farmer | nr Bakersfield | Kern Co | Bakersfield. |
| Loucks, Isaac | Miner | Kern Co | nr Havilah | Havilah. |
| Louis, Wm | Farmer | Walker's Basin | Kern Co | Havilah. |
| **Lowe, J P** | Watch maker | Bakersfield | Kern Co | Bakersfield. |
| Lucas, A | Farmer | nr Havilah | Kern Co | Havilah. |
| Lucas, James | Stockman | Kern Island | Kern Co | Bakersfield. |
| **Lucas, Wm H** | Ranchero | Cross Mountain | Kern Co | |
| Lundy, J M | Farmer | Kern Co | nr Bakersfield | Bakersfield. |
| Lundy, O J | Farmer | nr Bakersfield | Kern Co | Bakersfield. |
| Lynch, Danl | Miner | Havilah | Kern Co | Havilah. |

# WATERHOUSE & LESTER,

## IMPORTERS OF

# HARD-WOOD LUMBER

### AND ALL KINDS OF

## COACH, CARRIAGE AND WAGON MATERIALS.

IVES' HALF PATENT Steel and Iron Axles (Three grades or qualities) From the very best to a medium and low-priced Carriage and Buggy Axle.

BRIDGEPORT STEEL SPRINGS Half Patent Axles.

Concord and Kinsley Axles, —AND—

A Full Line of Carriage Hardware and Malleables.

**SARVEN PATENT WHEELS,**
BUGGY, CARRIAGE AND EXPRESS BODIES AND CARRIAGE PARTS.

Exclusive Sale on the Pacific Coast for

**CLARKE'S ADJUSTABLE**

## CARRIAGE UMBRELLA

### AND SUN SHADE,

Which is Cheaper, Lighter and Pleasanter than a Buggy Top, and can be adjusted in an instant;

AND

### WOOLSEY'S
## Patent Wheels.

Nos. 122 and 124 Market Street, and 19 and 21 California Street,

SAN FRANCISCO;

17, 19 and 21 SEVENTH STREET, between I and J, SACRAMENTO.

NEW YORK OFFICE, 121 and 123 FRONT ST., NEW YORK.

## DIRECTORY OF KERN COUNTY. 231

| Name. | Occupation. | Place of Business. | Residence. | Town or P. O. |
|---|---|---|---|---|
| Martin, R P | Miner | Kern Co | nr Havilah | Havilah. |
| Martin, T P | Miner | Kern Co | nr Kelsoe | Havilah. |
| Mason, Edmund | Miner | nr Sageland | Kern Co | Sageland. |
| Maude, A C | Farmer | Kern Island | Kern Co | Bakersfield. |
| May, F P | Farmer | nr Bakersfield | Kern Co | Bakersfield. |
| May, R C | Farmer | New River | Kern Co | |
| Mayo, C H | Farmer | nr Bakersfield | Kern Co | Bakersfield. |
| Mecham, Geo | Teamster | Kern Co | nr Kern Island | Bakersfield. |
| Meachem, R | Laborer | Kern Co | nr Bakersfield | Bakersfield. |
| Means, R | Miner | Kern Co | nr Havilah | Havilah. |
| Means, Thos A | Farmer | Bakersfield | Kern Co | Bakersfield. |
| Medlin, L L | Trader | Kern Co | Tehichipa | Tehichipa. |
| Melvin, Homer | Stock raiser | Long Tom | Kern Co | Bakersfield. |
| Melvin, R T | Saloon | Caliente | Kern Co | Caliente. |
| Melvin, R T | Farmer | Weldon | Kern Co | Weldon. |
| Menzel, W | Butcher | Kern Co | Havilah | Havilah. |
| Merrill, S P | Miner | Kern Co | nr Havilah | Havilah. |
| Meyers, Joseph | Merchant | Linn's Valley | Kern Co | Glenville. |
| Meyer, Wm | Saloon | Allen's Camp | Kern Co | Caliente. |
| Mills, Alexander | Miner | Kern Co | nr Long Tom | Bakersfield. |
| Mills, Jr, A | Well borer | Bakersfield | Kern Co | Bakersfield. |
| Mills, P | Farmer | Kern Co | nr Kern Island | Bakersfield. |
| Mills & Hodgkins | Well borers | Bakersfield | Kern Co | Bakersfield. |
| Miller, John | Miner | Havilah | Kern Co | Havilah. |
| Miller, B F | Farmer | Kern Co | nr Tehichipa | Tehichipa. |
| Miller, G | Miner | nr Piute | Kern Co | |
| Miller, H T | Hotel keeper | Kern Co | Tehichipa | Tehichipa. |
| Miller, J P | Tailor | Kern Co | Havilah | Havilah. |
| Miller, J W | Farmer | nr Linn's Valley | Kern Co | Glenville. |
| Miller, James E | Stock raiser | Weldon | Kern Co | Weldon. |
| Miller, Robert | Miner | nr Kelsoe | Kern Co | Havilah. |
| Miller, W W | Miner | nr Kelsoe | Kern Co | Havilah. |
| Milliken, G | Miner | nr Tehichipa | Kern Co | Tehichipa. |
| Millsaps, J T | Farmer | nr Tehichipa | Kern Co | Tehichipa. |
| Minter, Monroe | Farmer | nr Linn's Valley | Kern Co | Glenville. |
| Mirander, J | Farmer | Kern Co | nr South Fork | Weldon. |
| Mitchell, B F | Miner | nr Havilah | Kern Co | Havilah. |
| Mitchell, J W | Farmer | Kern Co | nr Kernville | Kernville. |
| Mix, A A | Physician | French Hotel | Bakersfield | Bakersfield. |
| Monahan, J J | Printer | Kernville | Kern Co | Kernville. |
| Montgomery, Elias | Carpenter | Delano | Kern Co | Delano. |
| Montgomery, E | Restaurant | Caliente | Caliente | Caliente. |
| Montgomery, M M | Blacksmith | Kern Co | Sageland | Sageland. |
| Montorya, R | Farmer | Bakersfield | Kern Co | Bakersfield. |
| Moran, James | Farmer | nr Bakersfield | Kern Co | Bakersfield. |
| Morden, J G | Miner | nr Havilah | Kern Co | Havilah. |
| Morgan, J A | Farmer | Tehichipa | Kern Co | Tehichipa. |
| Morgan, H H | Miner | Kern Co | nr Tehichipa | Tehichipa. |
| Morgan, Isaac | Miner | Kern Co | nr Sageland | Sageland. |
| Morham, F | Carpenter | Kern Co | Havilah | Havilah. |
| Morter, John | Farmer | New River | Kern Co | |
| Moore, Anderson | Miner | Kern Co | nr Havilah | Havilah. |
| Moore, B C | Farmer | nr Linn's Valley | Kern Co | Glenville. |
| Moore, Martin | Farmer | Walker's Basin | Kern Co | Havilah. |
| Moore, W H | Machinist | Kern Co | Bakersfield | Bakersfield. |
| Moore, Walter | Carpenter | Bakersfield | Kern Co | Bakersfield. |
| Morrall, W H | Farmer | Kern Co | nr Linn'sValley | Glenville. |
| Morris, H | Farmer | nr Bakersfield | Kern Co | Bakersfield. |
| Morrison, I N | Farmer | Linn's Valley | Kern Co | Glenville. |
| Moss, J T | Ranchero | nr Kernville | Kern Co | Kernville. |
| Mossman, Jas | Miner | Kern Co | nr Havilah | Havilah. |
| Moulinger, R | Miner | Kernville | Kern Co | Kernville. |
| Moyer, Wm | Saloon | Caliente | Kern Co | Caliente. |
| Muehe, Chas | Lodging house | Caliente | Kern Co | Caliente. |

# ANTONIO SCHIAPPA PIETRA,

### DEALER IN

# General Merchandise

## AND SHEEP-RAISER,

MAIN STREET, - SAN BUENAVENTURA,

VENTURA CO. CAL.

**Groceries, Dry Goods and Provisions,**

**READY-MADE CLOTHING, BOOTS AND SHOES,**

Cutlery, Fancy Goods, Patent Medicines,

Hardware, Tinware, Wines and Liquors,

CIGARS, TOBACCOS,

DRUGS AND CHEMICALS,

PAINTS AND OILS.

A Completely Stocked First-Class Country Store.

HAS ALSO A STOCK RANCH CONTAINING 12,500 ACRES, WELL ADAPTED TO GRAZING.

## DIRECTORY OF KERN COUNTY.

| NAME. | OCCUPATION. | PLACE OF BUSINESS. | RESIDENCE. | TOWN OR P. O. |
|---|---|---|---|---|
| Muehe, Chas | Miller | Bakersfield | Kern Co | Bakersfield. |
| Muehe, W | Miller | Kern Co | Bakersfield | Bakersfield. |
| Munn, Henry | Farmer | nr Havilah | Kern Co | Havilah. |
| Murphy, Patrick | Miner | nr Havilah | Kern Co | Havilah. |
| Murphy, Q | Miner | Kern Co | nr Kernville | Kernville. |
| Murphy, Thos | Miner | nr Long Tom | Kern Co | Bakersfield. |
| **Murray, J J** | Farmer | nr Tehichipa | Kern Co | Tehichipa. |
| Mury, Jas | Ranchero | nr Bakersfield | Kern Co | Bakersfield. |
| Myers, Jasper | Farmer | Kern Co | nr Kern Island | Bakersfield. |
| **Nadeau, Jos** | Cerro gordo fire co | Caliente | Kern Co | Caliente. |
| Nadeau, R | Superintendent do | Caliente | Los Angeles | Caliente. |
| Nagle, J G | Miner | nr Sageland | Kern Co | Sageland. |
| Narboe, J | Farmer | Kern Co | nr Tehichipa | Tehichipa. |
| **Narboe, P** | Stock raiser | Kern Co | nr Tehichipa | Tehichipa. |
| Narboe, P M | Farmer | nr Tehichipa | Kern Co | Tehichipa. |
| Nash, W | Miner | Kern Co | nr Kernville | Kernville. |
| Nations, I W | Blacksmith | Kern Co | Reservation | |
| Navarro, J | Laborer | nr Bakersfield | Kern Co | Bakersfield. |
| **Nead, John** | Carpenter | Kern Co | Havilah | Havilah. |
| Neckar, John | Miner | Kern Co | nr Bakersfield | Bakersfield. |
| Neeson, J H | Farmer | nr Havilah | Kern Co | Havilah. |
| Neese, S | Farmer | nr Walker's Basin | Kern Co | Havilah. |
| Neff, Bernard | Stone cutter | Kern Co | Havilah | Havilah. |
| **Neideraun, Jacob** | Cabinet maker | Kern Co | Bakersfield | Bakersfield. |
| Nelson, J | Hostler | Kern Co | Linn's Valley | Glenville. |
| Nelson, S P | Miner | nr Havilah | Kern Co | Havilah. |
| Nester, M E | Miner | nr Walker's Basin | Kern Co | Havilah. |
| **Neuffer, J G** | Sheep raiser | nr Linn's Valley | Kern Co | Glenville. |
| Nicoll, John | Farmer | Kern Co | nr South Fork | Weldon. |
| **Niedaraur J** | Furniture | 3d st | Bakersfield | Bakersfield. |
| Niles, J E | Farmer | Kern Co | nr Walker's Basin | Havilah. |
| Niles, J H | Mail carrier | Kern Co | Bakersfield | Bakersfield. |
| **Noble, H** | Farmer | nr Bakersfield | Kern Co | Bakersfield. |
| Norris, B | Farmer | nr Tehichipa | Kern Co | Tehichipa. |
| Norton, Danl | Carpenter | Kern Co | Bakersfield | Bakersfield. |
| **Norton, J B** | Carpenter | Kern Co | Bakersfield | Bakersfield. |
| Nye, Chas H | Miner | Kernville | Kern Co | Kernville. |
| Ober, Geo K | Farmer | Panama | Kern Co | Panama. |
| O'Brien, J E | Miner | Kern Co | nr Walker's Basin | Havilah. |
| O'Brien, John | Miner | nr Walker's Basin | Kern Co | Havilah. |
| **O'Brien, John** | Farmer | Kern Co | nr Willow Spring | |
| O'Connor, J | Miner | nr Havilah | Kern Co | Havilah. |
| O'Donnell, Edwd | Farmer | Kern Co | nr Bakersfield | Bakersfield. |
| O'Haloran, J | Miner | Kern Co | nr Kernville | Kernville. |
| O'Hare, Peter | Miner | nr Bakersfield | Kern Co | Bakersfield. |
| O'Laughlin, J | Miner | Kernville | Kern Co | Kernville. |
| **Olds, H P** | Propr james hotel | Bakersfield | Kern Co | Bakersfield. |
| O'Neal, H | Saloon keeper | Kern Co | Havilah | Havilah. |
| Orioden, Jefferson | Miner | nr Kernville | Kern Co | Kernville. |
| Orioden, M | Farmer | nr Walker's Basin | Kern Co | Havilah. |
| Oriot, Edmund | Miner | nr Sageland | Kern Co | Sageland. |
| **Ormsby, C B** | Ranchero | Kern Co | nr Bakersfield | Bakersfield. |
| Ossa, A de la | Ranchero | Kern Co | nr Bakersfield | Bakersfield. |
| Otterman, Thos J | Miner | Kernville | Kern Co | Kernville. |
| Ownby, J P | Carpenter | Kern Co | Linn's Valley | Glenville. |
| **Owen, S M** | Stock raiser | Panama | Kern Co | Panama. |
| Owen, Wm | Miner | Kern Co | nr Havilah | Havilah. |
| Oyler, John F | Hotel keeper | Kern Co | Keysville | |
| **Packard, N R** | Merchant | Caliente | Kern Co | Caliente. |
| Packard, W | Farmer | nr Kernville | Kern Co | Kernville. |
| Paine, E D | Laborer | Kern Co | nr Bakersfield | Bakersfield. |
| Palmer, R | Miner | Kern Co | nr Kelsoe | Havilah. |
| **Paluis, E C** | Ranchero | nr Bakersfield | Kern Co | Bakersfield. |
| Park, H C | Book keeper | Bakersfield | Kern Co | Bakersfield. |

# WEED FAMILY WEED

The great improvements that the WEED FAMILY SEWING MACHINE COMPANY have made on their Machines in the last year, enables them to put before the public the BEST FAMILY Machine in the market. See them before purchasing elsewhere.

## T. H. PORTER,
Agent for Lake and Napa Counties.

## A. MEAD & CO.,
152 NEW MONTGOMERY STREET, SAN FRANCISCO,
General Agents for the Pacific Coast.

## DIRECTORY OF KERN COUNTY. 235

| Name. | Occupation. | Place of Business. | Residence. | Town or P. O. |
|---|---|---|---|---|
| Park, H J | Miner | Kern Co | nr Havilah | Havilah. |
| Parkhurst, D W | Contractor | Tehichipa | Kern Co | Tehichipa. |
| Pascal, C | Miner | Kern Co | nr Havilah | Havilah. |
| Pascoe, Henry | Farmer | nr Linn's Valley | Kern Co | Glenville. |
| Pascoe, Jeptha | Farmer | Kern Co | nr Linn's Valley | Glenville. |
| Patterson, J M | Farmer | Kern Co | nr South Fork | Weldon. |
| Patty, T N | Farmer | Tehichipa | Kern Co | Tehichipa. |
| Paull, Crockett | Grocer | Linn's Valley | Kern Co | Glenville. |
| Payne, W | Miner | nr Linn's Valley | Kern Co | Glenville. |
| Peasely, R K | Farmer | Kern Co | nr Tehichipa | Tehichipa. |
| Peet, D E | Miner | nr Kernville | Kern Co | Kernville. |
| Pemberton, J C | Farmer | nr Kernville | Kern Co | Kernville. |
| Pemberton, W | Farmer | nr Kernville | Kern Co | Kernville. |
| Pendleton, A B | Engineer | Kern Co | Havilah | Havilah. |
| Pennoyer, J F | Wheelwright | Kernville | Kern Co | Kernville. |
| Pensinger, J | Teamster | Kern Island | Kern Co | Bakersfield. |
| Peregoy, B P | Miller | Kern Co | Linn's Valley | Glenville. |
| Peters, Chas | Farmer | Tehichipa | Kern Co | Tehichipa. |
| Peterson, N P | Miner | nr Kernville | Kern Co | Kernville. |
| Pettys, J E | Trader | Kern Co | Bakersfield | Bakersfield. |
| Peyton, T B | Farmer | Kern Co | nr Linn's Valley | Glenville. |
| Phippeny, H | Farmer | Bakersfield | Kern Co | Bakersfield. |
| Piepmire, E A F | Miner | Kern Co | nr Piute | Piute. |
| Pierce, Uriah W | Farmer | nr Linn's Valley | Kern Co | Glenville. |
| Pike, John | Miner | Kern Co | nr Sageland | Sageland. |
| Pinley, J | Farmer | nr Tehichipa | Kern Co | Tehichipa. |
| Pinnell, George | Miner | Kern Co | nr Long Tom | Bakersfield. |
| Polkingham, T | Miner | nr Kernville | Kern Co | Kernville. |
| Pope, C A | Peddler | Kern Co | Havilah | Havilah. |
| Pope, W H | Barber | Bakersfield | Kern Co | Bakersfield. |
| Potillo, J D | Laborer | nr Kernville | Kern Co | Kernville. |
| Potts, Hiram | Farmer | nr Bakersfield | Kern Co | Bakersfield. |
| Powell, W A | Engineer | Kern Co | Walker's Basin | Havilah. |
| Powell, D A | Engineer | Walker's Basin | Kern Co | Havilah. |
| Powell, P S | Farmer | nr Linn's Valley | Kern Co | Glenville. |
| Powers, Wm H | Stable keeper | Bakersfield | Kern Co | Bakersfield. |
| Prater, E B | Prospector | Kern Co | Havilah | Havilah. |
| Pratt, W C | Farmer | Kern Co | nr Bakersfield | Bakersfield. |
| Prewitt, E | Farmer | nr Bakersfield | Kern Co | Bakersfield. |
| Prewett, James | Farmer | Linn's Valley | Kern Co | Glenville. |
| Prewitt, J, Jr | Teacher | Kern Co | Kern Islai d | Bakersfield. |
| Purcell, Michael | Blacksmith | Kern Co | Bakersfield | Bakersfield. |
| Pyle, J F | Miner | nr Long Tom | Kern Co | Bakersfield. |
| Quinn, Thos J | Farmer | Tehichipa | Kern Co | Tehichipa. |
| Quarrier, Wm M | Farmer | Fort Tejon | Kern Co | Tejon. |
| Rackliff, B C | Miner | Kern Co | nr Havilah | Havilah. |
| Raguin, G W | Farmer | nr South Fork | Kern Co | Weldon. |
| Ramey, M | Laborer | Kern Co | nr South Fork | Weldon. |
| Randall, P | Farmer | Kern Island | Kern Co | Bakersfield. |
| Rankin, W | Ranchero | Kern Co | nr Walker's Basin | Havilah. |
| Randolph, Hamilton | Millwright | Kern Co | Bakersfield | Bakersfield. |
| Rathbone, Geo C | Laborer | Kernville | Kern Co | Kernville. |
| Rawling, J S | Miner | nr Havilah | Kern Co | Havilah. |
| Raymond, F S | Jeweler | Kern Co | Havilah | Havilah. |
| Reading, E M Y | Druggist | Kern Co | Bakersfield | Bakersfield. |
| Reading, H A | Farmer | | Kern Co | |
| Reed, Andrew | Miner | Kern Co | nr Greenhorn | Kernville. |
| Reeder, L R | Farmer | Kern Co | nr Bakersfield | Bakersfield. |
| Reed, S E | Blacksmith | Kern Co | Linn's Valley | Glenville. |
| Reed, Theron | Lawyer | Kern Co | Havilah | Havilah. |
| Reed, Wm C | Speculator | Bakersfield | Kern Co | Bakersfield. |
| Reeg, Geo | Farmer | Kern Co | nr Tehichipa | Tehichipa. |
| Reid, G P | Miner | Kern Co | nr Kelsoe | Havilah. |

# DOWN WITH MONOPOLY.
## The Grangers' Favorite
### AND CHAMPION OF THE WORLD.

IS NOISELESS, SEWS FASTER, RUNS LIGHTER,
AND HAS GREATER MECHANICAL SIMPLICITY
THAN ANY OTHER MACHINE IN THE WORLD.
THE WINNER AT LONDON, 1862; PARIS, 1867; VIENNA, 1873.

## WHEELER & WILSON,
### Improved Draw-Feed Sewing Machine!
IS THE ONLY LOCK-STITCH WITHOUT A SHUTTLE.

#### DISTINGUISHED HONORS.

WORLD'S EXPOSITION, VIENNA, Nov. 1, 1873.—"The Emperor of Austria has conferred the Imperial Order of Francis Joseph on the Hon. Nathaniel Weeeler, President of the celebrated Wheeler & Wilson Sewing Machine Company of New York.

The Best is the Cheapest. Buy no machine until you have seen the New "Draw-Feed Wheeler & Wilson." It will last a lifetime. Every Purchaser made a perfect operator. ALL MACHINES GUARANTEED.

### Sold on Easy Terms.

SPECIAL ATTENTION GIVEN TO ORDERS SENT TO

## E. W. HARRAL, No. 20 Geary Street, San Francisco.

# DIRECTORY OF KERN COUNTY. 237

| NAME. | OCCUPATION. | PLACE OF BUSINESS. | RESIDENCE. | TOWN OR P. O. |
|---|---|---|---|---|
| Reid, J C............ | Farmer............. | Kern Co................... | nr Linn's Valley...... | Glenville. |
| Reine, Guillaume ... | Farmer ............. | Kern Co.................... | Kern Island............ | Bakersfield. |
| Reinhart, C H....... | Carpenter .......... | Kernville............... | Kern Co................ | Kernville. |
| **Reinstein, P** ........ | Harness............ | Caliente................. | Caliente............... | Caliente. |
| Reische, T ........... | Miner ............... | Kern Co................... | New El Dorado....... | |
| Remington, S O ..... | Miller ............... | Kern Co.................. | Havilah................. | Havilah. |
| **Rena, Jose**........... | Farmer ............. | nr Bakersfield......... | Kern Co................ | Bakersfield. |
| Rhodes, E J.......... | Teacher............. | Kern Co................... | Canfield................ | Bakersfield. |
| Rhodes, R M......... | R R employee..... | Delano.................... | Kern Co................ | Delano. |
| **Rhymes, J J**........ | Farmer ............. | nr Linn's Valley...... | Kern Co................ | Glenville. |
| Rice, J E............... | Farmer ............. | nr Havilah.............. | Kern Co................ | Havilah. |
| Rice, S M.............. | Teamster........... | nr Havilah.............. | Kern Co................ | Havilah. |
| Richards, Thos...... | Farmer ............. | nr Kernville........... | Kern Co................ | Kernville. |
| **Richardson, John**.. | Saloon keeper.... | Tehichipa............... | Kern Co................ | Tehichipa. |
| Riddle, Jos .......... | Farmer ............. | nr South Fork......... | Kern Co................ | Weldon. |
| Riley, J A............. | Miner ............... | Bakersfield............. | Kern Co................ | Bakersfield. |
| **Riley, J R**............. | Phys'n & drugg't | Chester Ave............ | Bakersfield........... | Bakersfield. |
| Ringualt, J H.,...... | Laborer............. | Kernville............... | Kern Co................ | Kernville. |
| Rings, J ................ | Farmer ............. | Kern Co................... | nr Walker's Basin... | Havilah. |
| **Riser, T A**............ | Carpenter......... | Kernville............... | Kern Co................ | Kernville. |
| Rison, R A............. | Miner ............... | nr Havilah.............. | Kern Co................ | Havilah. |
| Rivers, Harry....... | Lumber............. | Kern Co................... | Kern Island............ | Bakersfield. |
| **Robb,** —.............. | Lumber............. | Bakersfield............. | Kern Co................ | Bakersfield. |
| Robb, H D............. | Farme............... | Panama.................. | Kern Co................ | Panama. |
| Robb, Jno S.......... | Farmer ............. | Westfield................ | Kern Co................ | |
| Roberts, J V......... | Farmer ............. | nr South Fork......... | Kern Co................ | Weldon. |
| **Roberts, H** .......... | Carpenter ......... | Kern Co................... | South Fork............ | Weldon. |
| Roberts, Thos ...... | Farmer ............. | Kern Co................... | nr Bakersfield........ | Bakersfield. |
| Roberts, W H....... | Miner ............... | nr Sageland............ | Kern Co................ | Sageland. |
| Robertson, J H...... | Teamster........... | nr Tehichipa........... | Kern Co................ | Tehichipa. |
| Robertson, S ........ | Laborer............. | Tehichipa............... | Kern Co................ | Tehichipa. |
| **Robinson, B F**...... | Farmer ............. | nr Havilah.............. | Kern Co................ | Havilah. |
| Robinson, S........... | Farmer ............. | Kern Co................... | nr Havilah............. | Havilah. |
| **Robinson, H**......... | Saloon............... | Caliente................. | Caliente................ | Caliente. |
| Rogers, A............. | Miner ............... | nr Bakersfield......... | Kern Co................ | Bakersfield. |
| Rogers, Jesse....... | Teamster........... | Kern Co................... | nr Bakersfield........ | Bakersfield. |
| **Rogers, L S** ......... | Physician .......... | Kern Co................... | Bakersfield........... | Bakersfield. |
| Rolf, Alfred........... | Wheelwright..... | Kern Co................... | Havilah................. | Havilah. |
| Roper, F............... | Lumber............. | Bakersfield............. | Kern Co................ | Bakersfield. |
| Rose, A E.............. | Miner ............... | nr Havilah.............. | Kern Co................ | Havilah. |
| Rosemyer, J V...... | Ranchero .......... | Kern Co................... | Tejon Ranch.......... | Tejon. |
| **Ross, G B** ............ | Saloon............... | Caliente................. | Caliente................ | Caliente. |
| Roth, E................. | Merchant........... | Kern Co................... | Bakersfield........... | Bakersfield. |
| Rothrock, G H...... | Mechanic........... | Bakersfield............. | Bakersfield........... | Bakersfield. |
| Rothstein, E. ........ | Miner ............... | nr Kernville........... | Kern Co................ | Kernville. |
| Rupp, John........... | Gardener........... | Kern Co................... | Walker's Basin...... | Havilah. |
| Russell, C............. | Vaquero............ | Kern Co................... | Cummin's Valley.... | Tehichipa. |
| **Russell, S A** ........ | Carpenter.......... | Kernville............... | Kern Co................ | Kernville. |
| Rush, Frank......... | Farmer ............. | nr Havilah.............. | Kern Co................ | Havilah. |
| Rutledge, P.......... | Farmer ............. | Woody's................. | Kern Co................ | |
| Ryan, Jas............. | Miner ............... | nr Havilah.............. | Kern Co................ | Havilah. |
| Ryan, John........... | Farmer ............. | nr Walker's Basin... | Kern Co................ | Havilah. |
| **Sageley, R B**........ | Assessor ............ | Kern Co................... | Havilah................. | Havilah. |
| Said, B R.............. | Carpenter .......... | New River.............. | Kern Co................ | |
| Salazar, P............. | Farmer ............. | nr San Emidio......... | Kern Co................ | Bakersfield. |
| Sanders, J H........ | Farmer.............. | nr Greenhorn.......... | Kern Co................ | Kernville. |
| Scarff, J P............ | Farmer ............. | Tehichipa............... | Kern Co................ | Tehichipa. |
| **Schlachter, T**....... | Brewer.............. | 2d st...................... | Bakersfield........... | Bakersfield. |
| Schnall, H............. | Farmer ............. | nr Greenhorn.......... | Kern Co................ | Kernville. |
| Schubert, J M....... | Moulder............ | Kern Co................... | Walker's Basin...... | Havilah. |
| **Schuetzler, J M**..... | Wine grower...... | Kern Co................... | Walker's Basin...... | Havilah. |
| Schwerr, C E........ | Miner ............... | nr Havilah.............. | Kern Co................ | Havilah. |
| Scobie, James....... | Farmer ............. | Agua Caliente......... | Kern Co ............... | Caliente. |
| **Scott, David**......... | Farmer . ........... | Kern Co................... | nr Linn's Valley..... | Glenville. |

| Name. | Occupation. | Place of Business. | Residence. | Town or P. O. |
|---|---|---|---|---|
| Scott, Robert | Miner | Kernville | Kern Co | Kernville. |
| Scott, Richardson | Miner | Kern Co | nr Havilah | Havilah. |
| Sebring, A | Miner | Havilah | Kern Co | Havilah. |
| Seibert, Chs | Farmer | Kern Co | nr Cummin's Valley | Tehichipa. |
| Sewall, J | Laborer | Kernville | Kern Co | Kernville. |
| **Sewall, T C** | Farmer | Woody's | Kern Co | |
| Seymour, H | Farmer | nr Bakersfield | Kern Co | Bakersfield. |
| Shackleford, B | Vaquero | Kern Co | nr Tehichipa | Tehichipa. |
| Shackleford, D | Farmer | nr Tehichipa | Kern Co | Tehichipa. |
| **Shannan, B** | Carpenter | Kern Co | Bakersfield | Bakersfield. |
| Sharp, W | Miner | nr Bakersfield | Kern Co | Bakersfield. |
| Shaw, J B | Moulder | Kernville | Kern Co | Havilah. |
| Shelby, Danl | Farmer | nr Bakersfield | Kern Co | Bakersfield. |
| **Sheldon, John** | Blacksmith | Kern Co | Bakersfield | Bakersfield. |
| Sheres, Samuel | Laborer | Panama | Kern Co | Panama. |
| Sheridan, James | Miner | Caliente | Kern Co | Caliente. |
| Short, J W | Blacksmith | Kern Co | Bakersfield | Bakersfield. |
| Short, W H | Farmer | Kern Co | Kern Co | |
| **Shultz, E G** | Farmer | New River | Kern Co | |
| Shults, J C | Farmer | nr Kern Island | Kern Co | Bakersfield. |
| Sidles, Henry | Blacksmith | Kern Co | Bakersfield | Bakersfield. |
| Sillman, L H | Farmer | Kern Co | Bakersfield | Bakersfield. |
| **Simon, Jacob** | Miller | Kern Co | Havilah | Havilah. |
| Simmons, F | Farmer | Tehichipa | Kern Co | Tehichipa. |
| Sinclair, D W | Merchant | Kern Co | Havilah | Havilah. |
| Smith, A H | Stock raiser | Kern Co | Temple Ranch | |
| Smith, A P | Miller | Kern Co | Bakersfield | Bakersfield. |
| Smith, A T | Miner | nr Long Tom | Kern Co | Bakersfield. |
| Smith, C G | Farmer | Kern Co | nr Bakersfield | Bakersfield. |
| **Smith, David** | Druggist | Bakersfield | Kern Co | Bakersfield. |
| Smith, E L | Clerk | Bakersfield | Kern Co | Bakersfield. |
| **Smith, Geo V** | Lawyer | Bakersfield | Kern Co | Bakersfield. |
| Smith, J E | Blacksmith | Kern Co | Bakersfield | Bakersfield. |
| Smith, J F | Farmer | Kern Co | nr Tehichipa | Tehichipa. |
| **Smith, J M** | Farmer | nr Tehichipa | Kern Co | Tehichipa. |
| Smith, J W | Carpenter | Kern Co | Bakersfield | Bakersfield. |
| Smith, R W | Vaquero | Kern Co | nr Long Tom | Bakersfield. |
| Smith, T H | Farmer | nr South Fork | Kern Co | Weldon. |
| Smith, V B | Miner | nr Long Tom | Kern Co | Bakersfield. |
| **Smith, W H** | Printer | Kern Co | Havilah | Havilah. |
| Smithwick, E | Farmer | Kern Co | nr Linn's Valley | Glenville. |
| Smithwick, T P | Farmer | nr Linn's Valley | Kern Co | Glenville. |
| Snodderly, E S | Farmer | Kern Co | nr Bakersfield | Bakersfield. |
| Sohn, P | Shoe maker | Caliente | Kern Co | Caliente. |
| **Sork, L** | Butcher | Kern Co | Bakersfield | Bakersfield. |
| Spencer, Hubbard | Farmer | nr Tehichipa | Kern Co | Tehichipa. |
| Spinney, G | Farmer | Kern Co | nr Bakersfield | Bakersfield. |
| **Sprague, G F** | Eclectric phys | Arlington House | Bakersfield | Bakersfield. |
| Springer, B | Butcher | Caliente | Kern Co | Caliente. |
| Spurgeon, Aaron | Farmer | nr Bakersfield | Kern Co | Bakersfield. |
| **Spurgeon, G J** | Blacksmith | Kern Co | Bakersfield | Bakersfield. |
| Staff, W W | Miner | Kern Co | nr Havilah | Havilah. |
| Stalle, W E | Blacksmith | Kern Co | Tejon | Tejon. |
| **Staples, G H** | Merchant | Kern Co | Kernville | Kernville. |
| Staples, F H | Miner | nr Kernville | Kern Co | Kernville. |
| Stark, S J | Farmer | Kern Co | nr Tebichipa | Tehichipa. |
| Starkey, L | Laborer | Kern Co | nr Bakersfield | Bakersfield. |
| Starr, W C | Blacksmith | Kern Co | Havilah | Havilah. |
| **Stearns, W W** | Contractor | Kern Co | Kernville | Kernville. |
| Steel, Andrew | Machinist | Kern Co | Tejon | Tejon. |
| **Steele, David** | French hotel | Bakersfield | Kern Co | Bakersfield. |
| **Stephens, A L** | Builder | Kern Co | Bakersfield | Bakersfield. |
| Stephens, E | Farmer | Bakersfield | Kern Co | Bakersfield. |
| Stephens, G Van S | R R employee | Caliente | Kern Co | Caliente. |

# DIRECTORY OF KERN COUNTY. 239

| Name. | Occupation. | Place of Business. | Residence. | Town or P. O. |
|---|---|---|---|---|
| Stephens, W | Miner | nr Bakersfield | Kern Co | Bakersfield. |
| Stephenson, J | Farmer | Kern Co | nr Tehichipa | Tehichipa. |
| Stephenson, M R | Farmer | Tehichipa | Kern Co | Tehichipa. |
| Stevenson, H | Stock raiser | nr Kernville | Kern Co | Kernville. |
| Stockton, I D | Farmer | nr Kern Island | Kern Co | Bakersfield. |
| Stoel, M J | Millwright | Kern Co | Bakersfield | Bakersfield. |
| Stine, P W | Farmer | Kern Co | nr Bakersfield | Bakersfield. |
| Stone, W L | Stageman | Bakersfield | Kern Co | Bakersfield. |
| Stordenburgh, T A | Lawyer | Kernville | Kern Co | Kernville. |
| Stover, J H | Carpenter | Kernville | Kern Co | Kernville. |
| Strainler, H D | Farmer | Kern Co | nr South Fork | Weldon. |
| Strauss, G | Miner | Kern Co | nr Tehichipa | Tehichipa. |
| Stricklang, H | Miner | ur Kernville | Kern Co | Kernville. |
| Strong, C L | Miner | Kern Co | nr Kernville | Kernville. |
| Stubbs, James | Farmer | Delano | Kern Co | Delano. |
| Suedden, S | Miner | Kern Co | nr Kernville | Kernville. |
| Sullivan, C | Ranchero | Tehichipa | Kern Co | Tehichipa. |
| Sullivan, F H | Farmer | Kern Co | nr Linn's Valley | Glenville. |
| Sumner, J W | Miner | nr Kernville | Kern Co | Kernville. |
| Suviate, R | Blacksmith | Kern Co | Panama | Panama. |
| Swan, Jas | Lumberman | Kern Co | South Fork | Weldon. |
| Swift, R | Farmer | New River | Kern Co | Bakersfield. |
| Swiggart, T C | Trader | Kern Co | Tehichipa | Tehichipa. |
| Swinney, Wm G | Farmer | Westfield | Kern Co | Bakersfield. |
| Tarlton, P | Miner | nr Sageland | Kern Co | Sageland. |
| Tarwater, G T | Miner | Sageland | Kern Co | Sageland. |
| Tassara & Castagneto | Fruit store | Caliente | Kern Co | Caliente. |
| Tassara, Augt | Fruit store | Caliente | Caliente | Caliente. |
| Tate, John | Laborer | nr Bakersfield | Kern Co | Bakersfield. |
| Taylor, A L | Teamster | nr Kernville | Kern Co | Kernville. |
| Taylor, J S | Teamster | nr Bakersfield | Kern Co | Bakersfield. |
| Taylor, R R | Farmer | Kern Co | nr Tehichipa | Tehichipa. |
| Taylor, Thos | Farmer | nr Bakersfield | Kern Co | Bakersfield. |
| Taylor, W A | Farmer | nr Tehichipa | Kern Co | Tehichipa. |
| Taylor & Giles | Blacksmiths | Tehichipa | Kern Co | Tehichipa. |
| Templeton, B S | Stock raiser | Kern Co | South Fork | Weldon. |
| Thomas, J N | Blacksmith | Kern Co | Bakersfield | Bakersfield. |
| Thompson, G W | Miner | nr Tehichipa | Kern Co | Tehichipa. |
| Thompson, J H | Blacksmith | Walker's Basin | Kern Co | Havilah. |
| Thompson, Jas | Miner | Kern Co | nr Long Tom | Bakersfield. |
| Thompson, Jas | Farmer | Kern Co | nr Long Tom | Bakersfield. |
| Thompson, J P | Stage driver | Kern Co | Bakersfield | Bakersfield. |
| Thompson, S B | Engineer | Kern Co | Kernville | Kernville. |
| Thompson, T | Laborer | Kern Co | nr Bakersfield | Bakersfield. |
| Thompson, W H | Farmer | Kern Co | nr Cummin's Valley | Tohichipa. |
| Thurman, F M | Stock raiser | Kern Co | Tehichipa | Tehichipa. |
| Thurman, S D | Farmer | nr Tehichipa | Kern Co | Tehichipa. |
| Tibbett, E | Farmer | Kern Co | nr Bakersfield | Bakersfield. |
| Tibbett, P | Trader | Kern Co | Bakersfield | Bakersfield. |
| Ticknor, Benj | Farmer | nr Kelsoe | Kern Co | Havilah. |
| Tilley, J L | Miner | nr Kernville | Kern Co | Kernville. |
| Tilley, Thos | Miner | Kern Co | nr Kernville | Kernville. |
| Timberlake, H C | Engineer | Kern Co | Havilah | Havilah. |
| Tives, J H | Blacksmith | Kernville | Kern Co | Kernville. |
| Todd, H L | Miner | Kern Co | nr Havilah | Havilah. |
| Totty, J S | Farmer | nr South Fork | Kern Co | Weldon. |
| Towery, J R | Farmer | Kern Co | nr Linn's Valley | Glenville. |
| Tracy, F A | Stock raiser | Kern Co | Bakersfield | Bakersfield. |
| Trainer, W H | Miner | nr Walker's Basin | Kern Co | Havilah. |
| Treon, H W C | Miner | nr Kernville | Kern Co | Kernville. |
| Tresize, Wm | Miner | Kern Co | nr Kernville | Kernville. |
| Tribble, J R | Clerk | Kern Co | Linn's Valley | Glenville. |
| Troy, Danl | Stock raiser | Kern Co | Bakersfield | Bakersfield. |

# BAKER & HAMILTON,

**13 to 19 Front St.** | **9 to 15 J St.**

SAN FRANCISCO. | SACRAMENTO.

MANUFACTORY

**Sweepstake Plow Co.**
**San Leandro.**

CAUTION.—We are the only importers of the genuine Buffalo Pitts Threshers. There are numerous imitations, and purchasers should be certain to see that all have our name on them if they desire the genuine.

**Ames Threshing Engine.**

PITTS "GENUINE" BUFFALO THRESHER.

The Ames Portable and Threshing Engines are made with special reference to the requirements of this Coast.

Our terms are liberal, and we are determined not to be undersold.

## WE HAVE THE
# BEST STOCK OF HARDWARE ON THE COAST.

SOLE AGENTS FOR Gem Sowers, Cahorn Sowers, Bain Wagons, Sweepstake Spring Wagons.

Pitts Buffalo Powers, Baxter Engines, Burr-Stone Grist Mills, Non-pareil Grist Mills.

THE CELEBRATED CHAMPION SELF-RAKE REAPER AND MOWER.

**Sweepstake and Eureka Gang Plows.**
The Sweepstake Plow Co. make the best Gangs in the world. Universally esteemed superior to all others. Send for list.

THE "BAIN" WAGON.

The Sweepstake Single-Gear Headers as sold by us are the best in the State. The improvements are adapted to this Coast, and the Header is complete in every respect. Made to cut from 10 to 24 feet.

The "Bain" is the only wagon which will stand the dry climate of California. Every wagon sold gives perfect satisfaction, and is a model of neatness and beauty, combined with strength.

We are sole agents for
THE GENUINE
**Haines Headers.**

SEND FOR OUR
**CATALOGUE.**

**SWEEPSTAKE SINGLE-GEAR HEADERS.**

## DIRECTORY OF KERN COUNTY. 241

| Name. | Occupation. | Place of Business. | Residence. | Town or P. O. |
|---|---|---|---|---|
| Troy, Jerome | Farmer | Kern Co | Lower Kern River | |
| Troy, L. | Sheep raiser | nr Bakersfield | Kern Co | Bakersfield. |
| Tucker, A P | Miner | Kern Co | nr Long Tom | Bakersfield. |
| Tucker, H J | Miner | nr Long Tom | Kern Co | Bakersfield. |
| Tungate, — | Sample room | Bakersfield | Kern Co | Bakersfield. |
| Tungate, G W | Teamster | Kern Co | nr Havilah | Havilah. |
| Tungate, J B | Miner | Kern Co | nr Havilah | Havilah. |
| Turman, J M | Teamster | Sageland | Kern Co | Sageland. |
| Turner, James | Plumber | Allen's Camp | Kern Co | Caliente. |
| Turner, S | Farmer | nr Linn's Valley | Kern Co | Glenville. |
| Tyler, M A | Farmer | nr Tehichipa | Kern Co | Tehichipa. |
| Tyler, Hial | Miner | Kern Co | Cross Mill | |
| Underwood, J | Stock raiser | Kern Co | South Fork | Weldon. |
| Valles, L C | Laborer | Kern Co | nr Walker's Basin | Havilah. |
| Valencia, C | Farmer | nr Bakersfield | Kern Co | Bakersfield. |
| Valenzuela, E | Vaquero | Kern Island | Kern Co | Bakersfield. |
| Van Buskirk, R | Shoe maker | Kernville | Kern Co | Kernville. |
| Van Nostran, F M | Miner | nr Kernville | Kern Co | Kernville. |
| Van Noy, Z J | Miner | Kern Co | nr Greenhorn | Kernville. |
| Van Ormen, N | Engineer | Kern Co. | Bakersfield | Bakersfield. |
| Vascas, J J | Miner | Kern Co | nr Havilah | Havilah. |
| Vaughn, B | Brick maker | Linn's Valley | Kern Co | Glenville. |
| Vaughn, E | Farmer | nr Linn's Valley | Kern Co | Glenville. |
| Vaughn, O F | Farmer | Kern Co | nr Linn's Valley | Glenville. |
| Vaughn, T C | Farmer | nr Linn's Valley | Kern Co | Glenville. |
| Vaughn, W | Mason | Kern Co | Linn's Valley | Glenville. |
| Veach, J W | Laborer | Kern Co | nr Havilah | Havilah. |
| Veeder, C H | Attorney | Kern Co | Bakersfield | Bakersfield. |
| Veeder, J B | Teamster | nr Bakersfield | Kern Co | Bakersfield. |
| Voege, Peter | Miner | nr Havilah | Kern Co | Havilah. |
| Waldou, P J | Farmer | Kern Co | nr Kern Island | Bakersfield. |
| Walker, B F | Miner | Kern Co | nr Havilah | Havilah. |
| Walker, Edwd | Chair maker | Havilah | Kern Co | Havilah. |
| Walker, John | Miner | Kern Co | nr Havilah | Havilah. |
| Walker, L B | Farmer | Kern Island | Kern Co | Bakersfield. |
| Walker, Wm | Miner | Kern Co | nr Kernville | Kernville. |
| Walker, W B | Farmer | Kern Co | nr Kernville | Ker ville. |
| Wallace, J T | Laborer | nr Greenhorn | Kern Co | Kernville. |
| Wallace, Thos | Miner | Allen's Camp | Kern Co | Caliente. |
| Waller, Thos | Farmer | Kern Co | Linn's Valley | Glenville. |
| Walls & Ault | Saloon | Caliente | | Caliente. |
| Walls, D L | Saloon | Caliente | Caliente | Caliente. |
| Walser, D W | Stock drover | Havilah | Kern Co | Havilah. |
| Walters, John | Farmer | South Fork | Kern Co | Weldon. |
| Ward, Nelson | Hotel keeper | Kern Co | Tehichipa | Tehichipa. |
| Ward, R | Farmer | nr Kernville | Kern Co | Kernville. |
| Warren, F | Miner | Kern Co | Paso Flat | |
| Warren, R A | Miner | Havilah | Kern Co | Havilah. |
| Watson, Henry | Miner | Greenhorn | Kern Co | Kernville. |
| Watson, Thos H | Teamster | Bakersfield | Kern Co | Bakersfield. |
| Watson, J R | Farmer | nr Sageland | Kern Co | Sageland. |
| Watts, G W | Miner | nr Kernville | Kern Co | Kernville. |
| Wattiez, L | Hotel keeper | Kern Co | Havilah | Havilah. |
| Wear, S C | Farmer | nr Bakersfield | Kern Co | Bakersfield. |
| Weaver, Jno L | Farmer | New River | Kern Co | Bakersfield. |
| Weaver, P M | Farmer | New River | Kern Co | Bakersfield. |
| Webb, C H | Miner | Kern Co | White River | Bakersfield. |
| Webb, Jas | Hostler | Kern Co | Kernville | Kernville. |
| Webb, J F | Miner | Kernville | Kern Co | Kernville. |
| Weier, W F | Miner | nr Bakersfield | Kern Co | Bakersfield. |
| Weil, J & Co | Gen merchandise | 3d st | Bakersfield | Bakersfield. |
| Welch, John | Farmer | Kern Co | nr Linn's Valley | Glenville. |
| Weldon, W B | Farmer | nr South Fork | Kern Co | Weldon. |
| Wells, M P | Teamster | Kern Co | nr Havilah | Havilah. |

| Name. | Occupation. | Place of Business. | Residence. | Town or P. O. |
|---|---|---|---|---|
| Welsh, M............ | Miner ............ | Kern Co ............ | nr Havilah............ | Havilah. |
| Welsh, W W........ | Miner ............ | nr Havilah............ | Kern Co............ | Havilah. |
| Werle, M............ | Teamster........ | Kernville ............ | Kern Co............ | Kernville. |
| Wesley, J B ........ | Shoe maker ........ | Kern Co............ | Kernville ............ | Kernville. |
| West, W ............ | Teamster ........ | Kern Co............ | nr Havilah............ | Havilah. |
| **Westfall, S C**...... | Farmer............ | Kern Co............ | nr Bakersfield ........ | Bakersfield. |
| Weston, J ............ | Farmer............ | Kern Co............ | Kern Island............ | Bakersfield. |
| White, C D........... | Farmer............ | nr Bakersfield........ | Kern Co............ | Bakersfield. |
| White, C T........... | Farmer............ | Kern Co............ | nr Linn's Valley...... | Glenville. |
| White, Geo W....... | Laborer............ | Linn's Valley........ | Kern Co............ | Glenville. |
| White, J A........... | Miner ............ | nr Kernville............ | Kern Co............ | Kernville. |
| **White, J F**........... | Farmer............ | nr Tehichipa........ | Kern Co............ | Tehichipa. |
| White, W W......... | Teamster............ | nr Bakersfield........ | Kern Co............ | Bakersfield. |
| **Whitman, A T**..... | Insurance agent... | 3d st. & Chestnut Ave | 3d st............ | Bakersfield. |
| Wicker, C G......... | Farmer............ | nr Linn's Valley..... | Kern Co............ | Glenville. |
| Wicker, John......... | Farmer............ | Kern Co............ | nr Linn's Valley ..... | Glenville. |
| **Wickware, H A**..... | Dep postmaster... | 3d st.& Chestnut Ave | 3d st.& Chestnut Ave | Bakersfield. |
| Wickrond, S A....... | Clerk............ | Bakersfield............ | Kern Co............ | Bakersfield. |
| Wiggins, H L........ | Farmer............ | Kern Co............ | nr Tehichipa............ | Tehichipa. |
| Wiggins, J D........ | Farmer............ | nr Tehichipa........ | Kern Co............ | Tehichipa. |
| Wiggins, W C ....... | Farmer............ | Kern Co............ | nr Tehichipa............ | Tehichipa. |
| **Wilby, Wm**......... | Stock raiser........ | Kern Co............ | Tejon............ | Tejon. |
| Wilcox, S J......... | Miner ............ | Kernville ............ | Kern Co............ | Kernville. |
| Wilcoxen, I W....... | Blacksmith......... | Kern Co............ | Kernville ............ | Kernville. |
| **Wilkes, J A**......... | Farmer............ | nr Linn's Valley..... | Kern Co............ | Glenville. |
| Wilkes, J P........... | Farmer............ | nr Linn's Valley..... | Kern Co............ | Glenville. |
| Wilkes, T E........... | Farmer............ | nr Linn's Valley..... | Kern Co............ | Glenville. |
| Wilkes, W P......... | Farmer............ | nr Havilah............ | Kern Co............ | Havilah. |
| Wilkinson, N R...... | Carpenter............ | Kern Co............ | Bakersfield............ | Bakersfield. |
| **Wilkinson, W F**..... | Farmer............ | Kern Co............ | nr Walker's Basin... | Havilah. |
| Willard, O C.......... | Stone cutter........ | Kern Co............ | nr Kernville............ | Kernville. |
| Williams, Alex...... | Carpenter............ | Kern Co............ | Bakersfield............ | Bakersfield. |
| **Williams, E**......... | Miner ............ | Kern Co............ | nr Havilah............ | Havilah. |
| Williams, E T ...... | Miner ............ | nr Havilah............ | Kern Co............ | Havilah. |
| Williams, G H...... | Painter............ | Kern Co............ | Bakersfield............ | Bakersfield. |
| **Williams, D H**...... | Saloon............ | Havilah............ | Kern Co............ | Havilah. |
| Williams, John...... | Farmer............ | nr Bakersfield........ | Kern Co............ | Bakersfield. |
| Williams, J N ...... | Barber............ | Caliente............ | Caliente............ | Caliente. |
| Williams, J E........ | Farmer............ | Kern Co............ | nr Bakersfield........ | Bakersfield. |
| **Williams, L B**...... | Ranchero ............ | Kern Co............ | nr Tehichipa............ | Tehichipa. |
| Williams, Thos...... | Farmer............ | nr Walker's Basin... | Kern Co............ | Havilah. |
| Williams, T J........ | Miner ............ | nr Havilah............ | Kern Co............ | Havilah. |
| Williams, Wm....... | Farmer............ | nr Kern Island ........ | Kern Co............ | Bakersfield. |
| **Williams, W H**..... | Farmer............ | Kern Co............ | Bear Valley............ | Tehichipa. |
| Willis, D M........... | Farmer............ | nr Bakersfield........ | Kern Co............ | Bakersfield. |
| Wilson, A ............ | Miner ............ | nr Kernville............ | Kern Co............ | Kernville. |
| Wilson, G W........ | Farmer............ | Kern Co............ | nr Tehichipa............ | Tehichipa. |
| Wilson, J F........... | Miner ............ | nr Kernville............ | Kern Co............ | Kernville. |
| **Wilson, Henry**...... | Farmer............ | Hudson&Rosemeyers | Kern Co............ | Tejon. |
| Wilson, J B........... | Farmer............ | nr Cummin's Valley | Kern Co............ | Tehichipa. |
| Wilson, James N... | Farmer............ | Tehichipa............ | Kern Co............ | Tehichipa. |
| Wilson, Jno S....... | Carpenter............ | Kernville ............ | Kern Co............ | Kernville. |
| **Wilson, O B**......... | Farmer............ | Kern Co............ | nr Bear Valley........ | Tehichipa. |
| Wilson, W........... | Farmer............ | nr Bakersfield........ | Kern Co............ | Bakersfield. |
| Wilson, Wm......... | Miner ............ | nr Greenhorn......... | Kern Co............ | Kernville. |
| **Wilson, W M**....... | Teacher............ | Kern Co............ | Bakersfield............ | Bakersfield. |
| Wilson, Zion......... | Laborer............ | Kern Co............ | nr Bakersfield........ | Bakersfield. |
| Willow, Elias........ | Teamster............ | Bakersfield............ | Kern Co............ | Bakersfield. |
| Winham, W B ..... | Farmer............ | nr Linn's Valley..... | Kern Co............ | Glenville. |
| Winham, W B...... | Farmer............ | nr Tehichipa........ | Kern Co............ | Tehichipa. |
| **Winn, G**............ | Saloon keeper..... | Kern Co............ | Kernville ............ | Kernville. |
| Withington, R B..... | Ice dealer........... | Bakersfield............ | Kern Co............ | Bakersfield. |
| Withington, R W .. | Teamster........ | Kern Co............ | nr Havilah............ | Havilah. |
| Wittey, Ichabod V | Stock raiser........ | Kern Co............ | Lower Kern Island... | Bakersfield. |

| Name. | Occupation. | Place of Business. | Residence. | Town or P. O. |
|---|---|---|---|---|
| Woodward, G | Merchant | Kern Co | Bakersfield | Bakersfield. |
| Woody, S W | Farmer | nr Linn's Valley | Kern Co | Glenville. |
| Womble, Geo | Miner | Bakersfield | Kern Co | Bakersfield. |
| Wormuth, Wm | Miner | Bakersfield | Kern Co | Bakersfield. |
| Wrage, Wm | Farmer | nr Linn's Valley | Kern Co | Glenville. |
| Wright, Jno M | Teacher | Bear Valley | Kern Co | Tehichipa. |
| Wright, W C | Laborer | nr Sageland | Kern Co | Sageland. |
| Yarbrough, W | Farmer | nr Linn's Valley | Kern Co | Glenville. |
| Yoakum, W J | Merchant | Kern Co | Long Tom | Bakersfield. |
| Young, Franklin | Shoe maker | Kern Co | Tejon | Tejon. |
| Young, Geo | Stock raiser | Kern Co | Bakersfield | Bakersfield. |
| Young, Jas | Stock raiser | Kern Co | Tejon | Tejon. |
| Young, Saml | Ranchero | nr Tejon | Kern Co | Tejon. |
| Zimmerman, B | Blacksmith | Tehichipa | Kern Co | Tehichipa. |

# OTTO KAEDING & CO.

## SALOON,

### State Street, Santa Barbara, Cal.

#### THE BEST OF

### LIQUORS, WINES AND CIGARS

To be found south of San Francisco, are to be had at our bar. All kinds of Mixed and Fancy Drinks skillfully "hove" together by an expert "mixologer," especially engaged by the season to serve in this palate-tickling capacity. Whiskey Cocktails are his strong suit. "Eye Openers," "Hair Straighteners," "Pedal Progressors" and "Resurrection Draughts," specialties.

---

### Andrew J. Kraszynski,
# PROPRIETOR HOTEL,
## LYON'S STATION,
LOS ANGELES COUNTY,     CALIFORNIA.

## A FIRST-CLASS COUNTRY HOTEL
Unsurpassed by any in Southern California.

THE SLEEPING ROOMS are neatly furnished and well ventilated, and the Table is bountifully supplied from the best the market affords. Boarders taken by the week or month, at the usual rates.

## JAMES CASS,
# CAYUCOS LANDING,
### SAN LUIS OBISPO COUNTY, CAL.

General and Special Dealers in

## LUMBER, BUILDING MATERIALS,

Posts, Shakes, Shingles,

### DOORS, WINDOWS, LIME,

## AGRICULTURAL IMPLEMENTS, Etc.

Also, constantly on hand a large assortment of

### HARDWARE, GROCERIES, & GENERAL MERCHANDISE

I would also call the attention of the public to the fact that I have lately made improvements that will greatly facilitate the unloading and

## SHIPPING OF FREIGHT

And have perfected arrangements with

### GOODALL, NELSON & PERKINS,

For a regular visit of one of their steamers every eight days.

### SUITABLE WAREHOUSES HAVE BEEN ERECTED

FOR THE STORAGE OF GRAIN, ETC.

Additions will be made to wharf and warehouses as business increases or necessity demands. 22 miles from Paso Robles Hot Springs; 14 miles from Cambria, and 20 miles from San Luis Obispo, the County Seat.

### JAMES CASS.

# E. B. STOCKING,

PROPRIETOR OF THE

# MORO WHARF AND WAREHOUSE,

## Forwarding & Commission Merchant,

—DEALER IN ALL KINDS OF—

# FARM AND DAIRY PRODUCE.

TOWN PROPERTY FOR SALE.  AGENT FOR THE HARTFORD
FIRE INSURANCE COMPANY.

Moro, San Luis Obispo County, California.

# J. C. STOCKING,

# BLACKSMITH AND WAGON MAKER,

WHOLESALE AND RETAIL DEALER IN

# HARDWOOD LUMBER, IRON,

COAL, ETC., ETC.

ALL KINDS OF REPAIRING DONE WITH NEATNESS AND DISPATCH.

MORO, SAN LUIS OBISPO COUNTY, CALIFORNIA.

## W. J. BRADFORD,
## Blacksmith,
CARPENTERIA, SANTA BARBARA COUNTY, CAL.

**BLACKSMITHING, HORSESHOEING,
WAGON WORK, MACHINE WORK**

And Repairing of all kinds, done reasonably and with dispatch.

---

## L. CARTERI,
## HOTEL !
### STORE & FEED STABLE,
SANTA YNEZ, SANTA BARBARA CO., CAL.

Hotel well furnished and fitted. Table well supplied.

Sleeping apartments neat and comfortable.

Store fully stocked with new goods.

Stable roomy, with good corral. Feed for sale in large and small quantities.

---

## D. D. McCOY,
## HOTEL
### HUENEME
VENTURA COUNTY, CAL.

**Good Accommodations**

GOOD TABLE, GOOD BEDS,

Careful Attention and Perfect Comfort

---

## Joseph Middlemiss & Co.,
—Dealers in—
## REAL ESTATE!

Haley St., Santa Barbara, Cal.

Lands bought and sold. Town and county property.

Rents collected and Taxes paid.

County and Rancho maps to be found at our office.

## Haley Street, Santa Barbara.

A GENERAL DESCRIPTION

OF

# SAN BERNARDINO COUNTY.

---

SAN BERNARDINO COUNTY is bounded upon the North by Inyo County and the State of Nevada; on the East by the Colorado River; on the South by San Diego County; and on the West by the Counties of Kern and Los Angeles. It was

### ORGANIZED

In 1853, previous to which year it formed a portion of Los Angeles County. It derives its name from the old mission of San Bernardino, founded by a Mexican named Lugos, who once held by grant the entire magnificent valley of San Bernardino, cultivating it almost altogether by means of Indian labor.

This immense tract was purchased from the original grantee by Messrs. Rich and Hanks, in the year 1851. San Bernardino is the largest County in the State, covering an

### AREA,

According to Mr. Arthur Kearney, one of the County's most able chroniclers, of twenty-two thousand, four hundred and seventy-two square miles; an area embracing only two hundred and fourteen square miles less than the aggregated areas of Massachusetts, Connecticut and Vermont.

### ITS POPULATION

We are warranted in stating, by the authority before quoted, at about nine thousand, in the year 1874. The total value of

### REAL AND PERSONAL PROPERTY

represented in the County for the present year is about $2,000,000, or an excess of about $500,000 over the assessed valuation of last year. In this County, too, real estate is not assessed above one-fourth of its real value. The County is separated into

### TWO GREAT DIVISIONS,

By the San Bernardino range of mountains. The division to the Eastward lies within the valley of the Colorado River; is an arid waste, totally worthless for agricultural purposes, and almost, if not quite, uninhabitable. The other division occupies the space intermediate between the Western slope of the San Bernardino Range and the boundary line of Los Angeles County. This portion of the County has an area of two thousand square miles, nearly all of which is extremely fertile. These divisions present a wonderful contrast, one being the exact antithesis of the other in point of climate, topographical formation, adaptability of soil, and general resources.

The Southwestern slope is an elevated plain, well watered and fertile.

The Temescal Mountains, in which are the celebrated Tin Mines, are in this portion of the County. There is said to be an area here of one hundred square miles, permeated by veins of this ore. It is only partially developed, and not even fully explored.

Vineyards, orchards and well-tilled fields give abundant evidence of the richness of the soil in this portion of the County. It is especially noted for the excellence of some of the varieties of grapes produced, chief among which is the Cucamonga.

In all directions throughout the San Bernardino Range, agricultural settlements occupy the valleys. They are exceedingly prosperous; the soil yielding abundant crops.

## THE COAST RANGE

Covers about three millions of acres, large portions of which are valuable for grazing and mining purposes. The mountains and hills being heavily timbered, offer large lumbering advantages. Much of the finest land in the County has been owned in large tracts, old grants of the Spanish Government, some of them covering eleven square leagues. This, in time past, operated seriously against the advancement of the County, as the means of the ordinary settler were inadequate to the purchase of such enormous tracts. He was, therefore, obliged to take his modest means to other localities. This difficulty has long since been obviated, as the grants have, from time to time, been purchased and subdivided into farms of more reasonable dimensions.

Among the volcanic ranges in the Northern and Eastern portions of the County, the precious metals, both gold and silver, have been found in abundance; mining districts have been established, but so unfitted for habitation is that sterile locality, so impossible of obtainance are those primal necessaries of life, wood and water, that one after another have been abandoned, even the promise of untold riches, of known existence, being insufficient to induce the sturdy miner to undergo the hardships and privations of a region of such utter desolation.

This portion of the County presents undeniable evidence of its volcanic origin. It has been torn, wrenched, melted and fused by the gases generated and the fires which raged beneath. That it was afterwards subjected to the action of water, being, probably, submitted to the tide processes of the vast ocean for ages, there can be no doubt; at least that time was required to soften its rugged outline and remove its jagged excrescencies. Everywhere can be seen the dry beds of former water bodies, borne from the ocean at its final emersion. Upon all sides, one can mark extinct volcanoes, beds of pumice, fragments of lava; can find hot springs, sulphur deposits, and a thousand and one evidences of what existed in the past, as well as assure himself that the processes which occasioned the depression and uprisal of this vast section of country are simply smouldering—by no means extinct.

Vegetation here is very scanty, and differs radically from that of the other division of the County. A plant of the palm variety, termed the Yucca, is its most abundant growth. It attains a height ranging from five to fifteen feet. The extreme diameter of its stem, for the largest growth, is about one foot, having from two to five branches. Its leaves are similar in shape to a bayonet blade, and it has an exceedingly rough, rugged appearance, caused by the leaves, which depend close to its stem. It is almost the sole growth which could serve as fuel in this entire waste. The

## SODA LAKE

Lies in this section of the County. It is a glaring misnomer, which presents the wondrous anomaly of a lake without water. It receives the discharge of the Mojave, but retains none of its large supply, the water sinking through the alkaline soil with a rapidity equal to that of its influx.

San Bernardino County possesses an area of

## TIMBER LANDS

Measuring, approximately, seven hundred and twenty square miles. The growth consists of sugar, pitch and yellow pine; balsam, fir, cedar and spruce; together with some oak, alder and maple. When the railroad shall have carried into this region a representation of all the manufacturing industries, these vast timber reserves will prove a source of inexhaustible wealth. The

# DIRECTORY OF SAN BERNARDINO COUNTY.

## RESOURCES

Of this County are agricultural, pastoral and mineral. We place its mineral resource last in the schedule, not that it is in reality most unimportant, for, indeed, it is almost boundless; but it seems to us that a country truly prosperous, in the full sense of the term, must base its prosperity upon its agricultural interest, especially when it is favored in climate and soil, and has such facilities for irrigation as would tend to render a development of that interest a matter of ease, and crown all efforts in that direction with unqualified success.

## THE PRINCIPAL VALLEYS

Of this County are the San Bernardino, Rincon, Juapa, Chino, Las Ceirros, Jurupa, San Gorgonia and Uciapa.

San Bernardino, the principal valley, occupies the Southwestern portion of the County. It is about fifty miles in length, having a width of about twenty miles. On the East, North and South, it is skirted with lofty, timber-clad mountains. From these mountains descend into the valley innumerable streams, whose devious courses can be traced by the growths of willow, sycamore and other trees which fringe their banks, and cause the great plain to resemble the carefullly laid out pleasure domain of some railroad or stock-jobbing "Crœsus." The Santa Ana River, quite a large stream, traverses the entire length of the valley, which, thus sheltered and watered, could not be otherwise than the favored locality it is, both in the attractions presented by its unparalleled climate and the rich resources of its soil. Its products are widely diversified; nearly all known fruits, grain and vegetables are successfully and profitably cultivated, those indigenous to the tropics side by side with those transplanted from Northern climes. In this valley there are one hundred artesian wells; water being obtained at depths varying from seventy to two hundred feet. The County possesses good

## EDUCATIONAL ADVANTAGES.

It has twenty-one school districts, nearly all lying within the San Bernardino Valley.

The range of the thermometer is from 40° to 100°, the mean temperature, however, being from 60° to 65°.

In the County are three flouring mills, five steam saw mills and two planing mills.

At Holcombe and Bear Valleys, on the Northern side of the great peak of San Bernardino, are valuable placer and quartz mines, which have been worked with marked success for about fifteen years. Placer gold is also found in large quantities along Lytle Creek, a tributary of the Santa Ana.

## THE PRINCIPAL TOWNS

Of the County are San Bernardino, the County seat, Holcombe, Old San Bernardino, Rincon, Riverside, San Timoteo, Valverde and Ukipah.

The County seat is the only large town in the County; the others being mere agricultural or mining settlements, with the exception of Riverside, which is an enterprising, thriving little town.

## SAN BERNARDINO,

The County seat, is situated in the San Bernardino Valley. Its site is upon the level plain about five miles distant from the foot-hills. It is literally embowered, the pepper trees, willows and cottonwoods almost concealing it from the careless glance.

Its streets are spacious, its buildings substantial, and possessing an air of comfort rather than elegance. Everything attests to the thrift and general well-being of the community.

The town site was chosen and settled by the Mormons in 1847. The town was laid out after the usual plan of Mormon towns, in large blocks, sufficient to form a homestead for a family.

It lies across the route to the Southeast and into the great desert. It is also the central point where meet the various roads leading to the mining districts of Panamint, Hualapai, Death Valley, the Upper Colorado, Holcombe Valley, La Paz, Prescott and Yuma.

Thus, to add to the wealth and importance of the little city, both trade and travel are concentrated. The route of the Southern Pacific Railroad is surveyed through the town, leading, by way of the San Gorgonio Pass, to the Colorado at Fort Yuma. Much doubt is expressed regarding the immediate building of this road. The cars are running from Los Angeles beyond Spadra, leaving a distance of only twenty-four miles between this town and railroad connection. San Bernardino has a population numbering between thirty-five hundred and four thousand. Its population is rapidly increasing, as are also its business interests. The town was organized in 1869. There are six

## CHURCHES,

The Presbyterian, Methodist, Congregationalist, Mormon, Spiritualist and Catholic denominations being represented. The church structures are, some of them, costly buildings, but erected with greater regard to comfort and convenience than any elegance in architectural display. The

## NEWSPAPER INTEREST

Is represented by three sheets, the *Guardian*, *Argus* and *Advertiser*. The two former issue daily and weekly sheets. The latter has only a weekly issue. All the prominent

## SECRET SOCIETIES.

Have lodges here, and seem to be as prosperous as elsewhere throughout the State.

San Bernardino will, in the future, be one of the most prosperous of the inland cities of the State. Everything seems to indicate it. It is the point where converge all the interests of the County, all the industries of which pay her tribute. When the railroad is finally completed into Arizona, a new field will be open to her. The travel passing through to this new territory, as well as that flowing back, will add to her prosperity; while the producer in that new country, whatever be his product, will find his nearest market at her door.

## RIVERSIDE,

A post office town, and the seat of one of those thriving colonies, through the establishment of which, Southern California has attained, in a great part, its population, lies twelve miles Southwest from San Bernardino, twenty-eight miles from Spadra, the recent terminus of the Southern Pacific Railroad, and about fifty-eight miles from Los Angeles. It has an area of one square mile, and a population numbering between six and seven hundred.

The town lots contain, each, two and one-half acres; shade trees abound; the structures are neat and tasteful, and, judging from appearances, it is one of the most delightful little spots in the County.

The great natural adaptiveness of both soil and climate gave the cue for the establishment of the colony, capital having thus been induced to invest largely for the introduction of the only element needed to fully develop it.

The colony and town date only from 1871. In that year was built the work above referred to, the Riverside Irrigating Canal. Its construction was effected at the cost of $60,000, one year being required for its completion. It was finished in 1871.

The water is taken from the Santa Ana River. It has an extreme width at the top of twenty feet, narrowing to eight feet at the bottom. It flows four feet of water; is above fifteen miles in length, and we are informed is being extended still further; our informant fixing its beginning at Agua Mansa, its termination at the Hartshorn tract, some eight miles beyond Riverside.

There is scarcely any fruit, cereal or vegetable, the growth of which is ~~which is~~ not favored by the soil and climate of this "garden spot." With a growth proportional to its merits, it will some day be one of the leading colonies of the State.

## HOLCOMBE AND BEAR VALLEYS

Lie upon the North side of the San Bernardino mountains, in a wide plateau or broad valley, about thirty-five miles from the town of San Bernardino. The mines here, both quartz and placer, have periodically, since 1860, attracted considerable notice. The yield has been considerable, although they have, at times, been abandoned. They are now being vigorously worked, with flattering results.

## RINCON

Is a post office; the settlement a small one.

## VALVERDE COLONY

Is as yet somewhat prospective, although the advantages offered cannot but lead to an early and full development. It is situated upon the Mojave River, about forty miles North from the valley of San Bernardino. It has secured the entire water privilege of the Mojave, and needs but this adjunct to its fertile soil and favorable climate to render it a formidable rival, in the diversity of its products and its wondrous growths, to the most favored portions of the State.

## OLD SAN BERNARDINO

Is an agricultural settlement.

Thrifty settlements are also springing up in the valleys of Yucipa, San Timoteo and San Gorgonio.

## THE SLOVER MOUNTAIN COLONY

Possesses two thousand acres of excellent fruit and grain land, some three miles from the town of San Bernardino, being upon the proposed, and, in fact, surveyed line of the Southern Pacific Railroad. It is under the management of gentlemen well known in the County, whose connection with an enterprise is alone a sufficient guarantee of its legitimacy.

It is the intention to divide this tract into ten-acre lots, to be sold at low rates and on reasonable terms to actual settlers.

An irrigating canal is now in process of construction, which will convey water from the Santa Ana River in sufficient quantities to answer all the needs of the agriculturist. In addition to this, it is stated that an artesian well will be sunk upon every forty acres, by the projectors of this enterprise.

The colonies of this County offer advantages to the industrious cultivator of sufficient importance to prevent their being overlooked. With the possession of but small means, in these communities, one may, in a comparatively short time, rise to a condition of ease and independence, if not affluence. A small tract of twenty or thirty acres, planted with oranges, almonds, walnuts or figs, will, in the course of a few years, yield a fine revenue, requiring scarcely any investment beyond that of the necessary labor. Few such desirable ends are to be achieved, so safely and certainly, the investor incurring so little risk. We trust they may have a full share of that prosperity which they certainly seem to merit.

Santa Cruz,      Railroad Landing,      San Luis Obispo.

# SCHWARTZ, HARFORD & CO.,

—— DEALERS IN ——

## LUMBER

### POSTS, SHINGLES,
### MOLDINGS, WINDOWS,
### BLINDS, DOORS,

——AND ALL KINDS OF——

## Building and Furnishing
## LUMBER.

MAIN OFFICE--L. SCHWARTZ & CO'S BRICK BUILDING,

MONTEREY STREET, SAN LUIS OBISPO.

# DIRECTORY OF SAN BERNARDINO COUNTY. 257

| Name. | Occupation. | Place of Business. | Residence. | Town or P. O. |
|---|---|---|---|---|
| Abadie, F. | Miner | San Bernardino Co. | San Bernardino | S Bernardino. |
| Abbot, W A | Farmer | South of Riverside | Riverside | Riverside. |
| Abel, Jessie | Farmer | nr San Bernardino | San Bernardino | S Bernardino. |
| Abel, S L | Farmer | San Bernardino Co. | Riverside | Riverside. |
| Ables, B | Farmer | | Riverside | Riverside. |
| Acosta, Eduardo | Farmer | San Bernardino Co. | San Salvador | San Salvador. |
| Adams, John | Miner | nr San Bernardino | San Bernardino Co. | S Bernardino. |
| Adams, J W | Laborer | nr San Bernardino | San Bernardino Co. | S Bernardino. |
| Adley, Frank | Stage driver | San Bernardino Co. | Mojave | S Bernardino. |
| Aguilar, H | Carpenter | San Bernardino Co. | Temescal | Temescal. |
| Aitken, Wm | Farmer | San Bernardino | San Bernardino Co. | S Bernardino. |
| Aker, John | Teamster | San Bernardino | San Bernardino Co. | S Bernardino. |
| Akers, S M | Blacksmith | San Bernardino | San Bernardino Co. | S Bernardino. |
| Albia, P | Farmer | San Bernardino Co. | nr San Timoteo | S Bernardino. |
| Alder, S | Wagon maker | Main st | Vine st | Riverside. |
| Aldridge, D H | Farmer | nr San Bernardino | San Bernardino Co. | S Bernardino. |
| Alducto, J B | Farmer | nr San Bernardino | San Bernardino Co. | S Bernardino. |
| Allen, James | Blacksmith | | San Bernardino | S Bernardino. |
| Allen, H | Farmer | San Bernardino Co. | San Bernardino | S Bernardino. |
| Allen, J | Farmer | San Bernardino Co. | South of Riverside | Riverside. |
| Allen, Thos F | Miner | San Bernardino Co. | Lytle Creek | S Bernardino. |
| Allen, Legare | Teacher | | | S Bernardino. |
| Allen, R, Jr | Farmer | nr San Bernardino | San Bernardino Co. | S Bernardino. |
| Allen, Jacob | Physician | 7 Kelling's Block | 7th and California sts | S Bernardino. |
| Allen, Richard | Farmer | San Bernardino Co. | nr San Bernardino | S Bernardino. |
| Allen, John | Farmer | nr San Bernardino | San Bernardino Co. | S Bernardino. |
| Allen & Drew | Druggists | 3d st | San Bernardino | S Bernardino. |
| Allen, — | Druggist | 3d st | San Bernardino | S Bernardino. |
| Alexander, A P | Blacksmith | San Bernardino Co. | San Bernardino | S Bernardino. |
| Almasan, F | Blacksmith | San Bernardino Co. | San Bernardino | S Bernardino. |
| Alvarado, M | Laborer | San Bernardino Co. | nr San Salvador | San Salvador. |
| Alvarado, F | Farmer | San Bernardino Co. | nr San Salvador | San Salvador. |
| Alvarado, J J | Farmer | San Bernardino Co. | nr Chino | Chino. |
| Alvitrae, F | Farmer | San Bernardino Co. | nr San Salvador | San Salvador. |
| Alvitrae, A | Farmer | San Bernardino Co. | nr San Salvador | San Salvador. |
| Alvitraes, G | Butcher | San Bernardino Co. | San Bernardino | S Bernardino. |
| Amandell, — | General store | | San Bernardino | S Bernardino. |
| Ames, A M | Mason | San Bernardino Co. | San Bernardino | S Bernardino. |
| Ames, D A | Farmer | nr San Bernardino | San Bernardino Co. | S Bernardino. |
| Ames, J T | Merchant | San Bernardino Co. | San Bernardino | S Bernardino. |
| Ames, Ellis | Merchant | San Bernardino Co. | San Bernardino | S Bernardino. |
| Ames, E, Jr | Farmer | San Bernardino Co. | San Bernardino | S Bernardino. |
| Aucker & Co, L | General merch'se | 3d and Utah sts | | S Bernardino. |
| Anderson, M H | Teamster | San Bernardino Co. | San Bernardino | S Bernardino. |
| Anderson, J Y | Miner | San Bernardino Co. | nr San Bernardino | S Bernardino. |
| Anderson, R Jr | Teamster | nr San Bernardino | San Bernardino Co. | S Bernardino. |
| Anderson, A B | Farmer | San Bernardino Co. | nr San Bernardino | S Bernardino. |
| Anderson, John | S Bern'o brewery | cor 3d and Lake sts | San Bernardino | S Bernardino. |
| Andrew, John | Genl merchandise | 3d st | San Bernardino | S Bernardino. |
| Andrew, T D | Farmer | San Bernardino | San Bernardino Co. | S Bernardino. |
| Annabal, A | Farmer | Riverside | San Bernardino Co. | Riverside. |
| Antonio, F | U S restaurant | Salt Lake st | San Bernardino | S Bernardino. |
| Appodac, S | Laborer | San Bernardino Co. | nr San Salvador | San Salvador. |
| Arbon, R | Farmer | nr San Bernardino | San Bernardino Co. | S Bernardino. |
| Archuleta, Thos | Farmer | San Bernardino Co. | nr San Salvador | San Salvador. |
| Armor, J W | Laborer | San Bernardino Co. | San Bernardino | S Bernardino. |
| Armstrong, G C | Sawyer | nr San Bernardino | San Bernardino Co. | S Bernardino. |
| Arras, A | Farmer | San Bernardino Co. | Rincon | Chino. |
| Arvizo, J | Laborer | nr San Bernardino | San Bernardino Co. | S Bernardino. |
| Ashcroft, John | Farmer | San Salvador | nr San Salvador | San Salvador. |
| Ashcroft, Wm | Farmer | San Bernardino Co. | nr San Salvador | San Salvador. |
| Atencia, C | Farmer | San Bernardino Co. | nr San Salvador | San Salvador. |
| Atencio, A | Farmer | San Bernardino Co. | nr San Salvador | San Salvador. |
| Atencio, J M | Farmer | San Bernardino Co. | Agua Mansa | |

17

| Name. | Occupation. | Place of Business. | Residence. | Town or P. O |
|---|---|---|---|---|
| Atencio, G | Laborer | San Bernardino Co. | Agua Mansa | |
| Atencio, J M | Laborer | San Bernardino Co. | Agua Mansa | |
| Atherton, Isaac W. | Clergyman | 12 m S San Bern'd'o | Riverside | Riverside. |
| Atkinson, J J | Clerk | San Bernardino Co. | San Bernardino | S Bernardino. |
| Atkinson, J J | Gen merchandise. | San Bernardino Co. | Bear Valley | |
| Artensia, Jose | Laborer | San Bernardino Co. | San Salvador | San Salvador. |
| Atwood, D | Farmer | nr San Bernardino. | San Bernardino Co. | S Bernardino. |
| **Ayer, John** | Blacksmith | San Bernardino Co. | San Bernardino | S Bernardino. |
| Ayers, Jas C | Teamster | San Bernardino Co. | nr San Bernardino | S Bernardino. |
| **Baca, B** | Farmer | San Bernardino Co. | nr San Timoteo | S Bernardino. |
| Baca, E | Stock raiser | San Bernardino Co. | nr Riverside | Riverside. |
| Bucca, J | Farmer | San Bernardino Co. | nr San Salvador | San Salvador. |
| Baca, B | Farmer | nr San Bernardino | San Bernardino Co. | S Bernardino. |
| Baca, T | Farmer | | | S Bernardino. |
| Bacca, B | Farmer | nr San Bernardino | San Bernardino Co. | S Bernardino. |
| **Bacca, M** | Butcher | San Bernardino Co. | San Salvador | San Salvador. |
| Baca, Jose R | Laborer | | San Salvador | San Salvador. |
| Badilla, J M | Vaquero | San Bernardino Co. | Temescal | Temescal. |
| Badilla, F | Vaquero | San Bernardino Co. | Temescal | Temescal. |
| Baker, J H | Miner | San Bernardino Co. | Ivanpah | S Bernardino. |
| Baker, W W | Laborer | San Bernardino Co. | San Bernardino | S Bernardino. |
| **Baldes, J L** | Farmer | San Bernardino Co. | nr San Salvador | San Salvador. |
| Baldez, J | Laborer | nr San Bernardino | San Bernardino Co. | S Bernardino. |
| Baldwin, Allen R | Farmer | | | S Bernardino. |
| Baldwin, J | Farmer | San Bernardino Co. | San Salvador | San Salvador. |
| Baldwin, R | Farmer | nr San Bernardino | San Bernardino Co. | S Bernardino. |
| Baldwin, Wm | Farmer | nr San Bernardino | San Bernardino Co. | S Bernardino. |
| **Ball, E A** | Dairyman | San Bernardino Co. | San Bernardino | S Bernardino. |
| Ball, H W | Farmer | nr San Bernardino | San Bernardino Co. | S Bernardino. |
| Ball, S S | Farmer | San Bernardino Co. | nr San Bernardino | S Bernardino. |
| Bank of San Bernardino | | 4th st | San Bernardino | S Bernardino. |
| Banks, J S | Miner | San Bernardino Co. | San Bernardino | S Bernardino. |
| Banford, Wm | Laborer | San Bernardino Co. | nr San Bernardino | S Bernardino. |
| Barbor, V | Laborer | San Bernardino Co. | San Salvador | San Salvador. |
| Bardin, J T | Miner | San Bernardino Co. | nr San Bernardino | S Bernardino. |
| **Barnes, Thos J** | Farmer | Martin's | Martin's | S Bernardino. |
| **Barnum, S** | Blacksmith | San Bernardino Co. | San Bernardino | S Bernardino. |
| Barresses, J D | Farmer | San Bernardino Co. | nr San Salvador | San Salvador. |
| Barr, Geo | Farmer | San Bernardino | San Bernardino Co. | S Bernardino. |
| **Barton, B** | Physician | San Bernardino Co. | San Bernardino | S Bernardino. |
| Barton, W A | Carpenter | San Bernardino Co. | San Bernardino | S Bernardino. |
| Bates, John | Miner | San Bernardino | San Bernardino Co. | S Bernardino. |
| Bateman, J M K | Teacher | | | S Bernardino. |
| Battles, D | Farmer | South of Riverside | San Bernardino Co. | Riverside. |
| Baxter, G W | Miner | San Bernardino Co. | Bellville | S Bernardino. |
| Bayly, Geo Weldon | Farmer | | | S Bernardino. |
| Beal, I | Ranchero | San Bernardino Co. | San Bernardino Co. | S Bernardino. |
| Beal, S C | Teamster | nr San Bernardino | San Bernardino Co. | S Bernardino. |
| Bean, J S | Farmer | nr San Bernardino | San Bernardino Co. | S Bernardino. |
| Beckstead, E | Farmer | San Bernardino Co. | San Salvador | San Salvador. |
| Beers, H M | Farmer | South of Riverside | San Bernardino Co. | Riverside. |
| Beiswinger, L A | Jeweller | San Bernardino | San Bernardino | S Bernardino. |
| **Beita, G** | Farmer | San Bernardino Co. | nr San Salvador | San Salvador. |
| Befil, J | Laborer | San Bernardino Co. | nr San Bernardino | S Bernardino. |
| Befil, J D | Laborer | San Bernardino Co. | San Salvador | San Salvador. |
| Bfiil, J | Farmer | | nr San Salvador | San Salvador. |
| Belarde, Quirino | Farmer | | San Salvador | San Salvador. |
| **Delarde, F** | Farmer | San Bernardino Co. | nr San Salvador | San Salvador. |
| Bell, James | Laborer | San Bernardino | San Bernardino | S Bernardino. |
| **Bellamy, G W** | Farmer | nr San Bernardino | San Bernardino Co. | S Bernardino. |
| Bemis, H | Farmer | nr San Bernardino | San Bernardino Co. | S Bernardino. |
| Bemis, Chas | Farmer | nr San Bernardino | San Bernardino Co. | S Bernardino. |
| **Bemis, Wm** | Farmer | nr San Bernardino | San Bernardino Co. | S Bernardino. |

## DIRECTORY OF SAN BERNARDINO COUNTY. 259

| Name. | Occupation. | Place of Business. | Residence. | Town or P. O. |
|---|---|---|---|---|
| Bemis, S............. | Farmer............ | San Bernardino Co.... | nr San Bernardino... | S Bernardino. |
| Bemis, E............. | Farmer............ | nr San Bernardino... | San Bernardino Co... | S Bernardino. |
| **Bemis, A**............. | Farmer............ | San Bernardino....... | San Bernardino Co... | S Bernardino. |
| Benninger, John..... | Saloon............ | 3d st.................... | 3d st.................... | S Bernardino. |
| Benson, Alfred W... | Farmer............ | ........................ | ........................ | S Bernardino. |
| Benson, I H......... | Teamster.......... | nr San Bernardino... | San Bernardino Co... | S Bernardino. |
| Benson, J M, Jr..... | Farmer............ | nr San Bernardino... | San Bernardino Co... | S Bernardino. |
| Benson, S B......... | Teamster.......... | nr San Bernardino... | San Bernardino Co... | S Bernardino. |
| Benson, A B......... | Farmer............ | San Bernardino Co... | nr San Bernardino... | S Bernardino. |
| Beony, John......... | Farmer............ | nr San Bernardino... | San Bernardino Co... | S Bernardino. |
| **Berge, S**............. | Newsprs & prdcls | 3d st.................... | San Bernardino...... | S Bernardino. |
| Bergel, S............. | Teacher............ | San Bernardino Co... | San Bernardino...... | S Bernardino. |
| Berlarde, A......... | Laborer............ | San Bernardino Co... | San Salvador......... | San Salvador. |
| Berlarde, I......... | Farmer............ | San Bernardino Co... | nr San Bernardino... | S Bernardino. |
| **Berlarde, P**......... | Farmer............ | San Bernardino Co... | nr San Salvador...... | San Salvador. |
| Berlarde, V......... | Farmer............ | San Bernardino Co... | Agua Mansa.......... | |
| Bermudas, P......... | Laborer............ | San Bernardino Co... | San Bernardino...... | S Bernardino. |
| Bermudas, J......... | Carpenter......... | San Bernardino Co... | San Bernardino...... | S Bernardino. |
| Bermudez, Jose..... | Farmer............ | ........................ | ........................ | S Bernardino. |
| Bermudas, M....... | Farmer............ | nr San Bernardino... | San Bernardino Co... | S Bernardino. |
| Bernal, E............. | Farmer............ | San Bernardino Co... | nr San Timoteo...... | S Bernardino. |
| Berry, Jas........... | Farmer............ | San Bernardino Co... | nr Chino................ | Chino. |
| Berry, J S........... | Laborer............ | San Bernardino Co... | San Bernardino...... | S Bernardino. |
| **Berry, Jno Francis** | Farmer............ | ........................ | ........................ | S Bernardino. |
| Berringer, John..... | Farmer............ | ........................ | ........................ | S Bernardino. |
| Bessant, James..... | Farmer............ | nr San Bernardino... | San Bernardino Co... | S Bernardino. |
| **Bessant, J**........... | Farmer............ | San Bernardino Co... | San Bernardino...... | S Bernardino. |
| Bessant, I........... | Farmer............ | San Bernardino Co... | San Bernardino Co... | S Bernardino. |
| Bessant, S........... | Farmer............ | nr San Bernardino... | San Bernardino Co... | S Bernardino. |
| Bethel, A............. | Carpenter......... | San Bernardino Co... | San Bernardino...... | S Bernardino. |
| **Biays, Jos**........... | Merchant.......... | San Bernardino Co... | San Bernardino...... | S Bernardino. |
| **Biays, John M**..... | Stove, tin & hdwr | 3d st.................... | San Bernardino...... | S Bernardino. |
| Bickmore, Jno R... | Farmer............ | ........................ | ........................ | Riverside. |
| Bickmore, E......... | Farmer............ | San Bernardino Co... | San Salvador......... | San Salvador. |
| **Bickmore, S**........ | Farmer............ | San Bernardino Co... | nr San Salvador...... | San Salvador. |
| Binkley, Wm F.... | Saddler............ | ........................ | ........................ | S Bernardino. |
| Bingham, Edwd A.. | Laborer............ | San Bernardino....... | San Bernardino Co... | S Bernardino. |
| Binkley, F........... | Teamster.......... | nr San Bernardino... | San Bernardino Co... | S Bernardino. |
| Birch, G R.......... | Farmer............ | San Bernardino....... | San Bernardino Co... | S Bernardino. |
| Bitschnan, J......... | Baker.............. | San Bernardino Co... | San Bernardino...... | S Bernardino. |
| Bixler, F............. | Farmer............ | South of Riverside... | San Bernardino Co... | Riverside. |
| Bixler, M F......... | Mason.............. | ........................ | ........................ | S Bernardino. |
| Blackburn, A C..... | Cooper............. | San Bernardino....... | San Bernardino Co... | S Bernardino. |
| **Blankenbeker, J L** | Farmer............ | ........................ | ........................ | S Bernardino. |
| Blanche, C.......... | Fruiterer.......... | ........................ | ........................ | S Bernardino. |
| **Blair, S F**........... | Farmer............ | South of Riverside... | San Bernardino Co... | S Bernardino. |
| Blair, F P........... | Teamster.......... | nr San Bernardino... | San Bernardino Co... | S Bernardino. |
| **Bledsoe, R E**....... | Farmer............ | nr San Bernardino... | San Bernardino Co... | S Bernardino. |
| Bledsoe, N C....... | Notary............. | r 4&6 Anderson's bldg | ........................ | S Bernardino. |
| Bledsoe, W K...... | Farmer............ | nr San Bernardino... | San Bernardino Co... | S Bernardino. |
| Bledsoe, N C....... | Farmer............ | San Bernardino Co... | nr San Bernardino... | S Bernardino. |
| **Bledsoe, J H**....... | Attorney........... | San Bernardino Co... | San Bernardino...... | S Bernardino. |
| Bledsoe, H......... | Farmer............ | San Bernardino Co... | San Bernardino...... | S Bernardino. |
| Block, —........... | Saddler............ | Riverside............. | San Bernardino Co... | Riverside. |
| Block, C S.......... | Farmer............ | San Bernardino Co... | San.Timoteo.......... | S Bernardino. |
| Blohm, A............ | Grocer............. | San Bernardino Co... | Mountain Mill........ | S Bernardino. |
| Blow, Robt Thos.... | Clerk............... | ........................ | ........................ | S Bernardino. |
| Blum, Simon........ | Clerk............... | ........................ | ........................ | S Bernardino. |
| **Borchardt, B**...... | Merchant.......... | San Bernardino Co... | Riverside............. | Riverside. |
| Boreham, W....... | Blacksmith........ | San Bernardino Co... | Bairdstown.......... | Bairdstown. |
| Boreham, Wm Jno | Dairyman.......... | ........................ | ........................ | S Bernardino. |
| **Boren, Christia & Shoap**........ | Real estate........ | Boren's block........ | San Bernardino...... | S Bernardino. |
| Boren, Wilfred..... | Cigars, etc......... | ........................ | San Bernardino...... | S Bernardino. |

| Name. | Occupation. | Place of Business. | Residence. | Town or P. O. |
|---|---|---|---|---|
| Boren, Wm | Blacksmith | San Bernardino Co | San Bernardino | S Bernardino. |
| Boren, B M | Farmer | San Bernardino Co | nr San Bernardino | S Bernardino. |
| Boren, A D | Real estate | 4th st | San Bernardino | S Bernardino. |
| Boren, E D | Farmer | San Bernardino Co | nr San Bernardino | S Bernardino. |
| Boren, B C | Farmer | San Bernardino Co | San Bernardino | S Bernardino. |
| Boren, W A | Clerk | San Bernardino Co | San Bernardino | S Bernardino. |
| Bormer, Wm | Sawyer | | | S Bernardino. |
| Bosshard, H | Carpenter | San Bernardino Co | San Bernardino | S Bernardino. |
| Bottoms, John J | Farmer | | | S Bernardino. |
| Bowland, — | Druggist | 3d st | San Bernardino | S Bernardino. |
| Bowland & Craig | Druggists | 3d st | San Bernardino | S Bernardino. |
| Bowland, F P | Clerk | San Bernardino Co | San Bernardino | S Bernardino. |
| Bowlden, C R | Farmer | nr San Bernardino | San Bernardino Co | S Bernardino. |
| Boyd, James | Farmer | 3 m N E Riverside | San Bernardino rd | Riverside. |
| Boyd, James Hill | Merchant | | | S Bernardino. |
| Brace, Rodney | Wagon maker | | | S Bernardino. |
| Bradford, Wm | Farmer | San Bernardino Co | nr San Bernardino | S Bernardino. |
| Bradford, Wm A | Laborer | San Bernardino | San Bernardino | S Bernardino. |
| Bradnibb, J | Farmer | South of Riverside | San Bernardino Co | S Bernardino. |
| Bragg, B F | Physician | San Bernardino | San Bernardino Co | S Bernardino. |
| Brageletton, J A | Livery stable | 3d st, opp P O | San Bernardino | S Bernardino. |
| Bridger, Jos | Farmer | San Bernardino Co | nr Chino | Chino. |
| Bright & Van Doren | Carriage makers | 3d st, opp W, F & Co | | S Bernardino. |
| Bright, — | Carriage manfcty | 3d st | San Bernardino | S Bernardino. |
| Bright, Joseph S | Blacksmith | | | S Bernardino. |
| Brunyel, John | Tailor | | | S Bernardino. |
| Brinkmeyer, H | Saloon | 3d st | | S Bernardino. |
| Brinkmeyer, H | Miner | San Bernardino | San Bernardino Co | S Bernardino. |
| Broadbeck, John | Miner | | | S Bernardino. |
| Brocker, H | Furniture | 3d st | San Bernardino | S Bernardino. |
| Brocker & Reinhold | Furniture | 3d st | San Bernardino | S Bernardino. |
| Brodhus, — | Mfr carrgs & wgns | Utah st | San Bernardino | S Bernardino. |
| Broderibb, Edward | Farmer | | | Riverside. |
| Brooke, J F | Farmer | San Bernardino Co | nr San Bernardino | S Bernardino. |
| Brooke, S | Blacksmith | San Bernardino Co | nr San Bernardino | S Bernardino. |
| Brooks, D W | Contractor | Utah st | San Bernardino | S Bernardino. |
| Brooke, S | Farmer | San Bernardino Co | nr San Bernardino | S Bernardino. |
| Brooks, Jas S | Carpenter | San Bernardino Co | San Bernardino | S Bernardino. |
| Brooke, H C | Conveyancer | San Bernardino Co | San Bernardino | S Bernardino. |
| Brooke, Robt A | Farmer | | Mojave | S Bernardino. |
| Brush, D | Farmer | San Bernardino Co | nr San Bernardino | S Bernardino. |
| Brush, I | Farmer | San Bernardino Co | nr San Bernardino | S Bernardino. |
| Brush, J | Farmer | nr San Bernardino | San Bernardino Co | S Bernardino. |
| Bruin & Sherwin | Prs Starke's hotel | 3d st | 3d st | S Bernardino. |
| Brunn & Roe | General mdse | 3d st, cor Utah | San Bernardino | S Bernardino. |
| Brunn, L | Merchant | San Bernardino Co | San Bernardino | S Bernardino. |
| Brown, E G | Justice peace | 1 m N E Riverside | San Bernardino rd | Riverside. |
| Brown, John, Jr | Notary public | 3d st | San Bernardino | S Bernardino. |
| Brown, Jerry | Farmer | | | S Bernardino. |
| Brown, Chas W | Teacher | | | S Bernardino. |
| Brown, John B | Clerk | | | S Bernardino. |
| Brown, John | Teacher | San Bernardino Co | San Bernardino | S Bernardino. |
| Brown, Jas | Farmer | San Bernardino | San Bernardino Co | S Bernardino. |
| Brown, B P | Farmer | nr San Bernardino | San Bernardino Co | S Bernardino. |
| Brown, Jos | Ranchero | San Bernardino Co | San Bernardino | S Bernardino. |
| Brown, H L | Teamster | nr San Bernardino | San Bernardino Co | S Bernardino. |
| Brown, L C | Farmer | nr San Bernardino | San Bernardino Co | S Bernardino. |
| Brown, H | Lumberman | San Bernardino Co | San Bernardino | S Bernardino. |
| Brown, J | Toll road keeper | San Bernardino Co | San Bernardino | S Bernardino. |
| Browne, T V | Druggist | San Bernardino Co | San Timoteo | S Bernardino. |
| Brownhardt, B | Clerk | | | S Bernardino. |
| Brownhardt, Samuel | Clerk | | | S Bernardino. |

DIRECTORY OF SAN BERNARDINO COUNTY. 261

| Name. | Occupation. | Place of Business. | Residence. | Town or P. O. |
|---|---|---|---|---|
| Bryant, Wm | Farmer | San Bernardino Co... | nr San Bernardino... | S Bernardino. |
| Bryant, S H | Farmer | San Bernardino Co... | nr San Bernardino... | S Bernardino. |
| Bryant, Jas | Farmer | nr San Bernardino... | San Bernardino Co ... | S Bernardino. |
| Buck, Wm Henry | Musician | | | S Bernardino. |
| Buck, Wm Henry | Cook | | | S Bernardino. |
| Buck, S A | Carpenter | San Bernardino Co... | San Bernardino Co... | S Bernardino. |
| Buchanan, J A | Farmer | nr San Bernardino... | San Bernardino Co... | S Bernardino. |
| Burke, C W | Cattle dealer | San Bernardino Co... | San Bernardino... | S Bernardino. |
| Burmudez, M | Farmer | San Bernardino... | nr San Timoteo... | S Bernardino. |
| Burnham, D H | Farmer | Riverside | 7th st | Riverside. |
| Bustamente, D | Ranchero | San Bernardino Co... | nr San Salvador | San Salvador. |
| Burt, B D | General mdse | Main st | 7th st | Riverside. |
| Burt, J W | Hostler | San Bernardino Co... | Cocomongo | Cocomongo. |
| Burruel, J | Farmer | San Bernardino Co... | nr San Salvador | San Salvador. |
| Burton, Geo I | Farmer | nr San Bernardino... | San Bernardino Co... | S Bernardino. |
| Bustameute, M | Farmer | nr San Bernardino... | San Bernardino Co... | S Bernardino. |
| Butherruth, T | Baker | San Bernardino Co... | Ivanpah | S Bernardino. |
| Button, M E | Teamster | nr San Bernardino... | San Bernardino Co... | S Bernardino. |
| Button, S B | Teamster | San Bernardino... | San Bernardino Co... | S Bernardino. |
| Buttles, Frank | Clerk | | | S Bernardino. |
| Byrne, Jas | Laborer | San Bernardino Co... | San Bernardino... | S Bernardino. |
| Byrne, Mathew | General mdse | 3d & Utah sts | | S Bernardino. |
| Cable, H G | Farmer | nr San Bernardino... | San Bernardino Co... | S Bernardino. |
| Cadd, D | Farmer | nr San Bernardino... | San Bernardino Co... | S Bernardino. |
| Cadd, Joseph | Farmer | | | S Bernardino. |
| Cahill, D | Miner | nr San Bernardino... | San Bernardino Co... | S Bernardino. |
| Caldwell, S | Carpenter | San Bernardino Co... | San Bernardino Co... | S Bernardino. |
| Caldwell, E | Farmer | 1½ m N Riverside... | Fruit st | Riverside. |
| Caldwell, James P | Lawyer | | | S Bernardino. |
| Caldwell, J H | Blacksmith | San Bernardino Co... | San Bernardino... | S Bernardino. |
| Caley, Wm | Engineer | San Bernardino Co... | San Bernardino... | S Bernardino. |
| Caley, Wm & Co | Lumber | | San Bernardino... | S Bernardino, |
| Caleff, P M | Farmer | ¾ m N Riverside... | San Bernardino... | Riverside. |
| Cameron, Jas | Minister | San Bernardino Co... | San Bernardino... | S Bernardino. |
| Campbell, John | Stage driver | San Bernardino Co... | San Bernardino... | S Bernardino. |
| Campbell, Jno A | Miner | San Bernardino Co... | San Bernardino... | S Bernardino. |
| Campbell, W C | Farmer | San Bernardino Co... | nr San Salvador | San Salvador. |
| Campbell, W L | Farmer | San Bernardino Co... | nr San Bernardino... | S Bernardino. |
| Campbell, J R | Farmer | nr San Bernardino... | San Bernardino Co... | S Bernardino. |
| Campbell, Jos | Teamster | San Bernardino Co... | nr Chino | Chino. |
| Cantwell, T J | Merchant | San Bernardino Co... | Camp Cady | |
| Carleton, Geo D | Nursery | Riverside | San Bernardino... | Riverside. |
| Carter, G | Clerk | San Bernardino Co... | San Bernardino... | S Bernardino. |
| Carter, J T | Miner | nr San Bernardino... | San Bernardino Co... | S Bernardino. |
| Carter, B | Teamster | San Bernardino Co... | San Bernardino Co... | S Bernardino. |
| Carter, L S | Farmer | nr San Bernardino... | San Bernardino Co... | S Bernardino. |
| Carter, T W | Farmer | San Bernardino Co... | nr San Bernardino... | S Bernardino. |
| Carter, Richd James | Miner | San Bernardino Co... | San Bernardino... | S Bernardino. |
| Carter, Chas | Farmer | nr San Bernardino... | San Bernardino Co... | S Bernardino. |
| Carter, J C | Farmer | nr San Bernardino... | San Bernardino Co... | S Bernardino. |
| Carter, D | Miner | San Bernardino Co... | Mountain Mill | S Bernardino. |
| Carter, J M | Farmer | nr San Bernardino... | San Bernardino Co... | S Bernardino. |
| Carter, A A | Farmer | San Bernardino Co... | nr San Bernardino... | S Bernardino. |
| Carter, D | Farmer | nr San Bernardino... | San Bernardino Co... | S Bernardino. |
| Carter, A | Farmer | nr San Bernardino... | San Bernardino Co... | S Bernardino. |
| Carleton, G D | Nurseryman | ¾ m N Riverside | San Bernardino Road | Riverside. |
| Caro, L | Merchant | San Bernardino Co... | San Bernardino... | S Bernardino. |
| Carlton, Geo D | Dairyman | | | S Bernardino. |
| Carpenter, F | Saloon keeper | San Bernardino Co... | San Bernardino... | S 'Bernardino. |
| Carpenter, D | Farmer | San Bernardino Co... | nr San Bernardino... | S Bernardino. |
| Case, J F | Farmer | nr San Bernardino... | San Bernardino Co... | S Bernardino. |
| Case, J H | Farmer | San Bernardino Co... | nr San Bernardino... | S Bernardino. |
| Case, G C | Farmer | nr San Bernardino... | San Bernardino Co... | S Bernardino. |
| Case, W W | Farmer | nr San Bernardino... | San Bernardino Co... | S Bernardino. |

## L. L. PAULSON'S HAND-BOOK AND

| NAME. | OCCUPATION. | PLACE OF BUSINESS. | RESIDENCE. | TOWN OR P. O. |
|---|---|---|---|---|
| Casta, M................ | Farmer................ | San Bernardino Co... | nr San Timoteo........ | S Bernardino. |
| Castillo, T............ | Stock raiser......... | North of Riverside... | San Bernardino Co... | Riverside. |
| Castillo, A............ | Silversmith.......... | San Bernardino Co... | San Bernardino........ | S Bernardino. |
| Castillo, M............ | Farmer................ | San Bernardino Co... | Agua Mansa............ | |
| Castillo, B............ | Farmer................ | San Bernardino Co... | nr San Salvador...... | San Salvador. |
| Castillo, B............ | Laborer............... | San Bernardino Co... | nr San Salvador...... | San Salvador. |
| Castillo, J............ | Farmer................ | San Bernardino Co... | nr Chino............. | Chino. |
| Castillo, del M...... | Laborer............... | San Bernardino Co... | nr San Salvador...... | San Salvador. |
| Castillo, del G...... | Laborer............... | nr San Bernardino... | San Bernardino Co... | S Bernardino. |
| Casteel James N.... | Farmer................ | ...................... | ...................... | Riverside. |
| Casteel, J O.......... | Farmer................ | nr San Bernardino... | San Bernardino Co... | S Bernardino. |
| Cate, J P.............. | Miner................. | nr San Bernardino... | San Bernardino Co... | S Bernardino. |
| Cave, James W..... | Farmer................ | ...................... | ...................... | S Bernardino. |
| Cave, W P............ | Carpenter............ | San Bernardino Co... | San Bernardino...... | S Bernardino. |
| Cave, J P............. | Farmer................ | San Bernardino Co... | nr San Bernardino... | S Bernardino. |
| Cavruro, R........... | Farmer................ | San Bernardino Co... | Temescal.............. | Temescal. |
| Chacon, D............ | Farmer................ | San Bernardino Co... | nr San Salvador...... | San Salvador. |
| Chamberlain, P..... | Physician............ | Anderson's Building. | San Bernardino...... | S Bernardino. |
| Channey, M.......... | Farmer................ | San Bernardino Co... | San Bernardino Co... | S Bernardino. |
| Chapman, S ......... | Farmer................ | San Bernardino Co... | nr Riverside ........ | Riverside. |
| Chapelle, Francisco | Farmer................ | 15 m E S Bernardino | San Timoteo.......... | S Bernardino. |
| Chapman, F T....... | Farmer................ | San Bernardino Co... | nr San Bernardino... | S Bernardino. |
| Charbivilla, J....... | Laborer............... | nr San Bernardino... | San Bernardino Co... | S Bernardino. |
| Chenhall, N ......... | Merchant............. | San Bernardino...... | San Bernardino Co... | S Bernardino. |
| Chilson, S A......... | Farmer................ | San Bernardino Co... | nr Temescal.......... | Temescal. |
| Chilson, E L......... | Farmer................ | San Bernardino Co... | nr Temescal.......... | Temescal. |
| Chipman, M E ...... | Farmer................ | San Bernardino Co... | nr San Bernardino... | S Bernardino. |
| Choate, Nehemiah.. | Merchant............. | San Bernardino...... | San Bernardino Co... | S Bernardino. |
| Christia, —  ......... | Attorney.............. | 4th st................ | San Bernardino...... | S Bernardino. |
| Clark, H .............. | Teamster............. | San Bernardino Co... | nr San Bernardino... | S Bernardino. |
| Clark, J P............ | Farmer................ | San Bernardino Co... | nr Chino............. | Chino. |
| Clark, C C ........... | Printer................ | San Bernardino Co... | San Bernardino...... | S Bernardino. |
| Clark, W S........... | Farmer................ | nr San Bernardino... | San Bernardino Co... | S Bernardino. |
| Clark, Geo R........ | Farmer................ | San Bernardino Co... | nr Cocomongo........ | Cocomongo. |
| Clark, I S............ | Farmer................ | San Bernardino Co... | nr Chino............. | Chino. |
| Clark, H M........... | Laborer............... | nr San Bernardino... | San Bernardino Co... | S Bernardino. |
| Clark, James C..... | Farmer................ | ...................... | ...................... | S Bernardino. |
| Clapp, J C .......... | Farmer................ | nr San Bernardino... | San Bernardino Co... | S Bernardino. |
| Clapp, J D .......... | Farmer................ | So of S Bernardino... | San Bernardino Co... | S Bernardino. |
| Clayton, J ........... | Teamster............. | San Bernardino Co... | nr San Bernardino... | S Bernardino. |
| Cleft, George H.... | Farmer................ | ...................... | ...................... | Riverside. |
| Cleine, F ............. | Farmer................ | San Bernardino Road | San Bernardino Road | Riverside. |
| Clemenson, Jas..... | Painter............... | San Bernardino Co... | San Bernardino...... | S Bernardino. |
| Clews, Jos .......... | Mason................. | San Bernardino Co... | San Bernardino Co... | S Bernardino. |
| Cline, H .............. | Engineer ............. | San Bernardino Co... | Chino................. | Chino. |
| Cline, D............... | Carpenter............ | San Bernardino Co... | San Bernardino Co... | S Bernardino. |
| Clusker, C C ........ | Miner................. | nr San Bernardino... | San Bernardino Co... | S Bernardino. |
| Clyde, A D .......... | Farmer................ | nr San Bernardino... | San Bernardino Co... | S Bernardino. |
| Clyde, E P........... | Farmer................ | nr San Bernardino... | San Bernardino Co... | S Bernardino. |
| Clyde, S D .......... | Farmer................ | nr San Bernardino... | San Bernardino Co... | S Bernardino. |
| Coan, E P ............ | Farmer................ | nr San Bernardino... | San Bernardino Co... | S Bernardino. |
| Coburn, James A... | Farmer................ | ...................... | ...................... | S Bernardino. |
| Coburn, J M ........ | Farmer................ | San Bernardino Co... | nr San Bernardino... | S Bernardino. |
| Cochran, R A....... | Assayer............... | San Bernardino Co... | Ivanpah............... | S Bernardino. |
| Cochrane, R......... | Farmer................ | nr San Bernardino... | San Bernardino Co... | S Bernardino. |
| Cock, C J............ | Butcher............... | San Bernardino Co... | San Bernardino...... | S Bernardino. |
| Coddington, D A... | Farmer................ | 12 m S S Bernardino | Riverside............ | Riverside. |
| Colby, Levi J....... | Merchant............. | 12 m S S Bernardino | Riverside............ | Riverside. |
| Cole, D M............ | Carpenter............ | San Bernardino Co... | San Bernardino...... | S Bernardino. |
| Cole, Chas Ira...... | Car driver........... | ...................... | ...................... | S Bernardino. |
| Cole, A............... | Laborer............... | San Bernardino Co... | nr San Bernardino... | S Bernardino. |
| Cole, J A............. | Farmer................ | San Bernardino Co... | nr San Bernardino... | S Bernardino. |
| Cole, H H............ | Farmer................ | San Bernardino Co... | nr San Bernardino... | S Bernardino. |
| Collins, C A ........ | Carpenter............ | San Bernardino Co... | San Bernardino...... | S Bernardino. |

# DIRECTORY OF SAN BERNARDINO COUNTY. 263

| NAME. | OCCUPATION. | PLACE OF BUSINESS. | RESIDENCE. | TOWN OR P. O. |
|---|---|---|---|---|
| Colman, A............ | Stone cutter........ | San Bernardino Co... | San Bernardino........ | S Bernardino. |
| Colton, C E........... | Freighter............. | San Bernardino Co... | San Bernardino........ | S Bernardino. |
| Comerford, D........ | Painter ................ | San Bernardino Co... | San Bernardino........ | S Bernardino. |
| Comstock, C B...... | Farmer ................ | San Bernardino Co... | Riverside................. | Riverside. |
| Condee, A ............ | Surgeon.... .......... | 3d st...................... | San Bernardino........ | S Bernardino. |
| Confer, A.............. | Butcher................ | San Bernardino Co... | San Bernardino........ | S Bernardino. |
| Congdon, J R....... | Farmer ................ | San Bernardino Co... | nr San Timoteo........ | S Bernardino. |
| Conklin, Wm Henry | Gardener ............ | .............................. | .............................. | S Bernardino. |
| Conn, U A............ | Ranch owner ...... | San Bernardino Co... | nr San Bernardino... | S Bernardino. |
| Conner, H............. | Groceries............. | 3d st...................... | San Bernardino........ | S Bernardino. |
| Cook, Thos .......... | Laborer............... | San Bernardino Co... | Lytle Creek............. | S Bernardino. |
| Cook, J W............. | Farmer ..... ......... | San Bernardino Co... | San Bernardino........ | S Bernardino. |
| Cooley, Geo......... | Farmer ................ | nr San Bernardino... | San Bernardino Co... | S Bernardino. |
| Cooledge, S A...... | Stock raiser......... | San Bernardino Co... | San Salvador.......... | San Salvador. |
| Cooper, John ....... | Farmer ................ | nr San Bernardino... | San Bernardino Co... | S Bernardino. |
| Coplea, C L.......... | Farmer ................ | San Bernardino Co... | nr San Bernardino... | S Bernardino. |
| Cornwall, L I........ | Gardener ............ | San Bernardino Co... | San Bernardino........ | S Bernardino. |
| Cornwell, J D....... | Farmer ................ | .............................. | .............................. | S Bernardino. |
| Cota, R................. | Ranchero............. | San Bernardino Co... | nr Chino................. | Chino. |
| Courtenay, I H...... | Painter ................ | nr San Bernardino... | San Bernardino Co... | S Bernardino. |
| Courtney, W T...... | Farmer ................ | nr San Bernardino... | San Bernardino Co... | S Bernardino. |
| Cover, P D............ | Farmer................. | South of Riverside... | San Bernardino Co... | Riverside. |
| Cover, T W........... | Farmer................. | South of Riverside... | San Bernardino Co... | Riverside. |
| Cover, J S............. | Farmer................. | South of Riverside... | San Bernardino Co... | Riverside. |
| Covington, J W..... | Farmer ................ | nr San Bernardino... | San Bernardino Co... | S Bernardino. |
| Covington, W D ... | Farmer................. | nr San Bernardino... | San Bernardino Co... | S Bernardino. |
| Covington, D A.... | Farmer ................ | nr San Bernardino... | San Bernardino Co... | S Bernardino. |
| Cowan, David L.... | Carpenter ........... | San Bernardino....... | San Bernardino........ | S Bernardino. |
| Cox & Banks........ | Groceries............. | 3d st...................... | .............................. | S Bernardino. |
| Cox, S C............... | Teamster ............ | San Bernardino Co... | nr San Bernardino... | S Bernardino. |
| Cox, A J................ | Merchant ............ | San Bernardino Co... | San Bernardino........ | S Bernardino. |
| Cox, J B ............... | Farmer................. | San Bernardino Co... | San Bernardino Co... | S Bernardino. |
| Cox, R R............... | Teamster ............ | San Bernardino Co... | nr San Bernardino... | S Bernardino. |
| Craft, M H............. | Farmer................. | nr San Bernardino... | San Bernardino Co... | S Bernardino. |
| Crag, S................. | Farmer................. | San Bernardino Co... | nr San Salvador ...... | San Salvador. |
| Crafts, G H............ | Farmer ................ | San Bernardino Co... | nr San Bernardino... | S Bernardino. |
| Craig, W .............. | Hotel keeper ....... | Riverside............... | San Bernardino Co... | Riverside. |
| Craig, Joseph....... | Gun store............. | 3d st...................... | San Bernardino........ | S Bernardino. |
| Craig, Joseph D.... | Tinner.................. | .............................. | .............................. | S Bernardino. |
| Cram, H................ | Farmer................. | nr San Bernardino... | San Bernardino Co... | S Bernardino. |
| Cramm, G ............ | Farmer ................ | nr San Bernardino... | San Bernardino Co... | S Bernardino. |
| Cram, J H ............. | Farmer ................ | nr San Bernardino... | San Bernardino Co... | S Bernardino. |
| Cram, S F............. | Farmer ................ | nr San Bernardino... | San Bernardino Co... | S Bernardino. |
| Crandel, S ........... | Farmer .... .......... | San Bernardino....... | San Bernardino Co... | S Bernardino. |
| Crandall, R .......... | Carpenter............ | San Bernardino Co... | San Bernardino........ | S Bernardino. |
| Crandale, L D ...... | Freighter.............. | San Bernardino Co... | San Bernardino........ | S Bernardino. |
| Crandall, C.......... | Farmer ................ | nr San Bernardino... | San Bernardino Co... | S Bernardino. |
| Crane, T............... | Livery stable ....... | 6th st..................... | 6th st..................... | Riverside. |
| Crane, L............... | Farmer................. | South of Riverside... | San Bernardino Co... | Riverside. |
| Craw, C J ............. | Teamster ........... | San Bernardino Co... | nr San Bernardino... | S Bernardino. |
| Craw, H L............. | Teamster............ | nr San Bernardino... | San Bernardino Co... | S Bernardino. |
| Craw, Geo A........ | Farmer ................ | nr San Bernardino... | San Bernardino Co... | S Bernardino. |
| Crawford, Robt.... | Farmer ................ | .............................. | .............................. | S Bernardino. |
| Crawford, E ........ | Miner .................. | nr San Bernardino... | San Bernardino Co... | S Bernardino. |
| Craw, O................ | Freighter.............. | San Bernardino Co... | San Bernardino Co... | S Bernardino. |
| Crevecveur, A B... | Farmer ................ | San Bernardino....... | San Bernardino Co... | S Bernardino. |
| Cridge, A............. | Farmer ................ | South of Riverside... | San Bernardino Co... | Riverside. |
| Criswell, W D...... | Farmer ................ | nr San Bernardino... | San Bernardino Co... | S Bernardino. |
| Criswell, C M...... | Farmer ................ | nr San Bernardino... | San Bernardino Co... | S Bernardino. |
| Christie, Robt J.... | Lawyer................ | .............................. | .............................. | S Bernardino. |
| Crittenden, J Wm.. | Carpenter............ | San Bernardino....... | San Bernardino........ | S Bernardino. |
| Crosby, B S.......... | Clergyman.......... | San Bernardino Co... | San Bernardino........ | S Bernardino. |
| Crolik, Wm ......... | Tailor................... | 3d st...................... | .............................. | S Bernardino. |
| Culbertson, J A..... | Farmer ................ | nr San Bernardino... | San Bernardino Co... | S Bernardino. |

# HARNESS & SADDLE MANUFACTORY.

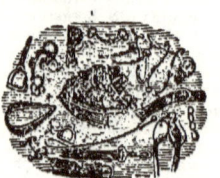  

## JOHN M. FOY,
Importer, Manufacturer, Wholesale and Retail Dealer in

### Saddlery and Harness of all kinds,

SULKY HARNESS, TROTTING HARNESS,

HEAVY DRAFT HARNESS,

### ROBES, BLANKETS,
AND WHIPS.

### GENUINE CONCORD HARNESS,

In fact, everything pertaining to a first-class Saddlery House.

---

THE VERY BEST GENUINE LOS ANGELES SADDLES.

The best brands of Saddle, Harness and Sole Leather always on hand and for sale, wholesale and retail.

HARNESS OILS, SOAPS AND BLACKING.

*REPAIRING PROMPTLY DONE.*

3rd STREET, BET. UTAH AND GRAFTON, SAN BERNARDINO, CAL.

Prices as Low as any house on the Coast.

DIRECTORY OF SAN BERNARDINO COUNTY. 265

| NAME. | OCCUPATION. | PLACE OF BUSINESS. | RESIDENCE. | TOWN OR P. O. |
|---|---|---|---|---|
| Cummings & Co, D W | Gen merchandise. | Bairdstown | Bear Valley | Bairdstown. |
| Cummings, H B | Miner | nr San Bernardino | San Bernardino Co | S Bernardino. |
| Cundiff, — | Groceries | San Bernardino | San Bernardino Co | S Bernardino. |
| Cundiff, — | Farmer | South of Riverside | San Bernardino Co | S Bernardino. |
| Cunningham, R F. | Genl merchandise | San Bernardino | San Bernardino Co | S Bernardino. |
| Cunningham, C P. | Physician | San Bernardino | San Bernardino Co | S Bernardino. |
| Cunningham, D G. | Dentist | 3d st | San Bernardino | S Bernardino. |
| Curtis, J W | Teacher | San Bernardino Co | San Bernardino | S Bernardino. |
| Curtis, R H | Printer | San Bernardino Co | San Bernardino | S Bernardino. |
| Curtis, W J | Attorney at law | 7 Kelling's Building | | S Bernardino. |
| Curtis, Wm | Farmer | nr San Bernardino | San Bernardino Co | S Bernardino. |
| Curry, A J | Lumberman | San Bernardino Co | nr San Bernardino | S Bernardino. |
| Curry, T | Tailor | San Bernardino Co | San Bernardino | S Bernardino. |
| Cureton, J J | Farmer | San Bernardino Co | nr San Bernardino | S Bernardino. |
| Cushing, S R | Engineer | San Bernardino Co | Bellville | |
| Daley, E W | Teamster | San Bernardino Co | nr San Bernardino | S Bernardino. |
| Daley, M | Teamster | San Bernardino Co | San Bernardino | S Bernardino. |
| Daley, E | Farmer | San Bernardino Co | nr San Bernardino | S Bernardino. |
| Daley, M L | Teamster | nr San Bernardino | San Bernardino Co | S Bernardino. |
| Daly, M | Farmer | West of Santa Ana | San Bernardino Co | Riverside. |
| Darracott, George | Photographer | | | S Bernardino. |
| Dates, L | Saddler | San Bernardino Co | San Bernardin' | S Bernardino. |
| Davis, Wm | Blacksmith | San Bernardino Co | San Bernardino | S Bernardino. |
| Davis, J A | Farmer | nr San Bernardino | San Bernardino Co | S Bernardino. |
| Davies, Wm | Miller | San Bernardino Co | San Bernardino | S Bernardino. |
| Davis, R A | Carpenter | San Bernardino Co | San Bernardino | S Bernardino. |
| Davis, C | Teamster | nr San Bernardino | San Bernardino Co | S Bernardino. |
| Davis, Mrs R A | Millinery | 3d st | San Bernardino | S Bernardino. |
| Davis, Wm Albert. | Farmer | | | |
| Davies, J | Farmer | San Bernardino Co | nr San Bernardino | S Bernardino. |
| David, D L | Farmer | San Bernardino Co | Bellville | |
| Davidson, J J | Farmer | San Bernardino Co | nr San Bernardino | S Bernardino. |
| Davenport, Noel | Book keeper | | | S Bernardino. |
| Day, Geo | Farmer | San Bernardino Co | nr Chino | Chino. |
| Decrow, I G | Teamster | San Bernardino Co | nr San Bernardino | S Bernardino. |
| Decrow, G | Farmer | San Bernardino Co | nr San Bernardino | S Bernardino. |
| Defley, F | Laborer | nr San Bernardino | San Bernardino Co | S Bernardino. |
| Dempsey, J H | Teamster | San Bernardino Co | San Bernardino Co | S Bernardino. |
| Depen, Wm | Miner | nr San Bernardino | San Bernardino Co | S Bernardino. |
| Du Pish, Edward | Barber | 3d st | 3d st | S Bernardino. |
| Devine, H | Printer | San Bernardino Co | San Bernardino | S Bernardino. |
| Dewitt, H L | Farmer | San Bernardino | San Bernardino Co | S Bernardino. |
| Dewitt, J | Farmer | San Bernardino Co | San Bernardino | S Bernardino. |
| De Witte, J | Teamster | nr San Bernardino | San Bernardino Co | S Bernardino. |
| Dias, Manuel, Jr | Farmer | 15 m E S Bernardino | San Timoteo | S Bernardino. |
| Dickey, D R | Physician | San Bernardino Co | San Bernardino | S Bernardino. |
| Dickson, W W | Teamster | San Bernardino | San Bernardino | S Bernardino. |
| Dickson, D | Teamster | San Bernardino Co | San Bernardino | S Bernardino. |
| Dillon, Wm J | Miner | San Bernardino Co | Lytle Creek | S Bernardino. |
| Donaly, Terens | Hostler | San Bernardino | San Bernardino | S Bernardino. |
| Donohoe, M | Farmer | San Bernardino | San Bernardino Co | S Bernardino. |
| Doston, H C | Farmer | San Bernardino Co | nr San Bernardino | S Bernardino. |
| Doston, E | Farmer | nr San Bernardino | San Bernardino Co | S Bernardino. |
| Dougherty, I L | Farmer | nr San Bernardino | San Bernardino Co | S Bernardino. |
| Dougherty, Jas | Farmer | nr San Bernardino | San Bernardino Co | S Bernardino. |
| Downey, A | Teamster | nr San Bernardino | San Bernardino Co | S Bernardino. |
| Downey, Wm A | Farmer | nr San Bernardino | San Bernardino Co | S Bernardino. |
| Down, J | Mason | Main st | San Bernardino Rd | Riverside. |
| Dowd, M F | Miner | San Bernardino Co | Ivanpah | S Bernardino. |
| Doyle, Jas | Cooper | San Bernardino Co | San Bernardino | S Bernardino. |
| Dozier, E F | Farmer | San Bernardino Co | nr Chino | Chino. |
| Drew, P G | Hardware | Utah st | | S Bernardino. |
| Drew, H L | Hardware | Utah st | | S Bernardino. |

| NAME. | OCCUPATION. | PLACE OF BUSINESS. | RESIDENCE. | TOWN OR P. O. |
|---|---|---|---|---|
| Drew, — | Druggist | 3d st | San Bernardino | S Bernardino. |
| Drew, Bros | Hardware | Utah st | | S Bernardino. |
| Drew, Thos S | Planter | San Bernardino Co | nr San Bernardino | S Bernardino. |
| Driggers, J J | Farmer | nr San Bernardino | San Bernardino Co | S Bernardino. |
| Dry, A | Lumberman | San Bernardino Co | nr San Bernardino | S Bernardino. |
| Duncan, N | Laborer | San Bernardino Co | Cocomongo | Cocomongo. |
| Durtee, M | Teamster | San Bernardino Co | nr San Bernardino | S Bernardino. |
| Dustin, C C | Farmer | nr San Bernardino | San Bernardino Co | S Bernardino. |
| Dustin, F | Farmer | nr San Bernardino | San Bernardino Co | S Bernardino. |
| Dustin, J H | Teamster | San Bernardino Co | nr San Bernardino | S Bernardino. |
| Dustin, J | Farmer | nr San Bernardino | San Bernardino Co | S Bernardino. |
| Dwyer, P | Laborer | San Bernardino Co | nr San Bernardino | S Bernardino. |
| Earl, Willard | Laborer | 15 m E San Bernar | San Timoteo | S Bernardino. |
| Easton, John | Teamster | San Bernardino | San Bernardino Co | S Bernardino. |
| Easton, George | Teamster | nr San Bernardino | San Bernardino Co | S Bernardino. |
| Eastman, A L Mrs. | Farmer | South of Riverside | San Bernardino Co | Riverside. |
| Eastman, Sanford | Physician | 12 m S San Bernar | Riverside | Riverside. |
| Edgar, James B | Farmer | San Bernardino Co | nr San Bernardino | S Bernardino. |
| Edgar, F M | Farmer | nr San Bernardino | San Bernardino Co | S Bernardino. |
| Edwards, T | Miner | nr San Bernardino | San Bernardino Co | S Bernardino. |
| Edwards, Wm P, Jr | Stationer | San Bernardino | San Bernardino Co | S Bernardino. |
| Egloff, J C | Blacksmith | San Bernardino | San Bernardino Co | S Bernardino. |
| Elisalde, Jesus | Ranchero | San Bernardino | San Bernardino Co | S Bernardino. |
| Eliania, F | Farmer | San Bernardino | nr San Bernardino | S Bernardino. |
| Embers, G | Miner | San Bernardino | nr San Bernardino | S Bernardino. |
| Emerson, D B | Farmer | San Bernardino Co | nr San Timoteo | S Bernardino. |
| Emery, J G Dr | Farmer | South of Riverside | San Bernardino Co | Riverside. |
| Emmons, H R Dr. | Phys & drug store | Main st | Riverside | Riverside. |
| Emmons, H R | Dry goods | San Bernardino | San Bernardino Co | S Bernardino. |
| Emich, C N | Hardware store | Jackson's blk, 3d st | San Bernardino Co | S Bernardino. |
| Emich & Sleppy | Hardware &stoves | San Bernardino | | S Bernardino. |
| Espinosa, Jose M | Farmer | | San Salvador | San Salvador. |
| Espinosa, Luciano | Laborer | San Bernardino Co | San Salvador | San Salvador. |
| Etu, F | Farmer | San Bernardino Co | nr San Salvador | San Salvador. |
| Evans, David Jones | Physician | San Bernardino | San Bernardino Co | S Bernardino. |
| Evans, J H | Farmer | nr San Bernardino | San Bernardino Co | S Bernardino. |
| Everett, John | Laborer | 12 m S San Bernar | Riverside | Riverside. |
| Everts, A | Farmer | San Bernardino Co | nr San Bernardino | S Bernardino. |
| Faburn, C S | Farmer | San Bernardino Co | nr San Bernardino | S Bernardino. |
| Farnsworth, W | Farmer | San Bernardino Co | nr San Timoteo | S Bernardino. |
| Faurol, I | Farmer | nr San Bernardino | San Bernardino Co | S Bernardino. |
| Fears, J M | Farmer | nr San Bernardino | San Bernardino Co | S Bernardino. |
| Feidler, C | Laborer | San Bernardino Co | San Timoteo | Bernardino. |
| Felter, Andrew J. | Farmer & lawyer | nr San Bernardino | San Bernardino Co | S Bernardino. |
| Felter, Jacob R | Clerk | San Bernardino | San Bernardino Co | S Bernardino. |
| Feliz, D | Saddle maker | San Bernardino Co | San Timoteo | S Bernardino. |
| Ferguson, John | Laborer | nr San Bernardino | San Bernardino Co | S Bernardino. |
| Ferris, F T | Civil engineer | Utah st | Utah st, bet 6th & 7th | S Bernardino. |
| Ferra, G | Farmer | San Bernardino Co | nr San Timoteo | S Bernardino. |
| Ferre, John | Farmer | nr San Bernardino | San Bernardino Co | S Bernardino. |
| Ferster, D S | Miner | San Bernardino Co | San Bernardino Co | S Bernardino. |
| Fernando, V | Farmer | San Bernardino Co | nr Chino | Chino. |
| Fessenden, B B | Teamster | 13th st | Riverside | Riverside. |
| Feudge, J | Printer | San Bernardino Co | San Timoteo | S Bernardino. |
| Filane, P | Farmer | San Bernardino Co | nr San Salvador | San Salvador. |
| Fillmore, D R | Farmer | nr San Bernardino | San Bernardino Co | S Bernardino. |
| Fisher, Wm H | Station keeper | San Bernardino | San Bernardino Co | S Bernardino. |
| Fitzhugh, S E | Farmer | nr San Bernardino | San Bernardino Co | S Bernardino. |
| Fizer, H M | Carpenter | San Bernardino Co | San Bernardino | S Bernardino. |
| Fleisher, W | Merchant | San Bernardino | San Bernardino Co | S Bernardino. |
| Flemming, Arthur | Real estate | Ruffen's building | San Bernardino | S Bernardino. |
| Fleming, A | Druggist | San Bernardino | San Bernardino | S Bernardino. |
| Flemming & Rose. | Searchers records. | Ruffen's building | San Bernardino | S Bernardino. |
| Flick, Oliver Jno | | San Bernardino Co | | S Bernardino. |

DIRECTORY OF SAN BERNARDINO COUNTY. 267

| NAME. | OCCUPATION. | PLACE OF BUSINESS. | RESIDENCE. | TOWN OR P. O. |
|---|---|---|---|---|
| Flinn, I............... | Farmer............. | San Bernardino Co... | San Bernardino........ | S Bernardino. |
| Flores, J............... | Silversmith........ | cor 3d & Salt Lake st |  | S Bernardino. |
| Foley, P........,.. | Saloon............... | Main st........ ......... | Main st....... ......... | Riverside. |
| Folks, S D........... | Carpenter........... | San Bernardino Co... | San Bernardino........ | S Bernardino. |
| Folks, S ........ ... | Merchant ....... .... | San Bernardino Co... | San Bernardino........ | S Bernardino. |
| Folks, Jessee......... | Carpenter........... | San Bernardino Co... | San Bernardino........ | S Bernardino. |
| Foot, George E...... | Teamster............ | San Bernardino Co... |  | S Bernardino. |
| Forbes, J L.......... | Farmer............. | nr San Bernardino... | San Bernardino Co... | S Bernardino. |
| **Forbes, J B**......... | Doctor ........ ..... | San Bernardino....... | San Bernardino....... | S Bernardino. |
| Ford, R M............ | Farmer............. | San Bernardino Co... | San Timoteo........ | S Bernardino. |
| Forsee, P A.......... | Printer......... ...... | San Bernardino Co... | San Bernardino........ | S Bernardino. |
| **Forsee, Jas**........... | Lawyer- ............. | San Bernardino Co... | San Bernardino........ | S Bernardino. |
| Fort, John B......... | Clerk............... | San Bernardino....... | San Bernardino........ | S Bernardino. |
| Foster, I S............ | Engineer ........... | San Bernardino Co... | Mountain Mill........ | S Bernardino. |
| Foster, T J........... | Teamster........... | San Bernardino Co... | San Bernardino........ | Chino. |
| Fowler, F M......... | Farmer ............. | San Bernardino Co... | nr Chino.............. | S Bernardino. |
| **Fowler, Geo A**....... | Farmer ........ ..... | San Bernardino Co... | nr San Bernardino... | S Bernardino. |
| Fowler, J T.......... | Teamster........... | San Bernardino Co... | nr San Bernardino... | S Bernardino. |
| **Fox & Condee**....... | Physicians .......... | 9 Kelting's blk, 3d st |  | S Bernardino. |
| Fox, W R ......... | Physician........... | Kelting bldg, 3d st... | San Bernardino........ | S Bernardino. |
| Fox, H................ | Riverside hotel.... | 7th and Orange sts... | 7th st................... | S Bernardino. |
| **Foy, J M**............... | Saddle & harness. | Court house blk, 3d st |  | S Bernardino. |
| Franklin, A J........ | Miner ............... | nr San Bernardino... | San Bernardino Co... | S Bernardino. |
| French, Wm......... | Farmer ............. | nr San Bernardino... | San Bernardino........ | S Bernardino. |
| Frescoes, A.......... | Farmer ............. | San Bernardino Co... | San Bernardino........ | S Bernardino. |
| Frink, J R............ | Farmer ............. | San Bernardino Co... | San Timoteo........ | S Bernardino. |
| Fuqua, I............... | Farmer ............. | San Bernardino Co... | Rincon................. | Chino. |
| Fulgham, B F....... | Teamster........... | nr San Bernardino... | San Bernardino Co... | S Bernardino. |
| **Furney, J**.............. | Blacksmith......... | San Bernardino Co... | San Timoteo........ | S Bernardino. |
| Gads, H C............ | Teamster........... | nr San Bernardino... | San Bernardino Co... | S Bernardino. |
| Garcia, David....... | Laborer............. |  | San Salvador......... | San Salvador. |
| Garcia, — ........... | Stock raiser........ | Riverside............. | San Bernardino Co... | Riverside. |
| **Garcia, J P**............ | Farmer ............. | San Bernardino Co... | nr San Salvador...... | San Salvador. |
| Garcia, J............. | Farmer ............. | San Bernardino....... | Agua Mansa......... | S Bernardino. |
| Garcia, M A......... | Farmer ............. | San Bernardino Co... | nr San Salvador...... | San Salvador. |
| Garcia, A............. | Laborer............. | San Bernardino Co... | nr San Salvador...... | San Salvador. |
| Garcia, E............. | Farmer ............. | San Bernardino Co... | nr San Salvador...... | San Salvador. |
| Garcia, Joseph Silveira | Merchant........... |  | Cocomongo........... | Cocomongo. |
| Garcio, Elicio....... | Laborer ... .......... |  | San Salvador......... | San Salvador. |
| Garcelon, G W...... | Fruiterer............ | Riverside............. | 7th st.................. | Riverside. |
| Garner, M B......... | Farmer.... ........... | San Bernardino Co... | nr San Bernardino... | S Bernardino. |
| Garner, J E.......... | Teamster........... | San Bernardino Co... | nr San Bernardino... | S Bernardino. |
| Garner, W W....... | Farmer ............. | nr San Bernardino... | San Bernardino Co... | S Bernardino. |
| **Garner, John**........ | Farmer ............. | San Bernardino Co... | San Bernardino........ | S Bernardino. |
| Garner, B F.......... | Farmer ............. | nr San Bernardino... | San Bernardino Co... | S Bernardino. |
| **Garner, John, Jr**.. | Farmer ............. | San Bernardino Co... | nr San Bernardino... | S Bernardino. |
| Gastello, J............ | Farmer ............. | San Bernardino Co... | nr San Bernardino... | S Bernardino. |
| Gates, E H........... | Farmer ............. | San Bernardino Co... | nr Chino.............. | Chino. |
| Geddes, Thomas..... | Farmer ............. | nr San Bernardino... | San Bernardino Co... | Riverside. |
| Gentry, D S.......... | Farmer ............. | San Bernardino Co... | nr San Bernardino... | S Bernardino. |
| **Gephardt, Adolph**. | Butcher............. | San Bernardino....... | San Bernardino........ | S Bernardino. |
| Gerard, C............. | Farmer ............. | nr San Bernardino... | San Bernardino Co... | S Bernardino. |
| **Getzendanner, E T** | Physician........... | San Bernardino Co... | Cocomongo ........... | Cocomongo. |
| Gibbs, W N.......... | Farmer ............. | San Bernardino Co... | nr San Bernardino... | S Bernardino. |
| Gibbons, Chas....... | Miner ............... | nr San Bernardino... | San Bernardino Co... | S Bernardino. |
| Gibson, James W... | Laborer ............. | 12 m S San Bernar... | Riverside.............. | Riverside. |
| Gibson, Jesse........ | Farmer ............. | nr San Bernardino... | San Bernardino Co... | S Bernardino. |
| **Gifford, Miles N**.... | Blacksmith......... | San Bernardino....... | San Bernardino........ | S Bernardino. |
| Gifford, L............ | Farmer ............. | San Bernardino Co... | nr San Bernardino... | S Bernardino. |
| Gilbert, J D.......... | Farmer ............. | nr San Bernardino... | San Bernardino Co... | S Bernardino. |
| Gilbert, Hiram H... | Saloon keeper...... | San Bernardino....... | San Bernardino........ | S Bernardino. |
| Gilbert, J A.......... | Miner ............... | San Bernardino Co... | nr San Bernardino... | S Bernardino. |
| Gilbert, J........... | Farmer ............. | San Bernardino Co... | nr San Bernardino... | S Bernardino. |

| NAME. | OCCUPATION. | PLACE OF BUSINESS. | RESIDENCE. | TOWN OR P. O. |
|---|---|---|---|---|
| Gilman, J M | Ranchero | nr San Bernardino | San Bernardino Co | S Bernardino. |
| Gleaves, James M | Druggist | San Bernardino | San Bernardino | S Bernardino. |
| Glenn, S S | Farmer | nr San Bernardino | San Bernardino Co | S Bernardino. |
| Glover, J B | Farmer | San Bernardino Co | nr San Bernardino | S Bernardino. |
| Goble, J | Farmer | nr San Bernardino | San Bernardino Co | S Bernardino. |
| Godcell, H | Attorney | 4 & 6 Anderson's Bdg | San Bernardino | S Bernardino. |
| Goldbaum, L | Merchant | San Bernardino Co | San Bernardino | S Bernardino. |
| Goldberg, H | Merchant | San Bernardino Co | San Bernardino | S Bernardino. |
| Goldkoffer, C F M | Brewer | San Bernardino Co | San Bernardino | S Bernardino. |
| Goldsmith, H C | Merchant | San Bernardino Co | Chino | Chino. |
| Gonzales, J | Laborer | San Bernardino Co | nr San Bernardino | S Bernardino. |
| Goodwin, J G | Carpenter | San Bernardino Co | San Bernardino | S Bernardino. |
| Goodwin, Frederic Le B | Lawyer | Argus Building | San Bernardino | S Bernardino. |
| Goodwin, — | Attorney | Kelting Block | San Bernardino | S Bernardino. |
| Goodcell, H | Farmer | nr San Bernardino | San Bernardino Co | S Bernardino. |
| Goodcell, H | Teacher | San Bernardino Co | San Bernardino | S Bernardino. |
| Good, J W | Miner | San Bernardino Co | Ivanpah | S Bernardino. |
| Goor, J | Carpenter | San Bernardino Co | San Bernardino | S Bernardino. |
| Gordon, John | Teamster | San Bernardino Co | nr Chino | Chino. |
| Gosa, P | Stock raiser | San Bernardino Co | San Salvador | San Salvador. |
| Gould, J F | Real estate agent | Argus Building | San Bernardino | S Bernardino. |
| Gould, John F | Printer | San Bernardino Co | San Bernardino | S Bernardino. |
| Gould, Wm H | Printer | San Bernardino Co | San Bernardino | S Bernardino. |
| Gould & Goodwin | Real estate agents | Argus Building | San Bernardino | S Bernardino. |
| Graham, D | Miner | nr San Bernardino | San Bernardino Co | S Bernardino. |
| Grant, James | Mail contractor | San Bernardino Co | | S Bernardino. |
| Grant, G W | Miner | San Bernardino | San Bernardino Co | S Bernardino. |
| Grant, Andrew V | Teamster | San Bernardino Co | | S Bernardino. |
| Grant, Edmund O | Farmer | nr San Bernardino | San Bernardino Co | S Bernardino. |
| Graves, I L | Teamster | San Bernardino Co | nr San Bernardino | S Bernardino. |
| Green, H S | Farmer | San Bernardino Co | nr San Salvador | San Salvador. |
| Green, G N | Teamster | San Bernardino Co | nr San Bernardino | S Bernardino. |
| Gregory, Wm | Farmer | nr San Bernardino | San Bernardino Co | S Bernardino. |
| Gregory, J | Farmer | San Bernardino Co | nr San Bernardino | S Bernardino. |
| Grenelle, B J | Carpenter | San Bernardino Co | San Bernardino | S Bernardino. |
| Greves, J P | Physician | San Bernardino Co | Riverside | Riverside. |
| Greves, J P | Notary & P M | Main st | Market st | Riverside. |
| Grice, — | Farmer | Riverside | San Bernardino Co | Riverside. |
| Grimes, J C | Farmer | nr San Bernardino | San Bernardino Co | S Bernardino. |
| Grucer, Charles | Farmer | nr San Bernardino | San Bernardino Co | S Bernardino. |
| Guien, Felipe | Laborer | San Salvador | San Salvador | San Salvador. |
| Gussen, S | Farmer | San Bernardino Co | nr Temescal | Temescal. |
| Haile, Smith | Freighter | San Bernardino | San Bernardino Co | S Bernardino. |
| Hale, N P | Jeweller | 101 3d st | San Bernardino | S Bernardino. |
| Hall, S B | Butcher | San Bernardino | San Bernardino Co | S Bernardino. |
| Hall, J Dr | Farmer | Riverside | San Bernardino Co | Riverside. |
| Hall, J E | Farmer | South of Riverside | San Bernardino Co | Riverside. |
| Hall, E | Stable keeper | San Bernardino Co | San Bernardino | S Bernardino. |
| Hale, Jesse | Farmer | San Bernardino Co | nr Temescal | Temescal. |
| Ham, G G | Teamster | San Bernardino Co | | S Bernardino. |
| Hamilton, Geo W | Apiarian | San Bernardino Co | San Bernardino | S Bernardino. |
| Hancock, J | Farmer | nr San Bernardino | San Bernardino Co | S Bernardino. |
| Hancock, A | Farmer | San Bernardino Co | nr San Bernardino | S Bernardino. |
| Hancock, S | Farmer | San Bernardino Co | nr San Bernardino | S Bernardino. |
| Hanes, S | Auctioneer | San Bernardino | San Bernardino Co | S Bernardino. |
| Harris, John C | Farmer | nr San Bernardino | San Bernardino Co | S Bernardino. |
| Harris, C J | Laborer | San Bernardino Co | nr San Bernardino | S Bernardino. |
| Harris, J M | Lawyer | San Bernardino Co | San Bernardino | S Bernardino. |
| Harris, B B | Attorney | Kelting's Block | San Bernardino | S Bernardino. |
| Harris, W A | Attorney | Kelting's Block | San Bernardino | S Bernardino. |
| Harris, W J | Farmer | San Bernardino Co | nr San Bernardino | S Bernardino. |
| Harris & Goodwin | Attorneys | Kelting's Block | San Bernardino | S Bernardino. |
| Harrison, Aaron | Farmer | nr San Bernardino | San Bernardino Co | S Bernardino. |

# DIRECTORY OF SAN BERNARDINO COUNTY.

| Name. | Occupation. | Place of Business. | Residence. | Town or P. O. |
|---|---|---|---|---|
| Harrod, W H | Sail maker | San Bernardino Co | Lytle Creek | S Berdardino. |
| Hart, Jas | Farmer | nr San Bernardino | San Bernardino Co | S Bernardino. |
| Hart, E | Farmer | South of Riverside | San Bernardino Co | Riverside. |
| Hartshorn, D W | Physician | Shur's Drug Store | San Bernardino | S Bernardino. |
| Hartley, C T | Farmer | South of Riverside | San Bernardino Co | Riverside. |
| Haskins, W | Farmer | San Bernardino Co | nr San Bernardino | S Bernardino. |
| Haskel, H W | Mechanic | San Bernardino Co | San Bernardino | S Bernardino. |
| Haswell & Peerson | Attorneys | Utah st | | S Bernardino. |
| Haswell, Geo F | Lawyer | San Bernardino Co | | S Bernardino. |
| Hathaway, A M | Painter | | San Bernardino Co | S Bernardino. |
| Hathawny, J | Farmer | San Bernardino Co | nr Chino | Chino. |
| Hathawny, H | Farmer | San Bernardino Co | nr Rincon | Chino. |
| Hawes, W A | Farmer | nr San Bernardino | San Bernardino Co | S Bernardino. |
| Hawker, T | Farmer | San Bernardino Co | nr San Bernardino | S Bernardino. |
| Hawley, Wm | Saloon | San Bernardino Co | San Bernardino | S Bernardino. |
| Hawley, L | Cooper | San Bernardino Co | San Bernardino | S Bernardino. |
| Harris, F M | Farmer | nr San Bernardino | San Bernardino Co | S Bernardino. |
| Haws, F M | Farmer | San Bernardino Co | nr San Bernardino | S Bernardino. |
| Hays, S T | Carpenter | San Bernardino Co | San Bernardino | S Bernardino. |
| Heaps, P W | Farmer | San Bernardino Co | nr San Bernardino | S Bernardino. |
| Heaps, Jos | Teamster | San Bernardino Co | nr San Bernardino | S Bernardino. |
| Heaps, Wm | Farmer | nr San Bernardino | San Bernardino Co | S Bernardino. |
| Heap, Jas | Farmer | San Bernardino Co | nr San Bernardino | S Bernardino. |
| Hedrick, J P | Farmer | San Bernardino Co | nr San Bernardino | S Bernardino. |
| Hedrick, C T | Miner | San Bernardino Co | Mountain Mill | S Bernardino. |
| Hoileman, Frederic | Farmer | nr San Bernardino | San Bernardino Co | S Bernardino. |
| Helmes, N B | Teamster | nr San Bernardino | San Bernardino Co | S Bernardino. |
| Hendricks, Wm | Farmer | San Bernardino Co | nr Chino | Chino. |
| Henderson, D | Farmer | nr San Bernardino | San Bernardino Co | S Bernardino. |
| Henderson, D G | Miner | nr San Bernardino | San Bernardino Co | S Bernardino. |
| Henderson, D | Trader | San Bernardino Co | San Bernardino | S Bernardino. |
| Henderson, W McD | Brakeman | San Bernardino Co | Riverside | Riverside. |
| Henderson, J M | Wagon maker | San Bernardino Co | San Bernardino | S Bernardino. |
| Hendew, Geo | Farmer | nr San Bernardino | San Bernardino Co | S Bernardino. |
| Henly, Thos | Farmer | nr San Bernardino | San Bernardino Co | S Bernardino. |
| Henry, Wm | Miner | San Bernardino Co | nr San Bernardino | S Bernardino. |
| Herd, Jas | Miner | San Bernardino Co | Ivanpah | S Bernardino. |
| Herreras, A | Miner | San Bernardino Co | Bellville | |
| Hetrick, D | Farmer | nr San Bernardino | San Bernardino Co | S Bernardino. |
| Hewes, J N | Teacher | San Bernardino Co | | S Bernardino. |
| Hickey, J C | Farmer | San Bernardino Co | Chino | Chino. |
| Hicks, W H | Lumberman | nr San Bernardino | San Bernardino Co | S Bernardino. |
| Hight, John P | Merchant | San Bernardino | San Bernardino Co | S Bernardino. |
| Hinds, J | Laborer | San Bernardino Co | nr San Bernardino | S Bernardino. |
| Hoag, A | Supt of construc'n | R Land Co | Riverside | Riverside. |
| Hoagland, L | Teamster | nr San Bernardino | San Bernardino Co | S Bernardino. |
| Hobbs, W A | Freighter | San Bernardino Co | Chino | Chino. |
| Hockhausen, J P | Butcher | San Bernardino | San Bernardino Co | S Bernardino. |
| Hoerlein, E | Painter | San Bernardino Co | San Bernardino | S Bernardino. |
| Hoyland, A A | Farmer | ur San Bernardino | San Bernardino Co | S Bernardino. |
| Holcomb, W F | Farmer | San Bernardino Co | nr San Bernardino | S Bernardino. |
| Holmes, D | Laborer | nr San Bernardino | San Bernardino Co | S Bernardino. |
| Holmes, A O | Engineer | San Bernardino Co | San Bernardino | S Bernardino. |
| Holmes, W | Mechanic | San Bernardino Co | San Bernardino | S Bernardino. |
| Homan, L | Saloon keeper | San Bernardino Co | San Bernardino | S Bernardino. |
| Hoose, I A | Book keeper | San Bernardino Co | San Bernardino | S Bernardino. |
| Horkous, Patrick | Clerk | San Bernardino | San Bernardino | S Bernardino. |
| Hornback, — | Carpenter | Riverside | ½ m E Riverside | Riverside. |
| Horowitz & Co., A | Gen merchandise | 3d st | | S Bernardino. |
| Horowitz, Abraham | Clerk | San Bernardino | San Bernardino | S Bernardino. |
| Horton, P J | Farmer | San Bernardino Co | San Bernardino | S Bernardino. |
| Houlton, A | Farmer | nr San Bernardino | San Bernardino Co | S Bernardino. |
| Hubble, G E | Farmer | San Bernardino Co | nr San Bernardino | S Bernardino. |
| Huckaby, S S | Farmer | San Bernardino Co | nr San Bernardino | S Bernardino. |

# Meyerstein & Co.

### SAN BERNARDINO.

## CITY OF PARIS,

*The Most Complete Stock of*

### DRY GOODS, CLOTHING,

BOOTS AND SHOES, HATS,

**CARPETS AND OIL-CLOTHS,**

*ETC. ETC.*

DIRECT IMPORTATIONS FROM THE EASTERN MANUFACTURERS.

---

# American Cash Store

WHOLESALE AND RETAIL

## Groceries and Provisions,

MINING

AND

### FARMING IMPLEMENTS,

LIQUORS,

Cigars, Tobacco, Etc., Etc.

Owing to our enormously large purchases, we are enabled to sell goods lower than any other house in Southern California.

---

## GENERAL STORE,

Riverside, San Bernardino Co., Cal.

*LYON & ROSENTHAL, Proprietors.*

### GROCERIES, PROVISIONS,

BOOTS AND SHOES,

**Dry Goods and Clothing,**

**CROCKERY, TINWARE,**

**HARDWARE, WOODENWARE,**

GLASSWARE.

All kinds of Country Produce bought at the highest market rates. The purchase of Wool a specialty.
Agent for Wells, Fargo's Express.

---

COMMISSION

# Lumber Dealer,

CORNER

Fourth and Salt Lake Sts.

SAN BERNARDINO, - - CAL.

DIRECTORY OF SAN BERNARDINO COUNTY. 271

| NAME. | OCCUPATION. | PLACE OF BUSINESS. | RESIDENCE. | TOWN OR P. O. |
|---|---|---|---|---|
| Hudson, Henry | Farmer | nr San Bernardino | San Bernardino Co | S Bernardino. |
| Hughes, W G | Farmer | nr San Bernardino | San Bernardino Co | S Bernardino. |
| Hughes, J W | Lumberman | nr San Bernardino | San Bernardino Co | S Bernardino. |
| Hughes, Joseph H. | Clerk | San Bernardino | San Bernardino | S Bernardino. |
| Humphrey, J P | Farmer | San Bernardino Co | nr San Bernardino | S Bernardino. |
| Hunt, A | Farmer | nr San Bernardino | San Bernardino Co | S Bernardino. |
| Hunter, P S | Farmer | nr San Bernardino | San Bernardino Co | S Bernardino. |
| Hunter, Wm H | Teamster | nr San Bernardino | San Bernardino Co | S Bernardino. |
| Huntington, H | Hotel keeper | Toll Road | San Bernardino Co | S Bernardino. |
| Huntington, H | Teamster | San Bernardino Co | nr San Bernardino | S Bernardino. |
| Huntley, Wm H | Lumberman | San Bernardino | San Bernardino | S Bernardino. |
| Hurley, W H | Teamster | nr San Bernardino | San Bernardino Co | S Bernardino. |
| Hurley, H | Hotel | Bairdstown | San Bernardino Co | Bairdstown. |
| Hunt, H H | Teacher | San Bernardino Co | Chino | Chino. |
| Huston, D T | Lumber merch't | San Bernardino Co | San Bernardino | S Bernardino. |
| Hutcheson, W M | Farmer | nr San Bernardino | San Bernardino | S Bernardino. |
| Iughan, Warren R | Horticulturist | nr San Bernardino | San Bernardino Co | S Bernardino. |
| Irvine, G P | Laborer | nr San Bernardino | San Bernardino Co | S Bernardino. |
| Isaac, John | Publisher | S B Argus | Utah st | S Bernardino. |
| Jacobs, Lewis | President | S B Bank | 4th st | S Bernardino. |
| Jacoby, Louis | Clerk | San Bernardino | San Bernardino | S Bernardino. |
| Jacob, L | Merchant | San Bernardino Co | San Bernardino | S Bernardino. |
| Jacoby, Albert | Merchant | San Bernardino | San Bernardino | S Bernardino. |
| Jacoby, Abraham | Merchant | San Bernardino | San Bernardino | S Bernardino. |
| Jackson, J M | Farmer | San Bernardino Co | nr San Bernardino | S Bernardino. |
| Jackson, S | Merchant | San Bernardino Co | San Bernardino | S Bernardino. |
| Jackson, Samuel | Farmer | nr San Bernardino | San Bernardino Co | S Bernardino. |
| Jaramillo, David | Laborer | San Bernardino Co | San Salvador | San Salvador. |
| Jaramillo, Antonio | Farmer | San Bernardino Co | San Salvador | San Salvador. |
| Jamarillo, J | Laborer | San Bernardino Co | nr San Salvador | San Salvador. |
| Jamarillo, L | Ranchero | San Bernardino Co | San Salvador | San Salvador. |
| Jaramillo, J | Farmer | San Bernardino Co | San Salvador | San Salvador. |
| Jaramillo, J | Laborer | San Bernardino Co | nr San Salvador | San Salvador. |
| Jaramillo, J J | Farmer | San Bernardino Co | nr San Salvador | San Salvador. |
| Jaramillo, F | Farmer | San Bernardino Co | San Salvador | San Salvador. |
| Jaramillo, J M | Farmer | San Bernardino Co | San Salvador | San Salvador. |
| James, J M | Lumberman | nr San Bernardino | San Bernardino Co | S Bernardino. |
| James, J T | Miner | nr San Bernardino | San Bernardino Co | S Bernardino. |
| James, D | Farmer | San Bernardino Co | nr San Bernardino | S Bernardino. |
| James, S | Teamster | nr San Bernardino | San Bernardino Co | S Bernardino. |
| Jamison, J B | Farmer | San Bernardino Co | nr Chino | Chino. |
| Jansen, L | Merchant | San Bernardino Co | Agua Mansa | |
| Jansen, C | Stock raiser | West of Rincon | San Bernardino Co | Riverside. |
| Jeffries, Thos | Laborer | San Bernardino | San Bernardino | S Bernardino. |
| Johnson, A | Cook | San Bernardino | San Bernardino | S Bernardino. |
| Johnson, W L | Farmer | nr San Bernardino | San Bernardino Co | S Bernardino. |
| Johnson, S H | Farmer | nr San Bernardino | San Bernardino Co | S Bernardino. |
| Johnson, J H | Carpenter | San Bernardino Co | San Bernardino | S Bernardino. |
| Johnson, F M | Teamster | San Bernardino Co | nr San Bernardino | S Bernardino. |
| Johnson, W C | Carpenter | Riverside | Vine st | Riverside. |
| Johnson, J F | Farmer | San Bernardino Co | San Bernardino | S Bernardino. |
| Johnson, N W | Farmer | nr San Bernardino | San Bernardino Co | S Bernardino. |
| Jones, A E | Farmer | San Bernardino Co | nr San Bernardino | S Bernardino. |
| Jones, S K | Farmer | San Bernardino Co | nr San Bernardino | S Bernardino. |
| Jones, E Mc V | Mason | San Bernardino Co | Ivanpah | S Bernardino. |
| Jones, J M | Farmer | San Bernardino Co | nr San Salvador | San Salvador. |
| Jones, J C | Teamster | San Bernardino Co | nr San Bernardino | S Bernardino. |
| Jones, J D | Farmer | nr San Bernardino | San Bernardino Co | S Bernardino. |
| Joubert, P | Laborer | San Bernardino Co | nr Cocomongo | Cocomongo. |
| Judson, I | Farmer | San Bernardino Co | nr San Bernardino | S Bernardino. |
| Judson, T | Farmer | nr San Bernardino | San Bernardino Co | S Bernardino. |
| Judson, Wm | Farmer | San Bernardino Co | nr San Bernardino | S Bernardino. |
| Kallman, George | Merchant | 25 m S W S Ber'no | Rincon | Chino. |
| Kane, D W | Painter | cor 4th & Grafton sts | San Bernardino | S Bernardino. |

| NAME. | OCCUPATION. | PLACE OF BUSINESS. | RESIDENCE. | TOWN OR P. O. |
|---|---|---|---|---|
| Karns, J | Blacksmith | San Bernardino Co | San Bernardino | S Bernardino. |
| Katz, J W | Merchant | San Bernardino Co | San Bernardino | S Bernardino. |
| Katz, — | Real estate | 3d st | San Bernardino | S Bernardino. |
| Kavanagh, N | Saloon keeper | San Bernardino Co | San Bernardino | S Bernardino. |
| Kearney, Arthur | Daily guardian | 3d st, Kelting's Blk | San Bernardino | S Bernardino. |
| Kearney, A | Teacher | San Bernardino Co | San Bernardino | S Bernardino. |
| Keenan, P | Clerk | San Bernardino Co | San Bernardino | S Bernardino. |
| Keiser, J H | Miner | nr San Bernardino | San Bernardino Co | S Bernardino. |
| Keith, Thos | Miner | San Bernardino Co | nr San Bernardino | S Bernardino. |
| Keller, F M | Farmer | San Bernardino Co | San Bernardino | S Bernardino. |
| Keller, W C | Farmer | San Bernardino | San Bernardino Co | S Bernardino. |
| Keller, H C | Farmer | San Bernardino Co | nr San Bernardino | S Bernardino. |
| Kellogg, B W | Farmer | San Bernardino Co | nr San Bernardino | S Bernardino. |
| Kelley, Horace A | Printer | San Bernardino Co | nr San Bernardino | S Bernardino. |
| Kelly, John | Trader | San Bernardino Co | San Bernardino | S Bernardino. |
| Kelley, Thos | Blacksmith | San Bernardino Co | San Bernardino | S Bernardino. |
| Kelly, J H | Teamster | San Bernardino Co | nr San Bernardino | S Bernardino. |
| Kelly, T H | Carpenter | San Bernardino Co | San Bernardino | S Bernardino. |
| Kelly, J A | Laborer | San Bernardino Co | Mountain Mill | S Bernardino. |
| Kelly, Jas | Painter | San Bernardino Co | San Bernardino | S Bernardino. |
| Kelting, S | Farmer | Riverside | San Bernardino Co | S Bernardino. |
| Kelting, J A | Lawyer | San Bernardino Co | San Bernardino | S Bernardino. |
| Kelting, S M | Farmer | San Bernardino Co | nr San Bernardino | S Bernardino. |
| Keniston & Brayelton | Livery stable | 3d st | San Bernardino | S Bernardino. |
| Keniston, — | Livery stable | 3d st, opp P O | San Bernardino | S Bernardino. |
| Kennedy, Kermeth McKenzie | Farmer | San Bernardino Co | nr San Bernardino | S Bernardino. |
| Kennedy, W D | Farmer | San Bernardino Co | nr San Timoteo | S Bernardino. |
| Kent, O F | Dairyman | nr San Bernardino | San Bernardino Co | S Bernardino. |
| Kenyon, W H | Farmer | San Bernardino Co | nr San Bernardino | S Bernardino. |
| Kerfoot, J F | Clerk | San Bernardino Co | San Bernardino | S Bernardino. |
| Kerfoot, E F | Farmer | nr San Bernardino | San Bernardino Co | S Bernardino. |
| Kerfoot, Walter | Farmer | San Bernardino Co | nr San Bernardino | S Bernardino. |
| Kerr, T | Farmer | Riverside | San Bernardino Co | Riverside. |
| Kibbe, Geo | Farmer | nr San Bernardino | San Bernardino Co | S Bernardino. |
| Kier, A | Farmer | San Bernardino Co | nr San Bernardino | S Bernardino. |
| Kier, A, Jr | Clerk | San Bernardino Co | San Bernardino | S Bernardino. |
| Kincaid, M | Farmer | San Bernardino Co | nr Cocomongo | Cocomongo. |
| King, Geo | Laborer | San Bernardino Co | nr San Bernardino | S Bernardino. |
| King, J C | Saddler | San Bernardino Co | San Bernardino | S Bernardino. |
| King, R H & Bro | Harness manufr | Stewart's Bl'g, 3d st | San Bernardino | S Bernardino. |
| King, J D | Bar keeper | San Bernardino Co | San Bernardino | S Bernardino. |
| King, R K | Saddler | San Bernardino Co | San Bernardino | S Bernardino. |
| Kinman, N | Stable keeper | San Bernardino Co | San Bernardino | S Bernardino. |
| Kinyon, J O | Farmer | nr San Bernardino | San Bernardino Co | S Bernardino. |
| Kinyon, G | Farmer | San Bernardino Co | nr San Bernardino | S Bernardino. |
| Kimball, N | Blacksmith | San Bernardino Co | San Bernardino | S Bernardino. |
| Kirkland, A | Blacksmith | San Bernardino Co | San Bernardino | S Bernardino. |
| Kissee, Robt Wm | Farmer | 15 m E San Ber'no | San Timoteo | S Bernardino. |
| Kissee, Huston | Farmer | 15 m E San Ber'no | San Timoteo | S Bernardino. |
| Klipper, J | Farmer | nr San Bernardino | San Bernardino Co | S Bernardino. |
| Knight, G | Farmer | San Bernardino Co | nr San Bernardino | S Bernardino. |
| Knight, E | Teamster | nr San Bernardino | San Bernardino Co | S Bernardino. |
| Knight, A | Lumberman | nr San Bernardino | San Bernardino Co | S Bernardino. |
| Knighten, W A | Teacher | San Bernardino Co | San Bernardino | S Bernardino. |
| Knowll, H | Cooper | San Bernardino | San Bernardino | S Bernardino. |
| Knox, John T | Merchant | San Bernardino | San Bernardino | S Bernardino. |
| Koch, Dr J C A | Physician | 3d st | San Bernardino | S Bernardino. |
| Kohn, Peter | Farmer | San Bernardino Co | | S Bernardino. |
| Kolman, Abram | Clerk | San Bernardino | San Bernardino | S Bernardino. |
| Kreitzner, John | Carpenter | San Bernardino Co | | S Bernardino. |
| Kreuter, Wm | Shoe maker | San Bernardino Co | San Bernardino | S Bernardino. |
| Kurtz, C | Farmer | San Bernardino Co | nr San Gorgono | S Bernardino. |

DIRECTORY OF SAN BERNARDINO COUNTY. 273

| Name. | Occupation. | Place of Business. | Residence. | Town or P. O. |
|---|---|---|---|---|
| Kurz, C............... | American bakery | 3d st...................... | San Bernardino........ | S Bernardino. |
| Laborey, L............ | Farmer............... | San Bernardino Co.. | nr San Bernardino... | S Bernardino. |
| Ladd, H C............ | Farmer............... | nr San Bernardino... | San Bernardino Co... | S Bernardino. |
| Lafarbe, L A......... | Stage driver........ | San Bernardino Co... | ................................. | S Bernardino. |
| Laird, Wm H......... | Farmer............... | ................................. | San Bernardino Co... | S Bernardino. |
| Lallie, P C............ | Cook ................. | San Bernardino....... | San Bernardino........ | S Bernardino. |
| Lamb, O............... | Teamster............ | San Bernardino Co... | nr San Bernardino... | S Bernardino. |
| Lamb, Jas............ | Farmer............... | San Bernardino Co... | nr San Bernardino... | S Bernardino. |
| Lambert, H........... | Miner................. | San Bernardino Co... | nr San Bernardino... | S Bernardino. |
| Lami, L................ | Carpenter........... | San Bernardino Co... | Cocomongo ........... | Cocomongo. |
| Lander, C A......... | Teamster............ | nr San Bernardino... | San Bernardino Co... | S Bernardino. |
| Lander, E............. | Farmer............... | nr San Bernardino... | San Bernardino Co... | S Bernardino. |
| Lane, A G............ | Teamster............ | nr San Bernardino... | San Bernardino Co... | S Bernardino. |
| La Neice, Jas........ | Bricklayer .......... | San Bernardino Co... | San Bernardino....... | S Bernardino. |
| Lapraix, W S........ | Machinist............ | San Bernardino Co... | Mountain Mill......... | S Bernardino. |
| Larew, J G........... | Farmer............... | San Bernardino Co... | nr San Bernardino... | S Bernardino. |
| Lathrop, A W....... | Farmer............... | San Bernardino Co... | nr San Bernardino... | S Bernardino. |
| Lathrop, A W....... | Farmer............... | San Bernardino Co... | nr San Timoteo...... | San Salvador. |
| Lathrop, Horace H. | Farmer............... | 28 m S S Bernardino | Temescal............... | Temescal. |
| Law, H................. | Laborer.............. | San Bernardino Co... | nr San Bernardino... | S Bernardino. |
| Lawson, Bros....... | Cigars, etc ......... | Utah st................. | San Bernardino....... | S Bernardino. |
| Lawson, Chas A.... | Merchant ........... | Utah st................. | San Bernardino....... | S Bernardino. |
| Lawson, J E......... | Merchant ........... | Utah st................. | San Bernardino Co... | S Bernardino. |
| Leach, Geo........... | Farmer............... | South of Riverside ... | San Bernardino Co... | Riverside. |
| Leach, Mrs........... | ........................... | Riverside.............. | San Bernardino Co... | Riverside. |
| Le Bar & Stone..... | Palace saloon...... | Davis' Building...... | 3d st...................... | S Bernardino. |
| Le Bar, John......... | Tax collector....... | San Bernardino....... | San Bernardino....... | S Bernardino. |
| Lee, B J................ | Laborer.............. | nr San Bernardino... | San Bernardino Co... | S Bernardino. |
| Lee, G M.............. | Farmer............... | nr San Bernardino... | San Bernardino....... | S Bernardino. |
| Lee, J T................ | Stock raiser ....... | San Bernardino Co... | nr San Bernardino... | S Bernardino. |
| Lee, Geo............... | Farmer............... | nr San Bernardino... | San Bernardino....... | S Bernardino. |
| Leffen, J T............ | Engineer............. | San Bernardino Co... | San Bernardino....... | S Bernardino. |
| Leffingwell, I........ | Farmer............... | San Bernardino Co... | nr San Timoteo...... | S Bernardino. |
| Leffingwell, H G ... | Farmer............... | ........................... | San Bernardino Co... | S Bernardino. |
| Leich, James........ | Miner................. | San Bernardino Co... | nr San Bernardino... | S Bernardino. |
| Leonard, B .......... | Teamster............ | San Bernardino Co... | San Bernardino....... | S Bernardino. |
| Leonard, M........... | Butcher .............. | San Bernardino....... | San Bernardino....... | S Bernardino. |
| Leonard, W M....... | Painter............... | San Bernardino....... | San Bernardino....... | S Bernardino. |
| Lester, C H........... | Prof of dancing .. | San Bernardino Co... | San Bernardino....... | S Bernardino. |
| Levy, Isaac H ...... | Real estate......... | 3d & Bernardino st... | San Bernardino....... | S Bernardino. |
| Lewis, W R .......... | Farmer............... | nr San Bernardino... | San Bernardino Co... | S Bernardino. |
| Lightfoot, W E W | Station keeper .... | nr San Bernardino... | San Bernardino....... | S Bernardino. |
| Lightner, A .......... | Cabinet maker..... | nr San Bernardino... | San Bernardino....... | S Bernardino. |
| Linder, Charles..... | Laborer.............. | San Bernardino....... | San Bernardino....... | S Bernardino. |
| Linder, C.............. | Restaurant ......... | 3d st...................... | 3d st...................... | S Bernardino. |
| Linn, G................. | Carpenter........... | San Bernardino Co... | San Bernardino....... | S Bernardino. |
| Linville, W J........ | Planing mill ....... | San Bernardino Co... | San Bernardino....... | S Bernardino. |
| Linville, Wm J..... | Farmer............... | San Salvador......... | San Salvador......... | San Salvador. |
| Lish, Geo W ........ | Teamster............ | San Bernardino Co... | nr San Bernardino... | S Bernardino. |
| Littlefield, Jos...... | Teamster............ | San Bernardino Co... | nr San Bernardino... | S Bernardino. |
| Logsden, M........... | Wagon maker..... | San Bernardino Co... | San Bernardino....... | S Bernardino. |
| Logsdon, Jos McG... | ........................... | San Bernardino Co... | ................................. | S Bernardino. |
| Long, John........... | Farmer............... | nr San Bernardino... | San Bernardino Co... | S Bernardino. |
| Long, R M............ | Wheelwright....... | San Bernardino Co... | San Timoteo.......... | S Bernardino. |
| Long, Thos .......... | Farmer............... | nr San Bernardino... | San Bernardino Co... | S Bernardino. |
| Long, W C............ | Teamster............ | San Bernardino Co... | San Bernardino Co... | S Bernardino. |
| Lopez, Eustacio.... | Ranchero ........... | San Bernardino Co... | San Salvador......... | San Salvador. |
| Lopez, F............... | Farmer............... | San Bernardino Co... | nr San Timoteo...... | San Salvador. |
| Lopez, J............... | Laborer.............. | San Bernardino Co... | nr San Bernardino... | S Bernardino. |
| Lord, G................. | Farmer............... | San Bernardino Co... | nr San Bernardino... | S Bernardino. |
| Lovato, D W......... | Farmer............... | San Bernardino Co... | nr San Bernardino... | S Bernardino. |
| Loveland, James S... | Lecturer............. | San Bernardino Co... | ................................. | Riverside. |
| Lovell, S O........... | Farmer............... | San Bernardino Co... | nr San Salvador ..... | San Salvador. |
| Lovell, Drury G.... | Teamster............ | San Bernardino Co... | ................................. | S Bernardino. |

| Name. | Occupation. | Place of Business. | Residence. | Town or P. O |
|---|---|---|---|---|
| Loveland, J S | Shoe maker | 7th st | 7th st | Riverside. |
| Lyon, Geo Bidwell | Farmer | nr San Bernardino | San Bernardino Co | S Bernardino. |
| Lyon, W | Gen merchandise | Main st | Main st | Riverside. |
| Lyon & Rosenthal | Gen merchandise | Main st | | Riverside. |
| Lujahn, E C | Merchant | San Bernardino Co | San Salvador | San Salvador. |
| Lujahn, A M | Farmer | San Bernardino Co | nr San Salvador | San Salvador. |
| Lytle, A | Farmer | nr San Bernardino | San Bernardino Co | S Bernardino. |
| Lythe, J H | Farmer | nr San Bernardino | San Bernardino Co | S Bernardino. |
| Mace, D W | Teamster | San Bernardino Co | San Bernardino | S Bernardino. |
| Machado, J | Shepherd | 28 m S W S Bern'no | Rincon | Chino. |
| Macovich, — | Chop house | San Bernardino | San Bernardino | S Bernardino. |
| Macovich, Petro | Laborer | San Bernardino | San Bernardino | S Bernardino. |
| Madison, R | Miner | nr San Bernardino | Ivanpah | S Bernardino. |
| Madrille, T | Laborer | nr San Bernardino | Agua Mansa | |
| Magee, — | Farmer | South of Riverside | San Bernardino Co | Riverside. |
| Mahen, J F | Farmer | San Bernardino Co | Rincon | Chino. |
| Mallo, J | Laborer | San Bernardino Co | nr San Salvador | San Salvador. |
| Malloy, Wm Edgar | Farmer | San Bernardino Co | nr San Bernardino | S Bernardino. |
| Mann, J | Farmer | South of Riverside | San Bernardino Co | Riverside. |
| Manson, Louis G | Clerk | San Bernardino | San Bernardino Co | S Bernardino. |
| Mansfield, F A | Farmer | San Bernardino Co | nr San Bernardino | S Bernardino. |
| Mapstead, J | Farmer | San Bernardino Co | nr San Bernardino | S Bernardino. |
| Margeston, Wm | Farmer | San Bernardino Co | nr San Bernardino | S Bernardino. |
| Margetson, F G J | Publisher | San Bernardino Co | San Bernardino | S Bernardino. |
| Marsh, A | Merchant | San Bernardino Co | Ivanpah | S Bernardino. |
| Marsh, Isaac | Hardware | Main st | Main st | Riverside. |
| Marshall, J | Farmer | San Bernardino Co | nr San Bernardino | S Bernardino. |
| Martinez, F | Vintner | San Bernardino Co | Riverside | Riverside. |
| Martos, J M | Carpenter | San Bernardino Co | San Salvador | San Salvador. |
| Martinez, J A | Farmer | San Bernardino Co | nr San Salvador | San Salvador. |
| Martinez, I | Farmer | San Bernardino Co | nr San Salvador | San Salvador. |
| Martin, A | Farmer | San Bernardino Co | nr Union | |
| Martin, A | Farmer | San Bernardino Co | nr San Salvador | San Salvador. |
| Martine, B | Laborer | San Bernardino Co | nr San Salvador | San Salvador. |
| Martin, Jose Pablo | Laborer | 88 m N E S Bern'no | Holcomb | Bairdstown. |
| Martin, E T | Mason | San Bernardino Co | Ivanpah | S Bernardino. |
| Martinez, S | Laborer | San Bernardino Co | nr San Salvador | San Salvador. |
| Martinas, J | Laborer | San Bernardino Co | nr San Salvador | San Salvador. |
| Martin, J H | Teamster | nr San Bernardino | San Bernardino Co | S Bernardino. |
| Martin, Geo | Farmer | San Bernardino Co | nr San Bernardino | S Bernardino. |
| Martin, M | Farmer | nr San Bernardino | San Bernardino Co | S Bernardino. |
| Mason, John | Farmer | nr San Bernardino | San Bernardino Co | S Bernardino. |
| Mathews, S B | Farmer | San Bernardino Co | nr Chino | Chino. |
| Mathes, W T | Bar keeper | San Bernardino Co | San Bernardino | S Bernardino. |
| Mathes, John | Farmer | nr San Bernardino | San Bernardino Co | S Bernardino. |
| Mathes, R F M | Farmer | San Bernardino Co | nr San Bernardino | S Bernardino. |
| Mathews, T J | Miller | San Bernardino Co | San Salvador | San Salvador. |
| Mathews, Samuel | Carriage trimmer | San Bernardino | San Bernardino | S Bernardino. |
| Mathews, B F | Justice of peace | Utah st | San Bernardino | S Bernardino. |
| Mattison, G H | Farmer | nr San Bernardino | San Bernardino Co | S Bernardino. |
| Mathews, B F | Farmer | San Bernardino Co | nr San Salvador | San Salvador. |
| Mattews, R | Farmer | San Bernardino Co | nr San Bernardino | S Bernardino. |
| Mayer, John | Farmer | San Bernardino Co | nr Riverside | Riverside. |
| Mayfield, John | Farmer | San Bernardino Co | nr San Bernardino | S Bernardino. |
| Mayhen, I | Farmer | San Bernardino Co | nr Chino | Chino. |
| Mayne, L | Miner | San Bernardino Co | nr San Bernardino | S Bernardino. |
| McCanel, A J | Farmer | nr San Bernardino | San Bernardino Co | S Bernardino. |
| McCall, John | Horse shoer | Utah st | San Bernardino | S Bernardino. |
| McCoy, W W | Farmer | nr San Bernardino | San Bernardino Co | S Bernardino. |
| McCoy, D | Farmer | San Bernardino Co | nr San Bernardino | S Bernardino. |
| McCoy, Geo | Laborer | San Bernardino Co | nr Mountain Mill | S Bernardino. |
| McCoy, D | Laborer | nr San Bernardino | San Bernardino Co | S Bernardino. |
| McCrary, W H | Farmer | San Bernardino Co | nr San Bernardino | S Bernardino. |
| McCrary, W | Farmer | San Bernardino Co | nr San Bernardino | S Bernardino. |

## DIRECTORY OF SAN BERNARDINO COUNTY. 275

| Name. | Occupation. | Place of Business. | Residence. | Town or P. O. |
|---|---|---|---|---|
| McCrary, V | Farmer | San Bernardino Co... | nr San Bernardino... | S Bernardino. |
| McCrary, J M | Farmer | nr San Bernardino... | San Bernardino Co... | S Bernardino. |
| McCray, J | Miner | San Bernardino Co... | Ivanpah | S Bernardino. |
| McCray, B C | Farmer | San Bernardino Co... | nr San Bernardino... | S Bernardino. |
| McDonald, W | Carpenter | San Bernardino Co... | San Bernardino | S Bernardino. |
| McDonald, James Wm | Printer | San Bernardino | San Bernardino | S Bernardino. |
| McDonald, Francis Wm | Laborer | San Bernardino | San Bernardino | S Bernardino. |
| McDonald, Mrs | Furniture store... | 50 3d st | San Bernardino | S Bernardino. |
| McDougall, Wm | Farmer | nr San Bernardino... | San Bernardino Co... | S Bernardino. |
| McDowell, R | Farmer | ¼ m N Riverside | San Bernardino Road | Riverside. |
| McDonald, A | Wheelwright | San Bernardino Co... | San Bernardino | S Bernardino. |
| McDonald, J | Carpenter | San Bernardino Co... | San Bernardino | S Bernardino. |
| McDowell, Jas | Farmer | nr San Bernardino... | San Bernardino Co... | S Bernardino. |
| McElvain, J | Teamster | nr San Bernardino... | San Bernardino Co... | S Bernardino. |
| McFarlane, Thos & Cochran | Livery stable | 3d st | | S Bernardino. |
| McFarland, Thos L | Miner | 180 m N S Bern'do... | Ivanpah | S Bernardino. |
| McGarroll, Wm | Mason | San Bernardino Co... | | S Bernardino. |
| McGinnes, J M | Teamster | nr San Bernardino... | San Bernardino Co... | S Bernardino. |
| McGowan, Thomas | Farmer | San Bernardino Co... | | S Bernardino. |
| McGuire, Patrick | Laborer | San Bernardino | San Bernardino | S Bernardino. |
| McIntyre, D | Farmer | nr San Bernardino... | San Bernardino Co... | S Bernardino. |
| McIntyre, A | Farmer | San Bernardino Co... | nr San Bernardino... | S Bernardino. |
| McKay, C | Laborer | San Bernardino Co... | San Bernardino | S Bernardino. |
| McKenney, A F | County clerk | San Bernardino Co .. | San Bernardino | S Bernardino. |
| McKee, J T | Farmer | nr San Bernardino... | San Bernardino | S Bernardino. |
| McKinney, H S | Book keeper | San Bernardino | San Bernardino | S Bernardino. |
| McKinzie, W L | Teamster | nr San Bernardino... | San Bernardino Co... | S Bernardino. |
| McKinners, B | Farmer | San Bernardino Co... | nr San Bernardino... | S Bernardino. |
| McMurry, B | Blacksmith | San Bernardino Co... | San Bernardino | S Bernardino. |
| McNalley, T | Lumberman | San Bernardino | nr Mountain Mill | S Bernardino. |
| McNew, Granville | Lumberman | San Bernardino | San Bernardino | S Bernardino. |
| McNew, J | Teamster | nr San Bernardino... | San Bernardino Co... | S Bernardino. |
| McPherson, Saml C | Farmer | San Bernardino Co... | | S Bernardino. |
| McQueen & Webbe | Hotel | 15 m S E San Bern'o | Box Springs | Riverside. |
| McQueen, A | Hotel | 15 m S E San Bern'o | Box Springs | Riverside. |
| McQueen, — | Stock raiser | 6 m E Riverside | San Bernardino Co... | Riverside. |
| Meacham, R | Laborer | nr San Bernardino... | San Bernardino Co... | S Bernardino. |
| Meagher, Martin | Laborer | San Bernardino Co... | | S Bernardino. |
| Mecham, J | Farmer | nr San Bernardino... | San Bernardino Co... | S Bernardino. |
| Medina, E | Laborer | San Bernardino Co... | Agua Mansa | |
| Medina, A | Laborer | San Bernardino Co... | Agua Mansa | |
| Meechum, D F | Teamster | nr San Bernardino... | San Bernardino Co... | S Bernardino. |
| Meechum, J | Farmer | nr San Bernardino... | San Bernardino Co... | S Bernardino. |
| Meechum, L | Farmer | nr San Bernardino... | San Bernardino Co... | S Bernardino. |
| Meechum, J | Farmer | nr San Bernardino... | San Bernardino Co... | S Bernardino. |
| Meechum, D | Carpenter | San Bernardino Co... | San Bernardino | S Bernardino. |
| Meehan, S G | Tinner | San Bernardino Co... | San Bernardino | S Bernardino. |
| Meck, S H | Miner | nr San Bernardino... | San Bernardino Co... | S Bernardino. |
| Mee & Co | Blacksmiths | San Bernardino | San Bernardino | S Bernardino. |
| Mee, Wm | Blacksmith | San Bernardino Co... | San Bernardino | S Bernardino. |
| Mee, S | Shoe maker | San Bernardino Co... | San Bernardino | S Bernardino. |
| Meintzler, W P | Butcher &packing | Boren's Building | 4th st | S Bernardino. |
| Meintzer, L & W P | Butchers & pack'g | Boren's Building | 4th st | S Bernardino. |
| Melendez, R | Servitor | San Bernardino Co... | San Bernardino | S Bernardino. |
| Melrose, Thos | Machinist | San Bernardino Co... | Temescal. | Temescal. |
| Mendez, Jose Maria | Laborer | San Salvador | San Salvador | San Salvador. |
| Mentzler, L | Butcher &packing | Boren's Building | 4th st | S Bernardino. |
| Merges, F | Millinery | Katz Building | San Bernardino | S Bernardino. |
| Messer, W H | Teamster | San Bernardino Co | nr San Bernardino... | S Bernardino. |
| Metcalf, H W | Farmer | South of Riverside... | San Bernardino Co.. | Riverside. |
| Metcalf, J F | Teamster | nr San Bernardino... | San Bernardino Co... | S Bernardino. |

| Name. | Occupation. | Place of Business. | Residence. | Town or P. O. |
|---|---|---|---|---|
| Meyers, A J | Farmer | nr San Bernardino | San Bernardino Co | S Bernardino. |
| Meyer, — | Saloon | Jackson's Block | San Bernardino | S Bernardino. |
| Meyerstein & Co. | Dry goods, etc | 3d st | | S Bernardino. |
| Meyer, D | Restaurant | 3d st | 3d st | S Bernardino. |
| Meyer & Linder | Occidental rest'nt | 3d st, Jackson's Blk | | S Bernardino. |
| Meyerstein, C | Merchant | San Bernardino Co | San Bernardino | S Bernardino. |
| Meyerstein, Cæsar | S B Bank cashier | 4th st | San Bernardino | S Bernardino. |
| Meyer, G W | Miner | nr San Bernardino | San Bernardino Co | S Bernardino. |
| Meyers, A J | Farmer | 1½ m N Riverside | Santa Ana River | Riverside. |
| Meyerstein, J | Merchant | San Bernardino Co | San Bernardino | S Bernardino. |
| Middleton, G | Shepherd | San Bernardino Co | nr San Bernardino | S Bernardino. |
| Migel, L | People's dollar sto | 3d st, Jackson's Blk | San Bernardino | S Bernardino. |
| Milburn, Jefferson | Farmer | San Bernardino Co | | S Bernardino. |
| Miller, J F | Bella union hotel. | 4th and Utah sts | San Bernardino | S Bernardino. |
| Mallard, N D | Farmer | South of Riverside | San Bernardino Co | Riverside. |
| Miller, Charles H | Farmer | | | S Bernardino. |
| Miller, J F | Blacksmith | San Bernardino Co | San Bernardino | S Bernardino. |
| Miller, C C | Civil engineer | 7th st | 7th st | Riverside. |
| Miller, J E | Farmer | nr San Bernardino | San Bernardino Co | S Bernardino. |
| Miller, Geo | Laborer | nr San Bernardino | San Bernardino Co | S Bernardino. |
| Miller, J | Farmer | South of Riverside | San Bernardino Co | Riverside. |
| Miller, A G | Painter | San Bernardino Co | San Salvador | San Salvador. |
| Milstead, J F | Teamster | San Bernardino Co | Mountain Mill | S Bernardino. |
| Mintzer, W H | Farmer | San Bernardino Co | nr San Bernardino | S Bernardino. |
| Molle, F | Farmer | San Bernardino Co | nr San Salvador | San Salvador. |
| Molle, J M | Farmer | San Bernardino Co | nr San Salvador | San Salvador. |
| Molle, Ja la L | Laborer | San Bernardino Co | nr San Salvador | San Salvador. |
| Molle, J de D | Farmer | San Bernardino Co | nr San Salvador | San Salvador. |
| Montoyo, F | Laborer | San Bernardino Co | nr San Salvador | San Salvador. |
| Montgomery, J W | Physician | San Bernardino Co | Riverside | Riverside. |
| Montovos, J A | Laborer | San Bernardino Co | nr San Salvador | San Salvador. |
| Moody, E P | Cabinet maker | Market st | 7th st | Riverside. |
| Moody & Warner | Cabinet makers | Market st | | Riverside. |
| Moore, H P | Farmer | South of Riverside | San Bernardino Co | Riverside. |
| Moore, W A | Teamster | San Bernardino Co | nr San Bernardino | S Bernardino. |
| Moore, M | Potter | San Bernardino Co | San Bernardino | S Bernardino. |
| Moore, Geo E | Saloon | 3d st | San Bernardino | S Bernardino. |
| Moore, C | Farmer | nr San Bernardino | San Bernardino Co | S Bernardino. |
| Moore, R B | Farmer | nr San Bernardino | San Bernardino Co | S Bernardino. |
| Moore, G E | Merchant | San Bernardino Co | San Bernardino | S Bernardino. |
| Moore, A J | Farmer | San Bernardino Co | nr San Bernardino | S Bernardino. |
| Mopes, John | Teamster | San Bernardino Co | Ivanpah | S Bernardino. |
| Morales, A | Blacksmith | San Bernardino Co | San Salvador | San Salvador. |
| Morgan, Saml C | Salesman | San Bernardino | San Bernardino | S Bernardino. |
| Morgan, J W | Saloon keeper | San Bernardino Co | San Bernardino | S Bernardino. |
| Morene, M | Laborer | San Bernardino Co | nr San Salvador | San Salvador. |
| Morris, G R | Miner | San Bernardino Co | Ivanpah | S Bernardino. |
| Morris, W T | Farmer | San Bernardino Co | nr San Bernardino | S Bernardino. |
| Morris & Preusse | Bricklayers | 4 doors S of 3d st | San Bernardino | S Bernardino. |
| Morris, John Milton | Bricklayer | San Bernardino | San Bernardino | S Bernardino. |
| Morris, G F | Farmer | San Bernardino Co | Cocomongo | Cocomongo. |
| Morris, W P | Laborer | San Bernardino Co | Riverside | Riverside. |
| Morrison, A | Teamster | San Bernardino Co | nr San Bernardino | S Bernardino. |
| Morrison, D | Farmer | nr San Bernardino | San Bernardino Co | S Bernardino. |
| Morrow, J R | Farmer | nr San Bernardino | San Bernardino Co | S Bernardino. |
| Morse, H | Teamster | nr San Bernardino | San Bernardino Co | S Bernardino. |
| Morse, J R | Lumberman | nr San Bernardino | San Bernardino Co | S Bernardino. |
| Morse, C E | Lumberman | San Bernardino Co | nr San Bernardino | S Bernardino. |
| Morse, J | Shingle maker | San Bernardino Co | San Bernardino | S Bernardino. |
| Morse, J, Jr | Laborer | nr San Bernardino | San Bernardino Co | S Bernardino. |
| Morse, W | Carpenter | San Bernardino Co | San Bernardino | S Bernardino. |
| Morse, J C | Bar keeper | San Bernardino Co | San Bernardino | S Bernardino. |
| Morse, C H | Brick moulder | San Bernardino Co | San Bernardino | S Bernardino. |
| Morton, S | Farmer | San Bernardino Co | nr San Bernardino | S Bernardino. |

# DIRECTORY OF SAN BERNARDINO COUNTY. 277

| Name. | Occupation. | Place of Business. | Residence. | Town or P. O. |
|---|---|---|---|---|
| Morton, B | Miner | San Bernardino Co | Ivanpah | S Bernardino. |
| Morton, W S | Restaurant keeper | San Bernardino Co | San Salvador | San Salvador. |
| Mosse, D E | Farmer | San Bernardino Co | nr Cocomongo | Cocomongo. |
| Mountain, John | Hotel keeper | San Bernardino | San Bernardino | S Bernardino. |
| Mowbray, M E | | San Bernardino Co | San Bernardino | S Bernardino. |
| Mullen, H P | Farmer | San Bernardino Co | nr San Bernardino | S Bernardino. |
| Mulvaney, M | Farmer | San Bernardino Co | nr San Bernardino | S Bernardino. |
| Munson, M | Miner | San Bernardino Co | nr San Bernardino | S Bernardino. |
| Murdock, A | Laborer | nr San Bernardino | San Bernardino Co | S Bernardino. |
| Murphy, M | Teamster | nr San Bernardino | San Bernardino Co | S Bernardino. |
| Murphy, J | Lumberman | San Bernardino Co | nr San Bernardino | S Bernardino. |
| Moya, Ysidro | Farmer | San Bernardino Co | nr San Bernardino | S Bernardino. |
| Moya, Ygnacio | Farmer | San Bernardino Co | nr San Bernardino | S Bernardino. |
| Myers, C | Farmer | San Bernardino Co | nr San Salvador | San Salvador. |
| Neal, Andrew J | Laborer | San Bernardino | San Bernardino | S Bernardino. |
| Nedo, F | Saddler | San Bernardino Co | San Bernardino | S Bernardino. |
| Newburg, O | Clerk | San Bernardino Co | San Bernardino | S Bernardino. |
| Newcomb, D | Farmer | ¾ m N Riverside | San Bernardino Rd | Riverside. |
| Newman, O N | Farmer | San Bernardino Co | nr San Salvador | San Salvador. |
| Newman, G O | Civil engineer | 7th st | 7th st | Riverside. |
| Newman, J B | Cigars | 3d st | San Bernardino | S Bernardino. |
| Nevers, A B | Farmer | San Bernardino | San Bernardino Co | S Bernardino. |
| Nichols, Willard M | Trader | San Bernardino Co | | S Bernardino. |
| Nicholson, J | Teamster | nr San Bernardino | San Bernardino Co | S Bernardino. |
| Nicholson, J A | Farmer | San Bernardino Co | nr San Bernardino | S Bernardino. |
| Nicholson, J | Mason | San Bernardino Co | San Bernardino | S Bernardino. |
| Nicholson, G | Miller | San Bernardino Co | San Salvador | San Salvador. |
| Nickerson, E A | Gunsmith | San Bernardino Co | San Bernardino | S Bernardino. |
| Nisbet, E A | Painter | San Bernardino | San Bernardino Co | S Bernardino. |
| Nisbet, A | Proprietor | S B Guardian | San Bernardino | S Bernardino. |
| Nish, Wm | Miner | nr San Bernardino | San Bernardino Co | S Bernardino. |
| Noble, John | Teamster | nr San Bernardino | San Bernardino Co | S Bernardino. |
| Noble, C D | Farmer | South of Riverside | San Bernardino Co | Riverside. |
| Noble, N | Farmer | San Bernardino Co | nr San Bernardino | S Bernardino. |
| Nogales, E | Farmer | San Bernardino Co | nr Temescal | Temescal. |
| Norcross, M S | Pottery | Market st | Riverside | Riverside. |
| Norega, M | Mechanic | San Bernardino Co | Temescal | Temescal. |
| Norias, E | Laborer | San Bernardino Co | nr San Salvador | San Salvador. |
| North, J W | Farmer | Riverside | Vine st | Riverside. |
| North, Edward | W U tel operator | Market st | Vine st | Riverside. |
| North, C | Livery stable | Utah st | San Bernardino | S Bernardino. |
| North, J W | Attorney | San Bernardino Co | Riverside | Riverside. |
| Norton, W H | Farmer | South of Riverside | San Bernardino Co | Riverside. |
| Nottage, E W | Coppersmith | San Bernardino | San Bernardino Co | S Bernardino. |
| Noyes, James Allen | Tinner | San Bernardino | San Bernardino | S Bernardino. |
| Oakey, Geo | Miner | nr San Bernardino | San Bernardino Co | S Bernardino. |
| O'Brien, John | Shoe maker | San Bernardino Co | San Bernardino | S Bernardino. |
| O'Connell, J P | Groceries | Utah st | San Bernardino | S Bernardino. |
| O'Connell, J P | Clerk | San Bernardino Co | San Bernardino | S Bernardino. |
| O'Connell, W | Farmer | San Bernardino Co | nr San Bernardino | S Bernardino. |
| O'Cacha, O | Gunsmith | San Bernardino Co | San Bernardino | S Bernardino. |
| Oliver, H | Farmer | nr San Bernardino | San Bernardino Co | S Bernardino. |
| O'Neil, John | Veterinary surg'n | Reich's Drug Store | San Bernardino | S Bernardino. |
| Ortega, J Y | Farmer | San Bernardino Co | nr San Salvador | San Salvador. |
| Ortega, J R | Laborer | San Bernardino Co | nr San Salvador | San Salvador. |
| Osborn, J | Farmer | San Bernardino Co | San Bernardino | S Bernardino. |
| Osborn, W S | Farmer | nr San Bernardino | San Bernardino Co | S Bernardino. |
| Osborne, P | Teamster | nr San Bernardino | San Bernardino Co | S Bernardino. |
| Osborne, J P | Farmer | nr San Bernardino | San Bernardino Co | S Bernardino. |
| Osburn, A J | Laborer | nr San Bernardino | San Bernardino Co | S Bernardino. |
| Otez, M | Farmer | San Bernardino Co | nr San Bernardino | S Bernardino. |
| Ousterhout, J D | Farmer | San Bernardino Co | | S Bernardino. |
| Oustolt, M M | Teamster | San Bernardino Co | nr San Salvador | San Salvador. |
| Outweros, J | Farmer | San Bernardino Co | nr Temescal | Temescal. |

| Name. | Occupation. | Place of Business. | Residence. | Town or P. O. |
|---|---|---|---|---|
| Packard, C E | Farmer | South of Riverside | San Bernardino Co | Riverside. |
| Packard, C | Farmer | San Bernardino | San Bernardino Co | S Bernardino. |
| Packer, I | Teamster | San Bernardino Co | nr San Bernardino | S Bernardino. |
| Padilla, Juan | Vaquero | 15 m E San Ber'no | San Timoteo | S Bernardino. |
| Page, J W | Miner | San Bernardino Co | Ivanpah | S Bernardino. |
| Pahlman, Mrs | Dress maker | 2d and Utah sts | San Bernardino | S Bernardino. |
| Paine, C R | Farmer | San Bernardino Co | nr San Salvador | San Salvador. |
| Paine, M. | Farmer | San Bernardino Co | San Bernardino | S Bernardino. |
| Pais, Jose Ignacio | Laborer | San Bernardino Co | San Salvador | San Salvador. |
| Paris, Bledsoe & Goodeell | Attorneys | 4 & 6 Anderson's Bdg | | S Bernardino. |
| Parish, C L | Farmer | nr San Bernardino | San Bernardino Co | S Bernardino. |
| Parks, A | Stock raiser | West of Santa Ana | San Bernardino Co | Riverside. |
| Parks, A F | Justice of peace | San Bernardino Co | San Bernardino | S Bernardino. |
| Parks, H C | Farmer | nr San Bernardino | San Bernardino Co | S Bernardino. |
| Parks, H | Stock raiser | West of Santa Ana | San Bernardino Co | Riverside. |
| Parker, Wm | Teacher | San Bernardino Co | Chino | Chino. |
| Parrish, Wm F | Farmer | San Bernardino Co | | S Bernardino. |
| Parrish, E K | Farmer | nr San Bernardino | San Bernardino Co | S Bernardino. |
| Parrish, Samuel | Farmer | San Bernardino | San Bernardino Co | S Bernardino. |
| Parrish, A L | Laborer | San Bernardino Co | San Bernardino | S Bernardino. |
| Parrish, E | Farmer | nr San Bernardino | San Bernardino Co | S Bernardino. |
| Parris, Andrew B | Attorney at law | with Co Superinten't | San Bernardino | S Bernardino. |
| Parsons, Thos M | Civil engineer | San Bernardino | San Bernardino Co | S Bernardino. |
| Parsons, W | Farmer | San Bernardino Co | nr Riverside | Riverside. |
| Passmore, E H | Stage driver | San Bernardino Co | San Bernardino | S Bernardino. |
| Parten, HughOwen | Merchant | San Bernardino | San Bernardino | S Bernardino. |
| Pattridge, Henry H | Miner | San Bernardino | San Bernardino | S Bernardino. |
| Pattridge & Berry | Saloon | Bairdstown | San Bernardino Co | Bairdstown. |
| Patterson, Levi H | Farmer | San Bernardino Co | | S Bernardino. |
| Patton, S S | Dentist | Main st | Riverside | Riverside. |
| Patton, J | Carpenter | Riverside | ½ m E Riverside | Riverside. |
| Potter, J D | Wagon maker | San Bernardino Co | San Bernardino | S Bernardino. |
| Paul, B L | Gardener | San Bernardino Co | | S Bernardino. |
| Paul, Wm | Teamster | | San Bernardino Co | S Bernardino. |
| Paul, Samuel | Farmer | San Bernardino Co | | S Bernardino. |
| Payne, H A | Blacksmith | nr San Bernardino | San Bernardino Co | S Bernardino. |
| Payne, W W | Shepherd | San Bernardino Co | nr San Bernardino | S Bernardino. |
| Peacock, D R | Carriage painter | San Bernardino | San Bernardino | S Bernardino. |
| Peacock, James C | Painter | San Bernardino | San Bernardino | S Bernardino. |
| Peacock, Dr J C | Druggist | San Bernardino | San Bernardino | S Bernardino. |
| Peacock, Edwin R | Painter | | San Bernardino Co | S Bernardino. |
| Pearce, Wm Burke | Miner | 14 m N W S Bern'o | Lytle Creek | S Bernardino. |
| Pearl, A H | Clerk | San Bernardino Co | San Bernardino | S Bernardino. |
| Pearson, John | Physician | San Bernardino Co | San Bernardino | S Bernardino. |
| Peck, W G | Laborer | San Bernardino Co | nr San Bernardino | S Bernardino. |
| Peck, Jas | Farmer | San Bernardino Co | nr Temescal | Temescal. |
| Peck, Orren | Carpenter | San Bernardino Co | San Bernardino | S Bernardino. |
| Peck, L R | Miner | nr San Bernardino | San Bernardino Co | S Bernardino. |
| Pendergrast, I W | Clerk | San Bernardino Co | Agua Mansa | |
| Pena, J | Farmer | San Salvador | San Bernardino Co | San Salvador. |
| Percy, John | Laborer | San Bernardino Co | nr San Bernardino | S Bernardino. |
| Perdew, A G | Farmer | San Bernardino Co | nr San Bernardino | S Bernardino. |
| Perdew, A | Merchant | San Bernardino Co | San Bernardino | S Bernardino. |
| Perdew, G F R B | Merchant | San Bernardino Co | San Bernardino | S Bernardino. |
| Perdew, W | Farmer | nr San Bernardino | San Bernardino Co | S Bernardino. |
| Perkins, C R | Farmer | San Bernardino Co | nr Temescal | Temescal. |
| Peerson, — | Attorney | Utah st | San Bernardino | S Bernardino. |
| Perigo, A | Farmer | San Bernardino Co | nr San Timoteo | S Bernardino. |
| Perigo, A | Farmer | nr San Bernardino | San Bernardino Co | S Bernardino. |
| Perratta, F | Farmer | San Bernardino Co | nr Temescal | Temescal. |
| Perres, Y | Farmer | San Bernardino Co | nr San Timoteo | San Timoteo. |
| Petrie, George W | Saloon | San Bernardino | San Bernardino | S Bernardino. |
| Perris & Isaac | Proprietors | S B Advertiser | San Bernardino | S Bernardino. |

## DIRECTORY OF SAN BERNARDINO COUNTY. 279

| Name. | Occupation. | Place of Business. | Residence. | Town or P. O. |
|---|---|---|---|---|
| Perris, —............ | Publisher............ | Utah st............ ........ | San Bernardino........ | S Bernardino. |
| Perris, Fredk Thos | Surveyor ........... | San Bernardino........ | San Bernardino........ | S Bernardino. |
| Perris, E T........... | Civil engineer...... | Utah, bet 6th&7th sts | San Bernardino........ | S Bernardino. |
| Petchner & Aldee... | Blacksmiths ....... | Main st............ ........ | ............................ | Riverside. |
| Petchner, F........... | Blacksmith ........ | Main st............ ........ | Almond st ............ | Riverside. |
| Peterson, Peter C... | Ranchero............ | San Bernardino Co... | San Salvador........ | San Salvador. |
| Peters, Thos........... | Stage driver........ | San Bernardino Co... | San Bernardino........ | S Bernardino. |
| Pettit, J H........... | Farmer ............ | nr San Bernardino... | San Bernardino Co... | S Bernardino. |
| Petty, W........... | Farmer ............ | San Bernardino........ | San Bernardino Co... | S Bernardino. |
| Phelps, J B........... | Mason ............ | Riverside............ | San Bernardino Co... | Riverside. |
| Phillips, H........... | Farmer ............ | San Bernardino Co... | San Bernardino........ | S Bernardino. |
| Pickens, N I........... | Nursery............ | Orange st...... ......... | Riverside............ | Riverside. |
| Pickering, Wm Price...... | Farmer ............ | San Bernardino........ | San Bernardino Co... | S Bernardino. |
| Pierce, E R........... | Carpenter............ | Olive st............ | Riverside............ | Riverside. |
| Pierce, Wm........... | Miner ............ | San Bernardino Co... | Ivanpah............ | S Bernardino. |
| Pike, J E........... | Farmer............ | nr San Bernardino... | San Bernardino Co... | S Bernardino. |
| Pike, J F........... | Farmer............ | San Bernardino Co... | nr San Bernardino... | S Bernardino. |
| Pike, A J........... | Farmer............ | nr San Bernardino... | San Bernardino Co... | S Bernardino. |
| Pike, W J........... | Farmer ............ | San Bernardino Co... | nr San Bernardino... | S Bernardino. |
| Pike, G C........... | Farmer ............ | nr San Bernardino ... | San Bernardino Co... | S Bernardino. |
| Pine, D........... | Hotel keeper ...... | San Bernardino Co... | San Bernardino........ | S Bernardino. |
| Pine, S C........... | Farmer............ | San Bernardino Co... | nr San Salvador ...... | San Salvador. |
| Pishon, N J........... | Farmer ............ | San Bernardino Co... | nr San Bernardino... | S Bernardino. |
| Pitcher, W........... | Farmer ............ | San Bernardino Co... | nr San Bernardino... | S Bernardino. |
| Pope, J D........... | Farmer ............ | nr San Bernardino ... | San Bernardino Co... | S Bernardino. |
| Poppett, R........... | Farmer ............ | nr San Bernardino ... | San Bernardino Co... | S Bernardino. |
| Porter, H R........... | Miner............ | San Bernardino Co... | Lytle Creek............ | |
| Porter, Silas Alex... | Carpenter ............ | San Bernardino Co... | ............................ | S Bernardino. |
| Potter, B F........... | Teamster............ | nr San Bernardino... | San Bernardino Co... | S Bernardino. |
| Poterill, C........... | Farmer ............ | San Bernardino Co... | nr San Bernardino... | S Bernardino. |
| Potts, D C........... | Farmer ............ | nr San Bernardino... | San Bernardino Co... | S Bernardino. |
| Powell, Dr J G.... | Dentist............ | San Bernardino........ | Utah st............ | S Bernardino. |
| Powell, L H........... | Blacksmith............ | San Bernardino Co... | San Bernardino........ | S Bernardino. |
| Pratt, James E...... | Grocer... ............ | cor 3d and Utah sts.. | ............................ | S Bernardino. |
| Pratt & Stewart...... | Groceries, etc...... | cor 3d and Utah sts.. | San Bernardino........ | S Bernardino. |
| Presley, Wm Henry | Carpenter............ | San Bernardino........ | San Bernardino........ | S Bernardino. |
| Preusse, H........... | Contractor ............ | 7 Brewery building.. | San Bernardino........ | S Bernardino. |
| Preusse, H........... | Draughtsman........ | Anderson's building. | Salt Lake st............ | S Bernardino. |
| Price, M M........... | Laborer ............ | nr San Bernardino... | San Bernardino Co... | S Bernardino. |
| Prieta, A........... | Farmer ............ | San Bernardino Co... | nr San Salvador...... | San Salvador. |
| Prieto, A........... | Laborer ............ | San Bernardino Co... | nr Temescal............ | Temescal. |
| Prieto, D A........... | Farmer ............ | San Bernardino Co... | nr San Timoteo........ | San Timoteo. |
| Prothero, E........... | Farmer ............ | nr San Bernardino... | San Bernardino Co... | S Bernardino. |
| Prothero, W........... | Farmer ............ | nr San Bernardino... | San Bernardino Co... | S Bernardino. |
| Prothero, E P...... | Farmer ............ | San Bernardino Co... | nr San Bernardino... | S Bernardino. |
| Prothero, John...... | Farmer ............ | San Bernardino Co... | San Bernardino Co... | S Bernardino. |
| Prothero, Jas........... | Farmer ............ | nr San Bernardino... | San Bernardino Co... | S Bernardino. |
| Pugh, E W........... | Shoe maker ........ | San Bernardino Co... | San Bernardino........ | S Bernardino. |
| Pyburn, Wm........... | Farmer ............ | San Bernardino Co... | nr San Timoteo........ | S Bernardino. |
| Quigley, Jas........... | Machinist............ | San Salvador............ | San Bernardino Co... | San Salvador. |
| Quigley, Hugh L.... | Carpenter............ | San Bernardino........ | San Bernardino Co... | S Bernardino. |
| Quintanna H........... | Farmer ............ | San Bernardino Co... | San Salvador............ | San Salvador. |
| Quintanua, M........... | Farmer............ | San Bernardino Co... | nr San Salvador...... | San Salvador. |
| Quintanna, J M...... | Laborer ............ | San Bernardino Co... | nr San Salvador...... | San Salvador. |
| Rabel, H........... | Farmer ............ | nr San Bernardino... | San Bernardino Co... | S Bernardino. |
| Ramirez, F........... | Laborer ............ | San Bernardino Co... | nr San Bernardino... | S Bernardino. |
| Randall, J T........... | Teamster............ | nr San Bernardino... | San Bernardino Co... | S Bernardino. |
| Ranne, B F........... | Farmer............ | Riverside............ | San Bernardino Co... | Riverside. |
| Rathburg, D........... | Farmer ............ | nr San Bernardino... | San Bernardino Co... | S Bernardino. |
| Raweiz, B........... | ............ | San Bernardino Co... | San Bernardino........ | S Bernardino. |
| Raymond, Frank C | Laborer ............ | San Bernardino Co... | ............................ | S Bernardino. |
| Raynor, Platt Augustus. | Broker............ | San Bernardino........ | San Bernardino........ | S Bernardino. |

| Name. | Occupation. | Place of Business. | Residence. | Town or P. O |
|---|---|---|---|---|
| Reavill, David | Farmer | San Bernardino Co.. | | S Bernardino. |
| Reber, Wm | Teamster | San Bernardino Co.. | nr San Bernardino | S Bernardino. |
| Redding, Patrick H | Gas fitter | San Bernardino | Martin's | S Bernardino. |
| Reed, Henry | Farmer | | San Bernardino Co.. | S Bernardino. |
| Reed, W C | Farmer | nr San Bernardino | San Bernardino Co.. | S Bernardino. |
| Reed, A | Shoe maker | San Bernardino Co.. | San Bernardino | S Bernardino. |
| Reed, T E | Farmer | nr San Bernardino | San Bernardino Co.. | S Bernardino. |
| Reeder, L F | Farmer | nr San Bernardino | San Bernardino Co.. | S Bernardino. |
| Reeder, J P | Farmer | nr San Bernardino | San Bernardino Co.. | S Bernardino. |
| Reedford, W | Teamster | San Bernardino Co.. | Ivanpah | S Bernardino. |
| Reese, L | Laborer | San Bernardino Co.. | nr San Bernardino | S Bernardino. |
| Reeve, R | Farmer | South of Riverside | San Bernardino Co.. | Riverside. |
| Reeve, R | Butcher | San Bernardino Co.. | Agua Mansa | |
| Reich, G A | Druggist | San Bernardino Co.. | San Bernardino | S Bernardino. |
| Reinhold, G | Furniture | 3d st | San Bernardino | S Bernardino. |
| Reinhold, J G | Builder | San Bernardino Co.. | | S Bernardino. |
| Rene, Dr G A | Physician | Reich's drug store | San Bernardino | S Bernardino. |
| Rennous, T J | Carpenter | San Bernardino Co.. | San Bernardino | S Bernardino. |
| Reve, G A | Physician | San Bernardino Co.. | | S Bernardino. |
| Rey, C H | Prof of dancing | San Bernardino Co.. | San Bernardino | S Bernardino. |
| Reynald, W | Baker | San Bernardino Co.. | San Bernardino | S Bernardino. |
| Reynolds, C | Farmer | nr San Bernardino | San Bernardino Co.. | S Bernardino. |
| Reynolds, S | Laborer | San Bernardino Co.. | nr San Bernardino | S Bernardino. |
| Reynolds, B M | Carriage maker | San Bernardino Co.. | San Bernardino | S Bernardino. |
| Rhine, I N | Blacksmith | San Bernardino Co.. | Agua Mansa | |
| Rice, M | Farmer | San Bernardino Co.. | nr Cocomongo | Cocomongo. |
| Richardson, J | Lumberman | San Bernardino Co.. | Mountain Mill | S Bernardino. |
| Riche, F L | Merchant | San Bernardino Co.. | Cocomongo | Cocomongo. |
| Rickard, W C | Carpenter | San Bernardino Co.. | | S Bernardino. |
| Rickman, A | Stock raiser | San Bernardino Co.. | nr San Bernardino | S Bernardino. |
| Ridge, R | Farmer | San Bernardino Co.. | nr San Bernardino | S Bernardino. |
| Ridley, E | Farmer | nr San Bernardino | San Bernardino Co.. | S Bernardino. |
| Riley, J C | Farmer | nr San Bernardino | San Bernardino | S Bernardino. |
| Rissinge, W A | Shoe maker | San Bernardino Co.. | San Bernardino | S Bernardino. |
| Rittlor, M | Store keeper | San Bernardino Co.. | San Bernardino | S Bernardino. |
| Rittner, J | Miner | nr San Bernardino | San Bernardino Co.. | S Bernardino. |
| Rivas, Casimiro | Laborer | San Bernardino Co.. | | San Salvador. |
| Riverside Land & Irrigation Co | | Main st | | Riverside. |
| Rives, Robt Wm | Farmer | 25 m S W San Ber.. | Rincon | Chino. |
| Roach, Wm | Artesian well borer | 3d st | San Bernardino | S Bernardino. |
| Robeads, W B | Farmer | San Bernardino Co.. | nr San Salvador | San Salvador. |
| Roberds, R T | Farmer | San Bernardino Co.. | Agua Mansa | |
| Roberts, J | Farmer | San Bernardino Co.. | Agua Mansa | |
| Roberts, C A | Farmer | San Bernardino Co.. | nr San Salvador | San Salvador. |
| Roberts, B | Farmer | San Bernardino Co.. | Agua Mansa | |
| Robert, George | Farmer | San Bernardino Co.. | nr San Bernardino | S Bernardino. |
| Roberts, H M | Stage driver | San Bernardino Co.. | | S Bernardino. |
| Roberts, Wm Henry | Miner | | San Bernardino Co.. | S Bernardino. |
| Robidoux, P | Farmer | San Bernardino Co.. | nr San Bernardino | S Bernardino. |
| Robidoux, A A | Farmer | nr Riverside | Riverside | Riverside. |
| Robinson, Wm Henry | Vaquero | San Bernardino Co.. | Mojave River | S Bernardino. |
| Robinson, M F | Farmer | nr San Bernardino | San Bernardino Co.. | S Bernardino. |
| Robinson, H G O | Miner | San Bernardino Co.. | nr San Bernardino | S Bernardino. |
| Roby, T | Laborer | San Bernardino Co.. | nr Chino | Chino. |
| Rochon, Z | Miner | San Bernardino Co.. | | S Bernardino. |
| Rodella, J B | Laborer | San Bernardino Co.. | nr San Bernardino | S Bernardino. |
| Rodden, W H | Boot maker | San Bernardino Co.. | San Bernardino | S Bernardino. |
| Rodgers, A C | Saloon | Kelting's Block | San Bernardino | S Bernardino. |
| Rodgers, A C | Harness maker | 3d st | San Bernardino | S Bernardino. |
| Rodgers, A | Saddler | San Bernardino Co.. | San Bernardino | S Bernardino. |
| Rodriguez, A | Laborer | San Bernardino Co.. | nr San Bernardino | S Bernardino. |
| Rodriguez, T | Silversmith | San Bernardino Co.. | San Bernardino | S Bernardino. |

| Occupation. | Place of Business. | Residence. | Town or P. O. |
|---|---|---|---|
| aquero | San Bernardino Co... | nr Temescal | Temescal. |
| erchant | San Bernardino Co... | San Bernardino | S Bernardino. |
| armer | South of Riverside... | San Bernardino Co.... | Riverside. |
| arpenter | San Bernardino Co... | Riverside | Riverside. |
| umberman | nr San Bernardino... | San Bernardino Co... | S Bernardino. |
| loon | 3d st | San Bernardino | S Bernardino. |
| ttorney | Over Ruffin & Biny's | San Bernardino | S Bernardino. |
| umber | San Bernardino Co... | San Bernardino | S Bernardino. |
| nker | San Bernardino Co... | San Bernardino | S Bernardino. |
| lversmith | San Bernardino Co... | San Bernardino | S Bernardino. |
| aborer | nr San Bernardino... | San Bernardino Co... | S Bernardino. |
| aborer | San Bernardino Co... | nr Chino | Chino. |
| eal estate | Ruffin's building | San Bernardino | S Bernardino. |
| iner | San Bernardino Co... | | S Bernardino. |
| en merchandise. | Main st | Main st | Riverside. |
| lacksmith | Utah st | San Bernardino | S Bernardino. |
| aborer | San Bernardino Co... | nr San Timoteo | S Bernardino. |
| arpenter | 7th st | 7th st | Riverside. |
| armer | South of Riverside... | San Bernardino Co... | Riverside. |
| inter | San Bernardino Co... | Mountain Mill | S Bernardino. |
| hysician | San Bernardino Co... | Agua Mansa | |
| lacksmith | San Bernardino Co... | San Bernardino | S Bernardino. |
| ttorney at law... | Anderson's building.. | San Bernardino | S Bernardino. |
| | San Bernardino Co... | Riverside | Riverside. |
| ock raiser | Riverside | San Bernardino Co... | Riverside. |
| ecretary | R L & I Co | Hotel | Riverside. |
| oves,tin& hrdwr | 3d st | San Bernardino | S Bernardino. |
| oves,tin& hrdwr | 3d st | San Bernardino | S Bernardino. |
| armer | San Bernardino Co... | nr Chino | Chino. |
| armer | North of Riverside... | San Bernardino | Riverside. |
| urseryman | 1 m N of Riverside... | San Bernardino Road | Riverside. |
| armer | San Bernardino Co... | San Salvador | Riverside. |
| urseryman | 1 m N of Riverside... | San Bernardino Road | Riverside. |
| ursery | North of Riverside... | San Bernardino Co... | Riverside. |
| aborer | San Bernardino Co... | | S Bernardino. |
| anufacturer | San Bernardino | San Bernardino | S Bernardino. |
| intner | 22 m W San Ber'no.. | Cocomongo | Cocomongo. |
| intner | San Bernardino Co... | Cocomongo | Cocomongo. |
| intner | San Bernardino Co... | Cocomongo | Cocomongo. |
| intner | San Bernardino Co... | Cocomongo | Cocomongo. |
| armer | San Bernardino Co... | nr San Salvador | San Salvador. |
| armer | San Bernardino Co... | nr San Salvador | San Salvador. |
| armer | San Bernardino Co... | Agua Mansa | |
| oulder | San Bernardino | San Bernardino | S Bernardino. |
| armer | San Bernardino Co... | nr San Salvador | San Salvador. |
| armer | San Bernardino Co... | nr San Salvador | San Salvador. |
| ttorney at law... | Kelting's block | San Bernardino | S Bernardino. |
| utcher | San Bernardino | San Bernardino | S Bernardino. |
| eamster | San Bernardino Co... | Ivanpah | S Bernardino. |
| Vines and liquors | San Bernardino | San Bernardino | S Bernardino. |
| aborer | San Bernardino Co... | nr San Timoteo | S Bernardino. |
| armer | San Bernardino Co... | nr Riverside | Riverside. |
| | | San Bernardino | S Bernardino. |
| rest R Land Co. | Main st | 7th st | Riverside. |
| ardener | Wilmington st | San Bernardino | S Bernardino. |
| armer | San Bernardino Co... | nr San Bernardino... | S Bernardino. |
| armer | nr San Bernardino... | San Bernardino Co... | S Bernardino. |
| armer | nr San Bernardino... | San Bernardino Co... | S Bernardino. |
| achinist | San Bernardino | San Bernardino Co... | S Bernardino. |
| mbroiderer | San Bernardino | | S Bernardino. |
| aloon | 3d st | 3d st | S Bernardino. |
| Vaiter | nr San Bernardino... | San Bernardino Co... | S Bernardino. |

L. L. PAULSON'S HAND-BOOK AND

| Name. | Occupation. | Place of Business. | Residence. | Town or P. O. |
|---|---|---|---|---|
| Schunemann, F..... | Blacksmith......... | San Bernardino........ | San Bernardino........ | S Bernardino. |
| Schuyff, J H........ | Blacksmith......... | San Bernardino Co... | San Bernardino........ | S Bernardino. |
| Scofield, G W....... | Farmer............. | nr San Bernardino... | San Bernardino Co... | S Bernardino. |
| Scott, Wm John..... | Farmer............. | nr San Bernardino... | San Bernardino Co... | S Bernardino. |
| Scott, Wm........... | Farmer............. | San Bernardino Co... | nr San Bernardino... | S Bernardino. |
| Scott, W M.......... | Teamster........... | San Bernardino Co... | nr San Bernardino... | S Bernardino. |
| Scrimgeour, Robt... | Farmer............. | nr San Bernardino... | San Bernardino Co... | S Bernardino. |
| Scrimgeour, R....... | Variety store...... | 3d st............... | San Bernardino........ | S Bernardino. |
| Scully, George...... | Laborer............ | San Bernardino Co... | ...................... | S Bernardino. |
| Scultz, E G.......... | Farmer............. | San Bernardino Co... | Chino................ | Chino. |
| Scybert, R.......... | Farmer............. | nr San Bernardino... | San Bernardino Co... | S Bernardino. |
| Sears, Jas........... | Farmer............. | San Bernardino Co... | nr Chino............. | Chino. |
| See, J W............. | Farmer............. | San Bernardino Co... | nr Riverside......... | Riverside. |
| Seeley, D............ | Farmer............. | nr San Bernardino... | San Bernardino Co... | S Bernardino. |
| Serrano, L........... | Farmer............. | San Bernardino Co... | nr Temescal.......... | Temescal. |
| Sexton, D............ | Farmer............. | San Bernardino Co... | San Bernardino........ | S Bernardino. |
| Seymore, C.......... | Lumberman......... | San Bernardino Co... | Mountain Mill........ | S Bernardino. |
| Shaber, Jacob F..... | Merchant........... | San Bernardino Co... | San Bernardino........ | S Bernardino. |
| Shackford, L C...... | Carpenter.......... | San Bernardino Co... | San Bernardino........ | S Bernardino. |
| Shackleford, W F.. | Wagon maker...... | San Bernardino Co... | San Bernardino........ | S Bernardino. |
| Shafer, Harry H.... | Agent.............. | ...................... | ...................... | S Bernardino. |
| Shaw, Rebecca...... | Dress maker........ | South of Riverside... | San Bernardino Co... | Riverside. |
| Shaw, W............. | Laborer............ | nr San Bernardino... | San Bernardino Co... | S Bernardino. |
| Shay, W A........... | Farmer............. | San Bernardino Co... | nr San Bernardino... | S Bernardino. |
| Shay, M.............. | Laborer............ | nr San Bernardino... | San Bernardino Co... | S Bernardino. |
| Shearer, M.......... | Farmer............. | nr San Bernardino... | San Bernardino Co... | S Bernardino. |
| Sheel, C.............. | Miner.............. | San Bernardino Co... | Ivanpah.............. | S Bernardino. |
| Sheldon, E M....... | Mason.............. | 1 m N E Riverside... | San Bernardino Road | Riverside. |
| Shelley, Pinckney.. | Engineer .......... | San Bernardino Co... | Martin's............. | S Bernardino. |
| Shelton, R........... | Dentist............. | San Bernardino Co... | San Bernardino........ | S Bernardino. |
| Sheperd, S........... | Farmer............. | San Bernardino Co... | nr San Bernardino... | S Bernardino. |
| Sherman, A.......... | Philadela brewery | 3d st............... | San Bernardino........ | S Bernardino. |
| Sherrill, W L........ | Farmer............. | South of Riverside... | San Bernardino Co... | Riverside. |
| Sherwin, —......... | Starke's hotel...... | 3d st............... | San Bernardino........ | S Bernardino. |
| Shields, C L......... | Laborer............ | San Bernardino Co... | nr San Bernardino... | S Bernardino. |
| Short, Wm........... | Farmer............. | ...................... | ...................... | S Bernardino. |
| Shoup, Christie & Boren............. | Attorneys.......... | Boren's block, 4th st | San Bernardino........ | S Bernardino. |
| Shoup, —........... | Attorney........... | Boren's block, 4th st | San Bernardino........ | S Bernardino. |
| Shugart, K D........ | Physician.......... | San Bernardino Co... | San Bernardino........ | S Bernardino. |
| Shur, F C............ | Drugs, glass, etc. | 3d st............... | San Bernardino........ | S Bernardino. |
| Simmons, J.......... | Farmer............. | nr San Bernardino... | San Bernardino Co... | S Bernardino. |
| Singleton, Wm...... | Farmer............. | San Bernardino Co... | nr San Bernardino... | S Bernardino. |
| Singleton, Jas....... | Engineer........... | San Bernardino Co... | San Bernardino........ | S Bernardino. |
| Sisemore, A......... | Laborer............ | San Bernardino Co... | San Bernardino........ | S Bernardino. |
| Slaughter, F M..... | Farmer............. | San Bernardino Co... | nr Chino............. | Chino. |
| Slavan & Hodgdon | Stable.............. | Bairdstown......... | San Bernardino Co... | Bairdstown. |
| Sleppy, N............ | Druggist........... | San Bernardino Co... | San Bernardino........ | S Bernardino. |
| Sleven, J G.......... | Miner.............. | San Bernardino Co... | Ivanpah.............. | S Bernardino. |
| Slinkard, W J....... | Farmer............. | San Bernardino Co... | nr San Bernardino... | S Bernardino. |
| Slosson, C B........ | Carpenter.......... | San Bernardino Co... | San Bernardino........ | S Bernardino. |
| Sloughter, E M..... | Shepherd.......... | San Bernardino Co... | nr Chino............. | Chino. |
| Smith & Cole....... | Wines and liquors | 3d, bet Utah&Grafton | ...................... | S Bernardino. |
| Smith, A R.......... | Butcher............ | Main st............. | Main st............... | Riverside. |
| Smith, A R.......... | Teamster........... | San Bernardino Co... | nr San Salvador..... | San Salvador. |
| Smith, Augustus Wm... | Painter............ | San Bernardino...... | San Bernardino........ | S Bernardino. |
| Smith, C K.......... | Teamster........... | San Bernardino Co... | nr San Bernardino... | S Bernardino. |
| Smith, D N.......... | Physician.......... | San Bernardino Co... | San Bernardino........ | S Bernardino. |
| Smith, E............. | Farmer............. | San Bernardino Co... | nr San Gorgonio..... | S Bernardino. |
| Smith, E............. | Physician.......... | San Bernardino Co... | San Salvador........ | San Salvador. |
| Smith, F M.......... | Farmer............. | nr San Bernardino... | San Bernardino Co... | S Bernardino. |
| Smith, John L...... | Saloon keeper..... | San Bernardino Co... | San Bernardino........ | S Bernardino. |
| Smith, J H.......... | Farmer............. | San Bernardino Co... | San Gorgonio........ | S Bernardino. |

## DIRECTORY OF SAN BERNARDINO COUNTY. 283

| Name. | Occupation. | Place of Business. | Residence. | Town or P. O |
|---|---|---|---|---|
| Smith, J P............ | Carpenter......... | San Bernardino Co... | Riverside............ ........ | Riverside. |
| Smith, J.................. ..... | Miner...... ......... | nr San Bernardino... | San Bernardino Co... | S Bernardino. |
| Smith, J.................. | Farmer............ | San Bernardino Co... | nr Cocomongo......... | Cocomongo. |
| Smith, I W............ | Physician............ | San Bernardino Co... | Rincon................... | Chino. |
| Smith, J S............ | Vaquero... ......... | San Bernardino Co... | nr San Bernardino... | S Bernardino. |
| Smith, I A............ | Farmer............. | nr San Bernardino... | San Bernardino Co... | S Bernardino. |
| Smith, Jas Horace.. | Shoe maker........ | San Bernardino...... | San Bernardino....... | S Bernardino. |
| Smith, W H... ...... | Farmer............ | nr San Bernardino... | San Bernardino Co... | S Bernardino. |
| Smith, W A........... | Teamster............ | San Bernardino Co... | nr San Bernardino... | S Bernardino. |
| Smithson, J B....... | Teamster............ | San Bernardino Co... | nr San Bernardino... | S Bernardino. |
| Smithson, W B..... | Farmer............. | San Bernardino Co... | nr San Bernardino... | S Bernardino. |
| Smidt, E............... | Farmer............ | nr San Bernardino... | San Bernardino Co... | S Bernardino. |
| Snapp, Rufus L..... | Saloon keeper...... | San Bernardino...... | San Bernardino...... | S. Bernardino. |
| Snow, J D......... | Farmer............ | nr San Bernardino... | San Bernardino Co... | S Bernardino. |
| Snow, G P............ | Farmer............. | San Bernardino Co... | nr San Bernardino... | S Bernardino. |
| Sollnberger, L M. | Nurseryman......... | San Bernardino Co... | San Bernardino...... | S Bernardino. |
| Somers, WmFrancis | Miner.......... ...... | ....................... | San Bernardino Co... | S Bernardino. |
| Sommer, Ernest.... | Merchant............ | cor 7th & Salt L sts... | cor 4th & Salt L sts.. | S Bernardino. |
| Sonder, J............... | Farmer ............ | San Bernardino Co... | nr San Timoteo........ | S Bernardino. |
| Southworth, Harvey .......... | Harness maker ... | 12 m S S Bernardino | Riverside.............. | Riverside. |
| Southworth, H...... | Farmer ............ | ¾ m N Riverside...... | San Bernardino rd... | Riverside. |
| Sparks, G W......... | Farmer ............ | nr San Bernardino... | San Bernardino Co... | S Bernardino. |
| Sparks, W T......... | Farmer............. | San Bernardino Co... | nr San Bernardino... | S Bernardino. |
| Spencer, A J........ | Farmer ......,..... | nr San Bernardino... | San Bernardino Co... | S Bernardino. |
| Spencer, M .......... | Farmer ............ | nr San Bernardino... | San Bernardino Co... | S Bernardino. |
| Spencer, A P......... | Machinist............ | San Bernardino Co... | San Bernardino...... | S Bernardino. |
| Spencer, D............ | Farmer ............ | nr San Bernardino... | San Bernardino Co... | S Bernardino. |
| Spicer, John.......... | Farmer ............ | San Bernardino rd.... | San Bernardino rd... | Riverside. |
| Springer, Theodore.. | Tourist .............. | ........................ | San Bernardino...... | S Bernardino. |
| Spival, J ............. | Lumberman......... | nr San Bernardino... | San Bernardino Co... | S Bernardino. |
| Stafford, Thos....... | Horse shoer ........ | San Bernardino...... | Mojave................ | S Bernardino. |
| Standefer, W R...... | Ranchero ........... | nr San Bernardino... | San Bernardino Co... | S Bernardino. |
| Stanfield, W T ...... | Farmer ............ | San Bernardino Co... | nr Chino............... | Chino. |
| Standifer, T ......... | Laborer............ | nr San Bernardino... | San Bernardino Co... | S Bernardino. |
| Stanley, H O......... | Act'g secretary ... | Riverside Land Co ... | Main st ............ | Riverside. |
| Staples, T.............. | Miner............. | San Bernardino Co... | nr San Bernardino... | S Bernardino. |
| Staples, Wm P...... | Clerk................ | San Bernardino Co... | San Bernardino...... | S Bernardino. |
| Starr, T C............. | Dentist............... | r 10 Keltings Block.. | 4th st ............... | S Bernardino. |
| Starr, Thomas...... | Farmer............ | nr Riverside.......... | San Bernardino Co... | Riverside. |
| Starke, A............. | Hotel keeper ...... | San Bernardino Co... | San Bernardino...... | S Bernardino. |
| Starke, Augustus H | Clerk ........ ....... | San Bernardino...... | San Bernardino...... | S Bernardino. |
| Stark, L................ | Farmer ............ | nr San Bernardino... | San Bernardino Co... | S Bernardino. |
| St Clair, A S......... | Physician .......... | San Bernardino Co... | San Bernardino Co... | S Bernardino. |
| Stebbins, — ........ | Farmer............ | South of Riverside ... | San Bernardino Co... | Riverside. |
| Steinbrenner, L ..... | Teacher............. | San Bernardino Co... | San Bernardino...... | S Bernardino. |
| Stevenson, S D ..... | Farmer ............ | San Bernardino Co... | nr Riverside........... | S Bernardino. |
| Stewart, H J ........ | Stock.............. | Chino Ranch . ....... | 7 m S E Spadra ...... | Spadra. |
| Stewart, — ........ ...... | Groceries, &c...... | cor 3d & Utah sts..... | San Bernardino....... | S Bernardino. |
| Stewart, C ........... | Watch maker....... | San Bernardino Co... | San Bernardino...... | S Bernardino. |
| Stewart, J............. | Farmer ........... | nr San Bernardino... | San Bernardino Co... | S Bernardino. |
| Stewart, J H ........ | Farmer ............ | nr San Bernardino... | San Bernardino Co... | S Bernardino. |
| Stewart, R............ | Farmer ........... | San Bernardino Co... | nr Riverside........... | Riverside. |
| Stewart, O............ | Farmer ........... | nr San Bernardino... | San Bernardino Co... | S Bernardino. |
| Stewart, C ........... | Farmer ............ | West of Santa Ana... | San Bernardino Co... | Riverside. |
| Stewart, W R........ | Laborer............ | San Bernardino Co... | Mountain Mill........ | S Bernardino. |
| St John, S W......... | Teamster............ | nr San Bernardino... | San Bernardino Co... | S Bernardino. |
| St John, S M......... | Farmer ............ | nr San Bernardino... | San Bernardino Co... | S Bernardino. |
| St Marie, J........... | Saloon............. | Main st............... | ........................ | Riverside. |
| St Marys, James... | Farmer............ | nr Riverside........... | San Bernardino Co... | Riverside. |
| Stoddard, S .......... | Farmer ............ | San Bernardino Co... | nr San Bernardino... | S Bernardino. |
| Stones, M............. | Lumberman ...... | San Bernardino Co... | nr San Bernardino... | S Bernardino. |
| Stones, J E........... | Farmer ............ | nr San Bernardino... | San Bernardino Co... | S Bernardino. |
| Stones, H N ......... | Farmer............. | San Bernardino Co... | nr Mountain Mill..... | S Bernardino. |

| NAME. | OCCUPATION. | PLACE OF BUSINESS. | RESIDENCE. | TOWN OR P. O. |
|---|---|---|---|---|
| Stones, Wm | Farmer | San Bernardino | San Bernardino Co... | S Bernardino. |
| Stones, W H | Farmer | San Bernardino Co... | nr San Bernardino... | S Bernardino. |
| Stone, — | Palace saloon | Davis Building | San Bernardino... | S Bernardino. |
| Stone, J H | Blacksmith | San Bernardino Co... | nr San Bernardino... | S Bernardino. |
| Stones, John S | Laborer | San Bernardino Co... | | S Bernardino. |
| Stone, Wm | Blacksmith | San Bernardino Co... | San Bernardino Co... | S Bernardino. |
| Stout, S M | Farmer | nr San Bernardino... | San Bernardino Co... | S Bernardino. |
| Stout, Wm | Farmer | San Bernardino Co... | nr Riverside | Riverside. |
| Strong, D S | Farmer | San Bernardino rd... | San Bernardino rd... | Riverside. |
| Strong, Samuel | Miner | San Bernardino Co... | | S Bernardino. |
| Stroup, Elliott | Cook | San Bernardino... | San Bernardino | S Bernardino. |
| Stuchberry, J | Farmer | San Bernardino Co... | nr San Bernardino... | S Bernardino. |
| Styles, A | Farmer | San Bernardino Co... | nr Riverside | Riverside. |
| Suhr, F C | Merchant | San Bernardino Co... | San Bernardino | S Bernardino. |
| Summons, J B | Farmer | San Bernardino Co... | nr San Salvador | San Salvador. |
| Swarthout, N | Farmer | San Bernardino Co... | nr Riverside | Riverside. |
| Swarthout, H | Farmer | nr San Bernardino... | San Bernardino Co... | S Bernardino. |
| Sweat, M F | Farmer | San Bernardino Co... | nr Riverside | Riverside. |
| Sweeney, R | Laborer | San Bernardino Co... | nr Mountain Mill | S Bernardino. |
| Sweitner, L | Teamster | nr San Bernardino... | San Bernardino Co... | S Bernardino. |
| Swift, A | Lawyer & not pub | 3d st | San Bernardino | S Bernardino. |
| Swift & Katz | Real estate | 3d st | San Bernardino | S Bernardino. |
| Swift, A Mrs | Restaurant | Keltings Block | San Bernardino | S Bernardino. |
| Swing, J W | Carpenter | San Bernardino Co... | San Bernardino | S Bernardino. |
| Swing, Randolph S | Lawyer | San Bernardino.. | San Bernardino... | S Bernardino. |
| Sykes, M L | Machinist | San Bernardino Co... | | S Bernardino. |
| Taft, D M | Farmer | nr San Bernardino... | San Bernardino Co... | S Bernardino. |
| Taggart, C G | Pianos & organs | 101 3d st | San Bernardino | S Bernardino. |
| Talbott, Francis | Carpenter | | San Bernardino Co... | S Bernardino. |
| Talbott, J A | Painter | San Bernardino... | San Bernardino Co... | S Bernardino. |
| Talmage, F de B | Teamster | San Bernardino Co... | Mountain Mill | S Bernardino. |
| Tate, J | Farmer | San Bernardino Co... | nr San Salvador | San Salvador. |
| Taylor, C | Teamster | San Bernardino Co... | nr San Bernardino... | S Bernardino. |
| Taylor, J | Farmer | San Bernardino Co... | nr San Salvador | San Salvador. |
| Taylor, J | Farmer | San Bernardino Co... | nr Chino | Chino. |
| Taylor, Jas | Baker | San Bernardino Co... | San Bernardino | S Bernardino. |
| Taylor, J W | Teamster | San Bernardino Co... | nr San Bernardino... | S Bernardino. |
| Taylor, M | Farmer | San Bernardino Co... | nr San Bernardino... | S Bernardino. |
| Taylor, Thos D | Laborer | San Bernardino Co... | | S Bernardino. |
| Thabare, Peter | Gardener | | San Bernardino Co... | S Bernardino. |
| Thomas, C L | Farmer | nr San Bernardino... | San Bernardino Co... | S Bernardino. |
| Thomas, E H | Farmer | San Bernardino Co... | nr San Bernardino... | S Bernardino. |
| Thomas, E H | Farmer | nr San Bernardino... | San Bernardino Co... | S Bernardino. |
| Thomas, E J | Teamster | San Bernardino Co... | nr San Bernardino... | S Bernardino. |
| Thomas, M F | Farmer | nr San Bernardino... | San Bernardino Co... | S Bernardino. |
| Thompkins, T | Farmer | San Bernardino Co... | nr San Bernardino... | S Bernardino. |
| Thompson, Geo | Farmer | nr San Bernardino... | San Bernardino Co... | S Bernardino. |
| Thompson, H N | Stage owner | San Bernardino Co... | | S Bernardino. |
| Thompson, Uriah | Farmer | nr San Bernardino... | San Bernardino Co... | S Bernardino. |
| Thomas, Mrs | Farmer | Riverside | San Bernardino Co... | Riverside. |
| Thomson, J W | Miner | San Bernardino Co... | San Bernardino | S Bernardino. |
| Thom, J C | Farmer | nr San Bernardino... | San Bernardino Co... | S Bernardino. |
| Thom, J | Farmer | nr San Bernardino... | San Bernardino Co... | S Bernardino. |
| Thomdike, C M | | 6th st | Riverside | Riverside. |
| Tibbets, J H | Watch maker | cor 3d & Grafton sts. | San Bernardino | S Bernardino. |
| Tibbetts, L C | Farmer | San Bernardino Co... | nr Riverside | Riverside. |
| Tibbetts, G M Mrs | Milliner | cor 3d & Grafton sts. | San Bernardino | S Bernardino. |
| Tice, Jas | Farmer | San Bernardino Co... | nr San Salvador | San Salvador. |
| Tidrou, Jos | Farmer | San Bernardino Co... | nr San Bernardino... | S Bernardino. |
| Tipton, J | Farmer | San Bernardino Co... | nr San Bernardino... | S Bernardino. |
| Tittle, W S | Carriage maker | Utah st, bet 2d & 3d | San Bernardino | S Bernardino. |
| Tittle & Brodhurs. | Carriage makers | Utah st, bet 2d & 3d | | S Bernardino. |
| Tobias, J T | Carpenter | Olive st | Riverside | Riverside. |
| Tobias, Theodore | Carpenter | 12 m S S Bernardino | Riverside | Riverside. |

## DIRECTORY OF SAN BERNARDINO COUNTY. 285

| Name. | Occupation. | Place of Business. | Residence. | Town or P. O |
|---|---|---|---|---|
| Tokinto, J ............ | Farmer ............ | San Bernardino Co... | nr San Salvador ...... | San Salvador. |
| Tolles & Fleming .. | Searchers of rec'ds | Court House........... | San Bernardino........ | S Bernardino. |
| Tolles, — ............ | Searcher of rec'ds | Court House........... | San Bernardino........ | S Bernardino. |
| Tomer, Wesley...... | Farmer ............ | Mountain ............ | Mountain ............ | S Bernardino. |
| Toming, Peter...... | Farmer ............ | San Bernardino....... | San Bernardino....... | S Bernardino. |
| Toros, T............. | Farmer............. | San Bernardino Co... | nr San Timoteo....... | S Bernardino. |
| Torres, T............. | Mail carrier....... | San Bernardino Co... | San Bernardino........ | S Bernardino. |
| Torrez, Juan........ | Merchant .......... | 15 m E S Bernardino | San Timoteo........... | S Bernardino. |
| Trautman, John..... | Merchant .......... | ..................... | ..................... | S Bernardino. |
| Traver, O............ | Clerk............... | San Bernardino Co... | Riverside............. | Riverside. |
| Treese, B ............ | Farmer ............ | nr San Bernardino... | San Bernardino Co... | S Bernardino. |
| Tribolet, Seigfried... | Plasterer ........... | San Bernardino....... | San Bernardino Co... | S Bernardino. |
| Trohiza, R ......... | Farmer ............ | San Bernardino Co... | nr Temescal.......... | Temescal. |
| Tripp, S V........... | Mason............... | San Bernardino....... | San Bernardino Co... | S Bernardino. |
| Trujillo, D ......... | Farmer ............ | San Bernardino Co... | nr San Salvador ...... | San Salvador. |
| Trujillo, T .......... | Stock raiser ....... | 3 m N Riverside ..... | San Bernardino Co... | Riverside. |
| Trujillo, Fernando.. | Laborer............. | ..................... | San Salvador ........ | San Salvador. |
| Trujillo, —... ...... | Stock raiser ....... | 3 m N Riverside ..... | San Bernardino Co... | Riverside. |
| Trujillo, Francisco D | Laborer ............ | ..................... | San Salvador ........ | San Salvador. |
| Trujillo, Juan....... | Laborer ............ | San Bernardino Co... | San Salvador ........ | San Salvador. |
| Trujillo, E ......... | Farmer ............ | San Bernardino....... | nr San Salvador ...... | San Salvador. |
| Trujillo, J........... | Farmer ............ | San Bernardino Co... | nr San Salvador ...... | San Salvador. |
| Trujillo, J........... | Farmer ............ | San Bernardino Co... | nr San Salvador ...... | San Salvador. |
| Trujillo, Ramon..... | Laborer............. | ..................... | San Salvador.. ...... | San Salvador. |
| Trujillo, R.......... | Carpenter.......... | San Bernardino Co... | San Bernardino Co... | S Bernardino. |
| Trumper, Valentine........... | G & S plater ...... | San Bernardino....... | San Bernardino Co... | S Bernardino. |
| Turner, James ...... | Butcher............. | Bear Valley.......... | San Bernardino Co... | Bairdstown. |
| Twogood, D C....... | Farmer ............ | San Bernardino Co... | Riverside............. | Riverside. |
| Twogood, A J....... | Farmer ............ | San Bernardino Co... | Riverside............. | Riverside. |
| Tyler, C H.......... | Miner............... | nr San Bernardino... | San Bernardino Co... | S Bernardino. |
| Tyler, C Y.......... | Farmer ............ | San Bernardino Co... | nr San Bernardino... | S Bernardino. |
| Tyler, Joseph B..... | Miner............... | Mountain ............ | Mountain ............ | S Bernardino. |
| Tyler, N W ........ | Carpenter.......... | San Bernardino Co... | San Bernardino....... | S Bernardino. |
| Tyler, S W.......... | Farmer ............ | San Bernardino Co... | nr San Salvador ...... | San Salvador. |
| Tyson, Jos........... | Miner............... | nr San Bernardino... | San Bernardino Co... | S Bernardino. |
| Vahle, John ........ | Carpenter.......... | San Bernardino Co... | San Bernardino....... | S Bernardino. |
| Valdez, C............ | Farmer ............ | San Bernardino Co... | nr San Bernardino... | S Bernardino. |
| Valdez, I............ | Farmer ............ | San Bernardino Co... | nr San Salvador ...... | San Salvador. |
| Valdez, J............ | Laborer............. | San Bernardino Co... | nr Cocomongo........ | Cocomongo. |
| Valdez, Jose La luz | Farmer ............ | ..................... | San Salvador.. ...... | San Salvador. |
| Valdez, J M ........ | Farmer ............ | San Bernardino Co... | nr San Bernardino... | S Bernardino. |
| Vale, M W.......... | Farmer............. | nr San Bernardino... | San Bernardino Co... | S Bernardino. |
| Vale, W A.......... | Photographer ..... | 3d st................. | ..................... | S Bernardino. |
| Vale, M............. | Farmer ............ | San Bernardino....... | San Bernardino Co... | S Bernardino. |
| Vale, W A.......... | Farmer ............ | San Bernardino Co... | nr Chino.............. | Chino. |
| Valenzuela, Jose.... | Farmer ............ | ..................... | San Salvador......... | San Salvador. |
| Valenzuela, J....... | Farmer ............ | San Bernardino Co... | nr Temescal.......... | Temescal. |
| Valentine, N D..... | Clerk ............. | San Bernardino Co... | San Bernardino....... | S Bernardino. |
| Valenzuela, J....... | Farmer ............ | San Bernardino Co... | nr San Salvador ...... | San Salvador. |
| Van Buren, —...... | Farmer ............ | San Bernardino Co... | San Bernardino....... | S Bernardino. |
| Van Decar, Ezra H | Lawyer ............ | San Bernardino....... | San Bernardino....... | S Bernardino. |
| Vanderenter, Frank | Trader ............. | 15 m E San Bernar.. | San Timoteo ........ | S Bernardino. |
| Vaudorn, — ....... | Carriage mnfr..... | 3d st................. | San Bernardino....... | S Bernardino. |
| Van Fleit, —....... | Farmer ............ | South of Riverside... | San Bernardino Co... | Riverside. |
| Van Leuver, A ...... | Farmer ............ | San Bernardino Co... | San Bernardino Co... | S Bernardino. |
| Van Leuvin, B...... | Farmer ............ | San Bernardino Co... | nr San Bernardino... | S Bernardino. |
| Van Leuven, F M.. | Farmer ............ | San Bernardino Co... | nr San Bernardino... | S Bernardino. |
| Van Lewin, J A..... | Teamster........... | San Bernardino Co... | nr San Bernardino... | S Bernardino. |
| Van Lewin, L....... | Farmer ............ | nr San Bernardino... | San Bernardino Co... | S Bernardino. |
| Van Leuvin, O...... | Farmer ............ | San Bernardino Co... | nr San Bernardino... | S Bernardino. |
| Van Loan, J ........ | Laborer.... ....... | nr San Bernardino... | San Bernardino Co... | S Bernardino. |
| Vanslyke & Sommer............ | Lumber dealers... | cor of 7th & Salt L sts | ..................... | S Bernardino. |

| Name. | Occupation. | Place of Business. | Residence. | Town or P.O |
|---|---|---|---|---|
| Vanslyke, W E | | 14 m N S Bernardino | 3d & Independ'ce sts | S Bernardino. |
| Van Tassell, N | Merchant | San Bernardino Co... | San Bernardino | S Bernardino. |
| Varley, A | Mason | San Bernardino Co... | San Bernardino | S Bernardino. |
| Vassar, W J | Farmer | nr San Bernardino... | San Bernardino Co... | S Bernardino. |
| Vassar, G L | Farmer | San Bernardino Co... | nr San Bernardino... | S Bernardino. |
| Vaughn, R W | Farmer | San Bernardino Co... | nr San Bernardino... | S Bernardino. |
| Via Alvaso, I M | Farmer | San Bernardino Co... | nr San Salvador | San Salvador. |
| Vial, R M | Farmer | San Bernardino Co... | nr San Bernardino... | S Bernardino. |
| Vice, D | Saloon | Bairdstown | San Bernardino Co... | Bairdstown. |
| Vickers, J F | Farmer | San Bernardino Co... | nr San Bernardino... | S Bernardino. |
| Vincent, J | Miner | San Bernardino Co... | nr San Bernardino... | S Bernardino. |
| Vine, B | Farmer | San Bernardino Co... | nr Chino | Chino. |
| Vines, G R | Farmer | San Bernardino Co... | nr Rincon | Chino. |
| Volck, Dr Stephen | Physician & farm | 1 m N Riverside | San Bernardino Road | Riverside. |
| Voorhies, N | Blacksmith | Market st | Market st | Riverside. |
| Voorhies, W | Teamster | San Bernardino Co... | nr San Bernardino... | S Bernardino. |
| Wagner, J H | Just of peace & col | 3d st | San Bernardino | S Bernardino. |
| Wagner, J H | Farmer | San Bernardino Co... | nr San Bernardino... | S Bernardino. |
| Wagner, J H | Farmer | nr San Bernardino... | San Bernardino Co... | S Bernardino. |
| Waite, L C | Attorney & notary | 3 m N E Riverside... | Riverside | Riverside. |
| Waite, Sidney P | Clerk & recorder. | 1 Court House Block | San Bernardino | S Bernardino. |
| Waite, S P | Painter | San Bernardino Co... | Rincon | Chino. |
| Wakefield, A J | Farmer | San Bernardino Co... | nr San Bernardino... | S Bernardino. |
| Wales, H | Farmer | San Bernardino Co... | nr San Timoteo | S Bernardino. |
| Walkinshaw, T B | Farmer | San Bernardino Co... | nr San Salvador | San Salvador. |
| Wall, B M | Teaming | San Bernardino Co... | San Bernardino | S Bernardino. |
| Wall, Chas Jones | Architect | San Bernardino | San Bernardino | S Bernardino. |
| Wall, S M | Teamster | San Bernardino Co... | Rincon | Chino. |
| Wall, W | Farmer | San Bernardino Co... | nr San Bernardino... | S Bernardino. |
| Wallace, A | Teamster | nr San Bernardino... | San Bernardino Co... | S Bernardino. |
| Wallace, H M | Farmer | San Bernardino Co... | Rincon | Chino. |
| Wallace, J W | Farmer | San Bernardino Co... | nr Rincon | Chino. |
| Wallace, R W | Farmer | nr San Bernardino... | San Bernardino Co... | S Bernardino. |
| Wallen, J V | Teamster | San Bernardino Co... | nr San Bernardino... | S Bernardino. |
| Walrod, Clarence J | Clerk | San Bernardino | San Bernardino | S Bernardino. |
| Walton, Wm Charles | Farmer | nr San Bernardino... | San Bernardino Co... | S Bernardino. |
| Ward, J J | Farmer | San Bernardino Co... | nr San Salvador | San Salvador. |
| Warren, L F | Cabinet maker | Market st | 7th st | Riverside. |
| Warren, A H | Farmer | nr San Bernardino... | San Bernardino Co... | S Bernardino. |
| Warren, A A | Farmer | San Bernardino Co... | Rincon | Chino. |
| Warren, M | Farmer | San Bernardino Co... | nr San Salvador | San Salvador. |
| Warren, P | Farmer | San Bernardino Co... | nr San Salvador | San Salvador. |
| Warren, Z K | Farmer | San Bernardino Co... | Rincon | Chino. |
| Waters, Byron | Attorney at law | 5 Court House | San Bernardino | S Bernardino. |
| Waters, B B | Student | San Bernardino Co... | San Bernardino | S Bernardino. |
| Waters, Frederick | Harness maker | San Bernardino | San Bernardino | S Bernardino. |
| Waters, J W | Farmer | San Bernardino Co... | nr Rincon | Chino. |
| Weaver, J | Miner | San Bernardino Co... | Lytle Creek | |
| Weaver, Wm | Teamster | nr San Bernardino... | San Bernardino Co... | S Bernardino. |
| Webbe, — | Stock raiser | 6 m E Riverside | San Bernardino Co... | Riverside. |
| Webber, M | Farmer | nr San Bernardino... | San Bernardino Co... | S Bernardino. |
| Webber, M W | Farmer | nr San Bernardino... | San Bernardino Co... | S Bernardino. |
| Webster, Jas | Farmer | San Bernardino Co... | nr San Bernardino... | S Bernardino. |
| Webster, J | Farmer | San Bernardino Co... | nr San Bernardino... | S Bernardino. |
| Webster, W | Farmer | San Bernardino Co... | nr San Bernardino... | S Bernardino. |
| Weeks, J | Farmer | San Bernardino Co... | nr San Bernardino... | S Bernardino. |
| Weeks, S | Farmer | San Bernardino Co... | Rincon | Chino. |
| Weeks, John | Farmer | San Bernardino Co... | nr San Bernardino... | S Bernardino. |
| Welch, J A | Farmer | San Bernardino Co... | nr San Bernardino... | S Bernardino. |
| Welch, J M | Teamster | San Bernardino Co... | San Bernardino | S Bernardino. |
| Wells, W | Teamster | San Bernardino Co... | nr San Bernardino... | S Bernardino. |
| West, J M | Farmer | San Bernardino Co... | Rincon | Chino. |
| West, P | Carpenter | San Bernardino Co... | San Bernardino | S Bernardino. |

# DIRECTORY OF SAN BERNARDINO COUNTY. 287

| NAME. | OCCUPATION. | PLACE OF BUSINESS. | RESIDENCE. | TOWN OR P. O |
|---|---|---|---|---|
| West, S.M............... | Farmer ............... | nr San Bernardino... | San Bernardino Co... | S Bernardino. |
| West, Thomas ...... | Farmer ............... | nr San Bernardino... | San Bernardino Co... | S Bernardino. |
| Whaley, H H & Co | Saloon................... | 3d st........................ | ............................... | S Bernardino. |
| Whaley, H H, Jr... | Clerk...................... | San Bernardino Co... | San Bernardino....... | S Bernardino. |
| Whaley, H H......... | Saddler................. | San Bernardino Co... | San Bernardino....... | S Bernardino. |
| Whaley, J T........... | Merchant ............ | San Bernardino Co... | San Bernardino....... | S Bernardino. |
| Wheaton, J ............ | Farmer ............... | San Bernardino Co... | nr San Bernardino... | S Bernardino. |
| Whetstone, H J...... | Laborer................ | nr San Bernardino... | San Bernardino Co... | S Bernardino. |
| Whisler, W V......... | Farmer................ | San Bernardino Co... | nr San Bernardino... | S Bernardino. |
| Whilby, W.............. | Farmer.................. | nr San Bernardino... | San Bernardino Co... | S Bernardino. |
| Whitfield, W........... | Farmer ................ | San Bernardino Co... | nr Cocomongo......... | Cocomongo. |
| White, Mrs Caroline | ............................. | ............................. | 6th st....................... | Riverside. |
| White, George H ... | Laborer................. | San Bernardino Co... | Riverside................. | Riverside. |
| White, O................. | Clerk..................... | San Bernardino Co... | San Bernardino....... | S Bernardino. |
| Whitlock, Dr A...... | Dentist ................ | 3d st........................ | San Bernardino....... | S Bernardino. |
| Whitlock & Cunningham..... | Dentists............... | 3d st........................ | San Bernardino....... | S Bernardino. |
| Whitlock, O............ | Farmer ............... | San Bernardino Co... | nr San Bernardino... | S Bernardino. |
| Whitesides, M ...... | Farmer ............... | San Bernardino Co... | nr San Bernardino... | S Bernardino. |
| Whiteman, R R..... | Farmer................ | San Bernardino....... | San Bernardino Co... | S Bernardino. |
| Whitman, C........... | Butcher ............... | San Bernardino....... | San Bernardino Co... | S Bernardino. |
| Whitton, A............. | Farmer ............... | San Bernardino Co... | nr San Bernardino... | S Bernardino. |
| Whytton, A N....... | Stock raiser ....... | San Bernardino Co... | San Bernardino....... | S Bernardino. |
| Wilber, C B ........... | Miner ................... | San Bernardino Co... | Holcomb Valley...... | Bairdstown. |
| Wilbur, J ................ | Farmer ............... | 3 m N E Riverside... | San Bernardino Road | Riverside. |
| Wilbur, John ......... | Engineer ............. | 12 m S S Bernardino | Riverside................. | Riverside. |
| Willard, F............... | Teamster.............. | nr San Bernardino... | San Bernardino Co... | S Bernardino. |
| Willis, Henry M... | Attorney............... | Court House........... | San Bernardino....... | S Bernardino. |
| Willis, J J ............... | Lumberman ....... | San Bernardino Co... | Mountain Mill......... | S Bernardino. |
| Willis, Stephen R.. | Carpenter ........... | San Bernardino...... | ............................... | S Bernardino. |
| Williams, H ........... | Merchant ............ | San Bernardino Co... | San Bernardino....... | S Bernardino. |
| Williams, O............ | Farmer ............... | nr San Bernardino... | San Bernardino Co... | S Bernardino. |
| Wilshire, G T ....... | Farmer................ | nr San Bernardino... | San Bernardino Co... | S Bernardino. |
| Wilson, B W.......... | Farmer ............... | San Bernardino Co... | nr San Bernardino... | S Bernardino. |
| Wilson, C............... | Farmer ............... | San Bernardino Co... | nr San Bernardino... | S Bernardino. |
| Wilson, Edgar Delos | Laborer................ | San Bernardino...... | ............................... | S Bernardino. |
| Wilson, Harvey..... | Laborer................ | San Bernardino...... | ............................... | S Bernardino. |
| Wilson, Henry...... | Laborer................ | San Bernardino Co... | nr San Bernardino... | S Bernardino. |
| Wilson, H A.......... | Minister ............... | San Bernardino Co... | San Bernardino....... | S Bernardino. |
| Wilson, J G........... | Farmer ............... | San Bernardino Co... | nr San Salvador...... | San Salvador. |
| Wilson, J................ | Farmer ............... | nr San Bernardino... | San Bernardino Co... | S Bernardino. |
| Wilson, J W .......... | Miner ................... | nr San Bernardino... | San Bernardino Co... | S Bernardino. |
| Wilson, J W.......... | U S assessor....... | San Bernardino Co... | San Bernardino....... | S Bernardino. |
| Wilson, L M ......... | Saloon ................. | San Bernardino...... | ............................... | S Bernardino. |
| Wilson, Luther M.. | Clerk .................... | San Bernardino...... | San Bernardino....... | S Bernardino. |
| Wilson, Lorenzo D | Attorney ............. | San Bernardino Co... | San Bernardino....... | S Bernardino. |
| Wilson, S F .......... | Laborer................ | San Bernardino Co... | nr San Bernardino... | S Bernardino. |
| Wilson, T J ............ | Doctor.................. | San Bernardino Co... | San Bernardino....... | S Bernardino. |
| Wilson, Wm ......... | Miner ................... | San Bernardino Co... | ............................... | S Bernardino. |
| Wilson, W............. | Laborer................ | San Bernardino Co... | nr Cocomongo......... | Cocomongo. |
| Winkler, Aug........ | Lunch room........ | 3d st........................ | San Bernardino....... | S Bernardino. |
| Winkler, D D......... | Shipwright........... | San Bernardino Co... | San Bernardino....... | S Bernardino. |
| Winkapaw, Robt M | Carpenter............ | San Bernardino...... | ............................... | S Bernardino. |
| Winters, Jas.......... | Laborer................ | nr San Bernardino... | San Bernardino Co... | S Bernardino. |
| Wise, A B .............. | Blacksmith.......... | San Bernardino Co... | San Bernardino Co... | S Bernardino. |
| Wise, A D.............. | Blacksmith ......... | San Bernardino...... | ............................... | S Bernardino. |
| Winslow, E............ | Farmer ............... | San Bernardino Co... | nr San Salvador...... | San Salvador. |
| Wiseman, J C ....... | Laborer................ | San Bernardino Co... | nr San Bernardino... | S Bernardino. |
| Wiseman, W C...... | Lawyer ................ | San Bernardino Co... | San Bernardino....... | S Bernardino. |
| Wixom, D H .......... | Laborer................ | San Bernardino Co... | nr San Bernardino... | S Bernardino. |
| Wixon, C W .......... | Harness maker ... | San Bernardino...... | San Bernardino Co... | S Bernardino. |
| Wixon, N J............ | Laborer ............... | nr San Bernardino... | San Bernardino Co... | S Bernardino. |
| Wixom, R.............. | Farmer ............... | San Bernardino Co... | nr Rincon ............... | Chino. |
| Wixom, W A......... | Lumberman ....... | San Bernardino Co... | nr San Bernardino... | S Bernardino. |

| Name. | Occupation. | Place of Business. | Residence. | Town or P. O. |
|---|---|---|---|---|
| Wolff, M | Merchant | San Bernardino Co | San Bernardino | S Bernardino. |
| Wood, E | Tel operator | San Bernardino Co | San Bernardino | S Bernardino. |
| Wood, F M | Farmer | San Bernardino Co | nr Chino | Chino. |
| Wood, G T | Farmer | San Bernardino Co | nr Chino | Chino. |
| Wood, T J | Carpenter | Riverside | Vine st | Riverside. |
| Wood, S | Miller | San Bernardino Co | San Bernardino | S Bernardino. |
| Woods, T | Farmer | San Bernardino Co | nr Chino | Chino. |
| Woodward, R de la | Farmer | nr San Bernardino | San Bernardino Co | S Bernardino. |
| Woodward, W de la | Farmer | San Bernardino Co | nr San Bernardino | S Bernardino. |
| Woolf, A | Merchant | San Bernardino Co | San Bernardino | S Bernardino. |
| Woolford, J | Blacksmith | San Bernardino Co | San Bernardino | S Bernardino. |
| Worley, B | Farmer | San Bernardino Co | Rincon | Chino. |
| Wozencraft, H H | Teacher | San Bernardino Co | San Bernardino | S Bernardino. |
| Wozencraft, O M. | Physician | San Bernardino Co | San Bernardino | S Bernardino. |
| Wozencraft, O M | Miller | San Bernardino Co | Rincon | Chino. |
| Wozencraft, Wm R | Teacher | San Bernardino Co | Mojave | S Bernardino. |
| Wright, W G | Planing mill | San Bernardino Co | San Bernardino | S Bernardino. |
| Wright, O L | Engineer | San Bernardino Co | San Bernardino | S Bernardino. |
| Wright, R R | Millwright | San Bernardino Co | San Bernardino | S Bernardino. |
| Wright, M V | Farmer | Riverside | San Bernardino Co | Riverside. |
| Yager, A H | Farmer | nr San Bernardino | San Bernardino Co | S Bernardino. |
| Yager, B C | S B marble works | Los A Stage Road | 2½ m San Bernardino | S Bernardino. |
| Yager, G W | Farmer | nr San Bernardino | San Bernardino Co | S Bernardino. |
| Yager, H | Farmer | nr San Bernardino | San Bernardino Co | S Bernardino. |
| Yager, I H | Lumberman | San Bernardino Co | nr San Bernardino | S Bernardino. |
| Ybarra, F | Farmer | San Bernardino Co | nr San Salvador | San Salvador. |
| Ybarra, D | Farmer | San Bernardino Co | nr San Bernardino | S Bernardino. |
| Ybarra, S | Farmer | San Bernardino Co | San Timoteo | S Bernardino. |
| Ybarra, S | Laborer | nr San Bernardino | San Bernardino Co | S Bernardino. |
| Yorba, R | Farmer | San Bernardino Co | nr Chino | Chino. |
| Young, Alexander McC | Mariner | San Bernardino Co |  | S Bernardino. |
| Young & Maicovich | Chop house | 3d st |  | S Bernardino. |
| Young, — | Chop house |  | San Bernardino Co | S Bernardino. |
| Young, D W C | Farmer | nr San Bernardino | San Bernardino Co | S Bernardino. |
| Young, Edward | Farmer | nr San Bernardino | San Bernardino Co | S Bernardino. |
| Young, Henry Danl | Boatman |  | San Bernardino Co | S Bernardino. |
| Young, J A | Farmer | San Bernardino Co | nr San Bernardino | S Bernardino. |
| Young, J R | Farmer | nr San Bernardino | San Bernardino Co | S Bernardino. |
| Yount, C | Farmer | San Bernardino Co | nr Chino | Chino. |
| Yount, David | Farmer | 25 m S W San Bern'o | Rincon | Chino. |
| Zabriskie, B | Farmer | San Bernardino Co | nr San Bernardino | S Bernardino. |
| Zimmerman, A | Farmer | San Bernardino Co | San Bernardino | S Bernardino. |
| Zimmerman, A | Farmer | nr San Bernardino | San Bernardino Co | S Bernardino. |

# W. J. LINVILLE,
## Planing Mill, Sash and Door Factory,
### TURNING, SCROLL-SAWING,
— AND A —
## GENERAL WOOD-WORKING BUSINESS.
UTAH ST., near 3rd, SAN BERNARDINO, CAL.

# A GENERAL DESCRIPTION

## OF

# LOS ANGELES CO.

Los Angeles County is by far the most desirable in point of climate and soil, the most advantageous in position, and the most prosperous in its relation with commerce and all the industries, of the Southern counties.

It is bounded upon the North by Kern County; South and Southwest by the Pacific ocean; on the Southeast by San Diego County; East by San Bernardino County, and West by the county of Ventura.

In outline it is very irregular, and contains about five thousand six hundred square miles, or three million five hundred and eighty-four thousand acres.

The county was organized in 1850.

The assessed valuation of property for 1874 was $12,080,366.

The Sierra Madre Mountains traverse the county through nearly its centre, forming slopes, valleys, and foot-hills, well adapted to stock-grazing. This mountain range forms a barrier between the fertile portion of the county, stretching towards the ocean, and the sandy waste, reaching on the North to the Colorado River.

For bee-culture, both slopes of this mountain range offer advantages such as are to be met with nowhere else in the United States.

The mountains are heavily timbered. The small valleys yield abundantly all kinds of vegetables and temperate climate fruits. The apples and plums, especially, are said to be excellent in quality, and much superior to those raised upon the foot-hills sloping towards the ocean.

For purposes of irrigation, Los Angeles County is amply provided with many and never failing streams. The principal streams are the Santa Ana, San Gabriel, Los Angeles, and Santa Clara Rivers. There are also quite a number of smaller streams, having their rise in the numerous canyons of the Sierra Madre, which furnish a very considerable supply of water. These flow into the valleys during the wet season, but do not reach the ocean, and in summer are generally dry.

The Santa Ana River has its rise in San Bernardino County, among mountains bearing the same name; flows southwesterly, irrigating the famed valley of San Bernardino, and cuts through the foot-hills near the county line, at a distance of about thirty-five miles from the ocean. Thence it continues, in the same direction, through the lower extremity of Los Angeles Valley, passing between the towns of Richland and Anaheim, emptying into the ocean between Anaheim Landing and Newport.

The San Gabriel has its source in the Sierra Madre Mountains. Its course is southerly into the El Monte Valley. This river loses its waters in the summer, but, as if to compensate, in rising again, forms two branches just where it is precipitated through the foot-hills on its way to the ocean. These two branches are designated as the old and new San Gabriel, and after fairly entering the valley, lie apart a distance of about three miles.

The Los Angeles River rises in the San Fernando Valley, and, trending toward the southeast, furnishes water for irrigating and domestic purposes to the city of Los Angeles and its vicinity. Generally during the wet season it extends some four or five miles south of the city. In unusually wet seasons, however, it forms a coalition with the old San Gabriel, at a distance of about fifteen miles from Los Angeles.

The Santa Clara River rises in the canyons of the mountains between the Sierra Madre on south and the Sierra Nevada on the north. Its course is southwesterly through Santa Clara Valley, only the northeast portion of which is in Los Angeles County, the remainder lying in Ventura.

That portion of the county lying southwest of the Coast Range, forms a series of plains nearly fifty miles in length by about twenty in width. The lower plain contains the valleys of Los Angeles, San Pedro, and Anaheim. It skirts the ocean, lying from five to forty feet above the tide level. From the ocean, away to the distance of from twenty-five to forty miles, the ascent is gradual to the base of the foot-hills. These plateaus contain the finest agricultural lands of the county, and comprise the most beautiful portions of the southern coast.

The soil and climate of the lower plains are very uniform. The soil is a brown, sandy loam, exceedingly rich in vegetable matter, a trifle harder and more mixed with clay in the bottoms and hollows, a trifle more-gravelly on the dividing ridges. Higher up in the foot-hills it becomes much harder, yet is not at all difficult to work when brought in contact with water. In some localities is quite an amount of alkali. The judicious cultivator will soon eradicate this by systematic working, though an abundance of this substance in the soil will render his labor for a time much less productive.

The sea breeze, which springs up between eight and ten o'clock A. M., during the summer season, blows from the Northwest, and imparts sufficient moisture to the atmosphere to prevent any oppressiveness from heat.

This combination of an extremely fertile soil with a climate unexampled for equability, endows Los Angeles with attractions greater than those of any other county of Southern California.

Grapes of all varieties and from all countries, thrive here luxuriantly. The Orange, Lemon, and Fig, and all semi-tropical fruits, attain perfection in growth, while the feasibility of irrigation renders a return of heavy crops in cereals and vegetables, a matter of certainty.

The extreme range of the thermometer is less here than in any portion of the United States or Europe, being 23° from January to July.

In the season of 1872, the Southern counties produced 4,500,000 oranges and 1,500,000 lemons. Since that year more energy and capital has been directed towards this production than ever before, and the yield of the past season must have been very much in advance of those figures.

Mr. B. D. Wilson is devoting himself to fruit and grape culture. His orchard and vineyard are located in the San Gabriel Valley. The orchard contains in the vicinity of two thousand orange trees in full bearing. The vineyard is widely known. Its product for the past year amounted to 75,000 gallons wine, and about 4,000 gallons brandy.

Gen. George Stoneman is engaged in the same culture in the same locality. His ranch, the Los Robles, contains four hundred and fifty acres, two hundred of which are devoted to vineyards, grape culture being his specialty. Fifty acres are used exclusively for orcharding, in which all kinds of fruit find place. Of orange trees there are twelve hundred; also lemon, lime, citron, fig, olive, apple, pear, peach, plum, nectarine, cherry, pomegranate, (1000), mulberry, and walnut, and each fruit in all its different varieties. There is a constant flow of about eight thousand gallons of water per diem, from two springs on this magnificent property.

We noticed here a rose, termed "Cloth of Gold," whose flower, in full bloom, measured fifteen inches in diameter. We also saw roses blooming upon stems thirty feet from the ground, of perfectly natural and healthy growth. The yield from the General's vineyard for the past year, produced about 20,000 gallons wine, and some 2,000 gallons brandy.

Mr. L. H. Titus owns the celebrated "Dew Drop" orchards, in this same vicinity. Of orange trees he has the enormous number of 2,850; lemon, 400; lime, 300; also a profusion of peach, pear, apricot, olive, nectarine, fig, pomegranate, apple and quince trees, besides ten acres of vineyard, with 10,000 vines. Surrounding the orchard is a live hedge of three quarters of a mile in extent. There is probably but one orange orchard in the country which will compare with that of Mr. Titus: that owned by Mr. Rose. These surpass the most famed orange groves of Italy, and are the finest in the world.

The Marengo Ranch, owned by Mr. F. P. Bacon, is situated seven miles Northeast from Los Angeles. It is a magnificent piece of property of 8,000 acres. Mr. B. has a vineyard of 40 acres in full bearing, and 150 acres of orchards, containing 1,500 orange trees and 800 walnut, besides lemon, almond, peach, pear, apple, and fig trees in good growth and in full and best varieties. The water facilities are excellent, sufficing both for irrigating and domestic purposes. The springs from which the water supply is derived, are at a sufficient elevation to force the water to any portion of the property. The ranch also comprises extensive timber lands with timber of the best quality, there being 300 acres of white oak, live oak, red and black oak. The elevation above the sea level is one thousand feet. The soil varies from a sandy and gravelly loam to a black adobe. Frost never visits this locality.

## COUNTY SCHOOLS.

The educational interests of Los Angeles County have not been allowed to suffer. The school fund for 1875 amounts to nearly $70,000. There are forty-four school districts in the county, independent of those in the city of Los Angeles. The course of instruction is as advanced as in schools of the same grade anywhere in the United States, the teachers being as carefully chosen with reference to their competency as moral and educational instructors. The school buildings are commodious, suitably located, well constructed, and substantial structures.

The well devised and effective school system of this county forms one of the chief attractions this locality offers to immigration, and has no doubt already made large additions to its population. The number of teachers employed is fifty-two, with a daily attendance of about 2,000 pupils.

## GRAZING.

Formerly the large and principal resource of this county was cattle-grazing. The miles upon miles of verdant pasturage formed a natural advantage which the Spaniard was prone to appreciate, and the opportunity was by no means neglected. Agriculture and the kindred industries, implanted and fostered only by the hand of an energy to which that nation is a stranger, have placed it as a resource, far in the background. Still the large importation of cattle and hides from this county amply attest that it still lingers among the industries, and forms one of the resources, though one of the least, of the county.

## LANDS.

Mr. Norman C. Jones has 5,000 acres in the most desirable portion of Los Angeles County, formerly known as the Rancho Azusita. It includes the old Mexican homestead; beginning where the San Gabriel River emerges, and extends westerly along the southern base of the San Gabriel Mountains to within four miles of the old Mission church and depot of the Southern Pacific Railroad. It is traversed for five miles by the Los Angeles and Independence Railroad. Mr. Jones is bringing water by a large canal from the San Gabriel River, to feed a reservoir of sixty acres, eighty feet in depth, sufficient, he states, to irrigate all the land to the Mission San Gabriel, seven miles distant. He this year plants 500 acres to corn. His land will be brought to market with a perfect water supply within a short time.

Mr. Geo. W. Freeman owns a very fine property near Tustin City, where there is some of the best land in the county.

Mr. B. D. Wilson has 400 acres of land in the immediate vicinity of Wilmington, which he is offering to sell in small lots of five, ten, and twenty acres, to actual settlers. The land is laid off in plots containing twenty acres, bounded by wide streets. The soil is a dark, sandy loam, exceedingly rich, and will produce all varieties of semi-tropical fruits, besides fruits and vegetables of temperate zones. Soft water can be obtained at a depth not exceeding twenty-four feet. These lots are to be sold at low rates, from one to five years time being granted, at legal interest. Mr. Wilson, in offering these bargains, is influenced by a desire to build up the town and surrounding country. Good schools are within a few minutes walk of any portion of this land.

## MINING.

Its mineral resources are, beyond question, very great and valuable. Some forty-two years since, in 1833, the first gold positively known to have been discovered in the State, was found in the valley of Santa Clara. But whether in that portion of the valley lying within the boundary of Los Angeles County, or in that belonging to the present county of Ventura, it is impossible for us to say. Both counties claim this honor, and it seems to be a question, the decision of which should be left to them.

Comparatively little attention has been given to developing the mineral wealth of this region, although expert miners have characterized it as comparable with the richest portions of the State. Mining organizations have been formed, with large amounts of paid-up capital, but for some reason the developments have not been commensurate. It is presumable, however, that no full developments have as yet been made. Many are looking anxiously to see what the next year or two will do for these mining interests. Certain it is, that in some localities, take the vicinity of San Fernando for instance, thousands of acres of as rich placer exist as ever were washed, from whence "pay dirt" has been carried four miles to water. This granted, what may not be effected with a profuse water supply, such as will be secured by the large ditches now being constructed?

At the head of the Santa Clara River, where is located the town of Soledad, veins of gold-bearing quartz are being worked at a large profit. Copper-bearing veins are also numerous in this locality. It is fair to presume, however, that, where base metal exists in juxtaposition with the precious metals, it will not be worked with profitable results.

On the Northeastern slope of the San Gabriel Range, bordering upon the Mojave Desert, large veins of copper as well as other minerals are found. Large beds of asphaltum are also here, and in the resources of the county the oil production forms a prominent feature. No excitement, but much strong feeling is evinced regarding the future oil developments of this region. The report of a body of United States engineers, some years since, which was adverse to the interests of this development, temporarily destroyed the confidence of those engaged in producing. This, together with the fact that the early experiments in refining did not terminate successfully, from the want of skilled labor, has occasioned the loss of some years and money to the pioneers in this enterprise. The value of it as a resource, however, if fully developed, with the positive assurance that nothing but persistent effort is necessary to effect the desired end, has been fully demonstrated. Operators think themselves warranted in proceeding, with the view of tapping some hidden vein or reservoir, and in engaging the services of a competent refiner. Some day, without doubt, they will triumph, and a new resource, fully developed and richly worthy of being thus characterized, will add to the already great wealth of this favored community. A large amount of capital and energy is now actively engaged in this enterprise, and the establishing of an oil exchange is talked of, for the exclusive manipulation of oil stocks.

## PRINCIPAL TOWNS.

The principal towns of Los Angeles County are Los Angeles, Anaheim, Wilmington, Downey City, Compton, Santa Monica, Soledad, El Monte, Los Nietos, Santa Ana, San Juan, San Fernando, San Gabriel, Spadra, and Orange; also Tustin City, Newport Landing, Duarte Settlement, Azusa, Artesia, Centinela Colony, Westminster Colony, Cienega,, and Ballona. Many of these are embryotic towns or settlements, and at the present time amount to but little, except prospectively.

## LOS ANGELES

Is the largest town and county-seat of Los Angeles County. It differs somewhat from most of the cities grown on California soil, even in its foundation, as the great majority of them are an outgrowth either of the peaceful missions or were ushered into life amidst the bustle and swagger of the military presidios. This site was selected by men who, tired of the monotony of the garrison, sick of the turmoil of strife, weary of the forced march and long night watch, pined for a life-long asylum, a home. Worn out and disgusted with a hard and unremunerative service, this spot they dedicated to their household gods, and the experience of nearly an hundred years of settlement has honored their choice.

The city site originally comprised some sixteen square leagues. It was reduced to four square leagues by a Land Commission appointed by act of Congress. It is situated in a narrow valley, less than a mile in width. The Los Angeles River flows through the San Gabriel plain, on the east of the city, furnishing abundance of water for irrigating purposes, through the medium of intersecting ditches ; also furnishing the supply needed by the inhabitants of the city for domestic purposes.

It is stated that there are forty miles of ditches devoted to the public use for irrigating purposes, conveying the water from the Los Angeles River and distributing it throughout the municipality. In addition to this, is about the same extent of private canals, constructed by owners of lands which take their water from the main ditches, diffusing it over their private grounds.

The valley in which the city of Los Angeles is situated, is formed on the west by low hills, buttresses of the Santa Monica Mountains, distant about forty miles ; and on the east by the rising land of the San Gabriel Plain.

Los Angeles city is one of the oldest in the State. The old Mexican portion of it extends about a mile up the valley, but it has lost its distinctive features. To a great extent the old adobe flat-roofed structures, smeared with asphaltum, surrounded with broad verandahs or high walls, have been jostled from existence to make way for the more sightly, pleasing, and convenient structures of the American.

In 1874, the population of Los Angeles was twelve thousand. Its increase since that date has, without doubt, been greater than that of any interior town of the State. For the same year it was assessed upon a valuation of its property at $4,700,000. It has at the present time in the vicinity of 15,000 inhabitants.

It is about twenty-one miles inland from the coast; San Pedro, or Wilmington, its more recent name, being its port of entry. It is altogether likely, however, that the new town of Santa Monica will hereafter receive a portion of the shipping business now granted alone to Wilmington, as it is a good port, and lies nearer to the city of Los Angeles.

## RAILROADS.

Five branches of the Southern Pacific Railroad center at Los Angeles, the Wilmington branch extending South twenty miles; the Anaheim extending Southeast thirty miles; the Spadra branch, fast increasing its extent, in an easterly direction, with San Bernardino as its immediate objective point; the San Fernando branch running twenty-one miles North, and the Santa Monica branch running some twelve or fourteen miles nearly due West. The management of the road is very highly spoken of, and both fares and freights are placed at such figures as seem to give general satisfaction.

## STAGE LINES.

The Coast Stage Line runs from Anaheim, (the nearest point of railroad connection with Los Angeles,) to San Diego by way of Santa Ana, Tustin City, San Juan Capistrano, Las Flores, San Luis Rey and Soledad. The coaches run daily, the fare is ten dollars, and the trip requires twenty-four hours. The Los Angeles and San Bernardino stages leave the former place daily for San Bernardino, connecting with the Southern Pacific Railroad at Spadra. Another line to San Bernardino runs its stages by way of Chino, Rincon and Riverside, carrying the United States Mails and Wells, Fargo & Co's Express. The days of departure from Spadra are Tuesday, Thursday and Saturday, at eight A. M. Two lines of Stages are also running to Panamint, the new mining district. From San Francisco to Los Angeles, one has the choice of four well conducted lines of transit. By water, the Goodall, Nelson & Perkins Steamship Line, or the vessels of the Pacific Mail Steamship Co. By land, the Southern Pacific Railroad and Coast Stage Line, and the Southern Pacific Railroad and Telegraph Stage Line.

The vessels of the Goodall, Nelson & Perkins Steamship Company ply between San Francisco and the Southern ports. Their vessels are well officered, and the character of their passenger accommodations above reproach.

Los Angeles has a High School, under the supervision of a gentleman having had many years' experience as a teacher. There are also eight graded public schools in the city, under the conduct of efficient teachers. The Sisters of Charity have a day and boarding school for young ladies, with fine grounds and costly buildings. St. Vincent's College is also located here, an institution of learning for males, but whether as supplementary to institutions granting degrees, or itself granting degrees, we do not know; it is conducted by the priests of the Mission Congregation.

Ten religious denominations are represented in the city, each having a large congregation. Many of the church edifices are finely constructed, handsome buildings, which add much to the appearance of the city. Los Angeles has an infirmary of good capacity, is fully represented in the various social, secret, and benevolent societies, has a public library, some three or four banks, street railways, public buildings which would do credit to any community, and, in fact, all the ameniities of existence usually only enjoyed to the full by the people of large cities.

## LOS ANGELES NEWSPAPERS.

In proportion to its population, no city in the State publishes a greater number of newspapers. It supports three dailies, each of which issue a weekly, the *Herald*, *Evening Express*, and *Star*. One semi-weekly, the *La Cronica*, and two weeklies, *The Mirror* and *Süd Cal. Post*, are also published. The dailies are published in English, the semi-weekly in Spanish, and the weekly in German. The Daily and Weekly *Herald* are among the leading papers of Southern California, and have at least as large a circulation as any of their cotemporaries. In addition to those already enumerated, there are also one weekly advertising sheet and two monthly publications, each of which has a large circulation.

The *Herald* has been actively engaged in furthering all legitimate immigration schemes, and has disseminated as much information among Eastern people regarding Southern California, as any paper in the State. We are indebted to the "*Herald* Pamphlet," issued by the *Herald* Publishing Company, for much intelligence which we could not otherwise have obtained without exceeding difficulty, and considerable expense.

Los Angeles, a New York or San Francisco in miniature, possesses the conveniences and advantages of those cities, though in less grand proportions; emulating their energy and comparing favorably with them in the possession of an enlightened enterprise, endowed with vigorous vitality.

## NURSERIES.

Los Angeles is, *par excellence*, the nursery county of the State. Among the most noteworthy nurseries of the county are those of Thos. A. Garey, D. C. Hayward, J. C. Wallace and J. M. Vignes. Mr. Garey is proprietor of the semi-tropical nurseries, in the environs of Los Angeles city, where he carries the largest and most complete stock in the State. He has full assortments of temperate climate fruit-trees, including apple, peach, pear, etc., beside the best varieties of semi-tropical fruit-trees.

The largest orange orchard in Southern California has recently been planted just south of Los Angeles, within and adjoining the city limits. The orchard covers one hundred acres, and comprises 7,500 four-year-old trees. These trees will all be budded the present season with some of the choicest varieties of orange now growing in the State. There are several grafted orange trees now bearing in this county, but there is not an orchard of grafted orange trees in the State. Grafted trees bear much earlier than seedlings, and of course the fruit is much superior. Between the orchard trees, above mentioned, is being planted out a large semi-tropical nursery, consisting of orange, lemon and lime trees. The nursery is about half planted, and will comprise 750,000 yearling trees, just taken from the seed beds and put out in nursery shape. This nursery and orchard is the property of the Co-operative Nursery and Fruit Company, of which Thos A.

Garey is President, and H. J. Crow Superintendent. Mr. Garey has a national reputation as a semi-tropical nurseryman; at the close of 1876 he will turn over his entire business to the company, whose nursery will then take the lead in that line of business on this coast. The grounds are situated between Main and San Pedro Streets, below Jefferson, and contain 298 acres. The San Pedro street railroad will soon be built to the corner of the nursery grounds.

D. C. Hayward is proprietor of the Richland Nurseries, located at Orange. He is making a specialty of grafted orange and lemon trees, and is keeping on hand a full variety of temperate climate fruit trees, as well as the eucalyptus species in many varieties, and ornamental tree stock of every kind; also all kinds of flowering shrubs.

The San Gabriel Nursery is owned and conducted by J. C. Wallace, and is one mile Northwest from the town of San Gabriel. This gentleman has orange trees in seven varieties, Australian blue gum trees, the Monterey cypress, and a full variety of ornamental and flowering shrubs, rose trees, etc. Northern fruit trees of every known description, as well as all varieties of the semi-tropics, are to be found here.

J. M. Vignes' nursery is situated three miles South of Los Angeles. It consists of thirty-five acres of most arable land, fifteen acres of which are planted entirely in trees. On his property are ten acres of bearing trees, and twenty acres of foreign vines. All standard varieties of fruit trees can be found here, as well as cuttings from all choice varieties of foreign grapes. Mr. V. also manufactures all brands of wine from his own grapes.

The Pacific Salt Works, owned and conducted by Mr. J. B. Trudel, are situated eighteen miles west of Los Angeles. These works can turn out in the neighborhood of from 2,500 to 3,000 tons of salt per annum, if worked to their full capacity. The salt is made by the process of solar evaporation, from six lagoons of a depth varying from six to eight inches. In addition, also, are ten large vats, yielding from four to five tons fortnightly. The yield from the lagoons is from 600 to 800 tons tri-annually. Fresh water is struck upon this property at a depth of twenty-three feet. The largest spring flows 10,000 gallons per diem, of excellent water. The article of salt produced here is pronounced equal to any offered for sale in the State.

## ANAHEIM

Is situated thirty miles from Los Angeles, and at a distance of twelve miles from the coast. It was founded in 1857.

This is one of the wealthiest and most successful colonies in the State. The property, which was purchased at $5.00 per acre, is now held at from $300 to $500 per acre. Over sixty vineyards are owned by the residents of this locality, all in good bearing, furnishing a product which has warranted the establishment of from six to eight wine-manufacturing establishments. Many orange and lemon groves are also in this settlement. All the fruits and grains in common growth in Southern California, are said to thrive well here. The soil is sandy and rich, and the climate invariably mild.

Anaheim contains two hotels, three church organizations, a graded school, with primary, intermediate and academic departments; two livery stables; eight stores and groceries; and above twenty shops and places of business not included in the above.

During last year over thirty buildings were erected, at an aggregate cost of $100,000. The railroad was recently completed to this town, connecting it with Los Angeles. A project is on foot to erect at this point an hotel, the total cost with the ground to amount to $40,000. A new ditch is also talked of, from the Santa Ana River, with capacity sufficient to irrigate 30,000 acres.

The land in the vicinity of Anaheim is well adapted to all agricultural purposes.

Anaheim Landing, on the coast, is the shipping point for this district.

## WILMINGTON

Was incorporated in the latter part of March, 1871. The town is one mile square, and has a population numbering about 650.

The soil of this vicinity is a dark, sandy loam, producing hay, corn, rye, oranges, potatoes, and all varieties of garden vegetables.

The manufacturing interest here is represented by a carriage shop, furniture factory, and wool-grading house.

The best of drinking water is obtained at a depth of four feet below the surface.

One newspaper, the *Wilmington Enterprise*, is published weekly.

It lies South from Los Angeles twenty-two miles, with railroad connection, two or three trains moving between these points each day. Anaheim lies to the East, twenty-four miles; Point San Pedro, four miles South.

The Wilson College is located here, established under the patronage of the Los Angeles South Methodist Conference, and incorporated in the fall of 1874.

Mr. B. D. Wilson granted to this institution ten acres of land with several buildings, those used formerly as the hospital and barracks for government soldiers. The college has a faculty composed of four professors, with an average daily attendance of seventy students.

There are several very tasteful residences here, those most worthy of mention being Mr. B. D. Wilson's and General Banning's. Mr. Wilson is devoting much attention to the growing of fruit and grapes upon his place. In front of his house he has 3,000 trees of the eucalyptus species, known as the Australian blue gum. It was also his intention to plant fifty acres to this variety, 400 trees to the acre; if he has not already done so, the project is simply delayed—not abandoned.

Wilmington is the shipping port for Los Angeles, San Bernardino, and Inyo counties, as well as portions of Arizona. The breakwater, constructed by the United States Government, is working satisfactorily, and the fact that a deep and permanent channel can be dredged is fully established.

In the near vicinity of Wilmington about 100,000 acres of land are held by speculative parties, who refuse to subdivide and sell to settlers on reasonable terms. This is a ruinous policy in a young community, as instead of attracting it will repel immigration, and through the communication of the disappointed immigrant with those contemplating immigration, the prejudice will be disseminated and many will be forewarned against such communities, which will result in their seeking homes elsewhere.

The Los Angeles and Wilmington Railroad gives employment to some two hundred men, at the Wilmington end of the road.

The railroad wharf is a finely constructed piece of work, 1,200 feet in length, with substantial warehouses.

The Co-operative Association has a fine wharf, built during the year, which, together with the warehouses, cost $20,000.

## DOWNEY CITY

Is the shipping port for the Los Nietos section, of which it is also the principal town. It was for some time the southern terminus of the Anaheim branch of the Southern Pacific Railway, previous to its continuation to Anaheim. Its population amounts to about 250. Its foundation was occasioned by the necessities of commerce. It is sustained by a rich outlying agricultural district.

The section of country termed Los Nietos lies in the valley of the San Gabriel River. It covers an extent of country about thirteen miles in length by ten in width. The land is level, with an uniform slope toward the ocean on the southwest; the soil is rich and strong, and the facilities for irrigation are unexcelled, the water of the San Gabriel River being sufficiently plentiful to irrigate more than twice the area of this valley.

We append some information relating to this section from a recent issue of the *Downey City Courier*:

Two crops can be and are frequently harvested in the same year—one of corn and one of barley. A large area of the valley is moist land, requiring no irrigation, and ample facilities are at hand to irrigate land which may require it. All the semi-tropical fruits flourish and do as well in our valley as in any other section of the county. Tobacco is now being cultivated quite extensively, and at this time gives promise of becoming a staple production and a leading industry. The sugar beet can, and would, be extensively cultivated were there a market for the production. By a test, made at the beet sugar refinery, at Sacramento, the beets grown in this valley were found to contain two per cent. more saccharine matter than those grown elsewhere.

The following are some of the exports by railway for four months, much of the produce of the valley having been sent to market by wagon:

JANUARY.—Corn, 6,177 sks., 726,426 lbs.; Rye, 170 sks., 19,560 lbs.; Barley, 856 sks; 88,529 lbs.; Bran, 55 sks., 3,891 lbs.; Meal, 112 sks., 4,050 lbs.; Potatoes, 10 sks., 1,026 lbs., Mustard Seed, 62 sks., 5,510 lbs.; Oats, 26 sks., 1,967 lbs.; Bees (stands), 40, 2,227 lbs.; Assorted Packages, 81 sks., 5,773 lbs.; Lumber, 1,000 feet, 3500 lb.; Hogs, 149, 47,240 lbs.; Total weight, 909,749 lbs.

FEBRUARY.—Corn, 8,064 sks., 906,759 lbs.; Barley, 282 sks., 27,077 lbs.; Ru. Barley, 150 sks., 18,035 lbs.; Potatoes, 44 sks., 4,385 lbs.; Crk. Corn, 228 sks., 22,615 lbs.; Bran, 101 sks., 5,942 lbs.; Meal, 1,033 sks., 37,175 lbs.; Assorted Packages, 68 sks., 7,955 lbs.; Lumber, 595 feet, 1,932 lbs. Total weight, 1,031,925 lbs.

MARCH.—Corn, 3,658 sks., 407,941 lbs.; Barley, 505 sks., 45,730 lbs.; Crk Corn, 232 sks.; 23,200 lbs.; Bran, 91 sks., 6,480 lbs.; Gra. Flour, 188 sks., 4,875 lbs.; Meal, 605 sks., 20,175 lbs.; Bales Hay, 110, 20,465 lbs.; Assorted Packages, 94, 7,167 lbs.; Ft. Lumber, 9,188, 32,188 lbs. Hogs, No., 735, 147,000 lbs. Total weight, 715,221 lbs.

APRIL.—Corn, 2,207 sks., 260,522 lbs.; Barley, 161 sks., 16,194 lbs.; Crk. Corn, 141 sks., 14,100 lbs.; Meal, 288 sks., 8,400 lbs.; Potatoes, 9 sks., 951 lbs.; Assorted Packages, 80 sks., 4,654 lbs.; Stds. Bees, 46, 2,808 lbs.; Lumber, 1,935 feet, 5,864 lbs. Total weight, 313,493 lbs.

## COMPTON

Is situated on the line of the Los Angeles branch of the S. P. R. R., twelve miles South from Los Angeles, and ten miles North from Wilmington.

The town derives its name from Mr. G. D. Compton, one of the pioneers in the settlement of the State, and an enterprising business man. This is a town of about seven years' growth, and within that time has grown up from a very wilderness to a prosperity which will be as lasting as it is thorough. It relies upon a fruitful soil for all the advantages which may accrue to it, and possesses many attractions of climate, etc.

The breeze from the ocean tempers the atmosphere, it being sufficiently removed from the coast to escape the fogs and dampness which the breeze does not carry so far inland.

Artesian water is obtained at the moderate depth of from ninety to one hundred and fifty feet; there are over seventy-five wells flowing in this locality.

Immediately in town the land is low, containing a good deal of alkali, with considerable adobe also. All the country to the West, however, is a rich loam, while on the East the soil is sandy, but rich.

All the cereals yield well, also potatoes and vegetables.

Mr. Compton is identified with the settlement, and is holding large tracts of unimproved land, for sale at from $20 to $40 per acre, in any desired quantity, of good quality.

The settlement comprises about one hundred families, and supports a graded school, with a daily attendance of one hundred pupils.

The town contains one hotel, store, post office, blacksmith shop, school-house, Methodist church, and the S. P. R. R. depot.

Two societies are represented here, the Good Templars and Grangers.

Liquor is excluded from the settlement.

## SANTA MONICA

Is the most delightful sea-side resort on the Pacific Coast. It lies sixteen miles Southwest from the city of Los Angeles, in a narrow valley opening on the sea, well grown with sycamore and oak.

It has been the custom for people from Los Angeles to visit this place in the summer season, taking tents and cooking utensils, spending days and weeks in its pleasant locality. During the summer just past lots were sold at auction, the sales being ready, at good prices. An hotel has been recently built of large capacity; also bath houses, a wharf, and the community is now an exceedingly active and hopeful one. The place has positive advantages as a port of entry, also, and bids fair to divide the shipping business with the port of Wilmington.

## EL MONTE

Was the first American settlement in the county. It is twelve miles East from Los Angeles, on the line of the Los Angeles railroad. The San Gabriel River bisects the town, forming two little villages, which are essentially one in every respect save this accident of topography.

Considered together, it contains two hotels, four stores, four blacksmith and wagon shops, four saloons, two churches, Baptist and Methodist; a good graded school, an express, telegraph and post office.

The farms are generally small, irrigation being unnecessary from the fact of the low-lying position of the land, and its consequent moisture.

Little attention is paid to the cultivation of cereals, with the exception of corn, potatoes being the principal product, it being more celebrated as a potato-raising country than any portion of Southern California.

The thermometer here sometimes reaches 100°, and in winter a thin ice is quite frequently seen.

Improved land is worth from $20 to $40 per acre.

The precinct has a population of about 1000.

## SANTA ANA

Is a prosperous and pretty village, thirty-three miles South from Los Angeles, eight miles distant from the ocean, and six from Anaheim. It was founded about 1871. The settlement contains about 15,000 acres, light adobe and sandy loam soil, about one-half of which is under cultivation. Irrigating ditches from the Santa Ana River convey an abundance of water for all purposes, and, as a provision against emergencies, about a dozen artesian wells have been sunk.

The location of Santa Ana could not be improved, and its prosperity is ably abetted by a rich surrounding soil and an equable climate, its average temperature for 1874 being 65°.

Just below here is the fertile district of Gospel Swamp. It is almost impossible to find general belief for the crop statistics coming from sections so rich in production as this and the Los Nietos districts, let them be ever so well attested. We forbear appending such information for this reason alone, and can only request the unbeliever, who is desirous of cultivating the quality known as credulity, to visit these localities during some harvest season.

Gospel Swamp land is worth from $75 to $100 per acre.

In the locality of Santa Ana, in fact, where the settlement is now situated, land which five years since could have been purchased at from $5 to $10 per acre, is now worth from $40 to $60.

The town has one hotel, four stores, and a good school.

## SAN JUAN CAPISTRANO

Is thirty miles from Anaheim, toward the coast, on the main road between Los Angeles and San Diego. The valley in which this town is situated, is about nine miles in length by less than one mile in width.

The San Juan, a never-failing stream, passes through its entire length, furnishing an abundant supply of water.

Rich grasses, fine timber and dense underbrush grow luxuriantly throughout the entire valley, attesting the richness of a soil which unfortunately is but little cultivated.

The population aggregates somewhere from six to eight hundred, made up almost exclusively of Indians, Mexicans and native Californians, there being comparatively few Americans or Europeans in the place. It is the most thoroughly Mexican town in the State, the prevailing architecture being the low, flat-roofed adobe structures, the streets being laid out without any regard to regularity.

THE SAN JUAN CAPISTRANO SPRINGS are twelve miles from the Old Mission or town of San Juan, on the stage road to San Diego. The springs have a very abundant flow of water; from some the water is as soft as rain-water. The variation in temperature is very great, ranging from nearly the freezing point to an extreme heat of from 90° to 130° Fahrenheit.

The ravines and canyons surrounding the springs, are profuse in the growth of trees and shrubbery, furnishing pleasant walks and drives. Their curative properties are highly spoken of.

## SAN FERNANDO

Was organized April 15th, 1874. The first regular passenger train reached the town from Los Angeles, the day the organization was effected. It is twenty-two miles North from Los Angeles. But little more than a year since the whole section was a vast sheep range, known as the San Fernando Grant. Identical with the completion of the railroad to this point, land was divided and sold in small tracts, and a town site laid out. The blocks are 400x600 feet, with streets from sixty to eighty feet wide. The railroad forms the Eastern boundary of the town.

The town site consists of about 11,000 acres, the old mission grounds being included. When founded, it contained but one house besides the mission buildings; it now has above thirty buildings. Water is furnished from a large spring one and one-quarter miles Northwest, with a capacity of about two hundred inches, the only living water in the valley in dry seasons.

The town contains two very good hotels, two merchandise stores, six saloons, one saddler's shop, two blacksmith shops, one shoe shop, one barber shop, one carpenter shop, and a feed stable.

The population numbers about one hundred and twenty-five. The school is at Lopez Station, two and one-half miles Northwest.

The elevation of San Fernando is 1,050 feet above Los Angeles; above the sea 1,210 feet. The distance to Wilmington is forty-two miles.

The Telegraph Stage line passes through here en route for Caliente, Kern County, one hundred and three miles distant. The stage is daily, with an extra three times per week.

The valley of San Fernando is about ten miles in width by twenty in length.

## SAN GABRIEL

Is on the line of railroad to Spadra. It is a small village, situated in a magnificent valley of the same name. This valley is the great grape and fruit-growing section, in which are so many famous orchards, mentioned elsewhere.

Near the boundary of the valley close upon the railroad station, is located the old mission of San Gabriel.

The village of San Gabriel contains a church, hotel, school, two or three stores, etc. In the valley are some of the finest residences in the county.

## SPADRA

Is situated in the valley of San Jose, which contains a population of about one thousand.

The San Bernardino branch of the S. P. R. R. has just been extended beyond this point, which for some time has enjoyed the commercial advantages usually resulting to a railroad terminus.

Spadra is thirty miles East from Los Angeles, and has grown up within the past year. It is quite a village, comprising a school-house, hotel, three stores, butcher shop, three blacksmith and wagon shops, and quite a number of dwellings. The valley in which it is situated is a beautiful and fertile one. Much is being done here in the way of growing fruit from the seed, and in introducing new exotic growths in trees.

## TUSTIN CITY

Is a pretty little village, the site of which was purchased by Mr. C. Tustin in 1867. The settlement in which the town is situated, is East of Santa Ana, and some twelve miles from the ocean, and comprises about sixty farms of from twenty to forty acres each.

It was founded about two years since. Water can be obtained by artesian wells, or by ditches from the Santa Ana River, but a short distance away.

The soil is a sandy loam, producing large quantities of cereals, of good quality. Tobacco is successfully cultivated.

There is a good school in the settlement, and three religious denominations are represented.

## NEWPORT LANDING

Accommodates, with respect to shipping facilities, all the country lying East of Santa Ana.

Quite a bay is formed here, by a little inlet, which small sailing vessels and some of the smaller coast-wise steamers can readily enter. Santa Ana lies eight miles away.

## DUARTE SETTLEMENT.

This settlement is in the upper San Gabriel Valley. It is sheltered from severe winds and frosts by the San Gabriel Mountains, at whose foot it lies. It embraces 2,000 acres of land; has a population of about one hundred, and a school with an average attendance of about thirty pupils. The settlement is about two years old. For fruit-growing, and for the purposes of the general cultivator, this locality cannot be surpassed. The San Gabriel River furnishes an almost inexhaustible water supply to this vicinity.

The land owned by Mr. Jones, referred to elsewhere, is in this neighborhood.

The San Gabriel mines are five or six miles above, in the canyon; their promise is favorable for large returns, the prospects being quite flattering.

This town is seventeen miles from Los Angeles, and five miles from El Monte railroad station.

## AZUSA

Settlement is about five years old, and occupies a valley by itself, or rather a continuation of the San Gabriel Valley, that portion lying East of the San Gabriel River. It is well sheltered on three sides: by the San Gabriel Mountains on the North, and a chain of hills on the East and South. It is about five miles from Duarte, and ten miles from El Monte. It embraces about twenty-four square miles, and in every respect is as lovely a valley as one could wish to see. In the valley is a profusion of trees, scattered throughout the landscape, singly and in groups. The trees are mostly oaks, and in addition to lending a charm to the surroundings, they furnish an ever ready supply for domestic uses, as well as for manufacturing interests. The water supply is derived from the San Gabriel River.

About one hundred farmers occupy and cultivate the valley, their farms averaging from forty to eighty acres.

Here is a post office, and a good public school.

The climate is excellent. The extreme range of the thermometer is from 34 to 98°.

The soil is very productive, and is a sandy loam unmixed with either alkali or adobe. The production here is marked by a diversity one seldom sees equaled, everything which is adapted to the climate and soil of Southern California finding representation. The Western portion of the valley is to be apportioned as a school district, which will be called " Walnut Grove."

## ARTESIA

Is a very young settlement, recently sold in blocks of forty acres, and in town lots, by the "Immigration and Land Co-operative Association." The tract embraces 3,500 acres. The soil is a sandy loam, rich, and irrigable through the instrumentality of artesian wells, which can be easily and cheaply sunk. It is seventeen miles from Los Angeles, and three miles South from Norwalk

DIRECTORY OF LOS ANGELES COUNTY. 301

station, on the Anaheim branch. Its location could not be improved upon. The association, mentioned above, took the initiative in the water prospecting, by sinking a well upon the plaza, and donating it to the town, whose existence is yet prospective. They also erected a building two stories in height, at a cost of $4,000, for school, church, and public purposes. Each room is 31 x 36 feet, while the building is surmounted by a tower fifty-two feet in height.

## WESTMINSTER COLONY

Is about half way between Anaheim and the ocean. It was organized by Rev. L. P. Webber, in 1871. To secure high character and harmony from the start, those only were invited to join it who would pledge themselves not to sell or make intoxicating liquors, and who could feel at home in a Presbyterian church and would assist in its support.

The Colony consists of about seventy-five families.

There are nearly one hundred artesian wells in the Colony and immediate vicinity, and three sets of well tools are kept constantly busy. The depth of the wells varies from sixty-five to nearly two hundred feet, and the average flow is sufficient to irrigate sixty acres.

The Colony has two stores, one a co-operative store, doing a large business with all the surrounding country, and the other a private enterprise also doing well and attracting a large trade. There is also a blacksmith, harness, butcher shop, and cabinet warehouse. Other trades are also represented. In location the Colony is the nearest settlement to Anaheim Landing and the proposed Bolsa Chica Wharf.

The high character of its people, the abundance of pure artesian water, with the good quality of its lands and temperate climate, all contribute to its rapid and healthy growth.

The area appropriated to the Colony is about 10,000 acres, much of which is perfectly adapted to fruit culture, and much specially adapted for dairy farms. Barley and corn give very large crops. Potatoes are made a specialty. Eggs and chickens are exported in very large quantities, probably in excess of any other single place on the Coast. Several dairies are also exporting butter and cheese, and a vegetable farm, conducted by Chinamen, supplies Anaheim in part and much of the surrounding country.

Anaheim is six miles distant, the coast seven. It has a good school house, averaging an attendance of one hundred pupils.

## CENTINELA COLONY,

A Land Company, has purchased 25,000 acres of the choicest farming and fruit land in the State, for colonization purposes. It touches the limits of Los Angeles city, and occupies an interval lying between it and the coast. It is almost exclusively valley land, and produces abundantly of all kinds of grain and semi-tropic fruits. Wheat has been grown upon this land, and orange and lime trees are now in full bearing, one orchard containing 8,000 orange, lime, lemon, and almond trees. A nursery, located here, contains about as many more in various stages of perfection.

The northern portion of the tract is watered by the Centinela Creek, and on any portion of it water can be obtained by boring from 25 to 50 feet.

The climate varies but little from 60° through the entire year.

It is the intention, in pursuance of the original scheme adopted by the colony, to distribute the land, with all improvements of orchards, stock, etc., among the shareholders, each share entitling the holder to a thousandth part of the whole.

Each shareholder purchased his land, including his share in the improvements, live stock, etc., at $12 per acre. A division is made of the land into 5, 10, 20, 40, 80 and 160-acre lots, which were to have been sold some months since. The excess of the amount realized from the sale above the cost of the land was to be divided among the shareholders.

Large grants were made by the company to found a college and schools. The charter of the association forbids the erection of saloons, or the sale of intoxicating liquors.

A railway, to extend through this land from Los Angeles to the ocean, is talked of.

### CIENEGA AND LA BALLONA.

These valleys are contiguous, and contain flourishing settlements. The Cienega is ten miles long and three in width. La Ballona is ten miles in length, with a width of four miles. The characteristics of soil and climate are similar in these valleys. Water lies near the surface, and the lands, sloping gently from the mountains to the sea, furnish fine stock ranges. Grains of all varieties flourish, and all kinds of fruit except the orange; also vegetables of every description.

### ORANGE

Lies six miles south from Anaheim. It embraces an extent of country five miles in width by ten in length. The Santiagos River runs diagonally through it. It is a level and beautiful tract, rich in soil, and possessing a natural moisture rendering it almost independent of artificial irrigation. The growth here is almost spontaneous; all fruits and grains thrive, achieving wonders in production.

The growth of the settlement has been very rapid; two years since there were scarcely ten houses in the settlement, where are now in the vicinity of two hundred.

The land is divided into blocks containing 40 acres.

The town has two churches, a good school, with three departments; a Grange store, express and post office, all centrally located. Saloons and the sale of liquors are tabooed.

The temperature is mild, the range of the thermometer being lowest 40°, highest 98°. There are no hurtful frosts, and tomatoes and tube-roses bloom all winter in the open air. Water facilities are ample.

Dr. A. B. Hayward's nursery is located here; Mr. James Huntington also has an interest of that character in the locality.

---

## ARMES & DALLAM,

Manufacturers and Wholesale Dealers in

# WOOD AND WILLOW WARE,

### BROOMS, BRUSHES & TWINES,

Paper Bags, Feather Dusters, Clothes Wringers, Matches, Etc.

SOLE AGENTS FOR F. N. DAVIS & CO'S BUILDING PAPERS.

### Nos. 215 AND 217 SACRAMENTO ST.

### SAN FRANCISCO.

# MEEKER, JAMES & CO.

IMPORTERS, WHOLESALE AND RETAIL DEALERS IN

## CARRIAGE & WAGON MATERIALS,

Embracing all the WOOD MATERIALS for the Manufacture of VEHICLES OF EVERY DESCRIPTION, also

## SARVEN'S PATENT WHEELS

WOODBURN CO'S MANUFACTURE.

Concord Axles, and Steel and Iron Half-Patent Axles; Thimble Skeins and Boxes for Wood Axles, Carriage Hardware and Malleable Irons.

**DOLE'S PATENT**

Hub-Boxing and Tenoning Machines and Hollow Augers.

Orders from the Country solicited. Catalogues and Price Lists sent on application.

**NEW BRICK WAREHOUSE, SOUTHEAST COR. OF**

**CALIFORNIA & DAVIS STREETS,**

SAN FRANCISCO.

---

# FLAX SEED AND CASTOR BEANS.

## PACIFIC OIL AND LEAD WORKS, SAN FRANCISCO,

ARE PREPARED TO

**FURNISH SEED,**

AND

Contract for Next Year's Crop of Flax Seed and Castor Beans,

At rates that, with proper cultivation on suitable land, will make them among the most profitable crops grown. For further particulars, address

## PACIFIC OIL AND LEAD WORKS,

**3 AND 5 FRONT STREET,**

P. O. BOX 1443. SAN FRANCISCO.

# THE
# Bank of San Bernardino

### Fourth Street, San Bernardino, Cal.

LEWIS JACOBS, - - - President.
CÆSAR MEYERSTEIN, - - Cashier.

## General Banking Business Transacted.

#### RECEIVE DEPOSITS AND ISSUE CERTIFICATES.

*Legal Tender Notes, Government Securities, County Scrip and Bonds Bought.*

**HIGHEST PRICES PAID FOR GOLD AND SILVER BARS.**

*DRAFTS DRAWN ON*

MERCHANTS' EXCHANGE BANK, SAN FRANCISCO,
KOUNTZ BROS., NEW YORK,
FARMERS' AND MERCHANTS' BANK, LOS ANGELES,
COMMERCIAL BANK, SAN DIEGO,
And all the Principal Towns of California and Europe.

## INTEREST ALLOWED ON TIME DEPOSITS.

## FASHION STABLES,

MACY, WILSON & CO., - Proprietors,

MAIN STREET, LOS ANGELES.

ON HAND AT ALL TIMES, A NEW AND FINE STOCK OF

# Fancy Top & Open Buggies

### Carriages and Mountain Wagons,

## BRAND-NEW STYLISH TURNOUTS,

#### MATCH TEAMS, SINGLE AND SADDLE HORSES.

The stock is unsurpassed by any Stable in the Interior of the State.

**PARTIES CONVEYED TO ANY PORTION OF THE COUNTRY.**

**TRANSIENT STOCK ATTENDED TO WITH CARE.**

**TERMS MODERATE.**

# VINE HILL VINEYARD

## Santa Cruz County, Cal.

# GEO. M. JARVIS,

### PROPRIETOR.

This famous Vineyard is on the South side of the Coast Range of mountains, about twelve hundred feet above the sea, and some ten miles distant from it. The climate is the best in the state. The view from the residence of Mr. Jarvis, embracing within its scope over ninety miles of land and sea, is pronounced by travelers to fully equal in picturesqueness the view from Vesuvius of the Bay of Naples.

The estate contains four hundred acres, of which about one hundred are devoted to the growth of Fruits, Nuts, etc., etc., the Grape being the main product; yet Apples, Pears, Peaches, Plums, Nectarines, Quinces, Cherries, Figs, Almonds, Chestnuts, Limes, Pomegranates and Oranges thrive, and bear abundantly in the open air.

The Proprietor uses great care in the manufacture of his

## WINE & BRANDY.

Having the best possible location, and having planted nothing but the choicest varieties of grapes, for Wine-making purposes, his advantages are superior. His cellars are very large, and are stocked with

## Grape, Apple, Peach and Cherry Brandies, with

## PORT, SHERRY, MUSCATELLE,

### ANGELICA, CLARET,

## BURGUNDY, WHITE WINE AND WINE VINEGAR.

He invites the inspection of the **TRADE and PUBLIC** generally to his large stock, and assures all his visitors a hearty welcome.

DIRECTORY OF LOS ANGELES COUNTY. 307

| Name. | Occupation. | Place of Business. | Residence. | Town or P. O. |
|---|---|---|---|---|
| Aaron, Arnold | Clerk | | | Los Angeles. |
| Aaron, A | Clerk | Los Angeles | Los A and Aliso sts. | Los Angeles. |
| Abbott, C A | Sheep raiser | Los Angeles Co | | Los Angeles. |
| Abbott, W A | Lumber dealer | | Los Angeles Co | San Joaquin. |
| Abbott, W | Undertaker | 16 Main st | 21 Main st | Los Angeles. |
| Abbott, Frank | Mason | Lexington | 12 m E Los Angeles | El Monte. |
| Abarta, P | Trader | Los Angeles Co | | Los Angeles. |
| Abarta, Jose | Barkeeper | | | Los Angeles. |
| Abelardes, T | Ranchero | Los Angeles Co | San Juan | San Juan. |
| Abelardes, J de G | Ranchero | Los Angeles Co | San Juan | San Juan. |
| Abernathey, A B | Salesman | 53 Main st | Main and Spring sts. | Los Angeles. |
| Abila, Manuel D | Vaquero | | | San Juan. |
| Abila, Eraino | Ranchero | | | Los Angeles. |
| Abila, P A | Ranchero | Los A Township | Los Angeles Co | Los Angeles. |
| Abila, J B | Vaquero | Los A Township | Los Angeles Co | Los Angeles. |
| Abila, J del C | Farmer | San Juan Precinct | Los Angeles Co | San Juan. |
| Abila, C | Vaquero | | | Los Angeles. |
| Abila, S | Laborer | Los A Township | Los Angeles Co | San Juan. |
| Abila, J | Farmer | San Juan Precinct | Los Angeles Co | San Juan. |
| Abila, J M | Ranchero | Los A Precinct | Los Angeles Co | Los Angeles. |
| Abila, P | Ranchero | Los A Precinct | Los Angeles Co | Los Angeles. |
| Abila, Antonio M | Laborer | | Los Angeles | Los Angeles. |
| Abila, Francisco | Farmer | Los A Township | Los Angeles | Los Angeles. |
| Abila, Enrique | Stock raiser | San Pedro Ranch | 2 m N Compton | Compton. |
| Abila, J M | Stock raiser | Dominigues Ranch | 4 m N W Compton | Compton. |
| Abila, P | Stock raiser | Dominigues Ranch | 3 m N W Compton | Compton. |
| Abila, Felipe | Ranchero | Los A Township | Los Angeles Co | Los Angeles. |
| Abila, B Y | Farmer | Los A Township | Los Angeles Co | Los Angeles. |
| Abila, P A | Farmer | Los A Township | Los Angeles Co | Los Angeles. |
| Abril, M | Laborer | Los A Township | Los Angeles Co | Los Angeles. |
| Acebedo, J C | Laborer | Los A Township | Los Angeles Co | Santa Ana. |
| Achor, A | Laborer | Los Angeles | Bull st | Los Angeles. |
| Acosta, Jesus | Farmer | Los Nietos Precinct | Los Angeles Co | Los Nietos. |
| Acosta, J | Laborer | | | Los Angeles. |
| Acosta, D | Laborer | | | Los Angeles. |
| Acosta, P | Cook | Los Angeles | Los Angeles | Los Angeles. |
| Acosta, Encarnacion | Farmer | | | San Gabriel. |
| Acouturier, L | Barkeeper | Los Angeles | Los Angeles | Los Angeles. |
| Acuna, Jose Maria | Laborer | | | Los Angeles. |
| Acuna, T | Laborer | | | Santa Ana. |
| Adams, George W | Laborer | | | Los Angeles. |
| Adams, Abram | Minister | | | El Monte. |
| Adams, Frank H | Miner | | | Santa Ana. |
| Adams, Edward | Painter | | | Los Angeles. |
| Adams, John | Laborer | | | Los Angeles. |
| Adam, R | Baker | Los Angeles | Los Angeles | Los Angeles. |
| Adams, J | Teamster | | | Los Angeles. |
| Adams, J | Blacksmith | Anaheim | Anaheim | Anaheim. |
| Adams, S M | Farmer | | | El Monte. |
| Adams, E | Laborer | | San Antonio | Downey. |
| Adams, A V R | Stock raiser | | Ballona | Los Angeles. |
| Adams, D E | Attorney | Los Angeles | Fourth st | Los Angeles. |
| Adams, John J | Porter | R R Depot | Flower st | Los Angeles. |
| Adam, F | Merchant tailor | 13 Spring st | Buena Vista st | Los Angeles. |
| Adams, A V | Farmer | San Bernardino Road | 1¼ m E Lexington | El Monte. |
| Adams, I | Farmer | El Monte Valley | 3 m S W Lexington | El Monte. |
| Addis, A F | Photographer | Los Angeles | 3 Beaudry terrace | Los Angeles. |
| Adkinson Wm M | Farmer | | | San Jose. |
| Adkinson, Jesse | Farmer | | Silver Precinct | Downey. |
| Adkinson, A D | Apiarian | Dalton Canyon | 5 m N E Azusa | Azusa. |
| Adolphe, P | Clerk | cor 5th & Hill sts | Los Angeles | Los Angeles. |
| Acdas, Mrs M | French laundry | 62 Los Angeles st | | Los Angeles. |
| Aerick, John | Teamster | | | Los Angeles. |
| Agala, Mariano | Farmer | | Los Angeles | Los Angeles. |

## L. L. PAULSON'S HAND-BOOK AND

| Name. | Occupation. | Place of Business. | Residence. | Town or P. O. |
|---|---|---|---|---|
| **Agrida, F** | Merchant | San Fernando | San Fernando | San Fernando. |
| Aguayo, G | Laborer | | | Los Angeles. |
| Aguayo, Ygnacio | Farmer | | Azusa | Azusa. |
| Aguary, Jose M | Farmer | Azusa Ranch | 1¾ m S W Azusa | Azusa. |
| Aguilar, Jose | Vaquero | | | San Juan. |
| Aguilar, Francisco | Laborer | | | Anaheim. |
| Aguilar, Leonardo | Blacksmith | Los Angeles | Los Angeles | Los Angeles. |
| Aguire, Rafael | Laborer | | | Los Angeles. |
| Aguilar, A | Laborer | | | Los Angeles. |
| Aguila, M | Carpenter | | | Los Angeles. |
| Aguilar, R A | Laborer | | | Anaheim. |
| Aguirre, J M | Laborer | | | Los Angeles. |
| Aguilar, J | Clerk | Los Angeles | Los Angeles | Los Angeles. |
| Aguilar, Casildo | Farmer | | | Los Angeles? |
| **Aguilar, B** | Ranchero | | | San Juan. |
| Aguirre | Mason | | | La Ballona. |
| Aguilar, Rosario | Vaquero | | San Juan | San Juan. |
| Aguilar, Ambrosio | Vaquero | | San Juan | San Juan. |
| Aguilar, A | Laborer | | | Anaheim. |
| **Aguilar, C** | Overseer C W W | Spring & 1st sts | 40 Upper Main st | Los Angeles. |
| Ahern, John | Laborer | | | Los Angeles. |
| Aiken James | Farmer | | | San Gabriel. |
| **Ailland, H** | Bakery | 10 Negro alley | Los Angeles | Los Angeles. |
| Alari, J J | Laborer | | | San Jose. |
| Albrecht, John | Blacksmith | Los Angeles | Los Angeles | Los Angeles. |
| **Albrecht, Tribelet** | Baker | Los Angeles | Los Angeles | Los Angeles. |
| Alcaras, J M de L A | Laborer | | | Los Angeles. |
| Aldania, Vicente | Laborer | | | Los Angeles. |
| Aldrich, L M | Clerk | Los Angeles | Los Angeles | Los Angeles. |
| Aldrich, H | Carpenter | | | El Monte. |
| Alencios, E | Laborer | | | San Jose. |
| Alenez, Miss A | Dress maker | 31 Upper Main st | Los Angeles | Los Angeles. |
| **Alexander, J W** | Farmer | | | Azusa. |
| Alexander, Robert | Laborer | | | Los Angeles. |
| Alexander, S H P | Carpenter | | | Los Angeles. |
| Alexander, James | Mechanic | | | Los Nietos. |
| **Alexander, D W** | Fwd Merchant | Wilmington | Wilmington | Wilmington. |
| Alexander, G C | Merchant | Wilmington | Wilmington | Wilmington. |
| **Alexander, F H** | Farmer | | | Los Angeles. |
| Alexander, B L | Laborer | | | Los Angeles. |
| Alexander, M | Laborer | | | Los Angeles. |
| Alexander, J B | Farmer | | | Los Nietos. |
| Alexander, David | Clerk | S C W Shipping Co | Wilmington | Wilmington. |
| **Alexander, T C** | Millman | Los Angeles | Los Angeles | Los Angeles. |
| Alexander, F | Laborer | Los Angeles | 27 Eternity st | Los Angeles. |
| Alexander, Mrs M | | Los Angeles | San Pedro st | Los Angeles. |
| Alipaz, M | Laborer | | | San Gabriel. |
| Alipas, Juan | Laborer | | | Los Angeles. |
| Allanson, H S | Clerk | Los Angeles | Los Angeles | Los Angeles. |
| Allanson H S | Freight agt | R R Depot | San Gabriel | San Gabriel. |
| Allen, Ethan | Farmer | | | Los Angeles. |
| Allen, Albert G H | Farmer | | Silver Precinct | Downey. |
| Allen, Henry | Farmer | | | Los Angeles. |
| Allen, James Daniel | Farmer | | | Los Angeles. |
| Allen, John Henry | Farmer | | | Old Mission. |
| Allen, Thomas | Laborer | | | Old Mission. |
| Allen, George | Laborer | | | Los Angeles. |
| Allen, Edgar | Teamster | | | Wilmington. |
| **Allen, O H** | Att'y at law | Los Angeles | Los Angeles | Los Angeles. |
| **Allen, A C** | Physician | Los Angeles | Los Angeles | Los Angeles. |
| **Allen, E** | Painter | Los Angeles | Los Angeles | Los Angeles. |
| Allen, J R | Freighter | | | Los Angeles. |
| **Allen, James E** | Harness maker | Los Angeles | Los Angeles | Los Angeles. |
| Allen, Robert W | Laborer | | Los Angeles | Los Angeles. |

## DIRECTORY OF LOS ANGELES COUNTY. 309

| Name. | Occupation. | Place of Business. | Residence. | Town or P. O. |
|---|---|---|---|---|
| Allen, Isaac C. | Farmer | | Los Angeles | Los Angeles. |
| Allen, Bartlett B. | Laborer | | Los Angeles | Los Angeles. |
| Allen, Robert | Engineer | Los Angeles | Los Angeles | Los Angeles. |
| Allen, G | | Main st | Olive, near 6th st. | Los Angeles. |
| Allen, Mrs E | | | Olive, bet 4th & 5th sts | Los Angeles. |
| Allen, L W | Minister | | Charity & 5th sts | Los Angeles. |
| Allen, Ethan | | | Pearl, bet 5th & 6th sts | Los Angeles. |
| Allen, J D | Bookkeeper | 21 Los Angeles st | Pearl, bet 5th & 6th sts | Los Angeles. |
| **Allen, Charles** | Harness maker | 115 Main st | First, near Main st. | Los Angeles. |
| Allen, J | Cabinet maker | 4 Temple st | Temple & Spring sts | Los Angeles. |
| Allen, J | Saloon keeper | 161 Main st | 161 Main st | Los Angeles. |
| **Allen, J C** | Shoe maker | Commercial st | Los Angeles Hotel | Los Angeles. |
| Allen, J R | Carpenter | Los Angeles | San Pedro st | Los Angeles. |
| **Allen & Herrick** | Saloon & stable | 161 Main st | | Los Angeles. |
| **Allen, G** | Butcher | Wilmington | Wilmington | Wilmington. |
| Allnez, Miss A | Dress maker | | | Los Angeles. |
| Allen, Isaac | Carpenter | | | Los Angeles |
| Allison, R | Farmer | | | El Monte. |
| **Allison, John** | Machinist | Los Angeles | Los Angeles | Los Angeles. |
| Allis, John M. | Minister | | | Anaheim. |
| Allison, John | Alaska saloon | 83 Los Angeles st | Los Angeles | Los Angeles. |
| Allmind, K | Laborer | San Felipe Road | 5 m N E Los Angeles | Los Angeles. |
| **Almazan, F** | Blacksmith | Los Angeles | 46 Eternity st | Los Angeles. |
| Almada, Joaquin | Saloon | Pico House | Los Angeles | Los Angeles. |
| Almeida, J | Wharf hand | C P R R Co | Wilmington | Wilmington. |
| Almendares, Miguel | Mason | | | Los Angeles. |
| Altiminarez, F | Farmer | | | San Fernando. |
| Altirimano, Y | Farmer | | | Los Angeles. |
| Altimirano, S | Laborer | | | Los Angeles. |
| Alvarado, Juan | Carpenter | | | Los Angeles. |
| Alvarado, Estevan | Laborer | | | Wilmington. |
| Alvarado, Antonio | Farmer | | | Los Nietos. |
| Alva, J G de | Laborer | | | Los Angeles. |
| Alvarez, F | Laborer | | | Santa Ana. |
| Alvarado, F | Ranchero | | | Los Angeles. |
| Alvarado, J de D. | Laborer | | | San Jose. |
| Alvarado, Y M A | Laborer | | | San Gnb Mis'n. |
| **Alvarado, Y** | Farmer | | | San Jose. |
| **Alvarado, Y M** | Farmer | | | San Jose. |
| Alvaraz, J A | Farmer | | | Los Angeles. |
| Alvarado, J G | Laborer | | | Los Angeles. |
| Alvarez, M | Laborer | | | La Ballona. |
| Alvares, D | Laborer | | | Los Angeles. |
| Alvarez, Manuel | Laborer | | | Los Angeles. |
| Alvares, Refugio | Laborer | | San Joaquin | Santa Ana. |
| Alvarez, Jose M F. | Farmer | | San Antonio | Downey. |
| Alvarez, S | Farmer | | Los Angeles | Los Angeles. |
| **Alvarado, F** | Ranchero | | Los Angeles | Los Angeles. |
| Alvarado, G | Vaquero | | | Los Angeles. |
| Alvarado, Antonio | Laborer | Los Angeles | 64 Los Angeles st | Los Angeles. |
| Alvarez, Francisco | Laborer | Los Angeles | San Pedro st | Los Angeles. |
| Alvarez, M | Butcher | Los Angeles | Bull st | Los Angeles. |
| **Alvarez, F** | Brewer | Phila. Brewery | Cor Fort & 9th sts | Los Angeles. |
| Alvarado, S | Laborer | Los Angeles | New High st | Los Angeles. |
| Alvarado, Mrs A | | | Alameda st | Los Angeles. |
| Alvarado | Farmer | San Bernardino Road | 4½ m N E Spadra | Spadra. |
| Alvarado, Mrs | Farmer | San Bernardino Road | 3½ m E Spadra | Spadra. |
| Alvarado | Farmer | San Bernardino Road | 3¼ m E Spadra | Spadra. |
| Alvarado | Farmer | San Bernardino Road | 3 m E Spadra | Spadra. |
| Alvarado, F | Laborer | | | Los Angeles. |
| Alvarado, J A | Farmer | | | Los Angeles. |
| Alviso, Ygnacio | Laborer | | | San Gabriel. |
| Alvitria, Francisco | Laborer | | | El Monte. |
| Alvitro, Anastacio | Laborer | | | Mission Viejo |

| Name. | Occupation. | Place of Business. | Residence. | Town or P. O. |
|---|---|---|---|---|
| Alviso, M. | Laborer | | | Santa Ana. |
| Alvitre, T. | Laborer | | | El Monte. |
| Alviso, Ygnacio | Farmer | | Santa Ana | Santa Ana. |
| Alviso, Domingo | Farmer | Dalton Ranch | 1 m N Azusa | Azusa. |
| Amadon, H C | Laborer | | | Los Angeles. |
| Amat, Rt Rev T | Bishop | Catholic Church | Los Angeles | Los Angeles. |
| Amestoy | Farmer | | | Los Angeles. |
| Ames, John M. | Candy mnfr | Los Angeles | Los Angeles | Los Angeles. |
| Ames, George | Carpenter | Los Angeles | 60 Spring st | Los Angeles. |
| Ames, John | Laborer | Los Angeles | Main st | Los Angeles. |
| Ames, D | Farmer | El Monte Valley | 1½ m S Lexington | El Monte. |
| Amillac, A. | Sheep farmer | | | Los Angeles. |
| Amons, Peter | Ranchero | | | Los Angeles. |
| Amsbury, C. | Merchant | Los Angeles | Los Angeles | Los Angeles. |
| Analla, Juan | Laborer | | | Los Angeles. |
| Ancouturier, L | Theatre saloon | Main st | Los Angeles | Los Angeles. |
| Anderson, S A | Farmer | | | Los Nietos. |
| Anderson, J L | Farmer | | Silver District | Downey. |
| Anderson, W B | Farmer | | | Azusa. |
| Anderson, G D | Farmer | | | Los Nietos. |
| Anderson, J A | Telegraph Op | | | San Jose. |
| Anderson, D | Wagoner | | | Los Angeles. |
| Anderson, J | Miner | | | Los Angeles. |
| Anderson, John Y. | Farmer | | Westminster Col | Westminster. |
| Anderson, J | Farmer | | | Anaheim. |
| Anderson, Joseph | Waiter | | | Los Angeles. |
| Anderson, James | Stone cutter | Los Angeles | Los Angeles | Los Angeles. |
| Anderson, J B | Laborer | Los Angeles Co | Los Angeles | Los Angeles. |
| Anderson, John C. | Carpenter | | | Los Angeles. |
| Anderson, W | Painter | | Los Angeles | Los Angeles. |
| Anderson, J W | Fruit raiser | | | Anaheim. |
| Anderson, David | Capitalist | | Main, st near 2d | Los Angeles. |
| Andersen, J A | Farmer | El Monte Valley | 3 m S Lexington | El Monte. |
| Anderson, J | Farmer | | Halfway House | Compton |
| Anderson, W | Farmer | | Halfway House | Compton |
| Andrade, Reyes | Farmer | | | San Gabriel. |
| Andrada, S | Laborer | | | San Gabriel. |
| Andrews, E P S | Blacksmith | Los Angeles | Los Angeles | Los Angeles. |
| Andrews, Moses W | Physician | | Silver Precinct | Downey |
| Andrews, William | Farmer | | | Los Angeles. |
| Andrews, J | Farmer | | | Los Angeles. |
| Andres, P | Laborer | | | Los Angeles. |
| Andrews, C | Farmer | | | Compton. |
| Andrew, G B | Laborer | Los Angeles | Los Angeles st | Los Angeles. |
| Andrew, John | Farmer | Los Angeles Co | Ducommon st | Los Angeles. |
| Andres, R | Laborer | Los Angeles | New High st | Los Angeles. |
| Andrado, V | Laborer | Los Angeles | New High st | Los Angeles. |
| Aneucher, F | Stock raiser | Los Angeles Co | 41 Aliso st | Los Angeles. |
| Angell, F R. | Deputy recorder | Court House | Franklin, nr Fort st | Los Angeles. |
| Angelo, J | Farmer | San Pedro Ranch | 1¼ m N E Compton | Compton. |
| Angier, L | Farmer | | | Los Angeles. |
| Angil, J | Blacksmith | Los Angeles | Los Angeles | Los Angeles. |
| Angle, C C | Laborer | | | Los Angeles. |
| Anglo, John | Farmer | | Halfway House | Compton. |
| Annillo, Joseph | Grocer | 7 Bath st | Los Angeles | Los Angeles. |
| Anthony, Mrs | Restaurant | Santa Monica st | Santa Monica st | Los Angeles. |
| Antunes, E | Grocer | 59 Los Angeles st | Los Angeles | Los Angeles. |
| Antunes, Miguel | Grocer | 59 Los Angeles st | Los Angeles | Los Angeles. |
| Antunes & Co | Groceries | 59 Los Angeles st | | Los Angeles. |
| Antonis, Miguel | Saddler | | | Los Angeles. |
| Antonio, Joseph | Wharf hand | S P R R Co | Wilmington | Wilmington. |
| Anzar, P E | Carpenter | | | Los Angeles. |
| Aockerblum, Fr | Soda mnfr | 1st bet M and L A sts | | Los Angeles. |
| Apablasa, Cayetano | Wheelwright | | | Los Angeles. |

## DIRECTORY OF LOS ANGELES COUNTY. 311

| NAME. | OCCUPATION. | PLACE OF BUSINESS. | RESIDENCE. | TOWN OR P. O. |
|---|---|---|---|---|
| Aphold & Reinert... | Coopers | 1st st nr Wilmington | | Los Angeles. |
| Aphold, H B | Cooper | 1st st | Fort st nr 4th | Los Angeles. |
| Apodaca, F | Laborer | | | Los Nietos. |
| Apodaca, Jose C | Laborer | | Anaheim | Anaheim. |
| App, C | Laborer | | | Los Angeles. |
| Apple, N L | Carpenter | | | Soledad. |
| Applewhite J | Teamster | | | El Monte. |
| Aragon, V | Laborer | | | Old Mission. |
| Araiza, Leocadio | Ranchero | | | Santa Ana. |
| **Araiza, R** | Ranchero | | | Santa Ana. |
| Araico, Jesus | Laborer | | La Ballona | Los Angeles. |
| Aramenta, Refugio. | Laborer | | | Los Angeles. |
| Aranjo, F | Laborer | | | Los Angeles. |
| **Arana, Jesus** | Farmer | Placeritas | 4 m N E Lyon Sta'n | Lyon Station. |
| Arata, M | Clerk | 112 Main st. | Los Angeles | Los Angeles. |
| Arballe, Francisco. | Laborer | | | Los Angeles. |
| **Arbon, Robert** | Farmer | | | San Jose. |
| **Arbon, Russell** | Blacksmith | Los Angeles | Los Angeles | Los Angeles. |
| Arce, Ramon | Laborer | | | Los Angeles. |
| Arce, Jose | Laborer | | | Los Angeles. |
| Arce, Julian | Fisherman | Wilmington | Wilmington | Wilmington. |
| Archuleta, Perfecto | Farmer | | | Los Angeles. |
| Archuleta, P A | Laborer | | | Old Mission. |
| Arcia, Roque | Laborer | | | Los Angeles. |
| Arcia, Lauriana | Vaquero | | | San Juan. |
| Arcia, M | Laborer | | | Los Angeles. |
| Arcia, J B | Laborer | | | San Juan. |
| Arcia, J | Vaquero | | | San Juan. |
| Arcia, Cosmo | Vaquero | | | San Juan. |
| Arcia, Vidal | Vaquero | | | San Juan. |
| **Ardant, Louis** | Blacksmith | Los Angeles | Los Angeles | Los Angeles. |
| Ardes, J Chambers | Farmer | | | Silver Precinct. |
| Ardis, John Dawson | Farmer | | | Los Nietos. |
| Ardis, Isaac L | Farmer | | Silver Precinct | Downey. |
| **Ardrada, D** | Farmer | | | Old Mission. |
| Arellanes, R | Farmer | | | Los Angeles. |
| Arema, Jose | Laborer | | | Los Angeles. |
| Arendt, J H | Carpenter | | | Wilmington. |
| Arenas, Juan | Mason | Los Angeles | Los Angeles | Los Angeles. |
| Arey, E A | Carpenter | Los Angeles | 67 1st st | Los Angeles. |
| Arey, E | Carpenter | S P R R Co. | Wilmington | Wilmington. |
| Argelar, Jesus | Laborer | Los Angeles | New High st | Los Angeles. |
| Arguello, F | Ranchero | | | Los Angeles. |
| Arguello, S | Vaquero | | | Los Angeles. |
| Arguello, Jose M | Ranchero | | Los Angeles | Los Angeles. |
| Ariesa, R | Farmer | | | Los Angeles. |
| Arinas, F | Laborer | | | San Jose. |
| Aritch, B | Laborer | Los Angeles | Old Aliso st | Los Angeles. |
| Ariza, A | Laborer | | | Los Angeles. |
| Armenta, Ramon | Laborer | | | Los Angeles. |
| Armearta, A | Laborer | Los Angeles | Mission Road | Los Angeles. |
| Armentes, J A | Laborer | | | Santa Ana. |
| Armentes, D | Laborer | | | Santa Ana. |
| **Armillo, J** | Merchant | Los Angeles | Los Angeles | Los Angeles. |
| Armor, S | Teacher | Los Angeles Co. | Alameda st | Los Angeles. |
| Armstrong, Wm | Miner | | | La Ballona. |
| **Armstrong, A T** | Farmer | | | San Joaquin. |
| Armstrong, W | Teamster | | | Los Angeles. |
| **Armstrong, G C** | Farmer | | | El Monte. |
| **Armstroug, Geo A** | Attorney at law | Los Angeles | | Los Angeles. |
| Arnett, S E | Farmer | | | San Jose. |
| Arnett, R S | Farmer | | | San Jose. |
| **Arnett, Robert** | Farmer | San Jose Creek | 2 m S W Spadra | Spadra. |
| Arnett, Samuel | Farmer | San Bernardino Road | 4 m N E Spadra | Spadra. |

| Name. | Occupation. | Place of Business. | Residence. | Town or P. O. |
|---|---|---|---|---|
| Arnold, E N | Blacksmith | Anaheim | Anaheim | Anaheim. |
| Arnold, Aaron | Clerk | Los Angeles | Los Angeles | Los Angeles. |
| Arnold, W S | Farmer | Lexington | 12 m E Los Angeles | El Monte. |
| Arnold, William S. | Millwright | Los Angeles | Los Angeles | Los Angeles. |
| Arnold, W Stanley | Millwright | | | Soledad. |
| Arnold, Albert E. | Merchant | | | Los Angeles. |
| Arnold, W | Farmer | Los Angeles Road | 1½ m S W Spadra | Spadra. |
| Arpin, J L | Saloon keeper | | | Los Angeles. |
| Arroqui, Juan | Sheep raiser | | Los Angeles | Los Angeles. |
| Arsaga, A | Cigar maker | | | San Gab Miss'n |
| Artigue, J | Stock raiser | | | Elizabeth Lake. |
| Arviso, J | Milkman | | | Los Angeles. |
| Arzaga, F M | Laborer | | | Wilmington. |
| Arzaga, L | Laborer | | | Los Angeles. |
| Arzaga, E | Tinner | | | Los Angeles. |
| Arzaga, A | Printer | | 25 Upper Main st | Los Angeles. |
| Arzaga, E | Grocery | 25 Upper Main st | | Los Angeles. |
| Asane, Jesus | Stock raiser | Placeritas | 4 m N E Lyon Sta'n | Lyon Station. |
| Asbrand, August | Surveyor | | | Los Angeles. |
| Asbrandt, A | Grocery | 6th and Spring sts | Los Angeles | Los Angeles. |
| Asedo, A | Laborer | | | Old Mission. |
| Asevedo, E | Barber | | | Los Angeles. |
| Asevedo, Emiliano | Barber | 42 Main st | 1st st | Los Angeles. |
| Ashdown, J E | Farmer | | | El Monte. |
| Ashe, William | Cooper | | | Anaheim. |
| Ashe, J E | Opr and exp cl'k. | S P R R Co | Wilmington | Wilmington. |
| Ashton, W H | Butcher | Los Angeles | Los Angeles | Los Angeles. |
| Ash, T J | Farmer | | | El Monte. |
| Askin, T J | Livery stable | 14 and 18 Main st | Los Angeles | Los Angeles. |
| Askin & Hewitt | Union liv'y stable | 14 and 18 Main st | | Los Angeles. |
| Aston, S | Miner | | | Los Angeles. |
| Asylum, Orphan | | Alameda st | | Los Angeles. |
| Atchison, J | Miner | | | Soledad. |
| Athearn, F W | Farmer | | | Santa Ana. |
| Athenour, A | Laundryman | Los Angeles | San Pedro st | Los Angeles. |
| Atkinson, W D | Farmer | | | San Jose. |
| Atkin, T J | Trader | | | Los Angeles. |
| Atkinson, James J | Farmer | San Gabriel Mission | | San Gabriel. |
| Atkinson, James | Clerk | San Gabriel | 9 m E Los Angeles | San Gabriel. |
| Atwell, Thomas | Miner | | | Los Angeles. |
| Atwell, T | | Los Angeles | 1st cor Spring st | Los Angeles. |
| August, W | Miner | | | Los Angeles. |
| Aune, E | Restaurant | 114 Main st | Los Angeles | Los Angeles. |
| Austin, Charles | Farmer | | | Los Angeles. |
| Austin, H C | U S register | | | Los Angeles. |
| Austin, Thaddeus R | Teacher | | | Los Angeles. |
| Austin, Olden | Miner | | | Los Angeles. |
| Austin, F B | Blacksmith | Los Angeles | Los Angeles | Los Angeles. |
| Austin, Henry S. | Stationer | Anaheim | Anaheim | Anaheim. |
| Austin, H S | Grain dealer | Los Angeles st | Los Angeles st | Anaheim. |
| Austin, C | Carpenter | Los Angeles | Olive st | Los Angeles. |
| Austin, H C | Real estate | Los Angeles | Figueroa st | Los Angeles. |
| Autennse, E | Merchant | Los Angeles | Los Angeles | Los Angeles. |
| Aveline, J B | Broker | Los Angeles | Los Angeles | Los Angeles. |
| Averill, A A | Farmer | | Silver Precinct | Downey. |
| Avilez, A | Laborer | | | Los Angeles. |
| Avila, Mrs D | | | Old Aliso st | Los Angeles. |
| Avise, Jesse | Teamster | | | El Monte. |
| Avis, Benjamin | Teamster | | | Los Angeles. |
| Avis, F | Teamster | | | Los Angeles. |
| Avis, J | Farmer | | | El Monte. |
| Avis, J H | Blacksmith | San Gabriel | San Gabriel | San Gabriel. |
| Avis, Jesse, Jr | Teamster | | | El Monte. |
| Avis, Ramon | Farmer | | Los Angeles | Los Angeles. |

## DIRECTORY OF LOS ANGELES COUNTY. 313

| Name. | Occupation. | Place of Business. | Residence. | Town or P. O. |
|---|---|---|---|---|
| Avis, A............ | Farmer............ | El Monte Valley...... | 3 m W Lexington ..., | El Monte. |
| Avis, Jesse............ | Farmer............ | San Gabriel Valley... | 1 m S W San Gabriel | San Gabriel. |
| Avis, B............ | Farmer............ | Ellis Station............ | 2 m W Lexington.... | El Monte. |
| Avis, J B............ | Hackman............ | Los Angeles............ | 182 Main st............ | Los Angeles. |
| Ayala, C............ | Laborer............ |  |  | Los Angeles. |
| Ayers, James J..... | Editor............ | L A Evening Express | New High st............ | Los Angeles. |
| Ayers & Lynch..... | Mng'rs Eve'g Ex | Temple Block............ | ,,............ | Los Angeles. |
| Ayllon, F............ | Farmer............ |  |  | San Juan. |
| Ayres, J J............ | Printer'............ | Los Angeles............ | Los Angeles............ | Los Angeles. |
| Azbill, J............ | Farmer............ |  |  | Anaheim. |
| Azbill, W T............ | Farmer............ |  |  | Anaheim. |
| Azbill, J............ | Farmer............ |  |  | Anaheim. |
| Baal, Henry............ | Miner............ | Los Angeles............ | Cruzalta st............ | Los Angeles. |
| Baasar, F............ | Distiller............ | Los Angeles............ | Los Angeles............ | Los Angeles. |
| Babcock, N J............ | Farmer............ | San Pedro Ranch.... | 1½ m N E Compton... | Compton. |
| Babcock, Newton J | Millwright............ |  |  | Los Angeles. |
| Baca, M C D............ | Laborer............ |  | San Jose............ | Spadra. |
| Bachman, H............ | Laborer............ |  |  | Los Angeles. |
| Backman, P............ | Backman House.. | Main st............ | Main st............ | Los Angeles. |
| Backs, F & J............ | Furniture............ | cor Los A and 2d sts... |  | Anaheim. |
| Backs, Joseph............ | Merchant............ |  | Anaheim ............ | Anaheim. |
| Backs, F............ | Merchant............ | Anaheim............ | Anaheim ............ | Anaheim. |
| Backman, P............ | Farmer............ |  |  | Florence. |
| Backman, Foster ... | Bookkeeper ...... | Los Angeles............ |  | Los Angeles. |
| Bacon, J............ | Farmer............ |  |  | San Juan. |
| Bacon, Frank............ | Vintner............ | San Gabriel Valley | 9 m N E Los Angeles | Los Angeles. |
| Bacon, C P............ | Farmer............ | nr San Gabriel............ | Los Angeles Co....... | San Gabriel. |
| Bacon, M A............ | Farmer............ |  |  | Los Nietos. |
| Bacon, F P............ | Farmer............ | San Gabr Township.. | Marenyo Ranch....... | Los Angeles. |
| Badger, Samuel...... | Laborer............ |  |  | Los Angeles. |
| Baer, J & Co............ | Saloon............ | Los Angeles............ | Los Angeles............ | Los Angeles. |
| Baer & Walden..... | Saloon............ | Commercial & L A sts |  | Los Angeles. |
| Baer, J............ | Saloon............ | Los Angeles st......... | Los Angeles............ | Los Angeles. |
| Baffort, P............ | Merchant............ | Los Angeles............ | Los Angeles............ | Los Angeles. |
| Bailey, W H............ | Farmer............ |  |  | Santa Ana. |
| Bailey, R J............ | Apiarian............ | San Gabriel Valley.. | 9 m N E San Gabriel | San Gabriel. |
| Bailey, S C............ | Laborer............ | Wilmington............ | Wilmington............ | Wilmington. |
| Bailey, Henry C..... | Farmer............ |  | Silver Precinct....... | Downey. |
| Bailey, F E............ | Carpenter............ |  |  | Los Nietos. |
| Bailey, H M............ | Jeweler............ | Main st............ | Los Angeles............ | Los Angeles. |
| Bailey, A............ | Justice of peace... | Enterprise Block......., | Anaheim ............ | Anaheim. |
| Bailey, Morris...... | Laborer............ |  | Anaheim ............ | Anaheim. |
| Bailey, Frank L..... | Clerk............ | Los Angeles............ | Los Angeles............ | Los Angeles. |
| Bailey, Henry M... | Jeweler............ | Los Angeles............ | Los Angeles............ | Los Angeles. |
| Bailey, Alexander.. | Mason............ | Anaheim............ | Anaheim ............ | Anaheim. |
| Bair, J W............ | Laborer............ | Silver Precinct...... | Silver Precinct....... | Downey. |
| Bajorgamez, O...... | Farmer............ |  | Old Mission............ | El Monte. |
| Bajorquez, Jesus..... | Farmer............ |  | Old Mission............ | El Monte. |
| Baker, E L............ | Miner............ |  |  | Los Angeles. |
| Baker, J............ | Laborer............ |  |  | Los Angeles. |
| Baker, M C............ | Mechanic............ | Los Angeles............ |  | Los Angeles. |
| Baker, F............ | Teamster............ |  |  | Los Angeles. |
| Baker, J H............ | Blacksmith............ | Los Angeles............ | Los Angeles............ | Los Angeles. |
| Baker, W............ | Laborer............ | El Monte Precinct... |  | El Monte. |
| Baker, S A............ | Stage driver............ |  |  | Los Angeles. |
| Baker, J H............ | Laborer............ | ':............ |  | Mission Viejo. |
| Baker, Seth A....... | Laborer............ |  |  | Los Angeles. |
| Baker, C W............ | Laborer............ |  |  | Los Angeles. |
| Bakely, C............ | Clerk............ | Los Angeles............ | Los Angeles............ | Los Angeles. |
| Baker, Edwin G..... | Farmer............ |  | Silver Precinct....... | Downey. |
| Baker, J G............ | Refiner............ | Lyon Station............ | Lyon Station............ | Lyon Station. |
| Bakepool, G............ | Teamster............ |  |  | Los Angeles. |
| Baker, S C............ | Farmer............ |  | Silver Precinct....... | Downey. |
| Baker, M S............ | Mechanic............ | San Felipe Road...... | 5 m N E Los Angeles | Los Angeles. |

| NAME. | OCCUPATION. | PLACE OF BUSINESS. | RESIDENCE. | TOWN OR P. O. |
|---|---|---|---|---|
| Baker, Mrs | Music teacher | 30 Spring st | Los Angeles | Los Angeles. |
| Baker, J H | Blacksmith | with C Roynal | Eternity st | Los Angeles. |
| Baker, Robert M | Shepherd | Anaheim | Anaheim | Anaheim. |
| Baker, R S | Sheep raiser | | | Los Angeles. |
| Baker, F | | Los Angeles | Olive st | Los Angeles. |
| Baker, G | Hackman | | Alameda and 1st sts | Los Angeles. |
| Baker, M C | Sew mach agent | 39 Spring st | 39 Spring st | Los Angeles. |
| Baker, S C | Laborer | 13 Aliso st | | Los Angeles. |
| Baker, V | Laborer | Los Angeles | Temple and 1st sts | Los Angeles. |
| Baker, E L | Fruit grower | with M Keller | Alameda st | Los Angeles. |
| Baldwin, Jeremiah | Distiller | Los Angeles | Los Angeles | Los Angeles. |
| Baldridge, James | Farmer | Azusa | 2¼ m S E Azusa | Azusa. |
| Baldridge, J | Farmer | | | Los Angeles. |
| Baldwin, John M | Surveyor | Los Angeles | Los Angeles | Los Angeles. |
| Baldwin, James C | Blacksmith | Los Angeles | Los Angeles | Los Angeles. |
| Baldy, Christian | Merchant | Los Angeles | Los Angeles | Los Angeles. |
| Baldy, John | Clerk | Los Angeles | Los Angeles | Los Angeles. |
| Baldonado, Felip | Vaquero | | | Los Angeles. |
| Baldy, Oscar C | Vet'ry Surgeon | cor Fort and 4th sts | cor Fort and 4th sts | Los Angeles. |
| Baldwin, J W | Carpenter | Los Angeles | Fort and Hill sts | Los Angeles. |
| Baldwin & Co, J M | Real estate | 79½ Downey Block | Los Angeles | Los Angeles. |
| Baldwin, J M | Real estate | 79½ Downey Block | Downey Block | Los Angeles. |
| Baldy, A J | Clerk | Los Angeles | Los Angeles | Los Angeles. |
| Baldy, J | Bookkeeper | 70 Main st | Fort and 5th sts | Los Angeles. |
| Bales, L | Farmer | | Silver Precinct | Downey. |
| Balencia, Mrs M | | | Bet 1st & 2d sts | Los Angeles. |
| Baley, — | Fruit grower | | Alameda st | Los Angeles. |
| Balensia, J J | Laborer | | | Los Angeles. |
| Balenzan, Dario | Mason | | | Los Angeles. |
| Ball, J W | Farmer | | Westminter Col | Westminster. |
| Ballerino, B | Farmer | | | Los Angeles. |
| Ballesteros, F | Vaquero | | | Los Angeles. |
| Ballard, John | Farmer | | | Los Angeles. |
| Ballasquas, A | Grocer | Bull and Eternity sts | Los Angeles | Los Angeles. |
| Ballard, E J | Carpenter | Los Angeles | U S Hotel | Los Angeles. |
| Ballisteros, J | Butcher | Los Angeles | Los Angeles | Los Angeles. |
| Ball, G W | Machinist | Los Angeles | Los Angeles | Los Angeles. |
| Ballard, E J | Carpenter | | Los Angeles | Los Angeles. |
| Ballisteras, F | Saddler | Los Angeles | | Los Angeles. |
| Banchet, Mrs R A | | | Main st | Los Angeles. |
| Bancroft & Thayer | Real estate | 21 Spring st | Spring st | |
| Bancroft, B H | Farmer | | | Anaheim. |
| Bancroft, Curtis A | Clerk | Los Angeles | Los Angeles | Los Angeles. |
| Bancroft, H L | Well borer | | Anaheim | Anaheim. |
| Bancroft, C A | | Los Angeles | Clarendon Hotel | Los Angeles. |
| Bandini, Alphedo | Student | | | Los Angeles. |
| Bandini, Mrs R A | | | 30 Main st | Los Angeles. |
| Bandini, A | Bookkeeper | 2 Arcada Block | 30 Main st | Los Angeles. |
| Bandini, Arturo M | Student | | | Los Angeles. |
| Banks, H J | Farmer | | | Los Angeles. |
| Bank, The Temple and Workman | | Spring and Main sts | | Los Angeles. |
| Bank, Los Angeles County | | Main st | | Los Angeles. |
| Bank, Farmers' and Merchants | | Main st | | Los Angeles. |
| Bank, John R | Druggist | | Silver Precinct | Downey. |
| Banman, Louis | Cooper | Los Angeles | | Los Angeles. |
| Banning, William L | Clerk | | | Wilmington. |
| Banning, P | Merchant | | | Wilmington. |
| Banning, P | Stock raiser | Los Angeles Co | Wilmington | Wilmington. |
| Banoit, B | Farmer | 9 m E Los Angeles | San Gabriel | San Gabriel. |
| Bant, J | Carpenter | 132 Main st | | Los Angeles. |
| Banta, P | Farmer | Los Nietos Precinct | | Los Nietos. |

## DIRECTORY OF LOS ANGELES COUNTY.

| Name. | Occupation. | Place of Business. | Residence. |
|---|---|---|---|
| Banyard, L S | Farmer | El Monte Township | |
| Banyard, D Jr | Farmer | | El Monte Precinct |
| Barber, W F | Carpenter | | |
| Barber, W R | Miner | | |
| Barber, John S | Farmer | | |
| **Barbey, J L** | Farmer | San Pedro Ranch | 1 m W Compton |
| Barber, W B | Laborer | Wilmington | Canal st |
| **Barbier, J P** | | Spring & Court sts | High st |
| Barber, R C | Tinsmith | Los Angeles | Los Angeles |
| Barce, W | Ship carpenter | Point San Pedro | Point San Pedro |
| Barclay, J | | Wilmington | Canal st |
| Barcus, William | Farmer | | |
| Bard, H V | Farmer | | |
| Barelas, Amado | Laborer | | |
| Barham, James F | Farmer | | |
| Barham, J F | | | |
| Barham, J H | Sheep raiser | | Anaheim |
| Barios, Jose Moreno | Stock raiser | | |
| Baric, J | Miner | | |
| Barker, E D | Farmer | | |
| **Barkneck, A** | Blacksmith | with Page & Gravel | San Pedro st |
| Barker, J | Farmer | | |
| Barker, William | Carpenter | | |
| Barker, T A | Laborer | | |
| **Barling, F** | Farmer | Azusa Ranch | 1¼ m N E Azusa |
| **Barlow, L L** | Farmer | Mission Road | 1 m W San Fernando |
| Barnes, J C | Farmer | | |
| **Baruch, Jacob** | Merchant | 2 m S Downey | Gallatin |
| Barnett, John W | Carpenter | | Silver Precinct |
| Barnes, Ambrose J | Farmer | | San Juan |
| Barnard, William C | Manufacturer | Los Angeles | Los Angeles |
| Barnes, J C | Farmer | | |
| **Barnes, J C** | Justice of Peace | Azusa Ranch | 1½ m E Azusa |
| **Barnes, L** | Farmer | Azusa Ranch | 1 m E Azusa |
| Barnes, William L | Farmer | | |
| Barnes, Larkin | Farmer | | |
| Barnes, Anderson | Farmer | | |
| Barnett, Edward L | Mechanic | | Silver Precinct |
| Barre, Juan | Speculator | Los Angeles | Los Angeles |
| Barrows, Henry D | Merchant | Los Angeles | Los Angeles |
| Barry, George Y | Farmer | | |
| Barron, Michael | Laborer | | |
| Barrows, Henry F | Clerk | Wilmington | Wilmington |
| Barreras, Jose D | Vaquero | | |
| Barry, John W | | | |
| Barron, William L | Carpenter | | |
| Barry, Edward S | Clerk | San Gabriel | San Gabriel |
| Barrett, Thomas | Teamster | | |
| Barry, G | Farmer | | |
| Barrey, J H | Cook | Los Angeles | Los Angeles |
| Barrere, J H | Cook | Los Angeles | Los Angeles |
| Barragan, R | Miner | | |
| Barreras, C | | | Bull st |
| **Barrows, H D & Co** | Stoves & hardware | 19 Los Angeles st | |
| **Barrows, J A** | Livery | Los Angeles | Jefferson st |
| **Barrows, H D** | Stoves & hardware | 19 Los Angeles st | San Pedro st |
| Barrett, Patrick | Laborer | | |
| Barrett, James | Miner | | Soledad |
| **Barrett, Charles** | Nurseryman | | Richland |
| Bartholomew, A W | Farmer | | |
| Bartlett, Robert | Laborer | | |
| Bartley, James | Baker | | |
| Bartlett, W G | Farmer | | |
| **Bart, E** | Tailor | 13 Spring st | Spring st |

| Name. | Occupation. | Place of Business. | Residence. | Town or P. O. |
|---|---|---|---|---|
| Bartley, James | Moulder | Los Angeles | Los Angeles | Los Angeles. |
| Barton, A H | Farmer | | Silver Precinct | Downey. |
| Bassett, Josiah | Ranchero | | | San Fernando. |
| Bassett, J M | Editor | L A Herald | | Los Angeles. |
| Basser, Emil | Farmer | | | Los Angeles. |
| Basques, Abram | Laborer | | | Los Angeles. |
| Basuirto, F | Shoe maker | Los Angeles | Bull st | Los Angeles. |
| Basye, R | Farmer | | | El Monte. |
| Bates, H C | Teacher | | | San Fernando. |
| Bates, Arastus T | Farmer | | | Santa Ana. |
| Bateman, G E | Mechanic | Los Angeles | Los Angeles | Los Angeles. |
| Bates, J R | Miner | | | Wilmington. |
| Bates, F M | Actor | | | Los Angeles. |
| Bates, P | Carpenter | S P R R Co | Wilmington | Wilmington. |
| Bateman, C | Machinist | Los Angeles | Upper Main st | Los Angeles. |
| Bath, A L | Carriage maker | Spring st | Cor Hill & 5th sts | Los Angeles. |
| Batty, C G | Mason | Los Angeles | Los Angeles | Los Angeles. |
| Batts, P | Carpenter | C P R R Co | Wilmington | Wilmington. |
| Bauchet, Raphael L | Farmer | | | Los Angeles. |
| Bauer, L | Laborer | | | Los Angeles. |
| Bauer, Jacob | Farmer | | | Anaheim. |
| Bauer, Brothers | City Market | Spring st near 3d | Los Angeles | Los Angeles. |
| Bauer, George | Boot maker | Los Angeles st | Anaheim | Anaheim. |
| Bauer, Bernard | Butcher | Los Angeles | Los Angeles | Los Angeles. |
| Bauer, A | Butcher | Los Angeles | Los Angeles | Los Angeles. |
| Baume, S | Farmer | Azusa | 2 m S W Azusa | Azusa. |
| Bavala, Antonio | Vaquero | | San Fernando | San Fernando. |
| Baxendale, W | Finisher | Los Angeles | Los Angeles | Los Angeles. |
| Baxley, R J | Apiarian | | | San Gabriel. |
| Baxter, W | Butcher | San Gabriel | San Gabriel | San Gabriel. |
| Baxter, John | Farmer | San Pedro Ranch | 2½ m N Compton | Compton. |
| Baxter, W | Butcher | Los Angeles | Los Angeles | Los Angeles. |
| Baxter, Reuben | Tinsmith | Los Angeles | Los Angeles | Los Angeles. |
| Baxter, R | Clerk | H Newmarks & Co | | Los Angeles. |
| Bayer, Joseph | Clerk | | | Los Angeles. |
| Bayers, Joseph A | Miner | | | Los Angeles. |
| Bayer, J | | Los Angeles | U S Hotel | Los Angeles. |
| Beach, Wilson | Farmer | | | Los Angeles. |
| Beach, W | Stock raiser | Spadra | 30 m E Los Angeles | Spadra. |
| Beach & Butler | Stock raiser | Spadra | 30 m E Los Angeles | Spadra. |
| Beall, Malcolm D | Teamster | | | El Monte. |
| Beal, J M | Real estate | Los Angeles | Downey block | Los Angeles. |
| Beall, W H | Teacher | Los Angeles | Los Angeles | Los Angeles. |
| Beall, W H | Com merchant | Aliso st | Los Angeles | Los Angeles. |
| Bean, Thomas A | Farmer | | | Los Angeles. |
| Bean, William H | Farmer | | | Compton. |
| Beane, C H | Journalist | | Los Angeles | Los Angeles. |
| Beanner, S | Hostler | Los Angeles | Los Angeles | Los Angeles. |
| Beane, Charles E | Notary public | 79½ Downey block | | Los Angeles. |
| Beardsley, James B | Farmer | | | El Monte. |
| Beardsley, N | Farmer | Azusa | 3 m E Lexington | El Monte. |
| Beardslee, Melvin | Wood chopper | | | Soledad. |
| Beardslee, W R | Farmer | El Monte | | El Monte. |
| Beardslee, D G | Laborer | | | El Monte. |
| Beardslee, E P | Teamster | | | El Monte. |
| Beardslee, O H | Farmer | | | El Monte |
| Bear, William | Laborer | | | Los Angeles |
| Bear, H A | Carpenter | | | El Monte |
| Beaudry, P | Capitalist | 13 High st | 13 High st | Los Angeles |
| Beaudoin, Cyprien | Carpenter | | | Los Angeles |
| Beauchamp, F G | Farmer | | | Downey |
| Bebee, A G | Carpenter | | | Anaheim |
| Beckwith, J | Farmer | | Westminster Col | Westminster |
| Beckley, John | Apiarian | | | Los Angeles |

## DIRECTORY OF LOS ANGELES COUNTY. 317

| NAME. | OCCUPATION. | PLACE OF BUSINESS. | RESIDENCE. | TOWN OR P. O |
|---|---|---|---|---|
| Beck, Thomas J | Farmer | | | Los Nietos |
| Beckley, H | Jeweler | Los Angeles | Los Angeles | Los Angeles |
| Becraft, John | Laborer | | | Los Angeles |
| Bedford, J C | Farmer | Silver Precinct | | Downey |
| Bedfno, T J | Stock dealer | | Old Mission | El Monte |
| Bedome, William | Farmer | | | Los Nietos |
| Bedolla, F | Laborer | | | Los Angeles |
| Bedoy, Lorenzo | Laborer | | | Los Angeles |
| Bedwell, A W | Farmer | | Anaheim | Anaheim |
| Beebe, Charles A | Bookkeeper | Los Angeles | Los Angeles | Los Angeles |
| Beebee, A G | Carpenter | Anaheim | | Anaheim |
| Beggs, W J | Printer | Los Angeles | Los Angeles | Los Angeles |
| Begin, A | Merchant | Los Angeles | Los Angeles | Los Angeles |
| Begue, P | Farmer | | | Los Angeles |
| Behasque, H & Co | Liquors | Los Angeles | Los Angeles | Los Angeles |
| Behn, Peter | Ranchero | | | Los Angeles |
| Behn, Mrs A | | Los Angeles | Sansevain st | Los Angeles |
| Behrendt, Casper | Merchant | Los Angeles | Los Angeles | Los Angeles |
| Beilnes, J P | Trader | Los Angeles | | Los Angeles |
| Bejorges, J G | Farmer | | | Los Angeles |
| Belarde, Ygnacio | Laborer | | | San Jose |
| Belasques, Ygnacio | Laborer | | | San Jose |
| Bell, David W | Ship carpenter | | | Los Angeles |
| Bell, Charles | Laborer | | | El Monte |
| Bell, Horace | Farmer | | | Los Angeles |
| Bell, A T | Saddler | Los Angeles | Los Angeles | Los Angeles |
| Bell, P D | Feed stable | San Fernando | San Fernando | San Fernando |
| Bell, W C | Laborer | Lexington | 12 m E Los Angeles | El Monte |
| Bell, George H | Carpenter | | | Los Angeles |
| Bell, A | Mason | Los Angeles | Los Angeles | Los Angeles |
| Belliard, P | Farmer | | | Los Angeles |
| Bellwood, J | Farmer | San Pedro Ranch | 1¼ m N Compton | Compton |
| Bellya, E | Boarding house | Wilson's College | Wilmington | Wilmington |
| Bellinger, M H | Teamster | San Pedro Ranch | 2½ m N Compton | Compton |
| Bell, G H | Architect | 6 Downey Block | Los Angeles | Los Angeles |
| Bell & Green | Harness maker | 115 Main st | | Los Angeles |
| Bellocq, Felix | Whitewasher | Los Angeles | Los Angeles | Los Angeles |
| Bellya, E | Farmer | | San Antonio | Downey |
| Belmal, J | Farmer | | | Los Angeles |
| Belou, A | Waiter | | | Los Angeles |
| Belt, William D | Farmer | | | Downey |
| Benbrook, C M | Wagon maker | Los Angeles | Los Angeles | Los Angeles |
| Bender, John | Farmer | Azusa Ranch | 3 m N E Azusa | Azusa |
| Bengough, Mrs E | Teacher | Los Angeles | Los Angeles | Los Angeles |
| Benites, Ramon | Laborer | | San Gabriel | San Gabriel |
| Benitez, O | Blacksmith | Los Angeles | Los Angeles | Los Angeles |
| Benitos, Ramon | Laborer | | | Los Angeles |
| Bennett, G W | Miner | San Gabriel Canyon | 14 m N Azusa | Azusa |
| Bennett, Hiram C | Farmer | | | El Monte |
| Bennett, Silas | Trader | | | El Monte |
| Bennett, M L | Farmer | | | Downey |
| Benner, John | Butcher | Los Angeles | Los Angeles | Los Angeles |
| Bennett, P | Laborer | | | Los Angeles |
| Bennett & Page | Planters' Hotel | L A & Centre sts | | Anaheim |
| Bennerscheldt, J | Tinsmith | Center st | Anaheim | Anaheim |
| Benoit, Bila | Orange merchant | San Gabriel | | San Gabriel |
| Bent, Henry K W | Silk raiser | | | Los Angeles |
| Bently, William P | Teamster | | | Los Angeles |
| Benton, Albert | Farmer | | | Downey |
| Bent, H K W | Postmaster | Spring st | Los Angeles | Los Angeles |
| Bently, S C | Farmer | | | Los Angeles |
| Benton, M A | Farmer | | | Los Angeles |
| Benz, Urich | Laborer | | | Anaheim |
| Beouf, M | Stock raiser | | | Los Angeles |

| Name. | Occupation. | Place of Business. | Residence. | Town or P. O. |
|---|---|---|---|---|
| Bequette, L L | Tanner | | | Los Nietos |
| Berdrega, Mrs F | | | Main, near High st | Los Angeles |
| Berg, Simon | Clerk | | | Los Angeles |
| Bermudes, Vicente | Laborer | | | El Monte |
| Bermudes, Juan | Laborer | | | El Monte |
| Bermudez, A | Laborer | | | Los Angeles |
| **Bernard, Novel** | Upholsterer | Los Angeles | Los Angeles | Los Angeles |
| Bernal, Alexo | Laborer | | | San Gabriel |
| **Bernal, J A** | Plasterer | Los Angeles | Los Angeles | Los Angeles |
| Bernstein, Joseph | Clerk | Los Angeles | Los Angeles | Los Angeles |
| Berntes, Alvino | Laborer | | San Gabriel | San Gabriel |
| **Bernhard, S** | Merchant | Los Angeles | Los Angeles | Los Angeles |
| Bernal, B | Laborer | | | El Monte |
| Bernardo, Juan | Brick maker | | | Los Angeles |
| Berry, J A | Groceries | Spadra | 30 m E Los Angeles | Spadra |
| Berry, William | Farmer | | | San Jose |
| Berry, J L | Farmer | | | Los Angeles |
| **Berry, D M** | Real estate | 32 Main st | San Pasqual | Los Angeles |
| Berran, W R | Collector | Los Angeles | Los Angeles | Los Angeles |
| **Berry, D M** | Real estate | Los Angeles | Los Angeles | Los Angeles |
| Bertheon, Eugene | Saloon keeper | Los Angeles | Los Angeles | Los Angeles |
| Berthelos, Frank | Saloon keeper | Los Angeles | Los Angeles | Los Angeles |
| **Berthon, E** | Architect | Main st | Los Angeles | Los Angeles |
| Bertrand, P | Cook | Los Angeles | Los Angeles | Los Angeles |
| **Bertrand & Pellefigue** | Butchers | Los Angeles | Los Angeles | Los Angeles |
| Bessara, Enrique | Laborer | | | Los Angeles |
| Bettis, William R | Clerk | Los Angeles | Los Angeles | Los Angeles |
| Bettis, Elijah | | Los Angeles | Los Angeles | Compton |
| Bettis, Phillip H | Farmer | | | Los Angeles |
| Bettis, J W | Carpenter | | | San Fernando |
| Bewley, James A | Teamster | | Westminster | Wesminster |
| Bewley, Jesse D | Farmer | | | Los Angeles |
| Beyne, Bertrand | Butcher | | | Los Angeles |
| **Bicknell, J D** | Attorney at law | 39-41 Temple Block | | Los Angeles |
| Bidlecorn, A D | Teamster | | | Los Angeles |
| Bidwell, Chas | Spinner | | | Los Angeles |
| Biggs, Alvin | Laborer | | | Los Angeles |
| Bildarrain, Jesus A | Druggist | | | Los Angeles |
| **Bilderrain, R** | Harness maker | Los Angeles | Los Angeles | Los Angeles |
| Bildarrain, A | Laborer | | | Los Angeles |
| Bilderback, Mrs D | | Works 86 Main st | | Los Angeles |
| Billegas, Pedro | Laborer | | | Los Angeles |
| Billings, James A | Stable keeper | | | Los Angeles |
| Biller, Bernard | Barkeeper | Los Angeles | Los Angeles | Los Angeles |
| Billon, Louis | Farmer | | | Los Angeles |
| Bills, Robert | Teamster | | | Los Angeles |
| **Bills, R** | Baggage express | 70 Main st | Cor Flower & 6th sts | Los Angeles |
| Bills, Charles | Teamster | | | Los Angeles |
| Bills, J A | Laborer | | | Los Angeles |
| Binauzer, Jacob | Laborer | | | Los Angeles |
| **Bluford, Henry L** | Real estate | Los Angeles | Los Angeles | Los Angeles |
| Bingham, Joseph | Farmer | | Wesminster Col | Westminster |
| Bingham, J | Farmer | | | Los Angeles. |
| Bingham, Joseph | Mechanic | | | Westminster. |
| Bingham, J | Farmer | | | Downey. |
| Birchett, F S | Farmer | | | Downey, |
| Birch, Albert W | Farmer | | San Joaquin | Santa Ana. |
| **Bird, Frank** | Stage driver | Tel Stage Line | San Fernando | San Fernando. |
| Bird, W | Fireman | S S P R R Co | Wilmington | Wilmington. |
| Bird, J P | Stage driver | | | Los Angeles. |
| **Borde, Francisco D** | Baker | Los Angeles | Los Angeles | Los Angeles. |
| Birmingham, P | Clergyman | | | Los Angeles. |
| Bise, S | Farmer | San Pedro Ranch | 1¼ m S W Compton | Compton. |

## DIRECTORY OF LOS ANGELES COUNTY. 319

| Name. | Occupation. | Place of Business. | Residence. | Town or P. O. |
|---|---|---|---|---|
| Bishop, H C | Mechanic | | | Los Nietos. |
| Bisson, J J | Laborer | | | Los Angeles. |
| Biss, Jesus | Farmer | | | El Monte. |
| Biswalter, Andrew | Gardener | | | Los Angeles. |
| Bitall, Lusero | Farmer | | | El Monte. |
| Bitter, D | Miller | Los Angeles | Los Angeles | Los Angeles. |
| Bittner, Andrew | Shoe maker | | | Anaheim. |
| Bixby, G F | Ranchero | | | Wilmington. |
| Bixby, John W | Carpenter | | | Wilmington. |
| Bixby, J | Stock raiser | Cerritos Ranch | 5 m N Wilmington | Wilmington. |
| Bixby, George | Stock raiser | Cerritos Ranch | 5 m N Wilmington | Wilmington. |
| Bixby, A S | Farmer | Bixby's Ranch | 5 m N Wilmington | Wilmington. |
| Bixby, John W | Stock raiser | Los Angeles Co | Wilmington | Wilmington. |
| Bixby, Flint | Farmer | Bixby's Ranch | 5 m N Wilmington | Wilmington. |
| Bixby, Miss E P | Teacher | | | Los Angeles. |
| Bixby, Jonathan | Ranchero | | | Compton. |
| Bixby, M | Ranchero | | | Wilmington. |
| Bixby, J A | Blacksmith | Wilmington | Wilmington | Wilmington. |
| Black, William | Farmer | | | El Monte. |
| Black, S B | Farmer | | | Downey. |
| Black, W | Farmer | | | El Monte. |
| Blackley, C | Laborer | | | El Monte. |
| Blackman, J T | Teamster | | | Los Angeles. |
| Blakey, R E | Miner | | | Azusa. |
| Blake, G S | Farmer | | | San Jose. |
| Blakeley, S | Farmer | | | Downey. |
| Blakeslee, S B | Farmer | | | El Monte. |
| Blake, W | Farmer | | | San Jose. |
| Blake, C H | Merchant | San Jose | San Jose | San Jose. |
| Blake, J O | Clerk | Los Angeles | Los Angeles | Los Angeles. |
| Bland, S | Teamster | | | Los Angeles. |
| Bland, Charles I | Stock raiser | | Silver District | Downey. |
| Blanchard, J W | Blacksmith | | | Soledad. |
| Bland, W A | Farmer | | Silver Precinct | Downey. |
| Blanco, P | Merchant | Los Angeles | Los Angeles | Los Angeles. |
| Bland, W A | | | | |
| Bland, James H | Real estate agent | Los Angeles | Los Angeles | Los Angeles. |
| Bland, J H | Attorney at law | 21 Temple Block | Los Angeles | Los Angeles. |
| Blanken, Herman | Druggist | Anaheim Drug Store | Anaheim | Anaheim. |
| Blanchard, J H | Attorney at law | 18 & 19 Temple Bl'k | | Los Angeles. |
| Bland, Andrew F | Carriage mnf'r | | Los Nietos | Los Nietos. |
| Blanchard, J H | Lawyer | Los Angeles | Los Angeles | Los Angeles. |
| Blanchard, J | Carpenter | | | Los Angeles. |
| Blanco, Secayo | Farmer | | | Los Angeles. |
| Blanc, August | Saloon keeper | Los Angeles | Los Angeles | Los Angeles. |
| Blasdell, S W | Farmer | | | San Gabriel. |
| Blathardt, J | Carpenter | | | Los Angeles. |
| Blickensderfer, R | Civil engineer | | Soledad | San Fernando |
| Bliss, Oliver H | Farmer | | | Los Angeles. |
| Bloom, T | Farmer | | | Los Angeles. |
| Blum, Simon | Clerk | Los Angeles | Los Angeles | Los Angeles. |
| Bobenrieth, J | Saloon keeper | Los Angeles | Los Angeles | Los Angeles. |
| Boege, H | Teamster | | | Anaheim. |
| Boege, T | Teamster | | | Anaheim. |
| Boer, M | Laborer | | | Santa Ana. |
| Boettcher, A | Blacksmith | Los Angeles | Los Angeles | Los Angeles. |
| Bogart, O H | Cashier | Pacific Bank | Los Angeles | Los Angeles. |
| Boge, H | Wine grower | | | Anaheim. |
| Bohanan, John | Saloon | Azusa | 22 m E Los Angeles | Azusa. |
| Bohanan, J P | Farmer | Azusa Ranch | 1½ m S E Azusa | Azusa. |
| Bohannan, G W | Farmer | Azusa Ranch | 1 m S Azusa | Azusa. |
| Bohannan, J B | Farmer | | | El Monte. |
| Bohn, W A | Druggist | | | Los Angeles. |
| Boivin, A | Laborer | | | Los Angeles. |

| Name. | Occupation. | Place of Business. | Residence. |
|---|---|---|---|
| Boile, John | Plasterer | Los Angeles | Los Angeles |
| Bojorquez, A | Farmer | | |
| Boland, T | Salesman | Los Angeles | Los Angeles |
| Bolan, N M | Laborer | | |
| Boldt, Henry | Vintner | | |
| Boldt, Christian | Laborer | | |
| Bondolfi, V | Laborer | | |
| **Bond, G W** | Carpenter | Front st | Front st |
| **Bon, J P** | Mason | Los Angeles | Los Angeles |
| Bonet, Mrs L | | | Upper Main st |
| **Bonesteel, C A** | Stationer | Main st | |
| **Bonnelle, Peter A** | Merchant | Los Angeles | Los Angeles |
| Bonnomazon, J | Dyer | Los Angeles | Los Angeles |
| Bonsal, J | Farmer | San Pedro Ranch | 1¼ m N W Compton |
| **Bonshey, A** | Watch maker | Los Angeles | Los Angeles |
| Bonticue, E | Miller | Los Angeles | Los Angeles |
| Booth, N B | Confectioner | | |
| Borchard | Stock raiser | Soledad | 28 m N E Lyon Sta'n |
| Borchard, F | Farmer | | Los Nietos |
| Borden, O H | Farmer | | |
| Boring, Henry | Laborer | | |
| **Borrowe, W** | Contracter | 36 Main st | Main st |
| Borrowe, William | Agent | Los Angeles | Los Angeles |
| Boschke, A | Dredger | Los Angeles Co | Wilmington |
| Bosshard, Jacob | Laborer | | |
| Bostwick, J A | Tinner | Los Angeles | Los Angeles |
| Bosworth, B | Sailor | | Wilmington |
| Boswell, R P | Farmer | | |
| Botcher, C | Teamster | | |
| Botello, R | Butcher | | |
| Boteller, J B | Farmer | | |
| Botiller, D | Ranchero | | |
| Botillier, F | Farmer | | |
| Butieller, A | Farmer | | |
| Botiller, M J | Ranchero | | |
| Botiller, J J | Laborer | | |
| Botillerez, Y | Teamster | | |
| Botiller, E | Carpenter | | |
| Botiller, J J | Laborer | | |
| Botiller, B | Ranchero | | |
| Botiller, Plutarco | Ranchero | | |
| Botiller, Felipe | Farmer | | |
| Botiller, Fredrico | Laborer | | Santa Ana |
| Botiller, Tadeo | Merchant | Los Angeles | Los Angeles |
| Bott, Rev Joaquin | Catholic priest | Mission Church | San Gabriel |
| Bottoms, J T | Farmer | | San Joaquin |
| Bourbon, R | Tailor | Los Angeles | Los Angeles |
| Boushey, Stephen | Miner | | |
| **Bousall, J C** | Brick maker | Los Angeles | Los Angeles |
| Bousseaz, C | Laborer | | |
| Bouton, Edward | Sheep raiser | | |
| Bovard, M M | Minister | M E Church | Compton |
| Bowers, J W | Tel operator | Lexington | 12 m E Los Angeles |
| Bowers, Jacob | Farmer | El Monte Valley | 1½ m N Lexington |
| Bower, J | Farmer | | |
| Bowes, P | Farmer | | |
| Bowers, J | Farmer | | |
| Bowen, Walter, Jr | Clerk | Los Angeles | Los Angeles |
| Bowler, C H | Drover | | |
| Bowman, F R | Laborer | | |
| Bowman, J | Farmer | | |
| Bowman, A J | Well borer | | |
| Bowman, W H | Farmer | | Duarte |
| Boyce, J E | Machinist | Los Angeles | Los Angeles |

## DIRECTORY OF LOS ANGELES COUNTY. 321

| Name. | Occupation. | Place of Business. | Residence. | Town or P. O. |
|---|---|---|---|---|
| Boyd, E............... | Farmer ................. | ................................. | ................................. | Los Angeles. |
| Boyd, E H........... | Farmer ................. | ................................. | ................................. | Los Nietos. |
| Boyett, Mrs E H.... | ................................. | ................................. | 6 Beaudry Terrace... | Los Angeles. |
| Boyle, J F............ | Farmer ................. | ................................. | ................................. | Downey. |
| Boyle, T............... | Barkeeper............ | Los Angeles............ | Los Angeles............ | Los Angeles. |
| Bracamontes, J..... | Shoemaker........... | Los Angeles............ | Los Angeles............ | Los Angeles. |
| Brackett, J W....... | Gardener ............. | ................................. | ................................. | Anaheim. |
| Bradley, P........... | Teamster............... | ................................. | ................................. | Los Angeles. |
| Bradley, G Z........ | Laborer................. | ................................. | ................................. | El Monte. |
| Bradford, M W..... | Farmer ................. | ................................. | ................................. | Los Angeles. |
| Brady, G............... | Clerk.................... | Los Angeles............ | Los Angeles............ | Los Angeles. |
| Bradley, W........... | Painter ................. | Los Angeles............ | Los Angeles............ | Los Angeles. |
| Brady, P............... | Farmer ................. | ................................. | ................................. | Compton. |
| Bradfield, J W...... | Teamster............... | ................................. | ................................. | Los Angeles. |
| Bradshaw, J ......... | Tailor .................. | ................................. | ................................. | Wilmington. |
| Bradley, R........... | Laborer................. | ................................. | ................................. | Los Angeles. |
| Bradshaw, Joseph... | Tailor .................. | Canal st ............... | Canal st ............... | Wilmington. |
| Bradley, C H....... | Furniture ............ | 86 Main st............. | 4th st................... | Los Angeles. |
| Brader, C ........... | Soda mnf'r.......... | Los Angeles............ | Los Angeles............ | Los Angeles. |
| Bradshaw, Frank... | Laborer................. | ................................. | ................................. | Los Angeles. |
| Bradley, Cyrus H. | Merchant.............. | Los Angeles............ | Los Angeles............ | Los Angeles. |
| Bramberry, —...... | Apiarian............... | Placeritas.............. | 4 m N E Lyon Sta'n | Lyon Station. |
| Braman, J B........ | Attorney at law... | Los Angeles............ | Los Angeles............ | Los Angeles. |
| Branet, M............. | Dep Zanjero........ | ................................. | ................................. | Los Angeles. |
| Brannan, M........... | Laborer................. | ................................. | ................................. | Los Angeles. |
| Branch, J D ........ | Farmer ................. | ................................. | ................................. | Los Nietos. |
| Branstetter, J....... | Farmer ................. | ................................. | ................................. | Los Angeles. |
| Brantua, J........... | Shoemaker........... | ................................. | Wilmington............ | Wilmington. |
| Brandle, F........... | Butcher................. | Los Angeles............ | Los Angeles............ | Los Angeles. |
| Branscomb, H...... | Farmer ................. | ................................. | Los Nietos............. | Los Nietos. |
| Brand, W ........... | Butcher ............... | Los Angeles............ | Los Angeles............ | Los Angeles. |
| Bray, T................. | Teamster............... | ................................. | ................................. | Los Angeles. |
| Breckington, Mrs.. | Dressmaker.......... | Centre st............... | Anaheim................ | Anaheim. |
| Bredeiger, George... | Barkeeper ........... | Los Angeles............ | Los Angeles............ | Los Angeles. |
| Breeson, J............ | Laborer................. | ................................. | ................................. | Los Angeles. |
| Bree, J................. | Laborer................. | ................................. | ................................. | Los Angeles. |
| Breer, L............... | Blacksmith........... | Los Angeles............ | Los Angeles............ | Los Angeles. |
| Breen, Barney...... | Laborer................. | ................................. | ................................. | Los Angeles. |
| Bremmerman, H... | Hotel keeper........ | ................................. | ................................. | Anaheim. |
| Brenigen, F H..... | Machinist.............. | Los Angeles............ | Los Angeles............ | Los Angeles. |
| Brennan, J J........ | Horse trainer....... | ................................. | ................................. | Los Angeles. |
| Brenna, E............. | Engineer............... | ................................. | ................................. | Los Angeles. |
| Breson, Joseph..... | Saloon ................. | 105 Main st ........... | Los Angeles............ | Los Angeles. |
| Brewster, B ........ | Farmer ................. | ................................. | ................................. | El Monte. |
| Brewster, A.......... | Farmer ................. | ................................. | ................................. | San Gabriel. |
| Brewer, J H......... | Farmer ................. | ................................. | ................................. | Los Angeles. |
| Brewer, James M... | Teamster............... | ................................. | El Monte .............. | El Monte. |
| Brial, L............... | Barber.................. | Canal st ............... | Canal st................ | Wilmington. |
| Brierly, J R......... | Teacher................. | ................................. | ................................. | Compton. |
| Brite, Levy........... | Laborer................. | ................................. | ................................. | Los Angeles. |
| Broaded, J W ..... | Blacksmith........... | Lexington............. | 12 m E Los Angeles. | El Monte. |
| Brock, Charles ..... | Laborer................. | ................................. | ................................. | Wilmington. |
| Brockman, G H... | Farmer ................. | ................................. | ................................. | Azusa. |
| Brodrick, Mrs R.... | ................................. | ................................. | Alameda st............ | Los Angeles. |
| Brodrick, W J...... | Books, etc ........... | Spring st............... | 216 Main st .......... | Los Angeles. |
| Brodrick & Co..... | Books, stationery. | Spring st............... | ................................. | Los Angeles. |
| Brode, C............... | Groceries.............. | 79 Spring st.......... | ................................. | Los Angeles. |
| Brohan, W A....... | Farmer ................. | ................................. | ................................. | Wilmington. |
| Bronson, A C...... | Farmer ................. | Ellis Station.......... | 1 m W Lexington.... | El Monte. |
| Bronson, Abram C. | Teacher................. | ................................. | ................................. | Mission Viejo. |
| Brookout, S.......... | Farmer ................. | ................................. | ................................. | Los Angeles. |
| Brooks, James W... | Carpenter............. | ................................. | ................................. | Los Angeles. |
| Brooke, Dr S W.... | Physician & surg | San Franco's Build'g | 240 Main st .......... | Los Angeles. |
| Brook, T............... | Farmer ................. | ................................. | ................................. | Los Angeles. |

## MAP OF PART OF LOS ANGELES COUNTY
SHOWING THE
# "ABEL STEARNS' RANCHOS!"
### 128,000 ACRES! 200 SQUARE MILES! FARMING LANDS!

For sale in Sections or Fractions, on Liberal Terms, by

**ALFRED ROBINSON, Trustee, 542 Market Street, cor. Montgomery,**
SAN FRANCISCO.

**Or Apply to WM. R. OLDEN, Anaheim, California.**

The Famous Colonies, ANAHEIM, WESTMINSTER, ARTESIA, &c., are on these Lands.

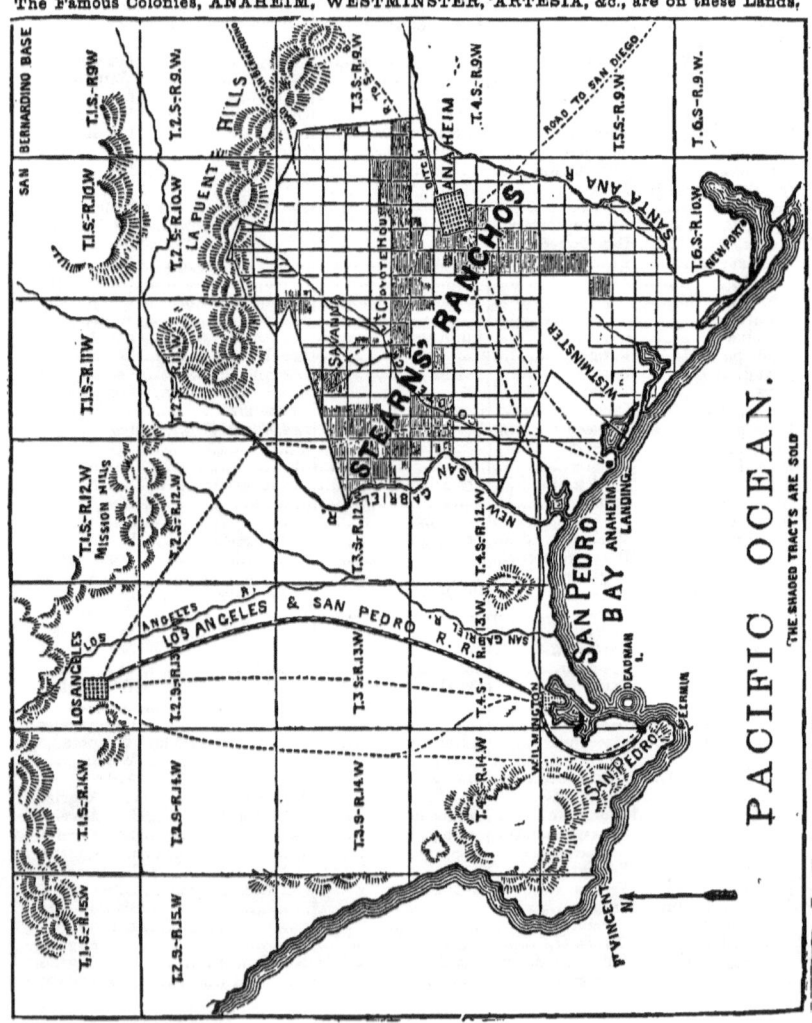

## DIRECTORY OF LOS ANGELES COUNTY. 323

| Name. | Occupation. | Place of Business. | Residence. | Town or P. O. |
|---|---|---|---|---|
| Brooks, W J | Shoemaker | | | Los Nietos. |
| Brooks, G C | | | | Wilmington. |
| Brooks, W H J | Searcher of rec'ds | Spring & Temple sts | Main st. | Los Angeles. |
| Brophy & Crowley | Blacksmiths | 1st st | | Wilmington. |
| Brophy, John | Blacksmith | 1st st | Wilmington | Wilmington. |
| Brophy, M | Stock raiser | Los Angeles Co | 6 m W Lyon Station | Lyon Station. |
| Brophy, Michael | Farmer | | | Los Angeles. |
| Brossmer, A | Carpenter | | | Los Angeles. |
| Brown, J C | Shoemaker | | | Los Nietos. |
| Brown, E | Laborer | Aliso Mills | Aliso st | Los Angeles. |
| Brown, Thomas | Carpenter | | | Santa Ana. |
| Brown, W H | Teamster | | | Los Angeles. |
| Brown, Peter | Laborer | | | Los Angeles. |
| Browner, W W | Printer | | | Los Angeles. |
| Brown, L | Laborer | | | Wilmington. |
| Brown, N A | Brewer | | | Los Angeles. |
| Brown, John | Laborer | | | Santa Ana. |
| Brown, D | Laborer | | | Azusa. |
| Brown, W R | | | | Downey. |
| Brown, William | Hunter | | | Los Angeles. |
| Brown, James | Tailor | | | Lor Angeles. |
| Brown, C B | Farmer | | | Los Angeles. |
| Brown, H | Barber | | | Los Angeles. |
| Brown, J | Laborer | | | Wilmington. |
| Brown, John | Farmer | | | Anaheim. |
| Brown, R | Miner | | | Los Angeles. |
| Brown, — | Farmer | Azusa Ranch | 1½ m N E Azusa | Azusa. |
| Brown, Robert | Farmer | | | Los Angeles. |
| Brown, Edward | Blacksmith | Wilmington | | Wilmington. |
| Brown, E | Laborer | | | Los Angeles. |
| Brown, G | Shoemaker | Los Angeles | Los Angeles | Los Angeles. |
| Brown, Samuel | Carpenter | | | Anaheim. |
| Brown, A J | Carpenter | | | Los Angeles. |
| Brown, John | Farmer | | | Anaheim. |
| Brown, J A | Cook | Los Angeles | Los Angeles | Los Angeles. |
| Brown, Mrs | | | Rebecca st | Wilmington. |
| Brown, W | Barkeeper | Canal st | Canal st | Wilmington. |
| Brown, R | Boarding house | San Pedro Bar | 4 m S Wilmington | Wilmington. |
| Brown, Rev T | Minister | | Wilmington | Wilmington. |
| Brown, W T | Forwarding clerk | S P R R Co | Canal st | Wilmington. |
| Brown, Mrs C | | | Olive st | Los Angeles. |
| Brown, Mrs B | Seamstress | | Olive st nr 4th | Los Angeles. |
| Brown & Co, N A | Phil'a Brewery | Los Angeles | Los Angeles | Los Angeles. |
| Brown, Mrs Flora | Milliner | Centre st | Anaheim | Anaheim. |
| Brown, R | Farmer | | Anaheim | Anaheim. |
| Brown, S | Blacksmith | Los Angeles | Los Angeles | Los Angeles. |
| Browning, W A | Law student | Los Angeles | Los Angeles | Los Angeles. |
| Brown, Edward E | Shoemaker | Los Angeles | Los Angeles | Los Angeles. |
| Brown, David M | Physician | | San Gabriel | San Gabriel. |
| Bruce, M D | Farmer | | | Los Angeles. |
| Bruggeman, H | Blacksmith | | San Jose | Spadra. |
| Brunning, H N | Clerk | | | Wilmington. |
| Brunson, A | Lawyer | Los Angeles | Los Angeles | Los Angeles. |
| Brunk, D D | Lawyer | Los Angeles | Los Angeles | Los Angeles. |
| Brundage, Mrs | | | Temple & B Vista sts | Los Angeles. |
| Brunk & Bruck | | | | Los Angeles. |
| Brunson & Hudson | Att'ys at law | 29 & 30 Temple Blk. | | Los Angeles. |
| Brunson, A | Att'y at law | 29 & 30 Temple Blk. | Figueroa & Adams sts | Los Angeles. |
| Brush, Joel C | Carpenter | | | Los Angeles. |
| Brush, J C | Contractor | 13 Downey Block | Hope st | Los Angeles. |
| Bruttig, Peter | Butcher | Los Angeles | Los Angeles | Los Angeles. |
| Bruttig, C | Gardener | Los Angeles | Los Angeles | El Monte. |
| Bryant, B S | Constable | El Monte Valley | 1 m E Lexington | Los Angeles. |
| Bryand, John | Painter | | | Los Angeles. |

324

L. L. PAULSON'S HAND-BOOK AND

| Name. | Occupation. | Place of Business. | Residence. | Town or P. O. |
|---|---|---|---|---|
| Bryant, Barney S... | Farmer | | | Los Angeles. |
| Bryant, Samuel H .. | Farmer | | | Los Angeles. |
| Bryall, Louis | Cook | | | Los Angeles. |
| **Bryan, John** | Blacksmith | Los Angeles | Los Angeles | Los Angeles. |
| Bryant, J L | Farmer | | | Florence. |
| Bryant, J J | Painter | Los Angeles | Los Angeles | Los Angeles. |
| Bryant, George | Stage driver | | | Los Angeles. |
| Bryel, Louis | Barber | | | Los Angeles. |
| Brymer, J | Laborer | | | Los Nietos. |
| Bryson, William | Plasterer | | | Los Angeles. |
| Buchanan, J W C . | Builder | | | Los Angeles. |
| Buchanan, S H | Carpenter | | | Los Angeles. |
| **Buck, Otho J** | Dairyman | Westminster Col. | Westminster Col. | Westminster. |
| Buck, R E | Farmer | | | Los Nietos. |
| Buckman, S S F | Teacher | Wilmington | | Wilmington. |
| **Buckley, J** | Coppersmith | | | |
| Buckley, W | Laborer | | | Los Angeles. |
| Buelna, Leandro | Laborer | | | Los Angeles. |
| **Buelner, Juan** | Cigar maker | Los Angeles | Los Angeles | Los Angeles. |
| **Buelna, J A** | Cigar maker | Los Angeles | Los Angeles | Los Angeles. |
| Buelner, Antonio | Laborer | | Anaheim | Anaheim. |
| Buelna, Manuel | Merchant | | Los Nietos | Los Nietos. |
| Buelna, Jesus | Waiter | | | Los Angeles. |
| **Buelner, Jose** | Merchant | Los Angeles | Los Angeles | Los Angeles. |
| Buettel, Frank | Tailor | Los Angeles | Los Angeles | Los Angeles. |
| Buet, A | Laborer | | | Los Angeles. |
| **Buhler, A** | Baker | Los Angeles | Los Angeles | Los Angeles. |
| Bullis, John Jay | Dairyman | | | Compton. |
| Bullis, Ormi | Farmer | | | Florence. |
| Bullis, John A | Farmer | | | Florence. |
| Bullis, J D | Butcher | | | Compton. |
| Bullis, J J | Farmer | | | Compton. |
| **Bullis, P H** | Farmer | San Pedro Ranch | 1½ m N E Compton | Compton. |
| **Bullis, J D** | Farmer | San Pedro Ranch | 1½ m N E Compton | Compton. |
| Bullis, Ormi | Dairy | San Pedro Ranch | 2½ m N Compton | Compton. |
| Bumiller, Charles.. | Grocer | | | Los Angeles. |
| **Bumiller, J** | Tobacconist | Los Angeles | Los Angeles | Los Angeles. |
| Bumuller, Fidel | Miner | | | Los Angeles. |
| Bunyard, B | Farmer | Azusa Duarte | 3 m E Lexington | El Monte. |
| Bunyard, D | Farmer | Lexington | 12 m E Los Angeles | El Monte. |
| Bunyard, L S | Farmer | Lexington | 12 m E Los Angeles | El Monte. |
| **Bunch, J P** | Gunsmith | El Monte | | El Monte. |
| Bunn, W | Carpenter | S P R R Co | Wilmington | Wilmington. |
| **Burbank, D** | Doctor | Los Angeles | Los Angeles | Los Angeles. |
| **Burbank, W** | Stock raiser | | | Los Angeles. |
| Burchard, D | Farmer | | | San Fernando. |
| **Burdick, Edson A** | Merchant | Los Angeles | Los Angeles | Los Angeles. |
| Burdick, Thomas H | Clerk | | | Los Angeles. |
| Burdick, Thomas | Farmer | | | Los Angeles. |
| **Burdick, T** | Farmer | San Bernardino Road | 4 m E Spadra | Spadra. |
| **Burdick, S** | Farmer | San Bernardino Road | 4 m E Spadra | Spadra. |
| Burdick, C | Farmer | | | Azusa. |
| **Burdick, H** | Merchant | Los Angeles | Los Angeles | Los Angeles. |
| Burden, D C | Farmer | | | Downey. |
| Burdick, H | Clerk | Sheriff's office | cor Spring & 2d sts | Los Angeles. |
| Burgess, Lewis | Farmer | | | Los Angeles. |
| Burgiss, Hiram | Farmer | | | Los Angeles. |
| **Burgess, R F** | Dentist | Main & Com'l sts | Los Angeles | Los Angeles. |
| Burkhardt, John V | Baker | Los Angeles | | Los Angeles. |
| Burkle, R | Farmer | | | Anaheim. |
| Burke, George W | Farmer | | | Downey. |
| Burke, Joseph H | Farmer | | | Los Nietos. |
| Burkle, Ferdinand | Laborer | | | Wilmington. |
| Burke, R | Teamster | | | Los Angeles. |

DIRECTORY OF LOS ANGELES COUNTY. 325

| Name. | Occupation. | Place of Business. | Residence. | Town or P. O. |
|---|---|---|---|---|
| Burke, M............... | Carpenter ............ | ............... ............... | ............... ............... | El Monte. |
| Burkhardt & Ebinger ......... | N Y Bakery ...... | Main st................. | ............... ............... | Los Angeles. |
| Burkhardt, A........ | Baker................ | Los Angeles......... | Los Angeles............ | Los Angeles. |
| Burlem, Edward..... | Laborer................ | ............... ............... | ............... ............... | Santa Ana. |
| Burlingame, H ...... | Farmer ............ | San Pedro Ranch.... | 1¼ m W Compton ... | Compton. |
| Burns, David......... | Farmer ............ | ............... ............... | ............... ............... | San Gabriel. |
| Burns, Elias James. | Farmer ............ | ............... ............... | ............... ............... | El Monte. |
| Burns, Martin........ | Teamster ........ | ............... ............... | ............... ............... | Los Angeles. |
| Burns, John ......... | Bricklayer............ | ............... ............... | ............... ............... | Los Angeles. |
| Burn, — ................. | Farmer ............ | Azusa Ranch........... | 2¼ m S W Azusa..... | Azusa. |
| Burns, Peter.......... | Miner............... | Azusa.................... | Azusa................... | Azusa. |
| Burnes, R.............. | Carpenter ............ | ............... ............... | ............... ............... | San Juan. |
| Burnam, W........... | Farmer ............ | ............... ............... | ............... ............... | Los Angeles. |
| Burns, P L........... | Blacksmith ........ | Wilmington............ | ............... ............... | Wilmington. |
| Burnham, Mrs R E | ............... ............ | ............... ............... | 3d & Polyxena sts.... | Los Angeles. |
| Burns, M L........... | Capitalist............. | ............... ............... | cor Hill & Fort sts... | Los Angeles. |
| Burns, J F............. | Collector............ | ............... ............... | Clarendon Hotel ...... | Los Angeles. |
| Burns, J Frank...... | Saloon.............. | SantaMonica Canyon | Santa Monica ......... | Los Angeles. |
| Burnett, P H......... | Banker................. | Pacific Bank ............ | ............... ............... | Los Angeles. |
| Burnham, J H....... | Machinist ............ | S P R R Co............. | Wilmington............. | Wilmington. |
| Burns, W............... | Carpenter ............ | ............... ............... | Anaheim............. | Anaheim. |
| Burruel, Desiderio... | Ranchero............ | ............... ............... | ............... ............... | Santa Ana. |
| Burruel, A............. | Laborer ............ | ............... ............... | ............... ............... | Santa Ana. |
| Burruel, T ............ | Shoe maker......... | ............... ............... | ............... ............... | San Juan. |
| Burrows, J............ | Laborer ............ | ............... ............... | ............... ............... | Soledad. |
| Burns, Joshua....... | Farmer ............ | ............... ............... | Anaheim ............ | Anaheim. |
| Burris, T................ | Farmer ............ | ............... ............... | Anaheim ............ | Anaheim. |
| Burton, C C.......... | Hair dresser ....... | 9 Spring st.............. | Spring st................ | Los Angeles. |
| Burtnett, Dr J N... | Physician & Surg | Faulkner's Hotel...... | Santa Ana .............. | Santa Ana. |
| Burt, George B ..... | Farmer ............ | ............... ............... | Wilmington ......... | Wilmington. |
| Busten, David ....... | Farmer ............ | ............... ............... | San Joaquin............ | Santa Ana. |
| Bush, William ....... | Farmer ............ | ............... ............... | ............... ............... | Santa Ana. |
| Bush, Charles W... | Doctor............... | Los Angeles............ | Los Angeles............ | Los Angeles. |
| Bush, John M........ | Ranchero........ | ............... ............... | ............... ............... | Anaheim. |
| Bush, John James.. | Farmer ............ | ............... ............... | ............... ............... | Santa Ana. |
| Bush, Abram L..... | Farmer ............ | ............... ............... | ............... ............... | Santa Ana. |
| Bush, Charles H... | Merchant............ | Los Angeles............ | Los Angeles............ | Los Angeles. |
| Bush, H M............. | Lithographer ...... | Los Angeles............ | Los Angeles............ | Los Angeles. |
| Bush, C H.............. | Watch maker....... | 79 Main st............... | Los Angeles............ | Los Angeles. |
| Bustamante, Jose.... | Miner ............. | ............... ............... | ............... ............... | Soledad. |
| Bustamante, F...... | Baker ............... | Los Angeles............ | ............... ............... | Los Angeles. |
| Bustamente, Jesus .. | Farmer ............ | ............... ............... | ............... ............... | Los Angeles. |
| Buster, F M ......... | Boarding house... | Wilson's College...... | Wilmington ......... | Wilmington. |
| Bustamente, Manuel | Laborer ............. | ............... ............... | Anaheim ............ | Anaheim. |
| Buster, Francis M... | Farmer ............ | ............... ............... | ............... ............... | Downey. |
| Bustamente, A...... | Farmer ............ | ............... ............... | Anaheim ............ | Anaheim. |
| Bustamente, S...... | Farmer ............ | ............... ............... | Anaheim ............ | Anaheim. |
| Bustamente, Jesus .. | Farmer ............ | ............... ............... | Anaheim ............ | Anaheim. |
| Butievas, Simon .... | Laborer ............ | ............... ............... | ............... ............... | Los Angeles. |
| Butler, George E... | Clergyman ......... | ............... ............... | ............... ............... | Los Nietos. |
| Butler, George R.... | Stage driver......... | ............... ............... | ............... ............... | Los Angeles. |
| Butler, George....... | Stock ............... | Spadra................... | 30 m E Los Angeles | Spadra. |
| Butler, Francisco... | Builder................ | ............... ............... | ............... ............... | Los Angeles. |
| Butler, F R........... | Miller ............... | Los Angeles............ | Los Angeles............ | Los Angeles. |
| Butler, J M............ | Farmer ............ | ............... ............... | ............... ............... | El Monte. |
| Butler, S A............ | R R employee...... | ............... ............... | ............... ............... | Los Angeles. |
| Butler, George....... | Switchman.......... | S P R R Co............. | Wilmington ......... | Wilmington. |
| Butterworth, E S... | Farmer ............ | ............... ............... | ............... ............... | Los Angeles. |
| Butterfield, S H..... | Teacher ............ | ............... ............... | ............... ............... | Downey. |
| Button, S B........... | Laborer ............ | ............... ............... | ............... ............... | Wilmington. |
| Byas, Pleasant...... | Carpenter ............ | ............... ............... | ............... ............... | El Monte. |
| Byrd, James D...... | Farmer ............ | ............... ............... | ............... ............... | Anaheim. |
| Byrd, W J............. | Farmer ............ | ............... ............... | Silver Precinct........ | Downey. |

J. C. MORGAN.                                                            JAS. MONROE.

# MORGAN & MONROE,

—— PROPRIETORS OF ——

# SANTA MONICA HOTEL

## LOS ANGELES COUNTY, CAL.

Only one hundred yards from the Depot and Wharf, at the Terminus of the Los Angeles and Independence R. R.

## A Roomy, Well-Conducted Hotel,

Capable of accommodating all visitors.

Extreme Care used in attending to the wants and comforts of Guests.

The most perfect facilities for

# SEA BATHING.

**BATH HOUSES** for those preferring them, and Bathing Suits furnished if desired.

DIRECTORY OF LOS ANGELES COUNTY. 327

| Name. | Occupation. | Place of Business. | Residence. | Town or P. O. |
|---|---|---|---|---|
| Byrne, Peter | Wheelwright | | | Wilmington. |
| Byrne, M J | Miner | | Azusa | Azusa. |
| Byrne, John | Baker | Los Angeles | Los Angeles | Los Angeles. |
| Cabanis, L G | | | | San Gabriel. |
| Cabanis, Mrs E S | Mantua maker | San Gabriel | 9 m E Los Angeles | San Gabriel. |
| Cabanis, L G | Notary public | 44 Temple Block | Los Angeles | Los Angeles. |
| Cabanis & Madegan | Brokers | Los Angeles | Los Angeles | Los Angeles. |
| Cable, J W | Teamster | | | Los Angeles. |
| Cabot, Charles | Agent | | | Los Angeles. |
| Cabot, C | Attorney | Temple Block | Los Angeles | Los Angeles. |
| Cadenas, Manuel | Laborer | | | Los Angeles. |
| Cadierque, F G | Speculator | | | Los Angeles. |
| Cadierque, M | Farmer | | | Los Angeles. |
| Cage, E H | Farmer | | | San Gabriel. |
| Cagin, S | Farmer | | | Los Angeles. |
| Cahn, Abram S | Merchant | Los Angeles | Los Angeles | Los Angeles. |
| Cahn, Nathan | Clerk | Los Angeles | Los Angeles | Los Angeles. |
| Caines, R | Plasterer | Los Angeles | Los Angeles | Los Angeles. |
| Cainarcho, T | Farmer | | | Los Nietos. |
| Cain, Michael | Teamster | | | Los Angeles. |
| Cain, Edward | Laborer | | | Los Angeles. |
| Calahan, Braxton | Farmer | | | Downey. |
| Caldwell, T A | Farmer | | | El Monte. |
| Caldwell & Bro | Merchandise | Spadra | 30 m E Los Angeles | Spadra. |
| Caldwell, Joseph | Farmer | Westminster Col | Westminster Col | Westminster. |
| Caldwell, A B | Merchandise | Spadra | 30 m E Los Angeles | Spadra. |
| Caldwell, T A | Merchandise | Spadra | 30 m E Los Angeles | Spadra. |
| Caldwell, J A | Farmer | Azusa | 2¼ m S W Azusa | Azusa. |
| Caldwell, J P | Farmer | | | El Monte. |
| Caldwell, A B | Farmer | | | San Jose. |
| Caley, T E | Teacher | Azusa Ranch | 1 m E Azusa | Azusa. |
| Calisher, Morris | Merchant | Anaheim | Anaheim | Anaheim. |
| Calisher, & Co, M | Merchandise | Anaheim | Anaheim | Anaheim. |
| Callaghan, James | Laundryman | Los Angeles | Los Angeles | Los Angeles. |
| Callahan, Edward | Farmer | | | San Gabriel. |
| Callahan, J | Laborer | San Gabriel | 9 m E Los Angeles | San Gabriel. |
| Callahan, W | Carpenter | San Gabriel | 9 m E Los Angeles | San Gabriel. |
| Callicott, W H | Engineer | S P R R Co | Wilmington | Wilmington. |
| Callumbe, W C | Miner | | | Los Angeles. |
| Callahan, John | Cook | Wilmington Ex | Canal st | Wilmington. |
| Calton, David | Farmer | | | Downey. |
| Caman, F | Carpenter | Los Angeles Co | Los Angeles Co | Los Angeles. |
| Camacho, L | Laborer | | | Los Angeles. |
| Cameron, A | Miner | | | Los Angeles. |
| Campbell, J T | Farmer | | | Azusa. |
| Campbell, S R | Blacksmith | Los Angeles | Los Angeles | Los Angeles. |
| Campbell, Joseph | Engineer | | | Los Angeles. |
| Campion, J S | Trader | | | Los Angeles. |
| Campbell, C B | Farmer | | | Downey. |
| Campe, C | Laborer | Wilmington | Wilmington | Wilmington. |
| Campos, F | Teacher | Los Angeles Co | Los Angeles Co | Los Angeles. |
| Campbell, A | Machinist | S P R R Co | Canal st | Wilmington. |
| Campbell, J H | Farmer | | | Downey. |
| Campbell, Irving | Druggist | Anaheim | | Anaheim. |
| Campion, W S | Teacher | Jan Juan | | San Juan. |
| Campbell, H | Agent | Los Angeles Town'p | Los Angeles Co | Los Angeles. |
| Campbell, B C | Farmer | | | Downey. |
| Campbell, D | Livery stable | 27 Aliso st | Sansevain st | Los Angeles. |
| Campbell, T P | Merchant | Los Angeles | Los Angeles | Los Angeles. |
| Campbell, A M | Minister | Los Angeles | Los Angeles | Los Angeles. |
| Campbell, Rev J M | Clergyman | Methodist Church | Fort st | Los Angeles. |
| Cannsave, Pierre | Stock raiser | | | Los Angeles. |
| Canalius, Thomas | Laborer | | | Wilmington. |
| Candle, Aurelius | Farmer | | | Downey. |
| Camillo | Barber | Los Angeles. Opp N. Temple st. | | Los Angeles. |

site the Court House.

| NAME. | OCCUPATION. | PLACE OF BUSINESS. | RESIDENCE. | TOWN OR P. O. |
|---|---|---|---|---|
| Candle, C R | Farmer | | | Los Nietos. |
| Can, Samuel | Tailor | Los Angeles | Los Angeles | Los Angeles. |
| Candill, T J | Farmer | | Anaheim | Anaheim. |
| Candill, C D | Farmer | | Anaheim | Anaheim. |
| Caneda, Juan | Laborer | | | Santa Ana. |
| Caneda, Jose S | Laborer | | | Los Angeles. |
| Canedo, Juan C | Vaquero | | | Compton. |
| Cane, Raphael | Farmer | | | Los Nietos. |
| Canedo, J | Farmer | | | Los Angeles. |
| Caneda, D | Musician | Los Angeles | Los Angeles | Los Angeles. |
| Canedo, F | Laborer | | | Los Angeles. |
| Canedo, D | Farmer | | | Los Nietos. |
| Cnedo, A | Vaquero | | | Los Angeles. |
| Canillo, S | Farmer | | | Los Angeles. |
| Canillo, J R | Farmer | | | Anaheim. |
| Canillo, E | Laborer | | | Los Angeles. |
| Canios, S | Laborer | | | Los Angeles. |
| Canillo, A E | Farmer | | | Los Angeles. |
| Canillo, W R | Farmer | | | Los Nietos. |
| Canillo, C | Laborer | | | Los Angeles. |
| Cannon, M | Laborer | | | Los Angeles. |
| Cannona, J G | Merchant | Los Angeles | Los Angeles | Los Angeles. |
| Cans, F | Laborer | | | Los Angeles. |
| Cantua, A | Laborer | | | Los Angeles. |
| Cape, W | Hotel proprietor | New High st | New High st | Los Angeles. |
| Capps, T J | Farmer | Azusa Ranch | 2 m S Azusa | Azusa. |
| Cappe, J | Liquor dealer | | | Los Angeles. |
| Capurro, A | Clerk | Los Angeles | Los Angeles | Los Angeles. |
| Capurro, J | Clerk | Los Angeles | Los Angeles | Los Angeles. |
| Carasco, F | Laborer | | | Los Angeles. |
| Caravajal, R | Farmer | | | Los Angeles. |
| Caravan, T | Stable keeper | Anaheim | Anaheim | Anaheim. |
| Carey, L A | Farmer | | Westminster Col | Westminster. |
| Carey, T | Farmer | | | Los Angeles. |
| Carey, J | Farmer | | Westminster Col | Westminster. |
| Carey, M | Blacksmith | S P R R Co | Canal st | Wilmington. |
| Carlile, W E | Steward | | | Los Angeles. |
| Carlin, J | Laborer | | | Los Angeles. |
| Carlyle, T | Laborer | | | Los Angeles. |
| Carlton, J J | Carpenter | | | Los Angeles. |
| Carlisle, T | Farmer | | | Los Angeles. |
| Carney, Isaac | Farmer | | Silver District | Downey. |
| Carpenter, Ira | Farmer | 6 m S E Los Angeles | San Antonio | Downey. |
| Carpenter, J A | Broom maker | | | Downey. |
| Carpenter, John T | Farmer | | | Los Angeles. |
| Carpenter, S | Farmer | | | Los Angeles. |
| Carpenter, P | Farmer | | | Los Angeles. |
| Carpenter, E B | Engineer | Los Angeles | Los Angeles | Los Angeles. |
| Carpenter, A | Sheep raiser | | | Orange. |
| Carpenter, J H | Farmer | | | Los Neitos. |
| Carpenter, J G | Farmer | | | Los Angeles. |
| Carpenter, F J | Farmer | | | Los Angeles. |
| Carpenter, F P | Farmer | | | Los Nietos. |
| Carriage, J A | Farmer | | | Los Angeles. |
| Carillo, F | Laborer | | | San Gabriel. |
| Carrillaga, M | Vaquero | | | Los Argeles. |
| Carrisosa, J M | Laborer | | | San Gabriel. |
| Carrasco, J | Vaquero | | | El Monte. |
| Carrosa, N | Laborer | | | San Gabriel. |
| Carrera, Y | Laborer | | | Los Angeles. |
| Carrasco, R | Laborer | | | Los Angeles. |
| Carrisosa, F | Laborer | | | San Gabriel. |
| Carrillo, P C | Laborer | | | Los Angeles. |
| Carr, James | Laborer | | | Los Angeles. |

# DIRECTORY OF LOS ANGELES COUNTY.

| Name. | Occupation. | Place of Business. | Residence. | Town or P. O. |
|---|---|---|---|---|
| Carrillo, D............ | Farmer............ | ............ | ............ | San Gabriel. |
| Carr, John S........ | Farmer............ | ............ | ............ | Los Angeles. |
| Carrillo, Felipe...... | Laborer............ | ............ | ............ | Los Angeles. |
| Carrillo, J C........ | Ranchero........... | ............ | ............ | Los Angeles. |
| Carreras, Rodolfo... | Refiner of oils...... | ............ | ............ | Los Angeles. |
| Carrissossa, Jesus... | Laborer............ | ............ | San Jose............ | Spadra. |
| Carroll, Patrick..... | Teamster........... | ............ | ............ | Los Angeles. |
| Carroll, Timothy.. | Farmer............ | ............ | Anaheim............ | Anaheim. |
| Carson, G............ | Tinsmith........... | ............ | ............ | Los Angeles. |
| Carson, S C........ | Laborer............ | ............ | ............ | Compton. |
| Carson, George..... | Stock raiser........ | Domingues Ranch.... | 7 m N Wilmington.. | Wilmington. |
| Carson, H............ | Sheep raiser........ | Domingues Ranch.... | 2½ m S Compton..... | Compton. |
| Carter, W T........ | Farmer............ | ............ | ............ | Downey. |
| Carter, C C........ | Farmer............ | ............ | ............ | San Fernando. |
| Carty, Thomas...... | Laborer............ | ............ | ............ | Wilmington. |
| Carthery, J......... | Laborer............ | ............ | ............ | Los Angeles. |
| Carter, N C........ | Speculator......... | Los Angeles............ | San Gabriel Valley... | Los Angeles. |
| Cartirer, P......... | Herder............ | ............ | ............ | Los Angeles. |
| Carter, S............ | Farmer............ | Azusa Duarte........ | 4 m E Lexington..... | El Monte. |
| Carter, G W........ | Hackman........... | ............ | ............ | Los Angeles. |
| Caruthers, W....... | Farmer............ | ............ | ............ | Los Nietos. |
| Cary, W H......... | Farmer............ | ............ | ............ | Compton. |
| Cary, L A......... | Farmer............ | ............ | ............ | Compton. |
| Casaday, M........ | Farmer............ | ............ | ............ | |
| Casad, Miss A H... | Teacher............ | ............ | ............ | Los Angeles. |
| Casey, James M..... | Farmer............ | ............ | San Joaquin......... | Santa Ana. |
| Casey, J W........ | Farmer............ | Azusa Ranch........ | 2 m N E Azusa...... | Azusa. |
| Casey, M............ | Blacksmith........ | C P R R Co........ | Wilmington........ | Wilmington. |
| Casey, T............ | Hostler............ | ............ | ............ | Los Angeles. |
| Casey, John........ | Farmer............ | Azusa Ranch........ | 2 m N E Azusa...... | Azusa. |
| Cash, S............ | Laborer............ | ............ | ............ | Los Angeles. |
| Cashion, J........... | Engineer........... | Los Angeles............ | Los Angeles............ | Los Angeles. |
| Cason, C............ | Restaurant prop'r | Main st............ | ............ | Los Angeles. |
| Casserly, J......... | Laborer............ | ............ | ............ | Los Nietos. |
| Cassidy, J J........ | Operator........... | Los Angeles............ | Los Angeles............ | Los Angeles. |
| Casseam, Pierre..... | Shepherd........... | ............ | Anaheim............ | Anaheim. |
| Cassiday, Patrick... | Bricklayer......... | Los Angeles............ | Los Angeles............ | Los Angeles. |
| Cassaque, C........ | Livery stable....... | Los Angeles st........ | Los Angeles............ | Los Angeles. |
| Cassady, Henry..... | Farmer............ | ............ | ............ | Anaheim. |
| Cassard, T......... | Farmer............ | ............ | ............ | Santa Ana. |
| Cassady, P,........ | Laborer............ | ............ | ............ | Los Angeles. |
| Castro, E........... | Harness maker...... | ............ | ............ | Los Angeles. |
| Castro, Francisco... | Laborer............ | Wilmington............ | Wilmington............ | Wilmington. |
| Castillo, S......... | Ranchero........... | ............ | ............ | Los Angeles. |
| Castro, L........... | Laborer............ | ............ | ............ | Los Angeles. |
| Castillo, R......... | Laborer............ | ............ | ............ | San Fernando. |
| Castruccio, Pietro... | Merchant........... | Los Angeles............ | Los Angeles............ | Los Angeles. |
| Castro, Mauricio.... | Laborer............ | ............ | ............ | San Gabriel. |
| Castro, M........... | Laborer............ | ............ | ............ | |
| Castro, J........... | Laborer............ | ............ | ............ | Los Angeles. |
| Castro, J D........ | Waiter............ | ............ | ............ | Los Angeles. |
| Castilla, J......... | Farmer............ | ............ | ............ | San Gabriel. |
| Castile, T.......... | Butcher............ | Los Angeles............ | Los Angeles............ | Los Angeles. |
| Castello, J......... | Laborer............ | ............ | ............ | San Jose. |
| Castillo, C......... | Laborer............ | ............ | Anaheim............ | Anaheim. |
| Castro, Mrs E..... | Dress maker........ | Los Angeles............ | Los Angeles............ | Los Angeles. |
| Caswell & Ellis.... | General merch'se | 80 and 82 Main st..... | ............ | Los Angeles. |
| Caswell, S B........ | Merchant........... | Los Angeles............ | Los Angeles............ | Los Angeles. |
| Cate, George........ | Farmer............ | ............ | ............ | El Monte. |
| Cates, A............ | Laborer............ | ............ | ............ | Los Angeles. |
| Cathcart, W M..... | Laborer............ | ............ | Silver Precinct........ | Downey. |
| Causet, L........... | Bar keeper......... | ............ | ............ | Los Angeles. |
| Cavarrubias, S..... | Carpenter.......... | ............ | ............ | Los Angeles. |
| Cave, McRea....... | Wool grower....... | ............ | San Joaquin......... | Santa Ana. |

E. P. F. TEMPLE.                          WM. WORKMAN.

# TEMPLE & WORKMAN,

## BANKERS,

TEMPLE BLOCK,   ·  ·   LOS ANGELES.

RECEIVE DEPOSITS, AND ISSUE THEIR CERTIFICATES, AND TRANSACT A

## GENERAL BANKING BUSINESS,

Draw on the London & San Francisco Bank (Limited), at San Francisco.

EXCHANGE FOR SALE ON

NEW YORK,          HAMBURG,
LONDON,            BERLIN AND
PARIS,               FRANKFORT.

Legal Tenders, Bullion, Gold Dust, and Government, State, County and City Bonds Bought and Sold. Receive Valuables for Safe Keeping.

## DIRECTORY OF LOS ANGELES COUNTY. 331

| NAME. | OCCUPATION. | PLACE OF BUSINESS. | RESIDENCE. | TOWN OR P. O. |
|---|---|---|---|---|
| Cawltren, C. | Mechanic | | | Los Angeles. |
| Caywood, J B | Laborer | | | San Gabriel. |
| Cayac, Louis C | Cook | Los Angeles | Los Angeles | Los Angeles. |
| Caystile, T J | Printer | 9 Temple st | Pose st | Los Angeles. |
| Cecil, J M | Farmer | | | El Monte. |
| Cecil, J N | Saloon | Lexington | 12 m F. Los Angeles. | El Monte. |
| Celalla, J J | Farmer | | | San Gabriel. |
| Celis, Jose M de | Artist | Los Angeles | Los Angeles | Los Angeles. |
| Celis, Adolfo | Laborer | | | Los Angeles. |
| Celis, E de, Jr | Real estate | | | Los Angeles. |
| **Celis, Juan** | Butcher | San Fernando Valley | 2½ m N W S Fern'do | San Fernando. |
| Coralis, J J | Laborer | | | Los Angeles. |
| Cereda, T | Fruit dealer | Los Angeles | Los Angeles | Los Angeles. |
| Cervantes, A | Vaquero | | | San Gabriel. |
| Chacon, J M | Ranchero | | | San Jose. |
| Chadsey, B | Carpenter | | | Los Angeles. |
| Chalfin, A S | Farmer | | | Los Angeles. |
| Champion, A A | Farmer | | | El Monte. |
| Chambers, H | Teamster | | | Compton. |
| **Champion, J D** | Farmer | San Bernardino Rd | 1¼ m E Lexington | El Monte. |
| Champlin, E W | Carpenter | | | |
| Champion, E H | Farmer | | | El Monte. |
| Chandler, W E A | Japanner | | | Wilmington. |
| Chaney, W W | Farmer | | | Downey. |
| Chanvin, A C | Groceries | 70 Main st | 153 Spring st | Los Angeles. |
| Chanel, Jacques | Blacksmith | | | Los Angeles. |
| **Chapman & Hutton** | Attorneys at law | Temple Block | | Los Angeles. |
| **Chapman, R H** | Attorney at law | Temple Block | Los Angeles | Los Angeles. |
| Chapman, A B | Attorney | Temple Block | 181 Main st | Los Angeles. |
| Chappell, W T | Farmer | | El Monte | El Monte. |
| Chappell, J B | Farmer | | | El Monte. |
| **Chappell, W** | Teamster | Lexington | 12 m E Los Angeles. | El Monte. |
| **Chappell, R D** | Teamster | Lexington | 12 m E Los Angeles. | El Monte. |
| **Chapman, W S** | Vintner | San Gabriel Valley | 13 m N E Los A | Los Angeles. |
| Chapman, J | Laborer | | | Los Angeles. |
| Chapman, O | Farmer | | | Los Angeles. |
| Chapman, C P | Farmer | | | Los Angeles. |
| **Chapin, H** | Farmer | | | Los Nietos. |
| Charles, H | Farmer | | | S J Capistrano. |
| Ohnse, F G | Laborer | | | Los Angeles. |
| **Chase, Reuben H** | Physician | Los Angeles | Los Angeles | Los Angeles. |
| Chase, Robert H | Miner | | | Los Angeles. |
| Chate, J W | Farmer | | | Los Nietos. |
| **Chauvin, A C** | Merchant | Los Angeles | Los Angeles | Los Angeles. |
| Chavez, Jose A | Farmer | | | Los Angeles. |
| Chavez, Ramon | Laborer | | | Los Angeles. |
| Chavis, J A | Farmer | | | Los Angeles. |
| Chavis, P | Ranchero | | | San Jose. |
| Chavis, G | Ranchero | | | Los Angeles. |
| Chaves, T | Laborer | | | Los Angeles. |
| **Chavis, Patricio** | Farmer | San Jose Valley | 4 m S W Spadra | Spadra. |
| Chavis, J M | Farmer | | | Los Angeles. |
| Chavanne, C G | Clerk | Los Angeles | Los Angeles | Los Angeles. |
| Chavis, J J A S | Vaquero | | Los Angeles Co | Spadra. |
| Chaves, J P | Ranchero | Los Angeles Co | near Spadra | Spadra. |
| Chavoya, J | Ranchero | near Los Angeles | Los Angeles Co | Los Angeles. |
| Chavis, R | Ranchero | near Los Angeles | Los Angeles Co | Los Angeles. |
| **Chavis, M** | Farmer | near Los Angeles | Los Angeles Co | Los Angeles. |
| Cheesman, M H | Farmer | near Downey | Los Angeles Co | Downey. |
| Cheney, Arthur H | Farmer | Los Angeles Co | near Downey | Downey. |
| Chenney, T S | Tanner | Downey | Downey | Downey. |
| Chenney, Tilford D | Tanner | | | Downey. |
| Cheny, C C | Farmer | near Downey | Los Angeles Co | Downey. |
| Chevallier, P F V | Druggist | Los Angeles | Los Angeles | Los Angeles. |

| Name. | Occupation. | Place of Business. | Residence. | Town or P. O. |
|---|---|---|---|---|
| Chevallier, V | Druggist | Main st | Los Angeles | Los Angeles. |
| Chick, Hiram | Laborer | | Los Angeles | |
| Childs, M W | Stoves & hardware | 21 Los Angeles st | 14 Los Angeles st | Los Angeles. |
| Chilson, Stephen L. | Farmer | near Downey | Los Angeles Co | Downey. |
| Chilson, Daniel G... | Farmer | near Santa Ana | Los Angeles Co | Santa Ana. |
| Childs, Marcus W.. | Merchant | Los Angeles | Los Angeles Co | Los Angeles. |
| Chilson, Daniel G... | Farmer | near Downey | Los Angeles Co | Downey. |
| Chilton, Raleigh,... | Farmer | near El Monte | Los Angeles Co | El Monte. |
| Chilson, H | Farmer | Azusa | 2 m S E Azusa | Azusa. |
| Chilson, Mrs | Farmer | Azusa | 2 m S E Azusa | Azusa. |
| Childs, O W | Merchant | Los Angeles | Los Angeles | Los Angeles. |
| Chism, William L.. | Teamster | Los Angeles Co | | Los Angeles. |
| Chism, Andrew | Barber | Los Angeles | Los Angeles | Los Angeles. |
| Chittenden, G W... | Farmer | Los Angeles | Anaheim | Anaheim. |
| Choate, Robert H.. | Merchant | Los Angeles | Los Angeles | Los Angeles. |
| Choate, Joseph | Teamster | Los Angeles Co | | Los Angeles. |
| Chopman, C | Vintner | near Los Angeles | Los Angeles Co | Los Angeles. |
| Chotean, L | Teamster | | Los Angeles Co | Los Angeles. |
| Choynski, Moritz... | Carpenter | Los Angeles Co | | Los Angeles. |
| Chrisco, Noah | Miner | | Los Angeles Co | Los Angeles. |
| Christopher, J M.. | Farmer | near Compton | Los Angeles Co | Compton. |
| Churm, B F | Laborer | Los Angeles Co | | Los Angeles. |
| Clancy, Dennis S... | Hotel keeper | Los Angeles | Los Angeles | Los Angeles. |
| Clancy, Thomas | Laborer | Los Angeles | | Los Angeles. |
| Clapp, John E | Bar keeper | Los Angeles | Los Angeles | Los Angeles. |
| Clapp, Daniel | Farmer | near Los Angeles | Los Angeles Co | Los Angeles. |
| Clark, Kenneth | Farmer | near Los Nietos | Los Nietos | Los Nietos. |
| Clark, George P... | Carpenter | Los Angeles Co | | Los Angeles. |
| Clark, J W | Justice & notary.. | Centre st.. | Anaheim | Anaheim. |
| Clark & Co, J W . | Gen merchandise.. | Centre st | | Anaheim. |
| Clarke, George J ... | Notary public | Downey Block | Los Angeles | Los Angeles. |
| Clarke, H | Att'y at law | r 3 & 4 Downey Blk. | Los Angeles | Los Angeles. |
| Clark, J M | Farmer | Westminster Colony. | | Westminster. |
| Clark, William | Farmer | Westminster Colony. | | Westminster. |
| Clark, F E | Farmer | near Los Angeles | Los Angeles Co | Los Angeles. |
| Clark, R C | Farmer | Silver Precinct | Silver Precinct | Downey. |
| Clark, William V. | Laborer | Compton | Compton | Compton. |
| Clark, A C | | Los Angeles Co | | Los Angeles. |
| Clark, Phares Allen | Merchant | Anaheim | Anaheim | Anaheim. |
| Clark, J | Laborer | Los Angeles Co | | Los Angeles. |
| Clarke, G R | | Los Angeles Co | | Los Angeles. |
| Clark, W | Reporter | Santa Ana | Los Angeles Co | Santa Ana. |
| Clark, P | Miner | Los Angeles Co | | Los Angeles. |
| Clark, M D | Farmer | near Los Angeles | Los Angeles Co | Los Angeles. |
| Claresy, J | Merchant | Los Angeles | Los Angeles Co | Los Angeles. |
| Clarke, Frank B.... | Farmer | near Los Angeles | Los Angeles Co | Los Angeles. |
| Clark, John C | Laborer | Los Angeles Co | | Los Angeles. |
| Clarebat, Charles | Laborer | | Los Angeles Co | El Monte. |
| Clark, James | Laborer | Los Angeles Co | | Wilmington. |
| Clark, James L | Teamster | | Los Angeles Co | Los Angeles. |
| Clark, A M M | Farmer | near El Monte | Los Angeles Co | El Monte. |
| Clark, W V C | Farmer | near Los Angeles | Los Angeles Co | Los Angeles. |
| Claude, Joseph | Miner | Los Angeles Co | | Los Angeles. |
| Clayton, P O | Minister | | Silver Precinct | Downey. |
| Clay, Levi | Farmer | near Azusa | Los Angeles Co | Azusa. |
| Clayton, John J.... | Stage driver | Los Angeles Co | | Los Angeles. |
| Clayton, W | Painter | Los Angeles | Los Angeles | Los Angeles. |
| Clement, Etienne | Baker | Los Angeles | Los Angeles | Los Angeles. |
| Clemenson, J J | Farmer | near El Monte | Los Angeles Co | El Monte. |
| Clement, Michel... | Vintner | near Los Angeles | Los Angeles Co | Los Angeles. |
| Clement, Edward J | Farmer | near El Monte | Los Angeles Co | El Monte. |
| Clemenson, John Sr | Farmer | Los Angeles Co | near El Monte | El Monte. |
| Cleveland, Hamilton | Farmer | Los Angeles Co | near Los Angeles | Los Angeles. |
| Cleveland, J | Farmer | Azusa | 2 m S E Azusa | Azusa. |

# DIRECTORY OF LOS ANGELES COUNTY. 333

| NAME. | OCCUPATION. | PLACE OF BUSINESS. | RESIDENCE. | TOWN OR P. O. |
|---|---|---|---|---|
| Clift, W............ | Stage driver....... | Los Angeles Co......... | ........................... | Los Angeles. |
| Clifton, Henry....... | Laborer ............. | ........................... | Los Angeles Co....... | Los Angeles. |
| Clifford, Patrick.... | Stair builder........ | Los Angeles........... | Los Angeles....... | Los Angeles. |
| Clifton, John P...... | Plasterer............ | Anaheim............... | Anaheim .......... | Anaheim. |
| Cline, J A............ | Hotel ............... | Los Angeles.......... | Los Angeles....... | Los Angeles. |
| Cline, Charles ....... | Plasterer............ | Los Angeles.......... | Los Angeles....... | Los Angeles. |
| Clinton, Edward M | Machinist........... | ........................... | ........................... | San Gabriel. |
| Clos, Ellis............. | Merchant ........... | Los Angeles.......... | Los Angeles....... | Los Angeles. |
| Close, Andrew J.... | Farmer ............. | Los Angeles Co...... | near Santa Ana..... | Santa Ana. |
| Clos & Lassere ...... | Grocers ............. | Los Angeles.......... | Los Angeles....... | Los Angeles. |
| Clough, T S......... | Farmer ............. | near Los Angeles..... | Los Angeles Co..... | Los Angeles. |
| Clough, Henry ...... | Carriage maker.... | Los Angeles.......... | Los Angeles....... | Los Angeles. |
| Clouse, George W. | Teamster ........... | Los Angeles Co...... | ........................... | El Monte. |
| Clove, Benjamin A | Farmer ............. | near Los Angeles..... | Los Angeles Co..... | Los Angeles. |
| Clyde, W............ | Bar keeper.......... | ........................... | ........................... | Wilmington. |
| Coalman, F C....... | Shoe maker ........ | Los Angeles.......... | Los Angeles....... | Los Angeles. |
| Conn, E P........... | Farmer ............. | near Los Nietos...... | Los Nietos......... | Los Nietos. |
| Cobler, Alpheus..... | Clerk................ | Los Angeles.......... | Los Angeles....... | Los Angeles. |
| **Cobler, Martin A**... | Speculator.......... | Los Angeles.......... | Los Angeles....... | Los Angeles. |
| Coblentz, J.......... | Wines & liquors.. | 71 Main st........... | Fort st............. | Los Angeles. |
| Cochran, R F ....... | Teamster ........... | Los Angeles Co...... | Los Angeles....... | ..................... |
| Cochrane, W A.... | Doctor .............. | Downey ............. | Downey ........... | Downey. |
| Cochran, Isaac N... | Farmer ............. | near Downey........ | Los Angeles Co..... | Downey. |
| Coffman, Charles A | Farmer ............. | near Los Angeles..... | Los Angeles Co..... | Los Angeles. |
| Cohen, Simon....... | Clerk................ | Los Angeles.......... | Los Angeles....... | Los Angeles. |
| **Cohen, Emanuel**.... | Merchant ........... | Los Angeles.......... | Los Angeles....... | Los Angeles. |
| Cohen, B ........... | Butcher............. | Center st ........... | Anaheim .......... | Anaheim. |
| **Cohen, Mrs H**....... | Milliner............. | Los Angeles.......... | Los Angeles....... | Los Angeles. |
| **Cohen & Davis**...... | Dry goods.......... | Los Angeles.......... | Los Angeles....... | Los Angeles. |
| Cohn, Max........... | Dry goods, &c... | Los Angeles st....... | Anaheim .......... | Anaheim. |
| Cohn, R ............. | Com merchant.... | Los A & Com'l sts... | 178 Main st....... | Los Angeles. |
| Cohn, Casper........ | Merchant ........... | Los Angeles.......... | Los Angeles....... | Los Angeles. |
| Cohn, Isaac.......... | Clerk................ | Los Angeles.......... | Los Angeles....... | Los Angeles. |
| Cohn, Louis......... | Merchant ........... | Los Angeles.......... | Los Angeles....... | Los Angeles. |
| **Cohn, Isidore**....... | Merchant ........... | Los Angeles.......... | Los Angeles....... | Los Angeles. |
| Cohn, Adolph....... | Clerk................ | ........................... | ........................... | Los Angeles. |
| **Cohn, S** .............. | Merchant ........... | Los Angeles.......... | Los Angeles....... | Los Angeles. |
| **Cohn, B** .............. | Merchant ........... | Los Angeles.......... | Los Angeles....... | Los Angeles. |
| Cohn, L.............. | Farmer ............. | ........................... | ........................... | Los Angeles. |
| **Cohn, K** .............. | Merchant ........... | Los Angeles.......... | Los Angeles....... | Los Angeles. |
| Coidarrens, Louis... | Barber .............. | Los Angeles.......... | Los Angeles....... | Los Angeles. |
| **Coin, J**............... | Ship carpenter..... | S P R R Co........... | Wilmington....... | Wilmington. |
| Coin, M A .......... | Farmer ............. | near Los Angeles..... | Los Angeles Co..... | Los Angeles. |
| Coin, F............... | Farmer ............. | near Los Angeles..... | Los Angeles Co..... | Los Angeles. |
| Colburn, Jacob E... | Blacksmith ........ | Los Angeles.......... | Los Angeles....... | Los Angeles. |
| Colder, William C. | Varnisher .......... | Los Angeles.......... | Los Angeles....... | Los Angeles. |
| Cole, Wallace D.... | Farmer ............. | ........................... | El Monte .......... | El Monte. |
| Coleman, G W..... | Teamster ........... | Los Angeles.......... | ........................... | Los Angeles. |
| Cole, Alexander..... | Laborer ............. | ........................... | Los Angeles Co..... | Los Angeles. |
| Cole, Lewis N....... | Miner................ | Los Angeles Co...... | Los Angeles Co..... | Los Angeles. |
| Cole, Benjamin F.. | Farmer ............. | near Downey........ | Los Angeles Co..... | Downey. |
| Cole, D R............ | Farmer ............. | Los Angeles Co...... | nr Los Angeles ,.... | Los Angeles. |
| **Cole, A J**............. | Machinist........... | S P P R R Co......... | Wilmington....... | Wilmington. |
| **Cole, G W**........... | Farmer ............. | nr Los Nietos....... | Los Angeles Co..... | Los Nietos. |
| **Cole, S**................ | Farmer ............. | Los Angeles Co...... | nr Los Nietos...... | Los Nietos. |
| **Cole, A T**............ | Farmer ............. | nr Downey.......... | Los Angeles Co..... | Downey. |
| Colgan, P H ........ | Cooper.............. | Los Angeles.......... | ........................... | Los Angeles. |
| Colima, N S ........ | Ranchero........... | ........................... | ........................... | Los Nietos. |
| Colima, J S.......... | Ranchero........... | ........................... | ........................... | Los Nietos. |
| Collins, W E........ | Farmer ............. | ........................... | ........................... | El Monte. |
| Collins, J P......... | Carpenter.......... | ........................... | ........................... | Anaheim. |
| Collins, Jeremiah... | Laborer ............. | ........................... | ........................... | Los Angeles. |
| Collins, Isaac Mc... | Farmer ............. | ........................... | ........................... | San Jose. |
| **Collins, M**........... | Bar keeper......... | Wilmington Ex ..... | Canal st ........... | Wilmington. |

# FARMERS' AND MERCHANTS' BANK

## OF LOS ANGELES.

### CAPITAL, - - $500,000

JOHN G. DOWNEY, - - - - President
ISAIAS W. HELLMAN, - - - - Cashier

### BOARD OF DIRECTORS:

| | | |
|---|---|---|
| JOHN G. DOWNEY, | F. LECOUVREUR, | M. KELLER, |
| I. M. HELLMAN, | CHARLES DUCOMMUN, | C. E. THOM, |
| JOHN S. GRIFFIN, | O. W. CHILDS, | ISAIAS W. HELLMAN. |

### EXCHANGE FOR SALE ON

New York, London, Dublin, Frankfort, Paris, Berlin and Hamburg.

RECEIVE DEPOSITS and ISSUE THEIR CERTIFICATES.

### BUY AND SELL

### Legal Tenders, Government, State, County and City Bonds

WILL ALSO PAY THE HIGHEST PRICE FOR

### GOLD AND SILVER BULLION.

ON ALL MONIES LEFT AS TERM DEPOSITS INTEREST WILL BE ALLOWED.

DIRECTORY OF LOS ANGELES COUNTY. 335

| Name. | Occupation. | Place of Business. | Residence. | Town or P. O. |
|---|---|---|---|---|
| Collins, P | Jeweler | | | Los Angeles. |
| Colling, B | Engineer | Wilmington | Canal st | Wilmington. |
| Collins, J | Blacksmith | | | Wilmington. |
| Collins, J J | Teamster | | Los Angeles | Los Angeles. |
| Collins, J W | Stage driver | | | Los Angeles. |
| Collins, David H | Farmer | | | Los Angeles. |
| Collins, Dennis | Waiter | | | Los Angeles. |
| Collins, Walter V | | | Los Nietos | Los Nietos. |
| Colman, J | Laborer | | Los Angeles | Los Angeles. |
| Colson, Jean B | Blacksmith | Los Angeles | Los Angeles | Los Angeles. |
| Colsom & Williams | Wagon makers | Los Angeles | Los Angeles | Los Angeles. |
| Coltom, C W | Carpenter | San Pedro Ranch | 1 m W Compton | Compton. |
| Compton & Binford | Real estate | Compton | | Compton. |
| Compton, G D | Real estate | San Pedro Ranch | 1 m W Compton | Compton. |
| Comstock, — | Farmer | San Pedro Ranch | 2 m S W Compton | Compton. |
| Condra, John | Farmer | | Los Nietos | Los Nietos. |
| Condit, M B | Farmer | | Azusa | Azusa. |
| Cone, Patrick | Brick maker | | Los Angeles | Los Angeles. |
| Congraves, J | Lumber | Spadra | 30 m E Los Angeles | Spadra. |
| Congdon, J R | Farmer | | | San Juan. |
| Congreve, J | Clerk | | | Los Angeles. |
| Conlan, A | Farmer | | | Los Angeles. |
| Conley, C C | Farmer | | | El Monte. |
| Conn, W | Teamster | | | Los Angeles. |
| Connolly, T | Laundryman | Los Angeles | Los Angeles | Los Angeles. |
| Conner, J D | Carpenter | | | Los Angeles. |
| Connelly, P | Farmer | | | Compton. |
| Connonado, J M | Laborer | | | Los Angeles. |
| Conrad, F | Cal Brewery | North st | Anaheim | Anaheim. |
| Conrad, M | Mason | | | Los Angeles. |
| Conrad, F | Brewer | | | Anaheim. |
| Conroy, J | Laborer | | | Los Angeles. |
| Contrillas, G | | | | Los Angeles. |
| Contreas, B | Miner | | | San Fernando. |
| Contreras, C | Mechanic | | | Los Angeles. |
| Contreras, Ramon | Farmer | | | Los Nietos. |
| Contreras, Y | Farmer | | | Los Nietos. |
| Contreras, F | Farmer | | | Los Nietos. |
| Contraras, L | Farmer | Placeritas | 4 m N E Lyon Stat'n | Lyon Station. |
| Contreas, I | Farmer | nr Azusa | Los Angeles Co | Azusa. |
| Contreas, J J | Laborer | Los Angeles Co | nr Los Nietos | Los Nietos. |
| Convers, M A | Farmer | | Soledad | San Fernando. |
| Conway, T | Brewer | Los Angeles | Los Angeles | Los Angeles. |
| Cook, W P | Farmer | Los Angeles Co | nr Los Nietos | Los Nietos. |
| Cook, C | Farmer | Los Angeles Co | Silver Precinct | Downey. |
| Cook, George | Stone mason | Los Angeles | nr Los Angeles | Los Angeles. |
| Cook, William | Farmer | Los Angeles Co | Silver Precinct | Downey. |
| Cook, Jefferson | Farmer | Los Angeles Co | Silver Precinct | Downey. |
| Cook, J G | Farmer | Los Angeles Co | nr Santa Ana | Santa Ana. |
| Cook, T H | Laborer | Los Angeles Co | | Los Angeles. |
| Cook, A | Teamster | Los Angeles Co | Los Angeles Co | Los Angeles. |
| Cook, A C | Farmer | Los Angeles Co | nr Los Nietos | Los Nietos. |
| Coombs, C C | Bookkeeper | Los Angeles | Los Angeles | Los Angeles. |
| Cooney, Thomas | Framer | Los Angeles Co | nr Los Angeles | Los Angeles. |
| Coons, George | Laborer | Los Angeles Co | | Los Angeles. |
| Cooper, M D | Farmer | Los Angeles Co | Silver Precinct | Downey. |
| Cooper, W F | Blacksmith | El Monte | El Monte | El Monte. |
| Cooper, J R | Laborer | Los Angeles Co | San Jose | Spadra. |
| Cooper, W | Farmer | Azusa Ranch | 2 m S W Azusa | Azusa. |
| Cooper, James | Farmer | San Bernardino Rd | 1½ m E Lexington | El Monte. |
| Cooper, J A | Farmer | Los Angeles Co | nr El Monte | El Monte. |
| Cooper, W P | Farmer | Los Angeles Co | nr El Monte | El Monte. |
| Cooper, T | Farmer | San Gabriel Valley | ½ m N San Gabriel | San Gabriel. |
| Cooper, I A | Farmer | San Gabriel Valley | ½ m N San Gabriel | San Gabriel. |

| Name. | Occupation. | Place of Business. | Residence. | Town or P. O. |
|---|---|---|---|---|
| Cooper, W James | Laborer | Los Angeles Co | | Los Angeles. |
| Cooper, Isaac W | Farmer | Los Angeles Co | nr Los Angeles | Los Angeles. |
| Copeland, C | Laborer | Los Angeles Co | | Los Angeles. |
| Copeland, Horace | Laborer | | Los Angeles Co | Los Angeles. |
| Copley, T | Contractor | 7 Front st | Los Angeles | Los Angeles. |
| Copley, T | Drayman | Los Angeles | Los Angeles | Los Angeles. |
| Copp, J | Farmer | Los Angeles Co | nr Azusa | Azusa. |
| Coralis, C | Laborer | Los Angeles Co | | Los Angeles. |
| Corbera, T | Laborer | | Los Angeles | Los Angeles. |
| Corbet, E N | Farmer | Los Angeles Co | Silver Precinct | Downey. |
| Corchoran, G M | Laborer | Los Angeles Co | Wilmington | Wilmington. |
| Cordova, Dolores | Farmer and stock | Cordova Ranch | 5 m N Lyon Station | Lyon Station. |
| Cordova, A | Laborer | Los Angeles Co | | Los Angeles. |
| Corea, Jesus | Farmer | Los Angeles Co | nr Santa Ana | Santa Ana. |
| Corea, G | Laborer | Los Angeles Co | | Los Angeles. |
| Corlue, W M | Farmer | Los Angeles Co | nr Los Nietos | Los Nietos. |
| Cornett, W L | Farmer | Los Angeles Co | nr Los Angeles | Los Angeles. |
| Cornbert, Joseph | Gardener | Los Angeles Co | | Los Angeles. |
| Corona, Jose Maria | Farmer | Los Angeles Co | nr Santa Ana | Santa Ana. |
| Coronides, G | Laborer | Los Angeles Co | San Jose | Spadra. |
| Corona, F | Laborer | Los Angeles Co | nr San Gabriel | San Gabriel. |
| Coronado, M | Farmer | Los Angeles Co | nr Los Angeles | Los Angeles. |
| Coronel, A F | Vintner | Los Angeles Co | nr Los Angeles | Los Angeles. |
| Coronel, M F | Farmer | Los Angeles Co | nr Los Angeles | Los Angeles. |
| Corrales, J | Laborer | Los Angeles Co | | Los Angeles. |
| Corriles, James L | Clerk | Los Angeles | Los Angeles | Los Angeles. |
| Correa, F | Laborer | Los Angeles Co | | Los Angeles. |
| Corsen, C | Farmer | Los Angeles Co | nr Los Angeles | Los Angeles. |
| Corvau, D C | Farmer | Los Angeles Co | nr Anaheim | Los Angeles. |
| Corwin, James | Minister | Compton | Compton | Compton. |
| Cosio, Francisco | Farmer | Los Angeles Co | nr Los Angeles | Los Angeles. |
| Coster, Samuel | Clerk | Los Angeles Co | Silver Precinct | Downey. |
| Cota, Antonio | Laborer | Los Angeles Co | | Los Angeles. |
| Cota, Damatio | Laborer | | Los Angeles Co | Los Angeles. |
| Cota, Manuel | Farmer | Los Angeles Co | nr Los Angeles | Los Angeles. |
| Cota, M N | Farmer | Los Angeles Co | nr Los Angeles | Los Angeles. |
| Cota, D | Laborer | Los Angeles Co | La Ballona | Los Angeles. |
| Cota, D | Ranchero | Los Angeles Co | nr Santa Ana | Santa Ana. |
| Cota, Jose J | Farmer | Los Angeles Co | nr Anaheim | Anaheim. |
| Cota, Salvador | Ranchero | Los Angeles Co | La Ballona | Los Angeles. |
| Cota, J S | Farmer | Los Angeles Co | La Ballona | Los Angeles. |
| Cota, Juan | Vaquero | Los Angeles Co | San Pedro | Wilmington. |
| Cota, Diego | Farmer | Los Angeles Co | nr Los Angeles | Los Angeles. |
| Cota, Leonarda | Farmer | Los Angeles Co | nr Santa Ana | Santa Ana. |
| Cottle, A | Farmer | Los Angeles Co | nr Los Angeles | Los Angeles. |
| Coulter & Harper | Stoves & hardw'e | 81 Main st | | Los Angeles. |
| Coulter, B F | Stoves & hardw'e | 81 Main st | Los Angeles | Los Angeles. |
| Courtney, W | Farmer | Los Angeles Co | nr Los Angeles | Los Angeles. |
| Courtney, W | Groceries | San Fernando | San Fernando | San Fernando. |
| Courdis, N | Deck hand | Steamer Los Angeles | Wilmington | Wilmington. |
| Conte, Germain | Dyer | Los Angeles | Los Angeles | Los Angeles. |
| Cover, T W | Farmer | Los Angeles Co | nr Los Angeles | Los Angeles. |
| Covell, L | Laborer | Los Angeles Co | nr San Gabriel | San Gabriel. |
| Cowden, F | Collector customs | Wilmington | Wilmington | Wilmington. |
| Cowles, E W | Engineer | Los Angeles | Los Angeles | Los Angeles. |
| Cowles, Miss M C | Clerk | P O Block | Hill st | Los Angeles. |
| Cox, John | Yard master | S P R R Co | Wilmington | Wilmington. |
| Cox, Simon B | Clerk | Los Angeles | Los Angeles | Los Angeles. |
| Cox, Thomas | Farmer | Los Angeles Co | nr Los Angeles | Los Angeles. |
| Cox, W B | Farmer | Los Angeles Co | nr Los Angeles | Los Angeles. |
| Cox, J C | Plasterer | Los Angeles | Los Angeles | Los Angeles. |
| Cox, G W S | Clerk | Los Angeles | Los Angeles | Los Angeles. |
| Coyle, Frank | Butcher | Los Angeles | Los Angeles | Los Angeles. |
| Crain, M H | Teamster | Los Angeles Co | Los Angeles | Los Angeles. |

## DIRECTORY OF LOS ANGELES COUNTY.

| Name. | Occupation. | Place of Business. | Residence. |
|---|---|---|---|
| Craig, Mary B. | Farmer | Los Angeles Co. | nr Anaheim |
| Craine, A J | Carpenter | Los Angeles Co. | Soledad |
| Crain, James E. | Farmer | | |
| Crain, William | Office boy | S P R R Co. | Wilmington |
| Craik, W R. | Clerk | Los Angeles | Los Angeles |
| Crall, H C. | Stone moulder | El Monte | El Monte |
| Cramp, N. | Baker | Los Angeles | Los Angeles |
| Cramer, S J | Stock raiser | Los Angeles Co. | nr San Gabriel |
| Cramer, T J B. | Teacher | Los Angeles Co. | San Gabriel |
| Cramer, J G B. | Farmer | El Monte Valley | 1 m E Lexington |
| Cran, G. | Farmer | Los Angeles Co. | nr Wilmington |
| Cram, H V. | Dairyman | Los Angeles Co. | nr Los Angeles |
| Crampton, Milton | Farmer | Los Angeles Co. | nr Los Angeles |
| Crandle, Joseph | Farmer | Los Angeles Co. | nr Los Angeles |
| Crane, Thomas | Laborer | Los Angeles Co. | nr Los Angeles |
| Crane, Francis O. | Laborer | Los Angeles Co. | San Fernando |
| Crane, James E. | Farmer | Los Angeles Co. | nr Anaheim |
| Crane, — | Apiarian | San Dimos Creek | 6 m N Spadra |
| Crandall, A. | Farmer | Los Angeles Co. | nr Los Angeles |
| Crandall, W | Hotel | Los Angeles Co. | San Joaquin |
| Crane, S L. | Farmer | Los Angeles Co. | nr Halfway House |
| Crane, J A | Farmer | Los Angeles Co. | nr Anaheim |
| Crawford, Edwin | Baker | Los Angeles | Los Angeles |
| Crawford, James S. | Dentist | Los Angeles | Los Angeles |
| Crawford, Terrel R. | Farmer | Los Angeles Co. | Silver Precinct |
| Crawford, J C. | Farmer | Los Angeles Co. | Silver Precinct |
| Creed, W R. | Laborer | Los Angeles Co. | |
| Creviston, Jacob C. | Miner | Los Angeles Co. | Soledad |
| Creluge, C | Merchant | | San Antonio |
| Crichton, David | Brewer | Los Angeles | Los Angeles |
| Crimmins, Denis | Gasfitter | Los Angeles | Los Angeles |
| Crimmins, John | Plumber | Los Angeles | Los Angeles |
| Crispin, Francisco | Shoe maker | Los Angeles Co. | Los Angeles |
| Crittenden, W E. | Laborer | Los Angeles Co. | |
| Crittenden, W. | Laborer | Point San Pedro | Point San Pedro |
| Crittenden, M | Farmer | Los Angeles Co. | Westminster Col. |
| Croix, F M de la | Trader | Los Angeles Co. | Los Angeles Co. |
| Cronin, William | Laborer | Los Angeles Co. | Los Angeles Co. |
| Crook, Edwin W. | Smith | Los Angeles | Los Angeles |
| Crooks, Oliver | Saloon keeper | San Gabriel | San Gabriel |
| Crosby, J | Baker | Los Angeles | Los Angeles |
| Crosby, W | Farmer | Los Angeles Co. | nr Los Angeles |
| Crosby, J B. | Barber | 8 Commercial st. | Los Angeles |
| Crowell, C T | Merchant | Los Angeles Co. | Silver Precinct |
| Crowther, W. | Wagon maker | Centre st. | Anaheim |
| Crowley, James | Laborer | Los Angeles Co. | Wilmington |
| Crow, Harry S. | Farmer | Los Angeles Co. | nr Los Angeles |
| Crowley, T. | Blacksmith | Wilmington | Wilmington |
| Crowell, E J | Engraver | Los Angeles | Los Angeles |
| Crowley, R. | Farmer | Los Angeles Co. | Silver Precinct |
| Crowley, James | Helper | S P R R Co. | Wilmington |
| Crowley, James | Blacksmith | 1st st | Canal st |
| Crozier, Abner B. | Farmer | Los Angeles Co. | nr Los Angeles |
| Crum, Almon | Carriage maker | Los Angeles | Los Angeles |
| Crump, William | Laborer | Los Angeles Co. | |
| Crump & Young | Bakers | Los Angeles | Los Angeles |
| Crusson, Jacob | Miner | Los Angeles Co. | Soledad |
| Cruz, Carlos | Carpenter | Los Angeles Co. | |
| Cruz, Santiago | Laborer | Los Angeles | Los Angeles |
| Cruz, Carlos | Mason | Los Angeles | Los Angeles |
| Cruz, Refugio | Laborer | | |
| Cruz, L J | Carpenter | | Los Angeles |
| Cruz, D. | Carpenter | Los Angeles Co. | Los Angeles Co. |
| Cubbon, J. | Farmer | Los Angeles Co. | nr Santa Ana |

| Name. | Occupation. | Place of Business. | Residence. | Town or P. O. |
|---|---|---|---|---|
| Cubbage, W | Trader | Los Angeles Co | El Monte | El Monte. |
| Cuellar, Thomas | Farmer | Los Angeles Co | nr Los Angeles | Los Angeles. |
| Cuen, Juan | Laborer | Los Angeles Co | | Los Angeles. |
| Culber, A S | Laborer | Los Angeles Co | Wilmington | Wilmington. |
| Cullen, C | Miner | Los Angeles Co | | Los Angeles. |
| Cummins, R | Farmer | Los Angeles Co | nr Los Angeles | Los Angeles. |
| Cummins, John M | Farmer | nr Los Angeles | Los Angeles Co | Los Angeles. |
| Cummings, James | Laborer | | Los Angeles Co | Los Angeles. |
| Cummings, George | Farmer | | Los Angeles Co | Los Angeles. |
| Cummings, Robert | Wagon maker | Los Angeles | Los Angeles | Los Angeles. |
| Cummings, W | Teamster | | Los Angeles Co | Los Angeles. |
| Cummings, D | Farmer | Los Angeles Co | nr Anaheim | Anaheim. |
| Cummings, Mrs M | Farmer | El Monte Valley | 3 m S Lexington | El Monte. |
| Cunningham, D | Laborer | | Los Angeles Co | Los Angeles. |
| Cunningham, C | Laborer | Los Angeles Co | Wilmington | Wilmington. |
| Cunningham, C | Farmer | San Jose Addition | 5 m N E Azusa | Azusa. |
| Cunningham, C | Farmer | Los Angeles Co | nr Los Angeles | Los Angeles. |
| Cunningham, W T | Farmer | Los Angeles Co | nr Los Angeles | Los Angeles. |
| Cunningham, R G | Dentist | Los Angeles | Los Angeles | Los Angeles. |
| Cunningham, R S | Dentist | 74 E Main st | Los Angeles | Los Angeles. |
| Cunze, Charles | Carpenter | | Anaheim | Anaheim. |
| Curley, S A | Farmer | Los Angeles Co | nr Los Angeles | Los Angeles. |
| Curley, J E | Farmer | Los Angeles Co | Los Angeles | Los Angeles. |
| Currier, G W | Clerk | Los Angeles | Los Angeles | Los Angeles. |
| Currier, A T | Farmer | San Jose Creek | 3 m S W Spadra | Spadra. |
| Curtis, Lewis A | Carpenter | Los Angeles Co | | Los Angeles. |
| Curtis, I O | Farmer | Los Angeles Co | nr Halfway House | Compton. |
| Curtis, B D | Teamster | | Anaheim | Anaheim. |
| Curtis, L | Distiller | Los Angeles | Los Angeles | Los Angeles. |
| Curtis, J F | Merchant | Los Angeles | Wilmington | Wilmington. |
| Cushing, J | Laborer | | El Monte | El Monte. |
| Cushion, Stephen | Fireman | Los Angeles | Los Angeles | Los Angeles. |
| Cushing, S | Laborer | | | Los Angeles |
| Cushing, John | Farmer | El Monte Valley | 2 m N Lexington | El Monte. |
| Cutlar, Robert | Dentist | Los Angeles | Los Angeles | Los Angeles. |
| Cuyas, Antonio | Hotel keeper | Los Angeles | Los Angeles | Los Angeles. |
| Daily, John | Laborer | | | Los Angeles. |
| Dailey, Daniel | Harness maker | Los Angeles | Los Angeles | Los Angeles. |
| Dakin, George H | Clerk | | Los Angeles | Los Angeles. |
| Daley, Mrs Sarah | Milliner | Los Angeles | | Los Angeles. |
| Daley, Thomas | Miner | | Los Angeles Co | Los Angeles. |
| Dalgalarrando, A | Laborer | Los Angeles Co | | Los Angeles. |
| Dallas, A | Farmer | Los Angeles Co | nr Halfway House | Compton. |
| Dalland, J | Farmer | nr Los Angeles | Los Angeles Co | Los Angeles. |
| Dalton, John | Laborer | Los Angeles Co | | Los Angeles. |
| Dalton, George J | Farmer | nr Los Angeles | Los Angeles | Los Angeles. |
| Dalton, Edwin H | Farmer | Los Angeles Co | nr Los Angeles | Los Angeles. |
| Dalton, Robert H | Clerk | Los Angeles Co | Los Angeles | Los Angeles. |
| Dalton, G B | Livery stable | Los Angeles | Los Angeles | Los Angeles. |
| Dalton, W T | Farmer | nr Los Angeles | Los Angeles Co | Los Angeles. |
| Dalton, G | Farmer | Los Angeles Co | nr Los Angeles | Los Angeles. |
| Dalton, W A | Farmer | Dalton Ranch | 1 m N Azusa | Azusa. |
| Dalton, Henry | Farmer | Dalton Ranch | 1 m N Azusa | Azusa. |
| Dalton, W A | Farmer | nr Azusa | Los Angeles Co | Azusa. |
| Daly, D | Hostler | Los Angeles Co | | Los Angeles. |
| Dameror, C F | Farmer | nr El Monte | Los Angeles Co | El Monte. |
| Damron, John S | Farmer | Los Angeles Co | Silver Precinct | Downey. |
| Damron, William Y | Farmer | Los Angeles Co | Silver Precinct | Downey. |
| Damron, John R | Farmer | nr Santa Ana | Santa Ana | Santa Ana. |
| Dana, A W | Surveyor | Los Angeles | Los Angeles | Los Angeles. |
| Dandien, Frederic | Farmer | nr Los Angeles | Los Angeles Co | Los Angeles. |
| Daniels, Seth | Miner | Los Angeles Co | | Los Angeles. |
| Daniels, James | Blacksmith | Los Angeles | Los Angeles | Los Angeles. |
| Daniel, B | Baker | Los Angeles | Los Angeles | Los Angeles. |

# DIRECTORY OF LOS ANGELES COUNTY. 339

| Name. | Occupation. | Place of Business. | Residence. | Town or P. O. |
|---|---|---|---|---|
| Daniels, R L | Clerk | Los Angeles | Los Angeles | Los Angeles. |
| Danskin, George | Fruit | Los Angeles Co | Westminster Col | Westminster. |
| Dantel, Charles | Barber | Los Angeles | Los Angeles | Los Angeles. |
| Darlinton, C A | Joiner | Los Angeles | Los Angeles | Los Angeles. |
| Darling, R S | Miner | Los Angeles Co | Los Angeles | Los Angeles. |
| D'Assonville, Virgilius | Doctor | | Anaheim | Anaheim. |
| Dassand, P | Hotel | Los Angeles | Los Angeles | Los Angeles. |
| Dass, E | Druggist | Los Angeles | Los Angeles | Los Angeles. |
| Dassinville, C | Druggist | Anaheim | 30 m S E Los A | Anaheim. |
| Davenport, Bailey McN | Farmer | Los Angeles Co | nr Santa Ana | Santa Ana. |
| Davenport, Jacob W | Farmer | Los Angeles Co | nr Santa Ana | Santa Ana. |
| Davies, Job Crocket | Farmer | San Gabriel Valley | nr San Gabriel | San Gabriel. |
| Davies, Edward A | Rope maker | Los Angeles Co | nr Los Nietos | Los Nietos. |
| Davis, Francis | Stabler | Los Angeles | Los Angeles | Los Angeles. |
| Davis, Joseph | Farmer | Los Angeles Co | Old Mission | El Monte. |
| Davis, Samuel J | Farmer | Los Angeles Co | nr Anaheim | Anaheim. |
| Davis, David | Teamster | Los Angeles Co | nr Anaheim | Anaheim. |
| Davis, William A L | Clerk | Los Angeles | Los Angeles | Los Angeles. |
| Davis, John R | Farmer | | Westminster Col | Westminster. |
| Davis, Charles W | Architect | Downey Block | cor 10th & Pearl sts | Los Angeles. |
| Davis, Francis M | Farmer | Los Angeles Co | Silver Precinct | Downey. |
| Davis, T J | Laborer | Los Angeles Co | Los Angeles | Los Angeles. |
| Davis, Francis C | Farmer | Los Angeles Co | El Monte | El Monte. |
| Davis & Brother | Merchant | Los Angeles st | Anaheim | Anaheim. |
| Davis & Co, R | Auctioneers | Los Angeles | Los Angeles | Los Angeles. |
| Davis, Jesse | Farmer | | Westminster Col | Westminster. |
| Davis, George M | Carpenter | Los Angeles | Los Angeles | Los Angeles. |
| Davis, David | Auctioneer | Los Angeles | Los Angeles | Los Angeles. |
| Davis, Mrs M | Dress maker | Los Angeles | Los Angeles | Los Angeles. |
| Davis, J W B | Carpenter | Los Angeles | Los Angeles | Los Angeles. |
| Davila, A | Silversmith | Los Angeles | Los Angeles | Los Angeles. |
| Davis, G | Merchant | 30 m S E Los A | Anaheim | Anaheim. |
| Davis, A R | Farmer | Los Angeles Co | nr Los Angeles | Los Angeles. |
| Davis, J J | Laborer | Los Angeles Co | Old Mission | El Monte. |
| Davidson, J P | Farmer | Los Angeles Co | nr Los Nietos | Los Nietos. |
| Davila, P Q | Farmer | Los Angeles Co | nr Santa Ana | Santa Ana. |
| Davis, P | Merchant | 30 m S E Los A | Anaheim | Anaheim. |
| Davis, H L | Doctor | Los Angeles Co | | Downey. |
| Davis, C K | Herder | Los Angeles Co | nr Santa Ana | Santa Ana. |
| Davis, M V B | Carpenter | Los Angeles Co | Los Angeles | Los Angeles. |
| Davis, John | Carpenter | 3 Spring st | 1st st | Los Angeles. |
| Davis, J L | Farmer | Azusa Ranch | 1¾ m S W Azusa | Los Angeles. |
| Davidson, Gen H D | | | Wilmington | Wilmington. |
| Davis, M | Farmer | Los Angeles Co | Silver Precinct | Downey. |
| Davis, G P | Miner | Los Angeles Co | nr Los Nietos | Los Nietos. |
| Davidson, G W | Farmer | Los Angeles Co | | Spadra. |
| Davis, I A | Farmer | Los Angeles Co | nr Los Nietos | Los Nietos. |
| Davis, O | Farmer | Los Angeles Co | | Downey. |
| Davis, T | Carpenter | Los Angeles Co | San Juan | Capistrano. |
| Davis, J H | Farmer | Los Angeles Co | nr Los Angeles | Los Angeles. |
| Davis, J L | Farmer | Los Angeles Co | nr El Monte | El Monte. |
| Davis, T E | Farmer | Los Angeles Co | nr Los Nietos | Los Nietos. |
| Davidson, A J | Merchant | Los Angeles | Los Angeles | Los Angeles. |
| Davis, J R | Farmer | Los Angeles Co | nr Westminster | Westminster. |
| Davis, J | Farmer | Los Angeles Co | nr Anaheim | Anaheim. |
| Davis, E | Farmer | Los Angeles Co | Green Meadows | Compton. |
| Davis, I E | Farmer | Los Angeles Co | nr Los Angeles | Los Angeles. |
| Davis, J W | Clerk | Los Angeles | Los Angeles | Los Angeles. |
| Davidson, C P | Farmer | Los Angeles Co | Silver Precinct | Downey. |
| Dawnst, Adrian | Carpenter | Los Angeles | Los Angeles | Los Angeles. |
| Dawson, R W | Farmer | Los Angeles Co | Azusa | Azusa. |
| Dawson, C | Farmer | Azusa Ranch | 1½ m N E Azusa | Azusa. |

| Name. | Occupation. | Place of Business. | Residence. | Town or P. O. |
|---|---|---|---|---|
| Dawson, R W | Farmer | Azusa Ranch | 1½ m N E Azusa | Azusa. |
| Dawson, T W | Trader | Silver Precinct | Silver Precinct | Downey. |
| Day, Alexander | Farmer | Los Angeles Co | San Jose | Spadra. |
| Day, I H | Carpenter | Los Angeles Co | Los Angeles | Los Angeles. |
| Day, D H | | Los Angeles Co | | Los Angeles. |
| Dean, John H T | Barber | Los Angeles | Los Angeles | Los Angeles. |
| Dean, A L | Farmer | nr El Monte | Los Angeles Co | El Monte. |
| Dearborn, Adolpho | Farmer | | | El Monte. |
| Dearing, W | Laborer | Los Angeles Co | | Santa Ana. |
| Dearing, R F | Farmer | Los Angeles Co | nr Los Angeles | Los Angeles. |
| Deaves, G | Hotel | Wilmington | Wilmington | Wilmington. |
| Deaver, George | Saloon | Canal st | Canal st | Wilmington. |
| Debois, Thomas | Cook | Los Angeles | Los Angeles | Los Angeles. |
| Decker, M | Farmer | Los Angeles Co | San Joaquin | Santa Ana. |
| Deckman, P W | Laborer | Los Angeles Co | | Los Angeles. |
| De Corse, Albert E | Druggist | Los Angeles | Los Angeles | Los Angeles. |
| Derois, Louis | Laborer | Los Angeles Co | | Los Angeles. |
| DeFennis, Henry | Farmer | San Fernando Valley | 4 m W San Fernando | San Fernando. |
| Dehare, Israel | Printer | Anaheim | Anaheim | Anaheim. |
| Delaney, P H | Farmer | Los Angeles Co | nr Los Angeles | Los Angeles. |
| Delano, T A | Farmer | nr Los Angeles | Los Angeles Co | Los Angeles. |
| Delgadillo, Antonio | Shoe maker | Los Angeles | Los Angeles | San Gabriel. |
| Demara, Jesus | Farmer | nr Los Angeles | Los Angeles Co | Los Angeles. |
| Demereaux, Claude | Laborer | Los Angeles Co | Los Angeles | Los Angeles. |
| Deming, J G | Miller | Los Angeles Co | Los Angeles | Los Angeles. |
| Dempster, Cornelius | Blacksmith | Los Angeles Co | Cerritos | Wilmington. |
| Denker, — | U S hotel | Main & Requena sts | | Los Angeles. |
| Denman, Z H | Carriage maker | | Los Angeles | Los Angeles. |
| Denman, J G | Sheep raiser | Los Angeles Co | Halfway House | Compton. |
| Dennison, W H | Farmer | Los Angeles Co | nr Los Angeles | Los Angeles. |
| Denny, W S | Cooper | Los Angeles Co | nr Azusa | Azusa. |
| Denny, A J | Carpenter | Dalton Ranch | 1 m N Azusa | Azusa. |
| Denton, H | Farmer | Los Angeles Co | Silver Precinct | Downey. |
| Dericot, Samuel | Farmer | Los Angeles Co | nr Santa Ana | Santa Ana. |
| Derrick, Alexander | Farmer | Los Angeles Co | nr Los Nietos | Los Nietos. |
| De Runks, Joseph | Gunsmith | 30 m S E Los A | Anaheim | Anaheim. |
| Des Antels, N | Livery stable | 14 Aliso st | | Los Angeles. |
| Des Granger, Otto | Farmer | Los Angeles Co | Anaheim | Anaheim. |
| De Shield, W J | Farmer | Azusa Ranch | 1½ m E Azusa | Azusa. |
| Desmond, Thomas | Laborer | | Los Angeles | Los Angeles. |
| Desmond, D | Hatter | Temple Block | Los Angeles | Los Angeles. |
| Destoup, J | Farmer | Los Angeles Co | nr San Fernando | San Fernando. |
| Devereaux, T | Tinner | Los Angeles Co | Los Angeles | Los Angeles. |
| Deviller, Oliver | Merchant | Los Angeles | Los Angeles | Los Angeles. |
| Devin, Joseph F | Contractor | | San Gabriel | San Gabriel. |
| Devire, J | Farmer | Los Angeles Co | Halfway House | Compton. |
| Dovine, J A | Teacher | Los Angeles Co | Los Angeles | Los Angeles. |
| Devine, M | Carpenter | Los Angeles Co | Los Angeles | Los Angeles. |
| Dewars, George W | Farmer | Los Angeles | Silver Precinct | Downey. |
| Dewey, Kimball & Co | Real estate | Los Angeles | Los Angeles | Los Angeles. |
| Dewey, S L | Merchant | Los Angeles | Los Angeles | Los Angeles. |
| Dewitt, A | Miner | Los Angeles Co | San Fernando | San Fernando. |
| Diaz, Luis | Laborer | Los Angeles Co | Los Angeles | Los Angeles. |
| Diaz, Justo | Laborer | Los Angeles Co | Los Angeles | Los Angeles. |
| Diaz, R | Laborer | Los Angeles Co | Los Angeles | Los Angeles. |
| Dickenson, James P | Farmer | Los Angeles Co | nr Los Angeles | Downey. |
| Dickerson, Martin | Farmer | Los Angeles Co | nr Los Angeles | Los Angeles. |
| Dickenson, Isaac J | Farmer | Los Angeles Co | nr El Monte | El Monte. |
| Dickson, F L | Laborer | Los Angeles Co | Los Angeles | Los Angeles. |
| Diez, V | Plasterer | Los Angeles | Los Angeles | Los Angeles. |
| Diffenderffer, G S | Book keeper | Los Angeles | Los Angeles | Los Angeles. |
| Diffenderffer, B W | Hack driver | Los Angeles | Los Angeles | Los Angeles. |

# DIRECTORY OF LOS ANGELES COUNTY. 341

| Name. | Occupation. | Place of Business. | Residence. | Town or P. O. |
|---|---|---|---|---|
| Dilley, F S | Farmer | Los Angeles Co | nr El Monte | El Monte. |
| Dilley, James V | Farmer | Los Angeles Co | Silver Precinct | Downey. |
| Dillon, Jeremiah | Laborer | Los Angeles | Los Angeles | Los Angeles. |
| Diller, Cristian | Shoe maker | Los Angeles | Los Angeles | Los Angeles. |
| Dillon & Kenealy | Dry goods | 18 Los Angeles st | | Los Angeles. |
| Dilley, D J | Teacher | Los Angeles Co | El Monte | El Monte. |
| Dille, G R | Teamster | Los Angeles Co | Los Angeles | Los Angeles. |
| Dimock, Dewitt C | Carpenter | Los Angeles Co | Anaheim | Annheim. |
| Dimond, E H | Clerk | Los Angeles | Los Angeles | Los Angeles. |
| Dinan, Lawrence W | Currier | Los Angeles | Los Angeles | Los Angeles. |
| Dingman, D J | Variety store | 36 Main st | 1st st | Los Angeles. |
| Diselhurse, Henry A | Carpenter | Los Angeles Co | Los Angeles | Los Angeles. |
| Ditts, David B S | Pearl worker | | Wilmington | Wilmington. |
| Dix, H M | Trader | Los Angeles Co | El Monte | El Monte. |
| Dixon, Joseph | Laborer | Los Angeles Co | Los Angeles | Los Angeles. |
| Doak, Edmond | Millinery | | St Charles Hotel | Los Angeles. |
| Dobbie, D | Farmer | Los Angeles Co | nr Los Angeles | Los Angeles. |
| Dobbie, Andrew | Miner | Los Angeles Co | Los Angeles | Los Angeles. |
| Dobson, R C | Jailor | Los Angeles | Los Angeles | Los Angeles. |
| Dochez, H L | Painter | Los Angeles | Los Angeles | Los Angeles. |
| Dockeveiler, H | Hotel | Los Angeles | Los Angeles | Los Angeles. |
| Dodge, Everett K | Merchant | | Half Way House | Compton. |
| Dodge, C L | Farmer | Los Angeles Co | Silver Precinct | Downey. |
| Dodson, William R | Farmer | Los Angeles Co | nr El Monte | El Monte. |
| Dodson, A M | Butcher | Los Angeles Co | Los Angeles | Los Angeles. |
| Dodson, W | Farmer | Los Angeles Co | nr Los Angeles | Los Angeles. |
| Dodson, J | Farmer | Los Angeles Co | Azusa | Azusa. |
| Dodson, A M | Butcher | Main st | Los Angeles | Los Angeles. |
| Dodson, Edward | Waiter | Los Angeles | Los Angeles | Los Angeles. |
| Dodson, John | Farmer | Lexington | 12 m E Los Angeles | El Monte. |
| Dodson, John | Farmer | Azusa Ranch | 2 m S W Azusa | Azusa. |
| Doherty, W | Boiler maker | Los Angeles | Los Angeles | Los Angeles. |
| Dohs, John | Barber | Los Angeles | Los Angeles | Los Angeles. |
| Dohs, Frederick | Barber | Los Angeles | Los Angeles | Los Angeles. |
| Doling, Timothy | Laborer | Los Angeles Co | Los Angeles | Los Angeles. |
| Domarguez, Cayetono | Laborer | Los Angeles Co | Los Angeles | Los Angeles. |
| Dominguez, Manuel | Laborer | Los Angeles Co | Los Angeles | Los Angeles. |
| Dominguez, Francisco | Laborer | Los Angeles Co | Los Angeles | Los Angeles. |
| Dominguez, Jose | Farmer | Los Angeles Co | nr Los Angeles | Los Angeles. |
| Dominguez, P E | Laborer | Los Angeles Co | | Compton. |
| Dominguez, F | Farmer | Los Angeles Co | nr Los Nietos | Los Nietos. |
| Dominguez, J C | Farmer | Los Angeles Co | nr Los Angeles | Los Angeles. |
| Dominguez, J D | Farmer | Los Angeles Co | nr San Fernando | San Fernando. |
| Dominguez, R | Teamster | Los Angeles Co | Wilmington | Wilmington. |
| Dominguez, D C | Laborer | Los Angeles Co | Los Angeles | Los Angeles. |
| Dominguez, P | Laborer | Los Angeles Co | Los Angeles | Los Angeles. |
| Dominguez, Donacioro | Farmer | Los Angeles Co | nr Santa Ana | Santa Ana. |
| Dominguez, C | Farmer | Los Angeles Co | nr Santa Ana | Santa Ana. |
| Dominguez, J M | Vaquero | Los Angeles Co | Los Angeles | Los Angeles. |
| Dominguez, Thomas | Laborer | San Juan | San Juan | San Juan. |
| Domingo, A | Druggist | Los Angeles | Los Angeles | Los Angeles. |
| Dominguez, M | Stock raiser | Dominguez Ranch | 2½ m S Compton | Compton. |
| Dominguez, E | Carpenter | 12 m W Los A | La Ballona | Los Angeles. |
| Dominguez, P S | Farmer | Los Angeles Co | La Ballona | Los Angeles. |
| Domingo, J A | Laborer | Los Angeles Co | Los Angeles | Los Angeles. |
| Dominguez, R | Farmer | Los Angeles Co | nr Los Angeles | Los Angeles. |
| Dominguez, A | Farmer | Los Angeles Co | nr Los Angeles | Los Angeles. |
| Dominguez, D | Farmer | Los Angeles Co | nr Los Angeles | Los Angeles. |
| Dominguez, P | Farmer | Los Angeles Co | nr San Fernando | San Fernando. |
| Domingo, J | Laborer | Los Angeles | Los Angeles | Los Angeles. |
| Donathan, William | Trainer | Los Angeles | Los Angeles | Los Angeles. |

| Name. | Occupation. | Place of Business. | Residence. | Town or P. O. |
|---|---|---|---|---|
| Donaldson, John M | Farmer | Los Angeles Co | nr Los Angeles | Los Angeles. |
| Donahue, P. | Carpenter | S P R R Co | Wilmington | Wilmington. |
| Donaleich, — | Sheep raiser | San Fernando Valley | 4 m W San Fernando | San Fernando. |
| Doncelance, P F | Mason | Los Angeles | Los Angeles | Los Angeles. |
| Donelson, J M | Stage line | cor Main & Market sts | | Los Angeles. |
| Donley, Felix | Farmer | | | Los Angeles. |
| Donley, G W | Miner | 30 m W San Fernando | Soledad | San Fernando. |
| Donohoe, P. | Laborer | Los Angeles Co | Wilmington | Wilmington. |
| Donohoe, John | Trainer | Los Angeles Co | Los Angeles | Los Angeles. |
| Donohoe, Patrick | Carpenter | Los Angeles | Los Angeles | Los Angeles. |
| Donovan, J. | Plasterer | Los Angeles | Los Angeles | Los Angeles. |
| Doody, Patrick | Laborer | Los Angeles Co | Los Angeles | Los Angeles. |
| Dooner & Sotell | Druggists | under Lafayette Hotel | | Los Angeles. |
| Dooner, R W | Reporter | Los Angeles | Los Angeles | Los Angeles. |
| Dorame, Masimo | Laborer | Los Angeles Co | Los Angeles | Los Angeles. |
| Dorlan, J D | Prin'l select sch. | Spring st, below 3d | Los Angeles | Los Angeles. |
| Dorman, G | Carpenter | Wilmington | Canal st | Wilmington. |
| Dorn, J | Farmer | Los Angeles Co | nr Los Nietos | Los Nietos. |
| Dorstine, J K | Printer | Wilmington | Wilmington | Wilmington. |
| Dosta, — | Laborer | Los Angeles | Los Angeles | Los Angeles. |
| Doster, J W | Farmer | Los Angeles Co | Silver Precinct | Downey. |
| Dotter & Bradley | Furniture | 86 Main st | | Los Angeles. |
| Dotter, John C | Furniture | 86 Main st. | 1st st | Los Angeles. |
| Dotter, C | Hatter | Los Angeles | Los Angeles | Los Angeles. |
| Doty, A | Laborer | Los Angeles Co | Los Nietos | Los Nietos. |
| Doud, L | Laborer | Los Angeles Co | Los Angeles | Los Angeles. |
| Dougherty, J L | Farmer | Azusa Ranch | 1½ m E Azusa | Azusa. |
| Dougherty, C | Farmer | Azusa Ranch | 1½ m E Azusa | Azusa. |
| Dougherty, James | Farmer | Azusa Ranch | 1 m E Azusa | Azusa. |
| Dougherty, R E | Clerk | Los Angeles | Los Angeles | Los Angeles. |
| Dougherty, J L | Farmer | | | Azusa. |
| Dougherty, James L | Farmer | | | El Monte. |
| Douglass, John W | Farmer | Los Angeles Co | nr Los Angeles | Los Angeles. |
| Dougherty, McNally | Laborer | Los Angeles Co | San Jose | Spadra. |
| Douglass, John W. | Farmer | Los Angeles Co | nr Los Angeles | Los Angeles. |
| Dougherty, Charles | Farmer | Los Angeles Co | nr El Monte | El Monte. |
| Dougherty, William J | Farmer | Los Angeles Co | nr El Monte | El Monte. |
| Dowling, J | Gardener | Los Angeles | Los Angeles | Los Angeles. |
| Downie, James | Painter | | | Los Angeles. |
| Downing, P H | Liv'y sta & saloon | Canal st | Wilmington | Wilmington. |
| Downs, F E | Farmer | San Bernardino Road | 1½ m E Lexington | El Monte. |
| Downey, J G | Farmer | Los Angeles Co | nr Los Angeles | Los Angeles. |
| Downey, P. | Clerk | Los Angeles | Los Angeles | Los Angeles. |
| Downing, P H | Clerk | San Pedro | San Pedro | Wilmington. |
| Doyharsabal, Jean | Farmer | Los Angeles Co | nr San Fernando | San Fernando. |
| Doyle & Silver | Barbers | Spring & Temple sts. | | Los Angeles. |
| Doyle, John | Barber | Los Angeles | Los Angeles | Los Angeles. |
| Dramer, John | Blacksmith | Los Angeles | Los Angeles | Los Angeles. |
| Drawsen, L H F | Butcher | 30 m S E Los A | Anaheim | Anaheim. |
| Dreury, Joseph H | Laborer | Los Angeles | Los Angeles | Los Angeles. |
| Dreux, P | Carpenter | Los Angeles | Los Angeles | Los Angeles. |
| Dreyfus, B | Merchant | 30 m S E Los A | Anaheim | Anaheim. |
| Drinkwater, N | Miner | Los Angeles Co | Los Angeles | Los Angeles. |
| Driscoll, H B | Laborer | Los Angeles | Los Angeles | Los Angeles. |
| Driver, G T | Miner | Los Angeles Co | Azusa | Azusa. |
| Drown, J W | Stock raiser | Los Angeles Co | El Monte | El Monte. |
| Drugon, John | Blacksmith | Los Angeles | Los Angeles | Los Angeles. |
| Drum, J | Clerk | Los Angeles | Los Angeles | Los Angeles. |
| Drum, T | Toll-gate keeper | San Fernando Cut | 2 m S Lyon Station | Lyon Station. |
| Dryden, W Jr | Farmer | Los Angeles Co | nr Los Angeles | Los Angeles. |
| Duarte, Mariano | Laborer | Los Angeles Co | San Jose | Spadra. |
| Duarte, Florencio | Borreguero | Los Angeles Co | San Jose | Spadra. |

## DIRECTORY OF LOS ANGELES COUNTY. 343

| Name. | Occupation. | Place of Business. | Residence. | Town or P. O. |
|---|---|---|---|---|
| Duarte, Jose G | Laborer | Anaheim | Anaheim | Anaheim. |
| Duarte, Jose Tomas | Vaquero | Los Angeles Co | San Gabriel | San Gabriel. |
| Duarte, A | Laborer | Los Angeles Co | Old Mission | Los Angeles |
| Duarte, J | Laborer | Los Angeles Co |  | San Gabriel. |
| Duarte, J A | Laborer | Los Angeles Co | Los Angeles | Los Angeles. |
| Duarta, V A | Farmer | Los Angeles Co | San Gabriel | San Gabriel. |
| Duarte, Jose J | Laborer | Los Angeles Co | San Gabriel | San Gabriel. |
| Duarte, Manuel | Laborer | 8 m E Los Angeles | San Gabriel | San Gabriel. |
| Duarte, M E | Laborer | Los Angeles Co | San Jose | El Monte. |
| Duarte, C | Laborer | Los Angeles Co | Santa Ana | Santa Ana. |
| Duarte, P | Laborer | Los Angeles Co | Santa Ana | Santa Ana. |
| Dubois, John B | Printer and publ'r | Los Angeles | Los Angeles | Los Angeles. |
| Dubordieu, B | Baker | Los Angeles | Los Angeles | Los Angeles. |
| DuBois, C G Mrs | Teacher | Los Angeles | Los Angeles | Los Angeles. |
| Ducasse, P L | Harness maker | Los Angeles | Los Angeles | Los Angeles. |
| Duckelburger, I R | Farmer | nr Los Angeles | Los Angeles Co | Los Angeles. |
| Ducommon, C L | Merchant | Los Angeles | Los Angeles | Los Angeles. |
| Dudley, John | Farmer | Los Angeles Co | nr Los Angeles | Los Angeles. |
| Duffey, John | Laborer | Los Angeles Co |  | Los Angeles. |
| Duin, Bernhard | Laborer |  | Los Angeles Co | Los Angeles. |
| Duin, Christian | Farmer | nr Los Angeles | Los Angeles Co | Los Angeles. |
| Dukes, C | Farmer | Azusa | 2 m S W Azusa | Azusa. |
| Dull, Henry J | Farmer | nr Soledad | Los Angeles Co | Soledad. |
| Dullahan, M | Drayman | Los Angeles Co | nr Los Angeles | Los Angeles. |
| Dumphrey, C | Engineer | S P R R Co | Canal st | Wilmington. |
| Dunbar, Edgar | Laborer | Los Angeles Co |  | Los Angeles. |
| Dunks, H H | Laborer | Los Angeles Co | Los Angeles | Los Angeles. |
| Dunlap, Jonathan D | Trader |  |  | Los Angeles. |
| Dunlap, Albert H | Ranchero | Los Angeles Co | Los Nietos | Los Nietos. |
| Dunlap, J D | Dep U S marshal | 55 Main st |  | Los Angeles. |
| Dunlap, J | Wheelwright | Los Angeles | San Joaquin | Santa Ana. |
| Dunlon, Thomas | Laborer | Los Angeles Co |  | Los Angeles. |
| Dunn, William B | Merchant | Los Angeles | Los Angeles | Los Angeles. |
| Dunn, Charles W | Foreman | Los Angeles | Los Angeles | Los Angeles. |
| Dunn, John A | Farmer | nr Los Nietos | Los Angeles Co | Los Nietos. |
| Dunn, J T | Farmer | nr Downey | Silver Precinct | Downey. |
| Dunsmore, J A | Farmer | nr Los Angeles | Los Angeles Co | Los Angeles. |
| Dunsmoor, C H | Dollar store | Spring st | Los Angeles | Los Angeles. |
| Dunsmoor Bros | Dollar store | Spring st |  | Los Angeles. |
| Dunsmoor, I A | Dollar store | Spring st | Los Angeles | Los Angeles. |
| Dunsmoor, A V | Farmer | nr El Monte | Los Angeles Co | El Monte. |
| Dupuy, E | Livery stable | Los Angeles | Los Angeles | Los Angeles. |
| DuPuy, G | Physician | Los Angeles | Los Angeles | Los Angeles. |
| Duran, E | Laborer | Los Angeles | Los Angeles | Los Angeles. |
| Duran, F | Laborer | Los Angeles | Los Angeles | Los Angeles. |
| Durfee & Reichard | Livery stable | Los Angeles |  | Los Angeles. |
| Durfee, C A | Dealer in horses | 14 Aliso st | 6th st | Los Angeles. |
| Durfee, J D | Farmer | Los Angeles Co |  | El Monte. |
| Durfee, G W | Farmer | Los Angeles Co | Old Mission | El Monte. |
| Durffee, G | Farmer | El Monte Valley | 3 m S W Lexington | El Monte. |
| Durffee, J D | Farmer | El Monte Valley | 3 m S W Lexington | El Monte. |
| Durgan, Pierce | Clerk | Los Angeles | Los Angeles | Los Angeles. |
| Durine, Ludwell | Blacksmith | San Jose | San Jose | Spadra. |
| Durrell, Josiah F | Farmer | Los Angeles Co | Half-way House | Compton. |
| Durrell, D N | Farmer | Los Angeles Co | Half-way House | Compton. |
| Durr, L | Vintner | Los Angeles Co | nr Anaheim | Anaheim. |
| Dutcher, N | Farmer | Los Angeles Co | Azusa | Azusa. |
| Dutcher, W H | Laborer | Los Angeles Co | Azusa | Azusa. |
| Dwyer, J R | Tobacconist | Los Angeles | Los Angeles | Los Angeles. |
| Dwyer, M | Laborer | Los Angeles | Los Angeles | Los Angeles. |
| Dyer, Thomas C | Butcher | Los Angeles | Los Angeles | Los Angeles. |
| Dyer, Samuel H | Farmer | Los Angeles Co | nr Anaheim | Anaheim. |
| Dye, G W | Hotel | Los Angeles | Los Angeles | Los Angeles. |
| Dye, J F | Carpenter | Los Angeles | Los Angeles | Los Angeles. |

| Name. | Occupation. | Place of Business. | Residence. | Town or P. O. |
|---|---|---|---|---|
| Dykes, Thomas | Laborer | Los Angeles Co | Los Angeles | Los Angeles. |
| Dyer, Jones J | Farmer | Los Angeles Co | nr Anaheim | Anaheim. |
| Eades, R | Farmer | Mud Spring Valley | 6 m N Spadra | Spadra. |
| Eads, Richard | Farmer | | | El Monte. |
| Eagan, John | Blacksmith | Spadra | 30 m E Los Angeles | Spadra. |
| Eagan, G C | General mdse | Spadra | 30 m E Los Angeles | Spadra. |
| Eames, S L | Farmer | Wilmington | 1st st | Wilmington. |
| Earnes, R L | R R agent | R R Depot | San Fernando | San Fernando. |
| Earl, James H | Miner | Los Angeles Co | | San Fernando. |
| Earley, W R | Locksmith | Los Angeles | Los Angeles | Los Angeles. |
| Easton, James H | Carpenter | | | Los Angeles. |
| Eastman, C J | Drayman | | | Los Angeles. |
| East, W T | Farmer | Los Angeles | nr San Antonio | Santa Ana. |
| Eaton, B S | Farmer | Los Angeles | nr San Gabriel | San Gabriel. |
| Eberle, John E | Miner | Los Angeles Co | | Los Angeles. |
| Ebinger, Louis | Baker | Los Angeles | Los Angeles | Los Angeles. |
| Ebner, George | Butcher | Wilmington | Wilmington | Wilmington. |
| Eccles, Robert | Plasterer | Westminster Col | Los Angeles Co | Westminster. |
| Eckert, R | Clerk | Los Angeles | Los Angeles | Los Angeles. |
| Eddy, Amos | Farmer | nr Compton | Los Angeles Co | Compton. |
| Eddy, James L | Mariner | | Los Angeles Co | Wilmington. |
| Edelman, A H Rev | Pastor | Hebrew Church | Los Angeles | Los Angeles. |
| Edgerton, G W | Carpenter | | | San Fernando. |
| Edgerton, R D | Teamster | Los Angeles Co | | Los Angeles. |
| Edger, W F | Doctor | Los Angeles | Los Angeles | Los Angeles. |
| Edington, J M | Farmer | Los Angeles Co | nr Los Nietos | Los Nietos. |
| Edmonds, Eugene | Teamster | Los Angeles Co | | Los Angeles. |
| Edwards, Elisha L | Farmer | Los Angeles Co | nr Downey | Downey. |
| Edwards, William | Teamster | Los Angeles Co | | San Gabriel. |
| Edwards, Hannibal | Farmer | Los Angeles Co | nr Los Angeles | Los Angeles. |
| Edwards, W W | Doctor | Downey | Downey | Downey. |
| Edwards, J | Teamster | Los Angeles Co | | Los Angeles. |
| Edwards & Hoff | General mdse | Spring st | | Los Angeles. |
| Edwards, W H | Farmer | | Westminster Col | Westminster. |
| Edwards, Samson | Farmer | nr Westminster | Westminster Col | Westminster. |
| Edwards, M M Mrs | Nurse | Los Angeles | Los Angeles | Los Angeles. |
| Edwards, John | Farmer | nr Westminster | Westminster Col | Westminster. |
| Edwards, Thomas | Farmer | nr Westminster | Westminster Col | Westminster. |
| Edwards, L E | Dress maker | Los Angeles | Los Angeles | Los Angeles. |
| Edwards, Frank | Clerk | Los Angeles | Los Angeles | Los Angeles. |
| Egan, Richard | Farmer | Los Angeles Co | nr San Juan | Capistrano. |
| Egan, John R | Blacksmith | Los Angeles | | Los Angeles. |
| Egan, George C | Farmer | Los Angeles Co | nr Los Angeles | Los Angeles. |
| Egan, J H | Clerk | Los Angeles Co | | Spadra. |
| Egert, George | Laborer | | Los Angeles Co | Wilmington. |
| Ehlers, Augustus | Miner | Los Angeles Co | | Los Angeles. |
| Ehlers, Edward | Clerk | Los Angeles | Los Angeles | Los Angeles. |
| Einsel, S G | Farmer | San Pedro Ranch | 2 m S W Compton | Compton. |
| Eldred, Albert | Speculator | Los Angeles Co | | Los Angeles. |
| Eldridge, Zorth | Farmer | nr Los Angeles | Los Angeles Co | Los Angeles. |
| Elillas, Andres | Saddler | El Monte | El Monte | El Monte. |
| Elisalde, Rafael | Laborer | Los Angeles Co | | Los Nietos. |
| Elisalde, Alfredo | Laborer | | Los Angeles Co | Los Nietos. |
| Elisalde, Eugenio | Laborer | Los Angeles Co | | San Gabriel. |
| Elisade, Jose | Laborer | | | Los Angeles. |
| Elizalde, Jose D | Laborer | Los Angeles Co | | Los Angeles. |
| Elizalde, Jose V | Ranchero | nr Los Angeles | Los Angeles Co | Los Angeles. |
| Ellis, J K | Tel operator | Lyon Station | Lyon Station | Lyon Station. |
| Ellis, Asa | Farmer | Ellis Station | 1 m W Lexington | El Monte. |
| Ellis, C J | Attorney at law | r 1 & 3 Downey Block | Los Angeles | Los Angeles. |
| Elliott, J M | Sec L A bank | 44 Main st | Hope, nr Temple | Los Angeles. |
| Ellis, Dr James | Physician | Hotel building | Anaheim | Anaheim. |
| Ellis, J | Laborer | Los Angeles Co | | Santa Ana. |
| Ellis, A | Mason | Los Angeles | Los Angeles | Los Angeles. |

## DIRECTORY OF LOS ANGELES COUNTY. 345

| Name. | Occupation. | Place of Business. | Residence. | Town or P. O. |
|---|---|---|---|---|
| Elliot, Sanders | Farmer | nr El Monte | Los Angeles Co | El Monte. |
| Elliott, John M | Clerk | Compton | Compton | Compton. |
| Ellis, Theodore | Student | Los Angeles | Los Angeles | Los Angeles. |
| Elliot, James Smith | Farmer | nr Downey | Los Angeles Co | Downey. |
| Ellis, Chas James | Lawyer | Los Angeles | Los Angeles | Los Angeles. |
| Ellis, Thos Jeff | Farmer | nr Downey | Los Angeles Co | Downey. |
| Ellis, John F | Merchant | Los Angeles | Los Angeles | Los Angeles. |
| Ellis, William | Farmer | nr El Monte | Los Angeles Co | El Monte. |
| Ellsworth, Frederick H | Farmer | Los Angeles Co | nr Compton | Compton. |
| Ellsworth, Chestlin O | Clerk | Wilmington | Los Angeles Co | Wilmington. |
| Elmer, Edward | Farmer | nr El Monte | Los Angeles Co | El Monte. |
| Embra, Chas | Laborer | Los Angeles Co | | Los Angeles. |
| Emery, Frank W | Farmer | nr San Gabriel | Los Angeles Co | San Gabriel. |
| Emerson, Hiram S | Carpenter | Los Angeles Co | | Wilmington. |
| Emery, George F | Farmer | nr San Gabriel | Los Angeles Co | San Gabriel. |
| **Emerson, F** | Apiarian | San Fernando Valley | 4 m N San Fernando | San Fernando. |
| Emmit, James | Shoe maker | Los Angeles | | Los Angeles. |
| Encinas, Jose E | Shepherd | | Los Angeles Co | Spadra. |
| Encinas, Francisco | Laborer | Los Angeles Co | | Los Angeles. |
| Encino, J Y | Laborer | | Los Angeles Co | Los Angeles. |
| Engelhardt, George | | Los Angeles Co | | Anaheim. |
| English, Robert | Farmer | nr Anaheim | Los Angeles Co | Anaheim. |
| Engle, William | Clerk | Los Angeles | Los Angeles | Los Angeles. |
| English, Louis L | Farmer | nr Santa Ana | Los Angeles Co | Santa Ana. |
| England, William I | Hotel keeper | San Fernando | Los Angeles Co | San Fernando. |
| English, Louis | Teamster | Los Angeles Co | | Capistrano. |
| English, Leavin | Farmer | nr Downey | Los Angeles Co | Downey. |
| English, Simeon V | Miner | Los Angeles Co | | Santa Ana. |
| Englander, Joseph | Harness maker | Los Angeles | Los Angeles | Los Angeles. |
| **English, F F** | Farmer | Los Angeles Co | nr Azusa | Azusa. |
| **England, R T** | Farmer | nr Azusa | Azusa | Azusa. |
| Enlors, B F | Carpenter | S P R R Co | Wilmington | Wilmington. |
| **Ennie, J S** | Farmer | Los Angeles Co | nr Los Angeles | Los Angeles. |
| Enriques, Manuel | Merchant | Los Angeles | Los Angeles | Los Angeles. |
| Enrinos, Carmel | Laborer | Los Angeles Co | | Los Angeles. |
| Entenener, Martin | Carpenter | Los Angeles Co | | Los Angeles. |
| **Ergenbright, O P** | Farmer | San Gabriel | 9 m E Los Angeles | San Gabriel. |
| Erkenbrock, Philip | Ranchero | nr El Monte | Los Angeles | El Monte. |
| Erkel, George | Trader | Los Angeles Co | Anaheim | Anaheim. |
| Ernst, Hieman | Merchant | Wilmington | Wilmington | Wilmington. |
| Ernst, I | Clerk | Canal st | Canal st | Wilmington. |
| Escaiche, Francis | Sheep raiser | nr Los Angeles | Los Angeles | Los Angeles. |
| Escalante, Ygnacio | Laborer | Los Angeles Co | | Los Angeles. |
| Eschrich, John K | Farmer | nr Los Angeles | Los Angeles | Los Angeles. |
| Escobedo, Clemente | Hatter | Los Angeles | Los Angeles | Los Angeles. |
| Escontrillas, Jose | Laborer | Los Angeles Co | | Los Angeles. |
| Eskridge, Benj R | Teacher | | Old Mission | El Monte. |
| Eslope, Jose | Farmer | nr San Gabriel | Los Angeles Co | San Gabriel. |
| Esmond, Thomas F | Carpenter | Los Angeles Co | | Wilmington. |
| Esparza, Jacinto | Shoe maker | Los Angeles | Los Angeles | Los Angeles. |
| Espinoza, Anastacio | Laborer | Los Angeles Co | | Los Angeles. |
| Espinosa, Juan | Shoe maker | San Gabriel | San Gabriel | San Gabriel. |
| **Espinosa, Jose A** | Farmer | Los Angeles Co | San Jose | Spadra. |
| Esquer, Ponciano | Laborer | Los Angeles Co | | Los Angeles. |
| Esquibel, Florenteno | Laborer | | Los Angeles Co | Los Angeles. |
| Estrada, Francisco | Vaquero | Los Angeles Co | Florence | Los Angeles. |
| **Estrada, Jose** | Blacksmith | Los Angeles | Los Angeles | Los Angeles. |
| Estrada, Francisco | Laborer | Los Angeles Co | | Los Angeles. |
| Estrada, Demetrio | Laborer | | Los Angeles Co | Los Angeles. |
| Estis, William H | Farmer | nr Anaheim | Los Angeles Co | Anaheim. |
| Etcheverry, Michael | Sheep raiser | nr Los Angeles | Los Angeles Co | Los Angeles. |
| **Euphrat, Dr F** | Physician & surg | Main st | Los Angeles | Los Angeles. |
| Evans, Bishop | Teamster | Los Angeles Co | | Los Angeles. |

| Name. | Occupation. | Place of Business. | Residence. | Town or P. O. |
|---|---|---|---|---|
| Evans, John | Builder | | Los Angeles Co | Los Angeles. |
| Evans, H W | Carpenter | Los Angeles Co | | Los Nietos. |
| Evans, Frank C | Butcher | Los Angeles | Los Angeles | Los Angeles. |
| Evans, Walter | Laborer | Los Angeles Co | | Los Angeles. |
| **Evans, James** | Farmer | Los Angeles Co | Cerritos | Wilmington. |
| Evey, David | Farmer | nr Anaheim | Los Angeles Co | Anaheim. |
| Evey, Edward | Farmer | Los Angeles Co | nr Anaheim | Anaheim. |
| Evers, Otto Theo | Laborer | Los Angeles Co | | Anaheim. |
| Everett, William F | Carpenter | | Los Angeles Co | Los Angeles. |
| Ewer, William A | Cook | Los Angeles Co | | Los Angeles. |
| Fader, G | Sailor | | Los Angeles Co | Los Angeles. |
| Fainey, J | Carpenter | Los Angeles Co | | Los Angeles. |
| Fainey, J | Miner | | | Wilmington. |
| Fair, James | Teamster | Los Angeles Co | | Los Angeles. |
| Falcenstein, R | Laborer | | Los Angeles Co | Los Angeles. |
| Fall, G M | Stage agent | Los Angeles Co | | Los Angeles. |
| Fanhart, J | Butcher | Los Angeles | Los Angeles | Los Angeles. |
| Farrington, R E | Farmer | nr Downey | Los Angeles Co | Downey. |
| **Fanning, Frank B** | Broker | Los Angeles | Los Angeles | Los Angeles. |
| Fanning, F B | Accountant | 1 Spring st | Los Angeles | Los Angeles. |
| Farley, Rev F | Catholic priest | Mission Church | San Gabriel | San Gabriel. |
| Farnsworth, O H | Carpenter | Los Angeles | Los Angeles | Los Angeles. |
| Farnham, Gilbert | Farmer | nr Los Angeles | Los Angeles Co | Los Angeles. |
| Farrell, Thomas | Waiter | Los Angeles | Los Angeles | Los Angeles. |
| Farris, James David | Farmer | nr Compton | Los Angeles Co | Compton. |
| Farris, Wm F | Farmer | Los Angeles Co | nr Compton | Compton. |
| Farris, George B | Farmer | nr San Juan | Los Angeles Co | Compton. |
| Farrell, William | Gasfitter | Los Angeles | Los Angeles | Los Angeles. |
| **Farris, J F** | Farmer | nr Florence | Los Angeles Co | Florence. |
| Farris, J D | Farmer | nr Los Angeles | Los Angeles Co | Los Angeles. |
| **Farrell, J** | Farmer | Los Angeles | nr Los Angeles | Los Angeles. |
| Farrar, G B | Farmer | nr Los Angeles | Los Angeles Co | Los Angeles. |
| Farrell, Wm | Gas fitter | 15 Court st | Los Angeles | Los Angeles. |
| Farrell, R S | Blacksmith | S P R R Co | Wilmington | Wilmington. |
| **Faucett, T M** | Farmer | Los Angeles Co | nr Downey | Downey. |
| **Faucett, Thomas** | Farmer | nr Los Angeles | Los Angeles Co | Los Angeles. |
| Fausnicht, Andrew | Wagon maker | Los Angeles | Los Angeles | Los Angeles. |
| Fawcett, Miles | Carpenter | Los Angeles Co | Westminster Col | Westminster. |
| Fay, John M | Clerk | Los Angeles | Los Angeles | Los Angeles. |
| Fay, Melvin Samuel | Laborer | Los Angeles Co | | Los Angeles. |
| Feeks, C Ellison | Farmer | nr San Gabriel | Los Angeles Co | San Gabriel. |
| Feelis, M | Carpenter | Los Angeles Co | | Los Angeles. |
| Felx, Julius I | Farmer | nr San Gabriel | Los Angeles Co | San Gabriel. |
| Felch, N | Butcher | Los Angeles | Los Angeles | Los Angeles. |
| Feliz, Jeromino | Laborer | Los Angeles Co | | San Gabriel. |
| Felis, J J | Laborer | Los Angeles Co | | Santa Ana. |
| Felis, E | Laborer | Los Angeles Co | | Spadra. |
| **Felis, J G** | Farmer | nr Los Angeles | Los Angeles Co | Los Angeles. |
| Fliz, Anastacio M | Ranchero | nr Los Angeles | Los Angeles Co | Los Angeles. |
| Feliz, Ramon | Laborer | Los Angeles Co | | Santa Ana. |
| Felix, Francisco | Carpenter | | Los Angeles Co | Los Angeles. |
| Feliz, Ramon Vejarde | Laborer | | Los Angeles | Los Angeles. |
| Feliz, Nicolas | Carpenter | | Los Angeles Co | Los Angeles. |
| Feliz, Jordan | Laborer | Los Angeles Co | | Spadra. |
| Feliz, Tomas | Ranchero | nr San Fernando | Los Angeles Co | San Fernando. |
| **Feliz, S** | Farmer | nr Los Angeles | Los Angeles Co | Los Angeles. |
| Feliz, Jose Jesus | Farmer | Los Angeles Co | nr Santa Ana | Santa Ana. |
| Feliz, Jose Jesus | Laborer | Los Angeles Co | | San Fernando. |
| Feliz, Anastacio | Laborer | | Los Angeles Co | Los Angeles. |
| Feliz, Martiniano | Carpenter | Los Angeles Co | | Los Angeles. |
| **Felkin, S I** | Harness maker | Los Angeles | Los Angeles | Los Angeles. |
| Fellows, David | Miner | San Gabriel Canyon | 14 m N Azusa | Azusa. |

DIRECTORY OF LOS ANGELES COUNTY. 347

| Name. | Occupation. | Place of Business. | Residence. | Town or P. O. |
|---|---|---|---|---|
| Felt, I W............ | Salesman ............ | San Gabriel............ | San Gabriel............ | San Gabriel. |
| Femmons, F......... | Carpenter............ | San Pedro Ranch.... | 1 m W Compton...... | Compton. |
| Fenell, J............... | Farmer .............. | Los Angeles Co........ | Silver Precinct......... | Downey. |
| Fennessy, James.... | Blacksmith ........ | Los Angeles............ | Los Angeles............ | Los Angeles. |
| Feraut, Pierre........ | Farmer .............. | Los Angeles Co........ | nr Los Angeles........ | Los Angeles. |
| Feraut, J ............. | Farmer .............. | Los Angeles Co........ | nr Los Angeles........ | Los Angeles. |
| Ferguson, William | Livery stable....... | Los Angeles............ | Los Angeles............ | Los Angeles. |
| Ferguson, Charles... | Farmer .............. | nr Spadra.............. | Los Angeles Co........ | Spadra. |
| Ferguson & Roe.... | Livery stable....... | Main st.................. | ............................ | Los Angeles. |
| Ferguson, J B...... | Coal dealer.......... | Spring & Court sts... | 9th st..................... | Los Angeles. |
| Ferlin, Auguste ..... | Ranchero ............ | nr Los Angeles........ | Los Angeles Co........ | Los Angeles. |
| Ferman, Louis...... | Cook .................. | Los Angeles............ | Los Angeles............ | Los Angeles. |
| Fernandez, Matias. | Laborer ... .......... | Los Angeles Co........ | ............................ | Los Angeles. |
| Ferrari, Louis ...... | Clerk................... | Los Angeles............ | Los Angeles............ | Los Angeles. |
| Ferrari, G............ | Merchant ............ | Los Angeles............ | Los Angeles............ | Los Angeles. |
| Ferris, C.............. | Farmer ............... | Los Angeles Co........ | nr Los Angeles........ | Los Angeles. |
| Ferre, James......... | Moulder .............. | Los Angeles............ | Los Angeles............ | Los Angeles. |
| Ferrot & Saentons | Butchers.............. | Los Angeles............ | Los Angeles............ | Los Angeles. |
| Fessender, A......... | Farmer ............... | nr Los Angeles........ | Los Angeles............ | Los Angeles. |
| Ficks, L............... | Farmer ............... | Los Angeles Co........ | nr Santa Ana.......... | Santa Ana. |
| Fidolin, V............ | Sheep raiser ........ | Los Angeles Co........ | nr Los Angeles........ | Los Angeles. |
| Fields, D W ........ | Farmer ............... | Los Angeles Co........ | nr Anaheim............ | Anaheim. |
| Fifield, George ..... | Teamster............. | Los Angeles Co........ | ............................ | Los Angeles. |
| Figueroa, Miguel.. | Farmer ............... | Los Angeles Co........ | nr San Gabriel........ | San Gabriel. |
| Figueroa, Feliciano | Farmer ............... | Los Angeles Co........ | nr San Gabriel........ | San Gabriel. |
| Figueroa, Gabriel... | Laborer ............... | Los Angeles Co........ | San Gabriel............ | San Gabriel. |
| Figueroa, Diego .... | Laborer................ | Los Angeles Co........ | Los Angeles............ | Los Angeles. |
| Figueroa, Belisario. | Laborer................ | ............................ | Los Angeles Co........ | Los Angeles. |
| Figueroa, Jeronimo | Gardener............. | Los Angeles Co........ | San Gabriel............ | San Gabriel. |
| Figueroa, P........... | Laborer................ | Los Angeles Co........ | ............................ | San Gabriel. |
| Figueroa, Jose....... | Laborer................ | ............................ | Los Angeles Co........ | Los Angeles. |
| Finch, Geo........... | Tailor ................. | 13 Spring st.......... | Spring st................ | Los Angeles. |
| Finch, James F..... | Farmer ............... | nr Compton............ | Los Angeles Co........ | Compton. |
| Fine, J C.............. | Farmer ............... | Los Angeles Co........ | nr Los Nietos.......... | Los Nietos. |
| Finley, Peter......... | Laborer................ | Los Angeles Co........ | ............................ | Compton. |
| Finly, J ............... | Farmer ............... | Los Angeles Co........ | Silver Precinct......... | Downey. |
| Finnell, Fountain... | Sheep raiser ........ | nr San Fernando..... | Los Angeles Co........ | San Fernando. |
| Fischer, Joseph..... | Farmer ............... | Los Angeles Co........ | San Joaquin........... | Santa Ana. |
| Fischer & Welch... | Brick makers....... | Anaheim............... | ............................ | Anaheim. |
| Fischer, J............. | Farmer ............... | nr Anaheim........... | Los Angeles Co........ | Anaheim. |
| Fischer, A............. | Musician ............. | Los Angeles............ | Los Angeles............ | Los Angeles. |
| Fish, Leander Wm | Electrician .......... | Los Angeles............ | Los Angeles............ | Los Angeles. |
| Fisher, E J........... | Clerk................... | Los Angeles............ | Los Angeles............ | Los Angeles. |
| Fish, James C....... | Carriage painter... | Los Angeles st........ | Anaheim................ | Anaheim. |
| Fisher & Thatcher | Jewelers............... | 67 Main st............. | ............................ | Los Angeles. |
| Fisher, L F........... | Publisher............. | Wilm'n Enterprise... | Canal st................. | Wilmington. |
| Fisher, Chas Sumner | Laborer................ | Los Angeles Co........ | Los Angeles............ | Los Angeles. |
| Fisher, Oliver B..... | Butcher................ | Los Nietos............. | Los Nietos............. | Los Nietos. |
| Fish, Lyman F...... | Farmer ............... | Los Angeles Co........ | Los Angeles............ | Los Angeles. |
| Fite, James C....... | Farmer ............... | Los Angeles Co........ | Silver Precinct......... | Downey. |
| Fithian, W........... | Farmer ............... | Los Angeles Co........ | nr Anaheim............ | Anaheim. |
| Fithian, Ephraim... | Farmer ............... | Los Angeles Co........ | nr Anaheim............ | Anaheim. |
| Fitzgerald, J M..... | Laborer................ | Los Angeles Co........ | ............................ | Los Angeles. |
| Fitzgerald, H M ... | Merchant............. | Los Angeles............ | Los Angeles............ | Los Angeles. |
| Fitz Gerald, Richd | Hostler................ | Los Angeles............ | Los Angeles............ | Los Angeles. |
| Fitzgerald, John.... | Laborer ............... | Los Angeles............ | Los Angeles............ | Los Angeles. |
| Fitzer, James........ | Farmer ............... | Los Angeles Co........ | nr Compton............ | Compton. |
| Fitz Patrick, D W | Merchant tailor.... | 15 Main st............. | Los Angeles............ | Los Angeles. |
| Fizer, H M........... | Carpenter............ | Los Angeles Co........ | Silver Precinct......... | Downey. |
| Flanagan, T J....... | Engineer.............. | Los Angeles............ | Los Angeles............ | Los Angeles. |
| Flanders, D P....... | Photographer....... | Los Angeles............ | Los Angeles............ | Los Angeles. |
| Flanders, S C........ | ........................... | ............................ | Los Angeles............ | Los Angeles. |
| Fleischman, Jacob | Farmer ............... | nr Los Angeles........ | Los Angeles Co........ | Los Angeles. |

| Name. | Occupation. | Place of Business. | Residence. | Town or P. O. |
|---|---|---|---|---|
| Fleishman, — | Stationery store | 50 Main st | Fort st | Los Angeles. |
| Fleishman, Henry | Merchant | Los Angeles | Los Angeles | Los Angeles. |
| Fleishman, Herman | Hotel keeper | Los Angeles | Los Angeles | Los Angeles. |
| Fleming, J H | Harness maker | nr Westminster | Wesminster Col | Wesminster. |
| Flemming, Wm Patton | Farmer | nr Downey | Silver Precinct | Downey. |
| Fletcher, E W | Merchant | Los Angeles | Los Angeles | Los Angeles. |
| Fletcher, E E | Farmer | Los Angeles Co | | Wilmington. |
| Fletcher, Nathan | Farmer | nr Los Angeles | Los Angeles Co | Los Angeles. |
| Fletcher, Nathan, Jr | Farmer | Los Angeles Co | nr Los Angeles | Los Angeles. |
| Fletcher, Morris | Laborer | Los Angeles Co | | Anaheim. |
| Flinn, Thomas | Laborer | Los Angeles Co | | Los Angeles. |
| Flint, Edward A | Engineer | Wilmington | Wilmington | Wilmington. |
| Flood, L | Farmer | San Pedro Ranch | 1 m S W Compton | Compton. |
| Flood, J A J | Farmer | San Pedro Ranch | 1 m S W Compton | Compton. |
| Flood, George | Farmer | San Fernando Miss'n | 2 m W San Fernando | San Fernando. |
| Flood, George W | Farmer | Los Angeles Co | nr Halfway House | Compton. |
| Flood, John Andrew, J | Farmer | Los Angeles Co | nr Halfway House | Compton. |
| Flores, M | Saddler | Los Angeles | Los Angeles | Los Angeles. |
| Flores, R | Laborer | Los Angeles | Los Angeles | Los Angeles. |
| Flores, V | Laborer | Los Angeles | La Ballona | Los Angeles. |
| Flores, James | Carp'r & blsmith | San Gabriel | 9 m E Los Angeles | San Gabriel. |
| Flores, G | Peddler | San Gabriel | 9 m E Los Angeles | San Gabriel. |
| Flores, Jesus | Miner | Los Angeles Co | | San Gabriel. |
| Flores, Santiago | Laborer | Los Angeles Co | | San Gabriel. |
| Flores, Jose Jesus | Laborer | | San Gabriel | San Gabriel. |
| Flores, Anastacio | Laborer | | Los Angeles Co | Los Angeles. |
| Flote & Cason | Oriental rest'nt | Main st | | Los Angeles. |
| Flote, B | Oriental rest'nt | Main st | Los Angeles | Los Angeles. |
| Flowers, Henry | Farmer | Los Angeles Co | nr Compton | Compton. |
| Floyd, T L | Farmer | Los Angeles Co | nr El Monte | El Monte. |
| Floyd, Frank | Farmer | Ellis Station | 2 m W Lexington | El Monte. |
| Floyd, R J | Farmer | Ellis Station | 1½ m W Lexington | El Monte. |
| Floyd, Robert J | Farmer | Los Angeles Co | nr El Monte | El Monte. |
| Fluhr & Gerson | Hotel | Los Angeles Co | Los Angeles | Los Angeles. |
| Fluhr, Chris | Lafayette hotel | Los Angeles | Los Angeles | Los Angeles. |
| Fluhr, Mary | Laundry | Los Angeles | Los Angeles | Los Angeles. |
| Flynn, B J | Tanner | nr Los Angeles | Los Angeles Co | Los Angeles. |
| Foch, C | Merchant | Los Angeles | Los Angeles | Los Angeles. |
| Fogle, H | Farmer | Los Angeles Co | Old Mission | El Monte. |
| Fogle, L | Farmer | Los Angeles Co | nr Halfway House | Compton. |
| Fogle, Henry | Farmer | El Monte Valley | 3 m S Lexington | El Monte. |
| Fogle, Andrew | Farmer | Los Angeles Co | nr Los Angeles | Los Angeles. |
| Fogo, Manuel J | Cook | Wilmington | Wilmington | Wilmington. |
| Foley, Danl J | Printer | Los Angeles Co | Los Angeles Co | Los Angeles. |
| Foley, Francis M | Laborer | Los Angeles Co | El Monte | El Monte. |
| Follen, Wm | Laborer | Los Angeles Co | | Los Angeles. |
| Folsom, Geo E | Ranchero | Wilmington | Wilmington | Wilmington. |
| Folsom, Chas D | Ranchero | Wilmington | | Wilmington. |
| Fonck, John Victor | Trimmer | Los Angeles | Los Angeles | Los Angeles. |
| Fontana, Carlo | S F restaurant | Centre & Clem'ne sts | | Anaheim. |
| Foote, N | Plasterer | Los Angeles | Los Angeles | Los Angeles. |
| Foran, G W | Clerk | Los Angeles | Los Angeles | Los Angeles. |
| Forbes, Paul | Check clerk | S P R R Co | Wilmington | Wilmington. |
| Forbush, E | Laborer | | Los Angeles Co | Los Angeles. |
| Forbes, C H | Teacher | Los Angeles | | Los Angeles. |
| Ford, J | Carpenter | | Los Angeles Co | Los Angeles. |
| Ford, A D | Miner | Azusa | Azusa | Azusa. |
| Ford, James | Farmer | San Gabriel | San Gabriel | San Gabriel. |
| Foreman, S | Butcher | San Gabriel | 9 m E Los Angeles | San Gabriel. |
| Forsman, Hugh | Farmer | Los Angeles Co | nr Los Nietos | Los Nietos. |

# DIRECTORY OF LOS ANGELES COUNTY. 349

| Name. | Occupation. | Place of Business. | Residence. | Town or P. O. |
|---|---|---|---|---|
| Forst, A............... | Proprietor hotel... | Ellis Station............ | 1 m W Lexington... | El Monte. |
| Foster, H............... | Farmer ............... | Los Angeles Co....... | nr Los Angeles......... | Los Angeles. |
| Foster, D............... | Farmer ............... | Los Angeles Co....... | nr Los Angeles......... | Los Angeles. |
| Foster, S C............ | Farmer ............... | Los Angeles Co....... | nr Los Angeles......... | Los Angeles. |
| Foster, Francisco A | Farmer ............... | Los Angeles Co....... | ............................... | Los Angeles. |
| Foster, Fernando ... | Blacksmith.......... | Los Angeles........... | Los Angeles........... | Los Angeles. |
| Foster, George W .. | Farmer ............... | Los Angeles Co....... | Silver Precinct....... | Downey. |
| Fouck, J L............ | Carriage trimmer | Wilmington........... | Wilmington........... | Wilmington. |
| Fountain, George... | Farmer ............... | Los Angeles Valley.. | 10 m S Wilmington.. | Wilmington. |
| Fourcade, P ......... | Sheep raiser....... | Los Angeles........... | nr Los Angeles......... | Los Angeles. |
| Fournier, F............ | Clerk.................. | Los Angeles........... | Los Angeles........... | Los Angeles. |
| Fournier, F............ | ........................... | ........................... | Los Angeles Co....... | Los Angeles. |
| Fourgirat, J........... | Laborer ............... | ........................... | Los Angeles Co....... | Los Angeles. |
| Fowler, H D.......... | Farmer ............... | ........................... | Silver Precinct....... | Downey. |
| Fowler, James...... | Farmer ............... | Los Angeles Co....... | ............................... | Los Angeles. |
| Fox, S C................ | Harness manufr... | 17 Front st............ | Pearl bet 7th & O'nge | Los Angeles. |
| Fox, Wm Henry.... | Carpenter........... | Los Angeles Co....... | Anaheim .............. | Anaheim. |
| Fox, John Joseph.. | Printer................ | Los Angeles Co....... | ............................... | Los Angeles. |
| Fox, John............. | Laborer ............... | ........................... | Los Angeles Co....... | Los Angeles. |
| Fraijo, P............... | Laborer ............... | Los Angeles Co....... | Old Mission ......... | El Monte. |
| Fraijo, G............... | Farmer ............... | ........................... | Los Angeles Co....... | Los Angeles. |
| Fraigo, Ysidro....... | Plasterer............. | Los Angeles........... | ............................... | Los Angeles. |
| Frame, G.............. | Farmer ............... | Los Angeles Co....... | Silver Precinct....... | Downey. |
| Franklin, B............ | Teamster............. | ........................... | Los Angeles Co....... | Los Angeles. |
| Frankel, M............ | Merchant............ | Downey ............:... | Silver Precinct....... | Downey. |
| Frankel, M E ....... | Merchant............ | Downey ............... | Silver Precinct ....... | Downey. |
| Frankel, C............ | Miner................... | ........................... | Los Angeles Co....... | Los Angeles. |
| Franklin, D C....... | Physician............. | Los Angeles........... | ............................... | Los Angeles. |
| Frank, J................ | Merchant............ | Los Angeles........... | Los Angeles........... | Los Angeles. |
| Franklin, F............ | Farmer ............... | Los Angeles Co....... | nr El Monte........... | El Monte. |
| Frame, D M.......... | Farmer ............... | Los Angeles Co....... | Silver Precinct....... | Downey. |
| Franklin, J T......... | Farmer ............... | Los Angeles Co....... | nr El Monte........... | El Monte. |
| Frank, Martin....... | Miner................... | Los Angeles Co....... | ............................... | Los Angeles. |
| Francis, John........ | Wharf hand......... | S P R R Co............. | Wilmington........... | Wilmington. |
| France, Jacob F..... | Carpenter........... | Los Angeles Co....... | ............................... | Los Angeles. |
| Franklin, D W C... | Dentist ............... | 11 Spring st........... | Los Angeles........... | Los Angeles. |
| Franklin, John....... | Farmer ............... | El Monte Valley...... | 3 m S Lexington...... | El Monte. |
| Franklin, Marshall.. | Farmer ............... | Los Angeles Co....... | ............................... | Los Angeles. |
| Franco, Pablo........ | Laborer ............... | ........................... | Los Angeles Co....... | Los Angeles. |
| Frankell, Samuel... | Merchant............ | Downey ............... | Silver Precinct ....... | Downey. |
| Franklin, Samuel... | Farmer ............... | Los Angeles Co....... | nr El Monte........... | El Monte. |
| Francisco, Manuel.. | Farmer ............... | Los Angeles Co....... | nr Wilmington ....... | Wilmington. |
| Franck, Adolph ..... | Butcher............... | Los Angeles........... | ............................... | Los Angeles. |
| Franklin, John....... | Farmer ............... | Los Angeles Co....... | nr El Monte........... | El Monte. |
| Frashier, G W ....... | Farmer ............... | Los Angeles Co....... | Compton .............. | Compton. |
| Frawley, Timothy .. | Boot maker......... | ........................... | Los Angeles........... | Los Angeles. |
| Frazier, Thos......... | Boot maker......... | Front st................ | Front st................ | Wilmington. |
| Frazer, Joseph M... | Teamster............. | Los Angeles Co....... | Silver Precinct....... | Downey. |
| Freeman, Royal L.. | Teacher............... | ........................... | Tustin City........... | Santa Ana. |
| Freeman, Geo W... | Farmer ............... | ........................... | Tustin City........... | Santa Ana. |
| Freer, Thos .......... | Farmer ............... | El Monte Valley...... | 1½ m N Lexington... | El Monte. |
| Freer, John........... | Farmer ............... | El Monte Valley...... | 1½ m N Lexington... | El Monte. |
| Freitas, J.............. | Wharf hand......... | S P R R Co............. | Wilmington........... | Wilmington. |
| French, L W ........ | Dentist ............... | 86 Main st............ | ............................... | Los Angeles. |
| French, C E.......... | Clerk.................. | Los Angeles Co....... | Santa Ana ........... | Santa Ana. |
| French, A T ......... | Locomotive eng... | S P R R Co............. | San Fernando........ | San Fernando. |
| Frend, S W........... | Clerk.................. | Los Angeles Co....... | ............................... | Los Angeles. |
| French, Loving W. | Dentist ............... | Los Angeles........... | Los Angeles........... | Los Angeles. |
| Freyer, J W........... | Farmer ............... | Los Angeles Co ...... | nr El Monte........... | El Monte. |
| Frier, T................. | Farmer ............... | Los Angeles Co....... | nr El Monte........... | El Monte. |
| Frimat, G.............. | Laborer ............... | Los Angeles Co....... | ............................... | Los Angeles. |
| Frink, E B............. | Clerk.................. | ........................... | Los Angeles Co....... | Los Angeles. |
| Froehlinger & Franck ............. | Butchers............. | Main st................ | ............................... | Los Angeles. |

| Name. | Occupation. | Place of Business. | Residence. | Town or P. O. |
|---|---|---|---|---|
| Frohling, Francis... | Blacksmith | | Los Angeles Co. | Los Angeles. |
| Frohliger, Wm H.. | Farmer | Los Angeles Co. | nr Los Nietos. | Los Nietos. |
| Froon, Eli | Farmer | Los Angeles Co. | San Gabriel | San Gabriel. |
| Frost, C | Farmer | | Los Angeles Co. | Los Angeles. |
| Fryer, R C | Farmer | Los Angeles Co. | nr El Monte | El Monte. |
| Fryer, Lyttleton M. | Farmer | | San Jose | Spadra. |
| Fryer, James M. | Farmer | Los Angeles Co. | San Jose. | Spadra. |
| Fryer, Jerry | Farmer | Los Angeles Co. | San Jose | Spadra. |
| Frymire, Walter.... | Laborer | Los Angeles Co. | San Jose | Spadra. |
| Fry, George Wm... | Nurseryman | Los Angeles Co. | | Los Angeles. |
| Fryer, J | Farmer | Spadra | 30 m E Los Angeles. | Spadra. |
| Fryer, R C | Farmer | Spadra | 30 m E Los Angeles. | Spadra. |
| Fryer, Jas | Farmer | Spadra | 30 m E Los Angeles. | Spadra. |
| Fuentez, J D | Laborer | Los Angeles Co. | Old Mission | El Monte. |
| Fullerton, C H | Waiter | Los Angeles Co. | Anaheim | Anaheim. |
| Fuller, A | Farmer | Los Angeles Co. | nr Los Nietos | Los Nietos. |
| Fuller, Albert L. | Carpenter | | Los Angeles Co. | Los Angeles. |
| Fuller, Chas. | Shepherd | Los Angeles Co. | nr Los Nietos | Los Nietos. |
| Fulton, Dr J E. | Physician | Downey City. | Downey City. | Downey. |
| Furlong, Luke. | Miner | Los Angeles Co. | nr Los Nietos | Los Nietos. |
| Furlong, R | Teacher | Los Angeles Co. | Silver Precinct | Downey. |
| Furlong, R | Farmer | | nr Florence. | Los Angeles. |
| Furman, G R | Farmer | Los Angeles Co. | nr Wilmington | Wilmington. |
| Furrey, Patrick | Stone cutter | Los Angeles | Los Angeles. | Los Angeles. |
| Furrey, Wm C | Hardware | 19 Los Angeles st | | Los Angeles. |
| Fury, William | Laborer | | El Monte | El Monte. |
| Gable, Geo. Wash... | Attorney | | Los Angeles | Los Angeles. |
| Gabriel, John Peter | Farmer | | Los Angeles Co. | Los Angeles. |
| Gaddy & Lewis, | Livery stable | Los Angeles st | | Anaheim. |
| Gaertner, E G. | Mining engineer | r 15 Downey Block | | Los Angeles. |
| Gage, A R | Carpenter | Los Angeles Co. | | Los Angeles. |
| Gage, J D | Farmer | Los Angeles Co. | nr Santa Ana. | Santa Ana. |
| Gage, Henry | | | Canal st | Wilmington. |
| Gage, D W | Sheep raiser | Los Angeles Co. | Canal st | Wilmington. |
| Gaillard & Savin... | Gen merchandise. | Los Angeles st | | Anaheim. |
| Guine, F | Teamster | Los Angeles Co. | | Los Angeles. |
| Gainier, P | Sheep raiser | Los Angeles Co. | nr Los Angeles | Los Angeles. |
| Gaines, J W | Joiner | | Los Angeles Co. | Compton. |
| Gaines, S M | Farmer | Los Angeles Co. | Green Meadows. | Compton. |
| Gaines, J W | Farmer | San Pedro Ranch. | 2 m S W Compton. | Compton. |
| Gaines, Robert | Butcher | Los Angeles. | Los Angeles. | Los Angeles. |
| Gains, John Wm | Stage driver | Los Angeles Co. | | Los Angeles. |
| Gaiter, Milton | Carpenter | Los Angeles Co. | | Los Angeles. |
| Gale, S | Farmer | Los Angeles Co. | nr Los Angeles | Los Angeles. |
| Galen, Antonio | Bartender | | Los Angeles Co. | Los Angeles. |
| Galinto, Desiderio. | Vaquero | | Los Angeles Co. | Los Angeles. |
| Galindo, Jesus | Laborer | Los Angeles Co. | | |
| Gallardo, Yginio | Laborer | | Los Angeles Co. | Los Angeles. |
| Gallardo, Francisco M | Farmer | Los Angeles Co. | | Los Angeles. |
| Gallardo, Feliz | Farmer | | Los Angeles Co. | Los Angeles. |
| Gallardo, Raphael | Farmer | Los Angeles Co. | Los Angeles. | Los Angeles. |
| Gallardo, Juan | Farmer | Los Angeles Co. | Los Nietos | Los Nietos. |
| Gallego, W | Laborer. | Los Angeles Co. | Los Angeles Co. | Los Angeles. |
| Gallego, G | Laborer | Los Angeles Co. | | Los Angeles. |
| Gallagher, T | Boot maker | Los Angeles Co. | | Los Angeles. |
| Gallagher, Patrick. | Laborer | Los Angeles Co. | | Los Angeles. |
| Galvin, Mrs B | Dress maker | | Los Angeles Co. | Los Angeles. |
| Gamble, D | Tinsmith | Los Angeles Co. | Los Angeles. | Los Angeles. |
| Gamble, Jno A | Carpenter | Los Angeles Co. | | Los Angeles. |
| Gamez, Francisco | Laborer | | Los Angeles Co. | Los Angeles. |
| Gammon, A J | Barkeeper | Los Angeles Co. | | Los Angeles. |
| Ganahl & McDaniels | Attorneys at law. | Downey Block | | Los Angeles. |

## DIRECTORY OF LOS ANGELES COUNTY.

| Name. | Occupation. | Place of Business. | Residence. |
|---|---|---|---|
| Ganahl, F | Lawyer | Los Angeles | Los Angeles |
| Gandot, E C | Farmer | Los Angeles Co | nr Los Angeles |
| Gammon, Thos | Laborer | | Los Angeles Co |
| Ganthier, F | Coffee & spice mls | 50 Los Angeles st | |
| Ganthier, Ferdinand | Manufacturer | | Los Angeles Co |
| Gara, Domingo | Vaquero | Los Angeles Co | Los Angeles Co |
| Garcia, Francisco | Mason | Los Angeles Co | Los Angeles Co |
| Garcia, Antonio | Laborer | Los Angeles Co | San Gabriel |
| Garcia, Anselmo | Blacksmith | Los Angeles Co | Los Angeles |
| Garcia, Jesus | Laborer | Los Angeles Co | Los Angeles |
| Garcia, Lauriano | Laborer | Los Angeles Co | Old Mission |
| Garcia, Antonio | Ranchero | Los Angeles Co | San Jose |
| Garcia, Francisco | Vaquero | Los Angeles Co | San Gabriel |
| Garcia, Rafael | Laborer | Los Angeles Co | Los Angeles |
| Garcia, Manuel | Merchant | Los Angeles Co | San Juan |
| Garcia, Juan B | Laborer | Los Angeles Co | San Jose |
| Garcia, Anacleto | Laborer | Los Angeles Co | Los Angeles |
| Garcia, Manuel | Laborer | Los Angeles Co | San Jose |
| Garcia, Rafael | Laborer | Los Angeles Co | San Gabriel |
| Garcia, Juan Jose | Laborer | Los Angeles Co | San Jose |
| Garcia, Jose Dolores | Merchant | Los Angeles Co | San Juan |
| Garcia, Salvador | Herdsman | Los Angeles Co | Los Angeles |
| Garcia, Jose | Laborer | Los Angeles Co | Los Angeles |
| Garcia, Jose de la lus | Laborer | Los Angeles Co | San Jose |
| Garcia, Gabriel | Laborer | Los Angeles Co | San Jose |
| Garcia, P | Farmer | Los Angeles Co | nr Los Angeles |
| Garcia, P | Farmer | Los Angeles Co | Silver Precinct |
| Garcia, D | Blacksmith | Los Angeles Co | Anaheim |
| Garcia, D | Farmer | Los Angeles Co | La Ballona |
| Garcia, J | Laborer | Los Angeles Co | |
| Garcia, J M | Cook | Wilmington | Wilmington |
| Garcia, Jackson | Wharf hand | S P R R Co | Wilmington |
| Garcia, P | Farmer | San Fernando Valley | 1 m N W San Fern'do |
| Garcia, P | Wharf hand | S P R R Co | Wilmington |
| Garcia, Juan | Farmer | San Bernardino Road | 4 m E Spadra |
| Garcia, Refugio A | Laborer | | Spadra |
| Garcia, Ayapito | Laborer | Los Angeles Co | |
| Garcia, Jose A | Laborer | Los Angeles Co | San Juan |
| Garcia, Ignacio de J | Laborer | Los Angeles Co | Old Mission |
| Garcia, Dolores | Livery stable | San Juan Capistrano | Los Angeles Co |
| Gard, George Edwin | Surveyor | Los Angeles Co | Los Angeles |
| Gardner, William | Mechanic | Los Angeles Co | Los Angeles |
| Gardner, J | Stage driver | Los Angeles Co | |
| Gardner, A L | Merchant | Los Angeles Co | Los Angeles |
| Gardner, O B | Miner | Los Angeles Co | nr Wilmington |
| Gardner, C A | Reporter | | Anaheim |
| Gardner, J S Dr | Physician & surg. | Clark's bldg | Anaheim |
| Garey, Thos A | Semi-trop nursery | San Pedro st | 2 m S City Hall |
| Garfias, E | Farmer | Los Angeles Co | Silver Precinct |
| Garfias, Manuel | Ranchero | Los Angeles Co | nr Los Angeles |
| Garibald, Jean | Merchant | Los Angeles | Los Angeles |
| Garibaldi, Joseph | Merchant | Los Angeles | Los Angeles |
| Garibaldi, Lorenzo | Groceryman | Los Angeles | Los Angeles |
| Garner, C | Painter | Los Angeles | Los Angeles |
| Garnier Bros | Sheep raisers | Coast Line Road | 9 m S San Fernando |
| Garnier, Camille | Stock raiser | Los Angeles Co | nr Los Angeles |
| Garrett, Robt S | Wheelwright | Wilmington | Wilmington |
| Garrett, Robert Odle | Farmer | Los Angeles Co | Silver Precinct |
| Garrett, R L | Wagon maker | 1st st | Willie st |
| Garvey, Richard | Miner | Los Angeles Co | |
| Gassagne, Charles | Hotel keeper | Los Angeles Co | Los Angeles |
| Gastelum, Leberato | Laborer | Los Angeles Co | |
| Gates, George | Miner | Los Angeles Co | Azusa |

352    L. L. PAULSON'S HAND-BOOK AND

| Name. | Occupation. | Place of Business. | Residence. | Town or P. O. |
|---|---|---|---|---|
| Gates, Thomas. | Miner | Los Angeles Co | Los Angeles | Los Angeles. |
| Gates, F | Farmer | Los Angeles Co | Silver Precinct | Downey. |
| Gates, W | Printer | Los Angeles Co | Santa Ana | Santa Ana. |
| Gates, B | Stock | Los Angeles Co | 4½ m W Lyon Stat'n | Lyon Station. |
| Gates, Solomon | Farmer | | Los Angeles Co | Los Angeles. |
| Gates, Bryant | Farmer | | San Vicente Ranch | Los Angeles. |
| Gaudry, A C | Cook | Los Angeles | Los Angeles | Los Angeles. |
| Gauns, S | Laborer | Los Angeles Co | | Los Angeles. |
| Gautt, Julius H | Farmer | Los Angeles Co | San Gabriel | San Gabriel. |
| Gavitt, Lorenzo D | Miller | | Los Angeles Co | Los Angeles. |
| Gay, E | Contracter | Los Angeles Co | | Los Argeles. |
| Gazaway, J R | Farmer | Los Angeles Co | nr El Monte | El Monte. |
| Gaze, Daniel W | Farmer | Los Angeles Co | Los Angeles | Los Angeles. |
| Gedge, John | Painter | | Los Angeles | Los Angeles. |
| Gee, — | Shoe maker | Canal st | Wilmington | Wilmington. |
| Geer, F M | Farmer | Los Angeles Co | nr Los Angeles | Los Angeles. |
| Geller, Wm Dr | Physician | Lexington | 12 m E Los Angeles | El Monte. |
| Geller, W Jr | Farmer | Los Angeles Co | nr El Monte | El Monte. |
| Geller, W | Physician | Los Angeles Co | El Monte | El Monte. |
| Gelsich, V | Physician | Los Angeles | Los Angeles | Los Angeles. |
| Genoud, J | Moulder | Los Angeles | Los Angeles | Los Angeles. |
| George, John | Farmer | Los Angeles Co | nr Los Angeles | Los Angeles. |
| George, Henry D | Sail maker | Los Angeles Co | San Juan | Capistrano. |
| George, Oscar | Farmer | Los Angeles Co | Los Angeles | Los Angeles. |
| George, Ethan Allen | Laborer | Los Angeles Co | | Los Angeles. |
| George, Gevhart | Farmer | Los Angeles Co | nr El Monte | El Monte. |
| Gerety, Patrick B | Laborer | Los Angeles Co | | Los Angeles. |
| Gerkins, Jacob F | Farmer | Los Angeles Co | nr Los Angeles | Los Angeles. |
| Gerkens, Henry | Hatter | Los Angeles | Los Angeles | Los Angeles. |
| German, J T | Wheelwright | Lexington | 12 m E Los Angeles | El Monte. |
| German & Goodwin | Wheelwrights | Lexington | 12 m E Los Angeles | El Monte. |
| Germain & Co, E | Grocers | Los Angeles | | Los Angeles. |
| Germain, E | Trader | Los Angeles Co | | Los Angeles. |
| Gerry, William | Laborer | Los Angeles Co | | Los Angeles. |
| Gerrish, L W | Broom maker | 60 Aliso st | | Los Angeles. |
| Gerson, C | Merchant | Los Angeles | Los Angeles | Los Angeles. |
| Giardo, Leandro | Farmer | Los Angeles Co | nr Los Angeles | Los Angeles. |
| Gibbins, John | Farmer | Los Angeles Co | nr Los Angeles | Los Angeles. |
| Gibbons, George | Miner | Los Angeles Co | Soledad | San Fernando. |
| Gibbens, James J | Trader | Los Angeles Co | | Los Angeles. |
| Gibbs, W | Farmer | Los Angeles Co | nr Los Angeles | Los Angeles. |
| Gibbs, A | Farmer | Los Angeles Co | nr San Gabriel | San Gabriel. |
| Gibbs, Albert | Farmer | San Gabriel | 9 m E Los Angeles | San Gabriel. |
| Gibbs, Geo C | Attorney | Los Angeles | San Gabriel | San Gabriel. |
| Gibney, O | Laborer | Los Angeles Co | | Wilmington. |
| Gibson, William S | Farmer | Los Angeles Co | nr Los Angeles | Los Angeles. |
| Gibson, George | Miner | Los Angeles Co | Soledad | San Fernando. |
| Gibson, Fielding W | Farmer | Los Angeles Co | nr El Monte | El Monte. |
| Gibson, C | Ranchero | Los Angeles Co | Silver Precinct | Downey. |
| Gibson, J M | Farmer | Los Angeles Co | Silver Precinct | Downey. |
| Gibson, A M | Farmer | Los Angeles Co | Silver Precinct | Downey. |
| Gibson, Charles | Farmer | Los Angeles Co | nr Wilmington | Wilmington. |
| Gibson, F J | Bartender | Los Angeles | Los Angeles | Los Angeles. |
| Gibson, F G | Farmer | Los Angeles Co | nr Florence | Los Angeles. |
| Gibson, H | Clergyman | Los Angeles Co | Florence | Los Angeles. |
| Gibson, F A | Clerk | Post office | | Los Angeles. |
| Gibson, C W | L A soap co | 1st st | | Los Angeles. |
| Gibson, Wm | Painter | Los Angeles | | Los Angeles. |
| Giddeon, J T | Farmer | Azusa Duarte | 3 m E Lexington | El Monte. |
| Giebel, Emil F G W | Clerk | Los Angeles | Los Angeles | Los Angeles. |
| Giese, Fred'k Jr | Druggist | Los Angeles | | Los Angeles. |
| Gildmacher, Levi | Butcher | Los Angeles | Los Angeles | Los Angeles. |
| Gillett, Thomas | Farmer | Los Angeles Co | nr Half-way House | Compton. |
| Gillet, Columbus | Farmer | Los Angeles Co | nr Los Nietos | Los Nietos. |

# DIRECTORY OF LOS ANGELES COUNTY. 353

| Name. | Occupation. | Place of Business. | Residence. | Town or P. O. |
|---|---|---|---|---|
| Gillett, Zachary | Farmer | Los Angeles Co | Silver Precinct | Downey. |
| Gillett, Winchester. | Farmer | Los Angeles Co | nr Los Nietos | Los Nietos. |
| Gillman, Joseph | Farmer | Los Angeles Co | nr San Gabriel | San Gabriel. |
| Gillman, Albert | Miner | Los Angeles Co | | Los Angeles. |
| Gillette, Jeffrey W. | Clerk | Los Angeles | Los Angeles | Los Angeles. |
| Gilliland, Edward P | Barber | Los Angeles | Los Angeles | Los Angeles. |
| Gill, A B | Farmer | Los Angeles Co | nr Anaheim | Anaheim. |
| Gilliland, E P | Barber | Los Angeles | Los Angeles | Los Angeles. |
| Gilland, N | Barber | Los Angeles | Los Angeles | Los Angeles. |
| Gillman, M L | Laborer | Los Angeles Co | | El Monte. |
| Gillette, J W | County recorder | Court House | Polyxena st | Los Angeles. |
| Gilman, J | Farmer | Los Angeles | Silver Precinct | Downey. |
| Gilmer, M A | Carpenter | Spadra | 30 m E Los Angeles. | Spadra. |
| Gilman, Albert H | Painter | Los Angeles | Los Angeles | Los Angeles. |
| Gilm, J J | Farmer | Los Angeles Co | Silver Precinct | Downey. |
| Gilroy, John | Bricklayer | Los Angeles | Los Angeles | Los Angeles. |
| Girard, J C | Saddler | Los Angeles | Los Angeles | Los Angeles. |
| Giraud, Martin | Laborer | Los Angeles Co | | Los Angeles. |
| Gird, Henry H | Farmer | Los Angeles Co | nr Los Angeles | Los Angeles. |
| Girod, Phillip | Laborer | | nr Los Angeles | Los Angeles. |
| Girtsen, John G | Farmer | Los Angeles Co | Santa Catalina | Santa Catalina. |
| Glancey, T | Publisher | 169 Main st | | Los Angeles. |
| Glassell, Andrew | Lawyer | Los Angeles | Los Angeles | Los Angeles. |
| Glassell, Andrew, Sr | Planter | Los Angeles Co | nr Los Angeles | Los Angeles. |
| Glassell, Wm T | Agent | Los Angeles Co | Richland | Orange. |
| Glasby, Jno C | Teamster | Los Angeles Co | | Los Angeles. |
| Glassell, A | Att'y at law | Temple Block | 166 Main st | Los Angeles. |
| Glassell, Chapman & Smiths | Attorneys at law | Temple Block | | Los Angeles. |
| Glenn, John | Farmer | Los Angeles Co | | Los Angeles. |
| Glidden, Chas C | Teamster | | Los Angeles Co | Los Angeles. |
| Glidden, E C | Peddler | Los Angeles Co | | San Gabriel. |
| Glinn, John | Farmer | Los Angeles Co | nr San Fernando | San Fernando. |
| Goatcher, William Jasper | Farmer | Los Angeles Co | nr Los Angeles | Los Angeles. |
| Gobey, E | Laborer | Los Angeles Co | | Los Angeles. |
| Godfrey, John F | Lawyer | Los Angeles | Los Angeles Co | Los Angeles. |
| Godfrey, J F | Attorney at law | Downey Block | | Los Angeles. |
| Godfrey & Ellis | Attorneys at law | Downey Block | | Los Angeles. |
| Godfrey, W | Photographer | Los Angeles | Los Angeles | Los Angeles. |
| Goethols, Charles | Machinist | Los Angeles Co | | Los Angeles. |
| Goldsworthy, John, Jr | Surveyor | Los Angeles | Los Angeles | Los Angeles. |
| Golden, Martin Joseph | Teacher | Los Angeles Co | Los Angeles | Los Angeles. |
| Goldbaum, Mitchell | Merchant | | Los Angeles Co | Los Angeles. |
| Goldbaum, Louis | Merchant | Los Angeles Co | | Los Angeles. |
| Goldsmith, Leopold | Merchant | Los Angeles Co | Azusa | Azusa. |
| Goldsmith, A | Gen merchandise | Azusa Ranch | 2½ m S W Azusa | Azusa. |
| Goldsworthy, J H | Farmer | Los Angeles | Westminster Col | Westminster. |
| Goldstein, Miss S | Fruit store | Main st nr 1st | 61 Spring st | Los Angeles. |
| Goldsmith, I | Cigars | 38 Main | | Los Angeles. |
| Goldsworthy, J | Mining engineer | 6 Downey Block | | Los Angeles. |
| Goldsworthy, J H | Miner | Los Angeles Co | | Anaheim. |
| Goldstein, S | Brewer | Los Angeles Co | Anaheim | Anaheim. |
| Goll, Franses, Jr | Farmer | Los Angeles Co | nr Los Angeles | Los Angeles. |
| Goll, Franses | Farmer | Los Angeles Co | nr Los Angeles | Los Angeles. |
| Gollmer, John | Painter | | Los Angeles | Los Angeles. |
| Gollmer, C | Painter | Los Angeles | | Los Angeles. |
| Gomez, Jose | Laborer | Los Angeles Co | | Los Angeles. |
| Gomez, Enrique | Laborer | | Los Angeles Co | Los Angeles. |
| Gomez, Jose Maria | Farmer | Los Angeles Co | nr Los Angeles | Los Angeles. |
| Gomez, Eugenio | Vaquero | Los Angeles Co | | Los Angeles. |
| Gomez, E | Laborer | | Los Angeles Co | Los Angeles. |

23

# PACIFIC SALT WORKS.

These Works are situated 18 miles west of Los Angeles, Los Angeles County, Cal.

The Salt is manufactured from six lagoons, of a depth of from six to eight inches, capable of evaporating from six to eight hundred tons of salt three times per year.

THERE ARE ALSO TEN LARGE VATS, WHICH YIELD FROM

## Four to Five Tons once in Two Weeks.

Fresh Water is had at a depth of twenty-three feet; one spring, probably the largest on the property, flows at the rate of 10,000 Gallons per day, the water being excellent in quality.

THE SALT PRODUCED HERE IS PRONOUNCED

## Equal to any offered For Sale
### IN THE STATE.

A fine house occupies a commanding site, with a good barn and other necessary buildings.

## DIRECTORY OF LOS ANGELES COUNTY. 355

| Name. | Occupation. | Place of Business. | Residence. | Town or P. O. |
|---|---|---|---|---|
| Gomez, M | Laborer | | Los Angeles Co | Los Angeles. |
| Goncalves, Sam | Wharf hand | S P R R Co | Wilmington | Wilmington. |
| Gonzales, R G | Painter | Los Angeles | | Los Angeles. |
| Gonzales, P | Laborer | | Los Angeles Co | Los Angeles. |
| Gonzales, Juan | Laborer | Los Angeles Co | | Los Angeles. |
| Gonzales, Edwardo | Laborer | Los Angeles Co | | Los Angeles. |
| Gonzales, Jose | Tailor | Los Angeles | Los Angeles | Los Angeles. |
| Gonzales, Felis | Laborer | Los Angeles Co | | El Monte. |
| Gonzalo, Fermin | Laborer | | Los Angeles | Los Angeles. |
| Gonzales, Estevan | Laborer | Los Angeles Co | La Ballona | Los Angeles. |
| Gonzales, Juanito | Laborer | Los Angeles Co | | Los Angeles. |
| Gonzales, Jose Rafael | Laborer | | Los Angeles | Los Angeles. |
| Gonzales, Antonio | Laborer | | Los Angeles | Los Angeles. |
| Gonzales, Cruz | Basket maker | Los Angeles | Los Angeles | Los Angeles. |
| Gonzales, Antonio C | Farmer | | nr Los Angeles | Los Angeles. |
| Gonzales, A | Sheep herder | Los Angeles Co | | Los Angeles. |
| Gonzales, F | Baker | Los Angeles | Los Angeles | Los Angeles. |
| Gonzales, E | Laborer | Los Angeles Co | San Jose | Spadra. |
| Gooch, J H | Carriage painter | Centre st | Anaheim | Anaheim. |
| Gooch, T L | Farmer | Los Angeles Co | Silver Precinct | Downey. |
| Gooch, J T | Farmer | Los Angeles Co | Silver Precinct | Downey. |
| Goodrich, Myron S | Clerk | Los Angeles | Los Angeles | Los Angeles. |
| Goodhue, Geo Wash | Laborer | Los Angeles Co | | Los Angeles. |
| Goodness, William | Carpenter | Los Angeles Co | Wilmington | Wilmington. |
| Goodwin, Leander C | Merchant | Los Angeles | Los Angeles | Los Angeles. |
| Goodnight, Thos B | Farmer | Los Angeles Co | nr Los Angeles | Los Angeles. |
| Good, Benj F | Farmer | | Los Angeles Co | Los Angeles. |
| Goodwin, Geo | Tailor | Los Angeles Co | San Joaquin | Santa Ana. |
| Goodwin, Patrick | Blacksmith | | Los Angeles Co | Los Angeles. |
| Goode, R | Teacher | Lopez Station | 2½ m N W San Fern'do | San Fernando. |
| Goodwin, E R | Wheelwright | Lexington | 12 m E Los Angeles | El Monte. |
| Goodman & Rimpau | Merchants | Anaheim | | Anaheim. |
| Goodrich, A J | Hack driver | Los Angeles | | Los Angeles. |
| Goodrich, B G | Farmer | Los Angeles Co | Silver Precinct | Downey. |
| Goodman, M L | Farmer | Los Angeles Co | Silver Precinct | Downey. |
| Goodwin, D B | Farmer | Los Angeles Co | Silver Precinct | Downey. |
| Gordon, John H | Tinsmith | | Los Angeles | Los Angeles. |
| Gordon, J T | Justice of peace | Dalton Ranch | 2½ m N Azusa | Azusa. |
| Gorinflo, William | Wine grower | Los Angeles Co | nr Los Angeles | Los Angeles. |
| Gorman, James | Farmer | | nr Los Angeles | Los Angeles. |
| Gormer, W F | Trader | Los Angeles Co | | |
| Goss, Willis Greenburg | Farmer | Los Angeles Co | nr Los Angeles | Los Angeles. |
| Goss, John | Farmer | Los Angeles Co | nr Los Nietos | Los Nietos. |
| Gosselin, Zotiqui | Coppersmith | Los Angeles | Los Angeles | Los Angeles. |
| Goss, William G | Peddler | San Pedro Ranch | 2½ m N E Compton | Compton. |
| Gothard, George | Farmer | | Westminster Col | Westminster. |
| Gould, Albert C | Laborer | Los Angeles Co | Los Angeles | Los Angeles. |
| Gould, Charles W | Deputy co clerk | | 3d st bet Fort & Sp'g | Los Angeles. |
| Gould & Blanchard | Attorneys at law | 18 & 19 Temple Blk | | Los Angeles. |
| Gould, W D | Attorney at law | 18 & 19 Temple Blk | | Los Angeles. |
| Gower, J T | Miner | Los Angeles Co | | Los Angeles. |
| Goyeneche, J | Farmer | Los Angeles Co | nr Los Angeles | Los Angeles. |
| Gozales, Genaro | Carpenter | Los Angeles | Los Angeles | Los Angeles. |
| Gracico, Blaz | Laborer | Los Angeles Co | Los Angeles | Los Angeles. |
| Gracia, J | Laborer | | Los Angeles Co | Los Angeles. |
| Graddy, M R | Laborer | Los Angeles Co | Silver Precinct | Downey. |
| Gradias, J | Laborer | Los Angeles Co | | Los Nietos. |
| Grady, Joseph T | Tinner | nr Los Angeles | | |
| Graff, John | Farmer | Los Angeles Co | nr Los Angeles | Los Angeles. |
| Graf, Herman | Cooper | Los Angeles | Los Angeles | Los Angeles. |

## L. L. PAULSON'S HAND-BOOK AND

| Name. | Occupation. | Place of Business. | Residence. | Town or P. O. |
|---|---|---|---|---|
| Graham, George | Painter | Los Angeles | Los Angeles | Los Angeles. |
| Graham, Geo Harvey | Laborer | Los Angeles Co | | Los Angeles. |
| Graham, F M | Stock raiser | Los Angeles Co | Silver Precinct | Downey. |
| Graham, H C | Nursery | Indiana Colony | 5 m N E Los Angeles | Pasadena. |
| Graham, W J | Architect | r 46 Temple Block | | Los Angeles. |
| Graham, J B | Farmer | Los Angeles Co | nr Los Nietos | Los Nietos. |
| Grallard, M | Laborer | Los Angeles Co | | Los Angeles. |
| Grand, R | Blacksmith | Los Angeles | Los Angeles | Los Angeles. |
| Grant, J N | Farmer | Los Angeles Co | nr El Monte | El Monte. |
| Granillo, Manuel | Laborer | Los Angeles Co | | Los Angeles. |
| Granillo, Santiago | Laborer | Los Angeles Co | | Los Angeles. |
| Grant, Thos B | Clerk | | Wilmington | Wilmington. |
| Grant, Robert W | Saddler | Los Angeles Co | Wilmington | Wilmington. |
| Granis, Laurence R | Laborer | Los Angeles Co | | Los Angeles. |
| Granges, J C | Civil engineer | | Anaheim | Anaheim. |
| Granadel, B | Bakery | | Los Angeles | Los Angeles. |
| Grandin, Egbert B | Farmer | Los Angeles Co | nr Los Nietos | Los Nietos. |
| Grant, Abram | Carpenter | | Los Angeles | Los Angeles. |
| Grand, S | Gen merchandise | Compton | Compton | Compton. |
| Grand & Co, S | Gen merchandise | Compton | Compton | Compton. |
| Grant, N | Farmer | Azusa Duarte | 6 m E Lexington | El Monte. |
| Graves, T A | Farmer | Los Angeles Co | Silver Precinct | Downey. |
| Graves, N | Farmer | Azusa Duarte | 4 m E Lexington | El Monte. |
| Graves, M | Apiarian | Azusa Ranch | 3 m N E Azusa | Azusa. |
| Graves, H S | Farmer | Azusa Duarte | 4 m E Lexington | El Monte. |
| Gravel, F E | Carriage mnf'r | | Los Angeles Co | Los Angeles. |
| Gray, James Andrew | Farmer | Los Angeles Co | nr El Monte | El Monte. |
| Gray, James H | Carpenter | Los Angeles Co | Los Angeles | Los Angeles. |
| Gray, Jacob W | Farmer | Los Angeles Co | nr Los Angeles | Los Angeles. |
| Gray, Thos Andrew | Farmer | Los Angeles Co | nr Los Angeles | Los Angeles. |
| Gray, William | Laborer | Los Angeles Co | Los Angeles | Los Angeles. |
| Gray, Thomas | Carpenter | Los Angeles Co | Los Angeles | Los Angeles. |
| Gray, John | Teamster | Los Angeles Co | San Fernando | San Fernando. |
| Gray, Josiah Holcomb | Farmer | Los Angeles Co | nr El Monte | El Monte. |
| Gray, David | Farmer | Los Angeles Co | nr El Monte | El Monte. |
| Gray, Jacob | Hotel keeper | Los Angeles | Los Angeles | Los Angeles. |
| Gray, Wm Henry | Justice of peace | Los Angeles | Los Angeles | Los Angeles. |
| Gray, Thos E | Physician | | Los Angeles | Los Angeles. |
| Gray, George R | Laborer | Los Angeles Co | | Los Angeles. |
| Grayson, James W | Laborer | | Los Angeles Co | Los Angeles. |
| Gray, George W | Teamster | Los Angeles Co | | Los Angeles. |
| Gray, Thos H | Printer | | Los Angeles | Los Angeles. |
| Gray, Austin N | Farmer | Los Angeles Co | San Antonio | Downey. |
| Gray, Joshua W | Stage driver | | Los Angeles | Los Angeles. |
| Gray, J H | Justice of peace | El Monte Valley | 1 m S Lexington | El Monte. |
| Gray, A S | Farmer | Los Angeles Co | nr Los Angeles | Los Angeles. |
| Gray, D J Jr | Carpenter | Los Angeles Co | | Los Angeles. |
| Gray, J | Sheep raiser | Los Angeles Co | nr Los Angeles | Los Angeles. |
| Graxiola, Juan | Laborer | | San Joaquin | Santa Ana. |
| Grazide, F | Sheep raiser | Los Angeles Co | nr San Jose | San Jose. |
| Greaves, J M | Painter | Los Angeles | Los Angeles | Los Angeles. |
| Greater, Edward E | Farmer | Los Angeles Co | Los Angeles | Los Angeles. |
| Grebe, Christopher | Clerk | | Los Angeles Co | Los Angeles. |
| Green, James Thos | Farmer | Los Angeles Co | Los Nietos | Los Nietos. |
| Green, Albert | Farmer | Los Angeles Co | Anaheim | Anaheim. |
| Green, Jose Maria | Painter | Los Angeles Co | Los Angeles | Los Angeles. |
| Greenbaum, Ephraim | Merchant | Los Angeles Co | Los Angeles | Los Angeles. |
| Greenleaf, E F | Doctor | Los Angeles Co | Santa Ana | Santa Ana. |
| Green, W G | Carpenter | Los Angeles Co | | Anaheim. |
| Green, L G | Barber | Los Angeles | Los Angeles | Los Angeles. |
| Green, H | Farmer | Los Angeles Co | nr Los Angeles | Los Angeles. |

## DIRECTORY OF LOS ANGELES COUNTY. 357

| NAME. | OCCUPATION. | PLACE OF BUSINESS. | RESIDENCE. | TOWN OR P. O. |
|---|---|---|---|---|
| Greening, E G | Farmer | Los Angeles Co | nr Los Angeles | Los Nietos. |
| Green, W H | Harness maker | Los Angeles | Los Angeles | Los Angeles. |
| Greeley, G E | Carpenter | Los Angeles Co | Silver Precinct | Downey. |
| Green, M | Teamster | Los Angeles Co | | Los Angeles. |
| Green, D R | Stage driver | Los Angeles Co | | Los Angeles. |
| Green, F | Laborer | Los Angeles Co | | Anaheim. |
| Green, Alfred D | Clerk | Los Angeles | | Los Angeles. |
| Greenwood, Alfred | Spinner | Los Angeles | | Los Angeles. |
| Green, A A | Teacher | Los Angeles Co | Spadra | Spadra. |
| Green, Perry M | Fruit grower | Indiana Colony | Hill Side Place | Pasadena. |
| Greenwode, Mrs S R | Farmer | San Gabriel | 9 m E Los Angeles | San Gabriel. |
| Green, — | Teacher | Mud Spring Valley | 6 m N Spadra | Spadra. |
| Greening, E J | Peddler | Lexington | 12 m E Los Angeles | El Monte. |
| Greenbaum, Mrs E | White house | Coml & Los A sts | | Los Angeles. |
| Green, E K | Agent for windm. | 34 Aliso st | | Los Angeles. |
| Green, E | Farmer | Los Angeles Co | nr Los Angeles | Los Angeles. |
| Gregg, J H | Farmer | Los Angeles Co | Coyote Ranch | |
| Gregory, J | Teamster | Los Angeles Co | | Anaheim. |
| Greholdo, N | Farmer | Azusa Ranch | ¾ m E Azusa | Azusa. |
| Gacjalva, Domingo | Laborer | Los Angeles Co | | Los Angeles. |
| Gresham, W D | Farmer | Los Angeles Co | nr Anaheim | Anaheim. |
| Gresham, John | Farmer | Los Angeles Co | Silver Precinct | Downey. |
| Gressard, Charles | Miner | Los Angeles Co | Los Angeles | Los Angeles. |
| Grey, Samuel | Teamster | Los Angeles Co | San Fernando | San Fernando. |
| Gribble, P V | Bar keeper | Los Angeles Co | Los Angeles | Los Angeles. |
| Grider, James | Farmer | Los Angeles Co | Los Angeles | Los Angeles. |
| Grider, Christopher H | Farmer | Los Angeles Co | nr Los Angeles | Los Angeles. |
| Grider, William Tobias | Farmer | Los Angeles Co | nr Los Angeles | Los Angeles. |
| Grider, Tobias Smith | Ranchero | Los Angeles Co | nr Los Angeles | Los Angeles. |
| Gridley, Cyprian | Farmer | Los Angeles Co | nr El Monte | El Monte. |
| Grider, T J | Farmer | San Pedro Ranch | ¼ m E Compton | Compton. |
| Griethe, A | Musician | Los Angeles Co | Silver Precinct | Downey. |
| Griffin, John S | Doctor | | Los Angeles | Los Angeles. |
| Griffeth, Elisha Emery W | Farmer | Los Angeles Co | nr El Monte | El Monte. |
| Griffin, John M | Farmer | Los Angeles Co | La Ballona | Los Angeles. |
| Griffin, William | Merchant | Los Angeles | Los Angeles | Los Angeles. |
| Griffin, John | Laborer | Los Angeles Co | | Los Angeles. |
| Griffith, John McK | Forwd. merchant | Los Angeles Co | Los Angeles | Los Angeles. |
| Griffin, Isaac | Laborer | Los Angeles Co | | Los Angeles. |
| Griffin, George A | Laborer | Los Angeles Co | Halfway House | Compton. |
| Griffin, L M | Dentist | Los Angeles Co | Anaheim | Anaheim. |
| Griffin, B | Farmer | Los Angeles Co | La Ballona | Los Angeles. |
| Griffin, P | Mason | Los Angeles Co | Anaheim | Anaheim. |
| Griffin, James E | Attorney | Los Angeles Co | Los Angeles | Los Angeles. |
| Griffin, Enoch | Farmer | Los Angeles Co | Ballona | Los Angeles. |
| Griffin & Berran | Employment off. | Los Angeles | Los Angeles | Los Angeles. |
| Griffith Lynch & Co | Lumber dealers | Alameda & 1st sts | | Los Angeles. |
| Grigulin, F | Laborer | Los Angeles Co | | Los Angeles. |
| Grimm, Edward M | Farmer | Los Angeles Co | nr El Monte | El Monte. |
| Grimaldd, W | Bookkeeper | Los Angeles Co | Los Angeles | Los Angeles. |
| Grinnard, S | Laborer | Los Angeles Co | | Los Angeles. |
| Griswold, John M | Carpenter | Los Angeles | Los Angeles | Los Angeles. |
| Griswold, Mrs J M | Dress maker | Los Angeles Co | Los Angeles | Los Angeles. |
| Griswold, D | Farmer | Westminster Col | | Westminster. |
| Griswold, S | Farmer | Westminster Col | | Westminster. |
| Griss, E | Jeweler | Los Angeles | | Los Angeles. |
| Grizalba, Malverto | Miner | Los Angeles Co | Azusa | Azusa. |
| Grizalva, Salvador | Laborer | Los Angeles Co | Los Angeles | Los Angeles. |
| Gronsse, Henry | Laborer | Los Angeles Co | Los Angeles | Los Angeles. |
| Grogan, Isom Thomas | Teamster | Los Angeles Co | Wilmington | Wilmington. |

# THOS. A. GAREY'S

# SEMI-TROPICAL NURSERIES,

## LOS ANGELES CITY, CAL.

The LARGEST and MOST COMPLETE STOCK OF TREES in the State.

I HAVE INTRODUCED AND AM NOW OFFERING A FINE STOCK OF GRAFTED AND BUDDED TREES, INCLUDING

## MALTA BLOOD, ST. MICHAELS NAVAL,

Tanqarine, Mandarin, Burgamot, Chuchu Pilos, Etc.

## LEMONS AND MEXICAN LIME TREES,

Well-Grown, Thrifty Los Angeles Orange Trees, in Large Quantities.

Also, a Full Stock of Temperate Climate Fruit Trees, including APPLE, PEACH, PEAR, Etc. Trees Packed for Transportation in the very best manner. Priced Catalogue sent free.

*Address me, P. O. Box 528, Los Angeles.*

THOS. A. GAREY, Proprietor.

# DIRECTORY OF LOS ANGELES COUNTY.

| Name. | Occupation. | Place of Business. | Residence. | Town or P. O. |
|---|---|---|---|---|
| Grote, S C | Teamster | | Los Angeles Co | Los Angeles. |
| Groux, D | Millwright | Los Angeles | Los Angeles | Los Angeles. |
| Grover, Edward | Teamster | Los Angeles Co | Wilmington | Wilmington. |
| Gruschenske, M | Merchant | Los Angeles | Los Angeles | Los Angeles. |
| Grunison, George | Laborer | Los Angeles Co | Los Angeles | Los Angeles. |
| Gryalva, A | Laborer | Los Angeles Co | San Jose | Spadra. |
| Grymes, G A | Cabinet maker | Los Angeles | | Los Angeles. |
| Guenette, F | Cigar dealer | Los Angeles | Los Angeles | Los Angeles. |
| Guenno, J D | Merchant | Los Angeles | Los Angeles | Los Angeles. |
| Guerro, Juan | Clerk | Los Angeles | | Los Angeles. |
| Guerero, Joseph | Car oiler | S P R R Co | Wilmington | Wilmington. |
| Guerrero, Francisco | Farmer | Los Angeles Co | nr Wilmington | Wilmington. |
| Guerrero, Francisco de P N | Printer | Los Angeles Co | Los Angeles | Los Angeles. |
| Guerrero, Blas Antonio | Laborer | Los Angeles Co | | Santa Ana. |
| Guerrero, Jose de la Luz | Blacksmith | Los Angeles Co | Wilmington | Wilmington. |
| Guess, John | Farmer | Ellis Station | 1 m W Lexington | El Monte. |
| Guess, John | Farmer | Los Angeles Co | nr El Monte | El Monte. |
| Guillen, Jesus | Laborer | Los Angeles Co | Old Mission | El Monte. |
| Guilgama, Luis | Farmer | | Santa Ana | Santa Ana. |
| Guillory, A | Blacksmith | Los Angeles | Los Angeles | Los Angeles. |
| Guillen, Mrs A M | Bakery | San Gabriel | 9 m E Los Angeles | San Gabriel. |
| Guillory, A | Wagon maker | River Shop | | Los Angeles. |
| Guilert, Mrs M | Dress maker | Los Angeles | Los Angeles | Los Angeles. |
| Guinn, Wm Harrison | Farmer | Los Angeles Co | nr El Monte | El Monte. |
| Guiol, Fred'k | Merchant | Los Angeles | Los Angeles | Los Angeles. |
| Guirra, M | Shoe maker | Los Angeles | Los Angeles | Los Angeles. |
| Guirado, Leandro | Ranchero | Los Angeles Co | Wilmington | Wilmington. |
| Guirado, Jean F | Farmer | Los Angeles Co | Los Angeles | Los Angeles. |
| Guirado, Bernardino | Merchant | Los Angeles Co | Los Nietos | Los Nietos. |
| Guiterrez, Isabel | Laborer | Los Angeles Co | | Los Angeles. |
| Gulick, T W | Dentist | 54 Main st | | Los Angeles. |
| Gulpen, Charles Van | Teacher | Los Angeles | Los Angeles | Los Angeles. |
| Guncas, Jean Pierre | Farmer | Los Angeles Co | | Los Angeles. |
| Gunther, L | Boot maker | Cor 3d & L A sts | Anaheim | Anaheim. |
| Guntelfinger & Co | Tanners | Alameda st | | Los Angeles. |
| Guntelfinger, George | Tanner | Alameda st | 1st st | Los Angeles. |
| Gusman, V | Saddler | Los Angeles | San Gabriel | San Gabriel. |
| Gustir, A | Laborer | | Los Angeles Co | Los Angeles. |
| Guthry, Robert Burns | Farmer | Los Angeles Co | Silver Precinct | Downey. |
| Gutierres, Felis | Ranchero | Los Angeles Co | Old Mission | El Monte. |
| Guzman, E F | Carpenter | Los Angeles Co | | Los Angeles. |
| Gwinn, Wm H | Farmer | Azusa Ranch | ½ m S W Azusa | Azusa. |
| Gwynn, Frederick K | Clerk | Los Angeles Co | Los Angeles | Los Angeles. |
| Haar, Henry | Baker | Los Angeles | Los Angeles | Los Angeles. |
| Haas, Abraham | Merchant | Los Angeles | Los Angeles | Los Angeles. |
| Hackett, H | Laborer | Los Angeles | Los Angeles | Los Angeles. |
| Hackman, John | Farmer | Los Angeles Co | nr Los Angeles | Los Angeles. |
| Haddin, J H | Farmer | | San Joaquin | Santa Ana. |
| Haddock, R W | Farmer | Los Angeles Co | Los Nietos | Los Nietos. |
| Hadley, Ebenezer | Surveyor | Los Angeles | Los Angeles | Los Angeles. |
| Hadley, Frank | Hack driver | Los Angeles | Los Angeles | Los Angeles. |
| Hafen, C | Farmer | Los Angeles Co | nr Los Angeles | Los Angeles. |
| Hagan, Charles | Farmer | Los Angeles Co | nr Los Angeles | Los Angeles. |
| Hageman, P H | Baker | Los Angeles | Los Angeles | Los Angeles. |
| Hahn, Daniel | Farmer | Los Angeles Co | nr Los Angeles | Los Angeles. |
| Haines, Rufus Rowe | Telegrapher | Los Angeles | Los Angeles | Los Angeles. |
| Haines, Edwin C | Trader | Los Angeles Co | Los Angeles | Los Angeles. |
| Haizlip, J | Farmer | San Pedro Ranch | 1¼ m N E Compton | Compton. |

L. L. PAULSON'S HAND-BOOK AND

| Name. | Occupation. | Place of Business. | Residence. | Town or P. O. |
|---|---|---|---|---|
| Halberstadt & Co. | Lumber dealer | Anaheim | | Anaheim. |
| Halberstadt, L | Farmer | Los Angeles Co | nr Los Angeles | Los Angeles. |
| Haley, John | Miner | Los Angeles Co | | Los Angeles. |
| Halesworth, W W | Farmer | Los Angeles Co | nr Los Angeles | Los Angeles. |
| Haley, Thomas | Laborer | Los Angeles Co | Spadra | Spadra. |
| Haley, Salisbury | Farmer | Los Angeles Co | nr Los Angeles | Los Angeles. |
| Hall, Thos S | Rev dept | Los Angeles | Los Angeles | Los Angeles. |
| Halleck, George | Waiter | Los Angeles | Los Angeles | Los Angeles. |
| Hall, Wm | Carpenter | S P P R R Co | Wilmington | Wilmington. |
| Hall, David F | Hotel | San Gabriel | 9 m E Los Angeles | San Gabriel. |
| Hall, N B | Laborer | Los Angeles Co | | Los Angeles. |
| Hall, David F | Merchant | Los Angeles Co | San Gabriel | San Gabriel. |
| Hall, John | Laborer | Los Angeles Co | Los Angeles | Los Angeles. |
| Hall, Wm Henry | Carpenter | Los Angeles Co | Wilmington | Wilmington. |
| Hall, George H | Laborer | Los Angeles Co | San Gabriel | San Gabriel. |
| Hall, George H B | Surveyor | Los Angeles | Los Angeles | Los Angeles. |
| Hall, Thomas | Farmer | Los Angeles Co | nr Los Angeles | Los Angeles. |
| Halpin, P | Watchman | S P R R Co' | Anaheim | Anaheim. |
| Halpin, P | Farmer | Los Angeles Co | nr Los Angeles | Los Angeles. |
| Halsell, William S | Farmer | Los Angeles Co | Silver Precinct | Downey. |
| Halstead, William G | Clerk | Los Angeles Co | Los Angeles | Los Angeles. |
| Ham, John B | Stage driver | Los Angeles | Los Angeles | Los Angeles. |
| Hames, H H | Horse trainer | Los Angeles Co | Los Angeles Co | Los Angeles. |
| Hamilton, Thomas | Laborer | Los Angeles Co | | Los Angeles. |
| Hamilton, Alex James | Clerk | Los Angeles | Los Angeles | Los Angeles. |
| Hamilton, H | Farmer | San Gabriel | 9 m E Los Angeles | San Gabriel. |
| Hamilton, Thos | Well digger | 110 Main st | | Los Angeles. |
| Hamilton, J W | Laborer | Los Angeles Co | | El Monte. |
| Hamilton, H | Publisher | Los Angeles | Los Angeles | Los Angeles. |
| Hamilton, C W | Teacher | Los Angeles Co | Old Mission | El Monte. |
| Hamilton, G W | Farmer | Los Angeles Co | Old Mission | El Monte. |
| Hamilton, Robt H | Teamster | Los Angeles Co | El Monte | El Monte. |
| Hamilton, Jesse C | Minister | Los Angeles | Los Angeles | Los Angeles. |
| Hamilton, James | Blacksmith | Los Angeles Co | Wilmington | Wilmington. |
| Hamilton, Chas | Carpenter | Los Angeles | Los Angeles | Los Angeles. |
| Hamilton, Samuel | Lawyer | Los Angeles | Los Angeles | Los Angeles. |
| Ham, Wm F | Farmer | Los Angeles Co | nr Los Angeles | Los Angeles. |
| Hamlin, Wm Pride | Miner | Los Angeles Co | Los Angeles | Los Angeles. |
| Hamlin, C C | Carpenter | Los Angeles Co | Los Angeles | Los Angeles. |
| Hammel, Geo W | Printer | Los Angeles | Los Angeles | Los Angeles. |
| Hammer, J C | Farmer | Azusa Duarte | 4 m E Lexington | El Monte. |
| Hammond, F A | Farmer | Los Angeles Co | San Joaquin | Santa Ana. |
| Hammer, Saml C | Farmer | Los Angeles Co | Azusa | Azusa. |
| Hammel & Denker | U S hotel | Main & Requena sts | | Los Angeles. |
| Hammel, George | U S hotel | Main & Requena sts | | Los Angeles. |
| Hammel, H | Hotel | Los Angeles | Los Angeles | Los Angeles. |
| Hammond, E M | Clerk | Los Angeles | Los Angeles | Los Angeles. |
| Hammes, Philip | Vintner | Los Angeles Co | Anaheim | Anaheim. |
| Hammel, Wm August | Merchant | Los Angeles | Los Angeles | Los Angeles. |
| Hammerton, Henry W | Farmer | Los Angeles Co | nr Los Nietos | Los Nietos. |
| Ham, G P | Teamster | Los Angeles Co | | Los Angeles. |
| Hampton, William | Farmer | | Silver Precinct | Downey. |
| Hancock, — | Laborer | Los Angeles Co | 7 m N Lyon Station | Lyon Station. |
| Hancock, M | Miner | Los Angeles Co | | Los Angeles. |
| Haneh, I | Mcht tailor | 4 Commercial st | | Los Angeles. |
| Hancock, Henry | Attorney | Los Angeles | Los Angeles | Los Angeles. |
| Hancock, Maranus | Laborer | Los Angeles Co | Los Angeles | Los Angeles. |
| Hancock, Thos D | Farmer | Los Angeles Co | nr Los Angeles | Los Angeles. |
| Hand, J R W | Farmer | Los Angeles Co | nr Los Nietos | Los Nietos. |
| Hanes, John Wm | Farmer | Los Angeles Co | nr El Monte | El Monte. |
| Hanks, John | Carpenter | Los Angeles | Los Angeles | Los Angeles. |

## DIRECTORY OF LOS ANGELES COUNTY. 361

| Name. | Occupation. | Place of Business. | Residence. | Town or P. O. |
|---|---|---|---|---|
| Hannon, Jeremiah C. | Farmer | Los Angeles Co | nr El Monte | El Monte. |
| Hanna, John | Farmer | Los Angeles Co | nr Anaheim | Anaheim. |
| Hannon, Michael | Farmer | Los Angeles Co | nr Los Angeles | Los Angeles. |
| Hannah, Newton M | Miner | Los Angeles Co | Los Angeles | Los Angeles. |
| Hannah, Newton M | Teacher | Los Angeles Co | Los Nietos | Los Nietos. |
| Hannon, J C | Farmer | El Monte Valley | 2 m N Lexington | El Monte. |
| Hannon, Dr J | Physician | Ellis station | 1 m W Lexington | El Monte. |
| Hannon, J | Farmer | Los Angeles Co | nr Los Angeles | Los Angeles. |
| Hause, George | Laborer | Los Angeles Co |  | Los Angeles. |
| Hansen, Henry | Seamen | Los Angeles Co |  | Los Angeles. |
| Hansen, J H | Farmer | San Pedro Ranch | 2½ m N Compton | Compton. |
| Hansen, Ole | Lighterman | Pt San Pedro | Pt San Pedro | Wilmington. |
| Hansen, C M | Laborer | Los Angeles Co |  | Los Angeles. |
| Hanshe, J B | Waiter | Los Angeles | Los Angeles | Los Angeles. |
| Hanser, J C F | Watch maker | Los Angeles | Los Angeles | Los Angeles. |
| Hanser, John | Carpenter | Los Angeles Co | Anaheim | Anaheim. |
| Hanson, P | Painter | Los Angeles Co | Anaheim | Anaheim. |
| Hanson, Harry | Carpenter | Los Angeles | Los Angeles | Los Angeles. |
| Hanson, George | Surveyor | Los Angeles | Los Angeles | Los Angeles. |
| Happ, C F | Carpenter | Los Angeles Co |  | Los Angeles. |
| Happ, Martin | Tailor | Los Angeles | Los Angeles | Los Angeles. |
| Harasztliy, Bela | Wine maker | Los Angeles Co | San Gabriel | San Gabriel. |
| Harbalt, James R | Laborer | Los Angeles Co | Los Nietos | Los Nietos. |
| Harding, Madison | Carpenter | Los Angeles Co | Halfway House | Compton. |
| Hardy, Louis William | Laborer | Los Angeles Co | Los Angeles | Los Angeles. |
| Harding, Wm C | Minister | Los Angeles | Los Angeles | Los Angeles. |
| Hardin, Wm Nelson | Doctor | Los Angeles Co | Anaheim | Anaheim. |
| Hardin, Asa | Miner | Los Angeles Co | Wilmington | Wilmington. |
| Hardin, Dr Wm R | Physician | L A & Sycamore sts |  | Anaheim. |
| Hardy, Mrs Mary | Dress maker | Los Angeles | Los Angeles | Los Angeles. |
| Harding, J R | Farmer | Los Angeles Co | nr Azusa | Azusa. |
| Hardy, K | Farmer | Los Angeles Co | nr Los Angeles | Los Angeles. |
| Hardgrave, I N | Farmer | Los Angeles Co | nr Los Nietos | Los Nietos. |
| Hare, A | Plasterer | Los Angeles | Los Angeles | Los Angeles. |
| Hare, M D | Constable | Temple st |  | Los Angeles. |
| Hargrave, Robt | Blacksmith |  | Los Nietos | Los Nietos. |
| Hargitt, Godfrey | Carpenter | Los Angeles | Los Angeles | Los Angeles. |
| Hargan, W G | Laborer |  | Los Angeles Co | Los Nietos. |
| Hargrave, Wm P | Farmer | Los Angeles Co | nr Los Nietos | Los Nietos. |
| Harmon, Henry H | Surveyor | Los Angeles | Los Angeles | Los Angeles. |
| Harmon, Ludwig | Cooper | Los Angeles | Los Angeles | Los Angeles. |
| Harmon, May & Co | Apiarians | San Fernando Valley | 4 m N San Fernando | San Fernando. |
| Harmon, James | Carpenter | Aliso Mills | Aliso st | Los Angeles. |
| Harmon, W C | Farmer | Azusa Ranch | 2½ m S W Azusa | Azusa. |
| Harned, Jacob A M | Stable keeper | Los Angeles | Los Angeles | Los Angeles. |
| Harper, William | Teamster | Los Angeles | Los Angeles | Los Angeles. |
| Harper, Samuel | Teamster | Los Angeles Co | Soledad | San Fernando. |
| Harper, Samuel | Stock | Soledad | 28 m N E Lyon St'n | Lyon Station. |
| Harper & Long | Hardware | 81 Main st |  | Los Angeles. |
| Harper, C F | Stoves & hardw're | 81 Main st |  | Los Angeles. |
| Harper, C H | Tinsmith | Los Angeles | Los Angeles | Los Angeles. |
| Harper, S | Stage driver | Los Angeles Co |  | San Fernando. |
| Harrigan, James | Blacksmith | Los Angeles Co | Wilmington | Wilmington. |
| Harriman, Henry | Miner | Los Angeles Co | Los Angeles | Los Angeles. |
| Harris, Andrew G | Farmer | Los Angeles Co | nr El Monte | El Monte. |
| Harris, William | Farmer | Los Angeles Co | Silver Precinct | Downey. |
| Harris, Jesse | Blacksmith | Los Angeles Co | San Jose | Spadra. |
| Harris, Archillas | Farmer | Los Angeles Co | nr El Monte | El Monte. |
| Harris, Leopold | Merchant | Los Angeles | Los Angeles | Los Angeles. |
| Harrison, George | Carver | Los Angeles | Los Angeles | Los Angeles. |
| Harris, John | Farmer | Los Angeles Co | Silver Precinct | Downey. |
| Harris, James | Farmer | Los Angeles Co | La Ballona | Los Angeles. |

**THE LEADING PAPER OF SOUTHERN CALIFORNIA,**

Is Published Every Morning Except Monday,

BY

THE LOS ANGELES CITY AND COUNTY

Printing and Publishing Company,

J. M. BASSETT, Editor and Manager.

OFFICE,

## Herald Steam Book and Job Printing House,

Spring St., opposite Court House.

**TERMS:**

| | |
|---|---:|
| Per Annum, by Mail or Express, - - - - - | $10.00 |
| Six Months,       "         "      - - - - - - | 6.00 |
| Three Months,  "         "      - - - - - - | 3.00 |
| Delivered by Carriers, per Week, - - - - - | 25 Cts. |

## THE WEEKLY HERALD

IS PUBLISHED EVERY SATURDAY MORNING.

**TERMS:**

| | |
|---|---:|
| One Year, by Mail or Express, Single Copy, - - - | $3.00 |
| Six Months,   "      "       "      - - - - | 1.75 |
| Three   "     "      "       "      - - - - | 1.00 |

## DIRECTORY OF LOS ANGELES COUNTY. 363

| NAME. | OCCUPATION. | PLACE OF BUSINESS. | RESIDENCE. | TOWN OR P. O. |
|---|---|---|---|---|
| Harris, C W | Carpenter | S P R R Co | Wilmington | Wilmington. |
| Harris, C H Rev | Clergyman | | Wilmington | Wilmington. |
| Harris, Samuel T | Printer | Los Angeles | Los Angeles | Los Angeles. |
| Harris & Jacoby | General merch'se. | Los Angeles | Los Angeles | Los Angeles. |
| Harris, Seth | Farmer | | Westminster Col | Westminster. |
| Harrington, O C | Laborer | Los Angeles Co | | Los Angeles. |
| Harris, E | Bartender | Los Angeles | Los Angeles | Los Angeles. |
| Harrington, J | Miner | | Los Angeles Co | San Fernando. |
| Harrington, D | Laborer | Los Angeles Co | | Los Angeles. |
| Harrison, Geo | Laborer | Los Angeles Co | Los Angeles | Los Angeles. |
| Harrison, T W | Farmer | Los Angeles Co | nr Santa Ana | Santa Ana. |
| Harron, T | Laborer | Los Angeles Co | Los Nietos | Los Nietos. |
| Harris, N J | Merchant | Los Angeles | Los Angeles | Los Angeles. |
| Harrington, J A | Teamster | Los Angeles Co | | Los Angeles. |
| Harter, George | Farmer | Los Angeles Co | Silver Precinct | Downey. |
| Hartlee, Chas Thos. | Farmer | Los Angeles Co | nr Los Angeles | Los Angeles. |
| Hartshorn, William | Mason | Los Angeles Co | Los Angeles | Los Angeles. |
| Harter, Charles | Shepherd | Los Angeles Co | Anaheim | Anaheim. |
| Hart, James S | Farmer | Los Angeles Co | Green Meadows | Compton. |
| Hart, J B | Saddler | Los Angeles | Los Angeles | Los Angeles. |
| Hartley, M De la F | Dairyman | Los Angeles Co | nr Los Angeles | Los Angeles. |
| Hartlee, B F | Farmer | Los Angeles Co | nr Los Angeles | Los Angeles. |
| Hart, James | Laborer | Los Angeles Co | | Los Angeles. |
| Hart, M L Miss | Sewing mach agt. | 60 Spring st | | Los Angeles. |
| Hartman & Haley | Attorneys at law. | Los Angeles | Los Angeles | Los Angeles. |
| Harvey, Edward | Farmer | Los Angeles Co | nr Los Nietos | Los Nietos. |
| Harvey, Mrs | Milliner | Los Angeles st | Anaheim | Anaheim. |
| Harvey, Thomas | Mason | Los Angeles Co | Anaheim | Anaheim. |
| Haseltien, George W | Carpenter | Los Angeles Co | | Los Angeles. |
| Haskins, H | Farmer | Downey's Ranch | 2½ m W Compton | Compton. |
| Haskill, K | Farmer | Azusa | 3 m N E Azusa | Azusa. |
| Haskin, D W | Blacksmith | Los Angeles | Los Angeles | Los Angeles. |
| Haskell, John C | Miner | Los Angeles Co | Los Angeles | Los Angeles. |
| Haskell, Joshua | Mason | Los Angeles Co | Los Angeles | Los Angeles. |
| Hasper, Henry | Laborer | Los Angeles Co | Los Angeles | Los Angeles. |
| Hasse & Asseveda | Barbers | 42 Main st | | Los Angeles. |
| Hasse, C | Hotel | Los Angeles | Los Angeles | Los Angeles. |
| Hass, C H | Farmer | Los Angeles Co | nr Los Angeles | Los Angeles. |
| Hastings, Walter | Carver | Los Angeles Co | Anaheim | Anaheim. |
| Hathorn, J G | Farmer | San Pedro Ranch | 1¼ m S W Compton | Compton. |
| Hathaway, Chas | | Los Angeles Co | | Los Angeles. |
| Hathaway, Chas D | Trader | Los Angeles Co | Los Angeles | Los Angeles. |
| Hathorn, Jacob G | Farmer | Los Angeles Co | Half-way House | Compton. |
| Hathorn, Freeman J | Wagon maker | Los Angeles Co | Wilmington | Wilmington. |
| Hatting, Richard A. | Carpenter | Los Angeles Co | Anaheim | Anaheim. |
| Hauch, Isaac | Tailor | Los Angeles | | Los Angeles. |
| Hauff, Frederick | Baker | Los Angeles Co | Los Angeles | Los Angeles. |
| Havanagh, Wm | Laborer | Los Angeles Co | | Los Angeles. |
| Havell, A H | Music teacher | 160 Main st | Los Angeles | Los Angeles. |
| Haverstick, John W | Farmer | Los Angeles Co | nr Los Angeles | Los Angeles. |
| Havens, John H | Farmer | Los Angeles Co | La Ballona | Los Angeles. |
| Havus, Benjamin | Farmer | Los Angeles Co | Silver Precinct | Downey. |
| Hawk, John F | Clerk | Los Angeles Co | | Los Angeles. |
| Hawkins, Eli W | Stock raiser | | Los Angeles Co | Los Angeles. |
| Hawkins, Marwin | Miner | Los Angeles Co | Los Angeles | Los Angeles. |
| Hawkins, John | Baker | 2nd st | 2nd st | Wilmington. |
| Hawks, E L Miss | Teacher | Los Angeles Co | | Los Angeles. |
| Hawkins, H A | Farmer | Los Angeles Co | nr Los Angeles | Los Angeles. |
| Hawley, — | Carpenter | Azusa | 22 m E Los Angeles. | Azusa. |
| Hawley, A T | Real estate | 15 Spring st | | Los Angeles. |
| Hawley & Beall | Com merchants | Aliso st | | Los Angeles. |
| Hawley, J F | Com merchant | Aliso st | | Los Angeles. |
| Hawley, John Milton | Farmer | Los Angeles Co | nr Los Angeles | Los Angeles. |

| Name. | Occupation. | Place of Business. | Residence. | Town or P. O. |
|---|---|---|---|---|
| Hawley, Everton W | Carpenter | Los Angeles Co | | Wilmington. |
| Haxall, Henry | Groceries | San Fernando Miss'n | 1½ m W San Fern'do | San Fernando. |
| Hayden, Martin | Butcher | Los Angeles Co | | Los Angeles. |
| Hayes, Stephen Thos | Wagon maker | Los Angeles | Los Angeles | Los Angeles. |
| Hayes, Russel T | Doctor | Los Angeles | Los Angeles | Los Angeles. |
| Hayes, Thomas | Machinist | Los Angeles | Los Angeles | Los Angeles. |
| Hayes, Thos. | Deputy sheriff | Wilmington | Wilmington | Wilmington. |
| Hayes, S T | Wagon maker | Ellis Station | 1 m W Lexington | El Monte. |
| Haynes, Joseph Green B | Farmer | Los Angeles Co | nr Los Nietos | Los Nietos. |
| Haynes, W | Farmer | Los Angeles Co | Silver Precinct | Downey. |
| Hayward, Albert B. | Doctor | Los Angeles | Los Angeles | Los Angeles. |
| Hazard, Amiel Mesick | Farmer | Los Angeles | Los Angeles | Los Angeles. |
| Hazard, H T | Attorney at law | 8 Downey Blk | 101 Spring st | Los Angeles. |
| Hazard, C. | Carpenter | Los Angeles | Los Angeles | Los Angeles. |
| Hazard, D | Teamster | Los Angeles Co | | Los Angeles. |
| Hazeltine, W Dr | Dentist | Spring & Temple sts. | | Los Angeles. |
| Hazlett, Thos Jeff | Laborer | Los Angeles Co | | San Fernando. |
| Headrick, Chas N | Teamster | Los Angeles Co | | Los Angeles. |
| Healey, Stephen | Farmer | Los Angeles Co | Silver Precinct | Downey. |
| Heanline, A | Carpenter | | Los Angeles Co | Los Angeles. |
| Heason, Wm | Laborer | Los Angeles Co | | Los Angeles. |
| Heath, Samuel Myers | Farmer | Los Angeles Co | nr San Gabriel | San Gabriel. |
| Heath, S M | Farmer | El Monte Valley | 1 m W Lexington | El Monte. |
| Heaver, Wm | Nurseryman | Los Angeles Co. | nr Los Angeles | Los Angeles. |
| Heberle, Jacob | Farmer | Los Angeles Co | nr San Fernando | San Fernando. |
| Hecklar, Jacob | Miner | Los Angeles Co | | Los Angeles. |
| Heer, Henry | Baker | Los Angeles | Los Angeles | Los Angeles. |
| Hefner, J | Farmer | Los Angeles Co | Elizabeth Lake | San Fernando. |
| Hefner, George | Cooper | Los Angeles Co | | Anaheim. |
| Hefte, Fred | Brewer | Los Angeles | Los Angeles | Los Angeles. |
| Heiliger, Isador | Speculator | Los Angeles | Los Angeles | Los Angeles. |
| Heiman & George. | Gen'l merchants | Anaheim | Anaheim | Anaheim. |
| Heiman, Richard | Merchant | Los Angeles Co | Anaheim | Anaheim. |
| Heiman, Charles | Clerk | Los Angeles | Los Angeles | Los Angeles. |
| Heinsch, H | Harness maker | Heinsch Blk | | Los Angeles. |
| Heinzeman & Co., C F | Druggists | 72 Main st | | Los Angeles. |
| Heinzeman, C F | Druggist | Main st | Los Angeles | Los Angeles. |
| Helbrandt, H | Wharf hand | S P R R Co | Wilmington | Wilmington. |
| Hellman, Isaiah M. | Merchant | Los Angeles | Los Angeles | Los Angeles. |
| Hellman, Herman W | Merchant | Los Angeles Co | Los Angeles | Los Angeles. |
| Hellwig, Henry | Clerk | Los Angeles | Los Angeles | Los Angeles. |
| Hellriegel, Jacob | Laborer | Los Angeles | | Los Angeles. |
| Hellman, Haas & Co. | Com merchants | 14 & 16 L A & Com sts | Main st | Los Angeles. |
| Hellman, H W | Com merchant | L A & Commercial sts | Main st | Los Angeles. |
| Hellman, I M | Capitalist | | 162 Main st | Los Angeles. |
| Hellman, J | Laborer | R R Depot | San Fernando | San Fernando. |
| Heller, A | Butcher | San Gabriel | 9 m E Los Angeles | San Gabriel. |
| Hellman, S | Books, etc | 95 Main st | 211 Main st | Los Angeles. |
| Heller, A | Butcher | Los Angeles | Los Angeles | Los Angeles. |
| Heller, S P | Merchant | Los Angeles | Los Angeles | Los Angeles. |
| Hellman, J W | Merchant | Los Angeles | Los Angeles | Los Angeles. |
| Hellman, I W | Cashier | F & M Bank | Main st. | Los Angeles. |
| Helms, Jonathan H | Laborer | Los Angeles Co. | | Los Angeles. |
| Helms, W | Miner | Los Angeles Co | | Los Angeles. |
| Hemerson, Charles. | Laborer | Los Angeles Co | | San Fernando. |
| Hemphill, J | Farmer | Los Angeles Co | nr Wilmington | Wilmington. |
| Henderson, J A | Hardware | 19 Los Angeles st | | Los Angeles. |

DIRECTORY OF LOS ANGELES COUNTY. 365

| Name. | Occupation. | Place of Business. | Residence. | Town or P. O. |
|---|---|---|---|---|
| Hendrick, James.... | Laborer | Los Angeles Co........ | .................................. | Los Angeles. |
| Henderson, D M... | Distiller | Los Angeles............. | Los Angeles............... | Los Angeles. |
| Henderson, F C..... | Lodging house.... | Los Angeles............. | Los Angeles............... | Los Angeles. |
| Hendricksen, G..... | Laborer | .................................. | Los Angeles Co........ | Santa Ana. |
| Henderson, W F.... | Miner | Los Angeles Co........ | Soledad..................... | San Fernando. |
| Henderson, J........ | Farmer | Los Angeles Co........ | nr Los Angeles......... | Los Angeles. |
| Hendrickson, Gordon ............... | Farmer | Los Angeles Co........ | nr Los Angeles......... | Los Angeles. |
| Henderson, David A | Laborer | Los Angeles Co........ | .................................. | Los Angeles. |
| Henne, Christian... | Brewer | Los Angeles............. | Los Angeles............... | Los Angeles. |
| Heninger, W K..... | Butcher.................. | San Gabriel............. | 9 m E Los Angeles... | San Gabriel. |
| Hennenfeld, P........ | Salesman............... | Silver Precinct........ | Silver Precinct.......... | Downey. |
| Henry, Alexander... | Laborer | Los Angeles Co........ | .................................. | Anaheim. |
| Henry, Jacob.......... |  | Los Angeles Co........ |  | Wilmington. |
| Henry, Wm Joseph | Trader.................... | Los Angeles Co........ |  | Los Angeles. |
| Henry, Stephen...... | Farmer | Los Angeles Co........ | nr Anaheim ............ | Anaheim. |
| Henriot, Mrs T...... | Teacher ................. | Los Angeles............. | Los Angeles............... | Los Angeles. |
| **Henry, W E** ........ | Wheelwright........ | Los Angeles Co........ | Silver Precinct.......... | Downey. |
| Herberger, Carl...... | Furniture ............. | 13 Aliso st............... |  | Los Angeles. |
| Hereford, Edward S | Farmer | Los Angeles Co........ | nr San Gabriel......... | San Gabriel. |
| Hereford, Ramon... | Ranchero .............. | Los Angeles Co........ | nr Los Angeles......... | Los Angeles. |
| **Hereford, James H** | Farmer | .................................. | Silver Precinct.......... | Downey. |
| Hereford, R P........ | Miner | Los Angeles Co........ |  | Anaheim. |
| **Herfuer William**... | Blacksmith.......... | Los Angeles........... | Los Angeles............... | Los Angeles. |
| Hericourt, Felix H. | Miner | Los Angeles Co........ |  | Los Angeles. |
| Herman, Joaquin... | Laborer.....*......... | Los Angeles Co........ |  | Los Angeles. |
| Hermon, Wm........ | Laborer | Los Angeles Co........ |  | Los Angeles. |
| Hermon, J ............. | Teamster............... | Los Angeles Co........ |  | Los Angeles. |
| **Hernandez, Guadalupe**....... | Shoe maker........... | Los Angeles............. | Los Angeles............... | Los Angeles. |
| Hernandez, Juan.... | Laborer | Los Angeles Co........ |  | San Fernando. |
| Hernandez, Jesus... | Ranchero ............. | Los Angeles Co........ |  | San Fernando. |
| Hernandez, D........ | Shoe maker........... | San Gabriel............ | 9 m E Los Angeles... | San Gabriel. |
| Hernandez, Juan ... | Engineer ............... | Los Angeles Co........ |  | Los Angeles. |
| **Hernandez, O**....... | Farmer ................... | Los Angeles Co........ | nr Los Angeles......... | Los Angeles. |
| Hernandez, J........ | Shoe maker........... | Los Angeles............ | Los Angeles............... | Los Angeles. |
| Hernandez, J C..... | Laborer | Los Angeles Co........ | San Jose................... | Spadra. |
| Hernandez, N........ | Laborer | .................................. | Los Angeles Co........ | Los Angeles. |
| Herrera, Ygnacio... | Peddler.................. | Los Angeles Co........ | .................................. | San Fernando. |
| Herrera, J ............. | Carpenter ............. | Los Angeles Co........ | San Jose................... | Spadra. |
| Herron, Thomas..... | Carpenter ............. | Los Angeles Co........ |  | Los Angeles. |
| **Herrick, Emery**.... | Merchant .............. | Los Angeles............. | Los Angeles............... | Los Angeles. |
| Herrick, H P........ | Wharfinger .......... | Los Angeles............. | Los Angeles............... | Los Angeles. |
| Herron, T ............. | Painter................... | Los Angeles............. | Los Angeles............... | Los Angeles. |
| Herrick, J ............. | Vaquero ................ | Los Angeles Co........ | Los Angeles............... | Los Angeles. |
| Herwig, Henry...... | Farmer ................... | Los Angeles Co........ | nr Los Angeles......... | Los Angeles. |
| **Herzog & Ruth**..... | Dry goods, etc..... | Los Angeles............. |  | Los Angeles. |
| Heslope, J ............. | Farmer................... | San Gabriel Valley... | 3 m N W San Gabriel | San Gabriel. |
| Hessinger, John .... | Saloon keeper...... | Los Angeles............. |  | Los Angeles. |
| Hester, James........ | Laborer | Los Angeles Co........ |  | Los Angeles. |
| Hester, Robert Allen | Machinist ............. | Los Angeles Co........ |  | Los Angeles. |
| **Hettenger, Charles** | Farmer | Los Angeles Co........ | nr Los Angeles......... | Los Angeles. |
| Heuer, William ..... | Bar keeper............ | Los Angeles............. | Los Angeles............... | Los Angeles. |
| **Hewett, Joseph**..... | Watchman ............ | S P R R Co............. | Wilmington............. | Wilmington. |
| Hewitt, E E........... | Supt ...................... | L A R R.................. | Hill st ...................... | Los Angeles. |
| Hewitt, J............... | Porter .................... | Los Angeles............ | Los Angeles............... | Los Angeles. |
| Hewitt, Abijah ...... | Miner | Los Angeles Co........ |  | Anaheim. |
| Hewitt, Orison P ... | Stock raiser ......... | Los Angeles Co........ | Silver Precinct.......... | Downey. |
| Hewitt, Eldridge E | Clerk..................... | Los Angeles Co........ | Wilmington............. | Wilmington. |
| Hewling, Isaac...... | Cooper................... | Los Angeles Co........ |  | Los Angeles. |
| Heyd, Louis........... | Laborer | Los Angeles Co........ |  | Los Angeles. |
| Heymann, Joachim | Ranchero .............. | Los Angeles Co........ | Azusa....................... | Azusa. |
| **Hibberts, William** | Farmer | Los Angeles Co........ | Old Mission.............. | El Monte. |
| Hicks, Augustus C.. | Lumber dealer..... | Los Angeles............. | Los Angeles............... | Los Angeles. |

# San Gabriel Nursery,

### J. C. WALLACE, Proprietor.

 **ONE MILE N. W. FROM SAN GABRIEL,**

**LOS ANGELES CO., CAL.**

### Trees ready for Delivery and Transplanting.

5,000 ORANGE,
5,000 LEMON,
2,000 POMEGRANITES,
Peach Trees in Seventy-three different varieties, maturing from May to January.
Also, Walnut, Apricot,

Cherry, Plum, Pear and Apple Trees, in all known varieties.
Bananas, Strawberries, Blackberries, Raspberries, Currants, and all kinds of Grapes.

### Trees Ready for Delivery during the Ensuing Year:

75,000 ORANGE, 4,000 LEMON, 2,000 POMEGRANATES; also, a full stock of all STANDARD FRUIT TREES, and SMALL FRUIT CUTTINGS.

## Orange Trees in Seven Varieties,

### GUM TREES AND CYPRESS,

AS WELL AS A FULL VARIETY OF

Ornamental and Flowering Shrubs, Rose Trees, Etc.

KEPT CONSTANTLY ON HAND.

---

**BLIGHT OR BUGS ON TREES UNKNOWN, AND ALL VARIETIES "TRUE TO NAME."**

| Name. | Occupation. | Place of Business. | Residence. | Town or P. O. |
|---|---|---|---|---|
| Hickman, Samuel... | Miner | Los Angeles Co | | Azusa. |
| Hickmott, John | Farmer | Los Angeles Co | nr San Juan | Capistrano. |
| Hickey, Isaac | Trader | Los Angeles Co | | Santa Ana. |
| Hickey, West Walker | Farmer | Los Angeles Co | near Santa Ana | Santa Ana. |
| Hickey, John Henry | Farmer | Los Angeles Co | San Joaquin | Santa Ana. |
| Hickey, Isaac Green | Farmer | Los Angeles Co | San Joaquin | Santa Ana. |
| Hicks, Leroy Jeff... | Farmer | Los Angeles Co | nr El Monte | El Monte. |
| Hickman, Andrew J | Bar keeper | Los Angeles Co | Wilmington | Wilmington. |
| Hicks, Rodolphus... | Laborer | Los Angeles Co | | Los Angeles. |
| Hicks, John D | Merchant | Los Angeles | Los Angeles | Los Angeles. |
| Hickox, Alfred | Farmer | Los Angeles Co | Silver Precinct | Downey. |
| Hicks, James | Harness maker | Los Angeles | Los Angeles | Los Angeles. |
| Hickman, Saml | Miner | San Gabriel Canyon | 14 m N Azusa | Azusa. |
| Hickman & Root... | Saloon | Los Angeles | Los Angeles | Los Angeles. |
| Hickmott, J | Farmer | Los Angeles Co | nr Los Angeles | San Juan. |
| Hiett, Henry J | Farmer | Los Angeles Co | nr Los Angeles | Los Angeles. |
| Higbie, A | Surveyor | Compton | Halfway House | Compton. |
| Higby, C C | Saloon keeper | Los Angeles | Los Angeles | Los Angeles. |
| Higgins, H | Stock raiser | San Pedro Ranch | 1½ m S W Compton | Compton. |
| Higgins, W M | Druggist | Lemon, cor Centre st | | Anaheim. |
| Higgins, Mrs A | Physician | Lemon, cor Centre st | | Anaheim. |
| Higgins, J P | Farmer | Los Angeles Co | Halfway House | Compton. |
| Higgins, William E | Farmer | Los Angeles Co | nr San Jose | Spadra. |
| Higgins, Philo W... | Farmer | Los Angeles Co | nr El Monte | El Monte. |
| Higgins, James | Farmer | Los Angeles Co | nr El Monte | El Monte. |
| Higgins, Wm Morris | Apothecary | Los Angeles | Los Angeles | Los Angeles. |
| Higgins, Harmon... | Farmer | Los Angeles | Halfway House | Compton. |
| Higgins, Samuel S.. | Farmer | Los Angeles Co | nr El Monte | El Monte. |
| Higgins, Josiah W.. | Printer | Los Angeles Co | Soledad | San Fernando. |
| Higley, Truman | Miner | Los Angeles Co | | Los Angeles. |
| Higuera, Lorenzo... | Laborer | Los Angeles Co | | Los Angeles. |
| Higuerra, Domingo | Laborer | Los Angeles Co | | San Gabriel. |
| Higuera, Dorateo... | Laborer | Los Angeles Co | Los Angeles | Los Angeles. |
| Higuera, Miguel | Laborer | Los Angeles Co | La Ballona | Los Angeles. |
| Higuera, Florencia | Vaquero | Los Angeles Co | nr Los Angeles | Los Angeles. |
| Higuero, M Y | Farmer | Los Angeles Co | Ballona | Los Angeles. |
| Higuera, H A | Laborer | Los Angeles Co | | Los Angeles. |
| Higuera, A | Ranchero | Los Angeles Co | nr Los Angeles | Los Angeles. |
| Hill, John Cyrus... | Farmer | Los Angeles Co | nr Los Angeles | Los Angeles. |
| Hill, Thomas W | Laborer | Los Angeles Co | | Los Nietos. |
| Hille, Chas Christie | Farmer | Los Angeles Co | nr Anaheim | Anaheim. |
| Hill, Jasper C | Book keeper | Los Angeles Co | Santa Ana | Santa Ana. |
| Hill, John James... | Farmer | Los Angeles Co | nr Anaheim | Anaheim. |
| Hill, William Henry | Butcher | Los Angeles Co | Anaheim | Anaheim. |
| Hiller, Horace | Book keeper | Los Angeles | Los Angeles | Los Angeles. |
| Hiller, Rudolph | Printer | Los Angeles | Los Angeles | Los Angeles. |
| Hill, Charles | Fireman | Wilmington | Wilmington | Wilmington. |
| Hill, Benj | Ship carpenter | Wilmington | Wilmington | Wilmington. |
| Hill, A | Wagon maker | Lemon st | Anaheim | Anaheim. |
| Hill, John J | Clerk | Anaheim | Anaheim | Anaheim. |
| Hill, John | Laborer | Los Angeles Co | | Los Angeles. |
| Hille, Charles | City bakery | Centre st | Anaheim | Anaheim. |
| Hillhouse, J T B | Engineer | Los Angeles | Los Angeles | Los Angeles. |
| Hill, Thos | | Los Angeles Co | | Los Angeles. |
| Hill, Rev Wm H... | Rector | Episcopal Church | Los Angeles | Los Angeles. |
| Hill, J C | Farmer | Los Angeles Co | nr Santa Ana | Santa Ana. |
| Hill, T T | Farmer | Los Angeles Co | nr Santa Ana | Santa Ana. |
| Hilmer, Charles | Farmer | Los Angeles Co | nr Los Angeles | Los Angeles. |
| Hilmes, Byron C | Laborer | Los Angeles Co | | Los Angeles. |
| Hilt, Howard F | Farmer | Los Angeles Co | nr Los Angeles | Los Angeles. |
| Hindes, John J | Saddler | Los Angeles Co | El Monte | El Monte. |
| Hinds, George | Butcher | Los Angeles Co | Wilmington | Wilmington. |

| Name. | Occupation. | Place of Business. | Residence. | Town or P. O. |
|---|---|---|---|---|
| Hinds, George | Butcher | Canal st | Wilmington | Wilmington. |
| Hinds, S S | Laborer | S P R R Co | Wilmington | Wilmington. |
| **Hinds, Chas D** | Watchmaker | Los Angeles | Los Angeles | Los Angeles. |
| Hinds, Wm Richardson | Carpenter | Los Angeles Co | | Los Angeles. |
| Hines, James R | Farmer | Los Angeles Co | nr Los Angeles | Los Angeles. |
| Hinman, Frank | Farmer | San Pedro Ranch | 2 m S W Compton | Compton. |
| Hinson, Alex | Wharf hand | S P R R Co | Wilmington | Wilmington. |
| Hinton, John R | Apiarian | Los Angeles Co | nr El Monte | El Monte. |
| Hirschberg, A | Clerk | Los Angeles | Los Angeles | Los Angeles. |
| Hirsch, J | Clerk | Los Angeles | Los Angeles | Los Angeles. |
| **Hitchcock, W L G.** | Farmer | El Monte Valley | 1¼ m N Lexington | El Monte. |
| Hitt, James D | Farmer | Los Angeles Co | nr Los Angeles | Los Angeles. |
| Hixon, W | Receiving clerk | S P R R Co | Wilmington | Wilmington. |
| Hoagland, Abram R | Teamster | Los Angeles Co | | |
| **Hodgdon, Andrew T** | Farmer | | San Joaquin Towns'p | Santa Ana. |
| Hodgkins, L R | Miner | | San Gabriel Mission. | San Gabriel. |
| **Hodges, John E** | Farmer | Los Angeles Co | nr Los Angeles | Los Angeles. |
| Hoffman, John Knox | Carpenter | Los Angeles Co | | Los Angeles. |
| Hoffner, Saml | Farmer & carpen | Spadra | 30 m E Los Angeles. | Spadra. |
| **Hoffman, Dr D B** | Physician | 17 Downey Block | Blackman House | Los Angeles. |
| Hoff, John V | | Los Angeles | Los Angeles | Los Angeles. |
| Hogan, Chas N | Wood carver | Los Angeles | Los Angeles | Los Angeles. |
| Hogan, J C | Farmer | San Pedro Ranch | 1¼ m W Compton | Compton. |
| Hogarth, E | Carpenter | Los Angeles | nr Compton | Los Angeles. |
| Holaday, George M | Farmer | Los Angeles Co | San Jose | Spadra. |
| Holbrook, Jno F | Tinsmith | Los Angeles | Los Angeles | Los Argeles. |
| Holderfield, Benj F. | Farmer | Los Angeles Co | Halfway House | Compton. |
| Holden, Henry | Carpenter | Los Angeles Co | | Los Angeles. |
| Holden, Geo W | Lather | Los Angeles | Los Angeles | Los Angeles. |
| Holden, James | Laborer | Los Angeles Co | | Wilmington. |
| Holdgate, S | Farmer | Los Angeles Co | Silver Precinct | Downey. |
| Holden, J O | Carpenter | | Los Angeles Co | El Monte. |
| **Hole, A W** | Farmer | Los Angeles Co | nr Florence | Los Angeles. |
| Hollinshead, Daniel | Carpenter | Los Angeles Co | | Los Angeles. |
| Hollinsworth, James | Farmer | Los Angeles Co | nr Los Nietos | Los Nietos. |
| Holly, Richard S | Farmer | Los Angeles Co | nr El Monte | El Monte. |
| Hollaway, J B | Attorney | Los Angeles Co | Los Nietos | Los Nietos. |
| **Holland, Danl** | Farmer | Los Angeles Co | nr Los Angeles | Los Angeles. |
| Holladay, L | Locomotive fire'n | Spadra | Spadra | Spadra. |
| Holladay, Thos | Farmer & consta. | Spadra | 30 m E Los Angeles. | Spadra. |
| Holland, H | Farmer | Azusa Duarte | 3 m E Lexington | El Monte. |
| Holmes, Joseph | Cook | Los Angeles Co | Wilmington | Wilmington. |
| Holmes, James | Engineer | Wilmington | Canal st | Wilmington. |
| **Holman, R** | Millwright | Aliso mills | Old Aliso st | Los Angeles. |
| **Holmes, Harry** | Farmer | | Cerritos | Wilmington. |
| Holmes, A C | Notary public | 26 Temple Block | | Los Angeles. |
| Holmes, Geo F | Carpenter | Los Angeles Co | | Los Angeles. |
| Holmes, D J | Farmer | Los Angeles Co | Silver Precinct | Downey. |
| Holmes, A C | Revenue collector | Los Angeles | Los Angeles | Los Angeles. |
| Holmes, James G | Machinist | Los Angeles Co | Wilmington | Wilmington. |
| Holmes, Chas A | Trader | Los Angeles Co | | Los Angeles. |
| Holmes, Joseph | Cook | Los Angeles Co | Los Angeles | Los Angeles. |
| **Holman, Woodford C** | Farmer | Los Angeles Co | Silver Precinct | Downey. |
| Holmes, James R | Farmer | Los Angeles Co | nr Los Angeles | Los Angeles. |
| Holst, Charles | Carpenter | Los Angeles Co | nr Anaheim | Anaheim. |
| Holt, Samuel Madison | Shepherd | Los Angeles Co | | San Gabriel. |
| Holt, Luther M | Printer | Los Angeles Co | Los Angeles | Los Angeles. |
| **Holyfield, Newton** | Farmer | Los Angeles Co | nr Los Nietos | Los Nietos. |
| Hoogstraten, John A | Laborer | Los Angeles Co | | Los Angeles. |
| Hooper, Thomas | Farmer | Los Angeles Co | nr Los Nietos | Los Nietos. |
| Hooper, Andrew J. | Farmer | Los Angeles Co | nr San Gabriel | San Gabriel. |

## DIRECTORY OF LOS ANGELES COUNTY. 369

| Name. | Occupation. | Place of Business. | Residence. | Town or P. O. |
|---|---|---|---|---|
| Hooper, W............ | Teamster............ | .................... | Los Angeles Co ...... | Wilmington. |
| Hoover, David...... | Farmer ............ | .................... | La Ballona............ | Los Angeles. |
| Hopkins, Henry ..... | Painter ............ | Los Angeles........ | Los Angeles............ | Los Angeles. |
| Hopkins, C H........ | Stationary engin'r | S P R R............ | Canal st............ | Wilmington. |
| Hopkins, A A........ | Stage driver........ | Los Angeles........ | Los Angeles............ | Los Angeles. |
| Hopkins, M.......... | Truckman............ | Los Angeles........ | Los Angeles............ | Los Angeles. |
| Hopper, John ........ | Trader............ | Los Angeles Co.... | .................... | El Monte. |
| Hopper, John ........ | Justice of peace.... | Lexington............ | 12 m E Los Angeles. | El Monte. |
| Hopper, J F ........ | Merchant............ | Los Angeles........ | Los Angeles............ | Los Angeles. |
| Horn, Robert S.... | Wagon maker...... | Los Angeles Co .... | El Monte ............ | El Monte. |
| Horn, Geo Henry... | Farmer............ | Los Angeles Co ...... | nr Anaheim............ | Anaheim. |
| Horn & Turner .... | Genl merchandise | Lexington............ | 12 m E Los Angeles. | El Monte. |
| Horn, A J ........... | Genl merchandise | Lexington............ | 12 m E Los Angeles. | El Monte. |
| Horton, J............ | Tinner............ | Los Angeles........ | Los Angeles............ | Los Angeles. |
| Horton, O ............ | Farmer............ | Los Angeles Co .... | nr Anaheim............ | Anaheim. |
| Horton, Wade H.... | Farmer ............ | Los Angeles Co .... | Silver Precinct........ | Downey. |
| Horton, Wade........ | Farmer ............ | Los Angeles Co .... | Silver Precinct........ | Downey. |
| Horton, Daniel B... | Carpenter ............ | Los Angeles Co .... | .................... | Los Angeles. |
| Horton, Orran...... | Farmer ............ | Los Angeles Co .... | Silver Precinct........ | Downey. |
| Horton, George B... | Farmer ............ | Los Angeles Co .... | Silver Precinct........ | Downey. |
| Horton, Marshall ... | Farmer ............ | Los Angeles Co .... | Silver Precinct........ | Downey. |
| Horton, George..... | Teamster .. ....... | Los Angeles Co .... | .................... | Los Angeles. |
| Hosmer, Frank...... | City sexton........ | Los Angeles........ | Los Angeles............ | Los Angeles. |
| Houghton, Wm Lake...... ............ | Farmer ............ | Los Angeles Co .... | nr Los Nietos............ | Los Nietos. |
| Hourtado, Augustin ............ | Farmer ............ | Los Angeles Co ...... | nr Anaheim............ | Anaheim. |
| Houston, Walter... | Farmer ............ | Los Angeles Co ...... | Silver Precinct........ | Downey. |
| Houston, Robert.... | Farmer ............ | Los Angeles Co ...... | nr El Monte............ | El Monte. |
| House, William H.. | Farmer ............ | Los Angeles Co ...... | nr Azusa ............ | Azusa. |
| House, Frank R .... | Conductor ............ | Los Angeles........ | Los Angeles............ | Los Angeles. |
| House, R F ......... | Conductor ............ | S P R R............ | Spadra............ | Spadra. |
| Houston, Robt...... | Farmer ............ | El Monte Valley...... | 1 m W Lexington ... | El Monte. |
| Housman, H ........ | Wagon maker...... | Los Angeles........ | Los Angeles............ | Los Angeles. |
| Howard, David C... | Farmer ............ | Los Angeles Co ...... | nr El Monte............ | El Monte. |
| Howard, James G... | Attorney............ | Los Angeles........ | Los Angeles............ | Los Angeles. |
| Howard, William... | Mariner ............ | Los Angeles Co...... | .................... | Wilmington. |
| Howard, Phinehas.. | Doctor............ | Los Angeles........ | Los Angeles............ | Los Angeles. |
| Howard, William H | Lumberman ............ | Los Angeles Co...... | .................... | Santa Ana. |
| Howard, Volney E. | Attorney............ | Los Angeles........ | .................... | San Gabriel. |
| Howard, Francis H | Doctor ............ | Los Angeles Co .... | San Gabriel............ | San Gabriel. |
| Howard, Henry H... | Farmer ............ | Los Angeles Co .... | nr Los Angeles........ | Los Angeles. |
| Howard, A J........ | Farmer ............ | 9 m E Los Angeles.. | San Gabriel............ | San Gabriel. |
| Howard, J G ........ | Attorney at law ... | 8 Downey Block.... | 240 Main st ............ | Los Angeles. |
| Howard, V E & F H | Attorneys at law. | Temple Block ............ | .................... | Los Angeles. |
| Howard & Hazard | Attorneys at law.. | 8 Downey Block........ | .................... | Los Angeles. |
| Howard, A J........ | Farmer ............ | Los Angeles Co.... | nr San Gabriel........ | San Gabriel. |
| Howard, G H........ | Doctor.. ............ | Los Angeles........ | Los Angeles............ | Los Angeles. |
| Howard, T W........ | Clerk............ | Los Angeles........ | Los Angeles............ | Los Angeles. |
| Howe, George...... | Farmer ............ | Los Angeles Co .... | nr Los Angeles........ | Los Angeles. |
| Howe, Converse .... | Clerk............ | Los Angeles Co .... | Westminster Col..... | Westminster. |
| Howes, James O.... | Farmer ............ | Los Angeles Co .... | nr Los Angeles........ | Los Angeles. |
| Howe, William...... | Laborer............ | Los Angeles Co .... | Wilmington............ | Wilmington. |
| Howe, A J............ | Physician ............ | .................... | Westminster Col..... | Westminster. |
| Howe, Philip........ | Physician ............ | .................... | Westminster Col ..... | Westminster. |
| Howe, J M............ | .................... | .................... | Westminster Col..... | Westminster. |
| Howe, John......... | Laborer............ | Los Angeles Co .... | Los Angeles............ | Los Angeles. |
| Howe, Converse .... | Teacher............ | .................... | Westminster Col..... | Westminster. |
| Howell & Co, W C | Sew mach agent... | Los Angeles........ | .................... | Los Angeles. |
| Howe, P............ | Physician ............ | Los Angeles Co .... | Florence ............ | Los Angeles. |
| Howell, L P........ | Doctor............ | Los Angeles........ | Los Angeles............ | Los Angeles. |
| Howe, John N...... | Printer............ | Los Angeles........ | Los Angeles............ | Los Angeles. |
| Howe, John......... | Farmer ............ | Placeritas ............ | 4 m N W Lyon Statn | Lyon Station. |
| Howison, Azra...... | Farmer ............ | Los Angeles Co .... | nr El Monte............ | El Monte. |

24

### Three Miles south from Los Angeles.

This fine Nursery comprises 35 acres of fine arable land, 15 of which are planted entirely in trees.

#### TREES READY FOR THIS YEAR'S DELIVERY:

10,000 ORANGE TREES, (best varieties), 2,000 LIME TREES, 2,000 LEMON TREES.

#### TREES READY FOR DELIVERY NEXT YEAR:

10,000 ORANGE, (best varieties), 2,000 LIME, 2,000 LEMON.

## TEN THOUSAND BEARING TREES,
### AND TWENTY ACRES OF FOREIGN VINES.

#### ALL STANDARD VARIETIES OF FRUIT TREES CONSTANTLY ON HAND.

FOR SALE, CUTTINGS FROM ALL CHOICE VARIETIES OF FOREIGN GRAPES; ALSO, ALL BRANDS OF WINES OF MY OWN MANUFACTURE.

**WE SELL AS LOW AS ANY ONE IN THE STATE.**

DIRECTORY OF LOS ANGELES COUNTY. 371

| NAME. | OCCUPATION. | PLACE OF BUSINESS. | RESIDENCE. | TOWN OR P. O. |
|---|---|---|---|---|
| Howland, Wm | Stock raiser | Catalina Island | Wilmington | Wilmington. |
| Howorton, A B | Stage driver | Azusa Ranch | 2½ m N Azusa | Azusa. |
| Hoxall, H | Merchant | | San Fernando | San Fernando. |
| Hoyt, Albert Henry | Merchant | Los Angeles Co | El Monte | El Monte. |
| Hoyt, C D | Veterinary Surg | Main st | | Los Angeles. |
| Hoyett, A H | Farmer | Lexington | 12 m E Los Angeles | El Monte. |
| Hubbard, William | Miner | Los Angeles Co | Los Angeles | Los Angeles. |
| Hubbard, Joseph | Farmer | Los Angeles Co | nr Los Nietos | Los Nietos. |
| Hubbard, H | Farmer | San Fernando Miss'n | 1½ m W San Fern'do | San Fernando. |
| Hubbell, Geo E | Farmer | | San Jose | Spadra. |
| Hubbard, H | Farmer | Los Angeles Co | nr Los Angeles | Los Angeles. |
| Hubbell, J C | Attorney | Los Angeles | Los Angeles | Los Angeles. |
| Huber, Jos Jr | Hardware, etc | 110 Main st | 220 Main st | Los Angeles. |
| Huber, Joseph Jr | Clerk | Los Angeles | | Los Angeles. |
| Huber, Chas Edward | Clerk | Los Angeles | | Los Angeles. |
| Huckaby, David | Farmer | Los Angeles Co | nr Santa Ana | Santa Ana. |
| Hudson, George | Farmer | Los Angeles Co | nr Los Angeles | Los Angeles. |
| Hueston, Adolph | Carpenter | Los Angeles | | Los Angeles. |
| Huey, James | Blacksmith | Spadra | 30 m E Los Angeles | Spadra. |
| Hudson, Albert | Law student | Los Angeles | Los Angeles | Los Angeles. |
| Hudson, Rodney Jas | Lawyer | Los Angeles | Los Angeles | Los Angeles. |
| Hudson, Rodney | Attorney at law | 29 & 30 Temple Blk | Spring st | Los Angeles. |
| Hudson, David D | Farmer | | San Joaquin | Santa Ana. |
| Hudson, J W | Cooper | Los Angeles | Los Angeles | Los Angeles. |
| Huff, Jesse | Wood cutter | Los Angeles Co | | Los Angeles. |
| Huff, L C | Farmer | Los Angeles Co | nr Soledad | San Fernando. |
| Hufsettler, Henry | Farmer | Los Angeles | nr El Monte | El Monte. |
| Huggins, John | Miner | Los Angeles Co | | Los Angeles. |
| Hughes, Francis John | Miner | Los Angeles Co | | Los Angeles. |
| Hughes, Henry L | Laborer | Los Angeles Co | | Los Angeles. |
| Hughes, Robt | Miner | Los Angeles Co | | Los Angeles. |
| Hughes, W C | Farmer | Los Angeles | nr Los Angeles | Los Angeles. |
| Hughes, I J | Teacher | Los Angeles Co | | Los Angeles. |
| Hughes, J | Plasterer | Los Angeles Co | Los Angeles | Los Angeles. |
| Huic, Jus M | Blacksmith | Los Angeles | Los Angeles | Los Angeles. |
| Hukill, J F | Wheelwright | Los Angeles Co | El Monte | El Monte. |
| Hulbert, John W | Carpenter | Los Angeles | Los Angeles | Los Angeles. |
| Hull, T C | General mdse | Co-operative store | Westminster | Westminster. |
| Hullman, H | Teamster | Los Angeles Co | | El Monte. |
| Hulton, Samuel O | Miner | Los Angeles Co | | Azusa. |
| Humbert, J | Saloon keeper | Los Angeles | Los Angeles | Los Angeles. |
| Humboldt, August | Wine maker | Los Angeles Co | | Anaheim. |
| Humel, V | Bakery | San Fernando | San Fernando | San Fernando. |
| Hummel, J H | Farmer | Azusa Ranch | 1½ m N E Azusa | Azusa. |
| Humphreys, F | Farmer | San Jose Valley | 1 m N W Spadra | Spadra. |
| Humphreys, M A | Farmer | Azusa | 2 m S W Azusa P O | Azusa. |
| Humphrey, Henry J | Clerk | Los Angeles Co | | Los Angeles. |
| Humphreys, D A | Farmer | Los Angeles Co | San Jose | Spadra. |
| Humphreys, M A | Farmer | Los Angeles Co | nr San Jose | Spadra. |
| Humphreys, Alex M | Farmer | Los Angeles Co | nr El Monte | El Monte. |
| Huneke, John | Laborer | Los Angeles Co | | Los Angeles. |
| Hunter, S | Ranchero | Los Angeles Co | nr Los Angeles | Los Angeles. |
| Hunter, W | Farmer | Los Angeles Co | nr Los Angeles | Los Angeles. |
| Hunter, J D | Farmer | Los Angeles Co | nr Los Angeles | Los Angeles. |
| Huntingdon, Gilbert | Miner | Los Angeles Co | | Anaheim. |
| Hunt, William B | Blacksmith | Los Angeles Co | | Los Angeles. |
| Hunter, Benj A | Machinist | Los Angeles Co | | El Monte. |
| Hunter, Jesse Jr | Farmer | Los Angeles Co | nr Los Angeles | Los Angeles. |
| Huntington, James | Farmer | Los Angeles Co | nr Santa Ana | Santa Ana. |
| Hunter, Asa | Ranchero | Los Angeles Co | nr Los Angeles | Los Angeles. |
| Hunter, Thos Gordon | Carpenter | Los Angeles Co | | Los Angeles. |
| Huqueney, Alex | Cooper | Los Angeles Co | | Los Angeles. |

372  L. L. PAULSON'S HAND-BOOK AND

| Name. | Occupation. | Place of Business. | Residence. | Town or P. O. |
|---|---|---|---|---|
| Hurd, James A | Horse trainer | Los Angeles Co | | San Gabriel. |
| Hurffman, Robert | Farmer | Los Angeles Co | nr El Monte | El Monte. |
| Hurlburt, William | Farmer | Los Angeles Co | nr El Monte | El Monte. |
| Hurley, Jeremiah | Farmer | | Anaheim | Anaheim. |
| Hurn, Alfred | Laborer | Los Angeles Co | | Los Angeles. |
| Hurst, J F | Carpenter | | Santa Ana | Santa Ana. |
| Huse, Edward F | Carpenter | Los Angeles Co | | Los Angeles. |
| Huskins, Samuel B | Carpenter | Los Angeles Co | | Los Angeles. |
| Hutchinson, Geo W | Farmer | Los Angeles Co | Silver Precinct | Downey. |
| Hutchinson, Charles Gates | Farmer | Los Angeles Co | | San Gabriel. |
| Hutchings, Joseph S | Ranchero | Los Angeles Co | Half Way House | Compton. |
| Hutchings, Hovey | Carpenter | Los Angeles Co | | Anaheim. |
| Hutchingson, A J | Farmer | San Bernardino Rd | 5 m N E Spadra | Spadra. |
| Hutchinson, Wm A | Farmer | | Silver Precinct | Downey. |
| Hutchinson, W M | Farmer | Los Angeles Co | nr Los Angeles | Los Nietos. |
| Hutton, A W | Attorney at law | Temple Block | 23 Fort st | Los Angeles. |
| Hyde, Wash | Painter | Los Angeles Co | | Los Angeles. |
| Hyer, Robert Henry | Barber | Los Angeles Co | | Los Angeles. |
| Hyue, C W | Farmer | Los Angeles Co | nr Santa Ana | Santa Ana. |
| Iler, S W | Pioneer hotel | S J Capistrano | San Juan | S J Capistrano. |
| Ingram, W R | Stage driver | Telegraph Stage Line | San Fernando | San Fernando. |
| Ingram, Joseph | Freighter | Los Angeles | Los Angeles | Los Angeles. |
| Ingram, C E | Miner | Los Angeles Co | Los Angeles Co | Los Angeles. |
| Inman, — | Farmer | Azusa | 1 m S W Azusa | Azusa. |
| Ironside, John B | General agent | Los Angeles Co | San Gabriel | San Gabriel. |
| Irwin, Robert | Farmer | Los Angeles Co | nr El Monte | El Monte. |
| Isbell, Thomas | Farmer | Los Angeles Co | nr Los Nietos | Los Nietos. |
| Isbell, James F | Farmer | Los Angeles Co | nr Los Nietos | Los Nietos. |
| Isby, George B | Farmer | Los Angeles Co | nr San Gabriel | San Gabriel. |
| Jackson, Seymour A | Farmer | Los Angeles Co | Old Mission | El Monte. |
| Jackson, Wm | Engineer | S P R R Co | Spadra | Spadra. |
| Jackson, Wm D | Drayman | Wilmington | 2nd st | Wilmington. |
| Jackson, Wm | Cook | Los Angeles Co | Los Angeles | Los Angeles. |
| Jackson, J G | Lumber dealer | Alameda & First sts | Los Angeles | Los Angeles. |
| Jackson, Geo H | Clerk | Los Angeles Co | Los Angeles | Los Angeles. |
| Jackson, C G | Coal dealer | Los Angeles Co | Los Angeles | Los Angeles. |
| Jackson, S | Farmer | Los Angeles Co | nr El Monte | El Monte. |
| Jackson, S P | Farmer | Los Angeles Co | nr Los Angeles | Los Angeles. |
| Jackson, R E | Carpenter | Los Angeles Co | Los Angeles | Los Angeles. |
| Jacoby, H | | Wilmington | nr Wilson's College | Wilmington. |
| Jacoby, N | General mdse | Canal st | Wilmington | Wilmington. |
| Jacobs, Thos | Farmer | | Tustin City | Santa Ana. |
| Jacoby, C | Merchant | Los Angeles | Los Angeles | Los Angeles. |
| Jaeciomzzi, J | Bar keeper | Los Angeles | Los Angeles | Los Angeles. |
| James, Evan | Farmer | Los Angeles Co | nr El Monte | El Monte. |
| James, Walter B | Blacksmith | Los Angeles | Los Angeles | Los Angeles. |
| James, Benj | Laborer | Pt San Pedro | Pt San Pedro | Wilmington. |
| James, David | Farmer | Los Angeles Co | nr Los Angeles | Los Angeles. |
| James, I T | Laborer | Los Angeles Co | Anaheim | Anaheim. |
| James, A | Farmer | Los Angeles Co | nr Los Angeles | Los Angeles. |
| James, J W | Farmer | Los Angeles Co | La Ballona | Los Angeles. |
| Jameson, W | Laborer | Los Angeles Co | Soledad | Spadra. |
| Jamison, Wm S | Farmer | Los Angeles Co | nr Los Angeles | Los Angeles. |
| Jamison, J B | Farmer | Los Angeles Co | nr Santa Ana | Santa Ana. |
| Jamison, W | Farmer | Los Angeles Co | Halfway House | Compton. |
| Jander, Leonard | Saddler | Los Angeles | Anaheim | Anaheim. |
| Janes, A M | Sewing mach agt | 60 Spring st | Los Angeles | Los Angeles. |
| Janseguy, Peter | Shepherd | Los Angeles Co | nr Los Nietos | Los Nietos. |
| Jaramillo, C | Farmer | Los Angeles Co | nr Los Angeles | Los Nietos. |
| Jared, L D | Farmer | Los Angeles Co | | Los Nietos. |
| Jargsdorff, C H | Foreman | S P R R Co | Wilmington | Wilmington. |
| Jason, A | Teamster | Wilmington | Wilmington | Wilmington. |
| Jasper, Samuel N | Farmer | Los Angeles Co | Santa Ana | Santa Ana. |

## DIRECTORY OF LOS ANGELES COUNTY. 373

| Name. | Occupation. | Place of Business. | Residence. | Town or P. O. |
|---|---|---|---|---|
| Jasper, Wm H...... | Farmer............ | Los Angeles Co...... | nr Santa Ana......... | Santa Ana. |
| Jaunesee, Louis..... | Farmer............ | Los Angeles Co....... | nr Los Angeles........ | Los Angeles. |
| Jeantel, John......... | Farmer............ | Azusa Ranch........... | 1½ m S W Azusa..... | Azusa. |
| Jeantel, Joseph..... | Farmer............ | Los Angeles Co....... | nr Azusa............... | Azusa. |
| Jenes, Candaleria... | Farmer............ | Los Angeles Co....... | nr Los Angeles........ | Los Angeles. |
| Jenkins, Joseph W. | Carpenter......... | Los Angeles Co....... | ........................... | Los Angeles. |
| Jenkins, Charles M | Printer............. | Los Angeles........... | Los Angeles........... | Los Angeles. |
| Jenkins, Wm Wirt | Farmer............ | Los Angeles Co....... | nr Los Angeles........ | Los Angeles. |
| Jenkins, James M.. | Machinist.......... | Los Angeles........... | Los Angeles........... | Los Angeles. |
| Jenkins, J ............ | Laborer............ | San Pedro Ranch..... | ½ m W Compton...... | Compton. |
| Jenks, M J .......... | Painter............. | S P R R Co........... | Wilmington........... | Wilmington. |
| Jenkins, W......... | Farmer............ | Los Angeles Co....... | nr Anaheim........... | Anaheim. |
| Jenns, S S........... | Teamster........... | Los Angeles Co....... | ........................... | El Monte. |
| Jennings, M H..... | Farmer............ | Los Angeles Co....... | nr Los Angeles........ | Los Angeles. |
| Jensen, Mads........ | Cabinet maker ... | Los Angeles........... | Los Angeles........... | Los Angeles. |
| Jeremias, Victor.... | Laborer............ | Los Angeles Co....... | ........................... | San Fernando. |
| Jeremias, Ramon... | Ranchero.......... | Los Angeles Co....... | nr San Fernando..... | San Fernando. |
| Jeremiah, S........... | Mechanic.......... | Los Angeles Co....... | San Jose.............. | Spadra. |
| Jeremias, J A....... | Farmer ............ | Los Angeles Co....... | nr San Fernando..... | San Fernando. |
| Jersey, R M......... | Carpenter.......... | Los Angeles Co....... | Los Angeles........... | Los Angeles. |
| Jimenez, Felipe..... | Laborer............ | Los Angeles Co....... | ........................... | Los Angeles. |
| Jimenez, Jose....... | Miner.............. | Los Angeles Co....... | ........................... | Los Angeles. |
| Johansen, T J...... | Wagon maker..... | Los Angeles........... | Los Angeles........... | Los Angeles. |
| Johannsen, J........ | Farmer............ | Los Angeles Co....... | nr Anaheim........... | Anaheim. |
| Johannsen & Grosser............. | Furniture.......... | Main st............... | ........................... | Los Angeles. |
| Johansen, Jacob ... | Cabinet maker ... | Los Angeles.......... | Los Angeles........... | Los Angeles. |
| Johnson, C R....... | Farmer............ | San Pedro Ranch..... | ½ m W Compton...... | Compton. |
| Johnson, J.......... | Ship carpenter.... | S P R R Co........... | Wilmington........... | Wilmington. |
| Johnson, F C....... | Butcher........... | Canal st.............. | Palas Verde Ranch .. | Wilmington. |
| Johnson, James C.. | Stock raiser....... | 20 m S Wilmington.. | Catalina Island...... | Wilmington. |
| Johnston, A......... | Physician ......... | Canal st.............. | Canal st.............. | Wilmington. |
| Johnson, G F ...... | Tel operator....... | Los Angeles........... | Los Angeles........... | Los Angeles. |
| Johnson, Joseph.... | Farmer............ | Los Angeles Co....... | Gallatin.............. | Downey. |
| Johnson, Mrs E M. | Dress maker....... | Los Angeles........... | 51 Fort st............ | Los Angeles. |
| Johnson, Mrs C .... | ....................... | ........................... | 38 Los Angeles st.... | Los Angeles. |
| Johnson, Mrs E.... | Grocery ........... | Arcadia st........... | Los Angeles........... | Los Angeles. |
| Johnson, J S........ | Wagon maker..... | Spring st............. | Los Angeles........... | Los Angeles. |
| Johnson, Frank..... | Laborer............ | Los Angeles Co....... | ........................... | Los Angeles. |
| Johnson, Wm C.... | Clerk .............. | Los Angeles Co....... | Los Angeles........... | Los Angeles. |
| Johnson, David S... | Laborer............ | Los Angeles Co....... | ........................... | Los Angeles. |
| Johnson, Henry H.. | Carpenter ......... | ........................... | Los Angeles Co....... | Los Angeles. |
| Johnson, James..... | Farmer............ | Los Angeles Co....... | nr Anaheim........... | Anaheim. |
| Johnson, Geo O..... | Musician........... | Los Angeles........... | Los Angeles........... | Los Angeles. |
| Johnson, E H ...... | Farmer............ | Los Angeles Co....... | nr Anaheim........... | Anaheim. |
| Johnson, J P........ | Carpenter.......... | Los Angeles Co....... | Los Angeles........... | Los Angeles. |
| Johnston, H McC... | Surveyor........... | Los Angeles........... | Los Angeles........... | Los Angeles. |
| Johnson, J J ........ | Farmer............ | Los Angeles Co....... | nr Santa Ana......... | Santa Ana. |
| Johnston, A R...... | Plasterer .......... | Los Angeles........... | Los Angeles........... | Los Angeles. |
| Johnson, G......... | Farmer............ | Los Angeles Co....... | nr Los Angeles....... | Los Angeles. |
| John, G ............. | Bar keeper........ | Los Angeles........... | Los Angeles........... | Los Angeles. |
| Johnson, P F ....... | Printer............. | Los Angeles Co....... | nr Los Angeles....... | Los Angeles. |
| Johnson, A J........ | Attorney........... | Los Angeles........... | Los Angeles........... | Los Angeles. |
| Johnson, F.......... | Teamster.......... | Los Angeles Co....... | Wilmington .......... | Wilmington. |
| Johnston, C G...... | Attorney........... | 41 Spring st......... | 41 Spring st......... | Anaheim. |
| Johnson, A L....... | Carpenter ......... | Los Angeles Co....... | Silver Precinct....... | Downey. |
| Johnson, L A ...... | Livery stable...... | Los Angeles........... | Los Angeles........... | Los Angeles. |
| Johnson, H......... | Laborer ........... | Los Angeles Co....... | Los Angeles........... | Santa Ana. |
| Johnson, T......... | Farmer............ | Los Angeles Co....... | Silver Precinct....... | Downey. |
| Johnson, Mrs E .... | Grocery ........... | Arcadia st........... | Los Angeles........... | Los Angeles. |
| Johnson, D H....... | Farmer............ | Los Angeles Co....... | nr Anaheim........... | Anaheim. |
| Johnson, R M....... | Stock raiser....... | Los Angeles Co....... | nr Los Angeles....... | Los Angeles. |
| Johnson, C A....... | Clerk .............. | Los Angeles.......... | Los Angeles........... | Los Angeles. |
| Johnson, W L ...... | Farmer............ | Los Angeles Co....... | Los Nietos........... | Los Nietos. |

## ESTABLISHED IN 1854.

### PIONEER
### HARNESS & SADDLE
### MANUFACTORY.

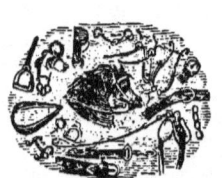  

# S. C. FOY,
Importer, Manufacturer, Wholesale and Retail Dealer in

### Saddlery and Harness of all kinds,
### SULKY HARNESS, TROTTING HARNESS,
### HEAVY DRAFT HARNESS.
### ROBES, BLANKETS,
### AND WHIPS.
### GENUINE CONCORD HARNESS,

In fact, everything pertaining to a first-class Saddlery House.

### THE VERY BEST GENUINE LOS ANGELES SADDLES.
The best brands of Saddle, Harness and Sole Leather always on hand and for sale, wholesale and retail.

### HARNESS OILS, SOAPS AND BLACKING.
### Repairing Promptly Done.
### No. 17 LOS ANGELES STREET, LOS ANGELES, CAL.
### Prices as Low as any house on the Coast.

## DIRECTORY OF LOS ANGELES COUNTY. 375

| Name. | Occupation. | Place of Business. | Residence. | Town or P. O. |
|---|---|---|---|---|
| Johnson, A | Wagon maker | Anaheim | Anaheim | Anaheim. |
| Johnson, W | Ranchero | Los Angeles Co | nr Los Angeles | Los Angeles. |
| Johnson, C F C | Sailor | | Wilmington | Wilmington. |
| Johnston, J A | Merchant | Los Angeles | Los Angeles | Los Angeles. |
| Johnson, J | Farmer | Los Angeles Co | nr San Juan | San Juan. |
| Johnson, W W | Clerk | Wilmington | Wilmington | Wilmington. |
| Johnston, Francisco de P | Trader | Los Angeles Co | | Los Angeles. |
| Johnson, William | Teamster | Los Angeles Co | | Los Angeles. |
| Johnson, John F C | Farmer | Los Angeles Co | nr Wilmington | Los Angeles. |
| Johnston, Peter | Farmer | Los Angeles Co | nr Los Angeles | Los Angeles. |
| Johnson, Charles R | Clerk | Los Angeles | Los Angeles | Los Angeles. |
| Johnson, Alexander | Farmer | Los Angeles Co | nr El Monte | Los Angeles. |
| Johnson, James | Carpenter | Los Angeles Co | | San Gabriel. |
| Johnson, Robert T | Farmer | Los Angeles Co | nr Los Angeles | Los Angeles. |
| Johnson, Santiago | Laborer | | | Los Angeles. |
| Jones, J M | Farmer | Los Angeles Co | Silver Precinct | Downey. |
| Jones, A | Doctor | Los Angeles Co | | Los Nietos. |
| Jones, C L | Farmer | Los Angeles Co | Silver Precinct | Downey. |
| Jones, H | Farmer | Los Angeles Co | Halfway House | Compton. |
| Jones, W W | Machinist | Los Angeles Co | Silver Precinct | Downey. |
| Jones, J G | Farmer | Los Angeles Co | Silver Precinct | Downey. |
| Jones, W S | Teamster | Los Angeles | | Los Angeles. |
| Jones, C A | Farmer | Los Angeles Co | nr Los Nietos | Los Nietos. |
| Jones, A | | | Wilmington | Wilmington. |
| Jones, H | Farmer | Los Angeles Co | nr El Monte | El Monte. |
| Jones, J | Merchant | Los Angeles | Los Angeles | Los Angeles. |
| Jones, T C | Teamster | Los Angeles Co | | Los Angeles. |
| Jones, F | Teamster | Los Angeles Co | Los Angeles | Los Angeles. |
| Jones, W S | Farmer | Los Angeles Co | nr El Monte | El Monte. |
| Jones, J C | Farmer | Los Angeles Co | nr Azusa | Azusa. |
| Jones, T | Barber | Los Angeles | Los Angeles | Los Angeles. |
| Jones, Dr M S | Physician | Santa Ana | Santa Ana | Santa Ana. |
| Jones, S K | Farmer | El Monte Valley | 3 m S Lexington | El Monte. |
| Jones, N C | Farmer | Azusa Duarte | 6 m E Lexington | El Monte. |
| Jones, W J | | San Gabriel | 9 m E Los Angeles | San Gabriel. |
| Jones, Edward | Justice of peace | San Gabriel Valley | 3½ m N San Gabriel | San Gabriel. |
| Jones, W H | | San Gabriel Valley | 3½ m N San Gabriel | San Gabriel. |
| Jones, Gilman | Soap manuf'r | Los Angeles | Los Angeles | Los Angeles. |
| Jones & Noyes | Auction & com'n | Temple Block | | Los Angeles. |
| Jones, G | Groceries | Los Angeles st | Los Angeles | Los Angeles. |
| Jones, Geo N | Auction & com'n | Temple Block | Los Angeles | Los Angeles. |
| Jones, M S | Physician | Los Angeles | Los Angeles | Los Angeles. |
| Jones, James N | Laborer | Los Angeles Co | | Los Angeles. |
| Jones, Wm Jasper | Wood chopper | Los Angeles Co | | San Gabriel. |
| Jones, John H | Teamster | Los Angeles Co | | Los Angeles. |
| Jones, Thomas George | Sailor | | | El Monte. |
| Jones, Ezra M | Farmer | Los Angeles Co | nr San Gabriel | San Gabriel. |
| Jones, Edward H | Merchant | Los Angeles Co | San Gabriel | San Gabriel. |
| Jonghin, Andrew | carriage maker | 34 Aliso st | Los Angeles | Los Angeles. |
| Joni, J | Sheep raiser | Los Angeles Co | nr Wilmington | Wilmington. |
| Jordon, E C | Printer | Los Angeles | Los Angeles | Los Angeles. |
| Jordan, R F | Teamster | Los Angeles | Los Angeles | Los Angeles. |
| Jordan, A Z | Merchant | Los Angeles | Los Angeles | Los Angeles. |
| Jordan, Luis | Merchant | Los Angeles | Los Angeles | Los Angeles. |
| Jordan, George M | Painter | Los Angeles | Los Angeles | Los Angeles. |
| Jost, George | Brewer | Los Angeles | Los Angeles | Los Angeles. |
| Joughin, Andrew | Blacksmith | San Juan | San Juan | Capistrano. |
| Juarez, F | Mason | Los Angeles Co | Soledad | San Fernando. |
| Judd, C E | Attorney | Los Angeles | Los Angeles | Los Angeles. |
| Judd, C E | Freight agent | S P R R Co | Canal st | Wilmington. |
| Juden, G W | Farmer | Los Angeles Co | Halfway House | Compton. |
| Judge, H M | Attorney at law | 55 Temple Block | | Los Angeles. |

| Name. | Occupation. | Place of Business. | Residence. | Town or P. O. |
|---|---|---|---|---|
| Judson, Gillette & Smiths | Attorneys at law | 39 Spring st | | Los Angeles. |
| Judson, A H | Attorney at law | 39 Spring st | Polyxena st | Los Angeles. |
| Judson & Adams | Attorneys at law | Los Angeles | Los Angeles | Los Angeles. |
| Jumaillieux, — | Fisherman | Wilmington | Canal st | Wilmington. |
| Jumalt, Mrs M | | | Alameda st | Los Angeles. |
| Junge, A | Druggist | Main st | Los Angeles st | Los Angeles. |
| Jung & Grump | Cala bakery | Main st | | Los Angeles. |
| Junguet, E | Laborer | Los Angeles Co | | Los Angeles. |
| Jurndo, V | Farmer | Los Angeles Co | nr San Juan | Capistrano. |
| Justice, Perry | Farmer | Azusa Ranch | ½ m S W Azusa | Azusa. |
| Justice, O T | Farmer | Azusa | 22 m E Los Angeles | Azusa. |
| Justice, Jesse | Farmer | Azusa | 22 m E Los Angeles | Azusa. |
| Justice, David | Miner | Azusa | 22 m E Los Angeles | Azusa. |
| Justice, W | Farmer | Los Angeles Co | Silver Precinct | Downey. |
| Justice, Elijah P | Teamster | Los Angeles Co | El Monte | El Monte. |
| Justice, Oliver T | Farmer | Los Angeles Co | Silver Precinct | Downey. |
| Kaiser, Chas | Engineer | Los Angeles | Los Angeles | Los Angeles. |
| Kalisher & Co, W | Gen mdse | Los Angeles | Los Angeles | Los Angeles. |
| Kalisher, Wolf | Merchant | Los Angeles | Los Angeles | Los Angeles. |
| Kalm, Maurice | Laborer | Los Angeles Co | | Los Angeles. |
| Kane, Daniel | Laborer | | Los Angeles Co | Los Angeles. |
| Karn, Jacob | Laborer | Los Angeles Co | | Los Angeles. |
| Karr, John | Laborer | | Los Angeles Co | Wilmington. |
| Katzenstein, Gus | Grotto saloon | cor Main & Com'l sts | Los Angeles | Los Angeles. |
| Katz, Benj | Saloon keeper | Los Angeles | Los Angeles | Los Angeles. |
| Kayer, James C | Merchant | Los Angeles | Los Angeles | Los Angeles. |
| Kearney, Patrick | Laborer | Los Angeles Co | | Los Angeles. |
| Keating, Nicolas | Laborer | Los Angeles Co | | Wilmington. |
| Keegan, John | Laborer | Los Angeles Co | | San Fernando. |
| Kee, Wong | Laundry | Canal st | Canal st | Wilmington. |
| Keen, Randolph | Teamster | Los Angeles Co | | Los Angeles. |
| Keenan, Hugh | Laborer | | Los Angeles Co | Los Angeles. |
| Keese, D | Steward | Los Angeles | Los Angeles | Los Angeles. |
| Kegel, Henry | Apiarian | Little Tejung Canyon | 5 m NE San Fernando | San Fernando. |
| Keich, F P | Engineer | Los Angeles | Los Angeles | Los Angeles. |
| Keith & Donahue | Stable keepers | Main st, below 1st | | Los Angeles. |
| Kelly, George | Plasterer | Los Angeles | Los Angeles | Los Angeles. |
| Kellar, M | Liquors | Alameda st | Los Angeles | Los Angeles. |
| Kellmer, C | Printer | Los Angeles | Los Angeles | Los Angeles. |
| Kell, Addison | Cabinet maker | | Westminster Col | Westminster. |
| Kell, William | Farmer | | Westminster Col | Westminster. |
| Kelley, T H | Laborer | Los Angeles Co | | Los Angeles. |
| Kelley, J | Laborer | Los Angeles Co | Old Mission | El Monte. |
| Kelleher, Michael | Engineer | Los Angeles | Los Angeles | Los Angeles. |
| Kellogg, Wm R | Speculator | Los Angeles | Los Angeles | Los Angeles. |
| Keller, Matthew | Wine grower | Los Angeles Co | Los Angeles | Los Angeles. |
| Kelley, James Vincent | Carpenter | Los Angeles Co | | Los Angeles. |
| Kelly, John | Laborer | Los Angeles Co | Silver Precinct | Downey. |
| Kelly, Charles | Laborer | Los Angeles Co | | Los Angeles. |
| Keller, William | Farmer | Los Angeles Co | Silver Precinct | Downey. |
| Kelly, Samuel S | Farmer | Los Angeles Co | nr Los Angeles | Los Angeles. |
| Kelly, Allen Christian | Miner | Los Angeles Co | | Los Angeles. |
| Kelly, James | Teamster | Los Angeles Co | | Los Angeles. |
| Kelly, William | Tanner | Los Angeles Co | | Santa Ana. |
| Keller, Jacob | Farmer | Los Angeles Co | nr Anaheim | Anaheim. |
| Kellogg, Benjamin F E | Farmer | Los Angeles Co | nr Anaheim | Anaheim. |
| Kelsler, James | Farmer | Los Angeles Co | nr Los Angeles | Los Angeles. |
| Kemp, James Clements | Cook | Los Angeles | Los Angeles | Los Angeles. |
| Kennedy, J W | Stock dealer | Los Angeles Co | nr Los Angeles | Los Angeles. |

# DIRECTORY OF LOS ANGELES COUNTY.

| Name. | Occupation. | Place of Business. | Residence. | Town or P. O. |
|---|---|---|---|---|
| Kennedy, Alexander | Farmer | Los Angeles Co | nr Los Angeles | Los Angeles. |
| Kennedy, James | Miner | Los Angeles Co | San Juan | Capistrano. |
| Kennedy James | Farmer | Los Angeles Co | nr Los Angeles | Los Angeles. |
| Kennedy, John | Tobacconist | Los Angeles | Los Angeles | Los Angeles. |
| Kent, Wm C | Mechanic | Los Angeles Co | | Los Angeles. |
| Keras, Jose | Farmer | Los Angeles Co | Old Mission | El Monte. |
| Kercheval, Albert F | Farmer | Los Angeles Co | nr Los Angeles | Los Angeles. |
| Kern, H E | Laborer | Los Angeles Co | nr Los Angeles | Los Angeles. |
| Kern, Paul | Vintner | Los Angeles Co | nr Los Angeles | Los Angeles. |
| Kerns, Thos Jeff | Farmer | Los Angeles Co | Silver Precinct | Downey. |
| Kerren, John | Ranchero | Los Angeles Co | nr Los Angeles | Los Angeles. |
| Kerren, W | Farmer | nr Anaheim | Los Angeles Co | Anaheim. |
| Kerren, Richard | Musician | Los Angeles | Los Angeles | Los Angeles. |
| Ketchum, Lawrence | Farmer | Los Angeles Co | nr Los Angeles | Los Angeles. |
| Kelter, Chas A | Farmer | Los Angeles Co | nr Los Angeles | Los Angeles. |
| Kevaul, Danl | Chemist | Los Angeles | Los Angeles | Los Angeles. |
| Kewen, Col E J C | Attorney | San Gabriel Valley | 2 m N W San Gabriel | San Gabriel. |
| Kewen & Howard | Attorneys | 8 Downey Block | | Los Angeles. |
| Keyes, Chas B | Justice of peace | Canal st | Canal st | Wilmington. |
| Keyes, Geo B | Genl mdse | Canal st | Canal st | Wilmington. |
| Keyes, Chas George | Clerk | Wilmington | Wilmington | Wilmington. |
| Kichline, Richd | Apiarian | San Fernando Valley | 4m N W San Fernando | San Fernando. |
| Kidd, Wm H A | Book keeper | Los Angeles | Los Angeles | Los Angeles. |
| Kiefhaber, F H | Blacksmith | Westminster Col | Westminster Col | Westminster. |
| Kilgore, William | Teamster | Los Angeles Co | Los Angeles | Los Angeles. |
| Kilray, J A | Way bill clerk | S P R R Co | Wilmington | Wilmington. |
| Kimball, N T | Blacksmith | Los Angeles | Los Angeles | Los Angeles. |
| Kimball, F W | Book keeper | Los Angeles Co | Los Angeles | Los Angeles. |
| Kimball, Chas H | Teacher | Los Angeles Co | Los Angeles | Los Angeles. |
| Kimball, M H | Auctioneer | Los Angeles | Los Angeles | Los Angeles. |
| Kimball, Geo H | Stock raiser | Los Angeles Co | nr Los Angeles | Los Angeles. |
| Kimball, John A | Journalist | Los Angeles | Los Angeles | Los Angeles. |
| Kimball, — | Sheep raiser | Alamitos Ranch | 7 m E Wilmington | Wilmington. |
| Kimble, T V | Farmer | San Pedro Ranch | 1m W Compton | Compton. |
| Kimball, Nathan | Blacksmith | Azusa | 22 m E Los Angeles | Azusa. |
| Kimball, Mark D | Clerk | San Gabriel | San Gabriel | San Gabriel. |
| Kincaid, Wiley W | Farmer | Los Angeles Co | nr El Monte | El Monte. |
| King, Norman Landon | Clerk | Los Angeles | Los Angeles | Los Angeles. |
| King, Edward | Teamster | Wilmington | Wilmington | Wilmington. |
| King, Morris Davis | Clerk | Los Angeles | Los Angeles | Los Angeles. |
| King, Henry | Blacksmith | Los Angeles | Los Angeles | Los Angeles. |
| King, John Daniel | Laborer | Los Angeles Co | Los Angeles | Los Angeles. |
| King, Samuel Houston | Trader | Los Angeles Co | El Monte | El Monte. |
| King, Andrew Jackson | Attorney | Los Angeles | Los Angeles | Los Angeles. |
| King, George H | Farmer | Los Angeles Co | nr Los Angeles | Los Angeles. |
| King, James Madison | Farmer | | | Los Nietos. |
| King, Fredk | Civil engineer | Los Angeles | Los Angeles | Los Angeles. |
| King, J M | Farmer | Los Angeles Co | Los Nietos | Los Nietos. |
| Kingsbury, Hiram | Farmer | Los Angeles Co | Florence | Los Angeles. |
| Kingsbury, Squire | Farmer | Los Angeles Co | nr Compton | Compton. |
| King, James H | Farmer | Los Angeles Co | Silver Precinct | Downey. |
| King, J W | Farmer | Los Angeles Co | Silver Precinct | Downey. |
| King, Saml B | Clergyman | | Westminster Col | Westminster. |
| King, Henry | Laborer | Los Angeles Co | Los Angeles | Los Angeles. |
| Kinney, John | Teamster | Los Angeles Co | Los Angeles | Los Angeles. |
| Kinney, Mrs E | Bdg house | Hill, bet 4th & 5th sts | | Los Angeles. |
| Kipp, James Brown | Carpenter | Los Angeles Co | Los Angeles | Los Angeles. |
| Kirby, Loring W | Farmer | Los Angeles Co | nr Anaheim | Anaheim. |
| Kirchler, Gottlieb | Blacksmith | Los Angeles | Los Angeles | Los Angeles. |
| Kirkland, Wm H | Farmer | Los Angeles Co | nr Los Angeles | Los Angeles. |

# "ALHAMBRA."

## 5, 10 and 20 ACRE LOTS,
## AT PRIVATE SALE.

Messrs. Wilson & Shorb now place on the market a few Five, Ten, and Twenty Acre Lots, on their beautiful tract,

NEAR SAN GABRIEL MISSION,

Where there is a fine supply of good water, brought on the tract by iron pipe, from a never-failing stream.

### FOR PARTICULARS APPLY TO

J. De BARTH SHORB, at Lake Vineyard,

NEAR THE PROPERTY, OR TO

C. CABOT, TEMPLE BLOCK, LOS ANGELES,

OR TO

B. D. WILSON, at Wilmington.

DIRECTORY OF LOS ANGELES COUNTY. 379

| Name. | Occupation. | Place of Business. | Residence. | Town or P. O. |
|---|---|---|---|---|
| Kirkpatrick, Wm John | Cooper | San Gabriel | San Gabriel | San Gabriel. |
| Kirkpatrick, Dr J C | Homœopathist | Backman House | Backman House | Los Angeles. |
| Kirsh, George | Butcher | Canal st | Canal st | Wilmington. |
| Kissel, Huston | Farmer | Los Angeles Co | nr San Gabriel | San Gabriel. |
| Kittilson, Andrew | Laborer | Los Angeles Co | Old Mission | El Monte. |
| Kittredge, Willard | Carpenter | Wilmington | Wilmington | Wilmington. |
| Kittredge, G | Bricklayer | Los Angeles | Los Angeles | Los Angeles. |
| Kittredge, W | Propr hotel | Railroad House | San Fernando | San Fernando. |
| Kittleston, A | Sheep raiser | El Monte Valley | 2½ m S W Lexington | El Monte. |
| Klaiber, William F | Brewer | | Los Angeles | Los Angeles. |
| Klein, George W | Mechanic | Anaheim | Anaheim | Anaheim. |
| Klockenbrinck, William | Clerk | Los Angeles | Los Angeles | Los Angeles. |
| Knapkle, Henry | Ditch tender | Anaheim | Anaheim | Anaheim. |
| Knight, G E | Farmer | nr Los Angeles | Los Angeles Co | Los Angeles. |
| Knipp, J | Farmer | nr Anaheim | Los Angeles Co | Anaheim. |
| Knott, Jonathan | Laborer | Los Angeles Co | Los Angeles | Los Angeles. |
| Knowlton, Charles | Farmer | Los Angeles Co | nr El Monte | El Monte. |
| Knowles, Horace Stanley | Painter | Los Angeles | Los Angeles | Los Angeles. |
| Knowlton, Chas | Hotel keeper | Los Angeles | Los Angeles | Los Angeles. |
| Knox, Geo Crockett | Civil engineer | Los Angeles | Los Angeles | Los Angeles. |
| Koch, Alfred | Laborer | Los Angeles Co | Los Angeles | Los Angeles. |
| Koch, Henry | Butcher | Los Angeles | Los Angeles | Los Angeles. |
| Koehler, J L | Miller | Los Angeles | Los Angeles | Los Angeles. |
| Kohler, William | Tailor | Los Angeles | Los Angeles | Los Angeles. |
| Kohler, August | Farmer | Los Angeles Co | Los Angeles | Los Angeles. |
| Koke, Charles Rudolph | Laborer | Los Angeles Co | nr Los Angeles | Los Angeles. |
| Koll, Frederick W | Farmer | Los Angeles Co | nr Santa Ana | Santa Ana. |
| Koller, Benjamin | Blacksmith | Los Angeles | Los Angeles | Los Angeles. |
| Konig, Wilhelm | Vintner | Los Angeles | nr Los Angeles | Los Angeles. |
| Korn, Frederick A | Farmer | Los Angeles Co | nr Anaheim | Anaheim. |
| Kouns, J R | Farmer | Los Angeles Co | Silver Precinct | Downey. |
| Kowell, Henry | Miner | | | Los Angeles. |
| Kraemer, Jonathan | Farmer | Los Angeles Co | nr Los Angeles | Los Angeles. |
| Krakewsky, M | Merchant | Los Angeles Co | San Juan | Capistrano. |
| Kralka, John Paul | Farmer | Los Angeles Co | Soledad | San Fernando. |
| Kraczynski, M | Prospector | Lyon Station | Lyon Station | Lyon Station. |
| Kraczynski, A J | Hotel and mdse | Lyon Station | Lyon Station | Lyon Station. |
| Kratt, August | Wool weaver | Los Angeles | Los Angeles | Los Angeles. |
| Krause, Chas J H | Carpenter | Los Angeles Co | Los Angeles | Los Angeles. |
| Krauth, John | Carpenter | Los Angeles Co | Los Angeles | Los Angeles. |
| Kreamer, Daniel | Farmer | Los Angeles Co | nr Anaheim | Anaheim. |
| Kremer, Maurice | Merchant | Los Angeles | Los Angeles | Los Angeles. |
| Kress, John | Mechanic | Los Angeles | Los Angeles | Los Angeles. |
| Kribs, Ludwig Wm | Carpenter | Los Angeles Co | Wilmington | Wilmington. |
| Krœger, H | Vintner | Centre st | Anaheim | Anaheim. |
| Krumdick, Henry | Steward | Los Angeles | Los Angeles | Los Angeles. |
| Krytser, Milton | Farmer | Los Angeles Co | nr Los Angeles | Los Angeles. |
| Kuhn, Henry | Baker | Los Angeles | Los Angeles | Los Angeles. |
| Kuhrts, Jacob | Merchant | Los Angeles | Los Angeles | Los Angeles. |
| Kuhrts, Martin H | Merchant | Los Angeles | Los Angeles | Los Angeles. |
| Kurtz, Joseph Dr | Physician | 72 Main st | Buena Vista st | Los Angeles. |
| Kyser, E F | Architect | Los Angeles | Los Angeles | Los Angeles. |
| Kysor & Mathews | Architects | r 12&13 Hellman Blk | | Los Angeles. |
| Kysor, B F | Architect | Hellman Blk | Los Angeles | Los Angeles. |
| Labory, A | Vintner | nr Los Angeles | Los Angeles Co | Los Angeles. |
| Laborni, J M | Laborer | Los Angeles Co | Azusa | Azusa. |
| Lacey, S | Upholsterer | Los Angeles | Los Angeles | Los Angeles. |
| Lacheval, P | Farmer | Los Angeles Co | Los Angeles | Los Angeles. |
| Ladd, Wm King | Farmer | Los Angeles Co | nr Anaheim | Anaheim. |
| Ladd, Jas King | Hostler | Wilmington | Wilmington | Wilmington. |

| Name. | Occupation. | Place of Business. | Residence. | Town or P. O. |
|---|---|---|---|---|
| Ladd, E A | Laborer | Los Angeles Co | Anaheim | Anaheim. |
| Ladd, J M | Farmer | Los Angeles Co | Silver Precinct | Downey. |
| Ladebaise, Jean | Laborer | Los Angeles Co | Los Angeles | Los Angeles. |
| La Dow, S W | Mechanic | Los Angeles | Los Angeles | Los Angeles. |
| La Fanchine, F R | Clerk | Los Angeles | Los Angeles | Los Angeles. |
| Lafontan, E | Stock raiser | Los Angeles Co | nr San Fernando | San Fernando. |
| Le Gas, Edgar T | Clerk | Los Angeles | Los Angeles | Los Angeles. |
| Lagomarsino, — | Farmer | Los Angeles Co | nr Los Angeles | Los Angeles. |
| Lake, J | Miner | Los Angeles Co | San Fernando | San Fernando. |
| Lake, Chas H | Laborer | Los Angeles Co | Los Angeles | Los Angeles. |
| Lakin, G M | Blacksmith | Los Angeles | Los Angeles | Los Angeles. |
| Lamasney, Wm | Merchant | Los Angeles | Los Angeles | Los Angeles. |
| Lamb, Chas Clarke | Deputy recorder | Los Angeles | Los Angeles | Los Angeles. |
| Lambard, Pierre | Sheep raiser | Los Angeles Co | nr Los Angeles | Los Angeles. |
| Lambourn & Co | Gen merchandise | La Punte mill | 3 m S E Lexington | El Monte. |
| Lambourn, F | Gen merchandise | La Punte mill | 3 m S E Lexington | El Monte. |
| Lamb, A D | Farmer | San Jose Addition | 5 m N E Azusa | Azusa. |
| Lamb, W D | Farmer | San Jose Addition | 5 m N E Azusa | Azusa. |
| Lamb, Wm | Farmer | Los Angeles Co | nr El Monte | El Monte. |
| Lambert, J S | Miner | Los Angeles Co | Los Angeles | Los Angeles. |
| Lamb, F | Farmer | Los Angeles Co | nr Los Angeles | Los Angeles. |
| Lambright, I G | Farmer | Los Angeles Co | nr Anaheim | Anaheim. |
| Lambourn, F | Teacher | Los Angeles Co | El Monte | El Monte. |
| Lamer, Amable | Blacksmith | Los Angeles | Los Angeles | Los Angeles. |
| Lami, L | Merchant | Los Angeles | Los Angeles | Los Angeles. |
| Lammert, Henry | Phil. brewery | New Aliso st | Los Angeles | Los Angeles. |
| Lamori, Victor | Cook | Los Angeles | Los Angeles | Los Angeles. |
| Lamouri, C J | Helper | S P R R Co | Wilmington | Wilmington. |
| Lammier, Fred'k A | Laborer | Los Angeles Co | Los Angeles | Los Angeles. |
| Lamure, L | Laborer | Los Angeles Co | Los Angeles | Los Angeles. |
| Lanbenheimer, C | Merchant | Los Angeles | Los Angeles | Los Angeles. |
| Lance, L | Laborer | Los Angeles Co | Los Angeles | Los Angeles. |
| Lancaster, David | Blacksmith | Los Angeles | Los Angeles | Los Angeles. |
| Lander, Wm H | Surveyor | Los Angeles | Los Angeles | Los Angeles. |
| Landon, H C | Stage driver | Los Angeles Co | Los Angeles | Los Angeles. |
| Landers, Capt | Boatman | Pt San Pedro | Pt San Pedro | Wilmington. |
| Lanehart, Thos S | Machinist | Los Angeles | Los Angeles | Los Angeles. |
| Lanfranco, M | Merchant | Los Angeles | Los Angeles | Los Angeles. |
| Langergen, — | Clerk | Anaheim | Anaheim | Anaheim. |
| Lang, J | Farmer | Los Angeles Co | Los Angeles | Los Angeles. |
| Lang, John | Miner | Soledad Road | 19 m N E Lyon Sta'n | Lyon Station. |
| Langenburger, A | Gen merchandise | Centre & Lemon sts | Centre & Lemon sts | Anaheim. |
| Langenberger, F W | Bookkeeper | Anaheim | Anaheim | Anaheim. |
| Lang, J | Dairyman | Los Angeles Co | Soledad | San Fernando. |
| Lanier, W B | Farmer | Los Angeles Co | nr Los Angeles | Los Angeles. |
| Lara, S | Laborer | Los Angeles Co | Los Angeles | Los Angeles. |
| Lario, P | Bricklayer | Los Angeles | Los Angeles | Los Angeles. |
| Laria, M | Laborer | Los Angeles Co | San Gabriel | San Gabriel. |
| Larkin, P | Laborer | Los Angeles Co | Los Angeles | Los Angeles. |
| Larned, C H | Farmer | San Gabriel Valley | 9 m N E San Gabriel | San Gabriel. |
| Lamour, C | Helper | S P R R Co | Wilmington | Wilmington. |
| Larson, Ed Chas | Farmer | Los Angeles Co | nr Los Angeles | Los Angeles. |
| Larson, S P | Fisherman |  | Los Angeles | Los Angeles. |
| La Rue, D J | Miner | Los Angeles Co | Soledad | San Fernando. |
| La Rue, B F | Farmer | Los Angeles Co | Silver Precinct | Downey. |
| Lascum, W | Farmer | nr Los Angeles | Los Angeles | Los Angeles. |
| Lassere, Joseph | Hotel keeper | Los Angeles | Los Angeles | Los Angeles. |
| Lassos, P | Saddler | Los Angeles | Los Angeles Co | Los Angeles. |
| Lassiere, A | Laborer | Los Angeles Co | Los Angeles | Los Angeles. |
| Latapie, J | Bar keeper | Los Angeles | Los Angeles | Los Angeles. |
| Lathrop, Frank Henry | Laborer | Los Angeles Co | Los Angeles | Los Angeles. |
| Latimer, Robt A | Minister | Silver Precinct | Silver Precinct | Downey. |
| Latourrette, Jules | Laundryman | Los Angeles | Los Angeles | Los Angeles. |

## DIRECTORY OF LOS ANGELES COUNTY. 381

| Name. | Occupation. | Place of Business. | Residence. | Town or P. O. |
|---|---|---|---|---|
| Lattimer, T R | Teamster | Los Angeles Co | Los Angeles | Los Angeles. |
| Laubersheimer, A | P M and druggist | Canal st | Willie st | Wilmington. |
| Laughlin, T | Orchardist | Alameda st | Los Angeles | Los Angeles. |
| Laughlin, S | Farmer | Los Angeles Co | nr Los Angeles | Los Angeles. |
| Laughlin, J | Farmer | nr Los Angeles | Los Angeles Co | Los Angeles. |
| Laughlin, P | Farmer | nr Los Angeles | Los Angeles Co | Los Angeles. |
| Laughlin, R | Farmer | nr Los Angeles | Los Angeles Co | Los Angeles. |
| Laughlin, V | Farmer | Los Angeles Co | nr. Los Angeles | Los Angeles. |
| Laukersheim & Co. | S F Wool Gr As'n | Coast Line Road | 9 m S San Fernando | San Fernando. |
| Laundy, Edwin | Clerk | Los Angeles | Los Angeles | Los Angeles. |
| Lauth & Co., Phil. | N Y brewery | 3rd st | | Los Angeles. |
| Lauth, P | N Y brewery | 3rd st | 3rd st | Los Angeles. |
| Laventhal, J | Merchant | Los Angeles | Los Angeles | Los Angeles. |
| Lavey, L | Merchant | Los Angeles | Los Angeles | Los Angeles. |
| Lavel, P | Laborer | Los Angeles Co | Los Angeles | Los Angeles. |
| Lavier, M | Laborer | Los Angeles Co | nr Los Nietos | Los Nietos. |
| Laventhal, E | Merchant | Los Angeles | Los Angeles | Los Angeles. |
| Lawlor, W B | Principal | Lawlor Institute | 168 Main st | Los Angeles. |
| Lawrence, W | Tanner | Los Angeles Co | Silver Precinct | Downey. |
| Lawry, E | Miner | Los Angeles Co | Los Angeles | Los Angeles. |
| Lawrence, Robert S | Publisher | Los Angeles | Los Angeles | Los Angeles. |
| Lawrence, E A | Farmer | Los Angeles Co | Los Nietos | Los Nietos. |
| Lawrence, L B | Physician | Soledad | Soledad | San Fernando. |
| Lawson, J J | Blacksmith | Los Angeles | Los Angeles | Los Angeles. |
| Lawson, W B | Mason | | Westminster Col | Westminster. |
| Lawton, A H H | Farmer | | | Los Angeles. |
| Lawton, D M | Carpenter | Los Angeles Co | Westminster Col | Westminster. |
| Lawton, C C | Farmer | Los Angeles Co | Halfway House | Compton. |
| Lawton, D W | Carpenter | Los Angeles Co | Halfway House | Compton. |
| Layman, W E | Farmer | nr Santa Ana | San Joaquin | Santa Ana. |
| Layman, C B | Laborer | Los Angeles Co | San Joaquin | Santa Ana. |
| Lazard, M | Merchant | Old Mission | Old Mission | El Monte. |
| Lazard, S | Merchant | Los Angeles | Los Angeles | Los Angeles. |
| Lazzere, D | Herder | Los Angeles Co | Los Angeles | Los Angeles. |
| Lazzarovich & Co, T | Groceries | Los Angeles | Los Angeles | Los Angeles. |
| Lazzarevich, J | Merchant | Los Angeles | Los Angeles | Los Angeles. |
| Leach, W | Farmer | Los Angeles Co | nr El Monte | El Monte. |
| Leahy, Patrick | Boot maker | Los Angeles | Los Angeles | Los Angeles. |
| Leahy, M | Vintner | Los Angeles Co | nr Los Angeles | Los Angeles. |
| Leahy, T | Merchant | Los Angeles | Los Angeles | Los Angeles. |
| Leal, Dr J H | Physician | Temple Block | Main st | Los Angeles. |
| Leal, J H | Physician | Los Angeles | Los Angeles | Los Angeles. |
| Leaming, C | Mining recorder | Lyon Station | Lyon Station | Lyon Station. |
| Leba, J M | Laborer | Los Angeles Co | Los Angeles | Los Angeles. |
| Leba, J R | Laborer | Los Angeles Co | Los Angeles | Los Angeles. |
| Leba, T | Saddler | Los Angeles | Los Angeles | Los Angeles. |
| Leblois, Eugene | Farmer | Los Angeles Co | nr Los Angeles | Los Angeles. |
| Lechler, G W | Tailor | Los Angeles | Los Angeles | Los Angeles. |
| Leck, L | Merchant | Los Angeles | Los Angeles | Los Angeles. |
| Le Clair, X | Laborer | Los Angeles | Los Angeles | Los Angeles. |
| Lecroq, Julius R | Gardener | | | Los Angeles. |
| Le Croq, Henry | Bakery | Santa Monica st | Los Angeles | Los Angeles. |
| Lecoq, Armand | Cook | Los Angeles | Los Angeles | Los Angeles. |
| Leconvreur, — | Surveyor | Los Angeles | Los Angeles | Los Angeles. |
| Lee Chung & Co | Merchants | Los Angeles | Los Angeles | Los Angeles. |
| Lee, P | Laborer | Los Angeles | Los Angeles | Los Angeles. |
| Lee, G A | Carpenter | Los Angeles | Los Angeles | Los Angeles. |
| Lee, W B | Farmer | nr El Monte | Los Angeles Co | El Monte. |
| Lee, W | Machinist | Los Angeles | Los Angeles | Los Angeles. |
| Leech, J | Farmer | Los Angeles Co | nr Los Angeles | Los Angeles. |
| Leese, Lewis V | Farmer | Los Angeles Co | nr Los Angeles | Los Angeles. |
| Lefeblive, Emile | Laundryman | Los Angeles | Los Angeles | Los Angeles. |
| Lofebre, Mrs J | Boarding house | Main st | Main st | Los Angeles. |
| Le Fern, J | Fruit dealer | Los Angeles | Los Angeles | Los Angeles. |

| Name. | Occupation. | Place of Business. | Residence. | Town or P. O. |
|---|---|---|---|---|
| Leffler, Blackburn | Clergyman | | Westminster Col | Westminster. |
| Leffler, Walter | Farmer | Los Angeles Co | Westminster Col | Westminster. |
| Lequia, Jose P | Laborer | Los Angeles Co | Santa Ana | Santa Ana. |
| Lehimas, J | Laborer | Los Angeles Co | | Los Angeles. |
| Lehman, M | Clerk | Los Angeles | Los Angeles | Los Angeles. |
| Lehman & Co | Upholsterers | 75 Downey Block | | Los Angeles. |
| Lehman, G | Renter | | Los Angeles Co | Los Angeles. |
| Lehman, A | Shoe maker | Los Angeles | Los Angeles | Los Angeles. |
| Leighton, Joseph | Laborer | Los Angeles Co | 7 m N Lyon Station | Lyon Station. |
| Leighton, J C | Teamster | Los Angeles Co | | Los Angeles. |
| Leihy, I M | Minister | | Santa Ana | Santa Ana. |
| Leiva, A | Laborer | Los Angeles Co | San Fernando | San Fernando. |
| Lelong, J | Laborer | Los Angeles Co | Old Mission | El Monte. |
| **Lelong, M, Jr** | Farmer | nr Los Angeles | Los Angeles Co | Los Angeles. |
| Le Masne, J | Ranchero | Los Angeles Co | nr Los Angeles | Los Angeles. |
| **Lemaire, Francisco** | Physician | Los Angeles | Los Angeles | Los Angeles. |
| Lemon, Wm | Farmer | San Pedro Ranch | 2½ m S W Compton | Compton. |
| Lenares, Felipe | Laborer | Los Angeles Co | nr Los Angeles | Los Angeles. |
| Lenares, Jose A | Laborer | Los Angeles Co | San Antonio | Downey. |
| Leomine, L | Stone cutter | Los Angeles | Los Angeles | Los Angeles. |
| Leonard, James E | Carpenter | Los Angeles Co | Los Angeles | Los Angeles. |
| Leonard, Albert T | Tinsmith | Los Angeles | Los Angeles | Los Angeles. |
| Leonard, Thomas H | Laborer | Los Angeles Co | Los Angeles | Los Angeles. |
| **Leonard, Chas E** | General mdse | San Fernando | San Fernando | San Fernando. |
| Leonard, E | Brewer | Los Angeles | Los Angeles | Los Angeles. |
| **Leonard, M** | Carriage maker | Los Angeles | Los Angeles | Los Angeles. |
| Leonard, J W | Laborer | Los Angeles Co | Wilmington | Wilmington. |
| Leonard, Geo D | Carpenter | | | Los Angeles. |
| Leonard, G F T | Carpenter | Los Angeles | Los Angeles | Los Angeles. |
| Leonard, J W | Boot maker | Los Angeles | Los Angeles | Los Angeles. |
| Leonis, J | Laborer | Los Angeles Co | San Fernando | San Fernando. |
| **Leonard, F W** | Farmer | Los Angeles Co | Silver Precinct | Downey. |
| Leora, J | Laborer | Los Angeles Co | Los Nietos | Los Nietos. |
| Le Prince, Victor A | Bar keeper | Los Angeles | Los Angeles | Los Angeles. |
| Lereque, J B | Carpenter | Los Angeles Co | | Los Angeles. |
| Lester, Wm | Plasterer | Los Angeles Co | San Pedro Ranch | Compton. |
| Leste, Joseph | Miner | San Gabriel Canyon | 14 m N Azusa | Azusa. |
| Lester, H C | Laborer | Los Angeles Co | Los Angeles | Los Angeles. |
| Leurent, A | Carpenter | | Los Angeles Co | Los Angeles. |
| Leveque, L | Laborer | Los Angeles Co | Los Angeles | Los Angeles. |
| Leverich, W B | Teamster | Los Angeles | Los Angeles | Los Angeles. |
| Levy, Noah | Merchant | Los Angeles | Los Angeles | Los Angeles. |
| **Levy, Simon** | Commission mcht | Aliso st | | Los Angeles. |
| Levy, M | Wines and liquors | 71 Main st | Fort st | Los Angeles. |
| **Levy & Coblentz** | Wines and liquors | 71 Main st | | Los Angeles. |
| Levy, L | Saloon keeper | Los Angeles | Los Angeles | Los Angeles. |
| Levy, D L | Clerk | Los Angeles | Los Angeles | Los Angeles. |
| Lewis, H E | Miner | Los Angeles | Los Angeles | Los Angeles. |
| Lewis, D C | Farmer | Los Angeles Co | nr El Monte | El Monte. |
| Lewis, J F | Farmer | Los Angeles | nr Los Angeles | Los Angeles. |
| Lewis, D | Farmer | nr El Monte | Los Angeles Co | El Monte. |
| Lewis, H | Farmer | Los Angeles Co | nr San Gabriel | San Gabriel. |
| **Lewis, H C** | Merchant | Los Angeles Co | Los Angeles Co | Wilmington. |
| **Lewis, Robert Wm** | Farmer | Los Angeles Co | El Monte | El Monte. |
| Lewin, Louis | Book store | Spring st | Aliso st | Los Angeles. |
| **Lewis, Jacob L** | Farmer | Los Angeles Co | El Monte | El Monte. |
| **Lewis, Wm S** | Farmer | San Pedro Ranch | 2½ m N E Compton | Compton. |
| Lewis, Leon T | Bill poster | Los Angeles | Los Angeles | Los Angeles. |
| Lowis, J M | Trader | Los Angeles | Los Angeles | Los Angeles. |
| **Lichtenberger, L** | Carriage manuf'r | Main st | Los Angeles | Los Angeles. |
| Lick, N | Teamster | Los Angeles Co | | San Gabriel. |
| Liebendelfer, D S | Painter | Los Angeles | Los Angeles | Los Angeles. |
| Lieber, J | Brewer | Los Angeles | Los Angeles | Los Angeles. |
| Liephart, J | Manufacturer | Los Angeles | Los Angeles | Los Angeles. |

## DIRECTORY OF LOS ANGELES COUNTY.

| Name. | Occupation. | Place of Business. | Residence. |
|---|---|---|---|
| Lieser, J................ | Laborer................. | Los Angeles Co....... | .......................... |
| **Liever, J**................ | Gunsmith............ | Los Angeles.............. | Los Angeles............ |
| Liehy, Isaac H...... | Printer................. | ............................. | San Joaquin........... |
| Lightfoot, F M...... | Farmer................ | Los Angeles Co......... | Silver Precinct........ |
| Lightfoot, F M...... | Teamster.............. | Los Angeles Co......... | Los Angeles............ |
| Ligon, W.............. | Farmer................ | Los Angeles Co......... | Halfway House....... |
| Lilly, D R............. | Laborer................ | Los Angeles Co......... | San Jose................. |
| Lilly, J R.............. | Constable............ | Spadra.................... | 30 m E Los Angeles. |
| Linares, M............ | Ranchero............. | Los Angeles Co......... | La Ballona............. |
| Linarez, P............. | Laborer................ | Los Angeles Co......... | San Gabriel............ |
| **Lincoln, L**............. | Farmer................ | Los Angeles Co......... | Silver Precinct........ |
| Lindeman, J D...... | Farmer................ | Los Angeles Co......... | nr Anaheim........... |
| Lindsay, J............. | Laborer................ | Los Angeles Co......... | Wilmington........... |
| Lindsey, J............. | Laborer................ | Los Angeles Co......... | Florence................ |
| **Lindenfeld, N**...... | Physician............ | Los Angeles.............. | Los Angeles............ |
| **Lindley & Thompson**...... | Attorneys............ | Los Angeles.............. | .......................... |
| Lindskow, M E..... | Laborer................ | Pt San Pedro........... | Pt San Pedro.......... |
| Ling, Robt A........ | Clerk................... | Los Angeles.............. | Los Angeles............ |
| Lion, J................. | Vaquero............... | Los Angeles Co......... | Los Angeles............ |
| Lion, C................ | Trader................. | Los Angeles.............. | Los Angeles............ |
| Lips, C C............. | Bookkeeper.......... | Los Angeles.............. | Los Angeles............ |
| Lipsis, Elias.......... | Agent.................. | ............................. | Los Angeles............ |
| **Lips, Craigue & Co** | Wines & liquors.. | 2 Arcadia Block........ | .......................... |
| Lisarrga, M........... | Farmer................ | Los Angeles Co......... | Old Mission........... |
| List, M................. | Laborer................ | Los Angeles Co......... | Los Angeles............ |
| Littlefield, J C...... | Editor.................. | Los Angeles.............. | Los Angeles............ |
| Little, A............... | Moulder............... | Los Angeles.............. | Los Angeles............ |
| Littlepage, C P..... | Mechanic............. | Los Angeles.............. | Los Angeles............ |
| **Littleboy & Davis**. | Druggists............. | 102 Main st............. | .......................... |
| Lloyd, James........ | Hostler................. | ............................. | .......................... |
| Lloyd, R............... | Carpenter............ | Los Angeles.............. | Los Angeles............ |
| Lobo, S................ | Vaquero............... | Los Angeles Co......... | San Jose................. |
| Lockman, J M...... | Sailor.................. | ............................. | Wilmington........... |
| Lockwood, G N..... | Printer................. | Los Angeles.............. | Los Angeles............ |
| **Locke, Eric**......... | Farmer................ | Los Angeles Co......... | nr Los Angeles........ |
| Lockwood, B B..... | Laborer................ | Los Angeles Co......... | Los Angeles............ |
| **Lockhart, L J**...... | Real estate.......... | Orange................... | Los Angeles Co....... |
| **Lockhart Bros & Parker**............. | Real estate.......... | Orange................... | .......................... |
| **Lockhart, T J**...... | Real estate.......... | Orange................... | Los Angeles Co....... |
| Lockwood, —....... | Laborer................ | Los Angeles Co......... | 9 m N Lyon Station.. |
| Loeb, L................ | Clerk................... | Los Angeles.............. | Los Angeles............ |
| **Logan, J**............. | Farmer................ | nr El Monte............. | Los Angeles Co....... |
| Logan, D H.......... | Teamster.............. | ............................. | Los Angeles Co....... |
| Logan, Mrs M...... | Dress maker......... | Los Angeles.............. | Los Angeles............ |
| Loge, Henry......... | Waiter................. | Los Angeles.............. | Los Angeles............ |
| Loiseau, P............ | Machinist............ | Los Angeles.............. | Los Angeles............ |
| Loller, J M........... | Actor................... | Los Angeles.............. | Los Angeles............ |
| Loman, M............ | Blacksmith........... | Los Angeles.............. | Los Angeles............ |
| Long, G............... | Sailor.................. | Wilmington............. | San Pedro.............. |
| Long, G E............ | Farmer................ | Los Angeles Co......... | Los Angeles............ |
| Long, B O............ | Trader................. | Los Angeles.............. | Los Angeles............ |
| Long, Jeremiah..... | Miner.................. | San Gabriel............. | Mission Precinct..... |
| **Long, Kong Fook**. | Merchant............. | Los Angeles.............. | Los Angeles............ |
| Longhery, Wm..... | Farmer................ | San Pedro Ranch..... | 1¾ m W Compton.... |
| Loobbers, Harmon. | Laborer................ | Los Angeles Co......... | Los Angeles............ |
| Loomis, Miles S..... | Farmer................ | Los Angeles Co......... | nr Los Angeles........ |
| Loop, C F............ | Minister............... | ............................. | Los Angeles............ |
| Loop, John........... | Notary public....... | Los Angeles.............. | Los Angeles............ |
| **Loop, C F**........... | Farmer................ | San Bernardino Road | 5 m N E Spadra...... |
| **Lopez, L**.............. | Ranchero............. | Los Angeles Co......... | La Ballona............. |
| Lopez, D.............. | Laborer................ | Los Angeles.............. | Los Angeles............ |
| Lopez, J............... | Carpenter............ | Los Angeles.............. | Los Angeles............ |

| NAME. | OCCUPATION. | PLACE OF BUSINESS. | RESIDEN |
|---|---|---|---|
| Lopez, G | Laborer | Los Angeles Co | Los Angeles. |
| Lopez, Valeutine | Farmer | Los Angeles Co | nr San Ferna |
| Lopez, R | Laborer | Los Angeles Co | Los Nietos |
| Lopez, J A | Ranchero | San Jose | San Jose |
| Lopey, J | Ranchero | nr San Fernando | Los Angeles |
| Lopez, F | Laborer | Los Angeles Co | |
| Lopez, R | Laborer | Los Angeles Co | La Ballona |
| Lopez, F | Ranchero | nr Los Angeles | Los Angeles |
| Lopez, V | Vaquero | Los Angeles Co | Los Angeles. |
| Lopez, B | Baker | Los Angeles | Los Angeles. |
| Lopez, Julius | Laborer | Los Angeles Co | San Fernand |
| Lopez, F | Laborer | Los Angeles Co | Los Nietos |
| Lopez, A M | Laborer | Los Angeles Co | La Ballona |
| Lopez, S | Saddler | Los Angeles | Los Angeles. |
| Lopez, A | Laborer | Los Angeles Co | San Jose |
| Lopez, J | Laborer | Los Angeles Co | Los Angeles. |
| Lopez, F | Farmer | Los Angeles Co | nr Los Angel |
| Lopez, J | Laborer | Los Angeles Co | Los Nietos |
| Lopez, M J | Stage driver | | Los Angeles. |
| Lopez, O | Farmer | Los Angeles Co | nr San Gabri |
| Lopez, F | Ranchero | Los Angeles Co | Soledad |
| Lopez, P | Laborer | Los Angeles Co | Los Angeles. |
| Lopez, F | Merchant | Los Angeles | Los Angeles. |
| Lopez, Jose Jesus | Laborer | Los Angeles Co | Los Angeles. |
| Lopez, Juan | Laborer | Los Angeles Co | Los Angeles. |
| Lopez, Miguel | Laborer | Los Angeles Co | Los Angeles. |
| Lopez, C | Farmer | Los Angeles Co | Old Mission. |
| Lopez, Jesus | Laborer | Los Angeles Co | Dominguez S |
| Lopez, T | Laborer | Los Angeles Co | San Gabriel |
| Lopez, J | Prop hotel | County Road | 2½ m N W Sa |
| Lopez, F | Farmer | San Gabriel Valley | San Gabriel |
| Lopez, S | Helper | S P R R Co | Wilmington |
| Lopez, D | Farmer | Azusa Ranch | ¾ m E Azusa. |
| Lopez, Jose | Farmer | Dalton Ranch | 1 m N Azusa |
| Lopez, N | Blacksmith | San Gabriel | 9 m E Los Ar |
| Lopez, Mrs J | Farmer | San Bernardino Road | 4½ m N E Sp |
| Lopez, C | Farmer | Los Angeles Co | La Ballona |
| Lopez, E | Laborer | Los Angeles Co | Soledad |
| Lopez, J | Laborer | Los Angeles Co | Halfway Hou |
| Lopez, C | Laborer | Los Angeles Co | Los Angeles. |
| Lopez, J de la Cruz | Ranchero | Los Angeles Co | nr Los Angel |
| Lopez, J S | Waiter | Los Angeles | Los Angeles. |
| Lopez, J E | Farmer | Los Angeles Co | N E San Fern |
| Lord, Walter S | Civil engineer | Los Angeles | Los Angeles. |
| Lord, Isaac W | Agent | Los Angeles | Fort st |
| Loredo, M | Laborer | Los Angeles Co | Los Angeles. |
| Lorenz, C | Vintner | Los Angeles Co | nr Anaheim. |
| Lorenzo, Marc | Miner | San Gabriel Canyon | 14 m N Azus |
| Loring, L A | Hotel keeper | Wilmington | Wilmington. |
| Los Angeles Library Association | | Main st | |
| Losen, E A | Cook | Los Angeles | Los Angeles. |
| Loughren, Wm | Farmer | Los Angeles Co | Compton |
| Louster, J | Laborer | Los Angeles Co | Los Angeles. |
| Lovell, A | Farmer | Los Angeles Co | Los Nietos |
| Lovenll, D G | Teamster | Los Angeles Co | |
| Lovejoy, David S | Clerk | Los Angeles | Los Angeles. |
| Lovo, S | Farmer | San Jose Valley | 1 m S W Spa |
| Lowe, A | Miner | Los Angeles Co | |
| Lower, L H | Farmer | nr Downey | San Antonio. |
| Lowe, B | Teamster | | Los Angeles |
| Lowery, Henry H | Barber | Los Angeles | Los Angeles. |
| Lowe, L H | Farmer | | Silver Precinc |
| Lowe, S J | Stoves &c | Centre st | Anaheim |

## DIRECTORY OF LOS ANGELES COUNTY. 385

| Name. | Occupation. | Place of Business. | Residence. | Town or P. O |
|---|---|---|---|---|
| Lowery, H H | Barber | 8 Commercial st | | Los Angeles. |
| Lowe, B N | Saloon | Spadra | 30 m E Los Angeles | Spadra. |
| Lucas, John Henry | Farmer | Los Angeles Co | La Ballona | Los Angeles. |
| Lucas, S | Baker | Los Angeles | Los Angeles | Los Angeles. |
| Lucky, Miss M C | Teacher | Los Angeles | Los Angeles | Los Angeles. |
| Lucky, Dr W T | Supt schools | Los Angeles | Los Angeles | Los Angeles. |
| Ludlow, Wm Evans | Clerk | Los Angeles | Los Angeles | Los Angeles. |
| Ludwig, J D | Miner | Los Angeles Co | Los Angeles | Los Angeles. |
| Luedke, R | Farmer | Los Angeles Co | nr Anaheim | Anaheim. |
| Luedke, R | Watchmaker | Centre st | Anaheim | Anaheim. |
| Luguet, Joseph | Farmer | Los Angeles Co | nr Los Angeles | Los Angeles. |
| Lugo, Jose D | Vaquero | Los Angeles Co | Los Angeles | Los Angeles. |
| Lugo, Gundalupe | Laborer | Los Angeles Co | San Antonio | Downey. |
| Lugo, D | Laborer | | Los Angeles Co | Los Angeles. |
| Lugo, A M | Farmer | nr Los Angeles | Los Angeles Co | Los Angeles. |
| Lugo, J A | Farmer | nr Los Angeles | Los Angeles Co | Los Angeles. |
| Lugo, J del C | Vaquero | Los Angeles Co | Los Angeles | Los Angeles. |
| Lugo, J L | Vaquero | Los Angeles Co | San Gabriel | San Gabriel. |
| Lugo, Francisco | Vaquero | Los Angeles Co | nr Los Angeles | Los Angeles. |
| Lugo, J C | Ranchero | Los Angeles Co | nr Los Angeles | Los Angeles. |
| Lugo, A M | Laborer | Los Angeles | Los Angeles | Los Angeles. |
| Lugo, J D | Laborer | Los Angeles Co | San Jose | Spadra. |
| Lugo, J A | Laborer | Los Angeles Co | San Jose | Spadra. |
| Lugo, Y | Vaquero | Los Angeles Co | Los Angeles | Los Angeles. |
| Lugo, V | Ranchero | Los Angeles Co | nr Los Angeles | Los Angeles. |
| Lugo, F | Ranchero | Los Angeles Co | nr Los Angeles | Los Angeles. |
| Lugo, M | Vaquero | Los Angeles Co | Los Angeles | Los Angeles. |
| Lugo, C | Ranchero | Los Angeles | nr Los Angeles | Los Angeles. |
| Luguin, Y | Blacksmith | Los Angeles | Los Angeles | Los Angeles. |
| Lung, Yan Wo | Merchant | Los Angeles | Los Angeles | Los Angeles. |
| Lung, Wa | Cigar factory | Commercial st | Los Angeles | Los Angeles. |
| Lunney, P | Farmer | Los Angeles Co | Los Angeles | Los Angeles. |
| Lunsford, J | Farmer | Los Angeles Co | Silver Precinct | Downey. |
| Luquet, Adolphe | Engineer | Los Angeles | Los Angeles | Los Angeles. |
| Lyman, George | Teamster | Los Angeles Co | Los Angeles | Los Angeles. |
| Lyman, Silvester | Farmer | | Westminster Col | Westminster. |
| Lyman, C C | Harness maker | Los Angeles | Los Angeles | Los Angeles. |
| Lynch, S J | Carpenter | Los Angeles | Los Angeles | Los Angeles. |
| Lynch, Gilbert | Farmer | Los Angeles Co | El Monte | El Monte. |
| Lynch, S J | U. brass foundry | Requina & Wilm'n sts | | Los Angeles. |
| Lynch, G | Farmer | Los Angeles Co | Los Nietos | Los Nietos. |
| Lynch, G | Laborer | Los Angeles | Los Angeles | Los Angeles. |
| Lynch, S J | Merchant | Los Angeles | Los Angeles | Los Angeles. |
| Lynham, T | Carpenter | Los Angeles | Los Angeles | Los Angeles. |
| Lynille, Theodore | Planter's hotel | cor L A & Centre sts | Anaheim | Anaheim. |
| Lyon, Saml M | Genl mdse | San Gabriel | 9 m E Los Angeles | San Gabriel. |
| Lyons, Early | Civil engineer | Los Angeles | Los Angeles | Los Angeles. |
| Lyon, Edward | Sheep raiser | Los Angeles Co | nr Wilmington | Wilmington. |
| Lyon, Perren | Farmer | | Westminster Col | Westminster. |
| Lyons, — | Sheep raiser | Alamitos Ranch | 7 m E Wilmington | Wilmington. |
| Lyons, Wm S | Sheep raiser | Alamitos Ranch | 7 m E Wilmington | Wilmington. |
| Lyons, David | Sheep raiser | Alamitos Ranch | 7 m E Wilmington | Wilmington. |
| Lyon, Sanford | Stock | Placeritas | 4 m N W Lyon Station | Lyon Station. |
| Lyon, J H | Carpenter | Los Angeles Co | Los Angeles | Los Angeles. |
| Lyon, S | Miner | Los Angeles Co | | Los Angeles. |
| Lyon, C | Ranchero | nr Los Angeles | Los Angeles | Los Angeles. |
| Lyons, I H | Laborer | Los Angeles Co | Los Angeles | Los Angeles. |
| Lyon, D | Ranchero | nr Wilmington | Los Angeles Co | Wilmington. |
| Lytte, M T | Speculator | Los Angeles | Los Angeles | Los Angeles. |
| Maag, C | Carpenter | Los Angeles Co | Los Angeles | Los Angeles. |
| Maben, S S | Stable keeper | Los Angeles | Los Angeles | Los Angeles. |
| Mabis, P | Laborer | Los Angeles Co | Old Mission | El Monte |
| Mabis, J M | Laborer | Los Angeles Co | Old Mission | El Monte. |
| MacChesney, Z J | Farmer | Los Angeles Co | nr Anaheim | Anaheim. |

| Name. | Occupation. | Place of Business. | Residence. | Town or P. O. |
|---|---|---|---|---|
| MacDonald, E | Miner | Los Angeles Co | | Wilmington. |
| Mace, W H | Attorney | Los Angeles | Los Angeles | Los Angeles. |
| Macerel, J | Speculator | Los Angeles | Los Angeles Co | Los Angeles. |
| Machado, R J de G. | Farmer | Los Angeles Co | La Ballona | Los Angeles. |
| Machado, J A E | Farmer | Los Angeles Co | La Ballona | Los Angeles. |
| Machado, F | Ranchero | Los Angeles Co | La Ballona | Los Angeles. |
| Machado, A | Farmer | Los Angeles Co | La Ballona | Los Angeles. |
| Machado, J I | Ranchero | Los Angeles Co | La Ballona | Los Angeles. |
| Machado, J J | Farmer | Los Angeles Co | La Ballona | Los Angeles. |
| Machado, P | Vaquero | Los Angeles Co | Los Angeles | Los Angeles. |
| Machado, B | Farmer | Los Angeles Co | La Ballona | Los Angeles. |
| Machado, J A | Ranchero | Los Angeles Co | nr Wilmington | Wilmington. |
| Machado, D | Ranchero | nr Los Angeles | Los Angeles Co | Los Angeles. |
| Machado, C | Farmer | Los Angeles Co | La Ballona | Los Angeles. |
| Machado, J D | Farmer | nr Wilmington | San Pedro | Wilmington. |
| Machado, Domingo. | Farmer | nr La Ballona | La Ballona | Los Angeles. |
| Mack, George C | Teacher | | Westminster Col | Westminster. |
| Mackney, J B G | Mechanic | Los Angeles Co | Los Angeles | Los Angeles. |
| Maclay, Moffitt & Leonard | Genl merchants | San Fernando | San Fernando | San Fernando. |
| Maclay, Charles | Speculator | SanFernandoMission | 1½ m W San Fernando | San Fernando. |
| Maclellan, D W | Clerk | Los Angeles | Los Angeles | Los Angeles. |
| Macumber, G | Farmer | Los Angeles Co | Silver Precinct | Downey. |
| Macy, O | Fashion stable | Main st | cor Macy & Bath sts | Los Angeles. |
| Macy, Wilson & Co | Fashion stable | Main st, opp Arcadia | | Los Angeles. |
| Madden, E | Engineer | S P R R Co | Canal st | Wilmington. |
| Maddux, G W | Farmer | Los Angeles Co | Los Nietos | Los Nietos. |
| Maddan, M | Sailor | | Wilmington | Wilmington. |
| Maden & Co, T E | Saloon | Santa Monica Canyon | | Los Angeles. |
| Maden; T E | Saloon | Santa Monica Canyon | Santa Monica | Los Angeles. |
| Madigan, A | Laborer | nr Los Angeles | Los Angeles Co | Los Angeles. |
| Madigan, M | Printer | Los Angeles | Los Angeles | Los Angeles. |
| Madison, J | Blacksmith | San Gabriel | Los Angeles Co | San Gabriel. |
| Madri, Santiago | Laborer | Los Angeles Co | Old Mission | El Monte. |
| Madri, E | Laborer | Los Angeles Co | Old Mission | El Monte. |
| Maglarie, P | Cook | Los Angeles | Los Angeles | Los Angeles. |
| Mahar, M | Drayman | Wilmington | Canal st | Wilmington. |
| Maher, P | Tinner | Los Angeles Co | La Ballona | Los Angeles. |
| Mahon, H Mc | Tailor | Los Angeles | Los Angeles | Los Angeles. |
| Mahoney, J | Laborer | Los Angeles Co | Los Angeles | Los Angeles. |
| Mailhean, Jean Marie | Shoe maker | Los Angeles | Los Angeles | Los Angeles. |
| Maine, D M | Saloon keeper | Spring st | Spring st | Los Angeles. |
| Major, C S | Printer | Los Angeles | Los Angeles | Los Angeles. |
| Malazewsky, A | Laborer | Los Angeles Co | | San Fernando. |
| Malagrin, C | Speculator | Los Angeles | Los Angeles Co | Los Angeles. |
| Malczewski, A | Capitalist | Los Angeles Co | Lyon Station | Lyon Station. |
| Malcom, Henry | Merchant | Wilmington | Wilmington | Wilmington. |
| Malom, W B | Farmer | Los Angeles Co | Halfway House | Compton. |
| Malcom, R McCoy | Carpenter | Los Angeles | Los Angeles Co | Los Angeles. |
| Maldini, A | Laborer | | Los Angeles Co | Wilmington. |
| Malgrant, C | Laborer | Los Angeles Co | Los Angeles | Los Angeles. |
| Mallard, J S | Merchant | Los Angeles | Los Angeles | Los Angeles. |
| Mallachowits, A | Farmer | Los Angeles Co | nr Los Angeles | Los Angeles. |
| Mulloy, P C | Farmer | Los Angeles Co | nr Los Angeles | Los Angeles. |
| Mallet, F | Cook | Los Angeles | Los Angeles | Los Angeles. |
| Maloney & Fennesy | Wagon makers | Los Angeles | | Los Angeles. |
| Malone, J | Farmer | Los Angeles Co | nr Los Angeles | Los Angeles. |
| Malone, R | Farmer | nr Azusa | Los Angeles Co | Azusa. |
| Malett, J | Laborer | Los Angeles Co | Los Angeles | Los Angeles. |
| Malone, O G | Farmer | nr Azusa | Los Angeles Co | Azusa. |
| Malone, P | Farmer | Azusa Ranch | 2 m N E Azusa | Azusa. |
| Malone, O J | Farmer | Azusa Ranch | 1½ m E Azusa | Azusa. |
| Malena, John | Tailor | 13 Spring st | Spring st | Los Angeles. |

DIRECTORY OF LOS ANGELES COUNTY. 387

| Name. | Occupation. | Place of Business. | Residence. | Town or P. O. |
|---|---|---|---|---|
| Maloney, Thos Frank | Farmer | Los Angeles Co | nr Los Angeles | Los Angeles. |
| Maloney, R | Carpenter | | Los Angeles Co | Los Angeles. |
| Malone, M | Teamster | Los Angeles Co | | Los Angeles. |
| Manchezo, F de J | Farmer | Los Angeles Co | San Jose | Spadra. |
| Manchester, J S | Farmer | Los Angeles Co | Halfway House | Compton. |
| Mandibles, A | Laborer | | Los Angeles Co | Los Angeles. |
| Mand, V | Saloon keeper | Los Angeles | Los Angeles | Los Angeles. |
| **Mandible, T** | Farmer | Los Angeles Co | San Jose | Spadra. |
| Mangin & Co, C | Machinists | 31 & 33 Spring st | | Los Angeles. |
| Mangin, C | Machinist | 31 & 33 Spring st | Los Angeles | Los Angeles. |
| Manjares, Jose C | Gardener | Los Angeles Co | nr Los Angeles | Los Angeles. |
| Manjores, J C | Laborer | | Los Angeles Co | San Fernando. |
| Manjares, J | Laborer | Los Angeles Co | | San Gabriel. |
| **Manning & Co, W S** | Real estate | Court st | Main st | Los Angeles. |
| Manning, S | Farmer | Los Angeles Co | nr Los Angeles | Los Angeles. |
| Mammie, Joseph P | Painter | Los Angeles | Los Angeles | Los Angeles. |
| Manning, J | Painter | 16 Court st | cor Spring & 1st st | Los Angeles. |
| **Manning, Thos F** | Plumber, etc | 32 Spring st | Los Angeles | Los Angeles. |
| Mannon, S E | Teacher | Los Angeles Co | Los Angeles | Los Angeles. |
| Mann, S B | Teamster | Los Angeles Co | | Wilmington. |
| **Manning, P** | Farmer | nr Downey | Silver Precinct | Downey. |
| Mann, W | Trader | Los Angeles | Los Angeles | Los Angeles. |
| Manning, W | Blacksmith | Los Angeles | Los Angeles | Los Angeles. |
| Manriques, J B | Laborer | Los Angeles Co | Old Mission | El Monte. |
| Manriques, M | Laborer | | Los Angeles Co | San Juan. |
| Manriques, Y | Farmer | Los Angeles Co | Old Mission | El Monte. |
| Manriques, A | Laborer | Los Angeles Co | San Juan | San Juan. |
| **Mauriques, J** | Farmer | Los Angeles Co | Old Mission | El Monte. |
| **Mauriques, P** | Farmer | Los Angeles Co | La Ballona | Los Angeles. |
| Manriques, J | Farmer | Los Angeles Co | La Ballona | Los Angeles. |
| Manriques, F | Farmer | Los Angeles Co | La Ballona | Los Angeles. |
| Manriques, J | Vaquero | | Los Angeles Co | San Juan. |
| Manriques, S | Laborer | Los Angeles Co | Old Mission | El Monte. |
| Manriques, F | Borregero | | Los Angeles Co | San Fernando. |
| Manzo, E | Shoe maker | Los Angeles | Los Angeles | Los Angeles. |
| Manzaneras, C | Laborer | Los Angeles Co | Old Mission | El Monte. |
| **Manzanera, V** | Farmer | nr San Gabriel | Los Angeles Co | San Gabriel. |
| Mappa, A G | Clerk | Los Angeles | Los Angeles | Los Angeles. |
| Marrassovich, L | Trader | Los Angeles | Los Angeles | Los Angeles. |
| Marbeuf, L | Restaurant | Main st | Los Angeles | Los Angeles. |
| Marbout, Louis | Restaurant keeper | Los Angeles | Los Angeles | Los Angeles. |
| Marcorich &Toppan | Restaurant | Los Angeles | | Los Angeles. |
| Mariona, V | Peddler | Los Angeles Co | Rebecca st | Wilmington. |
| Marinna, C | Teams'r & farmer | Placeritas | 4 m N E Lyon Sta'n | Lyon Station. |
| **Mariscal, O** | Ranchero | Los Angeles Co | nr San Gabriel | San Gabriel. |
| Marie, J | Sheep raiser | Los Angeles Co | nr Wilmington | Wilmington. |
| Marin, A | Store keeper | Los Angeles | Los Angeles | Los Angeles. |
| Mariano, L | Vaquero | nr Spadra | San Jose | Spadra. |
| Maricovitz, Peter | Laborer | Los Angeles Co | Los Angeles | Los Angeles. |
| **Marks, George** | Farmer | Azusa Ranch | 1 m S W Azusa | Azusa. |
| Marks, L | Merchant | Soledad | Soledad | San Fernando. |
| Markham, J M | Teamster | Los Angeles Co | Los Angeles | Los Angeles. |
| Marks, Max | Clerk | Los Angeles | Los Angeles | Los Angeles. |
| Markle, R | Drayman | Wilmington | 2nd st | Wilmington. |
| **Mark, G W** | Stock raiser | nr Los Angeles | Los Angeles Co | Los Angeles. |
| Marlow, M | Butcher | Los Angeles | Los Angeles | Los Angeles. |
| **Marlow, M** | Farmer | San Pedro Ranch | 1½ m N E Compton | Compton. |
| Maron, Y | Laborer | | Los Angeles Co | Los Angeles. |
| Maron, A | Carpenter | Los Angeles | Los Angeles | Los Angeles. |
| Maron, J J | Laborer | | Los Angeles Co | Los Angeles. |
| Maron, Rt | Laborer | nr Los Angeles | Los Angeles Co | Los Angeles. |
| Maron, J | Saddler | Los Angeles | Los Angeles Co | Los Angeles. |
| **Marora, H B** | Farmer | Los Angeles Co | San Antonio | Downey. |

| Name. | Occupation. | Place of Business. | Residence. | Town or P. O. |
|---|---|---|---|---|
| Maron, J A | Laborer | | Los Angeles Co | Los Angeles. |
| Marquez, S | Laborer | Los Angeles Co | La Ballona | Los Angeles. |
| Marquez, P | Laborer | Los Angeles Co | Los Angeles | Los Angeles. |
| **Marquez, B** | Farmer | Los Angeles Co | La Ballona | Los Angeles. |
| Marquez, J R | Laborer | Los Angeles Co | | Santa Ana. |
| Marquez, M | Laborer | Los Angeles Co | La Ballona | Los Angeles. |
| Marque, L | Laborer | Los Angeles Co | Los Angeles | Los Angeles. |
| Marquis, John | Clergyman | | Westminster | Westminster. |
| **Marquis, John F.** | Merchant | | Westminster Col | Westminster. |
| Marquis, Waldo H. | Clerk | | Westminster Col | Westminster. |
| **Marquez, J** | Farmer | Los Angeles Co | nr Los Nietos | Los Nietos. |
| Marquez, Señor | Farmer | | San Jose | Spadra. |
| Marquez, J F | Farmer | Los Angeles Co | nr Los Nietos | Los Nietos. |
| Marron, Patrick | Plasterer | Los Angeles | Los Angeles | Los Angeles. |
| **Marrow, J R** | Farmer | Los Angeles Co | Silver Precinct | Downey. |
| Marrow, J N | Farmer | Los Angeles Co | Silver Precinct | Downey. |
| **Marron, P** | Farmer | | Los Angeles Co | Los Angeles. |
| Marschalk, W H | Agent | Los Angeles | Los Angeles | Los Angeles. |
| Marshall, James | Laborer | Temple oil wells | 7 m W Lyon Station | Lyon Station. |
| **Marshall, J W** | Farmer | Azusa Ranch | 2 m S Azusa | Azusa. |
| **Marshall, L H** | Farmer | nr Los Angeles | Los Angeles Co | Los Angeles. |
| **Marshall, Chas M.** | Farmer | | San Joaquin | Santa Ana. |
| Marshall, Col | Farmer | San Dimas Creek | 6 m N Spadra | Spadra. |
| Marshall, W L | Attorney | Los Angeles | Los Angeles | Los Angeles. |
| Marshall, W | Farmer | nr Los Angeles | Los Angeles Co | Los Angeles. |
| Marshall, H M | Horse trainer | Los Angeles Co | | El Monte. |
| Marshall, T | Teamster | | Los Angeles Co | Wilmington. |
| **Marshall, James** | Farmer | Los Angeles Co | nr Los Angeles | Los Angeles. |
| Martin, John B | Farmer | Los Angeles Co | nr Los Angeles | Los Angeles. |
| Martinez, Francisco | Laborer | Los Angeles Co | Los Angeles | Los Angeles. |
| Marty, Andrew | Miner | Los Angeles Co | | Los Angeles. |
| **Martin, W C** | Hotel keeper | El Monte | El Monte | El Monte. |
| Martin, W T | Farmer | nr El Monte | Los Angeles Co | El Monte. |
| Martinez, D | Laborer | Los Angeles Co | San Gabriel | San Gabriel. |
| Martin, E | Blacksmith | Silver Precinct | Silver Precinct | Downey. |
| Martin, M W | Miner | Los Angeles Co | El Monte | El Monte. |
| **Martin, J H** | Farmer | Los Angeles Co | nr Los Nietos | Los Nietos. |
| **Martin, J W** | Farmer | Los Angeles Co | nr Los Nietos | Los Nietos. |
| Martinez, A | Vaquero | | Los Angeles Co | Los Angeles. |
| **Martinez, J** | Farmer | Los Angeles Co | San Jose | Spadra. |
| Martin, Nicholas | Saloon | Canal st | Canal st | Wilmington. |
| **Martinez, J A** | Farmer | Los Angeles Co | San Jose | Spadra. |
| **Martin, W H** | Farmer | Los Angeles Co | Halfway House | Compton. |
| Martinez, F | Vaquero | Los Angeles Co | Old Mission | El Monte. |
| Martinez, L | Laborer | Los Angeles Co | Los Angeles Co | Los Angeles. |
| Martin, E | Farmer | Silver Precinct | Silver Precinct | Downey. |
| Martinez, F | Laborer | Los Angeles Co | San Gabriel | San Gabriel. |
| Martin, J | Blacksmith | Los Angeles | Los Angeles Co | Los Angeles. |
| Martinez, J D | Farmer | Los Angeles Co | San Jose | Spadra. |
| **Martin, F J** | Farmer | nr Los Angeles | Los Angeles Co | Los Angeles. |
| Martinez, Simon | Laborer | Los Angeles Co | San Jose | Spadra. |
| **Martin, J H** | Farmer | El Monte Valley | 1 m E Lexington | El Monte. |
| Martin, Wm, Jr | Apiarian | San Jose Valley | 5 m N E Spadra | Spadra. |
| **Martin, J T** | Farmer | Azusa | 2½ m S E Azusa | Azusa. |
| **Martinez, Guadalupe** | Farmer | Los Angeles Co | Old Mission | El Monte. |
| **Martin, James J.** | Farmer | Los Angeles Co | San Joaquin | Santa Ana. |
| Martinez, Jose | Cigar maker | Los Angeles | Los Angeles | Los Angeles. |
| Martinez, J L | Laborer | Los Angeles Co | San Jose | Spadra. |
| Martin, C | Boot maker | Wilmington | | Wilmington. |
| Martinez, D | Laborer | Los Angeles Co | Old Mission | El Monte. |
| Martin, J R | Farmer | Los Angeles Co | Los Nietos | Los Nietos. |
| Martin, W G | Farmer | Los Angeles Co | San Joaquin | Santa Ana. |
| Martinez, J | Laborer | | Los Angeles Co | San Gabriel. |

DIRECTORY OF LOS ANGELES COUNTY. 389

| Name. | Occupation. | Place of Business. | Residence. | Town or P. O. |
|---|---|---|---|---|
| Martin, W E | Farmer | nr Downey | Silver Precinct | Downey. |
| Martinez, L | Farmer | nr Los Angeles | Los Angeles Co | Los Angeles. |
| Martinez, J. | Farmer | Los Angeles Co | nr Los Angeles | Los Angeles. |
| Martinez, J P de los A | Laborer | Los Angeles Co | San Jose | Spadra. |
| Martinez, F de S | Laborer | Los·Angeles Co | San Jose | Spadra. |
| Martinez, S | Farmer | Los Angeles Co | San Jose | Spadra. |
| Martin, C C | Carpenter | Los Angeles Co | Anaheim | Anaheim. |
| Martinez, J A | Vaquero | Los Angeles Co | nr Los Angeles | Los Angeles. |
| Martin, J | Farmer | nr Downey | Silver Precinct | Downey. |
| Martin, W | Miner | Los Angeles Co | | Los Angeles. |
| Martin, J A | Teacher | nr Anaheim | Los Angeles Co | Anaheim. |
| Martin, A | Farmer | nr Anaheim | Los Angeles Co | Anaheim. |
| Martinez, J | Waiter | Los Angeles | Los Angeles | Los Angeles. |
| Martinez, D J | Miner | Los Angeles Co | | Los Angeles. |
| Martin, C | Hotel keeper | San Juan | San Juan | San Juan. |
| Martsen, B | Clerk | Los Angeles | Los Angeles | Los Angeles. |
| Martinez, W S | Laborer | Los Angeles Co | | San Gabriel. |
| Martinez, M | Laborer | | Los Angeles Co | Azusa. |
| Mascarel, Jose | Wines and liquors | New Commercial st. | | Los Angeles. |
| Mascarel & Co, Jose | Wines and liquors | New Commercial st. | | Los Angeles. |
| Masias, M | Carpenter | Los Angeles Co | | Los Angeles. |
| Mason, H | Laborer | | Los Angeles Co | Los Angeles. |
| Massey, Gideon W. | Painter | Los Angeles | Los Angeles | Los Angeles. |
| Massey, H P | Farmer | Los Angeles Co | Silver Precinct | Downey. |
| Massey, T | Laborer | Los Angeles Co | Los Angeles | Los Angeles. |
| Masselin, Joseph | Sheep raiser | Los Angeles Co | nr Anaheim | Anaheim. |
| Massic, F | Cook | Los Angeles | Los Angeles Co | Los Angeles. |
| Mata, J | Shoe maker | Los Angeles | Los Angeles Co | Los Angeles. |
| Matfield, G H | Clerk | Los Angeles | Los Angeles | Los Angeles. |
| Mathias, Robt | Farmer | Los Angeles Co | Anaheim | Anaheim. |
| Mathews, W H | Architect | Hellman Blk | Los Angeles | Los Angeles. |
| Matlock, W M | Teamster | Los Angeles Co | Los Angeles | Los Angeles. |
| Mattison, E J | Farmer | Los Angeles Co | San Joaquin | Santa Ana. |
| Matthews, A P | | | Los Angeles | Los Angeles. |
| Matthews, J M | Farmer | Los Angeles Co | Pasadena | Pasadena. |
| Matthews, T | Teamster | Los Angeles Co | Wilmington | Wilmington. |
| Matthew, F M | Carpenter | Los Angeles Co | Los Angeles Co | Los Angeles. |
| Matthews, R | Laborer | Los Angeles Co | Los Angeles | Los Angeles. |
| Mauberret, Pierre | Shepherd | Los Angeles Co | | Los Angeles. |
| Maxey, L U Mrs | Farmer | Azusa Ranch | 1 m S W Azusa | Azusa. |
| Maxsen, B | Gen merchandise | | cor Main and Third sts | Los Angeles. |
| Maxwell, W F | Laborer | | Los Angeles Co | El Monte. |
| Maxwell, J | Farmer | nr El Monte | Los Angeles Co | El Monte. |
| Mayes, Edward | Gen merchandise | Lexington | 12 m E Los Angeles | El Monte. |
| Mayer, Lazarus | Saloon | Los Angeles | Los Angeles | Los Angeles. |
| Mayes, R H | Farmer | nr San Gabriel | Los Angeles Co | San Gabriel. |
| Mayer, J | Bricklayer | Los Angeles | Los Angeles | Los Angeles. |
| Mayet, L | Saloon keeper | Los Angeles | Los Angeles | Los Angeles. |
| Mayer, S J | Clerk | Los Angeles | Los Angeles | Los Angeles. |
| Mayer, W | Bricklayer | Los Angeles | Los Angeles | Los Angeles. |
| May, C A F | Brewer | Los Angeles | Los Angeles | Los Angeles. |
| Mayes, J A | Physician | Los Angeles Co | nr El Monte | El Monte. |
| Mayer, L | Tailor | Los Angeles | Los Angeles Co | Los Angeles. |
| Mayhew, J | Farmer | nr El Monte | Los Angeles Co | El Monte. |
| Mayo, F | Groceries | Canal st | Canal st | Wilmington. |
| Mazey, W W | Farmer | nr El Monte | Los Angeles Co | El Monte. |
| McAlpin, F C | Clerk | Los Angeles | Los Angeles | Los Angeles. |
| McAndrew, J | Farmer | | Los Angeles Co | San Gabriel. |
| McArthur, J | Wagon maker | Los Angeles | Los Angeles Co | Los Angeles. |
| McAuliffe, P M | Boiler maker | Los Angeles | Los Angeles | Los Angeles. |
| McAuliffe, M | Teamster | Los Angeles | Los Angeles | Los Angeles. |
| McAuliffe, R | Farmer | Los Angeles Co | Silver Precinct | Downey. |
| McCarty, O | Teamster | | Los Angeles Co | Los Angeles. |

| Name. | Occupation. | Place of Business. | Residence. | Town or P. O. |
|---|---|---|---|---|
| McCain, Chas | Laborer | | San Joaquin | Santa Ana. |
| McCarty, Peter S | Miner | Los Angeles Co | | Los Angeles. |
| McCarthy, E | Baker | Los Angeles | Los Angeles | Los Angeles. |
| McCabe, J | Laborer | Los Angeles Co | Los Angeles | Los Angeles. |
| McCarl, A J | Tanner | Los Angeles Co | Los Angeles | Los Angeles. |
| McCarthy, J | Sailor | | Los Angeles Co | Los Angeles. |
| McCarty, Peter | Laundryman | | | Los Angeles. |
| McCarthy, D | Laborer | | Los Angeles Co | Los Angeles. |
| **McCabe, B** | Farmer | San Pedro Ranch | 2 m S W Compton | Compton. |
| McCarthy, T | Tel operator | Los Angeles | Los Angeles | Los Angeles. |
| McChesney, J D | Clerk | Wilmington | Wilmington | Wilmington. |
| **McClay, David G** | Farmer | Los Angeles Co | San Joaquin | Santa Ana. |
| McClain, John | Farmer | | | Los Nietos. |
| **McClain, F** | Farmer | Los Angeles Co | nr Halfway House | Compton. |
| McClain, J | Farmer | Los Angeles Co | nr Los Angeles | Los Angeles. |
| McClellan, H | Agent | Los Angeles | Los Angeles | Los Angeles. |
| **McClelland, W J** | Farmer | Los Angeles Co | Los Nietos | Los Nietos. |
| McConnell, J R | Attorney at law | 39 & 41 Temple Blk | Los Angeles | Los Angeles. |
| McConnell, Bicknell & Rothchild | Attorneys | 39 & 41 Temple Blk | | Los Angeles. |
| McConnell & Judge | Attorneys | Los Angeles | | Los Angeles. |
| McCoy, James | Physician | | Westminster Col | Wesminster. |
| McCoy, Josiah | Farmer | Los Angeles Co | Westminster Col | Westminster. |
| McCoy, John J | Farmer | Los Angeles Co | Westminster Col | Westminster. |
| McComas, J E | Real estate agt | Compton | 1 m E Compton | Compton. |
| McComas, A | Farmer | San Pedro Ranch | ½ m E Compton | Compton. |
| McCormick, E F | Teamster | | Los Angeles Co | Los Angeles. |
| McCort, P | Laborer | Los Angeles Co | Los Angeles | Los Angeles. |
| **McCoy, J** | Farmer | Los Angeles Co | Silver Precinct | Downey. |
| McCormick, C | Painter | Los Angeles | Los Angeles | Los Angeles. |
| **McCormick, W** | Farmer | nr Downey | Silver Precinct | Downey. |
| **McCormick, I** | Farmer | Los Angeles Co | Azusa | Azusa. |
| McCoy, J | Farmer | Los Angeles Co | nr Los Angeles | Los Angeles. |
| McCraige, G D | Farmer | nr Downey | Silver Precinct | Downey. |
| McCristion, N | Minister | Los Angeles | Los Angeles | Los Angeles. |
| McCracken, W J | Farmer | nr Los Angeles | Los Angeles Co | Los Angeles. |
| McCrary, H | Farmer | El Monte Valley | 1 m W Lexington | El Monte. |
| McCrary, R K | Farmer | | Los Angeles Co | Los Angeles. |
| **McCraige, J L** | Farmer | nr Downey | Silver Precinct | Downey. |
| McCracken, T N | Farmer | Los Angeles Co | nr Los Angeles | Los Angeles. |
| McCrea, J | Clerk | Los Angeles Co | Los Angeles | Los Angeles. |
| McCulloch, E | Farmer | Los Angeles Co | Silver Precinct | Downey. |
| **McCuller, J** | Farmer | Los Angeles Co | Silver Precinct | Downey. |
| McCullough, John | Stock raiser | Los Angeles Co | | Los Angeles. |
| McCullough, R | Farmer | Los Angeles Co | nr Los Nietos | Los Nietos. |
| McDaniel, R H | Lawyer | Los Angeles | Los Angeles | Los Angeles. |
| **McDaniel, A B** | Farmer | nr El Monte | Los Angeles Co | El Monte. |
| **McDonald, W F** | Merchant | Los Angeles | Los Angeles Co | Los Angeles. |
| McDowell, Thos K | Teacher | Los Angeles Co | Los Angeles Co | Los Angeles. |
| McDonald, P | Laborer | Los Angeles Co | Wilmington | Wilmington. |
| **McDougall, F A** | Physician | Los Angeles | Los Angeles | Los Angeles. |
| McDonald, J J | Engineer | Los Angeles | Los Angeles | Los Angeles. |
| McDowell, Wm C | Clerk | Los Angeles | Los Angeles | Los Angeles. |
| **McDonald, John** | Boarding house | Los Angeles | Los Angeles | Los Angeles. |
| McDowell, A H | | | Westminster Col | Westminster. |
| McDonald, E N | Wool grader | Canal st | Wilmington | Wilmington. |
| McDonald, A S | Boots and shoes | 104 Main st | Los Angeles | Los Angeles. |
| **McDonald, A B** | Farmer | El Monte Valley | 1 m W Lexington | El Monte. |
| McDowell, E K | Farmer | El Monte Valley | 3 m S Lexington | El Monte. |
| McDonald, A H | Farmer | Los Angeles Co | nr Anaheim | Anaheim. |
| **McDonald, J G** | Farmer | nr Los Angeles | Los Angeles Co | Los Angeles. |
| McDougal, W | Fireman | Los Angeles | Los Angeles | Los Angeles. |
| McDowell, J | Farmer | Los Angeles Co | nr Anaheim | Los Angeles. |

DIRECTORY OF LOS ANGELES COUNTY. 391

| Name. | Occupation. | Place of Business. | Residence. | Town or P. O. |
|---|---|---|---|---|
| McDonald, N A | Conductor | Wilmington | Los Angeles Co | Wilmington. |
| McDonald, W P | Teacher | Los Angeles Co | Silver Precinct | Downey. |
| McElrath, J | Farmer | nr Los Nietos | Los Angeles Co | Los Nietos. |
| McFadden, J | Carpenter | Los Angeles | Los Angeles Co | Los Angeles. |
| McFadden, R | Farmer | Los Angeles Co | San Joaquin | Santa Ana. |
| McFadden, James | Farmer | Los Angeles Co | Anaheim | Anaheim. |
| McFadden, James | Farmer | Los Angeles Co | Westminster Col | Westminster. |
| McFadden, James A | Farmer | Los Angeles Co | Westminster Col | Westminster. |
| McFadder, A Mrs | Nurse | Los Angeles | Los Angeles | Los Angeles. |
| McFarlaud, A Dr | Physician | Compton | Compton | Compton. |
| McFadden, J D | Farmer | Los Angeles Co | nr Santa Ana | Santa Ana. |
| McFarland, H D | Clerk | Los Angeles | Los Angeles | Los Angeles. |
| McFadden, W M | Farmer | Los Angeles Co | nr Anaheim | Anaheim. |
| McFadden, J | Farmer | Los Angeles Co | nr Los Angeles | Los Angeles. |
| McFeely, Wm | Gardener | Los Angeles Co | Los Angeles | Los Angeles. |
| McFuqua, John | Farmer | Los Angeles Co | El Monte | El Monte. |
| McGaugh, P G | Laborer | Los Angeles Co | Silver Precinct | Downey. |
| McGarvin, L | Butcher | Los Angeles | Silver Precinct | Downey. |
| McGary, Samuel | Hostler | Los Angeles | Los Angeles | Los Angeles. |
| McGarvin, J | Butcher | Azusa | 2 m S E Azusa | Azusa. |
| McGaugh, J W | Farmer | Los Angeles Co | Silver Precinct | Downey. |
| McGeo, H | Teamster | | Los Angeles Co | Los Angeles. |
| McGee, A | Farmer | nr Los Angeles | Los Angeles Co | Los Angeles. |
| McGilvra & Bell | Feed stable | San Fernando | San Fernando | San Fernando. |
| McGilvra, John | Feed stable | San Fernando | San Fernando | San Fernando. |
| McGibbon, Wm A | Farmer | Los Angeles Co | Richland | Orange. |
| McGill, Rev James | Priest | St Vin Col | Los Angeles | Los Angeles. |
| McGibova, J | Teamster | Los Angeles Co | | Los Angeles. |
| McGlothlin, W M | Laborer | | Los Angeles Co | Los Angeles. |
| McGorry, T | Laborer | Los Angeles Co | Los Angeles | Los Angeles. |
| McGovern, F | Laborer | Los Angeles Co | Los Angeles | San Juan. |
| McGough, M J | Farmer | nr Downey | Silver Precinct | Downey. |
| McGrath, Albert | Machinist | Los Angeles | Los Angeles | Los Angeles. |
| McGrew, Chas O | Telegraph op | San Fernando | San Fernando | San Fernando. |
| McGrath, W | Laborer | Los Angeles Co | Anaheim | Anaheim. |
| McGregory, Henry | Stockman | Los Angeles Co | Los Angeles | Los Angeles. |
| McGregor, John | Laborer | Los Angeles Co | Los A Township | Los Angeles. |
| McGregory, W H | Farmer | Sunny Slope | 3 m N San Gabriel | San Gabriel. |
| McGrew, J D | Laborer | | Los Angeles Co | Los Angeles. |
| McGuire, J | Farmer | nr San Gabriel | Los Angeles Co | San Gabriel. |
| McGue, R K | Farmer | nr Los Angeles | Los Angeles Co | Los Angeles. |
| McIntire, A | Carpenter | Wilmington | Wilmington | Wilmington. |
| McIntosh, E | Painter | Los Angeles | Los Angeles Co | Los Angeles. |
| McIntire, J | Theatre saloon | Los Angeles Co | Los Angeles | Los Angeles. |
| McIntyre, Hugh | Laborer | Los Angeles Co | Los Angeles | Los Angeles. |
| McIlravey, J | Laborer | Los Angeles Co | Los Angeles | Los Angeles. |
| McIntosh, J | Laborer | Los Angeles Co | San Juan | Capistrano. |
| McKay, John | Miner | San Gabriel | 14 m N Azusa | Azusa. |
| McKenzie, R | Farmer | nr Azusa | Los Angeles Co | Azusa. |
| McKee, Dr J H | Physician & surg | 11 Spring st | 1st, bet Fort & Hill sts | Los Angeles. |
| McKee, W | | | Los Angeles | Los Angeles. |
| McKee, A S | Teamster | Los Angeles Co | El Monte | El Monte. |
| McKellar, D H | Farmer | nr Downey | Silver Precinct | Downey. |
| McKean, J D | Mechanic | Soledad | Soledad | San Fernando. |
| McKevit, M | Farmer | | Los Angeles Co | Los Angeles. |
| McKeon, J | Farmer | nr Los Angeles | Los Angeles Co | Los Angeles. |
| McKenzie, Kenneth | Painter | Los Angeles | Los Angeles | Los Angeles. |
| McKenzie, C | Barber | San Fernando | San Fernando | San Fernando. |
| McKellar, S A | Farmer | nr Downey | Silver Precinct | Downey. |
| McKeon, M | Tailor | Los Angeles | Los Angeles | Los Angeles. |
| McKenlay, S | Farmer | Los Angeles Co | nr Los Angeles | Los Angeles. |
| McKimm, Isaac | Machinist | San Gabriel min dist | | Azusa. |
| McKinnie, P C | Contractor | Centre st | Anaheim | Anaheim. |

| Name. | Occupation. | Place of Business. | Residence. | Town or P. O. |
|---|---|---|---|---|
| McKinnon, A........ | Farmer ............. | nr Los Angeles ....... | Los Angeles Co........ | Los Angeles. |
| McKinney, F H..... | Physician .......... | Los Angeles Co........ | nr Halfway House.... | Compton. |
| McKinney, J S...... | Wagon maker..... | Los Angeles Co........ | Halfway House........ | Compton. |
| McKoy, L S ......... | Farmer ..... ....... | Los Angeles Co........ | Silver Precinct ........ | Downey. |
| McLaughlin, W..... | Merchant ........... | Los Angeles............ | Los Angeles............ | Los Angeles. |
| McLain, G........... | Machinist.......... | Los Angeles............ | Los Angeles............ | Los Angeles. |
| McLaughlin, D...... | Miner ............... | Los Angeles Co........ | ........................ | Los Angeles. |
| McLaughlin, J B... | Harness maker ... | Wilmington........... | Wilmington ......... | Wilmington. |
| McLaughlin, —..... | Farmer .............. | San Fernando Miss'n | 1½ m W San Fern'do | San Fernando. |
| McLaren, — ........ | Farmer .............. | San Fernando Miss'n | 1½ m W San Fern'do | San Fernando. |
| McLain, Thos........ | Genl merchant ... | Lexington............. | 12 m E Los Angeles | El Monte. |
| McLaughlin, B...... | Wagon maker..... | Los Angeles............ | Los Angeles............ | Los Angeles. |
| McLanghlin, S F... | Blacksmith......... | Los Angeles............ | Santa Ana ........... | Santa Ana. |
| McLaughlin, J ..... | Farmer ............. | Silver Precinct........ | Silver Precinct........ | Downey. |
| McLaughlin, P...... | Laborer.............. | Los Angeles Co........ | Los Angeles............ | Los Angeles. |
| McLaughlin, — ..... | Farmer .............. | San Pedro Ranch .... | 2½ m N E Compton... | Compton. |
| McLellan, H........ | Insurance agent... | 61 Main st............. | 25 4th st................ | Los Angeles. |
| McLellan, B ........ | Clerk ................ | 61 Main st............. | Los Angeles............ | Los Angeles. |
| McLean, T........... | Teacher.............. | Los Angeles Co........ | El Monte ............. | El Monte. |
| McLean, W.......... | Plasterer............ | Los Angeles............ | Los Angeles............ | Los Angeles. |
| McLeod, A........... | Farmer .............. | Los Angeles Co........ | nr Los Angeles........ | Los Angeles. |
| McLoghlin, John P | Teamster ........... | Los Angeles Co........ | Los Angeles............ | Los Angeles. |
| McMahon, Philip D | Painter.............. | Los Angeles............ | Los Angeles............ | Los Angeles. |
| McMahon, H M.... | Tailor................ | Los Angeles............ | Los Angeles............ | Los Angeles. |
| McMaster, R........ | Laborer.............. | Los Angeles Co........ | Silver Precinct........ | Downey. |
| McManis, J R...... | Farmer .............. | Los Angeles Co........ | nr Los Angeles........ | Los Angeles. |
| McMahon, J E..... | Blacksmith......... | Wilmington .......... | Wilmington .......... | Wilmington. |
| McMenomy, J C... | Plumber............. | Los Angeles............ | Los Angeles............ | Los Angeles. |
| McMichael, J....... | Farmer ............. | Los Angeles Co........ | nr Azusa.............. | Azusa. |
| McMillan, D........ | Rest & lodging ho | Canal st............... | Canal st............... | Wilmington. |
| McMurray, J R .... | Clerk................ | Los Angeles............ | Los Angeles............ | Los Angeles. |
| McMullen, W G.... | Agriculturist ..... | nr Los Angeles........ | Los Angeles Co........ | Los Angeles. |
| McNally, T Y....... | Clerk................ | Los Angeles Co........ | Los Angeles............ | Los Angeles. |
| McNamara, M H... | Tinner .............. | Los Angeles Co........ | Los Angeles............ | Los Angeles. |
| McNamer, J P...... | Teacher............. | Los Angeles Co........ | Puente............... | El Monte. |
| McNamara, J....... | Plumber............. | Los Angeles............ | Los Angeles............ | Los Angeles. |
| McNaughton, A.... | Farmer ............. | Los Angeles Co........ | nr Santa Ana......... | Santa Ana. |
| McNamara, C...... | Waiter............... | Los Angeles............ | Los Angeles............ | Los Angeles. |
| McNeal, S T........ | Farmer ............. | Los Angeles Co........ | San Joaquin.......... | Santa Ana. |
| McNeal, A.......... | Laborer............. | ........................ | Los Angeles Co........ | Los Angeles. |
| McNelly, T......... | Farmer ............. | Los Angeles Co........ | nr Los Angeles........ | Los Angeles. |
| McNorton, John..... | Carpenter .......... | Wilmington........... | Wilmington .......... | Wilmington. |
| McNulty, H ....... | Farmer ............. | nr El Monte.......... | Los Angeles Co........ | El Monte. |
| McPherson, R...... | Teacher ............ | Los Angeles Co........ | Westminster Col..... | Westminster. |
| McPherson, W J... | Farmer ............. | ........................ | Westminster Col..... | Westminster. |
| McPherson, S...... | Teacher ............ | ........................ | Los Angeles Co........ | Westminster. |
| McPherson, W..... | Attorney............ | Los Angeles............ | Los Angeles............ | Los Angeles. |
| McQuirk, James... | Saloon............... | Los Angeles............ | Los Angeles............ | Los Angeles. |
| McQuillan, H ...... | Teamster............ | Los Angeles Co........ | Los Angeles............ | Los Angeles. |
| McQuaid, M B .... | Carpenter .......... | Los Angeles Co........ | Los Angeles............ | Los Angeles. |
| McRae, W.......... | Proprietor ......... | Caledonian Hotel .... | San Fernando ........ | San Fernando. |
| McRae, D........... | Proprietor ......... | Caledonian Hotel .... | San Fernando ........ | San Fernando. |
| McRae, W & D.... | Proprietors........ | Caledonian Hotel .... | San Fernando ........ | San Fernando. |
| McSwain, N B..... | Farmer ............. | ........................ | Compton ............ | Compton. |
| McSwain, L ....... | Farmer ............. | San Pedro Ranch .... | 1½ m S Compton..... | Compton. |
| McSwain, W T.... | Farmer ............. | nr Compton.......... | Los Angeles Co........ | Compton. |
| McSwain, N........ | Farmer ............. | nr Compton.......... | Los Angeles Co........ | Compton. |
| McVeigh, O......... | Boot maker ....... | Wilmington........... | Wilmington .......... | Wilmington. |
| Meade, T........... | Farmer ............. | Los Angeles Co........ | Silver Precinct........ | Downey. |
| Mead, J............. | Farmer ............. | Los Angeles Co........ | nr Los Angeles........ | Los Angeles. |
| Mead, E A.......... | Farmer ............. | Los Angeles Co........ | nr Anaheim.......... | Anaheim. |
| Meagher, James... | Carpenter .......... | Los Angeles Co........ | ........................ | Los Angeles. |
| Meci, F............. | Laborer............. | nr Los Angeles........ | Los Angeles Co........ | Los Angeles. |
| Medane, J .......... | Laborer............. | ........................ | Los Angeles Co........ | Los Angeles. |

# DIRECTORY OF LOS ANGELES COUNTY. 393

| NAME. | OCCUPATION. | PLACE OF BUSINESS. | RESIDENCE. | TOWN OR P. O. |
|---|---|---|---|---|
| Meek, S | Wheelwright | Wilmington | Wilmington | Wilmington. |
| Meeker, W H | Miner | Los Angeles Co | | Los Angeles. |
| Meeks, G | Farmer | Los Angeles Co | nr Los Angeles | Los Angeles. |
| Meeks, H C | Farmer | Los Angeles Co | Silver Precinct | Downey. |
| Meeks, C J | Farmer | nr Los Nietos | Los Angeles Co | Los Nietos. |
| Melbund, E P | Wharf hand | S P R R Co | Wilmington | Wilmington. |
| Melchert, A | Boot maker | Los Angeles | Los Angeles | Los Angeles. |
| Meldenson, M A | Merchant tailor | Centre st | Anaheim | Anaheim. |
| Melendy, G H | Miner | Los Angeles Co | | Los Angeles. |
| Melendrez, J D | Vaquero | | Los Angeles Co | Santa Ana. |
| Melendez, J | Vaquero | | San Gabriel | San Gabriel. |
| Melendrez, V | Laborer | Los Angeles Co | San Jose | Spadra. |
| Melendrez, R | Vaquero | | Los Angeles Co | Los Angeles. |
| Melendrez, M | Laborer | Los Angeles Co | La Ballona | Los Angeles. |
| Melendrez, Edwd | Vaquero | Los Angeles Co | San Jose | Spadra. |
| **Melhorn, A** | Farmer | Los Angeles Co | nr Los Angeles | Los Angeles. |
| **Mellus, J J** | Merchant | San Gabriel | San Gabriel min dist | Azusa. |
| Molles, C | Cook | Anaheim | Anaheim | Anaheim. |
| Mellus, Frank H | Carpenter | Los Angeles Co | | Wilmington. |
| Mellin, Wm | Foreman | S P R R Co | Wilmington | Wilmington. |
| Melrose, R | Clerk | Los Angeles Co | Anaheim | Anaheim. |
| **Melrose & Athearn** | Publishers | Anaheim Gazette | Los Angeles st | Anaheim. |
| **Melton, W J** | Farmer | | Los Nietos | Los Nietos. |
| Melville, H | Carpenter | Los Angeles Co | | Los Angeles. |
| **Melvin, Homer** | Stock raiser | Los Angeles Co | nr Los Angeles | Los Angeles. |
| **Melzer, Lewis** | General mdse | Lexington | 12 m E Los Angeles | El Monte. |
| Mencke, D | Farmer | Los Angeles Co | nr Anaheim | Anaheim. |
| Mendez, J B | Laborer | | Los Angeles Co | Los Angeles. |
| Mendes, Francisco | Ranchero | | La Ballona | Los Angeles. |
| Mendez, J | Laborer | nr Los Angeles | Los Angeles Co | Los Angeles. |
| Merdelbaum, C | Trader | Los Angeles Co | | Los Angeles. |
| Mendelson, L | Clerk | Anaheim | Anaheim | Anaheim. |
| Mondoza, J | Laborer | Los Angeles Co | Los Angeles Co | Los Angeles. |
| Mendozo, J Q | Laborer | Los Angeles Co | San Jose | Spadra. |
| Mendelson, M | Stage proprietor | Los Angeles st | | Los Angeles. |
| Mendez, F | Miner | San Gabriel Canyon | 14 m N Azusa | Azusa. |
| Mendibles, Luis | Vaquero | Los Angeles Co | nr Los Angeles | Los Angeles. |
| Mendez, Francisco | Laborer | Los Angeles Co | | Los Angeles. |
| Mendosa, R | Laborer | | Los Angeles Co | Los Angeles. |
| Mendibles T | Laborer | nr Los Nietos | Los Angeles Co | Los Nietos. |
| Menz, Frederick | Laborer | | | Los Angeles. |
| **Menz, Fritz** | N Y Brewery | 3d st | 3d st | Los Angeles. |
| Meranda, M | Farmer | Los Angeles Co | nr Los Angeles | Los Angeles. |
| Merandette, J P | Sheep herder | | Spadra | Spadra. |
| **Mercadante, N** | Merchant | Los Angeles | Los Angeles Co | Los Angeles. |
| Merchant, Thos B | Carpenter | | | Los Angeles. |
| **Mercer, Thos** | Farmer | San Felipe Ranch | 5 m N E Los A | Los Angeles. |
| Meredith, R A | Farmer | Los Angeles Co | nr El Monte | El Monte. |
| Merkel, W | Carpenter | | Los Angeles Co | Anaheim. |
| Murry, J P | | | Los Angeles Co | Wilmington. |
| Merrick, A N | Attorney | Los Angeles | Los Angeles Co | Los Angeles. |
| Merrill, S W | Carpenter | Los Angeles | Los Angeles Co | Los Angeles. |
| Merrill, J L | Musician | Los Angeles | Los Angeles Co | Los Angeles. |
| **Merritt, J I** | Farmer | | Westminster Col | Westminster. |
| Merrill, — | Clerk | Canal st | Canal st | Wilmington. |
| Morry, Judson L | Carpenter | Los Angeles Co | | Los Angeles. |
| Meserve, A R | Farmer | San Bernardino Road | 5 m N E Spadra | Spadra. |
| Mesmar, L | Hotel keeper | Los Angeles | Los Angeles | Los Angeles. |
| Mesmer, Louis | Wine cellar | under U S Hotel | Fort st | Los Angeles. |
| Mesquita, R | Laborer | Los Angeles Co | | Los Angeles. |
| Mesquita, L | Laborer | Los Angeles Co | | Los Angeles. |
| Messi, R J | Artist | | Los Angeles Co | Los Angeles. |
| **Messer, K** | Farmer | nr Los Angeles | Los Angeles Co | Los Angeles. |
| Messix, M | Farmer | Los Angeles Co | nr Los Angeles | El Monte. |

| NAME. | OCCUPATION. | PLACE OF BUSINESS. | RESIDENCE. | TOWN OR P. O. |
|---|---|---|---|---|
| Messenger, E.... | Farmer | Los Angeles Co. | nr San Gabriel | San Gabriel. |
| Messenger, Rev H H | Minister | Orange | Los Angeles Co | Orange. |
| Messenger, H H | Farmer | San Gabriel Valley | 1¼ m N W San Gab. | San Gabriel. |
| Metcalf, A | Farmer | Los Angeles Co | nr Anaheim | Anaheim. |
| Metcalf, W F | Farmer | Los Angeles Co | nr Anaheim | Anaheim. |
| Metz, J M | Vintner | Los Angeles Co | nr Anaheim | Anaheim. |
| Metzker, J | Stock raiser | Los Angeles Co | nr Los Angeles | Los Angeles. |
| Meyer, S | Merchant | Los Angeles | Los Angeles | Los Angeles. |
| Meyer, E | Merchant | Los Angeles | Los Angeles | Los Angeles. |
| Meyerstein, Herman | Merchant | Los Angeles | Los Angeles | Los Angeles. |
| Meyers, John | Butcher | Los Angeles st | Anaheim | Anaheim. |
| Meyer & Co, E | Dry goods | 53 and 55 Main st | | Los Angeles. |
| Meyer, M | Dry goods | L A and Comm'al sts | | Los Angeles. |
| Meyer, Victor | Farmer | Los Angeles Co | nr Los Angeles | Los Angeles. |
| Michaelis, M | Clerk | Los Angeles | Los Angeles | Los Angeles. |
| Michelbog, J | Saddler | Los Angeles | Los Angeles | Los Angeles. |
| Middleton, J B | Gasfitter | Wilmington | Wilmington | Wilmington. |
| Mier, J F | Farmer | Los Angeles Co | nr Los Angeles | Los Angeles. |
| Milenz, F E | Clerk | Los Angeles Co | Anaheim | Anaheim. |
| Miles, G F | Stock raiser | nr Anaheim | Los Angeles Co | Anaheim. |
| Miles, P C | Railroader | Wilmington | Los Angeles Co | Wilmington. |
| Miles, Chas E | Superintendent | L A W Co | cor Fort and 3d sts | Los Angeles. |
| Miles, David E | Farmer | Los Angeles Co | nr Anaheim | Anaheim. |
| Miles & Holbrook | Pipe workers | Los Angeles | Los Angeles | Los Angeles. |
| Miller, J P | Farmer | Los Angeles Co | Soledad | San Fernando. |
| Miller, E G | Clerk | Los Angeles | Los Angeles | Los Angeles. |
| Millross, A | Carpenter | Los Angeles | Los Angeles | Los Angeles. |
| Millard, W R T | Farmer | Los Angeles Co | Los Nietos | Los Nietos. |
| Miller, George | Restaurant keeper | Anaheim | Anaheim | Anaheim. |
| Miller, John S | Miner | Los Angeles Co | | Los Angeles. |
| Miller, Adam G | Painter | Los Angeles | Los Angeles | Los Angeles. |
| Milligan, S | Carriage maker | Los Angeles | Los Angeles | Los Angeles. |
| Millanes, S | Laborer | Los Angeles Co | | San Gabriel. |
| Miller, D W | Clerk | Los Angeles | Los Angeles | Los Angeles. |
| Miller, J | Marble worker | Los Angeles | Los Angeles | Los Angeles. |
| Miller, N | Miner | Los Angeles Co | | Los Angeles. |
| Milliken, E G | Millwright | Los Angeles Co | | Los Angeles. |
| Millard, H W | Farmer | nr Los Nietos | Los Angeles Co | Los Nietos. |
| Miller, J E | Minister | nr Silver Precinct | Silver Precinct | Downey. |
| Millen, Francis Frederick | Journalist | Los Angeles | Los Angeles | Los Angeles. |
| Millard, S Z | Farmer | San Pedro Ranch | 1 m S Compton | Compton. |
| Miller, T J | Farmer | San Pedro Ranch | 1 m E Compton | Compton. |
| Miller, J | Farmer | San Pedro Ranch | ½ m E Compton | Compton. |
| Miller, C | Watchman | S P R R Co | Spadra | Spadra. |
| Miller, John | Cook | Temple oil wells | 7 m W Lyon Station | Lyon Station. |
| Miller, Isaac Wm | Miner | San Gabriel Canyon | | Azusa. |
| Miller, Marion | Farmer | | San Antonio | Downey. |
| Mills, R H | Farmer | nr Anaheim | Los Angeles Co | Anaheim. |
| Miller, Taylor | Laborer | Los Angeles Co | | Los Angeles. |
| Miller, Geo | Laborer | Los Angeles Co | San Jose | Spadra. |
| Miller, D | Teamster | Los Angeles Co | El Monte | El Monte. |
| Miller, H | Vintner | Los Angeles'Co | Los Angeles | Los Angeles. |
| Miller, J B | Farmer | Los Angeles Co | Los Nietos | Los Nietos. |
| Miller, M M | Book keeper | Wilmington | Wilmington | Wilmington. |
| Miller, C G | Miner | | Santa Catalina | Wilmington. |
| Miller, F | Cook | Los Angeles Co | Los Angeles | Los Angeles. |
| Miller, N J | Laborer | Los Angeles Co | | Los Angeles. |
| Mills, A | Farmer | nr Tustin City | Tustin City | Santa Ana. |
| Mills, E T | Farmer | nr El Monte | Los Angeles Co | El Monte. |
| Miller, T W | Saloon | | Los Angeles Co | Los Angeles. |
| Millross, W | Joiner | Los Angeles Co | | Los Angeles. |
| Miller, J L | Farmer | Los Angeles Co | Half-way House | Compton. |
| Milner, J | Agent | Los Angeles | Los Angeles | Los Angeles. |

| NAME. | OCCUPATION. | PLACE OF BUSINESS. | RESIDENCE. | TOWN OR P. O. |
|---|---|---|---|---|
| Miner, Julius V | Machinist | Los Angeles | Los Angeles | Los Angeles. |
| Minor, C | Farmer | Los Angeles Co | nr Los Angeles | Los Angeles. |
| Minor, C L | Printer | Los Angeles | Los Angeles | Los Angeles. |
| Miranda, Jesus | Farmer | Los Angeles Co | nr Los Angeles | Los Angeles. |
| Miranda, Roman | Saddler | Los Angeles | Los Angeles | Los Angeles. |
| Mirande, G | Stock raiser | | Los Angeles Co | Los Angeles. |
| Mitchell, H M | Farmer | nr Los Angeles | Los Angeles Co | Los Angeles. |
| Mitchell, T F | Farmer | Los Angeles Co | Soledad | San Fernando. |
| Mitchell, Joseph Henry | Barber | Los Angeles | Los Angeles | Los Angeles. |
| Mitchell, William | Farmer | | Westminster Col | Westminster. |
| Mitchell, — | Miner | Placeritas | 4 m N E Lyon Stat'n | Lyon Station. |
| Mitchell, Thos | Stock raiser | Soledad | 4 m N E Lyon Stat'n | Lyon Station. |
| Mitchell, N H | Laborer | Los Angeles Co | Los Angeles | Los Angeles. |
| Mitrovich, G A | Merchant | Los Angeles | Los Angeles | Los Angeles. |
| Mitts, J | Farmer | Los Angeles Co | nr El Monte | El Monte. |
| Mock, J A | Farmer | Los Angeles Co | Silver Precinct | Downey. |
| Moffett, J McD | Miller | Los Angeles Co | Westminster Col | Westminster. |
| Moffitt, A B | General mdse | San Fernando | San Fernando | San Fernando. |
| Moffatt, T J | Laborer | Los Angeles Co | El Monte | El Monte. |
| Moiso, J | Merchant | Los Angeles | Los Angeles | Los Angeles. |
| Moiso & Co, J | Groceries | Los Angeles | Los Angeles | Los Angeles. |
| Molina, A | Farmer | nr Los Angeles | Los Angeles Co | Los Angeles. |
| Molina, L | Laborer | Los Angeles Co | Los Angeles | Los Angeles. |
| Molino, Alexander | Laborer | | San Jose | Spadra. |
| Mollett, W | Cabinet maker | Los Angeles | Los Angeles | Los Angeles. |
| Mollica, Vincenjo | Musician | Los Angeles | Los Angeles | Los Angeles. |
| Mollica, Francisco | Saloon keeper | Los Angeles | Los Angeles | Los Angeles. |
| Momassen, J | Butcher | Los Angeles | Los Angeles | Los Angeles. |
| Monahan, F | Conductor | S P R R Co | Canal st | Wilmington. |
| Moncoronel, V | Sheepherder | Los Angeles Co | | Los Angeles. |
| Mondran, V de | Teacher | Los Angeles Co | Los Angeles | Los Angeles. |
| Mondrau, F V C de | Real estate | Main st | Los Angeles | Los Angeles. |
| Moneda, J | Painter | Los Angeles | Los Angeles | Los Angeles. |
| Monk, C | Farmer | Los Angeles Co | nr Wilmington | Wilmington. |
| Monks, H G | Farmer | nr San Gabriel | Los Angeles Co | San Gabriel. |
| Monks, Wm | Stone mason | Los Angeles | Los Angeles | Los Angeles. |
| Monroy, A | Laborer | Los Angeles Co | San Jose | Spadra. |
| Monroe, W B | Cabinet maker | | San Jose | Spadra. |
| Monroe, A P | Farmer | | San Jose | Spadra. |
| Monroe & Co, Jas | Restaurant | | Los Angeles | Los Angeles. |
| Monroe, Henry R | Carpenter | Los Angeles Co | | Los Angeles. |
| Monroe, Jas | S Monica hotel | Front st | Front st | Santa Monica. |
| Monroe, John | Farmer | San Jose Valley | 6 m S E Spadra | Spadra. |
| Monroe, Andrew | Farmer | San Jose Valley | 6 m S E Spadra | Spadra. |
| Montgomery, H L | Farmer | Los Angeles Co | Half-way House | Compton. |
| Montgomery, T A | Farmer | Los Angeles Co | Silver Precinct | Downey. |
| Montana, B | Vaquero | | Los Angeles Co | Capistrano. |
| Montague, J | Laborer | Los Angeles Co | | Los Angeles. |
| Montana, J M | Laborer | | Los Angeles Co | Los Angeles. |
| Montague, N S | Farmer | nr Los Angeles | Los Angeles Co | Los Angeles. |
| Montana, J | Farmer | nr Los Angeles | Los Angeles Co | Los Angeles. |
| Montana, G | Laborer | Los Angeles Co | | Los Angeles. |
| Montgomery, T P | Farmer | Los Angeles Co | Silver Precinct | Downey. |
| Montijo, A | Farmer | Los Angeles Co | nr Los Angeles | Los Angeles. |
| Montolla, B | Trader | Los Angeles | Los Angeles | Los Angeles. |
| Montgomery, F E | Farmer | Los Angeles Co | Los Nietos | Los Nietos. |
| Montalla, R | Farmer | Los Angeles Co | San Jose | Spadra. |
| Montague, R | Farmer | Los Angeles Co | nr Los Angeles | Los Angeles. |
| Montgomery, W J | Farmer | nr Downey | Silver Precinct | Downey. |
| Montana, J J | Laborer | Los Angeles Co | Old Mission | El Monte. |
| Monteyo, M | Laborer | | Azusa | Azusa. |
| Montion, C | Laborer | Los Angeles Co | | Los Angeles. |
| Montgomery, C C | Laborer | Los Angeles Co | San Gabriel | San Gabriel. |

| NAME. | OCCUPATION. | PLACE OF BUSINESS. | RESIDEN |
|---|---|---|---|
| Montana, J | Laborer | Los Angeles Co | Wilmington |
| Montes, C | Laborer | Los Angeles Co | Los Angeles |
| Montijo, Y | Laborer | Los Angeles | Los Angeles |
| Montague, W H K | Farmer | Los Angeles Co | nr Los Angel |
| Montgomery, Jas A | Farmer | Los Angeles Co | Silver Precin |
| Montana, Francisco | Laborer | Los Angeles Co | |
| Montana, Pedro | Laborer | | Los Angeles |
| Montijo, Manuel | Laborer | Los Angeles Co | |
| **Moody, W** | Farmer | Los Angeles Co | nr Los Angel |
| Moody, A C | Carpenter | Los Angeles | Los Angeles |
| **Moody, W H** | Farmer | Los Angeles Co | nr El Monte |
| Moon, E P | Farmer | Los Angeles Co | Los Nietos |
| Mooney, Dana T | Clerk | Los Angeles | Los Angeles |
| Mooney & Dixon | Laundry | Los Angeles | Los Angeles |
| Mooney, D T | Laundry | Los Angeles | Los Angeles |
| Moore, T S | Laborer | | Los Angeles |
| **Moore, J A** | Farmer | Los Angeles Co | San Jose |
| Moores, O G | Farmer | Los Angeles Co | nr Los Nietos |
| Moore, J | Farmer | | nr Los Angel |
| Moore, P S | Farmer | Los Angeles Co | San Jose |
| **Moore, W** | Civil engineer | Los Angeles | Los Angeles |
| Moore, J A | Teamster | | Los Angeles |
| Moores, W | Minister | Los Angeles Co | |
| Moore, J | Horse trainer | | Los Angeles |
| **Moore, J** | Farmer | Los Angeles Co | San Jose |
| Moore, J J | Steward | Los Angeles | Los Angeles |
| Moore, J V | Farmer | Los Angeles Co | Halfway Hou |
| **Moore, R** | Farmer | Los Angeles Co | San Jose |
| Moore, C H | Farmer | Los Angeles Co | nr Los Angel |
| Moore, S S | Farmer | Los Angeles Co | San Jose |
| **Moore, C A** | Farmer | nr Los Angeles | Los Angeles |
| Moore, J | Miner | Los Angeles Co | |
| Moores, C W | Farmer | nr Los Nietos | Los Angeles |
| Moore, Isaac N | Farmer | Los Angeles | nr Los Angel |
| Moore, S T | Farmer | nr Downey | Silver Precin |
| Moore, P B | Laborer | | Los Angeles |
| Moores, J B | Farmer | nr Los Nietos | Los Nietos |
| **Moore, J S** | Farmer | Los Angeles Co | nr El Monte |
| Moore, B C | Farmer | Los Angeles Co | nr Los Angel |
| Moore, J J | Farmer | Los Angeles Co | nr Los Angel |
| Moore, J | Farmer | Los Angeles Co | nr Los Angel |
| Moore, J | Miner | Los Angeles Co | Silver Precin |
| Moore, S B | Steward | Los Angeles | Los Angeles |
| **Moore, Wm J** | Hotel keeper | Los Angeles | Los Angeles |
| Moore, Thos R | Hostler | Los Angeles | Los Angeles |
| Moore, Chas W | Wire weaver | Los Angeles | Los Angeles |
| **Moore & Pray** | Agents | Los Angeles | Los Angeles |
| Moore, Alfred | Auctioneer | 1 Court st | Los Angeles |
| **Moore & Kelleher** | Civil engineers | Temple st | Los Angeles |
| **Moore, Wm** | Restaurant | Commercial st | Wilmington & |
| Moore, L | Farmer | San Pedro Ranch | ½ m N Compt |
| **Moore, Francis** | Apiarian | Soledad Road | 15 m N E Lyo |
| Moore, Chas | Station keeper | Moore's Station | 6 m N Lyon St |
| Moore, J S | Farmer | El Monte Valley | 2 m S Lexingt |
| **Moore, Chas** | Hotel keeper | Los Angeles Co | San Fernando |
| **Moore, Wm Henry** | Brass foundry | Los Angeles | Los Angeles |
| Moquihan, S | Carpenter | Los Angeles Co | |
| Morales, J | Carpenter | Los Angeles | Los Angeles C |
| Morales, M | Vaquero | Los Angeles Co | Los Angeles |
| Morales, C | Laborer | Los Angeles Co | Los Angeles C |
| Morales, R | Laborer | Los Angeles | Los Angeles |
| Morales, A | Laborer | Los Angeles Co | |
| **Moran, J** | Vintner | Los Angeles Co | nr El Monte |
| **Moranno, M** | Ranchero | Los Angeles Co | nr Los Angel |

# DIRECTORY OF LOS ANGELES COUNTY. 397

| NAME. | OCCUPATION. | PLACE OF BUSINESS. | RESIDENCE. | TOWN OR P. O. |
|---|---|---|---|---|
| Moran, J | Clerk | Los Angeles | Los Angeles | Los Angeles. |
| Morales, L | Laborer | Los Angeles Co | | Los Angeles. |
| Morales, F | Laborer | Los Angeles Co | Old Mission | El Monte. |
| Morales, P | Laborer | | Los Angeles Co | Los Angeles. |
| Morales, Diego | Vaquero | Los Angeles Co | San Juan | Capistrano. |
| Morales, Leandro | Vaquero | Los Angeles Co | San Juan | Capistrano. |
| Morales, V | Bricklayer | San Gabriel | San Gabriel | San Gabriel. |
| Mora, A | Laborer | Los Angeles Co | San Gabriel | San Gabriel. |
| Morales, J J | Laborer | Los Angeles Co | Los Angeles | Los Angeles. |
| Mora, M | Laborer | nr Los Angeles | Los Angeles Co | Los Angeles. |
| Moran, Samuel | Painter | Los Angeles | Los Angeles | Los Angeles. |
| Mora, Juan | Laborer | | Old Mission | El Monte. |
| Morales, Sacramento | Laborer | | Los Nietos | Los Nietos. |
| Moreno, R | Farmer | Los Angeles Co | nr Los Angeles | Los Angeles. |
| Moreno, J J | Clerk | Los Angeles | Los Angeles | Los Angeles. |
| Moreno, C | Laborer | nr La Ballona | La Ballona | Los Angeles. |
| Moreno, J | Ranchero | Los Angeles Co | La Ballona | Los Angeles. |
| Moreno, F | Farmer | Los Angeles Co | nr Los Nietos | Los Nietos. |
| Moreno, F | Ranchero | Los Angeles Co | nr San Fernando | San Fernando. |
| Moreno, T | Farmer | Los Angeles Co | nr Santa Ana | Santa Ana. |
| Moreno, J | Plasterer | Los Angeles | Los Angeles | Los Angeles. |
| Moreno, G | Saddler | Los Angeles | Los Angeles | Los Angeles. |
| **Moreau, C** | Druggist | Los Angeles | Los Angeles | Los Angeles. |
| Moreno, J M | Clerk | Los Angeles | Los Angeles | Los Angeles. |
| **More, H C** | Blacksmith | Los Angeles | Los Angeles | Los Angeles. |
| Moreno, J | Laborer | Los Angeles Co | | Los Angeles. |
| Moreno, L | Laborer | Los Angeles Co | | Los Angeles. |
| Moreno, J J | Ranchero | | Los Angeles Co | Los Angeles. |
| Moreno, Wm H | Farmer | Los Angeles Co | nr Los Angeles | Los Angeles. |
| Moreno, J | Saddler | Los Angeles | Los Angeles | Los Angeles. |
| Moreno, R | Shovel maker | Los Angeles Co | Los Angeles | Los Angeles. |
| Moreton, W H | Farmer | Los Angeles Co | Halfway House | Compton. |
| Morey, R H | Mechanic | Los Angeles | Los Angeles Co | Los Angeles. |
| Moreno, Jose A | Bricklayer | Los Angeles | Los Angeles | Los Angeles. |
| Morel, John | Miner | Los Angeles Co | Old Mission | El Monte. |
| Moren, Geo C | Farmer | San Gabriel Valley | 1 m N San Gabriel | San Gabriel. |
| Moreal de Brevaus, Adolphe | Merchant | Los Angeles | Los Angeles | Los Angeles. |
| Morel, Joseph | Merchant | Los Angeles | Los Angeles | Los Angeles. |
| Moreno, Miguel | Laborer | Los Angeles Co | | Los Angeles. |
| **Morgan, C** | Farmer | Los Angeles Co | nr Santa Ana | Santa Ana. |
| **Morgan, E M** | Real estate | Los Angeles | Los Angeles Co | Los Angeles. |
| Morgan, A | Carpenter | Los Angeles | Los Angeles | Los Angeles. |
| Morgan, G L | Farmer | Los Angeles Co | nr Anaheim | Anaheim. |
| Morgan, Peter | Laborer | | | Los Angeles. |
| **Morgan, A** | Merchant | Los Angeles | Los Angeles | Los Angeles. |
| **Morgan, W P** | Farmer | Los Angeles Co | nr El Monte | El Monte. |
| Morgan, H J | Teacher | Los Angeles | Los Angeles | Los Angeles. |
| **Morgan, David** | | | Westminster Col | Westminster. |
| **Morgan, G W** | Real estate | 4 Temple Block | Charity st | Los Angeles. |
| **Morgan, J C** | S Monica hotel | Front st | Front st | Santa Monica. |
| **Morgan & Monroe** | S Monica hotel | Front st | Front st | Santa Monica. |
| Morillo, B | Vaquero | Los Angeles Co | San Juan | San Juan. |
| Morillo, S | Laborer | Los Angeles Co | Los Angeles | Los Angeles. |
| Morillo, J A | Vaquero | Los Angeles Co | Los Angeles | Los Angeles. |
| Morillo, M | Laborer | | Los Angeles Co | Los Angeles. |
| Morillo, J de la G | Farmer | nr Anaheim | Los Angeles Co | Anaheim. |
| Morillo, M | Laborer | | Los Angeles Co | Capistrano. |
| Morillo, Jesus | Laborer | | Anaheim | Anaheim. |
| Morlis, Wilpert | Tailor | 13 Spring st | Spring st | Los Angeles. |
| **Morrill, W H** | Farmer | nr Downey | Silver Precinct | Downey. |
| Morrow, H B | Farmer | Los Angeles Co | nr Los Angeles | Los Angeles. |
| Morris, W | Laborer | | Los Angeles Co | Los Angeles. |
| Morrill, J R | Laborer | nr Los Angeles | Los Angeles Co | Los Angeles. |

398　　　　　L. L. PAULSON'S HAND-BOOK AND

| Name. | Occupation. | Place of Business. | Residence. | Town or P. O. |
|---|---|---|---|---|
| Morrow, T J | Farmer | Los Angeles Co | Halfway House | Compton. |
| Morrison, J | Trader | Wilmington | Wilmington | Wilmington. |
| Morris, J | Clerk | Los Angeles | Los Angeles | Los Angeles. |
| Morrell, LaFayette | Farmer | Los Angeles Co | nr Anaheim | Anaheim. |
| Morrison, J | Farmer | nr El Monte | Los Angeles Co | El Monte. |
| Morrello, J | Farmer | Los Angeles Co | nr Anaheim | Anaheim. |
| Morrisey, J | Boot maker | Los Angeles | Los Angeles | Los Angeles. |
| Morris, H | Clerk | Los Angeles | Los Angeles | Los Angeles. |
| Morris, J L | Merchant | Los Angeles | Los Angeles | Los Angeles. |
| Morrow, J | Farmer | Los Angeles Co | San Jose | Spadra. |
| Morris, D B | Farmer | Los Angeles Co | Silver Precinct | Downey. |
| Morris, F Jas | Farmer | Los Angeles Co | nr Los Angeles | Los Angeles. |
| Morris, J Z | City assessor | | Alameda st | Los Angeles. |
| Morris, M | Farmer | San Pedro Ranch | Compton | Compton. |
| Morrison, John | Grocery | Canal st | Canal st | Wilmington. |
| Morrison, J K | Farmer | San Pedro Ranch | 2 m S W Compton | Compton. |
| Morrison, W A | Farmer | Azusa | 5 m E Azusa | Azusa. |
| Morris, Francis | Drayman | Los Angeles | Los Angeles | Los Angeles. |
| Morris, John | Laborer | Los Angeles Co | | Los Angeles. |
| Morris, Isaac N | Gas fitter | Los Angeles | Los Angeles | Los Angeles. |
| Morris, Chas C | Clerk | Los Angeles | Los Angeles | Los Angeles. |
| Morsch, F | Painter | 16 Court st | Spring st | Los Angeles. |
| Morsch & Maining | Painters | Los Angeles | Los Angeles | Los Angeles. |
| Morsser, John H | Farmer | Los Angeles Co | Gospel Swamp | Santa Ana. |
| Morton, J J | Farmer | Los Angeles Co | Halfway House | Compton. |
| Morton, V R | Carriage maker | Los Angeles | Los Angeles | Los Angeles. |
| Morton, Wm | Farmer | Los Angeles Co | Halfway House | Compton. |
| Morton, Henry | Clerk | Los Angeles | Los Angeles | Los Angeles. |
| Morton, Wm H | Dairy & farmer | San Pedro Ranch | 1 m N Compton | Compton. |
| Morton, John I | Dairy & farmer | San Pedro Ranch | 1 m N W Compton | Compton. |
| Moses & Co, I H | Real estate | 73 Downey Block | | Los Angeles. |
| Mosher, Wm C | Clergyman | Wilmington | Wilmington | Wilmington. |
| Mosher, W C | Teacher | San Gabriel Valley | 6 m N W San Grbr'l | San Gabriel. |
| Mosseman, C | Saloon keeper | Anaheim | | Anaheim. |
| Moss, W | Farmer | nr Los Nietos | Los Nietos | Los Nietos. |
| Moss, Joshua | | Los Angeles Co | Los Angeles | Los Angeles. |
| Mott, S H | Clerk | Los Angeles | Los Angeles | Los Angeles. |
| Mott, T D | | Los Angeles Co | Main st | Los Angeles. |
| Mouge, — | Farmer | Dalton Ranch | 1 m N Azusa | Azusa. |
| Moulton, E | Ranchero | Los Angeles Co | nr San Gabriel | San Gabriel. |
| Moulton, G | Mechanic | Soledad | Soledad | San Fernando. |
| Moulthrop, George | Locomotive eng | S P R R Co | Wilmington | Wilmington. |
| Moulthrop, W H | Tel operator | Depot | Spadra | Spadra. |
| Moulton, James | Laborer | Los Angeles Co | | Los Angeles. |
| Muldry, James | Laborer | | Los Angeles Co | Los Angeles. |
| Muldino, A | Engineer | S P R R Co | Wilmington | Wilmington. |
| Mulford, Joseph W | Engineer | Los Angeles Co | Wilmington | Wilmington. |
| Mulhall, T B | Dyer | Wilmington | Los Angeles | Wilmington. |
| Muller & Webber | Livery stable | Los Angeles | Los Angeles | Los Angeles. |
| Muller, Peter | Baker | Los Angeles | Los Angeles | Los Angeles. |
| Mullaly, Geo S | Laborer | Los Angeles Co | | Los Angeles. |
| Mullen, W | Shipwright | | Wilmington | Wilmington. |
| Mullins, W | Farmer | Los Angeles Co | Silver Precinct | Downey. |
| Mulligan, T | Saloon keeper | Los Angeles | Los Angeles | Los Angeles. |
| Muller, J | Laborer | Los Angeles Co | Los Angeles | Los Angeles. |
| Muller, Jacob | Butcher | Los Angeles | Los Angeles | Los Angeles. |
| Mullaly, T | Brick maker | Los Angeles | Los Angeles | Los Angeles. |
| Mulvaney, M | Butcher | Spadra | 30 m E Los Angeles | Spadra. |
| Mundell, I N | Blacksmith | Los Angeles | Los Angeles Co | Los Angeles. |
| Munoz, T | Saddler | Los Angeles | Los Angeles | Los Angeles. |
| Munoz, M | Laborer | | Los Angeles Co | Los Angeles. |
| Murnane, M | Saloon | San Fernando | San Fernando | San Fernando. |
| Murphy, C | Boiler maker | S P R R Co | Wilmington | Wilmington. |
| Murphy, J | Farmer | Downey Ranch | 2½ m W Compton | Compton. |

# DIRECTORY OF LOS ANGELES COUNTY. 399

| NAME. | OCCUPATION. | PLACE OF BUSINESS. | RESIDENCE. | TOWN OR P. O. |
|---|---|---|---|---|
| Murphy, P | Mason | Los Angeles | Los Angeles Co | Los Angeles. |
| Murry, R W | Laborer | | Los Angeles Co | Los Angeles. |
| Muth, Jacob | Tinsmith | Los Angeles | Los Angeles | Los Angeles. |
| Myers, Chas S | Bar keeper | Los Angeles | Los Angeles | Los Angeles. |
| Myers, A Van | Saloon | 17 Main st | Los Angeles | Los Angeles. |
| **Myers, W S** | Attorney at law | 31 Temple Block | Los Angeles | Los Angeles. |
| Myers, Chas S | Saloon | 17 Main st | Los Angeles | Los Angeles. |
| Myers & Myers | Bon ton saloon | 17 Main st | | Los Angeles. |
| Myers, S L | Cook | Los Angeles | Los Angeles | Los Angeles. |
| Myer, C | Clerk | Los Angeles | Los Angeles | Los Angeles. |
| **Myers, J H** | Stock raiser | Los Angeles Co | nr Los Angeles | Los Angeles. |
| Myers, John Wm | Plasterer | Los Angeles | Los Angeles | Los Angeles. |
| **Myres, John** | Sheep raiser | Los Angeles | nr Anaheim | Anaheim. |
| Nadeau, Joseph F | Carpenter | Los Angeles Co | | Los Angeles. |
| Nadeau, R | Freighter | | Los Angeles Co | Los Angeles. |
| **Napier, P N** | Fruit | Los Angeles Co | Westminster Col | Westminster. |
| Narbonne, N | Merchant | Wilmington | Los Angeles Co | Wilmington. |
| **Narbonne, N** | Stock raiser | Palos Verde Ranch | 2½ m N W Wilm'ton | Wilmington. |
| Nash, J | Farmer | Los Angeles Co | San Joaquin | Santa Ana. |
| Naud, E | Merchant | Los Angeles | Los Angeles Co | Los Angeles. |
| Naud, E | Wines & liquors | New Commercial st | | Los Angeles. |
| Nauendorf, F | Cooper | Anaheim | Los Angeles Co | Anaheim. |
| Navarro, T | Laborer | | Los Angeles Co | Los Angeles. |
| **Nava, T** | Farmer | Los Angeles Co | nr Los Angeles | Los Angeles. |
| Navarro, J | Laborer | | Los Angeles Co | Los Angeles. |
| Navarro, C R de | Laborer | | Los Angeles Co | Los Angeles. |
| Navarro, J A | Farmer | Los Angeles Co | Halfway House | Compton. |
| Navarro, J M | Laborer | Los Angeles Co | nr San Gabriel | San Gabriel. |
| Neal, W | Waiter | Los Angeles | Los Angeles Co | Los Angeles. |
| Neal, C | Teamster | | Los Angeles Co | Los Angeles. |
| Neal, M F | Saloon | Azusa | 22 m E Los Angeles | Azusa. |
| Nebelung, Max | Anaheim hotel | cor Centre sts | | Anaheim. |
| Need, T M | Laborer | | Los Angeles Co | Los Angeles. |
| Neel, F | Farmer | | Los Angeles Co | El Monte. |
| Neel, Wm S | Farmer | nr El Monte | Los Angeles Co | El Monte. |
| Negbaur, C H | Distiller | Los Angeles | Los Angeles Co | Los Angeles. |
| Neighbours, A W | Farmer | nr Los Nietos | Los Angeles Co | Los Nietos. |
| Neighbours, S M | Farmer | nr Los Nietos | Los Angeles Co | Los Nietos. |
| **Neitzke, Ernest** | Undertaker | 3 Spring st | 3 Spring st | Los Angeles. |
| **Neitzke & Wohlers** | Undertakers | 3 Spring st | | Los Angeles. |
| Neitze, E P | Clerk | Los Angeles | Los Angeles Co | Los Angeles. |
| **Nelson, A** | Farmer | Los Angeles Co | Halfway House | Compton. |
| Nelson, J | Carpenter | Los Angeles | Los Angeles Co | Los Angeles. |
| Nelson, Nicholas | Tailor | Los Angeles | Los Angeles | Los Angeles. |
| Nelson, W H | Teamster | | Los Angeles Co | Los Angeles. |
| **Nelson, A** | Farmer | nr Florence | Florence | Los Angeles. |
| Nerro, T | Carpenter | Los Angeles | Los Angeles Co | Los Angeles. |
| Nesbett, G H | Clerk | Downey | Silver Precinct | Downey. |
| Nenzel, R | Baker | Anaheim | Los Angeles Co | Anaheim. |
| Newall, Wm W | Painter | Los Angeles | Los Angeles | Los Angeles. |
| Newbell, S D | Farmer | | Silver Precinct | Downey. |
| Newbell, P H | Stock raiser | | Los Angeles Co | Los Angeles. |
| Newbauer, H | Merchant | Los Angeles | Los Angeles Co | Los Angeles. |
| Newbauer, Solomon | Clerk | Los Angeles | Los Angeles | Los Angeles. |
| **Newbauer, H** | Furniture | Spring st | | Los Angeles. |
| **Newcomb, R T** | Farmer | Los Angeles Co | Silver Precinct | Downey. |
| Newell, J | Farmer | nr Los Angeles | Los Angeles Co | Los Angeles. |
| Newkirk, Elias | Laborer | Los Angeles Co | Los Angeles | Los Angeles. |
| Newman, B | Farmer | Los Angeles Co | El Monte | El Monte. |
| **Newmark, H** | Merchant | Los Angeles | Los Angeles Co | Los Angeles. |
| Newmark, J | | Los Angeles | Los Angeles Co | Los Angeles. |
| Newmark, M A | Clerk | Los Angeles | Los Angeles Co | Los Angeles. |
| Newman, B | Farmer | El Monte Valley | 2 m S Lexington | El Monte. |
| **Newmark, M N** | General merch'se | Compton | Compton | Compton. |

| NAME. | OCCUPATION. | PLACE OF BUSINESS. | RESIDENCE. | TOWN OR P. |
|---|---|---|---|---|
| Newmark, Myer J. | Merchant | Los Angeles | Los Angeles | Los Angeles. |
| Newmark & Co, H. | Groceries | Los Angeles | Los Angeles | Los Angeles. |
| Newton, I | Farmer | | Los Angeles Co | El Monte. |
| Newton, J | Farmer | nr Los Nietos | Los Angeles Co | Los Nietos. |
| Newton, W | Farmer | Los Angeles Co | Silver Precinct | Downey. |
| Newton, G P | Miner | Los Angeles Co | Soledad | San Fernand |
| Newton, J C | Farmer | nr San Gabriel | Los Angeles Co | San Gabriel. |
| Nichols, L C | Clerk | Los Angeles | Los Angeles Co | Los Angeles. |
| Nichols, J G | Farmer | nr Los Angeles | Los Angeles Co | Los Angeles. |
| Nicholson, J | Farmer | Los Angeles Co | Silver District | Downey. |
| Nichols, Q | Barber | Los Angeles | Los Angeles Co | Los Angeles. |
| Nicholson, W | Farmer | Los Angeles Co | Silver Precinct | Downey. |
| Nichols, D B | Farmer | nr Los Angeles | Los Angeles Co | Los Angeles. |
| Nichelson, H | Farmer | nr Los Nietos | Los Angeles Co | Los Nietos. |
| Nichols, J A | Farmer | nr Los Angeles | Los Angeles Co | Los Angeles. |
| Nichols, Emory J | Pattern maker | Los Angeles | Los Angeles | Los Angeles. |
| Nichols, Ira | Carpenter | Los Angeles Co | | Los Angeles. |
| Nichols, J G, Jr | Stock raiser | nr Los Angeles | Los Angeles Co | Los Angeles. |
| Nichols, E P | Stage driver | | Los Angeles Co | Los Angeles. |
| Nickerson, C H | Teacher | Anaheim | Los Angeles Co | Anaheim. |
| Nickson, Albert | Laborer | Los Angeles Co | | Los Angeles. |
| Nickerson & Co, J. | Chinese emp office | Negro Alley & L A st | | Los Angeles. |
| Nicoles, E R | Farmer | Los Angeles Co | Richland | Orange. |
| Niedecken, H | Clerk | Los Angeles | Los Angeles Co | Los Angeles. |
| Niedecken, E | Merchant | Los Angeles | Los Angeles Co | Los Angeles. |
| Niedecken, A H | Merchant | Los Angeles | Los Angeles Co | Los Angeles. |
| Niemeyer, Henry | Farmer | Los Angeles Co | nr Los Angeles | Los Angeles. |
| Nieto, J J | Farmer | Los Angeles Co | nr San Gabriel | San Gabriel. |
| Nieto, D | Farmer | Los Angeles Co | Old Mission | El Monte. |
| Nietos, Jesus | Butcher | San Gabriel | 9 m E Los Angeles | San Gabriel. |
| Nimmo, John | Saloon | Santa Ana | Santa Ana | Santa Ana. |
| Nimmo, B F | Farmer | nr Los Angeles | Los Angeles Co | Los Angeles. |
| Nimmo, J | Farmer | Los Angeles Co | San Joaquin | Santa Ana. |
| Noceti, Antonio | Bricklayer | Los Angeles | Los Angeles | Los Angeles. |
| Noen, Feliciano | Farmer | Los Angeles Co | nr Los Angeles | Los Angeles. |
| Nolan, M | Teamster | | Los Angeles Co | Los Angeles. |
| Nolte, Frederick | Butcher | N Y City Market | | Los Angeles. |
| Noon, W | Butcher | Los Angeles | Los Angeles Co | Los Angeles. |
| Nordholt, W H | Carpenter | Los Angeles | Los Angeles Co | Los Angeles. |
| Nordlinger, S | Watch maker | 3 Commercial st | Los Angeles | Los Angeles. |
| Norton, Los Day | Clerk | Los Angeles | Los Angeles Co | Los Angeles. |
| Norton, — | Carpenter | S P R R Co | Wilmington | Wilmington. |
| North, J | Sea captain | Wilmington | Los Angeles Co | Wilmington. |
| Norton, S | Merchant | Los Angeles Co | Los Angeles Co | Los Angeles. |
| Norton, C | Merchant | Los Angeles | Los Angeles | Los Angeles. |
| Norton, M | Merchant | Los Angeles | Los Angeles | Los Angeles. |
| Norton, M | Attorney | Los Angeles | Los Angeles | Los Angeles. |
| North, W | Cook | Los Angeles | Los Angeles | Los Angeles. |
| Norton, I | Merchant | Los Angeles | Los Angeles | Los Angeles. |
| Norton & Co, I | Gen merchandise | Los Angeles | Los Angeles | Los Angeles. |
| Northcraft, James H | Tinner | Los Angeles | Los Angeles | Los Angeles. |
| North, James I | Sheep herder | nr Los Angeles | Los Angeles Co | Los Angeles. |
| Noyes & Durfee | Com merchants | Los Angeles | Los Angeles | Los Angeles. |
| Noyes, E W | Auction & comm | Temple Block | | Los Angeles. |
| O'Bannan, J | Farmer | nr Los Angeles | Los Angeles Co | Los Angeles. |
| O'Brien, J | Miner | nr San Gabriel | Los Angeles Co | San Gabriel. |
| O'Brein, M J | Priest | Los Angeles | Los Angeles Co | Los Angeles. |
| O'Brien, P | Laborer | | Los Angeles Co | Los Angeles. |
| O'Brien, J | Farmer | Los Angeles Co | nr Los Angeles | Los Angeles. |
| O'Brien, T | Laborer | Los Angeles Co | | Los Angeles. |
| O'Bryant, J B | Farmer | Los Angeles Co | nr Los Nietos | Los Nietos. |
| Ocampo, Ostiano | Laborer | | Los Angeles Co | Los Angeles. |
| O'Campo, Camilo | Laborer | Los Angeles Co | | Wilmington. |
| Ocana, Y | Laborer | nr Los Angeles | Los Angeles Co | Los Angeles. |

# DIRECTORY OF LOS ANGELES COUNTY. 401

| Name. | Occupation. | Place of Business. | Residence. | Town or P. O. |
|---|---|---|---|---|
| Ocano, J Y | Vaquero | | Los Angeles Co | Los Angeles. |
| Ocana, S | Laborer | | Los Angeles Co | Los Angeles. |
| Ocana, J J | Merchant | Los Angeles | Los Angeles Co | Los Angeles. |
| Ocano, G | Laborer | nr Los Angeles | Los Angeles Co | Los Angeles. |
| Ocana, F | Mason | Los Angeles | Los Angeles Co | Los Angeles. |
| Ocana, P | Laborer | | Los Angeles Co | Los Angeles. |
| Ocana, J | Vaquero | | Los Angeles Co | Capistrano. |
| Ochoa, J | Laborer | Los Angeles Co | San Gabriel | San Gabriel. |
| Ochoa, V | Laborer | Los Angeles Co | San Gabriel Mission | San Gabriel. |
| Ochoa, D | Laborer | Los Angeles Co | Old Mission | El Monte. |
| Ochoa, Jesus | Laborer | San Gabriel | | Azusa. |
| Ochoa, M | Laborer | nr San Gabriel | Los Angeles Co | San Gabriel. |
| Ochoa, Y | Laborer | Los Angeles Co | nr Azusa | Azusa. |
| Ochoa, Y | Laborer | Los Angeles Co | | San Gabriel. |
| Ochon, Antonio | Laborer | Los Angeles Co | Old Mission | El Monte. |
| Ochoa, A | Farmer | Dalton Ranch | Azusa | Azusa. |
| Ochoa, J | Farmer | Dalton Ranch | Azusa | Azusa. |
| **Oden, G W** | Wheelwright | Wilmington | Los Angeles Co | Wilmington. |
| **Oden, George W** | Stock | Los Angeles Valley | Wilmington | Wilmington. |
| **O'Donnell, P N** | L A foundry | cor Aliso & Garcia sts | | Los Angeles. |
| O'Donnell P N | Moulder | Los Angeles | Los Angeles Co | Los Angeles. |
| O'Donnell, G | Laborer | | Los Angeles Co | Los Angeles. |
| Oecjo, L | Laborer | Los Angeles Co | | Los Angeles. |
| **Oeflnger, M** | Farmer | | Anaheim | Anaheim. |
| O'Hair, J | Laborer | Los Angeles Co | | Los Angeles. |
| O'Harra, T B | Miner | nr Wilmington | Los Angeles Co | Wilmington. |
| Ojeda, B | Cook | Los Angeles | Los Angeles | Los Angeles. |
| O'Keefe, T F | Steward | Los Angeles | Los Angeles Co | Los Angeles. |
| O'Keefe, Patrick | Carpenter | Los Angeles Co | | Los Angeles. |
| **Oldenburg, Alex** | Civil engineer | Los Angeles | Los Angeles | Los Angeles. |
| **Olden, W R** | Ranchero | Anaheim | Los Angeles Co | Anaheim. |
| O'Leary, T J | Priest | Los Angeles | Los Angeles Co | Los Angeles. |
| Olquin, J | Laborer | | Los Angeles Co | Los Angeles. |
| Olinghouse, E | Freighter | Los Angeles | Los Angeles Co | Los Angeles. |
| **Oliver, J** | Physician | Los Angeles | Los Angeles | Los Angeles. |
| Olivera, J J | Laborer | | Los Angeles Co | Los Angeles. |
| Olivera, G | Farmer | nr Los Angeles | Los Angeles Co | Los Angeles. |
| Olivera, J | Laborer | Los Angeles Co | La Ballona | Los Angeles. |
| Olivera, S | Vaquero | | Los Angeles Co | Los Angeles. |
| Olivares, J del C | Laborer | Los Angeles Co | La Ballona | Los Angeles. |
| Olivera, J M M | Farmer | nr Los Angeles | Los Angeles Co | Los Angeles. |
| Olivera, M | Laborer | | Los Angeles Co | Los Angeles. |
| Olivares, J J | Vaquero | nr San Juan | Los Angeles Co | Capistrano. |
| Oliva, J A | Musician | Los Angeles | Los Angeles Co | Los Angeles. |
| Olivares, A M | Ranchero | nr San Juan | Los Angeles Co | Capistrano. |
| Olivares, F | Laborer | | Los Angeles Co | Los Angeles. |
| Olivera, A | Laborer | Los Angeles | Los Angeles Co | Los Angeles. |
| Olivares, T | Farmer | Los Angeles Co | La Ballona | Los Angeles. |
| Oliver, Francis | Hostler | Los Angeles | Los Angeles | Los Angeles. |
| Olivera, Andres | Laborer | Los Angeles Co | | Los Angeles. |
| Olivares, F | Laborer | | Los Angeles Co | Capistrano. |
| Olivera, Chas | Farmer | nr Los Angeles | Los Angeles Co | Los Angeles. |
| Olivares, G J | Vaquero | Los Angeles Co | | San Juan. |
| Olivares, U | Vaquero | | Los Angeles Co | Capistrano. |
| Olivera, B | Vaquero | Los Angeles Co | | Los Angeles. |
| Olivas, R | Laborer | | Los Angeles Co | Los Angeles. |
| Olivas, Jose | Laborer | Los Angeles Co | | Los Angeles. |
| Olivas, J de la T | Ranchero | nr Los Angeles | Los Angeles Co | Los Angeles. |
| Olivera, P | Vaquero | Los Angeles Co | | Los Angeles. |
| Olivares, Y | Vaquero | | Los Angeles Co | Capistrano. |
| **Olivas, Mrs S** | Dress maker | Los Angeles | Los Angeles | Los Angeles. |
| Olmstead, J C | Farmer | | Los Angeles Co | Los Angeles. |
| Olsen, L | Laborer | Los Angeles Co | | Wilmington. |
| Oman, Wm | Farmer | Domingues Ranch | 3 m N Wilmington | Wilmington. |

26

| Name. | Occupation. | Place of Business. | Residence. | Town or P. O. |
|---|---|---|---|---|
| Oman, Joseph | Fireman | S P R R Co | Wilmington | Wilmington. |
| O'Mara, T | Cook | Los Angeles | Los Angeles | Los Angeles. |
| O'Meara, E. | Laborer | | Los Angeles Co | Anaheim. |
| **O'Meara, R W** | Brewer | Los Angeles | Los Angeles | Los Angeles. |
| O'Melveny, H K S | Attorney | Los Angeles | Los Angeles Co | Los Angeles. |
| **O'Neale, P B** | Farmer | nr Los Angeles | Los Angeles Co | Los Angeles. |
| **O'Neal, P B** | Farmer | Los Angeles Co | Soledad | San Fernando. |
| O'Neale, H | Sheep raiser | | Los Angeles Co | Los Angeles. |
| O'Neil, J | Laborer | Los Angeles Co | Old Mission | El Monte. |
| **O'Neil, J S** | City laundry | 9th st | 9th st | Los Angeles. |
| O'Neil, John | Hostler | Los Angeles | Los Angeles | Los Angeles. |
| Onstott, Mrs E S | Teacher | Los Angeles | Los Angeles | Los Angeles. |
| Orcutt, Chas E | Tallyman | S P R R Co | Canal st | Wilmington. |
| Ordoque, L | Carpenter | Los Angeles | Los Angeles Co | Los Angeles. |
| Orduna, J M | Laborer | | Los Angeles Co | Los Angeles. |
| Orduna, A | Laborer | | Los Angeles Co | Los Angeles. |
| **O'Reily, J** | Blacksmith | Los Angeles | Los Angeles | Los Angeles. |
| O'Reilly, M J | Teacher | | La Ballona | Los Angeles. |
| Orio, N | Laborer | Los Angeles Co | nr Los Angeles | Los Angeles. |
| Orme, Dr H S | Physician | 74 Main st | Spring st | Los Angeles. |
| Ormsby, Wm H | Foreman | S P R R Co | Canal st | Wilmington. |
| Ormsby, W H | Farmer | nr Wilmington | Los Angeles Co | Wilmington. |
| Oroho, W | Teamster | | Los Angeles Co | Los Angeles. |
| Orosco, J | Laborer | | Los Angeles Co | Los Angeles. |
| Oroso, T | Laborer | nr San Gabriel | Los Angeles Co | San Gabriel. |
| Orr, John S | Carpenter | Los Angeles Co | | Los Angeles. |
| **Orr, M** | Farmer | San Pedro Ranch | ½ m W Compton | Compton. |
| **Orr, James** | Farmer | San Pedro Ranch | ½ m W Compton | Compton. |
| **Orr, Bros** | Apiarians | Los Angeles Co | 12 m Los Angeles | Los Angeles. |
| **Orr, Matthew** | Farmer | nr Compton | Los Angeles Co | Compton. |
| **Orr, R** | Farmer | nr Compton | Los Angeles Co | Compton. |
| **Orr, W W** | Farmer | nr Downey | Silver Precinct | Downey. |
| Orrick, T | Farmer | Los Angeles Co | Los Nietos | Los Nietos. |
| **Orrick, G W** | Farmer | Los Angeles Co | nr El Monte | El Monte. |
| Ortega, J M | Laborer | Los Angeles Co | | San Gabriel. |
| Ortega, R | Laborer | Los Angeles Co | nr San Gabriel | San Gabriel. |
| Ortes, M | Farmer | Los Angeles Co | Soledad | San Fernando. |
| Ortega, John A | Clerk | Los Angeles | Los Angeles | Los Angeles. |
| Ortega, Andres | Laborer | Los Angeles Co | | Wilmington. |
| Ortega, G | Laborer | Los Angeles Co | | Los Angeles. |
| Ortega, F | Butcher | San Gabriel | Los Angeles Co | San Gabriel. |
| Ortis, J | Laborer | nr Los Angeles | Los Angeles Co | Los Angeles. |
| **Orton, R** | Farmer | nr Downey | Silver Precinct | Downey. |
| Osburn, H W | Laborer | | Los Angeles Co | Los Angeles. |
| Osborne, W W | Miner | | Los Angeles Co | Los Angeles. |
| Osburn, W M | Freighter | | Los Angeles Co | Los Angeles. |
| Osburn, R B | Blacksmith | Los Angeles | Los Angeles Co | Los Angeles. |
| **Osborne, John** | Baggage express | W, F & Co's office | | Los Angeles. |
| Osburn, J | Teamster | nr Los Angeles | Los Angeles Co | Los Angeles. |
| Osejo, V | Laborer | Los Angeles Co | | Los Angeles. |
| Ossa, F de la | Farmer | nr San Fernando | Los Angeles Co | San Fernando. |
| Ossa, V de la | Laborer | Los Angeles Co | nr San Gabriel | San Gabriel. |
| Ossa, P de la | Laborer | nr San Gabriel | Los Angeles Co | San Gabriel. |
| Otis, T W | Agent | Los Angeles | Los Angeles Co | Los Angeles. |
| Ott, J | Cook | Los Angeles | Los Angeles | Los Angeles. |
| Ott, James D | Ag't An Ligh'r Co | Anaheim | Anaheim | Anaheim. |
| Otto, Henry | Carpenter | Los Angeles Co | | Los Angeles. |
| Outward, T M | Coachman | Los Angeles | Los Angeles Co | Los Angeles. |
| **Overton, David F** | Farmer | Los Angeles Co | Silver Precinct | Downey. |
| Owen, E H | Clerk | Los Angeles | Los Angeles | Los Angeles. |
| **Owens, H** | Farmer | Los Angeles Co | Silver Precinct | Downey. |
| Owens, R | Merchant | Los Angeles | Los Angeles Co | Los Angeles. |
| Owens, T H | Laborer | | Los Angeles Co | Los Angeles. |
| Owens, R | Farmer | | Los Angeles Co | Azusa. |

DIRECTORY OF LOS ANGELES COUNTY. 403

| Name. | Occupation. | Place of Business. | Residence. | Town or P. O. |
|---|---|---|---|---|
| Owen, T............ | Seaman............... | ....................... | ....................... | Wilmington. |
| Owen, J S........... | Farmer............. | nr Los Nietos ........ | Los Angeles Co........ | Los Nietos. |
| Owens, T............ | Farmer............. | nr San Gabriel........ | Los Angeles Co........ | San Gabriel. |
| Owens, C............ | Farmer............. | ....................... | Los Angeles Co ....... | Los Angeles. |
| Oxarart, S........... | Wool grower....... | nr Los Angeles........ | Los Angeles Co........ | Los Angeles. |
| Ozburn, J J......... | Farmer............. | nr Los Angeles........ | Los Angeles Co........ | Los Angeles. |
| Pachond, C.......... | Farmer............. | nr Los Angeles........ | Los Angeles Co........ | Los Angeles. |
| Pacheco, Mrs T..... | Washerwoman ... | Wilmington............ | Wilmington ........... | Wilmington. |
| Packard, S W....... | Distiller ............ | Los Angeles........... | Los Angeles........... | Los Angeles. |
| Packhurst, J........ | Laborer............. | Los Angeles Co ...... | Silver Precinct........ | Downey. |
| Packwood, L........ | Painter............. | Los Angeles........... | Los Angeles Co........ | Los Angeles. |
| Packer, E........... | Laborer............. | Los Angeles Co ...... | nr Azusa............... | Azusa. |
| Packard, Rev D T.. | Pas cong church.. | New High st.......... | ....................... | Los Angeles. |
| Packard, A G....... | Printer............. | Los Angeles........... | Los Angeles........... | Los Angeles. |
| Paddock, W A...... | Painter............. | Los Angeles Co ...... | El Monte............... | El Monte. |
| Paddilla, J M....... | Farmer............. | Los Angeles Co....... | nr Wilmington........ | Wilmington. |
| Paddilla, Jose M... | Farmer............. | San Gabriel........... | 9 E Los Angeles..... | San Gabriel. |
| Page, S L........... | Farmer............. | nr San Gabriel........ | Los Angeles Co........ | San Gabriel. |
| Page, R C........... | Farmer............. | Los Angeles Co ...... | San Joaquin........... | Santa Ana. |
| Page & Gravel...... | Carriage man'ftrs | Los Angeles........... | Los Angeles........... | Los Angeles. |
| Page, L E............ | Carriage man'ftr.. | Los Angeles........... | Los Angeles........... | Los Angeles. |
| Page, C M........... | Carpenter........... | Aliso Mills............. | Olive st................ | Los Angeles. |
| Paiester, N.......... | Ranchero ........... | ....................... | Los Angeles Co........ | Los Angeles. |
| Paine, M............. | Farmer............. | San Jose Addition.... | 6 m N E Azusa ...... | Azusa. |
| Paine, Lewis........ | Farmer............. | San Jose Addition.... | 6 m N E Azusa....... | Azusa. |
| Paine, John......... | Farmer............. | San Jose Addition.... | 6 m N E Azusa ...... | Azusa. |
| Palaski & Goodwin | Gen merchandise. | cor Coml & Main sts | ....................... | Los Angeles. |
| Palamoris, Thos .... | Farmer............. | San Bernardino Road | 4½ m E Spadra....... | Spadra. |
| Palamoris, F........ | Stock & farmer... | San Bernardino Road | 4½ m N E Spadra.... | Spadra. |
| Pallett, J R......... | Farmer............. | Los Angeles Co....... | nr Los Nietos.......... | Los Nietos. |
| Pallard, Thos ...... | Laborer............. | Los Angeles Co....... | ....................... | Los Angeles. |
| Pallacio, S.......... | Laborer............. | Los Angeles Co....... | ....................... | Los Angeles. |
| Pallett, G W A..... | Farmer............. | nr Los Nietos.......... | Los Nietos............ | Los Nietos. |
| Pallett, Thomas.... | Farmer............. | Silver Precinct........ | Silver Precinct........ | Downey. |
| Palle, John ......... | Farmer............. | Los Angeles Co....... | Los Nietos............. | Los Nietos. |
| Palmeut, A.......... | Farmer............. | Los Angeles Co....... | nr Anaheim............ | Anaheim. |
| Palmer, J C......... | Farmer............. | Los Angeles Co....... | nr Santa Ana.......... | Santa Ana. |
| Palmer, G M........ | Engineer ........... | Los Angeles Co....... | ....................... | Los Angeles. |
| Palmer, W A........ | Farmer............. | nr Los Angeles........ | Los Angeles ......... | Los Angeles. |
| Palmer, Miss R M.. | Teacher............ | Los Angeles Co....... | ....................... | Los Angeles. |
| Palmer, —.......... | Farmer............. | Azusa.................. | 2¼ m S W Azusa..... | Azusa. |
| Palomares, J F..... | Farmer............. | nr Spadra.............. | San Jose .............. | Spadra. |
| Pantoja, J........... | Laborer............. | Los Angeles Co....... | ....................... | Los Angeles. |
| Pantoja, Y.......... | Laborer............. | ....................... | Los Angeles Co........ | Los Angeles. |
| Para, A.............. | Laborer............. | Los Angeles Co....... | ....................... | Los Angeles. |
| Paraut, V........... | Sheep raiser........ | ....................... | Los Angeles Co........ | Los Angeles. |
| Parcels, H S........ | Farmer............. | Los Angeles Co....... | nr Los Angeles........ | Los Angeles. |
| Paredas, G.......... | Cook................ | Los Angeles........... | Los Angeles........... | Los Angeles. |
| Paroz, F............. | Laborer............. | ....................... | Los Angeles Co........ | Los Angeles. |
| Parhm, L............ | Farmer............. | nr Los Nietos.......... | Los Nietos ........... | Los Nietos. |
| Park, C T........... | Merchant .......... | Los Angeles........... | Los Angeles Co........ | Los Angeles. |
| Parker, R........... | Farmer............. | nr Los Angeles........ | Los Angeles Co........ | Los Angeles. |
| Parker, J B......... | Farmer............. | Anaheim .............. | Los Angeles Co ...... | Anaheim. |
| Parkhurst, J........ | Laborer............ | Los Angeles Co....... | Silver Precinct........ | Downey. |
| Parker, S ........... | Machinist.......... | Los Angeles........... | Los Angeles Co........ | Los Angeles. |
| Park, E D........... | Merchant .......... | Los Angeles........... | Los Angeles Co........ | Los Angeles. |
| Parker, L........... | Farmer............. | Los Angeles Co....... | nr Anaheim........... | Anaheim. |
| Parker, W.......... | Farmer............. | Los Angeles Co....... | nr El Monte........... | El Monte. |
| Parker, S ........... | Physician........... | Wilmington............ | Los Angeles Co........ | Wilmington. |
| Parker, John K..... | Photographer ..... | Los Angeles........... | Los Angeles........... | Los Angeles. |
| Parker, Geo W..... | Jeweler............. | Los Angeles........... | Los Angeles........... | Los Angeles. |
| Parker, Benj C.... | Capitalist........... | Los Angeles........... | Los Angeles........... | Los Angeles. |
| Parker, W M....... | Farmer............. | Los Angeles Co....... | nr Anaheim........... | Anaheim. |
| Parker, W.......... | Farmer............. | nr Los Nietos.......... | Los Nietos............ | Los Nietos. |

# Richland Nursery,

D. C. HAYWARD, - - - Proprietor.

### ORANGE, LOS ANGELES CO., CAL.

## Grafted ORANGE AND LEMON TREES

### A SPECIALTY.

## All kinds of Temperate Climate Fruit Trees,

### CYPRESS, GUM,

## And Ornamental Tree Stock of Every Variety.

**All Kinds of Flowering Shrubs,**

AS WELL AS EVERYTHING APPERTAINING TO THE STOCK OF
A FIRST-CLASS NURSERY.

DIRECTORY OF LOS ANGELES COUNTY. 405

| Name. | Occupation. | Place of Business. | Residence. | Town or P. O. |
|---|---|---|---|---|
| Parker, W E | Farmer | nr El Monte | Los Angeles Co | El Monte. |
| Parker, J Y | Farmer | Los Angeles Co | Los Nietos | Los Nietos. |
| Parker, W H | Farmer | nr El Monte | Los Angeles Co | El Monte. |
| Parker, C E | Carpenter | Wilmington | Los Angeles Co | Wilmington. |
| Park, W B | Butcher | El Monte | Los Angeles Co | El Monte. |
| Parker, J | Farmer | nr Downey | Silver Precinct | Downey. |
| Park, Mrs M E | Milliner | Main st | Los Angeles | Los Angeles. |
| Parker, Miss E | Dress maker | Centre st | Anaheim | Anaheim. |
| Parker, M F | Real estate | Orange | Los Angeles Co | Orange. |
| Parker, Mrs F A | School teacher | Spring st | Aliso st | Los Angeles. |
| Parker, O W | Music teacher | 66 Spring st | 66 Spring st | Los Angeles. |
| Parker, G R | Miller | Aliso Mills | Aliso st | Los Angeles. |
| Parker, — | Farmer | San Bernardino Road | 2½ m E Spadra | Spadra. |
| Parrish, E C | Farmer | nr El Monte | Los Angeles Co | El Monte. |
| Parra, R | Vaquero | | Los Angeles Co | San Juan. |
| Parra, Jr, M | Farmer | nr San Juan | Los Angeles Co | San Juan. |
| Parsons, H F | Carpenter | Los Angeles | Los Angeles Co | Los Angeles. |
| Parson, Howard | Carpenter | Wilmington | Wilmington | Wilmington. |
| Parson, T | Fisherman | Point San Pedro | Point San Pedro | Wilmington. |
| Partridge, E | Merchant | Los Angeles | Los Angeles | Los Angeles. |
| Passons, O P | Farmer | nr Los Nietos | Los Nietos | Los Nietos. |
| Patchell, I | Carpenter | Los Angeles | Los Angeles Co | Los Angeles. |
| Patrick, John | Slater | Los Angeles | Los Angeles | Los Angeles. |
| Patrick, J D | | 60 Spring st | | Los Angeles. |
| Patterson, J | Farmer | Los Angeles Co | nr El Monte | El Monte. |
| Patterson, E J | Cook | San Gabriel | Los Angeles Co | San Gabriel. |
| Patterson, W J | Farmer | nr Anaheim | Los Angeles Co | Anaheim. |
| Patten, B P | Teacher | Los Angeles | Los Angeles Co | Los Angeles. |
| Patterson, R T | Farmer | San Gabriel | Los Angeles Co | San Gabriel. |
| Patterson, C | Laborer | | Los Angeles Co | Los Angeles. |
| Patten, A V | Farmer | Los Angeles Co | nr El Monte | El Monte. |
| Patten, B P | Teacher | Los Angeles Co | Silver Precinct | Downey. |
| Patterson, Mrs P | Dress maker | Los Angeles | Los Angeles | Los Angeles. |
| Patterson, W J | Sheep raiser | | Westminster Col | Westminster. |
| Patton, C H | Car oiler | S P R R Co | Anaheim | Anaheim. |
| Patterson, W T | Merchant | San Gabriel Valley | 9 m N E San Gabriel | San Gabriel. |
| Paty, J R | Farmer | | Los Angeles Co | Santa Ana. |
| Paul, J | Miner | | Los Angeles Co | Wilmington. |
| Pauley, J | Laborer | Los Angeles Co | Old Mission | El Monte. |
| Paulsell, Newton | Farmer | Los Angeles Co | Silver Precinct | Downey. |
| Payne, H | Blacksmith | Anaheim | Los Angeles Co | Anaheim. |
| Payne, H T | Painter | Los Angeles | Los Angeles | Los Angeles. |
| Payne, D R | Teamster | Los Angeles Co | | Los Angeles. |
| Paynter, J W | Farmer | nr Los Angeles | Los Angeles Co | Los Angeles. |
| Paynter, Reece | Printer | Los Angeles | Los Angeles | Los Angeles. |
| Peacock, J C | Printer | Anaheim | Los Angeles Co | Anaheim. |
| Peacock, James C | Painter | Los Angeles | Los Angeles | Los Angeles. |
| Pearson, Miss Alice | Hair dresser | | 1st st | Los Angeles. |
| Pearson, P | Cook | Los Angeles | Los Angeles Co | Los Angeles. |
| Pearce, J B | Farmer | nr Los Nietos | Los Nietos | Los Nietos. |
| Peccaroni, J | Carpenter | El Monte | Los Angeles Co | El Monte. |
| Peck, E S | Farmer | Los Angeles Co | Silver Precinct | Downey. |
| Peck, Geo H | Co school supt | El Monte Valley | 1 m E Lexington | El Monte. |
| Peck, A M | Farmer | San Pedro Ranch | 1½ m S W Compton | Compton. |
| Peck, C A | Clerk | Los Angeles | Los Angeles | Los Angeles. |
| Peel, Mrs A R | Bdg house | 60 Spring st | 60 Spring st | Los Angeles. |
| Peel, B L | Merchant | Los Angeles | Los Angeles Co | Los Angeles. |
| Pegg, L | Painter | Los Angeles | Los Angeles Co | Los Angeles. |
| Pelfer, — | Farmer | San Fernando Miss'n | 2 m W San Fernando | San Fernando. |
| Pellegrin, P | Watch maker | Centre st | Anaheim | Anaheim. |
| Pellefigue, Peter | Butcher | Los Angeles | Los Angeles | Los Angeles. |
| Pena, Antonio | Laborer | Los Angeles Co | | Los Angeles. |
| Pena, J J | Laborer | Los Angeles Co | La Ballona | Los Angeles. |
| Pena, M | Miner | Los Angeles Co | | Los Angeles. |

| Name. | Occupation. | Place of Business. | Residence. | Town or P. O. |
|---|---|---|---|---|
| Pena, J............. | Boot maker........ | Los Angeles........... | Los Angeles......... | Los Angeles. |
| Pena, F.............. | Laborer.............. | ........................ | Los Angeles Co...... | Los Angeles. |
| Pender, S........... | Laborer.............. | Los Angeles Co....... | La Ballona............ | Los Angeles. |
| Pendleton, W B.... | Farmer............... | Los Angeles Co....... | Silver Precinct....... | Downey. |
| Pendleton, W H... | Farmer............... | Los Angeles Co....... | Silver Precinct....... | Downey. |
| Pendleton, A T ... | Farmer............... | Los Angeles Co....... | Silver Precinct....... | Downey. |
| Pendleton, W H... | Farmer............... | Los Angeles Co....... | Silver Precinct....... | Downey. |
| Penfold, Peter..... | Farmer............... | El Monte Valley...... | 3 m S Lexington...... | El Monte. |
| Penfold, John..... | Farmer............... | El Monte Valley...... | 3 m S Lexington ..... | El Monte. |
| Penfold, S ......... | Farmer ,............. | El Monte Valley...... | 1½ m S Lexington.... | El Monte. |
| Penland, J.......... | Farmer ,............. | Los Angeles Co....... | ............................ | Los Angeles. |
| Pennoyer, Edwin M | Confectioner....... | Los Angeles........... | Los Angeles.......... | Los Angeles. |
| Penpraise, P ....... | Miner.................. | ,......,................. | Los Angeles Co...... | Los Angeles. |
| Peoples, Mrs E..... | Music teacher...... | Los Angeles........... | Los Angeles.......... | Los Angeles. |
| Peppers, E........... | Teamster............. | ........................ | Los Angeles Co...... | Los Angeles. |
| Perasich & Co, N... | Groceries............. | Los Angeles........... | Los Angeles.......... | Los Angeles. |
| Peralta, Juan Pablo............... | Farmer................ | Los Angeles Co....... | Santa Ana............. | Santa Ana. |
| Peralta, R .......... | Laborer............... | ........................ | Los Angeles Co...... | Santa Ana. |
| Peralta, G .......... | Laborer............... | Los Angeles Co....... | San Gabriel.......... | San Gabriel. |
| Peralta, J A........ | Cook................... | Los Angeles........... | Los Angeles Co...... | Los Angeles. |
| Peralta, E........... | Laborer............... | ........................ | Los Angeles Co...... | Los Angeles. |
| Peralta, R A....... | Laborer............... | Los Angeles Co....... | ............................ | Santa Ana. |
| Peralta, Y........... | Laborer,.............. | Los Angeles Co ...... | ............................ | Los Angeles. |
| Peralta, C........... | Laborer............... | ........................ | Los Angeles Co...... | Los Angeles. |
| Peralta, F .......... | Laborer .............. | ........................ | Los Angeles Co...... | Santa Ana. |
| Perdew, W ......... | Farmer............... | nr El Monte.......... | Los Angeles Co...... | El Monte. |
| Perez, F.............. | Laborer............... | Los Angeles Co ...... | ............................ | San Gabriel. |
| Perez, P A.......... | Laborer............... | Los Angeles Co ...... | ............................ | Los Angeles. |
| Perella, R........... | Farmer ,............. | nr Los Angeles....... | Los Angeles Co...... | Los Angeles. |
| Perez, J.............. | Farmer ,............. | nr Los Angeles,....... | Los Angeles Co...... | Los Angeles. |
| Perez, J I........... | Laborer............... | Los Angeles Co ...... | San Gabriel Mission.. | San Gabriel. |
| Pores, A.............. | Laborer............... | Los Angeles Co ...... | San Jose............... | Spadra. |
| Perez, Manuel..... | Laborer............... | Los Angeles Co ...... | San Pedro............ | Wilmington. |
| Peres, J los S...... | Vaquero.............. | Los Angeles Co ...... | ............................ | San Gabriel. |
| Perez, Marino...... | Laborer............... | ........................ | Los Angeles Co ...... | Los Angeles. |
| Peroz, O............. | Laborer............... | ........................ | Los Angeles Co ...... | San Gabriel. |
| Perez, dual dei Esp Santo............... | Laborer............... | Los Angeles Co ...... | Old Mission.......... | El Monte. |
| Perez, A............. | Farmer............... | Los Angeles Co ...... | nr Los Angeles,...... | Los Angeles. |
| Perez, J A.......... | Ranchero............ | Los Angeles Co ...... | San Jose............... | Spadra. |
| Perez, Y............. | Vaquero.............. | ........................ | Los Angeles Co...... | Los Angeles. |
| Perez, J J........... | Laborer............... | Los Angeles Co ...... | ............................ | San Gabriel. |
| Perez, T............. | Laborer............... | Los Angeles Co ...... | San Jose............... | Spadra. |
| Perhall, Uriah .... | Farmer ............... | ........................ | Westminster Col..... | Westminster. |
| Perkins, James W. | Farmer .............. | Los Angeles Co ...... | Los Nietos........... | Los Nietos. |
| Perkins, F........... | Machinist............ | Los Angeles........... | Los Angeles Co ...... | Los Angeles. |
| Perosich, Nicholas. | Merchant ........... | Los Angeles........... | Los Angeles.......... | Los Angeles. |
| Perpich, A .......... | Restaurant.......... | Los Angeles........... | Los Angeles.......... | Los Angeles. |
| Perry, Richard..... | Saloon................ | Spadra ................ | 30 m E Los Angeles.. | Spadra. |
| Perry, M ............ | Bookbinder ........ | Downey Block........ | Los Angeles.......... | Los Angeles. |
| Perry, Woodworth & Co............... | Lumber dealers... | 76 Commercial st .... | ............................ | Los Angeles. |
| Perry, W H ........ | Lumber dealers... | 76 Commercial st .... | Sansevain st.......... | Los Angeles. |
| Perry, M ............ | Wharf hand........ | S P R R Co............ | Wilmington.......... | Wilmington. |
| Perry, M W........ | Printer ............... | Los Angeles........... | Los Angeles Co...... | Los Angeles. |
| Perry, W H......... | Furniture ........... | Los Nietos............ | Los Nietos........... | Los Nietos. |
| Perry, R C.......... | Farmer............... | Los Angeles Co ...... | nr El Monte.......... | El Monte. |
| Persing, W G....... | Carpenter........... | Silver Precinct ....... | Silver Precinct....... | Downey. |
| Pesche & Merz..... | Groceries............. | Los Angeles........... | Los Angeles.......... | Los Angeles. |
| Peschke, F W...... | Clerk.................. | Los Angeles........... | Los Angeles.......... | Los Angeles. |
| Peter, F L.......... | Teamster............. | Los Angeles Co....... | ............................ | Los Angeles. |
| Peters, James ..... | Farmer............... | Los Angeles Co....... | Westminster Col..... | Westminster. |
| Peters, Fritz ....... | Locksmith .......... | Los Angeles........... | Los Angeles.......... | Los Angeles. |

# DIRECTORY OF LOS ANGELES COUNTY. 407

| NAME. | OCCUPATION. | PLACE OF BUSINESS. | RESIDENCE. | TOWN OR P. O. |
|---|---|---|---|---|
| Peters, Frank E | Blacksmith | Los Angeles Co | Silver Precinct | Downey. |
| Peterson, C | Farmer | San Pedro Ranch | 1½ m S Compton | Compton. |
| Peterson, P | Wharf hand | S P R R Co | Wilmington | Wilmington. |
| Peters, James | Miner | Los Angeles Co | Anaheim | Anaheim. |
| Peterson, W | Laborer | Anaheim | Los Angeles Co | Anaheim. |
| Peterson, J W | | | Silver Precinct | Downey. |
| Peters, M A | Farmer | Los Angeles Co | nr Los Nietos | Los Nietos. |
| Petit, Wm H | Druggist | Los Angeles | Los Angeles | Los Angeles. |
| Petty, Wm H | Laborer | Los Angeles Co | | Wilmington. |
| Petty, N | Farmer | Los Angeles Co | nr Los Angeles | Los Angeles. |
| Peyregue, B | Stock raiser | | Los Angeles Co | San Fernando. |
| Peze, Adolphe | Merchant | Los Angeles | Los Angeles | Los Angeles. |
| Pfeiffenber & Shauer | Dry goods, etc | Los Angeles st | Los Angeles | Los Angeles. |
| Pfeiffenberger, Louis | Tailor | Los Angeles | Los Angeles | Los Angeles. |
| Pfeiffenberger, Franz | Laborer | Los Angeles Co | | Los Angeles. |
| Phelps, E M | Laborer | nr Wilmington | Los Angeles Co | Wilmington. |
| Phelps, J | Farmer | nr El Monte | Los Angeles Co | El Monte. |
| Phelps, E C | Clerk | Los Angeles | Los Angeles Co | Los Angeles. |
| Phelps, G | Miner | | Los Angeles Co | Los Angeles. |
| Phelps, E A | Civil engineer | Los Angeles | Los Angeles Co | Los Angeles. |
| Phelan, Thos | Farmer | Los Angeles Co | Los Nietos | Los Nietos. |
| Phelps, E M | Clerk | S P R R Co | Spadra | Spadra. |
| Phillips, J | Laborer | nr Wilmington | Los Angeles Co | Wilmington. |
| Philippi, J | Liquor dealer | Los Angeles | Los Angeles Co | Los Angeles. |
| Philbin, J | Vintner | nr Los Angeles | Los Angeles Co | Los Angeles. |
| Phillippay, W J | Laborer | Los Angeles Co | | Los Angeles. |
| Phillips, A R | Laborer | Los Angeles Co | | Los Angeles. |
| Phillips, M L | Book keeper | Los Angeles | Los Angeles Co | Los Angeles. |
| Phillips, J | Laborer | | Los Angeles Co | Los Angeles. |
| Phillips, S | Clerk | Los Angeles | Los Angeles Co | Los Angeles. |
| Philip, P | Real estate | 43 Main st | | Los Angeles. |
| Phillips, Peter | Apiarian | Little Tejunga Can'n | 7 m N E San Fern'do | San Fernando. |
| Phillips, A | Farmer | San Gabriel Valley | ½ m N E San Gabriel | San Gabriel. |
| Phillips, Lewis | Farmer & stock | Spadra | 30 m E Los Angeles | Spadra. |
| Phillips, Saml R | Stock raiser | Los Angeles Co | Los Nietos | Los Nietos. |
| Phillips, Hugh | Farmer | Los Angeles Co | | Los Angeles. |
| Picque, C V | Attorney | Los Angeles | Los Angeles Co | Los Angeles. |
| Pico, Andreas | Ranchero | San Fernando Mis'n | 1½ m W San Fer'do | San Fernando. |
| Pico, Romelo | Ranchero | San Fernando Mis'n | 1½ m W San Fer'do | San Fernando. |
| Pico, Francisco | Ranchero | Los Angeles Co | | Los Angeles. |
| Pico, P | Ranchero | nr Los Angeles | Los Angeles Co | Los Angeles. |
| Piepenburg, August | Musician | Los Angeles | Los Angeles | Los Angeles. |
| Piercy, Saml W | Clerk | Los Angeles | Los Angeles | Los Angeles. |
| Pierce, J | Farmer | nr Los Angeles | Los Angeles Co | Los Angeles. |
| Pierce, J B | Collector | Los Angeles Co | Anaheim | Anaheim. |
| Pike, G H | Ship joiner | Los Angeles Co | | Los Angeles. |
| Pilkington, Wm Henry | Farmer | Los Angeles Co | | Los Angeles. |
| Pina, F | Farmer | Los Angeles Co | Soledad | San Fernando. |
| Pinkham, Chas | Hostler | Los Angeles Co | Anaheim | Anaheim. |
| Pinney, E | Carpenter | Santa Ana | Los Angeles Co | Santa Ana. |
| Pinte, Simon | Tailor | Anaheim | Anaheim | Anaheim. |
| Piper, J N | Farmer | | Halfway House | Compton. |
| Piper, C | Clerk | Los Angeles | Los Angeles Co | Los Angeles. |
| Pitman, R J | Farmer | nr Los Angeles | Los Angeles Co | Los Angeles. |
| Pitscke, E | Farmer | nr Los Angeles | Los Angeles Co | Los Angeles. |
| Pitt, R D | Real estate | Downey Block | Los Angeles | Los Angeles. |
| Pitts, D C | Farmer | San Juan | San Juan | Capistrano. |
| Pittman, E | Cooper | Los Angeles Co | Silver Precinct | Downey. |
| Pitts, J M | Farmer | nr San Gabriel | Los Angeles Co | San Gabriel. |
| Plassan, J | Laborer | | Los Angeles Co | Los Angeles. |

## SPORTING MATERIALS.

### HENRY SLOTTERBEK,

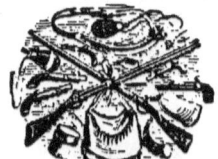

### GUNSMITH,

Dealer in

### GUNS, RIFLES, PISTOLS.

Guns, Rifles and Pistols made to order, the shooting of which cannot be excelled by those of any other make in the world.

Repairing of all kinds of Firearms done with neatness and dispatch, and work guaranteed in all cases.

No. 1 COMMERCIAL ST., near Main,
LOS ANGELES, CAL.

---

### JOHN LIEVER,
11 Commercial St.   Los Angeles.

### Guns, Pistols & Rifles,

Importer of every description of

### Firearms and Gun Materials,

Colt's, Smith & Wesson's, Sharp's, Henry's and Spencer's

### Rifles and Pistols.

Dixon's Powder Flasks, Shot Pouches.
Wostenholm's Pocket Cutlery,

Eley's Caps, Wads, and all kinds of Breech-Loading Ammunition, Fishing Tackle, Etc.

New work made to order. Repairing done in the best manner, and warranted to give satisfaction.

---

### SPURGEON BROS.

—DEALERS IN—

### DRY GOODS,

CLOTHING, BOOTS & SHOES.

### Groceries, Hardware,

Farming Implements, Etc..

CORNER FOURTH AND SYCAMORE STS.

**SANTA ANA, LOS ANGELES CO.**

CAL.

---

### Westminster Colony,

**10,000 ACRES,**

Between ANAHEIM and the OCEAN.

**BOUNDARIES ENLARGED.**

A Home for Presbyterians and others in Southern California. Church, Schools, and Co-operative Store.

**ARTESIAN WELL ON EVERY FARM.**

Unimproved Land, $18 to $30 Per Acre.

Farms, $25 to $125 Per Acre.

Address, Rev ROBERT STRONG, Supt.

WESTMINSTER, LOS ANGELES CO., CAL.

## DIRECTORY OF LOS ANGELES COUNTY. 409

| Name. | Occupation. | Place of Business. | Residence. | Town or P. O. |
|---|---|---|---|---|
| Plassant, C | Carpenter | Los Angeles Co | | Los Angeles. |
| Plato, D & G D | Gen merchants | Los Angeles st | | Anaheim. |
| Platt, Chas T | Farmer | Los Angeles Co | San Joaquin | Santa Ana. |
| Platt, Joseph C | Saloon | Los Angeles | Los Angeles | Los Angeles. |
| Pleasants, J E | Stock raiser | nr Los Nietos | Los Nietos | Los Nietos. |
| Poag, R | Pastor | Presb'n Church | Wilmington | Wilmington. |
| Poggi, R | Restaurant | Wilmington | Wilmington | Wilmington. |
| Polard, J | Wharf hand | S P R R Co | Wilmington | Wilmington. |
| Polaski, Saml | Clerk | Los Angeles | Los Angeles | Los Angeles. |
| Polhemus, E | Merchant | Anaheim | Los Angeles Co | Anaheim. |
| Polhemus, A A | Machinist | Los Angeles | Los Angeles | Los Angeles. |
| Polhemus, H D | Packet agent | Anaheim | Anaheim | Anaheim. |
| Polhamus, A A | Captain | S P R R Co | Wilmington | Wilmington. |
| Pollorena, Y | Laborer | | Los Nietos | Los Nietos. |
| Pollard, L C | Farmer | Los Angeles Co | Silver Precinct | Downey. |
| Pollard, R J | Wheelwright | Los Angeles Co | Silver Precinct | Downey. |
| Pollorena, G | Farmer | nr Los Nietos | Los Nietos | Los Nietos. |
| Polloreno, F | Farmer | nr Los Nietos | Los Nietos | Los Nietos. |
| Pollard, E | Farmer | San Gabriel Valley | San Gabriel | San Gabriel. |
| Pollard, Thos | Farmer | San Gabriel Valley | San Gabriel | San Gabriel. |
| Pollard, R J | Farmer | Azusa Ranch | 2 m S E Azusa | Azusa. |
| Pollard, L C | Farmer | Azusa | 22 m E Los Angeles | Azusa. |
| Polmer, James | Laborer | Los Angeles Co | | Los Angeles. |
| Polomares, J T | Ranchero | Los Angeles Co | San Jose | Spadro. |
| Polaski & Goodwin | Gen merchandise | Los Angeles | Los Angeles | Los Angeles. |
| Pony, Peter | Wagon maker | Los Angeles | Los Angeles | Los Angeles. |
| Ponyfourcat & Save | Hotel | Los Angeles | Los Angeles | Los Angeles. |
| Pool, Joseph | Carpenter | Los Angeles Co | | Los Angeles. |
| Poor, W F | Farmer | Westminster | Los Angeles Co | Westminster. |
| Poor, W Frank | Surveyor | Los Angeles Co | Westminster Col | Westminster. |
| Porter, W | Sailor | Wilmington | Los Angeles Co | Wilmington. |
| Portugal, A | Merchant | Los Angeles | Los Angeles Co | Los Angeles. |
| Portilla, I | Ranchero | nr Los Angeles | Los Angeles Co | Los Angeles. |
| Porter, W W | Miner | Los Angeles Co | | Los Angeles. |
| Porter, B F | Farmer | Anaheim | Los Angeles Co | Anaheim. |
| Porter, W | Farmer | nr Los Angeles | Los Angeles Co | Los Angeles. |
| Porter, Miss M S | Teacher | Los Angeles Co | | Los Angeles. |
| Porter, Fredrick | Farmer | | Westminster Col | Westminster. |
| Porter, F H | Farmer | | Westminster Col | Westminster. |
| Porter, A O | Capitalist | Indiana Colony | 5 m N E Los Angeles | Pasadena. |
| Porter, Calvin L | Farmer | | Florence | Los Angeles. |
| Potts, J | Laborer | | Los Angeles Co | Wilmington. |
| Potter, William | Laborer | | Los Angeles Co | Los Angeles. |
| Potter, W | Farmer | nr Anaheim | Los Angeles Co | Anaheim. |
| Potter, O M | Merchant | Los Angeles | Los Angeles | Los Angeles. |
| Potts, James Wm E | Farmer | Los Angeles Co | | Los Angeles. |
| Potts, J W | Merchant | Los Angeles | Los Angeles | Los Angeles. |
| Potts, A W | Clerk | Los Angeles | Los Angeles | Los Angeles. |
| Potter, W K | Miner | | Los Angeles Co | Los Angeles. |
| Potts, W H | Farmer | Los Angeles Co | nr Santa Ana | Santa Ana. |
| Potts, A W | Clerk | | cor Fort and 5th sts | Los Angeles. |
| Potter, Wm | Miner | San Gabriel Canyon | 14 m N Azusa | Azusa. |
| Potter, J C | Butcher | Azusa | 2 m N Azusa | Azusa. |
| Potts, J H | Farmer | Azusa Ranch | 3 m N E Azusa | Azusa. |
| Potuskey, — | Saloon | Comm'al & Main sts | | Los Angeles. |
| Potusky, Wm J | Bar keeper | Los Angeles | Los Angeles | Los Angeles. |
| Pouet, Mrs J | Milliner | Los Angeles | Los Angeles | Los Angeles. |
| Pouet, Victor | Undertaker | 66 Main st | New High st | Los Angeles. |
| Powell, J F | Farmer | Los Angeles Co | Soledad | San Fernando. |
| Powell, M A | Miner | Los Angeles Co | Soledad | San Fernando. |
| Powell, Wm | Marble cutter | Los Angeles | Los Angeles | Los Angeles. |
| Powell, Joseph L | Farmer | | San Jose | Spadra. |
| Prager, S | Merchant | Los Angeles | Los Angeles | Los Angeles. |
| Prager, Chas | Furnishing goods | Commercial st | | Los Angeles. |

| NAME. | OCCUPATION. | PLACE OF BUSINESS. | RESIDENCE. | TOWN OR P. O. |
|---|---|---|---|---|
| Pratt, A | Carpenter | Anaheim | Los Angeles Co | Anaheim. |
| Prator, J B | Miner | | Los Nietos | Los Nietos. |
| Pratt, L | Sheep herder | Los Angeles Co | | Los Angeles. |
| **Pratt, A W** | Watch maker | 39 Spring st | | Los Angeles. |
| **Pray, John M** | Blacksmith | Los Angeles | Los Angeles | Los Angeles. |
| Preciado, J | Farmer | El Monte | Los Angeles Co | El Monte. |
| Preciado, E | Laborer | | Los Angeles Co | Los Angeles. |
| Preciado, A | Laborer | nr San Gabriel | Los Angeles Co | San Gabriel. |
| Preciada, J M | Laborer | Los Angeles Co | | Los Angeles. |
| **Preston, C** | Surveyor | Los Angeles | Los Angeles | Los Angeles. |
| Priest, R | Laborer | nr El Monte | Los Angeles Co | El Monte. |
| Preston, J | Plumber | San Gabriel | Los Angeles Co | San Gabriel. |
| Presley, J M | Farmer | nr San Gabriel | Los Angeles Co | San Gabriel. |
| Preston, H | Farmer | Los Angeles Co | nr Los Angeles | Los Angeles. |
| **Preston, J C** | Farmer | Azusa Ranch | 2¼ m N E Azusa | Azusa. |
| **Preuss, E A, Jr** | Druggist | Los Angeles | Los Angeles Co | Los Angeles. |
| Preuss, E A, Jr | Clerk | 72 Main st | Spring st | Los Angeles. |
| Priciado, G | Laborer | Los Angeles Co | San Jose | Spadra. |
| Price, W | Laborer | Los Angeles Co | | Los Angeles. |
| Price, H | Farmer | Los Angeles Co | nr Los Angeles | Los Angeles. |
| Price, W W | Carpenter | Los Angeles Co | | Wilmington. |
| Price, J D | Farmer | El Monte | Los Angeles Co | El Monte. |
| **Price, L L** | Farmer | | Los Angeles Co | Los Angeles. |
| Price, W N | Farmer | Los Angeles Co | San Joaquin | Santa Ana. |
| Price, N | Cook | Los Angeles | Los Angeles Co | Los Angeles. |
| **Price, N H** | Farmer | Los Angeles Co | Silver Precinct | Downey. |
| Pridham, W | Exp agent | Main & Market sts | Main st | Los Angeles. |
| Pridham, G | Clerk | Los Angeles | Los Angeles Co | Los Angeles. |
| Pridham, Geo | | Los Angeles Co | | Los Angeles. |
| Priess, J F | Farmer | nr Los Angeles | Los Angeles Co | Los Angeles. |
| **Prindle, J W** | Farmer | Los Angeles Co | Silver Precinct | Downey. |
| Prince, Frederick C | Agent | Los Angeles | Los Angeles | Los Angeles. |
| Prior, Robert | Laborer | | Anaheim | Anaheim. |
| Procta, A A | Blacksmith | San Pedro Ranch | ½ m S E Compton | Compton. |
| Pronty, J | Farmer | Los Angeles Co | nr Los Angeles | Los Angeles. |
| Prost, Pierre J | Ship owner | Anaheim | Anaheim | Anaheim. |
| Proulx, C | Teamster | | Los Angeles Co | Los Angeles. |
| **Proudtey, J** | Sheep raiser | San Bernardino Road | 9 m E Lexington | El Monte. |
| **Pryor, P** | Ranchero | nr San Juan | Los Angeles Co | Capistrano. |
| Pryor, N | Vaquero | | Los Angeles Co | Los Angeles. |
| Puissegur & Bro | Bakers | Los Angeles | Los Angeles | Los Angeles. |
| **Pulaski, L** | Merchant | Los Angeles | Los Angeles | Los Angeles. |
| Pullen, E A | Painter | Anaheim | Los Angeles Co | Anaheim. |
| Pullman, J B | Miner | | Los Angeles Co | El Monte. |
| Pullman, John | Blacksmith | Los Angeles | Los Angeles Co | Los Angeles. |
| Purcell, T | Farmer | Anaheim | Los Angeles Co | Anaheim. |
| Purder, Jose | Laborer | | La Puente | El Monte. |
| Purdey, V K | Farmer | Azusa | 2 m S E Azusa | Azusa. |
| **Putman, H** | Farmer | nr Santa Ana | Los Angeles Co | Santa Ana. |
| Putman, F R | Farmer | nr Los Angeles | Los Angeles Co | Los Angeles. |
| Putnam, C C | Printer | Los Angeles | Los Angeles Co | Los Angeles. |
| Putnam, T B | Carpenter | Los Angeles | Los Angeles Co | Los Angeles. |
| Putney, A E | Machinist | Los Angeles Co | | San Gabriel. |
| Putnam, Henry E | Clerk | Los Angeles | Los Angeles Co | Los Angeles. |
| Putnam, John D | Teamster | Los Angeles Co | Anaheim | Anaheim. |
| **Pyeatt, A Mc C** | Farmer | nr Downey | Silver Precinct | Downey. |
| Queen, J P | Clerk | Los Angeles | Los Angeles Co | Los Angeles. |
| Quellien, G | Shoe maker | Los Angeles | Los Angeles Co | Los Angeles. |
| Quiros, Jose | Farmer | Los Angeles | Los Angeles Twp | Los Angeles. |
| Quill, J | Farmer | Los Angeles Co | Silver Precinct | Downey. |
| Quimby, H | Farmer | | Los Angeles Co | Los Angeles. |
| Quimby, F L | Farmer | nr Los Angeles | Los Angeles Co | Los Angeles. |
| Quinn, R | Shoe maker | Los Angeles | Los Angeles Co | Los Angeles. |
| **Quintana, J** | Farmer | Los Angeles Co | San Jose | Spadra. |

DIRECTORY OF LOS ANGELES COUNTY. 411

| Name. | Occupation. | Place of Business. | Residence. | Town or P. O. |
|---|---|---|---|---|
| Quinn, M F............ | Carpenter ......... | El Monte............... | Los Angeles Co....... | El Monte. |
| Quintano, J P....... | Laborer............. | nr Los Angeles........ | Los Angeles Co....... | Los Angeles. |
| Quintana, Manuel.. | Laborer............. | Los Angeles............ | ........................... | Los Angeles. |
| Quintana, A.......... | Farmer............. | Los Angeles Co....... | Los Angeles Twp.... | Los Angeles. |
| Quinteras, Jose D... | Laborer............. | Los Angeles Co....... | ........................... | Los Angeles. |
| Quinn, Richard...... | Laborer............. | Los Angeles Co....... | ........................... | Los Angeles. |
| Quinn, M F........... | Livery stable...... | Lexington............. | 12 m E Los Angeles. | El Monte. |
| Quinn, P J............ | Grange house...... | New Los Angeles st.. | nr 1st st................. | Los Angeles. |
| Quijada, R............ | Laborer............. | ........................... | Los Angeles Co...... | Los Angeles. |
| Quirollo, N............ | Shoe maker........ | Los Angeles............ | Los Angeles Co...... | Los Angeles. |
| Quirollo, B............ | Merchant ........... | Los Angeles............ | Los Angeles Co...... | Los Angeles. |
| Quizada, D............ | Shoe maker........ | Los Angeles............ | Los Angeles Co...... | Los Angeles. |
| Quyade, F............. | Farmer............. | Los Angeles Co....... | nr Los Angeles....... | Los Angeles. |
| Raab, David......... | Farmer............. | San Felipe Ranch.... | 5 m N E Los Angeles | Los Angeles. |
| Racine, A J........... | Merchant........... | Los Angeles............ | Los Angeles Co ..... | Los Angeles. |
| Racouillat, E L...... | Farmer............. | Los Angeles Co....... | nr Los Angeles....... | Los Angeles. |
| Radelfinger, S....... | Baker................ | Los Angeles............ | Los Angeles Co...... | Los Angeles. |
| Radford, E B........ | Farmer ............. | ........................... | Los Angeles Co...... | Los Angeles. |
| Radford, T............ | Farmer............. | Los Angeles Co....... | nr Halfway House... | Compton. |
| Radon, A.............. | Genl merchandise | La Punte Mill......... | 3 m S E Lexington... | El Monte. |
| Ragland, A S........ | Farmer............. | Los Angeles Co....... | Silver Precinct........ | Downey. |
| Ragsdale, R A ...... | Farmer............. | Los Angeles Co....... | Silver Precinct........ | Downey. |
| Raine, J B............. | Farmer ............. | nr Anaheim........... | Los Angeles Co....... | Anaheim. |
| Rains, E H ........... | Farmer............. | nr El Monte........... | Los Angeles Co....... | El Monte. |
| Rallales, J ............ | Vaquero............ | ........................... | Los Angeles Co...... | Los Angeles. |
| Rallales, J D ........ | Vaquero............ | ........................... | Los Angeles Co...... | Los Angeles. |
| Ralph, A............... | Mason............... | Los Angeles........... | Los Angeles Co...... | Los Angeles. |
| Ralphs, Richard .... | Brick mason....... | ........................... | Anaheim............... | Anaheim. |
| Ramage, WmJames | Teamster ........... | ........................... | Anaheim............... | Anaheim. |
| Ramirez, John R... | Printer.............. | Los Angeles........... | Los Angeles Co...... | Los Angeles. |
| Ramirez, A .......... | Farmer.............. | Los Angeles Co....... | nr Los Nietos......... | Los Nietos. |
| Ramirez, C........... | Farmer.............. | Los Angeles Co....... | nr Los Nietos......... | Los Nietos. |
| Ramirez, F B ....... | Editor............... | Los Angeles........... | Los Angeles Co...... | Los Angeles. |
| Ramirez, N........... | Laborer............. | Los Angeles Co....... | Mission Viejo......... | Los Angeles. |
| Ramitas, P........... | Farmer.............. | Los Angeles Co....... | Old Mission .......... | El Monte. |
| Ramirez, C........... | Barber .............. | Los Angeles........... | Los Angeles Co...... | Los Angeles. |
| Ramirez, L........... | Tinner .............. | Los Angeles........... | Los Angeles Co...... | Los Angeles. |
| Ramirez, R........... | Laborer............. | ........................... | Los Angeles Co...... | Los Angeles. |
| Ramirez, A M ...... | Tinner .............. | Los Angeles........... | Los Angeles Co...... | Los Angeles. |
| Ramirez, J M ....... | Farmer.............. | nr Los Nietos......... | Los Angeles Co...... | Los Nietos. |
| Ramirez, J........... | Laborer............. | Los Angeles Co....... | Old Mission........... | El Monte. |
| Ramirez, J C........ | Farmer.............. | Los Angeles Co....... | nr Los Nietos ........ | Los Nietos. |
| Ramos, P............. | Laborer ............. | Los Angeles Co....... | Old Mission .......... | El Monte. |
| Ramos, T............. | Laborer ............. | ........................... | Los Angeles Co...... | Capistrano. |
| Randall, S ........... | Carpenter........... | Anaheim .............. | Los Angeles Co...... | Anaheim. |
| Randall, L........... | Merchant........... | Los Angeles........... | Los Angeles Co...... | Los Angeles. |
| Randolph, J......... | Mechanic ........... | Los Angeles........... | Los Angeles Co...... | El Monte. |
| Randel, I S.......... | Teamster ........... | Los Angeles Co....... | ........................... | Wilmington. |
| Randell, J ........... | Carpenter........... | ........................... | San Fernando........ | San Fernando. |
| Randall, Josiah..... | Constable ........... | San Fernando ........ | San Fernando........ | San Fernando. |
| Rangel, R ............ | Laborer ............. | Los Angeles Co....... | San Jose............... | Spadra. |
| Rangel, F............. | Farmer.............. | Los Angeles Co....... | nr Los Nietos ........ | Los Nietos. |
| Rangel, J............. | Farmer.............. | Los Angeles Co....... | Old Mission........... | El Monte. |
| Rangel, G............ | Laborer ............. | ........................... | Los Angeles Co...... | Los Nietos. |
| Rankin, J ............ | Cook ................. | Los Angeles........... | Los Angeles Co...... | Los Angeles. |
| Rankin, W O ....... | Farmer.............. | Los Angeles Co....... | Silver Precinct........ | Downey. |
| Rankin, J T......... | Farmer.............. | El Monte.............. | Los Angeles Co...... | El Monte. |
| Ranney, R P........ | Farmer.............. | nr El Monte.......... | Los Angeles Co...... | El Monte. |
| Ranney, R........... | Nurseryman ....... | ........................... | Florence............... | Los Angeles. |
| Ranous, J S ......... | Farmer.............. | Los Angeles Co....... | Silver Precinct ....... | Downey. |
| Raphael, C .......... | Paints & oils....... | Requena st............ | ........................... | Los Angeles. |
| Raphael, H .......... | Painter.............. | Los Angeles........... | Los Angeles Co...... | Los Angeles. |
| Rappold, C.......... | Cooper............... | Los Angeles........... | Los Angeles Co...... | Los Angeles. |
| Rapp, C............... | Laborer ............. | ........................... | Los Angeles Co...... | Los Angeles. |

# CO-OPERATIVE CO.

⁓DEALERS IN⁓

# GENERAL MERCHANDISE,

## HARDWARE,

AGRICULTURAL IMPLEMENTS,

# GROCERIES, PROVISIONS, DRY GOODS

### BOOTS AND SHOES.

Westminster, Los Angeles Co., Cal.

DIRECTORY OF LOS ANGELES COUNTY. 413

| Name. | Occupation. | Place of Business. | Residence. | Town or P. O. |
|---|---|---|---|---|
| Rapp, Wm | Saloon | Main st | Los Angeles | Los Angeles. |
| Rasmussen-Muth, P V | Bee keeper | Los Angeles Co | nr Los Angeles | Los Angeles. |
| Rassmussen, B | Laborer | Los Angeles Co | Los Angeles Co | Anaheim. |
| Rawling, Wm D | Farmer | nr Los Angeles | Los Angeles Co | Los Angeles. |
| Rawson, J | Farmer | Los Angeles Co | Old Mission | El Monte. |
| Rawson, C B | Sheep raiser | nr San Juan | Los Angeles Co | Capistrano. |
| Ray, P H | Botanist | Los Angeles | Los Angeles | Los Angeles. |
| Raynal, Camille | Blacksmith | Los Angeles | Los Angeles | Los Angeles. |
| Rea, Thos | Farmer | Los Angeles Co | Halfway House | Compton. |
| Read, H | Merchant | Los Angeles | Los Angeles Co | Los Angeles. |
| Ready, R U | | | | Los Angeles. |
| Reavis, W S | Teacher | Los Angeles Co | Los Nietos | Los Nietos. |
| Reavis, A H | Teacher | Los Angeles Co | Los Nietos | Los Nietos. |
| Rebbick, G | Farmer | Los Angeles Co | nr Los Angeles | Los Angeles. |
| Rebbeck, B | Blacksmith | Los Angeles | Los Angeles Co | Los Angeles. |
| Rebbeck, H | Farmer | nr Los Angeles | Los Angeles Co | Los Angeles. |
| Reckman, P | Laborer | | Los Angeles Co | Anaheim. |
| Redding, P C | Teamster | | Los Angeles Co | Los Angeles. |
| Redding, J M | Cook | Wilmington | Los Angeles Co | Wilmington. |
| Reddick, John | Farmer | Los Angeles Co | Gallatin | Downey. |
| Redona, J | Silversmith | Los Angeles | Los Angeles Co | Los Angeles. |
| Redona, B | Saddler | Los Angeles | Los Angeles Co | Los Angeles. |
| Redona, F | Vaquero | Los Angeles Co | San Juan | Capistrano. |
| Reed, D A | Teacher | Los Angeles Co | | El Monte. |
| Reed, Asa D | Carpenter | | Los Angeles Co | Los Angeles. |
| Reed, John N | Farmer | Los Angeles Co | Silver Precinct | Downey. |
| Reed, John H | Farmer | Los Angeles Co | nr Anaheim | Anaheim. |
| Reeder, Thos | Miller | Los Angeles | Los Angeles | Los Angeles. |
| Reed, D H | Teacher | Ellis Station | 1 m W Lexington | El Monte. |
| Reed, Mrs John | Ranchero | San Bernardino Road | 7 m E Lexington | El Monte. |
| Reed, R | Farmer | Los Angeles Co | Silver District | Downey. |
| Reed, J | Ranchero | nr El Monte | Los Angeles Co | El Monte. |
| Reed, H T | Merchant | Los Angeles | Los Angeles Co | Los Angeles. |
| Reed, C | Teamster | Los Angeles Co | | Los Angeles. |
| Reed, J E | Teacher | Los Angeles | Los Angeles Co | Los Angeles. |
| Reeder, W | Farmer | Los Angeles Co | nr Santa Ana | Santa Ana. |
| Reese, J E | Policeman | Los Angeles | Los Angeles Co | Los Angeles. |
| Rees, Samuel | Book keeper | Los Angeles | Los Angeles Co | Los Angeles. |
| Reeves, S S | Farmer | Azusa Ranch | 1½ m S W Azusa | Azusa. |
| Reichard, J B | Miner | | Los Angeles Co | San Gabriel. |
| Reihm, H P | Blacksmith | Los Angeles | Los Angeles | Los Angeles. |
| Reina, Guillermo | Laborer | | Mission San Gabriel | San Gabriel. |
| Reinecke & Jones | Barbers | Los Angeles | Los Angeles | Los Angeles. |
| Reinecke, G | Barber | Los Angeles | Los Angeles | Los Angeles. |
| Reiser, — | Brewer | | Anaheim | Anaheim. |
| Reiser, T | Vintner | nr Anaheim | Los Angeles Co | Anaheim. |
| Reinert & Aphold | Coopers | 1st st | | Los Angeles. |
| Remes, C | Physician | Los Angeles | Los Angeles Co | Los Angeles. |
| Remington, J L | Laborer | Los Angeles Co | | Los Angeles. |
| Remler, M | Farmer | nr Los Angeles | Los Angeles Co | Los Angeles. |
| Rendon, A | Barber | Los Angeles | Los Angeles Co | Los Angeles. |
| Renaud, J M | Miner | Los Angeles Co | | Los Angeles. |
| Renaud, P | Laborer | | Los Angeles Co | Los Angeles. |
| Renina, S | Laborer | | Los Angeles Co | Los Angeles. |
| Repetto, A | Stock raiser | | Los Angeles Co | Los Angeles. |
| Repette, J | Merchant | Los Angeles | Los Angeles | Los Angeles. |
| Requena, M | Farmer | Los Angeles Co | nr Los Angeles | Los Angeles. |
| Reser, J | Farmer | Los Angeles Co | La Ballona | La Ballona. |
| Reyburn, J L | Clerk | El Monte | Los Angeles Co | El Monte. |
| Reyes, J Y | Ranchero | Los Angeles Co | La Ballona | Los Angeles. |
| Reyes, L | Laborer | Los Angeles Co | San Jose | Spadra. |
| Reyes, R | Laborer | Los Angeles Co | Old Mission | El Monte. |
| Reyes, J D | Farmer | Los Angeles Co | | Los Angeles. |

| Name. | Occupation. | Place of Business. | Residence. | Town or P. O. |
|---|---|---|---|---|
| Reyes, J | Laborer | | Los Angeles Co | Anaheim. |
| Reyes, P | Farmer | Los Angeles Co | nr Los Angeles | Los Angeles. |
| Reyes, F | Ranchero | Los Angeles Co | Old Mission | El Monte. |
| Reyes, B | Laborer | Los Angeles Co | La Ballona | Los Angeles. |
| Reyes, J | Vaquero | nr Santa Ana | Los Angeles Co | Santa Ana. |
| Reys, A | Ranchero | nr Los Angeles | Los Angeles Co | Los Angeles. |
| Reyer, Manuel | Laborer | Los Angeles Co | | Los Angeles. |
| Reyes, Guadalupe | Farmer | nr Los Angeles | Los Angeles Co | Los Angeles. |
| **Reyes, Francisco** | Farmer | Los Angeles Co | San Jose | Spadra. |
| Reyes, J J | Vaquero | Los Angeles Co | Old Mission | El Monte. |
| Reyes, J A | Farmer | nr Anaheim | Los Angeles Co | Anaheim. |
| Reyes, de la Jose | Laborer | Los Angeles Co | | Los Angeles. |
| **Reynolds, Chas** | Laundryman | Los Angeles | Los Angeles | Los Angeles. |
| Reynolds, J J | Pioneer hack line | 50 Main st | 37 Los Angeles st | Los Angeles. |
| Reynolds, Thos M | Laborer | Los Angeles Co | | Los Angeles. |
| Reynolds, Bernard, Jr | Hackman | Los Angeles | Los Angeles | Los Angeles. |
| **Reynolds, W P** | Druggist | Los Angeles | Los Angeles Co | Los Angeles. |
| Reynolds, S G | Farmer | nr Los Nietos | Los Angeles Co | Los Nietos. |
| Reynolds, J J | Stage driver | | Los Angeles Co | Los Angeles. |
| Reynolds, J B | Carpenter | Los Angeles | Los Angeles Co | Los Angeles. |
| Reynolds, W C | Farmer | nr Downey | Silver Precinct | Downey. |
| Reys, J P J | Ranchero | | Los Angeles Co | Los Angeles. |
| Rhea, S | Farmer | Los Angeles Co | Halfway House | Compton. |
| Rhoades, G | Farmer | San Pedro Ranch | 1¼ m N Compton | Compton. |
| Rhodes, H W | Farmer | | Los Angeles Co | Los Angeles. |
| Rhoades, G | Laborer | | Los Angeles Co | Wilmington. |
| Rhodes, J | Wagon maker | Los Angeles | Los Angeles Co | Los Angeles. |
| Rhyne, I N | Farmer | | Silver Precinct | Downey. |
| Riberra, Miguel | Laborer | | | Los Angeles. |
| **Ribial, F** | Sheep raiser | | La Ballona | Los Angeles. |
| Ricardo, Luis | Wharf hand | S P R R Co | Westminster | Wilmington. |
| Ricco, C | Hat maker | Los Angeles | Los Angeles Co | Los Angeles. |
| **Rice, J** | Hotel keeper | San Fernando | Los Angeles Co | San Fernando. |
| Rice, B B | Farmer | nr Los Angeles | Los Angeles Co | Los Angeles. |
| Rice, Wm | Farmer | nr Los Angeles | Los Angeles Co | Los Angeles. |
| Rice, B A | Farmer | Los Angeles | Los Angeles Co | Santa Ana. |
| Rice, J A | Ranchero | | Los Angeles Co | Capistrano. |
| Rice, G | Bar keeper | Los Angeles | Los Angeles Co | Los Angeles. |
| **Rice, J G** | Farmer | nr San Juan | Los Angeles Co | Capistrano. |
| Rice, M | Farmer | Los Angeles Co | Silver Precinct | Downey. |
| Rice, W | Farmer | nr Los Angeles | Los Angeles Co | Los Angeles. |
| Rice, H | Laborer | | Los Angeles Co | Los Angeles. |
| Rice, H B | Farmer | San Pedro Ranch | 1½ S W Compton | Compton. |
| **Rice, Francisco R** | Manufacturer | Los Angeles | Los Angeles | Los Angeles. |
| Rice, David M | Clergyman | | San Joaquin | Santa Ana. |
| Rice, Michael M | Painter | Los Angeles | Los Angeles | Los Angeles. |
| Rice, Robt | Bricklayer | Los Angeles | Los Angeles | Los Angeles. |
| Rice, Dolores | Laborer | Los Angeles Co | | Los Angeles. |
| Richardson, S | Vintner | San Gabriel Valley | 2 m W San Gabriel | San Gabriel. |
| Richmond, — | Laborer | S P R R Co | Wilmington | Wilmington. |
| Richardson, Cosmo B | Attorney | Los Angeles | Los Angeles | Los Angeles. |
| Richardson, M | Paper hanger | Los Angeles | Los Angeles | Los Angeles. |
| Richard, D A | Farmer | nr Anaheim | Los Angeles Co | Anaheim. |
| Richmond, J | Farmer | Los Angeles Co | nr Anaheim | Anaheim. |
| Richards, P | Saloon keeper | Anaheim | Los Angeles Co | Anaheim. |
| Richter, H | Farmer | Los Angeles Co | nr Anaheim | Anaheim. |
| Richardson, J | Farmer | Los Angeles Co | nr Los Angeles | Los Angeles. |
| **Richards, D** | Stable keeper | nr Los Angeles | Los Angeles Co | Los Angeles. |
| **Richardson, J** | Wagon maker | Spadra | San Jose | Spadra. |
| Richter, W M | Miller | Anaheim | Anaheim | Anaheim. |
| **Richardson, Dr N P** | Phys and surgeon | 14 Downey block | Los Angeles | Los Angeles. |
| Richardson, A | Hotel | Canal st | Wilmington | Wilmington. |

DIRECTORY OF LOS ANGELES COUNTY. 415

| Name. | Occupation. | Place of Business. | Residence. | Town or P. O. |
|---|---|---|---|---|
| Richardson, S L...... | Farmer............. | Azusa Duarte......... | 3 m E Lexington...... | El Monte. |
| Richardson, Mrs B. | Farmer............. | San Gabriel Valley... | 10 m N E San Gab... | San Gabriel. |
| Richardson, Levi... | Apiarian............ | Valley View........... | 8 m N San Gabriel... | San Gabriel. |
| Rickey, Wm.T...... | Carpenter.......... | Anaheim .............. | Los Angeles Co....... | Anaheim. |
| Ricker, E............. | Locomotive eng... | S P R R Co........... | Los Angeles.......... | Los Angeles. |
| Rickey, Wm A..... | Cabinet maker ... | Los Angeles.......... | Los Angeles.......... | Los Angeles. |
| Rickert, J B......... | Carpenter.......... |  | Los Angeles Co....... | Los Angeles. |
| Rickert, R H....... | Carpenter.......... | Los Angeles.......... |  | Los Angeles. |
| Rico, F............... | Laborer............. |  | Los Angeles Co....... | Los Angeles. |
| Rico, G.............. | Farmer............. | nr Los Angeles...... | Los Angeles Co....... | Los Angeles. |
| Ridenour, U B..... | Teamster........... | nr Los Angeles ...... | Los Angeles Co....... | Los Angeles. |
| Rieck, M F.......... | Tailor............... | Los Angeles.......... | Los Angeles Co....... | Los Angeles. |
| Ries, Wm........... | Farmer............. | Los Angeles Co...... | nr Los Angeles....... | Los Angeles. |
| Riese, A W......... | Farmer............. | nr Anaheim.......... | Los Angeles Co....... | Anaheim. |
| Riesgo, Mrs M..... | Dress maker...... | Los Angeles.......... | Los Angeles Co....... | Los Angeles. |
| Riffel, J L........... | Teamster........... |  | Los Angeles Co....... | Los Angeles. |
| Rigaud, J B......... | Stock raiser....... | nr Los Angeles...... | Los Angeles Co....... | Los Angeles. |
| Rigaud, Alphonse... | Seock raiser....... | Los Angeles Co...... | nr Los Angeles....... | Los Angeles. |
| Riggs, Garnett..... | Farmer............. | Los Angeles Co...... | Silver Precinct....... | Downey. |
| Riggs, R............. | Farmer............. | Los Angeles Co...... | Silver Precinct....... | Downey. |
| Riggs, J............. | Farmer............. | Los Angeles Co...... | Silver Precinct....... | Downey. |
| Riley, Wm.......... | Laborer............. | Los Angeles.......... | Los Angeles Co....... | Los Angeles. |
| Riley, T.............. | Printer.............. | Los Angeles.......... | Los Angeles Co....... | Los Angeles. |
| Riley, J.............. | Boot maker........ | Los Angeles.......... | Los Angeles Co....... | Los Angeles. |
| Riley, B.............. | Laborer............. |  | Los Angeles Co....... | Los Angeles. |
| Riley, Alexander... | Farmer............. | nr El Monte......... | El Monte............. | El Monte. |
| Riley, J M........... | Contractor......... | Main st............... | Main st............... | Los Angeles. |
| Riley, James........ | Store and stock... | Soledad road........ | 13 m N E Lyon Sta'n | Lyon Station. |
| Rimpau, T........... | Farmer............. | nr Anaheim.......... | Los Angeles Co....... | Anaheim. |
| Rinaldi, C R........ | Upholsterer........ | Los Angeles.......... | Los Angeles Co....... | Los Angeles. |
| Rinaldi, C R........ | Vintner............. | County road......... | 2½ m N W SanFernan | San Fernando. |
| Rinehart, W V..... | Los A soap co..... | 1st,belowAlameda sts |  | Los Angeles. |
| Rinehart, G B...... | Farmer............. | Los Angeles Co...... | nr El Monte......... | El Monte. |
| Ringle, G W........ | Laborer............. |  | Los Angeles Co....... | San Fernando. |
| Ring & Matthesen.. | Saloon............... |  |  | Los Angeles. |
| Rios, Pablo.......... | Laborer............. | Wilmington......... | 2d st............... | Wilmington. |
| Rios, Mrs Narcise... |  |  | 2d st............... | Wilmington. |
| Rios, J B............ | Vaquero............ |  | Los Angeles Co....... | Capistrano. |
| Rios, G.............. | Ranchero.......... | San Juan............. | Los Angeles Co....... | Capistrano. |
| Rios, Santiago...... | Laborer............. |  | Los Angeles Co....... | Los Angeles. |
| Eios, J S............. | Ranchero.......... | San Juan............. | Los Angeles Co....... | Capistrano. |
| Rios, Fernando..... | Wood chopper.... | Los Angeles Co...... | Los Angeles Co....... | Los Angeles. |
| Rios, J D............ | Vaquero............ |  | Los Angeles Co....... | Capistrano. |
| Rios, M.............. | Laborer............. |  |  | Capistrano. |
| Rios, M.............. | Carpenter.......... | Los Angeles.......... | Los Angeles Co....... | Los Angeles. |
| Rios, F............... | Cigar maker....... | Los Angeles.......... | Los Angeles Co....... | Los Angeles. |
| Rios, S............... | Farmer............. | Los Angeles Co...... | nr San Juan.......... | Capistrano. |
| Rios, A.............. | Farmer............. | Los Angeles Co...... | Old Mission.......... | El Monte. |
| Rios, P.............. | Laborer............. | Los Angeles Co...... |  | Los Angeles. |
| Rios, V.............. | Laborer............. |  | Los Angeles Co....... | Capistrano. |
| Riquelme, J J...... | Laborer............. | Los Angeles Co...... | Los Angeles Co....... | Los Angeles. |
| Risen, Wm......... | Shoe maker........ | San Gabriel......... | 9 m E Los Angeles... | San Gabriel. |
| Ritchie, S........... | Farmer............. | nr Anaheim.......... | Los Angeles Co....... | Anaheim. |
| Ritchy, U S......... | Farmer............. | nr Santa Ana........ | Los Angeles Co....... | Santa Ana. |
| Rius, I............... | Laborer............. |  | Los Angeles Co....... | Los Angeles. |
| Rius, G.............. | Ranchero.......... | nr Santa Ana........ | Los Angeles Co....... | Santa Ana. |
| Rivas, M............ | Laborer............. |  | Los Angeles Co....... | Los Angeles. |
| Rivas, F............. | Laborer............. |  | Los Angeles Co....... | Los Angeles. |
| Rivara, D........... | Merchant.......... | Los Angeles......... | Los Angeles Co....... | Los Angeles. |
| Rivas, M............ | Laborer............. | Los Angeles Co...... | San Jose............. | Spadra. |
| Rivas, J............. | Blacksmith........ | Wilmington ........ | Los Angeles Co....... | Wilmington. |
| Rivara & Vignolo... | Groceries........... | Los Angeles......... | Los Angeles......... | Los Angeles. |
| Rivara, D........... |  |  |  | Los Angeles. |
| Rivas, R............ | Farmer............. | Los Angeles Co...... | La Ballona........... | Los Angeles. |

| Name. | Occupation. | Place of Business. | Residence. | Town or P. O. |
|---|---|---|---|---|
| Rivera, Urbano | Ranchero | nr Los Angeles | Los Angeles Co | Los Angeles. |
| Rivera, Locasio | Vaquero | | San Juan | Capistrano. |
| Rivern, Felipe | Laborer | Los Angeles Co | Elizabeth Lake | San Fernando. |
| Rivera, Lino | Farmer | nr Los Angeles | Los Angeles Co | Los Angeles. |
| Rivera, J M | Laborer | | Los Angeles Co | Los Angeles. |
| Rivera, R | Vaquero | | Los Angeles Co | Los Angeles. |
| Rivera, Juan | Laborer | Los Angeles Co | La Ballona | LosAngeles. |
| Rivera, Pedro | Laborer | | Los Angeles Co | Los Angeles. |
| Rivera, Pablo | Farmer | Los Angeles Co | nr Los Angeles | Los Angeles. |
| **Riveria, F** | Wagon maker | Los Angeles | Los Angeles Co | Los Angeles. |
| **Rives, B E** | Physician | Los Angeles Co | Los Nietos | Los Nietos. |
| Rivera, J A | Laborer | Los Angeles Co | La Ballona | Los Angeles. |
| Rivers, R | Bricklayer | Los Angeles | Los Angeles Co | Los Angeles. |
| Riviere, B | Farmer | nr Los Angeles | Los Angeles Co | Los Angeles. |
| Rivera, A | Laborer | | Los Angeles Co | Los Angeles. |
| Robbins, O P | Farmer | nr San Fernando | Los Angeles Co | San Fernando. |
| Robbins, J | Butcher | Los Angeles | Los Angeles Co | Los Angeles. |
| **Robb, A G** | Merchant | Los Angeles Co | Westminster Col | Westminster. |
| Roberts, E S | Speculator | Los Angeles | Los Angeles Co | Los Angeles. |
| Robert, Francois | Tailor | Los Angeles | Los Angeles | Los Angeles. |
| Robertson, Chas H | Farmer | Los Angeles Co | San Joaquin | Santa Ana. |
| **Roberts, Dr J M** | Dentist | Centre st | Anaheim | Anaheim. |
| Roberts, H C | Miner | San Gabriel canyon | 3 m N Azusa | Azusa. |
| Roberts, W | | Los Angeles | Los Angeles Co | Los Angeles. |
| Roberts, J D | Farmer | nr San Juan | Los Angeles Co | Capistrano. |
| Roberts, E | Carriage trimmer | Los Angeles | Los Angeles Co | Los Angeles. |
| Roberts, J | Clerk | Los Angeles | Los Angeles Co | Los Angeles. |
| Robertson, T W | Farmer | Los Angeles Co | Silver Precinct | Downey. |
| **Robertson, J B** | Farmer | Los Angeles Co | Silver Precinct | Downey. |
| Robinson, N | Teamster | nr Los Angeles | Los Angeles Co | Los Angeles. |
| Robinson, A W | Farmer | nr Los Angeles | Los Angeles Co | Los Angeles. |
| Robinson, L | Miller | Santa Ana | Los Angeles Co | Santa Ana. |
| Robinson, W | Farmer | Los Angeles Co | Silver Precinct | Downey. |
| **Robinson, E T** | Farmer | | Los Angeles Co | Los Angeles. |
| Robinson, W W | Lumber | cor 1st & Alameda sts | cor 1st & Alameda sts | Los Angeles. |
| Robinson, — | Saloon and rest'nt | Spadra | 30 m E Los Angeles | Spadra. |
| Robles, S | Laborer | Los Angeles Co | Old Mission | El Monte. |
| Robles, P | Laborer | | Los Angeles Co | Los Angeles. |
| Rochford, H | Laborer | | Los Angeles Co | Los Angeles. |
| Rocha, A J | Farmer | Los Angeles | Los Angeles Co | Los Angeles. |
| Rocha, J J | Mason | La Ballona | La Ballona | Los Angeles. |
| **Rocha, Merajildo** | Farmer | | | Los Angeles. |
| Rocha, — | Carpenter | Wilmington | Canal st | Wilmington. |
| Rockwell, A W | Farmer | Los Angeles Co | Los Angeles | Los Angeles. |
| Roderiguez, Antonio | Laborer | | Old Mission | El Monte. |
| Roderiguez, Gregorio | Laborer | | | Los Angeles. |
| Roderiguez, Juan | Laborer | | La Ballona | Los Angeles. |
| Roderiguez, Albert | Farmer | | | Los Angeles. |
| Roderiguez, Vicente | Laborer | | | Los Angeles. |
| **Roderiguez, F** | Farmer | Dalton Ranch | 1 m N Azusa | Azusa. |
| Rodig, C A | Shoe maker | | | Los Angeles. |
| Rodrigo, Adolph | Carman | Los Angeles | Los Angeles | Los Angeles. |
| Rodriguez, O | Laborer | | Los Angeles Co | Los Angeles. |
| Rodriguez, Feliz | Laborer | | Los Angeles Co | Los Angeles. |
| Rodriguez, J F | Farmer | nr Anaheim | Los Angeles Co | Anaheim. |
| Rodriguez, F | Ranchero | nr Santa Ana | Los Angeles Co | Santa Ana. |
| Rodriguez, J | Ranchero | nr Santa Ana | Los Angeles Co | Santa Ana. |
| Rodrigues, J C | Vaquero | | Los Angeles Co | Los Angeles. |
| Rodriguez, J A | Laborer | Los Angeles Co | Old Mission | El Monte. |
| Roe, Watson W | Lather | Los Angeles | Los Angeles Co | Los Angeles. |
| **Roe, W B** | Merchant | Los Angeles | Los Angeles Co | Los Angeles. |
| **Roeder, L** | Carriage mnfr | Main st nr 1st | Main st | Los Angeles. |
| Roed, J | Ranchero | | Los Angeles Co | El Monte. |

## DIRECTORY OF LOS ANGELES COUNTY. 417

| Name. | Occupation. | Place of Business. | Residence. | Town or P. O. |
|---|---|---|---|---|
| Roesies, David | Carpenter | | | Los Angeles. |
| Rogers, R. | Farmer | Los Angeles Co | Halfway House | Compton. |
| Rogers, Walter E. | Saloon | Los Angeles | Los Angeles | Los Angeles. |
| Rogers, M | Laborer | | Los Angeles Co | Los Angeles. |
| Rogers, J | Farmer | nr El Monte | Los Angeles Co | El Monte. |
| Rogers, J J | Laborer | nr Wilmington | Los Angeles Co | Wilmington. |
| Rogers, B F | Farmer | Los Angeles Co | nr Anaheim | Anaheim. |
| Rogers, E H | Farmer | Los Angeles Co | Old Mission | El Monte. |
| Rogers, J | Farmer | Los Angeles Co | nr El Monte | El Monte. |
| Rogers, A W | Farmer | Los Angeles Co | Halfway House | Compton. |
| Rogers, J | Farmer | nr Los Angeles | Los Angeles Co | Los Angeles. |
| Rogers, G | Farmer | Los Angeles Co | nr Halfway House | Compton. |
| Rogers, T G | Farmer | nr Downey | Silver Precinct | Downey. |
| Rogers, S | Miner | Los Angeles Co | Half-way House | Compton. |
| Rogers, Thos H. | Farmer | nr Compton | Los Angeles Co | Compton. |
| Roge, Eugene | Carpenter | Los Angeles Co | | Los Angeles. |
| Rogers, Saml P | Farmer | nr Los Angeles | Los Angeles Co | Los Angeles. |
| Rogers, Danl R. | Farmer | Los Angeles Co | nr Los Angeles | Los Angeles. |
| Rogers, Alex H | Farmer | Los Angeles Co | | Los Angeles. |
| Rogers, M G | Farmer | Los Angeles Co | San Jose Township | Spadra. |
| Rogers, Matthew | Farmer | | Westminster Col | Westminster. |
| Rogers, Frank J. | Farmer | Los Angeles Co | Westminster Col | Westminster. |
| Rogers, Matthew | Farmer | Los Angeles Co | Westminster Col | Westminster. |
| Rogers, Henry | Farmer | Los Angeles Co | Westminster Col | Westminster. |
| Rogers & Potuskey | Grotto saloon | Comm'al & Main sts | | Los Angeles. |
| Rogers, — | Saloon | Comm'al & Main sts | | Los Angeles. |
| Rogers, David | Farmer | Los Angeles Co | Westminster Col | Westminster. |
| Rogers & Co, H Y. | Architects | Los Angeles | Los Angeles | Los Angeles. |
| Rogers, Rev J N | Preacher | | Wilmington | Wilmington. |
| Rogers, S | Farmer | San Pedro Ranch | 1¾ m S W Compton | Compton. |
| Rogers, H | Farmer | San Pedro Ranch | 1¼ m S Compton | Compton. |
| Rogers, — | Farmer | San Bernardino Road | 5 m N E Spadra | Spadra. |
| Rojas, G | Cigar maker | Los Angeles | Los Angeles Co | Los Angeles. |
| Rojo, F | Laborer | | Los Angeles Co | Los Angeles. |
| Roland, J | Ranchero | Los Angeles Co | San Jose | Spadra. |
| Rollins, H P | Miner | | Los Angeles Co | Los Angeles. |
| Rollin, Frederick E | Laborer | Los Angeles Co | | Los Angeles. |
| Roman, T | Blacksmith | Wilmington | Los Angeles Co | Wilmington. |
| Romero, J D | Vaquero | | Los Angeles Co | San Gabriel. |
| Romero, F L | Boot maker | Los Angeles | Los Angeles Co | Los Angeles. |
| Romero, M | Farmer | nr San Juan | Los Angeles Co | San Juan. |
| Romero, R | Boot maker | Los Angeles | Los Angeles Co | Los Angeles. |
| Romero, J | Laborer | | Los Angeles Co | Los Angeles. |
| Romero, Keyes | Farmer | Los Angeles Co | San Jose | Spadra. |
| Romero, J M | Soap maker | Santa Ana | Los Angeles Co | Santa Ana. |
| Romero, M | Laborer | | Los Angeles Co | Los Angeles. |
| Romero, G | Ranchero | nr Santa Ana | Los Angeles Co | Santa Ana. |
| Romero, J | Ranchero | nr San Fernando | Los Angeles Co | San Fernando. |
| Romero, J M | Farmer | nr Los Nietos | Los Angeles Co | Los Nietos. |
| Romero, D | Laborer | Los Angeles Co | Old Mission | El Monte. |
| Romero, A | Farmer | Los Angeles Co | Old Mission | El Monte. |
| Romero, J D | Laborer | | Los Angeles Co | Santa Ana. |
| Romo, Jose | Laborer | | Los Angeles Co | San Gabriel. |
| Romero, Louis L. | Miner | | | Los Angeles. |
| Romero, Jesus | Farmer | Los Angeles Co | nr Los Angeles | Los Angeles. |
| Romero, Antonio | Laborer | | Los Angeles Co | Los Angeles. |
| Romo, Jesus | Farmer | Los Angeles Co | nr Los Angeles | Los Angeles. |
| Romo, Refugio | Laborer | Los Angeles Co | | Los Angeles. |
| Romo & Co, Antonio | Star restaurant | Los Angeles st | | Anaheim. |
| Roonen, T | Blacksmith | S P R R Co | Wilmington | Wilmington. |
| Root, G R | Tinner | Los Angeles | Los Angeles Co | Los Angeles. |
| Roper, Wm | Harness maker | Los Angeles | Los Angeles | Los Angeles. |
| Rorden, C R | Farmer | Los Angeles Co | nr Anaheim | Anaheim. |
| Rosas, R | Vaquero | Los Angeles Co | Old Mission | El Monte. |

## L. L. PAULSON'S HAND-BOOK AND

| Name. | Occupation. | Place of Business. | Residence. | Town or P. O. |
|---|---|---|---|---|
| Rosas, V | Farmer | Los Angeles Co | Halfway House | Compton. |
| Rosby, W | Clerk | Los Angeles | Los Angeles | Los Angeles. |
| Rosenbaum, G H | Farmer | San Juan | Los Angeles Co | Capistrano. |
| Rose, Fredk Wm | Cook | Los Angeles | Los Angeles | Los Angeles. |
| Rose & Ferguson | Livery stable | Main st | | Los Angeles. |
| Rosenthal&Russek | Dry goods, etc | Los Angeles | Los Angeles | Los Angeles. |
| Rose, Alex | Wharf hand | S P R R Co | Wilmington | Wilmington. |
| Rose, L J | Vineyard | Sunny Slope | 12 m N E Los A | Los Angeles. |
| Rose, Amon | Farmer | Los Angeles Co | Silver Precinct | Downey. |
| Rose, T H | Teacher | Los Angeles | Los Angeles Co | Los Angeles. |
| Rosenthal, I | Clerk | Los Angeles Co | La Ballona | Los Angeles. |
| Rose, H W | Clerk | Los Angeles | Los Angeles Co | Los Angeles. |
| Rose, J S | Plasterer | Los Angeles Co | Silver Precinct | Downey. |
| Rose, G W | Farmer | nr Downey | Silver Precinct | Downey. |
| Ross, Alex | Confectioner | Los Angeles | Los Angeles Co | Los Angeles. |
| Ross, E M | Attorney | Los Angeles | Los Angeles Co | Los Angeles. |
| Ross, Josiah | Farmer | Los Angeles Co | nr Santa Ana | Santa Ana. |
| Ross, S P | Farmer | Los Angeles Co | nr El Monte | El Monte. |
| Ross, Samuel | Farmer | nr Santa Ana | Los Angeles Co | Santa Ana. |
| Ross, P P | Farmer | Los Angeles Co | nr Anaheim | El Monte. |
| Ross, H | Laborer | | Los Angeles Co | Los Angeles. |
| Ross, Jacob | Farmer | Los Angeles Co | nr Santa Ana | Santa Ana. |
| Ross, W W | Physician & surg | 82 and 84 Main st | | Los Angeles. |
| Ross, J | Wharf hand | S P R R Co | Wilmington | Wilmington. |
| Roth, P N | Merchant | Los Angeles | Los Angeles Co | Los Angeles. |
| Roth, T F | Painter | Los Angeles | Los Angeles Co | Los Angeles. |
| Roth, E | Merchant | Los Angeles | Los Angeles | Los Angeles. |
| Rothchild, J M | Attorney at law | 39 & 41 Temple Blk | | Los Angeles. |
| Rothschild, M | Butcher | | 6th st | Los Angeles. |
| Rothschild & Nolte | Butchers | Los Angeles | Los Angeles Co | Los Angeles. |
| Roth, E D | Gen merchandise | Main st | Wilmington st | Los Angeles. |
| Roth & Co, P N | Gen merchandise | Main st | Wilmington st | Los Angeles. |
| Rourke, B | Laborer | | Los Angeles Co | Los Angeles. |
| Rourke, J | Jockey | Los Angeles | Los Angeles Co | Los Angeles. |
| Roussin, Germain | Nurseryman | Los Angeles Co | nr Los Angeles | Los Angeles. |
| Roussene, D | Laborer | | Los Angeles Co | Los Angeles. |
| Rowal, Jose | Farmer | nr Los Angeles | Los Angeles Co | Los Angeles. |
| Rowan, T E | County treasurer | Los Angeles | Main st | Los Angeles. |
| Rowan, F | Blacksmith | Los Angeles | Los Angeles Co | Los Angeles. |
| Rowen, C H | Barber | Los Angeles | Los Angeles Co | Los Angeles. |
| Rowell, L D | Farmer | Los Angeles Co | | Los Angeles. |
| Rowe, G W | Broom maker | Los Angeles | Los Angeles Co | Los Angeles. |
| Rowe, S | Laborer | Los Angeles | Los Angeles Co | Los Angeles. |
| Rowe, A | Farmer | Los Angeles Co | San Joaquin | Santa Ana. |
| Rowland, J | Farmer | nr El Monte | Los Angeles Co | El Monte. |
| Rowland, W R | Farmer | Los Angeles Co | nr El Monte | El Monte. |
| Rowland, W | Carriage maker | San Gabriel | Los Angeles Co | San Gabriel. |
| Rowland, Thos | Ranchero | San Bernardino Road | 8 m E Lexington | El Monte. |
| Rowland, Mrs Juan | Ranchero | San Bernardino Road | 9 m E Lexington | El Monte. |
| Rowland, Mrs C M | Ranchero | San Bernardino Road | 6 m E Lexington | El Monte. |
| Rubio, Antonio | Farmer | San Gabriel | 9 m E Los Angeles | San Gabriel. |
| Rubio, Jesus | Farmer | San Gabriel | 9 m E Los Angeles | San Gabriel. |
| Rubio, J | Farmer | Los Angeles Co | Los Angeles | Los Angeles. |
| Rubio, T | Farmer | | Los Angeles Co | Los Angeles. |
| Rubio, A | Vintner | nr Los Angeles | Los Angeles Co | Los Angeles. |
| Rubottom, W W | Rubottom hotel | Spadra | 30 m E Los Angeles | Spadra. |
| Rubottom, J D | Farmer | Los Angeles Co | San Jose | Spadra. |
| Rucker, L F | Saloon | Los Angeles | Los Angeles Co | Los Angeles. |
| Rucker, Mrs M P | Dress maker | Los Angeles | Los Angeles Co | Los Angeles. |
| Rudolph, Edward | Jeweller | Los Angeles | Los Angeles Co | Los Angeles. |
| Ruelas, G | Laborer | | Los Angeles Co | Los Angeles. |
| Ruggles, A | Farmer | El Monte Valley | 1 m W Lexington | El Monte. |
| Ruis, Genaro | Laborer | | La Ballona | Los Angeles. |
| Ruis, S | Laborer | Los Angeles Co | San Jose | Spadra. |

DIRECTORY OF LOS ANGELES COUNTY. 419

| Name. | Occupation. | Place of Business. | Residence. | Town or P. O. |
|---|---|---|---|---|
| Ruis, Juan | Laborer | | Los Angeles Co | Los Angeles. |
| Ruis, Abram | Laborer | | Los Angeles Co | Los Angeles. |
| Ruis, Jose | Laborer | Los Angeles Co | Los Angeles Co | Santa Ana. |
| Ruis, J M | Farmer | Los Angeles Co | nr Los Angeles | Los Angeles. |
| Ruis, J D | Laborer | | Los Angeles Co | Los Angeles. |
| Ruis, J E | Laborer | Los Angeles | Los Angeles Co | Los Angeles. |
| Ruiz, R | Vaquero | Los Angeles Co | Wilmington | Wilmington. |
| Ruiz, Rafael | Laborer | | | Wilmington. |
| Ruiz, Juan | Laborer | | Los Angeles Co | Los Angeles. |
| Ruiz, M E | Ranchero | Los Angeles | Los Angeles Co | Los Angeles. |
| Ruiz, P | Farmer | nr Los Nietos | Los Nietos | Los Nietos. |
| Ruiz, N | Wood cutter | Los Angeles Co | Los Angeles Co | Los Angeles. |
| Ruiz, J A | Laborer | | Los Angeles Co | Los Angeles. |
| Ruiz, A | Ranchero | nr Los Angeles | Los Angeles Co | Los Angeles. |
| Ruiz, D | Laborer | | Los Angeles Co | Los Angeles. |
| Ruiz, J N | Laborer | | Los Angeles Co | Los Angeles. |
| Ruiz, F | Farmer | Los Angeles Co | nr Los Angeles | Los Angeles. |
| Ruiz, P | Laborer | | Los Angeles Co | Los Angeles. |
| Ruiz, S | Vaquero | | Los Angeles Co | Los Angeles. |
| Ruiz, D | Farmer | Los Angeles Co | nr Los Nietos | Los Nietos. |
| Ruiz, S C | Vaquero | | Los Angeles Co | Los Angeles. |
| Ruiz, J M | Laborer | | Los Angeles Co | Los Nietos. |
| Ruiz, J | Vaquero | | Los Angeles Co | Los Angeles. |
| Ruiz, Jose | Laborer | | Los Angeles Co | Los Angeles. |
| Rulo, L L | Farmer | nr Los Angeles | Los Angeles Co | Los Angeles. |
| Rumble, W S | Mining engineer | room 15 Downey Blk | Los Angeles | Los Angeles. |
| Rumble & Gaertner | Mining engineers | room 15 Downey Blk | Los Angeles | Los Angeles. |
| Rumble, Walter I | Surveyor | Los Angeles | Los Angeles Co | Los Angeles. |
| Rumppe, J | Baker | Los Angeles | Los Angeles Co | Los Angeles. |
| Rusher, John | Agent | Los Angeles | Los Angeles | Los Angeles. |
| Rushmore, F | Laborer | Los Angeles Co | nr Los Angeles | Los Angeles. |
| Rusher, J M | Farmer | nr El Monte | Los Angeles Co | El Monte. |
| Rush, G D | Baker | Los Angeles | Los Angeles Co | Los Angeles. |
| Russell, Hiram S | Real estate | Los Angeles | Los Angeles | Los Angeles. |
| Russell, Miss E | Teacher | Los Angeles Co | | Los Angeles. |
| Russell, J | Miner | Los Angeles Co | Soledad | San Fernando. |
| Russell, L M | Farmer | nr Wilmington | Los Angeles Co | Wilmington. |
| Russell, W H | Engineer | Los Angeles | Los Angeles Co | Los Angeles. |
| Russell, G L | Farmer | Los Angeles Co | nr Santa Ana | Santa Ana. |
| Russ, J N | Teacher | Los Angeles | Los Angeles Co | Los Angeles. |
| Russell, R B | Farmer | Los Angeles Co | Halfway House | Compton. |
| Russell, J | Farmer | Los Angeles Co | nr Halfway House | Compton. |
| Russeck, Max | Merchant | Los Angeles | Los Angeles | Los Angeles. |
| Russell, M C | Farmer | Los Angeles Co | Old Mission | El Monte. |
| Russell, M J | Farmer | Los Angeles Co | Old Mission | El Monte. |
| Rust, J | Farmer | nr Anaheim | Los Angeles Co | Anaheim. |
| Rust, G | Farmer | Los Angeles Co | nr Anaheim | Anaheim. |
| Ruthard, Chas | Carver | Olive st | Olive st | Los Angeles. |
| Ruth, W J | Lather | Los Angeles | Los Angeles Co | Los Angeles. |
| Rutherford, R H | | Santa Ana | Los Angeles Co | Santa Ana. |
| Rutschman, J | Brewer | Anaheim | Los Angeles Co | Anaheim. |
| Ryan, Paul | Foreman | Los Angeles | Los Angeles | Los Angeles. |
| Ryan, James E | Rigger | | San Pedro | Wilmington. |
| Ryan, Edward R | Stage driver | Los Angeles Co | | Los Angeles. |
| Ryder, — | Laborer | Point San Pedro | Point San Pedro | Wilmington. |
| Ryan, A W | Farmer | nr Los Nietos | Los Angeles Co | Los Nietos. |
| Ryan, M E | Laborer | Los Angeles Co | | Los Angeles. |
| Ryan, G | Farmer | Los Angeles Co | Silver Precinct | Downey. |
| Ryan, T H | Machinist | Los Angeles | Los Angeles Co | Los Angeles. |
| Ryan, J H | Farmer | Los Angeles Co | nr Santa Ana | Santa Ana. |
| Ryckelton, J | Miner | Los Angeles Co | Los Angeles Co | Los Angeles. |
| Ryder, B F | Cooper | Los Angeles | Los Angeles Co | Los Angeles. |
| Ryerson, C | Butcher | Los Angeles | Los Angeles Co | Los Angeles. |
| Sabalita, T | Laborer | | Los Angeles Co | Santa Ana. |

| Name. | Occupation. | Place of Business. | Residence. | Town or P. O. |
|---|---|---|---|---|
| Sabichi, F | Clerk | Los Angeles | Los Angeles | Los Angeles. |
| Sackett, T D | Teamster | Los Angeles Co | Silver Precinct | Downey. |
| Sacriste, Chas F, Jr | Manufacturer | Los Angeles | Los Angeles | Los Angeles. |
| Saez, J B | Farmer | Los Angeles Co | nr Los Angeles | Los Angeles. |
| Sainor, A J | Laborer | Los Angeles Co | Silver Precinct | Downey. |
| Saine, F | Laborer | | Los Angeles Co | Los Angeles. |
| Sainsevain, M | Vintner | Los Angeles | Los Angeles Co | Los Angeles. |
| Saiz, Jose Maria | Laborer | Los Angeles Co | | Los Angeles. |
| Saiz, Ysidro | Laborer | | Los Angeles Co | Los Angeles. |
| Salazar, J M | Laborer | nr Wilmington | Los Angeles Co | Wilmington. |
| Salazar, D | Laborer | nr Los Angeles | Los Angeles Co | Los Angeles. |
| Salazar, J | Laborer | nr San Gabriel | Los Angeles Co | San Gabriel. |
| Salare, Constantine | Restaurateur | Los Angeles | Los Angeles | Los Angeles. |
| Salazar, R | Farmer | nr Los Nietos | Los Angeles Co | Los Nietos. |
| Salcido, J | Laborer | nr Los Angeles | Los Angeles Co | Los Angeles. |
| Saldana, J | Laborer | nr Los Angeles | Los Angeles Co | Los Angeles. |
| Sale, J | Farmer | nr San Juan | Los Angeles Co | Capistrano. |
| Salez, Manuel | Ranchero | Los Angeles Co | San Antonio | Downey. |
| Sales, S | Laborer | Los Angeles Co | Old Mission | El Monte. |
| Salgado, J | Laborer | nr Los Angeles | Los Angeles Co | Los Angeles. |
| Salgardo, A | Laborer | | Los Angeles Co | Los Angeles. |
| Salis, S | Farmer | nr El Monte | Los Angeles Co | El Monte. |
| **Salisbury, Jno C** | Merchant | Los Angeles | Los Angeles | Los Angeles. |
| Salisbury & Whittaker | Hay & grain | Los Angeles | | Los Angeles. |
| Salla, M | Laborer | nr Los Angeles | Los Angeles Co | Los Angeles. |
| Sallaza, J J | Peddler | San Gabriel | 9 m E Los Angeles | San Gabriel. |
| Salorsano, G | Vaquero | Los Angeles Co | nr La Ballona | Los Angeles. |
| Salorsono, R | Laborer | | Los Angeles Co | Los Angeles. |
| Salside, A | Laborer | Los Angeles Co | nr Los Angeles | Los Angeles. |
| Salter, H | Farmer | nr San Juan | Los Angeles Co | Capistrano. |
| Salter, E M | Farmer | Los Angeles Co | nr Santa Ana | Santa Ana. |
| Sambrano, G | Ranchero | Los Angeles Co | San Jose | Spadra. |
| Samis, Jesse | Farmer | | San Joaquin | Santa Ana. |
| Samis, D H | Farmer | Los Angeles Co | San Joaquin | Santa Ana. |
| **Samis, Daniel H** | Farmer | | Westminster Col | Westminster. |
| Samorano, Ramon | Farmer | Los Angeles Co | | San Fernando. |
| Samorano, L A | Laborer | nr Los Angeles | Los Angeles Co | Los Angeles. |
| Sampson, W | Cook | Los Angeles | Los Angeles Co | Los Angeles. |
| Sanborn, T D | Clerk | Los Angeles Co | Old Mission | El Monte. |
| Sanborn, C A | Shoe maker | Los Angeles | Los Angeles Co | Los Angeles. |
| Sanchez, A | Laborer | nr Los Angeles | Los Angeles Co | Los Angeles. |
| Sanchez, J | Farmer | | Los Angeles Co | Los Angeles. |
| Sanchez, J M | Ranchero | Los Angeles Co | Old Mission | El Monte. |
| Sanchez, E | Ranchero | | Los Angeles Co | Los Angeles. |
| Sanchez, J A | Carpenter | Los Angeles Co | | Los Angeles. |
| Sanchez, A M | Ranchero | Los Angeles Co | San Jose | Spadra. |
| Sanchez, I | Laborer | Los Angeles Co | La Ballona | Los Angeles. |
| Sanchez, T A | Ranchero | Los Angeles Co | nr Los Angeles | Los Angeles. |
| Sanchez, J R | Laborer | Los Angeles Co | Old Mission | El Monte. |
| Sanceda, F | Laborer | | Los Angeles Co | Los Angeles. |
| **Sanchez, M** | Farmer | Los Angeles Co | nr Los Angeles | Los Angeles. |
| Sanchez, R | Laborer | Los Angeles Co | | Los Angeles. |
| **Sands, S R** | Farmer | Los Angeles Co | Silver Precinct | Downey. |
| Sanders, P | Farmer | nr Santa Ana | Los Angeles Co | Santa Ana. |
| Sandoral, A | Bar keeper | Los Angeles | Los Angeles Co | Los Angeles. |
| Sands, W W | Bar keeper | Los Angeles | Los Angeles Co | Los Angeles. |
| Sandoral, Juan P | Laborer | Los Angeles Co | | Los Angeles. |
| Sand, J | Laborer | Los Angeles Co | | Los Angeles. |
| Saner, Louis | Clerk | Los Angeles | Los Angeles | Los Angeles. |
| **Sanford, Cyrus** | Farmer | | La Ballona | Los Angeles. |
| Sanford, Wm | Seaman | Los Angeles Co | | Wilmington. |
| Sanford, E M | Ranchero | nr Los Nietos | Los Angeles Co | Los Nietos. |
| **Sanger & Bell** | Architects | 6 Downey Block | | Los Angeles. |

DIRECTORY OF LOS ANGELES COUNTY. 421

| Name. | Occupation. | Place of Business. | Residence. | Town or P. O. |
|---|---|---|---|---|
| Sanguineti, G B.... | Merchant ............ | Los Angeles............ | Los Angeles Co........ | Los Angeles. |
| Sanger, C E.......... | Architect .............. | 13 Downey Block..... | Main st................... | Los Angeles. |
| Sanor, A J............. | Farmer ............... | San Pedro Ranch...... | 1¼ m E Compton...... | Compton. |
| Santons, L............ | Laborer................ | ............................... | Los Angeles Co........ | Los Angeles. |
| Santonge, J........... | Well borer .......... | Compton................... | Compton ............... | Compton. |
| Santong, J A.......... | Painter .............;... | Los Angeles............ | Los Angeles ........... | Los Angeles. |
| Santa Cruz, P........ | Laborer................ | .............................. | Los Angeles Co........ | Los Angeles. |
| Sarcey, G W.......... | Farmer ............... | Los Angeles Co....... | Silver Precinct........ | Downey. |
| Sasido, J F............ | Laborer................ | Los Angeles Co........ | Old Mission............ | El Monte. |
| Satter, A................ | Cooper................. | Los Angeles............ | Los Angeles Co........ | Los Angeles. |
| Satter & Bayer..... | Wines, etc .......... | Main & Requena sta.. | ............................. | Los Angeles. |
| Sauceda, A............. | Laborer................ | ............................... | Los Angeles Co....... | Los Angeles. |
| Saunders, J B...... | Physician............ | Los Angeles............ | Los Angeles Co ...... | Los Angeles. |
| Savage, J H.......... | Watchman........... | S P R R Co.............. | Canal st ................ | Wilmington. |
| Savage, Wm......... | Harness maker ... | Los Angeles Co....... | ............................. | Wilmington. |
| Savage, J M......... | Farmer ............... | Los Angeles Co....... | nr Los Nietos.......... | Los Nietos. |
| Save, Bertrand..... | Hotel keeper ....... | Los Angeles............ | Los Angeles ........... | Los Angeles. |
| Savin, Alexander... | Clerk .................. | Los Angeles............ | Los Angeles............ | Los Angeles. |
| Sawyer, Wm ........ | Railroad emp........ | Los Angeles............ | Los Angeles............ | Los Angeles. |
| Saxon, Thos A...... | Teacher .............. | ............................... | La Ballona.............. | Los Angeles. |
| Saxton, Edwin S... | Farmer ............... | Los Angeles Co....... | .............................. | Anaheim. |
| Scales, J C............ | Professor ............ | Wilson's college...... | Wilmington ........... | Wilmington. |
| Scarring, J ............ | Teamster ............ | nr Los Angeles........ | Los Angeles Co ...... | Los Angeles. |
| Schaffer, H O G.... | Gunsmith ............ | Los Angeles............ | Los Angeles Co ...... | Los Angeles. |
| Schallmo, S........... | Butcher............... | Los Angeles............ | Los Angeles Co ...... | Los Angeles. |
| Schad & Falkenau.. | Books&stationery | Los Angeles............ | Los Angeles............ | Los Angeles. |
| Schaeffer & Stengel | Gardeners........... | Wilmington st......... | ............................. | Los Angeles. |
| Scheider, J K........ | Farmer ............... | Los Angeles Co ...... | La Ballona.............. | Los Angeles. |
| Scheerer, H........... | Tinner ................ | Los Angeles Co ...... | Los Angeles............ | Los Angeles. |
| Schenk, A ............. | Vintner................ | nr Anaheim............. | Los Angeles Co ...... | Anaheim. |
| Schieck, D ............ | Teamster ............ | Los Angeles Co....... | .............................. | Los Angeles. |
| Schiller, P............. | Butcher............... | Los Angeles............ | Los Angeles Co....... | Los Angeles. |
| Schindler, H......... | Boot store............ | 52 Main st.............. | Los Angeles............ | Los Angeles. |
| Schlotterbeck, H.. | Gunsmith............ | Los Angeles............ | Los Angeles Co ...... | Los Angeles. |
| Schlebitz, A........... | Farmer ............... | Los Angeles Co...... | nr Los Angeles ........ | Los Angeles. |
| Schlesinger, Louis. | Merchant ........... | Los Angeles............ | La Ballona.............. | Los Angeles. |
| Schlesinger J........ | Clerk................... | Los Angeles............ | Los Angeles Co ...... | Los Angeles. |
| Schmidt, G L........ | Clerk .................. | Los Angeles............ | Los Angeles Co ...... | Los Angeles. |
| Schmidt, Henry .... | Blacksmith.......... | Lexington.............. | 12 m E Los Angeles | El Monte. |
| Schmidt, Fred....... | Baker ................. | Los Angeles............ | Los Angeles............ | Los Angeles. |
| Schmidt, D............ | Laborer ............... | Los Angeles Co....... | nr Anaheim ............ | Anaheim. |
| Schmidt, A............ | Carriage maker.... | Los Angeles............ | Los Angeles Co....... | Los Angeles. |
| Schmidt, H............ | Carpenter............ | San Gabriel............ | Los Angeles Co....... | San Gabriel. |
| Schmidt, T E ....... | Vintner................ | Anaheim ............... | Los Angeles Co ...... | Anaheim. |
| Schmidt, H J........ | Laborer................ | nr Los Angeles........ | Los Angeles Co ...... | Los Angeles. |
| Schneider, P......... | Blacksmith.......... | Los Angeles Co....... | Soledad.................. | San Fernando. |
| Schneider, N......... | Boot maker ......... | Los Angeles............ | Los Angeles Co ...... | Los Angeles. |
| Schneider, J ......... | Farmer ............... | Los Angeles Co....... | nr La Puenta........... | El Monte. |
| Schneider, John .. | Merchant ........... | Los Angeles............ | Los Angeles............ | Los Angeles. |
| Schnorrenberg, Joseph.............. | Bar keeper.......... | Los Angeles............ | Los Angeles............ | Los Angeles. |
| Schnickner, F....... | Miner.................. | Los Angeles Co....... | Los Angeles Co....... | Azusa. |
| Schooler, H W...... | Farmer ............... | Los Angeles Co....... | nr Los Angeles........ | Los Angeles. |
| Schreck, J ............ | Laborer............... | Los Angeles Co....... | Los Angeles............ | Los Angeles. |
| Schrambing, D...... | Laborer ............... | ............................... | Los Angeles Co....... | Los Angeles. |
| Schumaker, J....... | Merchant ........... | Los Angeles............ | Los Angeles............ | Los Angeles. |
| Schusterick, F...... | Saloon keeper...... | Los Angeles............ | Los Angeles Co ...... | Los Angeles. |
| Schultz, T............. | Clerk ,................. | Los Angeles............ | Los Angeles............ | Los Angeles. |
| Schulte, Wm ....... | Farmer ............... | .............................. | Anaheim................ | Anaheim. |
| Schwarz, M.......... | Brewer ................ | Los Angeles............ | Los Angeles............ | Los Angeles. |
| Schwer, J A ......... | Laborer............... | Los Angeles Co ...... | nr Los Angeles........ | Los Angeles. |
| Scott, J G.............. | Carpenter............ | Los Angeles............ | Los Angeles Co....... | Los Angeles. |
| Scott, W M........... | Harness maker.... | Los Angeles............ | Los Angeles Co ...... | Los Angeles. |
| Scott & Baker....... | Refiners............... | Lyon Station.......... | Lyon Station .......... | Lyon Station. |

| Name. | Occupation. | Place of Business. | Residence. | Town or P. O. |
|---|---|---|---|---|
| Scott, D C | Oil refiner | Lyon Station | Lyon Station | Lyon Station. |
| Scott, Wm H | Watch maker | Los Angeles | Los Angeles | Los Angeles. |
| Scott, Andres | Bricklayer | Los Angeles | Los Angeles | Los Angeles. |
| Scott, Robt W | Attorney at law | Centre st | Anaheim | Anaheim. |
| Scott, Miss H | Teacher | Los Angeles Co | | Los Angeles. |
| Scott, P M | Farmer | Los Angeles Co | La Ballona | Los Angeles. |
| Scully, T J | Farmer | | Los Angeles Co | Santa Ana. |
| Sculley, S T | Locomotive eng | S P R R Co | Los Angeles | Los Angeles. |
| Scymanski, J | Peddler | Los Angeles | Los Angeles Co | Los Angeles. |
| Seabury, J H | Miner | | Los Angeles Co | San Gabriel. |
| Seamans, Palmer L | Assayer | Los Angeles | Los Angeles | Los Angeles. |
| Seamans, J M | Jeweler | Los Angeles | Los Angeles | Los Angeles. |
| Seaman, I C | Clerk | Los Angeles | Los Angeles Co | Los Angeles. |
| Sears, N | Vaquero | | Los Angeles Co | El Monte. |
| Searles, J W | Miner | Los Angeles Co | Soledad | San Fernando. |
| Sears, T | Farmer | Los Angeles Co | nr Anaheim | Anaheim. |
| Sears, W | Farmer | Los Angeles Co | nr La Puenta | El Monte. |
| Sears, E | Farmer | Los Angeles Co | Old Mission | El Monte. |
| Searles, D | Miner | | Los Angeles Co | San Fernando. |
| Sears, M | Farmer | nr El Monte | Los Angeles Co | El Monte. |
| Seda, Mrs R | Groceries | New High st | Los Angeles | Los Angeles. |
| See, S M | Farmer | nr Los Nietos | Los Angeles Co | Los Nietos. |
| See, J | Farmer | Los Angeles Co | Los Nietos | Los Nietos. |
| See, R | Farmer | | Los Angeles Co | Los Nietos. |
| See, John S | Farmer | | Los Nietos | Los Nietos. |
| Seebold, L | Co surveyor | Court House | Los Angeles | Los Angeles. |
| Segars, M | Teacher | Los Angeles Co | San Joaquin | Santa Ana. |
| Selnya, Sebastian | Laborer | Los Angeles Co | San Joaquin | Santa Ana. |
| Selaya, P | Laborer | nr San Gabriel | Los Angeles Co | San Gabriel. |
| Selaya, J | Farmer | Los Angeles Co | Los Nietos | Los Nietos. |
| Seligman, M H | Furnishing goods | Commercial st | Los Angeles | Los Angeles. |
| Sellers, H | Blacksmith | Los Angeles | Los Angeles Co | Los Angeles. |
| Dell, F | Carpenter | Los Angeles | Los Angeles Co | Los Angeles. |
| Sell, G W | Engineer | Los Angeles | Los Augeles Co | Los Angeles. |
| Senger, D | Teacher | Los Angeles Co | Halfway House | Compton. |
| Sentour, J | Sheep raiser | Los Angeles Co | Los Angeles Co | Los Angeles. |
| Sentous, A | Baker | Los Angeles | Los Angeles | Los Angeles. |
| Sentous, Pierre | Stock raiser | Los Angeles Co | Los Angeles Co | Los Angeles. |
| Sepulveda, P | Laborer | nr Los Angeles | Los Angeles Co | Los Angeles. |
| Sepulveda, G | Ranchero | nr Wilmington | Los Angeles Co | Wilmington. |
| Sepulveda, A E | Ranchero | | La Ballona | Los Angeles. |
| Sepulveda, J C | Farmer | Los Angeles Co | La Ballona | Los Angeles. |
| Sepulveda, M | Farmer | Los Angeles Co | nr Los Angeles | Los Angeles. |
| Sepulveda, A B | Ranchero | | Los Angeles Co | Santa Ana. |
| Sepulveda, J A | Farmer | nr Los Angeles | Los Angeles Co | Los Angeles. |
| Sepulveda, Y | Attorney | Los Angeles | Los Angeles | Los Angeles. |
| Sepulveda, J L | Laborer | nr Wilmington | Los Angeles Co | Wilmington. |
| Sepulveda, J | Vaquero | | Los Angeles Co | Los Angeles. |
| Sepulveda, B | Stock | Palos Verde | 2 m W Wilmington | Wilmington. |
| Sepulveda, Mrs M | | Palos Verde | 2 m W Wilmington | Wilmington. |
| Sepulveda, Guadalupe | Stock raiser | Palos Verde | 2 m W Wilmington | Wilmington. |
| Sepulveda, Francisco | Stock raiser | Palos Verde | 2 m W Wilmington | Wilmington. |
| Sepulveda, Gregorio | Stock | Palos Verde | 2 m W Wilmington | Wilmington. |
| Sepulveda, Jose | Stock raiser | Wilmington | 2 m W Wilmington | Wilmington. |
| Sepulveda, Juan | Stock raiser | Wilmington | 2 m W Wilmington | Wilmington. |
| Sepulveda, Teofilo | Clerk | Los Angeles | Los Angeles | Los Angeles. |
| Sepulveda, S | Carpenter | Los Angeles Co | | Los Angeles. |
| Sepulveda, R | Laborer | nr Los Angeles | Los Angeles Co | Los Angeles. |
| Sepulveda, J D | Ranchero | Los Angeles Co | La Ballona | Los Angeles. |
| Sepulveda, J | Farmer | Los Angeles Co | nr Santa Ana | Santa Ana. |
| Sepulveda, J B | Ranchero | | Los Angeles Co | Wilmington. |
| Sepulveda, F | Ranchero | Los Angeles Co | La Ballona | Los Angeles. |

# DIRECTORY OF LOS ANGELES COUNTY. 423

| NAME. | OCCUPATION. | PLACE OF BUSINESS. | RESIDENCE. | TOWN OR P. O. |
|---|---|---|---|---|
| Sepulveda, V | Vaquero | | Los Angeles Co | Wilmington. |
| Sepulveda, J | Laborer | | Los Angeles Co | Los Angeles. |
| Serdam, J V | Borregero | Los Angeles Co | Los Angeles | Los Angeles. |
| Serrano, P | Laborer | nr Los Angeles | Los Angeles Co | Los Angeles. |
| Serrano, J | Laborer | Los Angeles Co | nr San Juan | Capistrano. |
| Serrante, C | Carpenter | Los Angeles | Los Angeles Co | Los Angeles. |
| Serrano, J A | Ranchero | nr Los Nietos | Los Angeles Co | Los Nietos. |
| Serrano, J A | Farmer | nr Los Angeles | Los Angeles Co | Los Angeles. |
| Serrano, Reyes | Farmer | Los Angeles Co | | Los Angeles. |
| Serrano, F | Ranchero | | Los Angeles Co | Capistrano. |
| Serrano, R T | Laborer | | Los-Angeles Co | Capistrano. |
| Serrano, J P | Farmer | Los Angeles Co | Capistrano | Capistrano. |
| Serrano, T | Laborer | Los Angeles Co | nr Los Angeles | Los Angeles. |
| Settle, M Geo, Sr. | Farmer | nr Los Nietos | Los Angeles Co | Los Nietos. |
| Settle, W H | Farmer | Los Angeles Co | Silver Precinct | Downey. |
| Settle, Newton T | Farmer | | Los Nietos | Los Nietos. |
| Sevestser, C C | Clerk | Anaheim | Los Angeles Co | Anaheim. |
| Severs, J | Farmer | Los Angeles Co | nr Los Angeles | Los Angeles. |
| Sex, W | Miner | Los Angeles Co | nr Los Angeles | Los Angeles. |
| Sexton, H | Farmer | Los Angeles Co | Silver Precinct | Downey. |
| Sexton, D P | Farmer | nr San Gabriel | Los Angeles Co | San Gabriel. |
| Seymour, J N | Blacksmith | Los Angeles | Los Angeles Co | Los Angeles. |
| Seymour, W B | Painter | Los Angeles | Los Angeles Co | Los Angeles. |
| Seymour, J H | Farmer | Los Angeles Co | Halfway House | Compton. |
| Seymour, John H | Grange store | 184 Main st | | Los Angeles. |
| Shaberg, H W | Bar keeper | Los Angeles | Los Angeles Co | Los Angeles. |
| Shackford, L C | Carpenter | Spadra | 80 m E Los Angeles | Spadra. |
| Shaffer, Fredr'k | Brewer | Los Angeles Co | | Anaheim. |
| Shaffer, P J | Farmer | Los Angeles Co | | Santa Ana. |
| Shafer, G McD | Farmer | Los Angeles Co | Los Nietos | Los Nietos. |
| Shannon, A M | Carpenter | Los Angeles | Los Angeles Co | Los Angeles. |
| Shang, H L | Saloon | San Fernando | San Fernando | San Fernando. |
| Shaner, Henry | Tailor | Los Angeles | Los Angeles | Los Angeles. |
| Shane, Peter | Farmer | Los Angeles Co | | Los Angeles. |
| Sharps, J H | Farmer | nr San Juan | Los Angeles Co | Capistrano. |
| Sharp, N | Farmer | Los Angeles Co | | El Monte. |
| Sharp, J | Minister | Los Angeles | Los Angeles Co | Los Angeles. |
| Sharp, D | Farmer | Los Angeles Co | nr Los Nietos | Los Nietos. |
| Sharp, G W | Ranchero | San Bernardino road | 1½ m E Lexington | El Monte. |
| Sharp, John | Farmer | San Pedro ranch | 1½ m S Compton | Compton. |
| Sharpe, H W | Blacksmith | Los Angeles | Los Angeles | Los Angeles. |
| Sharp, John English | Farmer | | Westminster Col | Westminster. |
| Sharp, D | Farmer | nr Los Angeles | Los Angeles Co | Los Angeles. |
| Shattuck, E | Farmer | Los Angeles Co | | Los Angeles. |
| Shaw, J | Farmer | Los Angeles Co | nr Los Angeles | Los Angeles. |
| Shaw, Albert C | Apiarian | Los Angeles | Los Angeles | Los Angeles. |
| Shaw, J F | Farmer | Los Angeles Co | Silver Precinct | Downey. |
| Shaw, A S | Contractor | Los Angeles Co | Soledad | San Fernando. |
| Shaw, R W | Farmer | Anaheim | Los Angeles Co | Anaheim. |
| Shea, James | Laborer | Los Angeles | | Los Angeles. |
| Sheetz, Z | Vintner | Los Angeles Co | nr Los Angeles | Los Angeles. |
| Sheets, — | Farmer | Los Angeles Co | | Wilmington. |
| Sheehan, M F | Printer | Los Angeles | Los Angeles Co | Los Angeles. |
| Sheffield, J A | Baker | Los Angeles | Los Angeles Co | Los Angeles. |
| Sheffield, J | Shoe maker | Los Angeles | Los Angeles Co | Los Angeles. |
| Shelton, J | Farmer | nr El Monte | Los Angeles Co | El Monte. |
| Shelton, — | Farmer | Azusa ranch | 1 m S Azusa | Azusa. |
| Shelton, John | Farmer | Azusa ranch | 1 m S Azusa | Azusa. |
| Shelton, L | Farmer | Azusa ranch | 1 m S Azusa | Azusa. |
| Shelley, T H | Expressman | Langenberger's store | Anaheim | Anaheim. |
| Shelton, J, Jr | Farmer | nr El Monte | Los Angeles Co | El Monte. |
| Shephard, S W | Rustler | Los Angeles | Los Angeles Co | Los Angeles. |
| Sheppard, R C | Farmer | Los Angeles Co | nr Los Angeles | Los Angeles. |

| Name. | Occupation. | Place of Business. | Residence. | Town or P. O. |
|---|---|---|---|---|
| Shepherd, C J | Tel operator | Los Angeles | Los Angeles Co | Los Angeles. |
| Sherwood, J F | Ranchero | nr Los Angeles | Los Angeles Co | Los Angeles. |
| Sherman, L S | Mason | Los Angeles | Los Angeles Co | Los Angeles. |
| Sherman, A | Cook | Los Angeles | Los Angeles Co | Los Angeles. |
| Sherwood, J F | Farmer | | Westminster Col | Westminster. |
| Sherwood, W | Laborer | | Los Angeles Co | Los Angeles. |
| Shields, C L | Laborer | | Los Angeles Co | Los Angeles. |
| Shipley, G W | Farmer | | Westminster Col | Westminster. |
| Shirley, B F | Farmer | Los Angeles Co | Silver Precinct | Downey. |
| Short, C R | Carpenter | | Los Angeles Co | Santa Ana. |
| Short, A S | Physician | Los Angeles | Los Angeles Co | Los Angeles. |
| Short, E | Farmer | Los Angeles Co | Silver Precinct | Downey. |
| Shorb, J DeB | Vintner | Mount & Lake vin'rd | 1½ m N San Gabriel | San Gabriel. |
| Shorey, S | Farmer | Azusa road | 2 m S E Azusa | Azusa. |
| Short, Mrs | Milliner | Los Angeles st | Anaheim | Anaheim. |
| Shorb, Dr A S | Homœopathist | Star Bldg, Spring st | cor Spring and 3d sts | Los Angeles. |
| Shores, Jno | Lumberman | El Monte | Los Angeles Co | El Monte. |
| Shores, H W | Laborer | nr Wilmington | Los Angeles Co | Wilmington. |
| Shortridge, C S | Harness maker | Los Angeles Co | Silver Precinct | Downey. |
| Short, J J | Hotel keeper | Los Angeles | Los Angeles Co | Los Angeles. |
| Shirley, B F | Ranchero | Los Angeles Co | La Ballona | Los Angeles. |
| Shortridge, C S | Farmer | Los Angeles Co | Silver Precinct | Downey. |
| Shrewsbury, L B | Farmer | Los Angeles Co | Halfway House | Compton. |
| Shrewsbury, L W | Farmer | | Los Angeles Co | Los Angeles. |
| Shrewsbury, A McC | Farmer | Los Angeles Co | Halfway House | Compton. |
| Shrewsbury, S | Farmer | Los Angeles Co | Halfway House | Compton. |
| Shrode, D S | Minister | nr El Monte | Los Angeles Co | El Monte. |
| Shrode, D K | Blacksmith | Los Angeles | San Jonquin | Santa Anta. |
| Shrode, W J | Farmer | Los Angeles Co | San Joaquin | Santa Ana. |
| Shropshire, J | Laborer | Los Angeles Co | San Jose | Spadra. |
| Shroad, D S | Blacksmith | Azusa Duarte | 3 m E Lexington | El Monte. |
| Shroeder, J C & Sons | Painter | Los Angeles | | Los Angeles. |
| Shupe, E | Laborer | | Los Angeles Co | Los Angeles. |
| Shugg, I | Farmer | Los Angeles Co | Los Nietos | Los Nietos. |
| Shwapshear, J | Farmer | Spadra | 30 m E Los Angeles | Spadra. |
| Sibits, W | Laborer | nr Los Angeles | Los Angeles Co | Los Angeles. |
| Sidwell, Jno Thos | Carpenter | Los Angeles Co | | Los Angeles. |
| Sidwell, W L | Farmer | nr Anaheim | Los Angeles Co | Anaheim. |
| Sievere, Henry | Farmer | Los Angeles Co | nr Los Angeles | Los Angeles. |
| Signoret & LePrince | Saloon | Los Angeles | Los Angeles | Los Angeles. |
| Signoret, F | Barber | Los Angeles | Los Angeles | Los Angeles. |
| Silvas, J A | Laborer | | Los Angeles Co | Capistrano. |
| Silva, M | Laborer | Los Angeles Co | San Jose | Spadra. |
| Silvas, Lucas | Laborer | nr San Gabriel | Los Angeles Co | San Gabriel. |
| Silvers, J M | Farmer | Los Angeles Co | Los Angeles Co | Capistrano. |
| Silvas, E | Laborer | | Los Angeles Co | Los Angeles. |
| Silves, A | Farmer | Dalton Ranch | 1 m N Azusa | Azusa. |
| Silves, R | Farmer | Dalton Ranch | 1 m N Azusa | Azusa. |
| Silva, J P | Laborer | Wilmington | Wilmington | Wilmington. |
| Silva, J V | Laborer | Wilmington | Wilmington | Wilmington. |
| Silva, Benj | Wharf hand | S P R R Co | Wilmington | Wilmington. |
| Silva, A | Wharf hand | S P R R Co | Wilmington | Wilmington. |
| Silvas, Jose Los Santos | Laborer | Los Angeles Co | | San Gabriel. |
| Silvia, T | Laborer | | Los Angeles Co | Anaheim. |
| Silvas, J | Laborer | Los Angeles Co | Old Mission | El Monte. |
| Silvas, J M | Laborer | | Los Angeles Co | San Gabriel. |
| Silva, F | Laborer | | Los Angeles Co | San Gabriel. |
| Silvas, J A | Laborer | nr San Gabriel | Los Angeles Co | San Gabriel. |
| Simard, T M | Physician | Los Angeles | Los Angeles | Los Angeles. |
| Simmons, J | | Los Angeles Co | Silver Precinct | Downey. |
| Simmons, W | Carpenter | Los Angeles Co | Silver Precinct | Downey. |
| Simms, A | Farmer | Los Angeles Co | nr San Joaquin | Santa Ana. |

DIRECTORY OF LOS ANGELES COUNTY. 425

| NAME. | OCCUPATION. | PLACE OF BUSINESS. | RESIDENCE. | TOWN OR P. O. |
|---|---|---|---|---|
| Simmons, John | Superintendent | Santa Anita Ranch | 7 m N E San Gabriel | San Gabriel. |
| Simms, Wm G | Printer | Los Angeles | Los Angeles | Los Angeles. |
| Simmons, Chas G | Horse trainer | Los Angeles Co | | Los Angeles. |
| Simmons, J | Porter | Los Angeles | Los Angeles Co | Los Angeles. |
| Simmons, H | Blacksmith | Los Angeles | Los Angeles Co | Los Angeles. |
| Simms, Chas | Physician | Los Angeles | Los Angeles | Los Angeles. |
| Simons, E B | Farmer | Los Angeles Co | Los Angeles Co | San Juan. |
| Simonds, S P | Confectioner | 5 Spring st | 5 Spring st | Los Angeles. |
| Simon, B | Clerk | Los Angeles | Los Angeles Co | Los Angeles. |
| Simpson, J S | Clerk | Los Angeles | Los Angeles Co | Los Angeles. |
| Simpson, W H | Cook | Los Angeles | Los Angeles Co | Los Angeles. |
| Simpson, F | Farmer | nr Los Angeles | Los Angeles Co | Los Angeles. |
| Sims, M | Farmer | Los Angeles Co | nr San Joaquin | Santa Ana. |
| Sing, So | Laundry | Canal st | Canal st | Wilmington. |
| Singer, J | Blacksmith | nr Los Angeles | Los Angeles Co | Los Angeles. |
| Sippel, G | Musician | Los Angeles | Los Angeles Co | Los Angeles. |
| Sippy, R | Watchman | S P R R Co | Spadra | Spadra. |
| Sippy, Wm | Engineer | S P R R Co | Spadra | Spadra. |
| Siprian, F | Laborer | Los Angeles Co | San Jose | Spadra. |
| Sitales, J M | Baker | Los Angeles | Los Angeles Co | Los Angeles. |
| Sitton, B M | Farmer | Los Angeles Co | Silver Precinct | Downey. |
| Sitton, S I | Farmer | Los Angeles Co | Silver Precinct | Downey. |
| Sittel, Caspar | Musician | Los Angeles | Los Angeles | Los Angeles. |
| Siwert, Fredk | Stock raiser | Los Angeles Co | San Joaquin | Santa Ana. |
| Sizer, Saml | Carpenter | Los Angeles Co | Westminster Col | Westminster. |
| Skidmore, E N | Farmer | Los Angeles Co | Silver Precinct | Downey. |
| Skidmore, W | Farmer | Los Angeles Co | Silver Precinct | Downey. |
| Skillings, E M | Teamster | Los Angeles Co | Soledad | San Fernando. |
| Skinner, J K | Carpenter | | Los Angeles Co | Los Angeles. |
| Slack, Wm T | Butcher | El Monte | Los Angeles Co | El Monte. |
| Slack, Wm | Farmer | El Monte Valley | 1 m S Lexington | El Monte. |
| Slack, Wm | Peddler | San Gabriel | 9 m E Los Angeles | San Gabriel. |
| Slaney, R | Merchant | Los Angeles | Los Angeles Co | Los Angeles. |
| Slathem, M A | Farmer | Los Angeles Co | Los Angeles Co | Azusa. |
| Slater, Wm | Carpenter | San Fernando | San Fernando | San Fernando. |
| Slauson, J S | Pres L A bank | 44 Main st | 10th st | Los Angeles. |
| Slaught, S H | Real estate | Los Angeles | Los Angeles | Los Angeles. |
| Slaney, W | Clerk | Los Angeles | Los Angeles Co | Los Angeles. |
| Sleeper, L | Farmer | nr Los Nietos | Los Angeles Co | Los Nietos. |
| Slert, J | Baker | Los Angeles | Los Angeles | Los Angeles. |
| Small, E | Carpenter | Los Angeles Co | | Los Angeles. |
| Small, C M | Clerk | Los Angeles | Los Angeles Co | Los Angeles. |
| Smart, J W | Farmer | Los Angeles Co | Halfway House | Compton. |
| Smart, H W | Miller | Los Angeles | Los Angeles Co | Los Angeles. |
| Smart, D P | Farmer | Los Angeles Co | Silver Precinct | Downey. |
| Smith, Albert G | Miner | | Los Angeles Co | Los Angeles. |
| Smith, John | Plasterer | Los Angeles | Los Angeles | Los Angeles. |
| Smith, Robt | Farmer | Los Angeles Co | nr Los Angeles | Los Angeles. |
| Smith, Wm Jno A | Painter | Los Angeles | Los Angeles | Los Angeles. |
| Smith, Samuel C | Mariner | | Los Angeles Co | Wilmington. |
| Smith, A G | Clerk | Anaheim | Los Angeles Co | Anaheim. |
| Smith, A | Photographer | Centre st | Anaheim | Anaheim. |
| Smith, I S | Attorney at law | 39 Spring st | Los Angeles | Los Angeles. |
| Smith, H M | Attorney at law | Temple Block | Los Angeles | Los Angeles. |
| Smith, Geo H | Attorneys at law | Temple Block | Fort st | Los Angeles. |
| Smith, Wm P | Machinist | Los Angeles | Los Angeles | Los Angeles. |
| Smith, Thomas | Painter | Los Angeles | Los Angeles | Los Angeles. |
| Smith, J | Farmer | nr San Gabriel | Los Angeles Co | San Gabriel. |
| Smith, B F | Farmer | nr El Monte | Los Angeles Co | El Monte. |
| Smith, L L | Teamster | Los Angeles Co | Los Angeles Co | Los Angeles. |
| Smith, J H | Bar keeper | Wilmington | Los Angeles Co | Wilmington. |
| Smith, H R | Carpenter | Los Angeles | Los Angeles Co | Los Angeles. |
| Smith, J P | Engineer | Los Angeles | Los Angeles Co | Los Angeles. |
| Smith, E | Broker | Los Angeles | Los Angeles Co | Los Angeles. |

| Name. | Occupation. | Place of Business. | Residence. | Town or P. O. |
|---|---|---|---|---|
| Smith, H. | Farmer | Los Angeles Co | nr Los Angeles | Los Angeles. |
| Smith, Mrs M C | Nurse | | | Los Angeles. |
| Smith, T H | Attorney at law | 28 Temple Blk | Fort st | Los Angeles. |
| Smith & Stephens | Attorney at law | 27 & 28 Temple Blk | | Los Angeles. |
| Smith, B F | Stage proprietor | Anaheim | Anaheim | Anaheim. |
| Smith, J S | Shepherd | nr Los Angeles | Los Angeles Co | Los Angeles. |
| Smith, W J | Farmer | Los Angeles Co | nr Anaheim | Anaheim. |
| Smith, R | Farmer | nr Los Angeles | Los Angeles Co | Los Angeles. |
| Smith, S C | Farmer | Los Angeles Co | Halfway House | Compton. |
| Smith, G | Teamster | Los Angeles Co | nr Los Angeles | Los Angeles. |
| Smith, A | Merchant | Los Angeles | Los Angeles | Los Angeles. |
| Smith, M | Farmer | Los Angeles Co | nr Los Nietos | Los Nietos. |
| Smith, C H | Farmer | nr Los Angeles | Los Angeles Co | Los Angeles. |
| Smith, F | Farmer | Los Angeles Co | Halfway House | Compton. |
| Smith, D R | Farmer | nr Los Angeles | Los Angeles Co | Los Angeles. |
| Smith, J F, Jr | Ranchero | nr Los Angeles | Los Angeles Co | Los Angeles. |
| Smith, I S | Merchant | Los Angeles | Los Angeles Co | Los Angeles. |
| Smith, R G | Baker | Wilmington | Los Angeles Co | Wilmington. |
| Smith, S D | Farmer | Los Angeles Co | San Jose | Spadra. |
| Smith, J T | Farmer | nr Los Angeles | Los Angeles Co | Los Angeles. |
| Smith, C F | Laborer | Los Angeles Co | nr Los Angeles | Los Angeles. |
| Smith, I J | Merchant | Los Angeles | Los Angeles Co | Los Angeles. |
| Smith, J | Laborer | nr Los Angeles | Los Angeles Co | Los Angeles. |
| Smith, B F | Stabler | Los Angeles | Los Angeles Co | Los Angeles. |
| Smith, C | Sailor | Anaheim | Los Angeles Co | Anaheim. |
| Smith, L E | Clerk | Anaheim | Los Angeles Co | Anaheim. |
| Smith, J M | Farmer | Los Angeles Co | nr Santa Anita | Santa Anita. |
| Smith, J | Farmer | nr Azusa | Los Angeles Co | Azusa. |
| Smith, H | Laborer | | Los Angeles Co | Los Angeles. |
| Smith, C | Stable | Los Angeles | Los Angeles Co | Los Angeles. |
| Smith, R J | Farmer | nr El Monte | Los Angeles Co | El Monte. |
| Smith, J | Farmer | Los Angeles Co | San Jose | Spadra. |
| Smith, L J | Clerk | Los Angeles | Los Angeles Co | Los Angeles. |
| Smith, A | Carriage maker | Los Angeles | Los Angeles Co | Los Angeles. |
| Smith, G H | Attorney | Los Angeles | Los Angeles Co | Los Angeles. |
| Smith, C M | Farmer | Los Angeles Co | Silver Precinct | Downey. |
| Smith, E T | Carriage maker | Los Angeles | Los Angeles Co | Los Angeles. |
| Smith, W | Teamster | Los Angeles Co | nr Los Angeles | Los Angeles. |
| Smith, W | Mason | Los Nietos | Los Angeles Co | Los Nietos. |
| Smith, N | Trader | Los Angeles Co | nr Los Angeles | Los Angeles. |
| Smith, W C | Physician | Los Angeles Co | Silver Precinct | Downey. |
| Smith, Dr I W | Physician | San Gabriel | 9 m E Los Angeles | San Gabriel. |
| Smith, C | Locomo fireman | S P R R Co | San Fernando | San Fernando. |
| Smith, Joseph | Farmer | Sunny Slope | 3 m N San Gabriel | San Gabriel. |
| Smith, J N | Farmer | Azusa Ranch | 1½ m N E Azusa | Azusa. |
| Smith, A G | Wharf hand | S P R R Co | Wilmington | Wilmington. |
| Smith, Fidel | Gardener | San Pedro Ranch | 1 m W Compton | Compton. |
| Smith, Wm | Farmer | Los Angeles Co | nr Los Angeles | Los Angeles. |
| Smith, Henry Clay | Painter | Los Angeles | Los Angeles | Los Angeles. |
| Smith, Abel G | Viniculturist | nr Anaheim | Anaheim | Anaheim. |
| Smith, J | Teamster | Azusa | 3 m N Azusa | Azusa. |
| Smith, Joseph | Teacher | Spadra | 30 m E Los Angeles | Spadra. |
| Smith, N | Farmer | San Bernardino Road | 1 m E Lexington | El Monte. |
| Smith, Theodore | Farmer | San Gabriel | 9 m E Los Angeles | San Gabriel. |
| Smith, W | Farmer | Ellis Station | 1 m W Lexington | El Monte. |
| Smith, Benj | Check clerk | S P R R Co | Wilmington | Wilmington. |
| Smizer, F | Carpenter | S P R R Co | Wilmington | Wilmington. |
| Smolley, C | Plasterer | Los Angeles | Los Angeles | Los Angeles. |
| Smoot, C | Farmer | Azusa Ranch | 1¼ m S W Azusa | Azusa. |
| Sneesly, D | Farmer | Los Angeles Co | La Ballona | Los Angeles. |
| Snee, M | Teamster | | Los Angeles Co | Los Angeles. |
| Snider, D | Gen merchandise | Ellis station | 1 m W Lexington | El Monte. |
| Snider, Peter | Farmer | El Monte Valley | 3 m S Lexington | El Monte. |
| Snodgrass, Benj J | Farmer | Los Angeles Co | nr Anaheim | Anaheim. |

| Name. | Occupation. | Place of Business. | Residence. | Town or P. O. |
|---|---|---|---|---|
| Snow, G W | Farmer | Los Angeles Co | nr Los Angeles | Los Angeles. |
| Snow, George T | Farmer | Azusa | 22 m E Los Angeles | Azusa. |
| **Snyder, Douglas** | Merchant | Los Angeles Co | El Monte | El Monte. |
| Snyder, Henry H | Farmer | nr Los Angeles | Los Angeles Co | Los Angeles. |
| **Snyder, Miss M L** | Dress maker | Los Angeles | Los Angeles | Los Angeles. |
| **Snyder, J H** | Farmer | Los Angeles Co | nr Los Angeles | Los Angeles. |
| Soeur, A | Butcher | Los Angeles | Los Angeles Co | Los Angeles. |
| Solacar, I | Saloon | Canal st | Canal st | Wilmington. |
| Solazar, Y | Laborer | nr Santa Ana | Los Angeles Co | Santa Ana. |
| **Solomon, D** | Merchant | Los Angeles | Los Angeles | Los Angeles. |
| Solarsaro, G | Laborer | Los Angeles Co | nr Los Angeles | Los Angeles. |
| Souerweid, A | Painter | Los Angeles | Los Angeles Co | Los Angeles. |
| Snoddy, W M | Teamster | Los Angeles Co | nr El Monte | El Monte. |
| Sonniechssen, Sonke | Shoe maker | Los Angeles | Los Angeles | Los Angeles. |
| Soper, Chas | Farmer | San Gabriel | 9 m E Los Angeles | San Gabriel. |
| Sopher, C M | Farmer | nr San Gabriel | Los Angeles Co | San Gabriel. |
| Sopher, Wm | Stage driver | Los Angeles Co | Los Angeles Co | Los Angeles. |
| Soques, Antonio | Laborer | | Los Angeles Co | Los Angeles. |
| Sorby, — | Farmer | San Bernardino Road | 5 m N E Spadra | Spadra. |
| Sorensen, D J | Ship builder | nr Los Nietos | Los Angeles Co | Los Nietos. |
| **Sorenssen, A** | Farmer | nr Los Nietos | Los Angeles Co | Los Nietos. |
| Sotelo, T | Laborer | | Los Angeles Co | Los Angeles. |
| Sotello, R | Vintner | Los Angeles | Los Angeles Co | Los Angeles. |
| Sotello, C | Laborer | | Los Angeles Co | Los Angeles. |
| Sotello, J de Dios | Laborer | | Los Angeles Co | Los Angeles. |
| Sotello, J | Vaquero | Los Angeles Co | | Los Angeles. |
| Sotelo, F | Laborer | nr Santa Ana | Los Angeles Co | Santa Ana. |
| Soto, M | Mason | Los Angeles | Los Angeles | Los Angeles. |
| Soto, Ramon | Farmer | Los Angeles Co | San Jose | Spadra. |
| **Soto, Trinidad** | Farmer | Los Angeles Co | San Jose | Spadra. |
| Soto, R | Laborer | Los Angeles Co | La Ballona | Los Angeles. |
| Soto, J | Laborer | Los Angeles Co | Old Mission | El Monte. |
| **Soto, M** | Farmer | Los Angeles Co | nr Los Angeles | Los Angeles. |
| Soule, George | Saloon | San Gabriel | 9 m E Los Angeles | San Gabriel. |
| Soule, Jean | Farmer | nr Los Angeles | Los Angeles Co | Los Angeles. |
| Southworth, A M | Ranchero | nr Los Angeles | Los Angeles Co | Los Angeles. |
| Southworth, J M | Farmer | nr Duarte | Los Angeles Co | Azusa. |
| **Soward, Chas** | Farmer | Azusa Duarte | 3 m E Lexington | El Monte. |
| Sorusen, H | Bdg house | Los Angeles | Los Angeles Co | Los Angeles. |
| Stevenson, A B | Farmer | nr El Monte | Los Angeles Co | El Monte. |
| **Spalding, Wm A** | Local editor | Los Angeles | Los Angeles | Los Angeles. |
| Spangler, W H | Superintendent | Temple oil wells | 7 m W Lyon Station | Lyon Station. |
| Sparks, Thos J | Farmer | nr Los Angeles | Los Angeles Co | Los Angeles. |
| **Sparks, O** | Farmer | Los Angeles Co | Silver Precinct | Downey. |
| Spean, J | Farmer | Los Angeles Co | nr Los Angeles | Capistrano. |
| Speake, S H | Clerk | Los Angeles | Los Angeles Co | Los Angeles. |
| Spelman, James | Steward | Anaheim | Anaheim | Anaheim. |
| Spencer, A M | Farmer | Los Angeles Co | Old Mission | El Monte. |
| Spencer, H H | Book keeper | Los Angeles | Los Angeles Co | Los Angeles. |
| Spence, John A | Miner | Los Angeles Co | | Los Angeles. |
| **Spencer, W H** | Blacksmith | Wilmington | Los Angeles Co | Wilmington. |
| Spencer, I E | | Los Angeles | Los Angeles Co | Los Angeles. |
| **Spiker, G** | Cigar maker | Los Angeles | Los Angeles Co | Los Angeles. |
| Spohn, P | Butcher | Los Angeles | Los Angeles Co | Los Angeles. |
| Spooner, A | Laborer | | Los Angeles Co | Los Angeles. |
| Spratt, J W | | Wilmington | Los Angeles Co | Wilmington. |
| Springer, C H | Farmer | nr Los Angeles | Los Angeles Co | Los Angeles. |
| Sproul, G H | Ranchero | nr Los Nietos | Los Angeles Co | Los Nietos. |
| Spurlock, Wm A | Agent | Wilson's College | Wilmington | Wilmington. |
| Spurgin, G | Farmer | Los Angeles Co | nr Santa Ana | Santa Ana. |
| Spurgin, W H | Farmer | nr Santa Ana | Los Angeles Co | Santa Ana. |
| Squires, J E | Farmer | nr Anaheim | Los Angeles Co | Anaheim. |
| Squires, E W | Farmer | Los Angeles Co | nr Halfway House | Compton. |
| Squires, H M | Farmer | Los Angeles Co | nr Santa Ana | Santa Ana. |

L. L. PAULSON'S HAND-BOOK AND

| Name. | Occupation. | Place of Business. | Residence. | Town or P. O. |
|---|---|---|---|---|
| Stackpole, J W | Jewelry | 3½ Spring st | | Los Angeles. |
| Stackpole, T W | Jewelry | 3½ Spring st | Spring st | Los Angeles. |
| Stack, M | Laborer | Los Angeles Co | | Los Angeles. |
| Stafford, Nelson O. | Mechanic | | San Joaquin | Santa Ana. |
| Stafford, E | Laborer | Los Angeles Co | | Los Angeles. |
| Stainsby, Joseph | Carriage maker | Los Angeles | Los Angeles | Los Angeles. |
| Stallcup, E D | Farmer | El Monte Valley | 1 m S Lexington | El Monte. |
| Stalee, A J | Teamster | nr Wilmington | Los Angeles Co | Wilmington. |
| Stamps, P N | Printer | Los Angeles | Los Angeles | Los Angeles. |
| Stamps, Chas F | Brickmaker | Los Angeles | Los Angeles | Los Angeles. |
| Stamps, Benj B | Hotel keeper | Los Angeles | Los Angeles | Los Angeles. |
| Stamper, J M | Teamster | Los Angeles Co | nr Los Angeles | Los Angeles. |
| Standlee, Joel W | Farmer | Los Angeles Co | Silver Precinct | Downey. |
| Stansfield, Geo R | Railroad house | Alameda st | | Los Angeles. |
| Stanway, Dr T S | Physician | 82 & 84 Main st | Hellman Block | Los Angeles. |
| Stanway & Ross | Physicians & surgs | 82 & 84 Main st | Los Angeles | Los Angeles. |
| Stanley, J Q A | Insurance agent | Los Angeles | Los Angeles | Los Angeles. |
| Stanford & Ramirez | Attorneys at law | Temple Block | Los Angeles | Los Angeles. |
| Stanlee, David W | Farmer | Los Angeles Co | Silver Precinct | Downey. |
| Standefer, J M | Farmer | nr El Monte | Los Angeles Co | El Monte. |
| Standefer, W W | Merchant | Los Angeles Co | Silver Precinct | Downey. |
| Standefer, W R | Farmer | nr El Monte | Los Angeles Co | El Monte. |
| Stanley, J | Farmer | nr Los Nietos | Los Angeles Co | Los Nietos. |
| Stanard, G | Farmer | nr Los Angeles | Los Angeles Co | Los Angeles. |
| Stanford, F | Attorney | Los Angeles | Los Angeles Co | Los Angeles. |
| Staples, J W | Carpenter | Los Angeles | Los Angeles Co | Los Angeles. |
| Stappenbeck, C | Carpenter | Los Angeles | Los Angeles Co | Los Angeles. |
| Staples, J F | Butcher | Los Angeles | Los Angeles Co | Los Angeles. |
| Starr, E | Printer | | Los Angeles Co | Los Angeles. |
| Starr, H | Miner | nr Los Angeles | Los Angeles Co | Los Angeles. |
| Stark, L | Farmer | nr Los Angeles | Los Angeles Co | Los Angeles. |
| Stark, R | Stock raiser | nr San Fernando | Los Angeles Co | San Fernando. |
| Stassfort, H | Tailor | Los Angeles | Los Angeles Co | Los Angeles. |
| Statler, T | Saloon keeper | Old Mission | Old Mission | El Monte. |
| St Clair, H S | Sheep raiser | nr Los Angeles | Los Angeles Co | Los Angeles. |
| Stearns, V J | Waiter | Los Angeles | Los Angeles Co | Los Angeles. |
| Stearns, W | Blacksmith | Los Angeles | Los Angeles Co | Los Angeles. |
| Stedman, J S | Shoe maker | Los Angeles | Los Angeles Co | Los Angeles. |
| Stearns, O | Mechanic | Los Angeles | Los Angeles Co | Los Angeles. |
| Stearns, C J | Clerk | Los Angeles | Los Angeles Co | Los Angeles. |
| Stedman, W H | Farmer | nr Los Angeles | Los Angeles Co | Los Angeles. |
| Steel, Mrs N | Dairy | San Pedro Ranch | 1½ m S W Compton | Compton. |
| Stedman, J C | Clerk | Wilmington | Los Angeles Co | Wilmington. |
| Steel, Wesley H | Farmer | Los Angeles Co | Silver Precinct | Downey. |
| Steel, H W | Farmer | nr Compton | Los Angeles Co | Compton. |
| Steel, T W | Farmer | Los Angeles Co | nr Los Angeles | Compton. |
| Steinart, J H | Genl merchandise | Azusa | 22 m E Los Angeles | Azusa. |
| Stein, Louis | Clerk | Los Angeles | Los Angeles | Los Angeles. |
| Steine, L H | Farmer | Los Angeles Co | Tustin City | Santa Ana. |
| Steinkamp, H A | Baker | Los Angeles | Los Angeles | Los Angeles. |
| Steinmann, Wm | Miner | Los Angeles Co | | Los Angeles. |
| Steinhauer, Bros | Boots and shoes | Downey Block | | Los Angeles. |
| Steinhart, A W | Clerk | Anaheim | Los Angeles Co | Anaheim. |
| Stephens, — | Livery stable | Temple & N High sts | Los Angeles | Los Angeles. |
| Stephens, Henry | Lumber | Los Angeles Co | Westminster Col | Westminster. |
| Stephens, Albert M | Attorney at law | 27 & 28 Temple Blk. | | Los Angeles. |
| Stephens, R | Laborer | Los Angeles Co | nr Los Angeles | Los Angeles. |
| Stephens, D G | Teamster | | Los Angeles Co | Los Angeles. |
| Stephenson, B V | Surveyor | San Fernando | Los Angeles Co | San Fernando. |
| Stephenson, G | Painter | Los Angeles | Los Angeles | Los Angeles. |
| Stern, D | Painter | Los Angeles Co | Los Angeles | Los Angeles. |
| Stevenson, H J | Civil engineer | 290 Downey Block | | Los Angeles. |
| Stevens, J | Laborer | nr Los Angeles | Los Angeles Co | Los Angeles. |

DIRECTORY OF LOS ANGELES COUNTY. 429

| NAME. | OCCUPATION. | PLACE OF BUSINESS. | RESIDENCE. | TOWN OR P. O. |
|---|---|---|---|---|
| Stevens, G............ | Miner................. | Los Angeles Co....... | Soledad................... | San Fernando. |
| Stevens, G W........ | Carpenter........... | Los Angeles........... | Los Angeles Co...... | Los Angeles. |
| Stevenson, F......... | Farmer .... .......... | nr Los Angeles....... | Los Angeles Co...... | Los Angeles. |
| Stevens, E ........... | Farmer ............... | Los Angeles Co....... | nr Los Angeles....... | Los Angeles. |
| Stevenson, W H ... | Carpenter........... | Los Angeles........... | Los Angeles Co....... | Los Angeles. |
| Stewart, Thomas.... | Laborer................ | Wilmington........... | Canal st.................. | Wilmington. |
| Stewart, Mrs A...... | Farmer ............... | El Monte Valley...... | 1 m E Lexington ..... | El Monte. |
| Stewart, R G......... | Mechanic ............ | Los Angeles Co....... | ............................ | San Fernando. |
| Stewart, James...... | Laborer................ | ............................ | Los Angeles Co....... | Los Angeles. |
| Stewart, Wm A..... | Engineer............. | Los Angeles........... | Los Angeles........... | Los Angeles. |
| Stewart, James ..... | Farmer................. | Los Angeles Co....... | Silver Precinct........ | Downey. |
| Stewart, J M......... | Farmer................. | Los Angeles Co....... | nr Los Angeles....... | Los Angeles. |
| Stewart, W P......... | .......................... | Los Angeles Co....... | Silver Precinct....... | Downey. |
| Stewart, J ............ | Painter ............... | Los Angeles........... | Los Angeles Co....... | Los Angeles. |
| Steward, C............ | Farmer................. | nr San Gabriel........ | Los Angeles Co....... | San Gabriel. |
| Stewart, T............. | Laborer................ | nr Wilmington....... | Los Angeles Co....... | Wilmington. |
| Stewart, R H......... | Miner................... | Los Angeles Co ..... | Los Angeles........... | San Fernando. |
| Stewart, J............. | Farmer................. | nr El Monte........... | Los Angeles Co....... | El Monte. |
| Stewart, J H......... | Blacksmith ......... | Los Angeles Co....... | Silver Precinct........ | Downey. |
| Stiles, W R............ | Bar keeper........... | Wilmington........... | Los Angeles Co....... | Wilmington. |
| Stine, J D ............. | Teamster.............. | Los Angeles Co....... | nr Los Angeles....... | Los Angeles. |
| Stine, E V ............. | Dairyman............ | Los Angeles Co....... | nr Los Angeles....... | Los Angeles. |
| St Jean, F S del..... | Miner................... | Los Angeles Co....... | nr Los Angeles....... | Los Angeles. |
| Stockwell, J H...... | Dairy................... | San Pedro Ranch.... | 1½ m N E Compton.. | Compton. |
| Stockton, Geo........ | Clerk.................... | Los Angeles........... | Los Angeles........... | Los Angeles. |
| Stockton, E........... | Farmer ................ | Los Angeles Co....... | Silver Precinct ....... | Downey. |
| Stockton, W McD.. | Farmer................ | nr San Gabriel........ | Los Angeles Co....... | San Gabriel. |
| Stockwell, J H...... | Farmer................. | Los Angeles Co....... | Halfway House...... | Compton. |
| Stoermer, A.......... | Gunsmith............. | Los Angeles........... | Los Angeles Co ..... | Los Angeles. |
| Stokes, Richd D..... | Purser.................. | Los Angeles........... | Los Angeles........... | Los Angeles. |
| Stokes, A S............ | Agent................... | Los Angeles........... | Los Angeles........... | Los Angeles. |
| Stoll, Henry W..... | Soda mnfr............ | Sansevain st........... | New Commercial st. | Los Angeles. |
| Stoll, S.................. | Barber.................. | Los Angeles........... | Los Angeles Co....... | Los Angeles. |
| Stoll, P.................. | Clerk ................... | Los Angeles........... | Los Angeles Co....... | Los Angeles. |
| Stoneman, Genl George.............. | Vintner ............... | Los Robles............. | 2 m N W San Gab... | San Gabriel. |
| Stoneman, —........ | Farmer ................ | Azusa.................... | 3 m S W Azusa....... | Azusa. |
| Stone, George M.... | Clerk.................... | Los Angeles........... | Los Angeles........... | Los Angeles. |
| Stonebarger, S....... | Miner................... | nr Los Angeles ...... | Los Angeles Co....... | Los Angeles. |
| Stone, J B ............. | Farmer ............... | nr Los Nietos......... | Los Angeles Co....... | Los Nietos. |
| Stone, E ................ | Carpenter ........... | Los Angeles........... | Los Angeles Co....... | Los Angeles. |
| St Ores, L.............. | Farmer ................ | Los Angeles Co ..... | Halfway House...... | Compton. |
| St Ores, A.............. | Farmer................. | Los Angeles Co ..... | Halfway House...... | Compton. |
| Stormer, L............. | Carpenter............ | nr Los Angeles ...... | Los Angeles Co....... | Los Angeles. |
| Story, T................. | Farmer ................ | Los Angeles Co....... | La Ballona.............. | Los Angeles. |
| Stout, J K ............. | Farmer ................ | Los Angeles Co....... | Silver Precinct........ | Downey. |
| Stratton, George.... | Farmer ................ | Los Angeles Co....... | nr Los Angeles....... | Los Angeles. |
| Strange, Saml....... | Farmer ................ | Los Angeles Co....... | nr San Gabriel........ | San Gabriel. |
| Stratton, Edward.. | Farmer ............... | nr Wilmington....... | Los Angeles Co....... | Wilmington. |
| Strader, J M.......... | Farmer ................ | Los Angeles Co ..... | Silver Precinct ....... | Downey. |
| Strahle, P.............. | Speculator........... | Los Angeles........... | Los Angeles Co....... | Los Angeles. |
| Strelitz, J.............. | Mcht tailor........... | 78 Main st.............. | 1st st...................... | Los Angeles. |
| Street, J................ | Driver.................. | nr Los Angeles ...... | Los Angeles Co....... | Los Angeles. |
| Strickland, I......... | Farmer ................ | Los Angeles Co....... | nr Azusa ................ | Azusa. |
| Strickland, R F ..... | Farmer ................ | nr Los Nietos ........ | Los Nietos.............. | Los Nietos. |
| Strobridge, Alanson | Farmer ................ | nr Santa Ana......... | Santa Ana.............. | Santa Ana. |
| Strong, Stephen .... | Farmer................. | Los Angeles Co....... | Silver Precinct........ | Downey. |
| Strong, Robert...... | Superintendent.... | Westminster Col..... | Westminster........... | Westminster. |
| Strong, J G............ | Farmer ................ | Los Angeles Co ..... | Silver Precinct........ | Downey. |
| Strong, H C .......... | Farmer ................ | Los Angeles Co ..... | Silver Precinct........ | Downey. |
| Strodthoff, D......... | Zanjero ............... | nr Anaheim ........... | Los Angeles Co....... | Anaheim. |
| Strong, R W.......... | Farmer ................ | nr El Monte............ | Los Angeles Co....... | El Monte. |
| Stroble, M F.......... | Civil engineer...... | Anaheim................ | Los Angeles Co....... | Anaheim. |
| Strong, H C........... | Farmer.................. | Los Angeles Co....... | nr Los Angeles....... | Los Angeles. |

| Name. | Occupation. | Place of Business. | Residence. | Town or P. O. |
|---|---|---|---|---|
| Strond, R............ | Blacksmith........ | nr Los Nietos......... | Los Angeles Co...... | Los Nietos. |
| Strunk, W C......... | Farmer ............. | Azusa ................. | 22 m E Los Angeles. | Azusa. |
| Strunk, G W......... | Mechanic ........... | Los Angeles Co...... | .......................... | Los Angeles. |
| Struck, J P........... | Farmer............... | nr El Monte........... | Los Angeles Co ..... | El Monte. |
| Struck, A............. | Miner ................. | ........................... | Los Angeles Co ..... | Anaheim. |
| Strunk, W C......... | Farmer............... | Los Angeles Co...... | nr Azusa............... | Azusa. |
| Stuart, J............... | Well borer........... | Compton............... | Compton............... | Compton. |
| Studszinski, S...... | Merchant ............ | Los Angeles.......... | Los Angeles Co...... | Los Angeles. |
| Stump, J K............ | Farmer............... | Los Angeles Co ..... | Halfway House....... | Compton. |
| Stump, J W .......... | Attorney at law... | r 4 Downey Block... | Los Angeles.......... | Los Angeles. |
| Sturgis, E G ........ | Farmer .............. | nr Los Angeles...... | Los Angeles Co...... | Los Angeles. |
| Sturhich, Thomas... | Laborer............... | Los Angeles Co...... | .......................... | Los Angeles. |
| Subita, A............. | Laborer............... | nr El Monte........... | Los Angeles Co...... | El Monte. |
| Suddey, Wm......... | Farmer ............... | El Monte Valley..... | 1½ m N Lexington... | El Monte. |
| Sudworth, John A.. | Miller ................. | Los Angeles Co...... | Anaheim............... | Anaheim. |
| Sullivan, Wm....... | Farmer ............... | nr Anaheim........... | Los Angeles Co...... | Anaheim. |
| Sullivan, F........... | Laborer............... | nr Wilmington........ | Los Angeles Co...... | Wilmington. |
| Sullivan, T........... | Farmer ............... | nr Los Angeles....... | Los Angeles Co ..... | Los Angeles. |
| Sullivan, M........... | Farmer ............... | nr Los Angeles....... | Los Angeles Co...... | Los Angeles. |
| Sullivan, D........... | Farmer ............... | Los Angeles Co...... | nr Los Angeles....... | Los Angeles. |
| Sullivan, J........... | Fireman.............. | S P R R Co........... | Anaheim .............. | Anaheim. |
| Sullivan, Simon.... | Blacksmith.......... | Los Angeles.......... | Los Angeles.......... | Los Angeles. |
| Sullivan, John ..... | Laborer............... | Los Angeles Co ..... | .......................... | Los Angeles. |
| Sullivan, J H ....... | Shepherd............ | .......................... | San Joaquin.......... | Santa Ana. |
| Summers, F.......... | Farmer ............... | Los Angeles Co...... | Silver Precinct....... | Downey. |
| Summers, J R....... | Mechanic............ | Los Angeles.......... | Los Angeles Co...... | Los Angeles. |
| Sumner & Nelson... | ........................... | 16 Spring st......... | .......................... | Los Angeles. |
| Suniga, R............. | Farmer ............... | Los Angeles Co...... | nr El Monte........... | El Monte. |
| Surdam, G............ | Laborer............... | Los Angeles Co...... | nr Los Angeles....... | Los Angeles. |
| Surhr, R K........... | Hotel keeper........ | Los Angeles.......... | Los Angeles Co ..... | Los Angeles. |
| Surrott, M............ | Farmer ............... | Los Angeles Co ..... | Halfway House...... | Compton. |
| Sutherland, Robt... | Waiter ................. | Los Angeles.......... | Los Angeles.......... | Los Angeles. |
| Sutton, J............. | Farmer ............... | nr El Monte........... | Los Angeles Co...... | El Monte. |
| Sutton, J T.......... | Farmer ............... | Los Angeles Co...... | Silver Precinct....... | Downey. |
| Sutton, J M.......... | Farmer ............... | nr El Monte........... | Los Angeles Co...... | El Monte. |
| Sutton, A L.......... | Farmer ............... | Los Angeles Co ..... | Silver Precinct ...... | Downey. |
| Sutton, F............. | Farmer ............... | San Fernando Valley | 7m S E San Fernando | San Fernando. |
| Sutton, J, Jr......... | Farmer ............... | nr Los Angeles....... | Los Angeles Co ..... | Los Angeles. |
| Swain, R P........... | Farmer ............... | Los Angeles Co...... | Silver Precinct....... | Downey. |
| Swain, W F.......... | Farmer ............... | Los Angeles Co...... | Silver Precinct....... | Downey. |
| Swain, B N.......... | Farmer ............... | Los Angeles Co...... | Los Nietos............ | Los Nietos. |
| Swanson, H F....... | Farmer ............... | Los Angeles Co...... | Silver Precinct....... | Downey. |
| Swan, W H.......... | Farmer ............... | Los Angeles Co...... | Los Angeles Co...... | Los Angeles. |
| Swanson, J W....... | Farmer ............... | Los Angeles Co...... | Silver Precinct....... | Downey. |
| Sweaney, M......... | Laborer............... | .......................... | .......................... | Los Angeles. |
| Sweetzer, C......... | Mariner .............. | Wilmington........... | Los Angeles Co...... | Wilmington. |
| Sweeney, E.......... | Laborer............... | Los Angeles Co...... | .......................... | Los Angeles. |
| Sweetman, Chas H.. | Carpenter ........... | .......................... | Los Angeles Co...... | Los Angeles. |
| Sweeny, O........... | Laborer .............. | Los Angeles Co...... | nr Compton........... | Compton. |
| Sweeney, J.......... | Tailor ................. | Los Angeles.......... | Los Angeles Co...... | Los Angeles. |
| Sweltzer, F.......... | Carpenter ........... | S P R R Co........... | Canal st............... | Wilmington. |
| Swift, F............... | Moulder.............. | Los Angeles.......... | Los Angeles Co...... | Los Angeles. |
| Swigart, T C........ | Hardware, etc...... | 110 Main st........... | Main st................ | Los Angeles. |
| Swigart & Huber.. | Hardware, etc...... | 110 Main st........... | .......................... | Los Angeles. |
| Swim, C.............. | Lighterman......... | Anaheim .............. | Los Angeles Co...... | Anaheim. |
| Switzer, C P ....... | Carpenter........... | Los Angeles.......... | Los Angeles Co...... | Los Angeles. |
| Switzler, John...... | Farmer ............... | Azusa Ranch......... | 2 m S W Azusa...... | Azusa. |
| Swope, R L......... | Farmer ............... | nr Los Angeles....... | Los Angeles Co...... | Los Angeles. |
| Sylva, Joseph P... | Check clerk ........ | S P R R Co........... | Wilmington........... | Wilmington. |
| Sylvas, Pio.......... | Vaquero.............. | .......................... | Los Angeles Co...... | Los Angeles. |
| Sylva, J.............. | Wharf hand ........ | S P R R Co........... | Wilmington .......... | Wilmington. |
| Sylvas, Y............ | Laborer............... | .......................... | Los Angeles Co...... | Los Angeles. |
| Sylva, V J........... | Laborer............... | Los Angeles Co...... | nr Wilmington........ | Wilmington. |
| Sylva, J P........... | Laborer............... | Los Angeles Co...... | nr Wilmington........ | Wilmington. |

DIRECTORY OF LOS ANGELES COUNTY. 431

| Name. | Occupation. | Place of Business. | Residence. | Town or P. O. |
|---|---|---|---|---|
| Taber, R............ | Farmer............ | Los Angeles Co........ | Silver Precinct......... | Downey. |
| Tabor, A G........... | Carpenter........ | Los Angeles............ | Los Angeles Co........ | Los Angeles. |
| Taenchell, A F..... | .................... | ....................... | Los Angeles Co........ | Los Angeles. |
| Taft, H........... | Traveler...  ......... | Los Angeles............ | Los Angeles Co........ | Los Angeles. |
| Taggert, J W........ | Prospector........ | Azusa Ranch....... | 2½ m N E Azusa...... | Azusa. |
| Talamandes, J...... | Laborer ............ | Wilmington........... | Wilmington........... | Wilmington. |
| Talamandes, L...... | Laborer............ | Wilmington........... | Wilmington ...  ....... | Wilmington. |
| Talamates, J T..... | Ranchero.. ........ | Los Angeles Co........ | La Ballona....  ........ | Los Angeles. |
| Talamantes, L....... | Farmer........... | Los Angeles Co........ | nr La Ballona......... | Los Angeles. |
| Talamantes, Jacinto | Laborer............ | ....................... | La Ballona........... | Los Angeles. |
| Talamantes, F....... | Laborer............. | nr Los Angeles........ | Los Angeles Co........ | Los Angeles. |
| Talbot, M W........ | Farmer............ | San Pedro Ranch..... | 1½ m N E Compton... | Compton. |
| Talbert, Henry...... | Porter............. | Los Angeles............ | Los Angeles Co........ | Los Angeles. |
| Talbott, J A......... | Printer........... | Los Angeles............ | Los Angeles Co........ | Los Angeles. |
| Talbert, H D....... | Farmer............ | Los Angeles Co........ | Silver Precinct......... | Downey. |
| Talbot, M W........ | ..................... | Los Angeles............ | Los Angeles Co........ | Los Angeles. |
| Talkington, Sun N.. | Farmer............ | nr Silver Precinct.... | Los Angeles Co........ | Downey. |
| Talkington, A A... | Farmer............ | Los Angeles Co........ | Silver Precinct ........ | Downey. |
| Tallant, E W....... | Farmer............ | San Gabriel............ | 9 m E Los Angeles... | San Gabriel. |
| Tallant, Eben W... | Farmer............ | Los Angeles Co........ | nr San Gabriel.. ...... | San Gabriel. |
| Tallant, Geo W.. ... | Ranchero.. ........ | nr San Gabriel......... | 4 m Los Angeles....... | San Gabriel. |
| Tam, James S........ | Clerk.. ............ | Los Angeles............ | Los Angeles............ | Los Angeles. |
| Tannehill, C B...... | Clerk............... | Los Angeles............ | Los Angeles Co........ | Los Angeles. |
| Tansey, J R......... | Minister ........... | Florence............... | Florence.............. | Los Angeles. |
| Tantiua, M.......... | Farmer ,........... | Los Angeles Co........ | nr El Monte.......... | El Monte. |
| Tapia, C............. | Farmer ............ | Los Angeles Co........ | nr Los Nietos.......... | Los Nietos. |
| Tapia, Antonia...... | Woodchopper.. .... | ....................... | Los Angeles Co........ | Los Angeles. |
| Tapia, Juan.......... | Laborer............ | Los Angeles Co........ | ....................... | Los Angeles. |
| Tapia, T............. | Laborer............ | ....................... | Los Angeles Co ...... | San Gabriel. |
| Tapia, J M.......... | Laborer............ | ....................... | Los Angeles Co........ | Los Angeles. |
| Tapia, S............. | Laborer ........... | Los Angeles Co........ | ....................... | Los Angeles. |
| Tapia, A............ | Laborer............ | ....................... | Los Angeles Co........ | San Gabriel. |
| Tapia, Francisco... | Farmer............ | Los Angeles Co........ | nr Los Angeles......... | Los Angeles. |
| Tapia, J A........... | Laborer............ | ....................... | Los Angeles Co........ | Los Angeles. |
| Tapia, C............ | Laborer ........... | Los Angeles Co........ | ....................... | Los Angeles. |
| Tapia, J J........... | Laborer ............ | ....................... | Los Angeles Co ...... | Los Angeles. |
| Tapia, M............ | Laborer............ | Los Angeles Co........ | ....................... | Los Angeles. |
| Tarbox & Curtis... | Brewers........... | Los Angeles............ | Los Angeles........... | Los Angeles. |
| Tarpin, Bernardo... | Laborer ............ | ....................... | Los Angeles Co........ | Los Angeles. |
| Tarr, C W........... | Minister........... | Compton ............. | Los Angeles Co........ | Compton. |
| Tarwater, B W..... | Farmer............ | Silver Precinct........ | Los Angeles Co....... | Downey. |
| Tasso, Guseppe..... | Farmer............ | Los Angeles............ | nr Los Angeles......... | Los Angeles. |
| Tatem, J W......... | Miner.............. | ....................... | Los Angeles Co ...... | Anaheim. |
| Tate, J H............ | Butcher........... | Los Angeles............ | Los Angeles Co........ | Los Angeles. |
| Taylor, J J.......... | Farmer............ | Los Angeles Co........ | nr El Monte.......... | El Monte. |
| Taylor, R B......... | Teamster .......... | ....................... | Los Angeles Co.... ... | El Monte. |
| Taylor, A........... | Farmer............ | nr Soledad............ | Soledad............... | San Fernando. |
| Taylor, James....... | Farmer............ | Los Angeles Co........ | nr Los Angeles......... | Los Angeles. |
| Taylor, Wm......... | Longshoreman ... | ....................... | Los Angeles Co ...... | Los Angeles. |
| Taylor, F M......... | Farmer............ | Los Angeles Co........ | Old Mission ......... | El Monte. |
| Taylor, J A......... | Farmer............ | nr El Monte.......... | Los Angeles Co ...... | El Monte. |
| Taylor, A........... | Farmer............ | nr El Monte.......... | Los Angeles Co ...... | El Monte. |
| Taylor, E S......... | Farmer............ | Los Angeles Co........ | nr El Monte.......... | El Monte. |
| Taylor, L H......... | Farmer............ | nr El Monte.... ...... | Los Angeles Co....... | El Monte. |
| Taylor, D........... | Painter............ | Los Angeles............ | Los Angeles Co........ | Los Angeles. |
| Taylor, J T......... | Miner.............. | Los Angeles Co—...... | Soledad.............. | San Fernando. |
| Taylor, G W........ | Farmer............ | ....................... | Los Angeles Co........ | Los Angeles. |
| Taylor, J D......... | Laborer........... | Los Angeles Co........ | ....................... | Anaheim. |
| Taylor, F........... | Farmer............ | nr El Monte.......... | Los Angeles Co........ | El Monte. |
| Taylor, W.......... | Restaurant ....... | Los Angeles........... | Los Angeles Co........ | Los Angeles. |
| Taylor, C E......... | Miner............. | Los Angeles............ | Los Angeles Co........ | Los Angeles. |
| Taylor, C D......... | Bookkeeper ....... | Los Angeles............ | Los Angeles Co........ | Los Angeles. |
| Taylor, C........... | Mechanic ......... | Los Angeles............ | Los Angeles Co........ | Los Angeles. |
| Taylor, E........... | Farmer............ | nr Los Angeles........ | Los Angeles Co........ | Los Angeles. |

L. L. PAULSON'S HAND-BOOK AND

| Name. | Occupation. | Place of Business. | Residence. | Town or P. O. |
|---|---|---|---|---|
| Taylor, W | Farmer | nr El Monte | Los Angeles Co | El Monte. |
| Taylor, D | Surgeon | Anaheim | Los Angeles Co | Anaheim. |
| Taylor, J | Farmer | Los Angeles Co | nr Santa Ana | Santa Ana. |
| Taylor, H | Mechanic | Los Angeles Co | Los Angeles Co | Los Angeles. |
| Teahan, John | Laborer |  | Los Angeles Co | Los Angeles. |
| Tedford, J T | Farmer | nr Santa Ana | Los Angeles Co | Santa Ana. |
| Tedford, W N | Farmer | nr Santa Ana | Los Angeles Co | Santa Ana. |
| Teed, M | Carpenter | Los Angeles | Los Angeles Co | Los Angeles. |
| Teel, G M | Farmer | Los Angeles Co | nr Anaheim | Anaheim. |
| Teel, A B | Farmer | Los Angeles Co | Old Mission | El Monte. |
| Teel, E A | Farmer | Los Angeles Co | nr Anahhim | Anaheim. |
| Teel, P | Farmer | nr Anaheim | Los Angeles Co | Anaheim. |
| Teffelmeyer, L | Stage driver |  | Los Angeles Co | Los Angeles. |
| Tell, Mrs Wm | Restaurant | Old Santa Monica | Old Santa Monica | Los Angeles. |
| Tell, W | Painter | Los Angeles | Los Angeles Co | Los Angeles. |
| Temple, F P F | Banker | Temple Block | Los Angeles | Los Angeles. |
| Temple, T W | Farmer | nr Los Angeles | Los Angeles Co | Los Angeles. |
| Temple, John | Laborer | Los Angeles Co |  | Los Angeles. |
| Tennison, J A | Lumberman | Los Angeles Co | Silver District | Downey. |
| Teodoli, E F | Propr | La Cronica | Los Angeles | Los Angeles. |
| Terrence, J M | Laborer | Los Angeles Co | Soledad | San Fernando. |
| Terri, Jean Pierre | Farmer | Los Angeles Co | nr Los Angeles | Los Angeles. |
| Terrel, Wm | Farmer | Spadra | 30 m E Los Angeles | Spadra. |
| Terrant & Pierre | Asphaltum roofs | High st |  | Los Angeles. |
| Tesch, Harmon | Blacksmith | Los Angeles | Los Angeles | Los Angeles. |
| Thatcher, L W | Jeweler | Los Angeles | Los Angeles | Los Angeles. |
| Thayer, J S | Real estate | 21 Spring st | Los Angeles | Los Angeles. |
| Thearer, M | Carpenter | Los Angeles | Los Angeles Co | Los Angeles. |
| Theile, Danl | Mariner |  | Los Angeles Co | Wilmington. |
| Theopile, N | Sheep raiser | Los Angeles Co | nr Los Angeles | Los Angeles. |
| Thomas, E N | Laborer |  | Los Angeles Co | Los Angeles. |
| Thomas, D H | Wheelwright | Los Angeles | Los Angeles Co | Los Angeles. |
| Thomas, W H | Miner |  | Los Angeles Co | El Monte. |
| Thomas, A | Farmer | Los Angeles Co | Halfway House | Compton. |
| Thompson, O D Jr | Farmer | nr Silver Precinct | Los Angeles Co | Downey. |
| Thompson, Thos | Laborer | Los Angeles Co |  | Los Angeles. |
| Thompson, A L | Lumberman |  | Los Angeles Co | Los Angeles. |
| Thompson, G | Blacksmith | Los Angeles | Los Angeles Co | Los Angeles. |
| Thomas, H C | Farmer | nr Los Angeles | Los Angeles Co | Los Angeles. |
| Thomas, E P | Farmer | nr Los Angeles | Los Angeles Co | Los Angeles. |
| Thomas, G P | Farmer | nr Los Angeles | Los Angeles Co | Los Angeles. |
| Thomas, J M | Farmer | Los Angeles Co | nr El Monte | El Monte. |
| Thomas, M B | Farmer | Los Angeles Co | nr Los Nietos | Los Nietos. |
| Thomas, H S | Farmer | nr Anaheim | Los Angeles Co | Anaheim. |
| Thompson & Waterman | Semi-trop nursery | San Pedro st | 2 m S Court House | Los Angeles. |
| Thompson & Clarke | Attorneys at law | 4 Downey block | Los Angeles | Los Angeles. |
| Thoun & Ross | Attorneys | Los Angeles | Los Angeles | Los Angeles. |
| Thompson Andrew | Farmer | Los Angeles Co | Westminster Col | Westminster. |
| Thomas, John | Farmer | nr Los Angeles | Los Angeles Co | Los Angeles. |
| Thomas, Nolan | Laborer | Los Angeles Co |  | Los Angeles. |
| Thompson, J W | Clerk | Spadra | 30 m E Los Angeles | Spadra. |
| Thom, Dr Wm A | Physician | San Gabriel | 9 m E Los Angeles | San Gabriel. |
| Thompson, I S | Farmer | Azusa Ranch | ½ m S W Azusa | Azusa. |
| Thompson, S G | Saloon & lodg ho | Canal st | Canal st | Wilmington. |
| Thompson, E R | Farmer | Azusa Ranch | 1½ m S W Azusa | Azusa. |
| Thomas, Wm H | Master mechanic | S P R R | Canal st | Wilmington. |
| Thompson, J S | Attorney at law | r 3 & 4 Downey Blk | Los Angeles | Los Angeles. |
| Thomas, T T | Prospector | Azusa | 2½ m N E Azusa | Azusa. |
| Thompson, U | Saloon keeper | Los Angeles | Los Angeles Co | Los Angeles. |
| Thomas, C C | Farmer | Los Angeles Co | nr Los Angeles | Los Angeles. |
| Thompson, D | Miner | Los Angeles Co | Los Angeles Co | Los Angeles. |
| Thompson, A | Blacksmith | Los Angeles | Los Angeles Co | Los Angeles. |
| Thompson, O D | Farmer | Los Angeles Co | Silver Precinct | Downey. |

## DIRECTORY OF LOS ANGELES COUNTY. 433

| Name. | Occupation. | Place of Business. | Residence. | Town or P. O. |
|---|---|---|---|---|
| Thompson, S S | Farmer | nr Los Nietos | Los Angeles Co | Los Nietos. |
| Thompson, C W | Laborer | | Los Angeles Co | Los Angeles. |
| Thomas, Jr, H B | Farmer | Los Angeles Co | Halfway House | Compton. |
| Thompson, J | Farmer | nr Los Angeles | Los Angeles Co | Los Angeles. |
| Thompson, T | Hotel keeper | Wilmington | Los Angeles Co | Wilmington. |
| Thompson, H | Laborer | | Los Angeles Co | Los Angeles. |
| Thompson, W F | Laborer | nr Los Nietos | Los Angeles Co | Los Nietos. |
| Thompson, W C | Painter | Los Angeles Co | Old Mission | El Monte. |
| Thom, C E | Attorney | Los Angeles | Los Angeles Co | Los Angeles. |
| Thomas, M G | Farmer | Los Angeles Co | Halfway House | Compton. |
| Thomas, H B | Farmer | Los Angeles Co | Halfway House | Compton. |
| Thompson, P | Clerk | Los Angeles | Los Angeles Co | Los Angeles. |
| Thompson, H | Engineer | El Monte | Los Angeles Co | El Monte. |
| Thompson, J F | Farmer | Los Angeles Co | nr Los Angeles | Los Angeles. |
| Thompson, Dr R M | Harness maker | nr Los Angeles | Los Angeles Co | Los Angeles. |
| Thompkins, G G | Farmer | nr Anaheim | Los Angeles Co | Anaheim. |
| Thompson, R E | Farmer | Los Angeles Co | nr Los Angeles | Los Angeles. |
| Thomas, M | Farmer | nr Los Angeles | Los Angeles Co | Los Angeles. |
| Thompson, W P | Upholsterer | Los Angeles | Los Angeles Co | Los Angeles. |
| Thompson, T | Carpenter | Los Angeles | Los Angeles Co | Los Angeles. |
| Thomas, J W | Farmer | Los Nietos | Los Angeles Co | Los Nietos. |
| Thomas, S W | Miner | | Los Angeles Co | Los Angeles. |
| Thompson, S G | Hotel keeper | Wilmington | Los Angeles Co | Wilmington. |
| Thompson, W W | Farmer | | Los Angeles Co | El Monte. |
| Thompson, W F | Farmer | Los Angeles Co | Silver Precinct | Downey. |
| Thompson, R | Farmer | nr Anaheim | Los Angeles Co | Anaheim. |
| Thomas, W H | Stock raiser | Los Angeles Co | San Antonio | Downey. |
| Thompson, S H | Blacksmith | Los Angeles | Los Angeles | Los Angeles. |
| Thomas, Adam G | Shepherd | | Anaheim | Anaheim. |
| Thomas, J J | Painter | Los Angeles | Los Angeles | Los Angeles. |
| Thomas, Wm | Farmer | nr Los Angeles | Los Angeles Co | Los Angeles. |
| Thomas, James | Farmer | nr El Monte | El Monte | El Monte. |
| Thompson, J W | Farmer | nr El Monte | El Monte | El Monte. |
| Thrift, W C | Farmer | Los Angeles Co | Silver Precinct | Downey. |
| Thurman, Columbus | Stock raiser | Los Angeles Co | La Puente | El Monte. |
| Thurman, R M | Farmer | nr El Monte | Los Angeles Co | El Monte. |
| Thurman, J | Farmer | nr El Monte | Los Angeles Co | El Monte. |
| Thurman, E A | Farmer | Los Angeles Co | nr El Monte | El Monte. |
| Thurman, A S | Farmer | nr El Monte | Los Angeles Co | El Monte. |
| Thurston, G W | Farmer | Los Angeles Co | Capistrano | San Juan. |
| Thurman, J S | Farmer | nr El Monte | Los Angeles Co | El Monte. |
| Thurman, E A | Sheep raiser | San Bernardino Road | 9 m E Lexington | El Monte. |
| Thurman, John Jr | Painter | Lexington | 12 m E Los Angeles | El Monte. |
| Thurman, John Sr | Farmer | Lexington | 12 m E Los Angeles | El Monte. |
| Thurman, R M | Farmer | Ellis Station | 1 m W Lexington | El Monte. |
| Tibbet, J H | Farmer | Los Angeles Co | Old Mission | El Monte. |
| Tibbet, J | Freighter | | Los Angeles Co | El Monte. |
| Tice, E G | Mason | Los Angeles | Los Angeles Co | Los Angeles. |
| Tichenal, W H | Farmer | Los Angeles Co | nr Santa Ana | Santa Ana. |
| Tichenal, W C | Farmer | Los Angeles Co | nr Santa Ana | Santa Ana. |
| Tichenal, J J | Farmer | | San Joaquin | Santa Ana. |
| Tierce, T R | Farmer | Los Angeles Co | Silver Precinct | Downey. |
| Tiernan, James | Laborer | | Los Angeles Co | Wilmington. |
| Tietz, G | Machinist | Los Angeles | Los Angeles Co | Los Angeles. |
| Tiffany & Co | Publishers | Los Angeles | Los Angeles | Los Angeles. |
| Tiffany, G A | Printer | Los Angeles | Los Angeles | Los Angeles. |
| Tiffany, G O | Farmer | nr Los Angeles | Los Angeles Co | Los Angeles. |
| Tighe, T | Bar keeper | Los Angeles | Los Angeles Co | Los Angeles. |
| Tillotson, Theodore | Farmer | Los Angeles Co | nr Los Angeles | Los Angeles. |
| Tillman, Chas W | Carpenter | Los Angeles | | Los Angeles. |
| Times, W | Farmer | Los Angeles Co | nr Los Angeles | Los Angeles. |
| Timms, A W | Hotel keeper | Point San Pedro | 4 m S Wilmington | Wilmington. |
| Tinker, Henry A | Laborer | Los Angeles Co | | Wilmington. |

28

| NAME. | OCCUPATION. | PLACE OF BUSINESS. | RESIDENCE. | TOWN OR P. O. |
|---|---|---|---|---|
| Tinker, R E............ | Mariner ............... | Wilmington............ | Los Angeles Co........ | Wilmington. |
| Tipton, John E...... | Farmer ............... | Heartsease House..... | 3 m E Lexington..... | El Monte. |
| Tisball, J F ......... | Farmer ............... | nr Los Nietos........... | Los Angeles Co........ | Downey. |
| Tishler, S .... ......... | Clerk.. ............... | Los Angeles........... | Los Angeles Co ...... | Los Angeles. |
| Titsman, G............ | Clerk ............... | Wilmington ........... | Los Angeles Co....... | Wilmington. |
| **Titus, L H**............ | Orange orchard... | Dew Drop............ | 11 m N E Los A...... | Los Angeles. |
| Toberman, J R...... | Agent ............... | Los Angeles........... | Los Angeles Co ...... | Los Angeles. |
| Tobias, J..... ......... | Peddler............... | Los Angeles........... | Los Angeles Co ...... | Los Angeles. |
| Tobin, Edward J ... | Clerk ............... | Los Angeles........... | Los Angeles............ | Los Angeles. |
| Tobias, J M............ | Clerk................. | Los Angeles........... | Los Angeles Co........ | Los Angeles. |
| Todd, A ................. | Carpenter .,....... | Wilmington .......... | Los Angeles Co....... | Wilmington. |
| Todd, Wm............. | ..................... | Los Angeles Co ..... | Halfway House....... | Compton. |
| Todman, C E........... | Laborer............... | ...................... | Los Angeles Co....... | Los Angeles. |
| Toffelmeir, J S ...... | Carpenter............ | Los Angeles Co....... | Halfway House....... | Compton. |
| Toffelmier, —........ | Wood & coal y'd | 49 Aliso st ..... ...... | Los Angeles............ | Los Angeles. |
| Toflemeyer, C........ | Brakeman ........ | S P R R Co........... | Canal st ............... | Wilmington. |
| Tolano, Gabriel ..... | Laborer................ | ........................ | Los Angeles Co....... | Los Angeles. |
| Tomasevich, M...... | Bar keeper......... | Los Angeles........... | Los Angeles Co....... | Los Angeles. |
| **Tomasini, A**.......... | Watch maker...... | Los Angeles........... | Los Angeles Co....... | Los Angeles. |
| Tompkins, W H..... | Farmer ............... | nr Los Angeles........ | Los Angeles Co....... | Los Angeles. |
| **Tompkins, George**. | Farmer ............... | Los Angeles Co....... | Westminster Col...... | Westminster. |
| Tonney, Geo W ...... | Bar keeper......... | Los Angeles........... | Los Angeles........... | Los Angeles. |
| Tonner, P C............ | Teacher............... | San Bernardino Road | 4 m E Spadra ........ | Spadra. |
| Tonsley, D............. | Carpenter............ | Los Angeles........... | Los Angeles Co....... | Los Angeles. |
| Toombs, W T ....... | Farmer ............... | nr Anaheim ........... | Los Angeles Co....... | Anaheim. |
| Toombs, T S ......... | Laborer................ | Los Angeles........... | Los Angeles Co....... | Los Angeles. |
| Torney, J W........... | Baker................. | Wilmington............ | Los Angeles Co....... | Wilmington. |
| Torres, S..... ......... | Laborer................ | ........................ | ........................ | Los Angeles. |
| Torres, U .... ......... | Laborer................ | ........................ | Los Angeles Co....... | Los Angeles. |
| Torres, A............... | Laborer................ | Los Angeles Co....... | ........................ | Santa Ana. |
| **Torrey, John Jr**...... | Farmer ............... | Los Angeles Co....... | Westminster Col...... | Westminster. |
| Town, R M............. | Ranchero ........... | nr Los Angeles........ | Los Angeles Co....... | Los Angeles. |
| Tracey, B E............ | Carpenter............ | S P R R Co......:..... | Wilmington ........... | Wilmington. |
| **Trafford, John**....... | Justice of peace... | Temple st............. | Los Angeles............ | Los Angeles. |
| Trainer, C C........... | Teamster ........... | Los Angeles Co ...... | Silver District......... | Downey. |
| Trapp, F M ............ | Farmer ............... | nr Los Angeles........ | Los Angeles Co....... | Los Angeles. |
| Trapp, J D............. | Farmer ............... | nr Los Angeles........ | Los Angeles Co....... | Los Angeles. |
| **Trapp, J** .............. | Farmer ............... | nr Los Angeles........ | Los Angeles Co....... | Los Angeles. |
| Trask, W C............ | Farmer ............... | Los Angeles Co....... | Silver Precinct........ | Downey. |
| Travis, T A............ | Farmer ............... | Los Angeles Co....... | nr Los Angeles........ | Los Angeles. |
| Travis, A............... | Farmer ............... | Los Angeles Co....... | nr Los Angeles........ | Los Angeles. |
| Treadwell, J B....... | Miner.................. | ........................ | Los Angeles Co....... | Los Angeles. |
| Trejille, J A ........ | Farmer ............... | Los Angeles Co....... | nr San Jose ........... | Spadra. |
| Trelles, T J............ | Carpenter............ | Los Angeles Co....... | Los Angeles Co....... | Los Angeles. |
| **Tripp, J R**............. | Farmer ............... | Los Angeles Co....... | San Pedro.........:... | Wilmington. |
| Tripp, R S.............. | Farmer ............... | Los Angeles Co....... | Silver Precinct........ | Downey. |
| Tripp, J B.............. | Farmer ............... | Los Angeles Co....... | Silver Precinct........ | Downey. |
| Trobridge, L L....... | Painter ............... | Wilmington ........... | Los Angeles Co....... | Wilmington. |
| Trojillo, Antonio ... | Farmer ............... | Azusa ................ | 1½ m S W Azusa...... | Azusa. |
| Trotter, A H.......... | Stock raiser ....... | nr Los Angeles........ | Los Angeles Co....... | Los Angeles. |
| Troxler, W F.......... | Clerk................. | Los Angeles........... | Los Angeles Co....... | Los Angeles. |
| **Trudel, J B**.......... | Salt mnfr............ | Los Angeles........... | Los Angeles Co....... | Los Angeles. |
| Trujillo, P............. | Vaquero ............. | Los Angeles Co....... | San Jose ............... | Spadra. |
| Trujio, J M............ | Laborer................ | ........................ | Los Angeles Co....... | Santa Ana. |
| Trujio, C............... | Laborer................ | ........................ | Los Angeles Co....... | San Gabriel. |
| Truman, J R ......... | Laborer................ | Los Angeles Co....... | Silver Precinct........ | Downey. |
| **Truman, Benj C**... | Publisher............ | D'ly Star,15 Spring st | Fort st ............... | Los Angeles. |
| Tryon, G G............ | Saw maker.......... | Wilmington............ | Los Angeles Co....... | Wilmington. |
| Tuch, N ............... | Gen merchandise.. | San Gabriel........... | 9 m E Los Angeles... | San Gabriel. |
| Tucker, J L............ | Farmer ............... | Los Angeles Co ..... | La Ballona............. | Los Angeles. |
| Tucker, J............... | Farmer ............... | Los Angeles Co....... | Silver Precinct........ | Downey. |
| **Tucker, Simeon**..... | Farmer ............... | Los Angeles Co....... | Westminster Col...... | Westminster. |
| Tuerdy, L D.......... | Stock raiser......... | Los Angeles Co....... | San Antonio............ | Downey. |
| Tufts, M P............. | Farmer .... ......... | Los Angeles Co...:... | San Jose............... | Spadra. |

DIRECTORY OF LOS ANGELES COUNTY. 435

| NAME. | OCCUPATION. | PLACE OF BUSINESS. | RESIDENCE. | TOWN OR P. O. |
|---|---|---|---|---|
| Tuler, E B | Farmer | nr El Monte | Los Angeles Co | El Monte. |
| Tullis, Woodford B | Watch maker | El Monte | Los Angeles | Los Angeles. |
| Tungate, W | Farmer | El Monte Valley | 2 m N Lexington | El Monte. |
| Tuorney, Henry J. | Clerk | Los Angeles | Los Angeles | Los Angeles. |
| Turner, D H | Farmer | Los Angeles Co | Halfway House | Compton. |
| Turney, Thos | Laborer | | Los Angeles Co | Los Angeles. |
| Turner, S | Trader | Los Angeles | Los Angeles Co | Los Angeles. |
| Turner, J C | Saloon keeper | Los Angeles Co | Silver Precinct | Downey. |
| Turner, H | Teamster | Los Angeles Co | Silver Precinct | Downey. |
| Turner, W F | Miller | Los Angeles | Los Angeles Co | Los Angeles. |
| Turner, J | Teamster | Los Angeles Co | Halfway House | Compton. |
| Turner, C B | Miller | Los Angeles | Los Angeles Co | Los Angeles. |
| Turner, W | Saloon keeper | Wilmington | Los Angeles Co | Wilmington. |
| Turner, G L | Stock raiser | nr Los Angeles | Los Angeles Co | Los Angeles. |
| Turner, G L | Auctioneer | Los Angeles | Los Angeles Co | Los Angeles. |
| Turner, Miss E M. | Books & station'y | Los Angeles | Los Angeles | Los Angeles. |
| Turney, N G | Physician | San Pedro Ranch | Compton | Compton. |
| Turner, H | Farmer | San Pedro Ranch | 2½ m N E Compton | Compton. |
| Turner, John | Miller | La Punte Mill | 3 m S E Lexington | El Monte. |
| Turner, Wm F | Gen merchandise. | Lexington, | 12 m E Los Angeles. | El Monte. |
| Tustin, C | Farmer | Santa Ana | Los Angeles Co | Santa Ana. |
| Tuttle, D W | Machinist | Los Nietos | Los Angeles Co | Los Nietos. |
| Tweedy, R | Farmer | Los Angeles Co | Halfway House | Compton. |
| Tweedy, W | Farmer | nr Los Nietos | Los Angeles Co | Los Nietos. |
| Tweedy, J | Farmer | Los Angeles Co | Halfway House | Compton. |
| Twichell, C C | Clerk | Los Angeles Co | | San Gabriel. |
| Twigg, W F | Farmer | Los Angeles Co | nr San Gabriel | San Gabriel. |
| Twiss, C W | R R agent | Compton | Compton | Compton. |
| Twiss, C P | Farmer | San Pedro Ranch | 1 m W Compton | Compton. |
| Twitchell, C C | Saloon | San Gabriel | 9 m E Los Angeles | San Gabriel. |
| Tyler, M F | Merchant | Los Angeles Co | Silver Precinct | Downey. |
| Tyler, M F | Proprietor | Jones Hotel | Lexington | El Monte. |
| Udall, J C | Miner | | Los Angeles Co | Los Angeles. |
| Ullman, S | Speculator | Los Angeles | Los Angeles Co | Los Angeles. |
| Ullman, D | Gasfitter | Los Angeles | Los Angeles Co | Los Angeles. |
| Ullyard, L R | Baker | Los Angeles | Los Angeles Co | Los Angeles. |
| Utterback, J | Farmer | Los Angeles Co | Silver Precinct | Downey. |
| Ulyard, Edward | Blacksmith | Los Angeles | Los Angeles | Los Angeles. |
| Ulyard, A | Baker | Los Angeles | Los Angeles Co | Los Angeles. |
| Upson, Frederick | Farmer | Los Angeles Co | nr Los Angeles | Los Angeles. |
| Urquides, Juan | Ranchero | nr Los Angeles | La Ballona | Los Angeles. |
| Urquides, C | Farmer | nr Los Angeles | Los Angeles Co | Los Angeles. |
| Urquides, Elanterio | Laborer | | Los Angeles Co | Los Angeles. |
| Urquides, G | Farmer | Los Angeles Co | nr Los Angeles | Los Angeles. |
| Urquides, Encarnarcion | | Los Angeles Co | nr Los Angeles | Los Angeles. |
| Urquides, J M | Ranchero | nr Los Angeles | Los Angeles Co | Los Angeles. |
| Urquides, A | Ranchero | Los Angeles Co | La Ballona | Los Angeles. |
| Urquides, F | Laborer | | Los Angeles Co | Los Angeles. |
| Urquides, T | Farmer | nr Los Angeles | Los Angeles Co | Los Angeles. |
| Urmstone, D | Farmer | Los Angeles Co | nr Los Angeles | Los Angeles. |
| Urton, N | Farmer | nr San Fernando | Los Angeles Co | San Fernando. |
| Vaca, Jose | Farmer | nr San Fernando | Los Angeles Co | San Fernando. |
| Vacca, J R | Laborer | Los Angeles Co | San Jose | Spadra. |
| Vache, E | Wines and cigars | | New Commercial st. | Los Angeles. |
| Vail, A E | Farmer | Los Angeles Co | nr Halfway House | Compton. |
| Valasquez, A | Boot maker | Los Angeles | Los Angeles Co | Los Angeles. |
| Valdez, Ramon | Dairyman | Los Angeles Co | nr Los Angeles | Los Angeles. |
| Valdez, Juan | Farmer | nr San Fernando | Los Angeles Co | San Fernando. |
| Valdez, P | Tailor | Los Angeles | Los Angeles Co | Los Angeles. |
| Valdez, J de los S | Laborer | Los Angeles Co | nr San Jose | Spadra. |
| Valdez, Jose | Laborer | Los Angeles Co | Los Angeles Co | Los Angeles. |
| Valdez, V M | Farmer | Los Angeles Co | nr Los Angeles | Los Angeles. |
| Valdez, J Y | Ranchero | Los Angeles Co | nr San Jose | Spadra. |

| NAME. | OCCUPATION. | PLACE OF BUSINESS. | RESIDENCE. | TOWN OR P. O. |
|---|---|---|---|---|
| Valdez, A M | Farmer | Los Angeles Co | nr La Ballona | Los Angeles. |
| Valdez, J C | Vaquero | | Los Angeles Co | Los Angeles. |
| Valdez, J E | Ranchero | nr Los Angeles | Los Angeles Co | Los Angeles. |
| Valdez, V | Laborer | Los Angeles Co | nr La Ballona | Los Angeles. |
| Valdez, A M | Laborer | | Los Angeles Co | Los Angeles. |
| Valdez, B | Vaquero | Los Angeles Co | nr La Ballona | Los Angeles. |
| Valdez, R | Farmer | Los Angeles Co | nr Los Angeles | Los Angeles. |
| Valdez, C | Laborer | Los Angeles Co | Los Angeles Co | Los Angeles. |
| Valdez, J | Bar keeper | Los Angeles | Los Angeles Co | Los Angeles. |
| Valdor, J A | Clerk | P O Block | Spring st | Los Angeles. |
| Valdez, Jose Jesus | Ranchero | Los Angeles Co | nr Los Angeles | Los Angeles. |
| Valdez, Francisco | Sheep raiser | Los Angeles Co | La Brea | Los Angeles. |
| Valdez, Teofilo | Ranchero | Los Angeles Co | La Brea | Los Angeles. |
| Valenzuela, E | Laborer | Los Angeles Co | | Los Angeles. |
| Valenzuela, J M | Laborer | Los Angeles Co | | Los Angeles. |
| Valencia, J M | Tailor | Los Angeles | Los Angeles Co | Los Angeles. |
| Valenzuela, R | Farmer | nr Los Angeles | Los Angeles Co | Los Angeles. |
| Valenzuela, D | Farmer | Los Angeles Co | nr La Ballona | Los Angeles. |
| Valenzuela, Juan | Ranchero | Los Angeles Co | nr Halfway House | Compton. |
| Valenzuela, T | Laborer | Los Angeles Co | | Los Angeles. |
| Valenzuela, J D | Laborer | Los Angeles Co | Los Angeles Co | Los Angeles. |
| Valenzuela, Jose | Farmer | nr Los Angeles | Los Angeles Co | Los Angeles. |
| Valencia, J M | Farmer | nr Los Angeles | Los Angeles Co | Los Angeles. |
| Valenzuela, F M | Vaquero | | Los Angeles Co | Los Angeles. |
| Valenzuela, G | Laborer | Los Angeles Co | | Los Angeles. |
| Valenzuela, J T | Vaquero | | Los Angeles Co | Los Angeles. |
| Valenzuela, J F | Farmer | nr Los Angeles | Los Angeles Co | Los Angeles. |
| Valenzuela, J M | Farmer | Los Angeles Co | nr San Jose | Spadra. |
| Valencia, B | Vaquero | Los Angeles Co | | Los Angeles. |
| Valencia, A | Laborer | | Los Angeles Co | Los Angeles. |
| Valenzuela, D | Merchant | Los Angeles | Los Angeles Co | Los Angeles. |
| Valencia, J | Farmer | nr Los Angeles | Los Angeles Co | Los Angeles. |
| Valenciana, M | Tailor | Los Angeles | Los Angeles Co | Los Angeles. |
| Valenzuela, I | Laborer | Los Angeles Co | | Los Angeles. |
| Valencia, G | Vaquero | Los Angeles Co | | Los Angeles. |
| Valenzuela, J | Gardener | Los Angeles | | Los Angeles. |
| Valenzuela, J de la Luz | Farmer | nr Los Angeles | Los Angeles Co | Los Angeles. |
| Valenzuela, R | Farmer | Los Angeles Co | nr San Jose | Spadra. |
| Valenzuela, B | Laborer | Los Angeles Co | nr La Ballona | Los Angeles. |
| Valencia, Jose | Ranchero | nr Los Angeles | Los Angeles Co | Los Angeles. |
| Valenzuela, J A | Vaquero | Los Angeles Co | | Los Angeles. |
| Valenzuela, Jose J | Laborer | | Los Angeles Co | Los Angeles. |
| Valenzuela, Alfredo | Laborer | Los Angeles Co | | Los Angeles. |
| Valenzuela, Felipe | Laborer | | Los Angeles Co | San Gabriel. |
| Valencia, Antonio | Laborer | Los Angeles Co | | Los Angeles. |
| Valencia, C | Saloon | San Gabriel | 9 m E Los Angeles | San Gabriel. |
| Valencia, Carlos | Painter | Los Angeles | Los Angeles Co | Los Angeles. |
| Valenzuela, L | Farmer | Los Angeles Co | nr La Ballona | Los Angeles. |
| Valenzuela, Juan | Farmer | Los Angeles Co | nr La Ballona | Los Angeles. |
| Valenzuela, J A | Vaquero | | Los Angeles Co | Capistrano. |
| Valenzuela, F S | Laborer | | Los Angeles Co | Los Angeles. |
| Valenzuela, M | Farmer | Los Angeles Co | nr La Ballona | Los Angeles. |
| Valencia, A | Laborer | Los Angeles Co | | Los Angeles. |
| Valencia, R R | Tinsmith | Los Angeles | Los Angeles Co | Los Angeles. |
| Valencia, M | Laborer | | Los Angeles Co | Los Angeles. |
| Valenzuela, V | Laborer | Los Angeles Co | nr La Ballona | Los Angeles. |
| Valenzuela, F | Farmer | Los Angeles Co | nr La Ballona | Los Angeles. |
| Valin, F | Wharf hand | S P R R Co | Wilmington | Wilmington. |
| Valison, D | Laborer | | Los Angeles Co | Los Angeles. |
| Valle, B | Butcher | Los Angeles | Los Angeles Co | Los Angeles. |
| Valla, Antonio | Merchant | Los Angeles | Los Angeles Co | Los Angeles. |
| Valle, Jose Ygnacio del | Farmer | Los Angeles Co | nr Los Angeles | Los Angeles. |

DIRECTORY OF LOS ANGELES COUNTY.    437

| Name. | Occupation. | Place of Business. | Residence. | Town or P. O. |
|---|---|---|---|---|
| Vallestero, Ramos | Laborer | | Los Angeles Co | Los Angeles. |
| Valpey, Geo W | Painter | Los Angeles | Los Angeles | Los Angeles. |
| Van Buren, George | Laborer | Los Angeles Co | | Los Angeles. |
| Van Doren, Saml M | Book keeper | Los Angeles | Los Angeles | Los Angeles. |
| Van Dusen, W S | Blacksmith | Los Angeles Co | Los Angeles | Los Angeles. |
| Van Dusen, C | Miner | | Los Angeles Co | Los Angeles. |
| Van Nuys, — | Supt S F homest. | Coast Line Road | 8 m S W San Fer'do | San Fernando. |
| Van Patten, E W | Clerk | Los Angeles | Los Angeles Co | Los Angeles. |
| Van Valen, Wm H | Stage agent | | | Los Angeles. |
| Van Valkenburg, H | Saddler | 1st st | Wilmington | Wilmington. |
| Vance, J | Farmer | Los Angeles Co | Silver Precinct | Downey. |
| Vance, G W | Farmer | nr Santa Ana | Los Angeles Co | Santa Ana. |
| Vantreso, B F | Butcher | Los Angeles | Los Angeles Co | Los Angeles. |
| Varelas, A | Farmer | nr Los Angeles | Los Angeles Co | Los Angeles. |
| Varela, Mrs | | | Wilmington | Wilmington. |
| Varela, — | Laborer | Wilmington | Wilmington | Wilmington. |
| Varela, M J | Painter | Los Angeles | Los Angeles | Los Angeles. |
| Varela, R | Laborer | Wilmington | Wilmington | Wilmington. |
| Varsulta, Ramon | Bricklayer | El Monte | Old Mission | El Monte. |
| Vasques, F M | Farmer | nr San Fernando | Los Angeles Co | San Fernando. |
| Vasquez, Chico | Stock | Soledad | 28 m N E Lyon Sta. | Lyon Station. |
| Vasquez, L | Laborer | | Los Angeles Co | San Gabriel. |
| Vassallo, F | Merchant | Los Angeles | Los Angeles Co | Los Angeles. |
| Vassar, G L | Farmer | Los Angeles Co | nr Los Angeles | El Monte. |
| Vassar, W J | Farmer | nr Los Angeles | Los Angeles Co | El Monte. |
| Vattat, P A | Clerk | Los Angeles | Los Angeles Co | Los Angeles. |
| Vaughn, C | Farmer | Azusa Ranch | 2 m S Azusa | Azusa. |
| Vaughn, S | Blacksmith | Los Angeles | Los Angeles Co | Los Angeles. |
| Vawtor, Edwin J | Farmer | Los Angeles Co | Pasadena | Pasadena. |
| Vega, T | Laborer | | Los Angeles Co | Los Angeles. |
| Vega, J J | Laborer | | Los Angeles Co | Los Angeles. |
| Vejar, Juan | Farmer | Los Angeles Co | nr Los Angeles | Los Angeles. |
| Vejar, Pablo | Ranchero | Los Angeles Co | San Jose | Spadra. |
| Vejar, P | Miner | Los Angeles Co | Los Angeles Co | Los Angeles. |
| Vejar, R N | Shepherd | Los Angeles Co | Los Angeles Co | Los Angeles. |
| Vejar, R | Farmer | Los Angeles Co | San Jose | Spadra. |
| Vejar, F | Farmer | Los Angeles Co | San Jose | Spadra. |
| Vejar, D | Ranchero | Los Angeles Co | nr Los Angeles | Los Angeles. |
| Velardes, Jose los Santos | Laborer | | Los Angeles Co | San Gabriel. |
| Velasco, J M | Laborer | Los Angeles Co | | Los Angeles. |
| Velasques, P A | Farmer | nr Los Angeles | Los Angeles Co | Los Angeles. |
| Velardes, L | Laborer | Los Angeles Co | | Los Angeles. |
| Velardes, T | Laborer | | Los Angeles Co | Los Angeles. |
| Velarde, J M | Farmer | Los Angeles Co | nr Los Angeles | Los Angeles. |
| Velarde, R | Farmer | Los Angeles Co | nr San Jose | Spadra. |
| Velasco, M | Laborer | Los Angeles Co | | Los Angeles. |
| Venable, J W | Farmer | Los Angeles Co | Silver Precinct | Downey. |
| Vera, M | Laborer | | Los Angeles Co | Los Angeles. |
| Verdugo, A | Vaquero | Los Angeles Co | | San Juan. |
| Verdugo, P | Ranchero | San Juan | Los Angeles Co | Capistrano. |
| Verde, L | Borregero | | Los Angeles Co | Los Angeles. |
| Verdugo, T | Laborer | Los Angeles Co | | Los Angeles. |
| Verdugo, J M | Ranchero | nr Los Angeles | Los Angeles Co | Los Angeles. |
| Verde, L | Laborer | | Los Angeles Co | Los Angeles. |
| Verdugo, V | Vaquero | Los Angeles Co | | Los Angeles. |
| Verdugo, L | Farmer | nr Anaheim | Los Angeles Co | Anaheim. |
| Verdugo, F | Laborer | | Los Angeles Co | Los Angeles. |
| Verdugo, P | Laborer | Los Angeles Co | | Los Angeles. |
| Verdugo, R A | Laborer | | Los Angeles Co | Los Angeles. |
| Verdugo, G A | Laborer | | Los Angeles Co | Los Angeles. |
| Verdugo, Q | Laborer | Los Angeles Co | | Los Angeles. |
| Vermadeo, V | Farmer | Los Angeles Co | nr Los Angeles | Los Angeles. |
| Verrill, T J | Millman | Los Angeles | Los Angeles Co | Los Angeles. |

| Name. | Occupation. | Place of Business. | Residence. | Town or P. O. |
|---|---|---|---|---|
| Verta, G | Farmer | nr Santa Ana | Los Angeles Co | Santa Ana. |
| Vickroy, W | Teamster | | Los Angeles Co | Wilmington. |
| Victory, J | Carpenter | Los Angeles | Los Angeles Co | Los Angeles. |
| Videla, F | Vaquero | Los Angeles Co. | | Los Angeles. |
| Vielle, L | Restaurant | Main st | Los Angeles | Los Angeles. |
| Vielle & Marbeuf | Hotel de princes | Main st, Downey Blk | | Los Angeles. |
| Viga, V | Laborer | Los Angeles Co. | | San Gabriel. |
| Vigela, J B | Vaquero | | Los Angeles Co | Los Angeles. |
| Vigil, Juan | Laborer | | Los Angeles Co | Los Angeles. |
| Vignon, J G | Gen mdse | San Jose Valley | 4 m S W Spadra | Spadra. |
| Vignolo, A | | Los Angeles Co. | | Los Angeles. |
| Vignes, J M | Nurseries | nr Los Angeles | Los Angeles Co | Los Angeles. |
| Vignes, V F | Laborer | Los Angeles Co | | Los Angeles. |
| Vigueri, J | Carpenter | San Gabriel | Los Angeles Co | San Gabriel. |
| Vijar, Juan C | Farmer | nr Los Angeles | Los Angeles Co | Los Angeles. |
| Villa, Abeline | Laborer | Los Angeles Co. | | Los Angeles. |
| Villalobos, J M | Blacksmith | San Gabriel | 9 m E Los Angeles | San Gabriel. |
| Villa, Ramon | Ranchero | nr Los Angeles | Ballona | Los Angeles. |
| Villancencio, J N | Gabarrero | Los Angeles Co. | | Santa Ana. |
| Villa, T | Laborer | | Los Angeles Co | Los Angeles. |
| Villa, F | Farmer | Los Angeles Co | nr La Ballona | Los Angeles. |
| Villa, M | Butcher | Los Angeles | Los Angeles Co | Los Angeles. |
| Villalobos, J del C | Saddler | Los Angeles | Los Angeles Co | Los Angeles. |
| Villa, M | Laborer | Los Angeles | Los Angeles Co | Los Angeles. |
| Villa, Jose Angel | Laborer | Los Angeles Co | | Los Angeles. |
| Villalobes, Joaquin | Shoe maker | Los Angeles | Los Angeles | Los Angeles. |
| Villela, F | Laborer | | Los Angeles Co | Los Angeles. |
| Villabobos, E | Boot maker | Los Angeles | Los Angeles Co | Los Angeles. |
| Villa, M | Ranchero | Los Angeles Co | nr La Ballona | Los Angeles. |
| Villa, J | Laborer | | Los Angeles Co | Los Angeles. |
| Villa, J V | Blacksmith | Los Angeles | Los Angeles Co | Los Angeles. |
| Vincent, C | Miner | Los Angeles Co | | Azusa. |
| Vincent, J | Carpenter | Los Angeles | Los Angeles Co | Los Angeles. |
| Virgin, Mrs | Farmer | Azusa Ranch | 2 m S W Azusa | Azusa. |
| Virgin, Benj J | Miner | Los Angeles Co | | Los Angeles. |
| Vise, N | Trader | El Monte | Los Angeles Co | El Monte. |
| Vise, H W | Farmer | nr El Monte | Los Angeles Co | El Monte. |
| Vogt, H | Carpenter | Los Angeles | Los Angeles Co | Los Angeles. |
| Voight, G | Farmer | Los Angeles Co | nr Los Nietos | Los Nietos. |
| Vonallmen, J H | Waiter | Los Angeles | Los Angeles | Los Angeles. |
| Von Plorices, Otto | Clerk | Los Angeles | Los Angeles | Los Angeles. |
| Von Piesen, Victor | Teamster | Los Angeles Co | | Los Angeles. |
| Vrooman, E W | Farmer | nr Los Angeles | Los Angeles Co | Los Angeles. |
| Votteler, C F | Laborer | | Los Angeles Co | Los Angeles. |
| Waddell, J | Shoe maker | Los Angeles | Los Angeles Co | Los Angeles. |
| Wade, T B | Agt and contractr | Court st | Alameda st | Los Angeles. |
| Wade, Wm | Clerk | Los Angeles | Los Angeles | Los Angeles. |
| Wadhams, C | Farmer | nr Los Angeles | Los Angeles Co | Los Angeles. |
| Wadsworth, C | Carpenter | Los Angeles | Los Angeles Co | Los Angeles. |
| Wagner, J C | Teamster | Los Angeles | Los Angeles Co | Los Angeles. |
| Wagner, J | Sheep raiser | nr Los Angeles | Los Angeles Co | Los Angeles. |
| Wagner & Wiggins | Groceries | Los Angeles | Los Angeles Co | Los Angeles. |
| Waibel, J | Vintner | nr Los Angeles | Los Angeles Co | Los Angeles. |
| Waite, A | Painter | Los Angeles | Los Angeles Co | Los Angeles. |
| Waittelle, Francisco | Farmer | Los Angeles Co | nr Los Angeles | Los Angeles. |
| Waite, Chas H | Laborer | | Los Angeles Co | Los Angeles. |
| Waldron, D Van K | Farmer | nr Los Angeles | Los Angeles Co | Los Angeles. |
| Walden, Charles | Bar keeper | Los Angeles | Los Angeles | Los Angeles. |
| Waldron, S A | Trader | Los Angeles | Los Angeles Co | Los Angeles. |
| Walker, J R | Butcher | Los Angeles | Los Angeles Co | Los Angeles. |
| Walker, R | Farmer | Los Angeles Co | nr Los Angeles | Los Angeles. |
| Walker, Robt S | Painter | Los Angeles | Los Angeles Co | Los Angeles. |
| Walker, H H | Farmer | Los Angeles Co | nr Los Nietos | Los Nietos. |
| Walker, B F | Merchant | Los Angeles | Los Angeles Co | Los Angeles. |

# DIRECTORY OF LOS ANGELES COUNTY. 439

| Name. | Occupation. | Place of Business. | Residence. | Town or P. O. |
|---|---|---|---|---|
| Walker, S N | Painter | Anaheim | Los Angeles Co | Anaheim. |
| Wallace, Wm | Engineer | Los Angeles | Los Angeles Co | Los Angeles. |
| Walls, G A | Plasterer | Los Angeles | Los Angeles Co | Los Angeles. |
| Wallace, T | Teamster | | Los Angeles Co | Los Angeles. |
| Waller, S R | Farmer | Los Angeles Co | Silver Precinct | Downey. |
| Wallace, James C. | Watch maker | Los Angeles | Los Angeles | Los Angeles. |
| Wall, Wm A | Laborer | Los Angeles Co | Soledad | San Fernando. |
| Wallace, J C | Nursery | San Gabriel Valley | 1 m N W San Gab | San Gabriel. |
| Wall, Edwd | Helper | S P R R Co | Wilmington | Wilmington. |
| Walsh, Danl P | Bar keeper | Los Angeles | Los Angeles | Los Angeles. |
| Walter, D L | Merchant | Los Angeles | Los Angeles Co | Los Angeles. |
| Walters, H W | Farmer | Los Angeles Co | nr Los Angeles | Los Angeles. |
| Walters, Geo | Store keeper | Los Angeles | Los Angeles Co | Los Angeles. |
| Walters, Thos | Laborer | Los Angeles Co | | Los Angeles. |
| Walton, F M | Farmer | nr Downey | San Antonio | Downey. |
| Walter, Wm | Bar keeper | Los Angeles | Los Angeles | Los Angeles. |
| Wattelet, Desoié | Carpenter | Los Angeles Co | | Los Angeles. |
| Walter, S | Mason | Los Angeles | Los Angeles Co | Los Angeles. |
| Wan, Sims | Chinese laundry | Los Angeles st | Anaheim | Anaheim. |
| Ward, J | Farmer | nr Los Angeles | Los Angeles Co | Los Angeles. |
| Ward, J L | Merchant | Los Angeles | Los Angeles Co | Los Angeles. |
| Wardell, S | Farmer | Los Angeles Co | nr Halfway House | Compton. |
| Ward, John | Laborer | | Anaheim | Anaheim. |
| Ward, James F | Miner | Los Angeles Co | | Los Angeles. |
| Ward, J L & Co | Com merchant | 8 Commercial st | Los Angeles | Los Angeles. |
| Ward, J L | Insurance agent | Main st | cor Main and 5th sts | Los Angeles. |
| Ward, E | Saloon keeper | Los Angeles | Los Angeles Co | Los Angeles. |
| Ward, Robt | Laborer | | Los Angeles Co | Wilmington. |
| Wardlow, D S | Farmer | Los Angeles Co | Silver Precinct | Downey. |
| Ware, H C | Farmer | Los Angeles Co | Half-way House | Compton. |
| Ware, John Wm | Barber | Los Angeles | Los Angeles | Los Angeles. |
| Warfield, S R | Farmer | Los Angeles Co | Capistrano | Capistrano. |
| Warling, O | Harness | San Fernando | San Fernando | San Fernando. |
| Warner, J | Baker | Wilmington | Los Angeles Co | Wilmington. |
| Warner, A F | Painter | Los Angeles | Los Angeles Co | Los Angeles. |
| Warner, Van Buren | Railroad employe | Los Angeles Co | | Los Angeles. |
| Warner, Henry L | Machinist | Los Angeles | Los Angeles | Los Angeles. |
| Warner, John M | Carpenter | Los Angeles Co | | Los Angeles. |
| Warner, J J | Notary public | 9 Temple Blk | Los Angeles | Los Angeles. |
| Warner, M A | Farmer | Los Angeles Co | Silver Precinct | Downey. |
| Warren, L | Laborer | | Los Angeles Co | Anaheim. |
| Warren, A L | Watchmaker | Los Angeles | Los Angeles Co | Los Angeles. |
| Warren, J M | Engineer | Wilmington | Los Angeles Co | Wilmington. |
| Warren, J | Teamster | | Los Angeles Co | Los Angeles. |
| Warter, Wm | Miner | Los Angeles Co | Soledad | San Fernando. |
| Wartenberg, H | Merchant | Los Angeles | Los Angeles Co | Los Angeles. |
| Wartenberg, L | Butcher | Anaheim | Los Angeles Co | Anaheim. |
| Washington, Geo | Freighter | Los Angeles | Los Angeles Co | Los Angeles. |
| Washburn, E A | Teamster | Los Angeles Co | Silver Precinct | Downey. |
| Waters, W W | Laborer | Los Angeles Co | Halfway House | Compton. |
| Waterman, Amos F | Attorney | Los Angeles | Los Angeles | Los Angeles. |
| Watkins, W K | Farmer | Los Angeles Co | San Joaquin | Santa Ana. |
| Watros, Wm S | Farmer | San Pedro Rauch | 1½ m S Compton | Compton. |
| Watson, J | Farmer | nr Santa Ana | Los Angeles Co | Santa Ana. |
| Watson, C W | Clerk | Los Angeles | Los Angeles Co | Los Angeles. |
| Watson, Thos | Teamster | Los Angeles Co | | Los Angeles. |
| Watson, Jacob | Farmer | Los Angeles | San Joaquin | Santa Ana. |
| Watson, Benj M | Plumber | Los Angeles | Los Angeles | Los Angeles. |
| Watson, J W | Laborer | | Los Angeles Co | Los Angeles. |
| Watson, D J | Ranchero | nr Anaheim | Los Angeles Co | Anaheim. |
| Watson, H | Farmer | Los Angeles Co | nr Anaheim | Anaheim. |
| Watts, Chas H | Farmer | Los Angeles Co | San Pascual | San Pascual. |
| Waveberg, O H | Wharf hand | S P R R Co | Wilmington | Wilmington. |
| Way, S | Teamster | Lexington | 12 m E Los Angeles | El Monte. |

| Name. | Occupation. | Place of Business. | Residence. | Town or P. O. |
|---|---|---|---|---|
| Wayman, Henry... | Well borer......... | Los Angeles Co....... | Westminster Col...... | Westminster. |
| Wear, W B.............. | Farmer .............. | Los Angeles Co....... | nr El Monte............. | El Monte. |
| Weathersford, Wm | Farmer............... | nr Anaheim............. | Los Angeles Co....... | Anaheim. |
| Weaver, N................ | Shoe maker......... | Los Angeles........... | Los Angeles Co....... | Los Angeles. |
| Webber, S N............ | Minister............... | Anaheim ............... | Los Angeles Co....... | Anaheim. |
| Webber, J................ | Miner ................. | ............................. | Los Angeles Co....... | Los Angeles. |
| Webber, A............... | Farmer ............... | Los Angeles Co....... | nr Anaheim............. | Anaheim. |
| Webb, E D............... | Carpenter............ | Los Angeles........... | Los Angeles Co....... | Los Angeles. |
| Weberle, J............... | Farmer ............... | nr San Fernando...... | Los Angeles Co....... | San Fernando. |
| Weber, F................. | Supt Aliso mills.. | New & Old Aliso sts.. | Howard st............... | Los Angeles. |
| Webster, C.............. | Teamster.............. | ............................. | Los Angeles Co....... | El Monte. |
| Webster, W............. | Wagon maker..... | Los Angeles........... | Los Angeles Co....... | Los Angeles. |
| Webster, W B.......... | Farmer ............... | San Pedro Ranch..... | 2 m S E Compton.... | Compton. |
| Wedgwood, J.......... | Dentist................. | Los Angeles........... | Los Angeles Co....... | Los Angeles. |
| Weeks, Wm............. | Farmer ............... | Los Angeles Co ...... | Mission Viejo......... | |
| Wehmeyer, Henry.. | Vintner............... | nr Anaheim............. | Anaheim.................. | Anaheim. |
| Weid, I A................. | Farmer ............... | nr Los Angeles........ | Los Angeles Co....... | Los Angeles. |
| Weigle, Jno V.......... | Shoe maker......... | Los Angeles........... | Los Angeles Co....... | Los Angeles. |
| Weil, Jacob.............. | Laborer................ | Los Angeles Co....... | Anaheim................. | Anaheim. |
| Weingand, Fredk... | Saloon................. | Los Angeles........... | Los Angeles........... | Los Angeles. |
| Weinshank, Frank A............... | Tinsmith.............. | Los Angeles........... | Los Angeles........... | Los Angeles. |
| Weinshank, A......... | Butcher................ | Los Angeles........... | Los Angeles Co....... | Los Angeles. |
| Weitzel, F................ | Farmer ............... | Los Angeles Co....... | nr Los Angeles........ | Los Angeles. |
| Weixel, J................. | Bricklayer .......... | Los Angeles........... | Los Angeles Co....... | Los Angeles. |
| Welch. Whiting Wm... | | Los Angeles Co....... | | Los Angeles. |
| Welch, J G............... | Carpenter ........... | Compton................. | Compton.................. | Compton. |
| Welch, Jno.............. | Teamster.............. | ............................. | Los Angeles Co....... | Los Angeles. |
| Welch, J J................ | Farmer ............... | Los Angeles Co....... | nr San Joaquin........ | Santa Ana. |
| Weldt, Wm............. | Watch maker....... | Wilmington .......... | Los Angeles Co....... | Wilmington. |
| Wells, D W............. | Farmer'............... | nr Santa Ana.......... | Los Angeles Co....... | Santa Ana. |
| Welsh, John............ | Boiler maker....... | Los Angeles........... | Los Angeles........... | Los Angeles. |
| Wence, P................. | Carpenter............ | Wilmington .......... | Los Angeles Co....... | Wilmington. |
| Wendt, C................. | Boot maker ........ | nr Los Angeles........ | Los Angeles Co....... | Los Angeles. |
| Werdan, John H... | Blacksmith.......... | Downey................. | Silver Precinct........ | Downey. |
| Werder, H L............ | Vintner............... | nr Anaheim............. | Los Angeles Co....... | Anaheim. |
| Weston, B S............ | Mariner............... | Los Angeles Co....... | Catalina Island........ | Wilmington. |
| Westerling, J.......... | Sailor.................. | Anaheim................. | Los Angeles Co....... | Anaheim. |
| West, M E............... | Carpenter ........... | Los Angeles........... | Los Angeles........... | Los Angeles. |
| West, John.............. | Miner.................. | Los Angeles Co....... | San Gabriel............. | San Gabriel. |
| Westfield, J............. | Laborer................ | ............................. | Los Angeles Co....... | Los Angeles. |
| Westfall, Carl......... | Baker................... | Anaheim................. | Anaheim.................. | Anaheim. |
| West, J P................. | Farmer ............... | San Pedro Ranch.... | 1¼ m S W Compton.. | Compton. |
| Weston, B S............ | Stock raiser ........ | Palos Verde Ranch.. | 2¼ m N W Wilm'n.. | Wilmington. |
| Weston, E J............. | Architect ........... | 29 & 30 Temple Blk | ............................. | Los Angeles. |
| Westphal, J............. | Coppersmith ..... | Centre st................ | Anaheim.................. | Anaheim. |
| Weston, J................ | Saloon keeper.... | Los Angeles........... | Los Angeles Co....... | Los Angeles. |
| Westphal, J............. | Cooper................ | Anaheim ............... | Los Angeles Co....... | Anaheim. |
| Weston, B F............ | Sailor.................. | Wilmington .......... | Los Angeles Co....... | Wilmington. |
| Wetzel, M................ | Locomotive eng'r | S P R R Co............. | Anaheim................. | Anaheim. |
| Whaling, M............ | Attorney ............ | Los Angeles........... | Los Angeles Co....... | Los Angeles. |
| Whaling, M............ | | San Gabriel Valley .. | San Gabriel............. | San Gabriel. |
| Whare, John ......... | Farmer ............... | nr Westminster....... | Westminster Col...... | Westminster. |
| Wheeler,JohnOzias | Clerk ................... | Los Angeles........... | Los Angeles........... | Los Angeles. |
| Whelan, Wm.......... | Teamster.............. | ............................. | Los Angeles Co....... | Los Angeles. |
| Whiting, B C........... | Lawyer................ | Los Angeles........... | Los Angeles........... | Los Angeles. |
| Whittaker, J G........ | Store keeper........ | Los Angeles........... | Los Angeles Co....... | Los Angeles. |
| White, D R.............. | Farmer ............... | Santa Anita Ranch.. | 7 m N E San Gabriel. | San Gabriel. |
| Whitesides,—......... | Teamster.............. | Azusa ................... | 4 m N E Azusa......... | Azusa. |
| White, J P................ | Farmer ............... | Azusa Ranch ........ | 2 m S E Azusa......... | Azusa. |
| White, Rev A F....... | Pastor.................. | Presbyterian Church | Los Angeles........... | Los Angeles. |
| White, J S R............ | Farmer ............... | nr San Gabriel......... | Los Angeles Co....... | San Gabriel. |
| White, Thos ........... | Laborer................ | ............................. | Los Angeles Co....... | Los Angeles. |

# DIRECTORY OF LOS ANGELES COUNTY. 441

| NAME. | OCCUPATION. | PLACE OF BUSINESS. | RESIDENCE. | TOWN OR P. O. |
|---|---|---|---|---|
| Whistler & Jones | Groceries | Los Angeles | Los Angeles | Los Angeles. |
| Whisler, M | Gen merchandise | Los Angeles | Los Angeles | Los Angeles. |
| Whistler, M. | Farmer | nr El Monte | Los Angeles Co | El Monte. |
| Whiteman, R R | Farmer | Los Angeles Co | Halfway House | Compton. |
| Whitworth, J H | Farmer | Los Angeles Co | nr La Ballona | Los Angeles. |
| White, Chas | Clerk | Los Angeles | Los Angeles Co | Los Angeles. |
| Whitley, J K | Laborer | | Los Angeles Co | Los Angeles. |
| Whitterley, F P | Stock raiser | nr Wilmington | Los Angeles Co | Wilmington. |
| White, M C | Farmer | nr Los Angeles | Los Angeles Co | San Gabriel. |
| White, D R | Farmer | nr El Monte | Los Angeles Co | El Monte. |
| Whiteside, Wm | Farmer | nr Los Angeles | Los Angeles Co | Los Angeles. |
| White, T J | | Los Angeles | Los Angeles Co | Los Angeles. |
| Whitehorn, G W | Freighter | Los Angeles | Los Angeles Co | Los Angeles. |
| Whitworth, J | Farmer | Los Angeles Co | nr La Ballona | Los Angeles. |
| White, J S | Teamster | | Los Angeles Co | Los Angeles. |
| White, R N | Clerk | Anaheim | Los Angeles Co | Anaheim. |
| White, C E | Farmer | nr Los Angeles | Los Angeles Co | Los Angeles. |
| Whitley, F | Sheep raiser | nr Wilmington | Los Angeles Co | Wilmington. |
| White, M | Farmer | San Gabriel Valley | 3 m N W San Gab | San Gabriel. |
| Whitney, John | Carpenter | Aliso Mills | Old Aliso st | Los Angeles. |
| White, S L | Laborer | Wilmington | Canal st | Wilmington. |
| Whittley, Frank | Stock raiser | Catalina island | 20 m S Wilmington | Wilmington. |
| Whittaker, J G | Groceries | Commercial st | Los Angeles | Los Angeles. |
| Whiting & King | Attorneys at law | Los Angeles | Los Angeles | Los Angeles. |
| White, Stephen M | Lawyer | Los Angeles | Los Angeles | Los Angeles. |
| White, Danl | Laborer | | Los Angeles Co | Los Angeles. |
| Wicks, Moses, J | Planter | Los Angeles Co | nr San Gabriel | San Gabriel. |
| Wicks, M J | Fruit grower | San Gabriel Valley | 1 m N E San Gab | San Gabriel. |
| Wickham, F H | Teamster | | Los Angeles Co | Los Angeles. |
| Widney, J P | Physician | Los Angeles | Los Angeles Co | Los Angeles. |
| Widney, Wm W | Clerk | Los Angeles | Los Angeles Co | Los Angeles. |
| Widney, R M | Attorney | Los Angeles | Los Angeles Co | Los Angeles. |
| Wiggins, T J | Farmer | El Monte Valley | 3 m S W Lexington | El Monte. |
| Wilbar, A P | Surveyor | Los Angeles | Los Angeles Co | Los Angeles. |
| Wilby, B F | Teamster | | Los Angeles Co | Los Angeles. |
| Wilder, H F | Musician | Los Angeles | Los Angeles Co | Los Angeles. |
| Wildman, Perry | Hotel proprietor | Wilmington | Canal st | Wilmington. |
| Wiley, W H | Livery stable | Anaheim | Los Angeles Co | Anaheim. |
| Wiley, H C | Real estate | Los Angeles | 4th st | Los Angeles. |
| Wiley & Berry | Real estate | 32 Main st | Los Angeles | Los Angeles. |
| Wiley, Wm | Farmer | nr Los Nietos | Los Angeles Co | Los Nietos. |
| Wilkens, Claus | Farmer | Los Angeles Co | Anaheim | Anaheim. |
| Wilkinson, Wm | Stage driver | Los Angeles Co | Los Angeles | Los Angeles. |
| Wilkins, R H | Gen merchandise | Los Angeles | Los Angeles | Los Angeles. |
| Wilkerson, Wm | Miner | Los Angeles Co | 4 m N W Lyon Sta'n | Lyon Station. |
| Wilkins, N M | Teamster | Los Angeles Co | Silver Precinct | Downey. |
| Wilkinson, J W | Farmer | Los Angeles Co | nr La Ballona | Los Angeles. |
| Wilkenson, C | Farmer | nr Los Angeles | Los Angeles Co | Los Angeles. |
| Wilkinson, F O | Farmer | Los Angeles Co | nr Los Angeles | Los Angeles. |
| Wilkinson, Z | Farmer | nr Azusa | Los Angeles Co | Azusa. |
| Willite, Wm L | Farmer | Los Angeles | Los Angeles | Los Angeles. |
| Williams, W J | Farmer | nr Santa Ana | Los Angeles Co | Santa Ana. |
| Williams, John | Farmer | Mission San Gabriel | Los Angeles Co | San Gabriel. |
| Willams, — | Farmer | San Jose Valley | 1 m N W Spadra | Spadra. |
| Williams, John | Deck hand | Steamer Los Angeles | Wilmington | Wilmington. |
| Williams, Wm H | Land agent | 25 Temple Block | Los Angeles | Los Angeles. |
| Williams, Joseph L | Saloon | Temple Block | Los Angeles | Los Angeles. |
| Willson, A B | Farmer | Los Angeles Co | Westminster Col. | Westminster. |
| Wille, Charles | Cooper | North 2nd st | Anaheim | Anaheim. |
| Willey, Jno | Farmer | Los Angeles Co | nr Halfway House | Compton. |
| Williams, T S | Teamster | | Los Angeles Co | El Monte. |
| Williams, J | Farmer | nr Los Angeles | Los Angeles Co | Los Angeles. |
| Willson, R J | Laborer | Los Angeles Co | Silver Precinct | Downey. |
| Wills, J T | Minister | Los Angeles | Los Angeles Co | Los Angeles. |

| Name. | Occupation. | Place of Business. | Residence. | Town or P. O. |
|---|---|---|---|---|
| Williams, J F | Laborer | | Los Angeles Co | Los Angeles. |
| Williams, R | Teamster | | Los Angeles Co | Anaheim. |
| Williams, Frank | Laborer | Pt San Pedro | Pt San Pedro | Wilmington. |
| **Williams, M W** | Farmer | El Monte Valley | 3 m S Lexington | El Monte. |
| Willets, S | Farmer | San Pedro Ranch | 1½ m N E Compton | Compton. |
| Williamson, N | Farmer | Los Angeles Co | Silver Precinct | Downey. |
| Williams, J L | Clerk | Los Angeles | Los Angeles Co | Los Angeles. |
| Willoughby, Wm | Teamster | Los Angeles Co | Silver Precinct | Downey. |
| **Williams, R W** | Farmer | Los Angeles Co | nr El Monte | El Monte. |
| Willis, C C | Teamster | Los Angeles Co | | Anaheim. |
| Williams, D K | Carpenter | Anaheim | Los Angeles Co | Anaheim. |
| Willhart, W | Farmer | nr Los Angeles | Los Angeles Co | Los Angeles. |
| Willits, J L | Butcher | Los Angeles | Los Angeles Co | Los Angeles. |
| Williams, Fred | Laborer | Los Angeles Co | | Los Angeles. |
| Williams, R M | Trader | Los Angeles | Los Angeles Co | Los Angeles. |
| Willmott, J | | Los Angeles | Los Angeles Co | Los Angeles. |
| Williams, F G | Farmer | nr Los Angeles | Los Angeles Co | Los Angeles. |
| Willie, Carl | Cooper | Anaheim | Los Angeles Co | Anaheim. |
| Williams, P | Farmer | nr Los Angeles | Los Angeles Co | Los Angeles. |
| Wilmington Hook & Ladder Co | | Canal st | | Wilmington. |
| Wilson, C T | Hostler | Los Angeles | Los Angeles Co | Los Angeles. |
| Wilson, Geo Otto | Laborer | Los Angeles Co | | Los Angeles. |
| Wilson, Frank W | Laborer | Los Angeles Co | San Joaquin | Santa Ana. |
| Wilson, Joseph | Lawyer | Los Angeles | Los Angeles Co | Los Angeles. |
| **Wilson, B D** | Capitalist | Lake Vineyard | Wilmington | Wilmington. |
| **Wilson & Co, B D.** | Vintners | Lake Vineyard | | San Gabriel. |
| Wilson, A L | Farmer | Azusa Duarte | 3 m E Lexington | El Monte. |
| Wilson, John T | Fruit grower | San Fernando Valley | 4 m N San Fernando | San Fernando. |
| **Wilson, A A** | Attorney at law | 26 & 27 Temple Blk | | Los Angeles. |
| **Wilson, John** | Fashion stable | Main st | San Pedro st | Los Angeles. |
| **Wilson, S H** | Stock raiser | nr Los Angeles | Los Angeles Co | Los Angeles. |
| Wilson, J H | Laborer | | Los Angeles Co | Los Angeles. |
| Wilson, W M | Farmer | nr San Gabriel | Los Angeles Co | San Gabriel. |
| Wilson, A B | Farmer | Los Angeles Co | nr Los Angeles | Los Angeles. |
| Wilson, J A | Mariner | Wilmington | Los Angeles Co | Wilmington. |
| **Wilson, C N** | Attorney at law | 1 Temple Block | Los Angeles Co | Los Angeles. |
| **Wilson, Wm A** | Stock raiser | San Pedro Ranch | 1½ m S Compton | Compton. |
| Wilson, John | L fireman | S P R R Co | Spadra | Spadra. |
| Wilson, W A | Farmer | nr El Monte | Los Angeles Co | El Monte. |
| Wilson, R | Merchant | Los Angeles | Los Angeles Co | Los Angeles. |
| Wilson, P | Drayman | Los Angeles | Los Angeles Co | Los Angeles. |
| Wilson, J | Farmer | Los Angeles Co | Silver Precinct | Downey. |
| Wilson, F | Farmer | San Gabriel | Los Angeles Co | San Gabriel. |
| **Wilson, J H** | Farmer | Los Angeles Co | nr El Monte | El Monte. |
| **Wilson, D C** | Farmer | nr El Monte | Los Angeles Co | El Monte. |
| Wilson, G H | Laborer | | Los Angeles Co | Anaheim. |
| Wilson, J R | Farmer | nr Wilmington | Los Angeles Co | Wilmington. |
| Wilson, Wm | Carpenter | Los Angeles | Los Angeles Co | Los Angeles. |
| Wilson, J A | Teamster | | Los Angeles Co | Los Angeles. |
| Wilson, Geo | Merchant | Los Angeles | Los Angeles Co | Los Angeles. |
| Wilson, Benj | Laborer | | Los Angeles Co | Anaheim. |
| Wilson, Jno | Laborer | Los Angeles Co | | Anaheim. |
| Wilson, F | Renovator | Los Angeles | Los Angeles Co | Los Angeles. |
| Wilson, J B | Farmer | Los Angeles Co | nr San Gabriel | San Gabriel. |
| Wilson, O R | Actor | Los Angeles | Los Angeles Co | Los Angeles. |
| Wilson, J W | Farmer | nr San Gabriel | Los Angeles Co | San Gabriel. |
| Wilson, J F | Laborer | | Los Angeles Co | Los Angeles. |
| **Wilson, W R** | Farmer | nr San Gabriel | Los Angeles Co | San Gabriel. |
| Wilson, G | Farmer | Los Angeles Co | Silver Precinct | Downey. |
| Wilson, J | Farmer | Los Angeles Co | Silver Precinct | Downey. |
| **Wilson, J J** | Farmer | Los Angeles Co | Silver Precinct | Downey. |
| Wilson, C | Farmer | nr San Gabriel | Los Angeles Co | San Gabriel. |
| Wilson, J P | Farmer | Los Angeles | Los Angeles Co | Los Angeles. |

# DIRECTORY OF LOS ANGELES COUNTY. 443

| Name. | Occupation. | Place of Business. | Residence. | Town or P. O. |
|---|---|---|---|---|
| Wilson, G A | Dentist | El Monte | Los Angeles Co | El Monte. |
| Wiltfong, E | Gunsmith | Halfway House | Halfway House | Compton. |
| Winans, I C | Farmer | Los Angeles Co | nr Los Angeles | Los Angeles. |
| Winbigler, D N | Carpenter | Los Angeles | Los Angeles Co | Los Angeles. |
| Winchester, G B | Tailor | Wilmington | Los Angeles Co | Wilmington. |
| Winders, J W | Musician | Los Angeles | Los Angeles Co | Los Angeles. |
| Winder, W S | Sheep raiser | nr Los Angeles | Los Angeles Co | Los Angeles. |
| Winfrey, R H | Carpenter | El Monte | Los Angeles Co | El Monte. |
| Winn, G H | Laborer | | Los Angeles Co | Los Angeles. |
| Winston, H W | Farmer | Los Angeles Co | nr San Gabriel | San Gabriel. |
| Winston, L C | | Los Angeles | Los Angeles | Los Angeles. |
| Winston, Dr | Physician | San Gabriel canyon | 6 m N Azusa | Azusa. |
| Winston, J B | Hotel keeper | Los Angeles | Los Angeles Co | Los Angeles. |
| Winter, Saul H | Merchant | Los Angeles | Los Angeles | Los Angeles. |
| Winter, S | Farmer | Los Angeles Co | nr Wilmington | Wilmington. |
| Winters, Jno | Staging | | Los Angeles Co | Los Angeles. |
| Winters, J | Machinist | Los Angeles Co | Soledad | San Fernando. |
| Wise, Chas | Merchant | Los Angeles | Los Angeles | Los Angeles. |
| Wise, Dr K D | Phys and surgeon | 74 Main st | Main st | Los Angeles. |
| Wiseman, W C | Attorney at law | Canal st, nr Wharf | Wilson College | Wilmington. |
| Wiseman, M | Mariner | Los Nietos | Los Angeles Co | Los Nietos. |
| Witherow, Saml N | | Los Angeles | Los Angeles | Los Angeles. |
| Wittelshoeffer, J | Paints & oils | Requena st | Los Angeles | Los Angeles. |
| Wittelshoeffer & Raphael | Paints, oils, &c | Requena st | | Los Angeles. |
| Wittelshoeffer, I | Paints & oils | 4 Arcadia Block | Spring st | Los Angeles. |
| Witti, Emil | Farmer | nr Anaheim | Los Angeles Co | Anaheim. |
| Wohlers, G H | Undertaker | 3 Spring st | Los Angeles | Los Angeles. |
| Wolenberg, Jno Wm | Clerk | Los Angeles | Los Angeles | Los Angeles. |
| Wolfskill, L | Ranchero | nr Los Angeles | Los Angeles Co | Los Angeles. |
| Wolfe, B F | Farmer | Los Angeles Co | Silver Precinct | Downey. |
| Wolfski, L | Bar keeper | Los Angeles | Los Angeles Co | Los Angeles. |
| Wolf & Co | Fashion saloon | 61 Downey Block | | Los Angeles. |
| Wolf, R J | Saloon | Santa Monica canyon | Santa Monica | Los Angeles. |
| Wolfenstein, V | Photographer | Los Angeles | Los Angeles | Los Angeles. |
| Wolf & Gates | Saloon | Los Angeles | Los Angeles | Los Angeles. |
| Wolfskill, J W | Farmer | nr Los Angeles | Los Angeles Co | Los Angeles. |
| Wolf, G W | Farmer | Los Angeles Co | Silver Precinct | Downey. |
| Wollweber, Theo | Druggist | Apothecaries Hall | 3d st | Los Angeles. |
| Wood, N T | Farmer | Los Angeles Co | nr Santa Ana | Santa Ana. |
| Woodbury, G A | Farmer | nr Los Angeles | Los Angeles Co | Los Angeles. |
| Wood, J H | Farmer | Los Angeles Co | Silver Precinct | Downey. |
| Woodward, S K | Farmer | nr El Monte | Los Angeles Co | El Monte. |
| Woodworth, E J | Farmer | Los Angeles Co | nr San Gabriel | San Gabriel. |
| Woodworth, J D | Farmer | Los Angeles Co | nr San Gabriel | San Gabriel. |
| Wood, C H | Confectioner | Los Angeles | Los Angeles Co | Los Angeles. |
| Woodbury, James | Clerk | Los Angeles | Los Angeles | Los Angeles. |
| Wood, Fred W | Civil engineer | Los Angeles | Los Angeles | Los Angeles. |
| Woods, Henry H | Carpenter | Los Angeles Co | | Los Angeles. |
| Woodman, W W | Miner | San Gabriel Precinct | | San Gabriel. |
| Woodroofe, E | Blacksmith | Ellis Station | 1 m W Lexington | El Monte. |
| Woodworth, W | Lumber dealer | 76 Commercial st | San Pedro st | Los Angeles. |
| Woodington, — | Farmer | Los Angeles Co | Westminster Col | Westminster. |
| Worden, C H | Farmer | nr Los Angeles | Los Angeles Co | Los Angeles. |
| Wordsworth, J | Laborer | | Los Angeles Co | Los Angeles. |
| Workman, J M | Farmer | nr El Monte | Los Angeles Co | El Monte. |
| Workman, A | Farmer | nr San Fernando | Los Angeles Co | San Fernando. |
| Workman, Wm | Ranchero | San Bernardino Road | 5 m E Lexington | El Monte. |
| Workman, W H | Harness maker | 76 Main st | Los Angeles | Los Angeles. |
| Workman, Jos | Ranchero | San Bernardino Road | 3 m E Lexington | El Monte. |
| Workman, E H | Harness maker | 76 Main st | Los Angeles | Los Angeles. |
| Workman Bros | Harness makers | 76 Main st | | Los Angeles. |
| Workman, Mrs M | Lodging house | 150 Main st | 159 Main st | Los Angeles. |

| Name. | Occupation. | Place of Business. | Residence. | Town or P. O. |
|---|---|---|---|---|
| Workman, C | Laborer | | Los Angeles Co | Los Angeles. |
| Workman, W | Ranchero | Los Angeles Co | | El Monte. |
| Worms, Solomon | Watch maker | Los Angeles | Los Angeles | Los Angeles. |
| Worrell, J T | Printer | Los Angeles | Los Angeles Co | Los Angeles. |
| Worth, A F | Laborer | Wilmington | Los Angeles Co | Los Angeles. |
| Wouderly, Henry | Dairyman | nr Downey | San Antonio | Downey. |
| Wo Yot & Co | Merchants | Los Angeles | Los Angeles | Los Angeles. |
| Wright, J | Farmer | Los Angeles Co | La Ballona | Los Angeles. |
| Wright, A | Miner | | Los Angeles Co | Los Angeles. |
| Wright, J S | Farmer | Los Angeles Co | nr Halfway House | Compton. |
| Wright, G | Farmer | Los Angeles Co | nr Halfway House | Compton. |
| Wright, J S | Carpenter | Los Angeles Co | Soledad | San Fernando. |
| Wright, B C | Farmer | Los Angeles Co | nr Los Angeles | Los Angeles. |
| Wright, J | Farmer | Los Angeles Co | nr San Jose | Spadra. |
| Wright, R R | Farmer | Los Angeles Co | nr Los Angeles | Los Angeles. |
| Wright, C B | Farmer | Los Angeles | Halfway House | Compton. |
| Wright, B F | Teamster | | Los Angeles Co | Los Angeles. |
| Wright, Chas | Engineer | Los Angeles | Los Angeles | Los Angeles. |
| Wright, Matthew | Carpenter | Los Angeles Co | | Los Angeles. |
| Wright, John M | Teacher | Los Angeles | Los Angeles | Los Angeles. |
| Wright, Joseph | Justice of peace | San Jose | Spadra | Spadra. |
| Wright, Geo | Farmer | Azusa Ranch | 2¼ m N E Azusa | Azusa. |
| Wright, C B | Hotel | Compton | Compton | Compton. |
| Wright, C L | Farmer | Compton | Compton | Compton. |
| Wright & Mier | Saloon | Los Angeles Co | | Los Angeles. |
| Wright, James H | Saloon | Los Angeles | Los Angeles | Los Angeles. |
| Wright, C M | Stage agent | Los Angeles | Los Angeles Co | Los Angeles. |
| Wright, C C | Wine maker | Los Angeles | Los Angeles Co | Los Angeles. |
| Wright, M H | Staging | | Los Angeles Co | Los Angeles. |
| Wright, J H | Merchant | Los Angeles | Los Angeles Co | Los Angeles. |
| Wuitt, D K | Rope maker | Los Angeles | Los Angeles Co | Los Angeles. |
| Wurdische, R | Laborer | San Gabriel | 9 m E Los Angeles | San Gabriel. |
| Wyatt, B | Attorney | Los Angeles | Los Angeles Co | Los Nietos. |
| Wylie, E R | Farmer | Los Angeles Co | nr Los Nietos | Los Nietos. |
| Wynn, Saml | Painter | Los Angeles | Los Angeles | Los Angeles. |
| Yarnell, Geo | Printer | Los Angeles | Los Angeles Co | Los Angeles. |
| Yarnell, S | Farmer | Los Angeles Co | nr Santa Ana | Santa Ana. |
| Yarnell, J | Publisher | Los Angeles | Los Angeles Co | Los Angeles. |
| Yarnell, Caystell & Brown | Publishers | L A Weekly Mirror | Los Angeles | Los Angeles. |
| Yates, J E | Miner | Los Angeles Co | Soledad | San Fernando. |
| Yates, J | Laborer | | Los Angeles Co | Azusa. |
| Yates, G S | Farmer | nr Anaheim | Los Angeles Co | Anaheim. |
| Yates, O | Laborer | | Los Angeles Co | Los Angeles. |
| Yates, Jemes | Miner | San Gabriel canyon | 14 m N Azusa | Azusa. |
| Yates, G S | Carpenter | Los Angeles Co | Westminster Col | Westminster. |
| Ybarro, Miguel | Laborer | Los Angeles Co | Anaheim | Anaheim. |
| Ybarra, Marcos | Farmer | nr Los Angeles | Los Angeles Co | Los Angeles. |
| Ybarra, Jose Maria | Ranchero | | nr Los Angeles | Los Angeles. |
| Ybarra, Felipe | Laborer | | Los Angeles Co | Los Angeles. |
| Ybarra, Refugio | Vaquero | Los Angeles Co | | Los Angeles. |
| Ybarra, R | Ranchero | Los Angeles Co | San Jose | Spadra. |
| Ybarra, F | Vaquero | Los Angeles Co | | Los Angeles. |
| Ybarra, Y | Laborer | Los Angeles Co | San Jose | Spadra. |
| Ybarra, J P | Gardener | Los Angeles | Los Angeles Co | Los Angeles. |
| Ybarra, J L | Laborer | Los Angeles Co | | Los Angeles. |
| Ybarra, P | Vaquero | | Los Angeles Co | Azusa. |
| Ybarra, Jose | Laborer | | Los Angeles Co | Azusa. |
| Ybarra, L | Ranchero | Los Angeles Co | San Jose | Spadra. |
| Ybarra, J M | Vaquero | | Los Angeles Co | Los Angeles. |
| Ybarra, R | Laborer | Los Angeles Co | | Los Angeles. |
| Ybarra, J S | Ranchero | Los Angeles Co | San Jose | Spadra. |
| Ybarra, P | Farmer | Los Angeles Co | nr Los Angeles | Los Angeles. |
| Ybarra, Y | Ranchero | nr Los Angeles | Los Angeles Co | Los Angeles. |

DIRECTORY OF LOS ANGELES COUNTY. 445

| Name. | Occupation. | Place of Business. | Residence. | Town or P. O. |
|---|---|---|---|---|
| Ybarra, C A | Farmer | Los Angeles Co | nr San Jose | Spadra. |
| Yeary, A C | Farmer | Los Angeles | Los Angeles Co | Los Angeles. |
| Yescas, A. | Laborer | Los Angeles Co | | San Gabriel. |
| **Yocum, Dr J H** | Physician | Anaheim | Anaheim | Anaheim. |
| Yoes, Guillaume | Laborer | | Los Angeles Co | Los Angeles. |
| Yorba, A | Laborer | Los Angeles Co | | Santa Ana. |
| Yorba, J Y | Vaquero | | Los Angeles Co | Los Angeles. |
| Yorba, Bicente | Laborer | Los Angeles Co | | Santa Ana. |
| Yorba, Bautista | Farmer | Los Angeles Co | Old Mission | El Monte. |
| Yorby, Miguel | Laborer | Los Angeles Co | Los Angeles Co | Capistrano. |
| Yorba, T | Farmer | Los Angeles Co | San Jose | Spadra. |
| Yorba, Felipe | Farmer | nr Santa Ana | Santa Ana | Santa Ana. |
| Yorba, Jose de Jesus | Farmer | Los Angeles Co | nr Los Angeles | Los Angeles. |
| Yorba, D | Farmer | nr Los Angeles | Los Angeles Co | Los Angeles. |
| Yorba, A M | Laborer | | Los Angeles Co | Wilmington. |
| Yorba, T | Vaquero | Los Angeles Co | | San Gabriel. |
| Yorba, P | Farmer | Los Angeles Co | | Santa Ana. |
| Yorba, Marcus | Vintner | Los Angeles Co | nr Santa Ana | Santa Ana. |
| Yorba, J B | Laborer | Los Angeles Co | Old Mission | El Monte. |
| Yorba, Jose | Farmer | nr San Gabriel | Los Angeles Co | San Gabriel. |
| York, Albert | Clerk | Los Angeles | Los Angeles Co | Los Angeles. |
| Young, Joseph | Farmer | nr Orange | Richland | Orange. |
| Young, Alex R | Stable keeper | Los Angeles | Los Angeles | Los Angeles. |
| Young, Joaquin | Farmer | Los Angeles Co | Puenta | El Monte. |
| **Young, George** | Farmer | nr Orange | Richland | Orange. |
| Young, Miguel | Mechanic | Los Angeles | Los Angeles | Los Angeles. |
| Young, Jas | Shoe maker | Los Angeles | Los Angeles Co | Los Angeles. |
| Young, F M | Farmer | Los Angeles Co | nr El Monte | El Monte. |
| Young, J A | Miner | Los Angeles Co | | Los Angeles. |
| Young, J M | Carpenter | Los Angeles | Los Angeles Co | Los Angeles. |
| **Young, S.** | Farmer | Los Angeles Co | La Ballona | Los Angeles. |
| Young, J D | Farmer | Los Angeles Co | nr La Ballona | Los Angeles. |
| **Young, Horace D** | Nurseryman | Los Angeles Co | Westminster Col | Westminster. |
| Yslar, F | Laborer | Los Angeles Co | | Los Angeles. |
| Yudart, Francis | Clerk | Los Angeles | Los Angeles | Los Angeles. |
| Yunghaus, F | Shoe maker | San Fernando | San Fernando | San Fernando. |
| Yunge, A | Druggist | Los Angeles | Los Angeles Co | Los Angeles. |
| Zahn, Rev J C | Pastor | Ger Ch, Spring st | Los Angeles | Los Angeles. |
| Zamora, B | Laborer | | Los Angeles Co | Los Angeles. |
| Zedford, W H | Farmer | nr Santa Ana | Los Angeles Co | Santa Ana. |
| Zeigelmuller, J | Farmer | nr Los Angeles | Los Angeles Co | Los Angeles. |
| Zenn, J L | Vintner | nr Anaheim | Los Angeles Co | Anaheim. |
| Zerega, S | Merchant | Los Angeles | Los Angeles Co | Los Angeles. |
| Zimmerman, J | Laborer | | Los Angeles Co | Los Angeles. |
| **Zlun, John** | Ranchero | Los Angeles Co | Silver Precinct | Downey. |

WM. MEE.    SAMUEL BROOKE.    W. M. BOREN.

# MEE & CO.

## Blacksmith and General Repairing

### AND JOBBING SHOP,

UTAH ST.   -   SAN BERNARDINO, CAL.

*Repairing of all kinds of Agricultural Implements. Horse-shoeing, Etc.*

# LARKINS & CO.

## MANUFACTURERS OF CARRIAGES,

Rockaways and Doctors' Phætons,

**ALL KINDS OF JOBBING & CARRIAGE PAINTING**

*DONE AT SHORTEST NOTICE.*

### 631 and 633 HOWARD ST.

CORNER HUBBARD STREET,

SAN FRANCISCO.

# W. H. J. BROOKS,
## EXAMINER OF TITLES.

### ABSTRACTS OF TITLE

To RANCHES, COUNTY LANDS AND CITY LOTS, showing every transaction, from the earliest dates to the present time, prepared with accuracy and dispatch.

In the course of his business during the past year, Mr. Brooks has investigated the title of most of the ranches of this county, as well as many lots and tracts in the city. The abstracts of all these have been preserved, and form already quite a large collection.

He is also preparing a PROPERTY INDEX OF THE ENTIRE COUNTY OF LOS ANGELES, which, to the extent to which it is completed, affords an additional safe-guard, for certainty.

### Conveyancing in all its Branches.

OFFICE IN ALLEN'S BUILDING,

## CORNER SPRING AND TEMPLE STS.
(UP STAIRS) LOS ANGELES.

## LINFORTH, KELLOGG & CO.
### 3 & 5 FRONT STREET, S. F.
# Hardware & Agricultural Implements.

**GENUINE CHICAGO PITTS' THRESHER**
Manufactured by H. A. Pitts' Sons. The best constructed machine made.

**MANSFIELD PORTABLE STEAM ENGINES**, unsurpassed in merit by any, and superior to most all others.

**RUSSELL'S SELF-RAKE REAPER.**

**THE IMPROVED WOODS' EAGLE MOWER**

**MYERS' PLOW.**—This celebrated Gang, with a patent dove-tail share, requiring no bolts, no delay in replacing the shares, and needs only to be seen to prove its great merits **over all other Gang Plows in the world!** Warranted to give satisfaction or no sale.

**GARDEN CITY CLIPPER PLOWS AND CULTIVATORS.**—We have a full assortment of this only Cast Steel Plow that comes to the market, and the thousands now in use in California and Oregon prove their superiority.

Studebaker Farm and Spring Wagons; Eagle Hay Presses; Chisel Cultivators; Friedeman Harrows; Furst & Bradley Sulky Rakes; Seed Sowers; Feed Cutters, &c. And a full a line of Hardware and Cutlery. Rumsey's Force and Lift Pumps; Hydraulic Rams; Church, School and Farm Bells.

**PLEASE SEND FOR CATALOGUES AND PRICE LISTS.**

## A GENERAL DESCRIPTION

OF

# SAN DIEGO COUNTY

SAN DIEGO, the extreme Southern County of California, is bounded on the North by San Bernardino County; on the East by Arizona; on the West by the Pacific Ocean; and on the South by Lower California. It has an extreme length of one hundred and sixty-two miles, by a breadth of one hundred and two, giving

### AN AREA,

In square miles, of sixteen thousand, five hundred and twenty-four; or, in acres, ten million, five hundred and seventy-five thousand, three hundred and sixty. Of these acres, about two million, five hundred thousand are occupied by the Colorado Desert; of the residue, some four million may be said to be appropriated by the mountains and canyons; leaving a handsome remainder of four million, seventy-five thousand, three hundred and sixty acres, stretching out in fertile plain, or, as valleys, niched among the fastnesses of the Coast Range, fruitful in soil, irreproachable in climate, adapted to all the requirements of agriculture or grazing.

### THE POPULATION

In 1870 amounted to four thousand, nine hundred and fifty-one, since which time the increase is thought to have been fully one hundred per cent.

### THE ASSESSED VALUATION

Of property for the current year is upwards of three millions. Two branches of

### THE COAST RANGE

Extend across the entire County, from North to South, making three divisions, as distinct from one another, in soil, climate, and topography as though occupying different hemispheres.

### THE DIVISION

Bordering upon the coast forms a strip, in width about twenty-five or thirty miles, of undulating valleys and gently sloping or level plains. Nearly all this land is well fitted for agricultural and grazing purposes, and is, to a great extent, unoccupied. The San Diego, San Luis Rey, Santa Margarita, Sweetwater, and other streams irrigate this slope. They have their sources in the branches of the Coast Range, some flowing through the entire year, others running dry during the summer season.

### THE CENTRAL DIVISION

Is mountainous in character, is irregular in outline, and is about forty miles in width. It contains large tracts of good farming land, and the greater part of the finest grazing land in the County. Gold, silver, copper and other minerals have been found in both these ranges, at various points. The mountains have heavy forests of oak, fir, pine, and cedar.

The Santa Ysabel District is distant from the town of San Diego, in an Easterly direction, about seventy miles. It is a succession of broad table lands, lying between the two main ridges of the mountains, at an elevation of between three and four thousand feet above the sea level.

The loftiest peak of these mountain ranges is the San Jacinto, variously estimated at from five thousand to eight thousand feet in height. It is the most fertile and richest portion of the County, better adapted to agricultural purposes in both soil and climate, and richer in the greater variety of its resources. Wheat, barley, oranges and grapes are among its products. The most rapid and greatest developments made within the limits of the County are being effected in this locality.

## THE THIRD DIVISION,

Comprising the great Colorado Desert, lies Eastward of this mountain range. This desert extends to the borders of the State on the South and East. It is an arid plain, destitute of the slightest vestige of vegetation for miles along its Northern and Western borders. On the South and East, its soil finds fertility from contact with the waters of New River, which receives the overflow from the Colorado in time of freshets. The Gila and Colorado have their confluence near here, and upon the fact that the desert lies at a level below the waters of the gulf into which they empty, was once formed an irrigation scheme for reclaiming this waste district. Although the action of Congress was favorable to it, the project was abandoned. It is without doubt perfectly practicable, and will at some future day be carried into execution.

Near the boundary line towards Arizona, after crossing the New River, the appearance of the country undergoes a complete change. Instead of the shifting sand so recently left behind, there is a soil having a greyish tint, as firm and compact as brick, covered with a scanty growth of short, wiry grass, among which flourishes the cacti family in all its infinite and forbidding variety. The mesquite also grows luxuriantly in this district, giving it the appearance of a forest, as compared with the bare, sandy plains.

This is the storehouse from which the Indians of Arizona and Lower California draw their winter's supply of the nuts or beans of this tree.

The entire vicinity has a tropical appearance, the air being literally swarmed with paroquets, orioles, and other brilliant-plumaged birds.

## THE PRINCIPAL VALLEYS

Of this County are the Tia Juana, Otay, Jamul, Sweet Water, Cajon, San Pasqual, San Luis Rey, San Diegnito, Santa Maria, Santa Ysabel, Ballena, Monserrate, Milquatay, Santa Margarita, Temecula, Warner's Ranch, and Valle las Viejas.

## ITS PRINCIPAL RIVERS

Are of Sierra origin, and assist in irrigating the agricultural portions of the County. They are the Tia Juana, Otay, Sweet Water, Nacional, San Diego, San Diegnito, San Luis Rey and Santa Margarita. They generally fail during the dry season, although some of them present a water supply throughout the entire year. The wants of irrigation, beyond the supply thus naturally furnished, are subserved by artesian wells. The underground supply is abundant, the water being about the same temperature as rain. One well of good capacity is capable of furnishing all the water demanded by ten acres, under cultivation to fruit. A peculiar method of farming is resorted to in San Diego County, no less than elsewhere in Southern California. The rain-fall occurs within an unusually short period, subjecting them to a long interval of drought, but in any year the rainfall is sufficient to produce fair crops. Deep plowing is resorted to during the winter, the soil being thoroughly stirred. The earth thus retains its moisture for a much greater period than when the soil is only superficially broken. This moisture being retained, comparatively little rain is necessary to ensure an ample return in the product sought. Plowing and sowing occupies the interval from November to April.

## VEGETABLES

Are successfully cultivated, by a trifling amount of labor, in the direction of artificial irrigation. San Diego County has less rainfall than any other portion of the State, yet a smaller amount, if ocurring at the proper season, is necessary here to produce and mature grain and potato crops than elsewhere, it being stated that ten inches of rain will accomplish perfectly that which twenty inches fails in thoroughly effecting in the upper counties.

## THE CLIMATE AND SOIL

Of this County are adapted to all fruits of a tropical nature. The orange, lemon, citron and lime seem to thrive well, and while in the valleys the frost may prove, to a certain extent, inimical to their growth, on the table lands they will meet with no such drawback.

## THE OLIVE

Is raised in a perfection rarely met. The groves at the San Diego Mission yield more largely, and surpass in the size and the quality of their fruit those of any other locality. The trees are seventy-five years of age, but remain unimpaired in vigor and productiveness, are of thrifty growth, and yield a handsome income to their proprietors.

For olive culture this is without doubt one of the most favorable point in the United States. Much attention has been directed toward it for the past two years. In 1874, several thousand cuttings were planted in the vicinity of San Diego Bay.

## THE FIG

Is also a profitable fruit for the cultivator in these latitudes. The planting of such an orchard is attended with but little expense, and from three to four crops have been gathered in one season from the same tree. An additional argument for its cultivation is also offered, from the fact that the climate, owing to the peculiar atmospheric dryness, presents unusual facilities for curing fruits.

One of the leading industries of this County, is the

## BEE CULTURE.

The increase in the exportation in 1873, over that of the previous year, was one hundred thousand pounds, but a moderate increase after all, in comparison with what might be effected, did they exert themselves in this direction as fully as might be expected from the possession of advantages, which would seem to lead, by a natural process, toward what would be so easily accomplished.

## SHEEP-RAISING

Is also beginning to attract especial attention. The export of wool for the year of "73" was six hundred thousand pounds.

SALT is manufactured from the waters of the bay.

HIDES are shipped raw, there being no facilities for tanning in the County.

Were a moderate amount of capital devoted to the legitimate purpose of erecting a manufacturing interest here, San Diego might become something more than a point from which to demand raw material. She might manufacture her own sugar from the sugar beet, the product of her own soil, and send her shipments to market pocketing the profits, instead of sending away the raw material and importing the manufactured article. The same may be said regarding the wool product, and the hide supply. But all this and perhaps more is lingering within her near future.

## THE BAY OF SAN DIEGO,

Upon the Northeastern shore of which stands the present town of San Diego, the County seat, was discovered in 1542, by a Portuguese navigator, employed by the Spanish government. The ancient Pueblo covered the site of old San Diego as well as the present town. These two places, although generally considered to be identical, are separated by a distance of about four miles in the position of their settlements, although in the same municipality. This was the first settled portion of the State, the mission having been located in 1769.

San Diego, or Saint James, was selected as the name under which the new mission was established. That the locality still exists, and has given its name to both the County and the Bay, is no doubt altogether due to the fostering care of this, their tutelar saint.

The mouth of the harbor is about eighteen miles from the Mexican border. From here the distance to New York is four hundred and twenty-three miles less than from San Francisco. It also lies five hundred miles nearer China than San Francisco.

## THE TONNAGE

Of the port in 1874 was 208,476 as opposed to 160,815 in 1873, being a gain in one year of 47,661 tons.

Following are the arrivals at the port during the year of 1874 : steamers, 220; brigs, 2; barks, 5; schooners, 34; sloops, 11.

Imports during 1874..................................33,510 tons freight.
  "       "       "      ................................2,837,475 feet lumber.
  "       "       "      ...................................487,000 shingles.
  "       "       "      ...................................302,200 laths.
  "       "       "      ...................................130,125 shakes.
Exports for 1874...................................1,024,021 ℔s wool.
  "       "       "      ...................................431,498 " honey.
  "       "       "      ...................................155,000 " salt.
  "       "       "      ...................................84,000 " flour.
  "       "       "      ...................................63,554 gallons wine.
  "       "       "      ...................................31,600 " whale oil.
  "       "       "      ...................................8,431 hides.
  "       "       "      ...................................30,000 ℔s. castor beans.

The mean temperature is 45°, the prevailing winds being from the West and Northwest.

At the time of the discovery of the Bay by Juan Rodrigues Cabrillo, in 1542, as before referred to, the name given to it was San Miguel. It was thus characterized until changed to its present name, in 1769, at the establishment of the old San Diego Mission, by the Franciscan Fathers. San Diego Bay has an average depth of twenty-two fathoms water, at low tide. The length of the Bay is thirteen miles from the entrance to its head.

With the exception of San Francisco this is the most commodious and safest port of the Pacific. Its width at the entrance is between six and seven hundred yards, and anchorage is good.

The steamers of the

## GOODALL, NELSON & PERKINS S. S. CO.

Ply regularly between this and the port of San Francisco, doing the carrying in passengers and freight for this and all intermediate points along the coast.

## THE MAIL SERVICE

To Los Angeles, a distance of one hundred and thirty miles, is by tri-weekly stages; that to Fort Yuma, one hundred and eighty miles distant, by weekly stage. The old town of San Diego not ministering sufficiently to the commercial necessities of this progressive age, has been left to its tumble-down fate, its adobe structures have been abandoned to the conservatives, while the business element has reared for itself a new city, as American in its character as the old one was Spanish. Its situation is more advantageous, commercially speaking; its residences are tasteful, handsome structures, an ornament to the city and an evidence of the cultivated taste and prosperous condition of the owners.

## ITS WAREHOUSES

And other commercial and mercantile structures are commodious, and well adapted to the wants and uses of trade. Its wharves are extensive, and bear evidence of having been erected at large cost, nothing having been neglected which could add to their durability, or render them better fitted for the service to which they are dedicated.

## THE POPULATION

Of San Diego approximates closely to three thousand. The anticipated construction of the Texas Pacific Railway, of which this is the terminal point, has given an impulse to enterprise in every direction, buildings of every description have been pushed to completion, and the entire population seem to be energized by a strong feeling of hope and confidence in their immediate future. Whether this feeling will be an abiding one, remains yet to be seen. It is to be hoped that the recent complications in the affairs of the Texas Pacific will not lead to a postponement, even, of their projected enterprise. The water supply of the city is derived from an artesian well, the supply being abundant.

San Diego is well supplied with schools, both public and private, and the religious element is represented by six churches of the following denominations: Baptist, Presbyterian, Methodist Episcopal, Episcopal, Unity Society, and Roman Catholic. It is also fully represented with social, secret, and benevolent societies. Two daily and weekly papers are published here, the *Union* and *World*. They are objects of local pride, well conducted, and correspondingly successful.

## SAN LUIS REY,

So called in honor of Louis IX of France, a warrior of the time of the crusades, is near the harbor of that name, forty-five miles North of San Diego. It is situated in a beautiful valley of an area of twenty-five miles, through which passes the San Luis Rey river, a never failing stream. The old mission of the same name was situated in this valley some five miles distant, where now stands the town of Pala. The soil of the valley is very fruitful. The harbor of San Luis is insecure and little used.

## TEMECULA,

North from Pala about forty-five miles, is a town of some little importance. The town is located on the bank of the Santa Margarita. The vicinity is well adapted for grazing purposes.

## WARNER'S RANCH

Is a small town about forty-five miles from Temecula, in an easterly direction.

FORT YUMA, at the extreme Southeast corner of the State, is a military post. This is known as the Picachto mining district. Placer mines exist there to some extent. Mining is the principal resource of the settlers.

San Diego County, in its entirety, is rich in varied resources, which will find development only in a largely increased population.

# DIRECTORY OF SAN DIEGO COUNTY. 455

| Occupation. | Place of Business. | Residence. | Town or P. O. |
|---|---|---|---|
| irpenter | San Diego | San Diego | San Diego. |
| erchant | San Diego | San Diego | San Diego. |
| irpenter | San Diego | San Diego Co. | San Diego. |
| :torney | San Diego Co. | San Diego | San Diego. |
| aquero | nr Milpitas | San Diego Co. | San Luis Rey. |
| iborer | San Luis Rey | San Luis Rey | San Luis Rey. |
| :amster | San Luis Rey | San Diego Co. | San Luis Rey. |
| ock raiser | 20 m N E San Diego | Paguay | Poway. |
| aborer | nr San Pascual | | San Pascual. |
| leep raiser | San Diego Co. | Cajon | San Diego. |
| armer | nr Milquatay | San Diego Co. | Campo. |
| arpenter | San Diego Co. | Warner's Ranch | Warner's Rch. |
| armer | San Luis Rey | San Diego Co. | San Luis Rey. |
| iner | 70 m N E San Diego | Banner | Banner. |
| armer | nr San Luis Rey | San Diego Co. | San Luis Rey. |
| armer | nr Laguna | San Diego Co. | |
| armer | San Diego Co. | nr San Pascual | San Pascual. |
| arness maker | San Diego | San Diego Co. | San Diego. |
| aborer | San Diego Co. | San Luis Rey | San Luis Rey. |
| aborer | Santa Margarita | 5 m N San Luis Rey | San Luis Rey. |
| anchero | San Diego Co. | San Pascual | San Pascual. |
| anchero | nr Guatay | San Diego Co. | |
| :udent | San Diego Co. | San Diego | San Diego. |
| erchant | San Diego Co. | San Jacinto | San Jacinto. |
| ar builder | San Diego Co | San Diego | San Diego. |
| arpenter | San Diego Co. | San Diego | San Diego. |
| armer | nr National City | San Diego Co. | National City. |
| armer | nr San Diego | San Diego Co. | San Diego. |
| armer | San Diego Co. | nr San Jacinto | San Jacinto. |
| aborer | San Diego Co. | nr San Diego | San Diego. |
| hysician | Drug store | San Diego | San Diego. |
| aborer | nr Jamul | San Diego Co. | San Diego. |
| rug store | cor 5th and F sts | San Diego | San Diego. |
| iner | nr San Diego | San Diego Co. | San Diego. |
| ock raiser | San Diego Co. | San Diego | San Diego. |
| lacksmith | San Diego | San Diego Co. | San Diego. |
| aquero | 65 m N E San Diego | Temecula | Temecula. |
| armer | nr Milpitas | San Diego Co. | San Luis Rey. |
| anchero | San Diego Co. | nr San Pascual | San Pascual. |
| anchero | San Diego Co. | Penasquitas | |
| armer | nr Milpitas | San Diego Co. | |
| aborer | 15 m E Temecula | Aguango | Temecula. |
| anchero | San Diego Co. | Monserrate | Monserrate. |
| armer | 90 m N San Diego | San Jacinto | San Jacinto. |
| aquero | San Luis Rey | San Diego Co. | San Luis Rey. |
| aborer | 65 m N E San Diego | Julian | Julian. |
| armer | nr San Marcus | San Diego Co. | San Luis Rey. |
| eamster | San Diego Co. | nr Banner | Banner. |
| anchero | San Diego Co. | Los Coches | Campo. |
| anchero | San Diego Co. | nr Cajon | San Diego. |
| eacher | San Diego Co. | Bear Valley | San Pascual. |
| utcher | San Diego Co. | San Diego | San Diego. |
| lerchant | San Diego Co. | San Diego | San Diego. |
| armer | San Diego Co. | Milquatay | Campo. |
| aborer | San Diego Co. | nr San Diego | San Diego. |
| armer | 65 m N E San Diego | Julian | Julian. |
| armer | San Diego Co. | nr Paguay | Poway. |
| armer | San Diego Co. | Carriseto | |
| arpenter | San Diego Co. | San Diego | San Diego. |
| aborer | San Diego | San Diego Co. | San Diego. |
| armer | San Diego Co. | Milquatay | Campo. |

| NAME. | OCCUPATION. | PLACE OF BUSINESS. | RESIDENCE. | TOWN OR P. O. |
|---|---|---|---|---|
| **Andrews, J** | Farmer | San Diego Co. | nr San Diego | San Diego. |
| Andrews, Stiles Burr | Cook | San Diego | San Diego | San Diego. |
| Ansuna, J M | Ranchero | San Diego Co. | nr Monserrate | Monserrate. |
| **Antes, J H** | Farmer | nr San Pascual | San Diego Co. | San Pascual. |
| Aquilla, Innocencia | Ranchero | San Luis Rey | San Diego Co. | San Luis Rey. |
| Arguello, F | Ranchero | San Diego Co. | La Punta | San Diego. |
| Arguelez, Bernard | Sheep raiser | 65 N E San Diego | Julian | Julian. |
| Arguello, J A | Ranchero | San Diego Co. | La Punta | San Diego. |
| Arguello, Jose C | Ranchero | 10 m S San Diego | La Punta | San Diego. |
| **Armstrong, J** | Wood turner | San Diego Co. | Tia Juana | San Diego. |
| Armstrong, S | Miner | nr San Diego | San Diego Co. | San Diego. |
| Armstrong, Wm | Farmer | 50 m N E San Diego | Ballena | Ballena. |
| **Arnold, C M** | Real estate & ins. | cor 3d and E sts | San Diego | San Diego. |
| **Arnold & Choate** | Real estate & ins. | cor 3d and E sts | San Diego | San Diego. |
| Arnold, L | Dentist | San Diego Co. | San Diego | San Diego. |
| Arnold, P | Fruit dealer | San Diego Co. | San Diego | San Diego. |
| **Arrambide & Etcheverey** | Sheep raisers | Santa Maria Ranch | San Diego Co. | San Diego. |
| Arremicia, A | Vaquero | San Diego Co. | Temecula | Temecula. |
| Arthur, R W | Blacksmith | San Diego Co. | Julian | Julian. |
| Ashby, C H | Mariner | San Diego Co. | Temecula | Temecula. |
| Asher, J M | Farmer | San Diego Co. | National Ranch | National City. |
| Atkinson, H S | Miner | nr Banner | San Diego Co. | Banner. |
| **Atkinson, Samuel** | Carpenter | San Diego | San Diego | San Diego. |
| Audlum, J E | Laborer | nr San Diego | San Diego Co. | San Diego. |
| Avery, S | Manufacturer | San Diego Co. | San Diego | San Diego. |
| Ayers, C R | Farmer | Warner's Ranch | San Diego Co. | Warner's Rch. |
| **Ayon, A** | Hair dresser | San Diego Co. | San Diego | San Diego. |
| Ayleworth, E | Carpenter | San Diego Co. | Monument City | San Diego. |
| Babb, A J | Farmer | nr Paguay | San Diego Co. | Poway. |
| Baca, N | Farmer | San Diego Co. | nr San Luis Rey | San Luis Rey. |
| Bacca, J | Farmer | nr San Jacinto | San Diego Co. | San Jacinto. |
| Backman, P | Real estate agent | San Diego Co. | San Diego | San Diego. |
| Bagnall, G W | Painter | San Diego Co. | San Diego | San Diego. |
| **Bailey, Geo Henry** | Physician | 65 m N E San Diego | Julian City | Julian. |
| Bailey, C | Mariner | San Diego Co. | San Diego | San Diego. |
| **Bailey & Redman** | Livery stable | Julian | San Diego Co. | Julian. |
| Bailey, E | Mariner | San Diego Co. | San Diego | San Diego. |
| **Bailey, F M** | Miner | nr Banner | San Diego Co. | Banner. |
| Baily, D D | Miner | San Diego Co. | nr Banner | Banner. |
| **Bailey, Y N** | Farmer | San Diego Co. | Banner | Banner. |
| Baily, J O | Miner | nr Banner | San Diego Co. | Banner. |
| Bailey, R | Miner | San Diego Co. | nr San Diego | San Diego. |
| **Bailey, Robt** | Saloon | San Diego | San Diego Co. | San Diego. |
| Baily, T | Laborer | nr San Diego | San Diego Co. | San Diego. |
| **Baker, A C** | Attorney | Court House | San Diego | San Diego. |
| Baker, C | Farmer | San Diego Co. | nr Julian | Julian. |
| Barnes, G W | Physician | San Diego Co. | Ballena | Ballena. |
| **Balcom, R G & Co** | Grocery | cor 5th and D sts | San Diego | San Diego. |
| Balenzulu, C | Farmer | San Diego Co. | nr San Luis Rey | San Luis Rey. |
| Ballard, George | Bricklayer | 30 m N San Diego | San Pascual | San Pascual. |
| Ballard, T J | Stock raiser | nr San Diego | San Diego Co. | San Diego. |
| Bancroft, Wm E | Teamster | San Diego | San Diego | San Diego. |
| **Bandini, J B** | Farmer | San Diego Co. | nr San Luis Rey | San Luis Rey. |
| Bandines, J B | Ranchero | Last Chance | 8 m E San Luis Rey | San Luis Rey. |
| Bandini, J de la C | Farmer | nr San Diego | San Diego Co. | San Diego. |
| **Bank of San Diego** | | 6th st | San Diego | San Diego. |
| Banks, J | Farmer | nr Temecula | San Diego Co. | Temecula. |
| **Bannister, E** | Lawyer | San Diego Co. | San Diego | San Diego. |
| Bansi, F | Carpenter | San Diego Co. | San Diego | San Diego. |
| Barelas, Jose | Laborer | Santa Margarita | 6 m N San Luis Rey | San Luis Rey. |
| Barker, B E | Farmer | 20 m N E San Diego | Paguay | Poway. |
| **Barnes, G W, Dr** | Physician | cor 6th and G sts | San Diego | San Diego. |
| Barnes, James | Laborer | San Diego | San Diego | San Diego. |

DIRECTORY OF SAN DIEGO COUNTY. 457

| NAME. | OCCUPATION. | PLACE OF BUSINESS. | RESIDENCE. | TOWN OR P. O. |
|---|---|---|---|---|
| Baron, J............... | Ranchero........... | San Diego Co........... | nr Milquatay............. | Campo. |
| Barrelles, J............ | Ranchero.. .......... | San Diego Co........... | nr Los Flores............ |  |
| Barrett, J F.......... | Miner........ ......... | San Diego Co........... | nr San Diego.. ......... | San Diego. |
| Barrona, August..... | Miner ................ | 65 m N E San Diego | Julian..................... | Julian. |
| Barry, J W........... | Miner ................ | nr Julian................ | San Diego Co.......... | Julian. |
| Barslow, H............ | Laborer.............. | nr National City....... | San Diego Co.... ...... | National City. |
| Barton, Guy......... | Farmer ............... | 35 m E San Diego... | Valle de las Viejas... | Viejas. |
| Barton, R M......... | Farmer ............... | Valle de las Viejas... | San Diego Co.......... | Viejas. |
| Bashford, O L........ | Farmer ............... | San Diego Co........... | nr Julian.................. | Julian. |
| Basques, G............ | Ranchero............. | San Diego Co........... | nr Temecula........... | Temecula. |
| Battaile, T G ....... | Clerk.................. | San Diego Co........... | San Diego............... | San Diego. |
| Baty, A ............... | Farmer ............... | San Diego Co........... | nr Cajon................. | San Diego. |
| Baugh, W A......... | Farmer .... .......... | San Diego Co........... | nr San Diego........... | San Diego. |
| Bayer, John......... | Laborer............... | San Diego................ | San Diego............... | San Diego. |
| Bayly & Bidwell... | Machine shop....... | cor 8th & M sts........ | San Diego............... | San Diego. |
| Bayly, Henry P F.. | Moulder ............. | San Diego................ | San Diego............... | San Diego. |
| Baze, P A B......... | Farmer ............... | San Diego Co........... | nr Monument City... | San Diego. |
| Beardslee, W........ | Miner................. | San Diego Co........... | nr San Diego........... | San Diego. |
| Beavers, J............. | Farmer ............... | San Diego Co........... | nr San Diego........... | San Diego. |
| Becker, J H.......... | Mechanic............ | San Diego Co........... | San Diego............... | San Diego. |
| Beebe, T J............ | Carpenter............ | San Diego Co........... | San Diego ............. | San Diego. |
| Beers, Wm A........ | Merchant ............ | 4 m S San Diego..... | National City.......... | National City. |
| Beers, W A........... | Fruit & confect'y | 5th st..................... | San Diego............... | San Diego. |
| Begole, W A......... | Stoves & tinware | 5th st..................... | San Diego............... | San Diego. |
| Bejon, Louis........ | Millman.............. | 70 m N E San Diego | Banner ................... | Banner. |
| Bejar, F............... | Ranchero ........... | San Diego Co........... | nr Temecula........... | Temecula. |
| Bell, C ................ | Plasterer.............. | San Diego Co........... | Green Valley.......... | Stonewall. |
| Bell, J S............... | Farmer ............... | nr Banner............... | San Diego Co.......... | Banner. |
| Bell, Z E.............. | Mason................. | San Diego Co........... | San Diego............... | San Diego. |
| Benedict, L.......... | Miner ................. | nr San Diego........... | San Diego Co.......... | San Diego. |
| Bennett, I............ | Farmer ............... | San Diego Co........... | nr San Diego .......... | San Diego. |
| Bennett, T............ | Miner.................. | nr Tia Juana ........... | San Diego Co.......... | San Diego. |
| Bennett, W .......... | Farmer ............... | nr San Diego........... | San Diego Co.......... | San Diego. |
| Bensel, Chas Wm'.. | Machinist............ | San Diego............... | San Diego............... | San Diego. |
| Benson, J M ........ | Farmer ............... | 90 m N San Diego... | San Jacinto............. | San Jacinto. |
| Bentzel, H M....... | Miller ................. | San Diego Co........... | San Diego............... | San Diego. |
| Berdnge, J............ | Ranchero ........... | nr Monserrate ......... | San Diego Co.......... | Monserrate. |
| Berry, Jas............. | Farmer ............... | nr San Diegnito....... | San Diego Co.......... | San Diegnito. |
| Bertheau, Stephen... | Teamster............. | 60 m E San Diego ... | Milquatay............... | Campo. |
| Bertrand, E ........ | Farmer ............... | nr Yenigai.............. | San Diego Co.......... |  |
| Berthand, S........ | Miner.................. | San Diego Co........... | nr Milquatay........... | Campo. |
| Betson, J ............ | Clerk.................. | San Diego Co........... | San Diego............... | San Diego. |
| Bevington, H A .... | Farmer ............... | San Diego Co........... | nr San Jacinto......... | San Jacinto. |
| Bevington, R....... | Farmer ............... | nr San Jacinto......... | San Diego Co.......... | San Jacinto. |
| Bevington, W P... | Farmer ............... | nr San Jacinto......... | San Diego Co.......... | San Jacinto. |
| Bick, F................ | Farmer ............... | San Diego Co........... | nr Warner's Ranch.. | Warner's Rch. |
| Bicknell, A.......... | Clerk.................. | San Diego Co........... | Julian .................... | Julian. |
| Bidwell, James..... | Machinist............ | San Diego............... | San Diego............... | San Diego. |
| Bigard, Louis ...... | Sheep raiser........ | Cañada Aliso......... | 2 m S San Luis Rey. | San Luis Rey. |
| Bigelle, B............. | Vaquero ............. | nr Temecula........... | San Diego Co.......... | Temecula. |
| Billingsly, W C.... | Farmer ............... | San Diego Co........... | nr Ballena.............. | Ballena. |
| Birdsall, J D ....... | Proprietor........... | Lyon House........... | San Diego............... | San Diego. |
| Birdseye, E L....... | Farmer ............... | 16 m E San Diego... | Cajon..................... | San Diego. |
| Bixby, C.............. | Cooper................ | San Diego Co........... | San Diego............... | San Diego. |
| Bixlor, S.............. | Farmer................ | nr Paguay ............. | San Diego Co.......... | Poway. |
| Black, B F........... | Laborer............... | nr Ballena.............. | San Diego Co.......... | Ballena. |
| Black, S N........... | Miller ................. | San Diego Co........... | San Diego............... | San Diego. |
| Black, W............. | Lumberman......... | San Diego Co........... | Monument City....... | San Diego. |
| Blackman, Chas A. | Teamster ........... | San Diego............... | San Diego............... | San Diego. |
| Blackmer, E T ..... | Professor of music | San Diego Academy. | San Diego Co.......... | San Diego. |
| Blaisdell, S G ...... | Harness maker ... | 5th st..................... | San Diego............... | San Diego. |
| Blanco, P............. | Farmer................ | nr San Diego.......... | San Diego Co.......... | San Diego. |
| Blandin, J W........ | Farmer ............... | San Diego Co........... | nr National Ranch.. | National City. |
| Blattner, J ........... | Butcher............... | San Diego Co........... | San Diego............... | San Diego. |

# EXTRAORDINARY INDUCEMENT
## FOR PEOPLE SEEKING HOMES
—IN—
## SOUTHERN CALIFORNIA.

### FOR RENT OR SALE,
## CHOICE HOMES IN SAN GABRIEL VALLEY,
### ACKNOWLEDGED TO BE THE

most desirable portion of Los Angeles county, Southern California, are offered to persons of moral worth and industrious habits, on terms to satisfy the most fastidious and within the reach of men of moderate means. Having recently purchased

### 5,000 ACRES OF THE RANCHO AZUSITA,

Including the old Mexican homestead, beginning where the San Gabriel river emerges and extending Westerly along the Southern base of the San Gabriel mountains to within four miles of the Mission Church and Depot of the Southern Pacific Railroad, and is traversed for five miles by the location of the Los Angeles and Independence Railroad, which is now being rapidly constructed. This land is abundantly supplied with pure mountain water, for irrigating and domestic purposes, by means of a large ditch, extending from the San Gabriel river along the base of the mountain and down the Western and Southern boundary, from which the entire tract can be easily irrigated—rendering it practicable to produce abundant crops of grain, tobacco, melons, potatoes and vegetables of all kinds—planted at all seasons of the year. This fact was clearly demonstrated by the heavy frost early in last April, which visited localities in Los Angeles county with disastrous severity, while on locations on this grant of land, similarly situated to a large portion of the entire tract, the young potato and melon plants and the tobacco and tomatoes (here perpetual bearers) were not affected, and the old homestead vineyard and orchard, clothed in their new and well advanced foliage, escaped entirely, while the vineyards in the valleys below turned black from the blighting frost.

### TERMS.

Twenty acres of choice cleared land and one good work-horse or mule and water for irrigating and wood and water for domestic purposes, will be let to the head of a family or a single man until the 1st of January, 1876, for one-tenth of all the crops grown on the land. The mild and uniform climate, together with the widespreading live oaks, especially reserved for building sites, do away with the necessity of building houses until the rainy season begins, which is about the 1st of December and continuing, at intervals, for three months, but should parties desire to build temporary houses, I will reimburse them for the cost of material when vacated.

### TWO THOUSAND ACRES

Of this choice land, which is, by actual demonstration, as well adapted as any in Southern California to the successful culture of the banana, orange, lime, lemon, English walnut, grape and other fruits and vegetables, will be sold at

### PUBLIC AUCTION, ON THE 10th DAY OF JANUARY, 1876, IN TRACTS OF 10, 20 and 40 ACRES, AND ON EASY TERMS,

Thus affording persons seeking homes in our delightful county of varied soil and climatic influences, an opportunity of selecting localities for themselves and friends with a practical knowledge of all the surroundings, and in the meantime spend a delightful Summer and Fall at a moderate expense and send their children to a good public school, centrally located.

The adjacent mountains and mesa lands abound in quail, rabbits and other game, and their streams are filled with mountain trout. The thrifty farmers of the neighborhood can supply, at a moderate price, the forage, grain, milk and butter that may be required, and a grist mill, propelled by water-power, now in course of construction on the premises, will soon be completed.

Two years' experience in California has convinced me that the choice, well-watered lands in favorable localities are being sold at prices far inadequate to their intrinsic value, while dry lands that are destitute of irrigating facilities are dear at any price for agricultural purposes, the purchase of which by persons who are ignorant of the facts, blight the hopes and absorb the fortunes of many good men, which has a prejudicial effect on the large immigration now pouring into this favored country from all quarters. Hence it is I make this fair and liberal proposition, so that all who embrace it may not be deceived.

### NORMAN C. JONES, Valley View,
—NEAR SAN GABRIEL MISSION,—

**LOS ANGELES COUNTY,** - - **CALIFORNIA.**

DIRECTORY OF SAN DIEGO COUNTY. 459

| Name. | Occupation. | Place of Business. | Residence. | Town or P. O. |
|---|---|---|---|---|
| Blauvelt, C J | Engineer | San Diego Co | Julian | Julian. |
| Blinn, H | Farmer | San Diego Co | nr Tia Juana | San Diego. |
| Blue, Jacob S | Watch maker | San Diego | San Diego Co | San Diego. |
| Blum, L | Farmer | nr Monument City | San Diego Co | San Diego. |
| Bobio, G | Farmer | nr San Diego | San Diego Co | San Diego. |
| Bogan, John | Prop oc'al hotel | cor 4th & E sts | San Diego | San Diego. |
| Bogar, J | Miner | San Diego Co | nr San Diego | San Diego. |
| Bolan, P | Ranchero | nr Temecula | San Diego Co | Temecula. |
| Bonnin, A | Miner | nr San Diego | San Diego Co | San Diego. |
| Borden, G | Bricklayer | San Diego Co | San Diego | San Diego. |
| Borden, H W | Sheep raiser | San Luis Rey | 45 m N San Diego | San Luis Rey. |
| Borden, O H | Sheep raiser | San Luis Rey | 45 m N San Diego | San Luis Rey. |
| Borden, N H | Tinsmith | San Diego Co | San Diego | San Diego. |
| Borden, J S | Sheep raiser | San Luis Rey | 45 m N San Diego | San Luis Rey. |
| Bossung, W | Laborer | San Diego Co | Milquatay | Campo. |
| Botello, Narcisco | Clerk | 30 m N San Diego | San Pascual | San Pascual. |
| Bouschi, M & Co | Grocers | F st | San Diego | San Diego. |
| Bovet, P | Farmer | nr San Diego | San Diego Co | San Diego. |
| Bower, Geo H | Stage agent | San Diego Co | San Diego Co | San Diego. |
| Bowers, J M | Harness maker | San Diego Co | Cajon | San Diego. |
| Bowers, M | Farmer | San Diego Co | nr Julian | Julian. |
| Bowers, W W | Farmer | nr San Diego | San Diego Co | San Diego. |
| Boyce, Alexander | Tailor | San Diego | San Diego Co | San Diego. |
| Boyd, John | Waiter | San Diego Co | San Diego | San Diego. |
| Boyd, J B | Wh liquor dealer | cor 4th & K sts | San Diego | San Diego. |
| Boyd, J B | Student | San Diego Co | San Diego | San Diego. |
| Boyd, J M | Carpenter | San Diego Co | San Diego | San Diego. |
| Bracamonte, Leonardo | Farmer | 55 m N W S Diego | Monserrate | Monserrate. |
| Bradt, G G | Real estate | Horton's Bank Blk | San Diego | San Diego. |
| Brady, A M | Farmer | San Diego Co | nr San Diego | San Diego. |
| Brady, Chas Franklin | Farmer | 20 m NW San Diego | San Diegnito | San Diegnito. |
| Brady, D D | Farmer | San Diego Co | nr Paguay | Poway. |
| Brady, P | Boots and shoes | 5th st | San Diego | San Diego. |
| Brady, T | Merchant | San Diego Co | Julian | Julian. |
| Bradley, G | Ranchero | nr Ballena | San Diego Co | Ballena. |
| Braly, F E, Jr | Farmer | nr Julian | San Diego Co | Julian. |
| Branngarh, M | Brewer | San Diego | San Diego Co | San Diego. |
| Brannon, R S B | Farmer | San Diego Co | nr San Luis Rey | San Luis Rey. |
| Branson, D W | Farmer | San Diegnito | San Diego Co | San Diegnito. |
| Branson, L | Attorney | Horton's Bank Blk | San Diego | San Diego. |
| Bratton, N B | Farmer | nr San Diego | San Diego Co | San Diego. |
| Bratton, A N | Farmer | San Diego Co | nr Jamul | San Diego. |
| Bratton, S H | Farmer | San Diego Co | nr San Diego | San Diego. |
| Bratton, T | Farmer | San Diego Co | nr San Diego | San Diego. |
| Breed, D C | Merchant | San Diego Co | San Diego | San Diego. |
| Breen, John | Miner | 70 m N E San Diego | Green Valley | Stonewall. |
| Brewster, G | Carriage maker | San Diego Co | San Diego | San Diego. |
| Brian, J E | Miner | San Diego Co | nr San Diego | San Diego. |
| Briant, D W | Planing mill | San Diego Co | San Diego Co | San Diego. |
| Briant, D W | Ranchero | San Diego Co | nr San Diego | San Diego. |
| Brilligham, E P | Miner | nr Julian | San Diego Co | Julian. |
| Briseno, J N | Printer | San Diego Co | San Diego | San Diego. |
| Brittain, Joseph | Miner | 65 m N E San Diego | Julian | Julian. |
| Britton, W | Farmer | San Diego Co | nr Otay | San Diego. |
| Brooks, Horace | Laborer | San Luis Rey | 45 m N San Diego | San Luis Rey. |
| Brooks, H | Farmer | San Diego Co | nr San Luis Rey | San Luis Rey. |
| Brottiers, T | Stage driver | San Diego Co | San Diego | San Diego. |
| Brown, C | Laborer | San Diego Co | nr San Diego | San Diego. |
| Brown, Chas H | Lumberman | San Diego | San Diego Co | San Diego. |
| Brown, Geo Wiley | Painter | | San Diego | San Diego. |
| Brown, H H | Barber | 5th st | San Diego | San Diego. |
| Brown, John | Laborer | San Diego | San Diego | San Diego. |

460     L. L. PAULSON'S HAND-BOOK AND

| Name. | Occupation. | Place of Business. | Residence. | Town or P. O. |
|---|---|---|---|---|
| Brown, J................ | Farmer............... | San Luis Rey............ | San Diego Co........... | San Luis Rey. |
| Brown, J F............ | Engineer............. | San Diego Co........... | San Diego............... | San Diego. |
| Brown, J M........... | Farmer............... | nr San Diego........... | San Diego Co........... | San Diego. |
| Brown, J M........... | Farmer............... | nr San Luis Rey...... | San Diego Co........... | San Luis Rey. |
| Brown, P............... | Hostler............... | San Diego Co........... | nr San Diego.......... | San Diego. |
| Brown, R............... | Laborer............... | San Diego Co........... | nr San Diego .......... | San Diego. |
| Brown, R A........... | Farmer ............... | San Diego Co........... | nr Monument City... | San Diego. |
| Brown, Wm Wallace .. .......... | Clerk................. | San Diego............... | San Diego Co........... | San Diego. |
| Brownson, Louis... | Saloon keeper .... | 65 m N E San Diego | Julian................... | Julian. |
| Bruce, Thos ......... | Laborer............... | San Diego Co. ......... | nr San Diego .......... | San Diego. |
| Bruner, P............... | Farmer............... | nr Santa Teresa....... | San Diego Co........... |  |
| Bryan, N T ........... | Painter............... | San Diego Co........... | San Diego............... | San Diego. |
| Buck, Joshua S...... | Trader................ | San Diego............... | San Diego Co........... | San Diego. |
| Buck, J J......... .. | S D soap works.. | San Diego............... | San Diego Co........... | San Diego. |
| Buckley, Cornelius. | Farmer ............... | San Diego............... | San Diego Co........... | San Diego. |
| Bucklor, J............. | Coppersmith ....... | San Diego Co........... | San Diego............... | San Diego. |
| Bulencuela, Antonio | Ranchero ............ | San Diego Co........... | Mesa Grande Ballena | Ballena. |
| Bumes, Tillman A.. | Saloon keeper..... | San Diego............... | San Diego Co........... | San Diego. |
| Bundy, T .............. | Miner............... | Julian................... | San Diego Co........... | Julian. |
| Bunton, J H ......... | Miner................ | San Diego Co........... | nr Julian............... | Julian. |
| Bunton, W........... | Carpenter.......... | San Diego Co........... | Julian................... | Julian. |
| Burbeck, B Allen.. | Merchant........... | 10 m E San Diego ... | Spring Valley ......... | San Diego. |
| Burchfield, Jno E... | Laborer............... | San Diego Co........... | San Diego...., ......... | San Diego. |
| Burdsall, J D......... | Farmer ............... | nr San Diego........... | San Diego Co........... | San Diego. |
| Burgman, I........... | Farmer............... | San Diego Co........... | Burgman Ranch...... |  |
| Burkbridge, F....... | Miner................ | nr San Diego .......... | San Diego Co........... | San Diego. |
| Burkhart, J B........ | Carpenter.......... | San Diego Co........... | San Diego............... | San Diego. |
| Burleigh, E L ....... | Coach maker...... | San Diego Co........... | San Diego............... | San Diego. |
| Burns, D............... | Laborer............... | nr Julian............... | San Diego Co........... | Julian. |
| Burns, J................ | Laborer .............. | nr San Diego .......... | San Diego Co........... | San Diego. |
| Burns, P................ | Farmer............... | San Diego Co........... | nr San Diego .......... | San Diego. |
| Burnes, Till A...... | Saloon................ | cor 5th & K sts...... |  | San Diego. |
| Burns, T............... | Miner................ | San Diego Co........... | nr Banner............... | Banner. |
| Burr, Dr Edward.. | Physician........... | Old San Diego........ |  | Old San Diego. |
| Burris, J M ........... | Farmer............... | San Diego Co........... | nr Milquatay........... | Campo. |
| Burris, T .............. | Farmer ............... | nr Milquatay......... | San Diego Co........... | Campo. |
| Burris, J............... | Farmer............... | nr San Diego .......... | San Diego Co........... | San Diego. |
| Burroughs, D....... | Physician........... | San Diego Co........... | Julian................... | Julian. |
| Burton, H H......... | Farmer............... | San Diego............... | San Diego............... | San Diego. |
| Burton, J L........... | Farmer ............... | San Diego Co........... | Township 10............ |  |
| Burton, G ............. | Mechanic .......... | San Diego Co........... | Milquatay ............. | Campo. |
| Busch, Henry ...... | Painter............... | San Diego............... | San Diego Co........... | San Diego. |
| Bush, G W ........... | Farmer............... | nr San Diego .......... | San Diego Co........... | San Diego. |
| Bush, I H.............. | Farmer ............... | nr Julian............... | San Diego Co........... | Julian. |
| Bush, I H.............. | Farmer............... | San Diego Co........... | nr San Diego .......... | San Diego. |
| Bush, I J............... | Farmer ............... | San Diego Co........... | nr San Diego .......... | San Diego. |
| Bush, J................. | Farmer ...., ........ | nr San Luis Rey...... | San Diego Co........... | San Luis Rey. |
| Bush, T H............. | Merchant ........... | San Diego Co........... | San Diego............... | San Diego. |
| Bushyhead, E W.. | Printer............... | San Diego Co........... | San Diego............... | San Diego. |
| Butoros, J M......... | Laborer............... | nr San Diego .......... | San Diego Co........... | San Diego. |
| Butieres, M........... | Ranchero ........... | San Diego Co........... | nr San Felipe.......... |  |
| Butler, W H......... | Student.............. | San Diego Co........... | San Diego............... | San Diego. |
| Butler, Thomas..... | Brick layer......... | San Diego............... | San Diego............... | San Diego. |
| Butler, J............... | Laborer............... | San Diego Co........... | nr San Diego .......... | San Diego. |
| Buxton, T.............. | Mason................ | San Diego Co........... | San Diego............... | San Diego. |
| Caballo, J ............. | Vaquero ............ | nr San Luis Rey...... | San Diego Co........... | San Luis Rey. |
| Caillard, F........... | Carpenter .......... | San Diego Co........... | nr San Diego .......... | San Diego. |
| Callaghan, John..... | Miner................ | San Diego Co........... | San Diego............... | San Diego. |
| Callaway, O P ..... | Merchant ........... | San Diego Co........... | San Diego............... | San Diego. |
| Calsines, James B .. | Farmer ............... | 22 m E San Diego ... | Jamul.................. | San Diego. |
| Cambch, John....... | Sheep man ......... | San Diego Co........... | San Diego............... | San Diego. |
| Cambron, Thos J... | Farmer............... | 20 m N E San Diego | Paguay ............... | Poway. |
| Cameron, T........... | Farmer ............... | nr Milquatay.......... | San Diego Co........... | Campo. |

## DIRECTORY OF SAN DIEGO COUNTY. 461

| Name. | Occupation. | Place of Business. | Residence. | Town or P. O. |
|---|---|---|---|---|
| Campbell, J. | Wood chopper | | San Diego Co | |
| Campbell, J H | Farmer | nr San Diego | San Diego Co | San Diego. |
| Campbell, N H | Machinist | San Diego Co | Banner | Banner. |
| Campbell, P B | Carpenter | San Diego Co | Jamul | San Diego. |
| Campbell, S | Miner | nr San Diego | San Diego Co | San Diego. |
| Canada, J | Laborer | nr Los Flores | San Diego Co | |
| Canby, J P | Farmer | San Diego Co | nr San Diego | San Diego. |
| Cann, Allen | Teamster | 30 m N San Diego | San Pascual | San Pascual. |
| Cant, W | Farmer | San Diego Co | nr San Diego | San Diego. |
| Cantlin, M | Carpenter | San Diego Co | San Diego | San Diego. |
| Capron, J G | Gov mail con | San Diego Co | San Diego | San Diego. |
| Caravia, G | Grocer | cor 10th & K sts | San Diego | San Diego. |
| Carloa, A | Farmer | nr San Jacinto | San Diego Co | San Jacinto. |
| Carlton, W B | Horse shoer | cor E & 2d sts | San Diego | San Diego. |
| Carnahan, R | Carpenter | San Diego Co | Jamul | San Diego. |
| Carpenter, S H | Miner | nr Julian | San Diego Co | Julian. |
| Carr, C L | Collector | San Diego Co | San Diego | San Diego. |
| Carr, J P | Miner | San Diego Co | nr Julian | Julian. |
| Carrillo, Doroteo | Farmer | 55 m N W San Diego | Monserrate | Monserrate. |
| Carroll, A | Laborer | San Diego Co | nr San Diego | San Diego. |
| Carroll, C | Farmer | nr San Diego | San Diego Co | San Diego. |
| Carroll, E | Manufacturer | San Diego Co | San Diego | San Diego. |
| Carroll, Edward | Farmer | San Diego | San Diego | San Diego. |
| Carroll, James | Farmer | 90 m N San Diego | San Jacinto | San Jacinto. |
| Carroll, M D | Clerk | San Diego Co | San Diego | San Diego. |
| Carroll, R J | Miner | nr Banner | San Diego Co | Banner. |
| Carroll, Wm | Foundryman | San Diego Co | San Luis Rey | San Luis Rey. |
| Carruth, J | Farmer | nr Milquatay | San Diego Co | Campo. |
| Carruthers, Matthew | Farmer | San Diego | San Diego | San Diego. |
| Casbeer, J R | Farmer | San Diego Co | Spencer Valley | |
| Carter, R | Farmer | San Diego Co | nr Milquatay | Campo. |
| Carter, W | Laborer | nr San Diego | San Diego Co | San Diego. |
| Case, Hobert H | Farmer | San Diego | San Diego Co | San Diego. |
| Case, T A | Ranchero | San Diego Co | nr Temecula | Temecula. |
| Casey, M | Blacksmith | San Diego Co | San Diego | San Diego. |
| Casias, P | Farmer | nr Julian | San Diego Co | Julian. |
| Casilar, John | Fisherman | San Diego | San Diego | San Diego. |
| Casner, F M | Farmer | San Diego Co | Agua Caliente | Agua Caliente. |
| Casner, T J | Farmer | San Diego Co | nr Ballena | Ballena. |
| Casner, T J | Farmer | San Diego Co | Agua Caliente | Agua Caliente. |
| Casner, M | Farmer | nr Ballena | San Diego Co | Ballena. |
| Casner, M V | Farmer | nr Ballena | San Diego Co | Ballena. |
| Cassidy, A | Tidal observer | San Diego Co | San Diego | San Diego. |
| Cassidy, J | Laborer | nr San Diego | San Diego Co | San Diego. |
| Cassidy, Peter | Fireman | San Diego | San Diego | San Diego. |
| Cassorr, P | Sheep raiser | San Marcus | 12 m E San Luis Rey | San Luis Rey. |
| Casson, M H | Miner | nr San Diego | San Diego Co | San Diego. |
| Castanet, Baptiste | Farmer | 60 m E San Diego | Milquatay | Campo. |
| Castinero, F | Farmer | nr San Diego | San Diego Co | San Diego. |
| Castro, E | Farmer | nr Temecula | San Diego Co | Temecula. |
| Castro, Louis | Farmer | San Diego Co | nr Temecula | Temecula. |
| Castro, Lino | Farmer | San Diego Co | nr Temecula | Temecula. |
| Castro, Lucio | Farmer | 65 m N E San Diego | Temecula | Temecula. |
| Castro, Jose | Farmer | nr Temecula | San Diego Co | Temecula. |
| Castro, J S | Vaquero | nr San Diego | San Diego Co | San Diego. |
| Castro, J | Farmer | San Diego Co | nr Temecula | Temecula. |
| Castro, M | Farmer | nr Temecula | San Diego Co | Temecula. |
| Castro, Ramon | Farmer | 65 m N E San Diego | Temecula | Temecula. |
| Castro, Uriol | Farmer | 65 m N E San Diego | Temecula | Temecula. |
| Castro, Zacarias | Farmer | 65 m N E San Diego | Temecula | Temecula. |
| Caswell, A M | Fruit & confect'y | 5th st | San Diego | San Diego. |
| Caulkins, F N | Miner | nr Julian | San Diego Co | Julian. |
| Cave, Dr D | French dentist | 5th st, bet G &H | San Diego | San Diego. |
| Cave, McRea | Sheep raiser | Agua Hodienda | 8 m S San Luis Rey | San Luis Rey. |

# COMMERCIAL BANK
## ─OF─
# SAN DIEGO,
## CORNER OF 5th AND G STREETS.

A. H. WILCOX, - - - - - President.
E. F. SPENCE, - - - - - Cashier.
JOSE D. ESTUDILLO, - - - Ass't Cashier.

### ─DIRECTORS.─

A. H. WILCOX,                O. S. WITHERBY,
M. S. PATRICK,               RETURN ROBERTS,
JNO. G. CAPRON,              HIRAM MABURY,
JOHN FORSTER,                JAS. McCOY,
L. CHASE,                    GEO. A. JOHNSON,
            E. F. SPENCE.

*This Bank Receives Deposits, Loans Money, Buys and Sells Bills of Exchange, and Transacts a General Banking Business.*

## DRAFTS DRAWN ON NATIONAL GOLD BANK AND TRUST CO.

SAN FRANCISCO, AND

## First National Bank, New York.

EXCHANGE DRAWN ON

## Los Angeles, Santa Barbara, San Bernardino

And San Buenaventura.

EXCHANGE, PAYABLE IN THE PRINCIPAL EUROPEAN CITIES, FURNISHED. U. S. CURRENCY BOUGHT AND SOLD.

DIRECTORY OF SAN DIEGO COUNTY. 463

| NAME. | OCCUPATION. | PLACE OF BUSINESS. | RESIDENCE. | TOWN OR P. O. |
|---|---|---|---|---|
| Cenac, Bernard...... | Farmer .............. | 12 m S San Diego.... | Otay...................... | San Diego. |
| Chaffee, C L......... | Machinist........... | San Diego Co........... | Julian................... | Julian. |
| Chase & Leach...... | Attorneys ........... | Horton's Bank Block | San Diego............. | San Diego. |
| Chase, Charles A... | Druggist............. | N W cor 5th & F sts. | San Diego ............ | San Diego. |
| Chase, A J............ | Ins & real estate.. | 6th st....................... | San Diego............. | San Diego. |
| Chase, L............... | Attorney.............. | Horton's Bank Block | San Diego............. | San Diego. |
| Chambard, P F...... | Laborer................ | San Diego Co........... | nr San Diego......... | San Diego. |
| Chambers, A.......... | Miner.................. | San Diego Co........... | nr Julian............... | Julian. |
| Chambers, D T...... | Wool grower........ | San Diego Co........... | Warner's Ranch...... | Warner's Rch. |
| Chambers, J T ...... | Painter................ | San Diego Co........... | San Diego............. | San Diego. |
| Chambers, Matthew | Laborer................ | 16 m E San Diego... | Cajon.................... | San Diego. |
| Chamberlain, Henry W.......... | Clerk ................. | San Diego.............. | San Diego Co......... | San Diego. |
| Chamberlain, J..... | Farmer ............... | nr Monserrate........ | San Diego Co......... | Monserrate. |
| Chapin, J F........... | Ranchero............. | nr San Diegnito ..... | San Diego Co......... | San Diegnito. |
| Chastenay, B......... | Miner.................. | nr Milquatay.......... | San Diego Co......... | Campo. |
| Chesney, D .......... | Gardener............. | San Diego Co........... | San Diego............. | San Diego. |
| Chetwood, C H..... | Clergyman .......... | San Diego.............. | San Diego Co......... | San Diego. |
| Chisney, D............ | Laborer................ | San Diego Co........... | nr Santa Margarita... | San Luis Rey. |
| Choate, —............. | Real estate agent. | cor 3d and E sts..... | San Diego............. | San Diego. |
| Choate, D ............. | Merchant ............ | San Diego Co........... | San Diego............. | San Diego. |
| Chowning, Wm H. | Farmer ............... | 60 m E San Diego... | Milquatay............. | Campo. |
| Christensen, John P | Mason................. | 35 m N San Diego.. | Bear Valley.......... | San Pascual. |
| Christian, D G...... | Farmer ............... | San Diego Co........... | nr San Diego......... | San Diego. |
| Christian, H T ...... | Clerk .................. | San Diego.............. | San Diego Co......... | San Diego. |
| Christie, H........... | Baker.................. | San Diego Co........... | San Diego............. | San Diego. |
| Christman, Jacob... | Blacksmith.......... | San Diego Co........... | San Diego............. | San Diego. |
| Clark, D P ............ | Miner.................. | nr San Diego......... | San Diego Co......... | San Diego. |
| Clark, G T............. | Butcher............... | San Diego Co........... | San Diego............. | San Diego. |
| Clark, G N ............ | Farmer ............... | nr San Diego......... | San Diego Co......... | San Diego. |
| Clark, J E............. | Merchant ............ | San Diego Co........... | San Diego............. | San Diego. |
| Clark, J M............. | Merchant ............ | San Diego Co........... | San Diego............. | San Diego. |
| Clark, J W............. | Farmer ............... | San Diego Co........... | Cajon.................... | San Diego. |
| Clark, O B............. | Printer ................ | San Diego Co........... | San Diego............. | San Diego. |
| Clark, R G ............ | Fireman.............. | San Diego Co........... | San Diego............. | San Diego. |
| Clark, W J M........ | Fisherman .......... | San Diego Co........... | San Diego............. | San Diego. |
| Clarke, Wm.......... | Farmer ............... | nr San Diego......... | San Diego Co......... | San Diego. |
| Clark, Wm............ | Teamster ............ | San Diego Co........... | San Diego............. | San Diego. |
| Clayton, H ........... | Civil engineer..... | San Diego Co........... | San Diego............. | San Diego. |
| Clendennin, W...... | Farmer ............... | Valle de las Viejas... | San Diego Co......... | Viejas. |
| Cleveland, D......... | Attorney.............. | 6th st....................... | San Diego............. | San Diego. |
| Cleveland, R H..... | Farmer ............... | San Diego Co........... | nr San Diego......... | San Diego. |
| Clifton, Wm W..... | Farmer ............... | 60 m E San Diego... | Milquatay............. | Campo. |
| Cline, A D............. | Farmer . ............. | San Diego Co........... | nr Milquatay........ | Campo. |
| Cline, C................. | Farmer ............... | San Diego Co........... | Milquatay............. | Campo. |
| Cline, F P.............. | Farmer ............... | nr Milquatay.......... | San Diego............. | Campo. |
| Cline, James T...... | Farmer ............... | 60 m E San Diego ... | Milquatay............. | Campo. |
| Cline, Thos J ........ | Farmer ............... | nr Milquatay.......... | San Diego Co......... | Campo. |
| Cline, W F............. | Teamster ............ | San Diego Co........... | nr Milquatay........ | Campo. |
| Clizbe, E G............ | Farmer ............... | San Diego Co........... | nr San Diego......... | San Diego. |
| Clymer, F P.......... | Trader................. | San Diego Co........... | San Diego............. | San Diego. |
| Codder, W............ | Laborer................ | San Diego Co........... | nr San Diego......... | San Diego. |
| Coggin, J R........... | Farmer ............... | nr Monument City... | San Diego Co......... | San Diego. |
| Cohen, M.............. | Mcht tailor.......... | 5th st....................... | San Diego............. | San Diego. |
| Cohn, J A.............. | Shoe maker......... | San Diego Co........... | San Diego............. | San Diego. |
| Colderbank, Wm... | Teamster............. | San Luis Rey........ | San Diego Co ....... | San Luis Rey. |
| Cole, A A.............. | Laborer................ | San Diego Co.......... | nr San Diego......... | San Diego. |
| Cole, J L............... | Farmer ............... | nr San Diego......... | San Diego Co......... | San Diego. |
| Cole, J A............... | Farmer ............... | San Diego Co........... | nr Julian............... | Julian. |
| Coleman, T........... | Farmer ............... | San Diego Co........... | nr Julian............... | Julian. |
| Coleman, M A ...... | Stock raiser......... | San Diego Co........... | Milquatay............. | Campo. |
| Coleman, F........... | Stage driver........ | San Diego Co........... | San Diego............. | San Diego. |
| Collier, R.............. | Teamster............. | nr San Diego......... | San Diego Co......... | San Diego. |
| Collier, W W........ | Cabinet maker.... | San Diego Co........... | San Diego............. | San Diego. |

| Name. | Occupation. | Place of Business. | Residence. | Town or P. O |
|---|---|---|---|---|
| Collins, G A | Farmer | San Diego Co | nr San Jacinto | San Jacinto. |
| Combs, Henry | Farmer | San Luis Rey | San Diogo Co | San Luis Rey. |
| Combs, John | Sheep raiser | San Marcus | 8 m E San Luis Rey. | San Luis Rey. |
| Combs, John A | Ranchero | 55 m N W S Diego | Monserrate | Monserrate. |
| Commercial Bk of San Diego | | cor 5th and G sts | San Diego | San Diego. |
| Condee, Dr A | Physician | San Diego | San Diego Co | San Diego. |
| Condee, C H & Bro | Gen merchandise. | 5th st | San Diego | San Diego. |
| Condez, J | Vaquero | San Diego Co | San Luis Rey | San Luis Rey. |
| Condez, J | Farmer | nr San Ysabel | San Diego Co | |
| Conklin, — | Prop eve'g world | | San Diego | San Diego. |
| Conklin, N H | Attorney | 5th st, bet G and H | San Diego | San Diego. |
| Conly, E | Mason | San Diego Co | San Diego | San Diego. |
| Connell, J | Gen merchandise. | 5th st, opp C'l Markt | San Diego | San Diego. |
| Conners, R | Miner | San Diego Co | nr Banner | Banner. |
| Connors, J W | Musician | San Diego Co | San Diego | San Diego. |
| Conrad, Chas C | Teacher | San Diego Co | San Diego | San Diego. |
| Conroy, M | Farmer | San Diego Co | Lawson's Valley | San Diego. |
| Contreras, Jose M | Ranchero | 65 m N E San Diego | Temecula | Temecula. |
| Contreras, Lucas | Ranchero | 65 m N E San Diego | Temecula | Temecula. |
| Cook, E | Mariner | San Diego Co | San Diego | San Diego. |
| Cook, Geo | Waiter | San Diego Co | San Diego | San Diego. |
| Cook, Wm | Miner | nr Julian | San Diego Co | Julian. |
| Cook, Wm | Farmer | San Diego Co | nr Green Valley | Stonewall. |
| Coolidge, C C | Cabinet maker | San Diego Co | San Diego | San Diego. |
| Cooper, G A | Miner | nr San Diego | San Diego Co | San Diego. |
| Copeland, F | Surveyor | San Diego Co | National City | National City. |
| Copland, — | Sheep raiser | Sickman's Canyon | 9 m N San Luis Rey | San Luis Rey. |
| Corcoran, Michael | Dairyman | 4 m S San Diego | National City | National City. |
| Corder, Francis E. | Soap maker | San Diego Co | San Diego | San Diego. |
| Cork, Benjamin | Cook | San Diego | San Diego | San Diego. |
| Cosper, A A Mrs | Millinery store | 5th st | San Diego | San Diego. |
| Cota, C | Ranchero | San Diego Co | Valle de las Viejas | Viejas. |
| Cota, J | Vaquero | San Diego Co | nr San Diego | San Diego. |
| Cota, J J | Ranchero | San Diego Co | nr San Diego | San Diego. |
| Cota, R | Ranchero | nr San Diego | San Diego Co | San Diego. |
| Cothell, B | Druggist | San Diego Co | San Diego | San Diego. |
| Courtney, J | Laborer | San Diego Co | nr San Diego | San Diego. |
| Couts, W B | Farmer | San Luis Rey | 45 m N San Diego | San Luis Rey. |
| Couts, Mrs I B | Ranchero | Guajoma Ranch | 4 m E San Luis Rey | San Luis Rey. |
| Covert, H M | Farmer | San Diego Co | nr San Diego | San Diego. |
| Covert, F M | Ranchero | nr San Diego | San Diego Co | San Diego. |
| Cowles, A | Farmer | San Diego Co | nr San Diego | San Diego. |
| Cowles, F H | Miner | nr San Diego | San Diego Co | San Diego. |
| Cox, I H | Minister | San Diego Co | Jamul | San Diego. |
| Cox, M B | Farmer | 22 m E San Diego | Jamul | San Diego. |
| Coyne, J | Miner | nr Banner | San Diego Co | Banner. |
| Crabtree, J | Farmer | San Diego Co | Crabtree Ranch | |
| Craigue & Co, S W | Wines & liquors | cor 4th and K sts | San Diego | San Diego. |
| Craigue, S W | Proprietor | Horton House | San Diego | San Diego. |
| Craig, Samuel | Carpenter | San Diego | San Diego | San Diego. |
| Cram, J | Mariner | San Diego Co | San Diego | San Diego. |
| Crane, A | Merchant | San Diego Co | San Diego | San Diego. |
| Crannell, N | Tinsmith | San Diego Co | San Diegnito | San Diegnito. |
| Crannell, C | Bee raiser | San Diego Co | San Diegnito | San Diegnito. |
| Cravath, A K | Farmer | nr Paguay | San Diego Co | Poway. |
| Creekmur, Orville | Laborer | San Diego | San Diego | San Diego. |
| Creel, Robert | Farmer | 65 m N E San Diego | Julian City | Julian. |
| Crispell, A | Fisherman | San Diego Co | San Diego | San Diego. |
| Crombie, L J | Farmer | San Diego Co | nr San Luis Rey | San Luis Rey. |
| Cropper, A L | Farmer | San Diego Co | nr San Luis Rey | San Luis Rey. |
| Cropper, O L | Laborer | San Luis Rey | 45 m N San Diego | San Luis Rey. |
| Crosby, D S | Carpenter | San Diego Co | San Diego | San Diego. |
| Crosby, E | Farmer | nr San Diego | San Diego Co | San Diego. |

## DIRECTORY OF SAN DIEGO COUNTY.

| Name. | Occupation. | Place of Business. | Residence. | Town or P. O. |
|---|---|---|---|---|
| Crosthwaite, P...... | Under sheriff...... | San Diego Co......... | San Diego............. | San Diego. |
| Crouch, Herbert..... | Ranchero.......... | San Luis Rey......... | San Diego Co......... | San Luis Rey. |
| **Culver, C B**.......... | Apiarian........... | S L Rey Valley .... | 5 m E San Luis Rey | San Luis Rey. |
| Culver, C B........... | Groceries.......... | San Diego Co......... | San Diego............. | San Diego. |
| Cunningham, C E.. | Farmer............. | nr San Diego......... | San Diego Co......... | San Diego. |
| Cunningham, J..... | Laborer............ | nr San Diego......... | San Diego Co......... | San Diego. |
| **Cunningham, Thos** | Tel operator........ | San Diego............. | San Diego Co......... | San Diego. |
| Curel, J................ | Farmer............. | San Diego Co......... | nr Santa Teresa...... | |
| **Curey, Henry M** ... | Farmer............. | 12 m S San Diego.... | Tia Juana............. | San Diego. |
| Curley, Pedro........ | Ranchero.......... | San Diego Co......... | Valle de las Viejas... | Viejas. |
| Curley, Peter........ | Ranchero.......... | San Diego Co......... | nr San Diego......... | San Diego. |
| Currier, James...... | Farmer............. | 4 m S San Diego..... | National City......... | National City. |
| **Curry, Chas A**...... | Bar keeper......... | San Diego............. | San Diego............. | San Diego. |
| Curtis, W............. | Farmer............. | nr San Diego......... | San Diego Co......... | San Diego. |
| Cushman, G.......... | Teamster.......... | nr Ballena........... | San Diego Co......... | Ballena. |
| Daley, James Thos. | Miner.............. | 70 m N E San Diego | Banner City.......... | Banner. |
| Daley, Robert........ | Teamster.......... | San Diego Co......... | San Diego............. | San Diego. |
| **Daley, Robert**...... | Stabling........... | San Diego Co......... | San Diego............. | San Diego. |
| Dannell, M H........ | Farmer............. | nr San Diego......... | San Diego Co......... | San Diego. |
| Dannals, G M........ | Clerk............... | San Diego Co......... | Julian................. | Julian. |
| Darnall, N............ | Farmer............. | nr San Diego......... | San Diego Co......... | San Diego. |
| **Davis, Andrew J**... | Saddler............ | San Diego............. | San Diego............. | San Diego. |
| Davis, G.............. | Farmer............. | San Diego Co......... | nr National City..... | National City. |
| Davis, Geo........... | Miner.............. | San Diego Co......... | Banner............... | Banner. |
| Davis, James........ | Farmer............. | 35 m N San Diego... | Bear Valley.......... | San Pascual. |
| **Davis, T J**........... | Farmer............. | San Diego Co......... | nr San Diego......... | San Diego. |
| Davis, T W.......... | Farmer............. | San Diego Co......... | nr San Diego......... | San Diego. |
| Davis, W............. | Farmer............. | San Diego Co......... | nr Santa Teresa..... | |
| **Davis, W W**......... | Millwright.......... | San Diego Co......... | San Diego............. | San Diego. |
| Dean, George........ | Farmer............. | 70 m N E San Diego | Banner............... | Banner. |
| Dean, G W........... | Farmer............. | San Diego Co........ | nr San Diego......... | San Diego. |
| **Deaner, J G**.......... | Stage driver....... | San Diego Co......... | Milquatay............. | Campo. |
| Deaner, —........... | Stage line.......... | San Diego............. | San Diego Co......... | San Diego. |
| DeFrees, A........... | Printer............. | San Diego Co......... | San Diego Co......... | San Diego. |
| Degan, John......... | Miner.............. | 65 m N E San Diego | Julian................. | Julian. |
| **Delaney, J W**....... | Printer............. | San Diego Co......... | San Diego............. | San Diego. |
| Deleval, C............ | Miller.............. | San Diego Co......... | San Diego Co......... | San Diego. |
| **Deleval, C**........... | Wines and liquors | 5th and F sts......... | ......................... | San Diego. |
| Deming, G W........ | Teamster.......... | San Diego Co......... | nr Julian............. | Julian. |
| Dempsey, Joseph... | Laborer ........... | 35 m E San Diego... | Valle de las Viejas... | Viejas. |
| Dempsey, James.... | Currier............ | San Diego Co......... | San Diego............. | San Diego. |
| Dempsey, S.......... | Miner.............. | nr Banner........... | San Diego Co......... | Banner. |
| Dennio, Manuel..... | Teamster.......... | San Diego............. | San Diego Co......... | San Diego. |
| **Denniston, John**... | Farmer............. | 30 m N San Diego... | San Pascual......... | San Pascual. |
| Denslow, C.......... | Machinist.......... | San Diego Co......... | San Diego............. | San Diego. |
| Derrick, M........... | Farmer............. | San Diego Co......... | Walker's Valley..... | |
| DeRungo, J.......... | Laborer............ | San Diego Co......... | nr San Diego......... | San Diego. |
| **Deutler, Mrs A**..... | Boarding house... | ......................... | 5th st, above D...... | San Diego. |
| **Devin, J T**........... | Livery stable...... | San Diego Co......... | San Diego............. | San Diego. |
| Dewitt, David W... | Machinist.......... | San Diego............. | San Diego............. | San Diego. |
| Diablar, M........... | Farmer............. | nr Temecula......... | San Diego Co......... | Temecula. |
| Dickerman, C B..... | Teacher............ | San Diego Co......... | San Diego............. | San Diego. |
| Dickson, D........... | Teamster.......... | San Diego Co......... | San Jacinto......... | San Jacinto. |
| Dickson, J........... | Carpenter......... | San Diego Co......... | Julian................. | Julian. |
| **Dickson, John H R** | Barber............. | San Diego............. | San Diego............. | San Diego. |
| Dievendorff, Jno J.. | Clerk............... | San Diego............. | San Diego............. | San Diego. |
| **Dievendorff, H**..... | Gen merchandise. | 6th st................ | San Diego............. | San Diego. |
| Dievendorff, H...... | Machinist.......... | San Diego Co......... | San Diego............. | San Diego. |
| Dievendorff, C A... | Clerk............... | San Diego Co......... | San Diego............. | San Diego. |
| Dimond, C W....... | Farmer............. | San Diego Co......... | nr National City..... | National City. |
| Dimond, L W........ | Farmer............. | San Diego Co......... | nr National City..... | National City. |
| **Divendorff, J H**.... | Farmer............. | San Diego Co......... | San Diego............. | San Diego. |
| Divilbiss, W......... | Farmer............. | San Diego Co......... | nr Santa Teresa..... | |
| Dixon, D B.......... | Teamster.......... | San Diego............. | San Diego Co......... | San Diego. |

30

# Hotel and Bathing House

### FOOT OF BATH ST.; SANTA BARBARA.

This House has just been completed, and is now open for the reception of guests. It stands directly on the beach, and is provided with first-class facilities for taking either

## HOT OR COLD SALT WATER BATHS.

THE TABLE will be found to be good, the Rooms, airy and well furnished. The wants of guests will always receive immediate attention.

## SINGLE BATHS, 25 Cts.

All those desirous of availing themselves of the advantages of sea air and salt bathing, will find this house all that can be desired.

## MRS. A. M. BENNETT,
### PROPRIETRESS.

DIRECTORY OF SAN DIEGO COUNTY. 467

| NAME. | OCCUPATION. | PLACE OF BUSINESS. | RESIDENCE. | TOWN OR P. O. |
|---|---|---|---|---|
| Driscoll, Wm | Clerk | San Diego Co | San Diego | San Diego. |
| Doblier, C | Brewer | San Diego Co | San Diego | San Diego. |
| Dodson, N H | Lawyer | San Diego Co | San Diego | San Diego. |
| Dohs, C | Musician | San Diego Co | San Diego | San Diego. |
| Dolores, Jose | Farmer | 20 m N W San Diego | San Diegnito | San Diegnito. |
| Domingo, J N | Laborer | nr Penasquitas | San Diego Co | |
| Dorgan, John | Ranchero | San Diego Co | San Pascual | San Pascual. |
| Dougal, Chas E | Saddler | San Diego Co | San Diego | San Diego. |
| Dougherty, E | Merchant | San Diego Co | San Diego | San Diego. |
| Dougherty, E C | Shoemaker | San Diego Co | San Diego | San Diego. |
| Dougherty, Ezro W | Farmer | San Diego | San Diego Co | San Diego. |
| Dougherty, H H | Lawyer | Plaza | San Diego | San Diego. |
| Dougherty, H W | Farmer | San Diego Co | nr San Diego | San Diego. |
| Dougherty, J R | Miner | San Diego Co | nr Julian | Julian. |
| Dougherty, L | Farmer | nr Jamul | San Diego Co | San Diego. |
| Dougherty, P | Bricklayer | San Diego Co | San Diego | San Diego. |
| Dougherty, W | Farmer | San Diego Co | nr Jamul | San Diego. |
| Downs, J | Laborer | nr Julian | San Diego Co | Julian. |
| Down, A Jas | Farmer | San Diego | San Diego | San Diego. |
| Downs, Edward S | Teamster | San Diego | San Diego | San Diego. |
| Downs, O H | Carpenter | San Diego | San Diego | San Diego. |
| Downey, — | Restaurant | 5th st | San Diego | San Diego. |
| Doyle, E J | Contractor | San Diego Co | San Diego | San Diego. |
| Doyle, James | Teamster | San Diego | San Diego | San Diego. |
| Dozier, W G | Agt G N & P line | Company's Wharf | San Diego | San Diego. |
| Dranga, N Gabriel O | Farmer | 12 m San Diego | Tia Juana | San Diego. |
| Drugan, Peter | Farmer | San Luis Rey | San Diego Co | San Luis Rey. |
| Duarte, Simon | Laborer | San Diego | San Diego | San Diego. |
| Duarte, Ygnacio | Laborer | San Diego | San Diego | San Diego. |
| DuBose, W E | Farmer | nr Cajon | San Diego Co | San Diego. |
| Duffy, James | Bar keeper | San Diego Co | Julian | Julian. |
| Dulac, Juan | Sheep raiser | San Diego Co | 2½ m N San Luis Rey | San Luis Rey. |
| Duncan, B F | Farmer | San Diego Co | nr Monument City | San Diego. |
| Dunham, C | P M agent | Hartford Ins. Co | San Diego | San Diego. |
| Dun, I | Farmer | nr Cajon | San Diego Co | San Diego. |
| Dunn, S J | Paper hanger | San Diego Co | San Diego | San Diego. |
| Dunnels, S S | Merchant | San Diego Co | San Diego | San Diego. |
| Dunn, T | Mariner | San Diego Co | San Pascual | San Pascual. |
| Dunnells, S | Pr san diego hotel | cor F and State sts | San Diego | San Diego. |
| Duprez, J E | Saloon keeper | San Diego Co | Julian | Julian. |
| Duran, H | Ranchero | Paumosa Canyon | 9 m E San Luis Rey | San Luis Rey. |
| Durand, H | Ranchero | 55 m N W San Diego | Monserrate | Monserrate. |
| Durbon, Henry L | Teamster | 60 m E San Diego | Milquatay | Campo. |
| Dyche, G V | Ranchero | nr San Felipe | San Diego Co | |
| Dye, J S | Stock raiser | San Diego Co | Dyer Ranch | |
| Dyer, H C | Farmer | nr Julian | San Diego Co | Julian. |
| Engle, J S | Farmer | San Diego Co | nr Campo | Campo. |
| Eastwood, Wm L | Miner | 65 m N E San Diego | Julian City | Julian. |
| Eaton, Nathan A | Carpenter | 20 m N W San Diego | San Diegnito | San Diegnito. |
| Eaton, R R | Farmer | nr San Diego | San Diego | San Diego. |
| Early, J | Laborer | nr San Diego | San Diego Co | San Diego. |
| Eccles, J F | Speculator | San Diego Co | San Diego | San Diego. |
| Edwards, C J | Saddlery&harness | 5th st | San Diego | San Diego. |
| Edwards, Charles | Blacksmith | 70 m N E San Diego | Banner City | Banner. |
| Edwards, J T | Farmer | nr Potrero | San Diego Co | |
| Elbe, Julius | Cigars& fancy gds | Postoffice | San Diego | San Diego. |
| Ellis, C | Miner | nr Milquatay | San Diego Co | Campo. |
| Ellis, J | Miner | San Diego Co | nr Green's Valley | Stonewall. |
| Elliff, E G | Farmer | nr Julian | San Diego Co | Julian. |
| Elliott, Columbus W | Mechanic | 65 m N E San Diego | Julian | Julian. |
| Elliott, E W | Tradesman | San Diego | San Diego | San Diego. |
| Elliott, Joseph | Farmer | 12 m S San Diego | Tia Juana | San Diego. |
| Elliott, W | Farmer | nr Milquatay | San Diego Co | Campo. |
| Elliott, Wm | Miner | San Diego Co | nr Green Valley | Stonewall. |

# LIVERY and FEED STABLES,
## GUADALUPE, CAL.
### J. W. HUDSON, - - Proprietor.

*These Stables are now fitted up for a First-class Livery Business.*

## ANIMALS AND VEHICLES

*Taken on Livery by the Day, Week or Month, and cared for in the best possible manner.*

⌒ADJOINING THE STABLES ARE SPACIOUS⌒

## CORRALS AND SHEDS,

For the accommodation of Teamsters and others, at Moderate Charges. Hay and Grain kept constantly on hand for sale, Wholesale and Retail. The Public can rest assured that everything connected with the business will be attended to in a manner up to the times.

# DIRECTORY OF SAN DIEGO COUNTY.

| NAME. | OCCUPATION. | PLACE OF BUSINESS. | RESIDENCE. |
|---|---|---|---|
| Emery, Edward C. | Farmer | San Diego | San Diego |
| Emery, H L | Trader | San Diego Co | Green Valley |
| Emery, H E | Merchant | San Diego Co | Green Valley |
| Emery, W S | Farmer | nr San Diego | San Diego Co |
| Endees, G W | Miner | nr Julian | San Diego Co |
| Englehardt, J G | Miner | Julian | San Diego Co |
| **England, W J** | Cabinet maker | San Diego Co | San Diego |
| England, W J | Baker | San Diego Co | San Diego |
| English, C C | Miner | nr Julian | San Diego Co |
| Epperson, James H | Gardener | San Diego Co | San Diego |
| Espinosa, Manuel | Sheep herder | 90 m N San Diego | San Jacinto |
| **Espinosa, N** | Ranchero | nr San Pascual | San Diego Co |
| Esquivil, C | Laborer | San Diego Co | nr San Diego |
| Estrado, S | Ranchero | San Diego Co | nr Pala |
| **Estudillo, Jose G** | Asst cash Com B. | cor 5th & G sts | San Diego |
| Estudillo, J A | Ranchero | nr San Jacinto | San Diego Co |
| Estudillo, J M | Ranchero | San Diego Co | nr San Jacinto |
| Estudillo, F | Ranchero | San Diego Co | nr San Jacinto |
| Estudillo, S R | Ranchero | nr San Jacinto | San Diego Co |
| Evans, C L | Miner | San Diego Co | nr Julian |
| **Evans, J N** | Farmer | San Diego Co | nr San Ysabel |
| Evans, W | Teamster | nr San Diego | San Diego Co |
| Everett, J A | Farmer | nr Paguay | San Diego Co |
| Ewing, W A | | | |
| **Ewing, Wm** | Farmer | San Diego Co | nr San Diego |
| Falman, C | Mechanic | San Diego Co | San Diego |
| Farley, D | Farmer | San Diego Co | nr Julian |
| Farley, F E | Clerk | San Diego Co | Julian |
| Farley, Jos | Farmer | nr San Diego | San Diego Co |
| **Farley, Jos** | Printer | San Diego Co | San Diego |
| Farley, J T | Farmer | San Diego Co | nr San Diego |
| Farley, A | Farmer | San Diego Co | nr Tia Juana |
| **Farmer, L** | Hotel keeper | San Diego Co | San Diego |
| Farr, L | Laborer | San Diego Co | nr San Diego |
| Farrel, W | Blacksmith | San Diego Co | San Diego |
| Farwell, G | Expressman | San Diego Co | San Diego |
| **Faivre, J** | Real estate | 5th st | San Diego |
| Feeler, A L | Farmer | nr San Luis Rey | San Diego Co |
| Feeler, Frederic E | Farmer | 20 m N E San Diego | Paguay |
| Feeler, W A | Teamster | nr San Luis Rey | San Diego Co |
| **Felis, Jose M** | Saddle maker | 80 m N San Diego | Agunango |
| Fellheimer, J | Store keeper | San Diego Co | San Diego |
| Fellows, Wm | Laborer | Temecula Creek | 10 m N San Luis Rey |
| Fellows, W H | Farmer | nr Temecula | San Diego Co |
| Felsenheld, M | Shoe dealer | 6th st | San Diego |
| **Felsendhel, N C** | Dry goods | cor 6th & F sts | San Diego |
| Fenn, C M | Physician | 5th st | San Diego |
| Fenton, C M | Laborer | San Diego Co | nr San Diego |
| Ferris, C O | Sail maker | San Diego Co | San Diego |
| **Fessenden, C P** | Photographer | cor 5th & E sts | San Diego |
| Fessenden, F S | Artist | San Diego | San Diego |
| Fewingo, J | Miner | San Diego Co | nr Julian |
| **Fickas, Benj A** | Searcher of rec'ds | San Diego | San Diego Co |
| Fields, J B | Boot maker | San Diego Co | San Diego |
| Field, V F | Musician | San Diego Co | San Diego |
| Fike, D S | Bricklayer | San Diego | San Diego |
| Fischer, A W F | Farmer | 35 m N W San Diego | Monserrate |
| Fischer, J | Fruit dealer | San Diego Co | San Diego |
| Fisher, F W | Laborer | nr Paguay | San Diego Co |
| Fisher, C S | Laborer | nr San Pascual | San Diego Co |
| Fitzpatrick, F | Farmer | San Diego Co | nr Banner |
| **Fleischman, Jos J** | Farmer | San Diego Co | nr San Diego |
| Fleming, Patrick | Hostler | San Diego | San Diego |
| Fleshman, Jos J | Farmer | 35 m N San Diego | Bear Valley |

# SANTA BARBARA NURSERY

Seven Miles West of the City.

JOSEPH SEXTON - - - Proprietor,

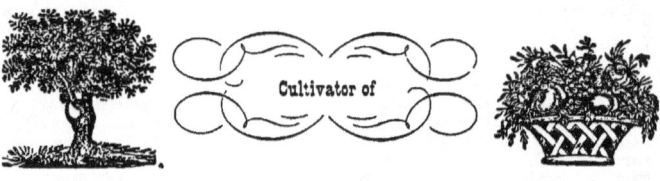

Cultivator of

# Fruit Trees, Pot Plants

—AND—

## HARDY EVERGREEN SHRUBBERY.

### DEPOT

Corner of Montecito and Castillo Streets,

Where persons can call and make their selections.

DIRECTORY OF SAN DIEGO COUNTY. 471

| NAME. | OCCUPATION. | PLACE OF BUSINESS. | RESIDENCE. | TOWN OR P. O. |
|---|---|---|---|---|
| Fletcher, G P | Farmer | nr San Luis Rey | San Diego Co | San Luis Rey. |
| Fletcher, G C | Farmer | nr San Luis Rey | San Diego Co | San Luis Rey. |
| Fletcher, W B | Farmer | nr San Luis Rey | San Diego Co | San Luis Rey. |
| **Fleurey, J M** | Sheep raiser | S L Rey Valley | 2½ m S W S L Rey. | San Luis Rey. |
| Flinn, J | Farmer | San Diego Co | nr Ranchita | |
| Flinn, W E | Farmer | nr Ranchita | San Diego Co | |
| **Floyd, G S** | Farmer | San Diego Co | San Diego | San Diego. |
| Fogge, C P | Hostler | San Diego Co | San Diego | San Diego. |
| Forest, P | Laborer | nr San Diego | San Diego Co | San Diego. |
| Forster, F P | Ranchero | Santa Margarita | 6 m N San Luis Rey | San Luis Rey. |
| Forster, J F | Ranchero | Santa Margarita | 6 m N San Luis Rey | San Luis Rey. |
| Forster, John | Ranchero | Santa Margarita | 6 m N San Luis Rey | San Luis Rey. |
| Forster, M A | Ranchero | Santa Margarita | 6 m N San Luis Rey | San Luis Rey. |
| Forster, M A | Farmer | San Diego Co | nr Los Flores | |
| **Forster, Thos** | Ranchero | nr Santa Margarita | San Diego Co | San Luis Rey. |
| Fort, J H | Hostler | San Diego Co | San Diego | San Diego. |
| **Foss, D R** | Farmer | San Luis Rey | 45 m N San Diego | San Luis Rey. |
| **Foster, Jas** | Blacksmith | San Diego Co | Pine Valley | |
| Foster, L J | Farmer | San Diego Co | nr San Diegnito | San Diegnito. |
| Foster, W F | Miner | San Diego Co | nr San Diegnito | San Diegnito. |
| **Foster, Geo S** | Carpenter | San Diego Co | San Diego | San Diego. |
| Fouts, J H | Farmer | nr Julian | San Diego Co | Julian. |
| Fox, C | Miner | nr Julian | San Diego Co | Julian. |
| Fox, C L | Laborer | nr San Diego | San Diego Co | San Diego. |
| **Fox, Chas J** | City engineer | 6th st, bet E and F | San Diego | San Diego. |
| Fox, C | Laborer | San Diego Co | nr San Diego | San Diego. |
| Francisco, C F | Teamster | San Diego Co | nr San Diego | San Diego. |
| **Francis, W H** | Real estate | Plaza | San Diego Co | San Diego. |
| Frary, A P | Farmer | nr Julian | San Diego Co | Julian. |
| **Frary & Shulz** | Gen merchandise | Main st | Julian City | San Diego. |
| Freeborn, Isaac S | Miner | San Diego Co | San Diego | San Diego. |
| Freeman, A A | Blacksmith | San Luis Rey | 45 m N San Diego | San Luis Rey. |
| Freeman, A J | Farmer | San Luis Rey | 45 m N San Diego | San Luis Rey. |
| Freeman, Frank | Farmer | 12 m S E San Diego | Monument | San Diego. |
| Freeman, T | Farmer | San Diego Co | Fort Yuma | Fort Yuma. |
| Freeman, John W | Laborer | San Luis Rey | San Diego Co | San Luis Rey. |
| Freeman, J B | Farmer | San Diego Co | nr Monument | San Diego. |
| Freeman, Wm F | Laborer | 65 m N E San Diego | Julian | Julian. |
| French, E | Ranchero | Monserrate | San Diego Co | Monserrate. |
| French, R | Miner | nr San Pascual | San Diego Co | San Pascual. |
| French, E D | Miner | nr San Pascual | San Diego Co | San Pascual. |
| **Frick, G** | Lumberman | San Diego | San Diego Co | San Diego. |
| **Friesenecker, A** | Brewer | San Diego Co | San Diego Co | San Diego. |
| Frimable, Marbon S | Book keeper | 70 m N E San Diego | Banner City | Banner. |
| Fripp, L V | Mason | San Diego Co | San Jacinto | San Jacinto. |
| Froom, E S | Carpenter | San Diego Co | Julian | Julian. |
| Fry, Andrew | Farmer | 70 m N San Diego | Agua Caliente | Warner's Rch. |
| **Fulkerson, E B** | Contractor | San Diego | San Diego Co | San Diego. |
| Fuller, T D | Farmer | nr San Diego | San Diego Co | San Diego. |
| Fullerton, R | Farmer | nr San Diego | San Diego Co | San Diego. |
| Fulton, W G | Painter | San Diego Co | San Diego | San Diego. |
| Furguson, C C | Farmer | nr Julian | San Diego Co | Julian. |
| Furlong, G J | Carpenter | San Diego Co | San Diego | San Diego. |
| Gable, W H | Miner | nr Julian | San Diego Co | Julian. |
| **Galasky, W J** | Gunsmith | San Diego Co | Sweetwater | San Diego. |
| Galaso, Dolores | Ranchero | 55 m N W San Diego | Monserrate | Monserrate. |
| Gale, W M | Farmer | San Diego Co | San Diego | San Diego. |
| Gale, J W & Co | Gen merchandise | cor 6th & F sts | San Diego | San Diego. |
| Gallagher, E | Miner | San Diego Co | nr San Diego | San Diego. |
| Gallagher, H | Hostler | San Diego Co | San Diego | San Diego. |
| Gallagher, P | Laborer | San Diego Co | nr San Diego | San Diego. |
| Gallego, G | Farmer | San Diego Co | nr Pala | Pala. |
| Gallespy, W | Gunsmith | San Diego | San Diego Co | San Diego. |
| **Gannon, Thos L** | Coach maker | 12 m S San Diego | Tia Juana | San Diego. |

## ISRAEL MILLER,

PRACTICAL

# Watchmaker

*Twenty Years in Succession,*

**STATE STREET, - - SANTA BARBARA.**

ALL KINDS OF

# JEWELRY

MADE TO ORDER.

Also Setting of every description done with neatness and dispatch.

**Watches, Clocks and Chronometers,**

Both Ancient and Modern,

Neatly cleaned and adjusted, and satisfaction guaranteed.

N. B.—All orders appertaining to the trade promptly attended to.

---

## J. C. CEBRIAN,

*Architect,*

## CIVIL ENGINEER

AND

## SURVEYOR,

STATE STREET,

SANTA BARBARA,

CAL.

---

## FRANK W. TWIST,

Wholesale and Retail Dealer in

# GROCERIES

**Crockery,**

WOOD & WILLOW WARE,

**COOK'S HALL,**

## STATE STREET,

SANTA BARBARA, CAL.

---

## UNION HOUSE.

Corner of

BATH & GUTIERREZ STS.

SANTA BARBARA,

CAL.

## F. R. DRAKE,

Proprietor.

DIRECTORY OF SAN DIEGO COUNTY. 473

| NAME. | OCCUPATION. | PLACE OF BUSINESS. | RESIDENCE. | TOWN OR P. O. |
|---|---|---|---|---|
| Garancio, J | Vaquero | nr Temecula | San Diego Co | Temecula. |
| Garcia, F | Farmer | nr Temecula | San Diego Co | Temecula. |
| Garcia, Jose | Sheep herder | 90 m N San. Diego | San Jacinto | San Jacinto. |
| **Garcia, Navarro** | Ranchero | Milpitas | 4 m E San Luis Rey | San Luis Rey. |
| Garcio, N | Mason | San Diego Co | Buena Vista | San Luis Rey. |
| Garcio, R | Laborer | nr Milpitas | San Diego Co | San Luis Rey. |
| Gardner, R | Teamster | San Diego Co | nr San Diego | San Diego. |
| Gardner, W | Machinist | San Diego Co | San Diego | San Diego. |
| Garican, J | Miner | nr Julian | San Diego Co | Julian. |
| **Gaskell, L H** | Merchant | San Diego Co | Campo | Campo. |
| Gaskell, S E | Postmaster | San Diego Co | Campo | Campo. |
| **Gass, A McK** | Merchant | San Diego Co | Campo | Campo. |
| Gassen, A G | Butcher | San Diego Co | San Diego | San Diego. |
| Gassen, C | Butcher | San Diego Co | San Diego | San Diego. |
| Gates, Mrs O W | Principal | Pt Loma Seminary | San Diego | San Diego. |
| Gatewood, W J | Attorney | Horton's Bk Block | San Diego | San Diego. |
| Geary, D | Farmer | San Diego Co | Jamul | San Diego. |
| Gray, John D | Druggist | San Diego | San Diego Co | San Diego. |
| Geddes, G | Trader | San Diego Co | San Diego | San Diego. |
| **Geiebnon, Fredk** | Saloon keeper | San Diego | San Diego Co | San Diego. |
| Gerety, P B | Sheep raiser | San Diego Co | Julian | Julian. |
| Gerull, Christopher | Mariner | San Diego | San Diego | San Diego. |
| Gibson, C | Ranchero | San Diego Co | nr San Diego | San Diego. |
| Gibson, Wm Thos | Musician | San Diego | San Diego Co | San Diego. |
| Giddens, John | Farmer | 65 m N E San Diego | Temecula | Temecula. |
| Gifford, E B | Blacksmith | San Diego | San Diego Co | San Diego. |
| Gifford, J T | Operator | Julian | San Diego Co | Julian. |
| **Gilbert, A H & Bro** | Lumber | cor J and Front sts | San Diego | San Diego. |
| Gilbert, A H | Lumber dealer | cor Front and J sts | San Diego | San Diego. |
| Gilbert, B T | Miner | nr Banner | San Diego Co | Banner. |
| **Gilbert, Chas G** | Lumber dealer | Front and J sts | San Diego Co | San Diego. |
| Gilbert, A H | Livery stable | San Diego Co | San Diego | San Diego. |
| Gilbert, E C | Farmer | San Diego Co | Banner | Banner. |
| Gilbert, J G | Miner | San Diego Co | nr Julian | Julian. |
| Gillam, Sylvester | Laborer | San Diego Co | San Diego | San Diego. |
| **Gillet, S R** | Sheep raiser | San Diego Co | Green Valley | Stonewall. |
| Gillis, G W | Farmer | nr San Diego | San Diego Co | San Diego. |
| **Gillingham, J W** | Builder | cor 4th and B sts | San Diego | San Diego. |
| Gillispie, Wm Jones | Blacksmith | 65 m N E San Diego | Julian | Julian. |
| Gilmore, John | Mariner | | San Diego | San Diego. |
| **Ginocchio, G** | Grocery | cor 5th and J sts | San Diego | San Diego. |
| Gilson, S | Teamster | nr Julian | San Diego Co | Julian. |
| Gladstone, Wm H | File cutter | San Diego | San Diego | San Diego. |
| Gleason, James | Shoe maker | San Diego | San Diego | San Diego. |
| Godall, A | Blacksmith | San Diego Co | San Diego | San Diego. |
| Goggins, James | Laborer | San Diego Co | San Diego | San Diego. |
| Goggins, W | Miner | San Diego Co | nr Julian | Julian. |
| Goff, L | Laborer | San Diego | San Diego Co | San Diego. |
| Gomez, S | Farmer | Pala | San Diego Co | Pala. |
| **Goldbaum, S & Bro** | Gen merchandise | San Luis Rey | 45 m N San Diego | San Luis Rey. |
| **Goldbaum, Simon** | Gen merchandise | San Luis Rey | 45 m N San Diego | San Luis Rey. |
| **Goldbaum, Louis** | Gen merchandise | San Luis Rey | 45 m N San Diego | San Luis Rey. |
| Goldbaum, S | Merchant | San Diego Co | Monserrate | Monserrate. |
| **Goldsmith, H** | Farmer | San Diego Co | nr San Diego | San Diego. |
| Golsh, A A C | Farmer | nr Monserrate | San Diego Co | Monserrate. |
| Golsh, A | Farmer | nr Monserrate | San Diego Co | Monserrate. |
| Golsh, X | Farmer | nr Monserrate | San Diego Co | Monserrate. |
| Gomes, Roman | Farmer | 50 m N San Diego | Pala | Pala. |
| Gonzales, Francisco | Farmer | 90 m N San Diego | San Jacinto | San Jacinto. |
| Goodfellow, P | Miner | San Diego Co | nr Julian | Julian. |
| **Goodwin, W G** | Painter | San Diego Co | San Diego | San Diego. |
| Goodrich, B | Farmer | nr Julian | San Diego Co | Julian. |
| Gordon, C H | Steward | San Diego Co | San Diego | San Diego. |
| **Gordon & Hazzard** | Genl merchandise | cor 6th & H sts | San Diego | San Diego. |

C. P. Sheffield.   N. W. Spaulding.   J. Patterson.

**PACIFIC**

# Saw Manufacturing Co.

17 and 19 FREMONT STREET,

SAN FRANCISCO.

Planing Knives, Curriers' Knives,

**SAW MANDRILS AND SAWS,**

OF EVERY DESCRIPTION,

On Hand and Made to Order.

French Band Saw Blades, Babbitt Metal, Fulled Raw-Hide Lacing, Files and Grindstones for Sale.

Repairing of all kinds Done at Short Notice.

**PACIFIC SAW MANUFACTURING CO.**

17 and 19 FREMONT ST. San Francisco.

# N. W. SPAULDING,

## SAW

# Smithing & Repairing

ESTABLISHMENT,

**17 & 19 Fremont Street,**

Near Market,

**San Francisco,**

MANUFACTURER OF

## SPAULDING'S

## INSERTED TOOTH

# CIRCULAR SAWS.

They have proved to be the Cheapest, Most Durable and Economical Saws in the World.

**DUPLICATE TEETH, $1 each.**

All Saws sold, or work done, warranted.

☞ *Send for Illustrated Circular and Price List.*

## DIRECTORY OF SAN DIEGO COUNTY. 475

| Name. | Occupation. | Place of Business. | Residence. | Town or P. O. |
|---|---|---|---|---|
| Gordon, J A | Manager | Horton House | San Diego | San Diego. |
| Gordon, J S | General mdse | cor 6th & H sts | San Diego | San Diego. |
| Gorman, T | Laborer | San Diego Co | nr San Diego | San Diego. |
| Gormley, P | Gardener | San Diego Co | San Diego | San Diego. |
| Grady, D | Teamster | nr San Luis Rey | San Diego Co | San Luis Rey. |
| Goss, T | Brick maker | San Diego Co | San Diego | San Diego. |
| Gradillas, R | Ranchero | San Diego Co | nr San Diego | San Diego. |
| Gradias, Francisco | Ranchero | San Luis Rey Valley | 4 m E San Luis Rey | San Luis Rey. |
| Gradias, Rafael | Ranchero | San Luis Rey Valley | 4 m E San Luis Rey | San Luis Rey. |
| Grady, Daniel | Teamster | 70 m N E San Diego | Green Valley | Stonewall. |
| Graham & Nugent | Genl merchants | San Diego Co | Bernardo | Bernardo. |
| Graham, P A | Farmer | San Diego Co | San Luis Rey | San Luis Rey. |
| Graham, Patrick A | General mdse | San Diego Co | Bernardo | Bernardo. |
| Graham, T W | Wind mill | cor 4th & H sts | San Diego | San Diego. |
| Grant, A S | Clerk | San Diego | San Diego Co | San Diego. |
| Graves, Lyman G | Farmer | 60 m N San Diego | Ballena | Ballena. |
| Graves, T A | Farmer | nr Milquatay | San Diego Co | Campo. |
| Gray, E C | Farmer | nr San Diego | San Diego Co | San Diego. |
| Gray, J D | Drug store | cor 5th and I sts | San Diego | San Diego. |
| Gray, T J | Blacksmith | San Diego Co | San Diego | San Diego. |
| Gray, J | Upholsterer | San Diego Co | San Diego | San Diego. |
| Granio, G | Farmer | nr San Jacinto | San Diego Co | San Jacinto. |
| Greaves, E G | Painter | San Diego Co | Milquatay | Campo. |
| Grebert, Harlow | Apiarian | 30 m N San Diego | San Pascual | San Pascual. |
| Grebe, Fredk C | Hotel keeper | San Diego | San Diego Co | San Diego. |
| Green, H | Butcher | San Diego Co | San Diego | San Diego. |
| Green, E L | Assessor | San Diego Co | San Diego | San Diego. |
| Green, Jas | Laborer | San Diego Co | nr Oak Grove | Oak Grove. |
| Green, Franklin W | Teamster | 65 m N San Diego | Julian | Julian. |
| Green, Jacob | Cook | 65 m N E San Diego | Julian | Julian. |
| Green, J W | Shoe maker | San Diego Co | San Diego | San Diego. |
| Greenanalt, David | Farmer | 65 m N San Diego | Julian | Julian. |
| Greenwood, W C | Farmer | San Diego Co | nr Green Valley | Stonewall. |
| Greenwood, B H | Farmer | Green Valley | San Diego Co | Stonewall. |
| Gregg, J H | Farmer | nr Marana | San Diego Co | |
| Gregg, W S | Merchant | San Diego Co | San Diego | San Diego. |
| Gregg, W S, Jr | Clerk | San Diego Co | San Diego | San Diego. |
| Gregg, A E J | Carpenter | San Diego Co | San Diego | San Diego. |
| Gregg, R Dr | Physician | 5th st | San Diego | San Diego. |
| Gregory, G | Miner | San Diego | San Diego Co | San Diego. |
| Gregory, E | Blacksmith | San Diego Co | San Diego | San Diego. |
| Gregory, F A | Farmer | nr Spring Valley | San Diego Co | San Diego. |
| Gregry & Trask | Shaving saloon | 5th st | San Diego | San Diego. |
| Griebnon, Fred | Saloon | San Diego | San Diego Co | San Diego. |
| Griffin, J | Farmer | San Diego Co | nr San Diego | San Diego. |
| Griffin, Wade | Farmer | San Luis Rey | 45 m N San Diego | San Luis Rey. |
| Griffin, H | Laborer | San Diego Co | nr San Diego | San Diego. |
| Griffin, James C | Farmer | San Luis Rey | 45 m N San Diego | San Luis Rey. |
| Griffin, James M | Farmer | San Luis Rey | 45 m N San Diego | San Luis Rey. |
| Griffith, F C | Butcher | San Diego Co | Julian | Julian. |
| Groesbeck, J | Constable | San Diego Co | San Diego | San Diego. |
| Grow, A L | Engineer | San Diego Co | Picacho | Fort Yuma. |
| Grumble, S H | Farmer | nr Milquatay | San Diego Co | Campo. |
| Grudius, Francisco | Laborer | San Diego Co | San Luis Rey | San Luis Rey. |
| Grudardo, Jesus | Laborer | Santa Margarita | 6 m N San Luis Rey | San Luis Rey. |
| Guavara, C | Soap maker | San Diego Co | San Luis Rey | San Luis Rey. |
| Guillaum, L | Mechanic | San Diego Co | Monument City | San Diego. |
| Guion, D | Dairy | Arizona Stables | San Diego | San Diego. |
| Guin, James Henry | Farmer | San Diego Co | National City | National City. |
| Gunn, Douglas | Publisher | San Diego Union | cor D & 4th sts | San Diego. |
| Gunn, Lewis C | Editor | San Diego | San Diego Co | San Diego. |
| Gunn, S M | Principal | San Diego Academy | San Diego | San Diego. |
| Gunn, E Le B | Principal | San Diego Academy | San Diego | San Diego. |
| Gunn, C | Machinist | Julian | San Diego Co | Julian. |

| HEYWOOD & HARMON, | B. F. CLAYTON, | W. S. HARRIMAN, |
| SAN FRANCISCO. | POINT SAL. | GUADALUPE. |

# HARRIMAN & CO.

## LUMBER MERCHANTS,

### POINT SAL LANDING

**AND**

### GUADALUPE, CAL.

DEALERS IN ALL KINDS OF

# LUMBER

**AND**

# BUILDING MATERIAL.

OREGON PINE, REDWOOD LUMBER,
SHINGLES, SHAKES, LATHS, PICKETS,
POSTS, FENCING, BLINDS,
WINDOWS, FLOORING, DOORS,
MOULDINGS, LIME, HAIR, ETC., ETC.

———o———

Having our own Timber Lands, Saw Mills and Sailing Craft, we are prepared to furnish better material at LOWER RATES than can be furnished by any other Lumber Dealers in the country.

———o———

### MAIN OFFICE

At LUMBER YARD, Guadalupe, Santa Barbara County, Cal.

———o———

ALL ORDERS PROMPTLY FILLED AND SATISFACTION GUARANTEED.

# DIRECTORY OF SAN DIEGO COUNTY. 477

| Name. | Occupation. | Place of Business. | Residence. | Town or P. O. |
|---|---|---|---|---|
| Gutekunst, John H | Blacksmith | 70 m N E San Diego | Banner | Banner. |
| **Guthrie, W H** | Carpenter | San Diego | nr San Diego | San Diego. |
| Guyrado, J | Teacher | San Diego Co | Santa Margarita | San Luis Rey. |
| Guzzler, L | Miner | Julian | San Diego Co | San Diego. |
| Hackett, Saml W | Mariner | | San Bernardo | Bernardo. |
| **Hale, J B** | Farmer | nr Julian | San Diego Co | Julian. |
| Hale, J M | Farmer | nr Julian | San Diego Co | Julian. |
| Haight, E G | Clerk | San Diego Co | San Diego | San Diego. |
| **Haight, J M** | Printer | San Diego Co | San Diego | San Diego. |
| Halland, P | Blacksmith | San Diego Co | San Diego | San Diego. |
| Halloran, W | Miner | San Diego Co | nr Banner | Banner. |
| Ham, G P | Farmer | nr Milquatay | San Diego Co | Campo. |
| Ham, J B | Laborer | nr San Diego | San Diego Co | San Diego. |
| Hamilton & Marston | Gen merchandise | cor 5th & J sts | | San Diego. |
| Hamilton, C S | Clerk | San Diego Co | San Diego | San Diego. |
| Hamilton, J | Teamster | San Diego Co | nr San Diego | San Diego. |
| Hamilton, Fred'k N | Clerk | San Diego | San Diego | San Diego. |
| Hamilton, J E | Farmer | San Diego Co | nr Santa Teresa | |
| **Hamilton, Martin D** | Farmer | 22 m E San Diego | Jamul | San Diego. |
| Hamilton, J A | Stage driver | San Diego Co | San Diego | San Diego. |
| Hammack, L W | Farmer | nr Julian | San Diego Co | Julian. |
| Hammell, C | Butcher | San Diego Co | Banner | Banner. |
| **Hammer, M B** | Druggist | San Diego | San Diego | San Diego. |
| Hamner, H A | Shepherd | San Diego Co | nr San Luis Rey | San Luis Rey. |
| Hancock, J C | Mariner | San Diego Co | Warner's Ranch | Warner's Rch. |
| Hand, S G | Farmer | nr Paguay | San Diego Co | Poway. |
| **Hanke, K T** | Farmer | nr San Diego | San Diego Co | San Diego. |
| Hanlon, J | Planing mill | cor 2d & G sts | San Diego | San Diego. |
| **Hansfelt, J** | Farmer | nr Catell Valley | San Diego Co | |
| Harbordt, F | Laborer | San Diego Co | nr San Diego | San Diego. |
| Hardin, A | Farmer | San Diego Co | nr Cajon | San Diego. |
| Hardin, J | Farmer | nr Cajon | San Diego Co | San Diego. |
| **Harper, E A** | Farmer | San Diego Co | nr San Diego | San Diego. |
| Harper, Nicholas C | Clerk | San Diego Co | San Diego | San Diego. |
| Harrington, J | Cook | San Diego Co | San Diego | San Diego. |
| Harrington, M | Hostler | San Diego Co | Banner | Banner. |
| Harris, L T | Farmer | San Diego | San Diego Co | San Diego. |
| **Harris, Enan** | Artist | San Diego Co | San Diego | San Diego. |
| Harris, Elijah | Farmer | nr Milquatay | San Diego Co | Campo. |
| Harris, J C | Farmer | San Diego Co | nr Milquatay | Campo. |
| Hart, G W | Farmer | nr San Luis Rey | San Diego Co | San Luis Rey. |
| Hart, R | Farmer | nr San Diego | San Diego Co | San Diego. |
| **Hartman, T & Son** | Attorneys | cor Front & F sts | San Diego | San Diego. |
| Hartman, — | Attorney | cor Front & F sts | San Diego | San Diego. |
| **Harvey, S G** | Merchant | San Diego Co | Julian | Julian. |
| Harvey, W W | Farmer | nr San Luis Rey | San Diego Co | San Luis Rey. |
| **Harvey, J S** | Merchant | San Diego Co | San Diego | San Diego. |
| Hatfield, A | Farmer | San Diego Co | nr Julian | Julian. |
| Hatfield, Chas Wm | Farmer | 65 m N E San Diego | Julian City | Julian. |
| **Hathaway & Foster** | Builders' goods | cor 4th & H sts | San Diego | San Diego. |
| **Hatleberg, J O** | Blacksmith | cor 8th & J sts | San Diego | San Diego. |
| Hattaram, W | Farmer | San Diego Co | nr San Diego | San Diego. |
| Hauck, Louis | Farmer | 35 m N San Diego | Bear Valley | San Pascual. |
| Hawkins, John | Apiarian | Temecula Creek | 10 m N San Luis Rey | San Luis Rey. |
| Hawkes, E | Miner | nr San Diego | San Diego Co | San Diego. |
| Hawyer, H W | Merchant | San Diego Co | Julian | Julian. |
| Hayden, Z | Farmer | nr San Diego | San Diego Co | San Diego. |
| Hayden, M D | Farmer | nr Milquatay | San Diego Co | Campo. |
| **Hayes, Benj** | Attorney | N W cor Plaza | San Diego Co | Old San Diego. |
| Hayes, I C & Co | Real estate | N W cor Plaza | San Diego Co | Old San Diego. |
| Hayman, J L | Farmer | nr San Diego | San Diego Co | San Diego. |
| Haynes, R S | Mechanic | San Diego Co | Milquatay | Campo. |
| Haynie, J | Farmer | nr Julian | San Diego Co | Julian. |

H. J. LAUGHLIN,                          H. DUTARD,
Guadalupe.                             San Francisco.

# H. J. LAUGHLIN & CO.

## GUADALUPE AND LA GRACIOSA,

### WHOLESALE AND RETAIL DEALERS IN

# GENERAL MERCHANDISE,

### GROCERIES AND PROVISIONS,

## DRY GOODS AND CLOTHING,

Hats, Boots, Shoes, Caps, Shawls, etc.,

Crockery, Glassware, Queensware and Hollowware,

### HARDWARE, TINWARE AND WILLOWWARE,

Wines, Liquors, Cigars and Tobacco.

### Agents for

# WELLS, FARGO & CO'S

## EXPRESS.

The Celebrated Bain Wagon, Eureka Gang Plow, Pitts' Genuine Buffalo Threshers, Ames' Threshing Engines, Champion Mower and Reaper, Hollingsworth Sulky Rake, Sweepstake Single-Gear Header, and the Improved Crandall Patent Spring Bed.

*Cash paid for Wool and Grain, and Advances made on all Consignments.*

## H. DUTARD,

# COMMMISSION MERCHANT,

### WHOLESALE DEALER IN

## Grain and Produce,

### 217 and 219 Clay Street, - - - San Francisco.

Refers to H. J. LAUGHLIN & CO.

## DIRECTORY OF SAN DIEGO COUNTY. 479

| Name. | Occupation. | Place of Business. | Residence. | Town or P. O. |
|---|---|---|---|---|
| Hazzard, George... | Gen merchandise. | cor 6th & H sts ........ | San Diego..... ........ | San Diego. |
| Hazzard, G W ....... | Merchant ... ......... | San Diego Co...... ..... | San Diego..... ......... | San Diego. |
| Hazen, K S ........... | Carpenter... .......... | San Diego Co.......... | San Diego..... .......... | San Diego. |
| Healy, E ............... | Harness maker ... | San Diego Co.......... | San Diego..... .......... | San Diego. |
| Heath, W ............. | Carpenter............. | San Diego Co.......... | San Diego........ ........ | San Diego. |
| Hedden, Geo ........ | Farmer ............. | San Diego Co.......... | nr San Diego...... | San Diego. |
| Hedden, Joel C...... | Laborer ............. | 35 m N San Diego.... | Bear Valley... ......... | San Pascual. |
| Heer, H ................ | Baker ..... .......... | cor 5th & J sts ....... | San Diego..... ,........ | San Diego. |
| Heenander, J ........ | Planing mill ...... | cor 9th & H sts........ | San Diego..... .......... | San Diego. |
| Heinrich, L ........... | Gunsmith.. .......... | San Diego Co.......... | San Diego..... .......... | San Diego. |
| Heinsohn, Claus J .. | Seaman........ ....... | ......................:..... | San Diego..... .......... | San Diego. |
| Helms, Chatam ..... | Farmer .......?..... | San Diego Co.......... | Agua Caliente......... | Warner's Rch. |
| Helms, H T ........... | Miner................ | nr Agua Caliente ..... | San Diego Co........... | Warner's Rch. |
| Henderson, J K ..... | Carpenter............ | San Diego Co.......... | Warner's Ranch...... | Warner's Rch. |
| Hendrick, E W ...... | Lawyer.... .......... | San Diego..... .......... | San Diego Co........... | San Diego. |
| Henry, A M........... | Farmer............... | nr Fort Yuma......... | San Diego Co........... | Fort Yuma. |
| Hensley, G B......... | Searcher of rec'ds | 5th st.................. | San Diego ..... ......... | San Diego. |
| Hensley, C... ......... | Carpenter ........... | San Diego Co.......... | San Diego ..... ......... | San Diego. |
| Hering, W H........... | Laborer................ | nr San Diego........... | San Diego Co........... | San Diego. |
| Herman, D C......... | Farmer.............,... | San Diego Co.......... | nr San Diego........... | San Diego. |
| Herrmann, D C..... | S F brewery ...... | 5th st, near K.......... | San Diego..... .......... | San Diego. |
| Hernon, Michael .. | Miner................ | 65 m N E San Diego | Julian............ ........ | Julian. |
| Hess, T P............... | Carpenter... ........ | Sah Diego Co.......... | nr San Diego .......... | San Diego. |
| Heuck, A............... | Teamster... .......... | San Diego Co.......... | nr San Diego .......... | San Diego. |
| Hicks, H B ............ | Farmer ............... | San Diego Co.......... | nr Centre Valley...... |  |
| Hickey, George S... | Clergyman........... | San Diego............. | San Diego Co........... | San Diego. |
| Hickey, T .............. | Trunk maker....... | San Diego Co.......... | San Diego............. | San Diego. |
| Higgins, T J........... | Real estate .......... | 5th st.................. | San Diego............. | San Diego. |
| Higgins, D W ........ | Farmer ............... | San Diego Co.......... | nr Monserrate ........ | Monserrate. |
| Higgins, H M......... | Real estate dealer | San Diego Co.......... | National City.......... | National City. |
| Highland, John N.. | Farmer ............... | 12 m S San Diego.... | Tia Juana............... | San Diego. |
| Highans, J............. | Farmer............... | nr Monserrate ........ | San Diego Co........... | Monserrate. |
| High, J E .............. | Miner................ | San Diego Co.......... | nr Monument.......... | San Diego. |
| High, W E ............ | Farmer.... ......... | nr Otay..... . ......... | San Diego Co........... | San Diego. |
| Hill, Ben P ............ | Farmer ............... | 16 m E San Diego ... | Cajon............... ........ | San Diego. |
| Hill, C J................ | Carpenter............. | Milquatay.............. | San Diego Co........... | Campo. |
| Hill, C N ............... | Farmer ............... | nr Jamul................ | San Diego Co........... | San Diego. |
| Hill, J W................ | Farmer............... | nr San Diego.......... | San Diego Co........... | San Diego. |
| Hill, N................... | Porter ................. | San Diego Co.......... | San Diego............. | San Diego. |
| Hill, R................... | Cabinet maker..... | San Diego Co.......... | Cajon................ ........ | San Diego. |
| Hill, W.................. | Farmer............... | nr Cajon ............... | San Diego Co........... | San Diego. |
| Hill, W G .............. | Farmer............... | nr Cajon ............... | San Diego Co........... | San Diego. |
| Himan, A ... ......... | Music teacher...... | 3d st.................... | San Diego............. | San Diego. |
| Hinchman, A F ..... | Attorney............. | San Diego Co.......... | San Diego............. | San Diego. |
| Hinds, E ..... .......... | Stock raiser......... | San Diego Co.......... | Julian................ ........ | Julian. |
| Hinds, R W........... | Farmer ............... | San Diego Co.......... | nr Monument City ... | San Diego. |
| Hinton, Gallagher & Co............... | Fashion stable..... | cor 2d & D sts......... | San Diego............. | San Diego. |
| Hinton, J B............ | Manager............. | Fashion Stable........ | San Diego ..... ......... | San Diego. |
| Hirschey, H B........ | Furniture ........... | 6th st.................. | San Diego............. | San Diego. |
| Hiscock, Almon..... | Merchant ........... | San Diego............. | San Diego Co........... | San Diego. |
| Hitchcock, G N...... | Lawyer............... | San Diego Co.......... | San Diego ..... ......... | San Diego. |
| Hite, T ................. | Farmer............... | San Diego Co.......... | nr Julian................ | Julian. |
| Hockensmith, P H.. | Farmer............... | nr Milquatay.......... | San Diego Co........... | Campo. |
| Hoeninghaus, A J .. | Laborer............... | San Diego Co.......... | nr San Diego........... | San Diego. |
| Hoffman, D B, Dr.. | Physician... ......... | cor 8th & G sts........ | San Diego............. | San Diego. |
| Hoffman, F W....... | Contractor.......... | San Diego Co.......... | San Diego............. | San Diego. |
| Hoffman, J............ | Miner................ | nr San Luis Rey...... | San Diego Co........... | San Luis Rey. |
| Hofman, Geo R ..... | Farmer ............. | 20 m N E San Diego | Paguay................ | Poway. |
| Hogue, — ............ | Saloon................ | 5th st.................. | San Diego............. | San Diego. |
| Hogue, T............... | Trader................ | San Diego Co.......... | San Diego ..... ......... | San Diego. |
| Hois, J D............... | Printer................ | San Diego Co.......... | San Diego............. | San Diego. |
| Hoke,—. ............... | Gasfitter ............ | 5th st.................. | San Diego............. | San Diego. |
| Hoke, J ................ | Miner................ | San Diego Co.......... | nr San Diego ......... | San Diego. |

## CORNER OF
## Ocean Avenue and I Streets,
## LOMPOC, CAL.

## LIGGETT & PORTER, Proprietors.

This is the first and only Hotel in Lompoc, and has

### Every Convenience

For the accommodation of the Traveling Public.

## BOARD

BY THE MEAL, DAY, WEEK OR MONTH.

## DIRECTORY OF SAN DIEGO COUNTY. 481

| Name. | Occupation. | Place of Business. | Residence. | Town or P. O. |
|---|---|---|---|---|
| Holcomb, B E | Farmer | nr San Pascual | San Diego Co | San Pascual. |
| Holden, J | Sailor | San Diego Co | San Diego | San Diego. |
| Holden, James | Farmer | San Diego Co | San Diego | San Diego. |
| Hollan, C M | Farmer | nr San Pascual | San Diego Co | San Pascual. |
| Hollister, O B | Miner | San Diego Co | nr Milquatay | Campo. |
| Hollister, D H | U S official | San Diego Co | San Diego | San Diego. |
| Holloway, C | Miller | San Diego Co | San Diego | San Diego. |
| Holloway, H C | Blacksmith | San Diego Co | San Diego | San Diego. |
| Holmes, H | Cook | San Diego Co | San Diego | San Diego. |
| Holm, Julius | Barber | Horton House | San Diego | San Diego. |
| Holmes, Wm | Laborer | San Diego Co | San Diego | San Diego. |
| Homer, S | Cook | San Diego Co | San Diego | San Diego. |
| Hook, J D | Teamster | San Diego | San Diego Co | San Diego. |
| Hooker, J B | Painter | San Diego Co | San Diego | San Diego. |
| Hooker, J B | Printer | San Diego Co | San Diego | San Diego. |
| Hopkins, Louis | Saddler | San Diego | San Diego Co | San Diego. |
| Hopkins, F M | Merchant | San Diego Co | Banner | Banner. |
| Hopkins, L B | Mining engineer | San Diego Co | Banner | Banner. |
| Hopper, J | Merchant | San Diego Co | Warner's Ranch | Warner's Rch. |
| Horan, Thos | Carpenter | San Diego Co | San Diego | San Diego. |
| Horan, Rich'd | Carpenter | San Diego Co | San Diego | San Diego. |
| Horan, W | Carpenter | San Diego Co | San Diego | San Diego. |
| Horgan, T | Plasterer | San Diego Co | San Diego | San Diego. |
| Hornbeck, J A | Farmer | nr San Diego | San Diego Co | San Diego. |
| Horrell, J W | Farmer | nr Agua Caliente | San Diego Co | Warner's Rch. |
| Horsefeldt, John | Butcher | San Diego | San Diego Co | San Diego. |
| Horton, Henry | Cooper | San Diego | San Diego Co | San Diego. |
| Horton, A E | Real estate | cor D and 3d sts | San Diego | San Diego. |
| Hotchkiss, A B | Attorney | San Diego Co | San Diego | San Diego. |
| Howard, M | Printer | San Diego Co | San Pascual | San Pascual. |
| Howell, W C | Apiarian | Temecula Creek | 10 m N San Luis Rey | San Luis Rey. |
| Howland, L L | Produce dealer | San Diego Co | Julian | Julian. |
| Hoyth, H | Apiarian | Temecula Creek | 10 m N San Luis Rey | San Luis Rey. |
| Hubby, H | Carpenter | San Diego Co | Fort Yuma | Fort Yuma. |
| Hubbert, P T | Farmer | San Luis Rey | 45 m N San Diego | San Luis Rey. |
| Hubbert, M | Farmer | San Diego Co | nr Julian | Julian. |
| Hubbell, Charles | Cashier | Bank of San Diego | 6th st, bet G and H | San Diego. |
| Hubbert, M | Farmer | San Luis Rey | 45 m N San Diego | San Luis Rey. |
| Hubling, Geo | Miner | nr Paguay | San Diego Co | Poway. |
| Hubling, H | Farmer | San Diego Co | nr Paguay | Poway. |
| Huborn, F | Farmer | San Diego Co | nr San Diego | San Diego. |
| Hudson, B J | Farmer | nr San Diego | San Diego Co | San Diego. |
| Huffman, J | Miner | San Luis Rey | San Diego Co | San Luis Rey. |
| Huft, Geo | Miner | nr Julian | San Diego Co | Julian. |
| Hughes, W G | Government guide | San Diego Co | San Diego | San Diego. |
| Humphreys, Thos & Son | Plumbers | 5th st | San Diego | San Diego. |
| Humphreys, George | Gas fitter | San Diego | San Diego | San Diego. |
| Humphreys, Thos | Plumber | San Diego | San Diego | San Diego. |
| Hungerford, B B | Miner | nr Julian | San Diego Co | Julian. |
| Hunsaker, N | Sheriff | San Diego Co | San Diego | San Diego. |
| Hunt, T | Laborer | San Diego | nr San Diego | San Diego. |
| Hunter, Jas | Farmer | nr San Diego | San Diego Co | San Diego. |
| Hunter, T T | Teamster | San Diego Co | nr Lawson's Valley | San Diego. |
| Hurlburt, J W | Carpenter | San Diego | nr San Diego | San Diego. |
| Hutchinson, E | Physician | San Diego | San Diego Co | San Diego. |
| Hyde, G | Lawyer | San Diego Co | San Diego Co | San Diego. |
| Hyland, J | Farmer | San Diego Co | nr San Diego | San Diego. |
| Hyland, C J | Farmer | San Diego Co | nr San Diego | San Diego. |
| Ihlstrom, L J | Laborer | nr San Diego | San Diego Co | San Diego. |
| Igams, I C | Miner | San Diego Co | nr Julian | Julian. |
| Iler, G | Blacksmith | San Diego Co | San Diego | San Diego. |
| Inden, J | Laborer | nr San Diego | San Diego Co | San Diego. |
| Ingraham, W | Farmer | nr Pala | San Diego Co | Pala. |

31

| Name. | Occupation. | Place of Business. | Residence. | Town or P. O. |
|---|---|---|---|---|
| Ingram, E............ | Miner............ ....... | San Diego Co........... | nr Monument City... | San Diego. |
| Isagrond, P........... | Merchant............ | San Jacinto... ......... | San Diego Co........... | San Jacinto. |
| Irving, W E........ | Ranchero .. ........... | Paumosa Canyon..... | 9 m E San Luis Rey | San Luis Rey. |
| Irving, W E........ | Ranchero ............ | San Diego Co........... | Monserrate............. | Monserrate. |
| Isidor, L...... ........ | Boot & shoe dealer | 5th st............ ........ | San Diego...... ........ | San Diego. |
| Israel, R D........... | Mariner............... | San Diego Co........... | San Diego........... | San Diego. |
| Ivey, John........... | Farmer ........ ....... | nr Julian.............. | San Diego Co........... | Julian. |
| Jackson, A........... | Farmer ........ ....... | San Diego Co........... | nr San Diego........... | San Diego. |
| Jackson, Geo........ | Farmer ............ | nr Santa Teresa....... | San Diego Co........... | |
| Jackson, J............ | Farmer ............ | San Diego Co........... | nr San Jacinto......... | San Jacinto. |
| Jackson, Thomas... | Farmer ............ | 65 m N E San Diego | Julian............. ........ | Julian. |
| Jacobs, G W......... | Ranchero ............ | nr San Diego........... | San Diego Co........... | San Diego. |
| Jaeger, L J F....... | Merchant............ | San Diego Co........... | Fort Yuma............. | Fort Yuma. |
| James, C A.......... | Farmer ............ | nr Julian.............. | San Diego Co........... | Julian. |
| Jamison, J H S..... | Teacher ............ | San Diego Co........... | San Diego............. | San Diego. |
| Jaramillo, A......... | Farmer ............ | San Diego Co........... | nr San Diego........... | San Diego. |
| Jean, J............... | Butcher............ | San Diego............. | San Diego Co........... | San Diego. |
| Jesse, Henry C...... | Teacher............ | San Diego Co........... | San Diego............. | San Diego. |
| Jewell & McLellan | Painters............ | 6th st............ ........ | San Diego............. | San Diego. |
| Jewell, —........... | Painter ............ | 6th st............ ........ | San Diego............. | San Diego. |
| Johnson, A........... | Farmer ............ | nr Julian.............. | San Diego Co........... | Julian. |
| Johnson, David A.. | Merchant............ | San Diego............. | San Diego Co........... | San Diego. |
| Johnson, Geo........ | Mariner............... | San Diego Co........... | San Diego............. | San Diego. |
| Johnson, Geo A..... | Mariner............... | San Diego Co........... | Penasquitas............. | |
| Johnson, J A........ | Mariner............... | San Diego Co........... | San Diego............. | San Diego. |
| Johnson, James..... | Miller............ ..... | 20 m N W S Diego.. | San Diegnito........... | San Diegnito. |
| Johnson, H C....... | Sea captain........... | San Diego Co........... | San Diego............. | San Diego. |
| Johnson, R....... ..... | Mechanic.. ........... | San Diego Co........... | San Diego............. | San Diego. |
| Johnson, T........... | Farmer ............ | San Diego Co........... | nr Ballena........... ..... | Ballena. |
| Johnson, Uriah...... | Carpenter........... | San Diego Co........... | San Diego............. | San Diego. |
| Johnson, W.......... | Ranchero............ | nr Monserrate......... | San Diego Co........... | Monserrate. |
| Jolly, A P........... | Coach maker...... | San Diego Co........... | San Diego............. | San Diego. |
| Jones, Charles....... | Laborer............ | San Diego Co........... | Ballena............. | Ballena. |
| Jones, B F........... | Hotel keeper......... | San Diego Co........... | Monserrate............. | Monserrate. |
| Jones, E L............ | Farmer ............ | San Diego Co........... | nr San Pascual........ | San Pascual. |
| Jones, J G........... | Hotel keeper......... | San Diego Co........... | San Diego............. | San Diego. |
| Jones, N....... ......... | Farmer............ | nr San Diego. ......... | San Diego Co........... | San Diego. |
| Jones, S A........... | Clerk............ ..... | San Diego Co........... | San Diego............. | San Diego. |
| Jones, T............... | Teamster............ | San Diego Co........... | nr Julian............. | Julian. |
| Jones, T E........... | Book keeper......... | San Diego Co........... | San Diego............. | San Diego. |
| Jones, Wm........... | Builder............ | San Diego Co........... | San Diego............. | San Diego. |
| Jones, W H.......... | Brewer............ | San Diego Co........... | San Diego............. | San Diego. |
| Jordan, Silas Robt.. | Teamster ........... | 65 m N E San Diego | Julian............. ........ | Julian. |
| Jorres, W............ | Carpenter........... | San Diego Co........... | San Diego............. | San Diego. |
| Journey, George.... | Asphiarian.. ........... | San Luis Rey Valley | 5 m E San Luis Rey. | San Luis Rey. |
| Journeay, G......... | Carpenter........... | San Diego Co........... | San Diego............. | San Diego. |
| Josset, J............... | Teacher............ | San Diego Co........... | San Diego............. | San Diego. |
| Judd, Thos A.. .'.... | Clerk............ ..... | San Diego Co........... | San Diego............. | San Diego. |
| Julian, A H.......... | Tinsmith............ | 5th st, bet H and I... | San Diego............. | San Diego. |
| Julian, A W......... | Miner............ ..... | nr Julian.............. | San Diego Co........... | Julian. |
| Julian & Conklin... | San diego world... | 5th st, Express Block | | San Diego. |
| Julian & Stutsman | Stoves & tinware.. | 5th st............ ........ | San Diego............. | San Diego. |
| Kalb, I N............. | Farmer ............ | San Luis Rey........... | 45 m N San Diego... | San Luis Rey. |
| Kalb, W............. | Hatter............ | San Diego Co........... | Green Valley........... | Stonewall. |
| Kampling, B......... | Hostler ............ | San Diego Co........... | San Diego............. | San Diego. |
| Kauffman, Chas T. | Saloon keeper...... | San Diego............. | San Diego Co........... | San Diego. |
| Kearney, J A........ | Grocer............ | San Diego Co........... | San Diego............. | San Diego. |
| Keating, M.......... | Painter ............ | San Diego Co........... | San Diego............. | San Diego. |
| Keiller, J............. | Laborer ............ | nr San Diego. ......... | San Diego Co........... | San Diego. |
| Keith, Alex P....... | Farmer ............ | San Diego Co........... | Ballena............. | Ballena. |
| Keith, H............. | Stage driver......... | San Diego Co........... | San Diego......,...... | San Diego. |
| Kelley, John........ | Hostler............ | San Diego............. | San Diego............. | San Diego. |
| Kelly, J............... | Farmer . ............ | nr Milquatay........... | San Diego Co........... | Campo. |
| Kelly, Jas............ | Miner............ | Julian............. ........ | San Diego Co........... | Julian. |

## DIRECTORY OF SAN DIEGO COUNTY. 483

| Name. | Occupation. | Place of Business. | Residence. | Town or P. O. |
|---|---|---|---|---|
| Kelley, Mat | Farmer | Ague Hodienda | 9 m S San Luis Rey | San Luis Rey. |
| Kelley, M | Blacksmith | San Diego Co | Deadwood | |
| Kelley, Peter | Miner | San Diego Co | Banner City | Banner. |
| Kelly, T | Tailor | San Diego Co | Julian | Julian. |
| Keniston, D | Farmer | San Diego Co | nr San Pascual | San Pascual. |
| Kenkead, W | Farmer | nr San Luis Rey | San Diego Co | San Luis Rey. |
| Kennedy, N | Mariner | San Diego Co | San Diego | San Diego. |
| Kennedy, P | Miner | San Diego Co | nr Banner | Banner. |
| Kennedy, S H | Farmer | nr Temecula | San Diego Co | Temecula. |
| Kennidy, J E | Farmer | nr San Jacinto | San Diego Co | San Jacinto. |
| Kennelly, E | Laborer | San Diego Co | nr San Diego | San Diego. |
| Kenniston, A M | Hotel keeper | San Diego Co | Oak Grove | Oak Gove. |
| Kerens & Mitchell | Proprs stage line | New Mex & Arizona | San Diego | San Diego. |
| Kerens, — | So pacific stage co | San Diego Co | San Diego | San Diego. |
| Kerren, J | Stock raiser | San Diego Co | Paguay | Poway. |
| Kerren, Wm | Ranchero | 20 m N E San Diego | Paguay | Poway. |
| Ketcham, M | Farmer | nr San Luis Rey | San Diego Co | San Luis Rey. |
| Kenppers, H J | Civil engineer | San Diego Co | San Diego | San Diego. |
| Keys, J A | Farmer | nr Milquatay | San Diego Co | Campo. |
| Kibbey, B F | Farmer | San Luis Rey | 45 m N San Diego | San Luis Rey. |
| Killebrew, J W | Farmer | San Diego Co | nr San Diego | San Diego. |
| Killen, H | Farmer | nr San Diego | San Diego Co | San Diego. |
| Kimball, G L | Real estate agent | San Diego Co | National City | National City. |
| Kimball, E N | Carpenter | San Diego Co | San Diego | San Diego. |
| Kimball, F A | Carpenter | National Ranch | San Diego Co | National City. |
| Kimball, Bros | Real estate | National City | San Diego Co | National City. |
| Kimball, L W | Carpenter | San Diego Co | National Ranch | National City. |
| Kimball, W C | Carpenter | San Diego Co | National City | National City. |
| Kincaid, E O | Farmer | San Diego Co | nr San Diego | San Diego. |
| King, D | Teamster | nr San Diego | San Diego Co | San Diego. |
| King, G V | Laborer | San Diego Co | nr San Diego | San Diego. |
| King, G T | | San Diego Co | San Diego | San Diego. |
| King, Geo | Mariner | San Diego Co | San Diego | San Diego. |
| Kingsbury, G | Miner | nr San Diego | San Diego Co | San Diego. |
| Kinon, M | Miner | San Diego Co | nr San Diego | San Diego. |
| Kinterro, A | Ranchero | San Diego Co | nr Monserrate | Monserrate. |
| Kirk, A L | Carpenter | San Diego Co | San Diego | San Diego. |
| Klauber, A | Merchant | San Diego Co | San Diego | San Diego. |
| Kitchen, A C | Farmer | San Luis Rey | 45 m N San Diego | San Luis Rey. |
| Kitterman, A | U S restaurant | 5th st | San Diego | San Diego. |
| Kitterman, H | Farmer | nr San Diego | San Diego Co | San Diego. |
| Knapp, Clark | Boarding house | San Diego Co | Julian | Julian. |
| Kneeland, E J | Ship carpenter | San Diego Co | San Diego | San Diego. |
| Knight, A J | Stage driver | San Diego Co | San Diego | San Diego. |
| Knight & Deaner | Stage proprietors | S D Jul & Banner S L | | San Diego. |
| Knight, Richd Henry | Farmer | San Diego Co | Ballena | Ballena. |
| Knowles, A P | Merchant | San Diego Co | San Diego | San Diego. |
| Knowlton, P | Dentist | San Diego Co | San Diego Co | San Diego. |
| Knox, Amaziah L | Farmer | San Diego | Cajon | San Diego. |
| Kolb, Jonathan | Farmer | San Luis Rey | 45 m N San Diego | San Luis Rey. |
| Kolb, J | Hatter | San Diego Co | Agua Caliente | Warner's Rch. |
| Kolb, James | Fruit stand | San Luis Rey | 45 m N San Diego | San Luis Rey. |
| Kolb, J F | Farmer | nr San Luis Rey | San Diego Co | San Luis Rey. |
| Kolb, I McD | Farmer | nr Agua Caliente | San Diego Co | Warner's Rch. |
| Koop, J H | Baker | 5th st | San Diego | San Diego. |
| Koster, P | Blacksmith | cor F & 4th sts | San Diego | San Diego. |
| Koster, Henry P | Blacksmith | San Diego Co | San Diego | San Diego. |
| Kramer, August | Merchant tailor | Plaza, opp Hort'n Hse | San Diego | San Diego. |
| Krause, E | Merchant | San Diego Co | San Diego | San Diego. |
| Kristeller, P | Shoe maker | San Diego Co | San Diego Co | San Diego. |
| Kuhner, Jacob | Butcher | San Diego | San Diego Co | San Diego. |
| Kurtz, D B | Carpenter | Santa Margarita | 6 m N San Luis Rey | San Luis Rey. |
| Kyle, James | Dyer | San Diego Co | nr San Diego | San Diego. |
| Kyle, S C | Hostler | San Diego Co | San Diego | San Diego. |

| NAME. | OCCUPATION. | PLACE OF BUSINESS. | RESIDENCE. | TOWN OR P. O. |
|---|---|---|---|---|
| Lacy, Wm | Architect | Commercial Bk Bdg | San Diego | San Diego. |
| Ladd, A | Blacksmith | San Diego Co | San Luis Rey | San Luis Rey. |
| Ladd, B J | Farmer | San Diego Co | nr San Luis Rey | San Luis Rey. |
| Lafayette, L T | Teamster | San Diego | San Diego Co | San Diego. |
| Lafon, Wm | Mechanic | San Diego Co | San Diego | San Diego. |
| Laley, W | Mechanic | San Diego Co | Campo | Campo. |
| Lancaster, A W | Farmer | San Diego | San Diego Co | San Diego. |
| Lancaster, Geo M | Farmer | 55 m NW San Diego | Monserrate | Monserrate. |
| Lancaster, J | Farmer | nr Temecula | San Diego Co | Temecula. |
| Lane, Wm | Farmer | 12 m S E San Diego | Monument City | San Diego. |
| Lang, J B | Miner | nr Banner | San Diego Co | Banner. |
| Lankhersheim, I | Flour mill | cor 12th & J sts | San Diego | San Diego. |
| Lamb, D | Farmer | San Diego Co | nr Cajon | San Diego. |
| Lamb, M | Mariner | San Diego Co | San Diego | San Diego. |
| Lambla, A | Restaurant | San Diego Co | San Diego | San Diego. |
| Lamkar, Wm H | Barber | 65 m N E San Diego | Julian | Julian. |
| Larkin, P | Miner | nr Milquatay | San Diego Co | Campo. |
| Larney, Nicholas | Laborer | San Diego Co | San Diego | San Diego. |
| Larsen, T | Wood & coal y'd | 5th st | San Diego | San Diego. |
| Larsen & Westcott | Truckmen | 5th st | San Diego | San Diego. |
| Larson, Peter S | Farmer | San Luis Rey | San Diego Co | San Luis Rey. |
| Larson, Thos | Teamster | nr San Diego | San Diego Co | San Diego. |
| Larson, Thos | Farmer | nr San Diego | San Diego Co | San Diego. |
| Lawrey, A G | Mason | San Diego Co | San Diego Co | San Diego. |
| Lawrey, Frank E | Clerk | San Diego | San Diego Co | San Diego. |
| Lawler, P Henry | Carpenter | San Diego Co | Cajon | San Diego. |
| Lawrence, A | Farmer | nr Milquatay | San Diego Co | Campo. |
| Lawrence, E | Farmer | nr Milquatay | San Diego Co | Campo. |
| Lawrence, F S | Agt W F & Co | 5th st | San Diego | San Diego. |
| Lawson, J | Farmer | San Diego Co | nr Lawson's Valley | San Diego. |
| Lawson, J J | Blacksmith | San Diego Co | Julian | Julian. |
| Leach, Wallace | Attorney | San Diego | San Diego Co | San Diego. |
| Leamy, J W | Porter | San Diego Co | San Diego | San Diego. |
| Leary, E A | Gardener | San Diego Co | San Diego | San Diego. |
| Le Brun, C | Miner | San Diego Co | San Diego | San Diego. |
| Leclaire, A H | Farmer | San Diego Co | Paguay | Poway. |
| Lee, A N | Miner | nr San Diego | San Diego Co | San Diego. |
| Lee, J A C | Clerk | San Diego Co | San Diego | San Diego. |
| Lehman, T | Merchant tailor | 5th st | San Diego | San Diego. |
| Lemon, Alex D | Lawyer | 4 m S San Diego | National City | National City. |
| Lent, W H | Farmer | San Diego Co | nr San Diego | San Diego. |
| Leonard, Jas | Painter | cor 2d and D sts | San Diego | San Diego. |
| Leppert, August | Farmer | 35 m N San Diego | Bear Valley | San Pascual. |
| Leslie, R | Merchant | San Diego Co | Julian | Julian. |
| Levet, J B | Carpenter | cor J and 8th sts | San Diego | San Diego. |
| Levi, Simon | Merchant | 65 m N E San Diego | Temecula | Temecula. |
| Lewelyn, W | Merchant | San Diego Co | San Diego | San Diego. |
| Leyton, F | Miner | San Diego Co | San Diego Co | San Diego. |
| Libby, B P | Farmer | nr San Luis Rey | San Diego Co | San Luis Rey. |
| Libby, E W | Farmer | San Luis Rey | 45 m N San Diego | San Luis Rey. |
| Libby, W E | Farmer | nr San Luis Rey | San Diego Co | San Luis Rey. |
| Libbey, W H | Farmer | San Luis Rey | 45 m N San Diego | San Luis Rey. |
| Likins, Joseph | Surveyor | San Diego | San Diego Co | San Diego. |
| Linley, James R | Physician | San Diego | San Diego Co | San Diego. |
| Lithgow, A | Farmer | nr San Diego | San Diego Co | San Diego. |
| Little, J O | Merchant | San Diego Co | San Diego | San Diego. |
| Little, J McD | Gardener | San Diego Co | San Diego | San Diego. |
| Little, W S | Lumberman | San Diego | San Diego Co | San Diego. |
| Littlefield, J A | Laborer | San Diego | San Diego Co | San Diego. |
| Littlepage, Louis Wright | Farmer | San Diego Co | Ballena | Ballena. |
| Littlepage, W C | Farmer | San Diego Co | nr Santa Teresa Sprg | |
| Littlepage, W W | Farmer | San Diego Co | nr Blackhouse Spr'g | |
| Livingston, J B | Farmer | San Diego Co | Sweet water | San Diego. |

DIRECTORY OF SAN DIEGO COUNTY. 485

| Name. | Occupation. | Place of Business. | Residence. | Town or P. O. |
|---|---|---|---|---|
| Llewelyn, D | Engineer | San Diego Co | San Diego | San Diego. |
| Lloyd, J | Blacksmith | San Diego Co | San Diego | San Diego. |
| **Lloyd, J S** | Engineer | San Diego Co | Julian | Julian. |
| Lloyd, W | Teamster | San Diego Co | nr San Diegnito | San Diegnito. |
| Llucia, Vincent | Baker | San Diego | San Diego Co | San Diego. |
| Locke, E G | Gen merchandise | San Luis Rey | 45 m N San Diego | San Luis Rey. |
| Locke, Joseph A | Civil engineer | San Diego | San Diego Co | San Diego. |
| **Locke & Wallace** | Gen merchandise | San Luis Rey | 45 m N San Diego | San Luis Rey. |
| Lockhart, B F | Merchant | San Diego Co | Warner's Ranch | Warner's Rch. |
| Lockling, L L | Civil engineer | cor 6th & E sts | San Diego | San Diego. |
| Logan, T | Hotel keeper | San Diego Co | San Diego | San Diego. |
| **Logan, Wm** | Farmer | San Luis Rey | San Diego Co | San Luis Rey. |
| Long, G W | Farmer | San Diego Co | nr San Diego | San Diego. |
| Long, Patrick | Miner | San Diego | San Diego Co | San Diego. |
| **Lopez, Dolores** | Laborer | Guajoma | 4 m E San Luis Rey | San Luis Rey. |
| Lopez, A | Ranchero | nr San Diego | San Diego Co | San Diego. |
| Lopez, F | Ranchero | nr San Diego | San Diego Co | San Diego. |
| Lopez, Jesus | Farmer | San Diego Co | nr Temecula | Temecula. |
| Lopez, Jose | Farmer | 70 m N E San Diego | Monserrate | Monserrate. |
| **Lopez, Jose** | Farmer | San Diego Co | San Diego | San Diego. |
| Lopez, J D | Ranchero | nr San Diego | San Diego Co | San Diego. |
| Lopez, L | Ranchero | San Diego Co | San Diego | San Diego. |
| Lopez, Miguel | Laborer | 35 m E San Diego | Valle de las Viejas | Viejas. |
| **Lopez, R** | Farmer | nr San Diego | San Diego Co | San Diego. |
| Lopez, Victor | Laborer | 70 m N E San Diego | Green Valley | Stonewall. |
| Lopez, Ygnacio | Ranchero | nr San Diego | San Diego Co | San Diego. |
| Lopez, Ygnacio | Laborer | San Diego Co | nr San Diego | San Diego. |
| Louis, Isidor | Shoe maker | San Diego Co | San Diego | San Diego. |
| Louis, M A | Miner | nr Banner | San Diego Co | Banner. |
| Love, J | Farmer | nr San Diego | San Diego Co | San Diego. |
| Loveland, H S | Miner | nr Julian | San Diego Co | Julian. |
| **Lovell, F B** | Briant's feed yard | cor 9th and I sts | San Diego | San Diego. |
| Lovett, J M | Millwright | San Diego Co | San Pascual | San Pascual. |
| Lowdine, W H | Cook | San Diego Co | San Diego | San Diego. |
| Lowell, F B | Teamster | San Diego Co | nr San Diego | San Diego. |
| **Lowenstein & Co** | Variety store | 5th st | San Diego | San Diego. |
| Lowenstein, E | Merchant | San Diego Co | San Diego | San Diego. |
| Lowenstein, H | Merchant | San Diego Co | San Diego | San Diego. |
| Lowenstein, Max | Merchant | San Diego Co | San Diego Co | San Diego. |
| Luce, Moses A | Attorney | San Diego | San Diego Co | San Diego. |
| **Luce & Porter** | Attorney | Commercial Bnk Blg | San Diego | San Diego. |
| Luckett, A T | Farmer | San Diego Co | nr Bolcan | |
| Luckett, A W | Merchant | San Diego Co | Green Valley | Stonewall. |
| Lugo, David | Farmer | San Diego Co | Ballena | Ballena. |
| Lugan, E | Cook | San Diego Co | San Diego | San Diego. |
| Lusero, J D | Vaquero | nr Julian | San Diego Co | Julian. |
| **Lush, T** | Bar keeper | San Diego Co | San Diego | San Diego. |
| Lynch, P | Laborer | nr San Diego | San Diego | San Diego. |
| Lynch, T | Laborer | San Diego Co | San Diego | San Diego. |
| Lynch, Thos | Laundryman | San Diego | San Diego Co | San Diego. |
| **Lyon, J J** | Searcher of rec'ds | 5th st | San Diego | San Diego. |
| Lyon, W C | Clerk | San Diego | San Diego Co | San Diego. |
| Lyons, G | Mechanic | San Diego Co | San Diego | San Diego. |
| Lyons, W | Blacksmith | San Diego Co | San Diego | San Diego. |
| **Lyons, J B** | Manager | Lyon House | San Diego | San Diego. |
| Lyons, J B | Farmer | San Diego Co | National City | National City. |
| Lyon, Isaac S | Carpenter | San Diego Co | San Diego | San Diego. |
| **Maybury, Hiram** | Capitalist | San Diego | San Diego Co | San Diego. |
| Maybury, S H | Farmer | San Diego Co | Township 9 | |
| Mace, R W | Miner | San Diego Co | nr Julian | Julian. |
| Machado, Jesus | Ranchero | Milpitas | 4 m E San Luis Rey | San Luis Rey. |
| McAlmond, C J | Mariner | San Diego Co | Milquatay | Campo. |
| McArthur, Peter | Clerk | San Diego | San Diego Co | San Diego. |
| McAuley, J | Farmer | nr Spring Valley | San Diego Co | San Diego. |

| Name. | Occupation. | Place of Business. | Residence. | Town or P. O. |
|---|---|---|---|---|
| McAuliffe, T F | Farmer | San Diego Co | nr San Diego | San Diego. |
| McCabe, J | Clerk | San Diego Co | San Diego | San Diego. |
| McCain, Geo | Farmer | San Diego Co | nr Milquatay | Campo. |
| McCain, John | Farmer | nr San Luis Rey | San Diego Co | San Luis Rey. |
| McCain, John | Farmer | San Diego Co | nr Walker's | |
| McCane, L | Farmer | nr Long Valley | San Diego Co | |
| McCain, Wm | Farmer | San Diego Co | San Bernardo | Bernardo. |
| McCann, John | Shoe maker | San Diego | San Diego Co | San Diego. |
| McCarthy, D O'C | Publisher | San Diego Co | San Diego | San Diego. |
| McCarthy, M J | Saloon keeper | San Diego Co | San Diego | San Diego. |
| McClain, John | Farmer | San Diego Co | nr San Diego | San Diego. |
| McClain, J W | Farmer | nr San Diego | San Diego Co | San Diego. |
| McCoy, John | Farmer | San Diego Co | nr Agua Caliente | Warner's Rch. |
| McCoy, Jas | Sheriff | San Diego Co | San Diego | San Diego. |
| McCormick, M C | Blacksmith | San Diego Co | San Diego | San Diego. |
| McCormick, W J | Merchant | San Diego Co | San Diego | San Diego. |
| McCrellish, A | Miner | San Diego Co | nr San Diego | San Diego. |
| McDaniel, E | Miner | San Diego Co | nr Julian | Julian. |
| McDonald & Co | Forwarding mchs | cor 6th & K sts | San Diego | San Diego. |
| McDonald, A | Wheelwright | San Diego Co | Milquatay | Campo. |
| McDonald, D | Laborer | San Diego Co | nr San Diego | San Diego. |
| McDonald, G W B | Stair builder | San Diego Co | San Diego | San Diego. |
| McDonald, H W | Seaman | San Diego Co | San Diego | San Diego. |
| McDonald, James | Mariner | San Diego Co | San Diego Co | San Diego. |
| McDonald, John | Farmer | San Diego Co | nr San Diego | San Diego. |
| McDonald, Michael | Laborer | San Diego Co | San Diego Co | San Diego. |
| McDowell, J | Farmer | San Diego Co | nr Mohave | |
| McDowell, Saml A | Miner | San Diego Co | Banner City | Banner. |
| McFarland, D F | Minister | San Diego | San Diego Co | San Diego. |
| McFarland, J R | Miner | San Diego Co | nr Sweetwater | |
| McGee, Wm | Farmer | nr Ballena | San Diego Co | Ballena. |
| McGonigle, D | Farmer | San Diego Co | nr San Diegnito | San Diegnito. |
| McGonigle, F | Farmer | nr Paguay | San Diego Co | Poway. |
| McGrath, Wm H | Tinner | San Diego | San Diego Co | San Diego. |
| McGregor, J | Carpenter | San Diego Co | Julian | Julian. |
| McGregor, W | Farmer | nr Julian | San Diego Co | Julian. |
| McGinness, James | Laborer | San Diego | San Diego Co | San Diego. |
| McGurck, E | Farmer | San Diego Co | nr San Diego | San Diego. |
| McHenry, W W | Farmer | nr Monument City | San Diego Co | San Diego. |
| McIntosh, D | Farmer | nr Ballena | San Diego Co | Ballena. |
| McIntosh, F | Boot & shoe dealer | Plaza | San Diego | San Diego. |
| McIntosh, F J | Shoe maker | San Diego Co | San Diego | San Diego. |
| McIntosh, J | Laborer | nr Milquatay | San Diego Co | Campo. |
| McIntyre, J L | County assessor | San Diego Co | San Diego | San Diego. |
| McKay, M | Miner | nr Banner | San Diego Co | Banner. |
| McKee, Wm F | Clerk | San Diego | San Diego Co | San Diego. |
| McKean, A B | Merchant | San Diego Co | Julian | Julian. |
| McKeane, G J | Laborer | San Diego Co | nr San Diego | San Diego. |
| McKellar, E | Hostler | San Diego Co | San Luis Rey | San Luis Rey. |
| McKenna, J | Laborer | San Diego Co | nr San Luis Rey | San Luis Rey. |
| McKinstry, G, Jr | Physician | San Diego Co | nr San Diego | San Diego. |
| McKnight, Henderson | Farmer | 70 m N E San Diego | Banner | Banner. |
| McLaren, J | Farmer | nr San Diego | San Diego Co | San Diego. |
| McLaughlin, D | Lather | San Diego Co | San Diego | San Diego. |
| McLaughlin, Wm | Miner | San Diego Co | San Diego Co | San Diego. |
| McLeavy, Thos | Grocer | 5th st | San Diego | San Diego. |
| McLellan, C R | Painter | 6th st | San Diego | San Diego. |
| McLellan, W S | Clerk | San Diego Co | San Diego | San Diego. |
| McLervy, J B | Laborer | San Diego Co | nr San Diego | San Diego. |
| McMellan, T | Farmer | nr Bolcan | San Diego Co | |
| McNealy, W T | Lawyer | San Diego Co | San Diego | San Diego. |
| McNeil, John | Teamster | San Diego | San Diego Co | San Diego. |
| McPherson, A W | Stage driver | San Diego Co | San Diego | San Diego. |

## DIRECTORY OF SAN DIEGO COUNTY.

| NAME. | OCCUPATION. | PLACE OF BUSINESS. | RESIDENCE. | TOWN OR P. O. |
|---|---|---|---|---|
| Morrillo, Eduardo.. | Laborer............ | San Diego Co......... | Agua Caliente......... | Warner's Rch. |
| Morrillo, A......... | Laborer............ | nr Santa Margarita... | San Diego Co......... | San Luis Rey. |
| Morine, Albert ...... | Moulder ........... | San Diego ............ | San Diego Co......... | San Diego. |
| Morron, J M........ | Ranchero........... | Buena Vista Ranch.. | 4 m S San Luis Rey | San Luis Rey. |
| Morron, S ......... | Ranchero .......... | Buena Vista Ranch.. | 4 m S San Luis Rey | San Luis Rey. |
| **Morrow, Richd**..... | Farmer ............ | San Diego Co......... | nr San Diego ......... | San Diego. |
| Morrow, Jos......... | Farmer ............ | nr San Luis Rey..... | San Diego Co......... | San Luis Rey. |
| Morse, C H......... | Carpenter.......... | San Diego Co......... | San Diego............. | San Diego. |
| **Morse, E W & Co**... | Carriages ......... | 6th st................ | San Diego............. | San Diego. |
| Morse, P........... | Clerk.............. | San Diego Co......... | San Diego............. | San Diego. |
| Mowsee, Danl P..... | Farmer ............ | San Diego Co......... | Ballena............... | Ballena. |
| Mulheron, M........ | Miner.............. | nr Banner........... | San Diego Co......... | Banner. |
| Mulkins, J W....... | Ranchero........... | San Diego Co......... | nr Green Valley ..... | Stonewall. |
| Mumford, J V ...... | Cutter............. | San Diego Co......... | San Diego Co......... | San Diego. |
| **Mund, S**............ | Merchant........... | San Diego Co......... | San Luis Rey......... | San Luis Rey. |
| Munge, N........... | Ranchero........... | San Diego Co......... | nr Temecula.......... | Temecula. |
| **Murdoch, H M**...... | Builder............ | San Diego Co......... | San Diego Co......... | San Diego. |
| Murphy, C.......... | Miner.............. | nr Banner........... | San Diego Co......... | Banner. |
| Murphy, Chas P..... | Moulder............ | San Diego............ | San Diego Co......... | San Diego. |
| **Murphy, F**.......... | Miner.............. | nr Julian........... | San Diego Co......... | Julian. |
| Murphy, John....... | Farmer ............ | San Diego ........... | San Diego Co,........ | San Diego. |
| Murphy, John....... | Laborer............ | nr San Diego ....... | San Diego Co......... | San Diego. |
| Murphy, Wm J..... | Waiter............. | San Diego Co......... | San Diego Co......... | San Diego. |
| Murray, J........... | Farmer ............ | nr San Diego ....... | San Diego Co......... | San Diego. |
| **Murray, J W**........ | Carpenter ......... | San Diego Co......... | Banner ............... | Banner. |
| Mussey, Albert W.. | Farmer ............ | San Diego Co......... | Cajon ................ | San Diego. |
| Myers, J............ | Farmer ............ | San Diego Co......... | nr Cajon............. | San Diego. |
| **Myers, J B**......... | Wood turner....... | San Diego Co......... | Cajon................. | San Diego. |
| Nairez, J M......... | Farmer ............ | nr San Luis Rey..... | San Diego Co......... | San Luis Rey. |
| Nash, Arthur H .... | Apiarian........... | San Diego ........... | San Diego Co......... | San Diego. |
| **Nash, F L**.......... | Clergyman.......... | San Diego Co......... | San Diego............ | San Diego. |
| Nash, J ............ | Gen merchandise. | cor 5th & J sts...... | San Diego Co......... | San Diego. |
| Natty, James ....... | Hatter ............. | San Diego ........... | San Diego Co......... | San Diego. |
| Navarro, E......... | Farmer ............ | San Diego Co......... | nr Pala.............. | Pala. |
| **Navarro, Jacinto** .. | Ranchero........... | San Luis Rey........ | 45 m N San Diego... | San Luis Rey. |
| Neal, Chas......... | Sailor ............. | San Diego ........... | San Diego Co......... | San Diego. |
| Neil, Chas.......... | Saloon ............. | San Diego............ | San Diego Co......... | San Diego. |
| **Neff, B F**........... | Sheep raiser....... | Sickman's Canyon... | 9 m N San Luis Rey | San Luis Rey. |
| Nelson, D W........ | Laborer............ | nr Jamul............ | San Diego Co. ....... | San Diego. |
| Nelson, D .......... | Laborer............ | San Diego Co......... | nr San Jacinto....... | San Jacinto. |
| **Nelson, N**........... | Cigars.............. | cor 5th & D sts...... | San Diego Co......... | San Diego. |
| Nelson, S .......... | Miner.............. | nr Green Valley .... | San Diego Co......... | Stonewall. |
| **Nesmith, L G**....... | Banker............. | San Diego............ | San Diego Co......... | San Diego. |
| **Nesmith, T L**....... | President........... | Bank of San Diego... | 6th st................ | San Diego. |
| Nevarro, J......... | Farmer............. | nr San Luis Rey..... | San Diego Co......... | San Luis Rey. |
| Nickels, Chas ...... | Stage driver........ | San Diego Co......... | Indian Wells ........ | Fort Yuma. |
| Niles, J M.......... | Mariner............ | San Diego Co......... | San Diego Co......... | San Diego. |
| Noble, John ........ | Farmer ............ | San Diego Co......... | San Bernardo........ | Bernardo. |
| Nobles, John........ | Teamster........... | San Diego Co......... | nr San Diego......... | San Diego. |
| Necochee, de J M... | Farmer. ........... | San Diego Co......... | San Jacinto.......... | San Jacinto. |
| **Noell, Chas P**....... | Merchant .......... | San Diego ........... | San Diego Co......... | San Diego. |
| Noonan, Daniel...... | Farmer. ........... | San Diego............ | Otay.................. | San Diego. |
| Normand, Alex...... | Shoe maker......... | San Diego Co......... | San Diego Co......... | San Diego. |
| Norris, W........... | Laborer............ | San Diego Co......... | San Diego ........... | San Diego. |
| Norris, W B ........ | Bag maker ......... | San Diego Co......... | San Diego ........... | San Diego. |
| North, J B.......... | Mariner............ | San Diego Co......... | San Diego ........... | San Diego. |
| Norton, Andrew A.. | Farmer ............ | San Diego Co......... | Bear Valley.......... | San Pascual. |
| **Norton, George M**.. | Salesman........... | San Diego Co......... | Julian City.......... | Julian. |
| Norton, W.......... | Cabinet maker ... | San Diego Co......... | San Diego ........... | San Diego. |
| Noyes, Alfred....... | Apiarian........... | San Diego Co......... | Tia Juana............ | San Diego. |
| **Nugent, Joseph L**.. | Genl merchant ... | San Diego Co......... | Bernardo............. | Bernardo. |
| Nunes, J ........... | Sheep herder....... | nr San Jacinto....... | San Diego Co......... | San Jacinto. |
| Oakes, G C ........ | Engineer........... | San Diego Co......... | San Diego ........... | San Diego. |
| Ober, W............ | Blacksmith......... | San Diego Co......... | San Diego ........... | San Diego. |

32

490  L. L PAULSON'S HAND-BOOK AND

| Name. | Occupation. | Place of Business. | Residence. | Town or P. O |
|---|---|---|---|---|
| O'Brien, D... | Miner... | nr San Pascual... | San Diego Co... | San Pascual. |
| O'Brien, J... | Laborer... | San Diego Co... | nr San Diego... | San Diego. |
| O'Brien, W... | Miner... | San Diego Co... | nr Julian... | Julian. |
| O'Campo, Francisco... | Ranchero... | San Luis Rey... | San Diego Co... | San Luis Rey. |
| O'Campo, Louis... | Farmer... | Santa Margarita... | 8 m N San Luis Rey.. | San Luis Rey. |
| O'Campo, Luis... | Farmer... | San Luis Rey... | San Diego Co... | San Luis Rey. |
| O'Connell, Dennis.. | Laborer... | San Diego... | San Diego Co... | San Diego. |
| O'Connell, D... | Farmer... | nr Paguay... | San Diego Co... | Poway. |
| O'Connor, D... | Miner... | nr Julian... | San Diego Co... | Julian. |
| O'Conor, Jas... | Laborer... | San Diego Co... | nr San Diego... | San Diego. |
| O'Conner, J J... | Porter... | San Diego Co... | San Diego... | San Diego. |
| Odel, C... | Miner... | nr Green Valley... | San Diego Co... | Stonewall. |
| O'Donahue, J... | Saloon keeper... | San Diego Co... | San Diego... | San Diego. |
| O'Donnell, B... | Laborer... | San Diego Co... | nr Julian... | Julian. |
| Ogden, W H... | Lawyer... | San Diego Co... | San Diego... | San Diego. |
| Olmstead, L... | Carpenter... | San Diego Co... | San Diego... | San Diego. |
| Olivera, J... | Farmer... | San Diego Co... | nr Temecula... | Temecula. |
| Olres, Jose... | Laborer... | Santa Margarita... | 6 m N San Luis Rey.. | San Luis Rey. |
| O'Meara, Edwd... | Mariner... | San Diego... | San Diego Co... | San Diego. |
| O'Neill, Henry... | Laborer... | San Diego... | San Diego Co... | San Diego. |
| O'Neill, H... | Mason... | San Diego Co... | San Diego... | San Diego. |
| O'Neil, P... | Farmer... | San Diego Co... | nr San Diego... | San Diego. |
| Opitz, J R... | Cigar store... | San Diego... | San Diego... | San Diego. |
| Ormed, H... | Paver... | San Diego... | San Diego Co... | San Diego. |
| Ormsbe, E... | Teamster... | San Luis Rey Valley | 5 m E San Luis Rey | San Luis Rey. |
| Ormsby, M E... | Farmer... | San Diego Co... | nr San Luis Rey... | San Luis Rey. |
| Ormsby, W W... | Saddler... | San Diego Co... | San Diego... | San Diego. |
| Orosco, A... | Ranchero... | nr San Pascual... | San Diego Co... | San Pascual. |
| Orr, James... | Laborer... | San Diego Co... | Green Valley... | Stonewall. |
| Ortega, F... | Laborer... | San Diego Co... | nr San Diego... | San Diego. |
| Ortega, J... | Ranchero... | San Diego Co... | nr Ecinitos... | |
| Ortega, Juan A... | Farmer... | San Diego Co... | Monserrate... | Monserrate. |
| Ortego, J... | Farmer... | San Diego Co... | nr San Diego... | San Diego. |
| Ortego, Jesus... | Sheep raiser... | Guajoma... | 4 m E San Luis Rey | San Luis Rey. |
| Orton, R J... | Farmer... | nr San Diego... | San Diego Co... | San Diego. |
| Osborn, E... | Farmer... | nr Pala... | San Diego Co... | Pala. |
| Osterloh, J... | Confectioner... | San Diego Co... | San Diego... | San Diego. |
| Osterhoudt, M S... | Solicitor... | San Diego Co... | Julian... | Julian. |
| O'Sullivan, Jeremiah... | Miner... | San Diego... | San Diego Co... | San Diego. |
| Osuna, D... | Ranchero... | nr San Diegnito... | San Diego Co... | San Diegnito. |
| Osuna, Juan... | Ranchero... | nr San Diegnito... | San Diego Co... | San Diegnito. |
| Osuna, Julio... | Ranchero... | nr San Diego... | San Diego Co... | San Diego. |
| Osuna, J D... | Ranchero... | nr San Pascual... | San Diego Co... | San Pascual. |
| Osuna, L... | Ranchero... | nr San Diegnito... | San Diego Co... | San Diegnito. |
| Osuna, R... | Ranchero... | San Diego Co... | nr San Pascual... | San Pascual. |
| Overbaugh, Allen... | Farmer... | San Diego... | San Diego Co... | San Diego. |
| Overmier, N... | Farmer... | nr San Pascual... | San Diego Co... | San Pascual. |
| Overmier, N... | Livery stable... | San Diego Co... | San Diego... | San Diego. |
| Owens, A J... | Brick layer... | San Diego Co... | San Diego... | San Diego. |
| Owens, B... | Miner... | San Diego Co... | nr Julian... | Julian. |
| Owens, J S... | Stock raiser... | San Diego Co... | nr San Jacinto... | San Jacinto. |
| Owings, Chas S... | Ranchero... | San Diego Co... | San Diego Co... | San Diego. |
| Packard, A... | Sailor... | San Diego Co... | San Diego... | San Diego. |
| Packar, J... | Cook... | San Diego Co... | San Diego... | San Diego. |
| Packard, P W... | Sailor... | San Diego Co... | San Diego... | San Diego. |
| Paine, C... | Farmer... | San Diego Co... | nr Paguay... | Poway. |
| Paine, H A... | Mechanic... | San Diego... | San Diego Co... | San Diego. |
| Palero, John... | Miner... | San Diego... | San Diego Co... | San Diego. |
| Palmer, O... | Miner... | San Diego Co... | nr San Diego... | San Diego. |
| Pardee, R S... | Farmer... | San Diego Co... | nr San Diego... | San Diego. |
| Parker, Benj Clarke... | Capitalist... | San Diego... | San Diego... | San Diego. |

## DIRECTORY OF SAN DIEGO COUNTY. 491

| Name. | Occupation. | Place of Business. | Residence. | Town or P. O. |
|---|---|---|---|---|
| Parker & Parker | Photographers | Foot of 6th st | San Diego Co. | San Diego. |
| Parker, Edwin | Miner | San Diego | San Diego Co. | San Diego. |
| Parker, Wm E | Druggist | San Diego | San Diego Co. | San Diego. |
| Parker, J C | Photographer | San Diego Co. | San Diego | San Diego. |
| **Park, Chas M** | Farmer | San Diego | San Diego Co. | San Diego. |
| Parks, D A | Farmer | San Diego Co. | Aguango | |
| Parra, A | Vaquero | nr Temecula | San Diego Co. | Temecula. |
| Parsons, B F | Blacksmith | San Diego Co. | San Diego | San Diego. |
| **Parsons, J O** | Farmer | San Diego Co. | nr Spring Valley | San Diego. |
| Parsons, J P | Miner | nr Julian | San Diego Co. | Julian. |
| Parsons, Jas | Hatter | San Diego Co. | San Diego | San Diego. |
| Parsons, T | Farmer | nr San Diego | San Diego Co. | San Diego. |
| Pascoe, James | Engineer | San Diego | San Diego Co. | San Diego. |
| Patrick, M S | | San Diego Co. | San Diego | San Diego. |
| Patterson, Henry W | Acrobat | San Diego | San Diego Co. | San Diego. |
| **Patton, John J** | Printer | San Diego Co. | San Diego | San Diego. |
| Paty, Henry Lee | Carpenter | San Diego | San Diego Co. | San Diego. |
| **Pauly, A & Sons** | Merchants | Horton House Plaza | San Diego | San Diego. |
| Pauly, A | Merchant | San Diego Co. | San Diego | San Diego. |
| Pauly, C W | Merchant | San Diego Co. | San Diego | San Diego. |
| Pauly, F N | Merchant | San Diego Co. | San Diego | San Diego. |
| **Pearson, M F** | Farmer | San Diego Co. | nr San Diego | San Diego. |
| Peck, E D | Miner | San Diego Co. | nr San Diego | San Diego. |
| Pedrovena, M | Ranchero | San Diego Co. | nr San Diego | San Diego. |
| Penio, L | Ranchero | San Diego Co. | nr Los Flores | |
| Perez, D | Vaquero | nr San Jacinto | San Diego Co. | San Jacinto. |
| Perez, J | Laborer | San Diego Co. | nr San Diego | San Diego. |
| **Perigo, W** | Cabinet maker | San Diego Co. | San Diego | San Diego. |
| Perin, M | Mechanic | San Diego Co. | San Diego | San Diego. |
| Peris, E | Vaquero | nr Guajome | San Diego Co. | San Luis Rey. |
| Peris, J | Vaquero | San Diego Co. | nr Guajome | San Luis Rey. |
| Perkins, Hiram | Miner | San Diego Co. | Banner City | Banner. |
| Perkins J P | Plasterer | San Diego Co. | San Diego | San Diego. |
| Perry, J F | Mariner | San Diego Co. | San Diego | San Diego. |
| **Perry, Robt D** | Farmer | San Diego Co. | San Diego | San Diego. |
| Peterson, Francis L | Farmer | San Diego Co. | San Diegnito | San Diegnito. |
| Peterson, James C | Farmer | San Diego Co. | San Diegnito | San Diegnito. |
| Peterson, L S | Seaman | San Diego Co. | San Diego | San Diego. |
| Peterson, Peter | Teamster | San Diego Co. | San Diego | San Diego. |
| **Peterson, R C** | Farmer | nr San Jacinto | San Diego Co. | San Jacinto. |
| Petty, J N | Steward | San Diego Co. | San Diego | San Diego. |
| **Phelan, John** | Ranchero | San Diego Co. | San Jacinto | San Jacinto. |
| Phelps, E C | Farmer | San Diego Co. | nr Spencer Valley | |
| Phillips, C R | Miner | San Diego Co. | nr San Diego | San Diego. |
| **Phillips, D T** | City attorney | 5th st | San Diego | San Diego. |
| **Phipps, George** | Farmer | San Diego Co. | San Diego | San Diego. |
| Piazza, Felippe | Farmer | San Diego Co. | Monument | San Diego. |
| Pico, Juan de la C | Farmer | San Diego Co. | nr Santa Margarita | San Luis Rey. |
| Pico, J M | Farmer | nr Santa Margarita | San Diego Co. | San Luis Rey. |
| Pico, Jose Antonio | Farmer | San Diego Co. | nr Santa Margarita | San Luis Rey. |
| Pico J de la C | Ranchero | nr San Jacinto | San Diego Co. | San Jacinto. |
| Pico, Jose A | Ranchero | San Diego Co. | nr San Jacinto | San Jacinto. |
| Pico, Pio, Jr | Farmer | San Diego Co. | San Jacinto | San Jacinto. |
| Pido, B | Farmer | nr Soledad | San Diego Co. | San Diegnito. |
| Pierce, C C | Miner | San Diego Co. | San Diego Co. | San Diego. |
| **Pierce, J M** | Farmer | San Diego Co. | nr San Diego | San Diego. |
| **Pierce, O** | Manufacturer | San Diego Co. | San Diego | San Diego. |
| Pierce, W W | Carriage maker | San Diego Co. | San Diego | San Diego. |
| Pierson, E | Farmer | San Diego Co. | nr San Diego | San Diego. |
| Pike, Moses D | Laborer | San Diego Co. | San Diego | San Diego. |
| Piley, H | Butcher | San Diego Co. | Monument | San Diego. |
| **Pino, L** | Ranchero | nr San Jacinto | San Diego Co. | San Jacinto. |
| Pittman, J H | Blacksmith | San Diego Co. | San Diego | San Diego. |
| Place, J | Farmer | nr Green Valley | San Diego Co. | Stonewall. |

| Name. | Occupation. | Place of Business. | Residence. | Town or P. O. |
|---|---|---|---|---|
| Plaisted, L H | Printer | San Diego Co. | San Diego | San Diego. |
| Podesto, G | Merchant | San Diego Co. | San Diego | San Diego. |
| Pohe, C | Blacksmith | San Diego Co. | San Diego | San Diego. |
| Polhemus, Jacob | Carpenter | San Diego Co. | San Diego | San Diego. |
| Pompa, Julian | Laborer | San Diego Co. | San Diego | San Diego. |
| Pond, J P | Laborer | San Diego Co. | Escondido | |
| Pond, J P | Miner | nr San Pascual | San Diego Co. | San Pascual. |
| Pope, Wm J | Farmer | San Diego Co. | Bear Valley | San Pascual. |
| Porter, — | Attorney | Commercial Bnk Blg | San Diego | San Diego. |
| Porter, J R | Painter | San Diego Co. | San Diego | San Diego. |
| Porter, R K | Farmer | nr San Diego | San Diego Co. | San Diego. |
| Portillo, J | Ranchero | San Diego Co. | nr San Felipe | San Diego. |
| Portman, Joseph | Miner | San Diego Co. | San Diego | San Diego. |
| Post, L | Physician | San Diego Co. | San Diego | San Diego. |
| Potter, M H | Sheep raiser | Agua Hodienda | 8 m S San Luis Rey | San Luis Rey. |
| Potter, S L R | Farmer | nr San Diego | San Diego Co. | San Diego. |
| Posnausky, N | Tailor | San Diego Co | San Diego | San Diego. |
| Powell, C S | Farmer | San Diego Co. | nr Milquatay | Campo. |
| Powell, J L | Farmer | nr Buena Vista | San Diego Co. | San Luis Rey. |
| Powell, James N | Miner | San Diego Co. | Julian City | Julian. |
| Powers, A R | Miner | nr Green Valley | San Diego Co. | Stonewall. |
| Powers, J L | Farmer | nr Monument City | San Diego Co. | San Diego. |
| Powers, O P | Miner | nr Julian | San Diego Co. | Julian. |
| Preston, P | Carpenter | San Diego Co. | Julian | Julian. |
| Price, D K | Farmer | San Diego Co. | nr Milquatay | Campo. |
| Price, Martin M | Teamster | San Diego Co. | nr San Diego | San Diego. |
| Price, Wm M | Farmer | San Diego | San Diego Co. | San Diego. |
| Price, R | Cabinet maker | San Diego Co. | San Diego | San Diego. |
| Price, W C | Mariner | San Diego Co. | Monument City | San Diego. |
| Puntney, J C | Miner | San Diego Co. | nr Banner | Banner. |
| Purdy, G | Mariner | San Diego Co. | San Diego | San Diego. |
| Putman, M D | Farmer | San Diego Co. | nr Julian | Julian. |
| Pyburn, W | Farmer | nr Milquatay | San Diego Co. | Campo. |
| Quackenbush, J L | Attorney | San Diego Co. | San Diego | San Diego. |
| Quakenbush, P H | Laborer | nr San Diego | San Diego Co. | San Diego. |
| Quigg, M J | Builder | San Diego Co. | San Diego | San Diego. |
| Quinlan, D | Car driver | San Diego Co. | San Luis Rey | San Luis Rey. |
| Quintana, Diego | Ranchero | San Diego Co. | Agua Caliente | Warner's Rch. |
| Quinteras, A | Vaquero | nr San Luis Rey | San Diego Co. | San Luis Rey. |
| Quirk, Andrew | Miner | San Diego Co. | Julian | Julian. |
| Quirino, J S | Vaquero | San Diego Co. | nr San Diego | San Diego. |
| Radley, Alfred D | Laborer | San Diego Co. | Aguango | |
| Raffl, G | Fancy goods | 5th st | San Diego | San Diego. |
| Ragan, G | Hostler | San Diego Co. | San Diego | San Diego. |
| Ragsdale, J | Printer | San Diego Co. | San Diego | San Diego. |
| Rainos, R | Farmer | nr San Jacinto | San Diego Co. | San Jacinto. |
| Ramirez, J | Laborer | nr San Diego | San Diego Co. | San Diego. |
| Randall, A C | Farmer | San Diego Co. | nr San Diego | San Diego. |
| Randall, M | Woodchopper | Julian | San Diego Co. | Julian. |
| Randolph, J N | Carpenter | San Diego Co. | San Diego | San Diego. |
| Ranken, L M | Mechanic | San Diego Co. | San Diego | San Diego. |
| Ranney, H L | Miner | San Diego Co. | nr San Diego | San Diego. |
| Ransom, W L | Printer | San Diego Co. | San Diego | San Diego. |
| Redding, M | Laborer | San Diego Co. | nr San Diego | San Diego. |
| Rehwoldt, A | Confectioner | San Diego | San Diego Co. | San Diego. |
| Redey, J | Farmer | San Diego Co. | nr Rincon | |
| Reed, A | Farmer | Kane Valley | San Diego Co. | San Diego. |
| Reed, D C | Attorney & ins agt | Plaza | San Diego | San Diego. |
| Reed, Frank | Mechanic | San Diego Co. | Banner City | Banner. |
| Reed, I L | Farmer | San Diego Co. | nr Temecula | Temecula. |
| Reed & Co, D C | Law & land office | Plaza | San Diego | San Diego. |
| Reed, R | Gen merchandise | nr Julian | San Diego Co. | Julian. |
| Reed, W | Farmer | San Diego Co. | Kane Valley | San Diego. |
| Reeder, Thos | Laborer | San Diego Co. | nr San Diego | San Diego. |

DIRECTORY OF SAN DIEGO COUNTY. 493

| Name. | Occupation. | Place of Business. | Residence. | Town or P. O. |
|---|---|---|---|---|
| Rees, B L............ ...... | Farmer............ ....... | San Diego Co........... | nr Sweetwater.......... | Poway. |
| Roetzke, Fredk............ | Ranchero ............... | San Diego Co ......... | Paguay........ ............ | San Diego. |
| Regensburger, S H. | Clerk........ ............ | San Diego Co........... | San Diego............. | San Diego. |
| Remsudo, P C, Dr. | Physician............ | 5th st................. | San Diego............ | San Luis Rey. |
| Renkhead, W........ | Miner............... | nr San Luis Rey...... | San Diego Co............ | San Diego. |
| Rennie, G............. ........ | Clerk................ | San Diego Co........... | San Diego............ | Monserrate. |
| Reyes, Ygnacio...... | Farmer ............ | San Diego Co........... | Monserrate.............. | San Diego. |
| Reynolds, C.......... | Sailor.............. | San Diego Co........... | San Diego.............. | San Diego. |
| Reynolds, Geo B... | Farmer .... ....... | San Diego Co........... | Jamul................ | San Diego. |
| Reynolds, H D...... | Miner................ | San Diego Co........... | nr San Diego........ | San Diego. |
| Reynolds, L G...... | Laborer............. | nr San Diego......... | San Diego Co. ......... | San Diego. |
| Reynolds, W E...... | Hostler..... ....... | San Diego Co........... | San Diego............ | San Jacinto. |
| Reys, Jas............ ...... | Laborer ........... | nr San Jacinto........ | San Diego Co........... | San Luis Rey. |
| Rias, M........... ...... | Farmer............. | San Diego Co........... | nr Santa Margarita... | Banner. |
| Rice, F B................. | Miner .............. | nr Banner......... ..... | San Diego Co........ ..... | Julian. |
| Richards, J H.. ..... | Miner ............. | San Diego Co........... | nr Julian............... | San Diego. |
| Richardson, John H | Painter.............. | 6th st, bet G and H... | San Diego............. | San Diego. |
| Richardson, J H.... | Book keeper........ | San Diego Co........... | San Diego............. | San Diego. |
| Richardson, S R...... | Farmer............. | nr Cajon ............ | San Diego Co........... | Monserrate. |
| Riche, S M........... | Farmer.............. | nr Monserrate.......... | San Diego Co............ | San Luis Rey. |
| Richey, A C........... | Apiarian ............ | Temecula Creek ...... | 10 m N San Luis Rey | San Diego. |
| Richter, G F W..... | Shell polisher...... | Block H, bet B & C sts | San Diego.............. | San Diego. |
| Rick, John E......... | Apiarian ............ | San Diego Co............ | San Diego............ | San Diego. |
| Rickey, J H..... ..... | Teamster........ | San Diego Co........... | San Diego............. | San Diego. |
| Rickwood, T........ | Miner............... | San Diego Co........... | nr San Diego........ | San Diego. |
| Ridee, John ........ | Carpenter ......... | San Diego Co........... | San Diego............ | San Diego. |
| Ridge, R........ ........... | Farmer............. | nr Monserrate.......... | San Diego Co.......... | Monserrate. |
| Ridley, O........ ........... | Farmer ............ | San Diego Co........... | nr Julian.......... . ..... | Julian. |
| Riedy, M........ ......... | Miner............... | San Diego Co........... | nr San Diego........ | San Diego. |
| Riggs, G......... .......... | Farmer ............ | San Diego Co........... | nr San Diego........ | San Diego. |
| Riggs, R............ ........ | Farmer ............ | San Diego Co........... | nr San Diego........ | San Diego. |
| Rimback, C............... | Ranchero ........... | nr Cajon............. | San Diego Co.......... | San Diego. |
| Rinedoller, J....... | Butcher............. | San Diego Co........... | San Diego.............. | San Diego. |
| Rios, J de la C...... | Miner ............. | nr San Jacinto........ | San Diego Co.......... | San Jacinto. |
| Rios, R............ .......... | Vaquero ........... | nr San Marcus......... | San Diego Co.......... | San Luis Rey. |
| Ripley, Ed............. | Saloon keeper..... | San Luis Rey......... | 45 m N San Diego ... | San Luis Rey. |
| Rivolen, Franklin... | Teamster............. | San Diego Co........... | Julian................ | Julian. |
| Robards, W A........ | Farmer............. | nr Julian........... ..... | San Diego Co.......... | Julian. |
| Roberson, W H...... | Farmer ............ | Kane Valley .......... | San Diego Co.......... | |
| Roberts, H C......... | Druggist........... | San Diego Co........... | San Diego............. | San Diego. |
| Roberts, L........... ...... | Machinist........... | San Diego Co........... | San Diego............. | San Diego. |
| Roberts, L L........ | Farmer ............ | San Diego Co........... | nr San Diego.......... | San Diego. |
| Roberts, W........ ...... | Laborer ........... | San Diego Co........... | nr San Diego......... | San Diego. |
| Robideaux, L........ | Farmer............. | nr San Jacinto......... | San Diego Co.......... | San Jacinto. |
| Robinson, A......... ........ | Farmer............. | nr Julian............. | San Diego Co.......... | Julian. |
| Robinson, Geo C... | Miner.......... ....... | San Diego Co........... | Banner City............ | Banner. |
| Robinson, G W D.. | Saloon keeper ..... | San Diego Co........... | Paguay............. ....... | Poway. |
| Robinson, W E...... | Merchant ........... | San Diego Co........... | San Diego............. | San Diego. |
| Robinson, W......... | Farmer.......... | San Diego Co........... | nr Valle de las Vie's | Viejas. |
| Robinson, W N...... | Clerk ............. | San Diego Co........... | Jamul................ | San Diego. |
| Rodgers, W........... | Miner............... | nr Banner............. | San Diego Co.......... | Banner. |
| Rodrigues, J ........ | Ranchero........... | nr San Pascual........ | San Diego Co.......... | San Pascual. |
| Rodriguez, R......... | Ranchero........... | nr San Diegnito........ | San Diego Co.......... | San Diegnito. |
| Rogers, B B........... | Machinist .......... | San Diego Co........... | San Diego............. | San Diego. |
| Rogers, B F........... | Farmer............. | nr Green Valley ...... | San Diego Co.......... | Stonewall. |
| Rogus, B B.......... | Carpenter ......... | San Diego Co........... | San Diego............. | San Diego. |
| Rollins, V E.......... | Miner............... | nr Julian............. | San Diego Co.......... | Julian. |
| Romere, P............ | Vaquero ........... | nr Temecula.......... | San Diego Co.......... | Temecula. |
| Romeros, Francisco | Laborer............. | San Luis Rey.......... | San Diego Co. ........ | San Luis Rey. |
| Romero, Felicano... | Vaquero ........... | nr Temecula.......... | San Diego Co.......... | Temecula. |
| Romero, Galvader.. | Farmer............. | San Diego Co........... | nr San Luis Rey....... | San Luis Rey. |
| Rooney, W ........ | Farmer............. | San Diego Co........... | nr National City...... | National City. |
| Rosa, J.............. ....... | Vaquero ........... | San Diego Co........... | nr San Diego.......... | San Diego. |
| Rose, E............ ......... | Carpenter ......... | San Diego Co........... | Julian.......... ....... .... | Julian. |

| Name. | Occupation. | Place of Business. | Residence. | Town or P. O. |
|---|---|---|---|---|
| Rose, L............... | Merchant.......... | San Diego Co.......... | San Diego............ | San Diego. |
| Ross, G H........... | Miner............... | nr Banner............. | San Diego Co........ | Banner. |
| Ross, John.......... | Farmer............. | San Diego Co.......... | nr Milquatay......... | Campo. |
| Ross, John G....... | Stage driver....... | San Diego Co.......... | San Diego............ | San Diego. |
| Ross, J T............. | Farmer............. | San Diego Co.......... | nr Banner............ | Banner. |
| Rosso, P.............. | Barber.............. | 6th st.................. | San Diego............ | San Diego. |
| Rothschild, A...... | Variety store...... | 5th st, bet G and H.. | San Diego............ | San Diego. |
| Rothschilds, S...... | Peddler............. | San Diego Co.......... | San Diego............ | San Diego. |
| Rouen, Louis A.... | Blacksmith........ | San Diego Co.......... | Temecula............ | Temecula. |
| Rowe, John.......... | Farmer............. | nr Julian............. | San Diego Co........ | Julian. |
| Rowe, J L............ | Farmer............. | San Diego Co.......... | nr San Diego......... | San Diego. |
| Rowe, W E........... | Miner............... | San Diego Co.......... | nr San Diego......... | San Diego. |
| Rouland, N P....... | Farmer............. | nr National City.... | San Diego Co........ | National City. |
| Royal, W W Dr..... | Physician.......... | J st..................... | San Diego............ | San Diego. |
| Rubio, N ............. | Silversmith....... | San Diego Co.......... | San Diego............ | San Diego. |
| Rudd, C G............ | Bookseller......... | San Diego Co.......... | San Diego Co........ | San Diego. |
| Rudolph, I........... | Farmer............. | San Diego Co.......... | nr Julian............. | Julian. |
| Ruis, Ambrosio..... | Laborer............. | San Diego Co.......... | San Diego Co........ | San Diego. |
| Ruiz, Jose F......... | Ranchero.......... | San Diego Co.......... | San Jacinto.......... | San Jacinto. |
| Ruiz, F............... | Ranchero.......... | nr Jamul............. | San Diego Co........ | San Diego. |
| Rusell, E A.......... | Farmer............. | nr Tia Juana......... | San Diego Co........ | San Diego. |
| Russell, Edwin M. | Jeweler............. | San Diego Co.......... | Banner City......... | Banner. |
| Russell, Geo W..... | Painter............. | San Diego Co.......... | San Diego Co........ | San Diego. |
| Russell, J............ | Clerk................ | San Diego Co.......... | San Diego Co........ | San Diego. |
| Russell, W........... | Farmer............. | San Diego Co.......... | nr Julian............. | Julian. |
| Ruth, Peter S....... | Clergyman........ | San Diego Co.......... | San Diego............ | San Diego. |
| Ruth, Theodore.... | Druggist........... | San Diego Co.......... | San Diego............ | San Diego. |
| Ryan, J .............. | Butcher............ | San Diego Co.......... | Banner............... | Banner. |
| Sabins, J F.......... | Carpenter.......... | San Diego Co.......... | Banner............... | Banner. |
| Sabiston, J.......... | Cook................ | San Diego Co.......... | San Diego............ | San Diego. |
| Sadler, E F.......... | Farmer............. | San Diego Co.......... | nr Milquatay........ | Campo. |
| Salgado, G........... | Ranchero.......... | nr Jamul............. | San Diego Co........ | San Diego. |
| Salis, G............... | Farmer............. | San Diego Co.......... | nr San Diegnito..... | San Diegnito. |
| Saloman, H.......... | Merchant.......... | San Diego Co.......... | San Diego............ | San Diego. |
| Sample, J A & Co.. | Hardware.......... | cor 5th & J sts....... | San Diego............ | San Diego. |
| Sample, James A... | Merchant.......... | San Diego Co.......... | San Diego............ | San Diego. |
| Sampson, S ......... | Miner............... | San Diego Co.......... | nr Julian............. | Julian. |
| San Diego Academy |  | cor 9th & G sts....... | San Diego............ | San Diego. |
| San Diego Mill Co. | Planing mill ..... | San Diego Co.......... | San Diego............ | San Diego. |
| Sanders, J........... | Farmer............. | San Diego Co.......... | nr San Jacinto...... | San Jacinto. |
| Sanders, R........... | Farmer............. | San Diego Co.......... | nr San Jacinto...... | San Jacinto. |
| Sandoval, J P....... | Ranchero.......... | San Diego Co.......... | nr Guatay........... |  |
| Sandoval, P......... | Ranchero.......... | San Diego Co.......... | nr Guatay........... |  |
| Sanford, O N........ | Civil engineer.... | San Diego Co.......... | San Diego............ | San Diego. |
| Sanguinette, A..... | Merchant.......... | San Diego Co.......... | San Diego............ | San Diego. |
| Sargent, B S........ | Painter............. | San Diego Co.......... | Cajon................. | San Diego. |
| Sarrail, Bernard... | Sheep raiser...... | San Diego Co.......... | nr San Diego........ | San Diego. |
| Saunders, Thos A.. | Farmer............. | San Diego Co.......... | Julian............... | Julian. |
| Savage, M ........... | Laborer............. | San Diego Co.......... | Julian............... | Julian. |
| Scarbourough, F G | Ranchero.......... | nr Cajon............. | San Diego Co........ | San Diego. |
| Schafler, M P....... | Merchant.......... | San Diego Co.......... | San Diego............ | San Diego. |
| Scheller, R........... | Book binder....... | 5th st.................. | San Diego............ | San Diego. |
| Scheppell, Fredk... | Farmer............. | San Diego Co.......... | Valle de las Viejas... | Viejas. |
| Schiller, Jacob...... | Clerk................ | San Diego Co.......... | San Diego............ | San Diego. |
| Schiller, J A........ | | San Diego Co.......... | San Diego............ | San Diego. |
| Schiller, R........... | Book binder....... | 5th st.................. | San Diego............ | San Diego. |
| Schiller, M.......... | Merchant.......... | San Diego Co.......... | San Diego............ | San Diego. |
| Schilling, I.......... | Saloon keeper.... | San Diego Co.......... | San Diego............ | San Diego. |
| Schilling, L......... | Barber.............. | San Diego Co.......... | San Diego............ | San Diego. |
| Schlappe, F......... | Farmer............. | nr Temecula........ | San Diego Co........ | Temecula. |
| Schlotterbeck, G... | Packer............. | San Diego Co.......... | San Diego Co........ | San Diego. |
| Schneider, A........ | Merchant.......... | San Diego Co.......... | San Diego............ | San Diego. |
| Schneider & Abegg | Book store......... | 5th st, near F....... | San Diego............ | San Diego. |
| Schnurpler, Henry.. | Miner............... | San Diego............ | Mesa Grande........ | Ballena. |

# DIRECTORY OF SAN DIEGO COUNTY. 495

| NAME. | OCCUPATION. | PLACE OF BUSINESS. | RESIDENCE. | TOWN OR P. O. |
|---|---|---|---|---|
| Schneth, H C | Merchant | San Diego Co | San Diego | San Diego. |
| Schneider, — | Bookseller | 5th st | San Diego | San Diego. |
| Schriever, W | Painter | San Diego Co | San Diego | San Diego. |
| Schroder, J | Farmer | nr San Diego | San Diego Co | San Diego. |
| Schroeppel, Gustav. | Musician | San Diego Co | San Diego | San Diego. |
| Schuler, Gustavus. | Merchant | San Diego Co | San Diego | San Diego. |
| Schwerer, F | Barber | San Diego Co | San Diego | San Diego. |
| Schwerer & Schneider | Hair dressers | 6th st | San Diego | San Diego. |
| Scott, C | Attorney | Plaza | San Diego | San Diego. |
| Scott, J | Coachman | San Diego Co | San Diego | San Diego. |
| Scott, Jos | Laborer | nr Cajon | San Diego Co | San Diego. |
| Scott, L | Carpenter | San Diego Co | San Diego | San Diego. |
| Scott, R L | Carpenter | San Diego Co | San Diego | San Diego. |
| Scranton, J R | Builder | San Diego Co | San Diego | San Diego. |
| Seamore, W B | Painter | San Diego Co | San Diego | San Diego. |
| Searl, H W | Farmer | San Diego Co | nr San Diego | San Diego. |
| Searl, L F | Farmer | San Diego Co | nr San Diego | San Diego. |
| Searl, O | Farmer | San Diego Co | nr San Diego | San Diego. |
| Seer, O | Barber | San Diego Co | Julian | Julian. |
| Segars, W | Laborer | nr Monument City | San Diego Co | San Diego. |
| Seely, A L | Farmer | San Diego Co | nr San Diego | San Diego. |
| Sellers, Eugene | Farmer | San Diego Co | Julian | Julian. |
| Selwyn, G | Blacksmith | San Diego Co | San Diego | San Diego. |
| Sepler, E L | Blacksmith | San Diego Co | San Diego | San Diego. |
| Serna, M | Farmer | San Diego Co | nr San Diego | San Diego. |
| Serres, P | Mason | San Diego Co | Pala | Pala. |
| Serrano, J | Butcher | San Diego Co | San Diego | San Diego. |
| Serrano, J A | Ranchero | nr Cordero | San Diego Co | |
| Serrano, L | Ranchero | San Diego Co | nr San Diego | San Diego. |
| Shaffer, M R | City assessor | Court House | San Diego | San Diego. |
| Shaffer, J | Coppersmith | San Diego Co | San Diego | San Diego. |
| Shannen, S | Sheep raiser | San Marcus | 8 m E San Luis Rey | San Luis Rey. |
| Shaw, A | Farmer | nr Julian | San Diego Co | Julian. |
| Shaw, F A P | Stage driver | San Diego Co | San Diego | San Diego. |
| Sherman, A | Farmer | San Diego Co | nr National City | National City. |
| Sherman, M | Inspector customs | San Diego Co | San Diego | San Diego. |
| Sherman, T | Plumber | San Diego Co | San Diego | San Diego. |
| Sherman, W | Mason | San Diego Co | San Bernardo | Bernardo. |
| Shillinger, J D | Clerk | San Diego Co | San Diego | San Diego. |
| Shore, E S | Farmer | nr Banner | San Diego Co | Banner. |
| Short, J | Waiter | San Diego Co | San Diego | San Diego. |
| Shoulder, F | Farmer | nr La Mesa | San Diego Co | |
| Shrode, W J | Farmer | nr San Luis Rey | San Diego Co | San Luis Rey. |
| Shuler, Gustavus | Brewer | San Diego Co | San Diego | San Diego. |
| Shulz, S | Merchant | San Diego Co | Julian | Julian. |
| Siddell, R | Farmer | San Diego Co | nr San Diego | San Diego. |
| Sidwell, W L | Blacksmith | San Diego Co | Julian | Julian. |
| Sierras, Ramon | Laborer | San Luis Rey | San Diego Co | San Luis Rey. |
| Sikes, Q | Farmer | nr San Pascual | San Diego Co | San Pascual. |
| Silvas, Isidro | Ranchero | nr San Pascual | San Diego Co | San Pascual. |
| Silvas, J M | Physician | San Diego Co | San Diego | San Diego. |
| Silvas, L | Ranchero | nr San Vincente | San Diego Co | |
| Simmons, Benj | Farmer | San Diego Co | Banner City | Banner. |
| Simons, John | Wood & coal dealr | San Diego Co | San Diego | San Diego. |
| Summers, John | Farmer | San Luis Rey | 45 m N San Diego | San Luis Rey. |
| Simmons, Jasper N | Farmer | nr Milquatay | San Diego Co | Campo. |
| Simons, D N | Agent | San Diego Co | San Diego | San Diego. |
| Simonds, H K | Carpenter | San Diego Co | Julian | Julian. |
| Simpson, J T | Farmer | nr Monument City | San Diego Co | San Diego. |
| Sinclair, J | Farmer | nr Milquatay | San Diego Co | Campo. |
| Sirey, G W | Farmer | San Diego Co | nr Oak Grove | Oak Grove. |
| Sisson, W F | Mariner | San Diego Co | San Diego | San Diego. |
| Sites, G W | Farmer | San Diego Co | nr Jamul | San Diego. |

| Name. | Occupation. | Place of Business. | Residence. | Town or P. O. |
|---|---|---|---|---|
| Sivering, Louis | Laborer | San Diego Co. | San Diego | San Diego. |
| Sizer, S. | Carpenter | San Diego Co. | San Diego | San Diego. |
| Skidmore, J E | Farmer | San Diego Co. | nr Julian | Julian. |
| **Skinner, Edw M** | Dealer dry goods. | 5th st | San Diego | San Diego. |
| Skinner, H C | Miner | San Diego Co. | San Diego | San Diego. |
| Slade, T P | Lawyer | San Diego Co. | Julian | Julian. |
| **Sloane, J** | Merchant | San Diego Co. | San Diego | San Diego. |
| Sloan, J C | Stock | Julian | San Diego Co. | Julian. |
| Smith, Angelo | Student | San Diego Co. | San Diego | San Diego. |
| **Smith, A** | Millwright | San Diego Co. | Tia Juana | San Diego. |
| Smith, C E | Laborer | San Diego Co. | nr San Diego | San Diego. |
| Smith, D | Farmer | San Diego Co. | nr San Diego | San Diego. |
| Smith, E J | Cabinet maker | San Diego Co. | San Diego | San Diego. |
| **Smith, F A** | Hotel keeper | San Diego Co. | San Diego | San Diego. |
| Smith, Harry | Blacksmith | San Diego Co. | Warner's Ranch | Warner's Rch. |
| Smith, Henry | Blacksmith | San Diego Co. | San Diego | San Diego. |
| Smith, Henry | Farmer | San Diego Co. | nr San Diego | San Diego. |
| Smith, H D | Stage driver | San Diego Co. | San Diego | San Diego. |
| Smith, Jas | Mariner | San Diego Co. | Julian | Julian. |
| Smith, John | Shepherd | nr Cajon | San Diego Co. | San Diego. |
| **Smith, J A** | Merchant | San Diego Co. | San Diego | San Diego. |
| Smith, P | Laundryman | San Diego Co. | San Diego | San Diego. |
| Smith, Sylvanus | Miller | San Diego Co. | San Diego | San Diego. |
| Smith, Wm | Stage driver | San Diego Co. | Oak Grove | Oak Grove. |
| **Smith, Wm** | Painter | San Diego Co. | San Diego | San Diego. |
| Smith, W J | Farmer | nr Santa Teresa | San Diego Co. | |
| Smith, W B | Cook | San Diego Co. | San Diego | San Diego. |
| Smith, W P | Miner | nr San Diego | San Diego Co. | San Diego. |
| **Smith, W E** | Manager | Western Union Tel. | cor D & 5th sts. | San Diego. |
| Smiley, C L | Carpenter | San Diego Co. | San Diego | San Diego. |
| Snow, N G | Mechanic | San Diego Co. | Julian | Julian. |
| Snyder, D H | Farmer | nr Julian | San Diego Co. | Julian. |
| **Snyder, Bramer F.** | Carriage maker | San Diego Co. | San Diego | San Diego. |
| Sohn, H S | Shoe maker | San Diego Co. | San Diego | San Diego. |
| **Solomon, H** | Merchant | San Diego Co. | San Diego | San Diego. |
| Somers, I S | Minor | nr Julian | San Diego Co. | Julian. |
| Soto, E | Ranchero | nr San Pascual | San Diego Co. | San Pascual. |
| Spaulding, D | Farmer | nr Ballena | San Diego Co. | Ballena. |
| Spear, A F | Carpenter | San Diego Co. | San Diego | San Diego. |
| **Speckler, Benj R.** | Farmer | San Diego Co. | Jamul | San Diego. |
| Speck, John C | Farmer | nr Milquatay | San Diego Co. | Campo. |
| **Spence, E F** | Cashier | Commercial Bank. | cor 5th & G sts. | San Diego. |
| Spencer, E R | Farmer | San Diego Co. | nr San Diego | San Diego. |
| Spencer, Isaac | Teamster | nr San Diego | San Diego Co. | San Diego. |
| **Spencer, James M** | Merchant | San Diego Co. | San Diego | San Diego. |
| Spinelli, Peter M | Clerk | San Diego Co. | San Diego | San Diego. |
| Spratt, H B | Merchant | San Diego Co. | Cannissa Creek | |
| Stafford, E F | Carpenter | San Diego Co. | nr Julian | San Diego. |
| Stanclift, J S | Farmer | San Diego Co. | Julian | Julian. |
| **Stanley, H H** | Millman | San Diego Co. | Julian | Julian. |
| Starkey, S | Farmer | nr Monument City | San Diego Co. | San Diego. |
| **Statler, S** | Real estate agent. | Plaza | San Diego | San Diego. |
| Stebbins, J T | Farmer | nr Paguay | San Diego Co. | Poway. |
| Stedman, R | Paper maker | San Diego Co. | San Diego | San Diego. |
| Stedman, R, Jr | Laborer | San Diego Co. | nr San Diego | San Diego. |
| Steele, E | Farmer | nr National Ranch | San Diego Co. | National City. |
| Steiner, — | Merchant | San Diego Co. | San Diego | San Diego. |
| **Steiner & Klauber** | Merchants | 7th st, cor I | San Diego | San Diego. |
| Steinman, J | Farmer | nr San Diego | San Diego Co. | San Diego. |
| Sterling, G E | Clerk | San Diego Co. | San Diego | San Diego. |
| Stevens, C F | News dealer | San Diego Co. | San Diego | San Diego. |
| **Stevens, J** | Blacksmith | cor 4th and F sts | San Diego | San Diego. |
| Stevens, S C | Farmer | San Diego Co. | nr Monument City | San Diego. |
| Stewart, D | Steward | San Diego Co. | San Diego | San Diego. |

## DIRECTORY OF SAN DIEGO COUNTY. 497

| Name. | Occupation. | Place of Business. | Residence. | Town or P. O. |
|---|---|---|---|---|
| Stewart, Edwd W. | Farmer | San Diego | San Diego Co. | San Diego. |
| Stewart, J C | Carpenter | San Diego Co. | San Diego | San Diego. |
| Stewart, O A | Dairyman | San Luis Rey | 45 m N San Diego | San Luis Rey. |
| Stewart, O A | Student | San Diego Co. | San Diego | San Diego. |
| Stewart, R M | Farmer | San Diego Co. | nr Julian | Julian. |
| Stewart, R | Teamster | nr Julian | San Diego Co. | Julian. |
| Stewart & Co, W W | Comm merchant | 5th st, nr P. M. Whf | San Diego | San Diego. |
| Stewart, W W | Merchant | cor 5th and J sts | San Diego | San Diego. |
| Stewart, W | Lawyer | San Diego Co. | San Diego | San Diego. |
| Stewart, Wm C | Engineer | San Diego Co. | San Diego | San Diego. |
| Stoekes, E | Carpenter | San Diego Co. | San Diego | San Diego. |
| Stockton, T C, Dr. | Physician | cor 5th and E sts | San Diego | San Diego. |
| Stokes, A | Ranchero | nr Santa Maria | San Diego Co. | |
| Stone, Bruce | Farmer | San Diego Co. | San Diego | San Diego. |
| Stone, C W | Farmer | San Diego Co. | nr San Pascual | San Pascual. |
| Stone, Francis | Ranchero | San Diego Co. | nr Los Coches | |
| Stone, Geo M | Farmer | San Diego Co. | nr San Diego | San Diego. |
| Stone, Geo | Agent | San Diego Co. | San Diego | San Diego. |
| Stone, J C | Farmer | nr San Diego | San Diego Co. | San Diego. |
| Stone, J P | Painter | San Diego Co. | San Diego | San Diego. |
| Stone, N M | Seaman | San Diego Co. | San Diego | San Diego. |
| Stone, R | Clerk | San Diego Co. | San Diego | San Diego. |
| Storm, W H | Farmer | San Diego Co. | nr Monument City | San Diego. |
| Storms, James P | Teamster | San Diego Co. | Lawson's Valley | |
| Story, George | Civil engineer | San Diego Co. | San Diego | San Diego. |
| Story, Joseph | Ranchero | San Diego Co. | Mission | |
| Stout, D | Miner | nr Banner | San Diego Co. | Banner. |
| Stout, F H | Blacksmith | 16 m E San Diego | Cajon | San Diego. |
| Stratton, James | Farmer | San Diego Co. | Julian City | Julian. |
| Strickland, Ney | Student | San Diego Co. | San Diego | San Diego. |
| Striplin, Abel M | Farmer | San Diego Co. | Bear Valley | San Pascual. |
| Striplin, S | Farmer | nr San Pascual | San Diego Co. | San Pascual. |
| Strong, D W | Physician | San Diego Co. | San Diego | San Diego. |
| Strong, J W | Carpenter | San Diego Co. | San Diego | San Diego. |
| Stroud, W B | Druggist | San Diego Co. | San Diego | San Diego. |
| Strudder, M | Farmer | nr Milquatay | San Diego Co. | Campo. |
| Studley, W B | Wheelwright | San Diego Co. | San Diego | San Diego. |
| Sullivan, D O | Lawyer | San Diego Co. | San Diego | San Diego. |
| Sullivan, Jerry | Farmer | nr San Diego | San Diego Co. | San Diego. |
| Sullivan, James | Laborer | San Diego Co. | San Diego | San Diego. |
| Sullivan, Jas | Clerk | San Diego Co. | San Diego | San Diego. |
| Sullivan, John A | Teamster | San Diego Co. | San Diego | San Diego. |
| Sullivan, J W | Miner | San Diego Co. | nr Julian | Julian. |
| Summers, J | Miner | nr San Luis Rey | San Diego Co. | San Luis Rey. |
| Swain, G W | Mechanic | San Diego Co. | Julian | Julian. |
| Swain, Wilson | Farmer | San Diego Co. | nr Julian | Julian. |
| Swain, W H | Plasterer | San Diego Co. | San Diego | San Diego. |
| Swain, W | Farmer | San Diego Co. | nr Julian | Julian. |
| Swan, George C | Farmer | San Diego Co. | National City | National City. |
| Swan, E H | Steam & gas fitter | San Diego Co. | San Diego | San Diego. |
| Swan, N P | Glover | San Diego Co. | San Diego | San Diego. |
| Swarthout, H | Farmer | San Diego Co. | nr Banner | Banner. |
| Sweeney, J P | Blacksmith | San Diego Co. | San Diego | San Diego. |
| Swift, Edward | Agent | San Diego Co. | San Diego | San Diego. |
| Swim, Jas | Farmer | San Diego Co. | Valle de las Viejas | Viejas. |
| Switzer, E D | Watch maker | 5th st, bet E and F | San Diego | San Diego. |
| Swycuffer, J | Farmer | nr Ballena | San Diego Co. | Ballena. |
| Syrnet, M | Teacher | San Diego Co. | Buena Vista | San Luis Rey. |
| Taggart, C P | Attorney | Plaza | San Diego | San Diego. |
| Talkington, J S | Farmer | nr Milquatay | San Diego Co. | Campo. |
| Talley, D | Farmer | nr Julian | San Diego Co. | Julian. |
| Tallman, E H | Carriages | 6th st | San Diego | San Diego. |
| Tannahill, John | Farmer | San Diego Co. | San Diego | San Diego. |
| Taney, E C | Carpenter | San Diego Co. | Julian | Julian. |

33

# Farm Lands

## FOR SALE!

### IN TRACTS TO SUIT PURCHASERS,

Located in San Luis Obispo County, 24 Miles south of the town of San Luis Obispo.

### DANA BROS.,   -   PROPRIETORS.

---

#### 37,700 ACRES OF CHOICE LAND.

| | |
|---|---|
| VALLEY LAND, | 17,000 Acres. |
| TIMBER LAND, | 3,000 Acres. |
| HILL, (or Grazing Land) | 17,700 Acres. |

---

The soil of more than one-half of this large tract is black adobe, the remainder being a sandy loam, suitable for Cereals, Potatoes, Beans, and all kinds of Vegetables.

On the adobe land are more than forty running streams, which never fail. There are also many springs. On any portion of the sandy soil, water can be had by digging to a depth of from fifteen to twenty feet. There is also a large lagoon on the property.

This land has been used chiefly for Stock Raising, there being at present, on the property, about 16,000 Sheep, producing six pounds of Wool, on the average. There are also about 2,500 head of Cattle, and 100 Horses.

The best of crops can be produced here, during the dryest year.

Land ranges in price from $20 to $100 per acre, any portion of which can be purchased on reasonable terms.

DIRECTORY OF SAN DIEGO COUNTY. 499

| Name. | Occupation. | Place of Business. | Residence. | Town or P. O. |
|---|---|---|---|---|
| Tasker & Hoke | Wood yard | 5th st, bet D and E | San Diego | San Diego. |
| Tasker, — | Plumber | 5th st | San Diego | San Diego. |
| Tasker, Jos | Waterman | San Diego Co | San Diego | San Diego. |
| Tapia, T | Farmer | nr Temecula | San Diego Co | Temecula. |
| Taylor, Jas | Cooper | San Diego Co | San Diego | San Diego. |
| Taylor, S B | Blacksmith | San Diego Co | San Diego | San Diego. |
| Taylor, T | Miner | San Diego Co | nr Julian | Julian. |
| Taylor, T L | Laborer | San Diego Co | nr San Diego | San Diego. |
| Tebbutt, John E | Carpenter | San Diego Co | San Diego | San Diego. |
| Terry, W W | Planing mill | San Diego Co | San Diego | San Diego. |
| Thing, Damon | Farmer | San Diego Co | Sweet Water Valley | San Diego. |
| Thomas, C | Farmer | nr Temecula | San Diego Co | Temecula. |
| Thomas, H H | Clerk | San Diego Co | San Diego | San Diego. |
| Thomas, John A | Farmer | San Diego Co | San Diego | San Diego. |
| Thomas, Wm | Seaman | San Diego Co | San Diego | San Diego. |
| Thomez, Thos | Tailor | San Diego Co | San Diego | San Diego. |
| Thompson, C | Farmer | nr San Pascual | San Diego Co | San Pascual. |
| Thompson, Gurden H | Carpenter | San Diego Co | San Diego | San Diego. |
| Thompson, J C | Gasfitter | San Diego Co | San Diego | San Diego. |
| Thompson, J F | Barber | San Diego Co | San Diego | San Diego. |
| Thompson, J O | Miner | San Diego Co | nr Julian | Julian. |
| Thompson, L K | Farmer | nr San Pascual | San Diego Co | San Pascual. |
| Thompson, M | Farmer | San Diego Co | nr Agua Caliente | Warner's Rch. |
| Thompson, R | Laborer | San Diego Co | nr San Diego | San Diego. |
| Thompson, V | Farmer | nr San Diego | San Diego Co | San Diego. |
| Thompson, W H | Miner | San Diego Co | nr San Pascual | San Pascual. |
| Thorman, H | Seaman | San Diego Co | San Diego | San Diego. |
| Thorn, J C | Farmer | San Diego Co | nr San Jacinto | San Jacinto. |
| Thorpe, Martin | Farmer | San Diego Co | Green Valley | Stonewall. |
| Thorpe, Roderick | Farmer | San Diego Co | Green Valley | Stonewall. |
| Thorpe, Wm | Farmer | San Diego Co | Green Valley | Stonewall. |
| Tibbitts, J H | Jeweler | 5th st | San Diego | San Diego. |
| Tibbitts, J H Mrs | Millinery | 5th st | San Diego | San Diego. |
| Tibbals, J S | Carpenter | San Diego Co | San Diego | San Diego. |
| Ticknor, Jason C | Merchant | San Diego Co | Bladen Mines | |
| Tiernan, Mrs | Milliner | Plaza | San Diego | San Diego. |
| Tiernan, J M | | Plaza | San Diego | San Diego. |
| Tiernay, Jas | Laborer | nr San Diego | San Diego Co | San Diego. |
| Tighe, Thos | Fruit vender | San Diego Co | San Diego | San Diego. |
| Tighe, W J | Market | Central Market | San Diego | San Diego. |
| Tilton, John | Laborer | San Diego Co | nr San Diego | San Diego. |
| Tilton, L | Mariner | San Diego Co | San Diego | San Diego. |
| Titcomb, J W | Miner | San Diego Co | nr Paguay | Poway. |
| Toothaker, C | Carpenter | San Diego Co | Julian | Julian. |
| Tomeney, R P | Teamster | San Diego Co | nr Spring Valley | San Diego. |
| Torres, Alex | Laborer | San Diego Co | San Jacinto | San Jacinto. |
| Townsend, J S | Clerk | San Diego Co | San Diego | San Diego. |
| Tracey, George | Laborer | San Diego Co | San Diego | San Diego. |
| Tracy, W W | Carpenter | San Diego Co | San Diego | San Diego. |
| Trask, P H | Barber | San Diego Co | San Diego | San Diego. |
| Trask, R | Blacksmith | San Diego Co | San Pascual | San Pascual. |
| Treanor, Geo W | Livery stable | cor 4th & E sts | San Diego | San Diego. |
| Treanor, J H | Clerk | San Diego Co | San Diego | San Diego. |
| Tribolet, G | Butcher | San Diego Co | San Diego | San Diego. |
| Trimmer, M | Harness maker | San Diego Co | San Diego | San Diego. |
| Trojillo, G | Blacksmith | San Diego Co | Santa Margarita | San Luis Rey. |
| Trout, Saml | Miner | nr San Diego | San Diego Co | San Diego. |
| Trujillo, Juan M | Farmer | San Diego Co | Temecula | Temecula. |
| Truman, A A | Blacksmith | San Diego Co | Warner's Ranch | Warner's Rch. |
| Turman, W F | Stock raiser | San Diego Co | Banner | Banner. |
| Tyner, H | Teamster | nr San Diego | San Diego Co | San Diego. |
| Turner, T M | Stock yard | San Diego Co | San Diego | San Diego. |
| Tweed, W | Farmer | nr San Diego | San Diego Co | San Diego. |

**DEALERS IN**

# REAL ESTATE

SAN BERNARDINO, CAL.

This is the Oldest and Most Reliable Real Estate Firm in San Bernardino.

**HAVE SOME OF THE MOST**

## DESIRABLE PROPERTIES

In the city and county for sale, always on hand. Parties desiring to purchase, should first consult this firm.

**RATES OF COMMISSION, FIVE PER CENT,**
Unless Special Terms are agreed upon.

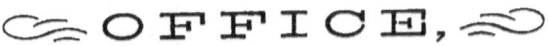

## OFFICE,

## KELTING'S BLOCK, THIRD STREET.

All Communications Promptly Answered.

DIRECTORY OF SAN DIEGO COUNTY. 501

| Name. | Occupation. | Place of Business. | Residence. | Town or P. O. |
|---|---|---|---|---|
| Tweed, Wm | Pioneer feed yard | 8th st | San Diego | San Diego. |
| Twiner, H W | Sheep raiser | Agua Hodienda | 8 m S San Luis Rey | San Luis Rey. |
| Tyler, Alvah | Teamster | San Diego Co | San Diego | San Diego. |
| Tyner, A | Teamster | nr San Diego | San Diego Co | San Diego. |
| Tyson, J W | Attorney | cor. Front and F sts | San Diego | San Diego. |
| Ulsaver, J | Hotel | San Diego Co | San Diego | San Diego. |
| Utt, L H | Ranchero | San Diego Co | nr San Luis Rey | San Luis Rey. |
| Valdez, C | Ranchero | nr Valle la Vieja | San Diego Co | Viejas. |
| Valdez, J | Farmer | San Diego Co | nr San Diego | San Diego. |
| Valdez, J L | Farmer | San Diego Co | nr San Jacinto | San Jacinto. |
| Valdez, J de la L | Farmer | nr San Jacinto | San Diego Co | San Jacinto. |
| Vail, J W | Miner | San Diego Co | nr San Diego | San Diego. |
| Valencia, J D | Ranchero | nr Temecula | San Diego Co | Temecula. |
| Valentine, E | Real estate agent. | San Diego Co | National City | National City. |
| Vance, Joseph | Manufacturer | San Diego Co | San Diego | San Diego. |
| Vanderwoort, J A | Milkman | San Diego Co | San Diego | San Diego. |
| Van, B | Carpenter | San Diego Co | San Diego | San Diego. |
| Van Curen, P | Blacksmith | San Diego Co | San Diego | San Diego. |
| Vanloon, C | Carpenter | San Diego Co | San Diego | San Diego. |
| Van Luren, S | Farmer | San Diego Co | nr San Jacinto | San Jacinto. |
| Van Mieter, A J | Farmer | San Luis Rey | 45 m N San Diego | San Luis Rey. |
| Van Matre, A J | Farmer | San Diego Co | San Luis Rey | San Luis Rey. |
| Van Riper, S W | Steam fitter | San Diego Co | San Diego | San Diego. |
| Van Schuyrer, E | Farmer | San Diego Co | San Diego Co | Monserrate. |
| Vasquez, Refugio | Laborer | San Diego Co | San Luis Rey | San Luis Rey. |
| Veal, Wm | Blacksmith | San Diego Co | Temecula | Temecula. |
| Veazie, E A | Merchant | San Diego Co | San Diego | San Diego. |
| Vedal, Pedro | Ranchero | San Diego Co | San Diego | San Diego. |
| Verlagne, Theo | Saloon keeper | San Diego Co | San Diego | San Diego. |
| Viberg, R L | Teamster | nr Julian | San Diego Co | Julian. |
| Villatin, J | Teamster | San Diego Co | nr San Diego | San Diego. |
| Vincent, Giles | Miner | nr Banner | San Diego Co | Banner. |
| Vincen, G M | Farmer | San Diego Co | nr Banner | Banner. |
| Vines, Solomon J | Teamster | San Diego Co | San Diego | San Diego. |
| Vollers, L | Farmer | nr San Diego | San Diego Co | San Diego. |
| Van Poser, H | Plasterer | San Diego Co | San Diego | San Diego. |
| Vosselnan, F | Farmer | nr San Diego | San Diego Co | San Diego. |
| Wadham, F E | Printer | San Diego Co | San Diego | San Diego. |
| Wadham, J F | Farmer | nr San Diego | San Diego Co | San Diego. |
| Wagner, C C | Gardener | San Diego Co | San Diego | San Diego. |
| Walden, W | Laborer | San Diego Co | nr San Diego | San Diego. |
| Walker, F M | Carpenter | San Diego Co | San Diego | San Diego. |
| Walker, Thos | Blacksmith | San Diego Co | National City | National City. |
| Walker, Wm James | Wheelwright | San Diego Co | San Diego | San Diego. |
| Wall, A E | Mariner | San Diego Co | San Diego | San Diego. |
| Wallace, A O | Market | Central Market | San Diego | San Diego. |
| Wallace, J | Miner | nr Milquatay | San Diego Co | Campo. |
| Wallace, W | Ranchero | nr Monserrate | San Diego Co | Monserrate. |
| Wallace, Wm | General mdse | San Luis Rey | 45 m N San Diego | San Luis Rey. |
| Wallack, D | Farmer | nr San Diego | San Diego Co | San Diego. |
| Walsh, John | Express driver | San Diego Co | San Diego | San Diego. |
| Walsh, John | Pilot | San Diego Co | San Diego | San Diego. |
| Walsh, N | Farmer | San Diego Co | Bear Valley | San Pascual. |
| Walsh, Robert | Miner | San Diego Co | nr San Diego | San Diego. |
| Walsh, T H | Carpenter | San Diego Co | San Diego | San Diego. |
| Walsh W J | Grocery | 5th st | San Diego | San Diego. |
| Walsh, Walter | Farmer | San Diego Co | nr San Diego | San Diego. |
| Walsh, W, Jr | Farmer | nr San Diego | San Diego Co | San Diego. |
| Walter, Oliver | Laborer | San Diego Co | San Diego | San Diego. |
| Walters, C A | Miner | nr Julian | San Diego Co | San Diego. |
| Wangeman, R | Pianos & organs | 5th st | San Diego | San Diego. |
| Ward, C H | Plasterer | San Diego Co | San Diego | San Diego. |
| Ward, E V | Farmer | San Diego Co | Cajon | San Diego. |

H. W. LITTLE.                       J. T. COCHRAN.

# LITTLE & COCHRAN,

—PROPRIETORS OF—

# NEW HALL,

## MONTEREY STREET,

## SAN LUIS OBISPO, - - CAL.

The above Hall is now open for entertainments. It is the largest Hall in the county, is most handsomely decorated, and is furnished with a magnificent Piano. The ventilation is perfect, the seating capacity large, and the seats comfortable. Several Dressing-rooms are conveniently located and fitted.

Traveling People are notified that this is the only Hall in San Luis Obispo having a Stage.

Messrs. Little & Cochran are also proprietors of the PALM SALOON, where the finest

## WINES, LIQUORS AND CIGARS

ARE ALWAYS TO BE HAD; ALSO TWO OF THE FINEST

### Phelan & Collender Billiard Tables

TO BE FOUND IN THE CITY.

DIRECTORY OF SAN DIEGO COUNTY. 503

| Name. | Occupation. | Place of Business. | Residence. | Town or P. O. |
|---|---|---|---|---|
| Ward, Henry J | Plasterer | San Diego Co | San Diego | San Diego. |
| Ward, J L | Farmer | nr Cajon | San Diego Co | San Diego. |
| Ward, R | Cabinet maker | San Diego Co | Milquatay | Campo. |
| Ware, H C | Hostler | San Diego Co | San Diego | San Diego. |
| Ware, J K | Druggist | San Diego Co | San Diego | San Diego. |
| Ware, L J | Farmer | San Diego Co | nr Monument City | San Diego. |
| Warner, Geo | Farmer | Cordero Valley | San Diego Co | |
| Warner, L | Carpenter | San Diego Co | San Diego | San Diego. |
| Warneck, A C | Confectioner | San Diego Co | San Diego | San Diego. |
| Warnock, S | Farmer | San Diego Co | nr Ballena | Ballena. |
| Warnock, W | Ranchero | nr Santa Teresa | San Diego Co | |
| Warring, G H | Teamster | nr San Diego | San Diego Co | San Diego. |
| Warren, H H | Farmer | nr Mesa Granda | San Diego Co | Ballena. |
| Washburn, C | Farmer | nr San Diego | San Diego Co | San Diego. |
| Watson, John | Carpenter | San Diego Co | San Bernardo | Bernardo. |
| Wattson, C C | Farmer | nr Paguay | San Diego Co | Poway. |
| Wattson, C R | Farmer | nr Paguay | San Diego Co | Poway. |
| Wayne, J C | Farmer | San Diego Co | nr San Diego | San Diego. |
| Webb, Dan'l F | Carpenter | San Diego Co | San Diego | San Diego. |
| Webb, G W | Trader | San Diego Co | Julian | Julian. |
| Webb, Sam'l F | Stock raiser | San Diego Co | Milquatay | Campo. |
| Webb, W | Farmer | San Diego Co | nr Carrisito | |
| Webster, W H | Teamster | San Diego Co | nr San Diego | San Diego. |
| Wedel, Philip | Brewer | San Diego Co | San Diego | San Diego. |
| Weed, A | Body maker | San Diego Co | San Diego | San Diego. |
| Weeger, E H | Fruit & confect'y | 5th st | San Diego | San Diego. |
| Wells, J B | Agent ætna ins co | San Diego | San Diego Co | San Diego. |
| Welsh, A | Farmer | nr San Diego | San Diego Co | San Diego. |
| Welty, Joseph | Hotel keeper | San Luis Rey | 45 m N San Diego | San Luis Rey. |
| Welty, R J | Lumberman | San Diego Co | Monserrate | Monserrate. |
| Wentworth, A C | Shipwright | San Diego Co | San Diego | San Diego. |
| Wentworth, Geo F | Constructor | San Diego | San Diego Co | San Diego. |
| Wentworth, Ira | Miner | San Diego Co | nr Julian | Julian. |
| Wenzel, W | Restaurant | 5th st | San Diego | San Diego. |
| Wenzel, Wm | Tinsmith | San Diego Co | San Diego | San Diego. |
| West, Peter | Farmer | San Diego Co | nr San Diego | San Diego. |
| Westcott, E | Miner | nr San Diego | San Diego Co | San Diego. |
| Wescutt, J W | Wagon manuf | cor 8th & J sts | San Diego | San Diego. |
| Wescott & Hattleburg | Wagon manufs | cor 8th & J sts | San Diego | San Diego. |
| Weston, Chas F | Millwright | San Diego Co | San Diego | San Diego. |
| Weston, Elijah | Farmer | San Diego Co | Otay | San Diego. |
| Whaley, T | Merchant | San Diego Co | San Diego | San Diego. |
| Wheeler, M G | Engineer | San Diego Co | San Diego | San Diego. |
| Whipple, Chas | Lawyer | San Diego Co | San Diego | San Diego. |
| Whipple, Chas | Miner | San Diego Co | San Diego | San Diego. |
| Whitaker, J C | Shoe maker | San Diego Co | San Diego | San Diego. |
| Whittaker, W | Wheelwright | cor 8th & L sts | San Diego | San Diego. |
| Whitcomb, H N | Farmer | San Diego Co | nr Julian | Julian. |
| White, Chas E J | Merchant | San Diego Co | San Diego | San Diego. |
| Whitfield, G | Druggist | cor 5th & E sts | San Diego | San Diego. |
| Whitmore, S | Teacher | San Diego Co | Otay | San Diego. |
| Whitney, E E | Clerk | San Diego Co | Tia Juana | San Diego. |
| Whitney, J H | Mason | San Diego Co | Oak Grove | Oak Grove. |
| Whitney, W J | Farmer | nr San Diego | San Diego Co | San Diego. |
| Whitney, W J | Carpenter | San Diego Co | San Diego | San Diego. |
| Wible, D F | Miner | San Diego Co | nr San Diego | San Diego. |
| Wicker, J | Carpenter | San Diego Co | San Diego | San Diego. |
| Wiggin, W S | Hotel keeper | San Diego Co | San Diego | San Diego. |
| Wilcox, A H | Pres com'l bank | cor 5th & G sts | San Diego | San Diego. |
| Wilcox, C | Mariner | San Diego Co | San Diego | San Diego. |
| Wilcox, H F | Farmer | San Diego Co | Ballena | Ballena. |
| Wilcox, L L | Miner | nr Julian | San Diego Co | Julian. |
| Wilcox, L F | Miner | San Diego Co | nr Julian | Julian. |

# White Sulphur Springs,

## SAN LUIS OBISPO CO., CAL.

LOCATED 14 MILES SOUTH OF SAN LUIS OBISPO, 12 MILES FROM STEAMER LANDING, AND 2 MILES FROM THE SANTA BARBARA STAGE STATION, ARROYO GRANDE.

---

### THIS WATER IS AN ABSOLUTE SPECIFIC FOR

Neuralgia, Rheumatism, Gout, Female Complaints, all Diseases of the Secretory Organs, Liver Complaint, Sick Headache, Erysipelas, Paralysis, Scrofula, Sore Eyes, Kidney Complaints,

**DYSPEPSIA, DISEASES OF THE STOMACH, AND ALL THOSE DISEASES WHICH HAVE THEIR ORIGIN IN THE IMPURITY OF THE BLOOD.**

---

### A HOTEL

For the accommodation of visitors, will soon be completed, large enough to comfortably entertain, in connection with the Cottages, one hundred guests, with good camping facilities for an innumerable host.

Mr. NEWSOM proposes to bring, in a race, sufficient water from the Arroyo Grande Creek to run a Twenty Horse-Power Engine all the year. This water-power he offers to anyone who will establish a manufacturing interest, he to take the value of the land and water interest in stock of the institution.

## DIRECTORY OF SAN DIEGO COUNTY. 505

| NAME. | OCCUPATION. | PLACE OF BUSINESS. | RESIDENCE. | TOWN OR P. O. |
|---|---|---|---|---|
| Wild, Jos | Mechanic | nr Monserrate | San Diego Co | Monserrate. |
| Wilder, A C | Moulder | San Diego Co | San Jacinto | San Jacinto. |
| Wilder, D O | Farmer | San Diego Co | San Jacinto | San Jacinto. |
| Wildy, H H | Attorney | Court House | San Diego | San Diego. |
| Willey, H I | Surveyor | San Diego Co | San Diego | San Diego. |
| Wiley, R C | Farmer | nr San Diego | San Diego Co | San Diego. |
| Wilkins, L A | Farmer | 12 m S San Diego | Tia Juana | San Diego. |
| Williams, Caleb | Farmer | nr San Diego | San Diego Co | San Diego. |
| Williams, C F | Physician | San Diego Co | San Diego Co | San Diego. |
| Williams, George | Restaurant | cor 5th & H sts | San Diego | San Diego. |
| Williams, H F | Wagon maker | San Diego Co | San Diego | San Diego. |
| Williams, J S | Physician | San Diego Co | San Diego | San Diego. |
| Williams, Jno J | Stock raiser | San Diego Co | Milquatay | Campo. |
| Williams, J S B | Miner | nr San Diego | San Diego Co | San Diego. |
| Williams, John | Saddler | San Diego Co | San Diego | San Diego. |
| Williams, Jas | Miner | nr San Diego | San Diego Co | San Diego. |
| Williams, M | Stage driver | San Diego Co | Milquatay | Campo. |
| Williams, Rich'd | Trader | San Diego Co | San Diego | San Diego. |
| Williams, W L | Miller | San Diego Co | San Diego | San Diego. |
| Williams, W W | Farmer | nr Jacumba | San Diego Co | San Diego. |
| Williamson, Geo | Stock raiser | San Diego Co | Julian | Julian. |
| Williamson, T | Farmer | San Diego Co | nr San Luis Rey | San Luis Rey. |
| Wilson, F R | Superintendent | San Diego Co | Julian | Julian. |
| Wilson, H | Station keeper | San Diego Co | Carrisa Creek | |
| Wilson, Jas | Mariner | San Diego Co | San Diego | San Diego. |
| Wilson, Jas | Clerk | San Diego Co | Warner's Ranch | Warner's Rch. |
| Wilson, Jere | Farmer | nr Warner's Ranch | San Diego Co | Warner's Rch. |
| Wilson, J C | Teamster | nr Agua Caliente | San Diego Co | Warner's Rch. |
| Wilson, Levi B | Attorney | San Diego Co | San Diego | San Diego. |
| Wilson, W | Blacksmith | San Diego Co | San Diego | San Diego. |
| Wiltshire, S | Wheelwright | San Diego Co | San Diego | San Jacinto. |
| Winans, Samuel | Locomotive eng | San Diego Co | San Diego | San Diego. |
| Winder, W A | Physician | Plaza | San Diego | San Diego. |
| Winder, Wm A | Miner | San Diego Co | nr San Diego | San Diego. |
| Winkapaw, J S | Caulker | San Diego Co | National City | National City. |
| Winter, Joseph | Baker | cor 4th & H sts | San Diego | San Diego. |
| Winter, L | Saloon keeper | San Diego Co | San Diego | San Diego. |
| Witham, J W | Carpenter | San Diego Co | San Diego | San Diego. |
| Witfield, C | Druggist | cor 5th & E sts | San Diego | San Diego. |
| Witfield, C G | Druggist | San Diego Co | San Diego | San Diego. |
| Witherby, O S | Ranchero | San Diego Co | nr San Diego | San Diego. |
| Wolf, L | Merchant | San Diego Co | Temecula | Temecula. |
| Wolf, M V | Farmer | Mountain Spring | San Diego Co | |
| Wolfsheimer, C | Clerk | San Diego Co | San Diego | San Diego. |
| Wolfsheimer, Chas & Co | Variety store | 5th st, bet G & H | San Diego | San Diego. |
| Wolfskill, J | Farmer | San Diego Co | nr Escondido | |
| Wood, A S | Civil engineer | San Diego Co | San Diego | San Diego. |
| Wood, A L | Farmer | nr Julian | San Diego Co | Julian. |
| Wood, C H | Printer | San Diego Co | Julian | Julian. |
| Wood, E D | Farmer | San Diego Co | nr Banner | Banner. |
| Wood, John | Farmer | San Diego Co | nr Julian | Julian. |
| Wood, R L | Stock raiser | Milquatay | San Diego Co | Campo. |
| Woods, A B | Carpenter | San Diego Co | San Diego | San Diego. |
| Woods, J McK | Farmer | nr San Diego | San Diego Co | San Diego. |
| Woods, M | Speculator | San Diego Co | Warner's Ranch | Warner's Rch. |
| Worthington, Geo | Farmer | nr San Jacinto | San Diego Co | San Jacinto. |
| Worthington, J G | Farmer | San Diego Co | nr San Diego | San Diego. |
| Worthington, W W | Farmer | San Diego Co | nr Temecula | Temecula. |
| Wrase, C | Saloon keeper | San Diego Co | San Diego | San Diego. |
| Wright, D H | Farmer | nr San Luis Rey | San Diego Co | San Luis Rey. |
| Wright, Edwd E | Cabinet maker | San Diego Co | San Diego | San Diego. |
| Wright, I A | Farmer | San Diego Co | nr Milquatay | Campo. |
| Wright, John S | Carpenter | San Diego Co | San Diego | San Diego. |

## HAMMERSCHLAG & LEVY,
### San Luis Obispo, Cal.

DEALERS IN

# GENERAL MERCHANDISE,

### FANCY GOODS, CHEMICALS,

### DRUGS, MEDICINES,

## PAINTS AND OILS, STATIONERY, ETC., ETC.

DRY GOODS, PROVISIONS, LIQUORS, TOBACCO AND CIGARS, BOOTS AND SHOES, HARDWARE, CROCKERYWARE, BLANKETS, CLOTHING, AND GENERAL FURNISHING GOODS.

### ARROYO GRANDE,

San Luis Obispo County, - - California.

—DEALER IN—

## GENERAL MERCHANDISE, DRY GOODS, DRUGS,
### MEDICINES, PAINTS, OILS, VARNISHES,

Provisions, Liquors, Tobacco and Cigars, Boots and Shoes, Hardware, Clothing and Gentlemen's and Ladies' Furnishing Goods.

*POST OFFICE IN THE STORE.*          *CALL AND EXAMINE.*

## DIRECTORY OF SAN DIEGO COUNTY.

| Name. | Occupation. | Place of Business. | Residence. | Town or P. O. |
|---|---|---|---|---|
| Wright, J C | Clerk | San Diego Co | San Diego | San Diego. |
| Wright, Orlando S | Physician | San Diego Co | San Diego | San Diego. |
| Wright, M C | Lumberman | San Diego Co | nr San Diego | San Diego. |
| Wright, R L | Trader | San Diego Co | San Diego | San Diego. |
| Wright, S E | Physician | San Diego Co | San Luis Rey | San Luis Rey. |
| Wright, Wm W | Carpenter | San Diego Co | San Diego | San Diego. |
| Yancey, J | Farmer | nr San Ysabel | San Diego Co | |
| Yandes, D | Restaurant | San Diego Co | San Diego | San Diego. |
| Yarncke, E F | Farmer | 7 m N San Pascual | Bear Valley | San Pascual. |
| Yenawine, S | Carpenter | San Diego Co | San Diego | San Diego. |
| Yorba, D | Farmer | San Diego Co | nr Santa Margarita | San Luis Rey. |
| Yorba, Gumecinto | Laborer | San Luis Rey | San Diego Co | San Luis Rey. |
| Yorba, Juan F | Farmer | San Luis Rey | San Diego Co | San Luis Rey. |
| Young, E | Teamster | San Diego Co | nr Monserrate | Monserrate. |
| Young, C L | Bar keeper | San Diego Co | San Diego | San Diego. |
| Young, J M | Furniture | cor 3d & G sts | San Diego | San Diego. |
| Young, J N | Seaman | San Diego Co | San Diego | San Diego. |
| Young, John N | Furniture | 5th st, nr H | San Diego | San Diego. |
| Zamarano, Jose A | Vaquero | 4 m S San Diegnito | Soledad | San Diegnito. |

## BLACKSMITH

—AND—

## WAGON SHOP,

Corner F and Fourth Streets,

SAN DIEGO, CAL.

**P. ROSTERT, PROPRIETOR.**

Uses the best Material, and does the most Perfect Work at Moderate Prices. Repairs promptly attented to. Horseshoeing a specialty.

## J. STEVENS,

## Carriage Manufacturer

**COR. E AND SECOND STS.**

SAN DIEGO, - - CALIFORNIA.

Made of Best Selected and Thoroughly Seasoned Timber, and warranted.

Jobbing, Carriage Trimming, Painting and Blacksmithing neatly done. Orders will receive prompt attention.

# J. C. ORTEGA,

### San Luis Obispo, Cal.

# School Books, Stationery

### SHEET MUSIC, CUTLERY,

## FANCY GOODS, NOTIONS, ETC.

# General News Agency.

### ⸺ALSO AGENT FOR ⸺

**PHŒNIX AND HOME INSURANCE CO'S,**
  **NORTH BRITISH AND MERCANTILE,**
    **IMPERIAL OF LONDON,**
      **QUEEN OF LIVERPOOL,**
**LONDON INS. INCORPORATED,**
  **COMMERCIAL UNION, OF LONDON,**
    **HARTFORD, OF CONNECTICUT,**
      **FIREMEN'S FUND, OF CALIFORNIA.**

POLICIES WRITTEN AND RENEWED IN THIS OFFICE.

Agent for the Coast Line Stage Company and Wells, Fargo & Co's Express. Western Union Telegraph Office in the Store.

# VENTURA HOUSE,

## Cor. of California and Santa Clara Sts.

San Buenaventura, — — California.

### W. D. HOBSON, Proprietor.

~THIS~

# HANDSOME NEW HOTEL

*IS NOW OPEN TO THE PUBLIC.*

IS FITTED UP IN GOOD STYLE, CENTRALLY LOCATED, COMMAND-
ING THE FINEST VIEW IN THE TOWN. NO EFFORTS WILL BE
SPARED TO MAKE IT A COMFORTABLE HOME FOR
TOURISTS AND INVALIDS, AS WELL AS
REGULAR BOARDERS.

**NO BAR KEPT ON THE PREMISES.**

# 40,000 ACRES OF LAND
## FOR SALE
### IN QUANTITIES TO SUIT PURCHASERS,

———CONSISTING OF———

## Improved Farms, Dairy Ranches and Unimproved Lands,

Comprising every variety of soil, from the best hill grazing to the richest bottom lands, suitable for raising all kinds of

### GRAIN, VEGETABLES, HOPS, SUGAR BEETS, TOBACCO & FRUITS

Large tracts susceptible of irrigation, almost without expense, magnificently watered by never-failing trout brooks, small lakes and springs. Plenty of live oak, willow and cottonwood timber.

Situated five miles south of San Luis Obispo, on the

### SANTA BARBARA STAGE ROAD,

And nine miles from the

## Best Harbor & Shipping Accommodations

Between San Francisco and San Diego.

TERMS.—Twenty per cent. cash, and ten years in which to make the balance of the payments, with yearly interest at ten per cent.

Also, a fine stock of Dairy Cows, Teams, Farming and Dairy Tools, Sheep and Hogs, with the land, if desired.

For further information and maps of the same, apply to

C. H. PHILLIPS,
At the Bank of San Luis Obispo, or
STEELE BROS.,
On the Rancho.

L. SCHWARTZ.                                H. LOOBLINER.

# L. SCHWARTZ & CO.

### San Luis Obispo, Cal,

~DEALERS IN~

## General Merchandise,

## FANCY GOODS,

## DRY GOODS, PROVISIONS,

### LIQUORS, TOBACCO, CIGARS,

## Boots, Shoes, Hardware, Cutlery,

### CROCKERYWARE, BLANKETS,

### CLOTHING, AND GENERAL FURNISHING GOODS,

Furniture, Bedding, and Household Furniture.

# The Bank of San Luis Obispo

SAN LUIS OBISPO, CAL.

**CAPITAL, - - - - $200,000.**

E. W. STEELE, PRESIDENT.         C. H. PHILLIPS, CASHIER

### DIRECTORS:

D. W. James,   Wm. L. Beebee,   E. W. Steele,   C. H. Phill,

P. W. Murphy.

### FINANCE COMMITTEE.

Geo. Steele,   J. P. Andrews,   Hugh Isom.

## EXCHANGE FOR SALE

On the principal cities in the United States, Europe, China, Japan and Australia.

Draw direct on the Bank of California, San Francisco, in Gold, Silver and Currency; or Agency of Bank of California, 33 Pine Street, New York, in Gold and Currency.

Deposits received, collections made, and a general banking business transacted. Interest paid on time deposits.

AGENCY FOR THE

**Liverpool and London and Globe Insurance Co.**

www.ingramcontent.com/pod-product-compliance
Lightning Source LLC
Chambersburg PA
CBHW021418300426
44114CB00010B/543